D1088454

# The Great
# Transition

RAYMOND L. GARTHOFF

# The Great Transition

## American-Soviet Relations and the End of the Cold War

THE BROOKINGS INSTITUTION
Washington, D.C.

Copyright © 1994
THE BROOKINGS INSTITUTION
1775 Massachusetts Avenue, N.W., Washington, D.C. 20036

*Library of Congress Cataloging-in-Publication data*

Garthoff, Raymond L.
  The great transition : American-Soviet relations and the end of the Cold War / Raymond
L. Garthoff.
    p. cm.    Includes bibliographical references and index.
  ISBN 0-8157-3060-8 — ISBN 0-8157-3059-4 (pbk.)
  1. United States—Foreign relations—Soviet Union. 2. Soviet Union—Foreign
relations—United States. 3. Cold War. I. Title.
E183.8.S65G38   1994
327.73047′09′048—dc20                                      93-48153
                                                            CIP

327.73
G-244

9 8 7 6 5 4 3 2 1

The paper used in this publication meets the minimum requirements of the American
National Standard for Information Sciences—Permanence of paper for Printed Library
Materials, ANSI Z39.48-1984

# ⒝ THE BROOKINGS INSTITUTION

The Brookings Institution is an independent organization devoted to nonpartisan research, education, and publication in economics, government, foreign policy, and the social sciences generally. Its principal purposes are to aid in the development of sound public policies and to promote public understanding of issues of national importance.

The Institution was founded on December 8, 1927, to merge the activities of the Institute for Government Research, founded in 1916, the Institute of Economics, founded in 1922, and the Robert Brookings Graduate School of Economics and Government, founded in 1924.

The Board of Trustees is responsible for the general administration of the Institution, while the immediate direction of the policies, program, and staff is vested in the President, assisted by an advisory committee of the officers and staff. The by-laws of the Institution state: "It is the function of the Trustees to make possible the conduct of scientific research, and publication, under the most favorable conditions, and to safeguard the independence of the research staff in the pursuit of their studies and in the publication of the results of such studies. It is not a part of their function to determine, control, or influence the conduct of particular investigations or the conclusions reached."

The President bears final responsibility for the decision to publish a manuscript as a Brookings book. In reaching his judgment on the competence, accuracy, and objectivity of each study, the President is advised by the director of the appropriate research program and weighs the views of a panel of expert outside readers who report to him in confidence on the quality of the work. Publication of a work signifies that it is deemed a competent treatment worthy of public consideration but does not imply endorsement of conclusions or recommendations.

The Institution maintains its position of neutrality on issues of public policy in order to safeguard the intellectual freedom of the staff. Hence interpretations or conclusions in Brookings publications should be understood to be solely those of the authors and should not be attributed to the Institution, to its trustees, officers, or other staff members, or to the organizations that support its research.

*There is nothing more difficult to take in hand, more perilous to conduct, or more uncertain in its success, than to take the lead in the introduction of a new order of things.*

NICCOLO MACHIAVELLI

# Foreword

THE END of the Cold War has created a new world, in which we are all seeking to get our bearings. Much has changed; the Soviet Union is no more, its place taken by Russia and other successor states. Yet even with these greatly changed conditions, history continues. American-Russian relations are a new phenomenon, but they can only be built on the foundation of the preceding stage of relations between the United States and the Soviet Union. That is one reason why it remains important to understand American-Soviet relations in their final decade, from 1981 to 1991.

There are other reasons as well. It is of intrinsic interest to know why and how the increased tensions of renewed Cold War in the early 1980s could move to a new if undeclared détente in the latter part of the decade. Still more, it is important to understand how the end of the division of Europe and the world, the end of the Cold War, could come in 1989–90 even while a communist-ruled Soviet Union continued to exist. Finally, there are lessons to be learned from both the American and the Soviet experiences of the 1980s that may be pertinent to relations between the United States and Russia, and more generally to international politics.

The author of this study, Raymond L. Garthoff, came to Brookings in 1980 after retiring from a long and distinguished career in government service. His first major study after resuming a career of scholarship was *Détente and Confrontation: American-Soviet Relations from Nixon to Reagan*, published in 1985—and now to appear in a revised and updated edition. The present volume, although it stands on its own, is a sequel to the earlier one.

The period from 1981 through 1991 encompasses the unexpected and significant transformation of American policy under President Ronald Reagan from confrontation in his first term to a new détente in the second. Even more unexpected and more far-reaching in its consequences was the emergence of a new Soviet leader, Mikhail Gorbachev, who was seeking to transform the Soviet

Union and its relationship with the rest of the world. He failed, spectacularly, in the attempt to restructure the Soviet economy and state, although he did end the communist monopoly on power. But he succeeded, also spectacularly, in his effort to bring an end to the Cold War.

This book, like its predecessor, provides an informed and comprehensive review of relations as they developed, from both the American and Soviet perspectives.

The author wishes to express his appreciation to the many people who, directly or indirectly, provided assistance based on their own participation in the events under review. Not all can be named but among those who provided information, comments, or both are, on the American side: Michael Beschloss, Lawrence Eagleburger, James Goodby, Harry Harding, Jr., Arthur Hartman, Ed Hewett, William Hyland, Robert Legvold, Jack Matlock, Jr., Paul Nitze, Mark Palmer, Richard Pipes, Condoleezza Rice, Thomas Simons, Walter Stoessel, Jr., and Thomas Watson, Jr. And on the Soviet side: Aleksei Arbatov, Georgy Arbatov, Aleksandr Bessmertnykh, Aleksandr Bovin, Fedor Burlatsky, Anatoly Chernyayev, Nikolai Chervov, Anatoly Dobrynin, Valentin Falin, Mikhail Gorbachev, Sergei Karaganov, Viktor Karpov, Andrei Kokoshin, Viktor Komplektov, Georgy Kornienko, Andrei Kortunov, Yegor Ligachev, Lev Mendeleyevich, Vladimir Petrovsky, Sergei Rogov, Georgy Shakhnazarov, Nikolai Shishlin, Sergei Tarasenko, Aleksei Vasiliyev, Vadim Zagladin, and Vitaly Zhurkin. The author is grateful to the staff of the Center for the Storage of Contemporary Documentation (TsKhSD) in Moscow and of the National Security Archive in Washington for their assistance in obtaining archival materials.

The author also wishes to thank Brookings Foreign Policy Studies director John D. Steinbruner for general support. Theresa Walker edited the manuscript; Melanie Allen, Diane Chido, Michael Levin, James Schoff, and Andrew Solomon verified the factual references; and Louise Skillings typed and retyped the manuscript many times. Julia Petrakis prepared the index. The author also acknowledges with sympathy the contributions of Brookings verifier Alison Ney, who died before the book was published.

This study was partially supported by the John D. and Catherine T. MacArthur Foundation, the Carnegie Corporation of New York, and the Andrew W. Mellon Foundation.

The views expressed in this book are solely those of the author and should not be attributed to the Brookings Institution, to its trustees, officers, or other staff members, or to the organizations that support its research.

BRUCE K. MACLAURY
*President*

*May 1994*
*Washington, D.C.*

# Contents

## II  A New Détente

## III  The End of the Cold War

       Chinese Policy                                                 624
       U.S.-Chinese Relations                                         629
       Sino-Soviet Relations                                          644
       Japan and East Asia                                            661
       Asia in American-Soviet Relations                             675


15.    Competition in the Third World                                678

       The Haig Doctrine, 1981–82                                     678
       The Reagan Doctrine, 1983–88                                   692
       The Soviet Role: On the Defensive, 1980–87                     716
       The "Gorbachev Doctrine," From Competition
         to Cooperation, 1988–91                                      733


V    Conclusions

16.    Retrospect and Prospect                                        751

       Looking Back: The Cold War in Retrospect                       751
       Looking Back: The Final Years of the Cold War                  757
       Looking Forward: American-Russian Relations in
         the Post-Soviet Era                                          778
       Looking Forward: International Relations in the
         Post–Cold War Era                                            793


       A Commentary on Sources                                        799

       Index                                                          803

# Introduction

HISTORY IS A seamless continuity, but it has significant turning points. The period covered by this study virtually defines itself. The year 1981 marked the advent of the Reagan administration, the last Cold War presidency in the United States, and a vintage one—with the most avowed anticommunist crusading policy in two decades. The new administration's stance also seemed to confirm to a reluctant Soviet leadership, blind to its own large share of responsibility, that the turn away from détente by the predecessor Carter administration a year earlier had indeed become the determined bipartisan policy of the United States.[1]

The reason for concluding this book at the end of 1991 is readily apparent. The end of the Cold War and the collapse of the Soviet Union and of communist rule marks a natural turning point, indeed a historic divide. American-Russian relations, and relations with the other successor states of the USSR, are grounded in what has occurred heretofore, but a new era has arrived. The years of a great transition, from renewed Cold War at the beginning of the 1980s through remarkable changes during the decade leading to the end of the Cold War by the beginning of the 1990s, are thus the theme of this book. This turning point is now history, albeit recent history. That history is also the inescapable foundation for what is now occurring and will evolve.

---

1. This analysis picks up the story from my earlier account of the rise and fall of the détente of the 1970s, covering 1969 through 1980, the years of the Nixon, Ford, and Carter administrations. See Raymond L. Garthoff, *Détente and Confrontation: American-Soviet Relations from Nixon to Reagan* (Brookings, 1985; revised edition, 1994). That study deals in depth with the period from 1969 through 1980; the 1985 edition also included a brief preliminary look at the period 1981-84. The revised edition has been updated to take account of new information, including recently declassified American and Soviet documents. It has also been revised to reflect perspectives derived from the demise of the Soviet Union and the end of the Cold War.

The present study seeks to provide a fairly detailed account of the development of relations from 1981 through 1991, based on the available record, including declassified materials and memoirs, supplemented by interviews with American and Soviet officials. The analysis, and in some details even the account, cannot yet be definitive. More information will become available, and time and the course of subsequent events will provide additional historical perspective. Enough is at hand, nonetheless, to make possible an informed picture of what happened in the dynamic American-Soviet relationship in this remarkable period of transition from renewed Cold War to a post–Cold War and post-Soviet world.

The United States and the Soviet Union were searching throughout the 1980s for a replacement for the détente of the 1970s. That relationship, after early promise, had attenuated over the second half of the 1970s and collapsed in the aftermath of the Soviet intervention in Afghanistan and the American reaction to that event at the close of the decade. During the 1980s, tension and diplomatic confrontation in the early years shifted gradually to a new relaxation of tensions in the second half of the decade.

In the United States, under President Ronald Reagan, the shift was remarkable. Neither supporters nor critics of the administration, who saw Reagan's hard line of confrontation and isolation in 1981-83, a rhetorical turn in 1984-85, and a new embrace of summitry and arms control negotiation from late 1985 through 1988, could have predicted the change. President George Bush in his first year followed a more measured middle course, maintaining the renewed dialogue but acting with more restraint in the pursuit of cooperation and arms control. But by the end of 1989 that course had already turned, and the revolutionary change in Eastern Europe and increasingly in the Soviet Union itself led to a radical transformation in U.S.-Soviet and East-West relations, occurring even before the revolutionary changes in the Soviet Union that took place from August through December of 1991.

Today, in the 1990s, it is already difficult to recall the very different historical context and nature of the U.S.-Soviet relationship of the 1980s. It is difficult to appreciate that statements and actions on both sides that may seem ordinary from the retrospective of a post-Soviet, post–Cold War world provoked tensions in their time. Today, when the sharpest criticisms of Soviet policies of the past are often voiced in Moscow, it is hard to put ourselves in the Soviet or American mindsets of a decade ago. While our present understanding of the past may benefit from knowing what history has brought about, our contemporary understanding of the political dynamics of that past era is more difficult to recreate. Yet it is essential to do so in order to understand the expectations, aims, and fears of political leaders at the time.

In the Soviet Union, the first half of the 1980s saw three transitions in the leadership, from Leonid Brezhnev through Yury Andropov and Konstantin Chernenko, all ailing, to the vigorous successor of a new generation, Mikhail Gorbachev. Moreover, besides changes in the leadership, other aspects of

Soviet domestic and foreign affairs made this a time of flux. Developments after 1985 by a changing collective ruling group under Gorbachev's leadership moved Soviet policy, at home as well as on the world arena, into new frontiers with fresh, in some cases radical, new approaches that permitted resolution of problems that previously seemed insoluble. By the end of the decade, the extent of the change in Soviet policy, and its growing impact, could not be doubted. But changes in the Soviet Union also included an intensifying economic decline and new political forces at work not controlled by the leadership in Moscow, and not pulling in any single direction. A desperate, abortive attempt by conservative forces to stop the rapid transformation of the Soviet Union led only to its more rapid disintegration. Boris Yeltsin, the first popularly elected president of Russia, came to power as Gorbachev's authority dissolved with the disintegration of Soviet authority. By the end of 1991, the Soviet Union (USSR) had ceased to exist, and the era of "U.S.-Soviet relations," in literal terms, came to an end.

During the first half of the 1980s, Reagan's political stance was the dominating factor in the relationship between the two countries. In most of the second half of the decade, Gorbachev's initiatives were of primary importance. By the early 1990s, however, events, rather than the choices of the leaders, had come to control the relationship.

A new, post–Cold War relationship began to develop at the beginning of the 1990s. While it is still early to predict its future course, and that would go beyond the purview of this book, the emergence of a new era is incontrovertible. The renewal of confrontation early in the 1980s and then the renaissance of détente in the second half of the 1980s bore witness to a changing mix of confrontational and cooperative elements in American-Soviet relations even before the disintegration of the Soviet Union. The important question had been the relative weight of one or the other in the mix.

During the years of Gorbachev's new thinking, the Soviet Union embarked on a significant path of cooperative security policies that was decisive in contributing to the end of the Cold War. For the first time since the end of World War II, by the beginning of the 1990s cooperation began to become dominant over rivalry. Yet serious internal difficulties within the former Soviet Union as the old union dissolved and since then, and American reactions to these developments, created complications. Even in the post-Soviet era, the relationship remains one with mixed positive and negative elements. Nonetheless, the new post–Cold War, post-Soviet situation holds promise not only for a more stable long-term relaxation of tensions between East and West (categories that no longer have much meaning), but even for moving beyond détente to an entente between the United States and Russia.

Developments within the two countries have always been important to the relationship between them, but in the 1990s the nature of radical change in the former Soviet Union is critical. The transformation of the entire Soviet system through an incompletely controlled chain reaction of deep political, social, economic, and ideological changes is a historical phenomenon without parallel. The relationships among Russia, Ukraine, Belarus, Kazakhstan, and the other successors of the former Soviet Union are not yet fully settled. Their course is bound to be rocky sometimes, and severe difficulties may arise with adverse reverberations on external relationships, including those with the United States.

Due attention must be given to the interaction of the policies of the two powers with each other, with other developments around the world, and how that affects the changing relations between them, as this study and my earlier one amply demonstrate.

Finally, the relationship between the United States and the Soviet Union (and since the end of 1991 between the United States and Russia), and the roles of each in the world, remains of special importance for the whole of world politics. Nevertheless the domination of the two powers and their rivalry in more than four decades of the Cold War have now passed. The nature of international relations has changed from the bipolarity of a political-military-ideological confrontation to a more complex multipolar political-economic-security relationship.

The purpose of this study is to see and describe from both the American and Soviet perspectives the unfolding of American-Soviet relations from the beginning of 1981 to the collapse of the Soviet Union at the end of 1991. An understanding based on such an approach is essential if in the future the United States and Russia are to understand each other and deal with conflicts of interest as well as identify and develop areas of common interest, including cooperative security.

Neither country alone can sustain increasing cooperation; either alone can lead both powers back into confrontation. Competition between rivals will at least in some measure remain; it can be controlled, but that will require constant effort. Currently, with the turn to a new relationship in the last decade of the twentieth century, it seems likely that American-Russian relations will develop over time into a more solidly based new era of mutual respect and accommodation. Irritants, however, will remain, and conceivably the relationship could revert to instability and tension. The future course will depend not only on policy preferences, but above all on domestic political developments—and diplomatic abilities—in both countries. Thus the challenge is not only between the powers, but within them; each must meet its internal developmental imperatives, as well as find paths of international accommodation and cooperative security. Although the challenge of the new era is unique, the historical setting is again the normal relationship between great powers; this is the natural state of world politics again after the great transition from the struggle of two superpowers in the world of the Cold War.

# I RENEWED CONFRONTATION

# 1 The Reagan Administration's Challenge, 1981–82

P RESIDENT  R ONALD  W.  R EAGAN and his key advisers entered office with confidence and optimism. While seeing a formidable Soviet challenge manifest in various forms around the world, they believed that a reinvigoration of American will, a reestablishment of American power, and a reaffirmation of American leadership of the Free World would meet that challenge. Not only the Democratic administration of Jimmy Carter but also the Republican administrations of Richard M. Nixon and Gerald R. Ford were believed to have been on the wrong track in foreign policy, above all by coming to terms with the Soviet Union in détente in the 1970s.

President Reagan's personal confidence had another source. He had long believed the American presidency was essentially inspirational, indicating broad general directions for policy rather than deciding concrete policy measures and carrying out policy. All modern presidents to some extent have seen the presidency as a political stage or arena, but only Reagan conceived of the president's role as essentially that of an actor, an actor for whom others arranged not only the production but also the script. Reagan "acted" the presidency for eight years.[1]

---

1. Reagan's political rise, starting with his first step as an actor giving a political speech for presidential candidate Senator Barry M. Goldwater in 1964, through his experience with a delegated administration of governance of California from 1967 to 1975, and in bids for the presidency as a marginal contender for the Republican presidential nomination in 1968 and a serious one in 1976, had earlier showed the power of a good public presence and scripted-speaking ability.

   Several of Reagan's political biographers have developed the point about his treatment of the presidency as an acting assignment, sometimes reflecting this theme in the titles of their books. See, for example, Bob Schieffer and Gary Paul Gates, *The Acting President: Ronald Reagan and the Supporting Players Who Helped Him Create the Illusion That Held America Spellbound* (E. P. Dutton, 1989); Michael Paul Rogin, *Ronald Reagan, The Movie* (Berkeley and Los Angeles: University of California Press,

## Anti-détente and Anticommunism

President Reagan's first comment on relations with the Soviet Union came in a revealing off-the-cuff reply to a question at his first press conference, on January 29, 1981. "Détente," he said, had been "a one-way street that the Soviet Union has used to pursue its own aims."[2] Asked about Soviet intentions, he said, "I don't have to think of an answer as to what I think their intentions are" because all Soviet leaders since the Revolution had "more than once repeated in the various Communist congresses they hold their determination that their goal must be the promotion of world revolution and a one-world Socialist or Communist state, whichever word you want to use." Moreover, he went on, they have "openly and publicly declared that the only morality they recognize is what will further their cause, meaning they reserve unto themselves the right to commit any crime, to lie, to cheat, in order to attain that [end]."[3] In later comments on criticism of this statement, Reagan in effect reaffirmed his sentiments and his continuing unawareness of the diplomatic impact of openly voicing them.[4]

In many other ways the new president and members of his administration freely expressed their very negative attitudes toward the Soviet Union. Reagan, for example, with characteristic overstatement declared that "the Soviet Union is the greatest violator today of human rights in all the world." In this same interview he adopted a distinction crafted by his UN Representative Jeane J. Kirkpatrick between "authoritarian" governments that do "not meet all of our principles of what constitutes human rights" but are pro-Western and anticommunist, on the one hand, and "totalitarian" communist states, on the other, "where there are no human rights."[5] And in a notable reference in 1983,

---

1987); Lou Cannon, *President Reagan: The Role of a Lifetime* (Simon and Schuster, 1991); and see Cannon, *Reagan* (Putnam's, 1982), and Garry Wills, *Reagan's America* (Doubleday, 1987).

2.    "The President's News Conference of January 29, 1981," *Weekly Compilation of Presidential Documents*, vol. 17 (February 2, 1981), p. 66. Hereafter *Presidential Documents*.

      This statement echoed one Reagan had voiced as early as 1976 in his challenge to President Ford. He said, "Détente, which started out worthily and with a good purpose, has become a one-way street." Quoted in Godfrey Sperling, Jr., "Candidates on the Issues: Reagan," *Christian Science Monitor*, June 3, 1976, p. 15.

3.    *Presidential Documents*, vol. 17 (February 2, 1981), pp. 66–67.

4.    "Interview with the President," March 3, 1981, *Presidential Documents*, vol. 17 (March 9, 1981), pp. 231–32; and "The President's News Conference of March 31, 1982," *Presidential Documents*, vol. 18 (April 5, 1982), p. 414.

5.    *Presidential Documents*, vol. 17 ( March 9, 1981), p. 235.

Reagan referred to the Soviet leaders as "the focus of evil in the modern world" and to their domain as an "evil empire."[6]

President Reagan's notorious disregard for concrete facts (in domestic as well as foreign affairs)[7] was evident in statements such as his reference to "the 10 commandments of Nikolai Lenin . . . guiding principles . . . and they're all there, that promises are like pie crust, made to be broken."[8]

---

6.  "National Association of Evangelicals," *Presidential Documents*, vol. 19 (March 14, 1983), p. 369.

    In this same address, Reagan recalled approvingly the words of a friend from the entertainment world in California who some years earlier had said, "I would rather see my little girls die now, still believing in God, than have them grow up under communism and one day die no longer believing in God." Reagan also equated the preaching of communist ideology to "the supremacy of the state," oblivious to the Marxist claim of the eventual withering away of the state, and more akin to Reagan's own antipathy to the role of the state (big government) in American life, as well as more applicable to the actuality of state domination of society in the Soviet Union than to its ideology.

7.  For a good sampling of President Reagan's egregious errors of fact in public statements, see Mark Green and Gail MacColl, *Ronald Reagan's Reign of Error* (Pantheon Books, 1984); on Soviet affairs see pp. 36–41, and on defense and arms control, pp. 42–48.

8.  "Second Anniversary of the Inauguration of the President," January 20, 1983, *Presidential Documents*, vol. 19 (January 24, 1983), pp. 77–78.

    The attribution of the name "Nikolai" to Vladimir Lenin (Vladimir Ulyanov), presumably originating from his early writing under the pseudonym "N. Lenin," has for some peculiar reason often been used by hard-line anticommunist Western commentators, and raises a flag as to a suspect source. Specialists on Soviet affairs, in and outside the U.S. government, were puzzled by Reagan's reference to the alleged "ten commandments," which were generally unknown. Apparently their origin was a Nazi propaganda fabrication that had made its way by professional anticommunists into right-wing publications of the kind read by Ronald Reagan. The fact that this odious charge was not a considered insult, but rather part of the personal intellectual baggage of the president of the United States, would scarcely have diminished its ominous implications in the eyes of the Soviet leaders even if they had been able to recognize the distinction.

    Later Reagan also referred in an interview to an alleged statement by Lenin that after taking Eastern Europe, Asia, and Latin America the United States would simply "fall into our outstretched hand like overripe fruit." "Foreign and Domestic Issues," September 9, 1985, *Presidential Documents*, vol. 21 (September 16, 1985), pp. 1062–63. This alleged quotation from Lenin also is spurious and has been traced to several publications of the John Birch Society, though it too may be a still earlier fabrication. See Karl E. Meyer, "The Elusive Lenin: Where Ronald Reagan Read of the Plot to Conquer America," *New York Times*, October 8, 1985, p. A30.

    Some years later, when the Soviet Union had dissolved, I found in the archive of the former Central Committee a once-secret September 1985 memorandum by Aleksandr Yakovlev and Leonid Zamyatin, then deputy Central Committee department chiefs, proposing a message to be delivered to the State Department by the Soviet ambassador protesting the "crude distortion of history" in this fraudulent attribution to Lenin by President Reagan in his speech of September 9 (erroneously cited as September 18 in the memo). TSKhSD (Center for the Storage of Contemporary Documenta-

From the standpoint of American-Soviet relations, the relevance of President Reagan's sentiments and abhorrence for communism, widely shared in the West and obviously anathema to the Soviet leaders, was twofold: what did it mean for American policy aims and actions, and what did the Soviet leaders see it as meaning for American policy? Reagan made clear what he regarded its policy relevance to be: he followed his reference to the Soviet leaders as the focus of evil with the remark that "if history teaches anything, it teaches that simple-minded appeasement or wishful thinking about our adversaries is folly" and urged his audience "to speak out against those who would place the United States in a position of military and moral inferiority," and he specifically assailed the idea of a nuclear freeze as "a very dangerous fraud" that would bring "merely the illusion of peace. The reality," he said, "is that we must find peace through strength."[9] When queried about his "focus of evil" remark some months later, he did say he would not repeat it, but he defended having stated it on the remarkable grounds of its impact on the Soviet leaders, notwithstanding their umbrage at the charge: "They really had to know and understand how we felt, what our views were and why we thought it necessary to build up our military defenses."[10]

There was a second element in Reagan's moral equivalent of a declaration of war on the focus of evil, apart from the uneasily associated declaration of a need for military strength. That was the call for a "crusade for freedom," announced before a somewhat stunned British Parliament in 1982. Again, in addition to an assault on communist totalitarianism, he noted that "even without our encouragement there has been and will continue to be repeated explosions against repression and dictatorships." Not only did Reagan challenge that none of the communist states in Eastern Europe had achieved "legitimacy," he also said that "the Soviet Union itself is not immune to this reality. Any system is inherently unstable that has no peaceful means to legitimize its leaders." Going beyond a challenge to a peaceful "competition in ideas," Reagan also declared that "while we must be cautious about forcing the pace of change, we must not hesitate to declare our ultimate objectives and to take concrete actions to move toward them. . . . So let us ask ourselves, 'What kind of people do we think we are?' And let us answer, 'Free people, worthy of

tion), Fond 4, Opis 29, Dokument 245, *O vrazhdebnykh vystupleniyakh prezidenta SShA* (On the Hostile Statements by the President of the USA), Secret, September 25, 1985, pp. 1–2.

9.   *Presidential Documents*, vol. 19 (March 14, 1983), pp. 368–69.
       Frequent injunctions against "appeasement" were sometimes specifically related to the Western experience with Hitler at Munich.

10.  "An Interview with President Reagan," *Time*, January 2, 1984, p. 37. Reagan repeated the same point in another interview soon after. See " 'There Is a New Feeling on the Part of the American People, . . .' " excerpts from an interview with President Reagan, *Washington Post*, January 22, 1984, p. A9.

freedom and determined not only to remain so but to help others gain their freedom as well'." Thus he called for a "global campaign for democracy," a "global campaign for freedom . . . a plan and a hope for the long term—the march of freedom and democracy which will leave Marxism-Leninism on the ash heap of history." This inspiring call for the world domination of democracy was not, however, clarified when the very next sentence continued, "And that's why we must continue our efforts to strengthen NATO [North Atlantic Treaty Organization]," and the one following reasserted that "our military strength is a prerequisite to peace" even though "the ultimate determinant in the struggle that's now going on in the world will not be bombs and rockets, but a test of wills and ideas . . . the forces of good ultimately rally and triumph over evil." "Let us now begin. . . . a crusade for freedom."[11]

A final element in President Reagan's personal view was that not only was the Soviet system ideologically bankrupt and therefore vulnerable, but that it was also stretched to the utmost by Soviet military efforts and therefore unable to compete in an intensified arms race. As he put it in a talk with some editors, "They cannot vastly increase their military productivity because they've already got their people on a starvation diet . . . if we show them [we have] the will and determination to go forward with a military buildup . . . they then have to weigh, do they want to meet us realistically on a program of disarmament or do they want to face a legitimate arms race in which we're racing. But up until now, we've been making unilateral concessions, allowing ours to deteriorate, and they've been building the greatest military machine the world has ever seen. But now they're going to be faced with [the fact] that we could go forward with an arms race and they can't keep up."[12] The Soviet system was indeed under growing strain, as would become increasingly evident throughout the 1980s. But most of the premises underlying Reagan's viewpoint were highly questionable: that the United States had not also been active in the arms competition and had been making unilateral concessions, that the Soviet Union was unable to match adequately a further American buildup, and that the Soviet Union would respond to such a buildup by accepting disarmament proposals that the United States would regard as "realistic" (that is, would favor the United States more than the SALT II Treaty that had been produced under the strategic arms limitations talks [SALT] conducted by the three preceding administrations but not ratified). But whatever their merit, they represented the thinking of the new president and his administration.

Some of the more zealous ideologues of the Reagan administration went further, even too far. Richard Pipes, a well-known hard-line anti-Soviet

---

11. President Reagan, "Address to Members of Parliament [London]," June 8, 1982, *Presidential Documents*, vol. 18 (June 14, 1982), pp. 764–70.

12. "Interview with the President," October 16, 1981, *Presidential Documents*, vol. 17 (October 26, 1981), pp. 1160–61.

academic, who had been brought to the White House as the Soviet and East European affairs specialist on the National Security Council (NSC) staff, had to be repudiated by the official spokesmen for the White House and the Department of State when he said that the "Soviet leaders would have to choose between peacefully changing their Communist system in the direction followed by the West or going to war. There is no other alternative and it could go either way."[13] (He was not rebuked for also saying "détente is dead.")[14]

President Reagan himself clearly set the general line on how the Soviet Union and its leaders were perceived, and the general aims of U.S. policy—to demonstrate American will and rebuild strength so as to compete aggressively with the Soviet Union and lead it to negotiate disarmament on U.S. terms in the Soviet Union's own interests. He did not, however, conceive or spell out a strategy for policy to achieve those general aims. Nor did Reagan's general attitude exclude a wide range of alternative policy courses that could have been implied. If the Soviet leaders were untrustworthy liars and the focus of evil, why should the United States negotiate with them? Or, should the United States pursue negotiations, with wary suspicion, tough verification proposals, and the pressure of its renewed arms programs to lead the Soviet leaders to accept American terms? Both views found expression within the administration.

President Reagan was determined to take a forthright stand opposing the Soviet Union. He not only believed that communism was evil, but that "the Soviet Union underlies all the unrest that is going on" in the world.[15] He seemed to believe that the main thing needed was simply for the United States to disabuse itself of notions that negotiations would resolve differences and that the Soviet Union could be dealt with as a normal negotiating partner, a view he considered naive and which he attributed to his three predecessors. Hence his belief that he needed to take an outspoken position in his early sharp criticisms of the Soviet system and leaders.

Reagan also had some unusual ideas about how the Soviet leaders viewed him. When asked that question during the closing days of the election campaign, he replied, "You see, they remember back, I guess [to] those union

---

13. See "U.S. Repudiates a Hard-Line Aide," *New York Times*, March 19, 1981, p. A8, quoting Pipes's statement from a Reuters interview.

  A few months later Major General Robert L. Schweitzer, the military assistant to National Security Adviser Richard V. Allen, was transferred from that post after making unauthorized inflammatory public comments that there was a "drift toward war" and that "the Soviets are on the move, they are going to strike," and that the United States was "in the greatest danger that the republic has faced since its founding days." See Michael Getler, "General Relieved of NSC Job after Unauthorized Speech," *Washington Post*, October 21, 1981, pp. A1, A7; and David Shribman, "Security Adviser Ousted for Talk Hinting at War," *New York Times*, October 21, 1981, pp. A1, A27.

14. Getler, *Washington Post*, October 21, 1981, p. A7.

15. Ronald Reagan, in a campaign address in June 1980, cited in Anthony Lewis, "Reagan on War and Peace," *New York Times*, October 20, 1980, p. A19.

days when we had a domestic Communist problem. I was very definitely on the wrong side for them."[16] Ronald Reagan's personal formative experience with "communists" was his participation in the Screen Actors Guild in struggles with American communist labor organizers of the late 1940s. He naively assumed the Hollywood experience and his role in it would also underlie the views of Soviet leaders in the 1980s, men whose experience at that time had been with Stalin's growing paranoia and a Cold War with the United States under a Democrat, President Harry S. Truman.[17]

Insofar as policy courses were concerned, Reagan's chief focus was on domestic affairs, dismantling oppressive "big government" in the United States.[18] A corollary would be unleashing American productive forces enchained by government bureaucracy, invigorating an economic revival. This economic surge would also serve a major foreign policy purpose by permitting the rebuilding of American military power, which he believed had been let slip toward or into inferiority. Restored American military power in turn would compel the Soviet leaders to desist from their support of international subversion and expansion. Such power might also permit negotiation from a position of strength, but its first role would be to discourage Soviet geopolitical advances such as had marked the second half of the 1970s.

---

16. Cited in "Men of the Year," *Time*, January 2, 1984, p. 23. On many other occasions President Reagan referred to his experience in the Screen Actors Guild, which clearly made an indelible impression on him.

17. At the time, Reagan believed that "the Russians sent their first team, their ace string, here to take us over [in Hollywood]." Cited from the *Los Angeles Times* (July 17, 1951) by Rogin, *Ronald Reagan, the Movie*, p. 27.

18. President Reagan's faith in free enterprise and deep antipathy to governmental regulation extended more broadly into foreign as well as domestic affairs. It was, for example, applied to questions of economic cooperation in the West and economic assistance to the developing world (although not to East-West trade). It was evident in a general disdain for the UN organization. Reagan's abandonment of the Law of the Sea negotiations in mid-1982 as they reached a climax after more than a decade of negotiation by the whole world community was a striking example of what can be called Reagan's preference for "the deregulation of international relations." This apt characterization was coined by a perceptive Soviet analyst; see G. A. Trofimenko, "Lessons of Peaceful Coexistence," *Voprosy istorii* (Questions of History), no. 11 (November 1983), p. 25. In the World Health Organization, in 1981 the United States was the only country opposing an infant food formula code designed to protect babies in developing countries, implementing an agreement that would end a six-year boycott of the Nestle Company; the vote was 118 to 1, and the reason was opposition to world government regulation of free enterprise. The United States refused to permit international organizations benefiting from U.S. financial support to help family planning efforts in the Third World involving birth control and abortions. The United States also refused to acknowledge jurisdiction by the International Court of Justice (the World Court) when it heard the complaint of Nicaragua against the United States for mining its ports, although it had no reservations about the World Court when it heard the case of Iranian seizure of the American Embassy in Tehran.

Reagan's disillusion with détente and belief that the United States needed to rebuild strength and reassert will against a perceived Soviet geopolitical challenge was widely shared. President Jimmy Carter had taken essentially the same stand in his last year of office after Afghanistan, but he had seemed pushed into it, whereas the stance came naturally with Ronald Reagan's view of the world. The wide public support for a post-détente policy of renewed containment was evident in such moderate "mainstream" organizations as the Council on Foreign Relations and the United Nations Association, each of which issued reports early in 1981 offering a framework for policy toward the Soviet Union in the 1980s with a strong endorsement of containment.[19]

Reagan's view went further. He not only saw specific geopolitical challenges, he saw a political avalanche. As he put it in a speech during the election campaign, "All over the world . . . the Soviets and their friends are advancing."[20] Moreover, many who had strongly supported Ronald Reagan's campaign and many who then entered his administration held even stronger views opposing détente and arms control that went well beyond vigilant containment. For example, about fifty members of the Committee on the Present Danger were named to senior positions in the Reagan administration in its first year, including (besides member Ronald Reagan himself), Assistant for National Security Affairs Richard V. Allen, CIA Director William J. Casey, UN Ambassador Jeane J. Kirkpatrick, Secretary of the Navy John F. Lehman, Jr., Arms Control and Disarmament Agency (ACDA) Director Eugene V. Rostow, Undersecretary of Defense Fred C. Iklé, Undersecretary of State James L. Buckley, Assistant Secretary of Defense Richard N. Perle, NSC staff expert on Soviet affairs Richard Pipes, arms negotiator Ambassador Paul H. Nitze, chairman of the Board of International Broadcasting (overseeing Radio Free Europe, RFE) Frank Shakespeare, and Conference on Security and Cooperation in Europe (CSCE) representative Ambassador Max M. Kampelman. Some of these later left, but Rostow was succeeded by fellow committee member Kenneth L. Adelman, and nonmember Alexander M. Haig was succeeded as secretary of state by George P. Shultz of the committee. Such organizations as the President's Foreign Intelligence Advisory Board and the General Advisory Committee on Arms Control and Disarmament were reconstituted with a

---

19. The Commission on U.S.-Soviet Relations sponsored by the Council on Foreign Relations prepared a report titled *The Soviet Challenge: A Policy Framework for the 1980s* (Council on Foreign Relations, May 1981); the UNA-USA National Policy Panel on US-Soviet Relations chaired by Governor William W. Scranton issued *US-Soviet Relations: A Strategy for the 1980s* (New York: United Nations Association of the United States of America, January 1981). Former aides of Henry Kissinger played a notably influential role in preparing both studies. Winston Lord, as president of the Council on Foreign Relations, was indirectly engaged in the first; William Hyland was a member, and Helmut Sonnenfeldt was principal drafter. Sonnenfeldt and Brent Scowcroft were members of the UNA panel.

20. "Reagan's Remarks to VFW," *Washington Star*, August 19, 1980, p. A3.

majority of their members drawn from the board of directors of the Committee on the Present Danger.


## The Vicar Sets Policy: "Restraint and Reciprocity"

The thrust of American policy toward the Soviet Union was never in doubt. The design of a policy and a strategy for implementing that policy was, however, subject to competing influences. Chief among these was the strong effort by Secretary of State Alexander M. Haig, Jr., to become the "vicar" of foreign policy and indeed to control the entire conduct of American international relations.

On January 6, in his first real discussion with president-elect Reagan, Haig had set forth his views that there must be a single manager or vicar coordinating the many facets of foreign policy and serving as the administration's spokesman on foreign policy. Haig indicates in his memoir account that Reagan "nodded after each point and agreed."[21] Haig believed he had been given the exclusive responsibility for foreign policy and, given Reagan's lack of experience or familiarity with the field, he planned to exercise that responsibility vigorously. Even before the inauguration, indeed on Haig's second day as secretary of state-designate, he had rather ostentatiously dismissed the Reagan transition team working on the State Department.[22]

On inauguration day, within minutes of the ceremony, Haig submitted to the president (through his counselor, Edwin M. Meese III) the draft of a proposed directive, National Security Decision Directive (NSDD)–1, assigning

---

21. Alexander M. Haig, Jr., *Caveat: Realism, Reagan, and Foreign Policy* (Macmillan, 1984), pp. 56–58. See also the text of Haig's own "talking paper" for that key meeting, later leaked to the press: "The Document That Sowed the Seed of Haig's Demise," *Washington Post*, July 11, 1982, pp. C1, C5. About Reagan's agreement to Haig's outline of his own broad role, Haig said he "had no doubts," although he later conceded that because of Reagan's "habitual cheery courtesy, it is at times difficult to know when he is agreeing or disagreeing, approving or disapproving." Haig, *Caveat*, p. 57.

22. See Haig, *Caveat*, pp. 56–72. Haig selected his dozen top associates well before inauguration but subsequently found that it took many weeks to overcome delaying tactics from conservatives on the Hill, such as Senator Jesse Helms, who used the pending nominations as leverage on other appointments. Haig's principal deputy was William P. Clark, whom he scarcely knew, and who was completely inexperienced in international affairs but who had the great advantage of being a long-time confidant of the president. It is still not clear on whose initiative Clark was given this post. Haig says it was his choice. Reagan's biographer Lou Cannon has stated that Richard Allen suggested Clark to Haig (after Edwin Meese and Michael Deaver had proposed it to Clark), and Haig picked up the idea because he wanted a sympathetic channel to the California clique in the White House. Lou Cannon, *President Reagan: The Role of a Lifetime* (Simon and Schuster, 1991), p. 190.

responsibilities in the field of national security. Haig, after consulting with Secretary of Defense Caspar W. Weinberger, Director of Central Intelligence William Casey, and National Security Adviser Richard Allen, had worked out in some detail the respective responsibilities of each and a structure for foreign policy decisionmaking confirming his dominant role. It was not, however, passed on to the president for approval—Meese and his closest associates in the White House staff, James A. Baker III and Michael K. Deaver, considered that Haig was making a "power play," attempting to steamroller a premature decision by the new president that would entail granting too much authority to the senior cabinet chiefs at the expense of the president (and of the White House staff). Moreover, Haig's eager attempt to get a quick delegation of authority was leaked to the press with disparaging connotations. Other memoranda from Haig to the president were also leaked.[23] A few weeks later in another flare-up based on a misunderstanding Vice President George H. W. Bush, rather than Haig, was announced to be responsible for "crisis management"—a key element of responsibility for foreign affairs—after Haig thought he had been assured by the president himself that rumors to that effect were incorrect.[24] NSDD-1 was not issued until a year later, and then in a considerably modified form.

Haig had tried too hard to get a clear early mandate for principal responsibility in the foreign affairs field. This was resented by suspicious White House advisers. Haig's desire for personal power was clearly an element in his motivation,[25] and he may have sensed the probable vacuum of strategic leadership from Reagan himself. But there was more: Haig, while serving in the White House in the Nixon and Ford administrations, had learned the need for central management of foreign policy. He had witnessed the successes, and failures, of Henry Kissinger's efforts, often depending significantly on control over the levers of policymaking or policy implementation. He had carefully brought the usual potential rivals of a secretary of state into the process—the

---

23. See Haig, *Caveat*, pp. 73–94, for his version of these events.
    According to Haig's account, he and Allen were accompanied by Weinberger and Casey when they met with Meese, Baker, and Deaver on inauguration day; Allen stated that only Haig and he met with Meese and Baker. See Haig, *Caveat*, pp. 76–77; and Richard V. Allen, "Foreign Policy and National Security: The White House Perspective," in Richard N. Holwill, ed., *Agenda '83, A Mandate for Leadership Report* (Washington: Heritage Foundation, 1983), p. 6.

24. Haig, *Caveat*, pp. 141–50.
    President Reagan in his memoir discussed Haig "going through the roof" over this assignment to the vice president, threatening to resign, and finally being mollified by a public statement by the president that Haig was his primary adviser on foreign affairs. Ronald Reagan, *An American Life* (Simon and Schuster, 1990), pp. 255–56.

25. Besides indirect indications in Haig's memoir, see Roger Morris, *Haig: The General's Progress* (Playboy Press, 1982), written by a former colleague of Haig on Kissinger's NSC staff.

national security adviser, the secretary of defense, and for good measure the director of central intelligence. But he had not understood the key role of the triumvirate of Reagan White House advisers who were to shield and influence the president in foreign affairs as well as all other areas—far more even than had H. R. Haldeman and John Ehrlichman in the Nixon White House. Reagan's White House triumvirate was especially suspicious of Alexander Haig, the one-time shadow of Henry Kissinger and later "acting president" in the dark final days of Nixon's travail, the "political" general, and more recently a presidential candidate himself. Minicrises arose constantly. Haig's breathless and bizarre declaration on national television on March 30, 1981, after President Reagan had been shot by a would-be assassin, "As of now, I am in control here, in the White House,"[26] did not help matters. The White House tended to view the vicar as a loose canon on the deck of the ship of state.

Haig was ambitious and sought power, but he also keenly appreciated the need to shape and manage a strategy of foreign policy. He saw himself not only as best qualified but indeed as the only one in the administration able to do so. He was in full agreement with President Reagan and others that it was necessary to build American economic and military power. But he saw these steps as means, not as an end in themselves. He understood that a posture, even "standing tall," is not a policy. He understood the need for a strategy of action, and ultimately for engaging with the adversary, to use American power by bringing it to bear on the conduct of the relations and in negotiation. He aimed to be a practitioner of power, as Kissinger had been, but under a strategy with greater stress on sticks than carrots, to carry forward what President Nixon began to call "hard-headed détente."[27]

In his address to the Republican National Convention in July 1980, Haig had echoed his mentor Kissinger's aim of a decade earlier: "The task ahead for this vital decade before us will be the management of global Soviet power."[28] Also in his convention address Haig had stressed a theme he was to repeat time after time as secretary of state: that over the last half of the 1970s the Soviet leaders had taken advantage of détente—and American administrations had let them do so—in a series of assaults on the world order by "illegal interventions,"[29] mostly by proxy, and that it was imperative to stop this advance.

---

26. For Haig's explanation, see *Caveat*, pp. 150–66.

27. See Richard Nixon, "'Hard-Headed Détente,'" *New York Times*, August 18, 1982, p. A21; and "A Call for 'Hard-Headed Détente'" *Time*, December 27, 1982, p. 18.

28. Quoted in "Sampler of Haig's Views," *New York Times*, December 18, 1980, p. B16.

29. By "illegal intervention" by the Soviet Union, Haig meant direct or indirect Soviet involvements in violent situations beyond the traditional sphere of Soviet hegemony in Eastern Europe. When asked by a puzzled reporter a few weeks after the administration had entered office what he meant by "illegal intervention," Haig explained that subversion and the creation of a local correlation of forces that justify intervention was

Haig placed the subject of Soviet involvement and expansion of influence in the Third World at the center of American-Soviet relations. He saw the Soviet pursuit of forceful expansion of its influence as aimed at securing strategic gains for the Soviet Union: "We must also recognize that Soviet interventions and meddling are not random. Moscow displays a keen interest in regions where there are strategic resources or routes vital to the economic well-being and political independence of the West. When the Soviet Union exploits local conditions for its own strategic aims, the problem is no longer local but a strategic threat to our own survival. We cannot ignore this threat." Consequently, "Illegal Soviet intervention calls into question the whole range of our relations with Moscow. It violates the restraint and reciprocity we seek in our relations" as well as making "a world order, governed by the rule of international law, all the more difficult to achieve."[30]

When the Reagan administration entered office in 1981, it inherited an ongoing covert assistance program supporting the *mujahedin* insurgents in Afghanistan. It continued, and gradually expanded, this program. Afghanistan was cited as an alarm bell on the Soviet threat. In the words of UN Ambassador Jeane J. Kirkpatrick, "The Soviet invasion impelled a widespread reassessment of the world situation based upon a new and more sober appreciation of the danger that the policies of the Soviet Union now pose to global stability and world peace." In addition, the invasion was said to have "marked a watershed in the postwar era, bringing to a definitive conclusion a period of optimism concerning the evolution of Soviet policy and intentions."[31] Incidentally, in this same speech in November 1981 Ambassador Kirkpatrick first referred to the Afghan *mujahedin* as "freedom fighters," an adaptation of the term first applied to the Hungarian rebels in 1956, and soon to be adopted by President Reagan

---

"longstanding classic Marxist strategy." Recently, however, in his view the Soviets had extended this strategy geographically: "We have witnessed a fundamental modification of the so-called Brezhnev doctrine which had historically been applied to areas within the sphere of Soviet interests and is now being applied in Africa, Southeast Asia, the Persian Gulf, and in this hemisphere. This is the crux of the core of the problem." See "Interviews at Breakfast Meetings," March 13, 1981, *Department of State Bulletin*, vol. 81 (May 1981), p. 11. (Hereafter *State Bulletin*.)

Haig's interpretation is subject to challenge on a number of points, not least that the Soviet Union had never spoken of applying the "Brezhnev doctrine" (which they did not even acknowledge) in those areas, that it applied in any case only to existing socialist states, and that Soviet-supported communist subversive and revolutionary activities around the world dated from 1917 and not the mid-1970s; but the point here is Haig's and the Reagan administration's perspective, rather than an evaluation of its validity.

30.  Secretary Haig, "Peaceful Progress in Developing Nations," May 24, 1981, *State Bulletin*, vol. 81 (July 1981), pp. 8–9.

31.  "Afghan Situation and Implications for Peace," Ambassador Kirkpatrick, November 18, 1981, *State Bulletin*, vol. 82 (January 1982), p. 57.

and others as a term applied to the Afghan insurgents, the Nicaraguan contras, and other opponents of radical regimes aligned with Moscow, to which the United States now gave assistance.[32]

While emphasizing a key Soviet role, Haig and others in the administration stressed Soviet use of "proxy" and "surrogate" forces. In speeches and other statements in 1981 and 1982, and in his later memoir, Haig repeatedly referred to Cuba, Libya, the Palestine Liberation Organization (PLO), Vietnam (frequently still "North Vietnam," an anachronistic designation), and Nicaragua as Soviet "proxies," "surrogates," or "clients." This lumping together of communist allies of the Soviet Union (incidentally having their own regional interests and aims), such as Cuba and Vietnam, with noncommunist independent actors on the world scene, such as Libya and the PLO, was an egregious error.[33] President Reagan, too, not only referred to "Qadhafi in Chad, Cuba in Angola, Cuba and East Germans in Ethiopia, in South Yemen, and of course, now the attempt here in our own Western Hemisphere" as actions involving "surrogates" of the Soviet Union, but he also spoke of Cuba, Libya, the PLO, "and others in the Communist bloc nations" in a way that suggested he did not realize that Qadhafi and the PLO were not communists.[34]

The blurring of Soviet relationships of support for various Third World countries and imputed control of those countries and direction of their actions was facilitated by a tendency by Haig and Reagan to see the national liberation struggle in various countries only as a device to serve Soviet geopolitical and strategic expansion. Haig was aware that there were serious problems in the Third World that could, and did, give rise to revolutionary situations. But once there was Soviet, Soviet-aligned, or local communist involvement or prospective gain (even if only by diminished Western influence), he saw the situation as converted into a Soviet offensive threat to the United States that must be countered. Thus, for example, "Grave though its plight might be, El Salvador was not merely a local problem. It was also a regional problem that threatened the stability of all of Central America, including the Panama Canal and Mexico and Guatemala with their vast oil reserves. And it was a global issue because it represented the interjection of the war of national liberation into the Western Hemisphere."[35] Such a contorted view of the interjection of a civil war from

---

32. See chapter 15.

33. For example, see Haig, *Caveat*, pp. 96, 109, 110, 172 and 220, and his statements of February 23, March 13, March 29, March 30, April 24, May 9, May 24, June 28 and October 29, 1981, *State Bulletin*, vol. 81 (April 1981), p. 15; (May 1981), pp. 1–2; (May 1981), p. 5; (May 1981), p. 9; (June 1981), p. 6; (June 1981), p. 11; (July 1981), pp. 8–9; (August 1981) pp. 51–52; and (December 1981), p. 28.

34. *Presidential Documents*, vol. 17 (March 9, 1981), pp. 229, 233.

35. Haig, *Caveat*, p. 118.

another hemisphere was possible only because Haig (and Reagan) saw the whole phenomenon as a "Soviet strategy of wars of liberation,"[36] rather than one of Soviet support for and exploitation for its own benefit of indigenous conflicts.

The administration went further in identifying the Soviet Union as (in Reagan's words of June 1980) the source of "all the unrest that is going on" in the world.[37] Haig began, literally from the administration's first days in office, to describe the Soviet Union as the sponsor of international terrorism. In his conception, the Soviet strategy encompassed two phases: an initial phase in Soviet selection of a "target" in which there are indigenous conditions for unrest, which the Soviets exploit by "terrorism, subversion and covert activity," and a later stage when they turn to a national liberation war in which they intervene with arms and proxy forces or even more direct action.[38] The view was a curiously naive image of the world, in which the Soviet Union selected, undermined, and then intervened with its strategy of national liberation, while the peoples of the countries involved were completely passive. Haig was aware that this construct of the Soviet strategy did not fully account for the local causes, even if he ignored local initiatives, but it provided at least a rationale for American interest in overriding any local interests that might coincide with or be aided by Soviet actions. "If we were to ignore that sophisticated [Soviet] approach and give them carte blanche in the so-called wars of liberation because of justified social conditions in a target country, we've adopted a formula for disaster."[39] In his view, possible Soviet gain overrode any "justified local conditions," or even regional considerations, insofar as the United States was concerned.

Soviet involvements and interventions in the Third World in the late 1970s, from Angola through Afghanistan, had been widely regarded in the United States as behavior not in keeping with détente. The Reagan administration not only shared this viewpoint but saw it as a challenge to the security of a Free World, especially to American influence and security. Secretary Haig in particular, but also President Reagan and other leading administration figures, frequently reiterated that view and listed up to six or eight situations that they saw as constituting a snowballing series of interventions by the Soviet Union or its proxies in the Free World (that is, in countries beyond the acknowledged Soviet bloc). Haig's list, which he recited with minor variation on more than a dozen occasions in 1981, comprised seven cases of Soviet or Soviet-sponsored direct or indirect aggression from 1975 through 1979: Angola (in 1975–76, mainly through Cuban proxy), Ethiopia (in 1977–78, mainly through the Cuban

---

36. Ibid., p. 106.

37. Cited in the *New York Times*, October 20, 1980, p. A19.

38. *State Bulletin*, vol. 81 (May 1981), pp. 16–17.

39. Ibid., p. 17.

proxy but with direct Soviet military participation), South Yemen (local communist coup in 1978), North Yemen (South Yemeni-supported incursions in 1979), Afghanistan (local communist coup in 1978), Kampuchea (Vietnamese invasion in late 1978), and finally Afghanistan again (direct Soviet military intervention in December 1979). All of these cases have been reviewed, most in some detail, in an earlier study.[40] In fact, the list was mixed, including some cases of local action where no Soviet role was demonstrated or even likely (the coups in South Yemen and Afghanistan in 1978), others where the initiative was by Soviet friends but on their own initiative (the South Yemeni-sponsored push into North Yemen, the Vietnamese invasion of Kampuchea, and even the initial Cuban aid to the MPLA [Popular Movement for the Liberation of Angola] in Angola). The only cases of clear Soviet involvement were support of the Angolan regime, recognized by the Organization of African Unity (OAU), aid to the Ethiopian government under attack from Somalia, and of course the quite different case of Afghanistan—the only one involving direct Soviet military intervention. The Soviet Union did see, and seize, several opportunities in the second half of the 1970s to extend its influence, but this did not constitute a coordinated Soviet expansionist drive gathering momentum. Nonetheless, that was increasingly the perception in the United States. This perception was not accompanied by recognition of the considerable U.S. efforts and successes in expanding its geopolitical influence in the 1970s, notably with China and Egypt.[41]

---

40. See Raymond L. Garthoff, *Détente and Confrontation: American-Soviet Relations from Nixon to Reagan* (Brookings, 1985, rev. ed., 1994); see chapter 15 on Angola, chapter 19 on most of the other cases, and chapter 26 on Afghanistan.

41. Curiously, Haig omitted the North Vietnamese takeover of South Vietnam in 1975, the two émigré Katangan incursions into the Shaba province of Zaire in 1977 and 1978 (which were comparable to the Kampuchean and North Yemeni cases), and even the Sandinista takeover in Nicaragua in mid-1979, although some other members of the administration did not.

   Haig was the best informed on foreign affairs of the senior members of the Reagan administration, but this was a relative matter. Haig displayed abysmal ignorance of the cases he was citing so confidently when he attempted to do more than list them. For example, in referring to the 1978 military coup in Afghanistan Haig said it was a *Soviet* intervention, in which the Soviets moved "to install a puppet leader a year before the actual invasion," and "the step from that, unchallenged [by the West], to the massive intervention of Soviet forces a year later is a very small step to take." See *State Bulletin*, vol. 81 (July 1981), p. 15. Compare that statement to the actual course of events in 1978 and 1979 discussed in detail in Garthoff, *Détente and Confrontation*, chapter 26. And the harassing border incursions into North Yemen, in which even South Yemeni direct participation was never clear, and where the Soviet preference was against the action, Haig depicted as an effort "to overthrow the government in Northern Yemen by the use of Southern Yemen forces and proxy forces shipped over from Ethiopia—Cubans and perhaps Ethiopians as well." *State Bulletin*, vol. 81 (November 1981), p. 70. There were Cuban advisers in South Yemen, but no forces shipped over from Ethiopia or involved in the incursions. And the 1978 coup (one of a series by factional rivals) in South Yemen

The important point was that the main impression of the administration (as of the Carter administration in its last years), and of the public, was that the Soviet Union and its associates had been "on the move," and that this seemed to represent a threatening pattern of expansion not in keeping with dtente. Haig described it as "an increasing [Soviet] proclivity to support change—either directly or indirectly—by rule of force, by bloodshed, terrorism, so-called wars of liberation." Haig continued, "At long last the American

---

in Haig's memory registered: "We saw a very heavy hand of Soviet activity in the original overthrow of the Southern Yemen regime" (p. 70). Compare with the account in Garthoff, *Détente and Confrontation*, chapter 19.

Beyond the cases of the late 1970s, Haig in his memoir recalled a whole series of historical developments in a skewed fashion: in looking back to the Korean War, rather than realizing that once the North Korean army had been defeated and driven from South Korea the United States decided to expand its objectives and seek also to occupy North Korea, precipitating the Chinese intervention, he recalled only that "we scaled down our objectives, put limits on the use of our power, and politicized the solution." (Haig, *Caveat*, p. 119.) He saw as the lesson of Vietnam: "If an objective is worth pursuing, then it must be pursued with enough resources to force the issue early." That comment was coupled with advice that El Salvador was crucial because it was "a symptom of dangerous conditions in the Americas—Cuban adventurism, Soviet strategic ambition" (p. 125). "When the rash of subversion broke out again in the Dominican Republic in 1965," Haig correctly noted, "President Johnson introduced 22,000 U.S. troops into the country." But he then added a remarkable non sequitur. "Only then did the Cubans and the Soviets flinch. They remained relatively quiescent until 1978" (p. 125). In fact, neither the Soviets nor the Cubans were involved in the Dominican Republic, and the Soviet leaders and the Cubans were sharply divided on support for revolutionary groups from 1964 through 1968.

Even when Haig himself had, or should have had, direct knowledge, his recalled account was grossly inconsistent with the record. On the Cienfuegos submarine base episode in 1970, Haig's account was distorted to give himself a decisive role in presenting an "ultimatum" with which the Soviets were said to have complied. (*Caveat*, p. 100; and see Garthoff, *Détente and Confrontation*, chapter 3.) And on the October 1973 Arab-Israeli war, Haig with exaggeration referred to a Soviet "ultimatum," a "threat to land airborne troops in the Sinai," and the U.S. alert of nuclear forces was said to have "persuaded Moscow to step back." (*Caveat*, pp. 142, 319–20; and see Garthoff, *Détente and Confrontation*, chapter 11.)

President Reagan's historical references were often even more distant from reality. To cite but one case: in his depiction, in the April 1978 coup in Afghanistan, "It was the Soviet Union that put their man as President of Afghanistan. And then their man didn't work out to their satisfaction, so, they came in and got rid of him and brought another man that they'd been training in Moscow and put him in as their President." From that oversimplified and misleading, but recognizable, reading of the situation in Afghanistan in 1978 and 1979, Reagan went on to draw a parallel with El Salvador in the 1980s: "Without actually using Soviet troops, in effect, the Soviets are, you might say, trying to do the same thing in El Salvador that they did in Afghanistan, but by using proxy troops through Cuba and guerrillas." (*Presidential Documents*, vol. 17 [March 9, 1981]), p. 230.) What "proxy troops"? Who was "their man"? Were the Soviets really trying to do "the same thing" in El Salvador that they did in Afghanistan? Presumably he meant acquiring a satellite, but a parallel between the two situations was not credible.

people have decided that this is no longer acceptable Soviet activity."[42] So long as "Moscow continues to support terrorism and war by proxy. . . . Only the United States has the pivotal strength to convince the Soviets—and their proxies—that violence will not advance their cause." American strength and determination would cause the Soviets to "respect reciprocity."[43]

This view underlay the stress placed by the Reagan administration, and above all by Haig, on disciplining the Soviet Union to respect the American conception of "restraint and reciprocity" within existing spheres of interest and hegemony, containing Soviet expansionist designs using force, locally and usually indirectly, but in the shadow of a relentless Soviet military buildup.

Haig was genuinely concerned about what he saw as the Soviet expansionist threat to vulnerable strategic areas of the Third World. He also saw a U.S. military buildup and militant containment as the most effective way to "discipline" the Soviets. In addition, Haig was aware that some elements in the administration, and still more among its constituents and supporters around the country, did not share his desire for a "hard-headed détente" but preferred a clean, hard line of confrontation and tended to be suspicious of negotiation. By taking the offensive, and, it was hoped, achieving early successes in a policy of opposing Soviet expansionism, Haig sought not only to stop the Soviets but also to build his credentials as a tough and effective anticommunist strategist so that, as both American power and Soviet awareness of the risks of pursuit of unilateral gains grew, he could later deal from a position of strength in negotiation.

One element of Haig's initiative was to match the more militant and ideological stand of the other members of the administration, such as Ambassador Kirkpatrick, by seizing and brandishing some themes embraced by the neoconservative cold warriors, in particular identifying the Soviet Union with international terrorism.[44] Thus at his first press conference, as noted earlier,

---

42. "Secretary Haig Interviewed for the *Wall Street Journal*," July 9, 1981, *State Bulletin*, vol. 81 (September 1981), p. 25. Hence, too, Haig criticized President Carter not only for failing to react more vigorously to these Soviet actions in the Third World but also for failing to comprehend the threat from "wars of liberation." See Haig, *Caveat*, p. 122.

43. Secretary Haig, "A New Direction in U.S. Foreign Policy," April 24, 1981, *State Bulletin*, vol. 81 (June 1981), p. 6.

44. A particularly influential event in mobilizing a major campaign stressing alleged Soviet ties to international terrorism was the Jerusalem Conference on International Terrorism sponsored by the Jonathan Institute of Jerusalem in July 1979. It brought together many journalists and commentators in the field including Senator Henry Jackson, retired Major General George Keegan, Yonah Alexander, Brian Crozier, Robert Moss, and Ray Cline. During the election campaign, in April 1980, another conference on terrorism under the same (but expanded) auspices held in Washington was addressed by Henry Kissinger, Richard Allen, who was to be the new national security adviser to the president, and Richard Pipes, the Soviet affairs member of the new NSC staff, and was attended by many leading neoconservatives including Norman Podhoretz, Midge Decter, and Ben Wattenberg.

Secretary Haig proclaimed that "international terrorism will take the place of human rights in our concern because it is the ultimate abuse of human rights" and stressed "Soviet activity in terms of training, funding and equipping . . . international terrorism."[45]

---

The Israeli contention that the PLO was a terrorist organization, rather than a national liberation movement some elements of which have engaged in terrorist acts, helped contribute to the conception espoused by the Reagan administration that blurred any distinction between terrorism and national liberation movements. *Commentary* magazine and other leading neoconservative groups began to stress Soviet connections with terrorism, as did such institutions as the Heritage Foundation, the Center for Strategic and International Studies then at Georgetown University, and a newly created Institute for Studies in International Terrorism at the State University of New York.

Soon after Haig's statement, in February 1981, a Subcommittee on Security and Terrorism under the Senate Judiciary Committee was established, chaired by Senator Jeremiah Denton, and including as members Senators John East and Orrin Hatch, all notably anti-Soviet hardliners. The subcommittee's first hearings on terrorism featured Arnaud de Borchgrave, Michael Ledeen, and Claire Sterling (whose book *The Terror Network* had just been published by Reader's Digest Press). The hearings were specifically directed to publicizing "Soviet and surrogate support for international terrorism."

45.  "Excerpts from Haig's Remarks at First News Conference as Secretary of State," *New York Times*, January 29, 1981, p. A10.

Haig had first made the claim of a close tie between the Soviet Union and international terrorism in his confirmation hearings, on January 14. See *On the Nomination of Alexander M. Haig, Jr., to be Secretary of State*, Hearings before the Senate Committee on Foreign Relations, 97 Cong. 1 sess. (Washington: Government Printing Office, 1981), pt. 2, pp. 74–75. Even earlier, in June 1979 on the occasion of his retirement as Supreme Allied Commander Europe—and four days after he narrowly escaped an assassination attempt in Belgium (by unidentified persons)—Haig had charged that Moscow and "the totalitarian regimes of the East" were largely responsible for the international "disease" of terrorism and upheaval, and "virulent forces" seeking change through violence. (See Michael Getler, "Soviets and Terrorist Activity: World of Shadow and Shading," *Washington Post*, February 7, 1981, p. 10.) In addition, just before his comments in January he had read advance proofs of Claire Sterling's forthcoming book, *The Terror Network*, putting the subject in the forefront of his mind. He was encouraged in this belief by Michael Ledeen, an enthusiastic advocate of the view that the Soviet Union was responsible for international terrorism (and a collaborator of Claire Sterling's). Haig soon brought Ledeen into the Department of State as a special assistant. See also footnote 47.

The idea that the Soviet Union was introducing some evil bacillus into the new world also appealed to President Reagan's image of reality. He saw an American duty to help fight "against the import or the export into the Western Hemisphere of terrorism, of disruption. And it isn't just El Salvador. That happens to be the target at the moment. Our problem is this whole hemisphere and keeping this sort of thing out." See *Presidential Documents*, vol. 17 (March 9, 1981), p. 229. And in an election campaign address in 1980 he had said, "Cuban and Soviet-trained terrorists are bringing civil war to Central American countries" and that "we must take a stand against terrorism in the world." *Washington Star*, August 19, 1980, p. A3.

Haig's claims, while congenial to Reagan, were not supported by the intelligence community in Washington, and this fact was quickly leaked.[46] In fact, immediately after Haig's January 28 press conference statement, he had been advised by the director of the Bureau of Intelligence and Research in the State Department that intelligence information did not support his contention. Haig was surprised and commented that he had just read the Sterling book. He was persuaded to request a formal national intelligence estimate by the intelligence community, which would draw together all information available.

The national intelligence estimate on Soviet support for international terrorism drafted by the Central Intelligence Agency (CIA) did not accord with Haig's claim. Director of Central Intelligence William Casey was disturbed by this finding and remanded the draft for revision.[47]

------

46. See Richard Halloran, "Proof of Soviet-Aided Terror Is Scarce," *New York Times*, February 9, 1981, p. A3; "CIA Said to Doubt Soviet Ties to Terrorism," *Washington Post*, March 29, 1981, p. A22; and Judith Miller, "U.S. Study Discounts Soviet Terror Role," *New York Times*, March 29, 1981, p. 4.

47. Casey reacted to the draft estimate by objecting that there was more on Soviet ties to terrorism in the Sterling book (*The Terror Network*) than in the estimate, and he wanted to know why. He was then advised that the CIA had played a part in supplying Claire Sterling with concocted misinformation for public propaganda, and that the book was not only unreliable but "tainted." One senior intelligence officer has said that Casey then said to use it anyway, but that has been questioned by others.

    Among Sterling's sources were Michael Ledeen and General Giuseppe Santovito, then chief of the Italian Military Intelligence and Security Service (SISMI), the latter soon removed when his membership in the P-2 secret Masonic lodge was discovered. One of SISMI's top operatives, Francesco Pazienza, a specialist on terrorism and a collaborator of Michael Ledeen, whom Ledeen had introduced to Haig, was ousted at the same time. As noted, Ledeen became a special assistant to Haig. See also chapter 3, footnotes 27 and 29, concerning Ledeen's (and Santovito's) role with respect to the alleged Bulgarian connection in the papal assassination plot. Ledeen also played a signal role later in generating the secret arms-for-hostages deal with Iran in 1985. See chapter 6, footnote 114.

    Apart from the fact that the findings of the draft estimate were not congenial to the convictions of Haig and Casey (and undoubtedly of many other members of the new administration, including Ronald Reagan), it was also argued that the intelligence professionals had defined the term "terrorism" too narrowly, that it should be applied more widely to use of violence, as in national liberation conflicts. Some analysts in the Defense Intelligence Agency (DIA) had disagreed with the CIA and the State Department from the beginning, and the DIA was permitted to draft a new version of the estimate. The DIA draft was, however, so extreme and ill-supported that it too was discarded, and new drafters at the CIA under senior review board member Lincoln Gordon, using broadened terms of reference, prepared a text that was finally, after eight months, found acceptable. The approved version did not say that the Soviets were directly fomenting international terrorism, but it did state that "the Soviets are deeply engaged in support of revolutionary violence worldwide," and that in turn national insurgencies that the Soviet Union "directly or indirectly" supported often "carry out

Apart from heightened attention to terrorism, the Reagan administration drastically reduced attention to human rights matters for the noncommunist (or, more precisely, the non-Soviet bloc) world. But the administration continued to flail Soviet treatment of dissidents. Most important, its general hard line against the Soviet system, rather than particular abuses, was equated with defense of human rights. As Assistant Secretary of State for Human Rights and Humanitarian Affairs Elliott Abrams put it, "By taking a strong stand against the Soviet Union, we are dealing with the human-rights problem wholesale rather than retail. The Soviet Union is the center of a Communist system that is the worst enemy of human rights."[48] In Reagan's words, the Soviet Union posed "the single greatest challenge to human rights in the world today."[49]

Haig sought to do more than take on the Soviet challenge verbally. An arena for early engagement in opposing Soviet expansion presented itself, and Haig seized it: Soviet-sponsored, Cuban-managed, Nicaraguan-supplied, communist-led terrorist-guerrilla insurgency in El Salvador. By no means did all agree with such a description of the civil war in El Salvador, but such a characterization reflected Haig's perception and fitted his purpose. Salvador was in America's backyard and far from the Soviet Union; it should be possible at minimal risk and cost to secure a victory that would demonstrate to all—to the Soviet leaders, to U.S. allies and others in the world, and to the American people—that American will and strength, reasserted, were effective in countering continuing Soviet efforts around the world to advance at American expense.[50]

---

terrorist activities as part of their larger programs of revolutionary violence." It omitted, however, the unchallenged statements of the first draft that "the Soviets have opposed international terrorist activity in public and, in private, have urged their own clients to avoid its use. . . . they do not encourage the use of terror by their third world clients." Quotation from the excerpts declassified and published in *Nomination of Robert M. Gates*, Hearings before the Select Committee on Intelligence of the United States Senate, 102 Cong. 1 sess., October 2, 1991 (GPO, 1992), vol. II, p. 439; and see *Nomination of Robert M. Gates to be Director of Central Intelligence*, U.S. Senate Executive Report 102-19, 102 Cong. 1 sess., October 24, 1991 (GPO, 1992), pp. 151–54.

This account is also based on information from several knowledgeable senior officials of the U.S. intelligence community. There are also brief corroborating accounts in Bob Woodward, *Veil: The Secret Wars of the CIA, 1981-1987* (Simon and Schuster, 1987), pp. 93–94, 124–29; and Joseph E. Persico, *Casey: From the OSS to the CIA* (Viking, 1990), pp. 220–21.

48. "'The Main Threat to Human Rights Is the Soviet Union,'" *U.S. News and World Report*, September 10, 1984, p. 39.

49. "Captive Nations Week, 1984," July 16, 1984, *Presidential Documents*, vol. 20, (July 23, 1984), p. 1031.

50. Some sources at the time high in the intelligence community have said that during the transition period in late 1980 or very early 1981 members of the incoming administration received intelligence from the chiefs of France's and Italy's intelligence services that the Soviet Politburo intended to "test" the new administration by unleashing a new insurgent offensive in El Salvador. The origin and provenance of this alleged intelligence is

The administration's actions with respect to the situation in Central America will be discussed later.[51] At this point it is sufficient to note that besides such actions the administration, especially Haig, launched a major campaign to highlight and attack the role of the Soviet Union and Cuba. The State Department issued a hastily prepared—and flawed—White Paper titled "Communist Interference in El Salvador" that called the situation in that country "a textbook case of indirect armed aggression by Communist powers through Cuba."[52] Diplomatic "truth squads" were sent to Western Europe to persuade America's allies of the role of the Soviet Union and other communists—although without notable success. Haig testified in open hearings in Congress that the Soviet Union had "major responsibility" for the spread of international terrorism and had a "hit list" for the "takeover of Central America"—Nicaragua, El Salvador,

---

not entirely clear, but it may well have been Michael Ledeen relaying a view held by his friends General Santovito, head of the Italian SISMI, and Alexandre de Marenches, then head of France's foreign intelligence service (SDECE) (perhaps at a meeting on December 9, 1980, in which Ledeen introduced Pazienza to Haig). The "intelligence" may well have represented an interpretation rather than information from a direct source, and it is in fact most unlikely that those services would have had a source able to recount such a Politburo decision. (Count de Marenches, removed from his position after eleven years by the new Mitterrand government later in 1981, had a penchant well-known in professional intelligence circles for frequently "predicting" dire Soviet actions, so that when on occasion these warnings coincided with real events he could then claim credit. One example was the Soviet intervention in Afghanistan in 1979.) The fact that the Salvadoran insurgents planned a new offensive was independently well known at that time, and the reported Soviet decision could not be corroborated or disproven by its occurrence. The American intelligence community had no information on such a Politburo decision on testing American resolve and none has ever come to light. But quite apart from this questionable intelligence report, Haig, and many members of the incoming administration (including Richard Allen), were in any event receptive to the idea that the Soviets would test their mettle and were determined to "pass" that test and to begin testing the Soviet resolve.

Count de Marenches also had a private meeting with President-elect Reagan in San Clemente on November 21, 1980, arranged by some of Reagan's ultraconservative California backers, in which Marenches is said to have warned Reagan not to trust the CIA. See Woodward, *Veil*, pp. 39–41.

51. See chapter 15.

52. *Communist Interference in El Salvador*, Department of State Special Report 80, February 23, 1981, reprinted in *State Bulletin*, vol. 81 (March 1981), p. 7. The report was filled with errors and misuses of captured documents cited as sources. The press soon pointed them out. The key articles were Jonathan Kwitny, "Tarnished Report? Apparent Errors Cloud U.S. 'White Paper' on Reds in El Salvador," *Wall Street Journal*, June 8, 1981, pp. 1, 5; Robert G. Kaiser, "White Paper on El Salvador Is Faulty," *Washington Post*, June 9, 1981, pp. A1, A14; and Juan de Onis, "U.S. Officials Concede Flaws in Salvador White Paper but Defend Its Conclusion," *New York Times*, June 10, 1981. p. A6. The principal author of the report was a Foreign Service officer named Jon D. Glassman, who readily acknowledged the haphazard preparation until he was advised not to respond to further press inquiries.

Honduras, and Guatemala.[53] He threatened unspecified American retaliation at "the source" of these eruptions, identified sometimes as Cuba and sometimes as the Soviet Union.[54]

This focal American counterchallenge in Central America also served Haig's general policy approach. In a series of speeches and other statements throughout the first year of the Reagan administration, Haig developed what he came to call the "four pillars" of American policy: developing American relations with the Soviet Union on the basis of "restraint and reciprocity," strengthening U.S. alliances, assisting in development of the Third World, and building American economic and military strength. All contributed to containment of Soviet expansion.

On May 9, Haig stated that "an insistence on restraint and reciprocity in East-West relations is the central theme of our foreign policy."[55] Moreover, "we must act to restrain the Soviet Union," because "it is Soviet reliance on force and the threat of force to create and exploit disorder that undermines the prospect for world peace today" (as well as threatening "Western strategic interests").[56] While the usual formula (also used occasionally by President Reagan and others) was "restraint and reciprocity," in a few cases Haig more specifically if less diplomatically made clear what he really meant: "greater *Soviet* restraint and greater *Soviet* reciprocity." He said, "Our pursuit of greater Soviet restraint and reciprocity should draw upon several lessons painfully learned over the past decade in dealing with the Soviet Union." And finally the

---

53.  See Bernard Gwertzman, "Haig Cites 'Hit List' for Soviet Control of Central America," *New York Times*, March 19, 1981, pp. A1, A10.

54.  Following earlier references in congressional testimony and in private interviews, Haig made public references to reacting "at the source," identifying Cuba as the subject on February 23 and 27, and the Soviet Union on March 13. See "Secretary Haig Interviewed for French Television," February 23, 1981, and "News Conference with British Press," February 27, 1981, *State Bulletin*, vol. 81 (April 1981), pp. 15, 22; and "Interviews at Breakfast Meetings," March 13, 1981, *State Bulletin*, vol. 81 (May 1981), p. 15.

      In his memoir, Weinberger has reported that as early as a preinauguration meeting of President Reagan and his future cabinet in December 1980, Haig had said that "it was quite clear we would have to invade Cuba and, one way or another, put an end to the Castro regime." Caspar W. Weinberger, *Fighting for Peace: Seven Critical Years in the Pentagon* (Warner Books, 1990), pp. 30–31.

      Haig later, when a candidate for the Republican presidential nomination in 1987, presented a very different evaluation even from his own memoir. He said the United States had "missed a diplomatic opportunity to work out a broad solution with the Soviet Union and Cuba in 1981 and 1982," and suggested we could have "offered Cuba incentives through an altered relationship with the United States." See James R. Dickenson, "Haig Hits Reagan Tax Cuts, Calls Defense Buildup 'Excessive'" *Washington Post*, October 20, 1987, p. A3.

55.  Secretary Haig, "NATO and the Restoration of American Leadership," May 9, 1981, *State Bulletin*, vol. 81 (June 1981), p. 11.

56.  Ibid.

other three pillars of American policy were seen ultimately as contributing to this one: "By rebuilding our strength, reinvigorating our alliances, and promoting progress through peaceful change, we are creating the conditions that make restraint and reciprocity the most realistic Soviet options."[57]

Haig did not, however, see the task of American policy solely as creating conditions to compel Soviet acquiescence in what Americans would regard as restraint and reciprocity. In a later address, he made clear where his approach differed from those (some in the Reagan administration, and some outside) who favored unalloyed confrontation of the Soviet Union. In April 1982, in one of his best (and last) policy statements, Haig said that "our enduring challenge is . . . to develop and to sustain a relationship with the Soviet Union which recognizes that the competition will proceed but constrains the use or threat of force." He deplored two extremes that have "distorted American foreign policy over the postwar period: First, that expressions of American goodwill and readiness to negotiate could somehow substitute for American strength and would move U.S.-Soviet relations from competition to cooperation; Second, that a posture of confrontation, a refusal to negotiate would somehow lead to capitulation by the other superpower."[58] The first of these was a straw man (no American leader, at least since Henry Wallace, had believed that goodwill alone would lead to cooperation and an end to competition). Haig certainly knew very well that it did not apply to Richard Nixon and Henry Kissinger and could scarcely have believed it of Jimmy Carter and Cyrus Vance. But the statement made the necessary antipode to a policy of confrontation, which did have its advocates in the administration. Moreover, Haig wanted to distance himself from the term "détente" even as he proposed a reformulated and toughened approach essentially based on the strategy of détente pursued throughout the 1970s.

Haig perspicaciously pictured the decade of the 1980s as one in which the Soviet Union would experience a transition in leadership and the need to face up to "greater economic difficulties and growing international isolation." Accordingly, "During this sensitive and dangerous period of changing superpower relationships, the United States must make clear to the Soviet Union that there are penalties for aggression and incentives for restraint." And "We will continue to probe Soviet willingness to engage in negotiations geared to achieve concrete results."[59]

---

57. Secretary Haig, "A Strategic Approach to American Foreign Policy," address to the American Bar Association, August 11, 1981, *State Bulletin*, vol. 81 (September 1981), pp. 11–13. Emphasis added.

58. Secretary Haig, "American Power and American Purpose," *State Bulletin*, vol. 82 (June 1982), p. 42.

59. Ibid., p. 43.

Haig had earlier stressed that "there must be a combination of incentives and disincentives—carrots and sticks, if you will."[60] He seemed unclear or at least unready to identify the carrots;[61] the sticks were much more evident. But in general terms he identified the incentives as well: "a broader relationship of mutual benefit," including "political agreements to resolve outstanding regional conflicts," "balanced and verifiable arms control agreements," and "the potential benefits of greater East-West trade"[62]—a list more than vaguely reminiscent of the détente strategy of Nixon and Kissinger. (The rhetoric surrounding the proposed new strategy was, of course, very different—with a strong accent on competition and containment and scarcely a hint of a structure of peace.)

Haig did not attempt to establish a formal charter for policy toward the Soviet Union. Indeed he opposed such an effort because it would require a consensus with those in the White House and Pentagon who favored a more confrontational stance. Only after his departure in June 1982 were efforts galvanized by Richard Pipes in the NSC staff to get a formal policy guidance on policy toward the Soviet Union and Eastern Europe. Thus the Reagan administration did not formalize its policy until late 1982 (just as Pipes departed to return to Harvard). NSDD-54 on Eastern Europe in August and NSDD-75 on the Soviet Union in January 1983 spelled out policy guidance. The guidance on Eastern Europe stressed differentiation, to favor movement either toward internal liberalization or greater independence from the Soviet Union in foreign policy, essentially continuing the policy conducted during the 1970s. NSDD-75 on the Soviet Union incorporated, but also expanded on and thereby changed, the policy line taken by Haig.[63]

The thrust of Haig's policy toward the Soviet Union was geopolitical: to wage a vigorous competition focused on containing and countering direct or indirect Soviet expansion beyond the Soviet bloc in Eastern Europe, but not to carry the challenge to Soviet rule in the Soviet Union or the bloc. This continued the line taken by Nixon and Kissinger, and largely although less consistently by Carter and Brzezinski. It also reflected the inclination of the profes-

---

60. *State Bulletin*, vol. 81 (September 1981), p. 25.

61. When asked by a *Wall Street Journal* interviewer, "What are the carrots?" he had replied in even more turgid prose than usual, "Some of those are yet to be clarified in the sense of what is the early period of an emerging dialogue," which presumably was intended to convey the idea that it was too early in an emerging dialogue with the Soviet leaders to identify the incentives, or at least to do so publicly. Ibid.

62. Ibid., p. 13.

63. Both documents remain classified, but their general line has been confirmed in unofficial interviews off the record. While completed in December 1982, NSDD-75 was not actually signed by the president until January 17, 1983. The existence of NSDD-75 was leaked to the press in early 1983; see Robert Toth, "Reagan Seeks to Sway Soviet Internal Policies," *Washington Post*, March 21, 1983, p. A3.

sionals in the Department of State.[64] Most of those who endorsed this version of containment had the aim not only of forestalling particular Soviet attempts to expand influence and control, but also of forcing the Soviet leaders to rethink their whole strategy—to make them face the consequences of their actions. Thus, for example, if the Soviet leaders found their actions in Afghanistan or their support for revolutions in Central America too costly in various respects, they would refrain from such advances in the future and perhaps withdraw from some present involvements.

In the summer of 1982, President Reagan authorized a major covert action program to support Solidarity underground and to destabilize the communist government in Poland.[65] Far less intrusive or extensive efforts were also directed at Czechoslovakia and Hungary, but in Poland a substantial and far-reaching effort was undertaken, in close coordination with the Vatican. It has now been confirmed that President Reagan and Pope John Paul II agreed at their meeting on June 7, 1982, to undertake clandestine collaboration in such an effort.[66] The CIA played a major role, directly and indirectly through the National Endowment for Democracy and the AFL-CIO. President Reagan and the pope, and their trusted emissaries (including former deputy CIA director Vernon Walters, and Cardinal Laghi, the Vatican representative in Washington), maintained an active role.[67] The United States and the Vatican shared intelligence and contacts, and the United States took Vatican advice on many

---

64. The Department of State encompasses professional foreign service officers, with varying views on particular issues, and political senior officials brought in by each administration. As evidenced by a considerable continuity and consistency in State Department views, reflected in the Haig and Shultz incumbencies, it is appropriate to speak of a State Department view in this case. In addition, the same officers often drafted speeches on Soviet policy made by Haig, Shultz, other senior State Department spokesmen, and at least initial drafts of some key policy statements by the president, thus contributing to a consistency and durability of such points as the call for "restraint and reciprocity." The contrast with divergent points of view in other speeches or spontaneous press conference statements by presidents, and sometimes by secretaries of state, reflects individual nuance—and sometimes much more.

65. CIA Director William Casey had already moved to prepare for such actions, including a confidential agency-to-agency agreement with the Israeli Mossad in April 1981 to finance stepped-up operations through its network in Eastern Europe, particularly in Poland. See Joseph E. Persico, *Casey: From the OSS to the CIA* (Viking, 1990), p. 236.

66. The most full account was by investigative reporter Carl Bernstein, "The Holy Alliance," *Time*, February 24, 1992, pp. 28–35. He was able to confirm and expand his main findings through on-the-record interviews with President Reagan, Judge William Clark, Alexander Haig, Richard Pipes, Edward Derwinski, Agostino Cardinal Casaroli, Pio Cardinal Laghi, and others.

67. By happenstance, most of the principal American officials involved were Roman Catholics—CIA Director William Casey, National Security Advisers Richard Allen and later William Clark, Secretary Haig, General Vernon Walters, and Congressman Edward Derwinski. Richard Pipes was born in Poland.

matters. While this covert action program did not bring down communist rule, it did keep Solidarity alive and prospering in Poland, and thus directly contributed to the need for the Polish government, and the Soviet leadership, to bring Solidarity back into the political process in 1989 when revolutionary change was possible under Gorbachev's new policy toward Eastern Europe and the world.[68]

Others in the Reagan administration, in the NSC staff, and the Pentagon, wanted to mount an even more direct challenge to the Soviet leaders on their own turf, so to speak. They wished to press political and economic competition into Eastern Europe and the Soviet Union itself even more vigorously, as well as containing Soviet expansionism; they wanted to "roll back" communism and not merely contain it. They also had little, or even negative, interest in negotiation; they believed the Soviet Union should be isolated, rather than brought into a network of interdependent ties with the West. And they were less interested in negotiating arms control, even negotiating from strength; they wished to put pressure on the Soviet Union through an intensified arms competition and retain and exercise American freedom to expand its military capabilities and options, with the aim of reasserting American primacy.[69]

Some of those who favored a hard-line stance toward the Soviet Union, and were eager to press economic, political, and ideological warfare against the USSR, were at the same time very cautious about even indirect use of American military power for containment. Secretary Caspar Weinberger, for example, and aides such as Undersecretary for Policy Fred Iklé and Navy Secretary John Lehman, Jr., were very cautious on any use or even deployment of U. S. military power in the Middle East and Caribbean in ways that Haig urged. (This attitude continued at least until after the successful invasion of Grenada in October 1983.) Some of the hard-line anti-Soviet specialists on the NSC staff (such as Richard Pipes and later John Lenczowski) also favored pressing ideological and economic warfare because of concern over Soviet military strength.

---

68. See chapters 9 and 13.

69. In addition to advocates of a confrontational line within the administration, even from 1981 there were criticisms from ardent supporters of Reagan on the right that his administration was not going far enough in pushing a hard line, a military buildup, and a political and ideological confrontation with the Soviet Union. These criticisms were heard from the neoconservatives around *Commentary* magazine, the Heritage Foundation, and the Committee on the Present Danger. See Norman Podhoretz, "The Future Danger," *Commentary*, vol. 71 (April 1981), pp. 29–47; Podhoretz, "The Neo-Conservative Anguish over Reagan's Foreign Policy," *New York Times Magazine*, May 2, 1982, pp. 30 ff; Walter Laqueur, "Reagan and the Russians," *Commentary*, vol. 73 (January 1982), pp. 19–26; and Committee on the Present Danger, *Is the Reagan Defense Program Adequate?* (Washington: Committee on the Present Danger, 1982).

    Most of these advocates of a more assertive American policy toward Eastern Europe and the Soviet Union, even within the administration, were not aware of the U.S. covert action program in Eastern Europe, in particular in Poland.

NSDD-75 was a compromise incorporating elements of both approaches. The main thrust of the directive, however, was pragmatic and geopolitical. It established three long-term objectives: to contain Soviet expansion and moderate Soviet international behavior; to encourage, by the limited means at the disposal of the United States, change in the Soviet system to greater liberalism over time; and to negotiate agreements that were in the interests of the United States. Thus it confirmed containment and circumscribed, although it did not eliminate, a confrontational approach. Although important qualifications were placed on the aim of encouraging change in the Soviet system, that aim remained. Negotiation was clearly affirmed, but decisions on whether, when, and what to negotiate remained to be resolved.

Some of the ambiguity in the president's directive reflected Reagan's ambivalence. He could usually be persuaded by someone like Haig or Shultz to take a geopolitical position, although his inner conviction and inclination were ideological.[70] Reagan was not disposed to take confrontational courses of action involving risks of a direct clash with the Soviet Union, nor were any of his principal advisers, but he held a confrontational attitude that often found rhetorical expression and that often competed with other considerations in the never-ending process of establishing concrete policy positions.

## Restoring American Military Strength

The new administration had moved promptly to request additional military outlays, wishing not only to begin augmenting military strength but also to underline the priority it would give to the task. Less than two weeks after entering office, Reagan approved an immediate increase of $32.6 billion in the defense budget over the $200.3 billion already requested by Jimmy Carter in his last week in office. That Carter request had represented a boost of $26.4 billion above the preceding year. So a massive increase was sought—and approved by Congress virtually intact. The most significant fact about the increase was that it had been decided on before obtaining requests from the military services—it was intended to signal the strong resolve of the new administration to build ("rebuild") military strength, and to cash in on the honeymoon with Congress to establish a high baseline for future percentage increases.[71] "Supply-side" military programming seemed the order of the day.

---

70. On the ideological impulse of Reagan and his administration, see Arthur Schlesinger, Jr., "Foreign Policy and the American Character," *Foreign Affairs*, vol. 62 (Fall 1983), pp. 1–16.

71. The most complete, and well-informed, account of this unusual decision on the size of the increase before even determining how it would be spent is in Nicholas Lemann, "Caspar Weinberger in Reagan's Pentagon: The Peacetime War," *Atlantic* (October 1984), pp. 71–73.

The first significant step was the exclusion from office in the administration and from significant influence of the most stridently alarmist wing of critics of the old order. Secretary of Defense Caspar Weinberger clashed with William Van Cleave, a hard-line professor from the University of Southern California and Nixon administration junior defense official who had headed the Reagan defense transition team. Van Cleave and a number of others seemed really to believe the idea of a dangerous "window of vulnerability" to Soviet attack, and they pressed for several expensive and disruptive quick-fix measures to shore up the strategic balance. They were not successful. Weinberger did, however, recruit some more subtle and durable hard-line associates, principally Undersecretary Iklé, Secretary of the Navy Lehman, and Assistant Secretary for International Security Policy Richard Perle, former long-time staff aide to Senator Henry M. Jackson of Washington and nemesis of détente. (Perle had been the driving force behind the Jackson-Vanik amendment, which undercut economic cooperation with the Soviet Union, and the Jackson amendment to the resolution approving SALT I that was later used to belabor SALT II.) All three were active members of the Committee on the Present Danger.[72]

As he took office, Weinberger said his mission was "to rearm America."[73] And Reagan indicated that he planned to increase the military budget share of federal spending from one-quarter to one-third of the total in three years.[74] Particular stress was placed on plans to expand the U.S. Navy.

Weinberger, in his first major statement on defense policy, in March 1981 cited "clear evidence of aggressive Soviet activity around the globe—including the training and support of terrorists; the use of military assistance and proxies, as in the case of El Salvador; the implicit threat of direct military intervention; and, in Afghanistan, actual invasion." He spoke of American "descent from a position of clear strategic superiority to the present perilous

---

David Stockman, the new director of the Office of Management and Budget (OMB), later related how he had agreed casually in January 1981 to base a planned 7 percent increase in the defense budget on the 1982 budget, without realizing at the time that that already incorporated the initial Reagan administration increases, and would involve a massive 10 percent increase over the last actual Carter budget, amounting in six years to a 160 percent increase, and a five-year defense budget totaling $1.46 trillion. David A. Stockman, *The Triumph of Politics: The Inside Story of the Reagan Revolution* (Avon, 1987), pp. 116–19.

Later research indicated that this massive increase, while unintended by Stockman, may have been deliberate on the part of William Schneider (the OMB official overseeing the defense account) and others. See Nicholas Lemann, "Calculator Error—or Calculated 'Error'?" *Washington Post*, July 10, 1986, p. A23.

72. Lemann, *Atlantic* (October 1984), pp. 74–76.

73. George C. Wilson, "Weinberger, in His First Message, Says Mission Is to 'Rearm America'" *Washington Post*, January 23, 1981, p. A3.

74. Richard Halloran, "Plan for Military Spending Is Major Shift for Peacetime," *New York Times*, February 19, 1981, p. B5.

situation." In support of the administration's massive planned increase in military programs, he argued that "it would be dangerously naive to expect the Soviet Union, if it once achieves clear military superiority, not to try to exploit their military capability even more fully than they are now doing." He supported this conclusion with the argument that "it is neither reasonable nor prudent to view the Soviet military buildup as defensive in nature," and "We must assume some rationale behind the Soviets' enormous allocation of resources to the military."[75] Apart from preventing Soviet attainment of strategic superiority, he also saw a requirement for what came to be called "horizontal" escalation: "We have to be prepared," he stated in another speech, "to launch counteroffensives in other regions and to exploit the aggressor's weaknesses wherever we might find them."[76]

Thus the defense policy of the Reagan administration, as well as its foreign policy, was geared to the assumption of a continuing Soviet strategy of geopolitical expansion by terrorist, proxy, and indirect or limited Soviet use of force. In several respects, however, defense policy pronouncements—and foreign policy pronouncements by Secretary of Defense Weinberger—were less well geared into national policy. Two weeks after the administration entered office, Weinberger had stated (without authorization) that the United States was going to proceed with deployment of the neutron warhead. The European allies were upset, and Haig was furious.[77] Then in April on a trip to Europe he alarmed many Europeans by gratuitous assaults on détente, a policy still held in Europe. In November there was an unseemly public dispute between Haig and Weinberger over whether NATO contingency plans included a possible demonstrative detonation of a nuclear weapon.[78] Apart from the fact neither was precisely correct, clearly public display of uncertainty over such a matter was unnerving.

President Reagan also contributed to European concerns when, in impromptu remarks in October, he seemed to envision a possible nuclear war limited to Europe.[79]

---

75. "Excerpts from Weinberger Statement on Military Budget Outlay," in *New York Times*, March 5, 1981, p. B11. Emphasis added.

76. Secretary Caspar W. Weinberger, "Requirements of Our Defense Policy," May 5, 1981, *State Bulletin*, vol. 81 (July 1981), p. 47.

77. See Haig, *Caveat*, pp. 86–87.
    In August, Reagan did decide to go ahead with production of neutron warheads, but holding them in the United States rather than deploying them in Europe. See Leslie H. Gelb, "Reagan Orders Production of 2 Types of Neutron Arms for Stockpiling in the U.S.," *New York Times*, August 9, 1981, pp. 1, 30.

78. Richard Halloran, "Haig Is Disputed by Weinberger on A-Blast Plan," *New York Times*, November 6, 1981, pp. A1, A13.

79. "Reagan Remark Stirs European Furor," *Washington Post*, October 21, 1981, p. A1; and Bernard Gwertzman, "Reagan Clarifies His Statements on Nuclear War," *New York Times*, October 22, 1981, pp. A1, A8.

On October 2, President Reagan unveiled his strategic military program.[80] He discarded the complex mobile MX intercontinental ballistic missile (ICBM) system devised under the Carter administration, and substituted deployment of a planned one hundred in existing silos (eventually cut back by Congress to fifty). He also resurrected the B-1 bomber and announced plans to build at least one hundred improved B-1B bombers. Some other elements of the plan, scarcely noted at the time, were also important, including a decision to deploy long-range nuclear-armed cruise missiles on attack submarines. But the controversial MX decision received most attention, and indeed continuing doubts and objections led the MX plan to be reconsidered and in flux for another eighteen months, and then to remain controversial for the years following.

In November 1981, the first defense policy guidances of the new administration were issued by the White House: NSDD-12 on command, control, communications, and intelligence (C³I), carrying forward on the basis of Presidential Directive (PD)–53 of the Carter administration; and NSDD-13 on nuclear weapon employment, basically reaffirming the doctrine set forth in PD-59 and PD-62 (and earlier in NSDM-242 of the Nixon administration). In March 1982, NSDD-26 on civil defense expanded on PD-41.[81]

The most important military policy directives of the Reagan administration were issued in the spring of 1982. Key among them was the annual "defense guidance" prepared in the Department of Defense and approved by the secretary. While an interim guidance had been prepared in 1981, the top secret, 136-page "Fiscal Year 1984-1988 Defense Guidance" approved in March 1982 represented the first considered strategic design of the Reagan administration. It also became the basis for a further presidential directive on strategy, NSDD-32, issued in mid-May.[82] Although constituting the most authoritative and highly secret strategic guidance, the substance of the 1984–88 Defense Guidance and in due course the entire document was promptly leaked. Moreover, the authenticity of the Defense Guidance and of direct quotations from it that appeared in the press was even confirmed. It is difficult to escape the conclusion that someone very senior in the Department of Defense wanted the thrust of the Defense Guidance to become generally known.[83] It provided a uniquely authoritative picture of the military policy of the Reagan administration.

---

80. "United States Strategic Weapons Program," October 2, 1981, *Presidential Documents*, vol. 17 (October 5, 1981), pp. 1074–75.

81. See Garthoff, *Détente and Confrontation*, chapter 22. NSDD-12, 13, and 26 remain highly classified.

82. This presidential strategic guidance (NSDD-32) remains highly classified and not officially acknowledged, but a public speech by William P. Clark on May 21, 1982, was based on it. See footnote 89.

83. The single most complete account appeared in Richard Halloran, "Pentagon Draws Up First Strategy for Fighting a Long Nuclear War," *New York Times*, May 30, 1982, pp. 1, 12.

The key change was to address requirements for waging protracted nuclear or conventional war with the Soviet Union, on the grounds that effective deterrence required effective war-fighting capabilities. Weinberger had stated a year earlier that he saw as "a primary mission of the Department [of Defense] to be prepared to wage war."[84] The new Defense Guidance spelled out the objective in general nuclear war: "Should deterrence fail and strategic nuclear war with the U.S.S.R. occur, the United States must prevail and be able to force the Soviet Union to seek earliest termination of hostilities on terms favorable to the United States."[85] It advocated "nuclear decapitation" of the Soviet political and military leadership and communication lines. In addition to forces "capable of supporting controlled nuclear counterattacks over a protracted period," the Defense Guidance stated that there was also a requirement for "a reserve of nuclear forces sufficient for trans- and post-attack protection *and coercion.*"[86]

Considerable attention was directed to the idea that the objective would be to prevail in case of war, an aim also stated in several authoritative public speeches. Weinberger said that it did not mean that the administration believed that a nuclear war could be "won," but he did not explain the difference between prevailing and winning.[87]

One of the new concepts (or old concepts given new attention) in the Defense Guidance and annual report statements was "horizontal escalation." As Weinberger put it, "We will not restrict ourselves to meeting aggression on its own immediate front . . . we must be prepared to launch counteroffensives in other regions and try to exploit the aggressor's weaknesses wherever they exist. If aggression by superior forces cannot be reversed where it occurs, we should not be confined to that particular arena."[88] The White House modified, but did not abandon, this approach. William Clark reaffirmed in 1982 that "the capability for counteroffensives on other fronts is an essential element of our strategy," although he went on to say that "it is not a substitute for adequate military capability to defend our vital interests in the area in which they are threatened."[89] Thus the objective became an added capability for stimulating

---

84. "Requirements of Our Defense Policy," May 5, 1981, *State Bulletin*, vol. 81 (July 1981), p. 47.

85. Quoted in George C. Wilson, "Preparing for Long Nuclear War Is Waste of Funds, Gen. Jones Says," *Washington Post*, June 19, 1982, p. A3. A slightly truncated version is also cited in Halloran, *New York Times*, May 30, 1982, p. 1.

86. Wilson, *Washington Post*, June 19, 1982, p. A3. Emphasis added.

87. Richard Halloran, "Weinberger Confirms New Strategy on Atom War," *New York Times*, June 4, 1982, p. A10.

88. Caspar W. Weinberger, "The Defense Policy of the Reagan Administration," address to the Council on Foreign Relations, New York, June 17, 1981, p. 5.

89. "Remarks of Judge William Clark, National Security Advisor to the President," Center for Strategic and International Studies, Georgetown University, May 21, 1982, transcript, Office of the Press Secretary, White House, p. 7.

new fronts to meet "aggression." While this was put in general terms in Weinberger's report to Congress in 1982, the Defense Guidance named specific potential targets for conventional riposte to a limited conventional attack: Cuba, Vietnam, and North Korea. How an American attack on North Korea would help in the case of, for example, a Soviet thrust into Iran was wholly inexplicable, not least because North Korea was scarcely an ally of the Soviet Union, as well as because a war in Korea would have severely taxed the United States, especially when it was involved in Iran. But most ominous was the Defense Guidance discussion not only of a political course of action to "develop more effective linkages with the people of East Europe so as to deny Soviet confidence in the reliability of its allies" but also to prepare military forces "to exploit political, economic and military weaknesses within the Warsaw Pact," although such special operations within Eastern Europe were mentioned explicitly only in the discussion of meeting Soviet aggression in Western Europe. But more broadly, and ambitiously, "United States conventional forces, in conjunction with those of our allies, should be capable of putting at risk Soviet interests, including the Soviet homeland."[90] This, it will be recalled, was the British and French strategy against Russia in mounting an offensive in the Crimea in 1854, best remembered for the ill-fated charge of the Light Brigade.

Less noted at the time, the Defense Guidance also covered several related, current, peacetime objectives. Most notably, it stated that the United States should develop weapons that were "difficult for the Soviets to counter, impose disproportionate costs, open up new areas of major military competition and obsolesce previous Soviet investment."[91] That represented a call to stimulate an arms race with emphasis on high technology in new areas of competition—such as space weaponry. Indeed, the Defense Guidance called for developing "space-based weapons systems." An antisatellite weapon was scheduled to achieve operational status by fiscal year 1987. The Defense Guidance also stated that no arms control agreements should be concluded that would prevent the United States from developing space-based weapons that would "add a new dimension to our military capabilities."[92]

A foreign policy application of the Defense Guidance of some importance was the statement that the trade policies of the West should put as much pressure as possible on a Soviet economy already heavily burdened with military spending.[93] This and other aspects of the Defense Department's strategy would become embroiled in continuing national policy disputes.

---

90. See Halloran, *New York Times*, May 30, 1982, p. 12.

91. Ibid, p. 12.

92. "U.S. Arms Plan Bared: Secret Nuclear Strategy Told," *Chicago Tribune*, January 17, 1983, p. 1.

93. Halloran, *New York Times*, May 30, 1982, p. 12.

Finally, one other military requirement identified in the Defense Guidance and given increasing attention over the next three years was the expansion and development of "special forces" for covert or counterinsurgency special operations. After an initial boost in 1981–82, another impetus was given after deepening involvement in Central America in 1983,[94] including Defense Department support to the CIA in its covert operations in Central America.[95] Also, in January 1983 the Rapid Deployment Joint Task Force established by President Carter was converted into the U.S. Central Command and given responsibility for the Southwest Asian-Persian Gulf area.

The defense buildup proceeded, but not without growing doubts as to its underlying strategic premises, economic sustainability, and military necessity.[96] The five-year program for 1982–86 totaled $1.5 trillion. In March 1983, President Reagan was sent a letter by six respected conservative former policymakers—five of them former secretaries of the treasury—arguing that the United States could not afford such heavy military spending: John B. Connally, William E. Simon, W. Michael Blumenthal, C. Douglas Dillon, Henry H. Fowler, and Peter G. Peterson.[97]

Apart from the MX missile (dubbed the Peacekeeper missile by the administration), few specific weapon systems were challenged. But widespread unease grew at the massive expenditures and uncertain results.

The saga of the MX was in some ways paradoxical. As one of the two major new weapons under development with greatest counterforce capability (the other being the Trident II or D-5 submarine-launched ballistic missile, SLBM), it might have been expected that the Reagan administration would embrace and expand the program of the Carter administration for deployment of 200 of these ICBMs, each carrying ten powerful and extremely accurate warheads. But objection to the Carter plans for a semimobile multiple protective shelter system, especially the local political opposition and hence objections of some of President Reagan's closest supporters in the states of Nevada and Utah

---

94. Richard Halloran, "Military Is Quietly Rebuilding Its Special Operations Forces," *New York Times*, July 19, 1982, pp. A1, A9; and Fred Hiatt, "U.S. Builds 3rd World Arms Role: Defense Planners Emphasize Use of 'Special Forces'" *Washington Post*, June 10, 1984, pp. A1, A19.

95. Jeff Gerth, "U.S. Military Creates Secret Units for Use in Sensitive Tasks Abroad," *New York Times*, June 8, 1984, pp. A1, A4.

96. For a good analysis, see Samuel P. Huntington, "The Defense Policy of the Reagan Administration, 1981-1982," in Fred I. Greenstein, ed., *The Reagan Presidency: An Early Assessment* (Johns Hopkins University Press, 1983), pp. 82–116.
   Even Haig later acknowledged that the surge in defense spending in 1981-83 had been "excessive." See James R. Dickenson, "Haig Hits Reagan Tax Cuts, Calls Defense Building 'Excessive'" *Washington Post*, October 20, 1987, p. A3.

97. Paul Taylor, "Former Cabinet Members Deplore 'Throwing Money at Defense,'" *Washington Post*, March 27, 1983, p. A3.

where deployment was planned, led to dropping that scheme. Several commissions and studies led to a series of proposals including one for new superhard silos in a "dense pack" deployment, an idea that died quickly. Finally, only in April 1983 did the last and most successful conservative bipartisan group, called the Scowcroft Commission after its chairman, retired Lieutenant General Brent Scowcroft, come up with a broad compromise solution. The most noteworthy aspect of the Scowcroft Commission's report was its refutation of the idea of a window of vulnerability. It also stressed the need to move in the future away from large ICBMs with multiple, independently targetable reentry vehicles (MIRVs)—but in a logical non sequitur nonetheless endorsed deploying one hundred MX missiles as an interim measure while developing a new small mobile ICBM (Midgetman).[98] Reagan endorsed the commission's findings and requested congressional support for deploying one hundred MX missiles.[99] The Scowcroft Commission was kept in being to monitor the strategic situation and to seek bipartisan support. It used this leverage, especially in a report in March 1984, to press the administration on arms control.[100]

Congressional opposition to deployment of the MX in any form, especially in potentially vulnerable silos, led to an extended political contest between Congress and the administration. The outcome of this long struggle over the MX was a compromise in May 1985 authorizing deployment of fifty missiles in Minuteman III silos.

The "threat" was reassessed in several other ways, not consistent in their findings and impact. Senior members of the Reagan administration in 1981 and early 1982 reiterated the theme that the strategic military power of the United States and the Soviet Union remained in rough equivalence or parity. The "relentless" Soviet buildup was frequently cited as threatening that balance but not as having upset it. As Secretary Haig put it in September 1981, "We have not lost the strategic balance that exists between the Soviet Union and ourselves. I like to think we still have a nodule of edge there. . . . What we have been dramatically pointing attention to is the fact that the trends . . . will become increasingly dangerous . . . if we don't take appropriate steps."[101]

Without realizing that he was saying anything new or controversial, President Reagan drastically revised the American assessment in an off-the-

98. See *Report of the President's Commission on Strategic Forces*, submitted to the president by chairman Brent Scowcroft, April 6, 1983, pp. 7–8, 15–18.

99. See "Transcript of Reagan Statement on Report of Strategic Forces Commission," *New York Times*, April 20, 1983, p. A22; "President's Commission on Strategic Forces," *Presidential Documents*, vol. 19 (April 25, 1983), pp. 563–66.

100. Letter from Chairman of the President's Commission on Strategic Forces Brent Scowcroft to the President, March 21, 1984, pp. 2–3, 9.

101. "Question and Answer Session, West Berlin," September 13, 1981, *State Bulletin*, vol. 81 (November 1981), p. 49. See also "Secretary Participates in Foreign Policy Conference," June 2, 1981, *State Bulletin*, vol. 81 (July 1981), p. 22.

cuff remark in March 1982. He stated, "The truth of the matter is that, on balance, the Soviet Union does have a definite margin of superiority." (He also said, "As you all know . . . [there is] a window of vulnerability," later directly refuted by the Scowcroft Commission.) Even such veteran hard-line critics of détente and alarmists on the military situation as Senator Henry M. Jackson, former secretary of defense James R. Schlesinger, and Zbigniew Brzezinski said they did not share Reagan's view, and even Weinberger had until then never claimed Soviet superiority.[102]

A much more significant reassessment occurred in 1983. The Central Intelligence Agency disclosed quietly in a routine congressional hearing in September 1983 that contrary to the claims of Secretary Haig and Secretary Weinberger (and the two preceding secretaries of defense) new and better intelligence had led to the conclusion that from 1976 through 1981 (later extended) Soviet defense outlays had fallen from the 4 to 5 percent a year real increases of the early 1970s to an average 2 percent increase, and that "procurement of military hardware [weapons]—the largest category of defense spending—was almost flat in 1976–81 . . . [and that trend] appears to have continued in both 1982 and 1983."[103] The "spending gap" stressed by the Reagan administration was deflated by its own intelligence estimates.[104] Yet the administration kept silent about the change and merely shifted to other arguments for its continuing military buildup.

Meanwhile, without direct correlation or measurable influence from these inconsistent indications of the relative military threat, American public opinion had undergone a significant shift. In the second half of the 1970s, public opinion polls showed a turning point in that a larger number of people believed the United States was spending too little on defense rather than too much. By the time of the 1980 election, public sentiment strongly supported an increase in American defense efforts. But from 1981 to 1982 a radical shift occurred. In 1981, more than half of those polled—51 percent—believed the

102. See Judith Miller, "Reagan's View on Lag in Arms Being Disputed," *New York Times*, April 2, 1982, pp. A1, A21; Hedrick Smith, "The Strategic Balance: An Adverse Impact among Allies Is Feared after Reagan Remark on Soviet Superiority," *New York Times*, April 2, 1982, pp. A1, A21; and Robert G. Kaiser, "Critics Dispute Reagan, Say Soviets Not Superior: 'Voodoo Arms Control' Assailed by Kennedy," *Washington Post*, April 2, 1982, pp. A1, A16.

103. Central Intelligence Agency, Office of Soviet Analysis, *USSR: Economic Trends and Policy Developments*, Joint Economic Committee Briefing Paper (September 14, 1983, pp. 8–11, 18). This briefing paper was presented by Robert Gates, the deputy director for intelligence, in open testimony before the Subcommittee on International Trade, Finance and Security Economics of the Joint Economic Committee, Congress, September 20, 1983. Gates told me that it had not been politically cleared with the White House.

104. See Raymond L. Garthoff, "The 'Spending Gap,'" *Bulletin of the Atomic Scientists*, vol. 40 (May 1984), pp. 5–6.

United States was spending too little on defense, 22 percent believed spending was about right, and only 15 percent believed too much was being spent. By 1982, in a sharp reversal, only 19 percent believed too little was being spent, 36 percent thought too much, and another 36 percent believed spending was about right.[105] In another poll in 1982, after President Reagan's remark, 41 percent believed the Soviet Union militarily superior to the United States, an equal 41 percent believed the two powers about equal, and only 7 percent believed the United States superior. By 1984 only 27 percent believed the Soviet Union superior, 57 percent believed the two about equal, and 10 percent believed the United States was ahead. The correlation of foreign policy judgments in such polls is not consistent. In 1984 two-thirds (67 percent) believed the Soviet Union had used détente to lull the United States and build up its military power, while at the same time a plurality of those same people believed détente in the Nixon-Kissinger period was better than the situation under Reagan (49 percent versus 37 percent who disagreed).[106]

Overall, the American public and Congress continued in 1981-82 to support some buildup in military strength, but increasingly in the years following they came to question both the premises for that policy and the results. Disclosures of wasteful Pentagon spending raised doubts about a policy defined most clearly by spending, rather than by the capabilities provided by that expenditure.

Ironically, the indexes of alleged declining strategic American capability so often cited in indictment of past administrations continued to decline: the number of strategic delivery vehicles, warheads, and megatonnage, as old B-52s and Titan and Polaris missiles were retired from the force. The new programs, including those set in train before the Reagan administration, were of course gradually bringing increased real capabilities.[107]

## Opening a Diplomatic Dialogue

Secretary Haig had not only moved quickly to establish his authority in Washington, he had also moved promptly to open a diplomatic dialogue with

105. Lawrence Kaagan, "Public Opinion and the Defence Effort: Trends and Lessons, The United States," *Defense and Consensus: The Domestic Aspects of Western Security*, Part I, Adelphi Paper 182 (London: International Institute for Strategic Studies, 1983), p. 15.

106. The Public Agenda Foundation in collaboration with the Center for Foreign Policy Development at Brown University, *Voter Options on Nuclear Arms Policy: A Briefing Book for the 1984 Elections* (New York: Public Agenda Foundation, 1984), pp. 20, 31.

107. For two useful analyses comparing the defense programs of the Reagan and Carter administrations, see Samuel F. Wells, Jr., "A Question of Priorities: A Comparison of the Carter and Reagan Defense Programs," *Orbis*, vol. 27 (Fall 1983), pp. 641–66; and John Allen Williams, "Defense Policy: The Carter-Reagan Record," *Washington Quarterly*, vol. 6 (Autumn 1983), pp. 77–92.

the Soviet leaders. In addition, he sought to establish American positions and take other actions designed to contribute indirectly to such a dialogue by impressing the Soviet leaders with American will and strength.

Haig's approach, and in general that of the administration, was however strongly influenced by a belief that the Soviet leaders would seek to test their mettle. Believing that the Soviet leaders had a strong expansionist inclination, and that earlier American administrations had often been tested and found wanting, they saw a need and an opportunity to impress the Soviet leaders with their toughness. This expectation had been buttressed by the idea that the Soviet leaders did indeed intend to "test" the new American administration.[108] This belief had not only further strengthened Haig's resolve to "win" in Central America but also to hang tough on the demand for Soviet restraint in the Third World as a precondition to developing any real diplomatic dialogue with the Soviets.

As Ambassador Anatoly F. Dobrynin arrived at the Department of State on January 29, 1981, for his first meeting with the new secretary of state, his car was stopped as it entered the basement of the department and required to drive to the main diplomatic entrance where "the flustered ambassador of the Soviet Union dismounted into a thicket of microphones and cameras," brusquely signaling the end to a decade of the privilege of the more private and discreet use of an inside entrance.[109]

Other gestures followed. On April Fools' Day, Academician Georgy A. Arbatov was denied a visa extension on grounds of reciprocity. The *Washington*

---

108. Caspar Weinberger in his memoir recalled a meeting of the Reagan cabinet-designees in Blair House in December 1980 in which he had the sense that "every one of us recognized the Soviets' tactic of testing a new President and the importance of their realizing that this new presidency would involve . . . a change in policy." See Weinberger, *Fighting for Peace*, p. 29.

109. Haig, *Caveat*, p. 101. As Haig explained it (pp. 101–02), the decision was made by Assistant Secretary George Vest, approving a proposal by the chief of the Soviet Affairs desk, Robert German, without having referred the question to Haig or even having informed him, and had been communicated to the Soviet Embassy. Just to be sure, Dobrynin's secretary had checked with Haig's office which, not knowing of the change, had said to park in the usual place. An officer from the Soviet desk who had been stationed at the entrance to the inside driveway barred the ambassador's car from entering there in conformity with the new instructions. (Information from Robert German and others.) While this explanation appears to be basically correct, I am told that no one from the Soviet desk alerted the press, so their ready presence remains unexplained.

Incidentally, the earlier practice had been intended not only as a courtesy to Dobrynin, but more importantly as a way of serving American interests in not having to account publicly for every visit of Dobrynin to the State Department.

Haig reverted to a practice of his mentor, Henry A. Kissinger, but not other secretaries of state, in making it a usual practice to meet alone with Dobrynin, without an American note-taker in attendance.

*Post* reported the next day that it had been told in explanation by a senior State Department official: "We're under pressure from the White House to flex our muscles every time we can" (at the Soviets).[110]

On May 12, American customs and FBI agents detained a departing Aeroflot airliner and seized its cargo on suspicion of violation of export control laws—only to find to their embarrassment that the cargo of electronic equipment had been legally and properly licensed. The Soviet Union denounced the action, saying with bitter hyperbole that "terrorism and banditry" had been raised to the level of official policy, while the White House countered with a disingenuous reply: "This has no connection with our foreign policy. It was not directed by the Department of State."[111]

American actions signaling the basis for the conduct of relations with the Soviet Union were, however, not consistent. Arguably the most important in intrinsic terms was a decision withdrawing an existing sanction. On April 24, President Reagan announced the end to the embargo on sales of grain and phosphates to the Soviet Union, the most economically effective and powerful of Carter's post-Afghanistan sanctions. This unilateral move conveyed the message that notwithstanding harsh rhetoric, and even geopolitical containment, the new administration was not prepared to accept the real sacrifice and domestic political discomfort of such a measure. The decision was not entirely unexpected; Reagan had not only denounced the measure when it was taken but in the electoral campaign had said he would reverse it. Haig, however, had fought (against strong opposition from some of the White House aides, especially Meese, and Secretary of Agriculture John Block) to delay the move. Haig saw the lifting of the embargo as a large "carrot" he hoped to yield (since for political reasons the president was determined to end it, and because U.S. allies were selling more grain) only in exchange for at least some Soviet commitment to restraint with respect to Poland, above all, or to support for revolutionary forces in the Third World. But Haig lost; the president would not wait for such diplomatic bargaining. When Haig called Dobrynin in to tell him, the Soviet ambassador inquired, "Are there any restrictions at all?" and Haig has recounted that he almost choked on having to indicate there were not, lamely stating only that "the decision *could* be affected by any surprise move on the part of your government." Even that was more than he was authorized to say.[112] Haig was so upset by this development that he compounded it by an unwise

---

110. Robert G. Kaiser, "Kremlin's Expert on U.S. Can't Prolong Visit Here," *Washington Post*, April 2, 1981, p. A2. See also Haig, *Caveat*, pp. 109–10.

111. Charles R. Babcock and Thomas O'Toole, "U.S. Seizure of Aeroflot Cargo Appears to Be Embarrassing Mistake," *Washington Post*, May 14, 1981, p. A18; and Robert Pear, "U.S. Seizes Devices in Soviet Jetliner's Cargo," *New York Times*, May 14, 1981, p. A9. Haig did not mention this event in his memoir.

112. Haig, *Caveat*, pp. 110–14. Emphasis added.

public statement. Fears of Soviet military intervention in Poland were mounting at that juncture, so Haig told the press the next day that if the Soviet Union invaded Poland, the administration would impose a total ban on all U.S. trade with the USSR, including an embargo on grain. Since the stated basis for Reagan's objections to the grain embargo had always been that it fell discriminately on American farmers, that objection would presumably become moot if the United States ever imposed a complete ban on exports to the Soviet Union. (In fact, since grain composed far and away the lion's share of American exports to the USSR, the real impact would still fall mostly on farmers.) While Haig felt that this position reflected an understanding he had with President Reagan on action in that contingency, clearly Reagan as well as his aides did not welcome having the American press filled with a message addressed to Moscow but also telling the American farmer and business executive that the ban might be reinstated even more broadly. The president's main purpose, after all, was to do something favorable for this important American constituency. So the press immediately reported White House "backgrounding" that Haig's statement did not represent the president's views and rumors of Haig's resignation.[113]

With the rather large exception of lifting the grain embargo, the main debate within the administration on economic relations with the Soviet Union was between the "pragmatists," especially Haig (and later Shultz), and the "ideological" cold warriors, such as Pipes and others in the NSC staff and Weinberger and Perle in the Defense Department. Haig and the pragmatists wanted to control trade but also to use it by linkage as a carrot to gain Soviet concessions such as restraint in the Third World. Pipes, Weinberger, and Perle wanted to wage economic warfare to strain the Soviet economy and polity.

In general, bilateral relations moved forward on a modest basis until December 1981 and the imposition of martial law in Poland. Grain sales talks in June led to an agreed Soviet purchase of 6 million tons by the end of September, followed by agreement in August on extension for one year of the existing agreement that would otherwise have expired at that time, pending negotiation of a new long-term agreement. A series of technical agreements from the 1970s due for renewal were also continued: agreements on scientific and technical cooperation in environmental protection, ocean studies, atomic energy, health, and artificial heart development. After the imposition of martial law in Poland, negotiations on a new, long-term grain agreement were suspended (although the existing one remained in force), new sanctions were placed on sales of gas and oil-processing equipment,[114] and the remaining technical agreements that came up for renewal up to mid-1982 (on space

---

113. Ibid., pp. 115–16.

114. The economic sanctions of 1982 and their repercussions in Europe are discussed in chapter 13.

cooperation, energy research, and the overall science and technology agreement) were allowed to lapse.

Bilateral relations, however, including arms control, were not at the center of official American interest. At their first meeting in January 1981, and subsequently, Dobrynin kept coming back to the question, how do the two governments "begin to develop a dialogue"? And above all, how could arms negotiations be resumed? Haig's reply was that "there could be no business as usual. The United States and the U.S.S.R. must, first of all, reach an understanding on standards of international conduct." In particular, "Moscow must control its client, Cuba, in this hemisphere. . . . The Administration," he said, "had to see some evidence of Soviet restraint. Then we could begin to think about dialogues on arms control, trade credits, technology transfer."[115]

As early as February 1981, Brezhnev indicated interest in a possible summit meeting, and Reagan and Haig had shown cool interest—hedging by indicating that Soviet restraint would be necessary first.[116] In March, Brezhnev initiated a correspondence with President Reagan. It was not answered for a month. When Reagan did write, it was in April on his own initiative while recuperating from the attempt on his life. When he told Haig he was thinking of writing a personal letter to Brezhnev (and in fact had already drafted one), Haig urged that the State Department draft it; the president took some drafting suggestions from the department, but rejected most. The letter is clearly Reagan's own and made a rather noble if naive plea for greater cooperation. He accompanied this personal letter, however, with a more formal official one, which among other things questioned "the USSR's unremitting and comprehensive military build up over the past fifteen years, a build up which in our view exceeds purely defensive requirements and carries disturbing implications of a search for military superiority." Needless to say, he received, in his own words, "an icy reply" from Brezhnev. Reagan comments in his memoir, "So much for my first attempt at personal diplomacy," and the correspondence lapsed, although owing to the official letter rather than to Reagan's personal diplomacy.[117]

---

115. Haig, *Caveat*, pp. 102–09.

116. See Bernard Gwertzman, "U.S. Shows Interest in Brezhnev's Plan," *New York Times*, February 24, 1981, p. A5; and Lee Lescaze, "Summit Interests Reagan," *Washington Post*, February 25, 1981, pp. 1, 3.

117. Reagan recited this in his memoir, which includes the cited excerpt from the still secret official letter, and the full text of his personal letter. See Reagan, *An American Life*, pp. 270–73.

  With respect to Haig's attempt to draft the letter, Reagan noted, "That was probably the first indication I had that it wasn't only other members of the cabinet and White House staff whom Al didn't want participating in foreign affairs. As I was to learn over the next year, he didn't even want me as the president to be involved in setting foreign policy—he regarded it as his turf. He didn't want to carry out the president's foreign policy; he wanted to formulate it and carry it out himself" (p. 270).

Dobrynin soon raised the prospect of a meeting of Haig and Gromyko in New York in September. "Can't we work out our differences?" he repeated. He stressed the importance of resuming the broken SALT dialogue (which Haig alluded to in his memoir only indirectly by saying that Dobrynin "suggested subjects for talks that were of interest to the U.S.S.R."). Haig's reply remained the same: "The key is illegal intervention. You must demonstrate goodwill if we are to discuss these matters [such as SALT]."[118]

Thus the diplomatic dialogue with the Soviet Union reflected the persistent stress in the public rhetoric of the new administration (especially Haig) on Soviet "restraint and reciprocity" in the Third World and toward Poland. Haig orchestrated the American side of the dialogue so that "every official of the State Department, in every exchange with a Soviet official, emphasized American determination that the U.S.S.R. and its clients—especially Fidel Castro and Qaddafi—must moderate their interventionist behavior, and that Poland must be spared."[119] "Our signal to the Soviets," Haig later stressed, "had to be a plain warning that their time of unresisted adventuring in the Third World was over, and that America's capacity to tolerate the mischief of Moscow's proxies, Cuba and Libya, had been exceeded."[120] He was determined that the Soviet leaders see the administration's determination and mettle and pass the "test" to which he believed the Soviets were subjecting it.

As Haig himself later characterized these statements of the position of the Reagan administration, "At this early stage there was nothing substantive to talk about, nothing to negotiate, until the U.S.S.R. began to demonstrate its willingness to behave like a responsible power. That was the basis of our early policy toward Moscow."[121]

The first high-level direct contact came in two Haig-Gromyko meetings in September 1981. These meetings too, however, were essentially a sparring exchange, reflected in the public release on the eve of the first meeting of a letter sent that day from President Reagan to President Brezhnev, pressing the Soviets again on Poland, Afghanistan, and Kampuchea (Cambodia), as well as on what was characterized as an "unremitting and comprehensive" Soviet military buildup. The president did express his desire for a "stable and constructive relationship" with the Soviet Union, built on "restraint and reciproc-

---

118. Haig, *Caveat*, p. 109. Other sources privy to the exchange have identified SALT as Dobrynin's chief interest.

     Incidentally, Dobrynin told Haig that the Soviets had taken Reagan's personal letter as a hopeful sign, but from Reagan's own later account it appears that he was never told that. Haig did not want to encourage a real Reagan-Brezhnev correspondence.

119. Ibid., p. 110.

120. Ibid., p. 96.

121. Ibid., p. 105.

ity."[122] Moreover, the United States had (under pressure from its European allies) made known its readiness in principle to begin negotiation on limiting intermediate-range theater nuclear forces. But in Haig's meetings with Foreign Minister Andrei A. Gromyko the still-born diplomatic dialogue did not advance perceptibly. That is hardly surprising, since in Haig's later words, "I said nothing to Gromyko in private that President Reagan and I had not said to the Russians in public."[123] The one concrete step was to inform Gromyko of U.S. readiness to open the talks on limiting intermediate-range nuclear forces (INF) before the end of the year.

Shortly before this meeting with Gromyko, Haig had commented, "I think the problem is not communication. The problem is that the Soviet leadership, thus far, has not liked what they have heard from this Administration." While professing interest in a dialogue, Haig added that it could only follow "some reining in, some restraint, if you will, of what has been 6 years of unacceptable Soviet international behavior."[124]

The United States had also not considered it necessary to send a new ambassador to Moscow for nine months; not until October 26, 1981, did Ambassador Arthur A. Hartman present his credentials. A respected professional, Hartman did not have Soviet affairs experience or command of the language, as had all earlier career foreign service officers sent to Moscow as chief of mission.

The United States was still biding its time while it hoped to impress the Soviet leaders with its determination and as it pressed forward with an American military buildup. A week after the first Haig-Gromyko meeting, the Department of Defense released a detailed slick-paper booklet called *Soviet Military Power* to persuade American and European publics of the extent of the relentlessly growing Soviet military threat.[125] A little over a week after that,

---

122. "President's Letter to President Brezhnev," Department Statement, September 22, 1981, *State Bulletin*, vol. 81 (November 1981), pp. 51–52.

123. See Haig, *Caveat*, pp. 229–34; quotation from p. 231.
    Haig had, however, prepared very carefully for the meeting. Indeed, to make an effective presentation, he conducted a rehearsal of the encounter, with an aide standing in for the Soviet foreign minister while Haig tried out his lines. Information from a close associate of Secretary Haig.

124. "Interview on 'Issues and Answers,'" ABC News, August 23, 1981, *State Bulletin*, vol. 81 (October 1981), p. 16.
    President Reagan and other key members of his administration seemed to regard "communication" with the Soviet Union as simply a matter of clearly and forcefully stating the U.S. position, with little or no consideration of the impact of such statements. This may have assuaged American doubts about whether we were being sufficiently forthright and forceful, but without calculation of effectively influencing Soviet views and actions it tended to be counterproductive to American interests. It seemed to make us "feel better" that we "called it as we saw it," but that was not effective diplomacy.

125. Department of Defense, *Soviet Military Power* (Washington, 1981), 99 pp. Revised and expanded editions were released in the spring of each year from 1983 through 1990.

the Department of State released a report on covert Soviet political and "disinformation" activities.[126]

Haig and other American officials throughout 1981 reiterated publicly and in private meetings with Dobrynin and others the serious negative effect on American-Soviet relations that would ensue if the Soviet Union intervened militarily in Poland. The problems in Poland must, it was stressed, be settled by the Poles. When Soviet direct intervention did not occur, but the Polish government itself instituted martial law, the American and Western position was thus somewhat disarmed. The United States did institute some economic sanctions, but again as in the case of Afghanistan, its European allies did not join in most of them.[127] American-Soviet bilateral relations generally were at such a low level of engagement that it did not prove possible to signal displeasure by any meaningful political action. There was nothing to cut back on.

In January 1982 Haig met again with Gromyko, although he curtailed it to only one brief session because of martial law in Poland. Then, in their third and last set of meetings in June, the only really new element was an angry query from Gromyko on the second day they met as to why Haig had not told him the day before of the pipeline sanctions announced overnight. Gromyko suggested Haig had either withheld the truth from him or did not speak for the U.S. government. The second alternative was no doubt mentioned as a rhetorical flourish, but Haig had to confess, "I'm afraid it is the latter." Less than a week later, Reagan requested Haig's resignation. And indeed the controversial pipeline sanctions decision evidently had been scheduled for an NSC meeting on June 18 when Haig, who was known to oppose it, would not be available.[128]

## Resetting Policy: "Strength and Dialogue"

Haig's departure stemmed from persisting psychological and bureaucratic disjunctions between the vicar and the White House and from policy clashes on European relations and Israeli-Arab relations—but not on the Soviet

---

While providing a great deal of factual data, the material was carefully selected to maximize the impression of Soviet military strength while downplaying relative American and Western strengths.

126. Department of State, *Forgery, Disinformation, and Political Operations*, Special Report 88, October 1981, reprinted in *State Bulletin*, vol. 81 (November 1981), pp. 52–55.

127. See chapter 13. The United States recognized that to suspend the recently convened INF arms control talks would be politically disadvantageous, so a potentially serious fissure in U.S.-Western European views on that score did not arise.

128. Haig, *Caveat*, pp. 312–13. William P. Clark was responsible for organizing the meeting for a time that Haig would not be present.

Union. The codification of an administration policy toward the Soviet Union after Haig's departure, and revisions in emphasis over time, did mark a substantial if gradual change. But initially, no change was evident or intended.[129]

The pattern of foreign ministerial meetings did not change with the change in the American incumbency. Secretary of State George P. Shultz met with Gromyko in late September and early October in New York. His aim was not to move toward agreements but to lay out American concerns. The list was basically the familiar one Haig had advanced at every meeting: Poland, Afghanistan, Kampuchea, Central America—but with a heavier emphasis on human rights. By virtue of being broadened beyond Haig's concentration on restraint in the Third World and Poland, it became even more a laundry list of American complaints, without real priorities (the first item was the continued detention of Jewish dissident Anatoly Shcharansky).[130]

In one important instance, however, the expression of American concern was made more concrete and was taken more seriously. In his meeting with Gromyko on September 28, Shultz made clear that the United States would not accept MiG fighter-bombers in Nicaragua.[131] The fact that this demand was made privately, and not subsequently leaked to the press, and that it represented a credible concern and a credible implied threat, led the Soviet leaders to take it seriously and to set aside plans that had been made to transfer such aircraft to Nicaragua through Cuba. The Soviet leaders took this action primarily out of prudence and respect for an American strategic interest in a neighboring area, and also because they believed it lent credibility to their warnings to the United States against escalating the types of weaponry made available to the insurgents in Afghanistan neighboring the USSR.[132]

Arms control negotiations resumed, without much enthusiasm in Washington, but at the urging of the State Department that at least the United States should go through the motions. Reagan acquiesced in new theater nuclear arms talks (now called intermediate-range nuclear forces [INF] talks) beginning in November 1981 in response to a rising peace movement in

---

129. For example, Shultz has noted that he approved Haig's action in cutting off Ambassador Dobrynin's automobile access to the State Department garage, permitting less conspicuous visits than use of the main entrance, which Shultz saw as a "remnant of détente." Shultz went a step further: upon learning that there was a direct phone line to the Soviet Embassy, he had it taken out because he "didn't see any use for it." George P. Shultz, *Turmoil and Triumph: My Years as Secretary of State* (Charles Scribner's Sons, 1993), p. 117.

130. See Ibid., pp. 122–23; and see Russell Watson and John Walcott, "What Reagan Should Do," *Newsweek*, November 22, 1982, p. 52.

131. See Shultz, *Turmoil and Triumph*, p. 121.

132. This tacit "reciprocity and restraint" in aiding and abetting opposition in respective spheres of influence was suggested privately by Soviet officials.

Europe. After growing public pressures in the United States itself, strategic arms talks (now renamed strategic arms reduction talks [START]) began in June 1982. While INF and START entered the diplomatic dialogue between Washington and Moscow, negotiations on specific issues were left to the delegations in Geneva. Neither separate, secret, back-channel SALT negotiations of the kind carried out by Kissinger from 1971 to 1976, nor an integrated second track of high-level negotiations as conducted by Cyrus Vance from 1977 through 1979, was instituted by the Reagan administration in its handling of INF and START.

A surprising offer by President Reagan on October 15, 1982, for the Soviet Union to buy up to 23 million tons of grain was widely recognized as an election ploy to please Midwestern voters on the eve of the midterm election. The Soviet leaders decided not to avail themselves of the offer.

As the first two years of the Reagan administration drew to a close, and coincidentally the death of Brezhnev ushered in a new leader and a reshuffled leadership in Moscow, the basis of American policy toward the Soviet Union remained rather unclear. Haig had sought to pursue a tough, pragmatic course stressing restraint on Soviet geopolitical conduct in the Third World as the main touchstone of American policy. The president, however, had overridden him and yielded to other considerations in treating the grain embargo (and later grain policy) neither as a stick nor as a carrot but as a derivative of American domestic politics. Similarly, the imposition of the Soviet gas pipeline sanctions (again over Haig's objection) against U.S. European allies' interests had represented a blow to efforts to build a stronger Western alliance consensus. And in his repeated ideological statements challenging Soviet legitimacy, Reagan had appeared to many (not only in the Soviet Union) to be calling for confrontation, rather than dialogue. Although arms control negotiations had resumed, the motivating element had transparently been European and American public opinion rather than any desire by the administration for negotiation or expectation of success. While there was "normal" diplomatic contact, as Haig later confirmed there was no real American interest in moving toward agreements; rather, the purpose in 1981 and 1982 was to hammer home to the Soviet leaders that negotiations would be possible only on the basis of Soviet "restraint and reciprocity" in the international arena—as defined in Washington. In the second half of 1982, after George Shultz had succeeded Alexander Haig, there was a somewhat smoother relationship between the White House and the State Department but no observable change in the conduct of U.S.-Soviet relations.

Brezhnev died on November 10, 1982. At the time of his death, long anticipated, there remained an unresolved debate in Washington on how the United States should respond to the contingency. Some in the administration had taken a hard line—the Soviet leadership would be weak, and the United

States should put pressure on it. Others believed the United States should encourage possibly more moderate tendencies in the leadership by affirming American desire to improve relations. Still others thought the best course was to stand back and see what happened in Moscow and leave it to the Soviets to demonstrate any readiness on their part for improvement in relations. The third course was chosen.[133]

Brezhnev's funeral in mid-November afforded Vice President Bush and Secretary Shultz an occasion to meet briefly the new Soviet leader, General Secretary Yury V. Andropov, but there was of course no opportunity for real discussion. Nor was there any real interest on the American side.[134]

A few days after Brezhnev's death, President Reagan said that the United States was waiting for "action, not just words" from the Soviet side to demonstrate an interest in improving relations. "For 10 years détente was based on words from them and not any deeds to back those words up . . . it takes two to tango."[135] In a speech a few days later lifting the pipeline sanctions and announcing (with considerable overstatement) a Western consensus on constraints on East-West trade, Reagan again stressed the need for building up American military strength, as well as for avoiding Western assistance to Soviet economic strength. While noting that the United States had "embarked upon a buildup of our defense forces" and that had "enabled us to propose the most comprehensive set of proposals for arms reduction and control in more than a quarter of a century" (another considerable exaggeration), he also stressed that "we still have a long way to go." Thus, "the process of restoring a proper balance in relations with the Soviet Union is not ended. It will take time to make up for the losses incurred in past years." As for the new leadership in the Soviet Union, "If they act in a responsible fashion, they will meet a ready and positive response in the West."[136] Shultz echoed this a few days later, saying that while he and Vice President Bush had been received with courtesy in Moscow at the

---

133. Information from interviews with administration officials.

134. Shultz in his memoir account made clear his own interest in sizing up Andropov, the long-time chief of the KGB, whom he saw as a "formidable adversary." Shultz commented that when George Bush, who had headed the CIA from November 1975 to January 1977, "joked about the fact that each had headed his country's intelligence service, I didn't find it humorous. I was uneasy about this new Soviet leader." See Shultz, *Turmoil and Triumph*, pp. 126–27.

    Soon after, on December 6 back in Washington, Ambassador Dobrynin asked to see Secretary Shultz and proposed launching a U.S.-Soviet dialogue "potentially at all levels." Shultz did not indicate that he was in a position to respond. Ibid., p. 127.

135. "The President's News Conference of November 11, 1982," *Presidential Documents*, vol. 18 (November 15, 1982), p. 1459.

136. "East-West Trade Relations and the Soviet Pipeline Sanctions," President Reagan's radio address to the nation, November 13, 1982, *Presidential Documents*, vol. 18 (November 22, 1982), pp. 1475–76.

funeral, and that might be construed by some as a favorable "signal," "the things that we are really looking for, after all the signaling has taken place, is the substance of change in [Soviet] behavior on important matters."[137] The United States was calling for Soviet deeds, not merely words, and it was testing the mettle of the Soviet leaders.

137. Secretary Shultz, "News Conference of November 18 [1982]," *State Bulletin*, vol. 83 (January 1983), p. 54.

# 2 The Response of the Brezhnev Regime, 1981–82

SOVIET POLICY in the world was always much more reactive and responsive than has generally been recognized in the West. During the 1970s the USSR did also show initiative in building détente with the United States and in pursuing efforts to expand its influence and presence in the Third World. In the first half of the 1980s, however, for several reasons, Soviet policy became even more reactive. One reason was the nature of changes in American policy and in the world. The American abandonment of détente left the Soviet Union little choice in its relations with the United States but to respond to a new American challenge, one perceived not only to include an intensified arms race and geopolitical containment but also to go beyond that into confrontation and a crusade directed at the very legitimacy and existence of the Soviet system and communist rule. At the same time, not only were there no new attractive opportunities in the Third World, but the Soviet Union was overextended in involvements in Africa and Asia, particularly by its commitment in Afghanistan, and economically in Cuba and Vietnam. Of at least equal importance, the Soviet Union throughout the first half of the decade was beset by internal challenges to the stability of the Soviet bloc by developments in Poland, persisting economic problems at home, and finally by the unsettled state of the Soviet leadership itself. The Soviet leader, President and General Secretary of the Communist Party of the Soviet Union Leonid I. Brezhnev, had been seriously ailing ever since the mid-1970s, and by 1981–82 at age 75 was barely able to function as even the nominal head of a small group of aging leaders. This situation had a very negative effect on policy, dampening any possibility for policy initiative or even effective reaction. In these declining years of Brezhnev's rule, continuing under the succeeding transitional leaderships headed by Yury V. Andropov and Konstantin U. Chernenko, and throughout the final years of a new reformational leadership under Mikhail S. Gorbachev, Soviet attention was absorbed by the internal political situation.

Reactive tendencies were intensified in 1980 as the détente of the 1970s with the United States collapsed. While a policy of waiting to see what might occur as a result of the American election may have seemed appropriate in Moscow in 1980 (as well as being the course of least resistance), the outcome of that election seemed to call for a new response. As fate would have it, the occasion for a new authoritative reaffirmation or change in the general line of Soviet policy came just at that juncture.

## The Twenty-sixth Party Congress

One of the products of the successful effort in the Brezhnev years to replace the uncertainties and arbitrary decisions that had become characteristic of First Secretary Nikita S. Khrushchev's style of politics was the regularization of meetings at five-year intervals of congresses of the Communist Party of the Soviet Union. Such regularization of this nominally fundamental party conclave was intended to ensure a sense of participation by wide circles of the party membership, to impart a feeling of steady and controlled forward movement of the party, and to provide a predictable and regular basis for timely reviews of the policy line and of the composition of the party leadership. Thus the twenty-sixth congress was expected to meet in the spring of 1981, and it would have required a weighty political decision to alter that schedule. The leaders did not select its timing because they were ready for new departures in policy.

The Twenty-sixth Party Congress opened on February 23 and concluded on March 3. The report of the Central Committee to the congress on domestic and foreign policy, presented by General Secretary Brezhnev on the first day, was the centerpiece and authoritative statement of the policy line. Brezhnev had intended the congress to represent a triumphant climax to his incumbency and to the central foreign policy line he had instituted: détente with the West, based on acknowledged parity of superpower status with the United States.

Even at the preceding congress in early 1976, reservations about détente—in particular, in relations with the United States—had been voiced by Brezhnev and others. Now, with the détente of the 1970s in collapse, Brezhnev's task was one of salvage and uncertain reassurance about the future. The Soviet leaders indeed faced a serious policy dilemma, one that was only partly reflected in their dilemma over public articulation of policy. The premises underlying the Soviet policy of détente and peaceful coexistence with the West while pursuing a competitive policy in the Third World needed review. While Brezhnev and his colleagues, having a supposedly "scientific" basis for policy, could never publicly admit to error and no doubt found it difficult to do so even among themselves, the course of events was not what they had expected. Moreover, not only were the premises of their policy line of the past ten years on détente now open to question, so too were they faced with difficult practical questions of how to deal with the current situation and the future.

The changed posture and policy of the leaders of the United States was only one of the unforeseen developments of the period since the early 1970s, but it was a central one and moreover one that readily permitted, even invited, the Soviet leaders to place the blame on the American leaders. As further events, and the unfolding of American policy, in the early 1980s confirmed the renunciation of a policy of détente by the United States, the Soviet leaders reluctantly accepted the need to recast their expectations for the future (and retroactively their own estimates in the past). In the early months of 1981, however, they had not yet reached the conclusion that détente with the United States was really dead. Notwithstanding some jolting early statements by President Ronald Reagan and members of his administration, the Soviet leaders continued to look for signs that the new administration would seek a modus vivendi. Some academicians and journalists privately expressed the hope, even the expectation, that Reagan would prove to be "another Nixon," a conservative "hard-line" Republican politician but one who would define American policy in pragmatic terms regardless of rhetorical anticommunism.[1] They expected stiffer terms on the strategic arms limitation talks (SALT), and perhaps more hard positions and tough bargaining on some other issues. Nonetheless, as one Soviet official put it, "Reagan may be more conservative and tough, but [in contrast to Carter] at least we'll know where we stand with him."[2] Consistency and pragmatism were expected, in contrast to Carter's ideological moralizing and shifts between détente and containment lines of policy. Indeed, wishful Soviet commentaries after the election even interpreted Reagan's victory as a repudiation by the voters of Carter's anti-Soviet, militarist, and anti-détente policies.[3]

Immediately following the American election, the new prime minister and Politburo member Nikolai A. Tikhonov, delivering the annual speech on the anniversary of the Bolshevik Revolution, expressed the leadership's "hope that the new administration in the White House will demonstrate a constructive approach toward relations between our two countries."[4] Brezhnev, a few days later, went on to state that "any constructive steps by the United States admin-

---

1.  I heard the hope that Reagan would become another Nixon and *revive* détente expressed by several leading Soviet academic figures and journalists in Moscow in October 1980, on the eve of the election. Other Western observers had similar experiences. Some Soviet analysts of American policy told me that they had learned to discount campaign rhetoric such as that employed by Reagan; they also saw Carter and his Democratic administration as having, after earlier vacillations, moved into an outright anti-détente and military containment strategy following Afghanistan.

2.  In a Moscow interview in October 1980.

3.  See T. Kolesnichenko, "USA: Results of the Elections," *Pravda*, November 6, 1980.

4.  Nikolai A. Tikhonov, "In Accordance with Lenin's Behests, Along the Path of October," *Pravda*, November 7, 1980.

istration in the sphere of Soviet-American relations and pressing world problems will meet with a positive response on our part."[5]

At the time of the Twenty-sixth Party Congress, the Reagan administration had been in office barely a month. Brezhnev noted first the deterioration in relations under the Carter administration. "Unfortunately, the previous administration in Washington placed its bets not on the development of relations and mutual understanding. Attempting to put pressure on us, they set about to destroy all that is positive, that with no little effort had been created in Soviet-American relations over the previous years. As a result, our bilateral relations in a number of respects were set back."[6] As examples, he noted the "freezing of the entry into force of the SALT II Treaty" and the American breaking off of several other arms control talks such as limitations on conventional arms transfers to third countries. The Soviet leaders reportedly had also planned a reiteration of Brezhnev's statement of January 28, offering a positive response to indication of constructive steps by the United States.[7] Instead, in response to such statements as Reagan's press conference comment on the alleged readiness of Soviet leaders to lie and cheat, and the charges of Soviet support for international terrorism by Secretary of State Alexander M. Haig, Jr., Brezhnev's report to the congress declared, "Unfortunately, since the change of leadership in the White House, openly belligerent statements and cries are still being heard from Washington seemingly deliberately calculated to poison the atmosphere of relations between our countries. All the same, we would like to hope that those who determine American policy today will in the final analysis be able to look at things more realistically."[8] There was quite a difference between the confident hope of the leadership statement on November 7 and the almost desperate hope against all available evidence in the statement of February 23.

Notwithstanding this early reaction to the initial statements of the Reagan administration, the Soviet leaders recognized, as Brezhnev put it at the congress, that "the international situation depends to a substantial extent on the policies of the Soviet Union and the United States," and (as he did not need or wish to make explicit) that Soviet policy toward the United States could not

---

5.   "Speech of L. I. Brezhnev," *Pravda*, November 18, 1980.

6.   "Report of the Central Committee of the CPSU to the Twenty-sixth Congress of the Communist Party of the Soviet Union and the Current Tasks of the Party in the Fields of Domestic and Foreign Policy," Report of General Secretary of the CC CPSU Comrade L. I. Brezhnev, *XXVI s"yezd Kommunisticheskoi partii Sovetskogo Soyuza, 28 fevralya-3 marta 1981 goda: stenograficheskii otchet* (The 26th Congress of the Communist Party of the Soviet Union, February 28–March 3, 1981: Stenographic Report) (Moscow: Politizdat, 1981), vol. 1, pp. 39–40.

7.   Information from a Central Committee member involved in the preparation of the report for the congress.

8.   Brezhnev, *XXVI s"yezd*, vol. 1, p. 40.

help but be substantially affected by U.S. policy toward the Soviet Union. He therefore went on to say, "The state of relations between us at the present time and the acute character of international problems requiring solution in our opinion dictate the need for a dialogue on all levels, and what is more an active dialogue. We are ready for dialogue. Experience shows that the decisive link is meetings at the highest level. This was true yesterday and it remains true today. The USSR wants normal relations with the United States."[9] This call for a summit meeting marked the Soviet leaders' first initiative to improve relations.

Before continuing a review of the development of Soviet thinking and policy toward the United States in 1981, it is necessary to look at a more general change in foreign policy as reflected at the Twenty-sixth Party Congress. It is useful to compare changes in the general approach taken in the previous three party congresses: in 1971 on the eve of détente, in 1976 in a period marking the onset of difficulties for détente, and in 1981 in the aftermath of its collapse.

The very structure of the discussion of foreign policy questions in the three reports is instructive. In 1976 and 1981 a section that had not been present in 1971 was devoted to relations with the capitalist countries. In 1981 it was reduced from third to fourth place in priority compared with 1976 and subtly reduced in other ways (the 1976 listing had referred to "development of relations," while in 1981 the more static term "relations" was used). In 1976 a separate section was devoted to "development of external economic ties" in the discussion of Soviet economic affairs, and this was dropped in 1981, with only brief discussion of that subject in the section on relations with the capitalist states. At the same time, while the relative prominence of developing ties with capitalist countries and special attention to economic ties were cut back from 1976 to 1981, the need for détente and arms control was highlighted in 1981. The most significant comparison, however, remained the sharp change from 1971 to both of the later congresses. In 1971 the report contained a section on "imperialism—enemy of the peoples and of social progress." There had also been reference to "repulsing the imperialist policy of aggression," a heading absent in 1976 but revived in modified form in 1981 as "opposition to the forces of aggression."[10]

---

9.    Ibid., p. 41. The published record shows applause followed the statement on a summit meeting.

10.   For the section headings dealing with external relations, see *XXIV s"yezd*, vol. 1, pp. 28, 38, 46; *XXV s"yezd*, vol. 1, pp. 28, 34, 39, 49, 51, 80; and *XXVI s"yezd*, vol. 1, pp. 22, 28, 33, 37, 43.
        There were also some changes on other aspects of Soviet foreign policy. Relations with the other socialist (communist) allies of the Soviet Union were always given highest priority in listing. References to the liberation struggle (in 1971) and to the world communist movement (specifically only in 1981), and to liberation movements and the world revolutionary process (the latter only in 1976) reflect the changing world scene and shifting Soviet interests. Similarly, in 1971 there had been no section on the liberated countries of the Third World, added and given high relative standing both in

The 1981 Central Committee report noted that "in the international sphere, the period under review [since 1976] was a complex, tempestuous time." The period was characterized as marked by an "intense struggle of two trends in world politics," one toward peace, détente, arms limitation, and the freedom of peoples; the other "undermining détente, boosting the arms race, a policy of threats and interference in other people's affairs." While reaffirming Soviet support for détente, peace, and arms limitation, the United States was held to be following a course of "undermining détente" and pursuing an arms race.[11] The geopolitical competition between the two powers in the Third World was depicted in ideological terms of supporting or opposing national liberation and progress.

Thus the international policy of the Communist Party of the Soviet Union was reaffirmed to be "a struggle to strengthen peace and deepen international détente," but in a context where this no longer represented a collaborative policy with the United States but one of competition and possible confrontation—owing, in the Soviet view, to the fact that "recently, those [in the United States] who oppose détente, arms limitation and improving relations with the Soviet Union and other countries of socialism have noticeably increased their activities." Indeed, these activities were seen to include not only an unprecedented military buildup but also "military doctrines dangerous to the cause of peace," including a doctrine of limited nuclear war. Nuclear parity, a "military-strategic balance," was said to prevail between the Soviet Union and the United States, and between the Warsaw Pact and NATO alliances, which "objectively serves the maintenance of world peace." Brezhnev reiterated that the Soviet Union had "not striven for and is not striving for military superiority. . . . But neither will we permit such a superiority to be established over us. Such attempts, as well as trying to talk to us from a position of strength, are absolutely futile." (At that point, the stenographic record noted "prolonged applause.") Brezhnev again stated that "to attempt to defeat each other in an arms race and to count on victory in a nuclear war is dangerous madness. (Applause.)"[12]

---

1976 and 1981. The 1981 report also noted that "the liquidation of colonial empires was virtually completed in the seventies." *XXVI s"yezd*, vol. 1, p. 21.

11. Ibid., pp. 20–21.

12. Ibid., pp. 21, 38, 40. The inclusion of the irrationality of any attempt to defeat the other side in an arms race, a new theme introduced to counter Reagan's comments on gaining from a competitive arms race, was thus tied to the irrationality of counting on victory in a nuclear war, a more fundamental question addressed earlier by Brezhnev and other Soviet leaders.

A senior Soviet official, the late Nikolai Inozemtsev, later said that the deliberations concerning the Twenty-sixth Party Congress led to a firmer decision by the Soviet leadership that indeed there could be no victors in a nuclear war, with important implications for Soviet military doctrine and for foreign policy and arms control policy.

While the party congress made the Soviet *position* clear, no clear *policy* for dealing with the challenge of an American administration that no longer supported détente was enunciated. One principal reason was that the policy of the Reagan administration was not yet clear. Was its rejection of détente rhetorical? What were the aims of the new administration toward the Soviet Union? That the element of competition would be high was clear, but it was not evident whether the new administration in Washington sought containment, confrontation, or even "hard-headed détente" without that name. Accordingly, the Soviet leaders settled down, uneasily, to probing to determine the answer.

At the extreme, there were evidently those at least in the Soviet intelligence establishment who took a dire view of American intentions, not excluding an early American military attack on one of the Soviet Union's allies (in particular, Cuba), or even on the Soviet Union itself. The basis for Soviet concern, even though in fact exaggerated, about a possible American attack on Cuba is clear. There was a real foundation for Soviet concern over U.S. covert political action in Eastern Europe, as we have seen, but not for apprehension about military action. Above all, the idea that the new American administration might actually attack the Soviet Union seems too far out of touch with reality to have been given credence. Nonetheless, a senior KGB officer then reporting to Great Britain (who defected and was spirited out of Moscow to England in mid-1985), Oleg Gordievsky, has stated that in May 1981 the KGB station in London, and presumably those in Washington, New York, and Western European capitals, declared an extraordinary alert for any indications of imminent American attack. Gordievsky provided important, accurate information on several other subjects and showed high reliability, so his report cannot be simply dismissed. Gordievsky, who by the time of his defection in mid-1985 had been named chief of the KGB station in London, stated that this special alert continued until late 1984. An intelligence alert is not the same thing as a military alert, and the Soviet Union did not alert its military forces at any time. Nonetheless, such an alert for possible indications of preparations for military action is extremely rare and therefore significant. The reason for invoking this alert by the KGB and GRU (military intelligence)—by decision of the Politburo—was not known to Gordievsky, and KGB officers in the field considered it extreme and unnecessary. Nonetheless, though still not explained, it implied a serious alarm in some quarters in Moscow about possible extreme American actions.[13]

---

13. The alert seems implausible, but given the unusually high credibility and direct knowledge of the source and documentary evidence Gordievsky supplied, it must be considered to have occurred. See the investigative reporting based on official American and British intelligence and other officials: Murrey Marder, "Defector Told of Soviet Alert: KGB Station Reportedly Warned U.S. Would Attack," *Washington Post*, August 8, 1986, pp. A1, A22; and Leslie H. Gelb, "K.G.B. Defector Helped the CIA Brief Reagan

The Soviet Union may have taken some measures to increase military readiness, although not a military force alert. There are indications that a decision may have been taken in 1981 to constitute, on a standby basis, plans for rapid emergency conversion to a wartime command arrangement with a Supreme High Command (VGK) and centralized command staff (Stavka), measures sought by Marshal Nikolai Ogarkov, the senior professional military man and chief of the General Staff.

These cautionary intelligence and military measures did not, however, reflect the debate over American policy and Soviet policy toward the United States that took place in the Moscow political establishment during these years.

There was some alarm on the margin, but an influential margin, of the Soviet political establishment. Ambassador Dobrynin, in an off-the-record comment in April 1982, said those years were the most dangerous time in his twenty years as ambassador in Washington, above all because there was no

---

before Summit Talks," *New York Times*, August 9, 1986, pp. 1, 4. I have confirmed the reported statements with Americans who personally participated in debriefing Gordievsky. Gordievsky also provided extensive detail on the actions taken by the London KGB station in accordance with the alert, including extensive (and ultimately unproductive) monitoring of the limousine movements of high British government leaders, U.S.-U.K. meetings, and even such things as the Greater London Council's blood donation drive—a possible indicator of medical stockpiling for anticipated war casualties.

In evaluating Gordievsky's credibility, it should be borne in mind that Gordievsky provided the information permitting the British to expel the entire London KGB Station—thirty-one diplomats and journalists. He also provided valuable information on Soviet policies, and by virtue of having handled arrangements for Gorbachev's visit to London in December 1984, an unusual vantage point for assessing the new Soviet leader. His reporting, passed in part to the Central Intelligence Agency by the British even before his defection, was found to be of sufficient interest that one report was among the very few informational reports on Soviet affairs passed to President Reagan by his National Security Council staff in 1982. In 1985 after his defection, on Prime Minister Thatcher's recommendation, Gordievsky's reports were made available to the United States, and CIA Director William Casey went to London to meet with him in October 1985, before the Geneva summit. Later, in February 1986, Gordievsky was flown to Washington to be debriefed by a select group of senior American intelligence and policy officials.

Gordievsky's report on the 1981–84 intelligence alert was not, however, made available to the United States until after he defected in 1985. Apparently the British regarded the report as implausible at a time that they had not disclosed the identity of their secret source to American intelligence, and the implications of it might have been taken by American officials as an indirect slap at the Reagan administration's confrontational style and policy.

See also Christopher Andrew and Oleg Gordievsky, *KGB: The Inside Story* (Harper Collins, 1990), pp. 583–605, for additional details on the alert. Gordievsky also supplied the texts of a number of instructions from KGB headquarters in 1983–84 on implementing the alert; for full translations see Christopher Andrew and Oleg Gordievsky, eds., *Instructions from the Centre: Top Secret Files on KGB Foreign Operations 1975-1985* (London: Hodder and Stoughton, 1991), pp. 67–90.

longer any trust between the two powers. The Soviet intelligence community not only took a dire view of American intentions but also reported more intense American military confrontational actions. For example, the Defense Ministry's journal specializing in foreign developments noted that "the activity of all forms of U.S. intelligence operations were activated particularly with the arrival of the new administration in the White House in January 1981."[14]

The American military buildup was a particular cause of concern. Marshal Nikolai Ogarkov and other military leaders were most emphatic, and while they no doubt cited a Western military threat as justification for their own calls for greater Soviet military efforts, they were almost certainly also disposed to believe their own propaganda—not unlike their Western counterparts such as Secretary Weinberger. Moreover, some of the civilian leaders who opposed a greater Soviet military buildup expressed their concern over the American programs. Politburo member Konstantin Chernenko, for example, in early 1982 said that the NATO arms buildup was "exceeding all reasonable limits" and was accompanied by nuclear war plans including first use of nuclear weapons and (allegedly) preemptive strikes. "This all," he concluded, "means that the process of militarization in the West has entered a new, much more dangerous phase."[15] Similarly, Andropov, responsible for the extraordinary intelligence alert, in mid-1982 publicly warned that "the administration in Washington is attempting to push the whole development of international relations on to a dangerous path . . . worsening the whole situation and intensifying the danger of war."[16] Some senior Soviet diplomats, who privately acknowledged that they did not share this extreme an assessment, commented that nonetheless some officials in Moscow indeed saw the United States as preparing for war.

Soviet official and academic advisers and commentators displayed both uncertainty and differences in their assessments of the new American administration and the prospects for Soviet-American relations. There was, of course, no divergence of view over the ideological assumption that the nature of the capitalist system inclined the imperialist powers, above all the United States, to a hostile and aggressive posture vis-à-vis the Soviet Union.[17] But while such

---

14. Col. A. Tsvetkov, "The United States—Placing Its Stake on Strengthening Espionage," *Zarubezhnoye voyennoye obozreniye* (Foreign Military Review), no. 8 (August 1981), p. 4.

15. "Meeting on International Solidarity, Speech of Comrade K. U. Chernenko," *Pravda*, February 7, 1982.

16. "Leninism—An Inexhaustible Source of Revolutionary Energy and Creativity of the Masses, Speech by Comrade Yu. V. Andropov on the Festive Meeting in Moscow Dedicated to the 112th Anniversary of the Birth of V. I. Lenin," April 22, 1982, *Pravda*, April 23, 1982.

17. For a clear statement of the ideological "analysis" and case for intensifying American aggressiveness see N. Kapchenko, "The General Crisis of Capitalism and the Growing Aggressiveness of Imperialism," *International Affairs*, no. 3 (March 1982), pp. 66–69.

ideological postulates were still not directly challenged, policy analysis had moved a long way toward more sophisticated understanding (not always correct but at least not precluding more sound analysis). There was a strong tendency for the policy analytic community in Moscow to take an optimistic view, especially at the beginning of a new American administration. Preelection rhetoric was discounted as a guide to a new administration's actual course of policy (and as a negative example, "that same old bankrupt Carter" was characterized as having come into office as a supporter of détente and disarmament, only to become "the instigator of a new cold war and another spiral in the arms race").[18] Before the inauguration, but after the new cabinet had been selected, an official in the Central Committee's International Information Department commented that the cabinet selections were "people of basically moderate views," and while he thought the new administration would take a "tough" stance, there were indications that it would see improvement of relations with the Soviet as a "foremost priority."[19] Particularly after Alexander Haig and Caspar Weinberger testified in nomination hearings, however, Soviet analysts criticized the nominees' stress on a military buildup and charged that they sought strategic superiority over the Soviet Union in order to place the Soviet Union in a disadvantageous position in strategic arms negotiations.[20]

Even several months after the Reagan administration had entered office, some prominent Soviet commentators continued to argue, in the words of Georgy Arbatov, that "few people would venture to draw a conclusion regarding the future policy of the new U.S. administration on the basis of the first statements of the president and secretary of state." He noted the traditional American allowance of the first hundred days to each new administration to set its course and added, "More cautious people have been speaking of six months or even a year. And skeptics have cited an even longer term." Arbatov's argument was not that the anti-Soviet attitudes of the leading figures of the Reagan administration reflected in their initial statements were unclear—"If they lacked anything, then it was political tact and courtesy rather than clarity." The reason Arbatov believed it was too early to evaluate the policy course of the new administration was "above all because their statements have still by no means bridged the gap between these politicians' long-known opinions and the present-day realities and specific conditions in our world, in which the United

---

18. V. Sisnev, "International Review: Change of Captain or Change of Course?" *Trud* (Labor), January 20, 1981.

19. Vitaly Kobysh and Aleksandr Bovin, "A Literary Gazette Dialogue: The Troubled World of the Eighties," *Literaturnaya gazeta* (Literary Gazette), January 1, 1981.

20. Oleg Anichkin, on "The International Situation: Questions and Answers," Radio Moscow Domestic Service, January 23, 1981, in Foreign Broadcast Information Service: *Daily Report, Soviet Union*, January 27, 1981, p. CC4. (Hereafter FBIS, *Soviet Union*.) See also A. Ptashnikov and A. Sokolov, "International Diary," Radio Moscow Domestic Service, January 12, 1981, in FBIS, *Soviet Union*, January 13, 1981, p. A2.

States will have to live and function." Arbatov argued that the reaffirmation of
the policy of détente by the Soviet Union at the party congress now faced the
American government with "the need to make a choice." He also stressed that
the leadership had not "let itself be provoked by certain statements by some
American leaders," as some believed ("some with regret, some with hope")
would be the case. "Others had probably fallen victim to their own propaganda,
coming to believe indeed that the Soviet Union had altered its course, had
retreated from détente and embarked on the path of 'expansion' and a race for
'military superiority'." He noted that the Soviet reaffirmation of a program for
deepening détente should not have been a surprise and in particular that
General Secretary Brezhnev had restated the Soviet position immediately after
the American election both publicly and privately (through Senator Charles
Percy, who had visited Moscow in late November, and was the new Republican
chairman of the Senate Foreign Relations Committee).[21]

The theme of Soviet restraint in the face of the early statements (such
as Reagan's allegation that the Soviet leaders sought a "world revolution" and
"reserve unto themselves the right to commit any crime, to lie, to cheat," and
other statements by Haig, Weinberger, and UN Ambassador Jeane J. Kirkpatrick cited in chapter 1) was also cited by others. Vitaly Kobysh referred to these
statements by "eminent representatives of the new Washington administration" as having "a bellicose, if not hysterical, note" and said, "We have been
accused of sins of which we are in no way guilty." Nonetheless, "We have not
succumbed to the provocation," and the Central Committee report adopted "a
firm, confident, but at the same time calm and moderate tone," which "we
believe has been [properly] interpreted as a sign not of weakness but of a sense
of responsibility in a matter too serious to let it be dominated not by reason and
a clear-cut line but by rhetoric and semantics." Kobysh concluded with a
remarkably frank statement, and plea to the United States: "The CPSU and the
Soviet Government really do believe that a dangerous situation has been created in the world and that the threat is too close to seek one-sided advantages
for oneself under these conditions, not to mention settling accounts with
anyone or fishing in troubled waters. If all this is understood correctly, if they
[the U.S. leaders] come halfway to meet us, an opportunity will be created for

---

21.  G. Arbatov, "A Difficult Choice," *Pravda*, March 9, 1981.
     Arbatov also noted that Brezhnev had "solemnly announced our loyalty to the
peace program formulated at the 24th and 25th CPSU Congresses" a year earlier—at
the Central Committee plenum in June 1980 after the Carter post-Afghanistan sanctions and virtual abandonment of détente. Arbatov, director of the Institute of the USA
and Canada, was promoted to full membership on the Central Committee at the
Twenty-sixth Party Congress (along with Nikolai N. Inozemtsev, head of the Institute of
the World Economy and International Relations). Arbatov personally played a part in
establishing the foreign policy line for the twenty-sixth congress, according to a knowledgeable Central Committee official who told me that at the time, shortly before the
congress convened.

resolving the gravest problems which seem insoluble today. In any event, we have had our say. It is now up to the other side to reply."[22]

Another Soviet commentator, a strong advocate of détente, Aleksandr Bovin, remarked that while the Twenty-fourth Party Congress (1971) presented "a program for the emergence of détente," and the Twenty-fifth Congress (1976) for "deepening and developing détente," the task after the Twenty-sixth Congress (1981) was "a program for saving détente."[23] Within a few weeks, however, Bovin had reached very pessimistic conclusions about the new American administration. By the end of March, he concluded that "the essential outlines of the new foreign policy course . . . have now become sufficiently visible. It is a harsh, conservative, power policy, it is a policy whose cornerstone comprises extremely primitive anticommunist concepts. . . . Anything [in the world] they do not like, anything that is contrary to the interests of imperialism, they say is all the result of the insidious actions of the Soviet Union. . . . A simple conclusion is drawn, the time for playing at détente is over, it is necessary to rearm immediately, it is necessary to strive for military strategic superiority over the Soviet Union, and on this basis impose the will of America the Great on the whole world."[24]

But Arbatov and some others continued to argue that while the intentions of the Reagan administration were clearly hostile, its ability to carry out policy was not clear. He argued that the Reagan administration included elements ranging from the extreme right to moderates and that "it is still impossible to say who will gain the upper hand. But U.S. history teaches that nearly every U.S. Government, whether it originated on the right or on the left, moves toward the center in the course of time." And "You cannot judge a U.S. Government on the first few months in office."[25] On May 4 Arbatov, after visiting the United States, in another major article in *Pravda* assessing the administration's first one hundred days, still argued for withholding a final judgment on the Reagan administration. He alluded to divergencies in judgment, saying that "some may hope" that American policy has not yet been formulated while "others may think differently" and concluded that the ques-

22. V. Kobysh, "Observer's Opinion: There Is No More Important Task," *Literaturnaya gazeta*, March 4, 1981.

23. "International Observers' Roundtable," Radio Moscow Domestic Service, March 1, 1981, in FBIS, *Soviet Union*, March 2, 1981, p. CC1.

24. A. Bovin, "International Panorama," Radio Moscow Domestic Service, March 29, 1981, in FBIS, *Soviet Union*, April 9, 1981, p. A2. Bovin repeated this same pessimistic evaluation on April 12 in another Radio Moscow broadcast and in three articles in *Izvestiya*, on April 10, 15, and 18.

25. Georgy Arbatov, interview with Paul Brill, in "Détente Is Not Dead," *De Volkskrant* (Amsterdam), March 16, 1981. Arbatov was perhaps more frank in this foreign interview; it surely did not serve Soviet propaganda purposes of painting the Reagan administration in dark colors.

tion "should be left open" for the time being. He noted, correctly, that President Reagan was giving priority to economic policy and observed "astonishingly few new actions or proposals" in foreign affairs. He questioned whether rhetoric could be regarded as policy, although he conceded that the declared aims of seeking military superiority and the "desire to switch relations with the USSR and the other socialist countries to the path of confrontation and a struggle for power" were indicators of the political views and *intentions* of the Reagan administration. "But," he continued to argue, "another fact remains no less a reality—the fact that intentions and desires alone are not enough to constitute a policy. Politics remains the art of the possible. And the possibilities, the realities of the modern world certainly do not leave a great deal of room for the imperial ambitions which the people in Washington today are pursuing with new force." Nonetheless, he concluded with a warning that "the continuation of the existing situation would itself pose grave dangers, particularly attempts to transform bombastic propaganda slogans into practical policy premises."[26]

This assessment was quite different from that of Bovin, for example, who not only had argued that the Reagan policy was clear but also that the new administration was beginning to "break up" the "fairly well developed structure of mutual relations which was formulated in dozens of different agreements" during the 1970s.[27] Both Arbatov and Bovin had been stalwart supporters of détente, and earlier both men had cautioned against the optimism of those who welcomed Reagan's election victory and hoped he would prove to be a new Nixon. The difference was that Bovin saw no opportunities for the Soviet Union to influence the new Reagan policy course, which he believed would be seriously pursued, while Arbatov saw more room for the Soviet Union in its own policy moves to take advantage of objective realities and to influence American policy and mitigate its undoubted anti-Soviet thrust and broader hegemonical aspirations.

The divergence among public assessments of Soviet commentators with access to policymakers reflected a similar uncertainty and variation in official Soviet thinking and policy approach.[28] All agreed that the key question

---

26. G. Arbatov, "The United States: One Hundred Days," *Pravda*, May 4, 1981. Among others expressing the Arbatov line on withholding judgment on the Reagan administration was Oleg Anichkin, an official of the International Information Department of the Central Committee. See Oleg Anichkin, "International Situation—Questions and Answers," Radio Moscow Domestic Service, March 27, 1981, in FBIS, *Soviet Union*, March 30, 1981, pp. CC9–10.

27. Bovin, FBIS, *Soviet Union*, April 9, 1981, p. A2.

28. For a particularly useful general analysis, see Franklyn Griffiths, "The Sources of American Conduct: Soviet Perspectives and Their Policy Implications," *International Security*, vol. 9 (Fall 1984), pp. 3–50.

was: "Will détente be continued or will it give way to confrontation, to antagonism fraught with conflict—that is the crucial question."[29]

The Soviet leaders had no alternative or "fall-back" to their advocacy of
détente. They kept hoping that the American leaders would eventually recognize that there was no viable alternative to peaceful coexistence and no advantage from confrontation. Hence they continued to wait for signs of a belated
recognition of this fact of life by the Reagan administration too. Soviet statements continued to repeat Brezhnev's call for dialogue made at the 1981 party
congress.[30] As noted earlier, Ambassador Anatoly F. Dobrynin, starting at his
first meetings with Secretary Haig, stressed the need for "dialogue."[31] This was
also the theme of Brezhnev's confidential letters to Reagan in March and May,
which reiterated the proposal for a summit meeting first advanced publicly at
the party congress.[32]

What did the Soviet leaders hope to accomplish through a dialogue?
Their agenda was clear, and it was headed by "military détente" and arms
limitation.[33] The Soviet leaders had expected the Reagan administration to seek
amendments to the SALT II Treaty. When, instead, it decided simply to reject
the treaty and did not move to resume strategic arms talks, the Soviets were
frustrated. Similarly, they proposed a mutual moratorium on intermediate-
range missile deployments in Europe and awaited at least a Western proposal
on arms limitation of intermediate-range nuclear forces (INF)—which did not
come until an intentionally nonnegotiable "zero option" proposal was made in
November 1981.[34] But the Soviet leaders did seek to respond to the American
agenda. Haig's stress on "restraint and reciprocity" in a code of international
behavior, though from the Soviet standpoint badly skewed and blindly one-
sided, at least identified an area for dialogue.

---

29. This statement of the issue is quoted from Vladlen Kuznetsov, "The Voice of Reason,"
    *New Times*, no. 11 (March 1981), p. 8.

30. For one important example, see I. Aleksandrov, "On the Policy of the New U.S.
    Administration," *Pravda*, March 25, 1981. "I. Aleksandrov" was a pseudonym often used
    by the leadership for authoritative but unofficial public statements.

31. See chapter 1.

32. The Soviet letter of mid-March has never been published. Following American publi-
    cation of a summary of Reagan's letter of April 24, the Soviets released and published
    the text of Brezhnev's reply letter of May 25; see "For the Sake of the Right to Life,"
    TASS, *Pravda*, November 22, 1981 (also published, after earlier release by the Soviet
    Embassy in Washington, in the *New York Times*, November 21, 1981, p. 25). The title
    of the article in *Pravda* was drawn from Brezhnev's counter to the American stress on
    human rights—the argument that the most basic human right was the right to life that
    was imperiled by the heightened risk of war from the arms race and increasing tension.

33. Again, see Aleksandrov, *Pravda*, March 25, 1981.

34. See chapter 12.

Most initial Soviet commentaries on the subject of working out a new international "code of conduct" were negative. The Soviet view on the eve of the change in U.S. administrations (and one optimistically stating the hope that "improvement of Soviet-American relations would give new impetus to the process of détente") was expressed by a leading Soviet diplomat-scholar, Vladimir Petrovsky, who stated, "There is no need to search for some kind of new rules of conduct, a so-called code of détente. . . . We already have such a code of détente." Petrovsky was referring to the Helsinki Final Act and other documents such as the Basic Principles agreement of 1972 with the United States. His objection to post-Afghanistan suggestions for such a code of conduct (citing codifications antedating the Reagan administration) was not only that they were not needed but that the authors of such proposals wanted to impose a double standard justifying American intervention while preventing Soviet activities around the world.[35]

This same objection clearly was seen to apply to the early comments by Haig on a code of conduct. Leonid Zamyatin, chief of the International Information Department of the Central Committee, on March 28 commented bitterly in response to what were taken as demands of the new administration for the Soviet Union to improve its international conduct as a precondition to a diplomatic dialogue: "If we speak of rules of behavior—which are being discussed in conversations in the United States—then the standards of behavior for each state, including the United States, are the UN statutes and the international agreements signed by the states," and "in many cases the United States does not now meet either of them."[36] A few days earlier, the Aleksandrov article in *Pravda* had also concluded that Washington was flagrantly violating "norms of international law" and had asked rhetorically, "Can interstate relations be built in such a fashion, will they not turn into a jungle?" But this was said as a criticism of American behavior, not as an argument that new norms were needed or possible.[37]

Most authoritatively, in the annual address on the anniversary of Lenin's birth, April 22, Politburo member Konstantin U. Chernenko declared that while "the Soviet Union firmly supports respect for generally accepted international norms. . . . We reject a 'code of conduct' that would throw mankind back into an age long past when the dictate of the imperialists . . . held undivided sway in international relations."[38]

---

35. V. F. Petrovsky, "The Struggle of the USSR for Détente in the 1970s," *Novaya i noveishaya istoriya* (Modern and Contemporary History), no. 1 (January–February 1981), pp. 6, 17–18, 20. This issue was signed to press on January 6, 1981.

36. Leonid Zamyatin, "Studio 9," Moscow Television, March 28, 1981, in FBIS, *Soviet Union*, April 8, 1981, p. CC5.

37. Aleksandrov, *Pravda*, March 25, 1981.

38. K. U. Chernenko, "Checking with Lenin, Acting in a Leninist Way," *Pravda*, April 23, 1981.

Some commentators, however, were more open to the possibility, and even the possible value and need, of working out clarified "rules of the game" with the United States. On the same day that Chernenko delivered his authoritative speech, Aleksandr Bovin in an interview in the Japanese press said that Moscow and Washington "may have to work out something like rules" for competition in the Third World and "devise means" to ease tension between them.[39] And on May 3, Bovin acknowledged that "some sort of code of conduct is indeed essential," and while the Soviet Union would not agree to give up assistance to national liberation movements and progressive states, "there must indeed be some rules" to prevent the world from becoming an "arena for clashes."[40]

By the time of Bovin's latter comment, a change had occurred in the official Soviet position. Only five days after Chernenko's speech, Brezhnev had directly addressed the question of a code of conduct in the Third World. He rejected establishment of spheres of influence or "any sort of 'rules' that would perpetuate imperialist brigandage." He reaffirmed Soviet support for "strict and complete observance of the principle of equality and generally recognized norms of international law in relations among all states," as contained in the UN Charter, the Helsinki Final Act, and the "well-known agreements in the 1970s between the USSR and the U. S."[41] What was new was a statement of five rules for U.S. and Soviet relations with the countries of the Third World: recognition of the right of each nation to make its decisions without outside interference; respect for territorial integrity; recognition of the right of each state "to equal participation in international affairs and to the development of relations with any country in the world"; complete and unconditional recognition of each state's sovereignty over its natural resources; and respect for nonaligned status where that is chosen. "This is the 'code of conduct' that we recognize and are always prepared to observe," and Brezhnev urged the United States to do the same.[42] He did not, however, propose the negotiation of a formal understanding.

Brezhnev's code of conduct was not strictly speaking a proposal, and its handling—even the occasion chosen—suggested a propaganda riposte rather than a diplomatic overture to the United States. It did not become a source of renewed Soviet-American dialogue. Although stated in neutral terms, it was intended to justify Soviet support for national liberation movements and devel-

---

39. "Interview with *Izvestiya* Editorial Committee Member Aleksandr Bovin," *Mainichi Shimbun* (Daily Newspaper), Tokyo, April 22, 1981.

40. A. Bovin, in "International Observers Roundtable," Radio Moscow Domestic Service, May 3, 1981, in FBIS, *Soviet Union*, May 4, 1981, pp. CC5–CC6.

41. "Speech of Comrade L. I. Brezhnev," *Pravda*, April 28, 1981. The occasion of this speech was a dinner in honor of Qadhafi.

42. *Pravda*, April 28, 1981.

opment of Soviet ties with newly independent countries without justifying American interference with those developments. It was an articulation and reaffirmation of the Soviet view of the code of conduct appropriate under détente, a challenge to the Reagan administration's attacks on Soviet behavior, and a counterattack against American actions in the Third World.

The principal Soviet commentaries made quite explicit these applications of the Soviet "code." The *Izvestiya* political commentator charged that the American proposed code of conduct was a front to cover American interference in Nicaragua, El Salvador, Namibia, and South Africa, and such proposals "run counter to the principles of the Soviet Union's foreign policy and are therefore absolutely unacceptable to it." Moreover, the Soviet proposed code drew on "the UN Charter, the Helsinki Final Act, and the USSR-U.S. agreements of the 1970s, which are now being flouted by the U.S. authorities because they prevent them from implementing a policy of hegemonism."[43] The *Pravda* political observer made similar points but drove home even harder the charges against American behavior and the U.S. effort to influence Soviet policy. He claimed, "Washington is attempting to fix the tag 'international terrorism' on any manifestation of the struggle for national liberation and social progress, and is trying to portray all world events and processes that are not to its liking as the result of 'Moscow's subversive activity.' That is not all. This spurious scheme is being used for the purpose of substantiating and consolidating a sharp turn in American policy—a shift away from détente toward confrontation. Since, it is said, the Soviet Union is to blame for all misfortunes, then until it agrees to behave differently and until it starts observing some 'rules of conduct' in relations with the young states of Africa, Asia and Latin America ('rules' drawn up, of course, to suit imperialist tastes), there can be no question either of peaceful coexistence or of talks on problems of curbing the arms race." He attacked this "resort once more to so-called 'linkage,' that is, to the setting of deliberately unacceptable preconditions." He also asked, "But what if the other side resorted to this logic? Imagine if the USSR were to say: Before talks can be initiated on the settlement of any urgent international problems, let the Western powers alter that element of their policy which definitely does not please the Soviet Union. . . . For instance, let the United States first withdraw its troops from a particular country, withdraw from particular military bases abroad. And let it cut off its support for particularly dictatorial terrorist regimes. Scarcely anyone would take this approach to negotiations seriously. Such attempts to disregard reality merely reveal their initiators as saboteurs of international cooperation and instigators of tension."[44]

---

43. V. Kudryavtsev, "Voice of Reason and Justice," *Izvestiya*, April 30, 1981.

44. Vsevolod Ovchinnikov, "For Equal Rights, against Arbitrariness," *Pravda*, May 5, 1981.
     Some members of the leadership were especially sensitive to the question of "linkage." Brezhnev had reacted strongly in remarks on April 7 ("Speech by Comrade L. I. Brezhnev," *Pravda*, April 8, 1981), and candidate Politburo member Boris N.

Notwithstanding this strong propaganda counterblast to the American propaganda campaign on Soviet Third World intervention, the Soviet leaders did not foreclose the possibility of working on the problem of devising "rules of the game" in the Third World through quiet diplomacy dealing with problem areas. But the main Soviet interest continued to be in "military détente"—controlling the arms competition and the risks of nuclear war. When Gromyko and Haig first met, in two sessions in September 1981, the Soviets proposed working out a new set of principles governing security relations, including reaffirmation of the principle of parity, equality, and equal security, and a pledge by each side not to seek military advantage over the other. While the practical effect of such a commitment might be questioned, the proposal was evidently a serious one. It was not made public.[45] It was not, however, picked up by the United States.

The Soviet leaders watched with mounting concern the American efforts to increase military spending and the avoidance of arms limitation negotiations. For their part, the Soviets kept up a steady barrage of propaganda on the subject of arms limitations. Their highest priority was on attempting to stop preparations for deployment of American intermediate-range nuclear missiles in Europe. The growth of public opposition in Western Europe, abetted and fed by the Soviet Union but by no means originated or controlled by it, did lead the United States and NATO to decide by May 1981 to open talks before the end of the year and to continue arms limitation talks on intermediate-range nuclear forces (INF) begun in November. The issue of INF deployment and the negotiations on INF continued to occupy a central place in Soviet attention until the deployment began and the talks ended in November 1983. But while the INF negotiation was a major undertaking, it was throughout an adversarial proceeding, and its only impact on relations in general was negative.[46] Similarly, although the United States agreed to resume strategic arms

---

Ponomarev, head of the International Department of the Central Committee, bitterly attacked the notion that the Soviet Union should be asked to "pay" for détente by giving up solidarity with the liberation movement in the Third World. B. Ponomarev, "On the International Significance of the XXVI Congress of the CPSU," *Kommunist* (Communist), no. 5 (March 1981), p. 14.

For a useful discussion, see Thomas N. Bjorkman and Thomas J. Zamostny, "Soviet Politics and Strategy toward the West: Three Cases," *World Politics*, vol. 36 (January 1984), pp. 210–13.

45. The general thrust of the proposal became known through a State Department off-the-record briefing after the Haig-Gromyko meetings. See Bernard Gwertzman, "Offer by Gromyko to Haig Reported," *New York Times*, October 1, 1981, p. A5. The approach has been confirmed to me by other knowledgeable State Department sources. Even after this public reference, the Soviet press remained silent on the initiative.

46. When the INF talks began, the Soviet side approached them with caution, waiting for the United States to take the lead, as it had done in SALT through the late 1960s and 1970s. But the United States proposed an extremely one-sided proposal, with a guarded

talks by mid-1982, at least from the Soviet perspective the United States never seriously pursued the negotiations with the aim of reaching agreement. These negotiations continued until the Soviets withdrew in November 1983.

The Soviet Union did undertake several unilateral initiatives in "military détente." In March 1982, Brezhnev announced a unilateral moratorium on further deployment of SS-20 missiles in Europe, although it had little impact in the West.[47] On June 15, in connection with the second UN General Assembly special session on disarmament, Brezhnev announced a unilateral Soviet pledge not to be the first to use nuclear weapons.[48] While this further stimulated Western reconsideration of the nuclear first-use issue, it too did not have broad political effect. And it did not lead to an East-West dialogue but to an exchange of propaganda charges between the two sides.

Soviet efforts to resume a real dialogue on security and arms control, in short, failed. In chapter 1, the development of bilateral relations in 1981–82 was reviewed from the standpoint of the evolution of American policy toward the Soviet Union. Soviet policy was effectively limited to reacting to American policy. The sudden replacement of Secretary Haig in June 1982 raised new questions in Soviet minds. One senior Soviet official, who had been optimistic that the slowly improving diplomatic dialogue would lead to a summit meeting later that year, reportedly said to a colleague that Haig's firing meant plans for a Brezhnev-Reagan summit were off.[49] Many Soviet officials had come to believe that despite Haig's hard line on terrorism and Central America, and in general on Third World involvements, he in fact represented the most prag-

---

position of its own, and the negotiations went nowhere. Gromyko reportedly wanted to take a more forthcoming stance in the INF negotiations in 1981–82, but Brezhnev and the Politburo consensus chose instead to support an alternative course advocated by Boris Ponomarev, party secretary and head of the Central Committee's International Department. Ponomarev believed political actions in Western Europe could build up pressures in the key NATO countries to stop the planned INF deployments by NATO, without major Soviet concessions in the INF negotiations. Vigorous Soviet propaganda efforts, open and covert, were launched, but the political action campaign failed completely by the end of 1983 when the deployments got under way.

There can be little question that such a Soviet decision was made. My source for the report of competing proposed courses by Gromyko and Ponomarev was a senior Central Committee official involved in the campaign.

47.  One reason that the Soviet SS-20 moratorium had little effect was that it came only after the Soviet Union had deployed so many SS-20s that it appeared to represent no real quid pro quo for a Western moratorium. The second reason (as discussed in chapter 1) was that the United States, during the following months, charged that the Soviet Union was failing to abide by its own moratorium. This charge, although widely accepted in the West, was based on ambiguities exploited by the United States rather than on Soviet noncompliance. This American action caused Soviet frustration and resentment.

48.  L. Brezhnev, "The Second Special Session of the UN General Assembly," *Pravda*, June 16, 1982. See further discussion in chapter 12.

49.  As told to me by a knowledgeable Soviet source present when the remark was made.

matic potential successor to Nixon and Kissinger in the Reagan administration. As earlier seen, this viewpoint was not entirely off the mark. Haig's removal, however, was not related to policy toward the Soviet Union, and his successor, George P. Shultz, picked up more effectively, in his low-key fashion, attempts to establish a basis for improving relations. This was not, however, immediately clear to Soviet observers who noted not only the imposition of stringent pipeline sanctions in retaliation for Polish martial law (which Haig had opposed, appreciating its adverse impact on the Western alliance) but also President Reagan's call for a crusade against communism (coincidentally occurring in the same month Haig was dismissed).

Probably only coincidentally with Haig's departure, by June 1982 President Reagan and his closest advisers had decided not to pursue a summit meeting. Reagan's very harsh attacks on the Soviet Union in his speech to the UN on June 17 signaled the change. Diplomatic exchanges gradually developing throughout 1981 and the first half of 1982, which by June Gromyko believed were heading toward a summit meeting in October, suddenly cooled, reflecting the changed American view. The Soviet belief that "the summit was off," although not owing to Haig's departure, was correct.

Soviet relations with the rest of the world were not governed by the impasse in relations with the United States and its turn to containment and, at least intermittently, toward confrontation. The serious situation in Poland in 1981–82 presented a special problem, but one that the Polish leader General Wojciech Jaruzelski eventually got under control without requiring Soviet direct intervention. Elsewhere, the Soviet Union reacted very cautiously and quietly to the Israeli invasion and occupation of southern Lebanon and clashes with Syrian forces there. In Central America, American charges notwithstanding, the Soviet role was minor and again cautious. Indeed, beginning with 1980, there were no Soviet initiatives to help its friends in the Third World. One Afghanistan was more than enough. And Cuba and Vietnam were more than enough of a drain on economic resources. Nicaragua was urged to be prudent and to repair its relations with the United States. Cuba, vaguely threatened by the United States, was given substantial arms to help deter an American attack and to reassure the Cubans, but it was not given assurances of more than moral support from the Soviet Union in a crisis. Soviet-American interactions around the world are examined later;[50] at this point, the relevant consideration is that the Soviet Union undertook no new initiatives involving itself further, although it did not yet abandon commitments earlier assumed.

While waiting for a positive American response on strategic security issues, being on guard against possible American hostile actions, and avoiding new involvements around the world, the Soviet leaders were increasingly preoccupied with the crisis in Poland, meeting internal economic (and related

---

50. See chapters 13, 14, and 15.

military resource) problems, and changes—first anticipatory and then actual—within the leadership itself.


## *The End of the Brezhnev Era*


Brezhnev's health had been faltering since 1975, and after Aleksei N. Kosygin and Mikhail A. Suslov died (in December 1980 and January 1982, respectively) the shifting alignment within the leadership came increasingly to absorb the attention of the Soviet leaders. A key event was the succession to Suslov as a party secretary of Yury V. Andropov in May 1982. By all evidence, Andropov, Foreign Minister Andrei A. Gromyko, and Defense Minister Dmitry F. Ustinov, long a "national security" cluster within the Politburo, formed a clique that influenced both policy and the later selection of Andropov as Brezhnev's successor. Andropov's move from the chairmanship of the Committee for State Security (KGB) back to the party apparatus, and as a member of the Secretariat of the Central Committee as well as of the Politburo, positioned him to be a contender for the succession to Brezhnev. The favorite of Brezhnev himself, Konstantin U. Chernenko, was a relatively recent addition to the Politburo (candidate membership in 1977 and full membership in 1978), and his main qualification was his many years as a loyal staff assistant to Brezhnev. During 1982 the former senior party secretary after Suslov's demise, Andrei P. Kirilenko, long believed to be Brezhnev's probable successor, declined in authority until he was removed from the Politburo on the eve of Brezhnev's death.

There was much below the surface in Soviet politics in 1982, including a developing anticorruption campaign aimed at friends of the Brezhnev family. But these aspects of political intrigue, while interesting, would digress from the political issues relevant to the development of Soviet policy toward the United States.[51]

The most pressing issues were related to economic affairs. The Central Committee plenum in May 1982 was devoted to problems of managing the economy and increasing productivity, particularly in food production and agriculture.[52] Economic issues, including reform, were clearly thought about not only in terms of technical alternatives and implications but also in light of

---

51. See Joseph Kraft, "Letter from Moscow," *New Yorker*, January 31, 1983, p. 105. Kraft's account on this point is based on an interview with the dissident intellectual Roy Medvedev. See also Ilya Zemtsov, *Andropov: Policy Dilemmas and the Struggle for Power* (Jerusalem: IRICS, 1983), pp. 63–98, especially pp. 76–79, for a detailed speculative kremlinological analysis of the struggle for power.

52. For the decrees of the May Central Committee plenum, see *Kommunist*, no. 9 (June 1982), pp. 3–63.

political implications for members of the leadership at a time of approaching succession to Brezhnev. But economic issues were also closely related to at least four major foreign policy and national security problems.

The Twenty-sixth Party Congress had declared that two contending lines now existed in world politics and had reaffirmed a policy of pressing for détente. But the congress had not offered a program or even a prediction on how Soviet relations with the West would develop. Political and economic relations with the West, most specifically trade but indirectly much more, could not be determined by unilateral Soviet decision. And after the American resort to economic sanctions at the end of 1981 following martial law in Poland, the uncertainties roused by the earlier economic sanctions imposed by the Carter administration after Afghanistan were intensified and autarchic tendencies reinvigorated.[53]

A second foreign policy problem, with economic and political aspects, was posed by Soviet involvement in the Third World. No one in the Soviet leadership, at any time after 1979, was tempted to seek new foreign involvements. But commitments inherited from earlier times remained and were economically demanding: Cuba, Vietnam, and Afghanistan were most costly but least susceptible to Soviet disengagement. There were, however, signs in the first half of the 1980s of debate over maintaining or curtailing economic (and related political) support for other countries of the Third World, particularly in Africa and the Middle East.

The third and fourth areas were related sides of the same security coin: military expenditure and possible limitations on military expenditure as a result of arms control limitations. Negotiated bilateral arms limitations, and reductions that would obviate the need for some unilateral programs drawing on economic resources, were only in part a question of Soviet choice. Decision depended equally on whether the United States was prepared to negotiate and agree on arms limitations. Beyond that question loomed the larger one of whether growing American military programs created a threat to the Soviet Union requiring increased Soviet military programs. This complex of questions—a perceived growing American military threat, economic resource constraints, and doubtful arms control prospects—became a central issue in Soviet policy over the next several years.

Articulate advocates in the Soviet military establishment, above all Marshal Nikolai Ogarkov, the senior deputy to Defense Minister Dmitry F. Ustinov and chief of the General Staff, presented a strong case for increasing investment in the Soviet military establishment. After the Carter administration in 1980 initiated a major upturn in American military spending and the SALT II Treaty was shunted aside, and before the Reagan administration entered

---

53. See Garthoff, *Détente and Confrontation*, chapter 27; and Bjorkman and Zamostny, *World Politics*, vol. 36 (January 1984), pp. 196–97.

office, Ogarkov had begun to argue that not only did the Soviet Union need to do more to meet particular American challenges but that the ultimate aim of imperialist policy was "to change the correlation of forces to the favor of imperialism" by acquiring "an overwhelming military superiority."[54] A few months after the Reagan administration had entered office, affirming its intention to build up American military power but before it announced a long-term program or a strategic doctrine, Ogarkov stressed the need for contingent preparations for wartime mobilization of the country.[55] He stressed the direct military threat posed by the American buildup of capabilities for a first strike, while other Soviet spokesmen for the most part saw the American intention as building its military strength in order to dictate its political will in arms negotiations and in other ways, in short as representing a serious American political-military challenge rather than a direct threat of military attack. Indeed, a difference between Ogarkov and Defense Minister Ustinov was apparent by mid-1981.[56] Ogarkov continued to stress the threat and the need for building

---

54. Marshal N. V. Ogarkov, "In the Interests of Raising Combat Readiness," *Kommunist vooruzhennykh sil* (Communist of the Armed Forces), no. 14 (July 1980), p. 25. (Hereafter *KVS*).

55. Marshal N. Ogarkov, "On Guard over Peaceful Labor," *Kommunist*, no. 10 (July 1981), pp. 89–91. Ogarkov continued to argue that imperialism was seeking "to reverse the wheel of history and secure its former dominance in the world, using any means and methods to this end," but he also went further to contend that "in fact, direct military preparations are being carried out on a broad front, the material preparation for a new world war is being carried out" (pp. 81, 83). He argued that "it is essential to convey to Soviet people in a more profound and better reasoned form the truth about the existing threat of the danger of war. It should not, of course, be overdramatized, but it is essential to show the seriousness of the contemporary international situation" (p. 91). He concluded by saying that "the *further* strengthening of the country's defense capability, of *increasing* the combat readiness of the Armed Forces, and of vigilance are constantly the focus of attention not only for military personnel but also for party and Soviet organs" (p. 91). While this meant, as he explicitly acknowledged, that "thanks to tireless concern of our party's Central Committee and of the Soviet Government, the Soviet Armed Forces have everything they need at their disposal," he was obviously also lobbying pretty strongly for increased efforts to ensure that the military would continue in the future to meet its requirements (p. 91).

56. In comparison to the above-cited article by Ogarkov, see Marshal D. F. Ustinov, "Against the Arms Race and the Threat of War," *Pravda*, July 25, 1981. Ustinov also blamed the United States for seeking military superiority and attacked Western concepts for waging limited nuclear war. But he stressed that American calculations to attain superiority were "built on sand," and the Soviet Union had the wherewithal to prevent the United States from attaining superiority. Ogarkov, in contrast, saw a need to argue vigorously for stronger Soviet measures to prevent American plans for attaining superiority from succeeding.

    Marshal Sergei Akhromeyev, then first deputy to Ogarkov, subsequently acknowledged this rift in his posthumous memoir. See S. F. Akhromeyev and G. M. Kornienko, *Glazami marshala i diplomata* (Through the Eyes of a Marshal and a Diplomat) (Moscow: Mezhdunarodnyye otnosheniya, 1992), pp. 29–30.

Soviet capabilities to ensure deterrence and to meet contingent wartime requirements in a protracted nuclear or nonnuclear war until he was suddenly relieved of his position some three years later.

Between the summer of 1981 and the beginning of 1983, Minister of Defense Marshal D. F. Ustinov and his four ranking deputies—Marshal N. F. Ogarkov, Marshal S. L. Sokolov, Marshal V. G. Kulikov, and General of the Army A. A. Yepishev—each published a booklet (in a series under the rubric "Implementing the Decisions of the XXVI CPSU Congress") issued by the Military Publishing House of the Ministry of Defense in 100,000 copies each.[57] While the titles and contents reflected the general responsibilities of each, altogether they represented a major military "pitch" for responding to the heightened American military threat.

Throughout the year, military leaders loyally supported continuing initiatives on arms control, including the controversial decision to renounce unilaterally the first use of nuclear weapons.[58] But there were many signs of restlessness over the USSR continuing to implement a military program under the eleventh five-year plan, which had been drawn up when the Soviet leaders believed that the SALT II Treaty would provide reliable parameters for the forces of the two sides and that a serious strategic arms limitation and reduction process would be under way.

Marshal Ogarkov and other military leaders understood very well that there were competing economic investment needs and limits on the availability of resources to meet the insatiable requirements for hedging to meet possible protracted nuclear and nonnuclear wars. Nonetheless, the perspective of military planners was bound to differ from that of Brezhnev and his colleagues on the Defense Council and Politburo who had a host of other economic—and political—considerations of equal importance.

---

57. Marshal D. F. Ustinov, *Sluzhim rodine, delu Kommunizma* (We Serve the Motherland, the Cause of Communism) (Moscow: Voyenizdat, 1982); Marshal N. V. Ogarkov, *Vsegda v gotovnosti k zashchite otechestva* (Always in Readiness to Defend the Fatherland) (Moscow: Voyenizdat, 1982); Marshal S. L. Sokolov, *Leninskii stil' v rabote voyennykh kadrov* (Leninist Style in Work with Military Cadres) (Moscow: Voyenizdat, 1983); Marshal V. G. Kulikov, *Kollektivnaya zashchita sotsializma* (Collective Defense of Socialism) (Moscow: Voyenizdat, 1982); and General of the Army A. A. Yepishev, *Ideyam partii verny* (True to the Ideas of the Party) (Moscow: Voyenizdat, 1981).

58. As noted earlier, in June Brezhnev made a unilateral pledge that the Soviet Union would not be the first to use nuclear weapons (*Pravda*, June 16, 1982). Four weeks later Marshal Ustinov followed with an article that admitted that questions had been raised about the timeliness and even the soundness of the decision and said that "it was no simple matter" to undertake that "unilateral commitment." He justified the decision in part on acceptance of the conclusion that a nuclear war would be a "universal catastrophe" and that the Soviet Union saw the "impossibility" of victory in a nuclear war. See Marshal D. F. Ustinov, "On Averting the Threat of Nuclear War," *Pravda*, July 12, 1982.

Some of the military leaders, in particular Marshal Ogarkov, were concerned not only by the American military buildup but also by the American abandonment of détente and strategic arms negotiations after they had brought themselves, and the Soviet military establishment and planning, in the 1970s to accept military détente and arms control. They were further troubled in the early 1980s by the unreadiness of Brezhnev, Ustinov, and the Soviet leadership in general to undertake the new military readiness and buildup measures they now believed necessary.

The development, and leaking into the public domain, of the new American Defense Guidance and other strategic policy documents in 1982, described in chapter 1, exacerbated the problem in Moscow. Fundamentally, though, the real problem for the Soviets was that having turned down their own military investment trend line in the late 1970s, they were now faced with an American upsurge in military spending accompanied by America's confident assertions of intentions to negotiate and, more vaguely but ominously, to act from positions of superior strength.

Again on the anniversary of the victory in Europe in World War II, in May 1982, Marshal Ogarkov took a stronger line than his chief, Minister of Defense Ustinov. Both officials attacked the American aim of gaining military superiority, but again Ogarkov singled out as "a particularly dangerous trend in the actions of American imperialism" what he again called "direct material preparation for a new war." And again he ended by stressing the "need" to "do everything to strengthen the defense capability" of the Soviet Union.[59] Ustinov, however, stressed that the Soviet Union would not allow the United States to attain superiority, that Soviet defense strength "deters the imperialist aggressors," and that the Communist Party "intends also in the future not to relax its concern for raising the defense capability of our country."[60] Ogarkov came close to saying an existing need to strengthen defense capability was not yet met; Ustinov assured his readership that the need had been met and would continue to be met by the Communist Party.[61]

---

59. Marshal Nikolai V. Ogarkov, "For the Sake of Peace and Progress," *Izvestiya*, May 9, 1982.

60. Marshal D. Ustinov, "The Feat of Liberation," *Pravda*, May 9, 1982.

61. There were other interesting and possibly significant differences. As in 1981, Ustinov gave more emphasis to Soviet initiatives in seeking arms control and détente, and Ogarkov to American rejection and disruption of arms control and détente. While Ustinov stressed the role of the Communist Party during World War II and at present, and repeatedly praised Brezhnev, Ogarkov gave less attention to both, and in his account of World War II he gave unusual attention and praise to Josef Stalin, the Supreme Command headquarters and the General Staff, and to its wartime leaders, Marshals G. Zhukov, A. Vasilevsky, B. Shaposhnikov, and A. Antonov—his own predecessors. The references to Stalin and Marshal Zhukov, while not unprecedented in recent years, were still highly unusual in a public statement by a military or political leader.

On October 27, 1982, in his last major political act, Brezhnev and the other Politburo members of the Defense Council met with an unprecedented assemblage of several hundred leading command personnel of the Soviet armed forces in the Kremlin.[62] Brezhnev opened by saying that he had accepted Ustinov's invitation for the meeting, and elsewhere in the speech gave special favorable reference to Ustinov, "our comrade-in-arms" (who, he said, "constantly reports to me about the state of our armed forces.") He also stressed his own attention to military matters: "And as for me, I too am constantly occupied with matters of strengthening the army and navy in the performance of my official duty, so to speak, and know how things are going with you."[63]

Brezhnev began by noting that two years had passed since the Twenty-sixth Party Congress and declared that "experience has confirmed the correctness of the appraisals and conclusions of the congress and the farsightedness of the decisions taken by it," while also noting that "new questions also appear which must be solved without delay." He repeated the theme earlier sounded at the congress on the clash of two lines in the world: a line for deepening tension and seeking military superiority and a line of détente. He went further by identifying the former as the line pursued by "the United States and those who go with it"; at the congress he had referred to "two tendencies," and while implying American support for the former, had not so directly cast the U.S. leadership as committed to that course. He then strongly reaffirmed the Soviet position, notwithstanding the intensifying conflict. "Our line," Brezhnev confirmed, "is for détente and strengthening international security. We shall not

---

Again after his removal as chief of the General Staff in 1984, Ogarkov wrote an article on the fortieth anniversary of victory in World War II in which he gave special praise to the Stavka headed by Stalin and the General Staff, which together "firmly and capably commanded the Soviet armed forces" in the war. Marshal N. Ogarkov, "An Unfading Glory of Soviet Arms," *KVS*, no. 21 (November 1984), p. 21.

62. The political leaders were not identified as members of the Defense Council, whose membership is not publicly divulged, but the six Politburo members attending were those believed to constitute its membership. They were, besides Brezhnev and Ustinov (the latter listed with the other political leaders and without mentioning his marshal's rank), Yury Andropov, Konstantin Chernenko, Andrei Gromyko, and Nikolai Tikhonov. Clearly, the intent was to show a united leadership backing Brezhnev up. Of the military participants, only the five senior deputies to Ustinov were listed: Marshal Nikolai Ogarkov (who was given special prominence), Marshal Viktor Kulikov, Marshal Sergei Sokolov, and General of the Army Aleksei Yepishev. The only other participant named was Deputy Prime Minister Leonid Smirnov, head of the important Military-Industrial Commission, the key link between the military and military industry; he was listed before the military leaders. The military leaders present included not only "leading" personnel of the Ministry of Defense but also the commanders, chiefs of staff, and deputy commanders for political affairs of the twenty military districts and groups of forces and the four naval fleets.

63. "Kremlin Meeting of Military Leaders," *Pravda*, October 28, 1982.

abandon it and shall step up our efforts and retain the initiative in international affairs."[64]

Brezhnev made clear continuing reliance on détente *and* defense. "The international situation makes it imperative for us to redouble or treble our efforts in the struggle for preserving peace, for reducing the danger of nuclear war which is hanging over mankind." At the same time, he stressed, "We are also obliged tirelessly to strengthen the defense of the country and maintain the greatest vigilance." Brezhnev did not downgrade the nature of the threat. He characterized American policy under the Reagan administration, as assessed by the Central Committee: "The ruling circles of the United States of America have launched a political, ideological, and economic offensive on socialism and have raised the intensity of their military preparations to an unprecedented level." He saw implications of this Reagan policy for Soviet diplomacy as well as military policy. He noted that the "adventurism" and the "egoism" of the American policy aroused concerns "in many countries, including those allied with the United States. In this situation," he also stressed, "it is very important, of course, how our relations with other countries shape up. Of no little significance are our relations with China." But while cautious, he held out hope in this connection by saying that "we must not ignore new moments, which are appearing."[65] The military, and above all Marshal Ogarkov, had in contrast stressed the increased military threat posed by the development of close American-Chinese relations.[66]

Brezhnev's statement to the assembled military leadership was important in several respects. First, although naturally not foreseen, it was his last major statement. In addition, the very convocation of this unusual assembly of the Soviet military command personnel, and the messages for them in Brezhnev's statement, demonstrated the mounting unease in the military establishment over what many evidently saw as a policy of equivocation and drift in the face of the military challenge being mounted by the Reagan administration. Brezhnev sought to meet this by clarifying for them and for the Soviet people as a whole (as the speech then appeared in *Pravda*) an updated Soviet assessment and affirmation of a line of response to American policy. Undoubtedly preparation for the meeting had required the Defense Council to reconsider carefully its military policy and foreign policy courses.

In speaking directly to the military concern over the allocation of resources to meet their requirements, Brezhnev gave reassurance laced with a reminder that the military establishment was also responsible for making the most of the share of resources given to it. He said, "The people spare nothing

---

64. Ibid.

65. Ibid.

66. For example see Ogarkov, *KVS*, no. 14 (July 1980), p. 26; and *Kommunist*, no. 10 (July 1981), p. 84.

to keep them [the Soviet armed forces] always up to the mark for their tasks. We equip the Armed Forces with the most modern arms and military equipment. The Central Committee of the Party takes measures so that you are not left in need." He then added an unusual counterpoint: "And the Armed Forces must always be worthy of this solicitude." Moreover, he shifted the focus from providing arms to the military, to requiring the military to make the most of what was provided. "The Soviet Army must be up to the mark in all respects: equipment, structure, methods of training. It must be up to its contemporary requirements. *And you, comrades, are responsible for that.*"[67]

Similarly, in addressing the question of "the further strengthening of the material base of the Armed Forces," he stressed the need not to lag, but again put the stress on others. "We expect that our scientists, designers, engineers, and technicians will do everything possible to resolve successfully all tasks in that connection."[68]

While not all specific decisions on Soviet military programs that may have been taken at that time are known, and Brezhnev and the collective leadership by late 1982 may have acceded to some requests by the military leaders for new programs, on the whole they did not. Overall, they continued to temporize and channel such decisions into ongoing preparation of the twelfth five-year plan covering the period 1986–90.

Brezhnev's speech did not address the question of the possibility of improving relations with the United States, although its thrust was certainly that the prospects for such improvement were not high. There had been continuing divergent evaluations of that possibility throughout 1981 and 1982. A number of such statements from the first months of the Reagan administration were cited earlier. Shortly before Brezhnev's speech, Leonid Zamyatin, head of the International Information Department of the Central Committee, had said that twenty months of the Reagan administration had "demonstrated that its policy is more militarist and reactionary than that of any other postwar Washington administration." It was said to have "completely broken with détente" and called for a "crusade" against the USSR aimed at "destroying socialism as a world system." He cited Reagan as declaring that "he believes the Soviet Union and the United States are in a state of war."[69] Other Soviet commentators also said it would not be realistic to expect any sharp changes for the better.[70] But some Soviet observers continued to seek to hold open the possibility of improving relations. Vadim Zagladin, another prominent Central

67. *Pravda*, October 28, 1982. Emphasis added.

68. Ibid.

69. Leonid Zamyatin, "Détente and Anti-détente: Two Tendencies in World Politics," *Literaturnaya gazeta*, September 29, 1992.

70. Spartak Beglov, "International Panorama," Moscow Television, October 9, 1982, in FBIS, *Soviet Union*, October 12, 1982, pp. A 1–2.

Committee official, commented to an Italian communist journalist in October that Moscow was "convinced of the possibility of an improvement, or at least a normalization, of Soviet-U.S. relations, and we hope for that."[71] Georgy Arbatov, head of the Institute of USA and Canada, also declared that the Soviet leadership had not "given up on Reagan."[72] These statements, however, were made to foreign journalists and may not have reflected serious interest or expectations by the leadership.

Most striking was a statement only two days later by Politburo member Konstantin Chernenko, who said that the Soviet Union sought "normalization and improvement" of Soviet-American relations and was "prepared to engage in businesslike and detailed negotiations, which must take account of the interests of both sides. And we are confident: if our partners cease living in a world of illusions, stop beguiling themselves with hopes of superiority, if they show high responsibility and political wisdom, then it will be possible to reach agreement on any question."[73] On the other hand, said Chernenko, "If Washington proves unable to rise above primitive anticommunism, if it persists in a policy of threat and dictate, well, we are sufficiently strong and we can wait. Neither sanctions nor belligerent posturing frighten us."[74] Chernenko made no reference to a need to strengthen Soviet defenses (nor to Brezhnev's speech). Similarly, at the UN General Assembly a few weeks earlier, Foreign Minister Andrei A. Gromyko had said that the Soviet Union was prepared to develop good relations with the United States, referring to statements authoritatively made at party congresses and before the Supreme Soviet.[75]

In the annual address on the anniversary of the Bolshevik Revolution on November 5, 1982, however, hard-line Politburo member Viktor Grishin stressed that while the Soviet Union was continuing to strive for peaceful coexistence and détente, "The U.S. ruling circles have taken it upon themselves to cancel all that was positive achieved during the 1970s, to bury détente and to

---

71. "The USSR at This Moment. We Talk with Zagladin: China, the USA, the Army, the Economy," Vadim Zagladin interviewed by Giulietto Chiesa, *L'Unita* (Unity), Rome, October 16, 1982, p. 8.

72. Reuters, September 28, 1982.

73. K. Chernenko, "The Fruitfulness of the Leninist Friendship of Peoples," speech in Tbilisi, October 29, 1982, in K. U. Chernenko, *Izbrannyye rechi i stat'i* (Selected Speeches and Articles) (Moscow: Politizdat, 1984), p. 553.

    Chernenko explained that he had been deputed to deliver this speech in place of Brezhnev, who was too heavily occupied in preparations for other meetings in Moscow. See "Comrade K. U. Chernenko's Speech," *Zarya vostoka* (Dawn of the East), Tbilisi, October 30, 1982. This impromptu explanation by Chernenko was omitted from the version of his speech later published.

74. Chernenko, *Izbrannyye rechi*, p. 554.

75. "Speech of A. A. Gromyko to the XXXVII Session of the UN General Assembly," *Pravda*, October 2, 1982.

revive the cold war." He emphasized the U.S. pursuit of "military superiority and of dictating political conditions to others from a position of strength." This policy "worsens and complicates the international situation and creates the danger of an outbreak of nuclear war, which would be disastrous for mankind." He recounted Soviet initiatives and efforts at arms control but gave no word of expectation or even hope of American return to détente or arms control. Rather, he stressed that "under conditions of heightened aggressiveness by imperialism our party is showing great vigilance and is doing everything necessary to strengthen the defense capability of the country." He cited the recent military conference with the participation of Brezhnev "and other party and state leaders."[76] And on November 7, in his brief speech at the parade in Red Square, Marshal Ustinov, while reaffirming the "Peace Program for the eighties" laid down by the Twenty-sixth Party Congress, had only one thing to say about relations with the United States: "The Soviet Union takes into consideration the fact that the aggressive forces of imperialism, above all the United States, have raised the intensity of their military preparations to an unprecedented level," and in addition have "unfolded a political, ideological and economic offensive against socialism." Consequently, the party shows "constant concern for strengthening the security of our country," and he too cited Brezhnev's participation and "precisely defined instructions" from the military conference as "a new manifestation of this concern."[77]

Both of these strands of Soviet thinking about the possibility of relations with the United States thus persisted throughout the first two years of the Reagan administration, which were coincidentally the last two years of the Brezhnev leadership. There was no doubt in Moscow that the Reagan administration was seeking military superiority and unwilling to grant military and political parity. But, as Chernenko had put it in his October speech, "We believe that sooner or later—and the sooner, the better—reason will triumph and the military threat will be averted."[78] Here, however, there was clearly not a unanimous view. The military leaders at least, and perhaps some of the political leaders, were less sanguine and more inclined to see a need to increase Soviet military programs to meet the military challenge. Brezhnev's stand at the meeting with the military command personnel showed appreciation of their concerns, and some—but not unequivocal or unlimited—readiness to meet the military requirements they saw. Soviet policy was thus poised at a time of decision when Brezhnev died. In his last statement, in a brief address at a Kremlin reception on the anniversary of the October Revolution, Brezhnev said, "The world is now living through not easy times. The broad offensive

---

76. "Continuing the Cause of Great October," *Pravda*, November 6, 1982.

77. "Speech of Comrade D. F. Ustinov," *Pravda*, November 8, 1982.

78. Chernenko, *Izbrannyye rechi*, p. 554. According to the transcript of the speech, this passage was greeted with "prolonged applause."

unleashed by the imperialists against socialism and the national liberation movement on all fronts has complicated the international situation. But it is not in the tradition of our party or of our people to retreat before difficulties." He reaffirmed both defense and détente. "We shall do all that is necessary so that . . . a potential aggressor would know that a crushing retaliatory strike would inevitably await him." But, at the same time, "The Soviet Union will continue persistently fighting for détente, for disarmament. We shall intensify our efforts to avert the threat of nuclear war."[79] He did not specifically address relations with the United States, nor did he delineate priorities for action by the Soviet Union on its dual course.

Brezhnev's legacy in national security policy was a policy of détente and arms control that had failed and one on defense at which the military was chafing. More fundamentally, the viability of the whole structure of Soviet society was increasingly undermined by obsolescence of the ideology undergirding internal as well as external policy, the economy as it began to fall more and more behind the demands of new technologies, and the polity geared to serve only the interests of a central bureaucratic leadership class, called the *nomenklatura*. But while many aspects of these failings were more or less recognized by some members of the leadership, the full extent of the failure of the system was not yet appreciated.

---

79. "Speech of Comrade L. I. Brezhnev," *Pravda*, November 8, 1982.

# 3 Renewed Dialogue Yields to New Tensions, 1983

IN HIS BRIEF remarks at the special Central Committee plenum in November 1982 that elected him the new general secretary of the party succeeding Brezhnev, Yury Andropov deferred to military concerns. "We know well," he said, "that peace with the imperialists is not for the asking. It can be safeguarded only by relying on the invincible might of the Soviet Armed Forces." He praised Brezhnev as "leader of the party and state, and Chairman of the Defense Council of the USSR" in ensuring that "the defense capability of the country would be up to contemporary requirements."[1] At the same time, by this very device, he reminded all that as the new leader of the party and state and chairman of the Defense Council *he* was now principally responsible for determining what was needed to meet such requirements.[2]

A joint statement by the Central Committee, the Presidium of the Supreme Soviet, and the Council of Ministers issued after the announcement of Brezhnev's death paraphrased Brezhnev's remarks of November 7, blaming the difficult international situation on "the attempts of aggressive circles of imperialism to undermine peaceful coexistence, to push peoples onto a course of enmity and military confrontation. But that cannot shake our determination to defend peace." As Brezhnev had, the statement stressed deterrence through the maintenance of capability for a crushing retaliatory strike and the continuation of a "struggle for détente and for disarmament."[3]

---

1.  "Speech of Comrade Yu. V. Andropov to the Plenum of the CC of the CPSU, November 12, 1982," *Kommunist* (Communist), no. 17 (November 1982), p. 7.

2.  Although not announced, when Andropov became general secretary of the party he also became chairman of the Defense Council and commander-in-chief of the armed forces. Information from a knowledgeable member of the Central Committee.

3.  "Address by the Central Committee of the CPSU, the Presidium of the Supreme Soviet of the USSR, and the Council of Ministers of the USSR to the Communist Party and to the Soviet People," *Kommunist*, no. 17 (November 1982), pp. 4–5.

In his first public statement, at Brezhnev's funeral a few days later, Andropov tilted this balance toward diplomacy and détente. The two predominant themes of this brief eulogy were raising the welfare of the people and peace. Apart from praising Brezhnev, who "struggled for the relaxation of international tensions and for delivering mankind from the threat of nuclear war," in looking to the future Andropov stressed, "We will always be loyal to the cause of the struggle for peace, for détente." He also repeated in close paraphrase the formula on deterrence used by the joint party-government statement, and then added, "We are always ready for honest, equal, and mutually adantageous cooperation with any state that desires it."[4]

In his first major address, on November 22, 1982, to another Central Committee plenum, Andropov set out Soviet policy in the most authoritative general statement since Brezhnev's report to the party congress in February 1981. It was his opportunity to reaffirm or modify the policy line laid down in the late Brezhnev years; he chose to stress continuity. He had more positive things to say about the prospects for improved relations with the West than had Brezhnev for a year or more before his death. Making a point of speaking collectively, he said, "We are deeply convinced that the Seventies, characterized by détente, were not—as is asserted today by some imperialist figures—a chance episode in the difficult history of mankind. No, the policy of détente is by no means a past stage. The future belongs to it."[5] Lest the Western leaders, particularly the Reagan administration, seek to take advantage of this expressed eagerness for détente, Andropov made clear the continuing Soviet rejection of attempts at linkage. "All," he said, "have an equal interest in preserving peace and in détente. Therefore statements in which a readiness to normalize relations is linked with a demand that the Soviet Union pay for it with some kind of preliminary concessions in altogether different fields do not, to say the least, sound serious." He reminded his listeners that the Soviet Union, after all, had levied no sanctions nor denounced treaties already signed. So he reaffirmed Soviet interest in reaching agreement, "but it must be sought on the basis of equal rights and reciprocity."[6]

Andropov's speech also represented the beginning of a new Soviet challenge to the United States to respond "with deeds, not words," although he did not use this expression at that time.[7] Later in his own brief tenure, and under his successor, this theme became more explicit.

---

4.    "Speech of Yu. V. Andropov at the Funeral Meeting, November 15, 1982," *Kommunist*, no. 17 (November 1982), pp. 11–12. Andropov also introduced one interesting new point not mentioned by Brezhnev or in the joint statement—"firmly defending the vital interests of our Motherland."

5.    "Speech of General Secretary of the CC of the CPSU Yu. V. Andropov to the Plenum of the CC of the CPSU, November 22, 1982," *Kommunist*, no. 17 (November 1982), p. 20. This passage was followed by applause.

6.    Ibid. Again, applause followed the statement on an equal interest in détente.

7.    Ibid. He noted, for example, that problems would not be resolved "if negotiations are held just for the sake of negotiations as, unfortunately, happens not infrequently."

Soviet officials have said that shortly before his death Brezhnev had been planning to take a harder line and propaganda counteroffensive in response to the Reagan administration's political and ideological crusade and (in the Soviet view) stalling tactics in the arms control talks, and that Andropov shelved this idea.[8] Whether these reports were accurate, it is clear that the Soviet position had become less optimistic by the close of Brezhnev's tenure. Andropov, however, was disposed to see for himself whether the Reagan administration was prepared to negotiate seriously and seek to lessen tensions.

## Andropov's Succession

The change of leadership led to a fresh assessment of prospects for dealing with the United States, in which varying points of view were again expressed. According to Georgy Arbatov, Brezhnev had said in remarks to the U.S.-USSR Trade and Economic Council in mid-November, not long before his death, "We are now at a crossroad, as it were, and will now have to decide where to go," referring to a challenge facing both countries.[9] Then, with Andropov's succession, there was a flurry of new attention to the state of American-Soviet relations. Arbatov acknowledged that "in the last few days many people's hopes regarding the prospects of Soviet-American relations have revived. The dramatic nature of the moment, when events are prompting reflection on the most serious problems perturbing people, may even have helped in a way." But while expressing hope, Arbatov cautioned that "we must be realists."[10]

Arbatov commented that the Soviet Union "assessed positively" Reagan's expression of condolences at the Soviet Embassy in Washington and the fact that the U.S. vice president and secretary of state went to Moscow for the funeral. He then commented: "We have carefully followed the words spoken in this connection and the good words we have greeted favorably. But if I were asked if I could assess these facts as evidence of the abandonment by the United States of a policy that in our country—I must be frank with you—is seen as a policy of Cold War and as a course of headlong arms race . . . I would

---

8.  See Dusko Doder, "Soviet Asks U.S. for Specific Moves," *Washington Post*, November 18, 1982, pp. A-1, A24, citing "well-informed Soviet sources." I, too, heard this from a well-placed member of the Soviet establishment some time later.

9.  Academician G. Arbatov, "We Are Not Losing Optimism: Trade and Politics in the Eighties," November 17, 1982, *Literaturnaya gazeta* (Literary Gazette), December 8, 1982.

10.  Ibid.

honestly say that as yet I have no answer." Although couching it as a hypothetical question, Arbatov, as the leading specialist on American affairs (and a close associate of Andropov's in the Central Committee Secretariat staff from the middle 1960s), undoubtedly *had* been asked that question. So his views and public indications of his assessment were of more than academic interest. He emphasized that the Soviet Union had always been in favor of "serious discussion of existing problems. It was not we who changed our line. It was not we who imposed trade sanctions, canceled flights, ended talks, and abandoned agreements." "Let's return to détente." He affirmed continuing close attention to any indications of American interest in improving relations. "We are of course carefully watching every good word and every good gesture from America. And I want to assure you that it will not be in vain, that it will be noticed and that decision-makers will pay attention to it. But the problem is this: You see, when a country that has virtually declared war on us—trade, economic, technological and political war—has accelerated the arms race and so forth, when that country wants to normalize relations, it certainly shouldn't do so by putting forward prior conditions and demanding of others that they first change their policy for the sake of normalization. Still less should it put forward ultimatums essentially demanding our capitulation on all fronts, demanding something it has been unable to obtain by the most shameless pressure. We will not do that, there must be no illusions [on that score]."[11]

A few weeks later, after President Reagan's speech of November 22, Arbatov engaged in a lively and informative discussion on Moscow television with Aleksandr Bovin. Arbatov noted that the speech was understood to have been addressed to the Soviet Union, as well as to the American people, and was the first major statement by the president since Andropov succeeded Brezhnev. In it, Reagan had announced his decision—after two years of equivocation and studies—to deploy 100 MX missiles with 1,000 warheads. Arbatov concluded from the speech that "President Reagan once more confirmed the U.S. course for military superiority." He vigorously refuted Reagan's claim that the United States had not threatened anyone when after World War II it had military superiority: "We well remember the Cold War and nuclear blackmail, the Caribbean [Cuban missile] crisis when the world found itself on the brink of war, and all of this was during those beneficial—from the point of view of the Americans, some Americans—days of American military superiority." He argued that "on the contrary, if history showed something convincing it was the fact that it was precisely parity . . . which insured more stable conditions and opened the opportunity for successful talks on disarmament."[12] As for the

---

11. Ibid.

12. G. Arbatov, on "Studio 9," Moscow Television, December 4, 1982, in Foreign Broadcast Information Service, *Daily Report: Soviet Union*, December 6, 1982, pp. CC7–8. (Hereafter FBIS, *Soviet Union*.)

future, Arbatov said bitterly that President Reagan had showed that "political extremism is not a thing of the past," nor of the political fringe: "He showed that primitive anticommunism and troglodyte anti-Sovietism are also not things that hide somewhere in corners and in the labyrinths of political life" but can be the "basis for state policy."[13]

Bovin, who described himself as by nature an optimist, said that "of course, talks with the Americans should be held . . . need to be held; compromises must be sought and something needs to be done." Nonetheless, his pessimistic prognostications since early 1981 on the position of the Reagan administration had deepened. Hence, despite his reaffirmed belief in the need for working together, he concluded that "judging by what is happening and judging by what I see, what is being said and done in Washington, I am nevertheless coming to the conclusion that we will not be able to agree on anything serious with the current administration."[14] This was too strong a conclusion for Arbatov, who, despite all his growing pessimism, believed it was necessary to continue to try. He rejoined: "I cannot say that there is no basis for such an opinion. . . . I feel that nevertheless it is not worth approaching this problem in this way . . . there is much that disposes one to be fairly pessimistic. However, I think that the policy we have seen to date—of closely following and looking for the smallest change in U.S. behavior, leaving the door constantly open, and if any changes of position actually occur it will never bypass this attention and be left unanswered—this policy was, is and will remain it seems to me the wisest, since we are talking about a very serious thing, about Soviet-U.S. relations, on which . . . very much depends in our political life today."[15] A few weeks later Arbatov said he had the impression that "common sense, which is a national trait of the Americans, is beginning to manifest itself in the United States." He cited the midterm congressional elections, which were a setback for Reagan, and "some movement toward realism in Congress." He expressed the hope that the coming year would become "a year of realism and that it would see a return to normal international relations based on the true perception of one's own interests." And he stressed the importance of arms limitations, because the arms race is "a waste of money for no good purpose. The Soviet

---

13. Ibid., p. CC11.

14. A. Bovin on "Studio 9," ibid., p. CC11.

In several later broadcasts and articles Bovin was somewhat more optimistic that "the opponents of détente in Washington are gradually beginning to give ground. . . . But at the moment it is difficult to say whether this will affect the essence of the foreign policy course or only its form." See A. Bovin, "Vremya" newscast, Moscow Television, December 30, 1982, FBIS, *Soviet Union*, January 4, 1983, p. CC2; Bovin, "Political Observer's Notes: Two Trends," *Izvestiya*, January 1, 1983; and Bovin, "Political Observer's Opinion: Impasse at the Crossroads," *Izvestiya*, January 20, 1983.

15. G. Arbatov, FBIS, *Soviet Union*, December 6, 1982, p. CC11.

Union and the United States could have used the funds consumed by the arms to solve their problems rather than waste them."[16]

The exchange between Bovin and Arbatov is of interest for comparing the views of these two important commentators at the end of 1982 with those they had expressed at the beginning of the Reagan administration two years earlier. What makes it of particular interest is the additional fact that both had been among a handful of party intellectuals serving as a "Group of Consultants" to the Central Committee Secretariat in the 1960s under Party Secretary Yury Andropov.[17] After Andropov returned to the Secretariat, and then succeeded Brezhnev, the weight given to the views of Bovin and Arbatov was assumed to have risen. Andropov himself, in a year-end interview, expressed interest in a summit meeting, properly prepared, and spoke up for "improving Soviet-American relations . . . we welcome everything that leads to this objective."[18]

There were, however, important elements in the Soviet establishment that viewed the state of Soviet-American relations with far less equanimity. Marshal Ustinov, in a meeting in early December with military leaders to discuss tasks stemming from the November Central Committee plenum, stressed "the increasingly dangerous character" of the international situation owing to the "aggressive policy of the United States," its "military preparations which have been raised to an unprecedented level," and the "military doctrines which stem from the strategy of 'direct confrontation' proclaimed by Washington and are directed at achieving military superiority over the Soviet Union and establishing U.S. world supremacy." These military doctrines were aimed ultimately at "'destroying socialism as a social and political system,' according to directives made public in Washington" (a reference to the leaked Defense Guidance). "Finally, the new 'crusade' against communism proclaimed by the president of that country serves the aim of achieving U.S. world domination. It means the political isolation and economic weakening of the USSR and its

---

16. G. Arbatov, Radio Moscow, December 31, 1982, in FBIS, *Soviet Union*, January 3, 1983, p. A3.

17. The consultants originated with Andropov's predecessor, Politburo member Otto Kuusinen, and the most prominent then was Fedor M. Burlatsky. He was later succeeded as head of the group by Georgy A. Arbatov. Other members included Georgy Kh. Shakhnazarov, by 1983 a deputy chief of the Central Committee Department for Liaison with the Communist Parties of the Socialist Countries, Oleg T. Bogomolov, head of the Institute of the Economics of the World Socialist System, Lev P. Delyusin, head of the China department of the Institute of Oriental Studies, Aleksandr Ye. Bovin, political observer for *Izvestiya*, Nikolai V. Shishlin, Gennady I. Gerasimov, and others. All were undogmatic "liberals" in the context of Soviet politics, and supporters of détente. Information from informed Soviet observers, including several of those named here.

18. "Replies by Yu. V. Andropov to Questions of the American Political Observer J. Kingsbury-Smith," *Pravda*, December 31, 1982.

friends. To this end an economic, political, and ideological assault against our country and other countries of the socialist community has been launched."[19]

Needless to say, Marshal Ustinov's speech did not refer to the "waste" of military outlays. He cited Brezhnev's October 27 statement that the "level of combat readiness of the Army and Navy should be even higher," and Andropov's speech to the Central Committee plenum declaring that "the Politburo has considered and considers it an obligation to provide the Army and Navy with all that is necessary, especially in the current international situation." For what was necessary, however, and for what was already available, he applied a different measure from the one Marshal Ogarkov had used, saying that "the military might of the Soviet Union is sufficient." He also stressed that "our might is subordinated exclusively to the aims of defense. . . . And our military doctrine is strictly defensive in character."[20] Marshal Ustinov also issued a detailed and considered refutation of President Reagan's claim at a news conference on November 22 that the Soviet Union had military superiority over the United States. He said, "Such assertions do not correspond to reality. They are calculated at deceiving the public and have the purpose of justifying the unprecedented U.S. military programs and aggressive doctrines. It is regrettable that such attempts to convince people of the existence of that which does not exist are made by the leader of a great power whose very position presupposes realism and responsibility in assessing reality." And in terms reminiscent of those used earlier by Marshal Ogarkov, Ustinov too now characterized the long-term American many-faceted strategic buildup as more ominous in purpose. "All this together can hardly be viewed as anything short of a program of preparations for an all-out nuclear war." But he said that although the actions of the United States and NATO compelled the Soviet Union and its allies to "maintain our defense capability at the necessary level," still "we are against military rivalry," and he closed by citing Andropov's call for agreements curbing the arms race.[21]

Such differences in focus and emphasis, with respect to assessments of both American policy and appropriate Soviet policy, continued. It would be too much to see them as representing a constant struggle between protagonists, but it would also be a mistake to ignore them. Contending Soviet views were, of course, affected by American rhetoric and actions.

---

19. "Up to the Level of New Tasks," Meeting of the Party Aktiv of the Order of Lenin Moscow Military District, *Krasnaya zvezda* (Red Star), December 8, 1982.

20. Ibid.

21. "Replies of the Minister of Defense of the USSR Marshal of the Soviet Union D. F. Ustinov to Questions of a TASS Correspondent," *Pravda*, December 7, 1982.

## Washington's Mixed Signals

An unusual development affecting American-Soviet relations arose just as Andropov was succeeding Brezhnev. Charges were raised of a possible "Bulgarian connection"—and by extension Soviet responsibility—in the case of the attempted assassination in May 1981 of Pope John Paul II. The charge was first levied by Claire Sterling, an American journalist in Rome who had written *The Terror Network*, in an article that appeared in the *Reader's Digest* in September 1982.[22] Then in November the Italian authorities arrested a Bulgarian civilian airline employee, and disclosed that the attempted assassin, Mehmet Ali Agca, had now claimed Bulgarian responsibility for the plot. Nonetheless, despite the administration's enthusiasm in claiming a Soviet tie to international terrorism, there was an unexpected reaction in Washington. Senior intelligence officials in Washington and Rome made clear that the CIA was skeptical of any Bulgarian-Soviet responsibility for the attempted papal assassination.[23] This led to angry recriminations from right-wing members of Con-

---

22. Claire Sterling, "The Plot to Murder the Pope," *Reader's Digest* (September 1982), pp. 71–84. The article received advance press notice; see "Soviet and Bulgarian Role Hinted In Shooting of the Pope by Turk," *New York Times*, August 17, 1982, p. A12. Sterling also served as expert consultant to a television special by Marvin Kalb, "The Man Who Shot the Pope," broadcast on NBC on September 21, 1982; the NBC special also incorporated the research of Paul Henze. On September 23 Sterling was interviewed on the subject on the Voice of America.

23. See Philip Taubman, "U.S. Officials See a Bulgarian 'Link,' But They Say Tie to Agca May Not Have Involved Pope," *New York Times*, January 27, 1983, pp. A1, A13; and many other articles, including those in the following footnote, and see William Safire, "You're On Your Own," *New York Times*, June 11, 1984, p. A19. Senior CIA officials told me the same thing privately.

    Casey himself pushed to find some support for a Bulgarian-Soviet connection, but acquiesced in the intelligence agencies' rejection of such a plot on the grounds of "insufficient evidence." Even so, when presenting this report to President Reagan, he reportedly told him, "You and I know better." See Joseph E. Persico, *Casey: From the OSS to the CIA* (Viking, 1990), pp. 286–88.

    The CIA prepared a number of reports on a possible Bulgarian-Soviet connection with the plot, one in 1983 that concluded it was unlikely, one in 1985 at Robert Gates's direction that had as its assignment to make the case for such a tie, and another he requested in 1985 that criticized both of the earlier studies. Large excerpts of these three studies and discussion of various views in the agency were made public in the congressional hearings on Gates's nomination to be director of the CIA in 1991. See *Nomination of Robert M. Gates to be Director of Central Intelligence*, U.S. Senate Executive Report 102-19, 102 Cong. 1 sess. (Washington: Government Printing Office, 1991), pp. 108–16, and for the texts see *Nomination of Robert M. Gates*, Hearings before the Select Committee on Intelligence of the United States Senate, 102 Cong. 1 sess. (GPO, 1992), vol. 2, pp. 336–71. Other parts of the testimony in vols. 1 and 2 of the hearings are also relevant. One statement submitted refers to a later national intelligence estimate not declassified, stating, "A sensitive NIE written in 1987 made it clear

gress and the press.[24] But the administration held firm to a skeptical aloofness from the charges. Only the hard-line departing National Security Council (NSC) adviser on Soviet affairs, Richard Pipes, remarked that to him "the evidence [was] very strong," and that if there was a Bulgarian conspiracy, it must have involved the Soviet KGB and its then head, Andropov. But Pipes, too, admitted that there was "a big 'if'," because "the Bulgarian connection has not been solidly made—and it is only inferential."[25]

Why did the Reagan administration take an uncharacteristically cautious stand and avoid comment on possible Bulgarian and Soviet responsibility—other than the CIA backgrounding stressing skepticism? Conservative critics believed it was owing to a growing "softness" on détente and interest in a possible summit meeting with Andropov—which would be out of the question if it turned out that Andropov had ordered the assassination of the pope. In fact, the reason was quite different, but one that the administration could not reveal without damage to itself. The original allegation of a "Bulgarian connection" by Claire Sterling was based in large part on materials supplied by Paul Henze, former CIA station chief in Turkey.[26] Subsequent accounts elaborating the alleged Bulgarian (and Soviet) connection included books and articles by Sterling, Henze, and Michael Ledeen, who had also supplied some of the material used in the earlier Sterling book before becoming a special assistant to Secretary of State Alexander Haig in the spring of 1981.[27] Although

---

that we still had no conclusive evidence of any Soviet involvement in the assassination attempt." *Nomination of Robert Gates*, Hearings, vol. 3, p. 80. That is the latest indication of official U.S. information and evaluation. Both the Russian and Bulgarian postcommunist governments, while disclosing and criticizing other actions of the earlier communist regimes, have said that there was no Bulgarian-Soviet connection with the assassination attempt.

24. For example, see William Safire, "'You Have No Proof'," *New York Times*, December 27, 1982, p. A19; Philip Taubman, "C.I.A. Inept on Pope Plot, D'Amato Says," *New York Times*, February 8, 1983, p. A3; and Niles Lathem, "Ron Blows Stack at CIA Over Pope Probe Foulup," *New York Post*, February 9, 1983, p. 7.

25. See Murrey Marder, "A Theory: Departing NSC Official Mulls a Soviet Role in Pope Plot," *Washington Post*, December 19, 1982, pp. A37, A42.

26. Taubman, *New York Times*, January 27, 1983, p. A12.

27. See Claire Sterling, *The Time of the Assassins: Anatomy of an Investigation* (Holt, Rinehart and Winston, 1983); Paul B. Henze, *The Plot to Kill the Pope* (Charles Scribner's Sons, 1983); and Michael Ledeen, "The Bulgarian Connection and the Media," *Commentary*, vol. 75 (June 1983), pp. 45–50.

   Ledeen later claimed to have warned Secretary Haig in early 1981 that the Soviets would attempt to kill the pope. Reuters dispatch, January 14, 1983. Ledeen himself, in one instance together with Arnaud de Borchgrave, had collaborated with the Italian military security service (SISMI) in 1980–81, then headed by General Giuseppe Santovito, and in particular with its expert on terrorism, Francesco Pazienza.

   Pazienza, by his own account, had supplied information to Sterling for her book on terrorism. Sterling conceded having discussions with General Santovito and Ledeen.

Sterling elaborately disclaims in the 1981 book any "access at all to the CIA while gathering material for this book,"[28] she had in fact been used as a conduit for CIA "black" (covert) propaganda and disinformation on alleged Soviet links with terrorism—whether she was aware of that fact or not.[29] Such a past connection, even if there was no clandestine CIA stimulation for her *Reader's Digest* charges of a Bulgarian connection in the papal assassination plot, was something that made the CIA very wary of now seeming to support the charge. The CIA was aware, at the least, that whereas allegations by a journalist raising public suspicions about a Bulgarian-Soviet connection were one thing, a full judicial proceeding was likely to bring out the truth. And to the best knowledge of American intelligence, although Agca probably *had* had a connection with the Bulgarian security service (*Darzhavna Sigurnost*) through his ties to the Grey Wolves (a right-wing Turkish terrorist group) and the underworld, there was no known Bulgarian (or Soviet) connection with the papal plot, and in fact many reasons to believe there had *not* been such a link.[30] Worst of all, the disclosure of a real American intelligence connection to the original charges would rebound to the discredit of the United States and could even lend credence to Soviet disinformation countercharges of secret *American* connections in the plot itself. Hence strict instructions were agreed upon at the NSC level that there be no comment by American officials in support of the charges of a Bulgarian-Soviet connection. Similarly, the CIA sought through discreet public disclosure of its own skepticism to distance itself from the taint of any earlier association with the origination of the charges. If the CIA was even more directly involved in planting the original Sterling story of a Bulgarian connec-

---

Pazienza, and his close associate Alexandre de Marenches, then chief of French secret intelligence, both stated that they had warned the Vatican of a Soviet plot six months before the attempted assassination. Pazienza later was accused by Agca of having in early 1982 offered him freedom from prison in exchange for implicating Bulgaria in the plot—as he later did. Pazienza, while denying that, volunteered the intriguing confirmation that he was involved in the case in other ways involving the spread of information on terrorism. See Jonathan Kwitny, "Tale of Intrigue: How an Italian Ex-Spy Who Also Helped U.S. Landed in Prison Here," *Wall Street Journal*, August 7, 1985, pp. 1, 12; Kwitny, "Tale of Intrigue: Why an Italian Spy Got Closely Involved in the Billygate Affair," ibid., August 8, 1985, pp. 1, 12; "Former Spy Says He Warned Vatican of Assassination Try," ibid., August 8, 1985, p. 12; Ralph Blumenthal, "Italian Ex-Agent Ordered Extradited from U.S.," *New York Times*, September 12, 1985, p. A12; and Philip Jenkins, "The Assassins Revisited: Claire Sterling and the Politics of Intelligence," *Intelligence and National Security*, vol. 1 (September 1986), pp. 459–471. See also chapter 1, footnotes 45, 47.

28. Claire Sterling, *The Terror Network* (Holt, Rinehart and Winston and Reader's Digest Press, 1981), p. 3.

29. This has been confirmed to me by several senior CIA officials, not for attribution. See also chapter 1, footnote 47.

30. Ibid.

tion, a plausible but unproved possibility, its interest in disengaging from the matter would evidently have been even stronger.[31]

Unofficial speculations by former American officials and other commentators on the implications of a Bulgarian-Soviet connection (if proved) for American-Soviet relations, especially once former KGB chief Andropov had become the Soviet leader, could not of course be prevented. Henry Kissinger, Zbigniew Brzezinski, and former ambassador Malcolm Toon were among those commenting on this impact and tending to accept a Bulgarian-Soviet connection.[32]

Judicial proceedings in Italy continued until the defendants were acquitted for insufficient evidence in March 1986, and the issue remained in the background, occasionally rising to public attention. It did not, however, have a strong or continuing impact on American-Soviet relations because the charges remained unproved and it became increasingly clear that Agca was not a credible source. What the issue did do, however, was to leave a residue of suspicion and stronger anti-Soviet sentiment in the minds of many Americans, and at the same time a strong suspicion in the Soviet leadership that the United States, despite its official restraint, was responsible for having stimulated the whole issue in its campaign of political warfare against the Soviet Union and communism.[33]

---

31. The senior CIA officials who confirmed that Sterling had been used to disseminate disinformation claiming Soviet connections with international terrorism would not (or could not) confirm or deny use of this same channel to plant the original story of a Bulgarian connection in the papal assassination plot. It may, however, have been very tempting to use a probable Bulgarian-Agca underworld connection as a base to launch suspicion-arousing disinformation about a Bulgarian-Soviet connection at a time when the suspicion would not have been expected to be subjected to juridical test.

32. Brzezinski went even further. After Italian judicial indictment, but before the trial, he also said it was "absolutely scandalous" that officials in the State Department and CIA were "unwitting, or in some cases, perhaps, even witting tools" in a campaign "pooh-poohing what turns out to be a very serious plot." See Bernard Gwertzman, "Papal Plot May Hurt U.S.-Soviet Ties," *New York Times*, October 31, 1984, p. A3.

33. The initial Soviet reaction was principally indignation and resentment at the "malicious campaign" and "provocative fabrications" by the "special [intelligence] services in some NATO countries" who "masterminded these allegations." Leonid Zamyatin, TASS, Radio Moscow, December 23, 1982, in FBIS, *Soviet Union*, December 23, 1982, p. P2; and see TASS, "Absurd Insinuations," Radio Moscow, December 17, 1982, in FBIS, *Soviet Union*, December 20, 1982, p. G1. Later, the Soviets began to make unwarranted charges of CIA involvement in the assassination plot itself. For one of the first, see Yury Soltan, Radio Moscow, January 11, 1983, in FBIS, *Soviet Union*, January 12, 1983, p. A6. Also, by July 1983, the KGB had fabricated letters allegedly sent by American Ambassador Maxwell Rabb in Italy in 1982 claiming credit for successfully linking Bulgaria to the assassination attempt. They were printed in *Pace e Guerra* (Peace and War), Rome, July 13, 1983.

Soviet officials have privately said that some in the Soviet political establishment interpreted the situation not only in terms of an American campaign to denigrate the

American policy following the 1982 midterm elections, and changes in leading personnel in the State Department and White House, seemed to be following an uncertain course. President Reagan continued to veer between inflammatory and constructive statements. On several occasions in late 1982 and early 1983 he stressed American desire for a "constructive relationship with the Soviet Union, based on mutual restraint, responsibility and reciprocity," while also criticizing Soviet violation of those principles in Afghanistan, Poland, and Kampuchea (Cambodia).[34] In an address to the nation on January 8, he again stressed that "we must learn from history. We all experienced the soaring hopes and then plunging disappointment of the 1970s, when the Soviet response to our unilateral restraint was to accelerate their military buildup, to foment violence in the developing world, to invade neighboring Afghanistan, and to support the repression of Poland. The lesson is inescapable. If there are to be better mutual relations, they must result from moderation in Soviet conduct." He noted "encouraging words" from the new leaders in Moscow, "But moderate words are convincing only when they're matched by moderate behavior." For our part, while skeptical and keeping our powder dry, "We stand ready to work toward solutions to all outstanding problems." He also reflected one of the pragmatists' main themes in conceding that "we do not insist that the Soviet Union abandon its standing as a superpower or its legitimate national interests," although from the Soviet standpoint he challenged those interests by also reaffirming the American position on Afghanistan, Poland, Kampuchea, and arms control.[35]

In his State of the Union address in January 1983, President Reagan even resurrected Nixon's phrase about a strategy for peace, and said that "at the heart of our strategy for peace is our relationship with the Soviet Union." Referring to the change in leadership in Moscow, he said, "We're prepared for a positive change in Soviet-American relations. But the Soviet Union must show by deeds as well as words a sincere commitment to respect the rights and sovereignty of the family of nations. Responsible members of the world community do not threaten or invade their neighbors. And they restrain their allies from aggression."[36]

In a speech to the American Legion in February, Reagan blasted American behavior in the 1970s as passive, reactive, and weak, saying that

Soviet Union, but more specifically to "get" Andropov by tying him to a Bulgarian plot against the pope even before Andropov became general secretary.

34. "The President's Trip to Latin America," November 30, 1982, *Weekly Compilation of Presidential Documents*, vol. 18 (December 6, 1982), p. 1545. (Hereafter *Presidential Documents*.)

35. President Reagan, "Radio Address to the Nation," January 8, 1983, ibid., vol. 19 (January 17, 1983), p. 25.

36. "The State of the Union," January 25, 1983, ibid., vol. 19 (January 31, 1983), p. 111. Reagan had also used the term "strategy for peace" on November 30, 1982, ibid., vol. 18 (December 6, 1982), p. 1545.

"America had simply ceased to be a leader in the world. . . . For too long, our foreign policy had been a pattern of reaction to crisis, reaction to the political agendas of others, reaction to the offensive actions of those hostile to freedom and democracy. . . . Too many of our leaders saw the Soviets as a mirror image of themselves," and engaged in policies based on wishful thinking. But the Soviet Union engaged in a massive military buildup while our military power declined. Now, as the United States was rebuilding its economic and military strength, it could restore balance. Productive relations with the Soviet Union would be possible based on "restraint and reciprocity."[37]

President Reagan also returned, however, to the theme of his address to the British Parliament the previous June, a "crusade for freedom." He reaffirmed an intention to wage vigorous ideological competition, and said that "we have forged the beginnings of a fundamentally new direction in American foreign policy."[38] And, indeed, the United States had embarked on a new intensified ideological propaganda campaign. In mid-January the president signed National Security Decision Directive (NSDD)–77, a directive to mount a coordinated campaign for "the management of public diplomacy."[39] A special cabinet-level planning and coordinating committee was established with National Security Adviser William P. Clark as chairman and Secretaries George Shultz and Caspar Weinberger, Director Charles Z. Wick of the United States Information Agency, and administrator Peter McPherson of the Agency for International Development as members. In addition, the administration requested $65 million from Congress to fund a new "Project Democracy" to support free labor unions and political parties overseas. Large increases in funding were requested for the Voice of America and Radio Free Europe, and Congress was again asked to authorize a new "Radio Marti" to broadcast to Cuba.[40]

The new propaganda program included intensified efforts directed at the Soviet Union and Eastern Europe. Nearly a year earlier, Haig had made clear that "just as the Soviet Union gives active support to Marxist-Leninist

---

37. "American Legion," February 22, 1983, ibid., vol. 19 (February 28, 1983), pp. 271–73.

38. Ibid., pp. 276–77.

39. The NSDD described public diplomacy as comprising "those actions of the U.S. Government designed to generate support for our national security objectives." This broad mandate was designed to cover a wide range of actions extending beyond public relations and propaganda.

40. The main facts of the new program were quickly leaked; see Bernard Gwertzman, "Reagan Intensifies Drive to Promote Policies in Europe," *New York Times*, January 20, 1983, pp. A1, A8; and see Gerald F. Seib, "Struggle for Ideas: Fearing Soviet Gains, U.S. Counterattacks in the Propaganda War," *Wall Street Journal*, May 17, 1983, pp. 1, 23.

Besides the Clark group (and four subordinate committees), a separate special committee was set up under Peter Dailey, Reagan's 1980 campaign advertising manager, and in 1983 ambassador to Ireland, to counter Soviet propaganda and gain support in Western Europe for the U.S. INF missile deployments.

forces in the West and South, we must give vigorous support to democratic forces wherever they are located—including countries which are now Communist." This formulation implied that such countries as were "now" communist might not remain so. He also had added an ominous edge to the idea of intensified competition (and "reciprocity") when he went on to say, "We want the competition of democracy and communism to be conducted in peaceful and political terms, but we will provide other means if the Soviet Union insists upon violent methods of struggle."[41] In addition, though of course not made public, the new intensified propaganda and political warfare campaign would also use "black" means, including unattributed disinformation.[42]

Having inaugurated an Afghanistan Day in March 1982, and a new annual Baltic Freedom Day in June 1982, President Reagan now also designated February 16, 1983, as Lithuanian Independence Day, and May 21 as National Andrei Sakharov Day. In another speech in February he also said: "In the struggle now going on for the world, we have not been afraid to characterize our adversaries for what they are. We have focused world attention on forced labor on the Soviet pipeline and Soviet repression in Poland and all the other nations that make up what is called the 'fourth world'—those living under totalitarian rule who long for freedom."[43]

In March 1983 President Reagan delivered two of the most significant statements of his presidency in terms of their impact on American-Soviet relations. First came his speech to the National Association of Evangelicals on March 8, in which Reagan reaffirmed a moral-ideological basis for policy toward the Soviet Union. Declaring the Soviet leaders to be "the focus of evil in the modern world," he also called for Americans not "to ignore the facts of history and the aggressive impulses of an evil empire . . . and thereby remove yourself from the struggle between right and wrong and good and evil." Reagan thus identified himself and the cause of anticommunism as the focus of good in the world. Relativism, any reading of history that did *not* place all blame on the Soviet side, that would "label both sides equally at fault" (or even unequally, but still finding both at fault) or "simply call the arms race a giant misunderstanding," was not only eschewed but in effect called immoral. True, he also said that "this doesn't mean we should isolate ourselves and refuse to seek an

---

41. Secretary Haig, "American Power and American Purpose," April 27, 1982, *Department of State Bulletin*, vol. 82 (June 1982), p. 43. (Hereafter *State Bulletin*.)

42. Information from knowledgeable officials.

    The public leaks did not disclose that William Casey was a member of the Clark group, nor that the man selected to be the executive staff director, Walter Raymond, Jr., was a veteran CIA officer experienced in covert operations who had been seconded to the NSC by Casey. Upon assuming his new "political" position on the NSC staff, Raymond retired from the CIA.

43. "Conservative Political Action Conference," February 18, 1983, *Presidential Documents*, vol. 19 (February 28, 1983), p. 262.

understanding with them."[44] But it became increasingly clear that any agreement would be expected to result from continuing efforts to build American strength, and Soviet recognition of that strength.

The second key statement followed on March 23, in what has become known as the Star Wars speech. In a major speech calling for support for the defense budget (and opposing the then current and popular nuclear freeze proposal, as he also had on March 8), Reagan proposed a change from the whole concept of mutual deterrence through assured capabilities for retaliation, which he conceded had prevented war for almost forty years, and its replacement by an effective strategic defense.[45] Without at this point examining the implications of this new departure, it should be noted that the threatened destabilizing effects of this initiative and its opening of a major new area of the arms race that had been quiescent since the Antiballistic Missile (ABM) Treaty of 1972 caused widespread disquiet in the West as well as in the Soviet Union.[46] The practical steps that were set in train marked an important new step in "deeds," not merely words, but actions intensifying the arms competition.

Although the catchy phrase Star Wars was a journalistic invention, this evocation of the popular futuristic "morality tale" film subtly and unintentionally fitted very well the Reagan image of the political universe, pitting death rays of a "force" for Good in battle against an "Evil Empire." The main reason for his sudden, and tenacious, attraction to the idea was a strong desire to escape the confines of mutual deterrence and mutual dependence for survival. President Reagan, wary of dealings with the communist leaders of the Soviet Union and restless over any need for mutual security, became captivated by a vision of strategic defenses able to liberate the United States from the need to rely upon mutual political accommodation, negotiated arms control, and reciprocal military restraint. And despite widespread misgivings and initial doubts in the United States that the initiative would become a serious military program, it did.

In the judgment of informed officials and observers the allure of restoration of the traditional invulnerability of the United States in the nuclear missile era remained only a vision and not a realistic prospect technologically, strategically, or politically. Moreover, the clearly predictable consequences of pursuing this will-o'-the wisp were not only negative but dangerous. Yet because it was at essence an ideological vision rather than a technological promise or a strategic design, it was impervious to arguments based on realities of technology and strategy. Cost was another matter, and eventually the extremely

---

44. "National Association of Evangelicals," March 8, 1983, *Presidential Documents*, vol. 19 (March 14, 1983), pp. 368–69.

45. "National Security," March 23, 1983, ibid., vol. 19 (March 28, 1983), pp. 442–48.

46. For discussion of the impact on arms control and the strategic balance, see chapter 12. Effects on U.S.-Allied relations are examined in chapter 13.

high costs of any conceivable program virtually precluded decision (by a future administration, in any case) to deploy an anti-missile system.[47]

Not all who followed and supported President Reagan in this quixotic quest shared the illusions of his vision; indeed, few even in his own administration did. But many supported it for various reasons: misplaced loyalty, cultivation of influence and power, political discipline, support for any military program, distrust or dislike for arms control and for any improvement in American relations with the Soviet Union, scientific challenge, and lucrative economic gain. Many sought strategic defenses as one element in a continuing arms competition by defending strategic missile forces. Of course, there was also a popular interest in real national population defense among those who were unaware of its unattainability and of the pernicious consequences of its pursuit.

In the course of describing the Soviet military buildup in his speech of March 23, President Reagan said that the Soviets had continued to increase their deployments of the SS-20 intermediate-range ballistic missile even though "a year ago this month, Mr. Brezhnev pledged a moratorium, or freeze, on SS-20 deployment." "Some freeze," he added ironically.[48] Three days later General Secretary Andropov responded that Reagan had "uttered a deliberate untruth in asserting that the Soviet Union does not observe its own unilateral moratorium."[49] In fact, although Reagan undoubtedly did not deliberately tell an untruth, he was wrong: the Soviets *did* abide by their moratorium. During the entire period of the moratorium (from March 1982 until it was ended in December 1983, when deployment of Pershing II missiles began) the Soviets did not in fact add any SS-20 launchers to the 243 existing (operational or under construction) that were facing Europe on the date the moratorium began. The Soviets had not, however, made clear that the moratorium applied to any additional *new* deployments and that they would not cut off construction under way; indeed the vagueness of their statements on this point implied a stop to deployment and even to construction right away. If the United States spokesmen had pointed out that the moratorium meant less than it seemed to promise, since the Soviets went on to complete 36 launchers under construction in

47.  For a good account of how Edward Teller and a few other determined scientists made a successful sales pitch to President Reagan see William J. Broad, *Teller's War: The Top-Secret Story behind the Star Wars Deception* (Simon and Schuster, 1992).

By the time of the Bush administration deployment of a comprehensive strategic antiballistic missile system was abandoned. The strategic defense initiative program as such, and its space-war components, were dropped by the Clinton administration early in 1993.

48.  *Presidential Documents*, vol. 19 (March 28, 1983), p. 444.

49.  "Replies of Yu. V. Andropov to Questions by a Correspondent of Pravda," *Pravda*, March 27, 1983.

This direct personal criticism of an American president by a Soviet leader was the first in many years and reflected growing Soviet pessimism on the possibility of dealing with the Reagan administration.

the European USSR (and 9 others facing Western Europe), that would have been one thing. But instead the administration argued that the moratorium was a "fraud," and (with reference to the fact of continuing deployment in Asia) argued that the SS-20 continued to be deployed despite the moratorium—although the Soviets had clearly stated that the moratorium applied only to SS-20 deployment facing Europe and not in Asia. The United States, seeking to maintain Western European support for the deployment of intermediate-range nuclear forces (INF), continued to argue that the Soviet Union was not exercising restraint, while the Soviets argued that it was doing so and further that the United States was lying in its charge of Soviet failure to abide by its own moratorium. The top leaders, Reagan and Andropov, had in effect accused each other of lying. No one in the two governments, however, publicly acknowledged the basis for the discrepant views.[50] The whole episode, minor in itself, illustrates the difficulty of dialogue when adversarial propaganda purposes are given priority.

In a third major speech in March, on arms control, Reagan stressed the "relentless military buildup" carried out by the Soviet Union over fifteen years, "acquiring what can only be considered an offensive military capability." Ominously, he continued in the very next sentence by saying that "all the moral values which this country cherishes . . . are fundamentally challenged by a powerful adversary which does not wish these values to survive." He therefore stressed a "commitment to peace through strength."[51]

Soon after, the President's Commission on Strategic Forces (better known as the Scowcroft Commission, after its chairman, Brent Scowcroft, a retired lieutenant general and Kissinger's successor as national security adviser under President Ford), reported its findings. Although established mainly to shore up bipartisan support for deployment of the MX missile, the more significant contribution of the commission's report was to quietly bury the lingering thesis that the United States faced a "window of vulnerability" in its deterrent force that might open a "window of opportunity" for a Soviet attack.[52]

---

50. See Raymond L. Garthoff, "That SS-20 Moratorium: Who Is Telling the Truth?" *Washington Post*, April 26, 1983, p. A19. The figure of 243 launchers facing Europe was confirmed as still valid, but with no reference to the moratorium, in a Department of Defense publication, *Soviet Military Power* (Washington, 1984), p. 51.

One may be sure that Reagan had simply been told that the Soviets kept on building SS-20s, and Andropov was told that the Soviets were observing their moratorium, and it is highly unlikely either understood the basis for the contradictory interpretations.

51. "Los Angeles World Affairs Council," March 31, 1983, *Presidential Documents*, vol. 19 (April 4, 1983), p. 484.

52. *Report of the President's Commission on Strategic Forces* (Washington, April 1983), 29 pp. See also *President's Commission on Strategic Forces*, Hearing before the Senate Committee on Foreign Relations, 98th Cong. 1 sess., May 11, 1983 (GPO, 1983), 34 pp.

Meanwhile, the diplomatic "dialogue," which had atrophied, was revived. Secretary of State Shultz undertook a thorough internal review of all aspects of U.S. relations with the Soviet Union as a basis for reconsidering policy. Shultz then began to move slowly but deliberately to build a constructive relationship; in his own later words, to try to turn the relationship "away from confrontation and toward real problem solving."[53] He began with a brief pitch to President Reagan at a New Year's party. But he still felt a need to determine whether Reagan was prepared to seek a more constructive relationship with Moscow. On January 19 he sent the president a memorandum outlining "U.S.-Soviet Relations in 1983," in which he proposed "an intensified dialogue with Moscow" at various levels, including an eventual summit if substance warranted. In this memorandum he first outlined the four-part agenda for relations that was to become the guide over the next five years: human rights, arms control, regional conflicts, and bilateral relations (including trade).[54] This agenda was seen as an alternative to letting the Soviet Union focus almost entirely on arms control. Shultz obtained approval to open a "careful dialogue" with Ambassador Anatoly Dobrynin and had an initial meeting in late January.

Reagan himself was, for the first time, becoming receptive to the idea of repairing relations with the Soviet Union. He felt a greater confidence in a growing American recovery under his administration. Moreover, over the Christmas 1982 holidays in Palm Springs, after consulting a few close friends, he had decided to run for a second term in 1984. While there was still two years until then, he had begun to think in campaign terms.[55] On Saturday, February 12, after an unusually heavy snowfall in Washington, the Reagans canceled plans to spend the weekend at Camp David, and on the spur of the moment invited George Shultz and his wife for dinner in the family quarters of the White House. Reagan said he had been fascinated by the television coverage of the secretary's trip to China, and—encouraged by Nancy—he wondered if he could not arrange to visit China and Russia. Shultz carefully responded that he thought such visits would be "a great idea if it comes about in the right way," that is, if it was prepared for by meaningful step-by-step improvements in relations. Shultz also told the president that, by chance, Dobrynin would be coming to see him at the State Department on the next Tuesday, and if Reagan wished, he could bring Dobrynin over to the White House. Reagan was enthusiastic, but wanted to keep the meeting secret.[56]

---

53. George P. Shultz, *Turmoil and Triumph: My Years as Secretary of State* (Charles Scribner's Sons, 1993), p. 159.

54. Ibid., pp. 159–62.

55. Information from a well-informed administration source in early 1984.

56. Shultz, *Turmoil and Triumph*, p. 164; and see Don Oberdorfer, *The Turn: From the Cold War to a New Era, The United States and the Soviet Union, 1983–1990* (Poseidon Press, 1991), pp. 15–17.

This chance relaxed private conversation between Reagan and Shultz helped to establish an important personal rapport. Perhaps most important was Shultz's realization that, in his words, "Ronald Reagan was much more willing to move forward in relations . . . than I had earlier believed." Shultz later mused that "if it hadn't snowed, the president would have gone to Camp David, and I would not have been invited to the White House to gain the insight and opportunity to help him engage directly with the Soviets."[57]

On February 15, when Dobrynin came to the State Department, he was told of the president's desire to meet with him, and they discreetly went to the White House through the little-used East Gate. It was Reagan's first meeting as president with Dobrynin or any Soviet official (apart from diplomatic functions and a brief courtesy call by Reagan to sign the condolence book at the Soviet Embassy after Brezhnev died). In a two-hour meeting (not long for diplomatic meetings, but unusually long for President Reagan) the president indicated his desire to improve relations and touched on a number of subjects. The one in which he showed the most interest concerned the fate of seven Pentecostal Christian Russians who, seeking to emigrate to the United States, had taken asylum in the American Embassy in Moscow in mid-1978 and were still there.[58]

The Soviet leaders were not convinced that Reagan had any real desire to improve relations, and they would not be convinced for the rest of the year for reasons that will become evident. Still, it seemed a small enough gesture to accede to the president's personal plea, and in April the Pentecostals were permitted to leave the embassy with assurances of no arrest, and by June they and other members of their extended families were allowed to leave the country.[59]

In early March Shultz submitted a new memorandum to the president, "U.S.-Soviet Relations: Where Do We Want to Be and How Do We Get There?" He noted that he had had several meetings with Dobrynin and saw "a few tentative signs of Soviet willingness to move forward on specific issues." Probably with an eye to the NSC hard-liners, but also expressing his own and Reagan's thinking, Shultz noted as a minimum objective of further exploration "to make clear that we are determined to resist Soviet efforts to use their growing military power in ways which threaten our security." But he also argued that there was "a chance to go beyond this minimum objective and make some progress toward a more stable and constructive U.S.-Soviet rela-

---

57. Shultz, *Turmoil and Triumph*, pp. 164, 167.

58. Ibid., pp. 164–67; and Oberdorfer, *The Turn*, pp. 17–20. Michael Deaver had enthusiastically supported the meeting with Dobrynin, as had Nancy Reagan; William Clark had opposed it.

59. Shultz, *Turmoil and Triumph*, pp. 167–71.

tionship over the next two years or so." He reiterated the four-part agenda. A meeting with the president was set for March 10.[60]

Shultz was surprised to find the meeting filled with people, some of whom (like hard-line staffers Richard Pipes and John Lenczowski) he did not even know. William Clark had arranged the meeting to let these hard-line experts weigh in against Shultz's cautious but forward proposals for engagement with the Soviets. Shultz let his anger show. The next day he told the president privately that he needed direction from him on Soviet relations, and Reagan told him to "go ahead." On March 16 Shultz submitted yet another memorandum to Reagan, "Next Steps in U.S.-Soviet Relations," proposing a wide-ranging series of gradual steps to improve relations. This time he met alone with the president on March 25, except for Clark, and recalled their discussion during the February snowstorm. Reagan made clear his desire to move ahead with a dialogue, and endorsed Shultz's suggestion that his testimony before the Senate Foreign Relations Committee (then scheduled for mid-April, later postponed until mid-June) would be the best vehicle to make public their new dialogue with the Soviet Union. Clark now understood that the president was serious.

Shultz saw this meeting as "critical," and as giving him "a green light to implement my policy—now the president's policy—step by step, with the potential for a real reversal of U.S.-Soviet relations. The process would be slow and laborious, I knew. But at least I was now in a position to start serious work on this relationship of vital importance and the full agenda of issues before us."[61]

A number of meetings between Shultz and Dobrynin were held during the first half of the year. The INF negotiations were one subject argued over in these talks. But Shultz also raised with Dobrynin the plan to open consulates in Kiev and New York, under way until it had been stopped by President Carter as a sanction after the Soviet occupation of Afghanistan, and the renewal of the cultural agreement, which had also been permitted by the United States to lapse after Afghanistan. Talks on other subjects, including ways of dealing with regional conflicts in Africa and with the situation in Afghanistan, were also renewed. In April Shultz was able to tell Dobrynin that the United States was ready to negotiate a long-term grain agreement.[62]

Ever since the formulation of NSDD-75 at the turn of the year, but especially in the January and March memorandums to the president and Shultz's discussions with the president as well as in their contacts with Soviet diplomats in Washington and Moscow, Shultz and the State Department had

---

60. Ibid., pp. 265–67.

61. Ibid., pp. 267–71.

62. Information from knowledgeable American and Soviet diplomatic officials. Shultz refers only in passing to these discussions in his memoir; see Shultz, *Turmoil and Triumph*, pp. 271–72.

been seeking to create a constructive *process* of developing relationship. Rather than work for specific accords, they sought to build a broadened agenda beyond arms control as a more solid base for relations than the failed détente of the 1970s, and to rely more on incremental steps than on dramatic but short-lived summit meetings that heightened expectations.

There were clearly problems, however, in coordinating and "signaling" policy statements, policy, and actions. Reagan's speech of January 8 had been drafted in the State Department, while those of March 8 and 23 obviously had not been. Although the assignment of pragmatic veteran Soviet affairs officer Jack Matlock to the NSC staff in May, succeeding the ideologically hard-line Richard Pipes, helped, it did not affect the ideological tenor of the president's speech-writing team, headed by Anthony Dolan. As Shultz later confirmed, neither he nor anyone else in the State Department was even aware of the "Evil Empire" and similar remarks before the president spoke.[63] Reagan himself seemed to see no relationship between such rhetorical utterances and American *policy* toward the Soviet Union, and he failed to see their negative impact on Soviet perceptions of American policy objectives.

Apart from rhetoric, while some steps the United States took indicated an interest in normalizing relations, others did not. On April 4 Reagan asked Congress for stiffer export control limits (at a time when U.S. trade with the USSR was down to about half the 1979 level). In April the United States also adopted new more stringent regulations controlling the movement of Soviet diplomats in the United States. And in May stricter visa requirements were imposed on citizens of the USSR and other communist countries.[64]

Through the spring and early summer Reagan became increasingly confident that the United States was making progress toward economic recovery, the growing defense budget was not under challenge, and at the Williamsburg Western economic summit in May alliance relations were clearly mended (after the damaging pipeline sanctions had been dropped). He increasingly gave signs of believing that the United States had now restored its strength enough to be able to negotiate with the Soviet Union.

Shultz believed that a new comprehensive statement of American policy toward the Soviet Union should be made to clarify the bases on which the United States was operating, and Reagan agreed. On June 15 Shultz made his major statement to Congress outlining American policy, in the most full exposition since Secretary Haig's address of August 11, 1981.[65] The statement was

---

63. Ibid., pp. 266–67.

64. The Soviets charged that these new discriminatory restraints on travel were violations of the provisions of the Helsinki Final Act Conference on Security and Cooperation in Europe (CSCE) calling for facilitating contacts and travel. Information from an informed American official.

65. As earlier noted, the original intention had been for Secretary Shultz to testify in mid-April; his testimony was postponed to June owing to scheduling difficulties.

carefully drafted in the State Department, with Matlock's help at the NSC, on the basis of the formal policy guidance reached by compromise in NSDD-75. Moreover, Shultz personally cleared the text with Reagan.[66] The statement reaffirmed the administration's tough line, demanding that the Soviet Union modify its behavior, at home and in Eastern Europe and in exercising "restraint" around the world, as a condition for improved relations, but it also affirmed American interest in dialogue and negotiation. This combination of a tough stance with an assertion of interest in dialogue was confusing to many.[67] It represented, in fact, the compromise reached in the formal policy guidance, but it also reflected Reagan's and Shultz's own thinking. It did represent a victory for *Realpolitik* pragmatists over doctrinaire ideologues. One can well imagine Haig—or Kissinger or Brzezinski—making this speech in 1983, but not the hard-line confrontationists in the Reagan Pentagon or NSC staff.[68] It set forth the basic policy of the Reagan administration on relations with the Soviet Union as it had evolved after the first two and a half years of the administration.

First of all, Shultz's statement recognized that "the management of our relations with the Soviet Union is of utmost importance. That relationship touches virtually every aspect of our international concerns and objectives—political, economic, and military—and every part of the world."[69]

Second, the Soviet Union was regarded as "a powerful . . . adversary" threatening both American interests and values. The United States therefore saw an obligation "to counter Soviet expansionism through sustained and effec-

---

The main statement made in the interim had been a little-noted speech by Undersecretary for Political Affairs Lawrence Eagleburger, "Review of U.S. Relations with the Soviet Union," February 1, 1983, *State Bulletin*, vol. 83 (March 1983), pp. 81–84.

66. Shultz, *Turmoil and Triumph*, pp. 276–80.

67. For example, the *New York Times* asserted the positive while the *Washington Post* stressed the negative, as reflected in their diverging headlines: Philip Taubman, "Shultz Testifies Rifts with Soviets Aren't Inevitable," *New York Times*, June 16, 1983, pp. A1, A16; and Don Oberdorfer, "Shultz Outlines Policy of Opposing Soviets," *Washington Post*, June 16, 1983, pp. A1, A20. See also Robert J. McCloskey, "Conflicting Reports on the Shultz Testimony," *Washington Post*, June 22, 1983, p. 1.

68. As Leslie Gelb subsequently reported (in "Expanding Contacts with Soviet: Shultz and Dobrynin Make a Start," *New York Times*, June 30, 1983, pp. A1, A12), members of the NSC staff had objected to three key points in the Shultz statement: that confrontation was not inevitable, that "gradual change" in the Soviet Union was possible, and that the United States was now sufficiently strong to begin a "constructive dialogue," but Reagan overrode their objections and approved those points.

There was one important change from the Nixon-Kissinger strategic approach; Shultz did not believe in "linkage," arguing that if it was in the interest of the United States to move in any instance, that possibility should not be made hostage to other aspects of U.S.-Soviet relations. See Shultz, *Turmoil and Triumph*, p. 278.

69. "U.S.-Soviet Relations in the Context of U.S. Foreign Policy," Secretary Shultz's Statement before the Senate Foreign Relations Committee, June 15, 1983, *State Bulletin*, vol. 83 (July 1983), p. 65.

tive political, economic, and military competition." Moreover, in addition to a "continuing Soviet quest for military superiority" the administration saw an "unconstructive Soviet involvement, direct and indirect, in unstable areas of the Third World," marked in the 1970s by major new forms of military intervention directly or through surrogates in Angola, Ethiopia, Indochina, and Afghanistan. The Soviet Union also was charged with an "unrelenting effort to impose an alien Soviet 'model' on nominally independent Soviet clients and allies," notably in Poland and its other "satellites," and in Afghanistan. In addition, for the first time the administration authoritatively charged that the Soviet leaders were guilty of a "continuing practice of stretching a series of treaties and agreements to the brink of violation and beyond"—in human rights, the Helsinki Final Act, and various arms control agreements.[70] But while the Soviet leaders were accused of bad conduct, they were not said to be evil.

The administration, said Shultz, did "not accept as inevitable the prospect of endless, dangerous confrontation with the Soviet Union." Despite ideological differences "we are not so deterministic as to believe that geopolitics and ideological competition must ineluctably lead to permanent and dangerous confrontation" nor "to regard mutual hostility with the U.S.S.R. as an immutable fact of international life."[71]

Containment, in the classical sense of the Truman Doctrine, Shultz said had been overtaken; "Soviet ambitions and capabilities have long since reached beyond the geographic bounds that this doctrine took for granted." Of course, he stated that "we have to make clear that we will *resist encroachments* on our vital interests and those of our allies and friends." Restraint must be instilled. "The policy of détente, of course, represented an effort to induce Soviet restraint." Although Shultz conceded that "some versions" of détente comprehended "the need to resist Soviet geopolitical encroachments," détente was based on expectations that "the anticipation of benefits from expanding economic relations and arms control agreements would restrain Soviet behavior. Unfortunately, experience has proved otherwise." Accordingly, the new post-détente American policy was "based on the expectation that, faced with demonstration of the West's renewed determination to strengthen its defenses, enhance its political and economic cohesion, and oppose adventurism, the Soviet Union will see restraint as its most attractive, or only, option."[72]

In an attempt to engage serious Soviet attention, Shultz's statement also included the important provision that "we will respect legitimate Soviet security interests and are ready to negotiate equitable solutions to outstanding political problems."[73] Although undoubtedly in practice a wide gap would

---

70. Ibid., pp. 65–67.

71. Ibid., p. 66.

72. Ibid., p. 67. Emphasis in original.

73. Ibid., p. 67.

remain between judgments in Washington and Moscow about precisely *what* constituted legitimate Soviet security interests, and equitable solutions, many (and not only in Moscow) had wondered whether the Reagan administration conceded that there were *any* legitimate Soviet security interests.[74]

Thus "peace must be built on strength." And, in what was intended to be the key element in the statement, Shultz declared that "having begun to rebuild our strength, *we now seek to engage the Soviet leaders in a constructive dialogue*—a dialogue through which we hope *to find political solutions to outstanding issues.*"[75] "Strength and realism," he said, "can deter war, but only direct dialogue and negotiation can open the path toward lasting peace."[76] The burden of choice was placed on "Brezhnev's successors" to "weigh the *increased* costs and risks of relentless competition against the benefits of a less tense international environment." In either case, "our parallel pursuit of strength and negotiation prepares us both to resist continued Soviet aggrandizement and to recognize and respond to positive Soviet moves."[77] Shultz subsequently characterized the essence of his statement, and of American policy, in two words: "strength and diplomacy."[78]

The Soviet leaders (as will shortly be seen) remained highly skeptical about whether this statement of policy marked any step forward in finding common ground. Coincidentally, the very next day Gromyko in a major policy review statement was sharply critical of American positions and policy.[79] Nonetheless, both sides, while wary, were prepared to advance the dialogue. The Soviets permitted Shultz's deputy, Kenneth Dam, to make an uncensored

---

74. The verbal acceptance of "legitimate national interests" of the Soviet Union (and even of its "standing as a superpower") had, as earlier noted, been included in President Reagan's brief remarks on January 8, 1983, and also in the statement by Undersecretary of State Lawrence Eagleburger a month later. See Eagleburger, *State Bulletin*, vol. 83 (March 1983), p. 82. These statements had not, however, carried the same context of invitation to a dialogue.

75. Shultz, *State Bulletin*, vol. 83 (July 1983), p. 66. Emphasis added.

76. Ibid., p. 69.

77. Ibid., p. 72. Emphasis added.

78. Secretary Shultz, "News Conference of June 22," *State Bulletin*, vol. 83 (August 1983), p. 6.
   Three days after his statement to Congress, Shultz met with Dobrynin and repeated the thrust of it privately, stressing that the administration was ready to negotiate and serious about wishing to improve relations.

79. One commentator described Gromyko's speech before the Supreme Soviet on June 16 as "in many ways like a mirror image" of Shultz's speech, only blaming the United States for all the tension in the world, while also expressing a desire to improve relations—and expecting the *other* side would make concessions in its behavior. See John F. Burns, "A Chill in the Kremlin," *New York Times*, June 17, 1983, pp. A1, A8.
   Gromyko's speech is discussed later in this chapter.

speech on Soviet television in late June. On June 26, as previously noted, the Pentecostalists who had taken refuge in the American Embassy in Moscow five years earlier were permitted to emigrate.

In June both the United States and the Soviet Union also modified their proposals in the strategic arms reduction talks (START), making at least a small step toward possible eventual agreement. And in Madrid, after almost three years of an acrimonious Conference on Security and Cooperation in Europe (CSCE) review conference, a compromise agreement was reached in July. Its main achievement was agreement to convene a conference on European confidence- and security-building measures and disarmament in Stockholm.

On July 28 a new five-year long-term grain agreement at a higher minimum level of 9 million tons a year was agreed upon, which provided a guarantee against cancellation under any future political embargo.[80] In late July Secretary Shultz and Commerce Secretary Malcolm Baldrige recommended the relaxation of controls on the export of gas and oil and pipelaying equipment originally imposed by Carter after Afghanistan. Despite opposition by Defense Secretary Weinberger, National Security Adviser Clark, and some NSC staff advisers, Reagan on August 20 approved the recommended relaxation of controls.

There continued to be some discordant developments. In the spring and again in August and September, Soviet and American diplomats were expelled for espionage—the first such cases made public since 1978.[81] On July 30 an American destroyer hailed and interrogated, and then trailed, a Soviet merchant ship approaching Nicaragua, in a legal but questionable display of close American monitoring.[82]

Nonetheless, in July, in confidential diplomatic discussions, the Soviets and Americans reached an agreement in principle to resume talks on the establishment of the new consulates and on a new cultural exchange agreement, cut off after Afghanistan, as Shultz had proposed to Dobrynin in March. This agreement was publicly announced on August 27. In further private talks

---

80. The agreement was publicly announced on that same day, although it was not formally signed until August 25 and did not go into effect until October. It replaced an earlier five-year agreement reached in 1976 but not renewed in 1982 because of a ban on negotiation imposed by Reagan as a sanction for martial law in Poland. Reagan lifted the ban in April, permitting the negotiations concluded in July.

81. See "Soviet Orders a U.S. Vice Consul Expelled as a Spy," and "U.S. Reveals Ouster of 2 Soviet Attaches within Last Month," *New York Times*, September 13, 1983, p. A12. At least some of these cases on both sides were flagrant, but public expulsion was not the only recourse.

82. Richard Halloran, "Pentagon Reports Encounter at Sea with Soviet Ship," *New York Times*, August 4, 1983, pp. A1, A9.

in August, the Soviets agreed to meetings of Shultz and Gromyko at Madrid on September 8 (when both would be there for a CSCE meeting), to be followed up on in New York when Gromyko came for the opening of the UN General Assembly.[83]

Andropov had revived presidential correspondence with a letter to Reagan on July 4. Reagan again wanted to write a personal reply, and did so (although he was persuaded by William Clark to delete a reference to arms reduction talks possibly leading to the complete elimination of nuclear weapons). His letter vaguely called for confidential communication. The Soviets were uncertain what to make of the letter, and responded by both a reserved "official" letter and a brief personal one from Andropov agreeing on the possible utility of confidential communications. Soon after, Shultz learned that a confidential channel of communication *had* been established earlier between Dobrynin and Clark, of which he was not aware, and Clark had tried to expand on his role in July by suggesting to the president that he, Clark, might travel to Moscow to pursue the U.S.-Soviet dialogue. When Shultz learned of this plan, and of several other things about which he had been uninformed, such as an intensification of U.S. covert paramilitary operations against Nicaragua and a secret visit by Clark's deputy Robert McFarlane to the Near East, topped off by press speculations downplaying Shultz's role and playing up Clark's, Shultz exploded and offered his resignation. Reagan talked him out of it.

On August 24 a reply was sent from Reagan to Andropov, again suggesting intensified dialogue, but again with no concrete proposals. These exchanges of July and August were not made public.[84]

Underlying all these moves was maneuvering for a possible summit meeting. Hints of interest from one side or the other had appeared from almost the outset of the new administration in 1981. Neither side wanted to appear to oppose a meeting, but both took refuge in statements on the value of a "prepared" summit meeting. By the summer of 1983 the possibility seemed greater than at any earlier time, although still uncertain. Clark was reported to be opposed, but James Baker and Michael Deaver were reported to believe it would bolster Reagan to have a summit meeting before the 1984 elections. Weinberger opposed a summit, in part because he suspected it would include some agreement on arms control. Shultz quietly favored the idea and sought to maneuver the course of developing relations in that direction, but he did not openly push it.

---

83. Information on the confidential exchanges was provided by knowledgeable U.S. officials.

84. See Oberdorfer, *The Turn*, pp. 37–42, 46–47; Shultz, *Turmoil and Triumph*, pp. 358–60; and Ronald Reagan, *An American Life* (Simon and Schuster, 1990), pp. 576–82.

## *Growing Soviet Disillusionment*

The discussion above has surveyed the development of American-Soviet relations in the first eight months of 1983 from the standpoint of U.S. policy. The salient developments from the Soviet perspective often had a different aspect. Thus in American eyes the United States placed particular attention on a gradual process of small steps to improve relations, and the main initiatives were Secretary Shultz's dialogue with Ambassador Dobrynin and Shultz's congressional testimony in June.

From the Soviet standpoint, the main development in 1983 (as in 1981 and 1982) was a steady continuing American military buildup while the United States conducted a holding action in the arms limitation talks. The Soviet Union continued to take initiatives in the arms control field from which it sought and gained some propaganda advantage: the unilateral pledge on no first use of nuclear weapons, draft treaties to ban antisatellite weapons and other weapons in space (a draft treaty in August 1981, and a revised version largely responsive to unofficial American criticisms in August 1983), and others. But the Soviet leaders also sought to engage the United States in a serious dialogue and negotiation, and in this they did not succeed.

The restraint that the new Andropov administration believed it had shown since November 1982 was met by an American one-two punch sequence in March 1983. As noted earlier, on March 8 President Reagan pronounced the Soviet Union an "evil empire," and indeed the "focus of all evil." Two weeks later in a strong pitch for his massive military program, he added the new element of a call for an impenetrable ballistic missile defense based on exotic new technologies, his Star Wars speech. Soviet commentators reacted with indignation and anger at the "evil empire" vilification, and the leadership observed the coincidental establishment of a major new propaganda program to carry out the president's political and ideological "crusade." But the touchstone was the military program of the administration. Andropov himself responded to the Star Wars speech. As a general conclusion, he said that "the present U.S. administration continues to tread an extremely perilous path. Issues of peace and war must not be treated so flippantly. All attempts at achieving military superiority over the Soviet Union are futile. The Soviet Union will never let that happen. . . . It is time they stopped thinking up one option after another in search of the best way of unleashing nuclear war in the hope of winning it. To do this is not just irresponsible, it is madness."[85] Thus

---

85. "Replies by Yu. V. Andropov to Questions from a Correspondent of Pravda," *Pravda*, March 27, 1983.

Andropov raised questions not only about the sincerity of Reagan's intentions but also about the rationality of his policy premises and conclusions.

On the specific idea of developing a defense against ballistic missiles, he conceded its superficial attraction, but saw the real U.S. purpose as "an intention to secure the potential with ballistic missile defenses to destroy the corresponding strategic systems of the other side, that is, to deny it the capabilities to mount a retaliatory strike, counting on disarming the Soviet Union in the face of the American nuclear threat."[86] A month later, Andropov again charged the United States with seeking a first-strike capability, and showed increasing impatience with the positions taken by the United States in the START and INF negotiations, as well as again expressing concern that the United States was broadening the arms race into space.[87]

The Soviets' reaction to Star Wars was more readily understood by Americans than their reaction to such things as a crusade against communism or calling the Soviet Union the focus of evil in the world. Such matters should not, however, be seen as merely a matter of rhetoric. Rhetoric, too, made an impact, notwithstanding Andropov's dismissive (and defensive) comment that the Soviet leaders were "realists enough not to pay attention to rhetoric."[88] The problem was not rhetoric, but perceptions of policy aims and intentions. And in this context the offending headline rhetoric not only offset the occasional soothing advocacy of dialogue but was seen as underlying and explaining what were perceived to be American actions. Moreover, as Andropov said just a few days after dismissing rhetoric, in referring to Reagan's call for a "crusade against communism," "Washington does not limit itself to mere words." He stressed "plans to gain military superiority over the USSR" and "brazen interference in the affairs of other countries." Indeed, he ascribed to the U.S. leadership a desire to gain "world domination" and said *"that* is the true root of evil perpetrated in the world" because of the risk of nuclear war.[89]

In contradistinction to this alleged (and perceived) American presumption of the possibility of war, Andropov asserted: "We proceed from the premise that the historical competition of the two social systems, the struggle of ideas, is quite a natural phenomenon stemming from the very fact of the existence of socialism and capitalism. But we are emphatically against this historical confrontation being directed against peaceful cooperation and even more so against switching to the plane of nuclear war."[90] Thus the questions of rhetoric, political competition, and stimulating the arms race were seen as ultimately joined. Although the ideological rivalry and competition of the two

---

86.  Ibid.

87.  "Replies by Yu. V. Andropov to the Journal *Der Spiegel* (FRG)," *Pravda*, April 25, 1983.

88.  Ibid.

89.  "Speech of Comrade Yu. V. Andropov," *Pravda*, May 4, 1983. Emphasis added.

90.  Ibid.

systems would continue under peaceful coexistence among states, *nothing* would justify nuclear war. "Under conditions when the whole of mankind is threatened by nuclear catastrophe, it is the duty of all who deal with making political decisions to put concern for the preservation of peace above *everything* else."[91]

This comment did not, of course, mean that the Soviet Union would be passive in the competition, but it reflected an important new emphasis in Soviet political-ideological strategy that Andropov had sounded in his very first policy speech and that his successors—above all Gorbachev—would take up as well. In setting the role of the Soviet Union in assisting the ideologically anticipated progressive revolutionary transformation of the world, Andropov had said, "We [the Soviet Union] exercise our main influence on the world revolutionary process through our economic policy."[92]

In remarks to the American visitor Averell Harriman, Andropov had also emphasized that just as the two countries had been allies in the war against Hitler, "the Soviet people and Americans now also have a common enemy— the threat of war . . . . awareness of this threat should become the common denominator inducing statesmen in the USSR and the United States to display reciprocal restraint and [should be] capable of becoming a basis for the concerted effort to find mutually acceptable accords." "Unfortunately," he continued, "we do not see the present American Administration displaying such a responsible approach. The policy aimed at gaining military superiority over the Soviet Union and dictating to it its terms has no future. It only crosses out the positive achievements earlier accomplished in relations between the USSR and the United States and undermines the foundations of trust between them. A situation has developed as a result which cannot but give rise to alarm."[93]

On the occasion of the anniversary of Lenin's birth, on April 23, the rising young party secretary and new Politburo member Mikhail Gorbachev was selected to present the leadership's annual policy address. His speech focused mainly on the economic and social development of Soviet society but partly also on the international situation. He emphasized not only that it was a time of "most acute ideological confrontation on the international scene," but that "the main reason for the deterioration of the international situation today is the adventuristic approach of the most aggressive forces of imperialism to the most important issue of contemporary times, the issue of war or peace." As a result of a profound crisis in the capitalist system, "the war party—to use Lenin's term—has gained the upper hand within the ruling circles" of the United States. He cited the Reagan administration's crusade against communism, psychological warfare, economic sanctions, "interference in the internal

---

91. Ibid. Emphasis added.

92. Andropov, *Kommunist*, no. 17 (1982), p. 19.

93. Radio Moscow, TASS, June 2, 1983, in FBIS, *Soviet Union*, June 3, 1983, p. A1.

affairs of the socialist states up to and including the mustering of a counterrevolutionary 'fifth column' in Poland," and above all the irresponsible pursuit of
an arms race. Nonetheless, he said there were "more realistic, sober tendencies
whose supporters are in favor of détente and cooperation," resisting "the more
aggressive tendencies of the ruling circles." And he reaffirmed that "the USSR
favors the elimination of tension in the international situation and normal, good
relations with all states, including the United States."[94] But certainly the speech
did not give its listeners and readers much reason to hope for any early
improvement, given the position ascribed to current "ruling circles" of the
United States.

The May Day slogans, always carefully considered by the party leadership, exhibited an interesting change in 1983: for the first time since 1967
precedence was given to foreign policy slogans over those dealing with domestic policy.

The Central Committee plenum in June 1983 provided the occasion
for a new stocktaking on Soviet policy in many spheres. Andropov's leadership
position was consolidated by his designation as chairman of the presidium of
the Supreme Soviet, "president" of the USSR. The most significant of a number of personnel changes, however, was the transfer of Politburo member
Grigory Romanov, the sixty-year-old long-time chief of the Leningrad party
machine and reported hard-line advocate of the "military-industrial complex,"
to become a party secretary—enhancing the possibility of his eventual succession to the party leadership. Konstantin Chernenko, passed over when Andropov was elected general secretary, also returned to a prominent second
place in the hierarchy at the plenum. The main focus of the meeting was on
ideological questions, rather than on the economy or foreign affairs, and included discussion of the preparation of a new party program to replace the one
adopted in 1961 at a time of Khrushchev's ebullient overoptimism.

At the Central Committee meeting, Andropov flatly declared the present historical period to be "marked by confrontation, unprecedented in the
entire postwar period by its intensity and sharpness, of the two diametrically
opposite world outlooks, the two political courses, socialism and imperialism."[95]
This comment was still short of stating that the Soviet Union and the United
States were on a collision course, and was put in terms of the ideological
conflict. Nonetheless, it was still a considerable escalation beyond the two
contending "trends," for and against détente, featured in Brezhnev's Twenty-
sixth Party Congress report in 1981 and Andropov's own initial statements in
November 1982. In speaking of relations between states, Andropov went on to

---

94. "Leninism Is a Living, Creative Teaching and Correct Guide to Action, Speech of
    Comrade M. S. Gorbachev at the Meeting in Moscow Celebrating the 113th Anniver-
    sary of the Birth of V. I. Lenin," *Pravda*, April 23, 1983.

95. "Speech of General Secretary of the CC of the CPSU Comrade Yu. V. Andropov,"
    *Kommunist*, no. 9 (June 1983), p. 5.

say that peaceful coexistence was the only possible course. He reaffirmed that the "military-strategic balance" was essential to peaceful coexistence and that Soviet military power was "a powerful deterrent to the aggressive aspirations of imperialist reaction." But he also stressed the need for arms reduction, which "would be a great benefit for all countries and peoples."[96]

Secretary Shultz's major address on American-Soviet relations coincidentally came on the same day as Andropov's speech to the Central Committee plenum. The next day, in an address to the Supreme Soviet, Gromyko presented a counterpoint (it was too early to represent a considered response). Gromyko had, in March, been named a first deputy chairman of the Council of Ministers, and had acquired even more stature as the principal member of the collective leadership in the field of international affairs.

Gromyko spoke of "the confrontation of two lines," one directed at preserving peace and the other undermining it, in a complex global situation "that can be described as stormy." He denounced at length American policy in the field of arms control, concluding, "It is becoming increasingly clear that the present American administration is pursuing a course not of reaching agreements, but of fulfilling its programs of building up strategic arms and deploying new medium-range missiles in Western Europe." Nonetheless, he said, "Concern for peace should be placed above everything else" and advocated détente. With respect to relations with the United States, Gromyko said: "We want smoother relations with the United States in the knowledge that this is important to prevent war. It is our conviction that the United States of America should also proceed from the objective necessity to have normal relations with the Soviet Union. The common interests of both countries would be served by removing the threat of nuclear catastrophe."[97] While stating this as Soviet policy, he did not express any direct judgment on the prospects for American agreement, and the tone of his report was hardly optimistic.

Military spokesmen, and many other commentators, continued to stress the negative. All Soviet leaders since early 1981 had expressed the conviction that the United States was seeking military superiority. There had, however, been differences in the policy implications drawn from that conclusion both for Soviet defense programs and for foreign policy positions. During 1983 Soviet political as well as military leaders came to be increasingly convinced, as Gromyko said, that the Reagan administration was not prepared to seek compromise agreements on arms control or indeed on other issues.

There still remained some optimists. Fedor Burlatsky, a long-standing advocate of détente, published an article in June 1983 in which he argued that

---

96.  Ibid., p. 15.

97.  "On the International Situation and the Foreign Policy of the Soviet Union, Speech of the First Deputy Chairman of the Council of Ministers of the USSR, Minister of Foreign Affairs of the USSR, [Supreme Soviet] Deputy A. A. Gromyko," *Pravda,* June 17, 1983.

despite "the White House's bombastic political rhetoric, the current crisis in Soviet-American relations will in the final analysis in one way or another" come back to détente. While acknowledging a "crisis of détente," he argued that the fundamental premise of the agreements of the early 1970s on the principles of Soviet-American relations had "not been shaken in the slightest degree"—the common need to "prevent mutual thermonuclear destruction." He argued that the "strategy of military superiority, first strike, limited nuclear war, and space defence is an irrational strategy from the standpoint of the interests of the USA itself." Moreover, "a conflict between our two countries would be disastrous. This means that neither side needs war. It cannot be a part of a rational military strategy either of the United States or the Soviet Union."[98]

Burlatsky then plunged into an aspect of Soviet-American relations rarely addressed. He stated that "there are perhaps two basic, fundamental contradictions between the two countries, one of which is the main one. This is the contradiction between the social and political systems. But does it follow from this that we must necessarily be enemies? The entire experience of the past refutes this. . . . The second source of contradictions may stem from the fact that we are the world's two mightiest powers. . . . People believe that both powers are vying with each other for leadership in the world. . . . A question arises in this connection: does the position of the two mightiest powers dictate the inevitability of a military hostility between them or the inevitability of a political rivalry? The answer is unambiguous: rivalry—yes, military hostility— no. . . . The Soviet Union has repeatedly declared: it does not want rivalry to assume the form of confrontation." He also argued that there exists "a vast field" of interests "where they could act as partners." Burlatsky concluded, in a statement that may have been directed at possible Soviet as well as American consideration, that "under no circumstances should the fundamental principles of Soviet-American relations shaped up in the 1960s–1970s be shaken." More- over, in a broad sweep he argued that "as regards partial, regional, and tempo- rary problems they must be viewed as partial, regional, and temporary. In each case they must be 'capsulated,' i.e., limited and localized like local anaesthesia. Only local anaesthesia and not general narcosis can preserve the living tissue of Soviet-American relations, mutual security, and mutual cooperation. In the past, too, Soviet-American relations knew their ups and downs, culminations and crises."[99]

Burlatsky's unusually frank acknowledgment of a bilateral superpower rivalry, as well as his optimism on the prospect of increasing cooperation as "partners," was certainly unusual in 1983, but it showed the range of opinion within the Soviet establishment.

---

98.  Fedor Burlatsky, "USSR-USA: Partners, Rivals, Enemies?—Reflections on the Funda- mental Principles of Soviet-American Relations," *Moscow News*, June 12–17, 1983.

99.  Ibid.

Meanwhile, within the Soviet leadership the question of military resource allocations continued to be a major issue. The year 1983, though occurring in the middle of implementation of the five-year plan approved in 1980–81, also saw the beginning of a serious formulation not only of the next five-year plan for 1985–90 but also of a master long-term plan. Immediate problems had been alleviated by a one-time improvement in productivity owing to Andropov's tightening of work discipline and to the first fairly good harvest in four years. But the longer-term problems of economic investment and resource allocation, severe enough for other reasons, were being aggravated by military pressures for new programs to offset the American buildup.

One sign of this persisting issue of military requirements and resource allocation—and a factor in stimulating it—was the more alarmist nature of the American military threat presented now by Marshal Ustinov as well as by Ogarkov and other senior military men, but also by Andropov, Gromyko, and other leaders.

Other developments in Soviet-American relations reinforced the growing Soviet pessimism on the prospect for improving relations. As noted, several Soviet diplomats in the United States, and American diplomats in the Soviet Union, were expelled as spies during 1983. In addition, during 1983 an unprecedented wave of arrests and expulsions of Soviet diplomats and spies also occurred in Western Europe and several other countries in the world, 135 in all.[100] The most extensive action was the expulsion in April of 47 Soviet officials by France. Most of the rest were expelled from other NATO countries, and a few from Japan, Australia, Thailand, neutral Switzerland, and Iran. Some American commentators suggested that this crackdown reflected stepped-up Soviet intelligence activity, whereas the Soviets claimed that it was an anti-Soviet campaign orchestrated by the United States. Although the actions may in some cases have been concerted, in other cases it may have snowballed or been coincidence. There certainly was widespread and evidently more aggressive Soviet political and industrial-technological espionage than in earlier years.[101] Even so, the Soviet leaders probably did see an American hand behind the wave of actions and concomitant anti-Soviet press commentary.

Some time in the summer of 1983 Soviet intelligence reported that the setback in the UN-sponsored talks seeking a settlement of the Afghanistan stalemate, caused by a suddenly recalcitrant Pakistani stand, had been the result of American influence. This report raised serious doubt in Moscow about

---

100. The 135 expulsions in 1983 compared with 49 in 1982 and 27 in 1981. See *Expulsions of Soviets Worldwide, 1984*, Department of State Foreign Affairs Note (Washington, January 1985), also presenting data for 1981, 1982, and 1983 cited above, p. 1.

101. As noted in chapter 2, the Soviet leaders instituted intensified intelligence collection in 1981, continued in 1982–83, because of heightened concern over U.S. political and military intentions and as part of their own preparation to meet a possible "threatening situation." In the early 1980s they found industrial-technological espionage lucrative.

the repeated declarations by the United States of its desire to resolve such regional conflicts.[102]


## KAL 007 and the Andropov Declaration


Without question, the most traumatic experience of the year, deeply affecting the course of Soviet-American relations, was the aftermath of the Soviet interception and shooting down of an intruding Korean Air Lines passenger airplane, KAL 007, on the night of August 31–September 1, 1983.

The world was startled by an announcement by Secretary of State Shultz on the morning of September 1 that only hours earlier a Korean Air Lines Boeing 747 with 269 people on board had been destroyed by a missile fired from a Soviet aircraft. Shultz stated that the United States "can see no explanation whatever for shooting down an unarmed commercial airliner, no matter whether it's in your airspace or not."[103] President Reagan expressed "revulsion at this horrifying act of violence," "this appalling and wanton misdeed,"[104] and used the event to slam home "the stark contrast that exists between Soviet words and deeds. What can we think of a regime that so broadly trumpets its vision of peace and disarmament and yet so callously and quickly commits a terrorist act to sacrifice the lives of innocent human beings? What could be said about Soviet credibility when they so flagrantly lie about such a heinous act? *What can be the scope of legitimate and mutual discourse with a state whose values permit such atrocities?*"[105] In an address to the nation on the incident two days later, Reagan referred to it as "an act of barbarism," a "massacre," a "crime against humanity," and spoke of the "savagery of their crime." He discussed a number of details of the incident and played excerpts from tapes of intercepted conversations of the Soviet pilot; he stated that "there is no way a pilot could mistake this for anything other than a civilian airliner."[106]

---

102. Information from Georgy Kornienko, then first deputy foreign minister. For discussion of the negotiations on Afghanistan see chapter 15.

103. Cited in *State Bulletin*, vol. 83 (November 1983), p. 66.

104. "Soviet Attack on Korean Civilian Airliner," September 1, 1983, *Presidential Documents*, vol. 19 (September 5, 1983), p. 1191.

105. "Remarks to Reporters," September 2, 1983, ibid., p. 1193. Emphasis added. On September 3 he repeated the contrast between Soviet words and deeds and referred to the act as "murder of innocent civilians" and an "inexcusable act of brutality." "Radio Address to the Nation," September 3, 1983, ibid., vol. 19 (September 12, 1983), p. 1197. Emphasis added.

106. "Radio Address to the Nation," September 5, 1983, ibid., vol. 19 (September 12, 1983), pp. 1199–1200.

Secretary Shultz's statement had been made as soon as American intelligence had ascertained beyond any doubt that the airplane had been shot down. Unfortunately, many of the allegations about the incident made by him, by President Reagan, and by other administration spokesmen even days later were based on unfounded assumptions or incorrect information. It later became clear that, contrary to the confident American charges, the Soviets had *not* known that it was a civilian airliner and indeed had believed (as shown in other taped interceptions not played by the president) that it was an American military reconnaissance aircraft.[107] Moreover, the U.S. government had infor-

---

107. The statement by Shultz, issued at about 10:40 A.M., had been hurriedly prepared by Undersecretary Lawrence S. Eagleburger and Assistant Secretary Richard R. Burt during the night and early morning so that Secretary Shultz could have the credit for the first, and tough, American statement. They succeeded in that aim but at heavy cost in other respects. The statement was cleared with the president (who was in Santa Barbara), but Shultz delivered it before the first meeting of Vice President Bush's Special Crisis Group at which some of the relevant intelligence—and, for example, information on the presence in the area of a U.S. military reconnaissance plane—first became known to the State Department. Shultz had asked for assurances on the facts, but the only real assurance he received was that a Soviet air defense fighter had shot the plane down. Yet in his statement and answers to questions he said there was "visual inspection" permitting the identification of the aircraft, that it had been continuously tracked for two and a half hours, and that the United States had no evidence of any Soviet warnings or attempts to get the plane to land. All of those answers were not only untrue, but at that time elements of the U.S. intelligence community knew them to be untrue.

   Even in his memoir years later, where Shultz correctly noted that he had opposed many extreme proposals of things to say or do in reaction to the incident, he evidently still had not realized the extent to which he and the president made untrue statements based on incomplete intelligence, and he even bridled at the fact that on the second day the CIA and the National Security Agency (NSA) stated that the Soviets may have believed the plane to be a reconnaissance intruder (as they had) and expressed his disbelief. See Shultz, *Turmoil and Triumph*, pp. 361–67, esp. p. 364.

   Five days after Shultz's announcement, when President Reagan addressed the nation in a major speech on "the murderous attack," he still stated that "there is no way a pilot could mistake this [a distinctive 747 silhouette] for anything other than a civilian airliner," which was not true. He played part of the tape of intercepted communications in which the Soviet pilot reported his actions and said "the target is destroyed." But he did not play other parts of the tape in which the pilot attempted repeatedly to communicate with the airliner, including by signal with cannon fire. Long before this speech, U.S. intelligence had established that the Soviet pilots believed the intruder was a U.S. military reconnaissance aircraft. Yet Reagan claimed to have "immediately made known to the world the shocking facts as honestly and completely as they came to us." The handling of the entire incident was not a good case study of candor on the American side, as well as on the Soviet side. For a remarkably thorough reconstruction of the story, see Seymour M. Hersh, *"The Target Is Destroyed"* (Random House, 1986).

   The final report issued by the International Civil Aviation Organization (ICAO) of the United Nations ten years later confirmed that the decision to shoot was based on Soviet error in believing the aircraft to be a U.S. reconnaissance intruder, not willful or

mation on the real situation before these inaccurate charges were hastily made—although at least in some cases not known by those who made them.[108]

The president and other senior officials thus buttressed charges of callousness and barbarity with allegations of deliberate Soviet action not supported by the facts. As one commentator later noted, there was "a frightening irony in all this: the president of the United States, relying on information that was wholly inaccurate and misleading, was accusing the other side of telling lies, and [yet] was perceived as being moderate in so doing."[109] And in the first American speech at the United Nations after the incident on September 2, the senior American delegate (in Jeane Kirkpatrick's absence) launched a sharp attack on the basis of a series of untrue statements (such as claiming that the Soviet interceptor pilot "had the Korean 747 in his sights, clearly identified as a civilian airliner"), in full ignorance of what was (and was not) known of the facts. The speech was not even cleared with anyone in Washington. Yet the United States representative triumphantly charged: "Let us call the crime for what clearly it is: wanton, calculated, deliberate murder."[110] The facts were not considered important; what was important was the opportunity to savage the Soviet leaders.

Even the tapes publicly played by the president were later found to have been both misread and selectively edited.[111] It was a tragedy, and the Soviet Union was responsible. To modify the analogy used by official American spokesmen, it may have been tragic justified homicide by virtue of perceived self-defense, or it may have been manslaughter by excessive use of defensive force. But it was not deliberate murder of innocent civilians or many of the other things so quickly and heatedly charged by senior American officials.[112]

The Soviet handling of the incident after the interception was extremely poor. At least initially this was caused by confusion and uncertainty in Moscow over the facts. Later, after the fact of the Soviet interception was clear, the Soviets continued for more than a week to use evasive language about their responsibility for the interception itself while completing their investigation. One unintended consequence was to make the Soviets appear guilty not only of

deliberate action against a civilian airliner. See Richard Witkin, "Downing of K.A.L. 007 Laid to Russian Error," *New York Times*, June 16, 1993, p. A7.

108. Hersh, *"The Target Is Destroyed"*, pp. 76–178, esp. 103–04, 117–18, 130–38.

109. Ibid., p. 131.

110. Cited ibid., p. 134.

111. Ibid., pp. 153–58, 161, 168–69, 171–73, 177.

112. For a dispassionate analysis of the incident, see Alexander Dallin, *Black Box: KAL 007 and the Superpowers* (University of California Press, 1985). For a well-informed exposé of the internal American handling (and mishandling) of the event, see Hersh, *"The Target Is Destroyed"*, pp. 35–191. See also Marilyn J. Young and Michael K. Launer, *Flights of Fancy, Flight of Doom: KAL 007 and Soviet-American Rhetoric* (University Press of America, 1988).

the interception but also of the wider range of charges levied by the United States. Subsequent much fuller explanations, particularly by Marshal Ogarkov on September 9, were too late to affect general impressions already formed in world public opinion. The Soviet political mishandling through delay and stubborn unwillingness to accept any responsibility thus compounded their initial military fumbling in the interception itself to make the Soviet case unconvincing.

Soviet charges that the KAL intrusion deep into Soviet airspace (a fact never challenged, despite a careless fleeting reference by Reagan on September 5 to "what they claim as their airspace") was a provocation, an American military intelligence collection flight using the hapless airliner, were not justified. The Soviet air defense command, however, had believed the aircraft to be an American reconnaissance intrusion into a strategic area. Moreover, there had been an unpublicized Soviet diplomatic protest of an American military reconnaissance intrusion in the area only months before the incident—and that fact at least bore witness to the Soviet belief, in that case founded, that such actions had been occurring.[113]

The American response, once the passion of outrage had been spent in denunciation, was moderate in terms of actions, mainly a suspension of Aeroflot flights to the United States. The administration therefore believed it had shown great restraint.[114] It had made a conscious effort to avoid getting out ahead of world reactions, and wanted to show that it was not acting from sudden disillusionment, as President Carter had after Afghanistan, but was proceeding on a steady course.[115] But the speed and intensity of denunciation made a deeply negative impression on the Soviet leaders and further persuaded them of American hostility, if not indeed provocation, in the whole incident—as did

---

113. That overflight was over one of the disputed islands north of Japan and occurred during a major U.S. Navy exercise in April 1983 simulating an American *offensive* against the Soviet forces and bases around the Sea of Okhotsk.

114. President Reagan was given a wide array of possible punitive actions, the most severe of which came from members of the White House and NSC staff. The most extreme was John Lenczowski, a Soviet affairs hard-liner on the NSC staff, who argued that some U.S. military action should not be ruled out, and he formally proposed consideration of a break in U.S.-Soviet diplomatic relations, or at least closing Soviet consulates and canceling such bilateral cooperation agreements as remained. (See Hersh, *"The Target Is Destroyed,"* pp. 122–23.) Others calling for a hard line included NSC staff officer Lt. Colonel Oliver North.

Among others, the Special Planning Group for Public Diplomacy (with W. Scott Thompson and staff director Walter Raymond) pressed more successfully for a hard propaganda campaign.

115. This contrast with the Carter administration had been made to me by senior officials in the State Department before it was explicitly made by Secretary Shultz in an address in October 1984. See Secretary Shultz, "Managing the U.S.-Soviet Relationship Over the Long Term," October 18, 1984, *State Bulletin*, vol. 84 (December 1984), pp. 1–5.

Reagan's successful subsequent use of the incident to lobby for his defense programs.[116]

The American reaction, although unquestionably grounded in genuine shock and anger, certainly also reflected the unconscious application of a double standard. For example, it stood in marked contrast to the reaction in a closely parallel case a decade earlier. In February 1973 a Libyan civilian Boeing 727 passenger aircraft, and clearly identified as such, was shot down by the Israeli Defense Forces for trespassing into a strategic area of Israeli airspace, with 108 innocent deaths. The Israelis, too, at first stonewalled on their responsibility. Then, there was not a word of American recrimination. Nor was that incident recalled when Reagan asked rhetorically, "Is this a practice of other countries in the world? The answer is no."[117]

Reagan and others repeatedly noted that "this is not the first time the Soviet Union has shot at and hit a civilian airliner when it overflew its territory,"

---

116. Even after the event a strong circumstantial case could be made that the airliner had been used for an American military reconnaissance mission. That does not mean that it was; from all available evidence it was not. But to anyone inclined to believe the worst case, as the Soviet leaders were by September 1983, not only could such a case be supported but it would seem compelling. Furthermore, that belief was psychologically reassuring because it tended to relieve the Soviet Union of responsibility for the tragic loss of life.

I was later told by Vadim Zagladin, a senior Central Committee official with responsibility for international affairs in late September 1983, that the Soviet Union had learned of a secret NSC decision to exploit the KAL issue against the Soviets for an entire year. While NSC officials have denied the existence of such a directive, the incident was deliberately exploited in the administration's "public diplomacy" propaganda campaign, and it is quite plausible that there was also some discussion of the benefit to the administration in keeping the issue alive for the midterm election a year hence.

The president's National Security Decision Directive providing guidance on handling the issue, NSDD-102, titled "U.S. Response to Soviet Destruction of KAL Airliner" was issued on September 5. The directive, with some deletions, was subsequently declassified under a Freedom of Information Act request. The directive makes crystal clear that the incident was viewed above all as an opportunity for prosecuting confrontational propaganda. In the words of the directive: "Soviet brutality in this incident presents an opportunity to reverse the false moral and political 'peacemaker' perception that their regime has been cultivating. This image has complicated the efforts of the Free World to illuminate the USSR's true objectives" (p. 2), and "This Soviet attack underscores once again the refusal of the USSR to abide by normal standards of civilized behavior and thus confirms the basis of our existing policy of realism and strength" (p. 1).

117. "Radio Address to the Nation," September 5, 1983, *Presidential Documents*, vol. 19 (September 12, 1983), p. 1199.

An even more embarrassing later example of the double standard used in judging the Soviet action was the attempt to exonerate the United States when in a not entirely dissimilar incident five years later the USS *Vincennes* shot down a civilian airliner on its regular charted course over international waters, killing all 290 passengers and crew. The official Soviet reaction was very restrained. See the discussion in chapter 8.

referring to another intrusion—coincidentally, also a KAL airliner—that penetrated deep into northern Russia on April 20, 1978, before being fired upon and
forced down.[118] But no one noted the case of a Seaboard World Airways DC-8
that had strayed some eighty to one hundred miles off course and overflew
some of the Kuril Islands, in the same vicinity as KAL 007, on June 30, 1968.
That plane, leased by the Department of Defense to carry American soldiers
from Seattle to South Vietnam, had responded to signals to land by Soviet
interceptors, and landed on Etorofu Island in the Kurils. The Soviets released
the airliner and all aboard with little delay, notwithstanding the military status
of the passengers. Recalling this case would not have jibed well with the
frequent administration claims (particularly when it became known that the
Soviets had *not* identified the KAL plane as a civilian airliner) that it made no
difference to the Soviets and stating or implying that they made a practice of
shooting down any intruder.

The Soviet leadership was stunned by both the KAL incident and the
world reaction to it. By all indications, although the Air Defense Headquarters
in Moscow was informed of the detection of an unidentified but probably
American military reconnaissance intruder and instructed action according to
standing operating procedures, no one in the party and government leadership
was even aware of the shooting down of the aircraft until well after it occurred.
Indeed, it has been plausibly reported that members of the Politburo did not
even know of the incident until Secretary Shultz announced it in Washington in
his harsh indictment.[119] In any event, as the Soviet leaders were still learning

---

118. Ibid. For the best account of the 1978 incident, see Hersh, *"The Target Is Destroyed"*,
  pp. 3–15.

119. A well-placed senior party official in Moscow informed me of this in late September
  1983; while it cannot be confirmed, it is plausible. He also stated that Andropov had
  been informed only after the plane had been shot down. Andropov was not in Moscow,
  but in a rest and recuperation sanatorium in Kislovodsk.
    The highest-level military officer notified before the interception was a senior
  officer, probably the chief of staff, of the PVO (Air Defense Forces) in Moscow. When
  the chief of the General Staff and other senior defense officers first learned of the
  incident is not known. As the incident unfolded, only after the second and deepest
  intrusion occurred, over Sakhalin Island, did the deputy commander of the Far East
  Military District responsible for air defense, in Khabarovsk, reportedly call Air Defense
  headquarters in Kalinin (near Moscow), report the intrusion, and request instructions.
  A senior officer was summoned by the duty officer, probably the chief of staff of the Air
  Defense Forces (PVO), Colonel General Semen F. Romanov, and left the matter in
  the hands of the regional command to deal with on the basis of established procedure.
  The Khabarovsk commander then instructed the PVO field command on Sakhalin to
  follow standard rules of operating procedure and also ordered visual inspection and
  verification that it was a hostile reconnaissance plane. Despite strenuous efforts, the
  interceptors were unable to identify the plane. Finally, the order to shoot it down was
  made by the Sakhalin air defense commander even without positive identification of the
  plane. Within seven months, General Romanov was reassigned to a less responsible post

just what had happened, they came under fierce public assault from the American administration. This reinforced their inclinations to admit to nothing, and to charge the United States with sending the airplane into their sovereign territorial airspace for nefarious purposes and then attempting to cast the blame on them. Soviet equivocation for six days over the fate of the aircraft (they said it had been tracked until it disappeared "in the direction of the Sea of Japan") before admitting it had been shot down did not lend credence to their story, although such reticence was in keeping with other precedents in dealing with uncomfortable incidents.[120]

Although it is virtually certain that the airplane was believed to be an American reconnaissance plane at the time it was shot down, it is less certain that, once it became known after the shootdown that the aircraft was in fact a Korean Boeing 747 off course, the Soviet political and military leaders continued to believe it had been on an intelligence collection mission. It is, however, probable that most continued to believe it. For one thing, there is to this day still no *conclusive* other explanation for the deep off-course penetration, although there are theories of navigational error, some one of which is probably correct. Moreover, the Soviets saw a strong plausible circumstantial case to support their contention. This is *not* to say that such a case was conclusive and that the plane was on a reconnaissance mission. But the case was sufficiently convincing, especially to those disposed to accept the conclusion, that the Soviet leaders believed it.[121] That is important in gauging their reaction to the American charges of wanton murder.

A transcript of the Politburo meeting of September 2, chaired by Chernenko in Andropov's absence, has now been made public. It is a fascinating document and shows very clearly that the members of the Politburo (including Gorbachev and Ryzhkov) were then unanimous in believing that the Soviet action in shooting down the plane was fully justified, and many expressed

---

and soon after died, possibly by suicide. Reportedly, within four months the Khabarovsk deputy for the air force and air defense was replaced, as was the Sakhalin air defense commander. The Soviets did not, however, acknowledge openly their dissatisfaction with the handling of the incident by the Air Defense Forces.

Hersh, *"The Target Is Destroyed"*, pp. 163–64, 230–37, gives a slightly different but generally similar account.

120. For example, while the circumstances were quite different, the United States had also equivocated and given a false cover story for four days after a U-2 was shot down near Sverdlovsk on May 1, 1960, until Soviet leader Nikita S. Khrushchev publicly announced that the pilot had been captured alive. Then President Dwight D. Eisenhower admitted the reconnaissance penetration and accepted responsibility. See Michael R. Beschloss, *Mayday: Eisenhower, Khrushchev and the U-2 Affair* (Harper and Row, 1986), pp. 37–66, 243–59.

121. See Hersh, *"The Target Is Destroyed"*, pp. 132–33, 175–76; and Dallin, *Black Box*, pp. 57–87.

the belief that the deep incursion had been an American provocation. In summing up the agreed-upon conclusion, Chernenko picked up a view earlier expressed by Ustinov and Gromyko that the United States was now using the incident to cast doubt upon and distract world opinion from constructive Soviet initiatives and peaceful policy. In his words, "We should proceed firmly on the basis that this violation [of Soviet airspace] constitutes a deliberate provocation by imperialist forces aimed at distracting the attention of the world public from the major peace initiatives put forward by the Soviet Union."[122]

Soviet official statements, press commentaries, and notably discussions by senior military men appeared in abundance, but no statement came from Andropov or any other political leader for four weeks. Instead, since the subject was deemed to concern American military intelligence collection and Soviet defensive military reaction, Marshal Ogarkov was given the responsibility for the principal presentation of the Soviet position, which he did very competently in a briefing and news conference for foreign correspondents on September 9.[123]

While the KAL incident stirred up anti-Soviet sentiment in the United States, it was at least equally responsible for unleashing anti-American sentiment in the Soviet press.[124] Many accounts related the incident to Reagan's "crusade," and noted his use of the incident to gain support for his military program in Congress.

Georgy Arbatov rejected the argument that the KAL incident had spoiled a "thaw beginning in Soviet-U.S. relations." As for the course of gradual improvement of relations by small steps that Secretary Shultz had in fact been pursuing, Arbatov dismissed it by saying that "the administration had nothing in mind except a number of ruses that it perhaps needed in view of the upcoming election campaign in 1984." Arbatov saw Reagan's policy as a "militaristic course" that he claimed was "aimed at U.S. domination of the world."[125] A Central Committee official agreeing with him went on to add, "When Reagan declares socialism, and primarily the Soviet Union, to be the focus of evil, he is not simply spilling out his hatred toward us, the Soviet people, and socialism; he

---

122. The full text of the transcript, which is accepted as authentic, originally top secret, was released and published under the heading "Secrets of the Politburo," *Rossiskiye vesti* (Russian News), August 25, 1992.

123. See "Transcript of Soviet Official's Statement and Excerpts from News Session," *New York Times*, September 10, 1983, p. 4.

124. To cite but two examples, see the article by the new director of the Institute of the World Economy and International Relations, Aleksandr Yakovlev, "Taking the Bit between Its Teeth," *Izvestiya*, October 7, 1983; and Arkady Sakhnin, "The Second Pretender," *Literaturnaya gazeta*, October 5, 1983. The meaning of the latter title was the second pretender or claimant to world hegemony—Reagan, the first having been Adolf Hitler.

125. G. Arbatov, "Studio 9," Moscow Television, October 1, 1983, in FBIS, *Soviet Union*, October 3, 1983, pp. CC8–9.

is also proclaiming an official course of his administration: a line directed at a multifaceted and large-scale confrontation between systems."[126] Arbatov concluded that the Reagan administration was making "an attempt to use one tragic incident in order to take a number of steps along the path toward a far greater tragedy," meaning the risk of nuclear war.[127]

The KAL incident demonstrated vividly how deeply relations between the two countries had plunged. Each was only too ready to assume the worst of the other and rush not only to judgment but also to premature indictment. The United States (as evidenced in bipartisan congressional expression, as well as administration statements) seemed almost to welcome in the tragedy an opportunity to belabor the Soviet Union with hasty charges of savage barbarity. The Soviet leaders, in response as well as to fend off the charges, accused the United States not only of callous recklessness in what they continued to affirm had been an illegal reconnaissance intrusion but also of political provocation and hostile exploitation of the tragedy. While Americans focused their outrage on the consequences of the Soviet military action, the Soviets focused on the facts of deep penetration of their sovereign airspace (presumably) for espionage, and of the immediate U.S. seizure of the initiative in using the incident to mount sharp attacks on the Soviet system. Each side thus converted its ready suspicions and worst assumptions about the other into accusations that could not be proved or disproved, but tended to be believed by its own side and bitterly resented by the other. The upshot was to seriously set back American-Soviet, and Soviet-American, relations.[128]

Shultz and Gromyko met on September 8 in Madrid for a ministerial level meeting at the closing of the CSCE review conference. Their meeting had been envisaged as the start of a new productive set of bilateral talks, planned to culminate in a meeting between Gromyko and Reagan in Washington after the usual Shultz-Gromyko meeting in New York in September, and perhaps lead to a summit. Instead, there had been a harsh debate in Washington over whether Shultz should even meet with Gromyko, and when they met sharp recriminations were exchanged between the two men, each believing himself and his country deeply wronged by the other.[129] Then the United States refused to

---

126. V. Kobysh, ibid., p. CC10. The FBIS translation has been modified to refer to "the focus of evil," using Reagan's words, rather than an awkward and incomprehensible FBIS retranslation as "a concentration of evil."

127. G. Arbatov, ibid., p. CC11.

128. In the aftermath of the KAL incident the Senate in September accepted an amendment by Senator James A. McClure calling on the president to issue a report each year on Soviet compliance with arms control agreements, establishing the legislative basis for the reports issued in January 1984 and subsequently. See chapter 12 for further discussion of the arms control compliance issue.

129. See Shultz, *Turmoil and Triumph*, pp. 365, 367–70; Oberdorfer, *The Turn*, pp. 57–61; and A. A. Gromyko, *Pamyatnoye* (Memoirs), vol. 2 (Moscow: Politizdat, 1988), pp. 237–43.

permit Gromyko's plane to land at any of the New York area airports, so Gromyko—for the first time in many years—did not attend the UN General Assembly at all, much less meet with Shultz or Reagan.[130] A long chill followed in official contacts and relations.

President Reagan, for his part, seemed to enjoy again being liberated as a crusader against the evil empire. On September 10 he proudly recalled the widely criticized statement he had made at his first press conference in January 1981, that the Soviet leaders "reserve unto themselves the right to commit any crime, to lie, to cheat," and he went on to say, "I hope the Soviets' recent behavior [the KAL incident] will dispel any lingering doubt about what kind of regime we're dealing with."[131]

American attention was soon absorbed first by the tragic loss of the lives of 241 U.S. Marines in Beirut, and then by the success of the American occupation of Grenada. Days after the American invasion of Grenada, Reagan in remarks to the Heritage Foundation said that containing Soviet expansion was not enough: "We must go on the offensive with a forward strategy for freedom." Recalling his address to the British Parliament in 1982, he said, "We must . . . work for the day when the peoples of every land can enjoy the blessings of liberty." He reaffirmed a Manichean view: "The struggle now going on in the world is essentially the struggle between . . . what is right and what is wrong."[132] What would later come to be called the Reagan Doctrine had been espoused, resurrecting a policy of the "rollback" of communist rule.[133] The measured, if tough, policy framework seeking dialogue and negotiation set forth by Shultz in June seemed to have disappeared.

The KAL incident, and in particular the strong American psychological warfare offensive launched on its foundation and the instinctive defensive counterattack by the Soviet leaders, came just as Andropov was entering a period of severely limited ability to perform his leadership role. Then, on its heels, came an activation of the American "crusade" against socialism: a challenge to the legitimacy of communist rule in Eastern Europe and even in the Soviet Union itself. That, in turn, was rapidly followed by a direct American military attack overwhelming the weakest aspiring "socialist" regime, Grenada.

---

Gromyko in his memoir said that was "the most sharp meeting of all I had with fourteen U.S. secretaries of state" over nearly half a century (p. 243).

130. This decision was actually made by the governors of New York and New Jersey, but no one in Moscow could believe it was not an action directed by, or at least approved in, Washington.

131. "American International Broadcasting," September 10, 1983, *Presidential Documents*, vol. 19 (September 19, 1983), p. 1225.

132. "Heritage Foundation," October 3, 1983, ibid., vol. 19 (October 10, 1983), pp. 1383–84.

133. See chapter 15.

The first of these developments, in September 1983, was scarcely noted in the United States. But it made a substantial and negative impact in the Soviet Union. Vice President George Bush, in a speech in Vienna, took the occasion (to the embarrassment of his neutral hosts) to launch a tirade against Soviet hegemony in Eastern Europe. While generally restating American policy toward the area, he declared that "Soviet violation of these obligations [Yalta] is the primary root of East-West tensions today," a considerable overstatement in the nuclear age. Bush also referred to the "brutal murder" of the 269 victims of the KAL incident, which he described as not "civilized" behavior in the "European tradition." Indeed, he claimed that Russia was not really European—had not experienced the Renaissance, the Reformation, the Enlightenment—while stressing the European roots of the United States. Overall it constituted a direct and gratuitous challenge to Russia and to the Soviet Union.[134]

The Soviet leaders (and others; the speech was criticized in the Western European press, and privately by Allied diplomats) had no way of knowing that the speech was *not* a deliberate and considered policy statement. As a prepared speech by the vice president of the United States it became, of course, a statement of American policy. But it had not been designed as such. In fact, the speech, as originally drafted in the Department of State, did not even *mention* the Soviet Union! Bush asked his own speechwriter to write a new speech because he wanted one that would resound well in the United States, and in particular one that would reinforce a tough image to favorably impress conservative politicians who considered Bush too moderate. The result was filled with anti-Soviet (and anti-Russian) rhetoric. The State Department officials concerned with Soviet and European affairs were appalled. Efforts to persuade the vice president's speechwriter to make extensive changes were only marginally successful. Finally, the assistant secretary for European affairs, Richard Burt, arranged a meeting with Bush to request reconsideration and changes. Some were made, but as was evident the thrust of the speech and many offensive elements remained. Thus an important statement of U.S. policy was made on the basis of domestic political considerations by the vice president and his speechwriter against the advice of the Department of State.[135] And

---

134. "Address at the Hofburg, Vienna, Sept. 21, 1983," *State Bulletin*, vol. 83 (November 1983), pp. 19–23, pp. 20, 22, 23, for the references quoted here.

   Bush even carried his assault on Russian culture to the point of citing an unsubstantiated historical anecdote (from a Czech émigré writer) alleging that "Russian soldiers on the loose in Warsaw" [subduing rebellion in 1863] had hurled the piano of the late Frederic Chopin from a fourth floor window, and "Today . . . the entire culture of Central Europe shares the fate of Chopin's piano" (p. 20).

   See chapter 13 for further discussion of the impact of the speech as a statement of U.S. policy toward Eastern Europe.

135. The personal interview by an assistant secretary with the vice president was a sign of the seriousness with which the officials of the State Department viewed the matter, although they did not carry the issue to the secretary or the president. One principal

Bush directly tied the KAL incident into this crusading attack on the legitimacy of Russia's European cultural heritage as well as the legitimacy of any Soviet role in Eastern Europe, and for good measure claimed—incorrectly—that the Soviet "monopoly of intermediate-range nuclear missiles" was a "new element" in the balance of power.[136] To the Soviet leaders, the Reagan administration was perceived as pulling out all the stops in a concerted drive on all fronts—political, propaganda, and military—to further its political-military offensive against the Soviet Union.

A month later came the American invasion of Grenada and the replacement of the fractured socialist regime there by a pro-American one (elected a year after the American intervention). The Grenada story is reviewed in chapter 15 in the context of the American-Soviet competition in the Third World. In the present context, it is sufficient to note that Andropov's warnings about the political reality of rhetoric seemed to the Soviet leaders to be demonstrated by the American attack on Grenada: the crusade against socialism was not merely rhetoric, and the readiness to use military power was curbed only by countervailing military power. American policy and action, not merely rhetoric, seemed to be increasingly geared to confrontation.

On September 28 an unusually formal statement by Andropov, as chief of both state and party, was issued on behalf of the Soviet leadership. It represented the first definitive and authoritative overall evaluation of the policy of the Reagan administration by the Soviet leadership. While precipitated by the KAL incident, the evaluation presented had been building up for a long time. The statement opened with these words:

The Soviet leadership deems it necessary to inform the Soviet people, other peoples, and all who are responsible for determining the policy of states, of its assessment of the course pursued in international affairs by the current U.S. administration. In brief, it is a militarist course that represents a serious threat to peace. Its essence is to try to ensure a dominating position in the world for the United States of America without regard for the interests of other states and peoples.[137]

---

reason for concern was recognition that the speech would be badly received in Western Europe, especially in Austria, the neutral locale of the speech. The other main reason was a recognition that the speech would antagonize the Soviets to no useful purpose.

Information on the whole incident was provided by knowledgeable officials of the Department of State and White House staff.

136. Ibid., p. 22. Soviet medium- and intermediate-range ballistic missiles had been deployed since 1959 and had been a "monopoly" since 1963; the SS-20 was a modern replacement for obsolescent SS-4 and SS-5 missiles. Bush's staff had not even checked the basic facts.

137. "Statement by General Secretary of the CC of the CPSU, Chairman of the Presidium of the Supreme Soviet of the USSR Yu. V. Andropov," *Pravda*, September 29, 1983. The statement was read on Soviet radio and television on September 28 and later reprintings give it that date.

I was in Moscow when the statement was issued and can attest to the electrifying, and sobering, effect it had. Several Soviet officials in conversations noted the unusual prominent format as well as the significant content.

The most revealing indication of the change from Andropov's own earlier position on giving a little more time for the American administration to come around to a recognition of realities was the remarkable conclusion, stated almost as self-criticism: "If anyone had any illusions about the possibility of an evolution for the better in the policy of the present American administration, recent events have dispelled them once and for all."[138] Although this did not mean that the Soviet leaders were giving up on any conduct of relations with the United States, it did mean that henceforth they were even less inclined to base their own policy on any expectation of the possibility of serious negotiation or agreement with the United States.

The statement described "the sophisticated provocation organized by the U.S. special services, using a South Korean airplane" as "extreme adventurism in policy." It noted that the "Soviet leadership has expressed its regret at the loss of life," but described it as "the result of this unprecedented, criminal act" and said it was "on the conscience of those . . . who conceived and implemented this provocation, and who literally the next day hastened to force colossal military appropriations through congress and are now rubbing their hands with satisfaction."

Andropov's statement criticized the basic tendency of the Reagan administration to "transfer ideological contradictions to the sphere of interstate relations," which, he contended, was "inadmissible" in the nuclear age. "Transforming the confrontation of ideas into a military confrontation would cost all mankind too dearly. . . . Beginning with the bogey of a 'Soviet military threat' they have now reached the point of declaring a 'crusade' against socialism as a social system. . . . But wishes and capabilities are far from being the same thing. No one can reverse the course of history. The USSR and the other socialist countries will continue to live and to develop." The statement emphasized that it was not just a matter of rhetoric, but these ideas were being "preached by the leaders of a major power and are not simply being proclaimed verbally but are also being implemented in practice."

While taking umbrage at the rhetoric—the "unseemly spectacle when the leaders of a country like the United States resort to . . . abuse mingled with hypocritical sermons on morality and humanity," with "the tone being set by the U.S. president himself"—the leadership's statement said that "of course, malicious attacks on the Soviet Union arouse in us a natural sense of indignation, but we have strong nerves, and we don't build our policy on emotions. It is

---

138. Ibid. Although cast in hypothetical terms to avoid admission of earlier unjustified optimism, the way the judgment was formulated made clear the reluctance in reaching that conclusion but also its definitive nature. A Central Committee official told me that although that particular statement would not have been made except for the American handling of the KAL incident, the new evaluation had been building up for a long time.

founded on common sense, realism, and profound responsibility for the destiny of the world."

Soviet dedication to peace and to curbing the arms race was contrasted to "U.S. policy, the increasing militarization of which is also manifested in reluctance to hold any serious negotiations and to reach agreement. . . . our partners in the Geneva talks are certainly not there to reach an accord." The American purpose in Geneva was to "procrastinate and then begin deploying Pershing II ballistic missiles and long-range cruise missiles in Western Europe." But "if the U.S. nuclear missiles appear on the continent of Europe this will be a step of fundamental dimensions."

The statement also declared defensively that the Soviet "desire to reach agreement should not be taken by anyone as a sign of weakness." And in the context of the U.S. military buildup, the statement specifically addressed concerns at home: "The Soviet people may be sure that our country's defense capability is at such a level that anyone would be ill-advised to stage a trial of strength." "For our part," the statement continued, "we do not seek such a trial of strength. . . . Responsible statesmen have one option—to do everything to prevent nuclear catastrophe. Any other position is shortsighted and, what is more, suicidal."

Soviet policy was reaffirmed, notwithstanding this assessment of American policy. "For the Soviet leadership, the question of what line to pursue in international affairs even in the present tense situation does not arise. Our policy is directed, as before, at preserving and strengthening peace, détente, curbing the arms race, and broadening and deepening cooperation among states."[139]

In some respects, the fact that for nearly three years the Soviet leaders had not made such a clear and strong negative evaluation of the policy of the Reagan administration and the prospect of negotiation with it was remarkable. This point was made from an unexpected quarter by an informed observer. Former secretary of state Haig commented in 1984 that the Soviet turn to a harsh line against the Reagan administration came "three years after the most unprecedented criticism from the United States. Believe me, it wasn't a tit-for-tat response. The Soviets stayed very, very moderate, very, very responsible during the first three years of this administration. I was mind-boggled with their patience. They were genuinely trying. What they hadn't faced up to was what it would really take to convince us." He thus conceded that the administration bore "some responsibility" for the Soviet turn to a harder line, and that the Soviet leaders had "concluded that they are going to feed fire with fire."[140]

The Soviet leaders saw subsequent events as confirming their hardening evaluation. In October the United States had used military force in Gre-

---

139. Ibid.

140. Roy Gutman, "Bad Tidings: The World According to Haig," *Newsday Magazine*, August 12, 1984, pp. 14–22. Quotations from pp. 18–19.

nada. The strong American propaganda campaign alleging Soviet use of Grenada as a proxy revolutionary base was so far removed from reality that the Soviet leaders assumed it must reflect American malevolence rather than ignorance, and saw it as a pretext for an American expansion of influence. This impression was fortified by a strident speech by CIA Director William Casey on October 29 at Westminster College in Fulton, Missouri, following the action on Grenada. Westminster was the site of Winston Churchill's famous speech on the Iron Curtain that signified the beginning of the Cold War. Casey called for a more sustained policy, including military assistance to "our friends" in the Third World, saying it would be "the principal U.S.-Soviet battleground for many years to come."[141]

The Soviet vice president (first deputy chairman of the Supreme Soviet Presidium) and candidate Politburo member Vasily Kuznetsov, engaging in turn in hyped rhetoric, said soon after the U.S. occupation of Grenada, but within a broader frame of reference, that the American leadership was "nurturing delirious plans for world domination" and "pursuing a 'policy with no brakes' in international affairs," and that such actions were "pushing mankind to the brink of catastrophe."[142] The Soviet press compared Reagan to Hitler.[143]

In November the final Soviet deep concessions on intermediate-range missiles—offering to reduce Soviet missiles facing Europe to lower levels of missile launchers and warheads than before the SS-20 deployment had begun—were rejected, and the American deployment began.

The Soviet reappraisal of relations and the hardening of line reflected in the Andropov statement of September 28 had not been based on a considered reexamination of how to *manage* Soviet-American relations. The precise implications and application of the new line had not been worked out. Similarly, although the contingent decision had been made to break off the INF talks once American missile deployment began, there had been no final decision on whether also to break off the stalemated START talks.

In November Andropov—resting at a sanatorium in Kislovodsk—held a conference with a number of key officials from the Central Committee and Ministry of Foreign Affairs dealing with Soviet-American affairs. The decision to withdraw from the INF—and START—negotiations once U.S. missile deployment began was confirmed. In addition, it was decided to increase the pressure on the United States and Western European governments by stressing

---

141. George Lardner, Jr., "Third World Strategy Offered," *Washington Post*, October 30, 1983, p. A5. The quotation is not from that article but from the CIA public affairs transcript of the speech, p. 14.

142. Cited in "Order for the City of Russian Glory [Novgorod]," *Pravda*, October 30, 1983.

143. By coincidence, on August 11 Secretary of Defense Caspar Weinberger had first made such a comparison, saying the Soviet threat was at least as great as the threat from Hitler. See "Inquiry. Topic: National Defense, 'The Soviets' Threat as Great as Hitler's,'" Interview with Caspar Weinberger, *USA Today*, August 11, 1983, p. A9.

to the publics of those countries the increased risk of war caused by the American and NATO persistence in its decision to proceed with the new missile deployments. The new Soviet offsetting deployments would also be publicized. Finally, it was decided to point up the unsatisfactory nature of Soviet-American relations by reducing to a trickle any and all bilateral contacts and business.[144]

Within only a few weeks, it became necessary to revise this approach, in part because it began to prove counterproductive in the West but also because of Andropov's sinking health. The leadership wanted to keep its options a little more open as the succession came nearer. In December the Soviets agreed to resume both technical talks on upgrading the hot line and talks on delimiting the Soviet-U.S. maritime boundary between Siberia and Alaska. But the chill in relations, though mitigated, remained.

Besides curtailing diplomatic contacts,[145] and breaking off arms control negotiations, other aspects of Soviet-American relations also suffered. For example, Soviet press commentary on the United States became increasingly hostile and vituperative. An editor of *Pravda* told me that a general "quota" of favorable reference to the United States in that important newspaper, which had reached 60 percent in the early 1970s and even 80 percent at the peak in the mid-1970s, by then (late 1983) was down to near "zero." Whether that was literally correct, shifts of that general magnitude, up and then down, certainly occurred.

Intermittently for several years there had been harassment and occasional terrorist acts against Soviet missions and personnel in the United States, especially by members of the Jewish Defense League. After the KAL incident there were a number of demonstrations and vandalism directed against the Soviet mission in New York. On December 12 a bomb was thrown into the grounds of the Soviet UN Mission at Glen Cove, New York. The Soviet leaders were unpersuaded that such acts could not be prevented.

The debate among Soviet analysts and commentators continued. In an article in October Aleksandr Yakovlev, newly chosen to succeed the late Nikolai Inozemtsev as head of the Institute of the World Economy and International Relations, took issue with "certain political and public figures," unidentified, who were "inclined to consider that which is happening in U.S. international policy today as an accident of history, an irrational moment, derived from the personal characteristics of President Reagan." While something of a straw man, that image was the foil for his conclusion that although Reagan's own contribution and responsibility for "such a rapid destruction of the structure of international cooperation" was great, basically he was representing the American

---

144. The Kislovodsk conference has not been previously reported. Information from knowledgeable Soviet officials.

145. In Moscow in October 1983 a senior official in the Ministry of Foreign Affairs told me an "in" joke, that Ambassador Dobrynin in Washington should apply for unemployment compensation because he now had so little to do.

ruling circles that had intentionally steered onto this new course of confrontation, militarism, and pursuit of world domination.[146]

Others, including Georgy Arbatov, while sharply condemning the course pursued by the Reagan administration, continued to stress the cyclical nature of American foreign policy and guardedly held open the prospect that even the Reagan administration, like that of John F. Kennedy, could see the error of its hard-line policy and could change.[147] And Aleksandr Bovin, in sharp contradistinction to Yakovlev, saw the Reagan administration as "at variance with the thrust of the historical process," and bound to be succeeded by a renaissance of more "realistic" elements in the American establishment that would again recognize the imperatives and "realities of the nuclear-missile age" and the need for coexistence and recognition of "the legitimate interests of the Soviet Union."[148]

This was the state of the debate in October and November when the last major clash of the year occurred: the American rejection of the final Soviet proposals for reducing Soviet intermediate-range missiles in return for not deploying new American missiles in Europe, the beginning of deployment, and the Soviet walkout from the talks. The Soviet decision to break off the INF talks was taken because the Soviet leaders saw no better alternative. Having threatened to take this action, they could not afford to have it be shown as a bluff. Given the evolving Soviet view, even as briefly illustrated in this account, the Soviet decision to walk out of the INF—and START—strategic arms talks in Geneva in November clearly reflected a Soviet assessment that the negotiations had no favorable prospect because the United States was not serious about reaching agreement. The INF negotiations were at the end of the road, with no promise of any agreement that would satisfy the objective they had set, to prevent the NATO deployment by offering reductions in Soviet forces. And in START there had been no significant movement on the American side; moreover, the American interest in SDI posed a new question about the very feasibility of strategic arms limits and reductions. No useful result was seen from continuing either negotiation. On November 25 *Pravda* carried another "statement" by Andropov, this time blasting the United States and NATO for the deployment of the INF missiles and ominously referring to the "dangerous consequences of that course."[149]

146. Yakovlev, *Izvestiya*, October 7, 1983.

147. G. A. Arbatov, "Thoughts on the Jubilee (Commemorating the Fiftieth Anniversary of the Establishment of Diplomatic Relations between the USSR and the United States)," *SShA: Ekonomika, politika, ideologiya* (USA: Economics, Politics, Ideology), no. 11 (November 1983), pp. 3–15. (Hereafter *SShA.*)

148. A. Bovin, "Fifty Years—What Is Next?" *Izvestiya*, November 16, 1983.

149. "Statement of the General Secretary of the CC of the CPSU and Chairman of the Presidium of the Supreme Soviet of the USSR Yu. V. Andropov," *Pravda*, November 25, 1983.

Thus failure of the INF negotiations had a far-reaching effect on Soviet-American relations,[150] although this fact was not fully realized in Washington. In Moscow, the decision to break off the arms talks was taken not only because the talks were considered to have reached a dead end but also in the hope this action would shock Western opinion into forcing a change in the U.S. arms control position. That was a serious miscalculation. Instead, it gave the administration in Washington the opportunity to blame the Soviet leaders for the fact that the arms negotiations were broken off and to stand pat on its position. More basically, the fact that the Soviet leaders had made so much of the issue of INF deployment now magnified their failure to prevent it. The successful beginning of INF deployment in late 1983 thus became a major defeat for Soviet diplomacy.

The Soviet political campaign against the INF deployment, waged from 1979 through 1983 with increasing intensity, had an important side effect of which neither side was aware. I have noted the Soviet leaders' rising concern over American policy intentions and actions, and their mounting concern from 1981 over the increased danger of war. This concern also extended deeply into Soviet society.[151] But the government community in Washington, focusing above all on the contest with Moscow over the deployment of INF missiles in Europe, was disposed to dismiss all indications of Soviet alarm over a growing danger of war as part of a controlled Soviet propaganda campaign to raise Western European concerns and opposition to deployment. Although there was such a propaganda campaign, there was *also* real concern in the Soviet Union stemming from much more than the missile deployment issue, and expressed in ways far removed from influencing Western opinion, as the discussion in this chapter shows. Yet this reality was not seen in Washington, and this very fact added to the gap in mutual understanding.

On November 5 the annual address on the anniversary of the Bolshevik Revolution was given by Politburo member Grigory Romanov. The analysis presented in his speech, which as a statement on behalf of the leadership was cleared by the Politburo, reflected the stress on increased tension and danger of war. Romanov cited the Andropov September statement, calling it "a document of enormous political significance" containing "a deep and principled

---

150. In October 1983, a confidential Central Committee letter was read to party meetings explaining that the INF agreement proved not possible, the talks were a failure, and that consequently no improvement in relations with the United States was in prospect. See Dusko Doder, *Shadows and Whispers: Power Politics inside the Kremlin from Brezhnev to Gorbachev* (Random House, 1986), p. 197.

151. A Communist Party chief in a remote agricultural region I visited soon after the KAL incident and the Andropov statement of September 1983 told me how, after a local party meeting called to discuss that statement, several women had come to him in tears asking if war with America was inevitable and if their sons would have to die. There were other such reports. See Raymond L. Garthoff, "Now Get Ready for the Real Crisis," *Washington Post*, November 6, 1983, pp. D1, D4.

appraisal of the present international situation." He characterized that situation in his own words in alarming terms. "Comrades," he said, "the international situation at present is white hot, thoroughly white hot." Moreover, he said that "perhaps never before in the postwar decades has the atmosphere in the world been as tense as it is now." The cause of this dangerous tension was that "imperialism has not given up its hopes of restoring the positions it has lost. . . . Confirmation of this lies in the unprecedented growth in the aggressiveness of the policy of U.S. imperialism everywhere in the globe." Specifically, he stressed the deployment of missiles in Europe. But, he added, "the question of the new American missiles in Europe is a most important link but still only one link, in the anticommunist and antidemocratic strategy of those who today rule in the White House and aspire to rule the whole world." He also stressed the arms race, and especially the desire to extend the arms race into outer space, plans for modernizing NATO military forces, "subversive activities," and "blatant military intervention" in Grenada and in efforts to overthrow the government in Nicaragua. "The 'crusade' proclaimed by Reagan is not targeted only against the Soviet Union and the other socialist countries," although that clearly was Romanov's central concern. "The cynical provocation using the South Korean airliner and the dirty racket the imperialists stirred up around it," he added, "have shown for the umpteenth time that the American reactionaries are ready to commit any crime, even the most vile, to work up tension."[152]

What was the Soviet response? Romanov's speech developed two lines of response. For one thing, "the development of events in the world arena requires of us the very highest vigilance, self-possession, firmness, and unflagging attention to strengthening the defense capability of the country." At the same time, "the Soviet Union does not intend to retreat from its policy of peace" and "the road of détente, peaceful coexistence, and disarmament."[153]

Another important statement late in the year was made by Politburo member and Defense Minister Marshal Dmitry Ustinov. Addressing in December an unusual major convocation of Soviet war veterans under the auspices of the Ministry of Defense, Ustinov stressed the United States' attempt to break the "existing approximate military-strategic balance between the United States and the USSR," and Soviet determination to take the necessary measures "so that the military balance would not be broken." He cited Andropov's statement as authoritatively describing the international situation. He stressed, "The 'crusade' proclaimed by President Reagan against socialism as a social system is in effect an expression not only of an ideology, but also of the real policy conducted by the ultrareactionary forces of the United States and those countries in the West aligned with

---

152. "The Great Vitality of the Ideas and Cause of October," *Pravda*, November 6, 1983.
153. Ibid.

them." He emphasized that "the Soviet people well remember the lessons of the last war and draw the necessary conclusions." Finally, he predictably drew as one conclusion the need for not only maintaining but "strengthening the defense capability of the country."[154]

Ustinov also, however, struck another note. He declared, "As you can see, comrades, the situation in the world is extremely tense. *But no matter how complicated the political-military situation, there is no point in overdramatizing it.*" He went on to say, "Soberly appraising the full seriousness of the current situation, one must see that imperialism is not all-powerful. And its threats do not frighten us. The Soviet people have strong nerves." And, continuing with a rare reference to the generational gap, "We people of the older generation have experienced much more trying times than these. *We will find enough strength and resources to stand up for our interests and those of our friends and allies!*"[155]

Some other military leaders were less ready to conclude that the main threat was in American attempts to "frighten" them. Marshal Ogarkov, for example, in an unusual article that appeared both in the military newspaper *Red Star* and the government organ *Izvestiya* shortly before Andropov's September "Statement," stressed "the sharply growing aggressiveness of international imperialism" headed by the United States and said, "In recent years their activity is strongly reminiscent of fascism in the 1930s. Armed with rude lies and slander, the United States and its allies have conducted a global offensive against socialism on all fronts, launching against us, as they openly declare, a new 'crusade.' The administration in Washington is nurturing the most evil plans." He cited evidence, including the "Fiscal Year 1984–1988 Defense Guidance," not only "an official document" but "prepared by the direction of the president of the United States," "the main aim of which is 'the annihilation of socialism as a socio-political system.' No more and no less!" And most ominous of all, "The forces of imperialism and reaction headed by the United States are strenuously pursuing the material preparation for a new world war. They have embarked directly on the creation of a global military coalition aimed against the Soviet Union and the socialist community as a whole. . . . The United States is intensively building up its strategic nuclear forces with a view to giving them the capability to inflict a 'disarming' nuclear strike on the

---

154. "The Address of Marshal of the Soviet Union D. F. Ustinov," *Krasnaya Zvezda*, December 15, 1983.

   Several categories of Soviet arms production were, in fact, increased during 1983 after a long hiatus in such increases, including production of military transport aircraft and tanks. Also in mid-1983 construction began on the first new nuclear weapon storage facility to be built in a decade. (Conventional ammunition production capacity had, after a decline in the latter years of the 1970s, again begun to expand in 1980–81 and continued.) Information from an informed American source.

155. Ibid. Emphasis added.

USSR." While describing such aims as illusory, he stressed the need for the Soviet Union to do more to ensure that they could not succeed. He cited the June 1983 Central Committee plenum as being "quite justified in setting the task of doing everything necessary to safeguard the country's security"—words that may have been intended to imply that not everything necessary had yet been done.[156]

These statements by Andropov, Romanov, Ustinov, and Ogarkov reflected the overall position—or range of positions—held by the leadership as the year drew toward a close. There were clearly differences among the leaders and in the political establishment as to actions that the Soviet Union needed to take. Romanov and Ogarkov, for example, were no doubt more enthusiastic in their calls for unflagging attention to strengthening defense, whereas some were probably more determined to persist in a détente and disarmament strategy. Under the circumstances, given American opposition, even a détente and disarmament strategy would of course be waged *against* the United States government. And even after all the remarks noted above, Romanov's speech had also included the statement that "we want to live as good neighbors with all states, and this includes the United States." If that was not feasible, Lenin was cited as authority for a policy of "let the American capitalists leave us alone, and we will leave them alone."[157] But clearly the Andropov Politburo had concluded that for the present the Reagan administration had no desire for a modus vivendi. In that circumstance, differences over the relative weight to be given to various aspects of Soviet policy, and over the degree of military threat and extent of continuing Soviet military preparations, remained to be resolved.

In early November the United States and its NATO allies carried out an unusually extensive and high-level military exercise, called Able Archer 83, testing the command and communications procedures for the release and use of nuclear weapons in case of war. Although such exercises were not unusual, this particularly sensitive operation came at a time of heightened tension and nervousness in high intelligence circles in Moscow. Moreover, for the first time it included some top political leaders; initially it was to have included President Reagan, Vice President Bush, and Secretary Weinberger, although their participation was dropped owing to some awareness in Washington of the tense Soviet mood. Reagan himself, after being briefed on the exercise, remarked that he considered it "a scenario for a sequence of events that could lead to the end of civilization as we know it."[158]

---

156. Marshal N. Ogarkov, "A Reliable Defense for Peace," *Izvestiya*, and *Krasnaya zvezda*, September 23, 1983.

157. *Pravda*, November 6, 1983. Similarly, Marshal Ogarkov had reaffirmed a Soviet policy of "peace and détente" and "preventing a new war." *Izvestiya*, September 23, 1983.

158. Oberdorfer, *The Turn*, p. 65, citing Robert McFarlane on the decision not to include the top political leaders in the exercise, and on Reagan's comments. (McFarlane had succeeded Clark as national security adviser just two weeks before the exercise.)

Oleg Gordievsky, then the deputy KGB chief in London—and also a spy for Britain—soon thereafter reported that at the height of the week-long exercise on November 8–9, the Moscow KGB "Center" had sent flash telegrams calling urgently for all information relating to possible U.S. preparations for an imminent nuclear strike on the Soviet Union. He said many veteran KGB officers did not share the belief in KGB headquarters that such an attack might be about to be launched, but the alarm in Moscow was real.[159] Soviet military doctrine had long held that a possible design for launching an attack would be the conversion of an exercise simulating attack into a real attack. Some Soviet interceptor aircraft in East Germany were observed by Western intelligence to have been placed on high alert, but in general the Soviet alarm seems to have been held to the top intelligence leaders.[160] British intelligence passed Gordievsky's reports to the CIA, and apparently at least one other well-placed U.S. intelligence source in Eastern Europe also reported similar information. Gordievsky also reported that Soviet intelligence had, erroneously as it turned out, reported some real movement of NATO troops during Able Archer.[161]

Initially, McFarlane discounted these reports as Soviet scare tactics when he presented them to President Reagan. But early in 1984 a more extensive U.S. intelligence review concluded that the Soviet leaders probably had had a real and serious concern.[162] Reagan himself was perplexed but disturbed to learn that the Soviet leaders could imagine the possibility of an American attack, and this contributed to his desire for face-to-face contact with Soviet leaders, as he said in his memoir. As will be seen, this influenced his thinking in the weeks and months ahead.[163]

---

159. See Christopher Andrew and Oleg Gordievsky, *KGB: The Inside Story* (Harper Collins, 1990), pp. 583, 598–600; and Christopher Andrew and Oleg Gordievsky, eds., *Instructions from the Centre: Top Secret Files on KGB Foreign Operations, 1975-1985* (London: Hodder and Stoughton, 1991) pp. 85–88.

160. Knowledge of the 1983 Able Archer alarm was very closely held. In interviews, among others having no knowledge of it were then First Deputy Chief of the General Staff Marshal Sergei Akhromeyev, First Deputy Foreign Minister Georgy Kornienko, and First Deputy Chief of the International Department of the Central Committee Vadim Zagladin. Mikhail Gorbachev has told me the matter never came to the Politburo.

161. Andrew and Gordievsky, *KGB*, p. 599.

162. Oberdorfer, *The Turn*, pp. 66–67, again citing interviews with McFarlane. As Oberdorfer notes, a study by the President's Foreign Intelligence Advisory Board six years later concluded that there had probably been a serious concern over possible U.S. attack.

Another source has informed me that, upon learning of the alarmed Soviet reaction, McFarlane commented excitedly, "We got their attention!" and then added more soberly, "Maybe we overdid it." While this report is not confirmed, it is plausible.

163. See the discussion in chapter 4. For his memoir reference, see Reagan, *An American Life*, pp. 588–89.

A clear sign of the Soviet concern was evident in a statement by Minister of Defense Marshal Ustinov just days after Able Archer. On November 19, by which time the Soviet alarm had subsided, he remarked: "The dangerous character of military exercises conducted in recent years by the U.S. and NATO draws attention. They are characterized by vast scope and *it becomes more and more difficult to distinguish them from the real deployment of armed forces for aggression.*"[164]

The special tension engendered by Able Archer 83 dissipated, but the general tension remained.

November 1983 was the fiftieth anniversary of the establishment of U.S.-Soviet diplomatic relations. There was little to celebrate. In an exchange of brief letters Reagan made the minimum gesture of expressing the "hope that we can [both] recommit ourselves to working constructively on the problems before us."[165] The Soviet letter, from the Presidium of the Supreme Soviet of the USSR, expressed its dedication "to the development of equitable, mutually advantageous relations."[166] Shultz and Dobrynin also met twice to resume some contact, but no significant exchanges occurred.

As the year drew to a close, the most optimistic assessment was a very guarded statement by Georgy Arbatov. After strongly criticizing American policy, he reaffirmed the Soviet desire to see relations improve, but said it was up to the United States whether they would; one could pick a quarrel, but it took two to have good relations. Whether the United States would improve relations with the Soviet Union he said would depend mainly on constraints of economic and political "reality," on the good sense of the American people, and on whether such facts would be "sufficient to strengthen the realistic element in U.S. policy." By late 1983 not all Soviets still accepted the existence of a "realistic element" even potentially able to influence U.S. policy.[167]

The most authoritative statement of the Soviet position on relations with the United States appeared in a formal resolution of the Supreme Soviet, "On the International Situation and the Foreign Policy of the Soviet State," issued on December 29, and published on December 30. It specifically en-

---

164. Member of the Politburo of the CC CPSU, Minister of Defense of the USSR, Marshal of the Soviet Union D. F. Ustinov, "To Struggle for Peace, To Strengthen Defense Capability," *Pravda*, November 19, 1983, p. 4. Emphasis added.

   Ustinov's words were cited in a confidential General Staff analysis of NATO 1983 exercise. See Colonel L. V. Levadov, "Results of the Operational Training of NATO Joint Armed Forces in 1983," *Voyennaya mysl'* (Military Thought), no. 2 (February 1984), p. 67. That analysis mentioned, but did not feature, Able Archer 83 (p. 70).

165. "50th Anniversary of U.S.-Soviet Relations," *State Bulletin*, vol. 84 (January 1984), p. 53.

166. For the Soviet text see ibid., p. 53.

167. Interview of Georgy Arbatov by Atanas Atanasov, "The USSR Unswervingly Follows the Path of Detente and Peace," *Rabotnichesko delo* (The Workers' Cause), Sofia, December 30, 1983; also in FBIS, *Soviet Union*, January 3, 1984, pp. A2–3.

dorsed the Andropov statements of September 28 and November 24 and expressed "serious anxiety over the acute exacerbation of the world situation caused by the increased militarization and aggressiveness of the imperialist forces, primarily the United States." Particular attention was given to U.S attempts to achieve military superiority and deny the Soviet Union military parity, "whatever the consequences," and to the policy of intervention around the world under the Reagan Doctrine.[168]

Perhaps most indicative was a TASS commentary on December 31 aimed at puncturing a State Department press conference comment reporting hopefully on the forthcoming meeting of Secretary Shultz with Gromyko in Stockholm at the opening of the multilateral Conference on Disarmament in Europe. TASS objected that "American official circles are spreading optimistic statements, apparently designed to create an impression that despite the deployment of Pershing II and cruise missiles in Europe, which is an extremely dangerous step against the cause of peace, things are going as if nothing has happened," thus "playing on the natural hopes of people for a better future in the coming year."[169]

The year ended with American-Soviet relations severely strained. For the first time in fifteen years there were no strategic arms control negotiations under way. Most important, not only had efforts to restore a dialogue been dashed but confidence—especially from the Soviet side—was at a new low. In addition, Andropov's health was failing fast, and the renewed succession process in Moscow was the central focus of attention there. Soviet relations with the United States could become an issue in political maneuvering in Moscow.

---

168. "Resolution of the Supreme Soviet of the USSR 'On the International Situation and the Foreign Policy of the Soviet State' " *Izvestiya*, December 30, 1983.

169. TASS, Radio Moscow, December 31, 1983, in FBIS, *Soviet Union*, January 3, 1984, p. CC6.

# 4 Wary Exploration of Improved Relations, 1984

JANUARY 1984 marked the beginning of President Ronald Reagan's campaign for reelection, a dominating element in foreign as well as domestic policymaking. Reagan himself, and at least as important, the triumvirate of White House advisers—Edwin Meese, James Baker, and Michael Deaver—were therefore responsive when in mid-December George Shultz proposed a major address by the president laying out the lines of American policy toward the Soviet Union as it would be depicted for the year ahead, including the election campaign. The KAL incident, the Soviet walkout from the arms control talks on intermediate-range nuclear forces (INF) and strategic arms reduction (START), and the virtual breakdown in high-level communication with the Soviet leaders would be swept aside and overtaken by a new presidential declaration of readiness to "meet the Soviets halfway." In addition, Reagan was concerned, if uncomprehending, over the intelligence reports of serious high-level alarm in Moscow in late 1983 about the possibility of an American attack, and he wanted to reaffirm American determination to reduce the risk of war, while remaining strong.[1]

## Reagan's New Rhetoric

Reagan's speech was delivered on January 16, 1984. The speech was drafted mainly in the State Department, consistent with National Security

---

1. Late in 1983, and again in early 1984, Reagan was advised by Director of Central Intelligence William Casey that the NATO exercise Able Archer in November 1983, which simulated nuclear release procedures, had caused genuine alarm in the KGB and presumably in other upper reaches of the Soviet leadership (Casey was relying mainly on information supplied by double-agent Oleg Gordievsky; see chapter 3). President Reagan alluded indirectly to this event in his memoir, where he admits being surprised to have learned that the Soviet leaders were genuinely afraid of an American attack. See Ronald Reagan, *An American Life* (Simon and Schuster, 1990), pp. 588–89.

Decision Directive (NSDD)–75, but resolving the ambiguities and contradic-tions in the official guidance in favor of an accent on negotiation and not confrontation. The increased cooperation between the White House and the State Department (exemplified in drafting the speech) reflected in part the fact that a career foreign service officer with considerable Moscow experience, Jack Matlock, had since the fall of 1983 been responsible for Soviet affairs on the National Security Council (NSC) staff.

Reagan stressed American strength and will. "I believe," he said, "that 1984 finds the United States in the strongest position in years to establish a constructive and realistic working relationship with the Soviet Union. We've come a long way since the decade of the seventies, years when the United States seemed filled with self-doubt and neglected its defenses, while the Soviet Union increased its military might and sought to expand its influence by armed forces and threat." He credited his administration with having "halted America's decline," and with economic, military, and political recovery. He also introduced a novel explanation for the recent "strident rhetoric from the Kremlin," namely, "America's recovery may have taken Soviet leaders by sur-prise. They may have counted on us to keep weakening ourselves."[2]

One of the main themes in the address was building "credible deterrence." By identifying the purpose of rebuilding American military power with deterrence, Reagan reaffirmed long-standing American policy more clearly than his administration had on some other occasions. More-over, he reaffirmed the basic theme of détente and peaceful coexistence (although of course not in those terms) when he said that "we should always remember that we [the United States and the Soviet Union] do have com-mon interests and the foremost among them is to avoid war and reduce the level of arms. There is no rational alternative but to steer a course which I would call credible deterrence and peaceful competition." He then added, "And if we do so, we might find areas in which we could engage in construc-tive cooperation." Later in the speech, indeed, he described American policy toward the Soviet Union as "a policy of credible deterrence, peaceful competition, and constructive cooperation," representing a challenge for Americans as well as for the Soviets.[3]

While stressing that "deterrence is essential," Reagan recognized that "deterrence is not the beginning and end of our policy toward the Soviet Union." He then came down strongly on the pragmatic side of the continuing internal debate within his administration, adding, "We must and will engage the Soviets in a dialog as serious and constructive as possible—a dialog that will serve to promote peace in the troubled regions of the world, reduce the level of

---

2. "Soviet-American Relations," January 16, 1984, *Weekly Compilation of Presidential Documents*, vol. 20 (January 23, 1984), p. 41. (Hereafter *Presidential Documents*.)

3. Ibid., pp. 41, 44.

arms, and build a constructive working relationship" with the Soviet Union. He stressed the need for "realism, strength, and dialog." "Realism means we must start with a clear-eyed understanding of the world we live in. We must recognize we are in a long-term competition. . . . Strength and dialog," he said, "go hand in hand, and we're determined to deal with our differences peacefully through negotiations." While recalling the ideological differences and competition between the two sides, "The fact that neither of us likes the other system is no reason to refuse to talk;" indeed, "Living in this nuclear age makes it imperative that we do talk."[4]

Reagan raised the problem of Third World conflicts but with a remarkable shift from the first two years of his administration. While briefly mentioning that many of these conflicts had been "exploited by the Soviet Union and its surrogates," he recognized that "most of these conflicts have their origins in local problems." Moreover, the main thrust of concern in the statement was not with Soviet expansion but with "the risk of larger confrontations" developing out of such local conflicts, and the main emphasis was therefore placed on "concrete actions that we both can take to reduce the risk of U.S.-Soviet confrontation in these areas." The broader aim was "to find ways to reduce, and eventually to eliminate, the threat and use of force in solving international disputes." The geopolitical challenge, while not absent, was muted. Instead, "A durable peace also requires ways for both of us to defuse tensions and regional conflicts."[5]

In place of the geopolitical confrontation and containment stressed by Haig, the main emphasis in this policy statement was on arms control, not only on reducing nuclear arms (a goal Reagan frequently avowed) but also on "reducing the risk of war, and especially nuclear war," which was said to be "priority number one" not only in arms control but "in our approach to negotiations."[6]

The speech, however, raised a major new problem in this field: questions about compliance and possible violations of arms control agreements reached in the past. "In recent years," said Reagan, "We've had serious concerns about Soviet compliance with agreements," and "There's been mounting evidence that provisions of agreements have been violated and that advantage has been taken of ambiguities in our agreements." This reference carried ominous potential implications for arms control and for the whole course of dialogue and negotiation. Either the actuality of intentional violations, or a belief by one side in violations not intended (or perceived) by the other, could

---

4.   Ibid, pp. 41, 43.

5.   Ibid., pp. 42, 44. In the last quotation above, the words "defuse tensions" have been used rather than the words "diffuse tensions" used, evidently in error, in *Presidential Documents*; the predelivery text used the word "defuse" and that better carries the meaning.

6.   Ibid., p. 43.

undermine future negotiations. Reagan stated that the United States "must take the Soviet compliance record into account, both in the development of our defense program and in our approach to arms control." He did not, however, say that it made arms control impossible, and he stated that "in our discussions with the Soviet Union, we will work to remove the obstacles which threaten to undermine existing agreements and a broader arms control process."[7]

With the important exception of flagging the issue of Soviet compliance with arms control agreements, Reagan's speech of January 16, 1984, marked a rather dramatic shift from earlier policy statements, one moving much further in the direction already taken in the speech by Secretary Shultz in June 1983.[8] By design, Secretary Shultz followed with a speech in Stockholm, at the opening of the Conference on Disarmament in Europe (CDE), an offspring of the Conference on Security and Cooperation in Europe (CSCE), the very next day.[9] If Reagan had made the same speech in January 1981 or 1982, or even January 1983, rather than not until January 1984, it could have given a positive impetus to the development of American-Soviet relations. The main problem with its effect in January 1984 was not the content but the context. This will become clearer when the development of the Soviet perspective has been spelled out.

The exception to the positive thrust of the speech was no accident. In accepting the State Department initiative and draft speech, Reagan and his advisers sought at the same time to balance this move toward the pragmatists with at least a nod to the conservative ideological anticommunists. Thus one week after the speech, as foreshadowed in it and in press leaks, the administration issued a "Report to the Congress on Soviet Noncompliance with Arms Control Agreements." The president's message to Congress and an unclassified fact sheet were made public, and a more detailed classified report was also submitted to Congress. While responsive to an earlier request from Congress,

---

7.  Ibid., pp. 42–43.

8.  Ibid., pp. 44–45. The most original and striking passage in the speech was drafted by Reagan himself, a few paragraphs imagining a meeting of four ordinary American and Soviet people "Ivan and Anya" and "Jim and Sally," who talked about personal interests of daily life, illustrating that "common interests cross all borders." While to many it seemed naive, it reflected a new personal outlook by Reagan.

     One reason for Reagan's new readiness to humanize the Russians and desire to seek real contact was the influence of an American writer on Russian culture and history, Suzanne Massie. Just after Christmas 1983 she met with President Reagan for what was to be the first of a number of meetings over the next four years. She succeeded in stirring Reagan's interest in the Russians as people and not merely as stereotyped communist automatons. Massie's influence reinforced Nancy Reagan's urgings to seek a rapprochement.

9.  "Secretary Shultz Visits Europe: Statement at the CDE, Stockholm," January 17, 1984, *Department of State Bulletin*, vol. 84 (March 1984), pp. 34–36. (Hereafter *State Bulletin*.)

the coincidental release of the report with the speech on policy toward the Soviet Union "covered" the president, with those seeking improved relations and negotiation and with those opposing these aims.[10]

The Soviets for their part echoed the president's own call for "deeds, not words" in their skeptical reaction to the January speech.[11] In response to the charges of Soviet noncompliance and violation of existing agreements, the Soviets submitted their own list of charges of American violations (mixing, as had the American list, old and recent, serious and not serious, charges).[12]

Secretary Shultz and Foreign Minister Andrei Gromyko used the occasion of the opening of the CDE Conference in Stockholm in January 1984 to meet privately. This meeting restored communication between them to the guarded jousting level of their first meeting in September 1982 (their only meeting in the interim was the extremely acrimonious exchange at Madrid following the KAL incident). In a five-hour meeting, they discussed a wide range of issues, and officials later described the meeting as "serious" and a step forward in a dialogue. Although Gromyko's public speech had been tough, he was more conciliatory in this private exchange. He proposed resuming the mutual and balanced force reductions (MBFR) negotiations on conventional arms on March 16, thus indicating that the suspension of INF and START did not represent a Soviet policy of boycotting all arms control talks, and Shultz

---

10. For the text see "Soviet Noncompliance with Arms Control Agreements," January 23, 1984, *Presidential Documents*, vol. 20 (January 30, 1984), pp. 73–77.

    The juxtaposition of the "soft" speech and the "hard" noncompliance report was the result of maneuvering within the administration and Congress. Hard-line Senators (Jesse Helms, Steven Symms, and James McClure), who had sponsored the legislation calling for the report (overwhelmingly supported in Congress), pressed the White House in early January for prompt release after they learned of the impending soft speech. The White House, also pressed by Richard Perle and other hard-liners in the Department of Defense and the Arms Control Disarmament Agency, compromised by selectivity in winnowing down the senators' long lists of charges of violations (Symms, for example, argued that there had been thirty-two violations of the SALT treaties alone). The president's Noncompliance Report alleged seven violations or probable violations of six arms control agreements. Incidentally, the formal congressional request had asked for a report on Soviet compliance or noncompliance, but the president's report neglected to report general compliance and was gratuitously titled a report on Soviet "noncompliance."

    Two well-known hard-line commentators stressed the tactical advantage seen in the administration's two-pronged approach in these words: "President Reagan's buttery peace appeal to the Russians coincided with his charge of Soviet cheating on nuclear treaties, giving him trump cards for the 1984 campaign the Democrats will find hard to top." Rowland Evans and Robert Novak, "The Week Reagan Played His Trump," *Washington Post*, January 18, 1984, p. A21.

    For discussion of the arms control compliance issue, see chapter 12.

11. See K. U. Chernenko, "The People and the Party Are United," *Pravda*, March 3, 1984.

12. "The United States Is Violating Its International Commitments," *Izvestiya*, January 30, 1984, provides the text of the Soviet aide memoir presented to the Department of State.

sensed that he was searching for a new approach to reopen strategic arms talks. Also, the very fact of the exchange demonstrated that the Soviet "big chill" of the previous four months was attenuating. In addition, a useful exchange on the Middle East concluded with agreement to continue discussions of that problem area at the assistant secretary (deputy minister) level. Shultz and Gromyko in effect began at Stockholm to renew the process of dialogue abruptly forestalled at Madrid by the KAL incident.[13]

Yury Andropov's death on February 9, 1984, after a long incapacitation, provided a fleeting opportunity for Vice President George Bush to meet yet another new Soviet leader when he met General Secretary Konstantin U. Chernenko at the funeral. But there was no active pursuit of the new "serious and constructive dialogue" promised in the president's January speech.[14] There was, to be sure, an unpublicized exchange of presidential correspondence, with letters from Chernenko on February 23 and March 19, and replies by Reagan on March 7 and April 16. A hiatus followed until June. The most productive aspect was the beginning of development of discussions between Secretary Shultz and Ambassador Anatoly Dobrynin on March 7, when Shultz conveyed the president's letter. While these early exchanges did not lead to any concrete results, they did represent an improvement in atmosphere over the chill of late 1983.[15]

Diplomatic talks on the question of reopening negotiation of a cultural and scientific exchange agreement and on opening consulates in Kiev and New York continued in the spring. So did quiet diplomatic discussions of regional problems in southern Africa, the Persian Gulf, and the Middle East. These talks had begun in December 1983 and included meetings of Secretary Shultz with Ambassador Dobrynin, and Ambassador Arthur Hartman with Foreign Minister Gromyko. Yet the Department of State, at the same time, decided to abolish its section dealing with U.S.-Soviet exchanges since there was so little for it to do.

Secretary Shultz decided to use the occasion of a change in the Soviet leadership to launch a high-level review of U.S. policy toward the Soviet Union. National Security Adviser Robert McFarlane supported this move, and in a memorandum to the president on February 24 he cited a letter received from

---

13. Based on interviews with informed officials, in part reviewed by George P. Shultz, *Turmoil and Triumph: My Years as Secretary of State* (Charles Scribner's Sons, 1993), pp. 469–71.

14. As after Brezhnev's death, only this time with less debate, the administration decided to take a positive stance, open to improving relations, and not to attempt to play on Soviet weakness at a time of transition.

15. Ambassador Dobrynin had informed Shultz on January 3, in response to Shultz's query in December, that the Soviet Union was indeed serious about a dialogue. (Shultz, *Turmoil and Triumph*, p. 465.) The letters followed the Shultz-Gromyko meeting of January, and focused mainly on arms control (pp. 473–74).

Chernenko the day before, which called for a dialogue and suggested that there might now be an "opportunity to put our relations on a more positive track." Reagan was enthusiastic and wanted to begin exploration of a possible summit.[16] An NSC meeting on March 1 launched the renewed effort to establish a dialogue.

An ill-conceived attempt to establish a back channel to the Soviet leadership, however, failed. Retired Lieutenant General Brent Scowcroft, President Gerald Ford's national security adviser and a respected figure, was traveling to Moscow on March 8 as a member of the Dartmouth Conference private group of foreign policy specialists for unofficial exchanges with Soviet counterparts. McFarlane and several other White House advisers (including Vice President Bush) decided on a back-channel approach to Chernenko, the new Soviet leader. They believed in "going to the top," and some wanted to bypass Foreign Minister Gromyko, whom they viewed as a hard-liner. Scowcroft was therefore given a letter from Reagan to be presented to Chernenko. The Soviet leaders, no doubt especially veteran Politburo member and First Deputy Prime Minister Gromyko, were suspicious of this unusual request for General Scowcroft to see General Secretary Chernenko, and they instead suggested that he meet with one of Gromyko's deputies, Viktor Komplektov, to transmit the letter. Scowcroft declined. The upshot was that the Soviet leaders believed the United States was trying to sow discord in their midst, Reagan believed he had been rebuffed in an attempt to improve relations, and a move intended to provide a step forward in relations instead became a source of new suspicion and disenchantment.[17]

---

16. See Don Oberdorfer, *The Turn: From the Cold War to a New Era, the United States and the Soviet Union, 1983–1990* (Poseidon Press, 1991), pp. 81–82.

17. See Francis X. Clines, "Scowcroft Pessimistic on Soviet Ties," *New York Times*, April 10, 1984, p. A3; and Rowland Evans and Robert Novak, "The Kremlin Brushoff," *Washington Post*, April 11, 1984, p. A21. Clines is, however, in error in reporting the Soviet official to whom Scowcroft was referred as First Deputy Foreign Minister Georgy Kornienko; it was Deputy Foreign Minister Viktor Komplektov, who normally handled relations with the United States. See also Shultz, *Turmoil and Triumph*, pp. 473–74.

From off-the-record discussions of the incident with American and Soviet officials, it is clear that the attempted ploy was well intended but ill-conceived and clumsily handled by the White House. In an unpublicized meeting of Secretary Shultz with Ambassador Dobrynin just a few days earlier, Shultz—uninformed on the plan at that point—did not of course advise Dobrynin of it. When Moscow queried Dobrynin he could only say he knew nothing of the matter. Ambassador Hartman did discuss the matter with Gromyko, but this did not dispel suspicions. Of course, neither Dobrynin nor any official in Moscow would have colluded in an attempt to cut Gromyko out, so to whatever extent that was an objective it was unattainable and should not have been attempted. The State Department understood the reasons for the failure of the probe, but the White House staff and especially President Reagan did not.

Other irritants also arose in American-Soviet relations. In March mines laid off Nicaragua by the United States damaged a Soviet tanker and caused casualties among the crew. The Soviet Union registered a vigorous protest over the action, blaming "mercenaries and terrorists" armed by the United States. The United States regretted the loss of life but rejected the protest and blamed "Soviet encouragement of conflict in Central America and the Caribbean."[18] The United States later acknowledged publicly in congressional debate the responsibility of the CIA for the mining, which did involve American manufacture of the mines and their deployment by Latin American mercenaries hired by the CIA to support the Nicaraguan counterrevolutionary contras trained and supported by the United States.[19] The United States did not, however, make such an acknowledgment to the Soviet Union. At about the same time, a Soviet submarine and an American aircraft carrier collided in the Sea of Japan, but neither side protested or made an issue of the accident.[20]

Other minor occurrences not directly involving the Soviet Union also contributed to a pattern of incidents raising tension. In January, near the Nicaraguan border, an American helicopter was fired upon and forced down in Honduras, killing the pilot. Shultz promptly went on television and charged: "It is unacceptable to fire from one country to another country and end up killing some people," and the White House spokesman called the action "reckless and unprovoked." In an unfortunate parallel to American charges in the KAL incident, it soon turned out that the helicopter had, albeit inadvertently, penetrated Nicaraguan airspace, that the only firing from one country to another had been by American-armed contras, that the helicopter's American identification insignia was—perhaps intentionally—obscured by mud, and that hostile actions in the area by contras had provoked the action.[21] And in April, an American helicopter was reportedly fired on by Czech fighters when it strayed about ten kilometers into Czechoslovakia.[22]

Incidents of a political nature also began to trouble relations. In several incidents beginning in mid-April and continuing into August 1984, American

---

18. See John F. Burns, "Moscow Holds U.S. Responsible for Mines Off Nicaragua's Ports," *New York Times*, March 22, 1984, pp. A1, A4.

19. See "Explosion over Nicaragua," *Time*, April 23, 1984, p. 16, and Leslie H. Gelb, "Officials Say C.I.A. Made Mines with Navy Help," *New York Times*, June 1, 1984, p. A4.

20. Richard Halloran, "Soviet Sub and U.S. Carrier Collide in Sea of Japan," *New York Times*, March 22, 1984, p. A6.

21. Richard Cohen, "Isn't This the Way the Soviet Leaders Talk to Their People?" *Washington Post*, January 16, 1984, p. A2.

22. Fred Hiatt, "Pentagon Says Its Copter Violated Czech Airspace," *Washington Post*, April 27, 1984, p. A32. West German border guards who witnessed the action stated that the American helicopter was escorted back to the border by the Czech fighters but not fired upon.

officials and visitors in Leningrad were harassed by Soviet "citizens" and police.[23] Yelena Bonner, wife of Soviet dissident Andrei Sakharov, after meeting
with U.S. Embassy officers and giving them a letter requesting asylum for
herself after Sakharov would begin a planned hunger strike, was accused of
"plotting" with the embassy to mount an anti-Soviet campaign in the West that
would exploit the hunger strike by Sakharov.[24] Concern over Sakharov's health
(and even life) and over Bonner's subsequent restraint from travel did spur
strong criticism in the United States. In June the National Academy of Sciences
canceled scheduled talks on a new exchange agreement in a show of concern
over Sakharov.[25] Meanwhile, on April 30 a departing Soviet scholar, Sergei M.
Kozlov, who had been visiting in the United States on the exchange program,
exhibited erratic behavior and uncertainty about whether he wanted to return
to the Soviet Union. The United States acted with high visibility to ensure that
he not depart unless he really wanted to; Assistant Secretary of State Richard
Burt personally rushed to the airport. After several weeks (during which time it
became clear the Russian had mental health problems), Kozlov declared in the
presence of American officials that he wanted to return to the Soviet Union and
was permitted to depart.[26] Meanwhile, renewal of an educational exchange
agreement between the American Council of Learned Societies and the Soviet
Academy of Sciences was held up by the Soviets until Kozlov was permitted to
depart.

A Soviet Academy of Sciences delegation invited to the United States
for unofficial talks with American scientists in early May was reportedly allowed
to come only after Politburo debate and decision, and with a strict injunction
against any meetings with U.S. officials. The reason was to avoid lending
credence to American claims of business as normal. One unanticipated consequence, however, was to prevent its head, Vice Chairman of the Academy of
Sciences Yevgeny Velikhov, from accepting an invitation from Secretary of
State Shultz to meet and discuss possible arms control on antisatellite and space
weapons—a subject in which the Soviets were greatly interested.[27]

---

23. John M. Goshko, "'Harassment' in Leningrad Leads to U.S. Warning for Travelers,"
    *Washington Post*, August 7, 1984, p. A10.
24. Dusko Doder, "Soviets Accuse U.S., Dissident of Plot," *Washington Post*, May 5, 1984,
    p. A1, A23.
25. Cristine Russell, "U.S. Science Academy Cancels Moscow Meeting in Support of
    Sakharov," *Washington Post*, June 9, 1984, p. A14.
26. Bernard Gwertzman, "U.S. Lets Russian Depart for Home," *New York Times*, June 7,
    1984, p. A7.
27. The Politburo consideration, with Ustinov and Gromyko reportedly opposed and
    Mikhail Gorbachev in favor, with Chernenko brokering a compromise, cannot be
    confirmed and may be Moscow gossip or disinformation. The delegation was, however,
    instructed to avoid contact with U.S. officials, and the invitation from Secretary Shultz

The most striking and significant development was the Soviet decision, announced on May 8, not to participate in the Olympic Games in Los Angeles. The Soviet Union was, reluctantly, followed by its Warsaw Pact allies (except Romania) and by such other close allies as Cuba and Vietnam. The Soviet action was justified by alleged connivance of the American authorities in a wide-ranging campaign whipping up "anti-Soviet hysteria" and organizing provocative activities directed at the Soviet Olympic delegation, and American actions were said to belie assurances to ensure the "security" of their people.[28] Undoubtedly the general low state of American-Soviet relations contributed to the Soviet decision. So, presumably, did an element of retaliation for the American Olympic boycott of 1980. In addition, some Western observers speculated that the Soviets may have thought the action would rebound negatively on President Reagan, although it did not. Soviet officials at the time, however, privately acknowledged that the withdrawal would not serve Soviet propaganda or political interests in the United States but was undertaken despite that fact.

While we do not know the mix of considerations that led the Soviet leaders, evidently only shortly before the announcement, to make their decision, clearly their announced reason was a major one. While they may not have been concerned over security from life-threatening terrorist acts, at the least they did fear anti-Soviet demonstrations and attempts to instigate defection. The Soviet charge that "extremist organizations" had been openly aiming to create "unbearable conditions" for the Soviet sports delegation had a great deal of truth to it. Considerable publicity had been given to plans to saturate the area with anti-Soviet propaganda, and it had been announced that vigorous efforts would be made to induce defection, including boasts of prepared "safe houses" for defectors. A "Ban the Soviets Coalition" of émigré nationalist and other groups had vowed to make life miserable for the Soviets. The coalition warned that Soviet participation could "result in acts of violence against their athletes," which the Soviets construed as a scarcely veiled threat.[29]

---

was tendered and declined. Information from U.S. officials and members of the Soviet Academy of Sciences delegation.

28. The text of the Soviet National Olympic Committee statement, as well as extensive American speculative commentary, is in the *New York Times*, May 9, 1984, pp. A1, A16, A17.

29. The coalition later claimed that this was not a threat; while technically it was not, the Soviet interpretation was not unreasonable. See David W. Balsiger, "No Olympic Threats," *Newsweek*, November 5, 1984, p. 8, for a letter from the director of the coalition.

The Soviet press also took umbrage at a letter to the head of the coalition from Assistant to the President Michael Deaver expressing sympathy with the coalition's views. See *Krasnaya zvezda* (Red Star), April 6, 1984.

At an unpublicized meeting on April 27, the State Department had assured the Soviet embassy on physical security and offered to discuss security measures but had rejected Soviet complaints and dismissed their concerns about political harassment.[30] Moreover, there had been public statements by American officials sympathetic to the campaign. And the annual presidential proclamation of Captive Nations Week was scheduled to occur on the eve of the Olympics. As a Soviet official told me at the time, "Every day, overshadowing the Olympic contests themselves, there would have been news and pictures of anti-Soviet demonstrations." No doubt they also feared some highly publicized defection. In any event, the Soviet leaders decided to abstain from participation in the Olympics for some combination of reasons relating to the state of the Soviet-American relations, and this decision thus reflected and further contributed to the chill in relations.

Throughout the election year 1984 the Reagan administration sought to counter criticisms from various American and other Western quarters that it was not trying or not able to maintain and improve relations with the Soviet Union. While the administration countered that the Soviet side was recalcitrant, it also had to show signs of a forthcoming American approach and maintain that business as usual *was* proceeding. This mix of themes was not always easy to manage.

In early April, President Reagan reiterated the main themes of his January speech: realism, strength, and dialogue. He reaffirmed that the highest challenge was "to reduce the risk of nuclear war and to reduce the levels of nuclear armaments." Seeking further to overcome the impression created earlier in his administration of a proclivity to prepare for the contingency of waging war, he affirmed that "a nuclear war cannot be won and must never be fought." To be sure, he used that conclusion, and the further observation that "merely to be against nuclear war is not enough to prevent it," as the basis for a strong reassertion of the need for maintaining military strength for deterrence.[31] He also reaffirmed containment and the need to build "stability in troubled and strategically sensitive regions" of the world and claimed that while local tensions often have indigenous sources, "throughout the 1970's, increased Soviet support for terrorism, insurgency, and aggression, coupled with a perception of weakening U.S. power and resolve, greatly exacerbated these tensions." He listed Kampuchea, Afghanistan, Angola, Ethiopia, and Central America as Soviet (and Cuban) actions, as well as the Iranian holding of American hostages and Libyan coercion in Africa. Finally, the one new element

---

30. Bernard Gwertzman, "U.S. Calls the Soviet Complaints a 'Classic Case' of Distortion," *New York Times*, May 15, 1984, p. A13. I was told by a Soviet official that the American reply had been "It's a free country." While true, under the circumstances this response was scarcely calculated to reassure the Soviets.

31. "American Foreign Policy Challenges in the 1980s," April 6, 1984, *State Bulletin*, vol. 84 (May 1984), pp. 1–6.

in his speech—obviously keyed to the election—was an appeal to "restore bipartisan consensus in support of U.S. foreign policy"—meaning, of course, in support of the policy of his administration.[32]

At about the same time Secretary Shultz gave a speech on "Power and Diplomacy in the 1980s" in which he accented heavily the need for the United States to operate from a position of military strength because "the hard reality is that diplomacy not backed by strength is ineffectual." Moreover, "By the accident of history, the role of world leadership fell to the United States," and since the United States is "the world's strongest free nation . . . hopes for a better world rest in great measure, inevitably, on our shoulders." Not quite in the bipartisan spirit of which President Reagan spoke, he also tore from its context and characterized Carter's view that "our fear of communism was 'inordinate' " as "a counsel of helplessness that substantially underestimates the United States and its ability to influence events."[33]

On the fortieth anniversary of the Allied landing at Normandy, Secretary of Defense Caspar Weinberger, in quoting a D-Day speech by General Dwight D. Eisenhower, deleted a passage in which Eisenhower had paid tribute to our gallant Russian ally. This gratuitous retrospective censorship of history was not only unnecessarily offensive to the Soviets but also did no credit to the American administration.

In June, following a public appeal by Republican Senate leaders Howard H. Baker, Jr., and Charles H. Percy to hold a summit meeting, President Reagan declared himself willing "to meet and talk any time" with Chernenko. Reagan, who himself had repeatedly insisted that any summit meeting must be well prepared, said now that it was the Soviets who were insisting on a "carefully prepared agenda."[34]

On a trip to Europe, Reagan covered all bets. On June 2 in Ireland he departed from reminiscences of his Irish heritage to stress that "the free world faces an enormously powerful adversary . . . a strong and aggressive military machine"—and that "we seek negotiations with the Soviet Union, but unfortunately we face an empty chair."[35] Two days later, after lengthy praise of his administration's arms control efforts, he proposed as a concession to the Soviet

---

32. Ibid., pp. 3, 5.

33. "Power and Diplomacy in the 1980s," April 3, 1984, *State Bulletin*, vol. 84 (May 1984), pp. 12–13.
   Four months later, Shultz gave another speech on the same theme, this time saying that "negotiations and diplomacy not backed by strength are ineffectual at best, dangerous at worst." Secretary Shultz, "Diplomacy and Strength," August 20, 1984, *State Bulletin*, vol. 84 (October 1984), pp. 18–20.

34. "The President's News Conference of June 14, 1984," *Presidential Documents*, vol. 20 (June 18, 1984), p. 877.

35. "Remarks at University College, Galway," Ireland, June 2, 1984, ibid., vol. 20 (June 11, 1984), p. 822.

approach to enter discussions "on reaffirming the principle not to use force." This was intended as a sign of concession to encourage negotiation.[36] He also said, "We seek to build confidence and trust with the Soviets in areas of mutual interest" but claimed that "the Soviet response has been disappointing . . . self-imposed isolation."[37]

In the same speech, however, Reagan also recalled his appeal in Europe two years earlier for "a crusade for freedom. . . . And now it is underway." In speaking of "the struggle between freedom and totalitarianism" he spoke at length of American efforts in Central America and also quoted a recent dissident Czechoslovak Charter 77 statement and Lech Wałęsa, the Polish Solidarity leader, and proffered "a forward strategy for freedom." And in a peroration, all four of the places of struggles he chose to mention were communist states: "All across the world today—in the shipyards of Gdansk, the hills of Nicaragua, the rice paddies of Kampuchea, the mountains of Afghanistan—the cry again is liberty."[38] Stirring to many, perhaps inspiring, but a "strategy for freedom" more keyed to liberation through confrontation than to containment or negotiation.

On June 16 Reagan signed a proclamation observing the annual Captive Nations Week, as mandated by Congress twenty-five years earlier. He denounced the "Communist totalitarianism" of the Soviet Union as "the single greatest challenge to human rights in the world today" and attacked what he referred to as a Soviet "relentless drive to conquer more and more lands" in Asia and Central America. He appealed for American support to the "freedom fighters" in Afghanistan and in Nicaragua.[39]

One week later, Secretary Shultz seemed to echo Haig's early charges, declaring that "the Soviet Union and its clients" supported terrorists "worldwide." He acknowledged official Soviet denunciation of terrorism as an instrument of state policy but claimed "a wide gap between Soviet words and Soviet actions" and that "the Soviets use terrorist groups for their own purposes." Shultz did acknowledge a distinction in expressing American sympathy for "those who strive for freedom and democracy" but said the United States would "oppose guerrilla wars where they threaten to spread totalitarian rule," which would of course cover any case where the Soviet Union or its "clients"

---

36. President Reagan had indicated U.S. readiness to consider a nonuse of force agreement in a letter to Chernenko in April, in the course of their private exchanges. In June he decided to make this same offer publicly, without disclosing the earlier confidential discussions. Information from an informed senior official.

37. "Address to a Joint Session of the National Parliament," Dublin, Ireland, June 4, 1984, *Presidential Documents*, vol. 20 (June 11, 1984), p. 833.

38. Ibid., pp. 832–36.

39. See David Hoffman, "Reagan Revives Anti-Soviet Rhetoric," *Washington Post*, July 17, 1984, p. A3, and see "Captive Nations Week, 1984," *Presidential Documents*, vol. 20 (July 23, 1984), pp. 1031–34.

aided a liberation or revolutionary movement, given expressed views on Soviet ability to manipulate such groups.[40] Shultz's speech thus converted a renewed Western concern over combating terrorism (following a fatal shooting from the Libyan embassy in London and other acts such as the assassination of a group of senior officials of South Korea in Burma, none involving the Soviet Union), into another element of American-Soviet confrontation.[41]

In economic relations, the administration declared: "Our policy is not one of economic warfare against the Soviets. We do not seek the 'collapse' of the Warsaw Pact economies." But in reaffirming that "the Administration believes in trade between the West and the communist nations," a rather large and imprecise exception was reaffirmed: "We want to avoid economic exchanges, particularly transfers of technology, that contribute to the military potential of the U.S.S.R. and its allies or that subsidize the heavily militarized Soviet economy and thus alleviate their difficult resource allocation decisions."[42] Moreover, this statement represented official administration policy as articulated by the Department of State. As seen in the Defense Guidance issued in 1982 (and unchanged in 1984), the Department of Defense had a very restrictive view of what would *not* contribute to Soviet military potential. The real question, constantly readdressed as new occasions for decision arose, was

---

40. "Terrorism: The Challenge to the Democracies," June 24, 1984, *State Bulletin*, vol. 84 (August 1984), pp. 32–33. The conference, in Washington, was sponsored by the Jonathan Institute of Jerusalem.

      Shultz also strongly criticized the notion that "one man's terrorist is another man's freedom fighter," yet examples he gave of acts of violence against civilian noncombatants would cover contras blowing up power plants in Nicaragua as well as guerrillas blowing up power plants in El Salvador.

41. On April 3, the White House issued a secret directive on dealing with terrorism, NSDD-138. In accordance with that directive, the administration had sought five new laws to assist in combating terrorism, for example, making the taking of hostages a federal offense, and prohibiting the training and support of terrorists. The administration had also pressed for and obtained agreement on a "Declaration on International Terrorism" by the seven Western leaders at the London economic summit in June. But the Western declaration, the American legislation, and testimony by Secretary Shultz before Congress in support of the legislative requests had made no mention of the Soviet Union. See Shultz, "Terrorism: The Problem and the Challenge," June 13, 1984, *State Bulletin*, vol. 84 (August 1984), pp. 29–30. See also the useful background account by Leslie H. Gelb, "Administration Debating Antiterrorist Measures," *New York Times*, June 6, 1984, p. A6.

      In October, Shultz returned to the theme of preemptive action against terrorists, and again stressed the alleged Soviet role and connections. See "Terrorism and the Modern World," October 25, 1984, *State Bulletin*, vol. 84 (December 1984), pp. 12–17.

42. W. Allen Wallis, Undersecretary of State for Economic Affairs, "Review of East-West Economic Relations," statement before the Subcommittee on Europe and the Middle East of the House Foreign Affairs Committee, March 29, 1984, Department of State, Current Policy No. 567, p. 1.

not whether the United States had declared economic war but whether it was waging an undeclared economic war.

By 1984, differences between the administration's view of technology controls in East-West trade and the views of the Western European countries, papered over in the agreement of November 1982 that ended the pipeline sanctions, were again simmering. So, too, were recurrent conflicts within the administration in Washington. Hard-liners in the Department of Defense, mainly Richard Perle and Fred Iklé, continued to press for tighter restrictions (and a stronger Pentagon role in deciding control issues). In the summer and fall of 1984, agreement was reached among the Western powers on guidelines in the particularly sensitive and thorny area of computer technology (and telephone switching, important to military command and control) for the period through 1988. Serious differences remained, however, over the question of those restrictions after that date and over other restrictions. The United States continued to impose stiffer controls on American trade than the agreed Western constraints.

The Soviets sought to lean over backward to avoid contributing to the Reagan administration's attempt to persuade the American public that relations with the Soviet Union were normal. Visiting Soviet scholars and scientists, many with important party or government connections, declined several opportunities in May to meet unofficially with administration officials. Nonetheless, an exception was made in the meeting of the U.S.-USSR Trade and Economic Council in late May, led by Deputy Minister of Foreign Trade Vladimir N. Sushkov.

By June, the Soviets began to resume normal bilateral relations. Chernenko resumed the presidential correspondence, in abeyance for nearly two months, with a letter on June 6. Soon after, Dobrynin told Shultz that the way was again open to resume steps in bilateral relations, the course both he and Shultz had seen as the most promising foot in the door for resuming a real dialogue. In June–July a delegation of eleven Soviet journalists and editors from the Union of Journalists visited the United States for ten days as guests of the American Society of Newspaper Editors, with a return visit by a dozen Americans to the Soviet Union in August-September. This was only the second time such an exchange of visits had occurred, and the previous occasion had been twenty years earlier.

President Reagan carried forward his campaign to demonstrate the interest and ability of his administration in improving relations with the Soviet Union. On June 27 in remarks to an unofficial American Conference on U.S.-Soviet Exchanges, Reagan mentioned no fewer than sixteen proposals for agreements on cooperation in various areas—most of them renewals of earlier agreements, a number of them already advanced in discussions, and some simply references to recent ongoing activities. Thus while somewhat inflated, the thrust of the message was to present an image of the administration as forthcoming and actively pursuing improved relations. In the president's own words, "So, as you can see, we've offered comprehensive and sensible proposals to improve the U.S.-Soviet dialog and our working relationship." He was careful to add, "It's still too early to judge the results," but his pitch was that the United States under his administration was actively doing its part.[43]

Among the subjects mentioned, one that was under active discussion was the opening of new consulates general in Kiev and New York. Another was negotiation of a new cultural exchange agreement to replace the one that expired in 1979. A series of other agreements were coming up for renewal or had recently been renewed, including cooperation in devising measures to protect the environment, on housing techniques, in the health field, on agricultural techniques, on oceanographic research, and a broad agreement on facilitating economic, industrial, and technical cooperation. A fishing agreement had been extended in April, and later (in July) the United States lifted a ban, imposed after Afghanistan, on Soviet fishing in U.S. waters. Similarly, talks on resolving a difference over the demarcation of the maritime boundary between the two countries in the Bering Sea west of Alaska were resumed in July. Naval officers had met in Moscow in May under the U.S.-Soviet Incidents at Sea Agreement, signed in Moscow in 1972, and agreed on its continuation. Talks between the U.S. Coast Guard and the Soviet maritime rescue authorities on emergency search and rescue at sea were planned. The only really new proposal, mentioned for the first time, was a comparable space rescue consultation with a joint simulated space rescue mission.

Reagan mentioned that progress had been made on talks on upgrading the "hot line" direct communications link, and agreement was reached on July 17. Two other U.S. proposals had not been considered necessary by the Soviet side, upgrading the technical communications of our respective embassies and a joint military communications link. Another proposal that had not yet led to real talks concerned consultations in the event of a nuclear terrorist threat or incident.[44]

The president did not mention another proposal privately advanced earlier in the year for exploring the possibility of regular contact between defense officials of the two countries to increase mutual understanding. This potentially useful forum for dialogue was regarded by the Soviet leaders with caution and as premature given the poor general state of relations.

As in his January speech and on most such occasions, Reagan chose to complement his offer of a hand in dialogue with a slap by the other hand.[45]

---

43. "Conference on U.S.-Soviet Exchanges," June 27, 1984, *Presidential Documents*, vol. 20 (July 2, 1984), p. 945.

   In a Freudian slip, President Reagan said the United States had taken steps to "remove," corrected then to "revive," a series of bilateral agreements.

44. The status of the various proposals summarized above, as of June 1984, was discussed in "Fact Sheet: U.S.-Soviet Bilateral Relations," White House, Office of the Press Secretary, June 27, 1984. It was not published in *Presidential Documents*.

45. As in January, the *New York Times* and the *Washington Post* accented different aspects of the speech; see Steven R. Weisman, "Reagan Outlines Steps to Improve Ties with

"When Soviet actions threaten the peace or violate a solemn agreement or trample on standards fundamental to a civilized world, we cannot and will not be silent." He mentioned several leading dissidents, including Sakharov and the imprisoned Anatoly Shcharansky, and charged Soviet violation of the Helsinki Final Act. "The people of the Soviet Union," he said, "pay a heavy price for the actions of their government." And in implicit recognition that a number of the steps now being taken were reversals of sanctions by the Carter administration in 1980, he argued defensively that these actions are "not a signal that we have forgotten Afghanistan." (He did not note that some of the talks resumed had also been cut off for a time by him after the KAL incident the preceding September.) Finally, he also did relate the prospects for "improving dialog, reducing arms, and solving problems" to Soviet realization that "the attempt to spread their dominance by using military power as a means of intimidation" was a strategy that would not work.[46]

Two days after President Reagan's speech, the Soviet leaders advanced a proposal for negotiations "to prevent militarization of outer space," including "complete renunciation of antisatellite systems" and a reciprocal moratorium on testing "space weapons." They proposed to begin negotiations in Vienna in September. Initially presented by Ambassador Dobrynin to Secretary Shultz on the morning of June 29, it was published by the Soviet government on the very next day.[47] No doubt to the surprise of the Soviet leaders (and of almost everyone in Washington), National Security Adviser Robert C. McFarlane rushed through a positive (but loaded) American reaction the same day the proposal was presented. The prompt U.S. response was an attempt to convert the Soviet proposition into a wide-open discussion of resuming negotiations on strategic and intermediate-range arms (START and INF), as well as to discuss "feasible negotiating approaches which could lead to verifiable and effective limitations on antisatellite weapons." The U.S. was "prepared to meet" in September but to discuss a quite different agenda—omitting space weapons other than antisatellite weapons (that is, excluding the Star Wars strategic ballistic missile defense systems), and offering only to try to agree on "limita-

---

Moscow," *New York Times*, June 28, 1984, pp. A1, A12; and Lou Cannon, "Reagan Uses Speech to Castigate Soviets, Propose Non-Arms Pacts," *Washington Post*, June 28, 1984, pp. A17, A27. This had also been true of the interpretation by the two newspapers of testimony by Secretary Shultz in June 1983.

Cannon quoted one unidentified official as conceding, "There are different voices in this administration and different points of emphasis in this speech." Another stated that the speech reflected the views of the Soviet affairs experts in the administration who incorporated "a message for the Soviets" that "we want to improve relations but only if they're ready to improve their conduct."

46. "Conference on U.S.-Soviet Exchanges," *Presidential Documents*, vol. 20 (July 2, 1984), pp. 945–46.

47. "Statement of the Soviet Government," *Pravda*, June 30, 1984.

tions," not a ban, on space weapon systems, as well as bringing in the INF and START talks from which the Soviet Union had withdrawn.[48]

Speculation at the time as to why the Soviet leaders had made this proposal was bereft of the important fact that confidential exchanges on this subject had been going on since March in messages between Reagan and Chernenko, and for some weeks between Shultz and Dobrynin. Reagan had authorized Shultz (through McFarlane) to engage in these discussions but without informing Secretary of Defense Weinberger. The Soviets apparently concluded that rather than negotiate with a counterpart whose position could be undermined at any time, it was better to get the United States to show its hand. Some in Moscow no doubt expected a rejection, but some may have hoped for acceptance. They clearly did not, however, anticipate the response they received.

Negotiations continued for another month or so, but although the United States drew back somewhat on its efforts to use the Soviet initiative to force them back into START and INF, it continued to stress the relationship between defensive and offensive arms limitations. Moreover, the gap remained as great as ever on the other two points: was the aim to prevent all weapons in space or merely to limit one class of space weaponry? And should a moratorium on antisatellite testing be instituted? Again, the upshot seemed only to confirm a difference between the two sides on that issue, to abort the talks, and to lead to charges by each side that it really wanted negotiations while the other did not. Nevertheless, the discussions on the subject suggested some real interest on both sides.

Generally, Congress continued to defer to Reagan's programs. The MX continued to be held on a tight leash with minimal production and deployment authorized and funded, and doubts about the Star Wars strategic defense initiative and antisatellite programs in the absence of the efforts at arms control were growing. The National Endowment for Democracy, set up in 1983 as a channel for waging the struggle of ideas, had stirred further doubts by such actions as providing funds to Polish political dissidents and supporting one of the candidates in the Panamanian election. In August the new funding request of $31.3 million for the endowment was cut to $18.5 million, and the planned distribution to the Republican and Democratic parties was prohibited.[49]

In a chance incident in August, President Reagan's casual approach and sense of humor precipitated renewed concerns about his underlying attitudes. In testing a microphone before a radio broadcast on August 11, he jokingly remarked: "My fellow Americans, I am pleased to tell you I have

---

48. "United States-Soviet Union Negotiations," June 29, 1984, *Presidential Documents*, vol. 20 (July 2, 1984), p. 958.
    See also Shultz, *Turmoil and Triumph*, p. 477.

49. See Walter Goodman, "Congress Assails Democracy Group," *New York Times*, August 15, 1984, p. A21.

signed legislation to outlaw Russia forever. We begin bombing in five minutes."[50] Reagan's levity over a matter of such gravity evoked widespread criticism, especially in Western Europe. The Soviet Union objected to the
president's "invective, unprecedentedly hostile to the U.S.S.R. and dangerous
to the cause of peace," saying "Such behavior is incompatible with the high
responsibility borne by leaders of states, particularly nuclear powers, for the
destinies of their own peoples and of all mankind." They also used the occasion
to pummel the United States for "doctrines of limited and protracted nuclear
wars" and "military-political plans for securing U.S. world domination." But
while the Soviets sought to exploit the incident for propaganda, it also stirred
real concerns they had about Reagan's underlying attitude and policy. They
probably did believe it when they said that it was "a manifestation of the same
frame of mind that has already been formulated officially in calls for a 'crusade.'"[51] The incident soon faded away, but it left another deposit on the
accumulated residue of doubts in the minds of many as to Reagan's sincerity in
his repeated election year calls for "dialogue" and protestations of interest in
improving relations.[52]

On the occasion of the fortieth anniversary of the Warsaw Uprising
against the German occupation, President Reagan declared that the United
States would not passively accept "the permanent subjugation of the people of
Eastern Europe." He also rejected "any interpretation of the Yalta agreement
[of 1945] that suggests American consent for the division of Europe into
spheres of influence." Finally, he challenged communist rule in Eastern Europe and said "what happened in Poland is one sign that the tide is turning."[53]

Despite these continuing statements carrying forward political pressure and propaganda against the Soviet Union, Reagan also moved to continue
his new approach of seeking a dialogue. On August 13, Shultz reported to
Reagan that Gromyko was coming to New York for the opening of the UN
General Assembly in September, and there had been unofficial hints he would

---

50. "Tapes Pick Up Reagan Joke about Soviets," *Washington Post*, August 13, 1984, p. A6.
    Reagan responded to the widespread criticism with yet another quip four days
    later, when he greeted a group of visitors to the White House by saying that he had to
    go to a cabinet meeting, but that he certainly was "not going to bomb Russia in the next
    five minutes." Steven R. Weisman, "President Jokes about War Quip," *New York Times*,
    August 17, 1984, p. A3.

51. "TASS Statement," *Pravda*, August 16, 1984. See also Yuri Zhukov, "The President's
    'Nuclear Joke,'" *Pravda*, August 15, 1984.

52. The incident also raised a question about possible inadvertent generation of a crisis by
    such events. In response to reports of Reagan's statement, a relatively low-level Soviet
    commander in the Far East reportedly alerted his troops, although his order was swiftly
    countermanded. See "Brief Alert Reported in Soviet after Quip by the President," *New
    York Times*, October 13, 1984, p. A2.

53. "Fortieth Anniversary of the Warsaw Uprising," August 17, 1984, *Presidential Docu-
    ments*, vol. 20 (August 20, 1984), pp. 1132–33.

like to be invited to see Reagan in Washington. Shultz was careful to note that he was not recommending such a step but merely calling the opening to Reagan's attention, and that it would resume a contact not maintained since Afghanistan. Reagan was immediately responsive and said he would like to have such a meeting.[54] This decision was supported by the inner White House team of Baker and Deaver (and Nancy Reagan).

The president chose his address to the UN General Assembly on September 24 as the occasion to present the culminating statement of his new policy line. In a statesmanlike tone and brimming with conciliation, the speech avoided even a single direct criticism of the Soviet Union. The man who had called the Soviet leaders "the focus of evil in the modern world" now appealed to those same leaders in maudlin terms: "For the sake of a peaceful world . . . let us approach each other with ten-fold trust and thousand-fold affection."[55]

The most important passage in the speech, although not the most noted in commentaries, was Reagan's statement that "America has repaired its strength. . . . We are ready for constructive negotiations with the Soviet Union."[56] This was the most categorical statement he or other senior members of his administration had made that the rebuilding of American power, which he had considered a necessary foundation for real negotiation, had now been accomplished, and that it was therefore possible to look ahead and to go forward into negotiations.

In discussions within the administration since June a consensus was reached (at least among President Reagan, Secretary Shultz, and National Security Adviser McFarlane) that the United States had indeed now repaired its strength sufficiently to be able to enter negotiations confidently. Shultz and McFarlane had in fact been taking this position since mid-1983. Weinberger throughout that time was wary of the effect of any public acknowledgement of U.S. strength on congressional support for a sustained buildup. He also was not sympathetic to negotiations with the Soviet Union.[57]

In fact, the United States had not been nearly as weak as President Reagan and others in his administration believed in 1981, nor had the nation become that much stronger by 1984. Nonetheless, if those were their perceptions, or even only their publicly expressed view, they provided a rationale for the shift in stance.[58]

---

54. Shultz, *Turmoil and Triumph*, p. 480.

55. "United Nations: Address before the 39th Session of the General Assembly," September 24, 1984, *Presidential Documents*, vol. 20 (October 1, 1984), p. 1359.

56. Ibid., p. 1356.

57. Information from a senior administration official.

58. Diehard advocates of building American military power and dealing with the Soviet Union only from superior strength, rather than in negotiations based on mutual advantage, began to criticize the Reagan administration for its military and foreign policy. A

In the speech, Reagan cited the Austrian State Treaty of 1955 and the Berlin accord of 1971 as examples of the kind of agreements he hoped to see in the future. While he stressed arms control, he conspicuously did not cite any of the arms control agreements of the 1960s or 1970s as examples. Rather than harp on the stalemated START and INF talks of 1981–83, he proposed to "extend the arms control process" by building an "umbrella," under which various talks and agreements might fit, a "road-map" to guide efforts in the arms control area over the next twenty years. He also expressed readiness to "discuss a wide range of issues of concern to both sides, such as the relationship between defensive and offensive forces and what has been called the militarization of space."[59] He also called for mutual restraint. This could be a constructive step, although the Soviet leaders were suspicious that it meant only a U.S. use of its Star Wars programs as leverage to seek to impose one-sided Soviet reductions in strategic offensive forces.

The most general political proposal was for institutionalizing regular ministerial cabinet-level meetings on a wide agenda of problems facing the two countries, "including the problem of needless obstacles to understanding." The president also proposed "periodic consultations at policy level about regional problems."[60]

The speech was certainly conciliatory but not soft. It was accepted by the president virtually as drafted in the State Department. The overriding question—in Washington, and still more in Moscow—was whether the speech really represented a changed view by the president or merely election campaign "mood music."

In a brief encounter with Gromyko in New York on September 23, President Reagan told him he wanted "nothing less than a realistic, constructive, long-term relationship with the Soviet Union."[61] He repeated much the same message when he saw Gromyko alone briefly four days later on his first visit to the White House since September 1978, during which they exchanged

report of the Committee on the Present Danger now sharply criticized the Reagan administration for allowing a further deterioration in military strength, claiming that "the gap between U.S. and Soviet military capabilities continues to grow." See Committee on the Present Danger, *Can America Catch Up? The U.S.-Soviet Military Balance* (Washington, 1984), p. v. One author of the report was William Van Cleave, who had headed the Reagan transition team at the Defense Department in 1980 but been passed over for a senior post in the new administration. Van Cleave commented on Reagan's September statement about the United States having the strength to negotiate. He said the United States "obviously did *not* have enough" strength. See Walter Pincus, "Defense Buildup Failing, Group Says," *Washington Post*, December 1, 1984, p. A14. Emphasis added.

59. *Presidential Documents*, vol. 20 (October 1, 1984), p. 1357.

60. Ibid., pp. 1358, 1356.

61. Cited by Francis X. Clines, "Reagan, Meeting with Gromyko, Asks for Closer Ties," *New York Times*, September 24, 1984, p. A13.

views on how to grapple with the problem of negotiating nuclear arms reductions.[62] Meanwhile Gromyko had met with Shultz, and in his address to the UN General Assembly on September 27 had made a fairly tough but straightforward statement of the Soviet position, the most important element of which was a restatement of the Soviet view that "it is precisely concrete deeds and not verbal assurances that can lead to normalization of the situation in our relations with the United States."[63] And the president's speech had represented only verbal assurances.

Several other developments tended, perhaps unjustifiably, to cast doubt on the sincerity or steadfastness of the turn by the Reagan administration toward dialogue and negotiation instead of confrontation. On the eve of the president's speech, he proclaimed a National Peace through Strength Week, a formality of no real significance except that it lent a presidential aura to a right-wing internal propaganda drive by the anti-détente Coalition for Peace through Strength and American Security Council.[64]

The Republican Party platform for the 1984 election, adopted only shortly before by a convention completely dominated by President Reagan, had also declared that the Soviet Union's "globalist ideology and its leadership obsessed with military power make it a threat to freedom and peace on every continent" and implied that Soviet expansionism was responsible for virtually every disturbance of the peace around the world. It rejected as an "illusion" that the Soviet leaders could share our aspirations. And despite President Reagan's earlier abandonment of avowal for a goal of military superiority, it promised to keep the United States "stronger than any potential adversary."[65]

Even before Gromyko's visit, the press reported that the White House had decided that it could "poison the atmosphere" for the talks if it released a report of the General Advisory Committee on Arms Control and Disarmament, collecting a large batch of alleged Soviet violations of arms control agreements since 1958. Therefore the White House would defer release. But an unclassified version of the report was released soon after, on October 10.

Most bizarre was the leaking to conservative news columnists of the substance of a memorandum written by Herbert E. Meyer, vice chairman of the CIA's National Intelligence Council and a political appointee of Director William Casey, saying that the Soviet empire had "entered its terminal phase,"

62. Shultz, *Turmoil and Triumph*, pp. 483–84, and on Shultz's discussions with Gromyko, p. 485. Gromyko's account of the meeting, and the Soviet perspective, is discussed later in this chapter.

63. "Address by A. A. Gromyko to the XXXIX Session of the UN General Assembly," *Pravda*, September 28, 1984.

64. "National Peace through Strength Week: Statement by the President," September 22, 1984, *Presidential Documents*, vol. 20 (October 1, 1984), p. 1350.

65. "Excerpts from Platform Adopted by Republican Convention," *New York Times*, August 22, 1984, p. A18.

and the period ahead "will be the most dangerous that we have ever known." While the memorandum cited CIA research on many internal problems in the Soviet Union, intelligence professionals privately made clear that they had nothing to do with the alarmist memorandum. Its purpose seemed to have been to help Casey buttress the administration's opposition to any economic or technological cooperation or trade with the Soviet Union, so as not to prop up a faltering regime but force its leaders to turn their energies inward. The memorandum had been written a few months earlier, and the leak was timed to precede closely Gromyko's White House visit.[66]

In an important but little-noted address in mid-October Secretary Shultz discussed the administration's approach toward managing relations with the Soviet Union. He spelled out more fully the basis for the policy of "realism, strength, and negotiation" set forth in his testimony of June 1983 and President Reagan's speeches of January and September 1984. He reaffirmed the three objectives set forth in NSDD-75 (without reference to the directive), with emphasis on the first and last—containment and negotiation—and not on changing the Soviet system. Thus, "We must be able to deter Soviet expansionism at the same time as we seek to negotiate areas of cooperation and lower levels of armaments." The task was seen as "to persuade Soviet leaders that continued adventurism and intransigence offer no rewards . . . to choose, instead, a policy of greater restraint and reciprocity."[67]

In the past, Shultz argued, the United States had focused either on strength or on negotiation. In a repudiation of one hard-line school he said that "we reject the view that we should become strong so that we need not negotiate. . . . Nor do we agree with the view that negotiated outcomes can only sap our strength." Rather, "Our premise is that we should become strong so that we are able to negotiate." He also broadened the purpose of negotiation beyond a common interest in survival: "U.S.-Soviet negotiation has as its purposes both

---

66. See Rowland Evans and Robert Novak, "Danger Warning," *Washington Post*, September 7, 1984, p. A17; and Michael J. Bonafield, "CIA Says Soviets in Terminal Phase," *Washington Times*, September 21, 1984, p. 1. The CIA reactions were privately conveyed to other news reporters. A similar memorandum from Meyer written the preceding December had not leaked.

An account stemming from Meyer suggested that it was Casey who had leaked the memo, because he liked it and thought it made the CIA "look good for a change." See Joseph E. Persico, *Casey: From the OSS to the CIA* (Viking, 1990), pp. 348–49.

The Meyer memorandum was also followed by a national intelligence estimate, prompted by concerns over a possible Soviet preelection "October surprise" challenge of some kind to the Reagan administration shortly before the election. This official intelligence estimate not only dispelled excessive fears of such a Soviet initiative in October 1984 but also quashed the main thrust of the Meyer memorandum. It did not leak.

67. Secretary Shultz, "Managing the U.S.-Soviet Relationship Over the Long Term," October 18, 1984, *State Bulletin*, vol. 84 (December 1984), p. 5.

to avert dangerous confrontations and to reach agreements that are in our mutual interest," and his aim included "eventually forging a more constructive relationship." He again repudiated "linkage."[68]

Finally, Shultz expressed the optimistic view that "the way is wide open to more sustained progress in U.S.-Soviet relations than we have known in the past" and said, "Our discussions with Mr. Gromyko lead me to conclude that the Soviets are interested in continuing our dialogue and in exploring ways to enrich that dialogue and turn it into concrete results."[69]

In late October and November diplomatic exchanges on possible new arms control negotiations revived. After a series of meetings between Secretary Shultz and Ambassador Dobrynin, Foreign Minister Gromyko and Ambassador Hartman, and an exchange of letters between President Reagan and President Chernenko, it was announced on November 22 that Shultz and Gromyko would meet in Geneva on January 7 and 8, 1985, to work out the precise terms of reference for a new arms negotiation on nuclear and space weapons. The breakthrough followed a renewed private expression of interest by Reagan after his reelection, and Soviet decision to test that interest. Also on November 28 American and Soviet experts met in Moscow to discuss nuclear non-proliferation, long a subject of recognized common interest.

On the same day that Reagan had privately written to Chernenko, November 7, the State Department had publicly spoken of "real possibilities" for improving relations. On November 25, National Security Adviser McFarlane made a speech in which he said the United States planned to be "flexible and constructive" in arms negotiations—but coupled that comment with an incongruous suggestion that the Soviet Union was scarcely a fit negotiating partner. In his words, from the experiences of the 1970s, "We learned that Soviets violate treaties. We learned that they bargain very hard; that compromise is really an alien concept to them."[70]

In other fields new irritants in American-Soviet relations arose or resurfaced. In September five Alaskans in a boat strayed into Soviet territorial waters. After being held several days, they were released and returned. Also in September, a Soviet scientist in the United States under an exchange program defected; a prominent Soviet journalist, Oleg Bitov, who had defected in Italy a year earlier redefected to the Soviet Union; and at the beginning of November Svetlana Alliluyeva, Stalin's daughter, returned to the Soviet Union after seventeen years in the United States and Britain. In October, for the first time an FBI agent was charged with espionage for the Soviet Union.

---

68. Ibid., pp. 4, 3, 5.

69. Ibid., p. 4.

70. Quoted in James F. Clarity, "U.S. Called Ready to be 'Flexible' at Talks on Arms," *New York Times*, November 26, 1984, p. A1, A11.

Somewhat more consequential for the course of American-Soviet relations was a flare-up of speculation on the alleged Bulgarian-Soviet connection in the papal assassination plot after the Italian prosecutor's report was released in October. While the U.S. government held to its noncommittal stand, some prominent former officials were less cautious, and there was press speculation about the impact on relations if the Bulgarians were found guilty.[71] And on the Soviet side, the press persistently insinuated American involvement in the late October assassination of Indian Prime Minister Indira Gandhi, even after Secretary Shultz at the funeral upbraided Prime Minister Nikolai A. Tikhonov.[72]

All in all, the state of relations, warily warming but marked by persisting corrosive suspicion, was exemplified by a small incident late in the year. A stranger with a Russian accent delivered a package at the gatehouse of the Washington Navy Yard, addressed to Vice Admiral James A. Lyons. A military bomb squad, called to investigate, saw an X-ray picture of "two liquid-filled cannisters," and the package was duly destroyed by a small explosive device. The remains disclosed that it had contained two bottles of premium Russian vodka, a present from the Soviet naval attaché's office to Admiral Lyons, who had headed the U.S. Navy delegation to the annual U.S.-Soviet meeting on preventing incidents at sea that year.[73]

As the Reagan administration faced the electorate in the fall of 1984, it claimed to seek a dialogue and negotiations on arms control and other issues, from a stalwart position of reviving military power and political and economic strength. Inability to achieve more progress with the Soviet Union was depicted as solely owing to Soviet intransigence. The democratic contender, Walter F. Mondale, former vice president, charged that the Reagan administration had not done enough in pursuing arms control, had converted Third World problems into East-West confrontations, and was not effective in dealing with the Soviet Union. He pointed out that Reagan was the first president since Herbert Hoover not to have met with his Soviet counterpart. He did not, however, offer a clear and coherent alternative policy toward the Soviet Union.[74]

---

71. For representative reporting, see Bernard Gwertzman, "Papal Plot May Hurt U.S.-Soviet Ties," *New York Times*, October 31, 1984, p. A3.

72. See Serge Schmemann, "Soviet Press Steps Up Hints of Involvement by the U.S.," *New York Times*, November 2, 1984, p. A18; and William Claiborne, "Moscow Seen Continuing Propaganda: Hints of U.S. Role in Gandhi Death Expected to Go On," *Washington Post*, November 8, 1984, pp. A29, A30, A31.

73. See Fred Hiatt, "Navy Yard Guards Say 'Nyet' to Gift," *Washington Post*, December 21, 1984, pp. A1, A10. Background information supplied by knowledgeable sources.

74. In remarks at the opening of his formal campaign, Mondale leaned over so far to dispel impressions of being soft that he sounded virtually indistinguishable from Reagan: "I have no illusions about the Soviet Union. It's a police state. Their leaders are paranoid. They've built up their military way beyond defensive needs. They're arming proxies.

By the time of the presidential election, the American people—and the Soviet leaders—were left with the question as to whether Ronald Reagan was serious in his protestations of desire for dialogue, negotiation, and improvement of relations with the Soviet Union. While most of the American people were prepared to give him the benefit of the doubt, the Soviet leaders were not. Nonetheless, they had no choice but to wait and see, and they kept their options open.

President Reagan himself, and most Americans, saw the strength of the United States being restored, took pride in American power, believed in "peace through strength," and saw successful containment of Soviet expansionist tendencies that they believed had been active from 1975 through 1979,[75] although the nettlesome situation in Central America remained unstable. Reagan also saw his policy as challenging the Soviet Union in Eastern Europe and around the world, but a peaceful challenge in accordance with the view that, as Shultz put it, "The tide of history is with us."[76] In the campaign, Reagan claimed, "We made it plain we're not out to change their system. We're certainly not going to let them change ours. But we have to live in the world together." This was, conceding his sincerity, certainly not something that had been "made plain" in the first four years of his administration.[77] While there were disturbing doubts in the minds of many, perhaps most, Americans as to whether President Reagan was really doing all he could and should to reduce tensions with the Soviet Union and seek arms control agreements, other considerations predominated and there was not sufficient doubt about the general thrust of his foreign policy to prevent his reelection by an overwhelming majority.

---

They're training terrorists. In Poland, in Afghanistan, in Cambodia, in Syria, they're using their power ruthlessly. And if they threaten our vital interests, or our allies, our country must always be ready to use military force to check them." His one complaint was that "today we're not talking with them." (Besides endorsing summit meetings Mondale did propose regular meetings of cabinet officers—an idea that received public notice only when Reagan proposed the same thing nine months later.) From the official transcript of "The 1984 Campaign," Washington, National Press Club, January 3, 1984, pp. 4–5.

75. Curiously, the Reagan administration did not make this a major theme. While the principal reasons for Soviet inactivity were actually not related to U.S. policy, Reagan might have advanced the claim more strongly. It was mentioned occasionally in 1982 and again during the 1984 election campaign. See Secretary Haig, "Interview on 'Meet the Press'" March 28, 1982, *State Bulletin*, vol. 82 (May 1982), p. 37; Secretary Shultz, "Secretary Interviewed for *U.S. News and World Report*," published November 8, 1982, *State Bulletin*, vol. 82 (December 1982), p. 19; and Shultz, "Managing the U.S.-Soviet Relationship over the Long Term," October 18, 1984, *State Bulletin*, vol. 84 (December 1984), p. 4.

76. Shultz, "Diplomacy and Strength," *State Bulletin*, vol. 84 (October 1984), p. 19.

77. "Peace and War: Exclusive Interviews on Where They Stand—Reagan, Realism with Soviets, Patience in Mideast," *U.S. News and World Report*, October 22, 1984, p. 29.

As the first term of Reagan's presidency ended, several questions remained to be answered. Would Reagan make a real effort to negotiate, especially on arms control, and if he did, would his administration hold together in making such an effort? Would its members understand the Soviet perspective well enough to be able to negotiate effectively? Beyond that formidable set of unanswered questions was a second series. Were the Soviet leaders still prepared for negotiation, would they recognize and accept a serious Reagan interest in dialogue and negotiation, and would they understand the American perspective well enough to negotiate effectively? For Soviet policy had been in flux, seeking to react to an uncertain policy from Washington and to serve Soviet interests under growing internal economic and political stress and change.

## The Chernenko Interregnum

On February 9, 1984, Yury V. Andropov died. Four days later, Konstantin U. Chernenko succeeded him as general secretary of the Communist Party of the Soviet Union and head of the collective leadership. Chernenko, like Andropov, had strongly supported the policy of détente with the West developed during the Brezhnev period. Chernenko thus inherited a situation of mismatch between a policy of détente and a reality of confrontation, much as had Andropov, but with tension even more aggravated and very strong doubts in Moscow about possible accommodation given the posture of the Reagan administration.

Chernenko was a party bureaucrat who had been propelled to the upper reaches of the leadership only through Brezhnev's patronage. But after Andropov's illness and death, even though Chernenko was also aging and ailing, he was the neutral choice of the other leaders several of whom had ambitions but were not yet in a position to seek the top position. The man favored by Andropov as his successor, who had been serving as chairman of Politburo meetings in Andropov's absence for several months, was the much younger Mikhail S. Gorbachev. Gorbachev was given the honor of nominating Chernenko and was unofficially regarded as the "second secretary," but it was clear that several other Politburo members with seniority (in particular Viktor Grishin and Grigory Romanov) would like to challenge him for the next succession.

Chernenko was not a political thinker or strategist, but he had been a faithful supporter of détente under Brezhnev and had supported Andropov, whose course he pledged in his acceptance speech to follow. At the same time, he was less committed than Andropov in his final months to a hard line against the United States and more prepared to test the possibilities for resuming a dialogue.

Beginning with Reagan's speech of January 16, 1984, as discussed above, the United States had begun to present a more moderate image and express interest in improving relations. The shadow of the KAL incident had lifted more quickly in the United States than it did in the Soviet Union. The January 16 speech was described, by as presumably well-disposed a source as any in the Soviet Union, the editorial board of the journal *USA*, as reiterating, "Washington's previous intention to conduct Soviet-American talks from a position of strength" accompanied by "bombastic rhetoric" alleging an interest in peace and curbing the arms race.[78]

In one of his last acts, Andropov (or, more accurately, the collective leadership in his name) had given the initial Soviet reaction to Reagan's speech. In an interview in *Pravda*, the Soviet reply was: "There is no need to convince us of the usefulness and expedience of dialogue. This is our policy. But the dialogue should be conducted on an equal basis, and not from a position of strength, as proposed by Ronald Reagan." It stated that the American leadership had given no indication of realizing the need to change its previous "negative approach," and his speech "does not contain a single new idea, a single new proposal" on limiting missiles in Europe or any other issue. "It is by practical deeds that we will judge whether the United States has serious intentions of conducting a dialogue with us."[79]

Chernenko, in his first address to the Central Committee as the new general secretary, restated Soviet dedication to peaceful coexistence and interest in "peaceful, mutually advantageous cooperation with states of all continents. We are for the peaceful resolution of all disputed international problems through serious, equal and constructive negotiations. The USSR will fully cooperate with all states which are prepared to assist through practical deeds to reduce international tension and to create an atmosphere of trust in the world." He also disavowed Soviet interest in military superiority while maintaining Soviet defense capability at the level of "sufficiency" for deterrence, having in view "the threat to mankind created today by the reckless, adventurist actions of the aggressive forces of imperialism."[80] In stressing the need for "practical deeds" Chernenko picked up the theme of Andropov's January interview.

On the following day, meeting with Vice President Bush, who attended Andropov's funeral, Chernenko stated that "Soviet-American relations should be built on a foundation of equality and equal security, consideration for one another's legitimate interests, and non-intervention in one another's internal

---

78. "Chronicle of Soviet-American Relations (December 1983–February 1984)," *SShA: Ekonomika, politika, ideologiya* (USA: Economics, Politics, Ideology), no. 4 (April 1984), p. 110. (Hereafter *SShA.*)

79. "Answers of Yu. V. Andropov to Questions from the Newspaper *Pravda*," *Pravda*, January 25, 1984.

80. "Speech of Comrade K. U. Chernenko," *Pravda*, February 14, 1984.

affairs. A show of willingness on the American side to adhere to these principles would allow for the improvement of relations between the two countries."[81]

Chernenko laid out his main policy lines more completely in his Supreme Soviet election speech, on March 2, on domestic and foreign policy. His entire discussion of foreign policy was concentrated on prevention of nuclear war, with a strong continuing stress on the importance of arms control but with no estimate of the practical prospect for agreements.

"Recent years," said Chernenko, "as you know have been marked by a sharp escalation of the policy of the most aggressive forces of American imperialism—a policy of undisguised militarism, pretensions to world domination, resistance to progress." The American military role in Lebanon, threats to Syria, the occupation of Grenada, "the undeclared war against Nicaragua," and "the conversion of Western Europe into a launching pad for U.S. nuclear missiles targeted on the USSR and its allies" were cited as examples.[82]

From this charge, Chernenko drew two conclusions. First, for defense: "All this forces us to pay the greatest attention to strengthening the defense of our country. The Soviet people do not want an arms buildup but arms reduction by both sides. But we are obliged to provide sufficiency for security of our country and our friends and allies. This is exactly what is being done. All should know that no military adventures will ever succeed in catching us off-guard, that no potential aggressor can hope to escape a crushing retaliatory strike."[83]

Chernenko hastened to balance this affirmation of continuing attention to defense sufficiency (which he asserted was already in hand) with a call for increased efforts at détente and arms control. "At the same time, the very complexity of the current situation obliges us to double and treble our efforts in pursuing a policy of peace and international cooperation. . . . Détente has deep roots. . . . Curbing the nuclear arms race is of course of crucial significance for peace and international security."

Chernenko took note of the new 1984 posture of the Reagan administration but with strong reservations on whether it meant any change of course. "The U.S. administration has recently begun to speak out with peaceful-sounding statements, calling for a 'dialogue.' The whole world has noted the sharp contradictions between these statements and everything the current U.S. administration has said, and above all has done and continues to do, in its relations with the Soviet Union. Assurances of its good intentions can be taken seriously only if they are backed up by real deeds."

---

81. Cited in *SShA*, no. 4 (April 1984), p. 111.

82. "Speech of Comrade K. U. Chernenko," *Pravda*, March 3, 1984.

83. Ibid. This speech was made before an audience of citizens in the Kuibyshev electoral district of Moscow. The heaviest applause (described as "stormy, prolonged applause") followed Chernenko's statement on deterrence through the capability for inevitable retaliation against any attacker.

Chernenko then cited four things on which the United States could take concrete action: ratification of the underground nuclear weapons test and peaceful explosions treaties signed nearly a decade earlier and resumption of the talks on a comprehensive nuclear test ban that the United States had broken off in 1980, agreement on renunciation of the militarization of outer space, a mutual freeze on American and Soviet nuclear weapons, and a ban on the use of chemical weapons.

Chernenko also called for agreement of the nuclear powers on prevention of situations threatening nuclear conflict, renunciation of nuclear war propaganda, no first use of nuclear weapons, no use of nuclear weapons against nonnuclear countries that have no nuclear weapons on their territory, creation of nuclear-free zones, prevention of nuclear weapon proliferation, and reduction of nuclear weapons with a view to their eventual elimination. This proposed "code of conduct" for the nuclear powers was stated as a more general objective and was not addressed specifically to the United States. None of these proposals were new, and some were clearly geared to Soviet political propaganda. Nonetheless, they too contributed to the centrality of the issue of prevention of nuclear war in Chernenko's foreign policy platform.[84]

A stream of statements along this same general line was issued by Chernenko throughout the year, sometimes echoed by other leaders. For example, on several occasions in April and May Chernenko called for a "turn from confrontation to détente," implying and occasionally stating that "the development of events can be turned from confrontation to détente" and saying that the Soviet Union was "ready for a dialogue," while seeking signs of American seriousness by deeds as well as words.[85]

Chernenko's stress on pursuing a policy of détente was not directly challenged. Nonetheless there were signs that not all members of the leadership shared his continued belief that the United States might come around to serious dealings with the Soviet leaders, at least under an administration led by President Reagan. There were also continuing debates over the "sufficiency" of the Soviet military programs to meet the challenge posed by the tremendous United States military buildup.

One divergent reaction was illustrated in an article by Valentin Falin. By tracing American political and military policy through the entire postwar period, he tied Reagan's pursuit of military superiority to earlier Cold War policy and military planning. His argument was clear: "The [U.S.] claim to a 'leading role' based on superiority is no joking matter." He cited the declassified *Dropshot* U.S. war plan of 1949 and other contingency war plans based on

---

84. Ibid.

85. For example, see Chernenko's message of March 30 (in *Pravda*, April 2, 1984), speech of April 29 (*Pravda*, April 30, 1984), and speech of May 10 (*Pravda*, May 11, 1984). The references to the fact that events can be turned to détente, and readiness for dialogue, appeared in the speech of April 29, 1984.

an American nuclear superiority as evidence of a continuing U.S. intention to gain and use military superiority either directly or indirectly to gain world domination. Incidentally, in a mirror-image parallel to an argument frequently made in the United States with respect to *Soviet* policy, Falin said, "The military factor acquires an ever greater significance in the eyes of Washington as the U. S. economic and political importance in the world shows a relative decline."[86]

Falin, and many Soviet commentators and officials, considered that "détente entered a period of crisis in the United States" as a result of "the prospects of a stabilization of international relations on the basis of military parity." While he placed his argument in part on the greed of the military-industrial complex, he also asserted, "Military parity undoubtedly clips the claws of aggressive doctrines . . . and has devalued the policy of confrontation. . . . The vigilant eye of the custodians of imperialist dogmas perceived a 'disintegrating' influence of nuclear parity between the USSR and the United States." Falin saw refusal by American ruling circles to accept military parity and renounce a policy of pressure based on positions of strength as the cause of American renunciation of détente. Moreover, he saw this as a continuing battle in which realists in Washington continued to lose. "This is why the germs of wisdom that Franklin Roosevelt tried to implant in American politics, the flashes of balance that seemed to gleam in John Kennedy, and the elements of political realism that became evident during Richard Nixon's time were crushed, stifled and rejected by the militant factions of imperialism. . . . The policy of peaceful coexistence is not to their liking. They crave an American leadership that would confirm a right on the United States to disregard the rights of others."[87]

Falin, and those in the Soviet leadership who shared his perspective, thus concluded, "The doctrine of direct confrontation adopted by the Reagan administration is oriented toward exerting pressure over the entire world, toward achieving 'escalation dominance' for the United States through the deployment of first-strike weapons, and to provoking and fanning conflicts for the satisfaction of Washington's military-political objectives." The president's NSDD-32 directive of May 1982 "required the armed forces to prepare both

---

86.  Falin was first deputy chief of the International Information Department of the Central Committee from 1978 to 1983. His removal in January 1983 was the subject of speculation in the West, but several well-placed Central Committee officials have told me that his removal was occasioned by an incident in his personal life, rather than a political difference. He remained an influential commentator as the political observer for *Izvestiya*, and later he became the chief of the International Department of the Central Committee from 1988 to 1991.

His article appeared in the principal theoretical and political journal of the Central Committee. See Valentin Falin, "Yesterday in Today's Washington," *Kommunist*, no. 8 (May 1984), pp. 114–25; the quotations are on pp. 119, 120.

87.  Ibid., pp. 121, 122.

for a protracted non-nuclear war and a victorious nuclear war." And most critical of all, "Imperialism has decided to limit both the time and the space for the USSR, and for all of world socialism, to just five minutes for contemplation in a crisis situation . . . to threaten and to wage war if Weinberger's dream of gaining the upper hand without resort to arms is not achieved."[88]

Falin's analysis was far from the most dire among Soviet commentaries. It has been cited at some length as an important representative line of Soviet thinking at the time. It was difficult to persuade those who held such a view that the imperialist ruling circles in the United States were now prepared to settle for parity, arms control, reduction of tensions, and at least coexistence if not détente.

Another example illustrates the concern of the Soviet leaders about the American political and ideological offensive. Leonid Zamyatin, the chief of the International Information Department of the Central Committee, responded to Reagan's remarks to the Irish Parliament in June 1984 expressing a readiness to begin talks with the Soviet leaders. He began by recalling Reagan's words to the British Parliament just two years earlier, proclaiming a "crusade" against socialism. "Washington's leaders declare they are for dialogue. But what they really want is not dialogue, but talks about dialogue. In practice, they proceed on the basis of the concept of strength, of nuclear superiority." "Judging from its actual deeds rather than its propaganda rhetoric, Washington does not want an end to the arms race, arms limitations, the transition to a military balance at lower and lower levels, and an improvement of the international situation."[89]

Indeed, not only were the Reagan administration's protestations of desire to improve relations suspect, they were often seen as dangerous. "This combination of the frankly militarist thrust of the Pentagon's numerous programs and demagogic statements about the readiness to 'improve relations with the USSR' cannot fail to cause alarm." "The adventurism of the U.S. administration's policy is an inseparable part of global ideological warfare against the Soviet Union, the other socialist countries, and the national liberation movements. . . . Ideological warfare against the USSR and the other countries of the socialist community has never ceased. But now it has taken on the status of state policy and is pursued by increasingly sophisticated methods, using all forms of disinformation." After reviewing in some detail the stepped-up American propaganda programs by the United States Information Agency (USIA) and other similar activities, Zamyatin related this activity directly to efforts at subversion in the socialist countries and "the transfer of the ideological confrontation to the sphere of interstate relations."[90]

---

88. Ibid., pp. 122, 125.

89. Leonid Zamyatin, "The 'Crusade' Goes On: Washington's So-Called 'New' Course," *Literaturnaya gazeta* (Literary Gazette), July 18, 1984.

90. Ibid.

Perceiving the Reagan administration's "peace campaign" of 1984 as an attempt to mislead public opinion, the Soviet leaders sought to expose and refute its claims. As noted in chapter 3, the Soviet Union had imposed a general freeze on bilateral relations in November 1983 and had intensified it in May 1984 (at which time it also withdrew from the Olympic Games). Less than two months later, in late June, it relaxed this stance and resumed negotiations on several matters of common interest.[91] But the Soviets continued to blame the United States for failing to make possible more serious moves.

The Soviets had made themselves vulnerable to American charges by having broken off the arms talks in Geneva on intermediate arms (INF) and strategic arms (START) at the end of 1983. Attempts to blame the United States for the end of those talks were bound not to be convincing to most people in the West. Thus the Soviet leaders saw themselves as aggrieved but unable to make their point. Indeed, contrary to the Soviet purpose, the Soviet walkout from INF and START and deprecation of the new Reagan peace rhetoric had gone a long way toward taking pressure off Washington to be more forthcoming in seeking arms control agreements. In addition, by taking the position that the Soviet Union would not resume those negotiations while American INF deployments in Europe continued (or even remained), the Soviet leaders had made their position to a large extent hostage to American decision. Finally, the Soviet campaign, especially in Europe, to stir up alarm over the deployments and over new Soviet counterdeployments said to be required to offset the new American missiles backfired badly. It had little effect in Western Europe and virtually none in the United States, while unexpectedly stirring up negative reactions and resentment in Eastern Europe[92] and alarm in the Soviet Union itself. But this was a position the Soviet leaders could not, in their view, reverse without suffering a still greater defeat. And they saw no alternative.[93] Moreover, they did see the Western missile deployment as increasing risks of war in a crisis.

The Soviet press had begun to stress the increasing danger of war after Andropov's March 1983 press interview, and after the KAL incident and

---

91. The Soviet resumption of normal bilateral business followed soon after the *Time* magazine issue featuring Gromyko depicted him on its cover, and in the article, as responsible for Moscow's new hard line. He, and the collective leadership, may have decided that a broad freeze was counterproductive. See "Moscow's Hard Line," *Time*, June 25, 1984, pp. 22–28, and cover.

92. See Robert English, "Eastern Europe's Doves," *Foreign Policy*, no. 56 (Fall 1984), pp. 51–55.

93. Some officials in the Foreign Ministry and in institutes of the Academy of Sciences saw the self-defeating nature of the Soviet stand and believed there was an alternative, but they were mostly silent or were not listened to at the time. Four or five years later, many would acknowledge the error of the policy and some could claim to have seen it. But that did not affect the situation in the early to mid-1980s.

Andropov's September 1983 formal statement, alarm over war became severe among the Soviet public.[94] For example, there was an unusual outpouring of letters to the editors of various journals from concerned Soviet citizens.[95] By late 1983 and early 1984 it was found necessary for several leaders to stress that the situation was serious but should not be overdramatized. As noted earlier, Marshal Ustinov in addressing a large convention of veterans in December 1983 had said, "As you see, comrades, the situation in the world is extremely tense. But no matter how difficult the political-military situation, there is no point in overdramatizing it. . . . Soberly appraising the full seriousness of the current situation, it is necessary [for us] to see that imperialism is far from all-powerful."[96]

Most dramatic was a disclosure and public reassurance by Chernenko. In a public speech in April he mentioned that in view of "the aggravated international situation" the Central Committee was receiving many letters that proposed extending the normal five-day work week and establishing a fund for contributions for the defense of the country. He expressed sincere appreciation but reassured everyone that "our economic potential and new technical means which enhance the efficiency of defense allow us reliably to ensure the security of the Soviet state and its allies without resort to such measures." He also offered further reassurance, "The planned socioeconomic programs for the development of the country and for enhancing the standard of living of the Soviet people will also be systematically implemented."[97]

Setting a new foundation for internal policy was, of course, an important matter for both the Andropov and Chernenko leaderships. One new task, first set under Brezhnev at the Twenty-sixth Party Congress in 1981 and continued under his successors, was revision of the Communist Party program. This program has been basically revised only twice since the first one was formulated at the time of the founding of the Bolshevik faction of the Russian Social-Democratic Party in 1903. The second program was adopted in 1919,

94. See the discussion in chapter 3, and see Vladimir E. Shlapentokh, "Moscow's War Propaganda and Soviet Public Opinion," *Problems of Communism*, vol. 33 (September–October 1984), esp. pp. 91–93. The author was a leading public opinion expert in the Soviet Union who emigrated shortly before writing this analysis.

95. Ibid., p. 93. In separate conversations with several Soviet editors and officials of the Central Committee in September and October 1983, I was told of the outpouring of deep public concern over the heightened danger of war as expressed in letters and remarks at local party meetings. Early in 1984 Fedor Burlatsky also wrote about an outpouring of letters to the editors of the important sociopolitical newspaper of the Soviet Union of Journalists, *Literary Gazette*, expressing great concern over the possibility of war. See F. Burlatsky, "1984: What Does It Hold in Store for Mankind?" *Literaturnaya gazeta*, January 14, 1984, p. 15.

96. "Address by Marshal of the Soviet Union D. F. Ustinov," *Krasnaya zvezda*, December 15, 1983. Other aspects of this address are discussed in chapter 3.

97. "Speech of Comrade K. U. Chernenko," *Pravda*, April 30, 1984.

soon after the Communist Party had taken power in Russia, and the country was still in the throes of the civil war. The third was in 1961, under Nikita S. Khrushchev. The revision in the 1980s was planned as a revised version of the third program rather than an entirely new program, but extensive and significant changes were expected that could have a bearing on Soviet foreign policy and Soviet-American relations, as well as on Soviet ideology and internal development.

Chernenko, who had shared responsibility for this task with Andropov even before succeeding him, in April 1984 made an important statement before the Central Committee drafting group preparing the revised version. In this guidance he stressed the need to be less optimistic on the timing of the eventual collapse of capitalism.

Unquestionably, the Program must contain a characterization of the course of the historical competition between socialism and capitalism. We have no doubt at all that in the final account socialism will win in this competition and that the correlation of forces in the international arena will be steadily changing in favor of socialism and peace. This must be clearly expressed. However, while emphasizing the historical doom of contemporary capitalism, we must take into consideration that even under the conditions of its general crisis it still retains substantial and far from exhausted reserves for development.[98]

He then added a very interesting observation: "It is extremely important, comrades, not to lose what science and practical life define in brief as 'proportion.' " Similarly, he urged presenting "a general picture of the processes that are changing the social structure of the world," but "in large and expressive strokes, with no attempts to anticipate details of future global developments." The one point he selected to stress was "the striving to prevent a nuclear catastrophe." And he noted that "the problems of peace and war and, in fact, all global problems, do not exist by themselves" but are inseparable from the class struggle in the world. "The Program must clearly define the significance of the struggle for peace under the circumstances of the increased threat of war."[99]

Chernenko did not need to point out to his select audience that he was proposing to delete a prediction of the impending collapse of capitalism and triumph of communism in the world, which had "prematurely" been included in the 1961 program. In effect he put off to the indefinite, distant future the still doctrinally anticipated eventual triumph of communism and proposed concentrating on more immediate problems of internal development.[100] Besides his

---

98. "Speech by K. U. Chernenko at the Session of the Commission of the CC CPSU on Preparation of the New Text of the Program of the CPSU, April 25, 1984," *Kommunist*, no. 7 (May 1984), p. 7.

99. Ibid., pp. 7–8.

100. This change met some resistance, or at least raised questions, within the Soviet political establishment. In a later statement, in September 1984, Chernenko defended the need

very general mention of a "solidarity" with manifestations of the revolutionary process around the globe, he emphasized, as noted above, the prevention of nuclear war.[101]

The major current problems of internal policy, apart from political maneuver for the next succession, concerned economic issues. These, in turn, were seen as closely related to the general state of tension with the United States and the prospects for agreement on arms limitation and reductions. And these prospects seemed poor; negotiations were no longer under way.

While deflating expectations on arms control and stressing lack of serious American interest, at least some of the Soviet leaders, including Chernenko, did hope that some progress could be made. An area of particular concern was the American development of antisatellite and antimissile space weaponry. Soviet proposals in 1981 and 1982, even before President Reagan's Star Wars speech, and in 1983 after it, had been ignored by the United States. During the spring of 1984, however, Secretary Shultz had begun to discuss the subject with Ambassador Dobrynin. The Soviets may have known, or at least suspected, that this exploration was being conducted with White House approval but without the Pentagon's knowledge or benefit of a formal government mandate. The Soviet leaders were highly suspicious that Shultz might hold out tentative lines of agreement and thus learn the Soviet position and extract concessions, while later the administration would repudiate his position. This was one argument in Moscow for making a public Soviet proposal for such talks. If the American commitment to them was so fragile that it could not stand up to the light of day and if the president was not prepared to take a position and enforce it, it was better to learn that sooner rather than later.[102]

A second reason for some urgency in raising the issue of banning space weapons was the U.S. program for testing a new antisatellite system in space in the fall. Thus rather than await the outcome of the American election, if there

---

for a more realistic prognosis and program. "We must," he said, "proceed from existing realities." He claimed widespread "unconditional support," but he added, "At the same time, in talking with people, looking at letters, one sometimes comes across the question: Are we not pushing back the communist perspective? The answer to this question is simple and unequivocal: of course not. On the contrary, we are doing everything possible to bring that time closer. But it is possible to bring it closer in one way only—by resolving the entire complex of large and complicated problems related to the various stages of the first phase of the formation of communism." "Affirm the Truth of Life and the High Ideals of Socialism, Speech by Comrade K. U. Chernenko," *Pravda*, September 26, 1984.

101. The revised party program was planned for presentation to the Twenty-seventh Party Congress in the spring of 1986, and the final version will be further discussed in that context. See chapter 6.

102. Information from informed Soviet and U.S. officials. See also John Newhouse, "The Diplomatic Round: Talks About Talks," *New Yorker*, vol. 60 (December 31, 1984), pp. 42–44.

was any possibility of gaining agreement on a moratorium on testing such weapons before a test series began, that was sufficiently important to give President Reagan whatever preelection credit there would be from a resumption of arms control negotiations. Moreover, if Reagan did feel there was an incentive in domestic political terms before the election, that might tip him to agreement on talks.

While some hoped for a positive American response, and some in the leadership saw it as perhaps a last chance for heading off space weapons, undoubtedly others—probably a majority—expected a negative American response again. But even that outcome could be used to demonstrate Soviet interest and American lack of interest in arms control. And so, on June 29, Ambassador Dobrynin proposed to Secretary Shultz a meeting in Vienna on September 18 to "prevent the militarization of outer space" by banning the testing or deployment of antisatellite and other weapons in space. Within hours, the Soviet government made its proposal public. Also within hours, the United States replied with an agreement to meet in Vienna in September. But while the United States agreed to discuss "verifiable and effective limitations on antisatellite weapons," it also added to the agenda discussion of ways to resume the stalemated INF and START talks. The Soviet Union swiftly turned down the American response as a rejection, despite U.S. characterization of it as an acceptance. For four weeks further discussions continued, and for several months desultory statements were made by the two sides, but the talks were not held.[103]

While the Soviets had undoubtedly been prepared for either an American acceptance or, more likely, rejection of their proposal, they evidently were not prepared for an American quasi acceptance tied to the question of resuming INF and START talks. In subsequent discussions the United States softened its position on resuming START and INF but insisted on the need for broader linkage of offensive and defensive arms limitations.[104] There were also

---

103. The American and Soviet press were filled with reportage on the proposals and counterproposals. For the original Soviet proposal, see "Statement of the Soviet Government," *Pravda*, June 30, 1984.

104. Along these lines, the American side introduced the argument that offensive strategic ballistic missiles *transit* space during their flight trajectory and should therefore be linked to space weapons in arms control consideration. The Soviet side vehemently objected to the U.S. position, not only because it ran counter to the Soviet position but because it resurrected an argument buried two decades earlier.

   In the late 1950s and early 1960s the United States had used the same argument against limited arms control agreements, including one that would ban nuclear weapons in space. Only when, in 1963, the United States abandoned its insistence on linkage was it possible for the two sides to agree on the ban on placing nuclear and other weapons of mass destruction in space (initially, in 1963, in the form of a jointly sponsored UN General Assembly resolution and parallel national declarations of intent, converted into a treaty obligation in the Outer Space Treaty of 1967). Thus one of the first concrete

two other important issues. One was the Soviet proposal of a moratorium on antisatellite tests during the talks. This was not initially presented as a condition for the talks, but the Soviets pressed hard for it. The final issue was the Soviet insistence that the goal of the talks be the banning of "a whole class of armaments—space attack systems, including antisatellite and anti-ballistic missile space-based systems, as well as any ground-, air-, or sea-launched system intended to hit targets in space."[105] The United States refused to consider anything more than limitations (not a ban) on antisatellite systems. The Star Wars initiative was not up for negotiation.[106]

All in all, the general Soviet impression was that the United States had attempted to parlay a weak variant of their space weapons ban into leverage on other disputed arms issues and thus prevented the negotiation. The general American impression was that the United States had been responsive, but that the Soviet Union would not take yes for an answer; in short, that the Soviet Union had not been serious. At the official level, many in Washington saw a clever Soviet ploy as having been successfully turned to American advantage, permitting talks to be averted. Even many who had favored the talks believed the Soviets had sought only a propaganda outcome or were too demanding. The space arms talks of the summer of 1984 thus became not only a nonevent but a further source of aggravation. Nonetheless, the episode did stir up consideration of the issue in Washington, and the U.S.-Soviet discussions, while not leading to agreement on talks, were not completely sterile.

Chernenko commented on U.S. policy and on relations with the United States in a *Pravda* interview at the beginning of September. He noted the speeches at the Republican Party convention and the platform adopted there as a source of "how the current U.S. administration views the world and what its intentions are. It must be said that the impression produced by all this is a depressing one." He concluded, "The political goals and, above all, the practical actions of those who determine the foreign policy line of the United

---

arms control agreements, reached two decades earlier in an early budding of détente, was based on American readiness not to link arms control issues on earth to issues of space weaponry—and now in 1984 the United States was returning to a Cold War argument to frustrate arms control. In light of the longer Soviet institutional memory, this particular point thus had very negative significance for the Soviets. Yet (according to participants interviewed) the American policymakers and their advisers were blissfully unaware of this whole aspect of the question. On the 1960s discussions see Raymond L. Garthoff, "Banning the Bomb in Outer Space," *International Security*, vol. 5 (Winter 1980–81), esp. pp. 33–34.

In his memoir account, Shultz noted that he had made the argument on ballistic missiles transiting space, but he was evidently still unaware of the history and connotation of that rhetorical argument. Shultz, *Turmoil and Triumph*, p. 475.

105. *Pravda*, June 30, 1984.

106. My account of the diplomatic discussions in July is based on confidential interviews with informed officials.

States are clearly geared to further dangerously fueling international tension. . . . Washington is flaunting its great power ambitions and exaggerated notions of America's role and place in the contemporary world with cynical frankness." Above all he saw an "obsession with force" and repeated the standard position, "The Soviet Union itself is not seeking military superiority over others, but will not allow anyone else to achieve superiority over it."[107]

Notwithstanding that grim evaluation of the Reagan administration's course, Chernenko nonetheless called for a "shift to a policy of realism, of common cause, of businesslike collaboration in the solution of the tasks confronting mankind." More specifically, Washington would have to "acknowledge the fact that our two states can conduct relations only on an equal basis, on the basis of consideration for each other's legitimate interests." And he reiterated Soviet "readiness for dialogue, for honest and serious talks."[108]

The annual meeting of the UN General Assembly in September provided the occasion for important speeches by President Reagan and Foreign Minister Gromyko and for the first meeting between Gromyko and Reagan. As earlier noted, this was the first time Gromyko had been to the White House since September 1978. What had been a usual occurrence in the 1970s now became a partial summit meeting, as Reagan made the most of the chance to show he was able to deal with the Soviets.[109] Gromyko, for his part, and his Politburo colleagues, felt that the action vindicated their position that the United States had to deal with the Soviet leaders and to accept them as equals, even though they also assumed Reagan was doing so for his own domestic political purposes.[110]

President Reagan's unusually conciliatory speech to the UN General Assembly on September 24 provided the backdrop to the events that followed in rapid succession. Two days later Gromyko met with Shultz and the next day with the challenging presidential candidate Walter F. Mondale. The same day,

---

107. "K. U. Chernenko's Replies to Questions of the Newspaper Pravda," *Pravda*, September 2, 1984.

108. Ibid.

109. Reagan prepared for this meeting with Gromyko by another discussion of Russia and the Russians with Suzanne Massie, a rehearsal of the meeting, and preparation of his own "talking points" for the meeting rather than taking those drafted by the State Department. Nancy Reagan enthusiastically supported this move, which was reflected in her active role at the reception for Gromyko.

110. See Gromyko's memoir on the latter point. A. A. Gromyko, *Pamyatnoye* (Memoirs) (Moscow: Politizdat, 1988), vol. 2, p. 255. Gromyko was personally pessimistic that any change by Reagan would improve relations with the Soviet Union. He also expected Reagan's reelection, as he had told visiting American political figure George McGovern on July 27 and therefore did not look forward to "productive" U.S.-Soviet relations for another four years. See Seth Mydans, "Gromyko Predicts Space Arms Talks Will Not Be Held," *New York Times*, July 30, 1984, p. 1.

September 27, the day before his meeting with Reagan, Gromyko made his speech to the General Assembly.

Gromyko was not deflected by the president's conciliatory rhetoric from delivering the message that the Soviet leadership sought to present to the leadership and public of the United States, the world, and the domestic Soviet public. He declared:

There is much truth in the assertion that the international situation depends directly on the state of Soviet-U.S. relations. Today, more than ever, our country stands for maintaining normal relations with the United States. And this is how these relations had been developing in general until the recent past, although not without ups and downs. And in the years of World War II they were actually the relations of allies.

In recent years these relations have been disrupted through the endeavors of Washington. No effort has been spared there to wreck all the gains that had been accomplished together and to undermine the confidence that had been built up earlier. What is more, they virtually flaunt their indifference to the reputation of the United States as a partner in international affairs. . . .

History does not begin on the day a particular U.S. administration comes into office. Those periods when the two powers joined their efforts to defeat fascism remain the best pages in the history of Soviet-U.S. relations. And those who determine U.S. policy today have a great deal to do if their words and the obligations they assume are to be trusted.

No attempt to substitute modifications in form for the substance of policy . . . can be meaningful. . . . The Soviet Union considers that it is precisely concrete deeds rather than verbal assurances that can lead to normalizing the situation in our relations with the United States. The USSR will not be found wanting.[111]

Gromyko also declared that the West had been responsible for beginning the Cold War by pursuing a "policy based on 'a position of strength' and 'brinksmanship.'" And when later "international relations were marked by budding cooperation between states with different social systems, as in the case of the period of détente, no effort was spared to undermine these positive processes." As a result, "The threat of war has grown and the foundations of world peace have become more shaky."[112]

Gromyko then made the centerpiece of his presentation the need to strive for the "key objective" and "goal of overriding importance"—"preventing a nuclear catastrophe." He stressed that it had proved possible to reach important accords, such as the ABM Treaty and the SALT I interim agreement, "when the U.S. side showed realism and the will for agreement on the basis of equality and equal security." But in the years that followed, "The tug of war among those deciding U.S. foreign policy has been won by the militaristically-minded

---

111. "Address by A. A. Gromyko at the XXXIX Session of the UN General Assembly," *Pravda*, September 28, 1984.

112. Ibid.

forces," and now "The central objective of U.S. policy is to try to gain military superiority."

Gromyko stressed, "It is futile and hopeless for anyone to expect to get ahead and gain military superiority under contemporary conditions. It is absolutely illusory to hope to win a nuclear war, whatever the nuclear war doctrines—whether global or limited, blitzkrieg or protracted."

Gromyko cited the nuclear "code of conduct" proposed by Chernenko in March, as well as a series of arms control proposals, including a ban on space weaponry (the "special urgency" of which he stressed), and a nuclear freeze. On the INF and START talks suspended almost a year earlier, he declared that it had been Washington's "deliberate intentions" to wreck those negotiations. He claimed, "We were told either to accept the U.S. position [in INF] or there would be no agreement. So there is no agreement." Looking to the future, Gromyko stated that the Soviet leaders have noted that "there are realistically-minded political figures and statesmen in the West, including in the United States" so a chance remained. And he said that "it is extremely important not to miss the chance."[113]

Particularly in comparison with President Reagan's speech to the United Nations a few days before, Gromyko's seemed tough. Secretary Shultz, who had prevailed on Reagan to make his conciliatory address, was particularly angered by the charges that the United States and NATO were responsible for the Cold War and by the generally harsh criticisms of United States policy.[114] While there may have been a basis to take umbrage at Gromyko's rhetoric, of greater significance was the implicit message that the Soviet Union wished to return to better relations with the United States (signaled by the three references to World War II alliance ties and cooperation),[115] and that the Soviet leaders had noticed the existence of "realistically-minded political figures and statesmen" who could recognize the need to work out a modus vivendi. (He was, however, deliberately ambiguous about whether such realism might be found within, or influencing, the current administration—an ambiguity that may have reflected different or uncertain judgments within the Soviet leadership.)

Gromyko's speech was also of interest because of his reference to "the period of détente" in the 1970s as a period in the past. While a recognition that détente between the two powers had long since ceased was only too evident, it

---

113. Ibid.

114. According to associates of Secretary Shultz in the State Department.

115. The third reference, not cited earlier, was especially revealing: Gromyko said that "the main lesson of World War II is that states must stand together in the fight against war," substituting a thesis of cooperative war prevention for the standard ideological claim that the main lesson of the war was the superiority of the victorious Soviet socialist system over the German capitalist one.

    The Soviet signal was apparently not recognized by American policymakers or their advisers, who reacted to the more contentious remarks.

had been the Soviet practice to refer to détente as a live, if dormant, relationship.

The meeting of President Reagan and Foreign Minister (and Politburo member) Gromyko, the day after Gromyko's speech, was given unusual attention in the United States because there had been no previous encounter by the president with Gromyko or any other Soviet leader. In their main talk, Reagan and Gromyko showed a propensity to discuss general principles. By his own later account, Gromyko bridled at and rebutted Reagan's simplistic charge that the Soviet Union sought above all to destroy the capitalist system in the United States and the West and, unless deterred by American military strength, might attack. Each side justified and defended its policy course. American participants believed that there had at least been a congenial harmony in agreeing on such goals as the reduction and eventual elimination of nuclear weapons and the importance of U.S.-Soviet cooperation in reducing regional and world tensions. Gromyko, however, concluded that the Americans were still just interested in talk. While no specific steps or areas of agreement were reached, none was really expected, although the Soviets had hoped to see a renewed consideration of space talks.[116]

After Gromyko's return to Moscow and report to his colleagues, the Politburo issued a cautious formal endorsement of his report. "A far-reaching exchange of views on key issues of Soviet-American relations and on the state of world affairs" was held, but it "did not reveal any signs that would attest to the real intention of the American side to adjust its policy course toward realism and peacefulness. Declarations of a general nature about the benefit of more constructive relations with the Soviet Union made by the American side are not backed by concrete deeds." Nonetheless, it reaffirmed "the readiness of the Soviet Union for serious, businesslike dialogue with the American side."[117]

In a nationwide television broadcast on the day of Gromyko's UN speech, before his meeting with Reagan, Chernenko had said that the Soviet Union was prepared "with reciprocity, to be an honest and well-intentioned partner, ready for the development of cooperation on the basis of equal rights and mutual advantage" with capitalist states. But this was a general comment (and accompanied by less reassuring promises such as "further strengthening the international positions of the Soviet Union and the entire socialist community," as well as "rebuffing the designs of aggressive imperialist circles").[118]

---

116. Information from participants. Much of this discussion was prefigured in the talks between Shultz and Gromyko.

   For Gromyko's account, see Gromyko, *Pamyatnoye*, vol. 2, pp. 255–61.

   John Newhouse reports that Reagan did hint at combining space weapons and strategic arms talks, and even some restraints on antisatellite weapons (ASAT) in that context. Gromyko did not respond. (*New Yorker*, December 31, 1984, pp. 46–49.)

117. "In the Politburo of the CC of the CPSU," *Pravda*, October 5, 1984.

118. "Speech of Comrade K. U. Chernenko," *Pravda*, September 28, 1984.

On October 16, in the midst of the American election campaign and shortly before the scheduled foreign policy debate between Reagan and Mondale, Chernenko granted a rare interview to the Moscow correspondent of the *Washington Post*. He not only reaffirmed Soviet desire for "good relations with the United States" but stated that "experience shows" that relations can be good, and that "there is no sound alternative at all to a constructive development of Soviet-U.S. relations." What was required was "a mutual desire to build relations as equals." But "In the past, we have already heard words about the U.S. administration's readiness for talks. But they have never been supported by real deeds." Nonetheless, "If what the president has said about readiness to negotiate is not merely a tactical move, I wish to state that the Soviet Union will not be found wanting. We have always been prepared for serious and business-like negotiations and have repeatedly said so."[119]

The heart of Chernenko's message was that Soviet-American relations could be improved if the United States would demonstrate a serious interest in reaching agreement on an equitable basis "at least on one of the essential questions" in arms control and reducing the risk of war. He repeated basically the same list of suggestions he had first made on March 2 and again on September 2, refined in October to the following four: ratification of the nuclear testing and peaceful nuclear explosions treaties signed in 1974 and 1976; a broad nuclear weapons freeze; a pledge of no first use of nuclear weapons; and an agreement on preventing the militarization of outer space. These he described as "practical steps" the United States could take. "Reaching agreement on them—or at least on some of them—would mean a real shift both in Soviet-U.S. relations and in the international situation as a whole."[120]

The proposed agreement to ban weapons in space had, as noted, been the subject of a month-long discussion that ended in disagreement, but it was a major issue the Soviets were determined to keep in the forefront of attention and on which they expected negotiations at some time. The nuclear freeze may have been included because it was an issue in the internal American debate, being favored by Mondale, but by the same token clearly was not something Reagan would accept. The no-first-use pledge was again not something on which positive U.S. response could be expected. The nuclear testing treaties were another matter. It would require no major reversal of stand for the Reagan administration to seek ratification of the treaties signed by Presidents Nixon

---

119. "Text of Chernenko Interview," *Washington Post*, October 17, 1984, p. A26. See also Dusko Doder, "Chernenko Says U.S. Holds Key to Arms Talks," *Washington Post*, October 17, 1984. pp. A1, A26.

120. Ibid. While clearly reflecting Chernenko's own views, in the interview Chernenko stressed that his answers (some in writing) reflected the collective view of the Soviet leadership. See Dusko Doder, "Fit-Looking Leader Jokes in Inner Sanctum," *Washington Post*, October 17, 1984, pp. A1, A26.

and Ford, although it might raise a question as to adequacy of provisions for verification. But on the basis of earlier confidential exchanges, the Soviet leaders had reason to hope this proposal might be taken up.

Most significant, in a way, was what Chernenko did not include. He did not mention the stymied START and INF talks, nor link any of these other arms control issues to the question of continuing U.S. deployment of intermediate-range missiles in Europe.

The American official response was to welcome the "constructive tone" of Chernenko's remarks but not to do more.[121]

Neither Chernenko's interview suggestions, nor indeed the subject of American-Soviet relations, figured in the foreign policy debate between Mondale and Reagan, or in the campaign more generally. While some American commentators speculated about possible Soviet attempts to influence the U.S. election, in fact the Soviet leaders were probably moved more strongly by efforts to keep open any possibilities for future development of relations than by temptations of tactical influence on the outcome. If domestic politics played any role in their decisions, they were more likely to be Soviet domestic politics than American ones.

Western speculation that Gromyko was "Comrade Cold War" and a hard-liner competing with Chernenko for leadership was wrong.[122] Gromyko did not visit Washington in a power play. And Chernenko's prominence in the series of speeches and interviews in September and October was not directed at offsetting Gromyko, although it did serve to reassert Chernenko's political authority.

Chernenko had been ill in July and August, and there were signs of increased maneuver among the Soviet leaders, who were looking to the eventual, and possibly not distant, succession. In particular, Mikhail Gorbachev seemed to be moving to enhance his position. By September and October Chernenko was back at work, and he moved to consolidate his position and to trim the sails of his putative successor.

The occasion for his television remarks of September 28 cited earlier had been the award to him of two high medals. Ustinov made the presentation. Of particular interest was Chernenko's stress on collective leadership. Chernenko, whether from modesty or for other reasons, commented that he saw in the award "an appreciation of our joint labor, approval, and support for the political course collectively worked out by the party," and his stress on the fact that the leaders were "armed with a clear and specific action program, to

---

121. See Bernard Gwertzman, "U.S. Praises Tone of Soviet Leader," *New York Times*, October 18, 1984, p. A11. Larry Speakes, the White House spokesman, made the response.

122. This view was held by some, but not all, professional Soviet affairs advisers in the administration.

which a very great contribution was made by my predecessors," Brezhnev and Andropov.[123] He clearly wanted, by endorsing them, to draw to his own current support their imputed sponsorship of the policies he was now espousing, including détente and a measured reaction to pressures for increasing defense expenditure.

While Ustinov on this occasion had been identified simply as a member of the Politburo, not also as minister of defense, he chose in his remarks to come down heavily on the defense issue and Chernenko's role. He stressed Chernenko's "tremendous attention" to "national security and the maintenance of the defense capability of the country at the appropriate level." He also referred to him as "the leader of the party and state, chairman of the Defense Council, and the supreme commander-in-chief."[124]

Only a month before, the collective leadership had taken another action that indirectly showed the sharpness of the continuing issue of defense allocation. On September 6 a simple announcement appeared on television and in the press that Marshal Nikolai V. Ogarkov had been relieved of his positions as first deputy minister of defense and chief of the General Staff of the armed forces, succeeded by his senior deputy, Marshal Sergei F. Akhromeyev. The decision was taken at the regular Politburo meeting that day and appeared to have been sudden.[125] While the reasons for Ogarkov's abrupt removal are not known, there is little question that they concerned matters of defense allocation. It appears from other sources that Ogarkov had become too self-confident as the top professional military leader, and he probably was too assertive and persistent in pressing his case after the political leadership had decided against his recommendation.[126] It is not known precisely which aspects of increased

---

123. "Speech of Comrade K. U. Chernenko," *Pravda*, September 28, 1984.

124. "Speech of Comrade D. F. Ustinov," *Pravda*, September 28, 1984. This was the first public acknowledgment by a Soviet leader that Chernenko was supreme commander-in-chief, an acknowledgment never publicly made during Andropov's tenure.

125. See "Chronicle," *Pravda*, September 7, 1984. Only the day before he was removed Ogarkov had seen off a departing Finnish military delegation, and he had been scheduled for a brief television interview by NBC "Today" in Moscow the following week.

   *Red Star*, incidentally, rather than use the two-sentence announcement of Ogarkov's relief and Akhromeyev's selection, ran a front-page article on Akhromeyev, showing a bemedaled photograph of him and omitting any reference to Ogarkov. "Marshal of the Soviet Union S. F. Akhromeyev—Chief of the General Staff of the Armed Forces of the USSR and First Deputy Minister of Defense of the USSR," *Krasnaya zvezda*, September 7, 1984.

126. Several Soviet officials privately indicated that Ogarkov had gotten "too big for his britches" and "acted in a non-party-like manner"—that is, was insufficiently disciplined in heeding the line.

   In what is certainly more than coincidence, on the day preceding Ogarkov's removal an editorial in *Pravda*, and on the day of his removal a similar editorial in the armed forces newspaper *Red Star*, strongly suggested that the party leadership had just

defense effort Ogarkov was pressing. In an interview in May he had stressed the need for more attention to advanced conventional weaponry, while suggesting strategic nuclear sufficiency,[127] but in various writings he had also stressed military and industrial wartime mobilization requirements, command and control, and a broad program to match the American buildup, including futuristic new weapons. In general, as noted earlier, he had been in the forefront of those portraying the increased military threat from the United States and NATO since 1980. There is no indication that Ogarkov was involved in factional political infighting. But the defense resource allocation issue was a continuing major economic and political issue, with important foreign policy implications.[128]

While resource allocation was constricted, the leadership agreed to take some new steps along the line of structural command changes advocated

---

rejected a proposal to reallocate resources from consumer programs to defense. *Pravda* stated, "Despite the current tense international situation, which requires diverting considerable resources to strengthening the security of the country, even thinking about cutting the broad social program laid down by the party at the XXVI Congress is not admissible." "For Soviet Man," *Pravda*, September 5, 1984. The next day *Red Star* fell into line, repeating almost exactly the same words (changing only "security" to "defense capability" of the country; the reference to the party congress was also dropped from this sentence but appeared in the preceding sentence and was directly linked). In one sense *Red Star* even went further, by referring to the social-economic program not only of the current economic five-year plan but also to be continued in the 1986–90 plan. "For the Good of the People," *Krasnaya zvezda*, September 6, 1984.

The language used in these editorial articles, clearly stemming from a party decision, had an august progenitor. In his March 2 Supreme Soviet election speech Chernenko had said that "we did not even think of cutting social programs," despite defense requirements, and this statement was quoted in a *Pravda* editorial on July 30. But the new formulation made clear that it was not admissible for *others*—like Ogarkov—to think of doing so either. Also Chernenko's reference had been to the past; the September references were in the present tense with a future application. Chernenko, *Pravda*, March 3, 1984; and "Party Solicitude in the Sphere of Services," *Pravda*, July 30, 1984.

127. "The Defense of Socialism: The Experience of History and the Present Day," interview with Marshal N. V. Ogarkov, *Krasnaya zvezda*, May 9, 1984. Ironically, in support of his plea, Ogarkov had quoted Chernenko as saying that "military men must . . . resolutely overcome any conservatism and inertia" and take as their slogan, "From a correct idea, fully armed with experience, to bold actions!" But he overestimated the permissible limits of bold actions.

128. It is, therefore, possible that while Ogarkov was not directly meddling in politics, his removal may have eased the position of Chernenko and other political leaders seeking to hold down arms outlays. In this connection, it may be relevant that Grigory Romanov, a reputed advocate of military-industrial interests, had left the country the day before the Politburo met on September 6, decided to remove Ogarkov, and announced the decision that same day. Dinmukhamed Kunayev, and probably Vladimir Shcherbitsky, two other conservative Politburo members, were also absent from the meeting, which took place soon after Chernenko had returned to work from an absence of a month and a half because of unreported illness.

by Ogarkov and other senior officers as a readiness measure. Indeed, Marshal Ogarkov himself was named to head a new Western theater of war command, and two similar new regional theater commands were established for the Southwest (the Balkans, the Turkish Straits, and the Mediterranean) and the South (the Caucasus facing Turkey and Iran, the Near East beyond, and the Iranian-Afghan-Pakistani sector). These three new superregional commands created in September–October 1984 complemented one established in the Far East in late 1978 after the Sino-American rapprochement.[129]

   In his first pronouncement as leader, Chernenko had reaffirmed to the Central Committee plenum in February 1984 the broad lines of defense policy set in the Brezhnev period and maintained also by Andropov. "We have no need for military superiority," said Chernenko, "but we will not permit the military balance to be upset. And let no one have the slightest doubt: we will also in the future see to it that we strengthen the defense capability of our country so that we have sufficient means to cool the hot heads of bellicose adventurists."[130] This statement was subsequently cited by many military and some other spokesmen, but of course it left open the question of "how much is enough" (or, how much is required). And while speaking of "strengthening" defense capability, Chernenko had implied no change from the past, saying, "We will *also* in the future see to it." Incidentally, in the Armed Forces Day statements soon following that plenum, while several leading marshals, including Ustinov, cited this statement, the defense minister went on to stress that it was "the Communist Party" that "determines the main directions for strengthening the defense capability of the country," and that military commanders are "conductors of party decisions."[131] Marshal Ogarkov, in contrast, in speaking of the military had said, "The CPSU Central Committee and the Soviet Government demand that we closely follow the development of the situation and that we persistently work on further strengthening the defense capability of the country."[132]

---

129. Marshal Akhromeyev later disclosed that the decision to create the regional theater commands was taken in the summer of 1984, and that there was much discussion that Ogarkov might be named commander-in-chief of the key Western command. See S. F. Akhromeyev and G. M. Kornienko, *Glazami marshala i diplomata* (Through the Eyes of a Marshal and a Diplomat) (Moscow: Mezhdunarodnyye otnosheniya, 1992), p. 30.

130. *Pravda*, February 14, 1984.

131. Marshal D. F. Ustinov, "Invincible and Legendary . . .," *Pravda*, February 23, 1984.

132. Marshal N. V. Ogarkov, address broadcast on Moscow domestic radio, February 23, 1984, in Foreign Broadcast Information Service, *Daily Report: Soviet Union*, February 24, 1984, p. V1. (Hereafter FBIS, *Soviet Union*.) Marshal V. G. Kulikov also omitted explicit reference to Chernenko and was much more vague in his reference that "we will continue to strengthen the defense capability of our country," as stated at the February plenum. Marshal V. G. Kulikov, "Guarding Peace and Labor," *Sovetskaya Rossiya* (Soviet Russia), February 23, 1984. Marshal Sergei Sokolov, who later succeeded Ustinov, cited Chernenko and quoted him precisely. He also stressed that "our party, its Central Committee, and the Soviet Government show tireless concern to maintain the

By the late fall of 1984 the Soviet leadership announced, for the first time in years, an increase in the published defense budget, of nearly 12 percent.[133] For other reasons, Western analysts believe that some modest increase in the rate of Soviet military outlays, steady since 1976, began in 1983 or 1984. The Soviet announcement, however, while perhaps reflecting an actual increase, was primarily a political sign to the West and to the Soviet people.

At the same time that the leadership decided to make a demonstrative increase in the declared defense budget, an effort was made to signal that this did not mean a radical shift. A major article stressed that one of the principal aims of the imperialists was to force an arms race on the Soviet Union with the aim of "undermining the economy of the Soviet Union and the other socialist states." In addition, it was said that the imperialists sought to build up their "material preparations for aggressive wars" but also to make "billion dollar profits."[134] The article then argued that the Soviet system did not require equal outlays in order to maintain a deterrent balance. Perhaps with an eye to the experience in Vietnam, the author argued that because of the aggressive nature of imperialist policy the U.S. armed forces are often used in distant areas "at enormous expense," and that in contrast "the Soviet economy is not burdened by such expenses." More basically, "In capitalist society, fundamentally irrational military expenditures become irrationality squared" because "the development and production of new types of weapons are increasingly often dictated not by the real requirements of the army but by the pursuit of orders and profits by the military-industrial complex." As for the Soviet Union, "Of course, the Soviet Union is compelled to take countermeasures to supply its armed forces with all that is essential. But our efforts do not go beyond the bounds of what is required to secure our defense, and our economic system makes it possible to do so more rationally [that is, economically]." Finally, "The military-strategic balance as a deterrent to American aggression is achieved not just by means of the funds allocated from the state budget to the Ministry of Defense. The balance in the final analysis is ensured by the real advantages possessed by socialism." Accordingly, "The hope of the enemies of socialism that it is possible to stifle the USSR economically is untenable both theoretically and in practice."[135]

---

defense capability of the USSR at the necessary level." Marshal S. Sokolov, "Always in Readiness, Always Alert," *Krasnaya zvezda*, February 23, 1984.

133. "On the State Budget of the USSR for 1985 and on the Implementation of the State Budget of the USSR for 1983, Report of the Minister of Finance Deputy V. F. Garbuzov," *Pravda*, November 28, 1984.

134. N. Voloshkin, "The Economic Front of Our Defense," *Novoye vremya* (New Times), no. 44 (October 26, 1984), p. 18.

135. Ibid., p. 19.
    Gromyko had made this same point in his White House discussion with President Reagan. See Gromyko, *Pamyatnoye*, vol. 2, p. 257.

And the author, while stressing readiness to do all that may be required to deter war "for the sake of preserving life on earth and socialism as a system," cited Chernenko on declining the offer in letters from the public to extend the work week as not necessary and went on to comment, "The Soviet Union, while ensuring the necessary level of defense capability, has not canceled or postponed a single one of the planned measures to improve the welfare of the citizenry over the past 10–15 years. Furthermore, even in the current rather tense conditions the party and the government have found ways."[136]

Debate within the Soviet establishment thus continued, but the Chernenko administration did not make the more drastic increases in military programs sought not only by Ogarkov but by many other military leaders.

Andrei Gromyko was selected to give the leadership's address on the anniversary of the Revolution on November 6. He restated Soviet aims in the international field in terms of "strengthening the international positions of world socialism" and at the same time "doing everything possible to check and remove the threat of war" and "to protect the security of the USSR and raise the defense capability of our country." His stress was on "the removal of the nuclear danger," which he said was "the main question of all." At the same time, he noted, "The international situation depends in many ways on the status of U.S.-USSR relations," which he characterized as "now in disarray," owing to what Washington had done "to wreck everything positive previously created by mutual efforts" in détente. He noted "recent statements heard from the American side about wishes to have more constructive relations with the USSR" and asked whether they represented "short-term considerations" (the presidential electoral campaign just ending) or "something more substantial. The reply to this question must be given by the United States itself, through practical deeds."[137]

Gromyko was harshly critical of American policy, "stubbornly pursuing a militarist course in international affairs," but he clearly saw the principal challenge as political-diplomatic rather than military. Of course, he declared that the Communist Party "devotes unflagging attention to strengthening the defense capability of the USSR and ensuring its security," but he also indicated emphatically that what was already being done met the need: "Our party and people are doing everything so that the valorous Soviet armed forces may have at their disposal everything necessary. . . . This is how it has been, this is how it is, and this is how it will be in the future too."[138]

---

136. Voloshkin, *Novoye vremya*, no. 44 (October 26, 1984), p. 20.

137. "Comrade A. A. Gromyko's Report 'Along the Path of October—Following a Course of Creation and Peace' at the Ceremonial Session Devoted to the 67th Anniversary of the Great October Socialist Revolution in the Kremlin Palace of Congresses, November 6, 1984," *Pravda*, November 7, 1984.

138. Ibid.

Following Gromyko's meeting with President Reagan in late September, even before the American election, the Soviet line seemed to have turned to giving every chance to the possibilities of a serious negotiation. Sharp criticisms likening Reagan to Hitler, for example, that had begun in late 1983 ceased in the fall of 1984. And diplomatic explorations picked up. On October 26 Shultz met with Dobrynin, and five days later Gromyko saw Ambassador Hartman. (At the funeral of Indira Gandhi, Shultz, accompanied by Senators Howard Baker and Patrick Moynihan, on November 4 met with Prime Minister Nikolai Tikhonov in New Delhi, but there was no substantive exchange.)

In Washington, a bureaucratic debate over the possible naming of a special high-level envoy took place in mid-November, but the idea was dropped after Shultz objected strongly. On November 17 the Soviet leader sent a message that seemed to offer a breakthrough, a message that "crossed" with one from Reagan of November 16, and this impression was strengthened in another Gromyko-Hartman meeting two days later. On November 22, agreement in principle was announced on new nuclear and space arms talks, the precise mandate to be worked out in a meeting of Shultz and Gromyko in Geneva on January 7–8, 1985.[139]

While the "agreement" marked a step forward, it was significant mainly as an indication that both sides wanted to resume negotiations rather than as an understanding on a basis for talks (an agreement would emerge even from the Gromyko-Shultz talks in January only in a very equivocal formulation that papered over deep differences and was not in fact a true agreement). Chernenko expressed Soviet readiness to search for solutions on the whole complex of international issues and said that the future would show whether the United States was prepared for "constructive talks."[140]

Soviet commentary following the U.S. election was cautious but generally open to the possibility of American readiness for serious negotiations. This was the position taken by Chernenko, and it found wide expression in the media. There remained considerable suspicion that Reagan's new rhetoric in 1984 calling for negotiation and improved relations was an expedient for electoral purposes. Some commentators, however, argued that even if this new tone was "merely a move in the election campaign," nonetheless "the appropriate words about peace were said," and now that Reagan had been reelected the American public expected the policy to be pursued and would be watching to see whether "practical deeds in American foreign policy" would match the rhetoric. "Common sense about the need—and, I would say, about the urgency—for realistic changes in American foreign policy and for curbing the arms race has clearly taken root in the United States. It has become much more

---

139. See Shultz, *Turmoil and Triumph*, pp. 499–500.

140. "K. U. Chernenko's Reception of N. Kinnock," *Pravda*, November 27, 1984.

difficult to refuse serious talks with the Soviet Union than it was in the past," in the words of a commentator for the party journal *Kommunist*.[141]

Not all Soviet commentary took this position. Leonid Zamyatin, chief of the International Information Department of the Central Committee, cited Reagan's 1984 campaign proclaiming a readiness for negotiations and desire to improve relations as an attempt "to brainwash international public opinion in an anti-Soviet, anti-communist spirit." He questioned how seriously these protestations could be taken when uttered by the same president who had said the Soviet Union is "an enemy with whom we are at war" and pursued as "the administration's strategic goal: the liquidation of socialism as a sociopolitical system."[142] Similarly, a commentator in the Armed Forces paper *Red Star* stressed that U.S. pursuit of military superiority and destabilization of the strategic situation was grounded in "the ideological principle of abandoning peaceful coexistence and waging a 'crusade' against socialism. Such principles cannot fail to raise alarm, however much they may have been camouflaged recently by the 'peace-loving' rhetoric coming from the White House."[143]

Differences in assessment of the prospects for fruitful negotiation with the United States in part stemmed from, and in part contributed to, divergent political and policy positions in the Soviet establishment and leadership.

Chernenko had returned to work in September, but his health continued to deteriorate and a struggle for the succession continued. There were several signs in October that Gorbachev's standing as putative successor was under challenge. On October 18, at an awards ceremony for Gromyko, for the first time during the Chernenko administration, Gorbachev's ranking fell below that of his rival Grigory Romanov. He also had been bypassed in favor of Dmitry Ustinov at an award ceremony for Chernenko on September 27. Then, on October 23, Gorbachev—long the Politburo member in charge of agricultural policy—was completely eclipsed at a Central Committee plenum on agriculture. On November 15, Gorbachev was unaccountably absent from a key Politburo meeting on the economic plan. And on November 6 and 7 there was a switch, with Romanov outranking Gorbachev on the sixth and Gorbachev

141. Vadim N. Nekrasov, on Radio Moscow's "International Observers' Roundtable," November 25, 1984, in FBIS, *Soviet Union*, November 26, 1984, p. CC2; and see Nikolai V. Shishlin, a consultant to the Central Committee, on Radio Moscow, November 2, 1984, in FBIS, *Soviet Union*, November 5, 1984, pp. CC7–8.

142. Leonid Zamyatin, "Washington's 'New' Orientation?" *Tribuna*, Prague, no. 44 (October 31, 1984), p. 3. He stressed further that at the head of a major political and psychological warfare campaign was "the U.S. president himself."

143. [Col.] L. Semeyko, "The United States in Pursuit of Military Superiority: A Gamble on Undermining Stability," *Krasnaya zvezda*, November 1, 1984. Colonel Semeyko remained a prominent military commentator even though retired and on the staff of the Institute of USA and Canada.

restored in standing the next day in published listings of the Politburo members attending annual ceremonies on the anniversary of the Revolution.

By December, however, Gorbachev had apparently recouped his standing. He made a major speech on ideology on December 10. Considerable prominence was given to his successful visit to Great Britain in mid-December. Although the death of Marshal Ustinov (and his succession by the politically insignificant, aging Marshal Sergei Sokolov) increased Romanov's Politburo role as a spokesman on the military resources issue, at Ustinov's funeral on December 22 Gorbachev was listed in his customary third place, preceding Romanov. In the nominations for the Supreme Soviet in late December Gorbachev was even tied with the second ranking leader, Prime Minister Nikolai Tikhonov, for the largest number of nominations after Chernenko. These small "Kremlinological" signs of changing status in the last three months of 1984 (and there were others) suggested intensified jockeying for power.[144]

Gorbachev's speech to the party conference on ideology was important, not only because it broadened the area of his evident competence and authority, and at this juncture marked a political rebound, but above all because it carried the seeds of far-reaching changes in ideology and policy that Gorbachev would institute in the next several years. For example, while the significance was not yet apparent, in this speech he introduced the concepts of basic "restructuring" (*perestroika*) and public openness (*glasnost*)—terms not yet familiar but soon to become so.[145]

Similarly, while Gorbachev's official visit to Britain on December 15–21 (cut short to return for Ustinov's funeral) was not the occasion for any pathbreaking negotiation or achievement, it marked a much more prominent role for Gorbachev on the world stage than had his one earlier official visit to a Western country (Canada in 1983). In a major speech in London on foreign policy, Gorbachev introduced a new theme later to be developed and applied to Soviet policy under his leadership, the idea that the Soviet Union and other countries of Eastern Europe and those of Western Europe inhabited a "common home." Emphasizing the need to abandon a military and confrontational frame of reference, he stressed "a common home . . . and not a theater of military operations."[146] No less important was Gorbachev's success in winning

---

144. For these and other Kremlinological clues on relative standing in the Chernenko period, see John W. Parker, *Kremlin in Transition* (Unwin Hyman, 1991), vol. 1, pp. 335–445. Such clues are not always valid, but those of the kind noted above tend to be indicative.

145. "Perfecting Developed Socialism and the Ideological Work of the Party in Light of the Decision of the June (1983) Plenum of the CC of the CPSU, An All-Union Practical-Scientific Conference: Vital Creativity of the People: Speech of Comrade M. S. Gorbachev," *Pravda*, December 11, 1984.

146. "Speech of M. S. Gorbachev to the British Parliament," *Pravda*, December 19, 1984. See in particular the discussion in chapter 13.

the confidence of Prime Minister Margaret Thatcher, who informed the world (and in a meeting with him soon after, Ronald Reagan) that Gorbachev was someone with whom the West could "do business."

Soviet politics were thus active in the last half of 1984 and promised to remain so as the leadership looked ahead to the next party congress and the next five-year plan, and to the succession to the ailing Chernenko, as well as to the question of whether there would be a change of line in the second Reagan administration and opportunities for real negotiation, or renewed intensification of confrontation.

# II  A NEW DÉTENTE

# 5  Gorbachev and the Geneva Summit, 1985

THE YEAR 1985 saw two important developments for American-Soviet relations: the accession to power of Mikhail S. Gorbachev in March, and the renewal of highest-level dialogue between the United States and the Soviet Union in the Geneva summit meeting between President Reagan and General Secretary Gorbachev in November. Of more equivocal significance was the resumption of arms control talks. As the year began, American-Soviet relations were on the course of an unsteady, gradual normalization of relations launched the previous year.

## Gradual Normalization

The meeting in Geneva between Secretary George Shultz and Foreign Minister Andrei Gromyko on January 7–8 resulted in agreement on a formula for the scope of the planned nuclear and space arms control talks (NST). Three concurrent sets of negotiations would be held, dealing with strategic offensive arms reductions (START), intermediate-range missile forces (INF), and strategic defense and space weapons. The formulation was, in one respect, a diplomatic achievement, but in another sense a mere postponement of difficulties, because it bridged unreconciled real and serious differences between the two sides. It was not until January 27 that agreement was reached to begin the negotiations in Geneva on March 12.

The much advertised January meeting was intended to end a year marked by the absence of arms control negotiation and to resume a broader diplomatic dialogue. There had been intense political, as well as internal bureaucratic, debates in Washington over this step. To allay suspicions, it was decided, on Shultz's recommendation, to send with him not only National Security Adviser Robert McFarlane, but also all the key bureaucratic contenders—Assistant Secretaries Richard Perle of Defense and Richard Burt of State, as well as Arms Control and Disarmament Agency Director Kenneth L. Adelman and special arms control advisers Paul H. Nitze and Lieutenant General Edward Rowny, the displaced chiefs of the defunct predecessor INF and START talks. Such an entourage did not encourage an intimate or far-reaching exchange between foreign ministers.

The U.S. strategic defense initiative and American allegations of possible Soviet violations of other arms agreements were discussed briefly. The main focus was on the important issue of the scope of the talks and revolved about the divergent views over banning weapons in space. Shultz also flagged the subject of human rights, as he did in all such encounters. But there was no real discussion of bilateral or world issues, and working out the formulation for the forthcoming arms control talks required all the available time.[1]

Coinciding with the Shultz-Gromyko meeting, Undersecretary of Commerce Lionel H. Olmer met in Moscow for talks January 8 through 10 with his counterpart Vladimir Sushkov in a working group preparing for a meeting in May of their ministers, Secretary of Commerce Malcolm Baldrige and Foreign Trade Minister Nikolai S. Patolichev, constituting the long dormant Joint U.S.-USSR Commercial Commission (which had last met in 1978).

There had been earlier steps to resume economic cooperation. Talks on renewal of exchanges on agricultural science and technology had brought Agriculture Minister Valentin K. Mesyats to the United States in December. Also in early December the unofficial U.S.-USSR Trade and Economic Council had met in Moscow, and the American cochairman, Dwayne O. Andreas, had been received not only by Patolichev, but also by Prime Minister Nikolai A. Tikhonov and by Politburo member Gorbachev.

While his deputy had been negotiating for talks to develop U.S.-Soviet trade, Secretary Baldrige in mid-January wrote a letter to Shultz, Defense Secretary Caspar Weinberger, Secretary of Energy Donald P. Hodel, NASA Administrator James M. Beggs, and National Security Adviser McFarlane complaining about a massive giveaway of U.S. government unclassified and declassified information to the Soviet Union. The fact of this letter of January 16 and its substance were leaked to the press by February 21, followed by a published article on the subject by Baldrige on March 4.

---

1.    See George P. Shultz, *Turmoil and Triumph: My Years as Secretary of State* (Charles Scribner's Sons, 1993), pp. 502–08.

National Security Decision Directive (NSDD)–153, providing instructions for the Shultz-Gromyko meeting, was sixteen single-spaced pages, with elaborate detail and background. NSDD-160 then set basic guidelines for the subsequent negotiations. Both have now been declassified: NSDD-153, "Instructions for the Shultz-Gromyko Meeting in Geneva," January 1, 1985, Secret; and NSDD-160, "Preparing for Negotiations with the Soviet Union," January 24, 1985, Secret.

Earlier, the U.S. International Trade Commission had in mid-December 1984 issued a report finding that the extent of "slave labor" used in making Soviet products imported into the United States was "negligible," thus defusing at least for a time an unofficial right-wing lawsuit to force the administration to impose import bans.[2]

Within the administration, however, the Departments of Defense and Commerce had been wrangling bitterly for more than two years over which should rule on high-technology exports to communist countries. On January 4, 1985, Reagan issued a decision through a memorandum by McFarlane giving Defense the authority to review computers, scientific instruments, and other such high-technology material with possible military applications.[3] Within Defense, Assistant Secretary Perle had won an earlier internal battle to handle the matter in that department.

Another dispute within the administration, with congressional interest as well, pitted the State Department against the FBI on the question of whether the United States should insist on reciprocity in the manning levels of the respective embassies in Moscow and Washington.

Among other steps in bilateral relations, consultations and negotiations continued quietly on several subjects. Talks on a possible renewed cultural exchange agreement and on opening additional consulates had resumed in mid-1984 and continued into the new year. At the end of November U.S.-Soviet talks on nuclear nonproliferation took place in Moscow. Talks between the Coast Guard and its Soviet opposite number began in January. On the diplomatic side, on February 19–20 a new exchange of views on the Middle Eastern situation was quietly held in Moscow at the deputy foreign minister-assistant secretary level.

The most prominent development in bilateral relations was the visit to the United States in early March of a Soviet parliamentary delegation headed, for the first time, by a full member of the Politburo, Vladimir Shcherbitsky.[4] This marked the first visit to the United States by any Soviet Politburo member (other than Foreign Minister Gromyko) since 1973. The visit included a meeting of Shcherbitsky with President Reagan on March 7. While uneventful, the visit and meetings went well. In their hour-long chat, President Reagan noted some of the ongoing talks toward normalization of relations. He also sought to allay Soviet suspicions by saying that the United States had no hostile intentions toward the Soviet Union, and to support that statement he argued that the

2.   Stuart Auerbach, "Few Imported Soviet Products Found Made by Slave Labor," *Washington Post*, December 20, 1984, p. A12.

3.   Fred Hiatt, "Pentagon Wins on Export Review," *Washington Post*, January 12, 1985, pp. A1, A18.

4.   The Russian version of his name, used in Soviet publications, will be used throughout; in Ukrainian his name (in transcription) was Volodymyr Shcherbytski.

United States had refrained from using its overwhelming power after World War II to impose its will. (This argument, convincing to most Americans, was not persuasive to Soviet leaders, who believed the United States did use its power to impose a whole international order favorable to American interests while "containing" the Soviet Union.) Shcherbitsky stressed the collaboration of the Soviet Union and the United States in World War II against a common foe and argued that today the two powers needed to collaborate against the common enemy of nuclear war.[5]

Relations with the Soviet Union were not foremost in Washington's attention in early 1985. The beginning of the second Reagan administration raised some questions as to whether priorities would change. There were, in addition, some personnel changes. In particular, James A. Baker III moved from being White House chief of staff to becoming secretary of the Treasury, changing places with the previous secretary, Donald T. Regan. Edwin Meese III moved to the Justice Department as Judge William Clark left government service. Michael Deaver left the White House and government service. Jeane Kirkpatrick, after earlier seeking and failing to become the national security adviser, left government service and was replaced as the U.S. representative to the United Nations by retired General Vernon A. Walters, who had been serving as a roving troubleshooter. The ardently conservative Patrick J. Buchanan came into the White House to serve as President Reagan's chief speech writer and communications adviser.

The administration placed its major emphasis on gaining support for its military budget, facing trouble after four years of easy riding. The MX intercontinental ballistic missile (ICBM) was in the forefront of debate. The president's strategic defense initiative (SDI) also remained controversial, and there was a fair amount of interest in the phenomenon of "nuclear winter," although the impact on defense programs was unclear.

President Reagan in his first press conference of the new year thus dealt with MX, SDI, continuing constraints of the unratified strategic arms limitation treaty (SALT II), charges of Soviet violations of arms control agreements, and aid to Nicaraguan insurgents. He did express the hope that the year 1985 would "emerge as one of dialog and negotiations, a year that leads to better relations between the United States and the Soviet Union."[6] And he welcomed the Geneva agreements on reopening arms talks. But when asked about a possible summit meeting with Konstantin Chernenko, he dismissed the idea: "To have a meeting, as I said before, just to have a meeting, doesn't make

---

5.   Information on the Reagan-Shcherbitsky discussion was provided by a senior U.S. government official privy to the exchange.

6.   "The President's News Conference of January 9, 1985," *Weekly Compilation of Presidential Documents*, vol. 21 (January 14, 1985), p. 31. (Hereafter *Presidential Documents*.)

any sense;" it wouldn't "make much sense simply to . . . have a meeting just to get acquainted."[7]

In his inaugural address on January 21, in counterpoint to his upbeat message on a renewal of faith in freedom in the United States and to his stress on "restoring our defense capability," President Reagan spoke of "those in the world who scorn our vision of human dignity and freedom. One nation, the Soviet Union, has conducted the greatest military buildup in the history of man, building arsenals of awesome offensive weapons." This, he argued, called not only for general American military efforts but for his SDI, a "security shield" in space, which he argued "would help demilitarize the arsenals of earth. It would render nuclear weapons obsolete."[8]

On February 1, the second "President's Report to Congress on Soviet Noncompliance with Arms Control Agreements" was sent to Congress.[9] Notwithstanding these reports, the administration was of course resuming arms negotiations. The administration argued that Soviet violations of agreements required the United States to be sure of its own military strength. In addition, Secretary Schultz argued that U.S. military strength "improves the prospects for successful [arms] negotiations."[10] He claimed that the MX missile in particular played "a pivotal role in advancing our arms control goals as well."[11] President Reagan credited "our determination to maintain a strong defense" with having "influenced the Soviet Union to return to the bargaining table."[12]

On February 5, the president issued a statement on the fortieth anniversary of the wartime Yalta Conference, citing the memory of that conference as "an episode of cooperation" with the Soviet Union, "but it also recalls the reasons that this cooperation could not continue." As for the present, he asserted that "the freedom of [Eastern] Europe is unfinished business."[13]

The State of the Union address on February 6 stressed American strength and resolve, in particular the SDI, and reasserted the renewed emphasis on waging the geopolitical competition through "support for freedom fighters." He justified this by declaring it to be "self-defense" and claimed it was

---

7.  Ibid., p. 35.

8.  "50th American Presidential Inaugural: Inaugural Address," January 21, 1985, ibid., vol. 21 (January 28, 1985), p. 69.

9.  See chapter 12 for discussion of the compliance issue.

10. "The Importance of the MX Peacekeeper Missile," February 26, 1985, *Department of State Bulletin*, vol. 85 (April 1985), p. 24. (Hereafter *State Bulletin*.)

11. Ibid.

12. "The State of the Union. Address Delivered before a Joint Session of the Congress," February 6, 1985, *Presidential Documents*, vol. 21 (February 11, 1985), p. 145.

13. "Yalta Conference. Statement on the 40th Anniversary," February 5, 1985, ibid, vol. 21 (February 11, 1985), p. 131. For further discussion of U.S. policy on Eastern Europe, see chapter 13.

"totally consistent with the OAS and UN Charters." But his appeal was for a crusade: "We must not break faith with those who are risking their lives—on every continent, from Afghanistan to Nicaragua—to defy Soviet-supported aggression."[14] This endorsement, encouragement, and direct support for various insurgencies against communist countries in the Third World, both overt and with additional covert assistance, came to be called "the Reagan Doctrine."[15] Nothing was said about American-Soviet relations.

Despite these confrontational elements, the uneven and inconsistent policy of gradual normalization of relations with the Soviet Union continued—and provoked criticism from the right for what to them seemed a de facto turn toward a renewed détente.[16]

In the Soviet Union, the early months of 1985 were concentrated above all on the clearly failing health of the third Soviet leader within a little more than two years. After December 27, 1984, Chernenko was seen but once in public, when he rose from his sickbed to be seen voting in the Supreme Soviet election on February 24, so feeble that he had to be almost carried. He had been unable to attend the funeral of his colleague Dmitry Ustinov in late December, had not been able to deliver his own election speech on February 22, and a meeting of the chiefs of the Warsaw Pact countries scheduled for January 15 had to be postponed.

Shcherbitsky's visit to the United States in early March was but one of a number of trips as various members of the Politburo traveled to the West to broaden their experience and acquaintance with the world. Gorbachev had a very well-received visit to Great Britain in December, Mikhail S. Solomentsev visited Paris to attend the French Communist Party Congress, Dinmukhamed A. Kunayev visited Turkey, Vitaly I. Vorotnikov went to Yugoslavia, candidate member Vladimir I. Dolgikh visited Southeast Asia, and Petr N. Demichev visited Algeria.

The first anniversary of Andropov's death on February 9 was marked by a stirring tribute in *Pravda*, breaking the pattern of silence enveloping deceased leaders. This article was a sign of the active role of Andropov-Gorbachev political forces against old Brezhnevite forces weakened by Chernenko's incapacitation. The new succession was under way.

---

14. *Presidential Documents*, vol. 21 (February 11, 1985), p. 46.

15. President Reagan never officially proclaimed a Reagan Doctrine. Following this initial endorsement of the idea by President Reagan, the neoconservative commentator Charles Krauthammer first christened this approach the "Reagan Doctrine" in *Time* magazine (April 1, 1985), p. 54. The policy, if not a formal doctrine, was espoused and practiced by the Reagan administration. See chapter 15.

16. In particular, see Norman Podhoretz, "The Reagan Road to Détente," *Foreign Affairs*, vol. 63 (1985), pp. 447–464.

## Gorbachev's Accession

In retrospect, Gorbachev's accession to power looked smooth and easy. But at the time there was a fierce struggle for the succession within the upper reaches of the party. As we have seen, in late 1984 there were signs of ups and downs in the political standing of the two younger aspirants, Gorbachev and Romanov.[17] In addition, in early 1985 rumors were planted that Viktor Grishin, the senior Politburo member in tenure and party chief of Moscow, had been designated to succeed the dying Chernenko. The rumor was no more than a trial balloon (probably by supporters of Grishin, or perhaps of Romanov, who reportedly hoped to become the compromise choice if Grishin and Gorbachev ended up in a deadlock).[18] But there were clear signs of an attempt to advance Grishin's candidacy. On February 22, when Chernenko was unable to appear in public and give his scheduled Supreme Soviet election speech, it was Grishin who announced the leader's inability to be there and said he had been asked by Chernenko to convey his greetings to the people. Two days later, when Chernenko was barely able to make a public appearance long enough to be photographed on Soviet television casting his vote, he was accompanied by Grishin. No other Politburo member was shown voting, so the message again was a visibly ailing Chernenko, with his closest colleague and presumed heir, Grishin. (In contrast, the Ministry of Foreign Affairs, headed by Gorbachev's backer Gromyko, had alerted Western correspondents in advance about the time they could observe Gorbachev casting his ballot.)[19]

When Chernenko died on the evening of March 10, the leadership moved quickly to resolve the succession issue. A Politburo meeting that night decided the matter, and it was then ratified by a hastily summoned Central Committee plenum the next day. Gorbachev's "unanimous" election was publicly announced less than twenty-four hours after Chernenko's death.

Although the succession was decided speedily, it was not done easily. Although there may have been a general understanding at the time of Chernenko's selection that Gorbachev would be next in line when he died, the question was still open. Both Romanov and Grishin had ambitions to succeed Chernenko. They hoped to have the support of Tikhonov, Kunayev, and Shcherbitsky (had he been in Moscow and not in the United States at the time).[20]

---

17. See chapter 4.
18. See Dusko Doder, *Shadows and Whispers: Power Politics Inside the Kremlin from Brezhnev to Gorbachev* (Random House, 1986), pp. 250–56.
19. Ibid., pp. 257–59.
20. According to an informed Soviet source, Gorbachev had originally been selected to lead the delegation to the United States to follow up his successful visit to Great Britain.

Gromyko took the initiative and nominated Gorbachev. The opposition collapsed and joined in making a unanimous nomination to the Central Committee.[21]

Gorbachev quickly identified himself with Andropov's legacy, but he began to exhibit much greater energy than Andropov had been able to muster in getting the country moving again.[22] Gorbachev moved quickly to get some of his new allies from the younger leaders who had been in the entourages of former party leaders Kirilenko and Suslov as well as Andropov and then moved to replace the mostly older Brezhnev and Chernenko conservatives. Within the year, Romanov, Grishin, and Tikhonov had been removed. It took longer (until the next year) to remove the entrenched Kazakh party leader Kunayev, and still longer (until 1989) for the Ukrainian leader Shcherbitsky. Even Grishin in Moscow proved difficult to dislodge.[23]

Gorbachev, however, was wary of leaving the Soviet Union when Chernenko's health was deteriorating so rapidly, and he declined, so Shcherbitsky was sent.

Gorbachev also reportedly successfully delayed Shcherbitsky's return from Washington until after the key meeting in Moscow.

21. While the transcript of the March 11, 1985, Politburo meeting is still classified at this writing, one Western writer was given the opportunity to read it and has reported the contents. See David Remnick, *Lenin's Tomb: The Last Days of the Soviet Empire* (Random House, 1993), pp. 519–20. Gromyko's unusually personal nominating speech, or at least a version of it, was published only a week after the meeting.

Apparently the eleven candidate Politburo members and five party secretaries were also present, although not entitled to vote. The support of most of them for Gorbachev, attested to by Yegor Ligachev (one of them), may have influenced the Politburo voting members, who simply supported Gromyko's nomination without a contested vote. It may be of significance that the official Soviet announcement of Gorbachev's election used the Russian word *edinodushno*, implying unanimity by acclamation, rather than *edinoglasno*, meaning by unanimous vote.

There may even have been more direct pressures; candidate member (and KGB chief) Viktor Chebrikov was reported to have made known that he had with him a dossier detailing Grishin's corruption. Boris Yeltsin says that many regional party secretaries, members of the Central Committee, had also made known their strong support for Gorbachev. For some of these reports, see Robert G. Kaiser, *Why Gorbachev Happened: His Triumphs and His Failure* (Simon and Schuster, 1991), pp. 80–85.

22. Gorbachev's forward-looking desire for innovation had long been evident. For example, soon after Andropov's passing Chernenko had set his sights on a steady, plodding course, calling for "relying on everything that has been accomplished earlier" ("Speech of Comrade K. U. Chernenko," *Pravda*, February 14, 1984). In striking contrast, Gorbachev in a statement at about the same time, with barely concealed reference to Andropov's beginning efforts, spoke of the need "to bolster and augment everything new and progressive that has recently become part of our societal life" ("Consolidate Achievements, Go Further, Increase Efficiency," *Izvestiya*, March 1, 1984).

23. Following a series of public disclosures of corruption and mismanagement in the Moscow party organization, a plenary meeting of that body on December 24, 1985, relieved Viktor Grishin, one of the senior Politburo members, from his position as first secretary of the Moscow City party committee. The TASS report mentioned that

There is little question but that the Politburo that selected Gorbachev, to say nothing of the Central Committee that elected him, as General Secretary expected him to be a forward-looking, active younger version of Andropov—a reformer in the limited sense of the term, not someone who soon would seek to transform the party and the country. Gorbachev himself had relatively modest initial ideas on what would be needed, and he muted even those in his words responding to Gromyko's nomination speech to the Politburo on March 11. He spoke of a need for greater "dynamism" in the economy and in foreign policy. And we know he realized substantial changes would be needed. But he still believed in reform and "acceleration" (his slogan for the first year, before it was replaced by *perestroika*). So he reassured his older, conservative colleagues, saying (according to the secret Politburo transcript), "We do not need to change policy. It is correct and it is true. It is genuine Leninist policy. We need,

---

"General Secretary of the Central Committee of the CPSU M. S. Gorbachev took part in the plenum's work," the only change of a regional party leader personally attended by Gorbachev. See "Plenum of the Moscow City Committee of the CPSU," *Pravda*, December 25, 1985.

What actually happened was far more dramatic than indicated by the brief announcement. As early as October, Grishin had attempted to defend himself in the press against charges that dishonest practices in Moscow's housing program had wasted large sums—although he had to admit the program's shortcomings, he himself had not been directly implicated. At the December 24 meeting, he unexpectedly—and initially successfully—fought to retain his position despite clear indications that the Secretariat of the Central Committee had sought his removal. When word of this action reached party headquarters, Gorbachev went at once to the Moscow party committee meeting and delivered a blistering indictment of Grishin's past failures—and expressed his and the new leadership's desire that Grishin be relieved. The Moscow party committee promptly reversed itself and ousted Grishin.

I learned of this event from a well-informed Soviet party source not long after it occurred. It was later confirmed by other sources. The only published account is slightly garbled, its author unaware that Gorbachev was not present when the first vote was taken; see Doder, *Shadows and Whispers*, pp. 300–01.

Grishin was replaced as Moscow party chief by Boris N. Yeltsin, a rising young leader from Sverdlovsk in Siberia. At a closed meeting with Moscow propagandists several months later, Yeltsin (in the interim promoted also to be a candidate member of the Politburo) solicited questions, submitted in writing. One of these reflected the latest antagonism felt by many old-line party machine members. It asked Yeltsin, who was seen as more bold in calling for change and in some respects as Gorbachev's "point man," "What do you think you are up to? Gorbachev simply needed his own man. Go back to Sverdlovsk before it is too late." Reading that question stirred the audience up, with cries of "shame." Yeltsin commented: "Don't worry comrades. I don't think this question comes from anyone in this audience. It was written by a sick person." From a leaked transcript of the meeting, a version of which (with slightly different translation) has been published in the British journal *Détente*; see "Can Moscow Believe in Yeltsin?" *Détente*, no. 7 (Autumn 1986), p. 4. Later, in 1987, Yeltsin went too far in criticizing the current leadership and was removed from the Moscow party post. By 1990, however, he had made a startling comeback outside of the party organization and was chairman of the Supreme Soviet of the Russian Republic.

however, to accelerate, to move forward, to disclose shortcomings and overcome them and realize our shining future."[24]

Gorbachev's highest priority in his first year in office was thus consolidation of his power and that of his "forward-thinking" allies in the new leadership. Closely related was preparation for the party congress, which was scheduled for February–March 1986.[25] Besides Gorbachev's report of the Central Committee to the congress, work had been under way since 1981 on a revision of the party program, unchanged since 1961 and badly in need of revision. This offered a unique opportunity for setting the party's line on basic ideological as well as policy lines for the intermediate and long term. Thus Gorbachev and his colleagues in the new leadership had an opportunity to shape the framework for policy for years ahead. Apart from these focal points for development during the first year ahead, the need to deal with growing social malaise, economic stagnation, and technological lag was increasingly urgent. "Acceleration," and later "reformation" (*perestroika*, more literally, "restructuring"), became the keynotes of this new policy approach. Internal affairs were thus unavoidably central to the attention of the new leadership.

Foreign policy could not, however, be ignored. For one thing, many of the principal internal problems were inseparable from external policy: What were the opportunities, and dangers, in increased foreign economic relations? Could the continuing heavy allocations of resources to the military (and especially of scientific-technological talent) be reduced, with arms control and force reductions, or would they need to be increased to meet a threat? Could the Soviet Union retrench on its commitments around the world, or did it need to expand them? Such questions concerned Soviet decisions on possible initiatives, but also on reactions and responses in an increasingly interdependent world.

In his first brief statement on foreign policy, on the day of his accession, the new general secretary reiterated the familiar overall framework of Soviet policy: strengthening the socialist community (the Soviet-led bloc, and China), supporting peoples' liberation and progressive development (in the

---

24. Remnick, *Lenin's Tomb*, pp. 519–20. The word "policy" instead of "politics" is used after "Leninist," and the word "accelerate" is used in place of "speedup" in variant translations changed here to accord with usage elsewhere.

25. In accordance with the party statutes, the interval between party congresses should not exceed five years, and that had been the practice for the past twenty-five years. It was, however, possible to hold a congress in less than five years. During the latter part of 1984, there were reports that the next congress might be held in 1985, and even that Chernenko, already ailing, might retire. No public announcement was ever made, and the reports have not been confirmed, but if that was the tentative plan it was abandoned in order to give Gorbachev a full year to prepare for "his" congress, in making personnel changes and otherwise.

   When the date of the Twenty-seventh Party Congress was set in April 1985, the opening date was February 25, 1986—coincidentally or otherwise, precisely the thirtieth anniversary of Khrushchev's secret speech denouncing Stalin's crimes.

Third World), and peaceful coexistence and détente with the capitalist powers (the United States, Western Europe, and Japan).[26] 

Soviet relations with the United States were addressed promptly by both governments. The start of the new arms control negotiations had earlier been scheduled for March 12. The United States offered to delay the opening, out of respect for Chernenko's passing, but the Soviet leadership preferred to proceed without delay. President Reagan decided not to attend Chernenko's funeral, but Vice President George Bush and Secretary of State Shultz represented the United States and also met with Gorbachev. The White House also disclosed that Bush was conveying an invitation from Reagan for a summit meeting.[27] Although Gorbachev did not accept the invitation on the spot (as he did with a similar invitation from France's President François Mitterrand), Bush said he was hopeful and that "if there ever was a time when we can move forward with progress in the last few years, I would say this is a good time."[28] Upon their return, Secretary Shultz spoke of "an opportunity for high-level dialogue," and said that the president believed it to be "a potentially important moment for U.S.-Soviet relations."[29]

President Reagan displayed his interest in a summit meeting in a series of statements in March. On March 14, even before Bush and Shultz returned, he had stated that he believed the Soviet leaders were in "a different frame of mind" about arms control and were "really going to try" to negotiate an agreement, although he attributed this willingness to the effect of the American military buildup, and he lobbied for the MX in the same remarks.[30] In a major

---

26. "Speech of Comrade M. S. Gorbachev, General Secretary of the Central Committee of the CPSU at the Plenary Meeting of the Central Committee of the CPSU on March 11, 1985," *Pravda*, March 12, 1985.

    Gorbachev, in contrast to his predecessor a year earlier, received all six Warsaw Pact leaders when they were in Moscow for the funeral. On April 26, Gorbachev's first major foreign treaty action, as previously planned, was signing a renewal of the Warsaw Pact for another twenty years.

27. President Reagan and his top advisers considered his attendance at the funeral but decided instead to offer the summit meeting. The president did personally visit the Soviet Embassy in Washington to present his condolences. In his decision to propose a summit, Reagan was influenced by Prime Minister Margaret Thatcher's favorable impression of Gorbachev from his visit to London, and by the feeling he was more than an interim leader with a "caretaker" mandate.

    Bush and Shultz had a very favorable impression of Gorbachev, as a serious, confident, and capable leader. See Shultz, *Turmoil and Triumph*, pp. 528–33; and Don Oberdorfer, *The Turn: From the Cold War to a New Era* (Poseidon Press, 1991), pp. 109–11.

28. "Vice President's Visit to Moscow: News Conference, Moscow, March 13, 1985," *State Bulletin*, vol. 85 (May 1985), p. 18.

29. "The Secretary: News Conference of March 15," ibid., vol. 85 (May 1985), p. 32.

30. "Magazine Publishers Association," March 14, 1985, *Presidential Documents*, vol. 21 (March 18, 1985), p. 301.

speech in Quebec, Canada, a few days later he declared: "We're ready to work with the Soviet Union for more constructive relations," and added, "We all want to hope that last week's change of leadership in Moscow will open up new possibilities for doing this."[31] And a few days later he said he thought it was "high time" that the two countries held a summit to improve relations.[32]

At the same time, Reagan not only reaffirmed assertive American positions and stressed the need for defense efforts, especially the MX missile, but he also renewed charges of Soviet violation of political and arms control agreements in the past from Yalta and the Helsinki Accord to SALT II and the ABM Treaty, claiming that "the Soviet record of compliance with past agreements has been poor."[33] And in this same address in Quebec, Reagan raised the banner of freedom movements in Afghanistan, Cambodia, Angola, Ethiopia, and especially Nicaragua. "The weight of the world," he said, "is struggling to shift away from the dreary failures of Communist oppression into the warm sunlight of genuine democracy and human rights."[34]

Soon thereafter he did say in an impromptu exchange that a summit meeting would be an appropriate time to discuss "mutual suspicions" about violations of arms control treaties, and he acknowledged that apparent violations were sometimes caused by differing interpretations. But these more measured comments on the question of compliance with arms control were not even officially published, and in any case they came too late to take the sharp edge off his strong public charges in Quebec.[35] *Pravda* had promptly asked: "Why did the President of the United States need to repeat such vicious and utterly groundless anti-Soviet fabrications at this precise moment? The answer is plain. The American president's statement is anything but a gratuitous emotional outburst; it is a considered move aimed at eliciting a specific political reaction: for example, casting a shadow over the progress of the Geneva talks, and giving advance 'justification' for the firmness of the U.S. position, especially on the question of 'Star Wars' calculated to militarize space; hampering the attainment of any accords with the Soviet Union that might improve the international atmosphere and serve to reduce the nuclear threat; breathing new life into circles hostile to the Soviet Union; and last, but not least, quelling

---

31. "Quebec City, Canada," March 18, 1985, ibid., vol. 21 (March 25, 1985), p. 322.

32. "The President's News Conference of March 21, 1985," ibid., p. 343.

33. "Quebec City, Canada," ibid, p. 322. In his Quebec speech, Reagan also distorted history to claim a Soviet interest in deploying ABM systems.

34. Ibid, p. 323.

35. See Hedrick Smith, "Reagan Suggests a Meeting in Fall," *New York Times*, March 26, 1985, p. A5. The remarks, in a breakfast session with reporters, were not published in the comprehensive official *Presidential Documents*.

hopes both in the United States and around the world for normalization of Soviet-U.S. relations."[36]

Nonetheless, the first reported meeting of the Politburo after Gorbachev's accession, on March 21, declared Soviet readiness to pursue détente with the Western countries, including the United States.[37] On that same day Foreign Minister Gromyko also received American Ambassador Arthur Hartman, and a Soviet trade delegation arrived in the United States. On March 24, Gorbachev wrote the first of what would be many private letters to President Reagan, expressing interest in a summit meeting.[38]

At this juncture a tragic incident occurred, placing a new tension on American-Soviet relations. On March 24, Major Arthur D. Nicholson, Jr., a member of the U.S. Military Liaison Mission in East Germany, was shot and killed while surreptitiously photographing Soviet military matériel through the window of a tank garage in a Soviet military facility. The legal issue turned on whether the facility was a posted, restricted-access area, as the Soviets claimed, or not, as the Americans claimed.[39] It was the first time in years that a military liaison officer was shot and killed, but the aggressive, semiallowed military reconnaissance activities of the respective Soviet, American, British, and French liaison teams had caused many incidents over the years. Shots had been fired in some cases; cars had been rammed. In 1984 a French observer was killed when his vehicle was rammed by an East German military truck. In 1982 a Soviet officer had been seriously injured when he was deliberately run down by an American vehicle in West Germany.

The Soviet Union promptly issued a statement expressing regret but placing responsibility on the American side. The United States charged that the Soviet action was "totally unjustified." Assistant Secretary of State Richard

---

36. T. Kolesnichenko, "Who Is This Intended for?" *Pravda*, March 21, 1985.

37. "In the Politburo of the CC CPSU," *Pravda*, March 21, 1985. Brief selective accounts of Politburo meetings were published regularly in *Pravda* after 1983.

38. See Shultz, *Turmoil and Triumph*, p. 534.

39. The agreement under which the Military Liaison Missions operated, the Huebner-Malinin Accord of 1947, allowed general freedom of travel in occupation zones of the other side, although it did forbid entry into "places of disposition of military units without escort or supervision," such areas normally indicated by posted restricted-area signs. It is curious that the Soviets would have failed to restrict access to a tank depot that had new technology material, but Major Nicholson may have thought he had found a loophole. Only three months earlier, incidentally, Nicholson had successfully carried out a daring exploit by penetrating another tank shed and photographing the interior of a Soviet tank during a New Year's Eve celebration by Soviet troops. See James M. Markham, "Slain U.S. Major Had One Exploit," *New York Times*, April 24, 1985, p. A7. On this occasion, he was trying to photograph new reactive tank armor on a T-72 tank.

Burt, who had contributed to the hasty American charges in the KAL incident in 1983, again said the Soviet action was tantamount to murder, and Secretary Weinberger immediately likened the incident to the KAL case, while other State Department officials said, "We're trying to avoid turning this into another KAL affair."[40] This time, President Reagan took the lead in curbing the impact of outrage on policy. He said that rather than making him unwilling to have a summit meeting with Gorbachev, the incident made him "more anxious to go to one."[41] He also wrote privately to Gorbachev, condemning the Nicholson incident but explicitly reconfirming interest in a summit meeting.[42]

On March 30, Secretary Shultz discussed the matter with Ambassador Anatoly Dobrynin. Shultz sought talks by the American and Soviet military commanders in Germany to work out arrangements to prevent such incidents in the future, and the Soviets agreed. On April 12 General Glenn K. Otis, and General Mikhail M. Zaitsev, the Soviet commander in Germany, met and agreed on some guidelines.[43] On April 16 the State Department released a joint

---

40. The pattern of the Nicholson incident does bear some similarity with the KAL incident, although in a different way than these comparisons implied. The precipitating factor was an external initiative (Major Nicholson's aggressive reconnaissance probing, and a deep incursion by a foreign aircraft) prompting a Soviet reaction, not a Soviet initiative. In both cases the Soviet reaction was excessive use of force resulting in tragic death. The Western (above all American) response was outrage, unleashing sharp, hostile, anti-Soviet indictment. The Soviets brazened it out, denying any fault and charging the other side with responsibility. That reaction fueled American indictment and punitive posture. The American perception of complete Soviet blame obscured such facts as the still unexplained deep incursion of the KAL plane into sovereign Soviet airspace and Soviet nonidentification of the intruder as a civilian airliner, or the risky intrusive nature of Major Nicholson's intelligence collection effort. The Soviet public reaction of injured innocence was accompanied by insistence of American blame and, in the case of the KAL, provocative intent.

    Nonetheless, after the KAL incident several Soviet air defense commanders were quietly sacked because the Soviet standard operating procedures and firm identification of the intruder had not been met. According to an unconfirmed report circulating in East Germany the Soviet sentry who shot Major Nicholson was court-martialed for not firing warning shots (that the Soviets had publicly claimed were fired). But neither side would admit any error in contributing to the undesired outcome, especially once the issue was promptly joined as a political confrontation.

41. For a roundup of reportage, including the reactions cited in this paragraph, see Bernard Gwertzman, "U.S. Plans to Seek Closer Soviet Ties in Spite of Slaying," *New York Times*, March 27, 1985, pp. A1, A11. The president's statement is in "Death of Major Arthur D. Nicholson, Jr., in the German Democratic Republic," March 25, 1985, *Presidential Documents*, vol. 21 (April 1, 1985), p. 363.

42. Shultz, *Turmoil and Triumph*, pp. 537–38.

43. This was the first time the two commanders had met. Earlier intermittent contacts between American and Soviet commanders, most sustained in the late 1970s, had been cut off by Washington as a political gesture after Afghanistan in 1980. Subsequent requests by General Otis's predecessor, General Frederick J. Kroesen, and by Otis to

statement worked out in Washington that indicated that the Soviet general had agreed that the Soviets would "not permit use of force or weapons against the members of our U.S. military liaison mission in the future." This reflected, but also distorted, the Soviet position and led to a Soviet public clarification that although indeed they agreed not to use force against members of the liaison missions, they reserved the right to use force if necessary against "unknown intruders."[44]

In retaliation for the incident, the United States expelled a Soviet army attaché in Washington, canceled a planned National War College visit to the Soviet Union, canceled official participation in a celebration of the fortieth anniversary of the linkup of the American and Soviet armies at Torgau in Germany in 1945, instructed Ambassador Hartman and the U.S. defense attachés in Moscow not to attend the military parade honoring V-E Day, and decided not to invite Soviet astronauts to a tenth anniversary celebration of the joint space flight of 1975. Furthermore, Secretary Weinberger, who consistently took a much more strongly negative stance than other administration leaders, in June curtailed the planned program for the scheduled U.S.-USSR naval meeting on incidents at sea, despite strong opposition from the U.S. Navy and the State Department and without White House clearance. In response the Soviets declined to attend, impinging on an agreement that had been signed while the United States was blockading Hanoi in 1972 and had not previously been interrupted even after the KAL incident.

These retaliatory measures were, however, regarded as insignificant and insufficient by hard-line anti-Soviet elements ranging from some members of the National Security Council (NSC) staff to conservative senators and columnists. Moreover, as in the case of the KAL, virtually no members of Congress were disposed to place themselves in jeopardy by appearing "soft" toward the Soviet Union on an incident involving an American death. On April 28, the House voted 394–2 to condemn the Soviet "murder" of Nicholson as inconsistent with the 1947 agreement on liaison missions, and on May 9 for good measure (in another "throw-away" vote for the record that they knew would not be implemented) by a 322–93 vote urged the president to declare the Soviet ambassador to the United States persona non grata unless the Soviet leadership formally apologized for the incident. Both measures died in the Senate.

Secretary Weinberger worked hardest to keep the Nicholson incident alive. Six months later he was still denouncing the Soviets for failure to apolo-

---

revive the contact had been turned down by the Department of Defense. The Soviet side throughout was prepared for such contacts and had earlier taken the initiative in reviving them in 1973 during the blossoming of détente.

    See also Shultz, *Turmoil and Triumph*, p. 535, on Weinberger's objection to any contact.

44. For a good account, see Gary Lee, "U.S., Soviets Dispute Shooting," *Washington Post*, May 14, 1985, p. A16.

gize, on the occasion of a special ceremony granting a rare posthumous promotion to lieutenant colonel to the late Nicholson. Two subsequent accidents involving Soviet and American military vehicles in July and September were briefly blown up by Weinberger before being acknowledged as simple accidents.[45]

The reactions to the Nicholson incident, visceral as well as considered, illustrate how brittle and tenuous the state of relations between the two countries had become.

---

45. On July 16 the Defense Department spokesman disclosed an incident three days earlier in which an American military vehicle was run into ("rammed," in the first account) by a Soviet vehicle. Weinberger commented that "we're extremely concerned about what appears to be the continuing nature of these episodes" and hinted that it was very "puzzling" how the accident could have occurred "unless it was intentional," although State Department officials at the same time said that available information strongly suggested reckless driving. See "U.S. Vehicle Is Hit in East Germany," *New York Times*, July 17, 1985, p. A10. (By curious coincidence, the driver of the American Land Rover was Sergeant Jessie Schatz, who had also been Major Nicholson's driver on March 24. The U.S. officer involved, Colonel Roland Lajoie, as a brigadier general three years later was made chief of the On-site Inspection Agency established to monitor the INF Treaty.)

   The American and Soviet military commanders met and easily resolved the issue. Within several days the Defense Department admitted that the collision was accidental. See "East Germany Crash Resolved," *New York Times*, July 24, 1985, p. A4. General Otis later commented, "It was quite obvious that the Soviets did not know who was in the [U.S.] vehicle," and that the Soviet military accepted that the accident was the fault of their driver, who had been severely disciplined. See "U.S. General Cites Soviet Assurances on Observers," *New York Times*, August 9, 1985, p. A5.

   On September 15, on "Face the Nation" national television, Secretary Weinberger suddenly disclosed yet another incident in which he claimed a Soviet military vehicle had deliberately bumped an American military vehicle to make it stop and then, when the driver got out to fix the truck, was held at gunpoint for hours and claimed that the Soviets "behaved in the same way in which they did in the incident in which Major Nicholson was killed and murdered." In fact, there had been an administration decision not to make the incident public because many of the facts were not yet clear. Weinberger's facts were largely an invention: the American military vehicle had gotten stuck and become ensnared in barbed wire near a Soviet communication installation. A Soviet military truck came along later at high speed and grazed the U.S. vehicle. Then the Soviet soldiers prevented the American occupants from leaving, but not at gunpoint, until a Soviet officer arrived, who verified their status. They then departed without incident. The Soviet side also promptly telephoned the American military mission headquarters and provided a detailed account and assurances that there was no problem. See Bernard Gwertzman, "U.S. Tones Down Version of East German Incident," *New York Times*, September 17, 1985, p. A12. It was not the Soviet side, but Weinberger, who behaved as he had in the Nicholson case. Several days later he defiantly repeated the word "intentional," even as he muttered inconsistently that "driver training is clearly indicated." See Bill Keller, "Bar More Russians, Weinberger Says," *New York Times*, September 20, 1985, p. A3.

Thus in the first few weeks after the accession of Gorbachev to leadership there were mixed indications of American policy interest. The president had signaled interest in a summit and stayed with that through the Nicholson incident. The president, however, had also personally resumed crusading rhetoric, charges of Soviet untrustworthiness, and reaffirmations of his SDI (in several addresses, including at Quebec). Moreover, there were clearly elements within the administration as well as outside of it who were only too eager to exploit the Nicholson case and any other incident to argue against any improvement in relations.

In his first public reaction to earlier American expressions of interest in a summit, Gorbachev used the vehicle of an interview in *Pravda* to disclose that there had been correspondence between the president and himself on the subject and that "both sides" had expressed a "positive attitude." Accordingly, the question was not whether, but when, and "time and place will be the subject of subsequent agreement." He also disclosed that the correspondence dealt more broadly with "finding joint ways of improving relations between the USSR and the United States, and giving them a more stable and constructive character." And he said he was "convinced that a serious impulse should be given to Soviet-American relations at a high political level," not only through meetings but by seeing that "the policies of the USSR and the United States are oriented not toward hostility and confrontation, but toward the search for mutual understanding and peaceful development." "Confrontation," he stressed, "is not an inborn defect in our relations. It is, rather, an anomaly. There is no inevitability that it should remain. We regard the improvement of Soviet-American relations not only as extremely necessary, but also as possible."[46]

Gorbachev acknowledged, "The relations between the USSR and the United States are an exceptionally important factor in international politics," although he commented that "we are far from viewing the world only through the prism of these relations." As to the current prospect, he said that "there is no simple answer. Some things give a basis for hope, but as before there is more than a little that raises alarm. . . . On the whole, relations remain tense." He noted the resumption of arms talks as positive but stressed that it remained to be seen whether they would lead to an agreement.[47]

Finally, Gorbachev used the same occasion to advance the first of a long series of unilateral arms control initiatives. He announced a six-month unilateral moratorium on deployment of intermediate-range missiles in Europe; if the United States joined, it would become permanent. This was not an attractive proposition to the United States and NATO since the Soviet Union had probably completed its own deployment, while NATO was still in the early

---

46. "Interview of M. S. Gorbachev with an Editor of the Newspaper *Pravda*," *Pravda*, April 8, 1985.

47. Ibid.

stages of its deployment. Ten days later, Gorbachev proposed a moratorium on all nuclear weapon testing, which the United States quickly rejected.

On April 10 Gorbachev received a visiting congressional delegation headed by Congressman Thomas P. (Tip) O'Neill, speaker of the House of Representatives. O'Neill conveyed a new letter and invitation from Reagan for a summit meeting. After the four-hour meeting, the Soviets released a partial account of Gorbachev's remarks, including the statement that "the world situation is disquieting, even dangerous, and a kind of ice age is being seen in relations between the USSR and the United States (at least until recently)," but that a real improvement could be made if both sides showed real "political will," and the Soviet side for its part had such will.[48]

On April 23, Gorbachev addressed a particularly important plenary meeting of the Central Committee, outlining for the first time his program for Soviet internal and foreign policy. For several years after that, references would be made to "the April plenum" (no one needed to ask of which year) as the turning point and a new starting point for a wide range of new lines of action. Among the new policy lines initiated at the plenum (but not made public) were a decision to reactivate a wide range of arms control and disarmament issues, a decision to make military doctrine more defensive and to limit the armed forces by criteria of sufficiency, and recognition of the need to disengage Soviet military forces from Afghanistan. These and other changes required further study and decisions on implementation, but a new approach to resolving them was taken at the April plenum.

The April plenum also formally announced the convening the next February of the forthcoming Twenty-seventh Party Congress, which would adopt a new revised party program for the first time in a quarter of a century.

Gorbachev reaffirmed the basic lines of foreign policy, for example, peaceful coexistence and détente, but often with a new twist—in that case, calling also for "civilized relations" between states.[49] It remained to be seen whether such rhetorical innovations portended changes in policy and action, but they certainly aroused expectations in the Soviet Union, and to a much lesser extent abroad.

While the Reagan administration had entered office with a high priority, at least in policy rhetoric, on disciplining Soviet global behavior, Gorbachev now maintained that moving beyond minimal peaceful coexistence to cooperation meant reining in the Reagan Doctrine. He argued that "civilized relations"

---

48. "Meeting of M. S. Gorbachev with the Speaker of the House of Representatives of the U.S. Congress," *Pravda*, April 11, 1985. On background and congressional reactions, see Seth Mydans, "Gorbachev, Receiving O'Neill, Urges U.S. to End 'Ice Age' in Ties," *New York Times*, April 11, 1985, p. A13.

49. "On the Convening of the 27th Congress of the CPSU and the Tasks Related to Its Preparation and Conduct, Speech of General Secretary of the CC CPSU M. S. Gorbachev," *Pravda*, April 24, 1985.

meant relations "based on genuine respect for the norms of intentional law." Beyond that, "It must be absolutely clear," he said, "that only if imperialism renounces attempts to resolve the historic contest between the two social systems by military means can international relations successfully be directed into a channel of normal cooperation." He assailed "claims by the United States of a 'right' to interfere everywhere," citing Grenada and Nicaragua. He also contended that there had been an intensification of imperialist subversive activity against socialist states in all spheres: political, economic, ideological, and military.

"The complexity of the international situation, the acuteness of tension, requires us to continue to give top priority to foreign policy matters."

Nonetheless, he reported that the Politburo, underlining that he was making a consensus statement of the leadership, believed that the agreements of "the period of détente" had not lost their significance and could still be built upon. In speaking of relations with the United States, "There is," he contended, "no fatal inevitability of confrontation of the two countries." Considering past successes and failures in relations between the two powers, he concluded that "the most rational thing is to look for ways to smooth out relations, to build a bridge of cooperation, but to build it from both sides."

Finally, in current affairs he reported that the first round of the new nuclear arms talks in Geneva had "given grounds for concluding that Washington was not following a course directed at agreement," in particular by not addressing the part of the earlier mandate concerning "the prevention of extending the arms race into space." He cautiously expressed the hope that the current American position would be "corrected" and reaffirmed Soviet readiness to reach mutually acceptable agreements.[50]

As the new Soviet leadership team headed by Gorbachev began to establish its position and to outline policy positions, the U.S. administration was in some disarray over its policy toward the Soviet Union. Notwithstanding the president's invitation to Gorbachev to attend a summit meeting, proffered without conditions, on April 8 the State Department spokesman said that "much serious work" was needed before such a meeting, and that a summit meeting must be "carefully prepared"—a qualification that had been used in the past to fend off suggestions for a summit meeting.[51] The White House chief of staff, Donald Regan, followed by saying, "We've always felt that there should be a lot of groundwork and an agenda set before any meeting between the leaders."[52] The next day National Security Adviser Robert McFarlane sought to

50. Ibid.

51. Bernard Gwertzman, "U.S. Renews Stress on Advance Plans for Summit Talks," *New York Times*, April 9, 1985, pp. A1, A10.

52. Gerald M. Boyd, "Reagan Aide Says an Agenda Must Precede Summit Talks," *New York Times*, April 10, 1985, pp. A1, A9.

clarify the admitted "ambiguity" in the U.S. position by distinguishing between "a meeting," which the president would welcome, and a full-fledged "summit meeting," which might take longer to prepare.[53]

At this juncture, with evident uncertainty and apparent disharmony, the U.S. government undertook in a series of meetings in the second half of April an unprecedented overall review of its policy toward the Soviet Union. Besides an effort to dispel the disarray, the change in leadership in Moscow and changed priorities in the White House led to this review. More precisely, the evaluation was intended to prepare for a meeting of Secretary Shultz with Foreign Minister Gromyko (set for May 14 in Vienna), to assess the first round in the arms talks (which ended with no visible progress on April 23), to provide guidance for an initial visit by Secretary of Commerce Malcolm Baldrige to Moscow (on May 21, ending a seven-year hiatus in such visits), and above all because the president was now for the first time thinking seriously of a summit meeting later in the year.

Secretary Shultz coincidentally published an article, "New Realities and New Ways of Thinking," in the journal *Foreign Affairs*, reflecting the fact that he had been seeking for more than a year to put relations on a more stable and productive, if still tough and cautious, path. Shultz proposed firmly resisting any Soviet encroachments, while holding open the door for constructive possibilities. In language similar to Kissinger's in the heyday of détente, he argued that the United States could gain not only a constructive relationship but also leverage "from creating objective realities that give the Soviets a growing stake in better relations with us across the board"—but then, instead of stressing incentives, or a mix of carrots and sticks as in the 1970s, he identified political, alliance, and military strength as the source of these objective realities and leverage.[54]

May 8, 1985, was the fortieth anniversary of the Allied victory over Nazi Germany. It provided (as Gorbachev had suggested in his first brief speech as the new party leader as early as March 11) an opportunity for the leaders of the two powers to find at least an historical accord, and Reagan and Gorbachev did exchange brief messages that recalled the wartime collaboration. Ambassador Hartman was also permitted to publish an article on the occasion. As noted earlier, Hartman did not, however, attend the victory parade ceremony because of the incident involving the death of Major Nicholson (and, for the same reason, American officials boycotted a joint Soviet-American ceremony at Torgau, Germany, two weeks earlier celebrating the wartime meeting of the two Allied armies).

53.  Gerald M. Boyd, "U.S. Aide Endorses Russian 'Meeting', If Not a 'Summit'" *New York Times*, April 11, 1985, pp. A1, A12.

54.  George P. Shultz, "New Realities and New Ways of Thinking," *Foreign Affairs*, vol. 63 (Spring 1985), pp. 705–21, quotation from p. 708.

During a visit to Western Europe, President Reagan recalled four earlier proposals for reducing tensions: improved military crisis communication links, meetings of leading defense officials, a nonuse-of-force declaration, and exchanging observers at military exercises.[55] It became known that Shultz would raise these points with Gromyko at their meeting, but Reagan raised them publicly first (on National Security Adviser McFarlane's recommendation) to give the president direct credit for an initiative it was hoped would offset Gorbachev's unilateral moratorium on INF missile deployment (on April 7) and proposed bilateral moratorium on nuclear testing (announced April 17).

As far as the Soviets were concerned, Reagan's rehash of peripheral confidence-building measures was seen as an attempt to distract attention from American marching in place on the strategic and space weapons negotiations. Moreover, the speech in which they were advanced, to the European Parliament at Strasbourg on the occasion of V-E Day, not only contained sharp attacks on the Soviet Union and actions attributed to it but also failed even to mention the Soviet Union as one of the wartime Allies.[56]

The Shultz-Gromyko meeting on May 14 was not very successful. The occasion for their getting together was the thirtieth anniversary of the Austrian State Treaty, one of the signal agreements in the thawing of the Cold War that followed Stalin's death. Both Shultz and Gromyko drew from that earlier experience encouragement for eventual agreement after long, patient negotiation, but there was little in their exchanges to provide encouragement. Neither side budged on the arms control issues, above all on space weapons (the American SDI). And neither wanted to appear too eager in taking the initiative to firm up a summit. Indeed Gromyko droned on for hours in a manner of negotiating behavior with which he was most familiar but which annoyed

---

55. "Address to a Special Session of the European Parliament," May 8, 1985, *Presidential Documents*, vol. 21 (May 13, 1985), p. 607.

56. Ibid.

    The Soviets were not the only ones offended. During President Reagan's speech he was booed, and many members walked out, over his intemperate criticisms of the Soviet Union ("arbitrary use of lethal force" against KAL 007 and "murder" of Major Nicholson) and idealization of American motivations (prompting cries of "Nicaragua"). Ibid., pp. 604–08.

    There had, in fact, been considerable infighting in the White House over the speech. An original draft by Patrick Buchanan had been even more rousing (more appropriate for delivery to "the American Legion in Philadelphia" than to the European Parliament in the off-the-record words of one official). McFarlane, Assistant Secretary Burt at State, and Michael Deaver sought to make the speech more "presidential" and more akin to a lofty address on postwar Europe. The upshot was that Donald Regan oversaw the later drafting, inserting McFarlane's reference to the four measures but keeping much of the hard-line rhetoric as well. See the well-informed account by Lou Cannon, "Reagan Aides Clash Over Europe Speech," *Washington Post*, April 30, 1985, pp. A1, A7.

Shultz.[57] (Even more important, Gromyko's old-style approach may also have led Gorbachev to consider reviving Soviet diplomacy with a new minister.)

At the last moment, McFarlane had added himself to the secretary's party (which also included Ambassador Hartman but not Ambassador Dobrynin or any equivalent to McFarlane on the Soviet side). Later information showed that if the Soviet side had announced acceptance of a preliminary or "get-together" summit meeting in New York in the fall, the Americans were prepared to offer some modest concessions on the arms talks (but not on the SDI).[58] The Soviets, however, were seeking substantive negotiation on space weaponry and a substantive summit. So there was no meeting of the minds.[59]

Nonetheless, there were some signs of improving relations. Gorbachev met with Secretary of Commerce Baldrige, saying it was "high time to defrost the potential of Soviet-American cooperation," and Baldrige described his visit not only as restoring high-level trade contacts (for the first time since Afghanistan) but as "part of President Reagan's effort to seek a more constructive working relationship with the Soviet Union."[60] No major new agreements were reached, but a month later a new exchange agreement on agricultural research and technology was signed, replacing one that had begun in 1973 and lapsed in 1980 after Afghanistan.

Periodic talks on regional issues held at the deputy minister-assistant secretary level continued. In February there had been talks on the Middle East, and in May on southern Africa. In June, Afghanistan was the subject of renewed talks (last held in late 1982). While no "breakthroughs" were made, or expected, the continuing quiet political dialogue on regional problems was recognized as useful by both sides. The renewal of these meetings at this time stemmed from a Soviet initiative but had been suggested earlier by President Reagan in his UN address the preceding September.

---

57. This account is based on information I obtained from participants, confirmed in part by Shultz, *Turmoil and Triumph*, pp. 563–64, and see Oberdorfer, *The Turn*, pp. 115–17.

58. The best-informed press account of the U.S. approach was Joseph Kraft, "The Big Two Mark Time," *Washington Post*, May 21, 1985, p. A19. See also Bernard Gwertzman, "No U.S.-Soviet Gain on a Summit Talk," *New York Times*, May 16, 1985, pp. A1, A14.

59. A participant in the meeting has provided a detailed account beyond what has appeared in the press. Shultz opened the discussion with a sharp reproach on the incident involving Major Nicholson's death, followed by strong representations first on imprisoned dissident Anatoly Shcharansky and then on exiled Andrei Sakharov. Then he provided "openings" hinting at a summit, which Gromyko chose to ignore. Gromyko concentrated on the arms talks, in particular calling for negotiations on weapons in space, as agreed on with Shultz in January but studiously avoided by the American delegation in Geneva.

60. See Celestine Bohlen, "'Defrost' Relations Gorbachev Asks, as Trade Talks Open," *Washington Post*, May 21, 1985, pp. A1, A22; and Serge Schmemann, "Trade Gain in Soviet Talks Seen," *New York Times*, May 22, 1985, p. D1.

On the same day that Shultz and Gromyko met, the American delegate at a conference in Ottawa on progress in human rights under the Helsinki CSCE (Conference on Security and Cooperation in Europe) process delivered a stinging indictment of Soviet (and Czechoslovak and Polish) compliance with the human rights provisions of the Helsinki Final Act, and declared that "we believe that performance in the field of human rights is inextricably linked to all aspects of improved bilateral relations." This was essentially a public attack paralleling Shultz's private stand to Gromyko. But the Ottawa political delegate, Richard Schifter, went further. In what was taken as an allusion to the arms control talks, he added that "our people have a right to wonder whether a country that fails to keep its word in matters unrelated to considerations of its security will do so when its security is at stake." A State Department official in Washington, queried on whether the United States was establishing a new condition for progress in arms control, was reported to have explained that the stance taken by the U.S. delegation in the Ottawa forum "did not necessarily follow set policy."[61] American policy still appeared to be in some disarray.

A few days earlier American retired astronaut Thomas P. Stafford quietly called on Ambassador Dobrynin to invite him to a National Academy of Sciences ceremony in July on the tenth anniversary of the joint U.S.-Soviet linkup in space. But the Reagan administration decided not to permit attendance by American officials, except from the National Aeronautics and Space Administration (NASA), because of the Nicholson incident.[62]

In June President Reagan equivocated on the question of whether to abandon the unratified but observed SALT II Treaty. He finally announced on June 10 steps that would leave the United States in compliance (deactivation of another Poseidon submarine), but with a strong hint that this would not necessarily continue. McFarlane openly spoke of later consideration of "options" on future compliance.[63]

In mid-June Reagan, reverting to a crusading anticommunist rhetoric, gave an interview broadcast by Radio Liberty and Radio Free Europe to the peoples of the Soviet Union and Eastern Europe. He not only declared that the United States would "demonstrate that communism is not the wave of the future" and "prevent the further expansion of totalitarianism throughout the world," long standard positions, but he also declared that America would "show the captive nations that resisting totalitarianism is possible." He also commented, "What the peoples of Eastern Europe choose to do to achieve their freedom, of course, is their own decision," but in all he seemed at least to bend

---

61.  See Christopher S. Wren, "U.S. Official Links Arms Control to Soviet Action on Human Rights," *New York Times*, May 16, 1985, p. A14.

62.  See Thomas O'Toole, "U.S. May Boycott Space-Linkup Event," *Washington Post*, May 16, 1985, p. A21.

63.  See Shultz, *Turmoil and Triumph*, pp. 567–70.

the long-standing American avoidance of instigation of open resistance to communist rule.[64]

Some other administration leaders had also sounded a harsh anti-Soviet note. CIA Director William Casey, in a little-noted public speech in May, had taken a very hard line on the Soviet global threat, in particular on the need to extirpate communist (Sandinista) rule in Nicaragua. Not only Afghanistan and Cambodia, but also Nicaragua, Angola, and Ethiopia were described as "occupied territories" responsible for "a holocaust comparable to that which Nazi Germany inflicted." It was vintage Cold War in style and substance: the only course and outcome envisaged was to defeat the communists everywhere.[65] Secretary Weinberger, similarly, at an international meeting of conservatives urged his audience not to be reticent in "spotlighting the inherent evil of the coercive and tyrannical system of our communist adversaries."[66]

Even Undersecretary of State for Political Affairs Michael H. Armacost, speaking in favor of intensified dialogue, argued that "the constraints on the U.S.-Soviet relationship are imposed not only by geopolitical rivalry but by the nature of the Soviet system."[67]

In June, reacting to several espionage cases (discussed later), Washington called for reducing the number of Soviet diplomats in the United States. Separately, the State Department announced plans to reduce the number of Soviet citizens employed by the American Embassy in Moscow.[68]

## Moving to the Summit

Against this less than auspicious drift in events, on July 3 it was announced in Washington and Moscow that President Reagan and General Secretary Gorbachev would meet in Geneva on November 19–20.[69]

64. See John M. Goshko, "Reagan Lashes Communism: Conciliatory Tone Dropped in Broadcast to Soviets, East Europeans," *Washington Post*, June 15, 1985, p. A17. The president's interview was not reproduced in *Presidential Documents*.

65. See Philip Geyelin, "Casey and the 'Focus of Evil' " *Washington Post*, June 17, 1985, p. A11.

66. Joanne Omang, "Weinberger Assails 'Inherent Evil' of Communism," *Washington Post*, July 26, 1985, p. A22.

67. Michael H. Armacost, "Reflections on U.S.-Soviet Relations," May 1, 1985, *State Bulletin*, vol. 85 (August 1985), p. 56.

68. See Ruth Marcus, "Soviet Diplomat Cut Considered," *Washington Post*, June 30, 1985, p. A18; and Joel Brinkley, "U.S. Embassy to Reduce Soviet Staff," *New York Times*, June 25, 1985, p. A3.

    As discussed in chapter 6, a larger wave of expulsions by both sides would occur in October 1986.

69. Shultz notes Dobrynin had conveyed the Soviet agreement on place and date of the summit on July 1; the announcement was then coordinated. Shultz, *Turmoil and Triumph*, p. 571.

Following the May meeting of foreign ministers, the Soviets had proposed a Moscow meeting, the American side proposed Washington, and in due course agreement was reached on Geneva. A firm agenda was not agreed on, and that was the primary focus for a planned meeting of Shultz with the new Soviet foreign minister, Eduard A. Shevardnadze, a party official new to international relations named on July 2 to succeed Gromyko (as the latter became "president," chairman of the Presidium of the Supreme Soviet of the USSR). Incidentally, on the same day that the Soviet-U.S. summit was announced, Moscow also announced a planned Soviet-French summit in France in October, giving second billing to the announcement of the later summit with Reagan.

The Soviet agreement to a summit meeting, without assurance of progress in the arms control negotiations, was not a decision easily reached in Moscow.[70] Divergent assessment of the prospects for change in American policy and possible improvement in U.S.-Soviet relations continued to be expressed in the Soviet political establishment. For example, on the question of continued American military buildup, Georgy Arbatov, director of the Institute of the USA and Canada, and some of his colleagues argued that the deficit and domestic political trends would rein in the administration's military spending.[71] Aleksandr N. Yakovlev, director of the rival Institute of the World Economy and International Relations, argued on the other hand that the hard-line course of the administration, and its military buildup, would continue unabated.[72] Both were full members of the Central Committee.

Again in June, in an interesting three-way roundtable debate, Yakovlev was highly pessimistic on the question of any political trend in the United States toward a more moderate and realistic course, and he argued that the United States and NATO leaders did not even rule out "unleashing war against the

---

70. It is tempting to speculate about the significance of the fact that the Soviet-U.S. summit was announced less than twenty-four hours after Gromyko's departure from his post heading the Ministry of Foreign Affairs. While no doubt both were decided at the same Politburo meeting, there is no evidence that Gromyko opposed the summit, as some have inferred. As earlier suggested, Gorbachev had probably concluded that a more flexible (and less independent) foreign minister was needed.

71. For example, see Georgy A. Arbatov on "Studio 9," Moscow Television, March 30, 1985, in Foreign Broadcast Information Service, *Daily Report: Soviet Union*, April 1, 1985, pp. cc14, 18–20 (hereafter FBIS, *Soviet Union*); and Andrei A. Kokoshin (a deputy director of Arbatov's institute), "Discussions on the Central Questions about U.S. Military Policy," *SShA: Ekonomika, politika, ideologiya* (USA: Economics, Politics, Ideology), no. 2 (February 1985), pp. 3–14. (Hereafter *SShA.*)

72. See Aleksandr Yakovlev, "Sources of the Threat and Public Opinion," *Mirovaya ekonomika i mezhdunarodnyye otnosheniya* (The World Economy and International Relations), no. 3 (March 1985), pp. 3–17. (Hereafter *MEiMO.*)

USSR." Fedor M. Burlatsky, the liberal political observer of the *Literary Gazette*, had challenged Yakovlev's contention that it would be advisable to be patient and wait for a more realistic American leadership. And the third participant in that discussion, first deputy chief of the International Department of the Central Committee Vadim Zagladin, not only argued that the common sense of the American people would prevail but also cited the example of détente under the conservative President Richard Nixon. He rebutted Yakovlev's extreme statement on military intentions and said that "the aim of directly unleashing nuclear war is now hardly part of Western plans."[73]

These divergent views on the prospects for American readiness to work for improved relations, or for controlling the arms race, were a major ingredient in the Soviet decision on whether a summit would be useful and warranted. The most important issue was arms control, and in particular whether—as they saw it—there was American readiness to give up a quest for military superiority through the American advantage in high technology by turning to weapons in space under the guise of a "strategic defense initiative."

On the whole, Soviet commentary was not very sanguine as to the outcome but was guided by the precept that "the risk of causing ourselves disadvantage by moving forward is less than the risk of inaction."[74]

On July 4, the Presidium of the Supreme Soviet sent congratulations to the United States on Independence Day, and Ambassador Hartman was given the opportunity to speak on Soviet television. On July 31, Shultz and Shevardnadze met at Helsinki on the occasion of the tenth anniversary of the signing of the CSCE Final Act. There was, however, little movement in positions.[75] More important was a Soviet initiative on the eve of the meeting, a unilateral moratorium on nuclear testing until the end of the year (later twice extended to the end of next year). The United States promptly declined a proposal to join the nuclear testing moratorium, but the Soviets generated a major campaign on the issue.

The United States decided to counter the burgeoning Gorbachev peace offensive by a rebuttal, rather than competition or engagement. On August 19, in a rare speech by National Security Adviser Robert McFarlane, the White House sought simultaneously to blame lack of success in arms negotiations, and more generally on improving relations, on the Soviet system and appealed to the Soviet leaders to change. Describing the current juncture as one of "considerable flux and introspection in the Kremlin," McFarlane

73.  See V. V. Zagladin, A. N. Yakovlev, and F. M. Burlatsky, "East-West: Civilized Relations. A Necessity? A Reality? A Utopia?" *Literaturnaya gazeta* (Literary Gazette), June 26, 1985.

74.  See G. A. Arbatov, "Prospects for Soviet-American Relations," *SShA*, no. 6 (June 1985), p. 46.

75.  This marked the first meeting of Shultz with Shevardnadze. See Shultz, *Turmoil and Triumph*, pp. 572–74.

stated that the Soviet leaders "deserve to know from whence we are coming if they are to reach coherent decisions. Perhaps by stating some of our frustrations we can shape their thinking. That is my purpose today."[76] And that direct address to the Soviet leaders was indeed the intention (although grounded in an assumption that the Soviets must be the ones to change). He acknowledged that Gorbachev had spoken of a need for a fresh look at shortcomings, but said we could not know whether real change was under way. He then argued that the Soviet Union had been responsible for stirring up arms competition in several areas relatively quiescent theretofore: chemical weapons, medium-range missiles, and even strategic defensive arms. He dismissed Soviet proposals for arms control and reductions in these and other areas as unrealistic. In one of the least controversial comments, he then said in apparent frankness: "In short, we're having a lot of trouble establishing a real dialogue." While reaffirming American readiness to meet the Soviet Union halfway, he went on to say that "without some change in the Soviet approach to security issues, in fact in the thinking that underlies it, I fear that even incremental improvements will be extremely hard to reach." He placed as a litmus test "practical measures," but he lacked precision or even coherence when he went on to explain that "the Soviet leadership should know that we have practical measures like Afghanistan, Cuba and Libya in mind." He expressed American self-confidence by adding that "there should be no doubt about the ability of the United States to deal with these difficulties when they are placed in our way." The problem was that "it makes improvement in other areas more difficult." He then made a pitch for internal change in the Soviet Union. And in conclusion he stated an American readiness "to take small steps forward," oddly coupled with a comment that "those who seek only small improvements often end up with none."[77]

McFarlane's speech was idiosyncratic and opaque. It was interpreted in the American press as pessimistic and drawing a "dark picture."[78] What the Soviets thought it meant is not clear. But actions in the next few days led to a sharper interpretation in the American press: "Reagan's Anti-Summit Arsenal," "U.S. Strategy of Toughness," "An Autumn of Confrontation," "U.S. Signals Hard-Nosed Approach to November Summit Talks."[79] The first measure that

---

76. "U.S.-Soviet Relations in the Late 20th Century," official White House transcript of an address in Santa Barbara by Robert C. McFarlane, August 19, 1985, p. 2.

77. Ibid., pp. 8, 9, 10, 12, 16.

78. See Gerald M. Boyd, "Soviet Must Shift on Major Issues, McFarlane Insists," *New York Times*, August 20, 1985, pp. A1, A11; and David Hoffman, "Reagan Adviser Pessimistic On Arms Control Prospects," *Washington Post*, August 20, 1985, p. A8.

79. Mary McGrory, "Reagan's Anti-Summit Arsenal," *Washington Post*, August 22, 1985, p. A2; Hedrick Smith, "U.S. Strategy of Toughness: A Counter to the Russians," *New York Times*, August 23, 1985, p. A7; and David Hoffman, "An Autumn of Confrontation: U.S. Signals Hard-Nosed Approach to November Summit Talks," *Washington Post*, August 22, 1985, pp. A1, A29.

drew this reaction was a White House announcement that the United States planned an early antisatellite (ASAT) weapon test in space, notwithstanding a unilateral Soviet moratorium on ASAT tests (announced in August 1983 but in effect since 1982). The United States was not interested in an ASAT ban.

On the following day the Department of State announced that the Soviet Union had been using an invisible chemical as an aid in tracking movements of American diplomats in Moscow to check on their contacts with Soviet citizens and that the chemical might be "potentially harmful" to health. "Spy dust," as it was promptly dubbed, was an intriguing new matter. But the American response (to a chemical technique the United States had known about for ten years, and with the possible health hazard uncertain and later definitively disproven) was soon being called "Spy Dust on the Summit Road," as a *New York Times* editorial put it.[80]

Not long after the spy dust episode, a number of espionage cases suddenly surfaced, drawing attention to that shadowy competitive strand of Soviet-American relations. Several cases had arisen earlier in the year, so the effect was a rising crescendo rather than a sudden new outburst. Early in the year it had been revealed that Arkady N. Shevchenko, a senior Soviet diplomat who had defected to the United States seven years earlier, had been an American spy for three years before that. But that was an old case. In March came the titillating trial of an attractive Russian emigré woman in California, Svetlana Ogorodnikov, who had seduced an FBI special agent, Richard W. Miller, into the dubious distinction of becoming the first FBI agent indicted for (and later convicted of) espionage. More significant was the arrest in Moscow in June and later execution of a Soviet engineer, Adolf G. Tolkachev, for spying for the United States, and the expulsion of American Embassy second secretary Paul C. Stombaugh as a CIA agent, when the two were caught red-handed. The full significance of this arrest became known only in September with the successful escape from the United States of a former CIA officer, Edward L. Howard, who had provided the information leading to the arrest of Tolkachev and probably several other American spies in the Soviet Union, as well as damaging disclosure of CIA personnel and techniques in Moscow. Meanwhile, the case of the long-time family spy ring headed by former Navy man John A. Walker, Jr., arrested in May, was being reported in detail.

In September, the United States released a well-grounded intelligence study detailing extensive Soviet technological espionage in the West.[81] Secretary Weinberger used the occasion to call for tighter entry curbs, reducing contacts with Soviet citizens, and reducing the number of Soviet diplomats in the United States to the lower level of American diplomats in the Soviet Union.

---

80.  "Spy Dust on the Summit Road," *New York Times*, August 23, 1985, p. A22.

81.  See *Soviet Acquisition of Militarily Significant Western Technology: An Update* (unattributed [Washington, CIA]), September 1985, 34 pp.

Two other remarkable cases of defection to the West of important Soviet intelligence officers were made public in September. Oleg Gordievsky, the KGB chief in London, had defected (and, in fact, had been spirited out of the Soviet Union) a few months earlier, but his defection became known when in September Britain expelled thirty-one Soviet spies from the country, including the entire twenty-five-man KGB station. At about the same time, the United States made known that on August 1 the deputy chief of a key KGB directorate in Moscow, Vitaly S. Yurchenko, had defected to the United States (while traveling in Italy). It was later disclosed that Yurchenko had tipped the United States off to Howard (and to William Pelton, a former National Security Agency man arrested in November). On November 2, however, Yurchenko slipped away from his CIA escort and redefected to the Soviet Embassy in Washington. Questions were raised as to whether he had been a "plant" and KGB operative feigning defection, although the weight of professional judgment was that he had been a genuine defector who had belated second thoughts and decided to return.[82] Not made public was the fact that two KGB officers then serving in the Soviet Embassy in Washington were secretly reporting to the FBI. One of them, Lieutenant Colonel Valery Martynov, had fallen under suspicion and was returned to Moscow with Yurchenko and then arrested upon his arrival.[83] More generally 1985 was an active year for intelligence and espionage revelations.[84]

---

82. Yurchenko subsequently made several disclosures and charges about alleged American intelligence attempts to exploit him while he was in American custody. He charged that attempts had been made to get him to use forged materials to implicate the Soviet Union in attempted subversion efforts in Central America. Yurchenko also claimed that the CIA attempted to persuade him to bear false witness at the Rome trial of Agca, alleging that as a high Soviet agent he had met Agca and paid him to assassinate the pope. If that charge is true, it would be a serious indictment of the CIA and the United States; if untrue, it would be a clever case of attempted Soviet disinformation. See "Lies Cooked Up by the CIA," *Moskovskaya pravda* (Moscow Pravda), August 9, 1986.

83. See Michael Dobbs and R. Jeffrey Smith, "From Inside the KGB: A Tale of Incompetence," *Washington Post*, February 21, 1993, p. A26.

84. For a sampling: in January the conviction of an American marine for attempting to sell secret information to the Soviet Union was made public; an Indian government spy ring supplying several communist and Western countries was uncovered in January; a Norwegian official was tried as a Soviet spy in February; a senior Soviet military intelligence officer defected in May; in July a CIA staff member in Ghana was arrested for disclosing to that country the names of Ghanaian officials that the United States had recruited as spies; in August a secretary of the president of West Germany was found to be an East German agent; the second-ranking West German counterintelligence officer fled to the East; and an East German spy for West Germany defected to the West. As noted above, Britain expelled thirty-one Soviet diplomats in September. And in the United States, besides the cases cited and disclosure of four other minor Soviet agents, in November a former CIA officer of Chinese ethnic origin, Larry Wu-Tai Chin, was discovered to have been a spy for communist China for thirty years, and a Jewish

These disclosures in the summer and fall in the American media, and to a lesser extent also in the Soviet press, of the espionage activities of the adversaries tended to heighten reciprocal suspicion and fear, even though that response did not impinge directly on the development of state relations.

There were also a number of "normalizing" developments. Secretary of Agriculture John Block visited Moscow in late August. The next month Gorbachev received a congressional delegation including nine senators led by Robert C. Byrd and Strom Thurmond, while Lev N. Tolkunov led a Soviet parliamentary delegation to the United States. In September the range of expert diplomatic talks on regional issues extended for the first time to a meeting on the Far East, and in October on Latin America as well.

In early September Gorbachev laid out his thinking about the summit and the course of Soviet-American relations in an unusually candid interview with *Time* magazine. He stressed the need for "an improvement in our relations, in relations between the two great nations on earth, nations on whom depends the very destiny of civilization," and said, "We will do all in our power to make the summit meeting instrumental in improving relations between the Soviet Union and the U.S."[85]

Gorbachev was, however, pessimistic in his evaluation: "Relations between our two countries are continuing to deteriorate, the arms race is intensifying, and the war threat is not subsiding. What is the matter?" He expressed puzzlement and "disappointment and concern" about why the United States rejected all arms control proposals, and above all seemed so intent on avoiding negotiation to prevent extension of the arms race into space. No doubt he hoped by the interview to influence American opinion, but he evidently also hoped to stimulate thinking on the matter and to present the Soviet viewpoint.[86]

The question of preventing weapons in space (the Soviet proposal) versus the SDI (the Reagan administration's strategic defense program de-

---

American naval intelligence analyst, Jonathan Jay Pollard, was arrested for spying for Israel, to the discomfort of both countries.

During 1985 the KGB also recruited a veteran CIA officer engaged in counterintelligence and knowledgeable about American intelligence operations against the Soviet Union, Aldrich Ames, although that successful penetration of the CIA did not become known until 1994.

85. "An Interview with Gorbachev," *Time*, September 9, 1985, pp. 26, 28. Also "M. S. Gorbachev's Replies to America's *Time* Magazine," *Pravda*, September 2, 1985.

86. *Time*, September 9, 1985, p. 23. Gorbachev's interview, though addressed to Americans, was simultaneously published in *Pravda* and given wide coverage. When the *Time* interviewers gave him an opening to criticize American actions more generally, suggesting that "the U.S. announcement of the ASAT test and the spy dust charges could hardly have been helpful" and asking "is this type of thing seriously damaging?" Gorbachev declined to pick up the criticisms and merely repeated Soviet desire and preparation to make the summit succeed. See ibid., p. 28.

pending on space weapons systems) was clearly the key issue for the strategic arms negotiation and for the summit. On September 19, the Geneva arms talks resumed after a summer recess with a session planned to last until November 6, just before the summit. In preparation for this round of negotiations, on September 16 Gorbachev convened an unusual special meeting with fellow Politburo members Gromyko, Shevardnadze, KGB chief Viktor M. Chebrikov, and Defense Minister Marshal Sergei L. Sokolov, with the three senior Soviet Geneva negotiators. Reagan also had a National Security Council (NSC) meeting on September 13 to review guidance worked out by the senior interagency group headed by McFarlane. The decision in Washington was not to budge on protecting the SDI. Soon after, on September 17, President Reagan in a nationally televised news conference went out of his way to state categorically that he would not curtail the SDI in exchange for Soviet reductions in offensive missiles.[87] Indeed, although the administration had stated that the SDI research and development program would be conducted in full compliance with the ABM Treaty, an unnamed White House "senior official" (McFarlane) in a background briefing two days later claimed that the Soviet "arms buildup" put "very much in question" the value of the ABM Treaty and that "it might be wise" to modify the treaty in the future.[88] A few weeks later, Secretary Weinberger characteristically made a more blunt statement implying that the United States should consider breaking with the ABM Treaty.[89]

The addresses by Secretary Shultz and Foreign Minister Shevardnadze to the UN General Assembly reflected the standoff between the two sides. Shultz expressed in moral-ideological terms the basis for the Reagan Doctrine, saying that "the reality of the democratic revolution" was "demonstrated by the rise of national liberation movements against communist colonialism: in Afghanistan, Cambodia, Angola, and other lands where, as in Nicaragua, people have organized in resistance to tyranny."[90] Shevardnadze in turn criticized as "inadmissible that states of Asia, Africa and Latin America should be regarded as someone else's sphere of 'vital' interests, as an arena for confrontation with

---

87. "The President's News Conference of September 17, 1985," *Presidential Documents*, vol. 21 (September 23, 1985), p. 1101.

88. David Hoffman, "U.S. Aide Says Soviet Buildup Puts ABM Pact 'in Question'" *Washington Post*, September 20, 1985, pp. A1, A24.

89. See "Strategic Defense and American Strategy," October 3, 1985, in *American Foreign Policy, Current Documents, 1985* (Department of State, 1986), pp. 63–67.
    In an internal Department of Defense memorandum on September 5 Weinberger ordered "all personnel, military and civilian" to provide "active" and "timely" support to the SDI as the "highest priority" Defense Department program.

90. "The Charter's Goals and Today's Realities: Secretary Shultz's Address before the UN General Assembly in New York City on September 23, 1985," *State Bulletin*, vol. 85 (November 1985), p. 9.

socialism," and said, "It is not the fault of the Soviet Union that local conflicts break out and are raging in various parts of the world."[91] Shevardnadze dwelt at greater length and with more of a positive thrust on arms control and disarmament issues and came up with a "positive" alternative to space weapons, calling for enhanced peaceful cooperation in space under the slogan "Star Peace." Shultz, speaking first, had dismissed Soviet concerns over the SDI as "propaganda," and said, "So let's get down to real business," implying that weapons in space were not serious business.[92] Both referred to the upcoming summit as an important opportunity, and each promised that his country would do all it could to make the meeting successful. But there was little to suggest any movement toward a meeting of the minds; it looked more like a propaganda duel.[93]

Secretary Shultz and Shevardnadze met on September 26 and again two days later, preceding and following a meeting with President Reagan. Although both sides described the talks publicly as "frank" and "useful," neither moved in its basic positions.[94] In the meeting with Reagan, however, Shevardnadze stressed the need to move on arms reductions and presented a letter from Gorbachev to Reagan that went beyond earlier Soviet offers. He proposed reductions of 50 percent in strategic offensive arms, to a level of 6,000 warheads, accompanied by agreement not to develop, test, or deploy "space-strike weapons." The president was adamant against giving up the SDI. Both the president and Shultz also stressed three other agenda items for the summit: human rights in the Soviet Union, regional conflicts, and bilateral U.S.-Soviet relations, but with no new initiatives on them. Shevardnadze also raised several more peripheral arms control proposals: undertakings not to create, produce, or deploy weapons based on new physical principles equivalent to nuclear weapons; not to deploy nuclear weapons on the territory of any country where they were not already deployed; not to increase military budgets and expenditures; and not to increase the numbers of military forces deployed beyond their national territories.[95]

91. "Address by E. A. Shevardnadze to the 40th Session of the UN General Assembly," *Pravda*, September 25, 1985.

92. *State Bulletin*, vol. 85 (November 1985), p. 12.

93. Although less is known of the specifics of Soviet decisionmaking, the Star Peace initiative, while perhaps sincere, was clearly intended as a propaganda rallying symbol. On the American side, the secretary's theme was directly in line with a White House decision just the day before by the McFarlane-Regan special committee on public diplomacy, charged with conducting propaganda, to stress the "seriousness" of U.S. arms positions and the "propaganda" nature of Soviet ones.

94. The meetings were not relaxed. In the first one, Shultz was accompanied by McFarlane and others and did not meet alone with Shevardnadze, as had usually been the case in meetings of the foreign ministers. Shevardnadze did not disclose what he would be presenting to the president.

95. Information from knowledgeable officials present or privy to the discussions. The main proposals, on 50 percent reductions and space weapons, were reported promptly in the

Shultz accepted an invitation to visit Moscow in early November for further presummit discussions. Meanwhile in October the Soviet delegation laid out its new proposals in specific terms. Gorbachev, visiting Paris on October 3, again drew attention to the intermediate-range missile issue, proposing direct talks with France and Britain over their nuclear missiles,[96] and announcing a unilateral reduction of deployed SS-20 missiles in the European zone to 243, the number there on June 1984 before the Soviets had increased deployments in the wake of the NATO deployment.[97]

American reactions to the proposed 50 percent reduction in strategic offensive arms, coupled with a ban on space weapons, ran the predictable gamut; on the same day, in the same newspaper, Paul C. Warnke contributed an article titled "It Can Be Done," while Norman Podhoretz titled his "Progress Is a Delusion."[98] There was much speculation about whether the president would, by the summit, decide to reach a "grand compromise" involving some significant constraint on weapons in space in exchange for deep reductions in Soviet offensive missiles, a possibility diminished but not fully dispelled by repeated statements by President Reagan and other members of the administration that the SDI was *not* a "bargaining chip."

On November 1, just a few days before Shultz's meeting with Shevardnadze, the United States announced a new proposal (really a counterproposal to Gorbachev's 50 percent reduction plan) for reductions to a series of sublimits on strategic offensive forces of roughly comparable overall reduction, but cutting and constraining Soviet ICBM forces most sharply.

The most significant development affecting the prospects for arms control, not only for reaching new agreements but even for retaining the keystone ABM Treaty, was a unilateral American reinterpretation of a key provision of that treaty. On October 2 six former secretaries of defense: Robert S. McNamara, Clark M. Clifford, Melvin R. Laird, Elliot L. Richardson, James R. Schlesinger, and Harold Brown, called on both the Soviet Union and the

---

press. Shultz in his memoir discussed only the strategic arms reductions, but he did note the good rapport that quickly developed between Reagan and Shevardnadze. Shultz, *Turmoil and Triumph*, pp. 576–77.

96. The proposal for talks with the European nuclear powers received a cool distancing from London and a rejection from Paris.

97. The Soviets had, in fact, withdrawn to inactive storage the 27 SS-20 launchers that they had augmented in the West. The number in the Far East was not changed, at 171 total. The United States continued, however, to speak of a grand total of 441 and to count the Soviet European total as 270, including the 27, right up to the time of accepting the official Soviet accounting in December 1987 when the INF Treaty was signed and the Soviet claim was validated.

98. Paul C. Warnke, "It Can Be Done," and Norman Podhoretz, "Progress Is a Delusion," *Washington Post*, October 6, 1985, p. D8.

United States to "avoid actions that would undermine the ABM Treaty."[99] Paradoxically, only four days later, in a "Meet the Press" television interview, National Security Adviser Robert McFarlane disclosed a new interpretation of a key provision of the ABM Treaty that would permit development and testing, though not deployment, of space-based ABM systems and components— theretofore believed banned by the treaty.[100] This sensational reinterpretation was immediately challenged by negotiators of the treaty and many others (including West German Chancellor Helmut Kohl and Prime Minister Margaret Thatcher of Great Britain, who sent personal letters). Within the administration, Secretary George Shultz objected strongly, and according to some reports, hinted at a threat to resign over the issue. In any case, a week later President Reagan decided on a compromise solution that deferred but did not defuse the issue: Shultz was authorized to state that the administration would continue to limit testing and development of the SDI according to the traditional "restrictive" interpretation of the treaty, even though it had decided that the "broader interpretation" was "fully justified." While not satisfying either side, this outcome calmed the immediate situation. But the administration had made no commitment on how long it would continue to abide by the restrictive interpretation.[101]

Some other developments in U.S.-Soviet relations were more encouraging. In particular, trilateral talks with Japan on cooperative measures to

---

99. "6 Ex-Secretaries of Defense Urge ABM Compliance," *Washington Post*, October 3, 1985, p. A20.

100. Robert C. McFarlane, "Meet the Press," October 6, 1985, transcript pp. 9–10. And see Don Oberdorfer, "White House Revises Interpretation of ABM Treaty," *Washington Post*, October 9, 1985, p. A21, following confirmation on October 8 by a "senior White House official."

    McFarlane had made public this convenient but highly dubious new interpretation before it had been thoroughly considered in the government, and without even having discussed it with President Reagan.

101. See Raymond L. Garthoff, *Policy versus the Law: The Reinterpretation of the ABM Treaty* (Brookings, 1987), for an account of these developments and analysis of the reinterpretation.

    In his memoir, Shultz indicated he was persuaded by Abraham Sofaer, the State Department legal adviser, that the broad interpretation was justified by the record (which Sofaer claimed incorrectly to have read in full), but he was appalled by the way no real decision had been made and engineered the compromise on handling the issue. See Shultz, *Turmoil and Triumph*, pp. 578–82.

    In a classified National Security Decision Directive (NSDD)–192 on October 11, 1985, President Reagan had specified that the restrictive interpretation of the treaty would continue to be applied only as long as the SDI "receives the funding support needed to implement its carefully crafted plan." NSDD-192, "The ABM Treaty and the SDI Program," October 11, 1985, Secret, p. 2. (Declassified August 22, 1990.)

    The Reagan administration's "reinterpretation" of the ABM Treaty was finally formally abandoned by the Clinton administration in July 1993.

enhance airline security in the North Pacific, to prevent further occurrences such as the KAL incident, reached agreement on October 8. Talks were then immediately opened by the United States and the Soviet Union on resumption of bilateral civil air connections.

Similarly, in late October, the Soviets allowed Andrei Sakharov's wife, Yelena Bonner, to travel to the United States for medical treatment, and they permitted a Jewish dissident, Irina Grivnina, and her family to emigrate.

Two other cases arose that directly involved the two countries. On October 24 a young Soviet seaman, Miroslav Medved, jumped into the Mississippi River and was returned to his ship by the Harbor Service. Only after he later was brought ashore and told U.S. officials he had changed his mind and wanted to return to the Soviet Union were the ship and he allowed to depart. A few days later a young Soviet soldier slipped into the grounds of the American Embassy in Kabul, Afghanistan, but he also decided to depart after being given assurances by the Soviet ambassador of no punishment.[102]

In the military sphere the United States seemed to the Soviets to be flexing its muscles. On top of a record military budget, the United States pushed its Pershing II missile deployments ahead of schedule, conducted the first antisatellite test against an object in space (on September 13), and launched a program for production of binary chemical weapons (including exaggerated claims about the Soviet chemical weapons program). Moreover, one American military movement in particular was regarded in the Soviet Union as intentionally provocative. The battleship USS *Iowa* cruised in the Baltic Sea, an unprecedented introduction of an American capital warship (armed with long-range cruise missiles) into that northern European sea. Although undeniably permissible, the Soviets saw the action as designed to place pressure on them before the summit by flaunting American military muscle in their backyard. Nonetheless, agreement was reached in early November to reschedule the annual naval talks on preventing incidents at sea that had been aborted in June by Secretary Weinberger's overreaction to the Nicholson incident. They were now set for mid-November, on the eve of the summit meeting.

The first tests of the new facsimile transmissions on the hot line were made.

As noted earlier, there had been a spate of espionage cases involving the two countries, in particular the spectacular redefection of Vitaly Yurchenko on the eve of Shultz's visit to Moscow. This did not, however, affect the political relationship between the two sides.

On October 24, in his address to the UN General Assembly, Reagan combined a plea for U.S.-Soviet dialogue and disarmament with renewed dedication to the Reagan Doctrine and Star Wars. He called for new arms

---

102. Shultz described both incidents, *Turmoil and Triumph*, pp. 583–85.

limitations, while again charging the Soviet Union with violations of past agreements.[103]

Shultz met with Shevardnadze on October 25 in preparation for his Moscow visit and provided a draft summit communiqué. This draft had been worked out by officers at the State Department and coordinated with the White House NSC staff, but Weinberger and his aides in Defense were still unaware of the draft. When they learned of it a few days later, Weinberger objected so strenuously that Reagan decided it might be better not to have any communiqué, and so instructed Shultz.[104] When Shultz told Dobrynin, he was taken aback.

As Shultz arrived in Moscow, *Izvestiya* printed the text of an interview with four leading Soviet journalists with President Reagan held several days earlier. The president's remarks were published, despite some strong criticisms of the Soviet Union; they were accompanied by a rebuttal by the journalists.[105] The airing in the Soviet media of frank and critical American views, above all by the president, was to some extent a further sign of the new "openness" of the Gorbachev leadership, and of its readiness to argue for its positions rather than merely to assert positions while withholding information on which they could be judged.[106] (Similarly, on November 9, a speech by Reagan addressed to the Soviet people, although not broadcast on Soviet radio or television and not given publicity, was not jammed.) Soviet commentary on Reagan's *Izvestiya* interview, while reiterating refutations of his position, also struck a positive note: "At the same time, it would be incorrect not to note the good things said by the president, about the fact that despite the differences in our systems we

---

103. "Address before the 40th Session of the General Assembly," October 24, 1985, *Presidential Documents*, vol. 21 (October 28, 1985), pp. 1291–96.

104. Shultz, *Turmoil and Triumph*, pp. 596–97; and Oberdorfer, *The Turn*, pp. 151–52.

105. "Interview with the U.S. President," *Izvestiya*, November 5, 1985; and G. Shishkin, V. Ovchinnikov, S. Kondrashov, and G. Borovik, "Apropos of R. Reagan's Interview," *Izvestiya*, November 5, 1985.

106. Besides prepared replies to written questions, President Reagan gave off-the-cuff replies to additional questions, providing a more lively exchange but unfortunately making many ill-prepared, incorrect, and even incredible comments. This provided opportunity for effective rebuttal by the Soviet journalists in their accompanying commentary. For example, Reagan claimed that the Soviet Union was "occupying" Angola, Ethiopia, and South Yemen; that the government of Grenada had asked for U.S. military assistance; that two Vietnamese states had been created by the 1954 Geneva Conference; that the United States had escalated its military involvement in Vietnam because U.S. military instructors were harassed by bombs in movie theaters and the like until they had to arm themselves for their own self-defense; that the Soviet strategic arsenal was "greatly superior to ours"; that "we have decided to supply weapons to neither side" in Angola (in his prepared statement); that the Soviet Union had first developed and tested an antisatellite system; and yet other invalid statements that the Soviet correspondents refuted.

must live in peace, that in a nuclear war there can be no victor, and that it is necessary to conduct a broad dialogue between the USSR and the United States. We value these words because we presume they represent evidence of an evolution in views."[107]

The Shultz meetings with Shevardnadze seemed to have gone smoothly but with no movement on either side. Shultz also was received by Gorbachev on November 5, and this meeting was unusually argumentative. After his fourteen hours of meetings with the two leaders, Shultz acknowledged on his departure that they had failed to narrow differences significantly.[108]

In fact, the talks demonstrated how very far apart the two sides were, not only in positions but even in understanding one another. Shultz was struck by Gorbachev's distorted stress on a "military-industrial complex" dominating American policy. The Soviet leaders, in turn, could see no evident American interest in reaching real agreement on the strategic arms issue but saw the United States focused on what they regarded as secondary or even irrelevant issues such as Soviet human rights practices and a bilateral cultural agreement. Shevardnadze, not surprisingly, challenged the new "broad" interpretation of the ABM Treaty. Gorbachev proposed a quick reduction of 200 to 300 ICBMs on each side as a public sign of earnest intention in arms reductions, but this was not picked up. Shultz, of course, had no authority to agree to such a proposal but also did not seem interested in exploring it.

We do not know whether Gorbachev was prepared to be more forthcoming if the United States had come forward with new proposals. On the American side, Shultz had been authorized by Reagan to raise the possibility of a large-scale ($3.5 billion) joint thermonuclear fusion energy research project if the talks went well. This idea had been developed between the White House and the Department of Energy, bypassing the Department of Defense (Weinberger's strong objection having been correctly anticipated). But Shultz did not raise the idea, nor did Reagan later at the summit.[109]

As noted, Shultz even had to back away from his earlier proposed draft communiqué, leaving open not only whether there would be a joint agreed-on statement but also whether the United States wanted one. The Soviets undoubtedly saw this as tactical pressure, not knowing it stemmed from internal differences within the U.S. administration and Reagan's preference to put such differences aside rather than resolve them.

---

107. Genrykh Borovik, "From the United States," Moscow Television ("Vremya" newscast), November 5, 1985, in FBIS, *Soviet Union*, November 6, 1985, p. A3.

108. See Shultz, *Turmoil and Triumph*, pp. 586–95, and Oberdorfer, *The Turn*, pp. 130–39. See also Bernard Gwertzman, "Shultz Reports Scanty Results in Soviet Talks," *New York Times*, November 6, 1985, pp. A1, A10.

109. Information on the Moscow talks was provided by informed American participants.

As a result of Shultz's Moscow visit, expectations of agreement at Geneva were scaled down by both sides. Nonetheless, both sides continued to prepare for the summit meeting with hope if also some trepidation.


## The Geneva Summit


As the Geneva summit approached, both Reagan and Gorbachev sought to prepare themselves as they looked forward to the first superpower summit meeting for each of them.

President Reagan and his staff launched into unprecedented preparations for the encounter. The White House organized three teams for Geneva preparations: a policy group cochaired by National Security Adviser McFarlane and Chief of Staff Regan, an interagency Soviet affairs group run by Jack F. Matlock, Jr., the senior NSC Soviet and European affairs adviser, and a public diplomacy group cochaired by McFarlane's deputy (and soon to be successor) Vice Admiral John M. Poindexter and Regan's deputy Dennis Thomas. Some twenty-five basic papers outlining Soviet history, politics, and the like were prepared.[110] Reagan himself talked with former presidents Nixon and Ford, with former national security advisers Zbigniew Brzezinski and Brent Scowcroft, and in addition to briefings with Department of State and CIA Soviet affairs experts, he also met with several nongovernmental Soviet affairs specialists.[111] Excerpts from a videotaped day-long conference of selected

---

110. Moreover, an account of these extensive preparations for the summit was leaked to the press to demonstrate the thoroughness of preparation. See Leslie H. Gelb, "Three Past Presidents May Brief Reagan," *New York Times*, November 5, 1985, p. A8; David Hoffman, "'Fine-Tuning' Reagan: Summit Briefers Have Hopes, Worries," *Washington Post*, October 6, 1985, pp. A1, A33; and Jeremiah O'Leary, "Reagan Studying Hard for Talks—And Lessons May Get Tougher," *Washington Post*, November 4, 1985, pp. A1, A10.

111. One of these, Suzanne Massie, an author of popular writings on Russian history and culture, commented afterward that Reagan "doesn't know anything about the [Soviet] people at all. He's in the same position as other Americans, despite all his advisors." Cited in Hoffman, *Washington Post*, October 6, 1985, p. A33. See also Lou Cannon, *President Reagan: The Role of a Lifetime* (Simon and Schuster, 1991), pp. 748–49.

     Reagan was much taken by Massie's colorful and vivid accounts of Russian history. As noted earlier, his first meeting with her had taken place in January 1984, as he first began to see the Soviet Union as something other than a movie-script villain. In all, he met with her eighteen times. Secretary Shultz in his memoir noted the impact of Massie's conversation on Reagan and disclosed that she usually also met with him after seeing the president; he, too, was impressed by the fact that she provided "a glimpse of a different Soviet reality from the one I read about in my secret briefing papers. There might well be a vast historic transformation developing." Shultz, *Turmoil and Triumph*, p. 720, and see p. 724.

American Soviet affairs experts was also prepared for the president, in lieu of meeting with them.

Reagan also talked with Arkady N. Shevchenko, the former Soviet diplomat who had spied for the United States and then defected in 1978. The most important source for special briefings was the former senior KGB officer Oleg Gordievsky, who was personally interviewed in London by CIA Director William Casey about six weeks before the summit; Casey then reported to Reagan. The main thing of interest to Reagan and his staff was Gorbachev himself, and Gordievsky as the deputy KGB station chief in London at the time of Gorbachev's visit to Britain in December 1984 had had close contact with him. Gordievsky had helped in a minor way to prepare Gorbachev for his first summit meeting with a senior Western leader, and now indirectly he helped to prepare Reagan for his meeting with Gorbachev.[112]

Adapting a technique that he had used in his presidential campaign debates in 1980 and 1984 and for formal news conferences, and for the Williamsburg summit of the Western powers of May 1983, Reagan went through a full-dress rehearsal (with Soviet affairs expert Jack Matlock standing in for Gorbachev). Reagan also studied videotapes of Gorbachev's visits to Britain and France, and of various speeches telecast in the Soviet Union (and taped by our Moscow Embassy).

As Reagan looked forward to his meeting with Gorbachev, a limited but interesting transformation occurred in his statements on the source and nature of the difficulties in American-Soviet relations.[113] Both in discussions with advisers and in public statements the president began to speak of "misunderstandings" and Soviet failures to understand America, U.S. peaceful intentions, and the benign purpose he had in mind in pursuing the strategic defense initiative. As the possibility for persuading Gorbachev in direct contact rose, so did Reagan's confidence that he could influence him and so too did his description of the problem. After all, one cannot reason with and persuade an impersonal "communist" leadership of an Evil Empire; but a flesh and blood

---

112. The Casey trip was arranged on the recommendation of Prime Minister Margaret Thatcher and was not publicly disclosed until nearly a year later. See Murrey Marder, "Defector Told of Soviet Alert," *Washington Post*, August 8, 1986, pp. A1, A22, and Leslie H. Gelb, "K.G.B. Defector Helped the C.I.A. Brief Reagan before Summit Talks," *New York Times*, August 9, 1986, pp. 1, 4.

113. One additional bizarre source should be noted. It has become known, first revealed by former White House chief of staff Donald Regan in 1988, that Nancy Reagan regularly consulted an astrologer, Joan Quigley, about President Reagan's official activities, particularly their timing but also their content. Ms. Quigley has disclosed that prior to the Geneva summit she strongly advised Reagan, through Nancy, of the need to approach Gorbachev with an entirely different outlook, not as an "evil empire" man but as a man open to ideas, and she predicted a successful summit if Reagan approached it with a proper attitude. See interview by Andrei Sidorin, "The White House Astrologer," *Ekho planety* (Echo of the Planet), no. 33-34 (August 11–24, 1990), pp. 28–29.

political leader, even if an adversary, can be influenced. And Reagan was above all confident in his ability as a "great communicator." On another plane, the president was similarly enthusiastic about the possibilities of really influencing Soviet thinking through greatly increased contacts, including exchanges involving thousands of students.

The official program called for only a brief, initial fifteen-minute meeting of the two leaders alone. But Reagan, without even telling most of his senior advisers, had discreetly worked out arrangements for more extensive private meetings, including preparing the fireplace for what later became known as "the fireside summit."

We know less about Gorbachev's preparations, but there are indications that they were not all that different from Reagan's. Gorbachev, too, was very confident in his ability and eager personally to take the measure of the American leader. Although he probably did not set up a full rehearsal of his coming drama, a senior Soviet official who accompanied Gorbachev to Geneva has privately said that the Soviet leader sought to anticipate Reagan's arguments and solicited the best arguments he might use that could be effective with Reagan.[114] Moreover, Gorbachev, in light of a comment he made to Reagan, had apparently viewed Reagan's 1942 Hollywood film "King's Row"— at the least he had been briefed enough to be familiar with its plot.

There were, of course, other elements of the preparation for the summit. Both sides had seen Shultz's visit to Moscow as a test of what might be expected—and both had been disappointed in the result. Gorbachev correctly understood Shultz's position to mean that the United States was not prepared to move on the SDI and would mount an offensive on Soviet involvement in the Third World. Reagan's UN speech of October 24 was also taken as a sign of a continuing attack on the Soviet Union, and this was mitigated only in part by the more forthcoming speech by the president from the White House on the eve of his departure for the summit.

President Reagan, in his speech of November 14 telecast to the American people, said, "My mission, stated simply, is a mission for peace . . . to build a foundation for lasting peace . . . in Geneva our agenda will seek not just to avoid war, but to strengthen peace." He voiced his new theme of reciprocally reducing misunderstanding: "We should seek to reduce the suspicions and mistrust that have led us to acquire mountains of strategic weapons." Moreover, he acknowledged that "nuclear weapons," not an evil adversary, "pose the greatest threat in human history to the survival of the human race" and reaffirmed that "a nuclear war cannot be won and must never be fought." Finally, "While it would be naive to think a single summit can establish a permanent peace, this conference can begin a dialog for peace."

---

114. Information from a conversation I had with this official a few months after the summit.

In contrast to his UN address, which had also avowed the aim of peace, Reagan did not launch into another attack on Soviet policies but instead stressed the need for greater American-Soviet contacts at all levels. "We're proposing the broadest people-to-people exchanges in the history of American-Soviet relations, exchanges in sports and culture, in the media, education, and the arts." Thus, "People of both our nations love sports. If we must compete, let it be on the playing fields and not the battlefields." And he saw such contacts as contributing to the reduction of misunderstanding: "If Soviet youth could attend American schools and universities, they could learn firsthand . . . that we do not wish the Soviet people any harm. . . . If American youth could do likewise, . . . *they* would learn that we're all God's children with much in common." Reagan and Gorbachev, in other words, should be able to find a modus vivendi; the summit "can be an historic opportunity to set a steady, more constructive course to the 21st century."[115]

On the eve of the summit meeting, a discordant note was introduced by the deliberate leak of a letter from Defense Secretary Weinberger to President Reagan intended to prevent agreement on any limitation of the SDI programs. Weinberger had failed in an attempt to be named part of the Geneva delegation—his efforts led White House Chief of Staff Don Regan, Robert McFarlane, and Shultz to work out arrangements that would exclude Weinberger, and the president had agreed.

Weinberger used an earlier White House directive of June 10 calling, pursuant to a congressional resolution, for an analysis of any Soviet violations of arms control treaties and their implications for U.S. defense programs, as the springboard for his letter. The State Department had not wanted to release a presidential report to Congress on alleged Soviet violations prior to the summit. But Weinberger not only submitted his report on November 13 but did so under the cover of an unclassified letter to the president in which he stressed the opportunity for the president to underline U.S. concern with strict compliance. But in this unclassified letter Weinberger also warned that at Geneva the president would come under "great pressure" to agree to continuing to observe SALT II constraints, to agree to restrictive interpretation of the ABM Treaty constraints and thereby limit SDI research and testing, and to accept language referring to the importance *both* sides attach to compliance—which, he argued, would indirectly imply U.S. acceptance that the Soviets did respect compliance.[116]

---

115. "United States-Soviet Summit in Geneva, Address to the Nation," November 14, 1985, *Presidential Documents*, vol. 21 (November 18, 1985), pp. 1399, 1402. Emphasis added.

116. The letter was promptly leaked to the *New York Times* and the *Washington Post*, and appeared just as the president arrived in Geneva. See "Weinberger Letter to Reagan on Arms Control," *New York Times*, November 16, 1985, p. 7, and "Text of Weinberger's Letter," *Washington Post*, November 17, 1985, p. A30, and accompanying articles of commentary.

The letter was clearly an attempt to "sabotage" the summit, as McFarlane (anonymously as a senior White House official) told the press. It was clearly an attempt to prevent any agreement that could even peripherally curb the SDI, but it also undercut the rationale for any arms control agreement. It was not an auspicious beginning for the summit.

As the two leaders met at Geneva, there was great public curiosity and interest in how they would interact and who would "win" on the disputed issues. Reagan and Gorbachev shared in this vision of a personalized joust of two standard-bearers. Each was confident of his own abilities and his brief, and each one hoped to be able not only to hold his own but to persuade the other. Although determined to be firm on principal positions, each also hoped to be able to bridge in part the gap between the two sides. Finally, without giving ground on major issues, both were determined that the summit be a success in the eyes of the world (and in particular to their own home constituencies).

The departure from the planned orchestration of a series of formal meetings with an array of attending officials, and the shift to half a dozen personal encounters of the two leaders amounting to five hours of private discussion, was critical to the fortunes of the summit.

By the afternoon of the first day Reagan also reluctantly reversed his earlier decision and agreed to a joint statement, the working out of which occupied most of the delegations' efforts to the very end. One subject that had been treated cautiously by officials of both sides was decided in a minute by the two leaders: Reagan invited Gorbachev to the United States, and Gorbachev at once accepted and invited Reagan to a return meeting in Moscow, which Reagan also promptly accepted. Although the shared expectation at the time was that these follow-on summits would occur in 1986 and 1987 respectively, in fact the timing was left open for later decision through diplomatic channels.

In terms of the public "scorecard," Gorbachev wanted the summit to concentrate on arms control, especially to curb the SDI and to maintain SALT II as well as new cuts, while Reagan wanted the agenda not to be limited to arms control but also to embrace three other areas: bilateral relations, regional trouble spots around the world, and human rights in the Soviet Union. The joint statement, and the concrete agreements reached, dealt mostly with arms control and bilateral relations but also had succinct but meaningful statements on the other two areas as well. On his scorecard, Reagan won hands down: although most of the discussion did focus on arms control, he gave up nothing on the disputed issues, and his four-part agenda was covered.[117] As a consequence, there was very little that anyone in Washington could object to,

---

117. Indeed, Reagan and his spokesmen seemed more determined to ensure victory on pursuing his four-point *agenda* than they were concerned about the result of the discussion of the four subjects.

For accounts of the summit discussions and preparation of the joint statement, see Shultz, *Turmoil and Triumph*, pp. 599–607; and Oberdorfer, *The Turn*, pp. 143–54.

even though hard-liners were uneasy and unhappy about the launching of a new dialogue with the Soviet Union. Even Weinberger's expressed concerns had been met, although his real desire that the United States not pursue arms control at all was not. The American press reflected the unanimous view that "Reagan had won" in the summit encounter.

Of particular importance, Reagan himself was buoyant over having successfully warded off Gorbachev's insistent efforts to encroach on the SDI, and over having done well in establishing a direct rapport and launching a dialogue without making concessions. His self-confidence was confirmed. And he now saw his adversary-partner not as an abstraction from an Evil Empire but as a live politician. Reagan was now confident in moving forward in relations with the Soviet Union.

Gorbachev had taken the greater risk in agreeing to a summit without prior agreement on any of the arms control measures sought by the Soviet side. Nor did he get any satisfaction at Geneva on the main ones: SDI and strategic arms reductions. Some in the Soviet establishment and leadership had been skeptical, and after Geneva some others who had been hopeful were disappointed. Nonetheless, despite the lack of success on concrete issues, Gorbachev had succeeded in restoring a dialogue. His aims in this direction had dovetailed with Reagan's tentative new line of engagement intermittently pursued in 1984–85 and doggedly pushed by Shultz since 1983.

In retrospect, it is clear that both sides gained from Gorbachev's determination to turn around the confrontation and resume dialogue, reducing greatly the tensions and dangers of the years 1981–83. The foundation had been laid for later summits, the INF Treaty, and a new détente (though not so labeled). This was the first summit in six years, only the second in ten. No one could have expected four more in Reagan's term. Reagan was more prophetic than he knew when he commented at the end of the summit meeting, "The real report card on Geneva will not come in for months or even years."[118]

Besides taking the measure of one another, the summit (and the preparations for it) was educational for both presidents in learning about the country and system of the other side. Gorbachev never again railed against the military-industrial complex running the United States as he had to Shultz in Moscow in early November. He learned that Reagan's views on SDI were, indeed, Reagan's own stubbornly held views.[119]

---

118. "Comments by 2 Leaders: 'Cooperation' for 'Hard Work Ahead'" transcript, in *New York Times*, November 22, 1985, p. A12.

119. These changes in thinking did not occur as sudden or complete reversals. For example, in his speech to the Supreme Soviet after the summit Gorbachev still referred to a "kind of order" given to Reagan by the Heritage Foundation before the summit and said "the president was instructed to continue the arms race." See "Report by Deputy M. S. Gorbachev General Secretary of the Central Committee of the CPSU," *Pravda*, November 28, 1985.

In concrete terms, the January mandate for the strategic arms talks was reaffirmed: "to prevent an arms race in space and to terminate it on earth, to limit and reduce nuclear arms and enhance strategic stability." Agreement was reached on "the principle of 50 percent reductions" in strategic nuclear arms, and the new idea of a separate "interim" INF agreement. The leaders reaffirmed intent to work for nuclear nonproliferation and for banning chemical weapons. The stalemated mutual and balanced force reductions (MBFR) conventional arms negotiations were kissed off with a single sentence reaffirming their "willingness to work for positive results," but they gave much more positive endorsement to the CDE (Conference on Disarmament in Europe) negotiations on confidence and security-building measures. They agreed, in a new move, to "study" possible expert-level risk-reduction centers to supplement the recently modernized hot line.[120]

Besides these steps in arms control, another element was included in the joint statement under the rubric of "security." The two sides "agreed that a nuclear war cannot be won and must never be fought." Moreover, "Recognizing that any conflict between the USSR and the U.S. could have catastrophic consequences, they emphasized the importance of preventing any war between them, whether nuclear or conventional." Finally, it was agreed that the two sides "will not seek to achieve military superiority."[121]

Much less attention was paid to this joint statement of military policy objectives in the United States than in the Soviet Union. The initiative for such a statement came from Gorbachev. Indeed, he is reported to have first raised the matter in his letter to Reagan presented by Shevardnadze in Washington on September 27. Reagan's own statement on no winners in a nuclear war in his November 14 presummit telecast to the American people provided the basis for the first point. The need to prevent any war was a Soviet proposal, as was the undertaking not to seek military superiority. Although the Republican Party platform of 1980 had called for regaining military superiority, Reagan as president had by 1984 explicitly settled for the standard of all other presidents since Nixon, to maintain parity rather than seek superiority. But apart from passing press coverage, no further U.S. attention was given to this element of the joint

---

120. "Joint Statement," November 25, 1985," *State Bulletin*, vol. 86 (January 1986), pp. 8–9.

   The initiative for nuclear risk reduction centers had come from Senators Sam Nunn and John Warner, who had personally presented the idea to Gorbachev in Moscow on a visit there in September, with administration approval. Their original idea had provided for joint U.S.-Soviet military manning of such centers in Moscow and Washington. The Pentagon had objected to joint manning, so the concept was scaled back to an adjunct to other communications channels before being presented to Gorbachev and before being incorporated in the Geneva joint statement. The only discussion at Geneva was in the framework of working out the statement. Later, the idea would become reality.

121. *State Bulletin*, vol. 86 (January 1986), p. 8.

statement, which was taken more as "background music" than as a significant or substantial matter.

Gorbachev in his postsummit remarks at Geneva to members of the press emphasized that "questions of war and peace, questions of survival, [are] at the center of world politics," and "I wanted to understand what the present U.S. administration's stand is on this cardinal question—the question of war and peace."[122] It was, after all, barely two years since "white hot" tensions had led Gorbachev's predecessor and mentor Andropov to declare that anyone who believed he could work with this same American administration had "illusions."

"Trust is not restored right away. It is a difficult process," said Gorbachev. "We have heeded the U.S. president's assurances that the United States is not seeking superiority and does not want nuclear war. We sincerely want these statements to be confirmed by deeds." And the joint statement on these matters is "of tremendous significance, if it is consistently implemented in practical steps."[123]

The Soviets considered these declaratory positions on prevention of war and renunciation of aspirations for superiority important in themselves but also believed they should be expressed in arms constraints and reductions. Gorbachev stressed to the Supreme Soviet on his return that from the first private meeting with President Reagan he had emphasized that the highest Soviet priority in going to Geneva was to deal with the most burning problem, "preventing nuclear war and curbing the arms race," and that the agreed-on understanding that a nuclear war cannot be won and must never be unleashed was among "the most important" of the achievements of the summit.[124]

The USSR Supreme Soviet in its resolution evaluating the summit considered as "of fundamental importance" the acknowledgment by both sides of the importance of preventing war and of not seeking military superiority.[125] This theme was reiterated in numerous Soviet media commentaries, including the military press.[126] Even conservative Politburo member Vladimir Shcherbitsky, who emphasized American belligerence, argued that the under-

122. "M. S. Gorbachev Press Conference at the Soviet Press Center in Geneva, November 21, 1985," *Kommunist*, no. 17 (November 1985), p. 19.

123. Ibid., pp. 25, 27.

124. "Report by Deputy M. S. Gorbachev, General Secretary of the Central Committee of the CPSU," *Kommunist*, no. 17 (November 1985), pp. 40, 43.

125. "Resolution of the USSR Supreme Soviet on the Results of the Soviet-American Summit Meeting in Geneva and on the International Situation," *Pravda*, November 28, 1985.

126. For example, see the editorial "Always on Guard, Always on Alert," *Zarubezhnoye voyennoye obozreniye* (Foreign Military Review), no. 1, January 1986, p. 6; and "A Meeting That Strengthened People's' Hopes," *Soviet Military Review*, no. 1 (January 1986), pp. 7–9.

taking in the joint statement was "of fundamental importance."[127] The only publicly expressed reservation was by Marshal Sergei Akhromeyev, chief of the General Staff. He commented sourly to the assembled deputies, "We are well aware that the other side did not by any means seek to make the problem of international security and nuclear and space arms the main problem for discussion." And after bitterly criticizing the U.S. positions on strategic arms and especially the SDI, he cautioned, "The commitment undertaken by the United States at the Geneva meeting not to seek military superiority over the Soviet Union is as yet only words."[128] This skepticism, however, was directed at the continuing U.S. military programs and stance on arms limitation, not at the conclusion that nuclear war was unwinnable. In a private conversation with a senior American retired general at almost the same time, Marshal Akhromeyev commented that the one real achievement of the Geneva summit was the agreement by President Reagan that there could be no winner in a nuclear war.[129]

Gorbachev went well beyond the jointly agreed language abjuring pursuit of military superiority. As he disclosed in his press conference in Geneva at the close of the summit, Gorbachev also expressed the conclusion that it would even be counterproductive to obtain strategic advantage. He said that "more than once, face to face and at plenary sessions, I tried to express our profound conviction that a lower level of security for the United States as compared to the Soviet Union would not be advantageous to us because it would lead to distrust and give rise to instability." He added that they were "counting on" a similar approach by the United States, but in any case he had also told the president that "in no event will we permit the United States to obtain military superiority over us." This, he commented, seemed to him "a logical way to put the question. Both sides must get used to the idea of strategic parity as the natural state of Soviet-American relations."[130]

Nor was this a position tailored for foreign consumption. Gorbachev reaffirmed the same point to the Supreme Soviet. "We do not base our policy [toward the United States] on a desire to encroach on the national interests of the USA. I will say more: we would not, for example, want changes in the strategic balance to our favor. We would not want this because such a situation would heighten suspicion of the other side and increase the instability of the general situation." And he again declared, "Things have developed in such a

---

127. "Comments on the Report of M. S. Gorbachev, Speech of Deputy V. V. Shcherbitsky," *Izvestiya*, November 28, 1985.

128. "Comments on the Report of M. S. Gorbachev, Speech of Deputy S. F. Akhromeyev," *Izvestiya*, November 28, 1985.

129. This conversation, with retired General David Jones, former chairman of the Joint Chiefs of Staff, took place in Moscow on November 26, 1985. I report it with his permission.

130. "M. S. Gorbachev Press Conference," *Kommunist*, no. 17 (November 1985), p. 20.

way that both our countries will have to get used to strategic parity as the natural state." He also used a then unfamiliar but later important formulation in relating this prevailing natural parity to defensive sufficiency. "It will be necessary to come to a common understanding on what level of arms on each side could be considered relatively sufficient from the standpoint of reliable defense. We are convinced that such a level of sufficiency is far lower than what the USSR and the United States now possess."[131]

Gorbachev had been interested in obtaining an American commitment not to pursue military superiority and to abjure any possibility to wage or win a nuclear war not only for its possible effect in restraining U.S. behavior but as a foundation for his own new definitions of security, strategic stability, and defense sufficiency—themes he noted for the first time in such a forum to the Supreme Soviet in November but would adumbrate at the more important forthcoming party congress in February 1986. These views also underlay the new campaign for nuclear and other disarmament he would launch in January.

At Geneva Gorbachev and Reagan had, as earlier noted, agreed on reducing strategic arms by 50 percent ("in principle"), and on an interim INF agreement (not yet negotiated). They had sharply disagreed on strategic defense and space weapons. Reagan had proposed agreement on conducting research on strategic defense "as permitted by, and in full compliance with, the ABM Treaty"—but evading the new divergence over interpretation of the treaty—and a "cooperative transition" to deployment of strategic defense. Gorbachev remained adamantly opposed to any strategic defense research and above all to any work on weapons in space.

Gorbachev did not, to the surprise of the U.S. side, press for recommitment to observing the never-ratified SALT II Treaty, nor did he call specifically for restoring the traditional interpretation of the ABM Treaty, nor did he propose an antisatellite ban. He wanted to concentrate attention on the SDI.

Gorbachev's principal arguments against the SDI were that it reflected or could give rise to a first-strike strategy, and that it would introduce weapons into space and open up possible space-strike weapons against an adversary. He repeated these themes in his press conference after the summit. At first Gorbachev believed Reagan to be an advocate of the SDI because of the strategic calculations and designs of a U.S. military-industrial complex and of general "ruling circles," whether to prepare for a possible attack on the Soviet Union, pressure the Soviets, or force them to spend themselves into bankruptcy. At Geneva he came to realize Reagan's devotion to the SDI was tenacious because he believed in it.

Reagan in turn was unable to persuade Gorbachev of the merits of the SDI but did come to appreciate that Gorbachev was sincerely concerned about "space-strike weapons," despite Reagan's assurances he wanted a shield, not a

---

131. "Report by Deputy M. S. Gorbachev," ibid., pp. 41–42.

sword. Reagan subsequently tried to get his administration to find some way to disabuse the Soviets of this concern. This could have been an important step. The bureaucracy later wrestled with possible arguments for the Geneva arms negotiations but was unwilling to curb the SDI research and development program in any way and therefore was not prepared to curb development of technologies adaptable to offensive weapon systems.[132]

Reagan was ill-served by his staff in their advising him at Geneva to try to make headway (or even to make debating points) by arguing to Gorbachev that "Soviet military doctrine has always stressed the value of defensive systems," and that Soviet scientists had been researching SDI technologies for fifteen years. He cited statements on strategic defense by former prime minister Aleksei Kosygin and former foreign minister Andrei Gromyko made in the mid-1960s. Gorbachev and his colleagues were indignant at these self-serving attempts to assign Soviet views on the basis of policy and doctrinal positions repudiated sixteen years earlier when the SALT negotiations began. They also objected to U.S. attempts to equate Soviet research consistent with the ABM Treaty with SDI objectives that were not. The American approach was feckless, based on poor understanding by advisers in an administration that had long ago lost the habit of substantiating statements before making them, under a president notorious for lack of interest in factual validity underlying his pronouncements.[133]

President Reagan was triumphant in his first weekly radio broadcast after returning from Geneva in assuring all that Gorbachev had failed in his "main aim" at Geneva, "to force us to drop SDI."[134] This was of course true, except that it understated the value to both sides of the other main aim of Gorbachev, shared by Reagan—to renew the U.S.-Soviet dialogue at the highest level.

As noted earlier, the Geneva summit also led to agreement to study the establishment of "risk reduction centers" in the two capitals and to work together toward strengthening nuclear nonproliferation, a ban on chemical

---

132. This attempt to find a way to allay Soviet concerns was described to me by participants. Shultz also discussed it briefly in his memoir; see Shultz, *Turmoil and Triumph*, p. 689.

133. I was informed of these statements of Reagan by knowledgeable Soviet diplomats, who were incensed at this approach. One can imagine Reagan's reaction if his predecessors' rejection of strategic defenses had been cited as an argument as to why he should not hold his view. I was aware from members of Reagan's NSC staff of their misreading of Soviet military doctrine on ABM defense, and their inability to differentiate between research bounded by accepted constraints and research intended to go beyond such constraints. Secretary Shultz, in a speech in Berlin three weeks later, in innocence and evident belief in the suitability of the argument, revealed publicly that Reagan had made these arguments. See "Berlin and the Cause of Freedom," by Secretary Shultz, *State Bulletin*, vol. 86 (February 1986), p. 30.

134. See Bernard Gwertzman, "Reagan Stresses 'Star Wars' Plan," *New York Times*, November 24, 1985, p. 17.

weapons, and agreement on confidence- and security-building measures at the Conference on Disarmament in Europe (CDE).

Arms control was not among achievements of the summit, but it remained at the heart of the dialogue. This was particularly true for the Soviet side. At the party congress three months later, despite the lack of progress on space and strategic arms, Gorbachev justified the resumption of a continuing summit dialogue to the Soviet political establishment because it would give "practical results on the most important directions in limiting and reducing arms."[135] This contention exaggerated the prospects for agreement and was to increase the pressures on Gorbachev as the Geneva arms talks failed to pick up momentum in the months following. It ensured a return bout on this issue at the next summit meeting.

Enough was discussed to warrant Reagan's claim that the other three agenda items he had pushed for were addressed. The sides agreed the least on the human rights question, formally only acknowledging "the importance of resolving humanitarian cases in the spirit of cooperation."[136] This was, however, the first time the Soviet Union had agreed to any statement implying that the subject was appropriate for U.S.-Soviet discussion, albeit as a matter of "humanitarian" concern rather than human "rights."

On regional issues, Reagan reiterated complaints about continuing Soviet intervention, directly in Afghanistan and indirectly through proxies in some other areas. Gorbachev took issue on such a characterization but was not confrontational. He did not raise the Middle East, as Reagan had anticipated. He did not react to an overbearing warning from Reagan that if the Soviet Union escalated its support and created any real threat to the United States in Nicaragua, the United States would crush it.[137] The quiet discussions of various regional issues at the assistant secretary (deputy foreign minister) level, under way since 1982, were formally endorsed by the two leaders in their joint statement: "Recognizing that exchanges of views on regional issues on the expert level have proven useful, they agreed to continue such exchanges on a regular basis."[138]

Most significant, although unmentioned publicly, Gorbachev responded to Reagan's routinely belligerent challenge on Afghanistan not by a routine defense of Soviet actions, or counterattack on U.S. support for the *mujahedin* or the contras, but by a matter-of-fact statement of concern and of

---

135. M. S. Gorbachev, *Politicheskii doklad tsentral'nogo komiteta KPSS XXVII s"yezdu Kommunisticheskoi partii Sovetskogo Soyuza* (Political Report of the Central Committee of the CPSU to the 27th Congress of the Communist Party of the Soviet Union) (Moscow: Politizdat, 1986), p. 88.

136. *State Bulletin*, vol. 86 (January 1986), p. 9.

137. Information from an American participant present at the session. Of course, the Soviet Union had no such designs and had even acted with circumspection in tacitly abiding by Shultz's warning in 1982 not to provide MiG fighter aircraft to Nicaragua.

138. *State Bulletin*, vol. 86 (January 1986), p. 9.

his desire to work constructively to deal with the Afghan problem and to withdraw Soviet forces. Although Reagan did not react, some of his advisers including Shultz, while wary and waiting to see concrete evidence of a new Soviet approach on Afghanistan, were encouraged by this stance.[139]

Agreements in bilateral relations, the fourth category, were modest and largely limited to agreement to expand educational and scientific exchanges and to open consulates general in Kiev and New York. Most of these were resumptions of plans or programs interrupted in 1980 in the aftermath of Afghanistan. A cultural agreement, in effect with renewals for two decades, had been permitted to expire at the end of 1979. Now, Secretary Shultz and Foreign Minister Shevardnadze signed a new one. The resuscitation of the consulates was also an agreement to pick up from the situation in early 1980 when the advance staffs of the two consulates, already in place, had been withdrawn. A new tripartite North Pacific Air Safety Accord, with Japan as the third member, signed a few days earlier, was made public at Geneva. This pact was designed to prevent such incidents as the tragic misdirection and downing of KAL 007 in 1983. Bilateral U.S.-Soviet air talks were held, and agreement was announced on November 23. Consultations on environmental protection were also to be initiated.

In effect, Reagan had told Gorbachev that if the Soviets were to give in on the SDI but agreed to strategic reductions, and were to pull back in regional conflicts and shape up on human rights issues, then the United States might be prepared to normalize relations—but even then there was no explicit promise of restoring normal most-favored-nation (MFN) trade status or access to credits.

In their remarks at the end of the summit conference, Reagan and Gorbachev expressed satisfaction and cautious optimism for the future development of relations and agreed to a future exchange of summit meetings. But both leaders also cautiously said this would require "deeds" ("concrete measures") and not merely "words."[140]

---

139. Confirmed by American and Soviet participants, this significant indication of a Soviet decision to disengage from Afghanistan was not widely briefed. The one correspondent who dug out and reported the story at the time was Don Oberdorfer, "Afghanistan, Arms Major Summit Themes," *Washington Post*, November 22, 1985, p. A9. The *New York Times* more cautiously reported that "there may have been some movement toward negotiation over the Soviet presence in Afghanistan." See "What Was Agreed On and What Was Not," *New York Times*, November 22, 1985, p. A1.

Some of Gorbachev's delegation quietly drew attention to and reinforced Gorbachev's comments on Afghanistan. Shultz told some reporters at the time, and mentioned in his later memoir, that he sensed a more serious interest by Gorbachev in withdrawal. Shultz, *Turmoil and Triumph*, p. 601.

See the discussion in chapter 15.

140. "Concluding Remarks," November 21, 1985, *State Bulletin*, vol. 86 (January 1986), p. 11.

The Geneva summit did not yet usher in a new détente. President Reagan reported in his homecoming address to Congress on the meeting that "the United States cannot afford illusions about the nature of the U.S.S.R. We cannot assume that their ideology and purpose will change. This implies enduring competition. Our task is to assure that this competition remains peaceful." And he sought to justify his five years as a time spent in "strengthening our economy, restoring our national will, and rebuilding our defenses and alliances," as a result of which "America is once again strong—and our strength has given us the ability to speak with confidence." But he saw the summit as a "fresh start," and as a result of it he and Gorbachev "understand each other better." "I gained a better perspective; I feel he did too."[141]

The Geneva summit for the first time fully and centrally brought Reagan into Shultz's strategy of diplomatic reengagement with the Soviet Union, the campaign he had initiated in 1983 and resumed in 1984–85. It thus gave a considerable boost to continuing pursuit of that approach.

Gorbachev's report to the Supreme Soviet a few days later was, indicatively, sandwiched in between discussion of the economic plans of the Soviet Union and a more general survey of Soviet foreign policy around the world. He had few accomplishments to report beyond the fact that the meeting had been held and a summit-level dialogue resumed. Gorbachev cited the assessment issued two days earlier by the Politburo calling the summit "an important event not only in our bilateral relations, but in world politics as a whole." And he added the comment that "the road to the Geneva dialogue was long and arduous for many reasons."[142] Indeed, the course of the six and a half years since Brezhnev had met President Carter in Vienna made that last meeting seem a long time ago. And Geneva, though in a limited sense a breakthrough, only brought the relationship back to its troubled and uneasy state before Afghanistan, at best a starting point for developing improved relations.[143]

For Gorbachev, of course, it represented recognition by the leader of the other superpower, who had not deigned to meet any of the three preceding Soviet leaders, and it was Gorbachev's first opportunity to meet an American president. It did reestablish a useful dialogue, as the future would confirm. But this result was less evident at the time to some in the Soviet Union, and Gorbachev's success at Geneva in relaunching a dialogue did not carry over to any success on what the Soviets saw as the crucial issue of the day: the American pursuit of the SDI.

---

141. "President's Address before a Joint Session of Congress, November 21, 1985," *State Bulletin*, vol. 86 (January 1986), pp. 13–14.

142. "Report by M. S. Gorbachev, General Secretary of the Central Committee of the CPSU," *Pravda*, November 28, 1985.

143. Shortly after the Geneva meeting, a senior Soviet diplomat who had been there remarked to me precisely that thought: "Geneva brings us back to 1979."

A month later, in an address at year's end to the ambassadors of the diplomatic corps in Moscow, Gorbachev remarked that the Geneva summit had led to "a certain warming up of the international climate," but he stressed that the renewed nuclear and space arms talks would determine whether the new year would justify hopes for curbing the arms race and reveal whether a true turning point had been reached.[144]

The Geneva summit meeting was duly praised by the NATO allies of the United States and the Warsaw Pact allies of the Soviet Union, as well as generally by the international community. Reagan personally reported to the NATO allies in a meeting in Brussels on his way home, and Gorbachev similarly met with the Warsaw Pact allies in Prague. Most European leaders, West and East, were pleased that Reagan now seemed personally committed to improving East-West relations. And the Western ones at least were also glad that Reagan had held his own so ably in dealing with Gorbachev, and that Gorbachev had risen to the occasion. NATO Secretary General Lord Carrington underlined that "Geneva is not the end of a process but, we hope, the beginning of a new and more constructive stage."[145]

Attention now turned to what would follow in this new and, it was hoped, more constructive stage.

## Postsummit Doldrums

As the frenetic diplomatic activity and massive media focus on the summit meeting dissolved, the momentum for developing U.S.-Soviet relations also subsided. In some, mostly secondary, areas of bilateral relations there was further action to carry out matters agreed on. At the working level (deputy assistant secretary of State and deputy chief of mission at the Soviet Embassy in Washington) some thirty cases of reunifying divided families were resolved. Discussions of the myriad details in setting up consulates continued. The nitty-gritty work began to implement the general provisions of the cultural exchange agreement signed in Geneva by Shultz and Shevardnadze. Even though the agreement had been the subject of continuing negotiation since August 1984, most implementing actions still needed to be worked out. Only now did work begin to design a joint program of cancer research for which no professional foundation had been laid.

On December 5, American and Soviet academic representatives (from the American Council of Learned Societies and the USSR Academy of Sciences) signed a new agreement on scholarly exchanges. Although not tied

---

144. "Meeting in the Kremlin: Speech of M. S. Gorbachev," *Pravda*, December 28, 1985.

145. Quoted by William Drozdiak, "Reagan Briefs Allies in Brussels: NATO Nations Hail Superpower Dialogue," *Washington Post*, November 22, 1985, p. A11.

directly to the summit accords, this agreement followed the spirit of the new budding cooperation. On January 15, 1986, U.S. Information Agency Director Charles Z. Wick arrived in Moscow for talks with cultural affairs chief Petr N. Demichev.

A Civil Aviation Agreement was initialed in November soon after the summit, with intention to restore Pan American and Aeroflot direct lines between the two countries. And on December 10 a direct civil air communication channel linking Khabarovsk and Anchorage, Alaska, under the tripartite North Pacific agreement, was announced.

The U.S.-USSR Trade and Economic Council met in Moscow in December 9–11, with the U.S. delegation headed by Secretary of Commerce Malcolm Baldrige, at this level for the first time since Afghanistan. The meeting went well, and Gorbachev received Baldrige and gave a speech urging increased Soviet-American trade. But the United States government made no move to normalize trade relations, either on MFN trade status or credits. U.S. exports to the Soviet Union remained only about 10 percent of Soviet imports from the nonsocialist world, and the Soviet Union's exports to the United States were only 2 percent of its exports to nonsocialist countries—on a par with Soviet exports to the Ivory Coast, as Gorbachev noted in his speech. The only significant development in nongovernmental action was a syndicated loan by four of the largest American (and one Canadian) banks, lending the USSR $400 million at low interest—the first such syndication since Afghanistan. In all, some steps were taken, but as Gorbachev correctly emphasized, the U.S. government had to do more if economic ties were to flourish.

The heavy publicity to the fireside summit (as Reagan had called it), and Reagan's enthusiasm for the meeting with Gorbachev and its outcome, helped to dispel the confrontational atmosphere in U.S.-Soviet relations—an atmosphere that Reagan had done so much to create with his calls for a "crusade" against an "Evil Empire." But not everyone welcomed this change or was prepared to accept it. On November 24 a conference of anti-Soviet neoconservatives (including Irving Kristol, Richard Pipes, and Elliott Abrams, the latter two from Reagan's first administration) met in New York. Calling themselves the Committee for the Free World, they clearly wanted to keep aloft the crusading banner, contending that the Geneva summit had not made any fundamental changes in U.S.-Soviet relations and clearly seeking to keep matters that way.[146] More significant, at the same time an official cultural affairs forum of the Conference on Security and Cooperation in Europe concluded six weeks of discussion in angry disagreement.[147]

---

146. See Robert Pear, "Push the Russians, Intellectuals Say," *New York Times*, November 25, 1985, p. A9.

147. See Jackson Diehl, "East-West Cultural Forum Ends Amid Angry Rhetoric: Soviets, U.S. Assail Lack of Geneva Spirit," *Washington Post*, November 26, 1985, pp. A1, A22.

President Reagan himself, in his annual speech on Human Rights Day (December 10), criticized the Soviet Union on several counts, particularly the war in Afghanistan. But his speech was less harsh and a less detailed indictment than in the past. He did reaffirm that "human rights will continue to have a profound effect on the United States-Soviet relationship as a whole."[148]

The Reagan administration did not see the sharp change in its stance that most observers did—some welcoming it, others grumbling over it. President Reagan himself saw the Soviet Union under Gorbachev coming around *because* of his policies of strength and confrontation. National Security Adviser Robert McFarlane stressed this point in a speech on December 9. "What was achieved in Geneva last month," he said, "would simply not have been possible without the firm foundation of his foreign policy as a whole, put in place over the last five years. There are new opportunities before us now not because the President is changing his approach but precisely because he *isn't* changing it." McFarlane even purported to see in Gorbachev's statement that the world had become more secure as a result of the summit, "a recognition, which the Soviet leadership did not have just a year or two ago, that the West will not be knocked off course by threats. That was the lesson of Geneva."[149] Apart from betraying a sense of vulnerability, this statement clearly indicated that the summit had not dispelled all misconceptions, if that was the "lesson" the Reagan administration drew from Geneva.

In arms control, the summit had registered no advance toward agreement, unless it did so by clarifying the basis and strength of divergent positions on space weapons and strategic defense. The START talks were scheduled to resume in mid-January 1986. Meanwhile, a few early steps in general in arms control seemed to reflect an unclear prospect.

The United States in early December had launched a satellite for ASAT testing, but on December 19 Congress banned further ASAT testing as long as the Soviet Union continued its unilateral moratorium.

Gorbachev offered, first in a private letter to Reagan on December 5 and two weeks later publicly, on-site inspection of nuclear test ranges to verify a nuclear test moratorium. The U.S. government was not interested.

Most important, and most discordant, was the issuance on December 23, 1985, of the third published presidential report to Congress, "Soviet Noncompliance with Arms Control Agreements."[150] Although the merits of the various charges varied greatly, the harsh tone and inclusion of many dubious

---

148. David K. Shipler, "Reagan Tempers His View on Soviet," *New York Times*, December 11, 1985, p. A11.

149. Robert C. McFarlane, "U.S. Foreign Policy: Opportunity and Risk," December 9, 1985, Current Policy No. 779 (Department of State, 1985), pp. 2, 4. Emphasis in original.

150. See *Documents on Disarmament 1985* (Washington: Arms Control and Disarmament Agency, 1989), pp. 935–54.

allegations raised serious questions in Moscow about the extent of real U.S. interest in arms control.[151] It strengthened the doubts, and the hand, of those who were convinced the United States was not seriously interested in arms limitations and reductions. And Gorbachev had failed at Geneva to obtain any American move toward resolving differences, above all on the space weapons and the SDI.

In the months following the Geneva meeting, the Reagan administration, satisfied that Gorbachev seemed to be coming around, saw no reason for new initiatives or still less for compromises in its stand.

Gorbachev, though by no means satisfied with the state of relations, saw no leverage to move Reagan. He decided to attempt to broaden the arms control agenda with a bold and sweeping new initiative. But his primary focus turned to the forthcoming party congress and the need to press for far-reaching new approaches in his own country in foreign policy and in domestic affairs. Soviet-American relations slid into the doldrums not because they did not remain crucial for the long term, but because there were no evident opportunities, and other needs in the short term were more pressing.

---

151. See chapter 12 for discussion of the verification and compliance issue.

# 6  Gorbachev, Reagan, and the Reykjavik Summit, 1986

THE KEY DEVELOPMENTS of 1986 were the party congress in Moscow early in the year that consolidated and further defined the policy line of the new leadership under Mikhail Gorbachev, and a second summit meeting of Gorbachev and Reagan. The unsuccessful pursuit of arms limitations and reductions given highest attention by the Soviet leaders, and the active pursuit of regional geopolitical competition given priority by the Reagan administration, dominated the uneasy development of relations between these two events and resulted in uncertainties for a number of months as to whether a second summit meeting would occur in 1986 and whether the dialogue launched at the Geneva summit would survive.

When a new summit meeting did take place, at Reykjavik in October, it was a spectacular failure in the immediate run, but it broke the mold and opened up new possibilities in arms control. As Gorbachev began to demonstrate "new thinking" and a new flexibility in internal and foreign policy, Reagan's standing and control of events in Washington were shaken late in the year by revelations in the Iran-contra scandal of duplicitous and unsuccessful foreign policy management. In retrospect, it is clear that the year marked a shift from Reagan's domination of the relationship to his sharing of at least an equal role with Gorbachev and his new approaches.

The first significant development in the new year was an initiative by Gorbachev to reanimate the field of arms control and disarmament. In a major formal "declaration," he offered a comprehensive program for elimination of all nuclear weapons by the year 2000 but framed to allow flexibility in the pursuit of more limited agreements.[1] Most initial American and other Western reaction addressed the dramatic call for eliminating nuclear weapons and saw the

---

1.  "Declaration of the General Secretary of the CC of the CPSU M. S. Gorbachev," *Pravda*, January 16, 1986.

speech as predominantly propaganda. There was no change in explicit Soviet linkage of strategic intercontinental arms reduction to a ban on the creation, testing, and deploying of space strike weapons, that is, U.S. renunciation of the strategic defense initiative (SDI). This led to a cautious and guarded American response. In fact, however, Gorbachev's initiative was intended as a serious opening to a basic improvement in relations through building confidence based on progressively greater arms limitation and reductions. He declared that verification would no longer be an obstacle to arms agreements. Moreover, for the first time the Soviet Union proposed a bilateral U.S.-USSR elimination of intermediate-range missiles in Europe, laying the basis for negotiation on intermediate-range nuclear forces (INF), leading by the end of the next year to the INF Treaty.[2]

Gorbachev may have been prepared to advance his broad disarmament program at Geneva, if Reagan had been more receptive. By unveiling it in January 1986, on the eve of resumption of the Geneva nuclear arms talks, he sought to revitalize and broaden the arms control agenda. (He also proposed a comprehensive nuclear test ban and a ban on chemical weapons, as well as reductions in INF and strategic arms.) Gorbachev may also have hoped for a more favorable American response that he could announce at the forthcoming party congress.[3]

## The Twenty-seventh Party Congress

The quinquennial congresses of the Communist Party of the Soviet Union from the 1950s through the 1980s performed some of the functions of the quadrennial American presidential elections. Even though there was no election by the population as a whole and no change of the top leader, the party congress focused the attention of the leadership at all levels, and of the country at large, on a reassessment and reaffirmation or change of what was long called in the Soviet Union "the general line" of policy, domestic and foreign. In considering developments on the Soviet side, the period covered by this study opened with the Twenty-sixth Party Congress in 1981—which proved to be the final such conclave of the Brezhnev era, as well as being the first attempt to

---

2. For a contemporary account noting these broader purposes and possibilities, including intermediate-range nuclear forces, see Raymond L. Garthoff, "The Gorbachev Proposal and Prospects for Arms Control," *Arms Control Today*, vol. 16 (January–February 1986), pp. 3–6.

3. A Soviet diplomat at the time told me that Gorbachev had been prepared to disclose and discuss the broader agenda at Geneva if Reagan had moved to compromise on the SDI. This, however, remains unconfirmed. Other Soviet officials later said that Gorbachev had hoped for a more positive response to use at the congress, and his comments there indicated disappointment at the reply he did get.

search out a new policy for relations with the United States in the period following the collapse of the détente of the 1970s.[4] After the extended process of transition chronicled in subsequent chapters, culminating in the accession of Gorbachev in early 1985, the fortuitous scheduling of the next congress in early 1986 provided an appropriate occasion for the new leadership to consolidate its control and stake out its own policy line (including final preparation of the new revision of the party program adopted a quarter of a century earlier).[5] It thus became an unusually important event and provides a useful window on the Soviet analysis of the world situation and policy guidelines that underlay the further development of Soviet foreign policy, including relations with the United States, in the second half of the 1980s. As we shall see, when the locus of real power shifted from the Communist Party to the institutions of the state in 1990, the next party congress and the very institution itself became less significant.[6]

The Twenty-seventh Party Congress opened on February 25, 1986, and concluded nine days later.[7] Gorbachev's leadership position was consolidated and unchallenged, although far from absolute, and more conservative elements, who were not excluded from influence, remained in the party establishment.[8] Gorbachev continued to show full confidence in his position as

---

4.   See chapter 2.

5.   By the party statutes, each congress was to be held no later than five years after its predecessor, providing leeway to hold it some time earlier than that. Although never made public or confirmed, Soviet party officials indicated at the time that a decision had tentatively been made by early 1985, shortly before Chernenko's death but well into his terminal illness, to hold the Twenty-seventh Party Congress in late 1985 and probably to use the occasion for a change in leadership if Chernenko were still alive but debilitated. After his death, however, Gorbachev and his colleagues decided to wait for the early spring of 1986 in order to use the longer interval to make personnel changes and prepare more fully their programmatic positions and decisions for the congress.

6.   See chapters 10 and 11.

7.   Whether coincidentally or more likely by unspoken design, the congress opened precisely to the day on the thirtieth anniversary of the landmark Twentieth Party Congress at which Nikita Khrushchev had in a famous secret speech unveiled the crimes of Josef Stalin and ushered in the "destalinization" of the party and its policies.

8.   Even before the party congress, as well as in changes attendant on the formal election of new leading party officials by the congress, Gorbachev and his allies effectively "packed" the key party Secretariat and removed most of his opponents and other Brezhnev holdovers from the Politburo. Grigory Romanov was removed in July 1985, Prime Minister Nikolai Tikhonov in September 1985, and Viktor Grishin in February 1986 on the eve of the congress. Some retired senior party chiefs were permitted to retain their seats on the Central Committee, in effect dividing those honorably retired (such as Tikhonov, Vasily Kuznetsov, and Boris Ponomarev) from those purged (Romanov and Grishin, most notably). Nonetheless in the broader membership of the Central Committee, and even among the new leaders, most were more conservative than Gorbachev (and especially more than he was to become).

preeminent within a collective leadership. General Secretary Gorbachev of course presented the Political Report of the Central Committee to the congress.[9] Although Gorbachev generally gave somewhat shorter speeches than his predecessors, the tradition of a very long programmatic report was retained. The most immediately evident difference from the preceding congress was the fact that, with a brief break near the middle, Gorbachev's vigorous delivery lasted five hours. The ailing Brezhnev in 1981 had only read the first six- and final seven-minute segments of a similar five-hour presentation, an unidentified reader filling in the remainder.[10] This contrast in a small but visibly evident way illustrated the change from a superannuated and slow leadership to a much more vigorous and dynamic leader.[11]

My present focus is on Soviet foreign policy, especially relations with the United States. Before turning to that specific subject, however, the broader vision of international relations presented in Gorbachev's report must be noted.

In the discussion of the preceding party congress held in 1981, a comparison of the Central Committee report with those given at the congresses of 1971 and 1976 showed interesting variations and changes in emphasis and policy interest but within an established general pattern.[12] The structure of thought and organization, as well as the content, of Gorbachev's report to the new congress marked a radical change from the previous pattern. The 1981 report had presented a major section, "On the International Policy of the Communist Party of the Soviet Union," comprising a progression of subordinate sections on relations with the world socialist system, the newly liberated

---

9.  In the past, the report had been called the "Accountability Report" (*otchet* in 1976 and 1981; *otchetnyi doklad* in 1971); the change to "Political Report" (*politicheskii doklad*) was intended to emphasize its authoritative nature. As in the past, a large part of the report dealt with economic questions and other aspects of social policy and the like, so the term clearly was not meant to designate narrowly "political" coverage.

10. The substitute presenter made occasional lame interjections, such as "Leonid Brezhnev notes," all excised in the published version, and even in a later Moscow Radio announcer's repeat reading of the entire speech.

11. Gorbachev himself, however, near the end of his presentation at one point skipped a paragraph on Lenin's precepts for drawing up such programmatic documents as the report, then paused and remarked in an ironic way, "It seems that I have left out a section of Lenin's fundamental thoughts about the approach to drawing up the program and they are worth recalling." His audience seemed uneasy about this rather casual reference to Lenin's fundamental thoughts. None of this was, of course, indicated in the subsequent broadcast or published versions. Still later, after coughing and hesitating at one point, he looked up and ad libbed, "It looks like the end is nigh." This time the audience reacted with laughter and merriment.

    These sidelights in the original delivery, broadcast on Moscow television, can be noted in "Gorbachev CPSU Central Committee Report," *Pravda*, February 26, 1986, in Foreign Broadcast Information Service, *Daily Report: Soviet Union*, February 26, 1986, p. 42, and February 27, 1986, p. 7. (Hereafter FBIS, *Soviet Union*.)

12. See chapter 2.

countries, the world communist movement, and then the capitalist states. In startling contrast, the 1986 report opened with a major section, "The Contemporary World: Basic Trends and Contradictions." Although the various elements in the previous reports were all at least noted, the entire framework as well as content was drastically revised. For example, in 1981 a separate section on Soviet relations with national liberation movements and newly independent nations of the Third World comprised thirty paragraphs, mentioning more than a dozen countries by name and discussing relations with some at length. It concluded with a promise of a consistent course by the Soviet Union "on strengthening the union of world socialism and the national liberation movement."[13] In 1986, there was no section on this subject, and the long discourse on the contemporary world had but three sentences of passing reference to the "anti-colonial revolutions and national liberation movement," with no country even named and no promise of support. Even references to the world socialist system were minimal. (In a later section, the Warsaw Pact and Council on Mutual Economic Assistance were mentioned, but no individual country other than China—omitting the 1981 discussions referring to each of the countries of Eastern Europe, Cuba, Vietnam, Mongolia, and North Korea.) Similarly, reference to the world communist movement was downgraded from a long section to three short perfunctory paragraphs.[14]

What took the place of these ideologically defined divisions of the world? What was the nature of the contemporary world presented as the foundation for Soviet policy attention?

The attention given to Soviet relations with the Western capitalist states, and above all the United States, continued to be highlighted. Much of this discussion, to be sure, was harshly critical of shortcomings, contradictions, and the aggressive nature ascribed to imperialism.[15] But when it came to Soviet relations with the imperialist powers of the capitalist world, the emphasis was on the possibility and need for peaceful coexistence and peaceful competition.

---

13.  Comrade L. I. Brezhnev, *XXVI s"yezd Kommunisticheskoi partii Sovetskogo Soyuza, 28 fevralya-3 marta 1981 goda: stenograficheskii otchet* (The 26th Congress of the Communist Party of the Soviet Union, February 28–March 3, 1981: Stenographic Report) (Moscow: Politizdat, 1981), vol. 1, p. 33.

14.  M. S. Gorbachev, *Politicheskii doklad tsentral'nogo komiteta KPSS XXVII s"yezdu Kommunisticheskoi partii Sovetskogo Soyuza* (Political Report of the Central Committee of the CPSU to the 27th Congress of the Communist Party of the Soviet Union) (Moscow: Politizdat, 1986), pp. 7–29. (Hereafter *Politicheskii doklad*.)

15.  No doubt Gorbachev and the other Soviet leaders at the time basically believed these criticisms. Furthermore, Gorbachev, in view of the unorthodox advocacy of the goals of global interdependence and international security he introduced elsewhere in the report, may have regarded such harsh criticism of capitalism as useful reassurance about his tough Leninist credentials to his conservative colleagues. Finally, strong criticism of the performance of the capitalist system may have been thought needed to offset the criticisms of *Soviet* economic performance elsewhere in the report.

The new element that dominated the report, in its discussion of the contemporary world and of Soviet policy, was global interdependence and the need for stable and mutual international security. The structure of the discussion, as well as the content, reflected this change in thinking. Instead of reflecting the image of Stalin's clash of two worlds, or even discussing separate socialist, developing countries and Western capitalist worlds, the discussion was about *one world*. And Gorbachev spoke about problems "on a global scale affecting the very foundation of the existence of civilization." Besides the crucial preeminent need to prevent a nuclear war, he noted pollution of the environment and depletion of natural resources. Most important, "One cannot resolve these global problems affecting all humanity by the efforts of any one state or group of states. For this cooperation on a global scale is required, a close constructive collaboration of the majority of countries."[16]

Gorbachev cited President Reagan's comment at Geneva that the Soviet Union and the United States would quickly find a common language if the earth were threatened by the arrival of extraterrestrial beings. "But," argued Gorbachev, "isn't a nuclear catastrophe a more real danger than a landing of unknown extraterrestrials? Is not the ecological threat a big enough threat? Don't all countries have a common interest in finding a sensible and fair approach to the problems of the developing states and peoples?" Indeed, he concluded that "the course of history, of social progress, requires ever more insistently establishing a *constructive, creative interaction among states and peoples on the scale of the entire world.* . . . Such interaction is essential in order to prevent a nuclear catastrophe, so that civilization should survive. It is essential in order that other worldwide problems that are growing more acute could be resolved jointly in the interests of all concerned."[17]

What of the continuing clash and competition of the socialist (communist) and capitalist (imperialist) worlds? Gorbachev purported to see "the vitality of Marxist-Leninist teachings convincingly confirmed," but he also noted that "any attempt to turn the theory by which we are guided into a collection of ossified schemes and prescriptions valid everywhere and under all circumstances is most definitely contrary to the essence and spirit of Marxism-Leninism." "We are," he said, "realists and are perfectly aware that the two worlds are divided by many things, and deeply divided. But we also see clearly that the need to resolve the most vital problems affecting all humanity must prompt them to combined action, awakening the heretofore unseen forces of self-preservation of mankind."[18]

---

16. Gorbachev, *Politicheskii doklad*, p. 23. Gorbachev had first spoken in this way about one world in an unpublished speech to a Central Committee plenum in October 1985. Information from Anatoly Chernyayev.

17. Ibid., p. 25. Emphasis in original.

18. Ibid., pp. 3–5, 25.

The central conclusion of this dilemma was that although the political and ideological competition of the two sides would continue, not only must it be contained within limits short of war, but it must also be combined with the exigencies of interdependence. In Gorbachev's own words: "The realistic dialectics of contemporary development consists of a combination of competition [*sorevnovaniye*] and opposition [*protivoborstvo*] between the two systems with the growing trend to interdependence of the states of the world community." And he spoke further of the "contradictory, but *interdependent and in many ways integral world that is taking shape*." This unprecedented disquisition on the emergence of global interdependence and an integral world, it should be recalled, was featured in the basic section of the Central Committee report on the main trends in the contemporary world, which was introduced by the statement that "it is possible to conduct a correct, scientifically based policy only with clear understanding of the key trends in current reality."

Gorbachev's report also featured a major section devoted to "The Basic Aims and Directions of the Party's Foreign Policy Strategy." At the outset, "the principal objective" of Soviet foreign policy was stated to be "to provide the Soviet people the opportunity to work under conditions of a stable peace and freedom." Throughout the entire elaboration of the report, a consistent emphasis on security dominated any other objective.

In the brief references to "progressive" change in the world, and explicitly to the world communist movement, "The Communist Party of the Soviet Union sees as its main international duty the successful progress of our country along the path opened up and laid down by [the] October [Revolution]." Thus the Soviet leaders saw their main "international duty" as communists not in assisting in the establishment of communist rule around the world but in developing the Soviet Union. Whether they were really that confident in the power of the example of their own successes may not be certain, but clearly the Soviet leaders had found an ideological justification for not risking the security of the Soviet Union in pursuit of revolutionary change in the world. They also provided ideological justification by recalling Lenin's rejection of "the theory of revolutionary war" advocated by some Bolshevik leaders seeking to carry socialism from Soviet Russia to other countries. Gorbachev cited this in the report, and added, "Today, too, we are firmly convinced that fueling revolutions from outside, and doubly so by military means, is futile and inadmissible."[19]

The only Third World country mentioned by name in Gorbachev's report was Afghanistan. And it was mentioned not as an example of revolutionary advance but as an instance of imperialist-supported counterrevolutionary challenge. Moreover, Gorbachev referred to the situation not in terms of its significance for revolutionary change in the Third World but as a threat to

---

19. Ibid., p. 25. Emphasis in original. See also pp. 7, 80, 93, 14.

Soviet security. Finally, he characterized Afghanistan as a "bleeding wound" and justified direct Soviet involvement (above all, to his primary audience, the members of the Communist Party and the Soviet people) not as a Soviet sacrifice to world revolutionary progress (although dispatched "at the request of the [Afghan] government") but because of "our vital *national interest*" in peaceful neighbors and "the *security* of our borders."[20] There is convincing evidence that this purpose was the overriding motivation of the Soviet leaders in deciding to intervene in 1979.[21] Reference to this past, direct, unilateral action in meeting a Soviet security imperative was, however, an exception to the main thrust of the report.

　　The central focus and theme of the entire discussion of Soviet foreign policy aims not only was on security but was couched in an unprecedented way. Although preventing nuclear war, achieving progress in disarmament, and promoting peaceful coexistence had been prominent Soviet aims also advanced in the reports to the three preceding party congresses, they were now said to be "the main line of the party's activity in the world arena" and were given a new context.[22] Gorbachev emphasized the new imperative by saying that "the world has become too small and too fragile for wars and for politics of force [*silovaya politika*]." The heart of Gorbachev's argument was the conclusion that *no nation can any longer find security in military power*, either in defense or deterrence. "The character of contemporary weapons," in Gorbachev's words, "does not leave any state hope of protecting itself by military-technical means alone, for example by creating even the most powerful defense."[23] And, while mutual deterrence was more effective than defense, "Security cannot indefinitely be based on fear of retaliation, that is on doctrines of 'deterrence' or 'intimidation.' "[24] Rather, "The task of insuring security increasingly is a political task, and can be resolved only by political means." Moreover, security can only be mutual with respect to security for the Soviet Union and the United States, and "if one takes international relations as a whole, can only be universal."[25] And building on the earlier discussion of global interdependence, he concluded his discussion of foreign policy by calling for "creation of a com-

---

20. Ibid., pp. 88–89. Emphasis added.

21. See Raymond L. Garthoff, *Détente and Confrontation: American-Soviet Relations from Nixon to Reagan*, rev. ed. (Brookings, 1994), chapter 26.

22. Gorbachev, *Politicheskii doklad*, p. 81. The words I have translated here as "the main line" (*magistral'noye napravleniye*) are far reaching; one official Soviet translation rendered them as "the fundamental direction."

23. Ibid., p. 83.

24. Ibid., p. 82. Gorbachev included both terms used in Russian for deterrence—the favorable one, *sderzhivaniye*, meaning restraint, and the critical one, *ustrashneniye*, meaning intimidation.

25. Ibid., pp. 81, 82.

prehensive system of international security"—military, political, economic, and humanitarian.[26]

In regard to relations with the United States, Gorbachev seemed a little defensive about the heavy emphasis placed on them. He stated: "The world, of course, is much larger than the United States. . . . And one must not in world politics lock in only on relations with any one country, even if it is especially important. That, as experience shows, only encourages a presumption of strength. But, naturally, we assign important significance to the state and character of relations of the Soviet Union and the United States." He continued, "Our countries have not a few common interests, and there is the objective imperative to live in the world at peace with one another, and to compete on an equal and mutually advantageous basis—but only equal and mutually advantageous."[27]

Although strongly advocating improvement of relations with the United States and the West in general, Gorbachev stressed that this of course required a readiness on both sides to do so. "We understand very well that by no means is everything up to us, that much will depend on the West, on the ability of its leaders not to lose sober reason at an important historical crossroads." And the prospect was clouded by developments in the United States. "The ruling circles of the United States have clearly lost a realistic orientation in this difficult period of history."[28] As a result of the fact that "the right wing group that has come to power in the United States and their main fellow-travellers in NATO have sharply turned from détente to a policy of military force," "never before in the postwar decades [that is, through the Cold War] has the situation in the world been so explosively dangerous, and consequently complex and unfavorable, as the first half of the 1980s." Hence the main question was: "Can the ruling centers of capitalism enter on the path of sober, constructive evaluation of what is going on? It would be easiest to reply: maybe yes, and maybe no. But history does not give us the right to such a prospective. We cannot accept 'no' to the question whether mankind will be or not be."[29]

---

26. Ibid., p. 83. The term rendered here as "comprehensive," *vseob"yemlyushchei*, could also be translated as "all-embracing" or even "universal."

   Gorbachev spelled out several measures and objectives for inclusion in such a system, including not only such predictable elements as arms limitations and reduction, confidence-building measures, and an end to economic discrimination and use of economic sanctions, but also "working for effective measures to prevent international terrorism," pooling efforts for peaceful exploration of space, and uniting divided families (ibid., pp. 82, 95–96.)

27. Ibid., p. 82. The expression I have rendered as "common interests" is literally "points of contact," a phrase used by Soviet officials to mean common positions or common interests. This sentence was followed by "extended applause"—although whether for the idea of cooperation with the United States, or for the repeated qualifier that cooperation was possible only on an equal basis, was not clear.

28. Ibid., p. 24.

29. Ibid., pp. 81, 25.

Despite the negative assessment of the stand of the Reagan administration to date, Gorbachev did reflect guarded optimism, based in particular on the recent summit meeting in Geneva. Accordingly, he said that "there appeared to be signs of a change for the better in Soviet-American relations," although cautioning that "the sharp chilling of the climate in the first half of the 1980s again reminded [us] that nothing comes on its own."[30] Indeed, in a late insertion in the report, Gorbachev noted that the Soviet leadership had just received two days earlier a negative reply from President Reagan to its latest arms proposals. And he stressed—in a theme to be reiterated throughout the year—that the significance of the next summit meeting, on which agreement had been reached at Geneva, was in the expectation that it would give "practical results to the most important directions of limiting and reducing arms." Not only would there be "no sense in carrying out empty talks," but Soviet-American talks must not be used as a cover for continuing the arms race. Yet also, earlier in the report, he had justified the course of seeking improved relations by saying that "it is necessary to seek, to find, and to use even the smallest chance, while it is still not too late, to break the trend of a growing military danger."[31]

This was the Soviet leadership's dilemma: how to pursue even a low-probability chance of a breakthrough in arms limitation with the United States without becoming party to a negotiating process that the American leaders could exploit to pursue the arms competition rather than to reach an agreement on constraints and reductions. And they had not found an answer to that dilemma.

The "new thinking," as it came to be called, reflected so clearly in Gorbachev's report to the party congress had not of course emerged all at once. Soviet academics and officials had been developing this new approach for years. Indeed, some elements had their roots in the Khrushchev post-Stalin thaw, although the new thinking was going far beyond those early manifestations. In the 1970s, as the East-West détente developed, so did thinking about a restructuring (*perestroika*) of international relations.[32] In the early 1980s, as détente gave way to renewed confrontation, there was increasing awareness that rigidity of Soviet thinking was an important factor, as well as Soviet actions such as the intervention in Afghanistan and deployment of SS-20 missiles facing Europe. This budding new thinking not only arose in academic institutes but also in the Communist Party's Academy of Social Sciences, the Central Committee staff, and in the Ministry of Foreign Affairs.[33] Nor was new thinking limited to

---

30. Ibid., p. 81.

31. Ibid., pp. 87, 88, 81.

32. See the discussion, and the references cited, in Garthoff, *Détente and Confrontation*, chapter 2.

33. See in particular Anatoly Gromyko and Vladimir Lomeiko, *Novoye myshleniye v yadernyi vek* (New Thinking in the Nuclear Age) (Moscow: Mezhdunarodnyye

Moscow intellectuals and the foreign affairs community. Eduard Shevardnadze has disclosed how he and Mikhail Gorbachev, as regional party leaders in the late 1970s, talked about the need for drastic change in the party's thinking and action in domestic as well as foreign affairs.[34]

Soon after Leonid Brezhnev's death, Yury Andropov quietly commissioned a large number of studies on possible new approaches, with which junior Politburo member Gorbachev, among others, became familiar.[35] Similarly, work on a revised party program, begun under Brezhnev in 1981, was pursued more seriously under Andropov and Chernenko. Even Chernenko in 1984 in a published guidance on drafting the program made clear that the prediction of the impending collapse of capitalism and triumph of communism that had "prematurely" been included in the previous (1961) program would be deleted. And in foreign affairs, he stressed the need for prevention of nuclear war.[36] The new revised program, adopted at the Twenty-seventh Party Congress, embodied many themes of the new thinking—although, as a document under review and consideration for several years, less completely than Gorbachev's Political Report of the Central Committee.[37]

---

otnosheniya, 1984); V. V. Zagladin and others, *Vopros vsyekh voprosov* (The Question of All Questions) (Moscow: Politizdat, 1985); and V. F. Petrovsky, *Sovetskaya kontseptsiya bezopasnosti* (The Soviet Conception of Security) (Moscow: Nauka, 1986). All were written before Gorbachev came to power; Gromyko was director of an Academy of Sciences institute and the son of the foreign minister, Lomieko was the elder Gromyko's son-in-law, Zagladin a senior Central Committee official, and Petrovsky a senior official in the Foreign Ministry. Among the leading academic new thinkers were Nikolai Inozemtsev, Georgy Arbatov, Yevgeny Primakov, and Vitaly Zhurkin.

34. Eduard Shevardnadze, *The Future Belongs to Freedom* (Macmillan Free Press, 1991), p. 26.

35. Several Soviet academic and political figures have confirmed this process. One of the few public references was by Gorbachev in a speech to leading scientific and cultural personnel in early 1989. While not specifically attributing the initiative to Andropov, he stressed that a process began "several years" before the key April 1985 Central Committee plenum at the start of his leadership. In an aside he asked Nikolai Ryzhkov how many studies had been undertaken, Ryzhkov said 110, and Gorbachev then repeated, "All of them belong to the period when the April plenum was still a long way off." And with reference to his participation, he added: "Indeed, I personally, among others, had occasion to meet many of you more than once to discuss these matters well before the April plenum." See "To Build Up the Intellectual Potential of Perestroika, Speech of M. S. Gorbachev," *Pravda*, January 7 (late ed.) and 8, 1989.

36. "Speech by Comrade K. U. Chernenko at the Session of the Commission of the CC CPSU on Preparation of the New Text of the Program of the CPSU, April 25, 1984," *Kommunist* (Communist), no. 7 (May 1984), pp. 7–8.

37. "CPSU Program New Edition Adopted by the 27th CPSU Congress," *Pravda*, March 7, 1986.

Shevardnadze has described very succinctly the foreign policy program underlying and applying those broad propositions. He has written that on the basis of the report to the party congress,

Our guidelines were precise: to stop the preparation for nuclear war; to move Soviet-American relations onto a track of normal, civilized dialog; to reject the dead, brutally rigid positions in favor of intelligent, mutually acceptable compromises; to move our affairs toward a balance of interests; to strive for the confinement of military capabilities to the level of reasonable sufficiency; to confirm the principle of comprehensive control and verification; to seek ways to end nuclear tests and dismantle the American and Soviet intermediate range missiles in Europe; to bring Soviet troops out of Afghanistan; to create a security system in Europe on the basis of the Helsinki process, radically cutting nuclear and conventional arms; to defuse regional conflicts, to normalize relations with China; to build relations with our neighbors on a basis of respect of their interests and the principles of noninterference in their internal affairs; to concern ourselves with global problems.

All this had to be embodied in a practical policy.[38]

Gorbachev himself, in a speech at a closed session to leading figures of the Ministry of Foreign Affairs three months later, referred to the report to the congress as providing "a profound analysis of world development and the basic trends in the foreign-policy activity of the Soviet state" and pleaded for members to take a "more realistic approach," based on "a more sober and broad evolution of concrete facts, rather than viewing everything only from the point of view of one's own [that is, Soviet] interests."[39]

New thinking, in new approaches and in underlying understanding, was much less advanced with respect to internal developments. The depth of the problems and the scope of necessary change, so striking in national and international security, were less well understood in regard to domestic economic and political reform, including the looming nationality problem. To some extent, failure to appreciate the extent of internal Soviet weakness facilitated the more radical approach to security and external affairs. For example, on the eve of his elevation to power Gorbachev in December 1984 in a speech to a party conference on ideology repeated a theme also sounded by Andropov in November 1982, that socialism (and the Soviet Union) "exerts its main

---

38. Shevardnadze, *The Future Belongs to Freedom*, p. 51.
   The guidelines may not have been quite so precise or clear in 1986 as Shevardnadze makes them in retrospect, but there is abundant evidence that most if not all of these important policy lines were envisaged at that early time.

39. Gorbachev's speech was not published until well over a year later, and then in a condensed form in the first issue of a new specialized journal of record of the Foreign Ministry. See "Time for Perestroika, Address of M. S. Gorbachev to the MID USSR, May 23, 1986," in *Vestnik Ministerstva innostrannykh del SSSR* (Bulletin of the Ministry of Foreign Affairs of the USSR), no. 1 (August 5, 1987), pp. 5–6.

influence on world development through its economic policy and its successes in the socio-economic field."[40]

The revised party program, while not contradicting the shift toward new thinking, was less far-reaching than Gorbachev's report. It reflected not only the extended collaborative editing process but also that strong conservative tendencies remained in the new collective leadership. There were other signs of this fact.

Despite his considerable successes in retiring conservative opponents, Gorbachev and his new team also had some setbacks. Most notably, an attempt in February to oust Politburo member Dinmukhamed A. Kunayev from his regional party base as first secretary of the Communist Party of Kazakhstan failed. In preparation for the round of republic party congresses preceding the national one, a Kazakh party official, acting as the agent of the central party Secretariat, strongly criticized Kunayev. To drive the signal home, this speech and its criticism were reported in *Pravda*. Even so, the Kazakh party machine— its members aware they would be purged along with their leader—defiantly kept him on. Instead, the official who had criticized Kunayev was removed! The criticism of Kunayev published in *Pravda* marked the first such direct criticism of a Politburo member who was not then promptly removed since the 1920s.[41] This episode showed there were limits to the power even of the general secretary and his Secretariat in Moscow and indicated that even within the Politburo there was caution against moving too strongly. Gorbachev and his colleagues did not want to force the issue, and they preferred to take more time to prepare the way.[42] Another entrenched conservative party chief of a republic, Vladimir Shcherbitsky of the Ukraine, was not even challenged at this time.

---

40. "True Work of the People: Report by Comrade M. S. Gorbachev," *Pravda*, December 11, 1984; and see "Speech of General Secretary of the Central Committee of the CPSU Yury Andropov to the Plenum of the CC CPSU, 22 Nov. 1982," *Pravda*, November 23, 1982.

41. D. Valovoi and A. Petrushov, "Kazakhstan: The Times Demand," *Pravda*, February 9, 1986. Valovoi was the deputy chief editor of Pravda.

42. In March, I asked a senior Central Committee official privately why Kunayev had not been ousted, since that clearly seemed to have been the intention. He acknowledged that the leadership wanted to remove him but explained it was harder to remove a party leader entrenched in one of the republics. It would take time. "Just wait six months or so, and you'll see," he said. In fact, it took a little longer, but nine months later, after intensive preparations, Kunayev was removed by the Kazakh party. Shortly before the end of the year he was replaced by a party official from Russia (discussed later in this chapter). Even then, recalcitrant members of the local party machine instigated riots in the capital city, Alma Ata, in a desperate (and unsuccessful) attempt to reverse or at least mitigate the purge; the effect was to speed it up. In the somewhat similar case of Grishin and the Moscow party machine, however, for Gorbachev and the majority of the collective leadership to have permitted Grishin to defy them would have been an intolerable display of weakness (see chapter 5).

Soviet relations with the United States were not a central issue in the internal Soviet political arena, although they were indirectly relevant in many ways. Gorbachev did not want to make himself politically vulnerable by appearing to give in to American terms for the relationship while failing to stand up for Soviet interests. Even when his new thinking and budding internal reform would move in directions that the United States would welcome, he did not want it to appear that his moves were responsive to American, rather than revalued Soviet, purposes. Above all, he could not appear to pursue his new advocacy of enlightened common security at the expense of perceived Soviet security interests. And on the greatest perceived security threat, the American SDI and its potential not only for blocking arms reductions but for increasing the risk of nuclear war, he had been entirely unsuccessful at persuading President Reagan at Geneva. This problem thus remained at the center of his agenda in relations with the United States.

## Reagan's Course

President Reagan was very pleased with his performance at the Geneva summit and with the policy course that welcomed dialogue and improving relations with the Soviet Union, as long as this could be obtained by Soviet concessions and movement toward American positions. Some of his team, in particular Defense Secretary Caspar Weinberger, were unhappy even at a limited rapprochement and reduction of tensions on that basis. Others, notably Secretary of State George Shultz, saw the new course as vindication of the gradual improvement of relations he had been seeking since 1983. But no one saw a need to change U.S. policy.

Gorbachev's major January 15 initiative to broaden and give momentum to disarmament was dismissed by the skeptics, and at best cautiously welcomed by some. It did not lead to any reappraisal, much less revision, of the American strategic arms positions.[43]

Even before Gorbachev's speech, in early January, Secretary Shultz through Ambassador Dobrynin had sounded out the Soviet leader on the possibility of holding the next summit meeting in Washington in June. The Soviets were, however, wary of agreeing to any meeting before there were signs of progress to break the stalemate over strategic arms control. Ambassador Dobrynin informally suggested September to allow more time for such prog-

---

43. Secretary Shultz, however, did see it as significant and an opening that the United States could use at least to push for zero INF. President Reagan was the most enthusiastic and recalled he had spoken to Gorbachev in their private chat in Geneva about working for a world without nuclear weapons. See George P. Shultz, *Turmoil and Triumph: My Years as Secretary of State* (Charles Scribner's Sons, 1993), pp. 699–702.

ress. In a meeting with visiting Senator Edward M. Kennedy in early February Gorbachev made clear that he would not commit himself to a summit date until he had a response from President Reagan and indication that progress on arms negotiations would justify a meeting.[44] Gorbachev renewed the direct exchange of letters with Reagan in a January 11 reply to Reagan's letter of December 7 dealing with a range of regional, humanitarian, and bilateral issues, but not the summit. Similarly, on January 15 he advised Reagan by letter of his forthcoming public initiative to seek a ban on nuclear weapons.[45]

Reagan resumed his dialogue on arms control, seeking to clear the way for a summit in two letters in February, the first (on February 6) replying to Gorbachev's of December and the second (on February 22) advancing some new proposals.[46] His proposals did not, however, move toward Gorbachev's initiatives on nuclear testing or, most important, signal any change on the SDI. Gorbachev so noted in a letter on April 2, amplified by comments orally conveyed by Ambassador Dobrynin. Although the full texts of the letters, and oral exchanges, are not available, from the excerpts released it seems that Gorbachev may have been signaling that even if the space weapons (SDI) issue could not be settled at that time, a major step forward toward banning nuclear testing might have been sufficient to justify a summit.[47] But there was no such breakthrough.

The private exchanges in correspondence between the two leaders were also reflected in part in public statements and leaks to the media. Gorbachev's statement to the party congress on February 25 that a summit was predicated on real progress in disarmament, "practical results," and that "there would be no sense in holding empty talks,"[48] annoyed the White House, which rejected such "linkage."[49] Even before that, Reagan administration spokesmen had been complaining to the press that, as they put it, "Moscow seems to be trying to obtain concessions on arms control in return for agreeing to a date" for the summit.[50] On March 6, President Reagan himself told news reporters at a

---

44. See Don Oberdorfer, "Kennedy Says Summit Tied to Arms Pact," *Washington Post*, February 9, 1986, p. A1.

45. See Ronald Reagan, *An American Life* (Simon and Schuster, 1990), pp. 649–51, providing excerpts of both letters. Reagan reacted negatively to Gorbachev's public initiative following the letter, rather than seeing the private message as courtesy advance notice of what would be in the speech.

46. Ibid., pp. 652–59, with extensive excerpts. See also Shultz, *Turmoil and Triumph*, pp. 707–09.

47. Ibid., pp. 660–64.

48. Gorbachev, *Politicheskii doklad*, p. 88.

49. See Michael R. Gordon, "U.S. Rules Out a Linkage of Arms and Summit Talks," *New York Times*, February 27, 1986, p. A8.

50. See Bernard Gwertzman, "U.S., Annoyed, Presses Soviet on a Date for Next Summit Meeting," *New York Times*, February 11, 1986, p. A12.

breakfast meeting that if Gorbachev wanted him to visit Moscow in 1987, he must make the arrangements to come to Washington in 1986, and that he wanted it in the summer because of his plans to be active in the fall election campaign.[51]

The funeral of assassinated Swedish Prime Minister Olof Palme provided an opportunity for Secretary Shultz to meet in Stockholm on March 15 with Soviet Prime Minister Nikolai Ryzhkov. The meeting, described by Shultz as "very frank," did not bring the sides closer together. Ryzhkov emphasized the need to address nuclear testing, stressing Gorbachev's declaration just two days earlier to continue a moratorium on nuclear testing as long as the United States also refrained from testing. The United States had promptly rejected that proposal and on March 22 underscored the point by carrying out another nuclear test. Not fazed, Gorbachev on March 29 proposed a summit meeting to agree on banning nuclear testing and extended the Soviet moratorium again despite the U.S. test. The United States promptly rejected the idea. Shultz soon after publicly expressed his dismay at the recent pattern of public Soviet and American statements and his hope that private diplomacy could again become the usual procedure; otherwise, he said, "We're not going anywhere."[52]

Shortly before his departure to assume his new position as a member of the party leadership in Moscow, Ambassador Dobrynin on April 8 met with President Reagan (at which time he transmitted Gorbachev's letter of April 2).[53] While no substantive agreement was reached, it was agreed that on May 14–16 Foreign Minister Shevardnadze would meet in Washington with Secretary Shultz to prepare for the summit—recommitting both sides to keep up efforts. On this same day, April 8, Gorbachev said he was placing no "preconditions" on a summit, which could take place if the "spirit of Geneva" were "revived."[54]

As the prospects for a second summit wavered, further steps were taken along lines of cooperation agreed on at Geneva. Meetings of regional experts (at the assistant secretary of state–deputy foreign minister level) were held: on March 6 on southern Africa, on June 10–11 on East and Southeast Asia, on June 26–27 on the Middle East, on September 2–3 on Afghanistan, and on August 26–28 on regional issues in general. Meetings of experts on banning chemical weapons met in Bern on March 5–6 and September 4–5, and

---

51. See David Hoffman and Walter Pincus, "President Presses Gorbachev for Action on Summit Plan," *Washington Post*, March 6, 1986, p. A1.

52. See Bernard Gwertzman, "Shultz Wants U.S. and Soviet to End Public Diplomacy," *New York Times*, March 31, 1986, p. A12.

53. See Don Oberdorfer, "Shultz and Dobrynin Discuss Summit," and "Dobrynin Farewell Talks Ease Tensions," *Washington Post*, April 8 and 12, 1986, p. A1.

54. "Speech of Comrade M. S. Gorbachev at a Meeting with Workers of the City of Togliatti," *Pravda*, April 9, 1986.

preliminary talks on nuclear risk reduction centers were held in Geneva on May 5–6 and August 25.

USIA Director Charles Wick's meetings in Moscow in January led to further talks and an agreement in August on thirteen educational, scientific, and cultural exchanges. These included the first exchange of high-school students (ten on each side) and of language teachers; health problems common to Alaska and Siberia; development of joint textbooks for language instruction; computer applications to elementary and secondary education; as well as an exchange of open visits and exhibitions of paintings. Soviet proposals for exchanges on research on fusion power, raised before the summit and with agreement at Geneva on their consideration, were shunted aside owing to objections by the Department of Defense, which proposed substituting cooperation on conventional fusion nuclear power plant safety, on which agreement was reached in August.

The Civil Aviation Agreement led to resumption of scheduled air service between the United States and the Soviet Union on April 29. Maritime talks began in March. The most novel and potentially useful step was an invitation by Defense Secretary Caspar Weinberger to the Soviet defense minister to visit the United States. Although such talks did not actually take place until two years later, the invitation was a start.

There was very little progress in developing economic relations. Oil and gas technology licensing was placed on a case-by-case review basis early in the year, but the United States moved very slowly on loosening the Western Coordinating Committee on export controls (COCOM) and unilateral U.S. controls. The United States reacted very negatively to Soviet expressions of interest in participating in the General Agreement on Tariffs and Trade (GATT) multilateral trade negotiations. The only exception to the cool American stance on trade was a decision, controversial within the Reagan administration, to subsidize American grain sales to the Soviet Union. Initially sponsored by Senator Robert J. Dole and sixteen other midwestern senators and supported by domestic affairs advisers in the cabinet, the proposal to subsidize Soviet grain purchases was strongly opposed by Secretaries Shultz and Weinberger. Nonetheless, President Reagan again, as he had in ending the grain embargo in 1981 over Haig's objection, decided in August to offer nearly 4 million metric tons of subsidized wheat to the Soviet Union to meet its quota under the long-term bilateral grain agreement signed in 1983. The administration was then embarrassed when the Soviet Union, taking advantage of a world grain supply glut, did not avail itself of the offer.

While summit diplomacy and arms negotiations remained stalemated, and economic and other contacts moved slowly and unevenly toward normalization, other events and actions by the two powers were moving in an adverse flow.

On March 7, in an unprecedented step, the United States ordered the Soviet Union to cut the staff of its diplomatic mission to the United Nations in New York from 275 to 170, phased over the next two years. The reason given was security against espionage, although the last public charge against a Soviet UN staff member had been three years earlier. Besides a strong diplomatic protest, the Soviets seized the first opportunity, only three days later, to arrest and expel an officer of the U.S. Embassy in Moscow, Michael Sellers, caught in a clandestine meeting with a Soviet source. Two months later another American Embassy staff officer, Erik Sites, was also arrested and declared persona non grata.[55] On June 20 it was the United States' turn; the arrest of Colonel Vladimir Izmailov, the Soviet air attache in Washington, was announced by the FBI in a publicized press conference. Further incidents, and a more important and different situation stemming from espionage charges, were to ensue in a few months, as will be discussed later.

Meanwhile, a more serious incident arose from an assertive American political use of military power, with a subsidiary intelligence aspect. On March 13, the USS *Yorktown*, a nuclear-missile-armed cruiser, and the USS *Caron*, a specially designed and outfitted intelligence-collection destroyer, deliberately entered Soviet territorial waters within six miles of the southern coast of the Crimea, despite Soviet warnings and signals to withdraw. It was routine for two U.S. warships to enter the Black Sea (usually twice a year) to show the flag and reaffirm their right to do so. The same two ships had been there on the last cruise in December 1965. What was not routine, indeed was without precedent, was for such ships to enter Soviet territorial waters. As soon as the Soviet Union publicly protested the action three days later, calling it "demonstrative, defiant and pursuing a clearly provocative aim," administration spokesmen insisted the action was "simply an exercise of the right of innocent passage." This explanation was challenged by many American experts, who saw no appropriate exercise of innocent "passage" through normal sea lanes, since the ships had had to go out of their way to enter those waters. Moreover, the passage was not "innocent," since the *USS Caron* was evidently collecting intelligence. The Law of the Sea Treaty, while the United States was not a signatory, had been accepted by the administration in 1983 as embodying customary international law in all respects except regarding rights of exploration of the seabed. This treaty (Section 3) states that "any act aimed at collecting information to the prejudice of the defense or security of the coastal State" is not consistent with innocent passage.[56]

---

55. Sellers was arrested on March 10, and the fact was announced by the Soviet Union on March 14. Sites was arrested on May 7, also while meeting a Soviet source, and the arrest was revealed by the Soviet Union on May 14.

56. See Rear Admiral Eugene J. Carroll, Jr., USN (ret.), "Black Day on the Black Sea," *Arms Control Today*, vol. 18 (May 1988), pp. 14–17, discussing a similar incursion in February 1988 as well as that of March 1986. See also three exchanges between Professors Alfred P. Rubin and Harry H. Almond, Jr., debating the issue in the *Naval War College Review*, vol. 41 (Autumn 1988), p. 110, 42 (Spring 1989), pp. 109–12, and (Autumn 1989), pp. 117–18.

Pentagon officials readily confirmed to news reporters that one purpose of the penetration of Soviet territorial waters was to collect intelligence, and the other was to assert their interpretation of innocent passage. They also declared that planned exercises in the Gulf of Sidra off Libya, to be held in a few days, would pursue the same objectives and also support the right to sail in international waters. Both actions had been approved by the Joint Chiefs of Staff and the secretary of defense. The loquacious officials were cited as saying both actions were also intended to bolster the president's appeal to Congress for an increase in military spending, which could be expected to follow incidents where the United States had "flexed its military muscle."[57]

When the "similar" naval exercises in the Gulf of Sidra led on March 24 to Libyan SA-5 antiaircraft missile firings, and retaliatory U.S. air strikes on those SA-5 sites and on several Libyan patrol vessels, the Soviets were further put off by the U.S. claims that the only purpose in the recent Black Sea episode was innocent exercise of innocent passage.[58] Moreover, when only a few weeks later, on April 14, the United States launched a bombing raid on several targets in Tripoli and Benghazi, in retaliation for a terrorist bombing incident in Berlin for which the Libyans were held responsible, the impression of intimidation created by the March actions in Sidra and the Black Sea the month before was strengthened.

The action against Libya seemed to fit an ominous pattern of new muscle-flexing by the American military in support of the Reagan Doctrine. Although the Soviet Union was not directly a target of the Reagan Doctrine, the Soviet leaders understood—correctly—that the United States was seeking not only to contain but to cut back Soviet influence around the world. Whether correctly or in exaggeration, they saw such actions as provocative American naval maneuvers close to Soviet shores, and not only in the Black Sea, as intimidation to prevent Soviet counteractions to the American use of military power in the Third World.

As noted in chapter 5, the Reagan Doctrine, or at least its foreshadowing, was evident in the Caribbean from the early days of the Reagan administration, and increasingly elsewhere as well. It was given new emphasis in the second Reagan administration notwithstanding the new readiness to deal with the Soviet Union.[59] Thus in his address on the State of the Union in early February, President Reagan proclaimed: "You are not alone freedom fighters. America will support you with moral and material assistance . . . to win freedom

57. See Richard Halloran, "2 U.S. Ships Enter Soviet Waters Off Crimea to Gather Intelligence," *New York Times*, March 19, 1986, p. A1; and William M. Arkin, "Spying in the Black Sea," *Bulletin of the Atomic Scientists*, vol. 44 (May 1988), pp. 5–6.

58. Incidentally, the lead ship in the U.S. naval force entering the Gulf of Sidra on March 22 was the USS *Caron*, recently back from its Black Sea adventures.

59. See also the extended discussion in chapter 15.

in Afghanistan, in Angola, in Cambodia, and in Nicaragua."[60] And in his formal message to Congress on that occasion, Reagan made clear that a new relationship with the Soviet Union based on "realism" meant *Soviet* realism in acquiescing to the American aim of "expanding," not merely defending, "the family of Free Nations."[61] The Soviet conception of détente and coexistence in Soviet-American relations in the 1970s had in fact been predicated on American acquiescence in progressive revolutionary change toward communism, with a nudge by the Soviet Union. The Reagan Doctrine of coexistence in the 1980s was predicated on precisely reversed roles, with an even more active American role in assisting revolutionary change away from communism.

On March 14, Reagan sent an unusual message to Congress devoted to the subject of regional conflicts around the world. This document represented, in effect, the charter for the Reagan Doctrine. Although recognizing disingenuously that "not every regional conflict should be viewed as part of the East-West conflict," he argued that "in the 1970s the challenge to regional security became—to a greater degree than before—the challenge of Soviet expansionism." Accordingly, he emphasized that "for the United States, these conflicts cannot be regarded as peripheral to other issues on the global agenda . . . and are a fundamental part of the overall U.S.-Soviet relationship." Moreover, "continuing Soviet adventurism in the developing world is inimical to global security and an obstacle to fundamental improvement of Soviet-American relations." The American aim was to change the actual situation in the Third World and "to convince the Soviet Union that the policies on which it embarked in the 70's cannot work."[62]

There was no hint of recognition that virtually coincident with this elaboration of the Reagan Doctrine, Gorbachev at the party congress had just presented a radically new Soviet view of the world that embraced the very reevaluation and change of course for Soviet policy that Reagan was calling for. The Reagan administration was unaware that it was essentially marshaling forces to knock down an open door.

To gain public and congressional support for arming "freedom fighters" around the globe, Reagan dramatized the Soviet role and challenge. For example, he sought to generate support for a record $320 billion military budget by referring to a "long history of Soviet brutality toward those who are

---

60. "The State of the Union," February 4, 1986, in *Weekly Compilation of Presidential Documents*, vol. 22 (February 10, 1986), p. 139. (Hereafter *Presidential Documents*.)

61. "America's Agenda for the Future. Message to the Congress. February 6, 1986," ibid., pp. 173–76.

62. "Freedom, Regional Security, and Global Peace," March 14, 1986, ibid., vol. 22 (March 24, 1986), pp. 356–64, passages cited from pp. 357, 358, 363.

   In his later memoir, Reagan candidly and casually acknowledged that for him the subject of "regional conflicts" was merely "a euphemism to describe Soviet adventurism" around the world. See Reagan, *An American Life*, p. 648.

weaker." He argued that in contrast to the 1970s when, he claimed, "One strategic country after another fell under the domination of the Soviet Union," "in these last 5 years, not one square inch of territory has been lost, and Grenada has been set free."[63] Throughout March, President Reagan also gave a series of speeches in support of a requested $100 million congressional authorization for funding the Nicaraguan contras filled with harsh anti-Soviet diatribes and exaggerated rhetoric about nefarious Soviet designs in the Americas.[64]

Nor were such statements President Reagan's rhetoric alone. Other statements, and actions, of the administration were no less strident and combative. On March 21, Reagan described "the continuing horror of the Soviet attempt to subjugate Afghanistan," ignoring talks under way to resolve the conflict there and withdraw Soviet forces, as he publicly proclaimed Afghanistan Day[65] and privately authorized another $300-plus million in "covert" military assistance (under an April 1985 intelligence finding publicly disclosed in June 1986).[66] On March 26, Attorney General Edwin Meese 3d, at the Khyber Pass, was carried away to the point of accusing the Soviet Union of "torture, rape and toxic gas, of famine, of scorched earth and genocide" as "part of a drive to dominate the entire world."[67] Four days later it was disclosed that Stinger antiaircraft missiles were to be supplied to the insurgents in Afghanistan.[68] At about the same time it was acknowledged publicly for the first time that the United States was, after a decade of congressionally imposed nonintervention, resuming military assistance to the UNITA insurgents in Angola, including supplying them with Stinger missiles.[69]

---

63. See his "Address to the Nation," February 26, 1986, *Presidential Documents*, vol. 22 (March 3, 1986), pp. 288, 286.

64. For example, see his "Address to the Nation," March 16, 1986, ibid., vol. 22 (March 24, 1986), pp. 371–75, and his "Radio Address to the Nation," March 22, 1986, ibid., vol. 22 (March 31, 1986), pp. 403–04.

65. "Afghanistan Day, 1986. Proclamation 5450. March 21, 1986," ibid., vol. 22 (March 24, 1986), p. 398.

66. See Leslie H. Gelb, "'85 Reagan Ruling on Afghans Cited," *New York Times*, June 19, 1986, p. A1.

67. The first of these quotations is in the transcript of his prepared address, obtained from his office in the Department of Justice. That transcript notes that "the speech as delivered may vary from this text." The latter quotation is from the Reuters dispatch based on actual delivery, adapted in "Meese Accuses Soviet [Union] of Afghan War Crimes," *New York Times*, March 27, 1986, p. A5.

68. See David B. Ottoway and Patrick E. Tyler, "U.S. Sends New Arms to Rebels," *Washington Post*, March 30, 1986, p. A1.

69. See Bernard Gwertzman, "President Decides to Send Weapons to Angola Rebels," *New York Times*, February 19, 1986, p. A1; and Rowland Evans and Robert Novak, "Stingers for Savimbi," *Washington Post*, March 31, 1986, p. A11.

Signs began to appear of the distorting effects of the gung-ho pursuit of the Reagan Doctrine on other U.S. objectives. For example, the United States had already been led by its covert program of support to Nicaraguan contras to engage in illegal terrorist actions such as mining civilian ports, and when that was uncovered, to draw back from a long tradition of American support for international institutions by withdrawing U.S. acceptance of the jurisdiction of the International Court of Justice in the case and refusing to participate in the proceedings. On June 27, the Court reached its final rulings, in favor of Nicaragua and condemning the United States for arming and sending the contras into Nicaragua, for mining Nicaraguan harbors, and for encouraging "acts contrary to general principles of humanitarian law" in producing the notorious assassination handbook for the contras. It rejected the U.S. claim of collective self-defense as justification for its support of the contras.[70]

Growing evidence was revealed, despite administration efforts first to stifle and then to downplay it, of the extensive involvement of the U.S.-supported Afghan insurgents in the drug trade.[71] In February, the State Department had reported to Congress that Afghanistan and the bordering tribal areas of Pakistan where the Afghan "freedom fighters" were congregated had become "the world's leading source of illicit heroin exports to the United States and Europe."[72] The United States had become so enamored of the Pakistani connection in supporting the Afghan insurgents that it also compromised its own policy on nuclear nonproliferation, turning a blind eye to active Pakistani pursuit of a nuclear weapon program (and blinking at the congressional requirement to certify that Pakistan did not yet "possess" a nuclear weapon). In June and July this action directly impinged on U.S.-Soviet relations. When the Soviet Union, sharing a parallel antiproliferation policy, warned Pakistan about its nuclear activities, the United States interceded privately with Moscow to warn the Soviets to keep hands off Pakistan.[73]

Some presumably fortuitous events also made American actions seem ominous to the Soviet leadership. Precisely at the time of the unprecedented U.S. incursion into Soviet territorial waters off the southern Crimea, Gorbachev was resting at his nearby leadership dacha at Livadia.[74] The action

---

70. For excerpts of the text see "International Court of Justice Final Ruling in Favor of Nicaragua," in *American Foreign Policy, Current Documents, 1986* (Department of State, 1987), pp. 768–71, and for the U.S. reaction, pp. 771–73.

71. For example, see Arthur Bonner, "Afghan Rebels' Victory Garden: Opium," *New York Times*, June 18, 1986, p. A1; and Peter Dale Scott and Jonathan Marshall, *Cocaine Politics: Drugs, Armies, and the CIA in Central America* (University of California Press, 1991).

72. Ibid.

73. See Bob Woodward and Don Oberdorfer, "Pakistan A-Project Upsets Superpowers," *Washington Post*, July 15, 1986, p. A1.

74. Two senior Soviet officials in Moscow told me this independently, at the time, in confidential tones. Mikhail Gorbachev in a later interview confirmed it to me.

thus seemed a direct slap at Gorbachev for holding back from a summit on American terms, and moreover raised questions in Soviet circles about whether Gorbachev had been too beguiled by Reagan's charm. A second event also was seen by some as a direct American slap at Gorbachev. On March 29, Gorbachev had renewed the moratorium on nuclear testing if the United States would follow suit. On April 8, when Ambassador Dobrynin paid his farewell call on President Reagan, he delivered Gorbachev's letter of April 2 extending a renewed plea to end nuclear tests. Two days later, the United States fired a new nuclear weapon test.

I have no doubt that Gorbachev's presence at a Crimean coastal dacha on March 13 was not known to U.S. military planners when they arranged the incursion. The resumption of nuclear testing just after the Soviet proposal was clearly a coincidence.[75] Nonetheless, it was not an incorrect Soviet reading of the events to see that the United States did not regard such an unprecedented naval incursion as inconsistent with the spirit of Geneva, and that America not only had no intention of restraining the SDI but also had no plan to curtail nuclear testing. Moreover, the new American détente did not include curbing assertive pursuit of the Reagan Doctrine of "neoglobalism" through flexing U.S. military muscle.

On April 15, in the immediate wake of the U.S. bombing raid on Libya, the Soviet Union canceled the planned May 14–16 meeting of Foreign Minister Shevardnadze and Secretary Shultz. The Soviet action was, in part, a minimum step in support of Muammar Qadhafi (and the only one they took). But it was more significant as an indication that Moscow was reassessing the prospects for cooperation with the United States that had seemed so promising in Geneva. An official "Soviet Government Statement" condemned American "neoglobalism" and gunboat diplomacy and claimed that "the latest actions of the United States convince even the few in the West who still had some illusions about the true intentions of the White House that its present course is a policy of aggression and provoking regional conflicts, a policy of perpetuating confrontation and balancing on the brink of war."[76] The language on dispelling

---

Gorbachev's presence at the time of the incident was not made public, as that would only have drawn attention to Soviet impotence.

75. In fact, the test had been long planned and was scheduled for April 8, the very day of Dobrynin's meeting with Reagan, but was postponed two days for technical reasons. See Walter Pincus, "Nuclear Test Postponed by Technical Problems," *Washington Post*, April 9, 1986, p. A19; Pincus, "U.S. Explodes Nuclear Device, Drawing Soviet Denunciation," *Washington Post*, April 11, 1986, p. A17; and Michael R. Gordon, "U.S. Carries Out a Disputed A-Test," *New York Times*, April 11, 1986, pp. A1, A8.

76. "Soviet Government Statement," *Pravda*, April 16, 1986.

any illusions was reminiscent of the Andropov "Statement" of September 1983, although this time implying that no one in the Soviet Union had had such illusions and tying the illusions to American expectations rather than to Soviet decisions on dealing with the United States. A Secret Central Committee Resolution of July 31 (whose authors included Shevardnadze, Dobrynin, and Yakovlev) emphasized that while the "immediate target of the policy of 'neoglobalism' now is mainly countries of the Third World," it really was directed above all at the Soviet Union and world socialism as a whole. It aimed "not only to stop the further spread and consolidation of positions of socialism around the world, but also to 'exhaust' the USSR and its allies, to disrupt the policy of acceleration of social-economic development of socialism both through a general arms race, and wearing it down in conflicts in different regions of the world."[77]

The picture looked bleak, but the Soviet leadership was not giving up on prospects for developing relations. Gorbachev, in a speech in East Berlin on April 21, again hit at American neoglobalism in Nicaragua, Angola, Afghanistan, and Cambodia and called the action against Libya "piracy." But in several speeches in April he balanced the need for a "new international atmosphere" with renewed emphasis on the need for progress in arms control.

On April 18, in a speech not then given the attention it deserved, Gorbachev proferred what he called "a serious offer of negotiations" for "a substantial reduction" of conventional forces in Europe, which could be verified by on-site inspection and would cover the whole area "from the Atlantic Ocean to the Urals."[78] This was followed up by a formal proposal along these lines by the Warsaw Pact at its next meeting, in Budapest on June 11, where a suggestion was made for a new forum, the Conference on Disarmament in Europe (CDE) under the Conference on Security and Cooperation in Europe (CSCE), instead of the more narrowly focused and long-stalemated mutual and balanced force reductions (MBFR) talks.[79] By offering verified substantial

---

77. TsKhSD (Center for the Storage of Contemporary Documentation; the former Central Committee Archive), Fond 3, Opis 102, Dokument 230: Postanovleniye TsK KPSS (Resolution of the Central Committee of the CPSU), *O merakh po usileniyu nashego protivodeistviya amerikanskoi politike 'neoglobalizma'* (On Measures to Strengthen Our Counteractions to the American Policy of "Neoglobalism"), July 31, 1986, Secret, p. 1 of the Resolution, p. 172 of the Archive file.

78. For example, contemporary reporting noted these new elements but reflected the jaded views of Western officials: "Diplomats here said the vaguely worded proposal did not appear substantially different from previous Soviet initiatives at the long-stalled [MBFR] East-West talks on conventional military force reductions in Vienna." Jackson Diehl, "Gorbachev Says U.S. Acts Hurt Ties, But Offers 'New Initiative' on Forces," *Washington Post*, April 19, 1986, p. A21.

79. "Warsaw Pact Appeal to the NATO States and All European Countries Concerning a Program for Reductions of Armed Forces and Conventional Arms in Europe," *Pravda*, June 12, 1986.

reductions in the European USSR as well as central Europe, this proposal lacked only one element (supplied two years later) to be compelling: an asymmetrical reduction disproportionately larger for the Warsaw Pact and the Soviet Union. The proposal represented dropping "the other shoe" so to speak, a proposed serious reduction in conventional arms to complement the elimination of nuclear arms proposed in January, although this was not generally recognized in the West at the time. Finally, an important development still under way in Soviet military doctrine was partly revealed in a reference in the Warsaw Pact that called for basing military doctrines and concepts of the alliances on "defensive principles" and maintaining a "balance of military forces at the lowest possible levels, the reduction of military potentials to the limits necessary for defense."[80] To be sure, this could still have been mere rhetoric, but in a few years it would be demonstrated to have been very significant.

A disastrous accident at a Soviet nuclear power station in Chernobyl in the Ukraine on April 26, not immediately acknowledged and without prompt alert to the Soviet population or to nearby countries, had international political as well as radioactive fallout. The Soviet leadership, badly misinformed at first by local officials who tried to minimize the danger and cover up the extent of the disaster, for a long time erred on the side of silence. Not only was the budding *glasnost* (openness) compromised, but the international interdependence of which Gorbachev had spoken so eloquently at the party congress now proved itself with a vengeance—and with an initially faltering Soviet response. Soviet slowness in meeting its obligations to inform others was partly a consequence of internal confusion and lack of information in Moscow. The Politburo first met on the matter only two days after the accident, at about the same time the first queries were received from Sweden (and met with an honest statement by the Foreign Ministry that they knew nothing about a nuclear accident).

There were justifiable complaints from neighboring countries, particularly in Scandinavia (and, less vocally, Eastern Europe) over the tardy notification and sketchy information. Even as the Soviet leadership was desperately trying to ascertain the true scope of the disaster and its consequences, and decide on countermeasures as well as how to advise other countries, Western media began to report all manner of unvalidated rumors. As the Soviet Union correctly reported two immediate deaths in the accident, the UPI (and many newspapers citing it) reported 2,000 dead. Other press reports (the *New York Post*) alleged as many as 15,000 deaths. Worse still, Radio Liberty and Radio Free Europe began reporting large death figures to Belorussia, Ukraine, Poland, and Hungary, contributing to the growing concern and even localized panic there. To some extent, the paucity of official Soviet information, especially in the early days, contributed to spawning speculations. So, too, did

---

80. Ibid.

over-eager Western press competition. But the Soviets discerned a Western plot to exploit this accident against them.

Several American leading figures contributed to the Soviet suspicions. As the *Washington Post* reported, "President Reagan and other top U.S. officials sought yesterday to mobilize world opinion against the Soviet Union for what the president called its 'stubborn refusal' to provide a full account." Reagan in fact charged that "the Soviets' handling of this incident manifests a disregard for the legitimate concerns of people everywhere."[81] Yet the Soviet account, while still very incomplete, was the beginning of what eventually became unprecedented Soviet disclosure on the whole situation. American leaders seemed determined to discredit whatever the Soviets said. Secretary Shultz rejected the Soviet explanation and said he was "willing to bet" that more than two people had died.[82] White House Chief of Staff Donald Regan described Moscow's handling of the accident "an outrage" that went far "beyond what civilized nations should do."[83] Arms Control Director Kenneth L. Adelman scoffed at the official death toll and lent a semiofficial aura to the unwarranted media speculations by offering his own estimate that deaths must be in the thousands. There seemed almost to be a replay of the Reagan administration's eagerness to think the worst of the Soviets and shoot from the hip in seeking to capitalize on it, as in the case of the KAL tragedy two and a half years earlier.

Gorbachev, when he could with confidence assure the Soviet public that the worst was over and provide an informed account, made a major television speech on May 14. In it he sought to reassure the population that the Soviet leadership had done its best, but he acknowledged errors. He sharply rebuked Western, and especially U.S., launching of "an unrestrained anti-Soviet campaign" with "dishonest and malicious lies" about "thousands of casualties, and the like," and (without specific reference to Radio Free Europe's broadcasts) attempts "to sow new seeds of mistrust and suspicion toward the socialist countries." He then sought to turn the tragedy to constructive aims by highlighting the lessons of the tragedy for "new thinking," international cooperation and security, and nuclear and other arms control. He proposed greater cooperation in the International Atomic Energy Agency (IAEA) in case of nuclear accidents and later followed up this proposal with concrete actions that led to a new IAEA agreement. He also emphasized the lesson of a need to prevent nuclear war and used the occasion to reaffirm yet another

---

81.  Lou Cannon and Hobart Rowen, "Chernobyl in Spotlight at [the Western Economic] Summit," *Washington Post*, May 4, 1986, p. A1.

82.  Bernard Gwertzman, "A New Face for Shultz: Tough and Hard-Hitting," *New York Times*, May 7, 1986, p. A14.

83.  R. W. Apple, Jr., "Change in Soviet Stance Expected after Accident," *New York Times*, May 5, 1986, p. A6.

proposal to ban nuclear testing—extending again the unilateral Soviet moratorium and suggesting a summit with President Reagan, perhaps in Hiroshima (or any European state), to agree on a ban.[84]

Many Soviet sources have attested to the major shock effect of the Chernobyl tragedy in the Soviet establishment, underlining the fact of international interdependence, the ecological dimension of security, and the need for *glasnost*, as well as for controlling all aspects of the nuclear threat.

A debate had developed in the United States over whether to continue to abide by the never ratified SALT II Treaty constraints. There was no major military reason not to do so. Advocates of arms control saw it as a useful mutual restraint being observed by both sides, while those who chafed under any arms control contended that the Soviet Union had violated the agreement and argued that the United States should jettison the "fatally flawed" treaty in any case. On May 27, President Reagan announced plans to decommission two older missile-launching submarines, which would keep the United States in conformity with SALT II levels for several months more, but he also emphasized that he was doing so for practical reasons rather than to comply with SALT II limits, which would no longer be considered binding. He also seemed to say that the United States might still abide by SALT II limits depending on what the Soviets did. His statement was at first variously interpreted, but two weeks later Reagan confirmed Secretary Weinberger's (and the Soviet) interpretation: the SALT II Treaty was "dead."[85]

In mid-June, Gorbachev delivered a major statement on Soviet internal development to the party Central Committee. He included a relatively brief but important section on international affairs, or more precisely, on arms control and disarmament. He drew attention to, but did not elaborate on, the Warsaw Pact proposals for arms reductions in Europe. But he zeroed in on the issues in the stalled Geneva nuclear and space talks with the United States. Not being able to point to any Western steps forward, he skillfully argued that standing pat would serve precisely the aims of those in the West who did not wish real progress, and thus, he said, U.S. intransigence required new Soviet approaches "to clear the road to a reduction of nuclear arms." He aired proposals already privately advanced and carried them further. He proposed

---

84. "M. S. Gorbachev's Address on Soviet Television," *Pravda*, May 15, 1986.

    The proposal to meet in Hiroshima was no doubt too clever and tended to undercut the fact that he was serious about the proposed ban.

85. See Michael R. Gordon, "Reagan Declares U.S. Is Dismantling Two Nuclear Subs," *New York Times*, May 28, 1986, p. A1; Don Oberdorfer, "U.S. Is 'No Longer Bound' By Salt II, Weinberger Says," *Washington Post*, May 29, 1986, p. A1; and David Hoffman, "Reagan Calls SALT II Dead; U.S. to Seek a 'Better Deal'," *Washington Post*, June 13, 1986, p. A1.

    Secretary of State Shultz had opposed the decision to abandon the SALT II constraints, but his view did not leak, and once the decision was made, Shultz publicly supported it. See Shultz, *Turmoil and Triumph*, p. 717.

agreement not to withdraw from the ABM Treaty for fifteen years, with ABM work on the strategic defense initiative (SDI) limited to "laboratory research" (not merely basic research). With respect to strategic arms, he proposed for the first time settling the intermediate-range (INF) systems separately from intercontinental systems (ICBMs, SLBMs, and heavy bombers), at a zero level in Europe for the United States and the Soviet Union, without including French and British INF forces (except that they should not be increased in number), and he agreed to freeze the number of Soviet INF missile forces in Asia. He also again made a plea for ending nuclear testing.[86]

President Reagan responded promptly and favorably. In a speech at Glassboro, New Jersey, site of President Lyndon B. Johnson's meeting in 1967 with Soviet Prime Minister Aleksei N. Kosygin, he acknowledged that in Geneva and in Gorbachev's speech the Soviets had made "a serious effort" in strategic arms control that could even represent "a turning point." At the same time, he continued to advocate a strategic defense "shield" in space and gave no sign of any willingness to compromise on the SDI.[87]

On June 23, Ambassador Yury V. Dubinin, the new Soviet envoy in Washington, called on the president for the first time and presented not only his credentials but also a letter from Gorbachev pressing for progress on arms control and reductions in order to justify a summit.

In the meantime, an American initiative had come from an unusual source: Defense Secretary Weinberger in June came up with the radical proposal to eliminate all ballistic missiles. He envisaged it as an alternative to Gorbachev's radical proposal for eliminating all nuclear weapons, not as a negotiable proposition, given the heavy Soviet reliance on ballistic missiles and American advantages in bombers and cruise missiles. But it appealed to Ronald Reagan. Shultz, too, welcomed the Weinberger proposal, especially as a way to "open up" the stalemated negotiations. The idea was then worked out in great secrecy from most of the Washington bureaucracy. By the time it had been worked out (and worked over), however, it bore little resemblance to the original simple idea so appealing to Reagan. Nonetheless, coupled with a protective proposition on the SDI, it was incorporated in a letter sent from Reagan to Gorbachev on July 25.[88]

---

86. "Report by M. S. Gorbachev, General Secretary of the CC of the CPSU, at the June 16 CC Plenum," *Pravda*, June 17, 1986.

87. "Remarks to the Graduating Class of Glassboro High School," June 19, 1986, *Presidential Documents*, vol. 22 (June 23, 1986), pp. 838–39.

88. For the most detailed and informed account of the proposal on eliminating ballistic missiles, see Oberdorfer, *The Turn*, pp. 169–74. See also Shultz, *Turmoil and Triumph*, pp. 719–23, 754. Reagan himself, in his memoir, did not provide the text of this message but instead briefly recited a greatly oversimplified version of what he had in mind. Reagan, *An American Life*, pp. 665–66.

Gorbachev and his colleagues saw the proposal as a step backward. The SDI provision called for reaffirmation of the ABM Treaty, an agreement of unlimited duration, for only five years. After that time, if there had not been agreement on a plan for joint sharing of strategic defenses and on elimination of all ballistic missiles, each side would be free to deploy ABM defenses. Gorbachev assigned to Shevardnadze's ministry the task of coming up with a package of new proposals, but with a concentration on a simple 50 percent reduction of ballistic missiles. He received the proposals while on vacation in the Crimea in August. But he was determined to find a way to present the ideas to Reagan directly and not, as he put it to an aide, "to keep [Soviet negotiator] Karpov living well in Geneva for three years."[89]

High-level experts met in Moscow on August 11–12 and Washington on September 5–6 to work on the nuclear and space arms issues but to little avail. The positions were too far apart not only on specifics but in their objectives. The only new step was adoption on August 13 by the American Congress, over the administration's strong objection, of a resolution mandating the United States to hold its actual military forces to the SALT II limits so long as the Soviet Union did so.

A wide range of bilateral contacts did continue, pursuant to American interest in not having a single-issue arms control focus for the summit and to Soviet interest in keeping the new détente alive. The Reagan administration wanted to build on what it saw as its success at Geneva in pushing on regional conflicts, human rights, and various bilateral issues. As noted earlier, there had been a series of meetings on regional conflicts, as well as various arms control issues other than the nuclear arms talks (chemical weapons; nuclear risk reduction centers; the Standing Consultative Commission; nuclear testing), and bilateral issues (trade, cultural relations, space cooperation). An important series of meetings was held in Washington, July 25–28, at the expert level, at which time a Soviet-proposed "work program" for the summit was accepted to facilitate preparations on all aspects of the planned meeting other than the central nuclear arms control issues. At the conclusion of these meetings, the United States agreed to receive Shevardnadze for talks with Shultz (and a meeting with President Reagan) on September 19–20, the presummit meeting

---

The proposals were elaborated in National Security Decision Directive (NSDD)–233 dated July 31 (although not circulated until August 16), which has now been declassified. Despite the date of the NSDD and its actual date of circulation, it called for consultations with Congress and the allies by July 23, and in fact President Reagan's letter to Gorbachev had been sent by July 25—long before all but a few of the interested government officials were even aware of it. See Poindexter's Memorandum for the Vice President, Secretary of State, Secretary of Defense and others dated August 16, and NSDD-233 itself, titled "Consultations on a Response to General Secretary Gorbachev," dated July 31, 1986, 6 pp., both Secret (Declassified November 27, 1992).

89. According to Anatoly Chernyayev, Gorbachev's chief foreign affairs aide, in a discussion on February 27, 1993.

originally scheduled for mid-May. But between this agreement at the end of July and the actual visit by Shevardnadze, in addition to the expected further preparatory meetings (in particular, at Soviet suggestion, a general discussion of regional conflict issues in Washington on August 26–28, and a meeting on Afghanistan in Moscow on September 2–3), a quite unexpected incident arose, clouding the summit prospects and Soviet-American relations more generally.

On August 23, the FBI arrested Gennady F. Zakharov, a Soviet scientist on the UN Secretariat staff, on a subway platform in New York on charges of espionage.[90] He had been caught red-handed with classified secret documents just handed over to him by a Guyanese machinist whom he had been cultivating as a source for three years. Zakharov, who did not have diplomatic immunity, was about to return to the Soviet Union after a four-year tour of duty. The arrest helped to bolster the U.S. claims of spying by Soviet UN employees.

The arrest was a setup, a "sting" operation. Zakharov had Soviet intelligence connections but was a coopted "spotter" who looked for and cultivated science students and other long-term-recruitment prospects for information on American technology. Other professional intelligence operatives, with diplomatic protection, would then handle actual espionage transactions—the standard Soviet (and American) practice. The Guyanese, named Leakh Bhoge, had never before given Zakharov any classified information (nor was classified information from any source found when Zakharov's apartment was thoroughly searched), and the three secret documents he handed Zakharov immediately before the FBI pounced had been given to him for that purpose by the FBI, with whom he was cooperating. The judge before whom Zakharov was arraigned denied bail, a departure from the standard practice under which Soviet personnel arrested for espionage were released on bail to the custody of the Soviet ambassador.

In Moscow, the timing and entrapment of the arrest looked suspiciously provocative. Gorbachev and the Soviet leadership undoubtedly assumed that the action had the blessing of figures high in the American administration, probably including the president. In fact, the arrest had been cleared but at the undersecretarial level; Reagan and Shultz knew nothing about it before it occurred. The Soviet leadership then authorized the KGB to set up and arrest an unofficial American in the Soviet Union to balance the scales. The KGB had an appropriate candidate: Nicholas Daniloff, an American of Russian descent, Moscow correspondent for *U.S. News and World Report*, about to end a five-year tour in the Soviet Union.

On August 30, Daniloff agreed to meet "Misha," a Soviet acquaintance from Central Asia, at a prearranged rendezvous site in a Moscow park. When

90. Most of the information in the paragraphs following appeared in the press, although not all at the time, confirmed and elaborated by official sources. The general impression conveyed by the media, however, was simply an arrest of a Soviet spy by the FBI.

they met, Misha handed Daniloff an envelope with information on a subject in which Daniloff had earlier expressed interest: Soviet military activities in Afghanistan. Daniloff was promptly arrested; the materials included a map and papers stamped *sekretno* (secret). Daniloff was also advised of other incriminating evidence of espionage. He was promptly permitted to call his wife and to receive visitors but was not released to the American Embassy.

There was great indignation in the United States at the arrest of an innocent American journalist, transparently linked to the arrest of a Soviet spy in the United States. Those elements in common—including entrapment, and the fact that neither Zakharov or Daniloff expected to be given secret documents—were not noticed. On September 5 President Reagan, based on assurances by CIA Director William Casey, wrote a letter to Gorbachev assuring him Daniloff was not an American spy. Two days later, National Security Adviser John Poindexter persuaded President Reagan to send a stiff message on the hot line—a misuse of that diplomatic channel.[91] On September 8, an article in *Izvestiya* provided information on other clandestine intelligence contacts in Moscow involving Daniloff. On September 12, on the basis of a Soviet suggestion, both Zakharov and Daniloff were released from prison into the custody of the respective ambassadors. On September 18, Gorbachev in an off-the-cuff interview said Daniloff was a spy caught in the act, a statement greatly angering Reagan after his personal assurance that Daniloff was not a CIA agent.

Shevardnadze's visit to Washington was not called off. On September 19 he saw Secretary Shultz and then President Reagan. Informed officials have disclosed that Shevardnadze laid out for Shultz a strong case that the Soviet Union was prepared to make against Daniloff in court if necessary.[92] By that time, Shultz had gradually learned many damning admissions from the CIA and other American sources.[93]

While Daniloff was not an American intelligence officer, he had been caught in a net of espionage intrigue long before his arrest. In January 1985, he had been given a sealed letter by an apparently dissident priest called Father Roman Potemkin, to be given to the American ambassador, and (contrary to his wife's advice) he did deliver it to a senior American Embassy officer. It contained an internal envelope addressed to CIA Director William Casey, and some materials of interest to the CIA station. In a second meeting in the embassy, he gave the CIA station chief, Murat Natbiroff, the telephone number of Father Roman. After he had been arrested, Daniloff was shown a letter

---

91. Shultz, *Turmoil and Triumph*, p. 732.

92. I was first advised of Shevardnadze's presentation by a Soviet diplomat, and his account was essentially confirmed by a State Department official. The press in due course learned most of the story as summarized in this paragraph but not the fact of the Shevardnadze presentation of it on September 19.

93. See Shultz, *Turmoil and Triumph*, pp. 728–43.

from a CIA station officer, Paul Stombaugh, to Father Roman introducing himself as a friend of "Nikolai" (Nicholas), and assuring him that the letter he had given to "the journalist" on January 24 [1985] had reached "the person you addressed it to," that is, CIA Director Casey. Linkage of Nicholas Daniloff to the CIA long before the incident with Misha was, even if its significance was distorted, thus quite real. As another former American correspondent in Moscow wrote about the case: "In effect the CIA had made a gift to the KGB of evidence so incriminating that even an American jury might well have concluded that Daniloff was hand in glove with the agency."[94]

Shultz was informed of the Daniloff-CIA linkage and also reportedly shown a KGB videotape of Daniloff's surreptitious maneuvering, ducking behind a large bush to ask for and receive the damning packet from Misha. This setup was of course buttressed by Daniloff's earlier contacts with and (if only partly witting) service as an intermediary for the CIA Moscow station.

Shultz and others, including above all the CIA, did not want a highly publicized court case that might even make Daniloff seem more guilty than Zakharov.[95] Even though Reagan had earlier vowed never to trade the Soviet spy for an innocent American, a deal was struck under which Daniloff was released on September 29, without being tried, and Zakharov released on September 30 after pleading *nolo contendere*.[96] This allowed one day of news coverage of Daniloff's release without apparent linkage. On the same day, September 30, it was announced that Soviet dissident Yury Orlov and his wife were being released to emigrate.

Also on September 30, with the Zakharov-Daniloff incident out of the way, it was announced that President Reagan and Gorbachev would hold an interim meeting at Reykjavik, Iceland, on October 11–12, to prepare for a later full-fledged summit. This was the outcome of a proposal by Gorbachev presented to Reagan by Shevardnadze on September 19. Acceptance had been prompt but conditioned on resolution of the Daniloff affair.

---

94. See Harrison E. Salisbury, "Russian Crimes and Punishments," *Washington Post Book World*, September 11, 1988, p. 5. See also Daniloff's later account, reviewed in this article by Salisbury. Nicholas Daniloff, *Two Lives, One Russia* (Houghton Mifflin, 1988).

95. Shultz had been advised by State Department Legal Adviser Abraham Sofaer that the Soviets had sufficient evidence not only to convict Daniloff in a Soviet court but to convict someone in an American court, a judgment backed up by Assistant Attorney General Stephen Trott. See Shultz, *Turmoil and Triumph*, p. 738.

96. The media in the United States were encouraged to note that Daniloff was freed without a trial, while Zakharov pleaded "no contest" to a charge and was then released. Although that is true, Daniloff's release was not because of a finding of innocence nor did Zakharov plead no contest to the charge of espionage but only to the charge of "receipt of classified documents"—something of which both he and Daniloff, to their shock, were "guilty."
See Shultz, *Turmoil and Triumph*, pp. 745–50.

The intense collaboration between Shultz and Shevardnadze in resolving the Zakharov-Daniloff issue and clearing the way for a summit was very important in developing both personal mutual trust and a conviction that many problems could be dealt with only by the two foreign secretaries.[97] There was even an immediate payoff: as a result of the successful turn in negotiations of September 9–20 on the Zakharov-Daniloff incident and the planned summit, Shevardnadze was able to give a green light to signature of an important agreement on confidence- and security-building measures.

The negotiations of the Conference on Disarmament in Europe (CDE) in Stockholm under the CSCE process received relatively little attention in the United States. Launched in January 1984, they received a boost during 1986 when the Soviet Union, in a series of steps, reluctantly agreed to set aside naval and air activities, and above all to accept far-reaching verification provisions including on-site inspection. On September 22, the Stockholm Document on confidence- and security-building measures was signed.[98]

Another indication of growing contact with a spirited exchange of views was an international Chautauqua conference held in Jurmala, Latvia, September 15–18. Like the more formal and important Stockholm agreement, this too was overshadowed in public attention by the Zakharov-Daniloff affair.[99]

Even after resolution of the Zakharov-Daniloff incident, and following the Reykjavik summit (to which we shall turn presently), espionage and security issues continued to complicate relations for some time. On September 2, the extremist Jewish Defense League, not satisfied with picketing an appearance under the cultural exchange program of the Moiseyev Dancers at the Metropolitan Opera House in New York, discharged a tear gas grenade in the auditorium. U.S. Information Agency Director Charles Z. Wick subsequently apologized, but in Soviet eyes the action reflected badly if not on American interest in developing cultural relations, then at least on American ability to carry them out.

On October 6, the State Department announced the establishment of an Office of Disinformation Analysis and Response to study Soviet "active measures" of disinformation and American countering measures.

American security investigators discovered in September that the new U.S. Embassy chancery under construction in Moscow was riddled with previously undiscovered listening devices. A Senate report in mid-October confirmed the seriousness of that situation and criticized laxity by the State Department in overseeing the construction.

---

97. The one key associate on whom Shevardnadze relied in this effort, then one of several deputies, was in 1991 to become his successor—Aleksandr Bessmertnykh. On the "bonding" effect of this experience for Shultz and Shevardnadze, see Oberdorfer, *The Turn*, pp. 179–82.

98. See chapter 13.

99. Shultz had to override hard-line opposition to American participation in the Chautauqua meeting because of the Daniloff affair. Shultz, *Turmoil and Triumph*, p. 736.

Meanwhile, at the height of the Zakharov-Daniloff affair, on September 17, the administration had tightened the screws on the drawdown of Soviet diplomatic and UN personnel, ordering twenty-five named officers from the Soviet UN mission out of the country. The Soviet Union retaliated by expelling five American diplomats from the Soviet Union in mid-October. The United States upped the ante by expelling five Soviet diplomats, and fifty more to reduce the number of the Soviet diplomatic personnel to equal the U.S. total of 251.[100] The Soviet Union, in return, expelled five more American diplomats and withdrew all 260 Soviet employees of the U.S. Embassy in Moscow, including the residence service staff as well as clerks, drivers, and all others. At this point, on October 23, both sides called a halt to the mutually debilitating exercise.

The Zakharov-Daniloff affair and other flare-ups of espionage and security issues did not derail the movement toward a new summit focused on arms control. As President Reagan later said in his memoir: "I don't believe the crisis over Daniloff's seizure ever brought either of us close to canceling the summit in Reykjavik. I think both Gorbachev and I felt the stakes were too high and acted cautiously to avoid torpedoing in advance whatever prospects we had of success in Iceland."[101]

## The Reykjavik Summit

The Reykjavik summit, cautiously advanced as an "interim summit" or preliminary meeting before the "real" summit in Washington foreseen at Geneva, was seen as such a routine working session that Nancy Reagan did not even accompany her husband on the trip. Yet the two-day weekend of meetings between Reagan and Gorbachev at Reykjavik became a startling and far-reaching exploration of possibilities for the drastic reduction or even elimination of nuclear weapons. The attempt, despite major efforts by both sides and unexpected agreements on many aspects of the problem, failed over the issue of strategic defenses. Some saw the results as a spectacular missed opportunity;

---

100. Almost all of the expelled Soviet Embassy and UN mission diplomats were intelligence officers, and the measure did severely impede Soviet intelligence activity. A Soviet KGB officer formerly serving in their Washington Embassy, Major Sergei Motorin, had been discovered to be a spy for the United States and was arrested in Moscow in early 1986. His arrest removed the reason for restraint on disclosure of the extent of American knowledge of Soviet intelligence personnel. This American intelligence penetration of the KGB was not, however, disclosed by either side for several years. See Michael Dobbs and R. Jeffrey Smith, "From Inside the KGB: A Tale of Incompetence," *Washington Post*, February 21, 1993, pp. A1, A26.

101. Reagan, *An American Life*, p. 674.

others as a perilous near disaster. For better or worse, the meeting was a historic near miss.

Gorbachev did not have a consensus in the Soviet leadership that would permit him to go to Washington for the regular summit meeting to which he had readily assented in Geneva. He had expected at least some forward movement on arms reductions by the American side. But as the months passed and the anniversary of Geneva drew nearer, it became clear that although Reagan was prepared to negotiate on his own terms, he was not disposed to seek a real compromise. And Gorbachev could not afford a second summit, much less going to Washington for it, without some substantial agreement. Reagan, however, could easily wait for the Soviet Union to come over to his terms. He was prepared for a summit with or without an arms agreement, and he would gain domestically either by showing that the Soviets had accepted his position or that they had not and that he would stand firm until they did. At the same time, Gorbachev needed a summit as well as an arms agreement to justify the changes in Soviet foreign and security policy that he considered necessary. Reagan did not plan any changes in policy and did not need a summit; he could easily rest on his open invitation and blame Soviet recalcitrance for the absence of one.

Gorbachev proposed the Reykjavik working summit because its risks and costs were less risky for him than a ceremonial visit to the United States, but he was still taking something of a gamble. He still needed to break the logjam and start new movement in the arms negotiations, and he correctly saw that the only way to do that was by engaging President Reagan personally. As Gorbachev and his advisers saw it, Reykjavik would be an interim summit but one where they would present a package with enough contingent concessions and new approaches to attract Reagan's interest. Gorbachev did not expect to negotiate the terms of an agreement with Reagan, still less to sign one, at Reykjavik, but his target was an agreement of the two leaders on substantive joint guidelines for their negotiators that could reactivate the process. To engage the president's personal attention and, it was hoped, gain a more favorable hearing, Gorbachev planned to propose his new package of proposals at the meeting itself. For this reason, the Soviet side did not follow the usual procedure of presummit disclosure of new proposals. But they did emphasize the nuclear arms issues.

President Reagan was relaxed about the forthcoming meeting. He expected some Soviet movement toward his positions. The American side did not have new proposals to advance. The Americans anticipated a new Soviet position on intermediate-range missiles, and preparation was focused on that area. The Soviet side in the arms talks had most recently discussed "token" INF deployments on the two sides in Europe, with a freeze on the existing Soviet deployments in Asia. The U.S. proposal prepared for Reykjavik would have set 200 INF missile warheads for each side: 100 each in Europe, and 100 each in the non-European USSR and the United States. To deflect Soviet (and congressional) proposals for negotiating a comprehensive test ban, the administration was preparing to submit the two limited-testing agreements of 1974 and 1976 for ratification, with reinforced verification. On the key subject of strategic offensive and defensive arms, the president intended to stand pat and see what Gorbachev would propose. The U.S. response would be worked out later in Washington.

These differences in aim and in expectations were evident in the makeup of the delegations. Gorbachev was accompanied not only by Raisa, undeterred by the prospect of a brief working summit in wintry Iceland, but by a large phalanx of political and military advisers. To the complete surprise of the American side, the chief Soviet negotiator turned out to be Marshal Sergei Akhromeyev, chief of the General Staff and first deputy defense minister. The United States had a much more limited delegation with no senior military representatives.

In the opening meeting (initially Gorbachev and Reagan alone, later joined by Shevardnadze and Shultz) Gorbachev took the initiative and laid out his package: a comprehensive set of proposals on strategic arms, intermediate-range missiles, and space weapons. He also urged a ban on nuclear testing. Although based on familiar Soviet positions, each part of the package contained some new concessions. On strategic missiles, Gorbachev accepted an equal 50 percent cut in the central systems, ICBMs, SLBMs, and heavy bombers, and for the first time agreed to include the Soviet heavy (SS-18) missiles in the cuts. (That night, Marshal Akhromeyev made the further concession of applying a full 50 percent cut to these heavy ICBMs.) The Soviet side also reluctantly agreed to exclude all American forward-based shorter-range systems capable of striking the Soviet Union from the "strategic forces" to be counted and limited.

On space and defensive systems, Akhromeyev reduced the proposed ABM Treaty nonwithdrawal commitment from fifteen to ten years (half the distance to Reagan's seven and one-half years, proposed in his letter of July 25). He dropped the Soviet demand that SDI research be banned, although he insisted such research be limited to the laboratory (coming much closer to the traditional narrow interpretation of the ABM Treaty). On INF, he dropped the demand that British and French weapons be frozen at existing levels, proposed zero U.S. and Soviet INF in Europe, and agreed to negotiate a limit on INF in Soviet Asia and the United States. He also dropped the earlier Soviet call for an immediate end to nuclear testing, while urging negotiations toward a comprehensive ban.

Although Reagan was wary about curbs on the SDI, Shultz (and some others, including Paul Nitze) were impressed with Gorbachev's concessions.[102]

---

102. The sweeping extent of the Soviet concessions was even greater, and had been more difficult to agree upon in Moscow than the Americans recognized. Marshal Akhromeyev, for example, in his posthumous memoir, has revealed that he contemplated resigning as chief of the General Staff over Gorbachev's decision to agree to equal

Reagan's presentation was by comparison weak, and Gorbachev expostulated over the "shopworn goods," old positions. Other subjects were also discussed, but none of any real significance. It was agreed that experts would meet that night.

A marathon meeting, with some intermissions to seek new instructions, lasted all night. Marshal Akhromeyev, chairing the Soviet group, was in full command of his delegation. Paul Nitze, on the American side, was more chairman of a collective delegation. The two expert teams made major progress on strategic arms reductions mainly because Akhromeyev was prepared to make decisions and concessions. No real advance was made on space weapons.

The next morning, Reagan and Gorbachev picked up where the experts had stopped and went on to agree on zero INF missiles in Europe, and 100 INF warheads each in Soviet Asia and the United States. The SDI, or issue of space weapon testing, remained intractable. The American delegation was prepared to consider a ten-year period of nonwithdrawal from the ABM Treaty but wanted compensating agreement that at the end of that time each side would be free to deploy ABM defenses. The Soviets were adamant; after all, the ABM Treaty is of unlimited duration; they envisaged the purpose of a ten-year commitment as reinforcement, not as a grace period before withdrawal. There was agreement to make the 50 percent cut in offensive arms during a five-year period.

During the lunch period, Shultz, Shevardnadze, and members of the two delegations met to continue efforts. During this period (through notes and whispered consultations) the American delegation came up with an idea Shultz advanced on a personal basis: introducing in this new context the idea of elimination of *all* ballistic missiles in the second five-year period, after the 50 percent cuts. But there was no change on space weapons. Reagan was quite prepared to accept the idea of elimination of all ballistic missiles (ICBMs and SLBMs) in ten years. Perle for Defense supported it; the representative from the Joint Chiefs of Staff, Lieutenant General John Moellering, was noncommittal. Gorbachev, when they met, was ready to "see and raise" the ante. He proposed eliminating all strategic nuclear weapons in the ten-year period. Reagan agreed, saying he would be ready to eliminate *all* nuclear weapons in ten years; Gorbachev agreed at once.

The proposed deal, however, collapsed over the terms of observance of the ABM Treaty. Gorbachev, clearly at the edge of his mandate from Moscow, continued to insist on limiting ABM research to the laboratory, and Reagan would not agree in effect to gutting the SDI. Reagan finally literally broke up the meeting over this issue—leaving up in the air what, if any, elements of

---

force levels dropping any compensation for American forward-based systems and NATO allied offensive arms capable of striking the Soviet Union. See S. F. Akhromeyev and G. M. Kornienko, *Glazami marshala i diplomata* (Through the Eyes of a Marshal and a Diplomat) (Moscow: Mezhdunarodnyye otnosheniya, 1992), pp. 108–09.

newfound agreement on many aspects of the arms issue could be salvaged and whether there could be any partial agreement.[103]

Reykjavik was an intense encounter, and the immediate let-down of failure caused disappointment and anger that was evident to the two thousand waiting media representatives. Nonetheless, within hours both sides were speaking not only of disappointment but also of great steps forward. In part this may have been psychological rebound; in part, on the American side, it was a defensive maneuver to avoid letting the blame for failure and missing a great

---

103. This account of the Reykjavik summit is based on interviews with several members of the U.S. and Soviet delegations. For informed accounts see Shultz, *Turmoil and Triumph*, pp. 751–80; Oberdorfer, *The Turn*, pp. 183–207, and *The Reykjavik Process: Preparation for and Conduct of the Iceland Summit and Its Implications for Arms Control*, Report of the Defense Policy Panel of the House Committee on Armed Services, 99 Cong. 2 sess. (Government Printing Office, 1987), pp. 1–23. And on the Soviet side, see Akhromeyev and Kornienko, *Glazami marshala i diplomata*, pp. 108–20.

Of particular value, the most complete record now available is the full Soviet transcript of the Gorbachev-Reagan sessions at Reykjavik, published by the Gorbachev Foundation in Moscow. See "From the Gorbachev Archives: Discussions of M. S. Gorbachev with R. Reagan at Reykjavik, October 11–12, 1986," *Mirovaya ekonomika i mezhdunarodnyye otnosheniya* (The World Economy and International Relations), nos. 4, 5, 7, 8 (April, May, July, August 1993).

Gorbachev was constrained by a Politburo decision establishing his negotiating position for the Reykjavik negotiations. Although he had dominated the Politburo decisionmaking and had great latitude (for example, on the discussion of strategic arms reductions and even elimination of nuclear weapons), the collective decision on ABM testing constraints meant that he did not have a free hand on that issue. No one knows whether he would have been prepared to make a further compromise if there had not been this constraint, but at the least it reinforced any reservations he may have had. I have discussed this issue with a number of Gorbachev's close associates (including Anatoly Chernyayev, his foreign policy aide; Aleksandr Bessmertnykh, the deputy foreign minister; Sergei Tarasenko, Shevardnadze's closest adviser; and Pavel Palazhchenko, Gorbachev's interpreter at Reykjavik). All express some uncertainty (and somewhat differing personal estimates) on whether Gorbachev had leeway for further compromise on this issue. Palazhchenko, for example, emphasized that Gorbachev had to be mindful of the Politburo consensus; he was, after all, "General Secretary, and not Emperor" (comment in a discussion on February 27, 1993). Marshal Akhromeyev, in his posthumously published memoir, noted that the decisions on the position to be taken at Reykjavik had been collective and unanimous, and that "it was agreed [*dogovoreno*] to hold firmly to the position that the ABM Treaty must be strictly observed by the parties in the form that it had been signed in 1972" (Akhromeyev and Kornienko, *Glazami marshala i diplomata*, p. 110). Gorbachev did not, however, use that formulation, but hewed to the established position of no ABM testing of space-borne systems except in the laboratory. Tarasenko (in discussion on February 27, 1993) said that Shevardnadze blamed Akhromeyev for not making clear to Gorbachev that there was a further "fallback," and this may be what he had in mind. It is, however, highly likely that the Politburo decision used the language of no testing except in the laboratory. Anatoly Dobrynin will cite the precise terms of the Politburo guidance for the meeting in his forthcoming memoir.

opportunity fall on Reagan's SDI. Two days after the summit, Reagan declared: "Believe me, the significance of that meeting at Reykjavik is not that we didn't sign agreements in the end; the significance is that we got as close as we did. The progress that we made would've been inconceivable just a few months ago."[104]

The Reykjavik near-agreement on eliminating all nuclear weapons (or all strategic nuclear weapons, if Reagan's offhand acceptance of the broader goal is set aside), or even all ballistic missiles—the U.S. proposal, reaffirmed as such after the meeting—came as a great surprise to everyone and a shock to many. In particular, U.S. allies were stunned by the apparent readiness of the American president to give up nuclear deterrence without any advance consultation. (The Joint Chiefs of Staff shared this dismay.) Short of that ultimate step, there was also some alliance grumbling, but divided views, over the U.S. readiness to agree to elimination of all INF missiles in Europe (particularly because in presummit consultation the U.S. representatives had declared the intention to retain a level of 100 as preferable to zero). But the allies were reluctant to appear to oppose progress in arms reductions, and there had been no agreements finally reached. It did, however, shake President Reagan's credibility as a stalwart of alliance defense and reinforce earlier indications of the priority he gave to acting unilaterally on the basis of his view of U.S. interests.

Gorbachev was deeply upset by the failure to shake Reagan on the ABM Treaty issue. At the same time, members of the Soviet delegation have said that he was impressed by Reagan's readiness to agree to zero INF missiles in Europe and even to entertain the idea of elimination of all nuclear weapons. Tactically, although Gorbachev gave vent to his disappointment and the failure of the American side to come prepared with some concessions to match those he offered, he too, like Reagan, had a stake in not letting it seem that the meeting had been a failure. In attempting to understand what to him seemed to be Reagan's inconsistency between a real desire for nuclear disarmament and a stubborn insistence on the SDI, Gorbachev reverted in his spontaneous Reykjavik press conference to his view that Reagan was "being held captive by this [military-industrial] complex" and hence "not free to take such a decision" strengthening the ABM Treaty at the expense of the SDI.[105] He said he received this impression from changes in Reagan's position after the breaks for consultation. This impression was undoubtedly reinforced after the meeting when the American administration first tried to deny that Reagan had ever

104. "Meeting with Soviet General Secretary Gorbachev in Reykjavik, Iceland. Remarks in a Meeting with Officials of the Department of State and the U.S. Arms Control and Disarmament Agency," October 14, 1986, *Presidential Documents*, vol. 22 (October 20, 1986), p. 1387. For a more defensive argument on the priority to the SDI, see his "Address to the Nation. October 13, 1986," ibid., pp. 1375–79.

105. "Press Conference of Mikhail Gorbachev," *Pravda*, October 14, 1986.

agreed to eliminating all strategic nuclear weapons and then two weeks later when the Geneva arms talks resumed and the United States withdrew its own proposal for eliminating all ballistic missiles in ten years.

Gorbachev, before departing from Reykjavik, stressed in this same initial press conference that a Washington summit could not be permitted to fail. What, he asked rhetorically, "would people think in the Soviet Union, in the United States, and all over the world. What sort of political leaders are heading those two great nations on which the fate of the entire world so greatly depends? They . . . have already held their third meeting but they cannot agree on anything. I think this would be simply a scandalous outcome with unpredictable consequences."[106] Gorbachev repeated his judgment about the controlling influence of the American military-industrial complex in a major television address to the Soviet people after his return to Moscow.[107]

The Politburo met on October 14 and issued a statement approving the positions taken by Gorbachev and focusing on the adamant U.S. stand on the ABM Treaty as "the sole cause" of the failure to reach agreement. The Reykjavik meeting was, nonetheless, hailed as "an important event in international life." The Politburo affirmed that "negotiations must continue" and that "it would be a fatal step to pass by the historic chance for cardinal solutions to the problems of war and peace. Everything must be done to make use of this chance."[108]

Although many commentaries continued to emphasize the American unreadiness to reach momentous agreements, the summit later was seen as having been an important step forward. Indeed, eight months later—even before a new breakthrough—one leading spokesman went so far as to describe Reykjavik as "a landmark in the development of the world."[109]

## The Aftermath

Whatever the later evaluations of the Reykjavik summit, in its immediate aftermath U.S.-Soviet relations and prospects for accord did not improve. As already noted, soon after the summit the United States reactivated the confrontation over espionage by expelling fifty-five Soviet diplomatic personnel. That action led Gorbachev to make a third television address on Reykjavik

---

106. Ibid.

107. "General Secretary of the CC of the CPSU M. S. Gorbachev on Soviet Television," *Pravda*, October 15, 1986.

108. "At the Politburo of the CC of the CPSU," *Pravda*, October 15, 1986.

109. Valentin Falin, "Studio 9," Moscow Television, June 4, 1987; see FBIS, *Soviet Union*, June 5, 1987, p. cc 2.

and its consequences. Gorbachev, on October 22, referred to his earlier expressions of hope that after reflecting on the unfinished business of Reykjavik, President Reagan would resume the dialogue constructively. But, he acknowledged, "Something quite different occurred. Beside the distortions of the whole picture of the Reykjavik talks . . . actions have been taken in recent days [the 55 expulsions] which, from a normal human viewpoint, simply look wild after so important a meeting at the level of the top leadership of the two countries." He continued, asking in reference to the United States:

> What sort of government is it, what can be expected from it on other matters on the international scene; what degree of unpredictability will its actions reach? It turns out that it not only has no constructive proposals on the key questions of disarmament, but it does not even have the desire to maintain an atmosphere essential for the normal continuation of a dialogue. . . . Every time a ray of light appears in attitudes toward the major questions of Soviet-U.S. relations, toward the settlement of questions that involve the interests of the whole of humankind, a provocation occurs calculated to wreck the possibility of a positive solution and to poison the atmosphere.[110]

This strong rhetorical stand was accompanied by a tightening of the strings on the "package" of concessions offered by Gorbachev at Reykjavik. This served two purposes: to defend against charges in Moscow that Gorbachev had given away too much for nothing in return and to restore some bargaining leverage with the United States while the Soviet side determined just what smaller package the United States *was* prepared to agree on.

Shultz and Shevardnadze met in Vienna on November 5–6 to try to pick up the pieces of the unfinished arms negotiation. In sharp contrast to Reykjavik, the entire top level of the U.S. political-military team traveled to Vienna, while the small Soviet team of experts was headed by Deputy Foreign Minister Viktor Karpov. Neither Marshal Akhromeyev nor any other senior military man was there. There was bitter disagreement over just what had been tentatively agreed on at Reykjavik as well as over the quid pro quo conditions for various concessions by one side or the other. By that time, not only had the Soviets decided to tighten the strings on their package approach but the United States had sought to pocket the Soviet concessions made at Reykjavik and moreover retreated from its own proposal on banning ballistic missiles. At the same time the United States continued to press such demands as subceilings on strategic forces. The result was a completely unsuccessful meeting.

The occasion for the meeting between Secretary Shultz and Foreign Minister Shevardnadze was a session at the level of foreign ministers of the CSCE. Although both men addressed the arms negotiations issue (in a rather confrontational manner) at the open CSCE meeting as well as in their private talks, the United States also launched heavy criticism of the Soviet Union's

---

110. "Speech on Soviet Television by M. S. Gorbachev, General Secretary of the CC of the CPSU," *Pravda*, October 23, 1986.

human rights practices, with Shultz citing President Reagan, "A government that will break faith with its own people cannot be trusted to keep faith with foreign powers."[111] Shevardnadze responded with an attack on the American expulsions of Soviet diplomats, saying it was "immoral to initiate a 'battle of expulsions' to suit one's election strategy or to placate 'hawkish' friends." He also argued Soviet support for human rights—including the right to work and free education, medical care, and social welfare—and proposed that a CSCE meeting on human rights be held in Moscow.[112]

By the time of the Shultz-Shevardnadze meeting, although only three weeks had elapsed since Reykjavik, two developments had begun to weaken and to distract the American side. On November 4, the Republicans lost control of the Senate in the midterm elections, portending a focus by a lame-duck Republican administration on the next presidential election. On the day before, and far more important in weakening the Reagan administration, a story appeared in a Beirut weekly disclosing covert American dealings providing arms to Iran for release of American hostages held in Lebanon. This story was soon substantiated, and it also became known that some of the financial returns from these dealings were then used illegally to support the Nicaraguan contras.

The Iran-contra story need not be reviewed here in any detail, but it became important to American politics and policy in several ways that had an important impact on U.S.-Soviet relations. First of all, it absorbed the attention of the Reagan administration. It became a continuing drama that would last through the remainder of his term. As the scandal unfolded, it soon led to resignations and shifts in the senior White House staff. In the first month alone, President Reagan's popularity declined in the polls from an approval level of 67 percent to 46 percent, with widespread belief in a cover-up and a loss of credibility of the president as well as members of his administration occurring.[113]

The tangled tale of official and semiofficial U.S. dealings with Israeli, Iranian, Saudi, American, and other arms dealers, intelligence agents, and international "operators" involved many senior officials. Among those directly implicated were former national security advisers Robert C. McFarlane and Vice Admiral John M. Poindexter (fired on November 24, along with his loose cannon National Security Council [NSC] staff associate Lieutenant Colonel Oliver North), and also CIA Director William Casey and others. Secretary of State Shultz and Secretary of Defense Weinberger, in contrast, had been

---

111. "Pursuing the Promise of Helsinki," address by Secretary Shultz at the Vienna CSCE meeting on November 5, 1986, *Department of State Bulletin*, vol. 87 (January 1987), p. 49.

112. "On the Meeting at Vienna, Speech of E. A. Shevardnadze," *Pravda*, November 6, 1986.

113. See Richard J. Meislin, "President Invites Inquiry Counsel; Poll Rating Dives—46% Approve Reagan's Work, Down 21 Points," *New York Times*, December 2, 1986, p. A1.

opposed to dealings proposed and were not fully informed as they nonetheless went forward. The initial focus was on trading arms to Iran, despite contravening American law and policy, in the hope of effecting release of Americans held hostage in Lebanon. Although this story was quickly traced back to 1985, its roots went back to 1980–81 when the new administration—and some of its members—had secretly approved or acquiesced in Israeli arms shipments to Iran (even before the inauguration).[114]

Only a month before the Iran arms deal became known, a contra support airplane had been shot down over Nicaragua on October 5 and a crew member captured. The extensive improper role of senior NSC staff members and some CIA officials in this supply of arms to the contras in contravention of the law was beginning to unfold when it was revealed that some of the ill-gotten profits from arms sales to Iran were being siphoned off and fed into this illegal support of the contras (and, briefly, commingled with a secret Swiss bank account for U.S. and Saudi aid to the Afghan *mujahedin* as well, which was covert but not contrary to American law).

The most serious casualty of this hemorrhage of disclosures of secret and sometimes illegal activity was the decline in credibility of the administration with the American people. The credibility of the United States, and in particular the Reagan administration, also suffered in the world. Allies, who had been startled by American unilateralism on arms and strategy as evidenced in the Star Wars SDI and at Reykjavik, were being subjected to a deceitful American double standard. While loudly lecturing them on the need to maintain strict arms embargoes against terrorist states such as Iran, the United States was quietly burrowing deep in such dealings. The purported idealism of the crusade for a free world was also not enhanced, although President Reagan continued to broaden this summons, declaring in a speech on November 18 that as Americans we were "true to our heritage of helping to hold out freedom's hand" and that it was "in our interest to stand with those who would

---

114. Michael Ledeen, who had alerted the Reagan administration in 1981 on alleged Soviet intentions to test its mettle (see chapter 1, footnote 50), and in 1981–82 on alleged Soviet involvements in international terrorism including the papal assassination plot (chapter 1, footnotes 45 and 47, and chapter 3, footnotes 27, 29, 30, 32), also played a signal role in generating the secret arms deal with Iran. Then a consultant to the NSC staff on antiterrorism, he met in Israel in April 1985 with the shady Iranian intelligence operative and arms merchant Manucher Ghorbanifar, and in May with Israeli Prime Minister Shimon Peres. To them, he represented himself as an emissary from the White House, while to the NSC staff he appeared as an emissary conveying proposals from the Israeli government and the Iranian go-between. See Charles R. Babcock, "Ledeen Seems to Relish Iran Insider's Role," *Washington Post*, February 2, 1987, pp. A1, A16; Stephen Engelberg, "A Consultant's Role in the Iran Affair," *New York Times*, February 2, 1987, p. A13; Shultz, *Turmoil and Triumph*, pp. 793–94; and for his own account, Michael A. Ledeen, *Perilous Statecraft: An Insider's Account of the Iran-Contra Affair* (Charles A. Scribner's Sons, 1988).

take arms against the sea of darkness."[115] Although the rhetoric soared, and furthermore was delivered in a speech before the Ethics and Public Policy Center, to many it sounded hollow in light of revelations of surreptitious American sales of arms to Iran to use against its own people as well as Iraq, and with the proceeds to buy arms covertly to supply insurgents against the recognized governments of Nicaragua and Afghanistan.

The Soviet leaders were less surprised and shocked by the Iran-contra revelations than were many others. Relations between the Soviet Union and the United States were not directly or necessarily involved. There were, however, some disquieting aspects of the affair from their standpoint. First of all, it reinforced concerns over doing business with the Reagan administration. The Soviet Foreign Ministry spokesmen stressed "duplicity" and said the affair "shows once again that the present [U.S.] administration is an extremely unreliable partner in international affairs." On the whole, although the Soviet Union did exploit the matter for propaganda, it did not give it major attention. Moreover, to cite the Foreign Ministry spokesman again, there were concerns that the U.S. administration "may resort to any risky action for the purpose of diverting attention from the inquiry into the scandal." And, said the spokesman, "we hope that the U.S. side will not take any rash actions which would complicate the already acute international situation," citing possible direct U.S. action against Nicaragua or Syria.[116]

The Soviet Union also had another, unexpressed, concern. A senior Soviet official later told me that President Reagan's speech of November 18, cited above, had been read in Moscow as ominous, portending a possible new thrust of the Reagan Doctrine against the socialist commonwealth in Eastern Europe. No one in the West had given it that interpretation, including its drafters (as they assured me). But on rereading the speech through apprehensive Soviet eyes one can readily see the reason for Soviet concern, even if unfounded. Reagan had referred yet again to "three decades of Soviet adventurism around the world," but he did so while posing the question about whether the Western failure to assist the Hungarian Revolution thirty years before "with arms" had been the correct reaction. "Can anyone truly say," he asked," it was in fact in our interest to stand by, hands folded, at the dying of the light in Hungary?"[117] Although he then raised and answered the question in the negative for Afghanistan, Angola, and Nicaragua, he had posed the question initially and untypically with respect to Eastern Europe. Moreover, his exam-

---

115. "Ethics and Public Policy Center. Remarks at the 10th Anniversary Dinner," November 18, 1986, *Presidential Documents*, vol. 22 (November 24, 1986), p. 1581.

116. "Pyadyshev Holds Foreign Ministry Conference," TASS, Radio Moscow, December 11, 1986, in FBIS, *Soviet Union*, December 12, 1986, p. cc 1.

117. *Presidential Documents*, vol. 22 (November 24, 1986), p. 1581.

ples of justified successful recent action were Libya and Grenada, direct uses of U.S. military power. And he had said, "We have no choice about the nature of the conflict, only about whether or not we recognize its nature" in introducing his reference to Hungary.[118] No doubt he meant that reference to be commemorative and rhetorical, but it did raise concern in Moscow.

The United States did, in some other ways, harden its position toward the Soviet Union. On November 21, Secretary of the Treasury James A. Baker III replied on behalf of the administration to a question posed earlier by conservative Representative Jack Kemp, stating for the first time that the United States would actively oppose any application by the Soviet Union for membership in the World Bank or the International Monetary Fund.[119] Until pressed to take a clear stand, the administration, although not prepared to support Soviet entry at that time, had in fact preferred to keep its options open.

Some American cooperative actions continued, including routine consultations on possible scientific and other exchanges with the Soviet Union. Other actions, however, were directed against the Soviet Union, including continued implementation of the Reagan Doctrine (the first Stingers shot down a Soviet aircraft over Afghanistan in October), and assertive military exercises. In September—at the height of the Daniloff crisis—a U.S. naval battle group, for the first time featuring the nuclear-missile-armed battleship USS *New Jersey*, passed through the Kuril Islands into the Sea of Okhotsk for an exercise simulating an attack on Soviet bases.

Meanwhile, the Soviet Union continued to develop relations with other powers. The Soviet Union sought in particular to activate relations with the countries of Asia.[120] In July, Gorbachev visited the Soviet Far East and made a major speech in Vladivostok addressing Asia and the Pacific area, especially China. He also sought, without success, to interest Asian countries in a security arrangement more or less analogous to the European CSCE process. In contrast to Brezhnev's call four years earlier for an Asian security arrangement transparently directed against China and the United States and its Asian alliances, Gorbachev urged inclusion of both China and the United States. Gorbachev also signaled initial steps to meet all three obstacles to improving relations that China had specified earlier. In January, Shevardnadze had visited Japan, and in November Gorbachev visited India.

The Soviet Union also moved to disengage from Afghanistan, although most observers in the West at that time remained skeptical.[121] Such disengage-

---

118. Ibid., p. 1580.

119. Hobart Rowen, "Baker: U.S. Would Oppose Soviet IMF Bid," *Washington Post*, November 22, 1986, p. C1.

120. See chapter 14 for more complete discussion of this subject.

121. See chapter 15. In mid-December 1986, Gorbachev summoned the new Afghan leader Najibullah to Moscow to tell him the Soviet Union would be withdrawing its troops from

ment would serve Soviet internal political purposes, as well as remove an irritant in relations with the United States, China, and many Asian and Middle Eastern countries. Pursuant to a promise made by Gorbachev at Vladivostok in July, six Soviet regiments were withdrawn from Afghanistan in the fall. There were, however, indications that the Soviet military had manipulated force movements in a way that circumvented the purpose; in the United States, this undercut the political signal Gorbachev had intended and even raised skepticism about his broader intentions.

With an eye to the Middle East, the Soviet Union took the first step toward restoring consular relations with Israel, and Foreign Minister Shevardnadze met with Israeli Prime Minister Shimon Peres in September when both men were in New York for the UN General Assembly.

Although no major steps were taken in regard to Europe, the Soviet Union was preparing to improve relations with the countries of Western Europe and, most significant for the long run, to establish a new relationship with the socialist countries of Eastern Europe.

Following a routine meeting of the government leaders of the member states of the Council of Mutual Economic Assistance (CMEA) in Bucharest, Gorbachev suddenly called an unplanned meeting of the party leaders of these countries in Moscow on November 10–11. Gorbachev used this occasion to inform the Eastern European communist leaders that they must take steps to restructure their own rule and gain legitimacy, and that the Soviet Union could no longer be expected to keep them in power. Without of course using the term (never one officially recognized), he was telling them that the Brezhnev Doctrine was dead.[122] Although the underlying basic change in Soviet policy would not become clear to the world for three years, it was a fundamental change. By the close of the decade it would lead to an end of communist rule in Eastern Europe, of the Warsaw Pact, of the division of Europe, and of the Cold War.

On December 11, the NATO foreign ministers meeting in Brussels issued their response to the Budapest Appeal of June and called for two sets of negotiations: one a new follow-on to the Stockholm agreement on further confidence and security-building measures, the other a negotiation between members of the NATO and Warsaw Pact alliances to eliminate disparities in major conventional arms from the Atlantic to the Urals and to establish conventional forces stability at lower levels. This led to new negotiations beginning early in the next year.

Internal developments in the Soviet Union included a preview of the ethnic unrest that within a few years would become a major internal political

---

Afghanistan within a year and a half to two years, whatever the outcome of the UN-sponsored negotiations.

122. Soviet debate and Politburo decisions leading up to this new policy line, and later development of the new position before its full unveiling in the fall of 1989, are discussed in chapter 13.

problem. The forced retirement of Politburo member Dinmukhamed Kunayev as party chief in Kazakhstan in December and his replacement by Gennady Kolbin, a party official from Russia, not Kazakhstan, gave rise to riots with ethnic overtones (as well as instigation and exploitation of the whole affair by local party conservatives). The volatile mixture of traditional versus reformist political considerations, central versus republican authority, and ethnic frictions fueled by growing economic problems was later to become a powerful factor in political instability in the Soviet Union. This was not, however, recognized at the time, and the possible warning signal was not adequately appreciated in Moscow.[123] At the end of 1986, political power in the USSR was stable, and the new leadership headed by Gorbachev was consolidating its hold.[124] Reagan's domestic troubles appeared at the time to be greater.

Soviet internal social change in 1986 as in 1985 had been focused on economic discipline, "acceleration" (the key word in this period), and initial references to a broader concept of "restructuring" (*perestroika*). Besides releasing such leading dissidents and Jewish émigrés as Anatoly Shcharansky in February and Yury Orlov (in settling the Daniloff affair) in September, and allowing them to go abroad, a major step was taken in December with the release of Academician Andrei Sakharov from internal exile in Gorky. Major changes in internal political life, however, remained for the near future.

American-Soviet relations at year's end remained in the slump into which they had fallen after the failure of the Reykjavik summit and of subsequent efforts by each side to revive arms negotiations on its own terms. In December, Jack Matlock, a career diplomat who had specialized in Soviet affairs (and since 1983 served as the Soviet expert on the NSC staff), replaced Arthur Hartman, who was retiring after seven years as the American ambassador in Moscow. This did not, however, portend or reflect any change in policy.

---

123. Shortly after these events, a Central Committee official (Nikolai Shishlin) told me that they had made a mistake in handling the replacement of Kunayev, primarily in bringing in an outsider from the Russian Republic rather than a local official. Kolbin was considered a Russian, although he was an ethnic Chuvash, but he was neither Kazakh nor had he lived in Kazakhstan. This was recognition of part of the problem, but only part. At the same time, the decision had not been capricious or thoughtless. The reason for bringing in an outsider *was* to break the pattern of local patronage and corruption.

124. While Gorbachev played a key role, and was clearly first among the leaders, most of his colleagues were not his selections or still less "his" men. As new and more far-reaching decisions on internal and external relations were faced, differences and divisions appeared among these leaders. Within a few years most of the new leaders of 1985–86 would follow their Brezhnevite predecessors into retirement. (Only in December 1986, on the occasion of what would have been Brezhnev's eightieth birthday, was the former leader first criticized by name in *Pravda*.) During 1985–86 substantial changes were made in the Ministry of Foreign Affairs under Eduard Shevardnadze's guidance. The changes among party officials most concerned with foreign relations took place to a greater extent than in most other areas and institutions. Shevardnadze was one of Gorbachev's closest associates.

When the American administration proposed an exchange of televised greetings between Reagan and Gorbachev, as had been done the year before, it was rebuffed as not warranted by the state of relations. "Why," asked Soviet Foreign Ministry spokesman Gennady Gerasimov, "should we create any illusions about our relations?"[125] On that sour note the year ended.

---

125. See Gary Lee, "Soviets Reject New Year's TV Exchange," *Washington Post*, December 31, 1986, p. A1.
    Reagan did broadcast a New Year's message to the Soviet people on the Voice of America, with the hope it would not be jammed (it was not). In it he regretted the rejection of the offer of an exchange of television greetings and referred to "common hopes" as well as "enormous differences between our two systems." "New Year's Message," December 31, 1986, *Presidential Documents*, vol. 22 (January 5, 1987), pp. 1681–83.

# 7 The INF Treaty and the Washington Summit, 1987

As the year 1987 opened, both Gorbachev and Reagan retained a strong interest in reaching an arms reduction agreement, but their expectations were tempered by failure at Reykjavik and in the weeks following to overcome their serious differences over developing space-based weapons. By year's end, despite continued failure to surmount this obstacle, a major arms reduction treaty had been concluded and celebrated at a full-fledged summit in Washington. That achievement was the central feature of U.S.-Soviet relations during the year, and it helped to carry the overall relationship forward on a path of reduced tensions and increasing rapport.

For the longer term, other developments that commanded the attention of the two leaders were also to have an important impact on the relationship, especially the process of internal change in the Soviet Union. Domestic developments in the United States, above all the drawn-out Iran-contra revelations, initially helped distract and absorb the attention of the American administration but later increased the attractiveness to it of summit diplomacy. Throughout the year, Gorbachev's position at home continued to strengthen against formidable resistance, while Reagan's position remained weakened if not threatened by the Iran-contra scandal and other domestic difficulties (including in October the worst stock market crash since 1929). The successful summit in Washington in December gave a strong boost to the two leaders, as well as to the U.S.-Soviet relationship. Gorbachev's standing, in particular, rose. At year's end, Gorbachev was chosen *Time* magazine's Man of the Year.

## Gorbachev on Two Fronts

Gorbachev continued in late 1986 and early 1987 to seek some way to engage the United States on strategic arms control, but his principal focus had to be on the internal development of the Soviet Union. His initial attempt in 1985–86 was to reinvigorate "Andropovism," to improve labor discipline and effectiveness and to "accelerate" the economy, and to increase popular support by bringing greater openness and public participation into traditional Soviet social-political life.[1] By the fall of 1986, Gorbachev was increasingly aware that this approach was not enough. In 1986 the slogan of "acceleration" (*uskoreniye*) was replaced by the much more far-reaching (if still ambiguous) "restructuring" (*perestroika*)—better rendered as "transformation," even "reformation"—of the economy but also of the society. *Glasnost*, openness through wider public information and expression, was encouraged.[2] By early 1987 this policy included opening up Soviet (largely Communist Party) history, renewed attention to Russian culture and history, and freer expression.[3] One important early sign of this relaxation was the release of most dissidents. The release and return to Moscow of Andrei Sakharov, the respected academician, in December 1986 was followed in early 1987 by the release of most of the political dissidents—some 140 in the first several weeks of the year, and more later. Most had been sentenced under Article 70, now rescinded, on charges of agitation and propaganda against the Soviet regime. A new policy of allowing greater religious freedom expanded on freedom of expression. Large numbers

---

1. One of the most resented, and failed, early "reforms" had been an antialcohol campaign reducing production of spirits, curtailing sales outlets and times, and forbidding sale of alcohol in restaurants before 2:00 p.m. The idea was particularly pushed by Yegor Ligachev, but Gorbachev had the responsibility (and took the heat of the public dissatisfaction; the *general'nyi sekretar'*—general secretary—was soon being jocularly and demeaningly called the *mineral'nyi sekretar'*—the mineral water secretary). The campaign was launched in May 1985, quietly downplayed by 1987, and so modified as to be essentially abandoned in September 1988. Although the campaign had somewhat reduced absenteeism and did lower the automobile accident rate, it also led to an increase in illicit moonshine production and sales, sharply cut government revenues, and caused wide public discontent. By cutting back vineyards for wine production, it also caused unemployment in the Nagorno-Karabakh Armenian-populated region of Azerbaijan, stimulating demands there for political change that led to local civil war.

2. Gorbachev had advocated *glasnost* in a party conference on ideology even before becoming general secretary, although at that time he clearly envisioned it as a tool for control over bureaucratic tendencies in the party, rather than a liberation of popular views to enlarge free democratic choice. See "The Live Creativity of the People, Speech of Comrade M. S. Gorbachev," *Pravda*, December 11, 1984. By 1987 his own "openness" to change was growing, but he almost certainly did not yet foresee *glasnost* as a force that would overwhelm the party. This was also true for Yury Andropov, who had introduced the term even before Gorbachev did.

3. For example, in January "Lenin's Testament," a memorandum in which the terminally ill Soviet leader Vladimir Lenin had criticized Josef Stalin's roughness and suggested removing him from his position as general secretary of the Party's Central Committee, was cited at length for only the second time in sixty years. (It had surfaced under Nikita Khrushchev's destalinization drive in 1956, before again disappearing into limbo.) See Yegor Yakovlev, "Farewell," *Moskovskiye novosti* (Moscow News), January 18, 1987.

of Jews and others denied exit began to be permitted to emigrate. Boris Pasternak's *Dr. Zhivago* and many other literary works of Soviet and émigré Russian writers whose works had been banned were now allowed to be published.

An important case given low key but open publication was the rehabilitation of an investigative reporter, Viktor B. Berkhin, who after publishing articles on local corruption had been arrested as recently as July 1986 by order of local party and KGB officials in the Ukraine. Moreover, the chief of the KGB, Viktor Chebrikov, personally signed an article in *Pravda* dismissing the local KGB chief responsible for Berkhin's wrongful arrest.[4] *Glasnost* about this case was intended to encourage the public—and bring home to the security forces—that the KGB was no longer above the law. Less than a month later, Lieutenant General Yury Churbanov, Leonid Brezhnev's son-in-law and a former top police official, was arrested for corruption.

Responsibility of everyone, not only security officials, was emphasized by publicity to a series of trials: in March of the maritime officers responsible for the tragic sinking of a large cruise ship, the *Admiral Nakhimov*, the previous August; in June of the former deputy minister of foreign trade, Vladimir Sushkov, for bribery; in July for those local officials responsible for the tragic nuclear power plant accident at Chernobyl; in August for those who had caused a serious train wreck.

In September 1986, in a speech in the south Russian city of Krasnodar, Gorbachev had first spoken of the "democratization" (*demokratizatsiya*) "of [Soviet] society and of all spheres of our life" as a priority.[5] At the time, the general assumption was that he meant greater *glasnost* and a participating role for the public but not real democratic elective choice.[6] But he had said that "much depends on how quickly restructuring occurs within the CPSU itself, within all its links from the primary party organizations to the Central Committee and Politburo." And later it was learned that soon after this statement, in late fall 1986, Gorbachev had tried to schedule a Central Committee plenum on political democratization and was unable to persuade the majority of his colleagues in the leadership. Several times (four, according to the Moscow correspondent of the Italian communist newspaper *L'Unita*) this plenum was postponed until it was finally held on January 27–28, 1987.

---

4.   V. Chebrikov, "Beyond the Limit," *Pravda*, January 8, 1987. The local party chief was also dismissed.

5.   "Speech by M. S. Gorbachev, General Secretary of the CPSU Central Committee, at a meeting with the Krasnodar Region Party Group," *Pravda*, September 20, 1986.

6.   The speech was little noted in the West, but a Soviet official immediately drew my attention to its significance.
     Perhaps not coincidentally, the regional party chief in the Krasnodar region was a strong conservative, later to become head of the conservative Russian Communist Party, Ivan Polozkov.

The January 1987 plenum marked Gorbachev's launching of a major political reform. *Perestroika*, initially focused on economic reform, now had a no less important political dimension. Gorbachev spoke in unprecedented frank terms with searing criticism for past party and state leadership. "At some point, the country began to lose momentum, difficulties and unresolved problems began to pile up, and there appeared elements of stagnation . . . a need for change was evidently overdue in the economy and in other fields . . . the Central Committee and the leadership of the country failed to see in time and in full the need for change and the danger of intensification of crisis phenomena in society."[7]

The plenum was important because it provided an opening wedge for the introduction of democratic procedures, but despite Gorbachev's efforts it did not actually decide to do so. He called for secret elections and multiple candidacies at all party levels from local districts to union republics, as well as local government and enterprises. There was, however, strong resistance in the Central Committee, and only a bland and ambiguous formulation on "improving" the mechanism for party elections appeared in its resolution. It also fudged on local government elections although there at least mentioning "a larger number of candidacies." Actual steps were taken gradually in the months ahead.

Gorbachev was also able to advance one of his supporters (Aleksandr Yakovlev) to candidate status in the Politburo and add one (Anatoly Lukyanov) to the Secretariat, but none to full Politburo membership.

Within two years there would be contested free elections for the national as well as republic and local legislatures, and in the Communist Party as well. But in 1987 Gorbachev still faced very strong opposition and resistance to any kind of far-reaching political or economic reform. Not wishing to await the normal span of time before the next party congress (in 1991), Gorbachev also proposed at the January plenum a party conference the following year (and although the matter was only decided later, there would be such a conference in June 1988).

A number of these steps in domestic policy were, at the time, seen with some suspicion in the West as cosmetic or peripheral corrections designed to make the Soviet Union look better abroad. In some cases the timing and even the nature of such actions did include considerations of impact on the outside world, but these changes were above all directed to an internal transformation of Soviet society and the Soviet polity. Even some steps that may primarily have been intended to influence external views often had an important domestic aspect. For example, in May the Soviet Union ceased jamming Voice of America Russian-language broadcasts (also unjammed during the détente of the

---

7.   "On Restructuring and the Party's Personnel Policy, Speech of General Secretary of the CC of the CPSU M. S. Gorbachev at the Plenum of the CC of the CPSU of January 27, 1987," *Pravda*, January 28, 1987.

1970s, but then jammed since 1980). This was part of a general pattern of normalization of external relations (jamming of BBC, Radio Beijing, and Radio Tirana had ceased earlier, and access to Kol Israel, Deutsche Welle, and later Radio Liberty followed). But such loosening of restrictions was also part of the pattern of growing internal *glasnost* that was building a foundation for democratization.

In retrospect, however, Gorbachev clearly failed to recognize two vital aspects of necessary political reform: a new definition of the division of authority between the republics and the Union center, and a need to deal with the growth of ethnic and national aspirations and frictions.

On the external front, in the absence of any movement from the Reagan administration, Gorbachev sought to stimulate Western public opinion. For example, he received a senior unofficial American delegation from the Council on Foreign Relations (including former secretaries of state Henry Kissinger and Cyrus Vance) for a frank discussion, in which they found Gorbachev "impressive" and sincere in his effort to effect major change.[8]

Gorbachev's most ambitious initiative in public diplomacy was the convening of an international forum "For a Nuclear-Free World, for the Survival of Humanity" in Moscow, which he personally addressed in the Kremlin on February 16. An effort was made to assemble not only inveterate optimists and peace seekers but people reflecting a wide spectrum of views, including skeptics and critics and cultural as well as political intellectuals, a group numbering about 1,000. In his address, Gorbachev for the first time characterized the developments under way in the Soviet Union as "essentially revolutionary changes . . . of immense significance for our society, for socialism as a whole, and for the entire world." He stressed the need for lasting peace in order to "concentrate on constructive efforts to improve our country." Although accepting the existence of nuclear deterrence, he criticized continued reliance on it because it placed undue weight on military means, on continued confrontation, and did not provide assurance against inadvertent or accidental war. He declared that the Soviet Union was prepared to renounce its status as a nuclear (super) power and to rely on mutual international security, to reduce other arms to a "minimal reasonable sufficiency" under a purely defensive military doctrine. All arms, he emphasized, were on the table for negotiation of reductions. He also emphasized the need to settle regional conflicts and to combat terrorism. In his peroration he spoke of a rising spiral of the arms race and of the exacerbation of regional and global problems (earlier he had attacked the strategic defense initiative [SDI] and a new strategic defense-offense dynamic). And he urged his listeners "not to waste more time on trying to outplay one

---

8.   "Report on the Council Delegation Visit to the U.S.S.R., February 2–6, 1987," remarks delivered to members of the Council on Foreign Relations on February 19, 1987, transcript (circulated by the Council on March 23, 1987), pp. 1, 5.

another and gain unilateral advantages. The stakes of the game are too high—the survival of humanity."[9]

By late February, Gorbachev decided that President Reagan was not going to limit the SDI or advance any new approach to strategic arms reduction, and that he must take the initiative.[10] He did so on February 28, in a speech proposing the elimination of all Soviet and U.S. intermediate-range nuclear forces (INF) in Europe, with no strings attached—not to strategic arms, the SDI, or even British and French intermediate-range forces.[11] He clearly had meant it two weeks earlier when he told the international forum that the stakes were too high to "waste more time on trying to outplay one another" in traditional arms control diplomacy.

In traditional terms, Gorbachev had capitulated to Reagan's attempts ever since the Geneva summit in 1985 (and in a broader sense since his proposal of a zero option in INF in 1981) to negotiate an elimination of U.S. and Soviet INF missiles in Europe. Reagan, hardly daring to believe it, welcomed the initiative three days later in his first White House press conference since the Iran-contra scandal had exploded four months earlier. He was disposed to credit the change not to Gorbachev's new thinking but to Western intransigence. And he rushed to "congratulate our allies for their firmness on this issue," reassuring them that "nothing is more important to the cause of peace than the credibility of our commitment to NATO."[12]

The INF element of the nuclear arms talks, at least, was back on track, although the negotiations would require most of the rest of the year. An INF agreement would have favorable and unfavorable aspects regarding Soviet

---

9.   "For a Nuclear-Free World, for Humanism in International Relations, Speech of M. S. Gorbachev," *Pravda*, February 17, 1987. I participated in the forum and can attest that Gorbachev's speech had a powerful impact on those present.

10.  In mid-January Gorbachev had sought to engage the American administration at a higher level in the stalled strategic arms talks by appointing the senior deputy foreign minister, Yuly Vorontsov, as head of the Soviet delegation concurrently with his ministerial post. The American response was simply to promote the same U.S. delegation chief, Max Kampelman, to counselor of the Department of State rather than to assign a more senior official. The sluggish American stance in the talks was not, in any case, Kampelman's responsibility, but that of the Reagan administration.

11.  Picking up from Reykjavik, Gorbachev proposed that the USSR retain INF missiles with one hundred warheads in Asia, and the United States one hundred in its national territory. The Soviet Union would also withdraw from Eastern Europe (East Germany and Czechoslovakia) the sub-INF range operational-tactical missiles (later termed SRINF, shorter-range INF) that it had deployed there in response to the NATO INF deployments. Finally, the Soviets proposed prompt negotiations on reducing and eliminating short-range missiles.

12.  "Intermediate-Range Nuclear Force Reductions," March 3, 1987, *Weekly Compilation of Presidential Documents*, vol. 23 (March 9, 1987), p. 204. (Hereafter *Presidential Documents*.)

strategic politico-military considerations. On the negative side, the Soviet Union would have to give up far larger numbers of missiles and launchers than the United States. Many NATO counterpart systems other than land-based missiles would not be reduced: sea-launched cruise missiles (SLCMs) and British and French sea-launched ballistic missiles (SLBMs) (and the small French land-based intermediate-range missile force). On the positive side, the NATO intermediate-range missiles, particularly the Pershing II, were seen as a serious military threat to Soviet missile and other command and control centers in Europe, including in the Moscow area (despite American claims that the range would not include Moscow). If these NATO systems were removed, the automaticity of escalation to all-out nuclear war would be greatly reduced. Gorbachev had to weigh these and other pros and cons, but he also saw what he regarded as a much more important purpose of achieving an INF treaty: reestablishing arms control and giving it new momentum. If President Reagan, the enemy of SALT II (and for that matter the ABM Treaty), whose administration had issued a series of reports charging Soviet noncompliance with virtually all existing arms control agreements, were to sign a new arms control agreement with the Soviet Union, the process would be relegitimized.

Meanwhile, Soviet military doctrine was being redefined to stress the prevention of war and a defensive doctrine should war nonetheless occur. Gorbachev in several speeches reasserted briefly the guidelines of "reasonable sufficiency" as a criterion for forces and a new defensive emphasis in doctrine and strategy, as first stated authoritatively in his report to the party congress in 1986. Besides his address to the international forum in February, he repeated these themes to domestic and foreign audiences. For example, only days after his address to the forum, he reassured a domestic audience that while "doing everything necessary to reliably guarantee our security . . . we shall not make a single step in excess of the demands and requirements of reasonable, sufficient defense."[13]

Most significant was a formal revision and statement of military doctrine issued by the Warsaw Pact on May 30, 1987.[14] This pronouncement incorporated both the redefinition of military doctrine to include the priority given to the prevention of war and the new emphasis on defensive doctrine and strategy. It represented the fruits of an early initiative by Gorbachev soon after he had come to power two years earlier, and thenceforth formed the basis for Soviet (as well as Pact) doctrine.[15]

Almost coincidental with the formal pronouncement on military doctrine, but unrelated to it, a chance occurrence gave Gorbachev the opportunity

---

13. "Restructuring—A Vital Cause of the Nation. Speech by M. S. Gorbachev to the Eighteenth Congress of Trade Unions of the USSR," *Pravda*, February 26, 1987.

14. "On the Military Doctrine of the Member States of the Warsaw Pact," *Pravda*, May 30, 1987.

15. For further discussion, see chapter 12.

to replace the aging minister of defense, Marshal Sergei Sokolov, with a younger and, it was hoped, more "perestroika-minded" general, General of the Army Dmitry Yazov—a selection made by jumping over at least a dozen more senior generals. The event precipitating Sokolov's retirement (and the firing of the deputy minister in command of air defense forces, Chief Marshal of Aviation Aleksandr Koldunov) was the extraordinary flight on May 28 of a light single-engine aircraft flown by a young West German from Finland unimpeded to a landing on Red Square just outside the Kremlin. A replacement of older military leaders had been under way since 1985 and would continue.

Military concerns were not, however, entirely overridden. On February 26, nuclear testing was resumed, ending the unilateral Soviet moratorium on nuclear testing in effect since July 1985—during which the United States had continued a vigorous weapon modernization program and carried out twenty-six tests.

At another Central Committee plenum on June 25–26, Gorbachev further strengthened his political position, promoting three supporters to full membership on the Politburo (party secretaries Aleksandr Yakovlev, Viktor Nikonov, and Nikolai Slyunkov) and reducing the role of his chief rival, Yegor Ligachev. (General Yazov, who had only been a candidate member of the Central Committee when elevated to the post of defense minister, was now also made a candidate Politburo member, the standing his predecessor had.) But though Gorbachev's authority was enhanced, his power in the sense of ability to make things happen remained circumscribed. He found the problems of radically transforming the massive Soviet economy, society, and polity daunting, and, as he had explicitly acknowledged for the first time at the January plenum, these problems were producing a genuine crisis.

Against this background of growing crisis at home Gorbachev had to maneuver to bring the United States around to an arms control agreement and hence achieve a political breakthrough to improved relations. And this task was also formidable.

## Reagan on Two Fronts

Although there were important differences in their situations and their purposes, Reagan and Gorbachev each faced problems on the internal and the foreign policy fronts.

The Iran-contra scandal continued to unfold and to make Reagan appear either deceiving or gullible, manipulative or manipulated, in cahoots or incompetent. His personal popularity, always high, suffered. Changes in his senior staff, though usually for the better, required new adjustments from which Reagan personally remained aloof. The late 1986 replacement of National Security Adviser Vice Admiral John Poindexter by Frank Carlucci was followed in February 1987 by replacement of Donald Regan as chief of the

White House staff by Howard Baker. William Casey, deeply implicated not only in Iran-contra but in broader uncontrolled covert activities, was terminally stricken by brain cancer and was replaced as director of Central Intelligence in early March by the former director of the FBI, William Webster. Patrick Buchanan joined a growing stream of right-wing conservative "Reaganauts" leaving the administration. In June, the hard-line Richard Perle left the Defense Department for private life.[16]

In January the White House released a forty-one-page paper called the *National Security Strategy of the United States*.[17] Permeated by a Cold War outlook, the discussion of the Soviet threat and of Soviet policy aims could have been written in the 1950s at the nadir of relations. There was no hint of recognition of Gorbachev's new thinking in this report: "Moscow seeks to alter the existing international system and establish Soviet global hegemony. These long-range Soviet objectives constitute the overall conceptual framework of Soviet foreign and defense policy." The relationship between the United States and the Soviet Union was said to be "essentially adversarial." The Soviet Union was said to have undertaken "an unprecedented military buildup that poses a continuing threat to the United States and our allies," "to execute its expansionist policies, the USSR has perpetuated a domestic political system of centralized totalitarian control," and to engage in such things as trade with the West "to obtain economic leverage, technology, and foreign exchange." In defiance of the early efforts of the intelligence community to be discriminatory and accurate, the paper argued that "the evidence of the relationship between the Soviet Union and the growth of worldwide terrorism is now conclusive" even though "the Soviets attempt to disguise such support by using middle men"— "Cuba, North Korea, Nicaragua, Syria and Libya, which deal directly with radical terrorists and insurgents." The only change ascribed to Soviet policy is that "the Soviet Union in recent years has become much more sophisticated in wielding the instruments of national power," such as trade, and in the use of "active

---

16.  Unrelated to these political changes in Washington, Ambassador Arthur Hartman completed his long tour in Moscow and returned in early 1987, to be succeeded in April by Ambassador Jack Matlock, who had been serving as the Soviet affairs expert on the National Security Council staff.

Incidentally, in late 1986 when Poindexter was replaced, Casey had urged President Reagan to name hard-line ex-Democrat Zbigniew Brzezinski again to the post, which he had held in the Carter administration. See George P. Shultz, *Turmoil and Triumph: My Years as Secretary of State* (Charles Scribner's Sons, 1993), p. 842. Carlucci was a much better choice, although initially he and Shultz clashed over such things as Carlucci's practice of meeting Dobrynin and other ambassadors in Washington without the knowledge of the State Department. See pp. 869–70, 877.

17.  This was intended to be the first of an annual series, similar to the series on *U.S. Foreign Policy for the 1970's* issued by President Richard Nixon from 1970 through 1973, and to the earlier classified annual *Basic National Security Policy* series issued by President Dwight Eisenhower throughout his presidency.

measures" such as disinformation.[18] All in all, the threat was portrayed in a way that almost made it seem that President Reagan was being duped by Gorbachev. The paper had little influence on policy, but it certainly bespoke the continued influence of ultraconservative forces in the Reagan administration.

Secretary of Defense Weinberger chose to launch a new campaign in January and February for initiation of SDI deployment and for "activating" the reinterpretation of the ABM Treaty advanced in October 1985. One aim may have been to move preemptively to forestall a major review then under way in the Senate of the reinterpretation of the ABM Treaty. In a meeting of the National Security Council (NSC) on February 3, Weinberger sought immediate presidential decision on deployment of an ABM system, in part justified by the broad interpretation of the treaty. Not only Secretary Shultz, but Admiral William J. Crowe, chairman of the Joint Chiefs of Staff, strongly objected. The idea was finally shelved following a public and congressional outcry and objections from European allies, including Prime Minister Margaret Thatcher of Britain, Chancellor Helmut Kohl of West Germany, Lord Peter Carrington, secretary general of NATO, and other allies including Japan and Canada.[19] Nonetheless, while the attempt to apply the broad interpretation and to make a decision on deployment failed, President Reagan's disturbing inclination to take these steps was disclosed through publication of a leaked copy of the transcript of the NSC meeting to the right-wing *Washington Times*.

The transcript of the NSC meeting showed that President Reagan had brushed aside the question of the ABM Treaty and of Soviet reactions. After Shultz had noted, "It's hard to say what the Soviets would do . . . some tests require broad interpretation of the ABM Treaty," Weinberger argued, "We shouldn't debate with the Soviets what can and can't be prohibited." Shultz contended, "We should see what we can find out . . . then negotiate with the Soviet Union." At that point, President Reagan showed his impatience with the intricacies of treaty constraints and negotiations impeding his SDI. According to the leaked transcript, he said, "Why don't we just go ahead on the assumption that this is what we're doing and it's right. . . . Don't ask the Soviets. Tell them."[20] Although Reagan deferred a deployment decision, the fragility of the

---

18. *National Security Strategy of the United States* (White House, 1987), pp. 6–7.

19. For a review of the matter, see Raymond L. Garthoff, *Policy Versus the Law: The Reinterpretation of the ABM Treaty* (Brookings, 1987), pp. 12–17; and Shultz, *Turmoil and Triumph*, pp. 870–73. Weinberger had first tried to sneak through a presidential decision by getting Patrick Buchanan to insert it in a draft of the State of the Union address. This attempt was foiled by the new national security adviser, Frank Carlucci, who insisted the matter be taken up by the National Security Council.

20. Gregory A. Fossedal, "NSC Minutes Show President Leaning to SDI Deployment," *Washington Times*, February 6, 1987, p. 10A. The authenticity of the minutes was never challenged.

ABM Treaty and arms control in general was evident.[21] More fundamentally, the episode showed how tenuous the idea of common security was in the United States under the Reagan administration, in contrast to Gorbachev's championing of the idea and his increasing readiness to act on it.

Although American receptivity to Gorbachev's offer of an INF agreement restored some prospect of an arms control agreement, another issue arose and quickly dominated American attention. A marine guard formerly posted at the U.S. Embassy in Moscow, Sergeant Clayton Lonetree, who had admitted violations of rules, was charged with espionage. The scandal, disclosed in January, quickly widened; in March another marine, Corporal Arnold Bracy, was also arrested, and the two were charged with permitting Soviet KGB agents into the embassy at night. Soon the entire contingent of twenty-eight marines in Moscow was replaced. Renewed attention was also given to the charges first advanced in 1985 about Soviet bugging of the new embassy building still under construction.

Although it became clear that several marines had violated instructions against fraternization with Soviet women, and Lonetree had revealed some confidential information, it was also eventually determined that he and Bracy had not admitted any Soviet agents into the premises, that invalid "confessions" had been obtained by impermissible means, and that the impression of a massive security failure was not valid. But the matter did not subside to its real dimensions for several months. In the meantime, a wide public and congressional outcry took place.[22] A Senate resolution, passed with seventy votes, called on Shultz not to go to Moscow for a planned meeting with Shevardnadze in April. He did go, promising to protest the Soviet action vigorously. In Moscow, Shevardnadze and Gorbachev himself authoritatively denied that Soviet agents had entered the embassy—as, indeed, the full American investigation later

---

21. Some other members of the administration also continued to press the issue. Deputy Director of the Central Intelligence Agency Robert Gates had slanted intelligence estimates to emphasize Soviet strategic defense efforts in a public speech in San Francisco on November 24, 1986, in order to boost support for the SDI. The result was that public commentary distorted what he had said. See Warren Strobel, "Kremlin Has Spent $150 Billion on its 'Star Wars,' CIA Estimates," *Washington Times*, November 26, 1986, p. 1. Gates had said that the United States estimated that the Soviet Union had spent that amount over the previous ten years on "strategic defense," but he did not make clear that by far the largest share had been spent on air defenses, not antimissile defense. He also stretched the official estimates and seemed to say more than his hedged words really stated. He contended that "taken together" various indications were "more significant and more ominous than any one considered individually," and that "cumulatively" they "suggest" that the USSR "may be preparing" an ABM defense of its national territory. Many intelligence analysts were shocked at his bending the facts and their estimates to leave a more ominous conclusion that would buttress the administration's political drive for the SDI.

22. Shultz reviews this well in his memoir; see Shultz, *Turmoil and Triumph*, pp. 879–83, 900.

concluded.[23] But from March to May, concerns about Soviet espionage tended to dominate the relationship in the eyes of the American public.

Soviet leaders strongly suspected that a minor indiscretion in the permanent competition of intelligence agencies had been intentionally blown into a major issue before Shultz's visit in order to hamstring improvement in relations.[24] There were other disquieting American actions in Soviet eyes. In February ABC television had aired *Amerika*, a film depicting the United States under Soviet occupation. (Gorbachev personally complained about that to the visiting notables of the Council on Foreign Relations.) On March 5, Deputy Secretary of State John Whitehead declared that the United States opposed Soviet membership in principal international economic institutions—the General Agreement on Tariffs and Trade (GATT), the World Bank, and the International Monetary Fund. On March 9, the Department of State denied visas to Soviet trade union officials to attend a conference to which they had been invited because they were communists. This was not a new issue, the AFL-CIO opposed any waiver of an old statute, but that was the rub—it was Cold War business as usual. On July 7, the State Department blocked a Soviet offer to sell space launch services. Meanwhile, in an incident not unlike the Black Sea intrusion of March 1986, a nuclear-powered cruiser, the USS *Arkansas*, deliberately (on May 17 and 21) entered Soviet territorial waters off Kamchatka in the Pacific, near the main Soviet naval base at Petropavlovsk.

President Reagan also kept up steady attacks on Soviet policy in Afghanistan and Nicaragua and made renewed charges of Soviet noncompliance with past arms control agreements.[25]

While Gorbachev, Shevardnadze, and other members of the Soviet leadership smarted at this tough line and may have seen a more hostile pattern to such events than was intended, they correctly understood that President Reagan was not repudiating a policy of continuing negotiation and development of relations. President Reagan himself, in a speech on the state of relations with the Soviet Union in April, made this clear. Though criticizing, almost in passing, the "recent disclosures of Soviet espionage against the United States Embassy," and what he still saw as the threat from a Soviet policy of "global expansionism" manifested in Afghanistan, Nicaragua, Angola, Ethiopia and Cambodia, these actions were now depicted as a declining threat. "If I had to characterize U.S.-Soviet relations in one word," he said, "it would be

23. See Don Oberdorfer, *The Turn: From the Cold War to a New Era, the United States and the Soviet Union, 1983–1990* (Poseidon Press, 1991), pp. 218–20.

24. The Soviets saw the "Spy Dust" charges just before the Geneva summit meeting in 1985, and the arrest of Zakharov shortly before the Reykjavik summit in 1986, as other recent examples of this pattern.

25. In particular, see "Regional Conflicts. Radio Address to the Nation," March 7, 1987, *Presidential Documents*, vol. 23 (March 16, 1987), pp. 235–36; and "Soviet Noncompliance with Arms Control Agreements," March 10, 1987, ibid., pp. 239–48.

this: proceeding. No great cause for excitement; no great cause for alarm. And perhaps this is the way relations with one's adversaries should be characterized."[26]

Reagan challenged the Soviets to move ahead on an INF agreement, commenting that the problem of "shorter range INF [SRINF] systems must be resolved in a way that protects allied security interests."[27] That very same day, coincidentally, Gorbachev in Prague proposed to deal with the SRINF issue by freezing and then cutting such systems.

When Shultz met with Shevardnadze and then Gorbachev on April 13 and 14, he conveyed the message that the United States must have the "right" to match the Soviets in SRINF—a category in which the Soviet Union had some 160 missile launchers operationally deployed. The United States had none. Gorbachev did not want a treaty that entailed larger Soviet reductions of INF systems, while sanctioning an American buildup in SRINF missiles. But in keeping with the aim of maximizing reductions of all nuclear systems, which he had made clear in his January 1986 speech, Gorbachev now proposed a solution—all right, the United States could match the Soviet Union, but the Soviet Union would come down to zero SRINF—that is, another zero in missiles in Europe, a "double zero," INF and SRINF. Shultz could not agree to what seemed to be a very generous offer because of allied sensitivities over such systems, but he could hardly object to the suggestion either, and he was left in the unenviable position of repeating that the United States must have the right to build *up* in order to equal the Soviet level.

On other arms control issues there was some backward movement by the United States. Shultz had been instructed to propose only a seven-year period of nonwithdrawal from the ABM Treaty instead of the ten years agreed on at Reykjavik. Discussions on interpretation of the ABM Treaty constraints on testing were not fruitful, despite Marshal Akhromeyev's presence and Soviet readiness to compromise, because Shultz had no authorization and Weinberger would have strongly objected to anything that brought agreement on this matter closer. Shultz had sought authority to discuss these matters, but President Reagan had decided against it.

---

26.  "Los Angeles World Affairs Council," April 10, 1987, *Presidential Documents*, vol. 23 (April 20, 1987), pp. 381, 383–84.
       The reason for Reagan's relatively balanced approach in his April 10 speech may have been a message he received from Prime Minister Thatcher following eleven hours of talks with Gorbachev during her visit to Moscow in March. She urged Gorbachev and Reagan to work things out and advised Reagan to help Gorbachev institute his *perestroika*. Information from an informed senior American official.

27.  Ibid., p. 383. SRINF missiles were defined as those with a range of 500–1,000 km, in distinction to INF missiles of 1,000–5,500 km, ICBM missiles of more than 5,500 km— and short-range systems under 500 km.

Gorbachev made clear his interest in a summit meeting to conclude an INF treaty *and* to agree on "key provisions" on strategic nuclear arms, space weapons, and nuclear testing. But there was no progress on these issues, nor did Gorbachev define what he meant by key provisions. Evidently he hoped to keep the pressure on for further negotiation in these areas, while not making a summit dependent on full agreement on anything beyond an INF treaty. Gorbachev also pressed for limitations on nuclear testing.

Shultz continued to hammer away at the issues of human rights in the Soviet Union (that is, the plight of Jews aspiring to emigrate) and regional conflicts (above all, Afghanistan). As noted earlier, he also brought up the alleged Soviet suborning of marines and penetration of the U.S. Embassy, which the Soviets firmly denied.[28]

One concrete agreement was signed, an accord on resuming cooperation in peaceful exploration of space, which had been in effect from 1972 to 1982, but, as a sanction against Soviet pressure on Poland, was not then renewed. The significance of Shultz's visit was in the steps toward arms control, in particular toward an INF agreement.

On the heels of Shultz's visit, a senior bipartisan congressional delegation chaired by House Speaker Jim Wright of Texas spent several days in Moscow and was given red carpet treatment. Gorbachev and a number of other Soviet leaders made a pitch for the INF double-zero approach and for limiting nuclear testing (the Soviet leaders included conservatives Yegor Ligachev and Vladimir Shcherbitsky, to show "bipartisan" Soviet support for arms control). The congressmen were favorably impressed.[29]

There was heated debate on the double-zero proposal among NATO leaders, with Chancellor Helmut Kohl most in favor and Prime Minister Margaret Thatcher most reluctant.[30] In discussions on the side at the Western economic summit meeting in Venice in June Reagan did side with Kohl.[31] (Incidentally, President Reagan was clearly not in a commanding role.) NATO formally approved the idea at its semiannual ministerial meeting on June 12.

Meanwhile, the Defense Department had reacted to the prospect of double zero in a different way. It proposed that the United States reserve the right to convert its Pershing II INF missiles into shorter-range SRINF missiles (of a new model, Pe-IB) and turn them over to the Germans—and in late June

---

28. On this range of arms control discussions, see Shultz, *Turmoil and Triumph*, pp. 884–96.

29. See Gary Lee, "Moscow Talks Offer Hope, with New Risk of Failure: Soviets Pin Future Relations on Shorter-Range Missile Offer," *Washington Post*, April 19, 1987, pp. A19, A24.

30. Chancellor Kohl was initially less sure, but on June 1 the coalition government he headed, pressed by Foreign Minister Hans-Friedrich Genscher, had decided to support zero SRINF, while excluding their own 72 Pe-IA SRINF missiles.

31. Ronald Reagan, *An American Life* (Simon and Schuster, 1990) pp. 685–86.

this objective became the U.S. proposal in Geneva. The Soviets not only objected adamantly but insisted that the United States dismantle its nuclear warheads for the seventy-two existing German Pe-IAs. In addition, there was an argument over where the United States could deploy its one hundred INF missiles, which were to be allowed to match the Soviet Union's retention of INF missiles with one hundred warheads deployed in Asia. Although it had been understood that the 100 U.S. INF missiles would be located in the United States rather than Europe, when American officials began to discuss their placement in Alaska, the Soviets objected. This would be a new deployment allowing the U.S. missiles to strike targets in the USSR, in contrast to Soviet reduction to thirty-three SS-20s (with ninety-nine warheads) of existing Soviet deployments in Asia unable to strike the United States.

On July 23, Gorbachev again took the initiative to break the impasse by proposing a global double zero, eliminating all INF and SRINF in Asia (and America) as well as in Europe.[32] Although not directly affecting the German Pe-IAs, it added momentum for a general ban (and Soviet negotiators made clear that no conversion of U.S. INF to German SRINF—nor ground-launched cruise missiles [GLCMs] to air-launched cruise missiles [ALCMs]—would be acceptable).

On August 26, Kohl announced Germany's willingness to destroy its Pe-IAs after U.S. and Soviet INF and SRINF missiles were eliminated. President Reagan publicly welcomed this move and later disclosed in his memoir that he had privately suggested to Kohl that he volunteer to eliminate the missiles in the interest of disarmament.[33] A dispute lingered over U.S. commitment to dismantle the seventy-two warheads for these missiles but was finally resolved by American agreement to do so when the missiles were dismantled.

While the negotiation of an INF treaty was proceeding from April to September, the broader development of U.S.-Soviet relations failed to advance, mainly because of a continuing dissonance in the objectives, strategy, and leverage of the two leaderships. President Reagan continued to express his readiness to negotiate, to meet at the summit, and to develop relations. At the same time, he criticized the Soviet Union sharply and called for it to change

---

32. "Answers of M. S. Gorbachev to Questions of the Indonesian Newspaper *Merdeka*," *Pravda*, July 23, 1987.

   Prior to Gorbachev's decision to agree on global-zero INF, Reagan and Shultz—though preferring that outcome—continued to advocate the compromise agreed on with the Soviet Union, allowing each side one hundred INF warheads deployed outside of and beyond range of Europe. On May 15, however, in an act of policy sabotage, Secretary of Defense Weinberger ignored Reagan's decision and engineered a NATO defense ministers' communiqué calling for global-zero INF—elimination of all INF missiles. See Shultz, *Turmoil and Triumph*, pp. 899–900.

33. Reagan, *An American Life*, p. 686.

many practices not only around the world, in regional conflicts, and in Eastern Europe but at home as well. As Gorbachev began to make more and more changes in these practices (almost always because he too saw a need for change and not because of Reagan's pressures), and also most of the concessions in negotiations, Reagan did not reciprocate but asked for more. Above all, on the few areas in which Gorbachev sought change by the United States, especially on space weapons and the SDI, but also in regional conflicts, Reagan was adamant. And the Soviet Union had very little leverage.

Thus Reagan continued in numerous speeches to call for Soviet disengagement from support to Nicaragua, Afghanistan, Angola, Cambodia, Ethiopia, and also Eastern Europe.

On June 12 in Berlin he grudgingly and cautiously said that "now the Soviets themselves may, in a limited way, be coming to understand the importance of freedom." But although he acknowledged that "we hear much from Moscow about a new policy of reform and openness," he also asked, "Are these the beginnings of profound changes in the Soviet state? Or are they token gestures, intended to raise false hopes in the West or to strengthen the Soviet system without changing it?" He challenged Gorbachev to make one "unmistakable" sign: "If you seek peace, if you seek prosperity for the Soviet Union and Eastern Europe, if you seek liberalization . . . Mr. Gorbachev, tear down this wall!"[34]

Reagan's challenge was broadened in a speech to the Captive Nations conference at the Ukrainian Catholic National Shrine in Illinois to call for a renunciation of the Brezhnev Doctrine "from the Baltic States through Bulgaria, from Vietnam to Ethiopia" (and, of course, Afghanistan, Angola, and Nicaragua).[35] And in his annual proclamation on Captive Nations week, while speaking of "peoples subjugated by Soviet imperialism," he said that "a struggle that began in Ukraine 70 years ago is taking place throughout the Soviet empire," in the past year not only in Eastern Europe but in "Kazakhstan, Latvia, Moldavia, and among the Crimean Tatars."[36]

A month later, Reagan spelled out his general strategic objectives as seeking to "break out of the stalemate of the Cold War . . . to dispel rather than to live with the two great darkening clouds of the postwar era: the danger of nuclear holocaust and the expansion of totalitarian rule." Those rather grandiloquent objectives were to be pursued by the two great Reagan doctrines (a term he did not use): "a new policy of helping democratic insurgents in their battle to bring self-determination and human rights to their own countries,"

---

34. "West Berlin. Remarks at the Brandenburg Gate," June 12, 1987, *Presidential Documents*, vol. 23 (June 22, 1987), pp. 658–59.

35. "Captive Nations Conference," July 24, 1987, ibid., vol. 23 (July 27, 1987), pp. 849–50.

36. "Captive Nations Week, 1987," July 17, 1987, ibid., vol. 23 (July 27, 1987), p. 827.

and "a transition to defensive deterrence" through the SDI.[37] He also added a new challenge to Gorbachev: not only to provide verification for arms control agreements but to reduce military secrecy. "It's time to show some *glasnost* in your military affairs. First, publish a valid budget of your military expenditures, just as we do. Second, reveal to the Soviet people and the world the size and composition of the Soviet Armed Forces. Third, open for debate in your Supreme Soviet the big issues of military policy and weapons, just as we do."[38]

Apart from the domestic political dividends to be expected from the Captive Nations rhetoric, these statements and many others were meant as a challenge to Gorbachev, even though Reagan did not expect them to be met. For the domestic front, the counterpart of the message was a replay of the Reagan message of earlier years: "A massive Soviet buildup throughout the 1970's had been met with inaction in the United States. . . . Meanwhile, in the Third World, Soviet adventurism had reached into countries like Afghanistan, Cambodia, Angola, and Nicaragua. Today, much has changed. We have built up our military, and the Soviets have responded to our new strength with a new willingness to talk seriously about arms reductions."[39] Although distorting history, this summary probably reflected a real historical impression held by Ronald Reagan himself and many others in the country.

Persistent public reaffirmation of the Reagan Doctrine compounded the problem that Gorbachev faced in responding to the challenge. Although Western observers tended to discount such "rhetoric" about American policy, the Soviet leaders took it very seriously. For one thing, they were becoming well aware of their internal weakness and vulnerability. For another, Gorbachev and his colleagues were sensitive to Western interference in their delicate process of internal transformation of the country under the policy of *perestroika*. Finally, Gorbachev and the reform element in the leadership (most forthrightly exemplified at the time by Boris Yeltsin, the new Moscow party chief) were personally, together with their policies, made politically vulnerable by charges of pandering or capitulating to Western pressures and demands. Gorbachev intended to disengage from Afghanistan and other Soviet commitments in the Third World, but he was seeking negotiated settlements. He intended to place relations with the countries of Eastern Europe on a new consensual basis, resting on independence. He intended to transform the Soviet Union itself. But not at Reagan's beck and call.

Although they avoided unproductive rhetorical counterpunches, the Soviet leaders did protest some American actions. Thus, while moving to

---

37. "Los Angeles, California. Remarks at a Luncheon," August 26, 1987, ibid., vol. 23 (August 31, 1987), pp. 965–67.

38. Ibid., p. 967.

39. "Soviet Union-United States Relations. Radio Address to the Nation," August 29, 1987, ibid., vol. 23 (September 7, 1987), p. 976.

remove the obstacle to arms control presented by the Soviet radar at Krasnoyarsk, constructed under the Brezhnev leadership in violation of a corollary provision of the ABM Treaty, the Soviets, in a formal protest on July 25, tried to draw attention to an arguably parallel U.S. violation in constructing a new similar early-warning radar at Thule. But when the United States brushed the issue aside there was nothing the Soviet Union could do about it. Similarly, although Reagan's rhetoric was not addressed, on July 30 the Soviets made a diplomatic protest over the presence of an officer of the U.S. Embassy at a public demonstration for the Crimean Tatars. Although the charge of American "instigation" of the protest was not justified, the Soviets were seeking to draw attention to external interference in domestic issues. Similarly, broadcasts by Radio Free Europe and Radio Liberty, charged with stirring up the situation in the Baltic States, were protested on August 24. What the Soviets did not publicly draw attention to, but was of great concern to them, was an increasing number of cases of infiltration of émigrés from the West, many belonging to groups associated with U.S. intelligence.[40]

Apart from the drumbeat of criticism of Soviet actions toward its own citizens and continuing involvements in Third World countries, there was little that the United States had to protest. Soviet missile test landings in the Pacific not far from Hawaii were protested in September. In an incident in East Germany in mid-September, an American soldier was wounded, but in sharp contrast to the Nicholson case two years earlier, the Soviets assumed some of the responsibility and promptly apologized.

Indeed, the Soviet Union continued to make many cooperative moves. On June 12, Gorbachev expressed readiness for joint calibration tests for nuclear tests that could verify a ban on virtually all tests, all down to one kiloton. On September 8, a U.S. congressional delegation, including experts, was

---

40. The Soviet leaders also considered the United States responsible at least indirectly, and some suspected directly, for several Afghan insurgent raids across the borders into the Soviet Union itself in March–April 1987. These raids were mounted by elements of Gulbuddin Hekmatyar's Hezb-i Islami *mujahedin* assisted by Pakistani military intelligence, probably in retaliation for Soviet transborder air attacks from Afghanistan against Afghan forces on Pakistan soil. See Olivier Roy, *The Lessons of the Soviet/Afghan War*, Adelphi Paper 259 (London: Brassey's for the International Institute of Strategic Studies, 1991), p. 22.

These Afghan incursions were a sensitive matter in the Soviet Union. After initial Western press reports, the Soviet leadership sought to calm any popular concerns by denying the reports in an account by a correspondent of *Pravda* (see N. Gladkov, "On a Calm Border: An Unsubstantiated Myth of 'Breakthrough' by Afghan Bandits into Soviet Territory," *Pravda*, May 21, 1987). A senior Soviet party official, however, some months later confirmed to me that such raids had occurred, and that this was regarded in high circles as a very negative development affecting Soviet-American relations. Even if exaggerated by this official to emphasize the point, such a reaction by the Soviet leadership would have been natural.

See the discussion in chapter 15.

granted access to the radar at Krasnoyarsk. The delegation's findings deflated the Reagan administration's ominous innuendos and charges of a possible ABM battle management radar but did not allay the charge of violation of the treaty provision on the siting of early-warning radars. In early October American and other Western experts were invited to visit the Soviet chemical weapon center at Shikhany. Clearly, Gorbachev *was* pursuing *glasnost* in military affairs, although not in response to Reagan's challenge of August 26.

Other actions, too, unannounced and publicly unnoted, reflected the Soviet unilateral efforts to ameliorate long-standing elements of confrontation. In the fall, Soviet ballistic missile submarine patrols off the U.S. coast were discontinued. And for the first time in a decade, there was no Soviet naval visit to the Caribbean (which set a new pattern). Overall Soviet naval activity beyond Soviet waters around the world, for the second year, declined.

American-Soviet bilateral diplomatic consultations, begun on a systematic basis after the Geneva summit, became routine, even if the results were not yet substantial. On March 17 Undersecretary of State Michael Armacost and First Deputy Minister of Foreign Affairs Yuly Vorontsov met in Moscow to discuss regional conflicts. On June 2 U.S. Information Agency Director Charles Wick again visited Moscow to discuss communication exchanges. On July 2 Deputy Foreign Minister Vladimir Petrovsky and U.S. Ambassador to the United Nations Vernon Walters discussed UN affairs and the Iran-Iraq Gulf conflict in Moscow. On July 6–7 Assistant Secretary Richard Murphy and Ambassador Vladimir Polyakov discussed Middle East issues. On August 23–25 Assistant Secretary Richard Schifter discussed human rights issues in Moscow. On September 10–11 talks on the Far East and Southeast Asia took place in Moscow, and on September 11 similar talks on Afghanistan took place in Geneva. On November 14, Deputy Secretary of State John Whitehead met with Deputy Foreign Minister Anatoly Adamishin on human rights, and on November 17–18 Undersecretary Armacost met again with First Deputy Minister Vorontsov on regional conflicts. Other meetings on many aspects of arms control were of course constantly under way.

## Toward a Summit

On September 15 Foreign Minister Shevardnadze, bearing a letter from Gorbachev for President Reagan, arrived in Washington for three days of intensive talks. With an INF agreement now clearly in view, Gorbachev made another impassioned plea for "bringing our positions closer together in a very real way" on another issue "even more important for the security of the USSR and the USA": "strategic offensive arms in space." This issue, he said, was "pivotal to the U.S.-Soviet strategic relationship, and hence to the entire course of military-strategic developments in the world." No longer was he asking for limiting ABM research to the laboratory but only "ensuring strict observance of the ABM treaty." Moreover, his reference to "strategic *offensive* weapons in space," a subject "with which you and I have come to grips after Reykjavik," also offered a way to seek constraints on such weapons, which Reagan insisted the United States was not seeking, at least insofar as compatible with allowable development of strategic defenses. And, he wrote, Shevardnadze had "all necessary authority" to discuss the matter in detail.[41] But Reagan would not or could not see such distinctions. He has described his reaction and response: "Once again I told Shevardnadze to tell Gorbachev we weren't going to give in on the SDI." Not only was Reagan stubbornly defensive about the SDI, but he also believed Gorbachev thought he would "buckle under to his demands on the SDI" because of his problems with the Iran-contra affair.[42] Reagan had, in fact, in preparation for Shevardnadze's visit, agreed to Caspar Weinberger's strong urging to make no compromises on strategic arms issues at all: on START issues or on space weapons and strategic defenses. This decision was a consolation award balancing his rejection of last-minute new efforts by Weinberger to seek exemption from the treaty of nonnuclear INF missiles and to use some INF missiles as boosters in SDI testing rather than destroying them as the draft INF agreement would require.[43]

The principal achievement of the meeting, announced with some fanfare, was anticlimactic: a cautious "agreement in principle to conclude a treaty" on global elimination of intermediate- and shorter-range missiles. The other main issue was also forward leaning but inconclusive: agreement on a summit between Reagan and Gorbachev to take place in the fall of 1987 at a date to be determined when Secretary Shultz would visit Moscow in October.[44]

It was also agreed that "full-scale, stage-by-stage negotiations" on nuclear testing would begin before December, aimed in the first instance at agreeing on further verification measures in order to ratify the Threshold Test Ban Treaty signed in 1974 and the Peaceful Nuclear Explosions Treaty of 1976. Although long overdue, this step at least began a new effort in nuclear testing negotiation, previously adamantly resisted by the Reagan administration.[45]

Finally, Shultz and Shevardnadze signed the first "arms control" agreement entered into by the Reagan administration—an agreement to establish Nuclear Risk Reduction Centers in Washington and Moscow to exchange information and notifications required by various arms agreements in order to

---

41. President Reagan has made public extensive excerpts from Gorbachev's letter in his memoir. See Reagan, *An American Life*, pp. 689–91.

42. Ibid., pp. 691, 687.

43. Information from informed administration sources.

44. "Joint Statement on Diplomatic Talks," September 18, 1987, *Department of State Bulletin*, vol. 87 (November 1987), p. 40. (Hereafter *State Bulletin*.)

45. "Joint Statement on Nuclear Testing Negotiations," September 17, 1987, ibid., p. 39.

reduce the risk of miscalculation or misunderstanding (but not to supplant the "Hot Line" Direct Communications Link reserved for heads of government, nor would the centers serve for crisis management).[46]

Some small steps forward were made in the strategic arms talks, and on INF the United States did finally agree to withdraw the nuclear warheads for the seventy-two German Pe-IA missiles when those missiles were dismantled—a small point but one of sufficient concern in Moscow to have warranted a plea from Gorbachev in his letter.

The *New York Times* editorialized on the announced agreement-in-principle on a zero-INF treaty by saying that Reagan and Gorbachev "show signs of trying to put Soviet-American relations on a steady course. Steadiness may not sound like much. But it has been the critical missing ingredient in the world's most important relationship."[47]

The steadiness that the *New York Times* saw was not yet in fact achieved. One illustration of the gap remaining was evident when Secretary Weinberger chose the concluding day of the Shevardnadze visit to announce his approval of demonstration and validation tests of a Star Wars space weapon system for the SDI.[48] Another sign was the continuing reluctance of Gorbachev to settle for a summit and signing of an INF treaty with no advances made toward agreement on strategic arms reductions linked with preservation of the ABM Treaty.

Gorbachev's letter, and Shevardnadze in private discussion with Shultz, also addressed several important matters apart from arms negotiations. Gorbachev made clear Soviet support for resolving regional conflicts, in particular by "national reconciliation," that is, compromise rather than victory for either side. Shevardnadze told Shultz alone, in confidence, that a firm political decision to leave Afghanistan had been made and that withdrawal would probably occur before the end of the Reagan administration's term. Shevardnadze sought American help in ensuring that Soviet disengagement not contribute to an Islamic fundamentalist takeover in Afghanistan. Shultz did not respond except to note American interest also in a neutral nonaligned Afghanistan.

---

46. "Text of Agreement [on Nuclear Risk Reduction Centers]," September 15, 1987, ibid., pp. 34–37.

The prospective INF Treaty was not universally welcomed. Not only hard-liners opposed to any arms agreement with Moscow, but also some conservative Atlanticists were alarmed (excessively, as it turned out) over possible weakening effects on the NATO alliance. Most prominent among former American officials were President Nixon, Secretary of State Henry Kissinger, Secretary Alexander Haig, National Security Adviser Brent Scowcroft, and UN Ambassador Jeane Kirkpatrick. See Shultz, *Turmoil and Triumph*, pp. 984–85, 988.

47. "To the Summit, and Beyond," *New York Times*, September 20, 1987, section 4, p. 26.

48. John H. Cushman, Jr., "Preliminary Tests Gain Approval in 'Star Wars'" *New York Times*, September 19, 1987, p. 7.

Shevardnadze also sought, and Shultz gave him, reassurance that the American military buildup in the Gulf was related to the crisis and would not be permanent. Finally, Shevardnadze also indicated that the Soviet Union was now prepared to be more forthcoming on humanitarian and human rights issues. After years of arguments over acceptance of American requests on individual cases, Shevardnadze now took the initiative: "Give me your lists."[49]

Only a few days after Shevardnadze's visit President Reagan addressed the UN General Assembly. Besides contending that "SDI has greatly enhanced the prospects for real arms reduction," Reagan belabored the Soviet Union at length for "the continuing Soviet occupation of Afghanistan. . . . There is no excuse for prolonging a brutal war or propping up a regime whose days are clearly numbered." He recalled having urged the Soviets to set a date for withdrawal, and he made a "pledge" that once the Soviet Union showed readiness for a genuine political settlement, the United States stood "ready to be helpful."[50]

This public pressure on Gorbachev over Afghanistan, though certainly in keeping with long-standing American policy, could only be taken in Moscow as a low blow. Five days earlier Shevardnadze had confidentially informed Shultz of the Soviet Union's decision to withdraw all of its troops from Afghanistan. Shultz had respected this confidence in holding the information closely, but he had of course told President Reagan. It now appeared in Moscow that Reagan was unnecessarily kicking the Soviets on their way out and setting himself up to claim credit for their decision.

The Soviet Union had cooperated in passing UN General Assembly Resolution 598 on settling the Iran-Iraq war, but it did publicly criticize U.S. naval involvement in the Gulf, which President Reagan noted with irritation in his UN address.[51]

American and Soviet government officials had been sounding one another out for some time on the idea of a meeting of the respective defense ministers, to pick up again an idea first tested in a side meeting at the Vienna summit in 1979. On September 22, Defense Secretary Weinberger wrote to Defense Minister Dmitry Yazov inviting him to visit Washington to discuss "a broad range of issues." General Yazov countered on September 30 with a proposal that they meet in Geneva at the planned session of the joint Standing Consultative Commission on arms control treaty issues. Weinberger did not like either the forum or the idea of being drawn into discussion of the interpretation of the ABM Treaty, so nothing came at that time of the general idea,

49. Shultz, *Turmoil and Triumph*, pp. 985–88.

50. "United Nations. Address before the 43rd Session of the General Assembly," September 21, 1987, *Presidential Documents*, vol. 23 (September 28, 1987), pp. 1055, 1053–54.

51. Ibid., p. 1053.

although it would soon return. Not long after, Weinberger decided to retire and was replaced by Frank Carlucci.

In another sphere, the Soviet Union moved ahead of the United States in demonstrating support for the United Nations by promising on October 15, in a reversal of years of practice, to pay all of its $197 million in arrears, including support for peacekeeping actions it had not supported. The United States was left the principal laggard in paying its due to the UN organization.

Secretary Shultz, accompanied by National Security Adviser Carlucci (by that time the secretary of defense-designate, but that fact was not yet publicly known), arrived in Moscow the evening of October 21 for two days of talks expected to wrap up arrangements for the summit. A large delegation of experts had accompanied him, and eight working groups were set up to deal with the wide range of matters planned to be on the summit agenda. The Soviet side sought not only to move forward on the nearly completed INF treaty draft, and the less complete START strategic arms reduction treaty, but also to negotiate toward further curbs on nuclear weapon testing. The discussions with Shevardnadze went fairly smoothly the first day, but when Shultz saw Gorbachev on October 23, he faced an unexpected obstacle.

Gorbachev returned to the theme that the strategic offensive arms and weapons in space were the central problem, the root problem, facing the Soviet Union and the United States. He again sought to tie a ten-year period of strict compliance with the ABM Treaty "as we both interpreted it and observed it before 1983," to reduced strategic forces, with subceilings as the United States had sought. Although somewhat less restrictive on ABM testing than the Reykjavik formula, in essence the proposition was the same. So, too, was the U.S. response, as Shultz quickly made clear. Gorbachev was prepared to retreat one step: rather than insisting on complete agreement on strategic and space weapons before a summit, he proposed at least agreement on "key provisions" on strategic and space weapons be completed in time to be signed by Reagan and himself at the summit.

Shultz could not agree to that, and for the first time envisaging that a summit meeting might not take place, he noted that the virtually completed INF Treaty could of course be signed by others than the two presidents. Gorbachev then drew back sufficiently to note that he had not said he would not go to Washington, only that there must be sufficient progress to justify a meeting. He implied that the INF Treaty alone was not a sufficient basis, because he did not propose a date for a summit. He closed by saying, "Both sides need to do some thinking. Clarify what should be done." He also commented that he would report to the Soviet leadership, and Shultz should report to the president.[52]

---

52. See Shultz, *Turmoil and Triumph*, pp. 993–1001; and Oberdorfer, *The Turn*, pp. 246–56. Gorbachev has now released a virtually verbatim transcript of the meeting, which is the fullest account. It confirms Shultz's brief review and provides flavor and detail. See

In the course of their disagreement over the relationship between strategic arms reductions and observance of the ABM Treaty limiting the SDI, Gorbachev suddenly interjected a strong complaint on an entirely new unrelated issue: American allegations of Soviet subversive "active measures" and disinformation. He waved a copy of a recently issued State Department report—which Shultz had never seen.[53] Not familiar with the report, Shultz defended it in general terms, but he took the offensive with other charges of his own, in particular complaining about the 1983 KAL incident as well as hitting the Soviet disinformation campaign alleging U.S. responsibility for devising and spreading the AIDS virus (which was featured in the report). In all, the acrimonious exchange did no credit to either side. Only later would it become clear why Gorbachev was so much on edge and in such a combative mood.[54]

Shultz returned to Washington (with a stop en route at NATO in Brussels) with the future of a summit undecided and the state of the relationship in disarray. Shultz did put the best face possible on the "constructive" nature of the exchanges and his hopes for prerequisite continuing progress, but it remained clear that an unexpected flareup over the old issue of space weapons had prevented expected agreement on a summit date.[55]

Only a week later did it become known that a serious political confrontation had occurred on the eve of Shultz's visit, October 21, at a Central Committee plenum. Although Gorbachev himself was not directly challenged, the collective leadership he headed had blown apart. The most ardent reformer, useful to Gorbachev as a forward scout and point man, Boris Yeltsin, launched a blistering attack on the leading conservative second-ranking member of the Politburo, Yegor Ligachev. The only personnel change made by the plenum was the retirement of conservative Geidar Aliyev, but clearly Yeltsin's days were numbered. Gorbachev, whether he wanted to or not (and after

---

"From the Gorbachev Archive (the Meeting of M. S. Gorbachev with U.S. Secretary of State G. Shultz, October 23, 1987)," *Mirovaya ekonomika i mezhdunarodnyye otnosheniya* (The World Economy and International Relations), no. 10 (October 1993), pp. 69–81. (Hereafter *MEiMO*.)

Gorbachev had also raised the subject of cooperation in the Persian Gulf in settling the Iran-Iraq war. Shultz expressed the American preference for cooperation over unilateral action and reaffirmed the reassurance given earlier to Shevardnadze that the large American military presence in the Gulf would diminish as the situation there normalized and the need for that presence diminished. See Shultz, *Turmoil and Triumph*, p. 996, and *MEiMO*, no. 10 (October 1993), pp. 74–75.

53. See *Soviet Influence Activities: A Report on Active Measures and Propaganda, 1986-1987* (Department of State, August 1987), a report prepared by an interagency committee chaired by a State Department officer and established pursuant to a congressional mandate to expose Soviet disinformation and propaganda measures.

54. See Shultz, *Turmoil and Triumph*, pp. 997–98; and Oberdorfer, *The Turn*, pp. 249–52.

55. See "News Conference, Moscow," October 23, 1987, *State Bulletin*, vol. 87 (December 1987), pp. 22–25, and other statements, pp. 25–31.

October 21 that was no longer clear), had to discipline him sharply. On November 11 Yeltsin was removed as Moscow party chief, and on February 18, 1988, he was dropped from candidate membership in the Politburo. Gorbachev had lost Yeltsin on his "left" and hence lost his preferred position at the center, balancing liberals and conservatives. Now Gorbachev faced the conservatives, and they were questioning his repeated concessions and compromises for agreements with the Americans who in turn ignored Soviet interests.

Gorbachev had been struggling since the first summit meeting in Geneva to overcome Reagan's tenacious fixation on a strategic defense initiative featuring unpredictable weaponry in space that threatened to undermine not only any accord on strategic arms reduction but even the strategic balance and mutual deterrence. For the months since he had conceded the need to negotiate a separate INF agreement he had also tried to get at least key provisions on strategic arms and space weapons. But even this was beyond grasp.

Reagan reacted with predictable equanimity. Although probably somewhat angered, or at least annoyed, he took the position that he was prepared for a summit if Gorbachev was but said, "A summit is not a precondition for progress on the agenda at hand."[56]

The Western reaction to the debacle in Moscow was general disappointment, with blame placed not on Reagan but on Gorbachev for overreaching, especially since he had conceded a separate INF agreement months earlier. Moreover, Gorbachev saw value not only in an INF accord as a legitimation of arms control but also in a summit meeting with Reagan where they could try again on space weapons and attempt to move the relationship forward in other ways. Evidently he was able to convince his colleagues in the leadership at least to go forward as earlier planned. Only three days after refraining from setting a summit date, Gorbachev gave in and sent Shevardnadze to Washington.

Shevardnadze arrived in Washington on October 30, with a letter from Gorbachev and agreement to set a summit for December 7. Gorbachev still sought key provisions on space and strategic weapons, but now he saw them as merely a subject for discussion at the summit rather than a prerequisite.[57]

The negotiations on verifying nuclear testing limits began on November 9, and negotiations on the INF agreement continued. On November 23–24 Shultz and Shevardnadze met in Geneva and resolved most of the remaining issues on the INF Treaty, although the last details (for example, whether U.S. inspectors could enter East Germany other than through East Berlin) were not resolved until December 5. More significant, real progress was made on the strategic offensive arms (START) agreement—facilitated by the fact that

---

56. "West Point, New York. Remarks to the Corps of Cadets," October 28, 1987, *Presidential Documents*, vol. 23 (November 2, 1987), p. 1236.

57. Shultz, *Turmoil and Triumph*, pp. 1001–02.

Weinberger had resigned. (Secretary Carlucci also fired a few hard-liners in the Department of Defense, notably Frank Gaffney, Richard Perle's chosen successor.) The pragmatic Lieutenant General Colin Powell had succeeded Carlucci as national security adviser. Also Kenneth Adelman, the hard-line director of the Arms Control and Disarmament Agency, resigned. To convey their new positions on START, including some concessions, the Soviets had reactivated a special confidential channel through the Soviet ambassador (initiated earlier under then-Ambassador Dobrynin), called CALYPSO.[58]

President Reagan continued in speeches to the American public as well as in addresses to his conservative constituency in particular (notably in a speech to the Heritage Foundation on November 30) to champion his summitry and the INF Treaty. At the same time he challenged Gorbachev strongly on Soviet internal affairs (such as religious freedoms) and military programs, as well as on Soviet involvement in Third World conflicts.[59]

The increasing cross-communication between the two countries was evident in the publication on November 3 by Harper and Row of a translation of Gorbachev's *Perestroika and the New Thinking for Our Country and the World*. Also, on November 30 NBC television carried an interview with Gorbachev, and four days later *Izvestiya* carried an interview with Reagan.

## The Washington Summit

As Reagan and Gorbachev posed for photographers before their first meeting, the elder host suggested they address one another by first names, "I'm Ron," to which his guest responded "I'm Mikhail." From then on, it was Ron and Mikhail. For all of the tension of the first meeting two years earlier, and the angry discord ending the second summit at Reykjavik the last time they met, the two men felt they were acquiring better understanding of each other and wanted to develop it.

The Washington U.S.-Soviet summit meeting on December 7–10 was the first in the American capital in fourteen years—and only the third ever (Brezhnev had come to Washington in June 1973 and Nikita Khrushchev in September 1959). They readily agreed to meet again in Moscow before the middle of 1988, whether or not a START agreement had by then been reached (it would not be, but they would meet). The seventy-six hours of the Washing-

---

58.  Ibid., p. 1004.

59.  See "Heritage Foundation," November 30, 1987, *Presidential Documents*, vol. 23 (December 7, 1987), pp. 1391–95; and see "Soviet Union-United States Relations. Radio Address to the Nation," November 28, 1987, ibid., pp. 1387–88.

Weinberger, after retiring, joined Nixon, Kissinger, and Scowcroft in opposing the INF Treaty, as did a group of conservative senators, notably Senator Dan Quayle.

ton summit were packed with developments, apart from the centerpiece, which was the ceremonial signing of the INF Treaty.

The summit covered the four-part agenda that the Reagan administration had made the obligatory framework for U.S.-Soviet relations. Besides arms control, which was a cooperative area (and one implicitly and correctly regarded as of particular interest to the Soviet Union), these items composed two areas of American challenge: human rights and regional conflicts (increasingly of interest to the Soviets as well). Finally the two sides addressed a catch-all of bilateral relations, including cultural and other exchanges, scientific and other cooperation, and economic and trade relations.[60] Gorbachev had a brief discussion with Director Charles Z. Wick of the U.S. Information Agency on the problem of disinformation and hostile propaganda, picking up from the confrontational discussion between Gorbachev and Shultz in October. This time, Gorbachev, more fully briefed, promised "no more disinformation" and assigned his Politburo associate (and overseer of the Propaganda Department of the Central Committee) Aleksandr Yakovlev to work with Wick to curb disinformation and enhance positive informational exchanges. This effort led to several productive meetings during the next two years and a sharp curtailment of disinformation activities such as the AIDS dissemination propaganda and forgeries.[61] Nonetheless the INF Treaty, and other arms control issues, dominated the meetings.

The INF Treaty was, by presidential direction, signed on December 8 at exactly 1:45 p.m. Washington time.[62] Although its terms and verification arrangements were complex and detailed (the treaty and annexes totaling 127 pages), the general provisions were simple: each side would, during the next three years, destroy all of its intermediate- and shorter-range land-based missiles and their launchers. As both Reagan and Gorbachev often stressed, in the words of their joint statement the treaty was "historic" because for the first time it would entail "the complete elimination of an entire class of U.S. and Soviet nuclear arms."[63]

---

60. Besides cited speeches by President Reagan and Secretary Shultz, see the policy statement earlier given by Undersecretary for Political Affairs Michael Armacost, "U.S.-Soviet Relations: Testing Gorbachev's 'New Thinking' " July 1, 1987, *State Bulletin*, vol. 87 (September 1987), pp. 36–38.

61. Those steps were noted in the next, and final, State Department report on Soviet propaganda and related "active measures." See *Soviet Influence Activities: A Report on Active Measures and Propaganda, 1987–1988* (Department of State, August 1989), p. 1.

62. The reason for this precision of timing, around which the schedule had to be arranged, was a mystery to almost everyone in both governments, including Secretary of State Shultz. See Shultz, *Turmoil and Triumph*, p. 1005. Only much later did it become known that the time had been selected as propitious by Nancy Reagan's astrologer.

63. See "Soviet Union-United States Summit in Washington, D.C.," joint statement, December 10, 1987, *Presidential Documents*, vol. 23 (December 14, 1987), p. 1494.
        See also Shultz, *Turmoil and Triumph*, pp. 1009–11.

Critics sought to downplay the significance of the agreement by pointing out that this action affected only about 5 percent of the nuclear arsenals of the two sides (roughly 50,000 warheads). And in the Soviet Union some critics also complained (publicly, in print—unprecedented in Soviet experience) because the Soviet Union had to destroy many more missiles than the United States.[64] But such criticisms failed to appreciate the psychological, political, and militarily strategic significance of the accord. The agreement meant not only reductions but the destruction of very recent and current arms. It eliminated not only an entire class of arms but those most likely to spur escalation to general nuclear war from any local hostilities that might erupt. Although such weapons might bolster deterrence of any deliberate decision to attack (the logic behind the NATO decision to deploy), they could also threaten key command centers in the Soviet Union (although not in the United States) and thus increase pressures for preemption in the absence of intention or desire to attack. This strategic concern on the Soviet side was sufficient to provide the support of the Soviet military leadership and permit Gorbachev's flexibility and concessions to gain agreement.

The second major feature of the INF Treaty, correctly deemed "historic," was its remarkably extensive and intrusive verification inspection and monitoring arrangements. It represented a real breakthrough after decades of Soviet refusal to countenance intrusive independent presence on its territory and to yield so much military secrecy. The extent of the breakthrough had become clear earlier in the year. In March the United States had proposed not only on-site inspections of the destruction of missiles, and perimeter monitoring of declared missile production facilities with partial inspection of the missiles themselves, but also challenge inspection any time and any place. To the surprise of most observers, the Soviets accepted and even proposed inspection of launch sites on the territories of other states and inspection of the interior of missile production facilities. The United States had second thoughts and partly rescinded its own proposal on "any time any place." By August the United States, to some extent on the defensive over verification, proposed reducing the scale of inspections. The provisions finally agreed on were extensive and expensive. The estimated cost for the United States alone was about $1 billion (some of the provisions were to last up to thirteen years).

The INF Treaty was a major success for President Reagan personally, as he alone may have believed in his proposal for a zero option for INF in 1981. It was unrealistic then. But with Gorbachev's new thinking, the option became

---

64. The Soviet Union was required to destroy 889 intermediate-range (LRINF) missiles, and the United States 677; the Soviet Union also had to destroy 957 shorter-range (SRINF) missiles, while the United States had only 169 to destroy. The numbers officially declared at the time of signing had varied slightly from these final figures.

possible, and with the two leaders' persistent support, the INF Treaty came into being.

The treaty was also a big success for Gorbachev. It showed the West that the Soviet Union was now serious about arms reduction, especially elimination of nuclear weapons, and was ready to apply *glasnost* to military security (through disclosures and verification). Above all, it showed that the new thinking about security was real. And it showed doubters at home, in the Soviet Union, that the United States could agree on a major reduction agreement.

The INF Treaty also served to relegitimate arms control, even with a conservative Republican administration under a president who had but a few years earlier railed against an Evil Empire. Looking to the future, Gorbachev sought to nail down strategic nuclear arms reductions with the Reagan administration to the maximum extent compatible with preserving Soviet security in the face of the unpredictable consequences of the SDI program. He therefore also sought to extract from Reagan the most assurance he could on preserving the ABM Treaty in order to build on these foundations with a successor administration. Finally, as Gorbachev and others in his entourage stressed, they hoped the INF Treaty and the Washington summit would lend momentum not only to arms control in the future but to transforming the political relationship between the two nations. They sought to dispel the image in the United States of the Soviet Union as an "enemy" and to demonstrate their real interest in peace.

Substantive negotiations on the START Treaty yielded some advances, through intense negotiations between negotiating teams headed, as at Reykjavik, by Ambassador Paul Nitze and Marshal Sergei Akhromeyev. They agreed, for example, that they would "find a mutually acceptable solution to the question of limiting the deployment of long-range nuclear armed SLCMs"—an American concession but qualified by Soviet concessions that SLCMs would not be included in the agreed-on strategic force ceilings, and that only nuclear-armed SLCMs would be limited. Several procedures for verification were agreed on, building on the INF breakthrough. Agreement was reached on an overall ceiling of 4,900 ballistic missiles within the agreed-on ceiling of 6,000 delivery vehicles.

The key issue on strategic arms, however, though again the subject of intensive discussion, was not brought closer to agreement: the ABM Treaty. At almost the last moment, the senior experts agreed on a formulation under which the two leaders "instructed their delegations in Geneva to work out an agreement that would commit the sides to observe the ABM Treaty, as signed in 1972, while conducting their research, development, and testing as required, which are permitted by the ABM Treaty, and not to withdraw from the ABM Treaty, for a specified period of time."[65] The tortured language and syntax

---

65. *Presidential Documents*, vol. 23 (December 14, 1987), p. 1495.
    See also Shultz, *Turmoil and Triumph*, pp. 1013–14.

reflected a serious continuing difference of position. Initially Reagan interpreted the language overeagerly to mean that this formulation "resolved" the dispute and meant that "we have agreed that we are going forward with whatever is necessary in the research and development [of SDI] without any regard to an interpretation of ABM."[66] It became necessary to correct this misimpression, for the press and for the president. What had happened was best captured by a homespun but apt comment by Geneva negotiator Max Kampelman: "They kicked the can down the road a piece." The issue was simply put off yet again.

Failure to reach any meeting of the minds of the two leaders on strategic defenses and space weapons, while not surprising, was a disappointment for Gorbachev and a continued obstacle to his flexibility in negotiating a START agreement. The only mitigating element was the internal American political process. On the eve of the summit, December 4, Reagan had been obliged to reluctantly sign legislation under which Congress mandated continued application of the traditional strict interpretation of the ABM Treaty (as well as cutting the SDI budgetary request by one-third). But he was determined not to make any such commitment to Gorbachev.[67]

The two leaders "welcomed" the opening of talks on nuclear testing a month earlier in accordance with their agreement on September 17 during Shevardnadze's visit to Washington. Although these talks focused on enhancing verification in order to ratify the threshold on testing agreed on in 1974, and which both in practice had been observing, the summit joint statement did cite the September agreement on subsequently "negotiating further intermediate limitations on nuclear testing leading to the ultimate objective of the complete cessation of nuclear testing as part of an effective disarmament process."[68] This was certainly a step forward from Reagan's earlier rejection in principle of negotiation on nuclear testing. But it was less of a change than it seemed to be. "Ultimate objectives," above all in disarmament, tend to be relegated to the indefinite future, and in this case the U.S. side drove the point home by adding language that tied the end of nuclear testing to the ultimate elimination of nuclear weapons.

Discussion of other arms control matters was limited and often pro forma, except that Gorbachev sought to convey the seriousness of his side in reductions in conventional forces, especially in Europe. He made this clear in

---

66. "Foreign and Domestic Issues," December 11, 1987, *Presidential Documents*, vol. 23 (December 14, 1987), p. 1508.

67. The Soviet delegation had tried to get the formulation of the joint statement to refer to the ABM Treaty "as signed and ratified" in 1972; Reagan's negotiators succeeded in getting "and ratified" dropped; although the meaning was not changed, the implicit reference to the Senate's understanding in the ratification process would have weakened the administration's position vis-à-vis Congress.

68. *Presidential Documents*, vol. 23 (December 14, 1987), p. 1496.

his televised report to the Soviet people upon his return to Moscow, where he emphasized the need to "sit down at the negotiating table and look for solutions . . . . [and] lay our cards on the table," and he said the Soviet Union was "prepared for the most drastic reductions."[69] When Gorbachev had made similar comments to Reagan, this extremely important opening was not pursued because the U.S. and NATO position was not yet formed. Soviet interest in deep conventional cuts would, indeed, become abundantly clear within a year or so. But because Gorbachev did not then, in December 1987, provide concrete proposals, his earnest plea for negotiation was underappreciated.[70]

Besides actively heading the Soviet arms control team in the summit negotiation, Marshal Akhromeyev accepted Admiral Crowe's invitation to visit the Joint Chiefs of Staff in the Pentagon (and, separately, also met with Secretary of Defense Carlucci). Akhromeyev showed interest in developing such military-to-military contacts, which had first been briefly discussed by Reagan and Gorbachev at Reykjavik. After the abortive efforts in September between Weinberger and Yazov, the Akhromeyev visit put such exchange visits back into active consideration, as would soon become evident.

Apart from arms control, while all bases were touched on Reagan's four-part agenda, the most important was discussion of the regional conflicts in Afghanistan and Nicaragua. This subject was given only brief and cryptic reference in the joint statement and in Gorbachev's later speeches. Reagan, in his address to the nation, while not informative on the discussions, did say that progress in resolving such conflicts was "essential to a lasting improvement in our relations."[71] The summit discussions were not, however, very successful. On Nicaragua, Reagan stated in his memoir that in a brief conversation, accompanied only by interpreters, he had told Gorbachev that it would "go a long way toward improving U.S.-Soviet relations" if he would cease shipping arms to Nicaragua, and Gorbachev had said he would.[72] When the subject was brought up at a working meeting, however, Gorbachev's response was rather different from Reagan's recollection. Gorbachev suggested both sides support the Contadora accords worked out by the Central American governments, and in the course of implementing them they would agree to stop supplying arms, except

69. "Press Conference of M. S. Gorbachev, General Secretary of the Central Committee of the CPSU," *Pravda*, December 12, 1987.

70. This was not a subject that the U.S. side was prepared to address, despite the fact that it would shortly become the subject of considerable American and European interest in the wake of the INF Treaty. In fact, Reagan was so ill-prepared that he could not carry the U.S. side of the discourse and Shultz had to step in, according to American officials present (and see Oberdorfer, *The Turn*, p. 263; and Shultz, *Turmoil and Triumph*, p. 1011).

71. "Soviet Union-United States Summit in Washington, D.C. Address to the Nation," December 10, 1987, *Presidential Documents*, vol. 23 (December 14, 1987), p. 1503.

72. Reagan, *An American Life*, p. 701.

light police-type weapons, to Nicaragua. In follow-up discussions, the Soviet position was made clear that under the accords *both* sides would stop supplying arms to the area, not only the Soviet Union to the Nicaraguan government, but the United States to the Nicaraguan contras and to other governments of Central America. When Reagan indiscreetly disclosed his version publicly on December 15, the Soviet Foreign Ministry spokesman promptly denied it and revealed the terms Gorbachev had alluded to in the official meeting. In addition, Reagan failed to raise with Gorbachev allegations by a high-level Sandinista defector that the Soviet Union was planning a major arms buildup. Though perhaps based on some Nicaraguan military maximum planning desiderata discussed with the Soviets, the alleged buildup was certainly not in the cards. But for whatever reason, immediately after the summit the defector was permitted to brief the press on his allegations, causing unwarranted suspicion of the Soviets in the United States and suspicion of the motives of the U.S. administration in Moscow. There was no buildup, and at the end of the next year the Soviet Union unilaterally cut off arms shipments to Nicaragua.

The discussion of Afghanistan was even more confused. Reagan in his address to the nation said, "I spoke candidly with Mr. Gorbachev on the issues of Afghanistan, Iran-Iraq, Cambodia, Angola, and Nicaragua."[73] In fact, he reiterated his call for the Soviets to stop assisting the governments of these countries. But there was inadequate discussion even to clarify positions. The Soviets had already made clear their intention to withdraw from Afghanistan, and to do so within twelve months, but they were in continuing negotiations under UN auspices over the terms of a settlement involving withdrawal. In those negotiations, the United States had pledged since December 1985 to end U.S. military assistance to the insurgents when Moscow withdrew its forces. Yet on the eve of the summit, when this idea was mentioned by a news correspondent, Reagan appeared to be hearing it for the first time and rejected the idea.[74] The official State Department spokesman publicly reaffirmed the position, but it was never thrashed out at the summit even though Reagan reportedly repeated his view—probably because the Soviet side and the State Department wanted the opportunity first to explain to him the whole complex of commitments of the various parties that had been built up over five years of negotiation, part of which was the U.S. commitment. Ultimately, of course, President Reagan had the deciding voice, and in January 1988 the United States repudiated the position it had taken in the UN negotiations. Gorbachev, instead of receiving greater U.S. assistance in facilitating Soviet withdrawal as he had hoped, was left with a much less favorable U.S. position than before. This

---

73. *Presidential Documents*, vol. 23 (December 14, 1987), p. 1503.

74. "Foreign and Domestic Issues," December 3, 1987, *Presidential Documents*, vol. 23 (December 7, 1987), p. 1428.

adverse turn was not a consequence of the summit, but the increased mutual "understanding" at the summit clearly did not include Afghanistan.[75]

On human rights, too, there was more of an argument than a dialogue. Reagan criticized the Soviets for not allowing more emigration of Soviet Jews, to which Gorbachev angrily retorted that if the United States was so keen on free movement of peoples, why did it keep out the Mexicans with armed patrols.[76]

These barbed exchanges kept the summit from being a full meeting of the minds. Moreover, there were many signs that Gorbachev and Reagan did not really understand the other's systems well. Gorbachev still believed Reagan was in part a puppet, or more kindly, a popular political spokesperson for the American military-industrial complex and conservative action groups such as the Heritage Foundation. Reagan still believed Gorbachev was someone who was making the best of a weak position rather than truly a new thinker. These judgments, though not without some foundation, were flawed. Similarly, Reagan believed the INF Treaty was evidence that his policy of strength coupled with negotiations had paid off. Yet if Gorbachev had not believed in a new conception of security he could and would simply not have agreed to the treaty.

Despite those shortcomings in mutual understanding, the dialogue between the two leaders, and between the two countries, was developing rather rapidly. Reagan's frequent jokes about Soviet life, often in poor taste and occasionally disrupting serious conversation, were less important than his genuine good humor and personal charm.[77] Similarly Gorbachev's sincerity was

---

75. See chapter 15.

76. See Oberdorfer, *The Turn*, pp. 258–59.

77. Beginning earlier in the year, and on many occasions, President Reagan commented to visitors, in speeches, to news reporters, and of course to his friend Mikhail that he had "a new hobby"—collecting jokes and anecdotes about the Soviet Union. Sometimes mildly amusing, the practice tended to remind one of an amiable elder relative who becomes obsessed with such a theme and must repeat it to everyone each time they meet. But the Soviets were often much offended. On several occasions the Soviet media would chide this practice. To cite but one example, shortly before the summit: "Funny? No, sad—and even somehow embarrassing for such a high-ranking orator. I do not think it suits the leader of a great country to churn out from a public rostrum scabrous, and by the way long out-dated, jokes about another great power, even less so on the threshold of a summit meeting." TASS observer Vladimir Chernyshev, Radio Moscow, November 17, 1987, in Foreign Broadcast Information Service, *Daily Report: Soviet Union*, November 18, 1987, p. 2.

The speech to which Chernyshev referred (without citing the jokes) was one given on November 16 to a conference of life insurance executives. Reagan confided about his new hobby and told several jokes including one that claimed the Soviets compared arms control treaties to diets: "The second day was always the best because that's when they broke them." And in claiming (incorrectly, and not as a joke) that the Soviets have "more than 10,000 scientists working on military lasers alone," he quipped, "We know this, and they know that we know, and we know that they know we know." The jokes

convincing and went a long way toward overcoming deeply instilled Cold War prejudices.

Gorbachev upon his return gave a highly positive report to the Politburo on the meeting as representing the first real contact and understanding.[78]

Gorbachev's personal popularity in the United States rose remarkably. An early postsummit poll showed a phenomenal 65 percent of Americans polled had a favorable impression of Gorbachev—higher even than Reagan's 61 percent. Some 77 percent approved of the way Reagan was handling relations with the Soviet Union, up 11 percent from a presummit poll and the highest yet in his presidency. Reagan's overall job approval rating rose from 50 to 58 percent, the best since Iran-contra broke.[79]

The successful atmosphere of the Washington summit, including the growing personal rapport between Ron and Mikhail (if not between Raisa and Nancy!), was also carried over to the extent possible by Gorbachev's use of the available occasions to meet and greet as many Americans as possible, including an impromptu stop in the middle of traffic in downtown Washington (to the consternation of security officials).

One meeting with an American was particularly important. Gorbachev had previously met Vice President George Bush only on the three occasions of the state funerals of his predecessors, Brezhnev in 1982, Andropov in 1984, and Chernenko in 1985. This time they had a breakfast meeting (not alone, but without the overshadowing presence of the president), and candidate Bush (who had included his campaign manager, John H. Sununu, in the meeting) used the fact of this meeting in his campaign. They also had a brief drive from the White House alone (with an interpreter) in which Bush reassured

---

brought laughter, but the Soviet critics had a point. See "American Council of Life Insurance," November 16, 1987, *Presidential Documents*, vol. 23 (November 23, 1987), pp. 1333–34.

At the summit, Reagan made a particularly bad *faux pas*. Just as Gorbachev was beginning to discuss seriously problems in the Soviet Union, Reagan interrupted to tell an inappropriate and demeaning anti-Soviet joke. Gorbachev flushed and went on to a different subject. Shultz has said he was "disturbed and disappointed" because Reagan's inept intervention was not only discourteous but also cut off a possibly important discussion. See Shultz, *Turmoil and Triumph*, p. 1011.

78. Gorbachev reported to a meeting of the Politburo on December 17, 1987.

Gorbachev's foreign affairs adviser, Anatoly Chernyayev, reading from the transcript of the Politburo session, said that Gorbachev had so described the meeting with Reagan, further remarking that while Reagan represented the most conservative element of the U.S. establishment, he also represented the human interests of the people. He also credited Soviet efforts to develop mutual understanding and the impact of such efforts on the American side. Chernyayev, in a meeting on February 26, 1993.

79. Richard Morin, "Post-Summit Poll Shows Reagan Gains," *Washington Post*, December 15, 1987, p. A1, A30.

Gorbachev of his desire, if elected president, to continue working toward improved U.S.-Soviet relations, an assurance that later became important.[80]

Consideration had been given to a possible meeting of Gorbachev with a joint session of Congress, but the administration abandoned the idea when some conservative members of Congress objected.

Gorbachev played to the people at every opportunity. And his engaging manner was very effective. Interviews with the man in the street found a wide range of views. Some people were still suspicious of the Russians or the communists, but many were charmed by Gorbachev and surprised to find he (or "the Russians") were "just like us." Most surprising was that even very conservative members of Congress were among those expressing their pleasant surprise at discovering Gorbachev to be flexible, open, and pragmatic. As one congressman said, "He's one of us—a political animal."[81] There was a touch of euphoria and "Gorbymania" in Washington and in the nation.

Not everyone was charmed. Some hard-line conservatives were very disappointed in Reagan, as well as suspicious and hostile toward Gorbachev. Not only were they afraid of the euphoria, but some believed Reagan had been taken in by "appeasing" pragmatists like Howard Baker, George Shultz, and Frank Carlucci, as well as by Gorbachev. Above all they saw Reagan's whole new policy direction as meaning that "conservative policies have been comprehensively abandoned." And as one prominent archconservative saw it, the INF Treaty "surrenders military and political domination of Western Europe to our enemy."[82] A body of moderate opinion, including Henry Kissinger and Brent Scowcroft, was concerned about the political impact of the INF Treaty in the absence of reduction of Soviet superiority in conventional forces in Europe. And quite a few moderates were concerned about the possible transient nature of the euphoria. But the hard-line opponents of improving relations were few, and their voices were shrill because they were an isolated extreme.

The administration, however, was not swept off its feet. Secretary Shultz, for all his determined effort since 1983 to improve relations, and despite acknowledgment that Soviet new thinking was of "potential importance," still

---

80. See chapter 9. Bush told Gorbachev he had been concealing his own moderate views and would have to take some tough positions to get elected, but Gorbachev should discount them. Gorbachev later referred to this conversation as the "most important talk Bush and I ever had." This episode was first disclosed in Michael R. Beschloss and Strobe Talbott, *At the Highest Levels: The Inside Story of the End of the Cold War* (Little, Brown and Company, 1993), pp. 3–4.

81. The quotation is in Joel Brinkley, "Soviet Visitor Is Turning On All His Charm," *New York Times*, December 10, 1987, pp. A1, A18. See also Marc Fisher and Lynne Duke, "Glasnost Winning Friends, Influencing People—Some Reluctantly," *Washington Post*, December 11, 1987, p. A36; and Saundra Saperstein Torry and John Mintz, "A Blase Washington Flips for Gorby," *Washington Post*, December 11, 1987, p. A32.

82. Howard Phillips, "The Treaty: Another Sellout," *New York Times*, December 11, 1987, p. A39. Phillips was the head of the once powerful Conservative Caucus.

declared that "there is nothing in the 'new political thinking' to date which suggests that the end of the adversarial struggle is at hand," rhetorically asking what did it mean for Eastern Europe, and Afghanistan, and asking with doubt if the Soviet Union would play a constructive role in settling regional conflicts.[83] President Reagan's own secret policy guidance for the summit, now declassified, stated, "While seeking concrete agreements in arms reductions which serve our national interests, we must not foster false illusions about the state of U.S.-Soviet relations," and "Our conduct at the Summit and the framing of its results must in no way complicate our efforts to maintain a strong defense budget and key programs like SDI; they must help us maintain support for the Contras, Mujahedin, UNITA, and the democratic resistance in Cambodia; and they must reinforce Alliance unity." By giving priority to the defense buildup and the Reagan Doctrine, the administration showed the still-limited place it was prepared to give to improving relations with the Soviet Union and to negotiations on arms and settlement of regional conflicts. In the concluding words of Reagan's guidance on objectives: "the Summit should seek simultaneously to codify progress in the U.S.-Soviet relationship, prepare the way for future progress, yet make clear where fundamental differences remain which block progress."[84]

In publicly summing up the accomplishments of the Washington summit and looking to the future, President Reagan in an exchange of farewell remarks noted the need for "a realistic understanding of each other's intentions and objectives, a process for dealing with differences in a practical and straightforward manner. . . . As a result of this summit, the framework for building such a relationship has been strengthened."[85] Gorbachev similarly emphasized they had put "the dialog between our two countries on a more predictable footing," which was "undoubtedly constructive," but he also noted that "there is still much work to be done and we must get down to it without delay."[86]

Though Gorbachev had in mind major new undertakings, it turned out that there was still work to do in "cleaning up" the agreements reached, as well as in attending to neglected areas (especially economic relations).

The INF Treaty had been completed so hastily that several minor problems occurred at the last moment—and even after the summit signing. The day before the signing, the Soviets failed to provide a glossy photograph of

83. "National Success and International Stability in a Time of Change," December 4, 1987, *State Bulletin*, vol. 88 (January 1988), p. 7.

84. National Security Decision Directive (NSDD)–288, "My Objectives at the Summit," signed Ronald Reagan, November 10, 1987, Secret, p. 2. (Declassified November 27, 1992.)

85. "Remarks on the Departure of General Secretary Mikhail Gorbachev," December 10, 1987, *Presidential Documents*, vol. 23 (December 14, 1987), p. 1500.

86. Ibid., p. 1501.

an SS-20 missile outside of its normal carrying canister. Six hours before signature they were able to supply one (sent by telephoto from Moscow). But the initial failure to have it led a few hard-liners to speak of a "violation" of the treaty even before it was signed. A better glossy photo was finally provided two weeks later. As the two sides were preparing the treaty and related documents for release to the public, it turned out that the Defense Department wanted to keep secret the detailed Memorandum of Understanding, which listed deployment locations by name and with precise geographic coordinates. Only when the Soviets indicated they planned to release the Russian language version did the Defense representatives on the U.S. side relent.[87]

There was also some initial concern when the number of SS-20 missiles declared by the Soviet Union was lower than the number estimated by the Defense Intelligence Agency, although within a range estimated by the Central Intelligence Agency. The number of Soviet cruise missiles and launchers, however, was higher. Ultimately it was concluded, and later inspections confirmed, that the Soviet declarations were correct. To the embarrassment of American officials, the official U.S. statement of its total stock of Pershing II missiles turned out to be inaccurate when sixteen more were discovered sidelined at a factory.[88]

The issuance of the fifth "Report on Soviet Noncompliance" submitted by the president to Congress on the eve of the summit had been at the least poor timing. Moreover, besides specific charges,some well grounded, others highly doubtful, the report included accusative innuendo, as it had in the past. Most notably, "The U.S. government reaffirms the *judgment* of the March 1987 Report that the *aggregate* of the Soviet Union's ABM and ABM-related actions . . . *suggests* that the USSR *may be preparing* an ABM defense of its national territory."[89] Quite apart from the tenuous, and indeed overstretched, nature of the basis for such an allegation, the charge was rather obviously self-serving coming from an administration that was avowedly seeking through its SDI to develop precisely an ABM defense of its national territory. The litany of charges was in part a legacy of the recently departed Defense Department team of

---

87. When this became publicly known, the U.S. reticence to apply *glasnost* led to explanations that there was concern over a possible terrorist attack if precise missile launch locations were publicly known. Privately, officials explained that there would be embarrassment when U.S. allies, in particular the Germans, learned that the United States had more Pershing II missiles in Germany than they had been led to believe.

88. After so often accusing the Soviet Union of cheating whenever an anomaly or error occurred, the United States was also embarrassed when it turned out that the coordinates for precise location of the missile factory at Magna, Utah, which the Soviets were going to inspect turned out to be in error—the coordinates would have put the factory in the middle of a lake, and the error was not discovered until the perplexed Soviets asked what was going on.

89. "Soviet Noncompliance with Arms Control Agreements," December 2, 1987, *Presidential Documents*, vol. 23 (December 7, 1987), p. 1417. Emphasis added.

Weinberger, Perle, and Gaffney. In recognition that the administration was signing a new major arms control agreement with the Soviet Union in the INF Treaty, the report did quietly drop a sentence that had appeared in previous reports to the effect that all past violations must be resolved before any new agreements would be signed.

Neither the Washington summit nor other developments during the year did much for U.S.-Soviet economic relations. Contrary to the expectations of many in the 1970s, in the 1980s economic ties were the caboose rather than the engine of détente.[90] The year opened with the lifting of an embargo on oil and gas drilling equipment (imposed nine years earlier in retaliation for the jailing of two Soviet dissidents released in 1979 and 1986). But from there on, movement was mostly retrograde. As the year ended, Congress was considering legislation that would place new constraints on trade with the Soviet Union, rather than relax existing curbs. There was no prospect of granting nondiscriminatory most-favored-nation (MFN) tariff treatment to the Soviets.

Nonetheless the climate in public opinion was clearly warming and given a boost by Gorbachev's visit. At the end of the year, *Time* magazine chose Gorbachev as Man of the Year.[91] And the *Bulletin of the Atomic Scientists* moved back the doomsday clock on its cover from three to six minutes before twelve (from the more dire timing set at the beginning of 1984), in recognition of the decreased tension and danger of war.

---

90. I owe this felicitous phrase to John Hardt of the Congressional Research Service.

91. The announcement was made December 27; the issue of *Time* featuring Gorbachev was dated January 4, 1988.

# 8   Culmination of the Reagan–Gorbachev Rapprochement, 1988

SURELY NO ONE in Washington or Moscow would have predicted when Ronald Reagan was sworn in as president in January 1981 that by the time he left office eight years later he would have set a record of five summit meetings with the Soviet leader, Mikhail Gorbachev, and carried a rapprochement with Moscow as far as any earlier attempt at détente. To be sure, by the time of the Washington summit in December 1987 this development was well advanced, and the final year of the Reagan administration did not see any major new achievements. Still, even as that year began, few would have predicted that Ronald Reagan, in Moscow, would repudiate any continuing validity to his earlier charge that the Soviet Union was an Evil Empire.

By 1988 the initiative in U.S.-Soviet relations had largely passed from Reagan to Gorbachev. Even the INF Treaty at the Washington summit was the product of Gorbachev's move to accept Reagan's earlier challenge. Reagan's administration essentially coasted through its final year, in domestic as well as foreign policy. Gorbachev, by contrast, while seeking to keep some momentum in foreign affairs, was embattled and preoccupied with his efforts to promote internal political and economic reform. Late in the year, however, he undertook a bold initiative on arms in Europe that reinvigorated his external policies.

## Reagan's Course on Relations with the Soviet Union

President Reagan had shown that he was ready to deal with Gorbachev and ready to improve relations with the Soviet Union—on his terms. Progress in relations came only in areas and to the extent that the Soviet side was prepared to accept U.S. positions. The rapprochement that developed from 1985 through 1988 stemmed from the fact that Gorbachev had been prepared to change Soviet positions and accept American ones. That, in turn, posed a domestic political problem for Gorbachev among those who saw the budding détente with the United States as based not on mutual recognition of interests but on Soviet capitulation. Among many other tasks in internal affairs, Gorbachev thus also faced the need to justify his external and security policies and demonstrate that they served Soviet interests. This necessity reinforced other reasons for him to pursue *glasnost* and new thinking in public Soviet discourse. It also required a dynamic and flexible foreign policy.

Reagan could, and did, in effect stand pat and wait for Gorbachev to come to him in those areas in which such movement was consistent with the revised and still changing Soviet policy. Reagan attributed Soviet change largely to American strength and firmness. Though not entirely wrong, this rationale was far from being the real motivation for Gorbachev's new thinking.

Reagan issued a second policy paper on "National Security Strategy of the United States" in January 1988. While more moderate and balanced than the first paper issued a year earlier, it also was permeated with a Cold War outlook. It stated that "in the Soviet Union we hear talk of 'new thinking' and of basic changes in Soviet policies at home and abroad. We will welcome real changes, but we have yet to see any slackening of the growth of Soviet military power, or abandonment of expansionist aspirations." Reagan's policy acknowledged that "as a result of changes in leadership style, the Soviet Union has succeeded in projecting a more favorable international image," but by referring to changes only in "style," it seemed to deny changes in substance, and by reference to "image," it cast doubt on the reality of the improvement. Indeed, although professing open-mindedness on the nature of the change, the new style of Soviet policy was said to pose "a new, continuing, and more sophisticated challenge to Western policy." But "whether recent changes constitute a real opportunity for more fundamental improvements in relations with the Soviet Union remains to be seen." And the emphasis was on keeping up our guard.[1]

Robert Gates, the deputy director of Central Intelligence, in a public speech at about the same time was even more emphatic. With a minimal genuflection to the administration's policy of improving relations, he contended that "while the changes under way offer opportunities for the United States and for a relaxation of tensions, Gorbachev intends improved Soviet economic performance, greater political vitality at home, and more dynamic diplomacy to make the U.S.S.R. a more competitive and stronger adversary in the years ahead." To rub it in, he continued, "We must not mislead ourselves or allow ourselves to be misled into believing otherwise." Moreover, even for the long run, omitting the possibility that more basic changes "remain to be seen," Gates

---

1. "National Security Strategy of the United States," *Department of State Bulletin*, vol. 88 (April 1988), pp. 1–31, quotations cited from pp. 1–2, 5. (Hereafter *State Bulletin*.)

flatly asserted that to the extent Gorbachev succeeded, "the United States will face in the 1990s and beyond a militarily powerful, domestically more vital and politically more adroit Soviet Union whose aggressive objectives abroad and essential totalitarianism at home remain largely unchanged."[2]

Even Secretary of State George Shultz, who had persisted with efforts to improve relations with the Soviet Union since 1983, in a key speech in February 1988 in presenting what he considered to be a "realistic appraisal of the nature of the Soviet society and its policies" saw the "ultimate goal" of a Soviet Union ready to deal with other countries and its own people "through dialogue rather than intimidation" as "distant," not "in the foreseeable future." Hence, he said, "I find it difficult to believe that our relations with the Soviet Union will ever be 'normal' in the sense that we have normal relations with most other countries." Thus "it seems unlikely that the U.S.-Soviet relationship will ever lose what always has been and is today a strongly wary and at times adversarial element."[3]

Unlike the year before, 1988 had opened with an exchange of televised New Year's greetings from Reagan to "the citizens of the USSR" and Gorbachev to "the American people," in which the main concrete element was the aim of seeking during the year to conclude a START treaty reducing strategic arms. (Gorbachev's message avoided any contentious issues; Reagan's sought to justify the strategic defense initiative (SDI) and called for resolving regional conflicts).[4] But as early as February 25, in an interview with editors of the *Washington Post*, Reagan said time was too short to reach a START agreement before the planned Moscow summit in late spring.[5] Gorbachev on

2.    Robert Gates's speech to the Dallas Council on World Affairs, excerpts cited in "Deputy at CIA Warns of Soviets," *Washington Times*, February 2, 1988, p. A3. Gates was quoted from an interview with similar views in Craig R. Whitney, "Does Tumult Imperil Gorbachev's Goals? Some U.S. Views," *New York Times*, March 2, 1988, p. A12. Gates's views on Gorbachev's objectives were not shared by many Soviet affairs analysts in the CIA and elsewhere, but they did reflect the views held by the Reagan administration.

      An even more dire interpretation was given by a former Soviet affairs expert on the Reagan administration's National Security Council staff, John Lenczowski. He saw the whole of the policies of *perestroika*, *glasnost*, and new thinking as sinister disinformation aimed at disarming the West. See Bill Gertz, "Expert Says Soviet Image Change Is Act," *Washington Times*, March 14, 1988, p. A3.

3.    "Managing the U.S.-Soviet Relationship," February 5, 1988, *State Bulletin*, vol. 88 (April 1988), pp. 39, 41, 40–41.

4.    See Lou Cannon, "Reagan, Gorbachev Urge Treaty," *Washington Post*, January 2, 1988, p. A1. For texts, see "President R. Reagan's New Year Message to the USSR," *Izvestiya*, January 2, 1988; and "Gorbachev's New Year's Address to the American People," on Radio Moscow, January 1, 1988, Foreign Broadcast Information Service, *Daily Report: Soviet Union*, January 4, 1988, pp. 10–11. (Hereafter FBIS, *Soviet Union*.)

5.    See Lou Cannon "Reagan: No Pact by Moscow Summit," *Washington Post*, February 26, 1988, p. A1.

March 11 and Foreign Minister Eduard Shevardnadze on March 23 both still spoke of the possibility of reaching an agreement, but it indeed proved a diminishing prospect.

Three important negotiating sessions between Shultz and Shevardnadze prepared for the planned summit and carried the brunt of most serious negotiation on other issues: the first on February 21–23, the second on March 21–23, and the third on April 21–24. Shultz (accompanied by Lieutenant General Colin Powell, the national security adviser) went to Moscow for the first session, which included a meeting between Shultz and Gorbachev and a discussion of economics between Shultz and Prime Minister Nikolai Ryzhkov.[6]

START issues were discussed, with the focus on verification. But progress was modest. The Soviets tried unsuccessfully to obtain a strengthened commitment to observe the ABM Treaty as signed in 1972. The two sides did agree to draw up additional verification protocols to the signed but yet unratified agreements of 1974 and 1976 curbing nuclear testing. Gorbachev attempted to stir up interest in the conventional arms talks, but Shultz was unable to do anything beyond agreeing that the mandate talks then in progress in Geneva be stepped up. Gorbachev also tried without success to argue against NATO plans for new military programs justified as "compensating" for the intermediate-range nuclear force (INF) missiles being destroyed. But though Shultz called the START issues "central," arms control issues were not the most pressing issue.

Afghanistan was of great concern to both sides, especially to the Soviets. The UN-sponsored Geneva negotiations were proceeding, and the Soviet Union had agreed to a relatively short period for withdrawal of its forces, but since the Washington summit a new problem had arisen—the United States had reversed its earlier position agreeing to the cessation of arms support for the *mujahedin* in exchange for Soviet withdrawal. This changed position was taken by President Reagan himself, who was unaware of the earlier U.S. agreement (made in December 1985).[7] Soviet efforts after the summit to get clarification of the U.S. position, and it was hoped restoration of the earlier stand, elicited ambiguous and finally negative response. Shevardnadze, arguing late into the first night of their talks, and then Gorbachev were unable to sway Shultz, who of course was bound by Reagan's position (reinforced by conservative Republican senators). Gorbachev nonetheless insisted that Shultz convey his view to President Reagan. He was naturally concerned about this American change, after the Soviet Union had already committed itself to withdrawal, at home as well as at Geneva.

---

6. See George P. Shultz, *Turmoil and Triumph: My Years as Secretary of State* (Charles Scribner's Sons, 1993), pp. 1095–96, for a brief account by Shultz.

7. See the discussion in chapter 15.

The two sides discussed other regional issues, including the Iran-Iraq war, Angola, Kampuchea, Central America, Korea, and the Middle East. Shultz remarked in a press conference at the end of the talks that "I don't think we have had such a detailed discussion before" on these regional issues, and that it had been "valuable."[8]

They also discussed human rights issues, or as the Soviets preferred to refer to the matter, humanitarian issues, with some strong differences but with greater Soviet confidence and willingness to address the subject than in the past. And Shultz met with Academician Andrei Sakharov to pay his respects.

Shultz and Shevardnadze signed a North Pacific fisheries agreement that opened up waters in the Soviet 200-mile zone for American fishermen. This joined other normalizing agreements being reached, including in mid-January a broader agreement covering a range of areas for scientific cooperation signed by the respective national academies of science.

Progress was also made in reducing Western Coordinating Committee (COCOM) restraints on trade with the Soviet Union. In February personal computers were stricken from the list of banned items. Later in the spring the United States further relaxed some of its own more stringent controls.

Subsequent Shultz-Shevardnadze meetings were planned for mid-March and mid-April to prepare for the summit. The two sides now agreed the summit meeting would be held whether or not a START agreement had been reached.

The established pattern of consultation at the assistant secretary of state-deputy foreign minister level continued, occasionally raised to include higher-level meetings. Thus in March Shevardnadze received Assistant Secretary Richard Murphy for discussions on the Middle East. In mid-April Deputy Minister Igor Rogachev and Assistant Secretary Gaston Sigur discussed East Asian and Pacific affairs. Also in mid-April Assistant Secretary Richard Schifter discussed human rights issues in Moscow. In May Assistant Secretary Chester Crocker had two sets of meetings with Deputy Minister Anatoly Adamishin on African affairs, especially on Angola and Namibia.

The most important and new departure was a meeting of Secretary of Defense Frank Carlucci with Minister of Defense Dmitry Yazov in Bern, Switzerland, on March 16–17. This was the first such meeting apart from a brief side-meeting of predecessors at the summit in Vienna in 1979, and was intended to inaugurate such meetings both between defense ministers and, separately, military chiefs of staff. The two men discussed military doctrine and policy, as well as in general terms conventional force reductions; they both expressed satisfaction with the meeting and committed themselves to continuing contacts at various levels.[9]

---

8.   Radio Moscow, February 22, 1988, in FBIS, *Soviet Union*, February 23, 1988, p. 20.

9.   Reagan and Gorbachev first discussed the idea of meetings of their defense chiefs at the Reykjavik summit in 1986. The attempt to arrange a meeting between Yazov and

There was also a considerable increase in congressional visits to the Soviet Union and in unofficial cooperation, including trials of nuclear testing detection equipment in January at both the Nevada and Semipalatinsk nuclear test ranges. New people-to-people contacts included an unprecedented civil air visit of eighty-seven people from Nome, Alaska, over the Bering Straits, to Providentya, on the Chukotsk peninsula.

Despite these many strands of developing contact and cooperation, not only did many differences remain, but also some new frictions arose. On February 12, only nine days before Secretary Shultz's visit to Moscow, the U.S. cruiser *Yorktown* and intelligence-collection destroyer *Caron* again intruded into Soviet territorial waters off the Crimea, just as these same two ships had done in March 1986 and as the cruiser *Arkansas* had done at Kamchatka in May 1987. Again, too, the Soviet Union lodged a vigorous diplomatic protest at the "provocative mission" and risk of a "dangerous incident." General Yazov protested these incidents to Carlucci when they met. The Soviets also escalated their reaction by arranging for the accidental minor scraping contact of smaller Soviet ships with both American warships, thus providing basis for complaint of the danger of such actions. The official U.S. contention that warships enjoy innocent passage through territorial waters is not supported by most Western legal opinion if such passage is not necessary for normal navigation, and particularly if it is used for electronic or other intelligence acquisition.[10]

Soon after Shultz's February visit, the Soviet Union also protested what it called "the sharply intensified subversive character" of broadcasts to the Soviet Union by the Voice of America.[11] Some broadcasts (and other American activities) may indeed have contributed to this and other Soviet complaints of U.S. interference. But these protests were largely engendered by Soviet sensi-

---

Weinberger in 1987 came to naught in part owing to Weinberger's desire not to discuss U.S. force plans, and not to meet in Geneva, site of arms control talks. He wanted Yazov to come to Washington. Bern was chosen as neutral ground; subsequent meetings would alternate between capitals.

Yazov took the occasion (after a hint from the American side) to express regret over the death of Major Nicholson in 1985 and to express readiness to discuss ways to prevent such incidents in the future. As noted below, the Soviet side also had some incidents to raise.

10. See the discussion in chapter 6, pp. 31–32.

    In other respects the U.S. Navy continued an aggressive pursuit of exercises close to the Soviet Union. For example, in 1988 U.S. aircraft carrier task forces, including two carrier task forces at once during the Seoul Olympics, entered the Sea of Japan on five occasions. This particularly riled the Soviet Navy because Moscow had postponed planned Soviet naval exercises in that area during the period of the Olympics. See Admiral of the Fleet V. Chernavin, "Problems of the Pacific: Restraint Must Be Reciprocal," *Krasnaya zvezda* (Red Star), December 7, 1988.

11. See the summary statement in *Vestnik Ministerstva innostrannykh del CCCP* (Bulletin of the Ministry of Foreign Affairs of the USSR), no. 6 (April 1, 1988), p. 27; the date of the protest was February 29, 1988. (Hereafter *Vestnik MID*.)

tivity to outbreaks of ethnic and nationalist violence, including a particularly bloody massacre of several dozen Armenians in Azerbaijan in late February and the growth of peaceful nationalist agitation in the Baltic states and elsewhere. It was still customary, as well as reassuring, to find foreign causes for domestic stresses.

Shevardnadze visited Washington on March 21–23 for talks with Shultz, and on March 23 with Reagan. At the conclusion of the talks the dates of the forthcoming summit were announced: May 29 through June 2. But while the same set of issues was again discussed, there was no real advance over the previous meeting the month before. Some procedural agreements on START were made, but no breakthroughs.[12]

The Soviet side had hoped that its urgings on Afghanistan would lead Reagan to reconsider, but the United States was adamant that it would not stop supplying arms to the *mujahedin* unless the Soviet Union stopped supplying the Kabul government.[13] A similar standoff remained on Soviet arms supply to Nicaragua and U.S. arms for other Central American states and the contras.

The Soviet side also did not succeed in getting the United States to do more than carry on in the talks on a new mandate for conventional arms reductions in Europe. American officials were inclined to recall the long disputes over data in the long-stymied talks on mutual and balanced force reductions (MBFR) and were not yet confident that Gorbachev really meant a full data disclosure and readiness for "balanced" (that is, greater Soviet) reductions. This American caution governed despite calls in Congress for conventional arms cuts to complement the INF nuclear arms reductions. At the end of the talks Shevardnadze remarked at his news conference, "Let me say, in all honesty, we were amazed at the response of our American partners. They have shown, to put it very mildly, no great enthusiasm to discuss the issue."[14]

Shultz and Shevardnadze formally opened the Washington Nuclear Risk Reduction Center (located in the Department of State) on March 23, in conjunction with a similar action in Moscow, thus activating the agreement they had signed on September 15, 1987. But there were no new agreements.

Trade relations had been low on the list of matters discussed in these foreign ministers' meetings, and would continue to be at later meetings and at the summit itself. The United States did, however, take steps in April to facilitate and expand trade. The new secretary of commerce, C. William Verity,

---

12. Shultz refers only to exchanges on Afghanistan; see Shultz, *Turmoil and Triumph*, p. 1090.

13. For a detailed and informed account of the discussions of Afghanistan at the February and March meetings, see Don Oberdorfer, *The Turn: From the Cold War to a New Era, the United States and the Soviet Union, 1983–1990* (Poseidon Press, 1991), pp. 274–77, 279–82.

14. "Press Conference of the Minister of Foreign Affairs of the USSR," March 23, 1988, *Pravda*, March 25, 1988.

Jr., had pushed for greater trade with the Soviet Union (as indeed he had done before being named to the post), and he was supported by Secretary Shultz and Secretary of the Treasury James A. Baker III, overcoming some remaining reluctance from the Defense Department. As a result, Reagan approved some modest steps forward.

From April 12 through 15 a meeting of the U.S.-USSR Trade and Economic Council was held in Moscow. The council was a mixed governmental-private group (the government members also meeting coincidentally as the Joint U.S.-USSR Commercial Commission, established in the earlier era of détente in 1973). Secretary Verity's delegation comprised some 550 American businessmen, and the Soviet delegation (on host ground) was about twice as large. They were feted at a banquet where Gorbachev made a substantial statement on trade policy, envisaging a "window of hope" for Soviet-American relations and urging more American trade and investment.

In an effort to stimulate long-term commerce, two trade consortia were established. The American Trade Consortium brought six major firms together: Eastman Kodak, RJR Nabisco, Archer Daniels Midland, Chevron, Johnson and Johnson, and Ford Motor Company (joined by Mercator Corporation, a small firm specializing in trade with the Soviet Union). All six were interested in exploring joint ventures and investment in the Soviet Union. Also, separately, Occidental Petroleum announced a joint venture to build two petrochemical plants in Ukraine. In addition, joint working groups were established to explore the marketing possibilities of American equipment for medical, construction, food processing, oil and gas, and consumer goods industries. Finally, there were discussions and plans for further contacts to familiarize Soviet agencies with legal aspects of investment and such adjuncts as insurance. The Soviet participants were keenly interested and almost overwhelmed to learn, for example, that private American enterprises had spent $109 billion on advertising in the preceding year (1987).[15]

On April 14 a series of accords on Afghanistan were signed in Geneva. Afghanistan and Pakistan signed two bilateral agreements on mutual relations and the repatriation of refugees, as well as the central Agreement on the Interrelationships for the Settlement of the Situation Relating to Afghanistan. The latter agreement was also signed by the United States and Soviet Union (Shultz and Shevardnadze) as "witnesses," and the two powers also signed a bilateral Declaration on International Guarantees.[16] The accords were the culmination of an active United Nations effort led from early 1982 on by the under secretary general for special political affairs, Diego Cordovez. They were a signal success in one important respect: facilitating a Soviet military with-

---

15. Data from an unpublished report of the proceedings and discussions with a participant.

16. For the texts see "Agreements on Afghanistan," *State Bulletin*, vol. 88 (June 1988), pp. 56–60.

drawal in the framework of a political settlement of external interventions in Afghanistan. They did not, however, despite their manifest intent and terms, end or even curtail external support for the contending Afghan parties, much less resolve the conflict among the Afghans. Through consciously understood and even articulated positions contravening the terms of the accords, Pakistan and the United States (among others) continued to host, arm, supply, and otherwise assist the Afghan *mujahedin*, and the Soviet Union continued to arm, supply, and support the Kabul regime.

The Afghan accords were thus a success for Gorbachev in providing cover for his troop withdrawal (announced to be completed within ten months, by February 14, 1989), but a failure in getting United States to agree to end support for the insurgency.[17]

When Shultz met with Shevardnadze and Gorbachev on April 21–24 in Moscow, there were no obstacles in the path of the approaching summit, but there were also no breakthroughs.[18] It was now not only evident that the START negotiations would not yield an agreement by the time the leaders met, but also doubtful that they would be able at the meeting itself to clear away any major roadblocks. Afghanistan was no longer an agenda issue, nor were other regional conflicts. Shultz and Gorbachev had a spirited exchange on human rights in the two countries. Unexpectedly for Shultz, Gorbachev at the outset had made a vigorous criticism of recent speeches by President Reagan on the Soviet Union, especially one made the day before (April 21) in Springfield, Massachusetts, which Shultz had not even seen.[19] Nor had it been regarded in Washington as particularly challenging the Soviet Union.[20] It had, in fact, implicitly discussed an improving relationship—but on the basis that American strength and resolve had paid off and that the Soviet Union was now more aware of the limitations of its own strength. That message was particularly sensitive for Gorbachev because of the internal opposition he was facing (which will be discussed further). Reagan had also gloated over the Soviet defeat in Afghanistan and rubbed it in that the United States was going to continue to arm the insurgents. Gorbachev was especially concerned that Reagan might be planning to sound such themes when he came to Moscow, and his strong protest was no doubt intended to dissuade Reagan from doing so. In addition, a

---

17. For discussion of the Afghanistan negotiations and settlement see chapter 15.

18. See Shultz, *Turmoil and Triumph*, pp. 1096–1100; and Oberdorfer, *The Turn*, pp. 282–92.

19. For the text see "Remarks to the World Affairs Council of Western Massachusetts in Springfield, Massachusetts," April 21, 1988, *Presidential Documents*, vol. 24 (April 25, 1988), pp. 503–07.

20. The speech, prepared by the conservative White House speech writers, had been cleared with the State Department at the last minute, with little time for review, and then the White House rejected some suggested changes. Secretary Shultz had been about to depart and was en route when the speech was delivered.

TASS account of the meeting featured Gorbachev's protest, so the domestic Soviet audience was evidently also in mind.

Shultz made brief visits to Ukraine and Georgia after his talks in Moscow, a new departure reflecting the growing importance of the ethnic and republic political factors in the Soviet Union.

In the days following, two U.S.-Soviet scientific cooperation agreements were signed. A protocol on cooperation in civil nuclear reactor safety was signed on April 26 by the Nuclear Regulatory Commission and the Soviet State Committee for the Utilization of Atomic Energy. On May 3 the National Aeronautics and Space Agency signed an agreement with the Soviet Institute for Space Research creating a joint working group on space astronomy and astrophysics and another on solar physics.

Shultz and Shevardnadze met in Geneva on May 11–12 for their final presummit discussions. They also signed an agreement specifying that the INF Treaty covered similar categories of intermediate-range weapons based on other physical principles, plugging a gap in the INF Treaty coverage. Before this meeting, Reagan had delivered a much more conciliatory speech on May 4, although still keeping pressure on the human rights issue. Gorbachev must have been only partly reassured about Reagan's intentions for public diplomacy in Moscow.

## *Gorbachev Embattled over* Perestroika

Over the first two to three years of his administration Gorbachev had successfully removed those colleagues who had opposed his accession to power, and even those from the old Politburo who had supported him. He had also made sweeping personnel changes in the party and government bureaucracies. Nonetheless, as his changes in concrete policy and even basic programs became more and more far-reaching, many of his own cohorts and personnel selections became conservatives, constituting a veiled opposition. Even his second in command in the party leadership, Yegor Ligachev, called into the central leadership by Gorbachev himself, had by 1988 become the leader of a powerful conservative constituency in the leadership. If 1987 had begun with a Central Committee plenum launching *demokratizatsiya* and *glasnost*, the February (17–18) 1988 plenum presented a much more conservative consolidationist line. Ligachev was, in fact, riding high and gave the main report to the Central Committee—the first time this had not been done by Gorbachev himself. Ligachev launched a scathing attack on excesses of *glasnost*, blasting the pernicious effects of rock music, the blackening of Soviet history, and the expressions of local nationalism in the Baltic states, Transcaucasia, and Central Asia. Gorbachev, too, gave a major speech on the second day of the plenum, strongly defending *perestroika* and *glasnost*, but he was clearly on the defensive and also considered it necessary to strike a middle position calling for balance in historiography and arguing for "Soviet patriotism" in place of local nationalism.[21]

The February plenum also removed Boris Yeltsin from candidate membership on the Politburo and named two new candidate members, Georgy Razumovsky, a liberal, and Yury Maslyukov, the new head of Gosplan. Although Maslyukov was widely considered at the time to be a "Gorbachev man," he and Oleg Baklanov, raised to become a party secretary, were primarily representatives of conservative industrial circles.

The more conservative line on *glasnost* stemmed from concerns in several quarters about letting the genie of uncontrolled free expression out of the bottle. General Dmitry Yazov had complained sharply in a mid-December 1987 meeting with writers, and again in a mid-January television interview, about articles (especially in the popular magazine *Ogonek*) considered to sully the honor of the Soviet military.

Party chiefs in the Baltic republics and Moldavia complained about the weakening of political discipline and the dangers of extremist nationalism in those republics as a result of *glasnost*. The first major protests over the Armenian-populated Nagorno-Karabakh enclave in Azerbaijan had occurred just a week earlier (February 11), and were to lead to a massacre of Armenians in Sumgait, Azerbaijan, ten days later. Both Ligachev and KGB chief Viktor Chebrikov had been publicly warning of the dangers of ethnic nationalism for several months. At the February meeting, for the first time Gorbachev called for a special plenum on the nationality issue.

Most disturbing, if only because of the implications for the planned party conference, a whole series of regional party plenums held from November 1987 through January 1988, intended to bolster *perestroika* and democratization, had in fact failed to have that effect and instead had strengthened the hold of party conservatives.

The mid-February plenum did not lead to a defeat for Gorbachev, but it clearly indicated the strength of the opposition to carrying *perestroika* beyond a point where it would remain safely under the control of the party machine. Gorbachev assumed a middle course partly because he, too, was concerned about excesses, but partly for tactical reasons. He continued to insist on the need for *glasnost* and democratization, as well as economic reform, for *perestroika*.

The opposition within the leadership also continued to do battle. On March 13 an extraordinary reactionary treatise was published in *Sovetskaya*

---

21. For the texts see "On the Course of Perestroika in Middle and Higher Schools and the Tasks of the Party in its Achievement," Report of Ye. K. Ligachev, Member of the Politburo and Secretary of the CC CPSU, *Pravda*, February 18, 1988; and "Revolutionary Perestroika—Ideology of Renewal, Speech of General Secretary of the CC CPSU M. S. Gorbachev at the Plenum of the CC CPSU of February 18, 1988," *Pravda*, February 19, 1988.

*Rossiya*, a conservative newspaper. Called "I Cannot Waive Principles," and attributed to an unknown Leningrad chemistry teacher named Nina Andreyeva, it not only bitterly and scathingly attacked *perestroika*, *glasnost*, and *demokratizatsiya*, but defended communist orthodoxy and even Stalin.[22] Clearly, some senior political figure had sponsored publication of this antireform diatribe. It appeared just as Gorbachev was leaving for a five-day state visit to Yugoslavia, and reform Politburo member Aleksandr Yakovlev for a meeting of communist party ideological heads in Mongolia.[23] For twenty days party propagandists and many local newspapers reprinted and used the article to rally conservative forces, with little real opposition. After Gorbachev and Yakovlev had returned, and only after two reportedly heated Politburo meetings on March 31 and April 4 (the first, at least, while Ligachev was away from Moscow), did *Pravda* on April 5 print an authoritative full-page editorial article blasting the Andreyeva article as the "ideological platform and manifesto of anti-perestroika forces."[24] Then a massive campaign by the reform camp was unleashed.

The upshot was a strong rebuff for the conservatives, especially Ligachev. But the episode had showed that there were powerful contending views in the leadership, and the paralysis of the reformers for three weeks was a disturbing sign.[25]

The divergent positions continued to appear. On April 13, while not criticizing *glasnost* directly, Chebrikov attacked subversive interference of foreign intelligence in Soviet affairs as being responsible for fanning nationalist unrest and hostility.[26]

---

22. Nina Andreyeva, "I Cannot Waive Principles," letter to the editorial office from a Leningrad VUZ lecturer, *Sovetskaya Rossiya* (Soviet Russia), March 13, 1988. Andreyeva originally sent a version of the letter to editors of *Pravda* and several other newspapers in September 1987, but none then published it. The letter as published had been revised, partly by Andreyeva and partly by the editors (and, according to some reports, by Ligachev personally, although he has denied responsibility).

23. This was not the first time that the opposition made public moves in Gorbachev's absence. In August-September of the year before, while Gorbachev was on vacation, the party media made a strong pitch for "collective leadership"—not a direct challenge but one reflecting the interests of the conservatives.

24. "Principles of Perestroika: Revolutionary Thinking in Practice," *Pravda*, April 5, 1988, 2d ed. *Sovetskaya Rossiya* was also compelled to reprint the *Pravda* article and to publish self-criticism for having printed the Andreyeva article.

25. At that time and later, several leading reformers told me how ashamed they were not to have mounted an immediate counteroffensive and said that they would be more resolute in the future.

26. "An Order on the City's Banner," speech by V. M. Chebrikov to a ceremonial meeting in Cheboksary, April 13, 1988, *Pravda*, April 14, 1988. Chebrikov also failed to mention the April 5 *Pravda* editorial, in contrast to most speeches by leaders at that time.

On May 7 a new political party called the Democratic Union was established by about one hundred liberals, including Sergei Grigoryants, a dissident in the past and now editor of a new unauthorized journal called *Glasnost*. Two days later, while the group was still meeting, the police cracked down and arrested fourteen people, including Grigoryants. He was released after a week in jail, but only a few days later his printing equipment was seized.

Gorbachev continued to press for more vigorous reform. Yeltsin, now out of the leadership (though still a member of the Central Committee), spoke up in support of Gorbachev's reform effort. Yeltsin was present at the May Day parade in Red Square (which included no military parade in 1988) but no longer among the leaders on the dais above Lenin's mausoleum.[27]

At a conference of top party leaders with media and cultural officials on May 7, reported in *Pravda* only four days later, Gorbachev pulled back somewhat from the anticonservative campaign launched on April 5. While strongly reaffirming the need to move forward with *perestroika*, an aim not challenged directly by Ligachev and the other conservative members of the party leadership, Gorbachev also called for unity and denied that *perestroika* threatened "the values of socialism."[28] He was at the same time working hard, but with only limited success, to get a stronger representation of liberal reformers named as delegates to the forthcoming party conference. At a Politburo meeting on May 19 (not publicized) and then on May 23 at a plenary session of Central Committee, "Theses" for the forthcoming party conference were approved (and published in *Pravda* on May 27). Ligachev publicly praised the theses on television that same evening, and it was clear they had been worked out in accordance with a liberal-conservative compromise. As part of a broader compromise, it soon became evident that Gorbachev had also given assurances that the party conference would not be used to elect a new Central Committee and purge conservative party officials.[29]

Meanwhile, a new degree of *glasnost* entered public discussion of foreign policy, sparked in particular by an article by historian Vyacheslav Dashichev on May 18. He not only criticized a number of past Soviet foreign policy moves but also showed unprecedented evenhandedness in attributing blame for the Cold War. He criticized Soviet "hegemonism" in relations with the countries of Eastern Europe and China. And he blamed Brezhnev for renewing the arms race in the 1970s instead of making a real success of détente with the United States. On a theoretical level, he reflected a traditional

27. I had obtained a special pass to enter Red Square and was surprised to encounter Yeltsin among the attendees, still privileged but far from the top leadership.

28. "Through Democratization to a New Image of Socialism, Meeting at the Central Committee of the CPSU," *Pravda*, May 11, 1988.

29. In a separate matter, however, the party chiefs of Armenia and Azerbaijan, Karen S. Demirchyan and Kyamran I. Bagirov, respectively, were sacked on May 21 for their inability to prevent or deal with the outbreaks of ethnic violence in those republics.

"Western" balance of power approach instead of the standard communist concept of a correlation of forces between two ideologically defined camps.[30] Later events were to show that this was the opening salvo in a new major debate. Other articles soon followed, criticizing such recent Soviet actions as the decisions in the 1970s to deploy SS-20 missiles and to intervene militarily in Afghanistan.[31]

The principal foreign policy move in this period preceding the party conference was Gorbachev's summit meeting with President Reagan.

## The Moscow Summit

The summit meeting in Moscow from May 29 to June 2 was a media extravaganza, high theater. President Reagan himself, who frequently oriented himself in such terms, declared at one point that he felt as though he had been dropped into a play. On this occasion, indeed, one of the principal American purposes—reinforcing President Reagan's own personal proclivities—was to meet and address the Soviet people to the fullest extent feasible, to sound a message and to project an image. Whereas Gorbachev's main interest was to negotiate, Reagan had no major negotiating objectives.[32]

---

30. Vyacheslav Dashichev, "East-West: The Search for New Relationships: On the Priorities of the Foreign Policy of the Soviet State," *Literaturnaya gazeta* (Literary Gazette), May 18, 1988.

　　Dashichev was identified simply as a doctor of history and professor. He was the head of the Foreign Policy Department of the Institute of the Economics of the World Socialist System and was the chief author of a confidential memorandum sent by the director of the institute, Oleg Bogomolov, to the leadership in January 1980 criticizing the Soviet intervention in Afghanistan. He also had been a career military man and was one of three prominent colonels on the General Staff purged in 1966 for defending a revisionist interpretation of the Soviet failure in meeting the German attack in 1941.

31. To note but a few other key early articles, see the report of a discussion by leading academic figures, "From a Balance of Forces to a Balance of Interests," *Literaturnaya gazeta*, June 29, 1988; Aleksandr Bovin, "Lets Break the Ice on Foreign Policy," *Moskovskiye novosti* (Moscow News), June 12, 1988; and Vadim Zagladin, "Precis of Party Conference Speech: The Priority of Trust," *Sovetskaya Rossiya*, June 23, 1988.

32. A detailed account and perceptive analysis of the Moscow summit is provided by Joseph Whelan, *Soviet Diplomacy and Negotiating Behavior—1980—90: Gorbachev-Reagan-Bush Meetings at the Summit*, Special Studies Series on Foreign Affairs Issues, vol. 3 (Washington: Government Printing Office, 1991), pp. 1–117. For documents and speeches see *State Bulletin*, vol. 88 (August 1988), pp. 1–45. See Shultz, *Turmoil and Triumph*, pp. 1101–06; for insights into the U.S. delegation's views see also Oberdorfer, *The Turn*, pp. 292–307.

　　President Reagan's secret National Security Decision Directive (NSDD)–305, "Objectives at the Moscow Summit," issued on April 26, 1988, has now been declassi-

The Soviet leadership sought to compete with the United States in displaying summit hospitality. With some pain, it bowed to Reagan's desire to meet with a group of dissidents, to make a featured visit to Patriarch Aleksei II at the recently restored Danilov monastery, and to address the students of Moscow University. The scale of the whole enterprise was impressive—necessarily, since the U.S. delegation and press entourage totaled some 700 people (overmatching the record delegation of 500 that had come to Washington from Moscow six months earlier).

Reagan's purpose, apart from a genuine personal interest in seeing the Soviet Union and meeting people there, was to gently prod Gorbachev by praising what he had already accomplished in reform while urging that he needed to do more, especially in the field of personal freedoms and human rights. This led to some defensive reactions by Gorbachev and by the Soviet bureaucracy (for example, curtailing media coverage of such matters as Reagan's meeting with dissidents and even his address to the students of Moscow University). From the American standpoint, nonetheless, this important facet of the summit was quite successful.

Reagan's speech to the students was especially good, well crafted and reflecting a broad understanding of Russian culture that drew on outside as well as State Department expertise, and on White House speechwriters tempered to the occasion. Even more impressive, and more unexpected, was Reagan's adept handling of questions and impromptu remarks on that and other occasions. He was relaxed, amiable, and human, qualities that especially for the Soviet audience were not expected and therefore had all the more favorable an impact.

Reagan himself, in turn, was affected by the experience. If this was the first time most Russians had seen an American president, it was also the first opportunity for him to see more than a handful of Soviet leaders and diplomats. And he, too, found that they were human and likable. When asked in Moscow whether he still thought the Soviet Union was the Evil Empire, Reagan unequivocally answered: "No. I was talking about another time, another era."

---

fied. It makes clear his primary objective was "to demonstrate the success of this Administration's approach to the Soviet Union based on the principles of strength, realism, and Western unity" and "to consolidate the gains made by this Administration on the four-part agenda with the Soviet Union." Reagan also sought "to press for further progress, particularly an attainment as soon as possible of a START agreement" on U.S. terms, as well as advances on Soviet "human rights performance" and "resolution of regional conflicts beyond Afghanistan." He also stressed the importance of "communicating directly with the Soviet people." The directive included a caution, especially for the Western European allies, to "guard against exaggerated expectations on the future pace and achievement of U.S.-Soviet relations or the reform process under way in the Soviet Union," although the United States was "willing to move forward as quickly as the situation allows." "Objectives at the Moscow Summit," White House, April 26, 1988, Secret, pp. 1, 3. (Declassified November 27, 1992.)

Gorbachev was so pleased by this remark that he referred to it in his own public farewell comments.

One wonders whether Reagan's conversion to belief in friendly relations might have come earlier had he visited Moscow sooner. It is not really possible to say. For one thing, during the first years of his term he really believed that the United States was weaker, and only from about 1984 did he seem sufficiently confident to seek better relations. Another factor was that in the early years he was surrounded by hard-line zealots, who had been replaced by conservative pragmatists in the second term.

As for the business at hand, the United States pursued its standard four-part agenda, stressing human rights but also including regional conflicts, arms control, and bilateral relations. The most visible, if ceremonial, act was signature by the two leaders of the protocol on exchange of instruments of ratification of the INF Treaty they had concluded in Washington. Some progress was also made in the START strategic arms negotiation, especially on mobile intercontinental missiles and air-launched cruise missiles. But this advance was not enough to give confidence that an agreement could be reached later in the year under the same U.S. administration. Shultz and Shevardnadze did sign secondary agreements reached on advance notification of ICBM test launchings (through the recently constituted Nuclear Risk Reduction Centers in the two capitals) and on joint experimentation on monitoring underground nuclear test limitations.

Several bilateral cooperative measures and other bilateral accords were signed, none of great importance, but all useful and instrumental to the growing pattern of cooperation. Agreements were concluded on fishing rights, cooperation in sea search and rescue, operational coordination in long-range radio navigation in the northern Pacific region, extension of the 1973 agreement on peaceful uses of nuclear energy, cooperation in transportation technology, expanded civil space cooperation, and extension of the general cultural exchange agreement, with greatly expanded student and teacher exchanges. In some areas the Soviets were prepared to go further than the Americans, for example in seeking a joint program for the exploration of Mars.

The strategy of small, gradual incremental steps building up the relationship between the two countries had been pursued by Secretary Shultz from early in his tenure. It was also the approach favored by Ambassador Anatoly Dobrynin, who recommended it to Gorbachev. In many ways the Moscow summit was the culmination of this approach, although it had taken Gorbachev's dramatic shift to accept the zero INF option to really provide impetus to the Washington and Moscow summits in 1987 and 1988, after the failure of Reagan to move on the SDI obstacle to a far-reaching START accord. At the Moscow summit, one administration spokesman referred to this approach as "coral-building," a very slow but steady accretion of small new increments of agreement eventually building a structure.

"Coral-building" satisfied Reagan's interests, but not Gorbachev's. As will be seen, after making unsuccessful efforts to move the American side to more dramatic advances at the summit, Gorbachev turned to dramatic unilateral action.

Although on regional issues the joint statement on the meeting merely noted the exchange of views (including "satisfaction" over the Geneva Afghan accords), the two sides reached an agreement on one important point: to support a resolution of the Angola and Namibia conflicts involving the withdrawal of all foreign (that is, Cuban) forces from Angola over the next twelve months. This agreement reflected a concession by the Soviet (and absent Cuban and Angolan government) side, and along with the ongoing withdrawal of Soviet troops from Afghanistan further demonstrated the sincerity of the renewed Soviet interest in resolving such regional conflicts through "national reconciliation."

Apart from American testing of the limits in pushing on the human rights issue and Soviet testiness and occasional flareups on that issue, and of course continuing differences on a number of START issues, only two subjects were really controversial. One was a Soviet effort to leap ahead on conventional force reductions in Europe, toward which Gorbachev tried on the first day and later to urge some dramatic move such as an agreement to a reduction of 500,000 men on each side. The U.S. delegation was not prepared for such an approach and was suspicious of any move other than one made in the routine multilateral "conventional stability talks" then under way in Geneva that were preparing a mandate for new negotiations on conventional forces in Europe. The Soviets, however, persisted in proposing a three-part program. First would be an exchange and verification of data on forces and arms; second, the removal of asymmetrical advantages on each side; and finally, cuts of one-half million men on each side. But the Americans were wary and preferred to set aside the whole issue, to Gorbachev's evident frustration.[33] The reasons for Gorbachev's strenuous, if unsuccessful, effort on this subject is discussed later.

The most controversial issue arose when the Soviet side introduced a brief statement of intentions on nonuse of force and nonintervention in the internal affairs of other states for inclusion in the planned joint statement. Work on this communiqué was begun at the outset of the meetings by senior officials (Deputy Foreign Minister Aleksandr Bessmertnykh and Assistant Secretary of State Rozanne Ridgway). The Soviets sought many such statements of principles or intentions, as they had in Washington in December. Again the U.S. side rejected most of them, including the one just mentioned. But on this issue, Gorbachev had personally given the proposed language to Reagan at their first meeting on May 29, and again pressed the matter with Reagan at the last major session on June 1. Gorbachev argued that they should now go beyond the

---

33. This detailing of the Soviet proposal has not been set forth in any of the accounts published to date, but was provided to me by an American participant and confirmed by Soviet participants.

renunciation of nuclear war and military superiority agreed to at Geneva in 1985 and reaffirmed at Washington. (At Washington, too, he had made such a pitch, arguing unsuccessfully for a statement on nonuse of force for intervention in the Third World, as a foundation for the then still forthcoming Soviet announcement on withdrawal of its forces from Afghanistan.)

Gorbachev's proposed statement read:

Proceeding from their understanding of the realities that have taken shape in the world today, the two leaders believe that no problem in dispute can be resolved, nor should it be resolved, by military means. They regard peaceful coexistence as a universal principle of international relations. Equality of all states, noninterference in internal affairs, and freedom of sociopolitical choice must be recognized as the inalienable and mandatory standards of international relations.

When Gorbachev had first given this paragraph to Reagan, the president commented that he liked it but wanted his advisers to look at it. They emphatically did not like it, and when the matter came up again Reagan told Gorbachev that, although he had "liked the tone of it, his advisers had objected to certain 'ambiguities.'" The delegations then broke to hold a caucus on the matter, and Reagan returned to reject the language despite sharp, even scornful, comments by Gorbachev. Gorbachev finally gave up, and the expert advisers drafted language once again paraphrasing the Geneva formulation and omitting all three new points in the Soviet draft.

Gorbachev really did find it difficult to understand why the Americans (Reagan's advisers, if not Reagan himself) were so adamant against a statement rejecting the use of military means to resolve disputes, affirming peaceful coexistence as a universal principle of international relations, calling for freedom of choice, and abjuring interference in the internal affairs of any state.

One reason for the strong U.S. objections, undoubtedly explained to Gorbachev but probably not impressing him, was that the Americans saw "peaceful coexistence" as a long-standing *Soviet* slogan, and moreover, in the view and memory of many American officials, one with negative "Cold War" adversarial connotations from its long history of being used to criticize various American actions and policies. In addition, the Americans believed that a very general injunction against any use of "military means" to resolve disputes would rule out not only aggressive actions but also necessary defensive uses of force (and might undercut support for necessary defense budgets). One objection that Gorbachev probably well understood but could not agree with was that the Soviets would certainly make use of the word "noninterference" to attack American support under the Reagan Doctrine for "freedom fighters." Finally, the whole paragraph, and in particular the reference to "peaceful coexistence," sounded to the Americans too much like the Basic Principles of Mutual Relations, signed in 1972 and associated with the Kissinger-Nixon détente of the 1970s, which the Reagan administration continued to deride despite its own budding undeclared détente.

These objections do not seem to me a sufficient basis for the Americans to have rejected the statement abjuring any use of military means to resolve disputes. Without a precise agreed-on definition of peaceful coexistence, it was not unreasonable to object to its characterization as a "universal principle of international relations"; nevertheless, the United States had held that coexistence in peace was necessary. It was unnecessarily awkward to object to an endorsement of freedom of choice and of noninterference in the internal affairs of other countries. Sometimes a charge of interference may be unjustly made; sometimes actions are interference and should not be undertaken. But the principle has been accepted in general international law and in the United Nations Charter, and indeed provided the basis for American objections to Soviet and Cuban actions on many occasions. The administration was, however, more concerned about protecting its own activities and freedom of action in furtherance of the Reagan Doctrine.

Gorbachev returned to the matter in his closing press conference statement, and it is clear that he had put high store in getting an indirect American endorsement of his "new thinking" on security policy in order to be able to move ahead more readily in his restructuring of Soviet foreign policy. He stressed the conclusions that "world problems are not to be solved by military means" but "must be solved by political means, on the basis of a balance of interests, on the basis of respect for social choice." He expressed deep disappointment that "the opportunity to take a big stride in shaping civilized international relations has been missed."[34] He then went on to express his regret also over the failure to move forward on conventional arms reductions in Europe. The Americans were perplexed at Gorbachev's persistence and the intensity of his reaction on both points—and failed to realize they were related in his mind and in his political strategy.[35]

The Americans also undervalued Soviet readiness to cooperate in defusing Third World regional conflicts. The success in reaching agreement in the negotiations on Angola was welcomed, but even added to the earlier Soviet decision to withdraw from Afghanistan, that agreement did not lead Reagan and Shultz to give full credit to Gorbachev's urgings for greater U.S.-Soviet cooperation in settling other regional conflicts through compromise on the basis of a balance of the interests of the parties.[36]

Both sides valued the development of continuing dialogue, manifested in the businesslike discussion of issues and indeed in the meeting itself. As Gorbachev summed it up in his parting remarks, "both of us have every reason to regard this meeting and your visit as a useful contribution to the development of dialogue between the Soviet Union and the United States." Noting that

---

34. "Press Conference of M. S. Gorbachev," *Pravda*, June 2, 1988.

35. This subject is further discussed later in this chapter.

36. *Pravda*, June 2, 1988.

President Reagan and he had been dealing with each other for three years, he observed that "we've come a long way."[37]

Reagan, in turn, commented in personal terms that he and Nancy wanted the Gorbachevs "to know that we think of you as friends," and asked Gorbachev to "tell the people of the Soviet Union of the deep feelings of friendship felt by us and by the people of our country towards them." He spoke of "hope for a new era in human history, an era of peace," and (referring to an earlier comment in St. George's Hall in the Kremlin about St. George, the dragon slayer) he said, "I would like to think that our efforts during these past few days have slayed a few dragons and advanced the struggle against the evils that threaten mankind—threats to peace and to liberty."[38] In one sense that may have been true, not least in his own remark disavowing the characterization of the current Soviet Union as the Evil Empire. And not least for the change in Reagan's own frame of reference. In his memoir the former president looked back on this occasion and revealed his own outlook when he said, "I knew the world was changing when we stood with the Gorbachevs in our box [at the Bolshoi Theater], with the Soviet flag on one side and ours on the other, and 'The Star-Spangled Banner' was played."[39]

Gorbachev did not, however, reciprocate by calling Reagan his friend, or refer to success in dragon slaying or in greeting a new era in human history. He was respectful and cordial, but his image of their accomplishments was somewhat different. He began by thanking President Reagan and his colleagues for their "cooperation, frankness and businesslike approach to the talks." After saying "we've come a long way," he went on to say, "Our dialogue has not been easy, but we have mustered enough realism and political will to overcome obstacles and switch the train of Soviet-U.S. relations from a dangerous track to a safer one." And he went on to add, "It has, however, so far been moving much more slowly than is called for by the real situation in both our countries and the world. . . . For our part, I can assure you we will do everything in our power to continue moving forward."[40]

And so the Moscow summit ended. On the way home Reagan gave a major speech at Guildhall in London, one strikingly different from the challenging speech in Helsinki on his way to Moscow (and, even more so, from his last speech in London in 1982 stridently calling for a new crusade against communism). This time Reagan spoke of Gorbachev as "a serious man, seeking

---

37. "The Visit of the President of the United States Is Concluded, Statement of M. S. Gorbachev," *Pravda*, June 3, 1988; and "Remarks at the Closing Ceremony for the Soviet-United States Summit in Moscow," June 2, 1988, *Presidential Documents*, vol. 24 (June 6, 1988), p. 733.

38. *Presidential Documents*, vol. 24 (June 6, 1988), p. 734.

39. Ronald Reagan, *An American Life* (Simon and Schuster, 1990), p. 711.

40. *Pravda*, June 3, 1988; and *Presidential Documents*, vol. 24 (June 6, 1988), p. 733.

serious reform," and of *glasnost* and *perestroika*, his latest Russian words. And he again came back to the images of the drama in which he had just played. "Imagine the President of the United States and the General Secretary of the Soviet Union walking together in Red Square, talking about a growing personal friendship, and meeting together average citizens, realizing how much our people have in common. It was a special moment in a week of special moments." Reagan also remarked, with cautious optimism (and with credit to Western policies), that "quite possibly, we're beginning to take down the barriers of the postwar era; quite possibly, we are entering a new era in history, a time of lasting change in the Soviet Union. We will have to see."[41]

## Gorbachev's New Foreign Policy Initiative

After his Moscow summit meeting with President Reagan, Gorbachev was confirmed in his conclusion that no new substantial move forward in relations with the West could be expected in the next year or more without some important new Soviet initiative. Relations were developing not badly, but he sought much more than mere continuation of an undeclared détente. Gorbachev sought a radical transformation of the relationship between the Soviet Union and the world outside as well as a radical transformation of the Soviet Union itself. Moreover, the two were inextricably connected.

Gorbachev most urgently faced the need to get a more firm grasp on the leadership within the country and to activate political democratization and economic reform, that is, to translate *perestroika* from a slogan into a real program with real results. He also sought to restructure relationships with the socialist countries in Eastern Europe, to dismantle the seemingly established but brittle edifice of the "socialist commonwealth," the Warsaw Pact and the Council on Mutual Economic Assistance (CMEA), and to create a more viable structure based on the real consent and real interests of those nations rather than on the artificial unity imposed by the Soviet Union and the discipline of a potential Soviet use of force. And finally, he sought to dismantle the division of Europe into two counterposed military alliances based on mutual deterrent military power to meet perceived reciprocal threats.[42]

---

41. "Remarks to Members of the Royal Institute of International Affairs in London, United Kingdom," June 3, 1988, *Presidential Documents*, vol. 24 (June 6, 1988), pp. 737, 735.
     Vice President Bush, not present in Moscow, was much less impressed, and a few weeks later publicly warned that "the Cold War is not over." See David Hoffman, "Bush Doubts Soviets Have Changed, Vice President Disagrees with Reagan's Assessment at Summit," *Washington Post*, June 8, 1988, p. A9; and David S. Broder, "Cold War 'Not Over' Bush Warns," *Washington Post*, June 30, 1988, p. A14.

42. See the discussion in chapter 13.

By mid-1988 it was clear that the mere enunciation of a goal of *perestroika* would not bring about the necessary changes in the beliefs and perceptions of other parties—necessary partners—to accomplish any of these three great transformations: at home, in Eastern Europe, or with the United States and Western Europe. The key would have to be a bold unilateral move by Moscow, sufficient to jar people into action and to launch changes that would then be picked up and carried on through new policies at home, as well as changes both in and with the countries of Eastern Europe and in negotiations with the West. A major unilateral Soviet reduction of conventional arms, especially those in central Europe, would begin the process of shifting internal Soviet priorities away from a militarized economy, would demonstrate that relations with Eastern Europe would be based on cooperation rather than compulsion, and by shaking Western assumptions about a potential Soviet military threat to the West and promising serious negotiations, could carry the process of demilitarizing the East-West relationship much further.

Gorbachev's complaint at the end of the Moscow summit that "more could have been achieved," as noted, specifically included disappointment that "it did not prove possible to reach agreement on the subject of talks on conventional weapons in Europe." Shevardnadze had tried to engage Shultz on this subject at Geneva in May, and Gorbachev had tried again at the summit, but to no avail. The problem was not that the United States opposed progress in this area, but that there were residual doubts and suspicions about what the Soviet leaders had in mind and also there had not yet been any high-level review and decision in the NATO alliance. So Reagan and Shultz had not been prepared to go beyond agreeing that the multilateral talks routinely under way should be carried forward. Gorbachev had disclosed in his June 2 statement of regret what he had tried to do: "The Americans did not accept our bold and entirely realistic plan consisting of three stages and integral parts directed at eliminating asymmetric and imbalance in Europe and a decisive transition toward the creation on the continent of a situation of nonoffensive structure of arms and armed forces at a considerably reduced level. I believe that a good opportunity has been missed to get things moving, lessening the danger of confrontation between the two most powerful alliances and thus enhancing international security."[43]

Gorbachev had earlier requested the Ministry of Defense and General Staff to study reductions and ways of implementing the new defensive doctrine adopted in 1987 and had encouraged outside academic institutes to explore the subject. In July, after the summit failure to engage the issue and after the party conference, Gorbachev directed the General Staff to draw up concrete plans for unilateral reductions ranging from several hundred thousand to a million

---

43. *Pravda*, June 2, 1988.

men, as well as for even greater subsequent reductions of forces and arms on a reciprocal negotiated basis.[44]

Before doing that, however, Gorbachev had to deal at the Nineteenth Party Conference with broader and more basic internal political reform.[45] As Gorbachev declared in his opening speech to the conference, "the reform of our political system" was the key issue.[46] Gorbachev had several objectives, most of which were not favored by the conservative majority of delegates, and it took considerable skill and some compromise to attain most of them. Because he was losing most battles in delegate selection in April and May, Gorbachev had made two principal concessions to get necessary support for his main reform measures. One was not to use the conference to change personnel, as he had originally planned to do.[47] The other was to agree that local party chiefs should also become chairmen of the corresponding local governments, as the price of the reform that shifted responsibility for most local rule from the party bureaucracy to elected local government councils (*soviets*). Many of the liberal reformers were very upset at this move, and in a step unprecedented since the 1920s, 209 (out of 4,991) delegates demonstratively voted against that measure.

Gorbachev nonetheless won a significant victory at the conference. He was able to weaken both the party bureaucracy *and* the government bureaucracy, and to place at least some popular control over the strengthened local

---

44. This statement is based on accounts of several senior Soviet officials, and partly confirmed by Marshal Sergei Akhromeyev in several articles in which he stated that the General Staff had been involved "from the start," in "the summer of 1988" and was based on a careful assessment of the military-political situation. See in particular two interviews: interview with Akhromeyev by Ezio Mauro, in *La Repubblica*, Rome, March 11, 1989, p. 11, and "Adviser to the Chairman of the Supreme Soviet of the USSR," interview with Marshal S. F. Akhromeyev by special correspondent Lieutenant Colonel N. Belan, *Krasnaya zvezda*, July 2, 1989.

45. When I saw Dobrynin at the Central Committee offices in early May, he emphasized that the upcoming party conference was far more important to future Soviet policy, by implication external as well as internal, than the forthcoming summit meeting with President Reagan. This was indeed the case; Gorbachev could not let his pursuit of new thinking in foreign affairs get too far out of line with both his power position and the line of internal policy.

46. "In the Course of Realization of the Decisions of the 27th Congress of the CPSU and the Tasks of Deepening Restructuring, Report of General Secretary of the CC CPSU M. S. Gorbachev at the 19th All-Union Conference of the CPSU, June 28, 1988," *Pravda*, June 29, 1988.

47. Gorbachev would not, in any case, have been able to purge all his conservative colleagues or even opponents. He had wanted to shift the blame by removing dead wood and those party machine men who were vulnerable. He almost certainly could not, however, have challenged Ligachev directly—Ligachev later told me that he would have been able to defeat any such direct challenge at the conference, and I believe that is correct. So, apparently, did Gorbachev, who trod much more carefully, keeping his eye on the possibilities for moving forward without a direct challenge to the party.

party chiefs, who now had to be popularly elected as local *soviet* chairmen. One reason for his agreement to this compromise was that he was planning precisely such a move himself, to become chairman of the Supreme Soviet of the USSR (president of the USSR), with increased powers for the post, while remaining general secretary of the Communist Party. And though the incumbent local, regional, and republic party chiefs' power would be enhanced, this move would weaken their opposition to the shift of power from the party machine to the elected *soviets*, at all levels. Local and regional party departments dealing with the economy would be abolished.

In addition to secret ballots and multiple candidacies for the governmental *soviets* at all levels (and a new Congress of People's Deputies on top of the Supreme Soviet) even party elections could now have contested elections and party leaders at all levels would have a limit of two five-year terms.

Broader political objectives were foreshadowed, including the creation of a "socialist state based on law," as well as democratic elections. All in all, Gorbachev did succeed in advancing political reform. In a Central Committee plenum held immediately after the conference, it was announced that party elections at local and regional levels would begin soon, and reorganization and reduction of the party apparatus would occur in the last months of that year. Also the elections of the new Congress of People's Deputies would be held in March 1989, and at its first session in May a new Supreme Soviet would be elected. Reforms to establish judicial independence would also be undertaken.

Perhaps most important, the publicity given to open debates (including again Ligachev and Yeltsin), as well as the measures approved, began to show the emergence of a new political culture. This action also again showed Gorbachev to be a master of political maneuver, identifying himself with the political center while advancing a radical reform.

The party conference dealt only briefly with international and security affairs, mainly in Gorbachev's own report. Gorbachev and especially Shevardnadze later, however, used what had seemed to be routine pronouncements by the conference approving the foreign policy lines to further enlarge the new thinking on external relations.

On July 25–28 the Ministry of Foreign Affairs held a "scientific-practical" conference on Foreign Policy and Diplomacy that greatly advanced the "new thinking" on international relations. It was the most important such occasion since a conference held in May 1986 soon after the Twenty-seventh Party Congress that was addressed by Gorbachev himself. But that one had been a closed conference within the ministry. This conference included wide participation by officials and academic figures as well as Foreign Ministry officials, and its proceedings were subsequently published. It was an offensive for *perestroika* and new thinking on relations with the outside world.

Shevardnadze greatly expanded on many of the themes Gorbachev had advanced at the Nineteenth Party Conference (most of which were little discussed at the conference and only cursorily noted in the resolutions adopted at its conclusion). He and several of his deputies, in speeches and in reports on the results of the congress, elaborated on the new conception of security and reliance primarily on political means of ensuring security; on freedom of choice (self-determination) of peoples; on the priority of general human interests over class interests; and on the need to base foreign relations on mutual advantage and to reconcile the national interests of states through a "balance of interests." One theme in particular was to become a focus for controversy in the leadership: the strong rejection of the long-held Soviet view that "peaceful coexistence" was a form of class struggle. Shevardnadze noted that this view had helped undercut the détente of the 1970s and that "in general equating interstate relations with class struggle is hard to combine with recognition of the real possibility and inevitability of peaceful coexistence as a supreme universal principle."[48] Without noting it, he undoubtedly had in mind the recent American refusal to include such a point in the summit communiqué because of the tainted past Soviet use of peaceful coexistence as a "form of the class struggle."

Shevardnadze's speech to the ministry conference, and those of his associates, made clear a more active role for the Ministry of Foreign Affairs in Soviet security and defense matters. No doubt having in mind problems that had arisen over negotiation of and even compliance with arms control agreements, he asserted, "Major innovations in the field of defense programming must pass by the Ministry of Foreign Affairs for verification that they correspond juridically with existing international agreements and declared political positions."[49]

Shevardnadze also raised a matter that, he correctly noted, "very rarely enters the field of vision of researchers," namely, "the image of a state as an important aspect of its existence in the international community, in the modern civilized world." He went on to speak even more bluntly about "the reputation of a country as a not unimportant element of foreign policy, as a component of state interests and national security."[50]

The ministry conference was a remarkable event in bringing the political leadership and Foreign Ministry into the area of *glasnost* on history and current policy and in making clear that such matters were no longer the

---

48. "The Scientific-Practical Conference of the Ministry of Foreign Affairs of the USSR on 'The 19th All-Union Conference of the CPSU: Foreign Policy and Diplomacy,'" *Vestnik MID*, no. 15 (August 15, 1988), pp. 32–34. The proceedings of the conference are also available in *Mezhdunarodnaya zhizn'*, no. 9 (September 1988), and its English-language version *International Affairs*, no. 10 (October 1988); above quotations from Shevardnadze in *International Affairs*, no. 10 (October 1988), pp. 13–15.

49. *Vestnik MID*, no. 15 (August 15, 1988), p. 36; and *International Affairs*, no. 10 (October 1988), p. 19.

50. *Vestnik MID*, no. 15 (August 15, 1988), p. 39; and *International Affairs*, no. 10 (October 1988), p. 23.

preserve of the Communist Party.[51] There was, as might have been expected, a reaction.

On August 5, while Gorbachev was absent from Moscow on his annual vacation in the Crimea, Yegor Ligachev took the occasion of a speech to a regional party group in Gorky (Nizhnii Novgorod) to challenge Shevardnadze (and implicitly Gorbachev) on the new course in foreign policy. He chose to mount a challenge for the first time in the foreign affairs field by reaffirming the traditional view that Soviet foreign policy is based on "the class nature of international relations," warning that "any other way of putting the matter only introduces confusion into the thinking of the Soviet people and our friends abroad." He also specifically endorsed support for "the national liberation struggle," while saying nothing about relations with the United States or the West.[52]

Ligachev was promptly rebutted by Aleksandr Yakovlev, who reaffirmed that "the thesis on the priority of common human values is valid precisely because it reflects an objective trend" in world development, above all in the necessity for coexistence in the nuclear age.[53] And on the anniversary of the Bolshevik Revolution, when Politburo member Nikolai Slyunkov delivered the leadership's annual address he gave an authoritative (if revisionist) ideological cachet to the new thinking by describing "the priority of common human values" as a "Leninist thought."[54]

Ligachev's opposition was sharply curtailed after a Central Committee plenum on September 30, when he was "put out to pasture," so to speak, shunted to the side as party secretary responsible for agriculture. At the same time Politburo members Andrei Gromyko and Mikhail Solomentsev were relieved, and Viktor Chebrikov was replaced as KGB chairman by a professional intelligence officer, Vladimir Kryuchkov. Thus the very group of Politburo members and candidate members to whom Gorbachev had owed his rise to power in 1985 (Gromyko, Chebrikov, Solomentsev, Ligachev) were now retired or removed from key positions in 1988, having become the new conservative wing.

At the same time the central party apparatus was shaken up by a drastic cut in the number of departments of the Central Committee Secretariat and by the creation of six "commissions" to oversee functional areas. Yakovlev was

---

51. In subsequent conversations, several academic participants in the conference referred to it in ways that made clear they were pleased to have been consulted and encouraged by the support for realistic scholarship on past and current history.

52. "For Deeds—Without Wavering," *Pravda*, August 6, 1988.

53. "In the Interests of the Country and Every People," *Pravda*, August 13, 1988 (reporting Yakovlev's speech in Vilnius on August 12).

54. "Deploy the Creative Forces of Socialism, Speech of N. N. Slyunkov at the Ceremonial Meeting Dedicated to the 71st Anniversary of the Great October Socialist Revolution in the Kremlin Palace of Congresses, November 5, 1988," *Pravda*, November 6, 1988.

named head of the commission on international affairs, and Ligachev and Chebrikov were shifted to nominal positions overseeing agriculture and legal affairs. The liberal party secretary Vadim Medvedev was raised to full Politburo membership and placed in charge of ideology in place of Ligachev, and Gorbachev's close associate Georgy Razumovsky took charge of personnel appointments.[55] The party *apparat* staff was drastically cut.

Some of the "new men" raised into the leadership in 1988 and presumed to be more malleable later turned into leaders of the abortive coup in 1991: Boris Pugo, named chairman of the party's Control Commission in place of Solomentsev; Vladimir Kryuchkov, who succeeded Chebrikov as head of the KGB; and Anatoly Lukyanov, raised to Politburo candidacy.

This major reshuffle of the party leadership and reorganization of the central party apparatus was all achieved in the plenary meeting on September 30 in less than an hour, with no debate. Gorbachev had publicly signaled the need to get *perestroika* moving in a speech on September 25, and he had worked out the changes in two Politburo meetings on September 26 and 27 (incidentally, in Ligachev's absence).

The formalities of changes in governmental posts were handled in a Supreme Soviet meeting called on short notice on October 1, notably the election of Gorbachev to be president (chairman of the presidium of the Supreme Soviet), succeeding Gromyko. Later the electoral and constitutional reforms, including new election procedures, creation of a Congress of People's Deputies, and enhanced authority for the president (as chairman of the Supreme Soviet rather than merely of its presidium), were all formally proposed and pushed through the Supreme Soviet on December 1.

Although there was some restiveness over the democratic reforms from conservative party leaders, both they and Gorbachev held to the compromise agreed on at the Nineteenth Party Conference. On various specific issues, some changes and compromises were made as a result of the debates and deliberations in October and November. The most controversial one to emerge, evidently not fully anticipated, concerned the relative power of the union and the republics—to become the key issue over the next three years. The main objections came from the party and government leaders of the Baltic republics, reflecting a growing popular pressure for greater independence. Though not fully resolved, these differences were partly compromised and partly deferred to later constitutional reform. Leaders and representatives of most republics (except Georgia and Armenia) strongly opposed the efforts of the Baltic representatives. As members of the conservative party machine they

---

55. At the level of candidate membership in the Politburo two Brezhnev-era holdovers were retired, Vladimir Dolgikh and Petr Demichev. They were replaced by Anatoly Lukyanov, Aleksandr Vlasov, and Aleksandra Biryukova. Anatoly Dobrynin was dropped as a party secretary and chief of the International Department, replaced by Valentin Falin. A month later, Dobrynin was named a foreign affairs adviser to Gorbachev.

understood the potential for disruptive nationalist movements in their own republics if the floodgates were opened. But for the time being the issue was papered over and deferred.

With the political reform partly implemented and on track, Gorbachev was able to turn to his planned major international initiative.

Gorbachev evidently decided after his successful Central Committee purge on September 30 that he would address the UN General Assembly as the best forum for his double-barreled global initiative.[56] He could, incidentally, now do so as president of the USSR, rather than as party leader. It was the first time that a Soviet leader had spoken to the UN since Nikita Khrushchev's crude harangue in 1960, on which occasion Khrushchev had taken off a shoe and pounded the table with it. There could have been no greater contrast.

Gorbachev's address reiterated many of the themes he had first systematically outlined to the party congress nearly three years earlier, but now he was addressing a world audience that could see accumulating evidence that Soviet policy was reflecting these new assessments and conceptions.[57] He reiterated the need for a new structure of international relations, and a new concept of security, in an interdependent world. He cited as an example of constructive political dialogue the change in Soviet-U.S. relations: "Look how our relations have changed." He noted the need for "deideologization" of interstate relations and spoke meaningfully of "the compelling necessity of the principle of freedom of choice"—"a universal principle to which there should be no exceptions." The full import of that strong affirmation would become clear a year later in Eastern Europe.[58] He also reaffirmed the need for settling international differences through "a balance of interests" and avoidance of violence.

Appropriate not only to the forum but also to the new thinking on international relations, Gorbachev stressed a rising role for the UN organiza-

---

56. At the time of Foreign Minister Shevardnadze's address to the UN General Assembly on September 27, or his talks with Shultz and Reagan on September 22–23 and a letter delivered then from Gorbachev to Reagan (all to be discussed later), there was no indication that Gorbachev would later come to New York. His intention to do so was first conveyed privately to the United States on November 13, five days after the U.S. national elections. Gorbachev may have had the idea earlier, but it seems to have been firmly decided upon only after the September 30 plenum.

57. For the speech and all quotations cited see "M. S. Gorbachev's Speech at the UN Organization," December 7, 1988, *Pravda*, December 8, 1988.

58. Gorbachev's UN speech also showed his failure to understand the relevance or consequences of freedom of choice in the *internal* Soviet political scene. In a different part of his speech, where he was describing the democratization of elections, he mentioned the task of working out the "interrelation between the central government and the republics, settling relations between nationalities on the principles of Leninist internationalism." This was not only a discordant and rare injunction of an ideological precept, but evidence of Gorbachev's failure to understand the depth of national feelings, especially in the republics.

tion. He declared a need for enhancing "the obligatory nature of international law for all states," resting "not on coercion, but on norms reflecting a balance of interests of states." He noted efforts under way in the USSR to "construct a socialist state based on the rule of law." And he proposed that the jurisdiction of the court in the human rights field be made obligatory for all states.[59] Gorbachev also stated that in accordance with "the Helsinki [CSCE] process," the Soviet Union was "examining an end to jamming of all foreign radio broadcasts to the Soviet Union."[60]

Even though Gorbachev's speech was a strong one, its important general message on Soviet policy outlook and approach did not receive the attention it should have had.[61] The impact was diminished by the heavy world attention given to the second, more tangible, element of his speech: announcement of a unilateral reduction of the Soviet armed forces by 500,000 men over the next two years, with particular attention to withdrawals and reductions of major forces and arms from Eastern Europe. The real significance of the half-million-men force reduction was not immediately evident because the overall force level was not given and the numerical personnel cut might have been made in ways not directly reducing the potential facing Europe. But Gorbachev's specific inclusion of the withdrawal and disbanding of six tank divisions from central Europe, including 50,000 men and 5,000 tanks, was militarily significant. In fact, it was a unilateral cut of about the size that Senator Sam Nunn and some others in the United States had indicated would be a worthwhile reduction to seek in negotiated bilateral reductions. In addition, Gorbachev noted that in all the Soviet forces in Europe would be cut by 10,000 tanks, 8,500 artillery pieces, and 800 combat aircraft. Reductions would also be made in Asia, he noted, including large withdrawals from Mongolia—long a sore point with the Chinese.

It would take some time for the West to see that these promised reductions were made and were indeed a stimulus for serious negotiations on

59. The Soviet Union had, the year before, proposed that the permanent members of the Security Council strengthen the International Court of Justice. The United States, in 1986, had by contrast withdrawn earlier acceptance of the Court's jurisdiction for certain categories and rejected its jurisdiction in the Nicaraguan case. In September 1988, the United States proposed to the Soviet Union that both countries accept jurisdiction for treaty interpretation in certain categories of international treaties accepted by both states. Gorbachev was now proposing greater widening of the role of the International Court.

60. In fact, jamming of the main radios still interdicted—Radio Liberty, Deutsche Welle, and Kol Israel—had ceased by December 1.

61. Secretary Shultz, however, at least in his later memoir, did note the importance of what he referred to as "the philosophical part" of Gorbachev's speech; see Shultz, *Turmoil and Triumph*, p. 1106.

still deeper reductions. But even at the time there was a general recognition that the Soviet Union was now talking with "deeds, not words" and was serious.

The Gorbachev initiative was far more sweeping than anyone in the West then appreciated. He was moving not only to reduce arms but to reduce the role of military power, not only to remove a perceived Soviet threat in Western eyes but to restructure Soviet relations with the countries of Eastern Europe, and not only to reduce military confrontation in Europe but to break down the political division of Europe. Indeed, not even all other members of the Soviet leadership were supportive of Gorbachev's new foreign policy. Ligachev later complained that Gorbachev's UN speech had not been "cleared" or even discussed in the Politburo. Nonetheless on December 28, the Politburo publicly pronounced its blessing on his UN speech.[62]

The Soviet military leadership had also accepted the force reduction and parallel decisions to agree in the forthcoming conventional arms negotiations to deep cuts greater on the Soviet and Warsaw Pact side. Marshal Sergei Akhromeyev's retirement as chief of the General Staff, which became known when Gorbachev was in New York, was widely but mistakenly taken as a sign of dissatisfaction with the reductions.[63] But the military had not fought the issue and had even agreed to cut 600,000 men.[64]

---

62. The record of the Politburo meeting is now available. See TsKhSD, Fond 89, Perechen' 42, Dokument 24, *Zasedaniye Politburo TsK KPSS 27–28 dekabrya 1988 goda* (Meeting of the Politburo of the CC CPSU, December 27–28, 1988), Top Secret, only copy (working transcript), archive, pp. 322–54 (on UN speech). Gorbachev and close colleagues were very satisfied; even Ligachev was cautiously supportive (pp. 347–49).

    Ligachev regarded this speech as a turning point in Gorbachev's shift from a prudent to a radical stance, and his objection was precisely on Gorbachev's conceptual turn away from communist orthodoxy to new thinking on foreign policy based on interdependence, freedom of choice, and balance of national interests. (From a personal conversation with the author on November 14, 1991.)

63. Akhromeyev's retirement resulted from his own desire. Gorbachev agreed but asked him to stay on until after the cut was announced. News of the retirement was "leaked" by a Soviet correspondent in the spirit of *glasnost'* after Akhromeyev mentioned it at a closed meeting with Soviet correspondents in the United States. The official notification of Akhromeyev's retirement appeared in *Krasnaya zvezda*, December 15, 1988.

64. See *Zasedaniye Politbyuro*, p. 342. There had been veiled debates, with some military leaders opposing unilateral reductions and some civilian institute experts advocating them. But the military leadership was resigned to the need for asymmetrical reductions, and in that context initiating the process with some substantial unilateral reduction made sense. For a good example of advocacy see Andrei Kozyrev (then a midlevel official in the Soviet Foreign Ministry, later the Russian foreign minister), "Confidence and the Balance of Interests," *Mezhdunarodnaya zhizn'*, no. 10 (October 1988), p. 10. For an early indication that reductions would be made, missed by most Western analysts, see General of the Army D. T. Yazov, "Qualitative Parameters of Defense Programming," *Voyennaya mysl'* (Military Thought), no. 9 (September 1988), p. 7, in which the defense minister listed "carrying out any reductions of

Gorbachev's UN speech and initiative on European arms reduction was intended to shape the agenda for the next year. Gorbachev also sought to use the occasion of his visit to New York to celebrate the relationship with President Reagan as the latter left the scene, and to boost a new relationship with President-elect Bush, about which he had some concern.

## The Fifth Summit: End of the Reagan-Gorbachev Era

On the same day that Gorbachev addressed the UN General Assembly he met with President Reagan and President-elect Bush. But before discussing this final brief meeting of the presidents, it is appropriate to review the course of U.S.-Soviet relations in the half year between the Moscow and New York meetings. Developments in relations were basically uneventful, and that is perhaps the most important thing to note. Negotiations on strategic arms reduction continued, but without either expectation or achievement of major advance. Negotiations also continued toward a ban on chemical weapons. Similarly, political consultations on various bilateral and regional issues continued. In mid-July Ambassador Jack Matlock conveyed a letter from Shultz to Shevardnadze and discussed with the latter the regional conflicts in the Iran-Iraq war and in Kampuchea. From August 31 to September 2 high-level expert talks were held in Moscow on a range of regional conflicts, with Undersecretary of State Michael Armacost meeting an array of deputy foreign ministers—Yuly Vorontsov, Anatoly Adamishin, Aleksandr Bessmertnykh, Viktor Komplektov, and Igor Rogachev. In mid-October Assistant Secretary Elliot Abrams met with Soviet Latin American affairs expert Yury Pavlov on Central America. In mid-November U.S.-Soviet consultations preceded the opening of four-power talks on Angola and Southwest Africa. In late November East Asian matters, especially Kampuchea (Cambodia), were again discussed at the level of Assistant Secretary Gaston Sigur and Deputy Foreign Minister Igor Rogachev.

Bilateral talks on other subjects also continued. Charles Wick, director of the U.S. Information Agency, met in Moscow with Aleksandr Yakovlev in September on exchange programs, and Shevardnadze received State Department policy planning chief Richard Solomon in early November. Successful talks among experts on cooperation in space exploration were also held in November.

The main new avenue of bilateral consultation was a series of meetings of top military leaders. Marshal Akhromeyev visited the United States as a guest of Admiral William Crowe, chairman of the Joint Chiefs of Staff, on July 6–11.

troops and arms" among the tasks related to fulfilling the instructions of the Nineteenth Party Conference.

A few weeks later, on August 1–4, Secretary of Defense Frank Carlucci visited General Yazov in Moscow. (During the latter visit Gorbachev also received Carlucci and urged that more be done on conventional arms reductions.) Both sides seemed well satisfied with these visits and consultations and agreed on a wider range of continuing contacts between their defense establishments. One Soviet radio commentator remarked during Carlucci's visit to Moscow: "There's been a painful process under way here of a reassessment of social values, overseas commitments, and domestic and foreign policy priorities. Our military are no exception. . . . the United States is dealing now with a different Soviet Union. In turn, we're dealing with a different America: less abusive, recalcitrant, and unyielding. Or so it seems."[65]

The only high-level contact during this period came when Gorbachev dispatched Shevardnadze to Washington in September to reinforce the dialogue for the transition to the next administration. Shevardnadze met with President Reagan, Vice President Bush, and Secretary Shultz. As Shevardnadze acknowledged in a press conference after he had met with Vice President Bush, "The meeting had been dominated by exchanges of opinion on how 'to preserve the level achieved in Soviet-American relations and secure their continued stability'."[66] In a letter that Gorbachev gave Shevardnadze to deliver to Reagan, he reviewed the bases for the improvement in relations since 1985 as "realism, a clearer awareness of the essence of our differences, and a focus on active search for possible areas where our national interests may coincide. Thus, we gave ourselves a serious intellectual challenge—to view our differences and diversities not as a reason for permanent confrontation but as a motivation for intensive dialogue, mutual appreciation and enrichment." And he concluded that "overall, we have been able to achieve fairly good results, to start a transition from confrontation to a policy of [mutual] accommodation." And he observed that "the main thing that made our common new policy a success is, above all, the fact that it reflects a gradually emerging balance of national interests."[67]

Not all developments were smooth or favorable. When on July 3 the cruiser USS *Vincennes*, fearing an Iranian attack, shot down an Iranian civil airliner over the Strait of Hormuz, killing all 290 passengers and crew, the Soviet press joined in the clamor of sharp criticism from many quarters. In contrast to the American reaction to the shootdown of a Korean airliner five years earlier, however, the Soviet official reaction was restrained.[68]

---

65. Pavel Kuznetsov, "Outlook," Radio Moscow, August 2, 1988, in FBIS, *Soviet Union*, August 3, 1988, p. 13.

66. TASS, Radio Moscow, September 23, 1988, in FBIS, *Soviet Union*, September 26, 1988, p. 15.

67. This letter was first disclosed and is printed in full in Reagan, *An American Life*, p. 717.

68. When queried on this relative restraint, Soviet spokesman Gennady Gerasimov commented that "the wild anti-Soviet howl raised by the U.S. Government and mass media

Past and current arms control verification and compliance issues also created problems. Even before the June summit, a dispute over verification procedures had delayed U.S. Senate consent to ratification of the INF Treaty. Later, new problems arose. On July 17 U.S. representatives were caught trying to sneak out nuclear rock samples and tools from a Soviet nuclear testing range.[69] In apparent retaliation, five days later the United States banned eight Soviet designated inspectors (who probably were intelligence officers). On August 11 the Soviets again officially protested the new U.S. large phased-array radars built at Thule, Greenland, and Fylingdales Moor, England, as violations of the ABM Treaty—clearly in response to renewed U.S. charges that the Krasnoyarsk radar was a violation. This issue was also the subject of confidential exchanges, even including an exchange of letters between Gorbachev and Reagan.[70]

On September 16, in a speech at Krasnoyarsk, Gorbachev offered the contentious radar there for international space research, an offer not accepted but broadened and reiterated in Gorbachev's December 7 UN address. Meanwhile, on October 27 the Soviet Union, while disputing U.S. charges of violation, agreed to destroy two other small radars located at Gomel and Moscow, again urging the United States to end the violations at Thule and Fylingdales Moor. President Reagan's response, inserted into a speech the next day, was to harp again on the Krasnoyarsk radar.[71] On December 2 the president submitted to Congress his annual report on Soviet "noncompliance" with arms control agreements, emphasizing the Krasnoyarsk radar issue.[72]

---

concerning the South Korean plane was a bad example, and we are not going to follow it." See FBIS, *Soviet Union*, July 5, 1988, p. 16.

There was a remarkable contrast. To be sure, there were substantial differences in the two cases: the U.S. action was taken in a zone of military action closely following some Iranian attacks at sea, so there was a rationale of self-defense for the U.S. ship's action, even if the decision was a serious error. Also, there were no Russian casualties in the 1988 incident in contrast to American casualties in 1983. Not all of the differences, however, were in the American favor: the Korean plane had flown far off course, intruding deeply into Soviet airspace, at night with poor visibility, and had been confused with U.S. military reconnaissance aircraft earlier in its flight, whereas the Iranian plane was on course and on time on its regularly scheduled flight over international waters in a designated air lane in excellent daylight visibility. Both cases were tragic errors.

69. The alleged actions did take place but apparently were the result of overzealousness by the individuals rather than a U.S.-authorized action. See R. Jeffrey Smith, "Soviets Catch U.S. Nuclear Inspectors," *Washington Post*, August 12, 1988, p. A1.

No comparable Soviet violations by inspectors are known to have occurred.

70. These letters have not been released.

71. "Remarks and a Question-and-Answer Session," October 28, 1988, *Presidential Documents*, vol. 24 (November 7, 1988), p. 1397.

72. "Letter to the Speaker of the House and the President of the Senate Transmitting the Report on Soviet Noncompliance with Arms Control Agreements," December 2, 1988, *Presidential Documents*, vol. 24 (December 5, 1988), pp. 1579–80.

In short, the Soviet side took some steps to remove the sources of U.S. concern over alleged arms violations, while attempting unsuccessfully to get some responsive American action. The compliance issues did not stop forward movement in arms control, but they did make it more difficult.[73]

Among the small events that sometimes capture American public attention, more than disputes over arcane details of arms agreements, was the saga, continuing over several days in late October, of two whales captured by the ice off Alaska—and ultimately rescued by Soviet icebreakers.

The meeting on Governor's Island between Presidents Reagan and Gorbachev was recognized to be more a ceremonial or courtesy meeting than one devoted to serious discussion. There was some interest in the fact that Vice President (and President-elect) Bush would also be there, but he was careful to stay in the background as vice president, not wanting either to upstage Reagan or yet to become involved in substantive talks with Gorbachev. He made it a point not to include his own designated secretary of state (James Baker) or national security adviser (Brent Scowcroft) in his own luncheon with Gorbachev. Gorbachev was content to stress continuity as his desire and expectation. Attention to the meeting was eclipsed by commentary on Gorbachev's announcement of the unilateral conventional arms cut.

In his final radio address on relations with the Soviet Union, just two days after Gorbachev's departure, President Reagan discussed his fifth summit meeting in generally upbeat terms. He acknowledged that "this has been a period of important change inside the Soviet Union," and welcomed Gorbachev's "vision" in his UN address. But Reagan still balanced such references with cautions. In approving the "promised" force reductions, he nonetheless noted that even after those "redeployments" were completed, "the Warsaw Pact will still have a large conventional advantage." And, clearly with no expectation of early change, he reaffirmed the "hope to see the day when all countries of Eastern Europe enjoy the freedom, democracy, and self-determination that their people have long awaited."[74]

Gorbachev had to cut short his visit on the day after his meeting with Reagan and return to the Soviet Union, in view of an earthquake disaster in

---

At their meeting on December 7, Gorbachev told Reagan that the Soviet Union would dismantle the Krasnoyarsk radar.

73. The merits of the charges of violation are of course of central relevance but not always clear-cut. The Soviet leaders understood that the Krasnoyarsk radar was a violation of the ABM Treaty provisions on placement of early-warning radars, and they were moving to resolve it. At the same time, they believed that the case against the U.S. radars at Thule and Fylingdales Moor was also valid. See chapter 12 for a fuller discussion.

74. "Radio Address to the Nation on Soviet-United States Relations," December 10, 1988, *Presidential Documents*, vol. 24 (December 19, 1988), pp. 1613–14.

Armenia, striking on the heels of renewed violence between that country and Azerbaijan.

One jarring action showed how far apart the two sides still were in efforts to move from confrontation to cooperation. On the day of Gorbachev's UN address and meeting with Reagan and Bush, the General Assembly voted on a resolution calling for international dialogue "on a comprehensive basis" to strengthen "the system of security laid down in the United Nations Charter." That anodyne resolution was what was left of a Soviet-sponsored call for the UN Secretariat to prepare a comprehensive system of international peace and security, a call supported in resolutions in 1986 and 1987, originally stemming from a Soviet proposal based on Gorbachev's call in his party congress speech for developing a comprehensive system of security. Yet even this anodyne version was *opposed* by two countries: the United States and Israel. Ninety-seven countries voted in favor and forty-five (including the other NATO countries) abstained. Moreover, even though it passed overwhelmingly, the fact that it had been gutted led to jubilation in U.S. and some other Western quarters. In the words of the *New York Times* report, "Western diplomats claimed a victory over the Soviet Union here today, saying they had stripped a major Soviet initiative of practical significance after a three-year struggle."[75]

New thinking still had a way to go in American policy.

In the final weeks of the Reagan administration, several closing developments were somewhat more encouraging.

On December 22 agreements were reached among Angola, Cuba, and South Africa (with the United States and the Soviet Union in the wings) for elections in Namibia, South African withdrawal from there and Angola, and Cuban military withdrawal from Angola. Secretary Shultz used the occasion to emphasize the importance of U.S.-Soviet cooperation.

In early January 1989 the thirtieth and final meeting of Shultz and Shevardnadze took place, when they attended a conference in Paris on banning chemical weapons. On January 17 Shultz in Vienna signed the CSCE Vienna Declaration, winding up that phase of CSCE meetings, and agreed that Moscow could be the site of a human rights conference in 1991. On that happy note, the Reagan-Gorbachev era in U.S.-Soviet relations came to an end.

---

75. Paul Lewis, "Diplomatic Gains Claimed by West," *New York Times*, December 9, 1988, p. A20.

# III THE END OF THE COLD WAR

# 9    The Bush Administration and Gorbachev, 1989

THREE DAYS AFTER his inauguration, on January 23, 1989, President George H. W. Bush called Soviet President Mikhail Gorbachev on the telephone, to thank him for a routine message of congratulation and to reassure him that the new administration would continue to seek to broaden cooperation and deepen understanding.[1] Gorbachev may not have needed the reassurance then as much as he did several months later, not because of any adverse turn in American policy but because of a rather long period of restraint from any new steps toward developing relations. Bush was not opposed to having better relations. But he and some of his closest advisers (including especially National Security Adviser Brent Scowcroft and his deputy Robert Gates) believed that President Ronald Reagan, if initially too bellicose, had become overly enthusiastic about his new relationship with Gorbachev in the last year or so of his

---

1.  President Bush may have been unaware of the fact, but he was making the first direct telephone call ever between an American president and a Soviet leader; all previous communications had been "buffered" by transmissions requiring (and permitting) time for deliberation (beyond that provided by translation). The idea for a telephonic rather than telegraphic connection for the "Hot Line" had been considered and rejected. Bush apparently on this occasion did not consider it necessary to recall his earlier confidential explanation of a need to appear to be more hard-line, for domestic political reasons, than he really was on the subject of relations with the Soviet Union. First made in December 1987 in Washington (see chapter 7), Bush had explicitly recalled and reaffirmed that explanation in an oral message through Shultz and Shevardnadze in September 1988 during the election campaign. Now, as president, he had less of an excuse—but also was in fact wary of too close and forthcoming a relationship. On the 1987 and 1988 explanations see Michael R. Beschloss and Strobe Talbott, *At the Highest Levels: The Inside Story of the End of the Cold War* (Little, Brown and Company, 1993), pp. 3–4, 9, 18.

administration.[2] They preferred to cool the ardor and tempo while reevaluating the situation.

George Bush was one of the most experienced recent presidents in the field of foreign affairs, having held a variety of relevant posts—member of Congress, U.S. representative to the United Nations, U.S. chief of mission in China, director of the Central Intelligence Agency, and of course Reagan's vice president for eight years.[3] His choice as secretary of state, James A. Baker III, while not so experienced in foreign affairs, was well grounded in domestic politics and policymaking and had Bush's personal confidence from long years of close association. Both men were conservative but pragmatic, less bound to ideological preconceptions than Reagan and most of his entourage (except George Shultz) had been, but also less inclined to sentimental ventures or, in Bush's betraying phrase, "the vision thing." They were prepared to accept demonstrable opportunities for improving relations with the Soviet Union but were not unduly predisposed to expect or to seek them.

While Bush and his senior advisers initially wanted to go slow on developing relations with the Soviet Union, they did not fail to recognize the importance of the American-Soviet relationship. On February 15, Bush issued National Security Review 3 (NSR)–3, a directive calling for a comprehensive review of U.S. policy toward the Soviet Union, to be completed in one month. He sought something looking well into the future, to the kind of relationship the United States might seek and have by the end of the decade. Many professional veterans from the previous administration, already surprised to learn that the new administration was moving to distinguish itself from its fellow-Republican predecessor, were suspicious that the call for a thorough review might portend a sharp change of policy and undo the progress in improving relations gradually made since 1984. Ambassador Jack Matlock, for one, in late February submitted three long cables from Moscow analyzing the

2.   Even as early as the Reagan-Gorbachev summit in June 1988 Vice President Bush had made known his more cautious assessment of Soviet policy and U.S.-Soviet relations. He publicly expressed the view that "the jury is still out" on Gorbachev's intentions, and said "I don't agree that we know enough to say that there is that kind of fundamental change . . . on the part of the Soviet Union." See David Hoffman, "Bush Doubts Soviets Have Changed, Vice President Disagrees with Reagan's Assessment at Summit," *Washington Post*, June 8, 1988, p. A9.

3.   Notwithstanding this wide-ranging service, Bush had never been closely involved in foreign policymaking; his experience was broad but not deep.
     Bush (Yale, 1948) was, incidentally, the first Ivy League president since John F. Kennedy, Franklin D. Roosevelt, and Woodrow Wilson. Baker (Princeton, 1952) followed George Shultz (Princeton, 1942), and many earlier predecessors including Cyrus Vance (Yale, 1939), Henry Kissinger (Harvard, 1950), and John Foster Dulles (Princeton, 1908). Others involved in U.S.-Soviet relations included George Kennan (Princeton, 1925), Charles Bohlen (Harvard, 1927), Allen Dulles (Princeton, 1914), William Colby (Princeton, 1940), McGeorge Bundy (Yale, 1940), Frank Carlucci (Princeton, 1952), and Zbigniew Brzezinski (Harvard PhD, 1953).

situation in the Soviet Union, Soviet external policy, and his recommendations for U.S. policy. On March 3, in Washington, he had an opportunity to make his case for greater political and economic engagement in order to have greater leverage and influence in a twenty-minute meeting with President Bush. He also urged an early summit meeting. But Bush was, at that time, noncommittal. Bush had, however, also been trying to educate himself, including arranging a seminar in mid-February with half a dozen academic specialists on Soviet affairs. The NSR-3 report, submitted on March 14, was cautious in its analysis and in its recommendations. It did conclude that Gorbachev's *perestroika* was in U.S. interests but mainly because it gave the United States leverage to help move the Soviet Union in directions the United States wanted it to go. Yet the review cautioned that the Soviet leaders still aspired to become a "more competitive superpower" and even found Gorbachev's desire for a "less confrontational" relationship "double-edged" because it could divide the Western alliance. Policy recommendations were neither bold nor specific. Although in many ways the policy review seemed to echo things that Bush, Scowcroft, and Baker had themselves been saying, it did not satisfy them. Scowcroft's staff set about to prepare a less bland policy directive. National Security Directive (NSD)–23 was the result, written in March, although not formally signed until September. It did at least contain one idea, cautiously advanced, that would be adopted: "containment was never an end in itself . . . [a] new era may now be upon us. We may be able to move beyond containment to a new U.S. policy that actively promotes the integration of the Soviet Union into the international system."[4]

On March 27, Secretary Baker, in an unusually frank interview with a correspondent of the *New York Times*, disclosed that Henry Kissinger had suggested negotiating an arrangement with the Soviet Union with respect to Eastern Europe—Soviet agreement to loosen its hold on Eastern Europe and permit greater liberalization, in exchange for Western agreement not to take advantage of such liberalization to the disadvantage of legitimate Soviet security interests. While describing the idea as "worthy of consideration," Baker also indicated it had not been adopted, mainly because Eastern Europe was liberalizing without the United States being party to any arrangement that would tend to normalize a continuing status there for the Soviet Union. The idea of such negotiation drew a storm of protest from Western and Eastern

---

4.   Beschloss and Talbott, *At the Highest Levels*, pp. 24–26, 33–34, 43–45, 69–70, including the quotations from NSR-3 and NSD-23.

There was even less to the theme of "beyond containment" than appeared. A senior White House staff official privately told me at the time that they did not mean that the time for containment had passed, it was still considered essential, only that they could now envisage the prospect for gradually and incrementally moving beyond it. Meanwhile, as Deputy National Security Adviser Robert Gates put it privately, "a pause" in policymaking was a good thing.

Europe and was quickly further disavowed. Kissinger was reported furious at this disclosure and sabotage of his proposal. One purpose of Baker's public disclosure of the idea was, in fact, to puncture speculation that Kissinger might become a power behind the scenes in the new administration's foreign policy.[5]

During the early months of 1989 Gorbachev had launched a process of democratization with free elections in the Soviet Union and pursuit of a "common European home" that by midyear had included summit visits to Britain, France, and Germany. But the first serious American-Soviet discussion between foreign ministers was not held until Secretary of State James A. Baker III went to Moscow on May 10–11.[6] By that time, even former President Reagan had joined many observers (not least in Moscow) restless over when—and even whether—President Bush was going to pick up the ball.[7] The Soviets had long made known their desire to move ahead.

Although Bush and Baker wanted to resume a dialogue with the Soviet leadership, they were not yet prepared to assume the initiative in any bold way. Indeed, they were still seeking to "test" Gorbachev.[8] Baker, therefore, apart from getting to know Shevardnadze, planned to concentrate mainly on pursuing the matter of Soviet aid to Nicaragua, while parrying anticipated Soviet objections to continuing U.S. military assistance to the Afghan insurgents now that Soviet troops had (on February 15, on schedule) completed their peaceful withdrawal from Afghanistan. Gorbachev had, in February, appealed to Bush in a confidential letter to join in sponsoring an international conference to end the warfare in Afghanistan, but Bush had declined. On March 27, Bush had written Gorbachev, just prior to a visit by Gorbachev to see Fidel Castro in Cuba,

---

5.  For further discussion see chapter 13. The article reporting the interview was Thomas L. Friedman, "Baker, Outlining World View, Assesses Plan for Soviet Bloc," *New York Times*, March 28, 1989, pp. A1, A6. For background and the report of Kissinger's reaction see Beschloss and Talbott, *At the Highest Levels*, pp. 14–21, 45–46.

    Kissinger had made the proposal to Bush even before his inauguration and had made clear his readiness to serve as the diplomatic conduit. Bush initially gave Kissinger leeway to take soundings on the possibility, but the administration later decided against the idea.

6.  Baker and Shevardnadze had met briefly March 7 at the CSCE meeting of thirty-five foreign ministers in Vienna, but not to hold serious talks.

7.  See Lou Cannon, "Reagan Is Concerned About Bush's Indecision," *Washington Post*, May 6, 1989, p. A21.

8.  See in particular the informed accounts by Don Oberdorfer, *The Turn: From the Cold War to a New Era, the United States and the Soviet Union, 1983–1990* (Poseidon Press, 1991), pp. 334–45; and Beschloss and Talbott, *At the Highest Levels*, pp. 56–68.

    Not mentioned in these accounts, Baker had prudently proposed (and the Soviet side had accepted) that key aides would meet several days before Baker and Shevardnadze, as well as accompanying them. This led to intense consultations that helped the two principals to understand each other's positions and to focus their discussion. (Information from one of the participants.)

hitting hard at what he saw as an inconsistency between Soviet and Cuban assistance to Nicaragua and Gorbachev's professed desire to cooperate in resolving regional conflicts.[9] On the eve of Baker's departure, Bush received a letter from Gorbachev with the unexpected and welcome word that the Soviet Union had ceased sending arms to Nicaragua at the end of the year.[10] Baker urged the Soviets to press the Sandinistas to hold free and fair elections in Nicaragua, and said that if they did, the United States would accept the outcome, even if it were a Sandinista victory. While not committing the Soviet Union, Gorbachev and Shevardnadze did later persuade the Sandinistas. The result was of course a defeat, and peaceful withdrawal from power, of the Sandinista government.

Baker also raised the subject of relations with the countries of Eastern Europe, reassuring the Soviet leaders that an announced visit in July by President Bush to Poland and Hungary would not be used against the Soviet Union.

Gorbachev, who saw Baker on May 11, talked at length on the progress of *perestroika*. He also emphasized again the importance of moving forward in the new talks on reducing conventional forces in Europe to equal levels for the two alliances, sought also to advance the idea of reductions in tactical nuclear weapons (not on the agreed agenda), and disclosed plans to announce a unilateral withdrawal of 500 Soviet tactical nuclear weapons from Eastern Europe. Baker asked, and was given, permission to disclose some of the details to his colleagues in the North Atlantic Treaty Organization (NATO), whom he was meeting the next day. He did so, and this gave the matter considerable press attention. Gorbachev himself promptly made his proposals public, and Baker felt he had been "set up" and exploited.[11]

In Baker's discussions with Shevardnadze and Gorbachev in May, it was also agreed (after Baker's proposal) that from then on transnational problems, such as global environmental concerns and narcotics trade and other international law enforcement issues should be added to the traditional four-element agenda for U.S.-Soviet high-level discussions: arms control, regional problems, human rights, and bilateral relations.

Shevardnadze also invited Baker to his home for a relaxed dinner, at which they began to develop a warm personal relationship based on mutual respect.

It was only a beginning, but not a bad one.

---

9.   Beschloss and Talbott, *At the Highest Levels*, p. 57.

10.   Oberdorfer, *The Turn*, pp. 338–39; and Beschloss and Talbott, *At the Highest Levels*, p. 59.

11.   Oberdorfer, *The Turn*, pp. 342–5; and Beschloss and Talbott, *At the Highest Levels*, pp. 65–68.
      On the substance of the new Soviet proposals, both accounts note the discussion of tactical nuclear weapons withdrawal, which at the time made the greatest impression on Baker, but not the more significant details on a reduction to equal specified levels of major types of conventional arms for the two alliances.

## Bush Cautiously Moves "Beyond Containment"

On May 12, in a speech at Texas A&M University, Bush finally un- veiled the results of his administration's four-month review of policy toward the Soviet Union. Though unobjectionable in its restatement of long-familiar American objectives, and in retrospect more prescient than even its authors knew ("we are approaching the conclusion of an historic postwar struggle between two visions"), it was still embarrassingly thin on initiatives or even on an agenda for U.S.-Soviet relations. Its most concrete proposal was for "Open Skies," that is, reciprocal aerial reconnaissance overflights, dusting off and reviving a proposal that was more meaningful when first made by President Dwight Eisenhower in 1955. Even that was couched as a challenge to Moscow (to "reveal their commitment to change"), as were his other hortatory calls for unilateral Soviet change—to "tear down the Iron Curtain," to "reduce Soviet forces," to "open emigration, open debate, open airwaves," and to "welcome the Soviet Union back into the world order." Within an astonishingly short span of a few years all of these and more would be done, but not because of any program identified in the speech or pursued in U.S. policy. The most successful new public theme introduced by the speech, and addressed mainly to the United States, was the call to move "beyond containment," the contribution of NSD-23. But the idea remained for the time being only articulation of an aspiration.[12]

Bush soon followed that address with two others on alliance policy and security. At Boston University he was still guarded, emphasizing an "obligation to temper optimism with prudence" and calling for NATO to "remain pre- pared." While welcoming steps Gorbachev was taking to transform the Soviet Union, Bush declared, "It is clear that Soviet 'new thinking' has not yet totally overcome the old."[13] Nor, evidently, had his own new thinking on relations with the Soviet Union totally overcome the old. At the Coast Guard Academy commencement he went further, building on the idea of going beyond contain- ment and explicitly endorsing *perestroika* (restructuring) in the Soviet Union. He affirmed that "our policy is to seize every—and I mean every—opportunity

---

12.  "Remarks at the Texas A&M University Commencement Ceremony," May 12, 1989, *Weekly Compilation of Presidential Documents*, vol. 25 (May 22, 1989), pp. 699–702. (Hereafter *Presidential Documents*.)

  Incidentally, the idea of resurrecting an "Open Skies" proposal was suggested to Bush only shortly before the speech by visiting Canadian Prime Minister Brian Mul- roney. It had not been "staffed," but it appealed to Bush. The first Washington interagency meeting to decide what the initiative meant did not take place until June 28—six weeks after the president's speech!

13.  "Remarks at the Boston University Commencement Ceremony," May 21, 1989, *Presi- dential Documents*, vol. 25 (May 29, 1989), pp. 747–49.

to build a better, more stable relationship with the Soviet Union," although—ever prudent—he balanced that statement with a reaffirmation in the same sentence, "just as it is our policy to defend American interests in light of the enduring reality of Soviet military power."[14]

Even some administration officials had characterized the new policy as "status quo plus," and although that was better than the status quo minus of the first four months, it was manifestly not enough. Bush himself, by now dissatisfied with the anodyne results of his administration's grand review of policy, and aware that Gorbachev planned to pursue new proposals, spurred closely held preparation of an initiative unveiled on May 29 in Brussels to reduce military forces in Europe. Quickly pushed through, it superseded the cautious stand-pat approach based on NATO bureaucratic review that had preceded Gorbachev's December 1988 announcement of significant unilateral conventional force reductions and even more significant proposals for negotiated asymmetrical reductions of Warsaw Pact arms to parity with NATO forces. Bush proposed 15 percent cuts in NATO and Warsaw Pact conventional arms and 20 percent cuts in U.S. and Soviet military personnel in Europe.[15] The initiative, the first of any consequence by the Bush administration, was well received at home, in Western and Eastern Europe, and by the Soviet Union.

Bush visited Poland and Hungary in July, and this trip made him more aware of the historic changes stirring there with Gorbachev's acquiescence and even encouragement.[16] Bush and Baker now understood that the key to political and economic liberalization for the countries of Eastern Europe was in encouraging the process with, rather than against, Moscow, and they realized that Gorbachev himself at least seemed prepared to facilitate change.[17] Even

---

14. "Remarks at the United States Coast Guard Academy Commencement Ceremony," May 24, 1989, ibid., pp. 766–69.

15. "Remarks Announcing a Conventional Arms Control Initiative," May 29, 1989, ibid., vol. 25 (June 5, 1989), pp. 781–86.
    Bush had initially wanted to announce cuts of 25 percent in manpower, but at the urging of the Joint Chiefs of Staff he scaled it back.

16. See chapter 13. President Bush's handling of this trip was much more successful than his first trip as vice president in 1983; see the discussion in chapter 3. A later trip in 1987 had been uneventful.
    NSC senior staff members, who privately acknowledged the thinness of the policy review on the Soviet Union, felt they had done better on Eastern Europe. But there was no real new administration policy line or initiative. Much of their attention had been devoted to assessing the damage to relations if the Soviet Union intervened to prevent the movement in the countries of Eastern Europe toward greater independence.

17. President Bush, in Poland on July 10, perhaps at this point still in part in challenge, cited Gorbachev's UN speech on "freedom of choice." See "Remarks to the National Assembly in Warsaw, Poland," July 10, 1989, *Presidential Documents*, vol. 25 (July 24, 1989), p. 1070.
    See the further discussion of policy toward Eastern Europe in chapter 13.

before he had returned to Washington, Bush decided that it was time to arrange a summit meeting with Gorbachev and wrote Gorbachev proposing a meeting. (Some of his advisers, notably Scowcroft, had opposed a summit.) Baker negotiated conditions for a summit in a series of meetings with Soviet Foreign Minister Eduard Shevardnadze (and his first deputy and later successor, Aleksandr Bessmertnykh) from late July into September, initiating a diplomatic contact of growing intensity. In all, Baker would meet Shevardnadze on six occasions in 1989 and nineteen in 1990. But in the summer of 1989 the process was still tentative.[18]

Meanwhile, other aspects of the relationship continued to develop, although fitfully. The United States had put the strategic arms talks on hold, and only at Baker's first visit to Moscow in May had it been agreed to resume the START talks in Geneva in mid-June. The twelfth annual meeting of the U.S.-USSR Trade and Economic Council in Washington in mid-May saw five new documents on cooperation but no real advance. President Bush in his Texas A&M speech on May 12 had agreed to work toward a "temporary waiver" of the Jackson-Vanik restrictions on trade if the Soviet Union were to "codify" its policy of freer emigration.[19] Although that was a modest advance over Baker's earlier general remark that the Soviet Union needed to do "more" before there could be relaxation of restrictions,[20] it only followed public recommendations for repeal of the constraints by former Congressman Charles A. Vanik and former Senator Adlai E. Stevenson (author of the other main restriction, the Stevenson amendment sharply limiting credit), and a number of Jewish organizations welcoming the greater permitted Jewish emigration. Trade was expanding but slowly.

The meetings of senior diplomats on regional problems proceeded— on the Middle East (April 11), Africa (June 3), the Asian-Pacific area (June 27–28), Afghanistan (August 2), and the Arab-Israeli conflict (November 17). Military visits also continued successfully, Admiral William J. Crowe, Jr., chairman of the Joint Chiefs of Staff, being received by Gorbachev on June 21 while

---

18. The most useful published sources providing a wealth of data and perceptive observations on the U.S.-Soviet high level diplomatic exchanges are Joseph G. Whalen, *Soviet Diplomacy and Negotiating Behavior—1988–90: Gorbachev-Reagan-Bush Meetings at the Summit*, prepared for the House Committee on Foreign Affairs (Washington: Government Printing Office, 1991); Beschloss and Talbott, *At the Highest Levels*; and Oberdorfer, *The Turn*.

    Baker and Shevardnadze met on July 29, while both were attending a conference in Paris on resolving the Cambodian conflict. On August 12 Bessmertnykh went to Washington for further discussions. As noted below, the key talks came in September.

19. *Presidential Documents*, vol. 25 (May 22, 1989), p. 702.

20. Don Oberdorfer, "Soviets Must Do More to Justify Lifting Trade Curbs, Baker Says," *Washington Post*, February 22, 1989, p. A20. Baker was testifying before the House Foreign Affairs Committee on the fiscal year 1990 budget request when he made this comment in response to a query.

spending ten days in the Soviet Union as a guest of his counterpart General of the Army Mikhail A. Moiseyev. Marshal Akhromeyev, now an adviser to President Gorbachev, visited the United States again in July and was received by President Bush and Secretary Cheney and appeared before a committee of Congress. When General of the Army Dmitry T. Yazov visited the United States October 2–7, it was the first visit ever by a Soviet minister of defense. The most significant in the long run, although seen almost as an amusing sideshow at the time, was an unofficial visit to the United States by Peoples' Deputy and ex-Politburo member Boris Yeltsin in September.

Two new items were added to the agenda of bilateral consultations. On April 28, discussions were held in Moscow on the activities of the United Nations and other international organizations, and in late June American and Soviet officials discussed cooperation in countering international terrorism.

Notwithstanding the favorable thrust of some of Bush's speeches, there were also counterpoints, not only in his own cautions and reservations, but also in other voices of the administration. Thus while Bush in May had welcomed and expressed support for Gorbachev's *perestroika*, his press spokesman, Marlin Fitzwater, on May 16 had reacted to an important and positive Soviet move, an announcement by Gorbachev that the Soviet Union would supply no more arms to Nicaragua, by suggesting it was only a gesture by a "drugstore cowboy." Vice President J. Danforth Quayle promptly (on May 19) endorsed Fitzwater's comment, saying there was "a bit of phoniness about the proposals" Gorbachev was making and dismissing them as "PR [public relations] gambits." Secretary of Defense Dick Cheney on April 29 had publicly predicted Gorbachev would fail with his reform. Deputy Secretary of State Lawrence Eagleburger on September 13 had said it was *not* "the task of American foreign policy" to ensure the success of Gorbachev's reforms. And despite Bush's initiative and the negotiations under way, on September 13 a senior White House official had replied to queries about a possible summit by saying that there was no hurry for a meeting. On September 18 Bush himself said he was "in no rush" for a summit.[21]

President Bush was, nonetheless, serious about relations with the Soviet Union. He received Shevardnadze in the White House on September 21, and Shevardnadze delivered a letter from Gorbachev. The key talks, however, were with Baker (fourth in their series) on the two days following. Baker had invited Shevardnadze to a scenic location near his own Wyoming ranch, at Jackson Hole in the Grand Tetons. This meeting, and especially the long plane ride out there from Washington, gave Baker and Shevardnadze the opportunity for extended conversation that was probably decisive in persuading Baker that Shevardnadze and Gorbachev were "for real," and that it was in the U.S.

---

21. Ann Devroy, "Bush Rebukes Critics of Arms Policy," *Washington Post*, September 19, 1989, p. A10.

interest to work together and to support them.[22] The Wyoming meeting led to several concrete steps moving forward in substantive negotiations on START and nuclear testing, a Soviet commitment to dismantle the Krasnoyarsk radar (built in a location not in accordance with the ABM Treaty), and above all agreement to announce a forthcoming summit meeting in Washington in May–June 1990.

Gorbachev and Shevardnadze had hoped to make a breakthrough on START by a major concession: the Soviet Union would be willing to sign a START treaty without an accompanying agreed constraint of space-based defense systems. Shevardnadze made this concession unilaterally and then asked for a much less far-reaching American step (and moreover one that many Americans had urged, including Ambassador Paul Nitze): agreement to hold separate talks to clarify the precise constraints imposed by the ABM Treaty, and hence to determine corresponding restraints on testing of the strategic defense initiative (SDI). Whether that would have been acceptable as a quid pro quo for the Soviet concession on START is uncertain, but in any event inasmuch as the Soviet request was not linked to that concession, Baker quickly rejected it. Shevardnadze was disappointed.

At the White House, Shevardnadze had made a second concession when he said that a "political decision" had been taken to dismantle the Soviet large phased-array early-warning radar near Krasnoyarsk in Siberia, which the United States had long been charging was a violation of the ABM Treaty. A month later when he announced this decision to the Supreme Soviet he explicitly acknowledged that it had been a violation. Although the location of that radar in the interior of the Soviet Union was a violation of the ABM Treaty corollary constraint limiting future deployment of such radars to the periphery of the national territory, and dismantling it was therefore not a "concession," the Soviet military had sought to resolve the future of that radar in conjunction with what they believed to be a comparable American violation of the same provision. The United States had built similar new phased-array early-warning radars at Thule, Greenland, and Fylingdales Moor in England—not along the periphery of U.S. national territory. Gorbachev had proposed such linkage in 1987. Shevardnadze threw aside that linkage and any leverage it may have provided to modify the American radar deployment or allow Krasnoyarsk also to be an exception. He did not even seek agreement to clarify the ABM Treaty

---

22. The plane ride provided better opportunity than the resort itself. While the majestic serenity of the mountains may conjure up an image of the two men relaxing with their boots resting on a low table in a secluded lodge, they were in fact accompanied by about 100 officials and 200 support staff. Shevardnadze had planned to fly out on his own Aeroflot jet, as was common practice by leaders of both countries, but Baker persuaded him to come on his DC-9 so that they would have the opportunity for long uninterrupted talks alone save for interpreters and personal aides.

For accounts with detail and flavor see Beschloss and Talbott, *At the Highest Levels*, pp. 109–12, 117–19; and Oberdorfer, *The Turn*, pp. 371–74.

provision that governed both the Soviet and American radars in question. Shevardnadze of course saw the issue as a major obstacle to far more important political aims (the U.S. Senate had made clear that START ratification would require prior resolution of the Krasnoyarsk radar violation). But he apparently had short-circuited the Moscow clearance process and acted on his own in getting Gorbachev's approval to make this further concession on the Krasnoyarsk radar.[23]

And on a third START issue, Shevardnadze also made a unilateral Soviet concession in agreeing to drop insistence on inclusion in a START treaty of limitations on sea-launched cruise missiles (SLCMs). Again, as with the START-ABM linkage, Shevardnadze sought a U.S. reciprocal lesser concession but failed to get it. He proposed a separate agreement limiting SLCMs, but Baker, sensitive to Pentagon objections, refused to agree. (The matter was settled later through agreement on a separate "politically binding" nontreaty limit as declared by each side and set far above U.S. or Soviet planned buildup.)

Thus from the American standpoint, and the standing of Baker in Washington, the meetings in Wyoming were a great success. From Shevardnadze's standpoint he had cleared away some obstacles to agreement but had obtained nothing from the United States in return for three substantial concessions. Soviet military dissatisfaction with Shevardnadze's negotiating was rapidly rising.

Baker did make an unexpected American concession on another arms control matter, one less central than START, but nonetheless another element on the arms agenda. The United States, Baker told Shevardnadze, was prepared to agree with the Soviet Union on a separate bilateral accord to reduce respective chemical weapons (CW) stockpiles by 80 percent, while negotiations continued in the multilateral forum for a comprehensive treaty banning CW. Shevardnadze promptly agreed. Bush had himself made the earlier U.S. proposal for a CW ban, and now his administration had a more proprietary interest in that subject than in merely completing the Reagan START negotiation. Two days later Bush unveiled the new (and now even more far-reaching) proposal, for a 98 percent reduction in U.S. and Soviet CW arsenals without awaiting conclusion of the comprehensive multilateral treaty ban on all CW weapons. And Shevardnadze the day following expressed readiness even for elimination of CW stockpiles of the two countries. As will be noted, an agreement for major bilateral CW reductions was reached by the May 1990 summit.

The Wyoming ministerial meeting, largely owing to the major Soviet concessions, did thus pave the way for the forthcoming summit.[24]

Secretary Baker, now convinced of the serious intent of Gorbachev and Shevardnadze to "restructure" relations with the United States and Soviet

---

23. On the radar issue, see the discussion in chapter 12.

24. For additional background on the Wyoming meeting, see Beschloss and Talbott, *At the Highest Levels*, pp. 117–21.

foreign policy more generally, as well as to seek genuine and far-reaching economic and political reform at home, began to change the thrust of American policy to meet and support this promising Soviet development. In virtually unnoticed testimony to the Senate Finance Committee on October 4, Baker presented a rare analysis and discussion of Soviet reform efforts. In contrast to many earlier experiences of doubt by members of the Reagan and Bush administrations, he credited what he now called "an extraordinary effort at internal reform" to Gorbachev from the beginning, 1985, and acknowledged that, as Gorbachev had said, it involved "a true 'revolution'" encompassing the political and juridical, as well as economic, spheres and foreign policy as well as internal policy. His prepared statement was short on American policy, but clearly his detailed account of Soviet reform was intended to lay a foundation for U.S. policy actions. He stressed that "the Administration wants *perestroika* to succeed," and that although the main efforts had to be made by the Soviet Union, the United States in pursuing its interests had a stake in the outcome and, by implication, should help: "our own national interest . . . does not exist in isolation from the events taking place in the Soviet Union." In his concluding paragraph, he referred to the recent Wyoming ministerial meeting as an example in practice of a policy of pursuing a "search for points of mutual advantage."[25]

On October 16, Baker made a major public address on that very theme, "Points of Mutual Advantage: *Perestroika* and American Foreign Policy."[26] Again, he credited the fact that "relations with the Soviet Union have improved considerably since 1985, when Mikhail Gorbachev launched what he called *perestroika*—a total restructuring of Soviet society, including Soviet foreign and defense policies." Although he still criticized residual Soviet policies in some respects, including some areas of regional conflict, he emphasized the favorable changes. And he stated that the president and he had concluded that they wanted Gorbachev's policies to succeed, "not because it is our business to reform Soviet society or to keep a particular Soviet leader in power—we can really do neither—but because *perestroika* promises Soviet actions more advantageous to our interests." And cooperation could be built on mutual advantage.

---

25. "U.S.-Soviet Relations: A Discussion of *Perestroika* and Economic Reform," *Department of State Bulletin*, vol. 89 (December 1989), pp. 20–26, quotations from pp. 20, 24, 26. (Hereafter *State Bulletin*.)

26. "Points of Mutual Advantage: *Perestroika* and American Foreign Policy," October 16, 1989, *State Bulletin*, vol. 89 (December 1989), pp. 10–14. All quotations in the paragraphs following are from this text.

    This speech was drafted by Baker's close aide and adviser Robert Zoellick, whom he had appointed Counselor of the State Department. Dennis Ross, named head of the Policy Planning Staff, was the other particularly close adviser on whom Baker relied heavily. These two confidants of the secretary also became the principal channel for the output of the entire State Department to Baker—to the annoyance of many senior career Foreign Service officers.

"We now have," he said, "a historic opportunity with the Soviet Union. We have the chance to leave behind the postwar period with the ups and downs of the cold war. We can move beyond containment to make the change toward better superpower relations more secure and less reversible. Our task is to find enduring points of mutual advantage that serve the interests of both the United States and the Soviet Union."

While noting that in the course of this search, "We must not succumb to a false optimism" prematurely, he argued that it would be "an equally great blunder" for the United States to be so suspicious and disengaged that it failed to "put *perestroika's* promise to the test."

Toward the end of his speech, Baker said, "We are prepared to provide technical assistance in certain areas of Soviet economic reform." While a secondary point and one not developed, this first indication of U.S. readiness to provide any kind of material assistance dominated the American press reaction.[27] (In the Soviet Union, by contrast, all major accounts led off with the reference to the "historic opportunity.")

Backgrounding and reporting noted that this did, indeed, represent a substantial change from the reserved stance of the first several months of the Bush administration.[28] Many articles noted the contrast with earlier-cited statements only a month before by Deputy Secretary of State Lawrence Eagleburger, and earlier by White House spokesman Marlin Fitzwater, Vice President Quayle, Secretary Cheney, and others. But the shift was, in fact, so sudden that poor coordination (as well as real differences) led to a new nearly simultaneous contradiction. Speaking in San Francisco on the day after Baker's speech and without having seen it, Vice President Quayle rejected the idea of U.S. help to Soviet reform efforts and said, "Let them reform themselves." And Quayle referred to a Soviet military buildup and policy in Afghanistan, Nicaragua, and elsewhere as "the darker side of Soviet foreign policy" and "just as real, just as significant as *perestroika*." "The Soviet Union," said the vice president, "remains our potential adversary." He did not, it seemed, see any points of mutual advantage. The press asked, "Whose voice is official?" President Bush tried to brush off any difference, but the matter was certainly not clarified when press spokesman Marlin Fitzwater said, "We all sing from the same song sheet, but there are several verses." Speculation was voiced that the president either was not in control or was cynically playing domestic politics with a matter of serious policy.[29]

---

27. For example, see Thomas L. Friedman, "U.S. Offers to Aid Gorbachev's Plan to Revamp System," *New York Times*, October 17, 1989, pp. A1, A15.

28. For example, see Thomas L. Friedman, "How Washington Shifted to Embracing Gorbachev," *New York Times*, October 22, 1989, p. A18.

29. See Ann Devroy, "Despite Speeches, Quayle and Baker Agree on Soviets, Aides Say," *Washington Post*, October 19, 1989, p. A24; and R. W. Apple, Jr., "Is Quayle Out of Tune on U.S. Soviet Policy?" *New York Times*, October 20, 1989, p. A14.

The dust had not settled before word was leaked that Baker had squelched a speech that Deputy National Security Adviser Robert Gates had planned to give suggesting that Gorbachev would not in any case succeed, thus seeming to cast doubt on any policy of cooperation.[30] Again, the press asked where President Bush was and where he stood.[31] Only days later Vice President Quayle again said that he still considered Gorbachev a Stalinist and was "not sure that [his] intentions have changed that much." And President Bush again waffled, declining to repudiate Quayle's comments.[32]

Meanwhile, in a major presentation on Soviet foreign policy to the Supreme Soviet, Shevardnadze claimed that "the Soviet-American dialogue has scaled new heights in terms of openness, businesslike intensity, the range of questions raised, and the degree of mutual understanding and amicability."[33] Of particular interest to American (and Soviet) audiences was that he also said that the Soviet military intervention in Afghanistan in 1979 had "violated norms of

30. Thomas L. Friedman, "Baker Blocks Expert's Speech about Gorbachev's Chances," *New York Times*, October 27, 1989, pp. A1, A10; and Don Oberdorfer, "Baker Blocked Speech by NSC Deputy on Gorbachev Reforms," *Washington Post*, October 28, 1989, p. A18.

  Just a year before, on October 14, 1988, Gates—then deputy director at the CIA—had given a speech expressing great caution and skepticism not only on the prospects for Gorbachev's success, but also on his motives and aims, provoking a sharp protest from Secretary of State George Shultz.

  Throughout the Bush administration, but most effectively in 1989, Gates (as deputy national security adviser) had reinforced the cautious nature of General Scowcroft and the president. He told colleagues that he believed Gorbachev was an "aberration" and would be succeeded by another old-line Soviet leader. In an earlier public speech in April he warned that Gorbachev was not irrevocably committed to reform, and in the White House he constantly expressed doubts about Gorbachev's real intentions and his political longevity. He therefore opposed Baker's line of support for Gorbachev's reforms. (For informed examples, corroborating what my own sources indicated, see Beschloss and Talbott, *At the Highest Levels*, pp. 25, 47, 99, 124–25; and Oberdorfer, *The Turn*, pp. 274, 334.)

  In September 1989, Gates was also responsible for establishing a very confidential contingency planning study of what options the United States might have if the Soviet political system were to collapse, a study that continued until early 1991. Baker did not oppose this effort at prudent policy planning, and his close aide Dennis Ross was a key participant. This exercise was successfully kept secret until disclosed by participants after Gorbachev (and Bush and Gates) were out of office and the Soviet Union had ceased to exist. See Don Oberdorfer, "U.S. Secretly Studied Possibility of Gorbachev Coup, Soviet Collapse," *Washington Post*, January 17, 1993, p. A42.

31. See the editorial, "On Moscow: The President Is Missing," *New York Times*, October 30, 1989, p. A18.

32. David Hoffman, "President Won't Dispute Quayle's Soviet Remarks," *Washington Post*, November 8, 1989, p. A20.

33. "Foreign Policy and *Perestroika*," Foreign Minister E. A. Shevardnadze's Report to the USSR Supreme Soviet, October 23, 1989, *Pravda*, October 24, 1989.

behavior, and gone against common human interests." Even more striking, he also acknowledged for the first time that the construction of the large early-warning radar near Krasnoyarsk was "frankly, a violation of the ABM Treaty" and said it would be dismantled.[34] The Soviet leadership was clearly moving to clear up past transgressions that still impeded the development of relations with the United States.

As earlier noted, in the spring talks on issues in the United Nations and other international organizations had begun to be held. This reflected the addition of the new, fifth category to the traditional four areas of dialogue: transnational world issues (such as global ecology, terrorism, and the like). In August, in a reversal of the trend in American policy under Reagan, the United States and the Soviet Union had agreed to accept binding arbitration of the International Court of Justice in disputes over interpretation of a number of treaties concerning terrorism, hijacking, drug smuggling, and the like. In November, this was taken further by the first ever U.S.-Soviet cosponsorship of a UN General Assembly Resolution calling on all nations to strengthen the United Nations in defending peace and human rights.[35]

Though still limited, the range of cooperation between the United States and the Soviet Union was widening.

## *Triumphs and Trials of* Perestroika

Gorbachev was determined to press forward on foreign relations, especially with the United States, but he was compelled in 1989 to give priority to internal affairs. In part this was his own preference, above all to press ahead with the incomplete program to democratize and institutionalize the shift to a civil society that he had envisioned at the Twenty-seventh Party Congress in March 1986 and launched at the Central Committee plenum in January 1987. The process of changing the party machine had been only partially realized at the Nineteenth Party Conference in June 1988. He was determined to carry this process forward in 1989 with the first popularly elected national Congress of People's Deputies and a new standing legislature, the reconstituted Supreme Soviet of the USSR. An equally important element of his program of fundamental social *perestroika*, to which however he failed to give equal attention and drive, was the faltering economic reform launched in 1987 and 1988. Finally, a third area of rising importance, the significance of which Gorbachev failed to recognize, was the rapid growth of ethnic friction, national feeling, and in some cases separatist independence sentiment.

---

34. Ibid.

35. Ethan Schwartz, "U.S., Soviets Team Up to Announce Their First Joint U.N. Resolution," *Washington Post*, November 4, 1989, p. A18.

A growing public malaise and dissatisfaction undergirded all of these separate but interrelated areas of internal affairs requiring policy decision and action. Cautious and skeptical interest in 1985 and 1986 in the new leadership and what it would mean for the general public had given rise by 1987 and 1988 to heightened expectations. But while intellectual circles continued to enjoy their ever-increasing opportunities for free thought and expression, by 1989 the general public was becoming disenchanted with unfulfilled expectations. Even growing political freedoms were offset by a declining economic situation and revived skepticism. While *glasnost* had brought out much new evidence of the failure of past promises by past leaderships, it was not bringing signs of delivery on the promises of the Gorbachev leadership.[36] Nor were successes in foreign policy seen as counterweight to failures at home.

Gorbachev began the year with a decision that implicitly reflected his awareness of growing popular disenchantment. A Central Committee plenum on January 10 selected the Communist Party's candidates for the forthcoming Peoples' Congress. (One-third of the seats were reserved for nominations by the Communist Party and certain other "public" organizations.) In keeping with the past, Gorbachev of course headed the party's list. But by that action, Gorbachev forfeited the opportunity (as well as the risk) to stand for popular election. He chose prudence over a political gamble that most Moscow observers thought he would have won.

Boris Yeltsin, by contrast, had no political future except as a popularly elected candidate and was spared such a choice. He did have a choice among any of some thirteen mostly "safe" seats in Moscow, Sverdlovsk, and elsewhere, and he decided to run for a Moscow "at-large" seat that gave him an opportunity to demonstrate his growing popularity. He won with nearly 90 percent of the votes, a little more than 5 million Muscovites—an impressive victory by any standard.

Conservative bureaucracies tried (unsuccessfully in the case of the Academy of Sciences, successfully in some other cases) to curb nomination of liberals for "organization" seats as distinguished from popularly elected candidates. But on the whole, the elections were free and were contested.

In the elections, held on March 26, some 80 percent of the Communist Party candidates won, but by the same token 20 percent, most with no opposition candidates, lost. For example, Yury F. Solovyev, the Leningrad party chief and a candidate member of the Politburo, with no opposing candidate, lost. (Voters had the right to cross out the name of the only candidate listed and vote against him; 130,000 voted against Solovyev and only 110,000 voted for him.) Gorbachev, who had tried in an off-the-cuff public comment on February 14 to

---

36. I was struck in January 1989, upon returning to Moscow after an absence of only a little more than six months, by the change in public mood. One extreme example was the declaration by a driver that "all the communist bastards ought to be lined up and shot." The only exception he would concede was Boris Yeltsin—made acceptable by standing up to the communist establishment and being attacked by them.

brush aside the question of a two- (or more) party system, nonetheless welcomed the public action in expressing its will even in rejecting some Communist Party candidates.

The Congress of People's Deputies, a new superlegislature intended to meet only twice a year for a few days, had 2,250 members, all (even the one-third nominated by the party and other official organizations) subject to election, in all by 170 million voters. Two-thirds of its composition, incidentally, was "white collar," mostly administrative and managerial personnel at all levels. The congress met on May 25, and its actions as well as its election meant a new experience in democracy for everyone. Before it ended its session on June 9, the congress elected the first standing legislature, a new Supreme Soviet of 542 members, as well as its chairman, the "president" of the country. Gorbachev won with 95 percent of the vote (against some ultraconservative blank ballots and a maverick self-nominated alternative candidate)—a more democratic result than previous automatic 100 percent votes of the old Supreme Soviet but again a long step away from a popular vote and mandate. Again, Gorbachev had not wanted to risk a low majority or even loss in a popular vote for the presidency, despite the advice of some of his aides. Sessions of the People's Congress, and initially of the Supreme Soviet, were telecast. In late June this practice was, however, discontinued because of massive distraction of interested citizens from their work—a reported 20 percent decline in productivity over the several weeks of daily television broadcasting to 200 million viewers over the entire country!

The congress, incidentally, included unprecedented direct and public criticism of Gorbachev, the Communist Party, and other sacrosanct institutions (including even the once-feared KGB). The congress initially failed to give Yeltsin a seat on the Supreme Soviet, but—with Gorbachev's assistance, in the face of public demonstrations—a parliamentary maneuver gave him a favorable vote. Many liberals failed to gain seats. There was an interesting groundswell of complaints from provincial and republic representatives that the Moscow delegates were taking more than their share of the time for debates.

By July an informal liberal reform faction of the Supreme Soviet, including Yeltsin, established itself as the Interregional Group of Deputies. By October, a smaller but active conservative or even reactionary group, Rossiya, was formed. Parliamentary politics was flourishing.

On October 24, the Supreme Soviet passed a new electoral law abolishing the one-third quota of reserved seats for nominations by the Communist Party and other organizations, making all seats open for competitive candidacies in the future. Democratic politics were flourishing too.

As Gorbachev was launching this major step in the democratization of the political life of the country and indirectly but deliberately reducing the role of the Communist Party machine, he also had to continue to deal with and through the old political institutions. As earlier described, he had moved in the latter half of 1988 to mute the role of the party Secretariat and other central organs. Now he went much further. On April 25, at a suddenly convened Central Committee plenum, he engineered a mass resignation of older and more conservative members from the Central Committee. In all, seventy-four full members and twenty-four candidate members of the Central Committee, and twelve members of the third-tier Central Auditing Commission, resigned. Only twenty-four candidate members were raised to full membership, so the size of the Central Committee fell to its lowest number in nearly two decades. (Clearly, Gorbachev would have liked to place more of his supporters in the committee, but by the rules a plenum between party congresses could only raise candidate members to full membership, and he only found twenty-four that he wished to promote.) The departure of one-fourth of the full members of the Central Committee included ten former Politburo and Secretariat members, including Andrei Gromyko, Geidar Aliyev, Boris Ponomarev, and Nikolai Tikhonov. (Some older members now out of other offices, however, declined to resign and remained members.) Thus Gorbachev was able in April 1989 to make many of the changes he had been unable to make the previous summer when he had been compelled to forgo making personnel changes at the party conference or at the September 1988 plenum. It should be noted that although Gorbachev had been able to replace some 40 percent of the old Brezhnev Central Committee at the Twenty-seventh Party Congress in 1986, many remained. Moreover, many allies of Gorbachev in 1985–86 were by 1989 opposed to the far-reaching reforms he was pursuing, most notably Yegor Ligachev, who had initially handled personnel matters for Gorbachev.

At the end of the frank exchanges at the plenum, Gorbachev sprang another surprise. He suddenly proposed to publish the full transcript of the proceedings—a practice not done in decades, and not of course expected when members had spoken.[37] His proposal carried.

On July 18, at a Central Committee conference of republic and province (*oblast*) party first secretaries, Gorbachev took head-on the challenge of the role of the party, seeking to "extricate" it from "a state of siege" by weakening democratic centralism and party discipline in order to encourage democratization, precisely the opposite of what the conservative party bureaucracy wanted. Even the partial published account of the proceedings made clear that there was sharp debate, with Ligachev openly leading the opposition to Gorbachev.

While Gorbachev was saying that the party must change to remain in an age of reform and democratization, Ligachev was arguing in effect that

---

37. One of those who had objected to Gorbachev's actions placing in question the leading role of the Communist Party and turning it into a mere debating society was Yury Solovyev, the Leningrad party chief who had failed popular election to the Congress of Peoples' Deputies (see *Pravda*, April 27, 1989). On July 12, Gorbachev personally went to Leningrad to officiate at a regional party meeting ousting Solovyev and replacing him with Boris Gidaspov.

democratic reform must be curbed to ensure the party's viability. Ligachev was the most outspoken Politburo conservative, but others too urged restoring authority of the party machine. Many of the regional party chiefs took a strongly conservative stand.

At a Central Committee plenum on September 19–20, convened for another purpose, Gorbachev again pushed through a purge of conservative members of the top leadership, larger than the previous September or any earlier occasion. Three full members of the Politburo—Viktor Chebrikov, Vladimir Shcherbitsky, and Viktor Nikonov—and two candidate members (one was Yury Solovyev, late of Leningrad) were dropped. Ligachev was kept, but now in virtual isolation. Two new full members (Vladimir Kryuchkov—Chebrikov's successor at the KGB—and Yury Maslyukov), two candidates, and four party secretaries were named. All were seen as more inclined to support reform, although several were later to become the new hard-line conservatives as the pace of *perestroika* became more revolutionary.

At another Central Committee plenum on December 9, two more reformers were added to the top leadership. There were still strong conservative voices, however, including the new Leningrad party chief Boris Gidaspov, who had been brought in by Gorbachev only five months earlier. A Russian Bureau of the Communist Party was also created to meet one of the demands advanced by conservatives at the September plenum. Gorbachev, who had been lukewarm to the idea, decided to head the bureau himself to prevent it from becoming a rival conservative forum.

In a major test of political strength in the new Congress of People's Deputies, as it opened its second session in December, political reformers proposed debate on the question of deleting Article 6 of the Constitution of the USSR, providing in the basic charter of the Soviet state that the "leading role" was taken by the Communist Party. Although Gorbachev had earlier voiced opposition to the idea of more than one party, some of his close advisers had come to favor the idea, and Gorbachev had shown himself much more open on the issue than most of his colleagues in the leadership. He did not support the proposal for a debate on such a constitutional amendment but also was not adamantly opposed to the possibility. The proposal was defeated on December 12 by a modest majority (1,138 to 839, with 56 abstentions), neither discouraging reformers for the future nor encouraging the traditionalists that the battle had yet been won.

Meanwhile, while pursuing his agenda of political democratization and fending off conservative party resistance, Gorbachev did not display equal adeptness in advancing economic reform. The year opened with a January 5 Politburo decision to retain central price control, postponing planned decentralization and relaxation because of concern over the social impact. A Central Committee plenum on agriculture in March put off the central issue of land ownership. Public confidence continued to drop. In July several hundred thousand miners went on strike, making demands for pay and working conditions and further political reform. Concessions were quickly granted on the former. When these promises were poorly kept, renewed strikes broke out in October. Less dramatic but more pervasive was a growing economic slowdown, greater than the year before. A large national budget deficit, acknowledged for the first time in October 1988, grew enormously in 1989. By November a draft law on property was passed for public discussion, but legislative action was deferred. Only on December 16 did Prime Minister Nikolai Ryzhkov propose an economic reform package, and then one roundly criticized by reformers as inadequate.

Gorbachev was well aware of the need for far-reaching economic reform, though not adequately aware of the growing urgency or of the full extent of the transformation needed. He was prepared to take major steps, but he believed it necessary first to have a democratic political structure in place and functioning to ensure public support for the privations that economic reform would entail. This may have been a serious, even fatal, error for *perestroika*, but not one based on doctrinal blinders or on opposition to deep economic change, as his position has sometimes been described. He seriously underestimated the consequences of procrastination and continued inaction, including a growing deficit, fall in productivity, and decline in public confidence.

The fourth trend in internal developments, stimulated by and in turn influencing favorable political and unfavorable economic trends, was the rise of regional and national sentiment, above all separatist sentiments in the western republics, in particular the three Baltic states, Moldavia, and the three Trans-caucasian states, and ethnic frictions there and elsewhere as well.

Gorbachev, and the leadership as a whole, greatly underestimated the revolutionary potential of the nationality issue, but insofar as they did recognize the existence of what they saw as a growing problem, the conservatives wanted to repress manifestations, while Gorbachev wanted to accommodate them and, he believed, thereby head off a more serious challenge. On some matters, however, Gorbachev was adamant. He had been incensed on his visit to earthquake-stricken Armenia in December 1988 by demonstrations for Armenian control over Nagorno-Karabakh. He may himself have made the decision to arrest the Karabakh committee. On January 14, a special committee in Moscow was appointed to administer the disputed territory in Azerbaijan (and did so until November, when it reverted to Azerbaijani administration).

On April 9, demonstrations in Tbilisi, capital of Georgia, were suppressed with excessive violence by the police and soldiers with riot gas and sharpened trenching shovels, resulting in twenty deaths and a mighty upsurge of Georgian independence sentiment. In May riots broke out in Turkmenistan, and in early June in Uzbekistan with deaths. The conflict in Uzbekistan stemmed from ethnic strife between native Uzbeks and Meskhetian Turks transferred there many years before. Only days later, rioting broke out in western Kazakhstan between Kazakhi and people of several nationalities of the

Caucasus who had earlier been brought there as supplementary labor. In July, there were serious disturbances and at least twenty-two deaths in Georgia, in fighting between Abkhazians and Georgians.

But much more serious were nonviolent but political steps taken by the Baltic states. Earlier stirrings for independence in the Baltic republics—Lithuania, Latvia, and Estonia—began to rise rapidly in 1989. The Lithuanian "Sajudis" popular front began to call for greater (if not yet complete) independence. The elections in March brought noncommunist proindependence "popular fronts" into majority control of all three Baltic republican legislatures. Gorbachev's December 1988 UN speech call for free choice, intended to open prospects for real independence in Eastern Europe, was cited in Lithuania. On May 18 Lithuania and Estonia, and on July 29 Latvia, passed legislation declaring their "sovereignty"—a step without immediate operative significance, but a clear indication of how things were heading and how rapidly.

The leadership had been wrestling with "the nationalities issue" since the party conference in mid-1988 and had twice scheduled special plenary meetings of the Central Committee only to postpone them. On July 1 Gorbachev addressed a speech to the issue, but apart from recognition of a growing problem, he did not offer any solution that would assuage the now politically active national groups.[38] At the root of the problem was a basic incompatibility of the idea of secession and independence with the widely ingrained acceptance of the indivisibility of the Soviet Union. But only a minority, even in the Baltic republics, was calling for complete independence. So the question of compromise solutions was still open and in varying degree appealed to Gorbachev and many others in the leadership. Some, however, were very leery of any compromise. Among the leaders actively engaged on the issue, Viktor Chebrikov, a Politburo member and party secretary, was most adamant. Nikolai Ryzhkov, besides being prime minister, was chairman of a Politburo commission on the matter, and more centrist in view. Party Secretary Vadim Medvedev, charged with ideology, was relatively liberal. But none of the leaders was disposed to think in terms of independence for the Baltic republics, to say nothing of any of the other republics. Moreover, there was real concern over "subversive" contacts with the West.[39]

---

38. "Address of the General Secretary of the Central Committee of the CPSU and Chairman of the Supreme Soviet of the USSR, M. S. Gorbachev on Central Television," *Pravda*, July 2, 1989.

39. Indications of high-level Soviet concern over subversive contacts and influences from the West are difficult to judge, because other purposes were also served by expressed concern. For example, Defense Minister Dmitry Yazov replied to a letter by two parliamentary deputies by citing published American references on financial assistance from the U.S. National Endowment for Democracy to groups in the Baltic states, Ukraine, and the Caucasus. His letter almost certainly reflected real concern but also political mobilization for countering such tendencies. See Yazov's letter, published in *Sovetskaya Rossiya*, December 26, 1990.

Gorbachev sought to meet the popular demands in the Baltic republics by offering substantial economic autonomy. First approved in principle by the Supreme Soviet in July, such autonomy was granted by a formal Supreme Soviet decree on November 27. But while economic considerations had played a role (especially in coopting much of the ethnic Russian population in Latvia and Estonia), and the three republics had begun to pass legislation seeking to provide economic autonomy, Gorbachev's assumption that greater economic independence would fulfill the aims of the majority of the population in the Baltic republics was flawed from the outset; it was too little, as well as too late.

On July 14 the Politburo approved a "draft platform" on nationality policy for the forthcoming (but again postponed) plenum. It was finally published as a draft for discussion on August 17.[40] The draft sought to balance its compromise by calling for stronger republics—*and* a stronger central government. The Central Committee finally met on the matter on September 19–20. The draft platform and the decisions of the plenary meeting were much too cautious and limited to meet the rising tide of independence sentiment in the western republics. By the fall, in addition to the three small Baltic republics, which had of course been independent from 1918–19 to 1940, Moldavia (reacquired in 1940) and, most significant by far, Ukraine had begun to show strong signs of popular interest in some degree of greater independence.[41]

On November 20 the USSR Supreme Soviet rejected party proposals for giving limited rights to the republics (211 to 149) on the grounds that greater concessions were needed. (As earlier noted, a week later it did approve extensive economic autonomy for the three Baltic republics.) But the year ended with the sharpest break within the Communist Party itself. On December 7, with support of the Lithuanian Communist Party, Article 6 of the Lithu-

---

The most clear evidence of high-level concern is a formerly Top Secret, now declassified, internal Central Committee report approved by the Politburo. Dated January 14, 1989, and specifically approved by Gorbachev, Yakovlev, and Shevardnadze as well as more conservative leaders, it was prepared by senior Central Committee officials and called upon the KGB and MVD not to permit social organizations "to use their international contacts to the detriment of the interests of the country and the aims of perestroika." It cited many specified cases, from late 1988, of contacts by Soviet citizens of the Baltic republics with U.S. émigré Balts, Radio Free Europe, and others with the aims of opposing Soviet and communist rule. For the full text, which has been authenticated, see "Secrets of the Politburo. Each Step of the Independent Social Organizations of the Baltics Was Covered by the Central Committee," *Rossiiskiye vesti* (Russian News), June 5, 1992.

40. "In the Politburo of the CC CPSU," *Pravda*, July 16, 1989; and "The Nationality Policy of the Party Under Contemporary Circumstances (Platform of the CPSU)," *Pravda*, August 17, 1989.

41. On September 8, a popular front organization called *Rukh* (Popular Movement for *Perestroika*) was created in the Ukraine, initially seeking greater economic independence.

anian Constitution (modeled on the same article of the USSR Constitution) according the "leading role" to the Lithuanian Communist Party was dropped. Thirteen days later on December 20, the Lithuanian Communist Party defied Moscow and declared independence from the Communist Party of the Soviet Union. Moreover, the Lithuanian party leadership avowed the aims of a "sovereign" Lithuania and "the restoration of Lithuanian statehood." Having assessed the depth of independence sentiment, the Lithuanian party under Algirdas Brazauskas had decided its only chance for the future was to match Sajudis in seeking political independence. A Central Committee plenum in Moscow on December 25–26 condemned the break by the Lithuanian Communist Party but was powerless to prevent it.

The Gorbachev leadership in Moscow had failed to appreciate the depth and seriousness of the challenge of nationalism in the Baltic states and potentially elsewhere. Compromises and concessions were made but never sufficient. It remains an unanswered question whether acknowledging the unique status of the three formerly independent Baltic states, and permitting their secession, might have eased the issue before it came to a complete breakup of the Soviet Union a mere two years later. Alone, it would not have been decisive, but coupled with other changes in policy it might have neutralized the Baltics rather than making them an engine carrying forward national aspirations in other Western areas that had never been independent, such as the western Ukraine, western Belorussia, and Moldavia. But it was not done, and the fiftieth anniversary of the Stalin-Hitler Pact of 1939 became an occasion for massive demonstration for a cause renewed, rather than an occasion for releasing the three republics from the union. It is, of course, easier to see such possibilities with hindsight, but the idea was widely bantered about in 1989 too.[42] It is also much clearer in retrospect that Gorbachev should have moved in 1988 or 1989, before the national movement had become stronger, to prepare and push through a new constitution or "union treaty" with greater authority for the republics.

In all fairness it must be observed that Gorbachev was facing a multifaceted political challenge. It was no accident that even the tepid concessions he offered on the nationality issue could only be made after his further purge of the conservative party machine at the September 19–20 plenum. This was also followed by the removal of Vladimir Shcherbitsky from leadership of the Ukrainian Communist Party, and his replacement by Vladimir Ivashko, in a plenum in Kiev personally presided over by Gorbachev, on September 28. But Gorbachev believed in "Soviet man," in an integrated existence among nation-

---

42. In a number of conversations with Soviet academic figures and Communist Party officials in the late 1980s, I (and I am sure others) warned my interlocutors that they were deluding themselves that the peoples of the Baltic republics would settle for less and were burdening the Soviet Union with a weakening influence with broad ramifications. But even as late as 1989 and 1990 many could not bring themselves to see that.

alities of the Soviet Union that transcended national particularities. He believed in respect for distinctive national cultures and history, economic autonomy, and national nondiscrimination in a "restructured" Soviet Union—and he believed most people, even in the Baltic republics, shared that goal.

Though these domestic developments were only indirectly related to Soviet-American relations, they became crucial to the evolution of the entire Soviet system. In the current run, they were essential elements of Gorbachev's policy environment. Policy toward the United States was not an issue. The Congress of People's Deputies in its first guidance on foreign policy in a Resolution "On the Main Lines of Domestic and Foreign Policy of the USSR" in June merely instructed the Soviet government to "seek further improvement in Soviet-U.S. relations," which it saw as "key to ending the arms race and strengthening world peace."[43]

While internal Soviet politics were volatile enough, other developments in Eastern Europe during 1989, above all in the year's final two months, had resounding implications both for Soviet internal policy and development and for East-West relations, including the Soviet-U.S. relationship.

## From Tremors to Upheaval in Eastern Europe

Gorbachev had been moving to lift the heavy dead hand of Soviet hegemonic control over the countries of Eastern Europe ever since he had entered office, though initially cautiously and gradually.[44] As within the Soviet Union, he believed that a true reform would lead enlightened free citizenry to reconfirm a "socialist choice." In his speech to the United Nations in December Gorbachev had reiterated his commitment to "freedom of choice" for all peoples, with "no exceptions."[45] Developments in Eastern Europe in 1989 were to put that commitment to the test.

By April 1989, President Wojciech Jaruzelski of Poland had opened round-table talks with the opposition and again legalized Solidarity (after a seven-year ban). In a free election for the Polish Senate, Solidarity won 99 of 100 seats—and even in the lower house of parliament, where communist predominance was presumed ensured by limited candidacies, voters rejected thirty-three of thirty-five party and government leaders by crossing out the names of unopposed candidates and denying them a majority. At the critical juncture in the ensuing negotiations on a coalition government in Warsaw, Gorbachev let Polish Communist Party chief Mieczysław Rakowski understand

---

43.  "On the Main Lines of Domestic and Foreign Policy of the USSR, Resolution of the USSR Congress of Peoples Deputies," *Pravda*, June 25, 1989.

44.  See the discussion in chapter 13.

45.  "Speech of M. S. Gorbachev at the United Nations," *Pravda*, December 8, 1988.

in a crucial telephone conference on August 22 that a line of national reconciliation should be followed. A Solidarity-led coalition government was formed, and the Soviet Union had acquiesced in the peaceful ouster of the communist government in the most important country in Eastern Europe.[46]

Hungary was next. The Hungarian Socialist Workers (Communist) Party abandoned Leninism, changed its name to the Hungarian Socialist Party, and changed the name of the country from the standard Soviet bloc term "people's republic" to simply "the Republic of Hungary." Again, no objection was raised by Moscow. But the critical case came in East Germany, soon after a visit by Gorbachev in early October to celebrate the fortieth (and, as it was to be, the last) anniversary of the German Democratic Republic. The aged dictatorial leader, Erich Honecker, was ousted by his own Politburo when he sought to use force to quell rising popular demonstrations. His successor, Egon Krenz, after consulting Gorbachev, finally on November 9 acceded to public demands and opened the infamous Berlin Wall. On the same day, when Bulgarian party chief Todor Zhivkov tried to fire his more moderate foreign minister, Petar Mladenov, Zhivkov himself was deposed. A week later, Czechoslovak party chief Miloš Jakeš was ousted.[47] The Eastern European bloc dominoes fell quickly; the last, and the only one to end in bloodshed, was the ouster of Nicolae Ceaușescu in Romania in December.

While liberals in Gorbachev's entourage were heartened by the sudden rapid collapse of the conservative old guard leaderships in Eastern Europe, there was concern over the further course of events in those countries and the impact on the Soviet Union itself. The three Baltic republics in May and July had declared their "sovereignty" and were increasingly moving toward an end to Communist Party leadership and the establishment of national independence. Moreover, in the midst of these developments was the example of massive popular demonstrations and brutal suppression in Tiananmen Square in Beijing, coincidentally immediately after Gorbachev's pathbreaking visit to China.

Gorbachev, and some others in the Soviet leadership to a greater degree, were also concerned about whether the United States would seek to take advantage of this time of vulnerability and flux in the socialist camp. President Bush had first proclaimed his interest in the countries of Eastern Europe on April 17—by coincidence, the very day of the formalities legalizing Solidarity in Warsaw.[48] And he followed with his visit to Poland and Hungary in

---

46. For a good summary and information from Rakowski's own unpublished memoir see Oberdorfer, *The Turn*, pp. 358–61.

47. Gorbachev had also probably given direct support to Mladenov, definitely in unseating Jakeš. See chapter 13.

48. "Encouraging Political and Economic Reforms in Poland," President Bush's address at Hamtramck, April 17, 1989, *State Bulletin*, vol. 89 (June 1989), pp. 3–5.

    Bush was, however, cautious in his proposals for American aid to the new signs of liberalization in Eastern Europe, initially proposing only $125 million over three years.

July (and, in Warsaw, cited Gorbachev's UN address on freedom of choice). Bush and Baker had decided that there were favorable prospects for the liberalization and even for democracy in Eastern Europe, but with the acquiescence of the Soviet leadership, rather than through a direct challenge to it. Bush was therefore reasonably circumspect in his statements while in Poland and Hungary. And Secretary Baker, when he saw Shevardnadze in Paris two weeks later (for a conference on Cambodia, on July 29), warned of the adverse consequences if force were to be used in Eastern Europe but also reassured the Soviet leader that the United States would not seek to take advantage of the situation to the security disadvantage of the Soviet Union. Shevardnadze, in reply, assured Baker the Soviet Union would not resort to force—as, indeed, it did not.[49]

Gorbachev continued throughout this process to reaffirm acceptance of freedom of choice for the Eastern European peoples, even if it meant an end of communist rule. At the Sorbonne during a visit to France, on July 5, following the fall of the Polish communist government, he again related freedom of choice to his conception of a common "European home" uniting Eastern and Western Europe.[50] He reiterated this stand in November in Rome after the fall of the Berlin Wall, again championing not only a common European home but also a "common civilization, in which the values of all mankind and freedom of choice hold dominion."[51]

The reorientation of Soviet policy and action in Europe was of course part of a still broader change in outlook and policy. There is now available a remarkable document, "On the Strategic Line of the USSR with Respect to the UN and Related International Organizations," approved by the Politburo on August 28, 1989. While prepared for the occasion of the then-forthcoming forty-fourth session of the UN General Assembly, the twenty-four-page secret document established a new general line of overall policy for the activities of all

---

Congress pushed for more, and spurred by the movement of events in November, authorized $938 million.

49. Information from an American source; and see Oberdorfer, *The Turn*, p. 360.

   American reassurance was not, however, consistent. In a classical example of policy inertia and poor coordination, the annual ritual "Captive Nations Week" (July 16–23), which coincided with Bush's visit to Eastern Europe (July 9–13), was written by inveterate cold warriors. Bush's proclamation referred to the "repression" of the "national consciousness" of the Baltic states—just as they were being permitted to regain a real voice; and in contrast to reality and Bush's statement in Europe, his proclamation intoned, "Even as we see rays of light in some countries [of Eastern Europe], we must recognize that brutal repression continues." See "Proclamation 5996—Captive Nations Week," July 6, 1989, *Presidential Documents*, vol. 25 (July 10, 1989), p. 1028.

50. "Seeking Common Criteria for Progress, Speech of M. S. Gorbachev," *Pravda*, July 6, 1989.

51. "Common Responsibility for the Fate of the World, Speech of M. S. Gorbachev," *Pravda*, November 30, 1989.

   See the further discussion in chapter 13.

Soviet institutions (with a coordinating role delegated to the Ministry of Foreign Affairs). The document, which bears all the hallmarks of its preparation by Shevardnadze's diplomatic team, was in effect the codification of new thinking relating to the UN and international cooperation in pursuit of common human interests in striking contrast to the Cold War confrontational approach of the preceding forty-four years.

The paper noted that the UN Charter had been predicated on cooperative pursuit of common human values. "The confrontation of the period of the 'Cold War,' however, long paralyzed the activity of the UN, and basically converted it into a forum for an exchange of polemical rhetoric." The Soviet approach formed in those years thus regarded the UN "almost exclusively as a propaganda tribune." Even after favorable tendencies began to develop in the world at the end of the 1960s, it was acknowledged, the Soviet Union failed to recognize the new potential of the United Nations. The April 1985 Central Committee plenum (in Soviet terms meaning the advent of the Gorbachev leadership) was credited with being the decisive turning point. "The radical change in the foreign policy course of the Soviet Union associated with new thinking and recognition of the reality of an integral interdependent world of our times permitted [us] to evaluate in a new way the significance and prospects for the activity of the UN and other instruments of international cooperation of states, to begin a decisive restructuring of our [policy] line relating to them." On this basis, the Soviet Union was working to strengthen the role of the United Nations.[52]

According to the document, "recognition of the necessity of regarding national security as a component part of international security is strengthening." Moreover, "with a gradual lessening of the role of the military factor in world politics, the significance of political means of resolving the most important international questions with reliance on the authority and capacities of the UN is growing." The Soviet withdrawal from Afghanistan was credited with having given a boost to UN efforts to resolve other regional conflicts, and more generally with having contributed to a growing rejection of use of force and increasing reliance on political means to resolve conflicts. The United Nations also was envisaged as able to play an increasing role in facilitating disarmament and confidence-building agreements and in active peacekeeping operations.

While imbued with idealism reflected in the new thinking, the Politburo decision on a new active support for the UN and other international

---

52. The document is in the former Central Committee archive, now the Center for the Storage of Contemporary Documentation (TsKhSD) and is located in TsKhSD, Fond 89, Perechen' 9, Dokument 26, *O strategicheskoi linii SSSR primenitel'no k OON i svyazannym s nei mezhdunarodnym organizatsiyam* (On the Strategic Line of the USSR with Respect to the UN and Related International Organizations), Central Committee document no. 164/177, excerpt from protocol no. 164 of the meeting of the Politburo, August 28, 1989, covering memo 2 pages, basic document 24 pp., quotations above from pp. 1–3 of the basic document.

organizations was also predicated on hard-headed pursuit of Soviet national interests. As the document made clear, this new strategic line of policy was conceived as "responsive to our long-term state interests." For one thing, the United Nations was seen as a valuable forum for major Soviet initiatives. In addition, Soviet status as one of the permanent members of the UN Security Council "presents wide opportunities for raising the role and influence of the USSR in world affairs through active participation in the search for resolving crisis situations in various regions with less cost." To be sure, support for UN peacekeeping activities, for example, could entail increased financial outlays, but it was noted "incomparably less than assistance in one or another form for parties to a conflict," and such savings should be shifted to meet these new expenditures. Indeed, more generally the costs of support to international organizations should, the document declared, be regarded as."a contribution to strengthening our security." In addition, because increased international cooperation would assist integration into the world economy, such expenditures would also constitute "an investment in our social-economic and scientific-technological progress."

Other important aspects of the new course of foreign policy were reflected, including the "deideologizing" of international politics and shift from confrontation to seeking a "balance of interests" among nations. Familiar aims of internal as well as international policy included disarmament, confidence-building measures, nonuse of force, conversions from military industry, downturn of military spending by applying a criterion of "reasonable sufficiency," and overcoming the "secrecy syndrome."

In pursuing the new increased reliance on cooperation in international organizations, a key role was assigned to regarding as "a long-term strategy the strengthening and broadening of constructive cooperation with the United States, and its translation into multilateral measures, without which it would be unrealistic to count on a practical raising of the effectiveness of international organizations and a realization of their decisions." Of course, it was also noted that the Soviet Union should "actively support and develop the interest in cooperation with us in international organizations displayed by the majority of Western European countries, Canada and Japan, without providing any basis for accusing the USSR of placing them in opposition to the United States and at the same time using them as a supplementary lever for pressure on the Americans." For the Third World, an active policy of support "in the spirit of the new political thinking" was advanced, cultivating multilateral international cooperation and discarding the practice of automatic voting in its support. Not a word appears about fraternal support for revolutionary or "progressive" countries. In contrast, "our own [Soviet] state interests" were said to be the key guideline in relations with those countries.

A "priority of strengthening the solidarity of the countries of the socialist community" was still included in this August 1989 policy guidance, but one could sense this priority was more from tradition than conviction. It was not, however, mere inertia. The unity of the bloc was even described as "less and less a synonym for identity" and would be "realized through a pluralism of interests and approaches to particular concrete questions on the international agenda." It was also noted pointedly that Romania, East Germany, and Cuba were lagging in "deideologization and democratization of politics." In another category, all that was said about the other major communist power was a laconic short sentence calling to "widen the sphere of mutual understanding with the People's Republic of China."

In a quite different category, and reflecting the attempt at controlled internal decentralization in pursuit of a new union treaty, attention was also devoted to broadening the international role of the constituent republics of the USSR. The document set the objective not only of reinforcing the role of the Ukrainian Soviet Socialist Republic and the Belorussian Soviet Socialist Republic, already members of the United Nations and some other organizations, but also of gaining acceptance for membership of other union republics of the USSR in various international organizations where their membership could be justified. Short of that, wider participation of representatives of the republics in Soviet Union delegations was called for. While in part the aim was no doubt to enhance Soviet influence, even more it was an attempt to accord with the new internal role of the constituent republics of the union.

Many aspects of the changing Soviet foreign policy and conduct of its relations were undergoing change. Decisions such as those in this document needed to be addressed not only in terms of guidance and objectives, but in numerous concrete decisions, many of which were more controversial within the Soviet political establishment. For example, there were economic, political, ideological, and military constituencies for and against changing Soviet relations with, say, Cuba to a new basis grounded in Soviet "national interests." Or, to note one other example of a different kind, there was a continuing tug-of-war between the Foreign Ministry and the KGB over the extent to which Soviet personnel working in international organizations and in Soviet delegations to them should be professional diplomats or intelligence officers. The Politburo decision of August 1989 made an indirect reference to this matter, and referred to an earlier decision, calling for "complete fulfillment, without exceptions, of the letter and spirit of the Central Committee instruction of April 14, 1988, both in the quantitative and qualitative aspects in preparing and sending qualified professionals for work in the UN and other organizations. The relationship to the international civil service must be placed on the level of the new political thinking and conducted in accordance with generally accepted international practice."[53] It is not clear whether American prodding on such matters through the earlier pressure to reduce the number of Soviet personnel in the United

---

53. Ibid., pp. 3–9, 18–23. I was told of the Foreign Ministry-KGB struggle over personnel by senior Soviet Foreign Ministry officials.

Nations, and expulsions of Soviet intelligence personnel by the United States and other countries, helped the new thinkers such as Shevardnadze. On balance, it probably did.

## The Malta Summit

Even before the announcement in September of a summit meeting planned for mid-1990, unknown to all but a handful of close aides Bush and Baker were already negotiating with Shevardnadze for a possible earlier, less formal, "interim" summit meeting. This idea was given further impetus by the rapid course of change in Eastern Europe over the summer and fall of 1989. On October 31, it was announced in Washington and Moscow that Bush and Gorbachev would meet on warships of the two countries in the Mediterranean on December 2 and 3, 1989. Described by Bush at the time as an "informal meeting in the interim before a real summit in June [1990]," the meeting at Malta marked an important step in developing closer American-Soviet relations.[54]

In the few weeks between the announcement of the "interim summit" and its actual occurrence, the revolutionary changes in Eastern Europe had dramatically swept aside the old order there, and with it much of the familiar Cold War framework for U.S.-Soviet relations. It was not easy to grasp immediately the full import of the change, but it was obvious that something of historic significance had taken place.

President Bush initially reacted to the developments in Eastern Europe with remarkable reserve. Indeed, he seemed almost too restrained in reacting to the dramatic opening of the Berlin Wall, the visible symbol of the division of Europe as well as Germany. But he did not want to add to the trauma of this event in Moscow. Most important, he did recognize that the changes in Europe now called for really moving "beyond containment," not only in rhetoric, and he set out to prepare for a concrete program and initiatives to go beyond containment in relations with the Soviet Union. Again, a small group of selected White House National Security Council (NSC) and State Department aides prepared the staff work in secrecy from the bureaucracy.

Like his predecessor, although with more diligence, Bush prepared for his first presidential summit with briefings, meetings, and a composite documentary film on Gorbachev, as well as checking on the work of his advisers in preparing an initiative in the field of bilateral relations rather than the usual field of arms control. Baker and Scowcroft tried also to work out a major new

---

54. The discussion of the Malta summit below draws on Raymond L. Garthoff, "The Mediterranean Summit," *Mediterranean Quarterly*, vol. 1 (Spring 1990), pp. 14–24.

arms reduction initiative concentrating on getting rid of MIRVed ICBMs, but with opposition from Defense Secretary Cheney and the Joint Chiefs of Staff that idea—and any new START initiative for Malta—was abandoned.[55]

The concrete business of the shipboard summit at Malta was thus primarily a "wrapping up" of matters under way before the Eastern European upheaval and only an incremental step in bilateral relations. But it also marked the beginning of a new stage in the U.S.-Soviet relationship.

Most political leaders feel a need for direct personal contact, and many believe that they are their own best exponents. Certainly this was true of both Reagan and Gorbachev, and the extraordinary transformation of American foreign policy toward the Soviet Union from the first to the second Reagan administrations would not have occurred without the summit meetings of 1985 through 1988. Bush, too, although less dependent than Reagan on such personal experience, by late July when planning began for an interim meeting wanted above all to establish a better understanding of and rapport with Gorbachev.

Gorbachev, for his part, had been impatient, and some of his advisers concerned, over the cool initial months of the Bush administration. Gorbachev wanted to resume a dialogue at the summit as soon as possible. Though the very fact of a meeting would revalidate his policy and be politically useful at home, its principal purpose from his standpoint was to engage Bush personally and to restore momentum to the process of normalizing and improving relations with the United States. In more specific terms, he sought to move forward the arms control agenda, to gain U.S. support for *perestroika* by ending discriminatory trade restrictions and facilitating Soviet integration into the world economic system, and to assure himself and others in the Soviet leadership that the United States would not seek to exploit the fast-moving situation in Eastern Europe to undercut Soviet security interests.

The meeting was clearly a success for both Bush and Gorbachev. The stature of each at home and in the world was enhanced. Moreover, the leaders placed U.S.-Soviet relations on a more even keel and steady course than they had enjoyed for a long time. At the same time, without carrying the comparison too far, the inability of the two superpower leaders to control or even to foresee the buffeting winds and seas that compelled a tactical change in their shipboard meeting plans symbolized the limits of their power in dealing also with elemental political changes such as those sweeping Eastern, Central, and, less dramatically, Western Europe.

---

55. For a more detailed informed account of Bush's preparations, see Beschloss and Talbott, *At the Highest Levels*, pp. 139–52.

There was no NSC meeting or discussion with Defense Secretary Cheney about the forthcoming Malta meeting, apart from his intervention to oppose the proposed initiative in MIRVed ICBMs.

The Malta meeting in historical perspective may be accorded the honor of symbolically representing the end of the postwar and Cold War world. It may even be seen as the first meeting to look ahead to a new relationship between East and West, a new Europe, and in some respects a new world. Although the Malta summit itself did not of course end the Cold War, it happened to take place at a time when a long-maturing process of change had suddenly leaped forward to reach a point where prospects for future cooperation could outweigh continuing competition, even though elements of both remained.

As President Bush said at Brussels, in characterizing his impression of Gorbachev's understanding, "He now sees that we want to have a cooperative, forward-leaning relationship with the Soviet Union."[56] It was important both that Bush himself should have so characterized American policy and that Gorbachev should have so seen it. And by all indications he did. Though there remained in each of the two countries doubts about the long-term intentions of the other, based on prudent caution as well as residual suspicions, there had been a growing awareness of real change and new prospects for normalization and even cooperation in the relationship. Even though some in Washington might still quail at the prospect, and some in Moscow as well, the two leaders and the two peoples seemed increasingly confident, and this confidence was grounded in new realities. As Gorbachev told Bush at Malta: "We don't consider you an enemy any more."[57]

The most immediate concerns on both sides, while not an issue between the two leaders, were eased by the confirmation of something that by then was evident: that the Brezhnev Doctrine of external socialist intervention was dead, and so too the Dulles Doctrine of external anticommunist rollback in Europe.

For all its potential and symbolic significance, Malta was in some other respects the "interim meeting" originally described by Bush. No agreements were concluded or even negotiated. Yet the meeting provided not only for a useful exchange of views but also for a joint resolve to press ahead in the strategic arms reduction talks (START), toward an interim U.S.-Soviet agreement to reduce sharply arsenals of chemical weapons, and of course toward an agreement on reducing Conventional Forces in Europe (CFE).[58]

President Bush used the occasion to advance bilateral economic relations "beyond containment." He commendably took the initiative, offering

---

56. "The President's News Conference in Brussels, Belgium," December 4, 1989, *Presidential Documents*, vol. 25 (December 11, 1989), p. 1892.

57. Oberdorfer, *The Turn*, p. 381. Shevardnadze later explained to Baker that this had not been an easy thing to say, and that conservatives in Moscow had criticized Gorbachev for giving in to the Americans, as well as losing Eastern Europe. Ibid.

58. In two areas, however, the United States rejected Soviet proposals. Gorbachev sought unsuccessfully to include an antisatellite ban as an objective in the nuclear and space arms talks, and Bush also declined to enter into talks on naval arms control.

steps to normalize trade relations through the prospective granting of most-favored-nation (MFN) status, thus removing discriminatory trade restrictions. He also promised to seek removal of legislative bars to credits. More broadly, Bush promised to support Soviet observer status in the General Agreement on Tariffs and Trade, thus helping to bring the Soviet Union into the world economic structure as its economic reform comes to warrant. As Gorbachev put it, their discussion provided "a political impetus that had been lacking for our economic cooperation to gain momentum." He was clearly pleased and reaffirmed the Soviet effort "to turn our economy sharply toward cooperation with other countries, so that it would be part and parcel of the world economic system."[59] These initiatives by Bush did not require congressional funding, although lifting the statutory restrictions on export credits and MFN status required congressional concurrence.

The most controversial area of discussion was the subject of regional conflicts, especially the matter of arms sent from Nicaragua to the insurgents in El Salvador. But the difference of view, while real, was also limited. Gorbachev agreed with Bush on free elections in Nicaragua, on opposing the transfer of arms to the Salvadoran rebels, and on resolving conflicts in the region by political means. Gorbachev explained that the Nicaraguans had given the Soviets assurances that they were not sending arms. Bush insisted, with good basis, that Nicaragua was still sending arms, but he accepted Gorbachev's account and blamed Daniel Ortega for lying to Gorbachev. Two months later, when the Sandinistas lost the election in Nicaragua, the Soviet Union supported the transition.

All in all, for an interim summit a good deal was done. But the most important direct consequence was the establishment of a confident dialogue between the two men. The rapport between them was evident in their collaborative fielding of questions at an unprecedented (if also unplanned) joint press conference at the conclusion of the meetings. The Malta summit did for Bush and Gorbachev what the air flight to Wyoming did for Baker and Shevardnadze, establishing genuine mutual respect and confidence.

One indicative example of new understanding occurred after Gorbachev privately complained at Bush's repeated references to the developments in Eastern Europe as a triumph for "Western" democratic values; Gorbachev said these were shared universal values that the Soviet Union now was affirming. Bush had not reflected on that distinction, or realized that his wording conveyed an unintended invidious and politically difficult connotation from a Soviet perspective.

In his remarks in Brussels en route home from the summit, where he met with the NATO allies, President Bush therefore referred to the need to end the division of Europe and of Germany in accordance with "values that are

---

59. "Replies of M. S. Gorbachev and G. Bush to Questions of Journalists," *Pravda*, December 5, 1989.

becoming universal ideals." And in his New Year's greetings to the Soviet people a few weeks later, he again referred to democratic and human (rather than Western) values. In Brussels, he also emphasized that Gorbachev's response to the situation in Eastern Europe, his acceptance of peaceful change, and his readiness to accept disproportionately larger conventional arms reductions in Europe "deserved" and indeed "mandated" new thinking on the part of the West as well.[60]

A new era was dawning. As Gorbachev put it at Malta, "The world is leaving one epoch, the 'Cold War,' and entering a new one."[61]

Two weeks later, in a symbolic step that would have seemed inconceivable at the beginning of the year, Shevardnadze paid a visit to NATO headquarters in Brussels. Clearly, the Cold War was fading fast.

Only a few weeks later, on December 24, in an extraordinary illustration of how rapidly and how far the changing situation in Eastern Europe had affected American thinking and U.S. policy toward the Soviet Union, Secretary of State James Baker said the United States would not object if the Soviet Union and its Warsaw Pact allies "felt it necessary to intervene [with military force] on behalf of the opposition" to the toppled Ceauşescu regime in Romania in order to prevent widespread bloodshed or defeat for the reformers.[62] The merits of making such an invitation to intervene were dubious, and it was not sought or appreciated in Moscow,[63] but it was a remarkable reflection of a basic shift in outlook toward seeing the Soviet Union as a force contributing to positive change in the world rather than assuming it to be a permanent source of destabilization and threat. It would have been hard to find a more striking example reflecting American recognition of the end of the Cold War.

Also on December 24, as the 1980s were ending, *Time* magazine, which two years earlier had picked Gorbachev as its Man of the Year, selected him for the even greater signal honor of Man of the Decade.

---

60. "Text of the [President's] Afternoon Intervention Delivered at North Atlantic Treaty Organization Headquarters in Brussels, Belgium," and "The President's News Conference," December 4, 1989, *Presidential Documents*, vol. 25 (December 11, 1989), pp. 1888, 1895.

61. *Pravda*, December 5, 1989.

62. See Don Oberdorfer, "Baker Implies U.S. Would Back East-Bloc Military Aid to Rebels; French, Dutch Would Support Soviet Role in Romania," *Washington Post*, December 25, 1989, p. A37.

63. The Soviet leaders had no desire or intention to intervene, and some officials darkly wondered if the United States was engaged in a subtle attempt at entrapment or perhaps indirect efforts to justify the recent American military intervention in Panama. Shevardnadze bluntly told Ambassador Matlock, when he raised the matter, that Baker's suggestion was "stupid," and that he categorically opposed any outside intervention in Romania. See Beschloss and Talbott, *At the Highest Levels*, pp. 170–71.

# 10   Ending the Cold War, 1990

DURING 1990, U.S. policy toward the Soviet Union shifted its focus from going "beyond containment" to the objective of moving "beyond the Cold War." In the wake of the Revolution of '89 in Central and Eastern Europe, the tasks of reunifying Germany and redefining European security came to the fore. Growing problems within the Soviet Union also increasingly came to affect Soviet, and American, policy and prospects for the future.

Presidents Bush and Gorbachev opened the year with an exchange of New Year's greetings in addresses to the peoples of the other country. Bush recapped the Malta meeting, reaffirming that the United States welcomed and supported "the dynamic process of reform in the Soviet Union," reassuring his listeners that "the West seeks no advantage from the extraordinary changes underway in the East." He alluded to East-West "sharing of democratic values" and hailed President Mikhail Gorbachev as "a good partner in peace." Gorbachev in turn noted that the two presidents agreed that "it was essential to get away from the Cold War" and that the future could open up "a period of genuine cooperation before us." He called for the new decade to be devoted "to drawing the United States and the Soviet Union closer together on the basis of universal human values and a balance of interests."[1]

Beneath this high plane of policy aspirations, genuine though they were, there also remained some people in both countries who were unsure whether this budding cooperation meant an end to competitive rivalry or merely a hiatus before renewed confrontation. In the Soviet Union there was a

---

1.   "New Year's Message to the People of the Soviet Union," January 1, 1990, *Weekly Compilation of Presidential Documents*, vol. 26 (January 8, 1990), p. 1. (Hereafter *Presidential Documents.*) Bush's message, broadcast by Radio Moscow, and Gorbachev's as recorded and delivered on Moscow television, are given in Foreign Broadcast Information Service, *Daily Report, Soviet Union*, January 2, 1990, p. 10. (Hereafter FBIS, *Soviet Union.*)

delayed shock reaction to the sudden loss of Soviet hegemony in Eastern Europe and of military parity in European alliances. But even in the United States, where the end of the Cold War certainly meant a drastically reduced threat, some people were still wary and suspected that the changed situation was too good to be true.

Two commentaries at the beginning of the year pointed up very nicely the range of reactions. Strobe Talbott, the Washington editor of *Time* magazine, in its first issue of the year presented a perceptive reevaluation of the new situation and a thoughtful analysis of how greatly the United States had exaggerated the Soviet threat during the Cold War. "A new consensus is emerging," he wrote, "that the Soviet threat is not what it used to be. The real point, however, is that it never was."[2] The other essay reflected stubborn clinging to the image of the enemy, not merely in terms of possible threats from an authoritarian nationalist alternative if Gorbachev should fail, but also depicting Gorbachev's own new thinking (and new action) as concealing an unalloyed determination to carry the Bolshevik conflict to the end, "awaiting the eventual re-emergence of conditions in which the presumed advantages in the management of conflict . . . will give Communist parties a decisive edge in dealing with a potentially fragmented world."[3] The author of the second view was Paul Nitze, and while Talbott was suggesting that the United States had exaggerated the Soviet communist peril for forty years, Nitze proudly harped back to the fundamental policy directive of the Cold War—National Security Council (NSC)–68 of 1950 (of which he had been a primary author) and not only suggested that its prescriptions had been valid for the past forty years but implied they would be for the next forty as well.

Within these two extremes, the political debate focused on two contending definitions of what was prudent and realistic. The Bush administration had clearly decided that the Cold War and confrontation in Europe were essentially over. It also saw a need for positive U.S. engagement to help move the Soviet Union into a new constructive relationship. As one aide to Baker put it, "If he [Gorbachev] is a man with a moving bottom line, then our policy should be to help him move where we want him to go."[4] In fact, the administration was moving cautiously and many felt too slowly. But the challenging view was that the administration was too prone to accept Gorbachev's new thinking and reform moves and was not sufficiently concerned about the enduring threat

---

2.   Strobe Talbott, "Rethinking the Red Menace," *Time*, January 1, 1990, pp. 66–72, quotation on p. 69.

3.   Paul H. Nitze, "Gorbachev's Plan for a Communist Comeback," *Washington Post*, January 10, 1990, p. A19.

4.   Thomas L. Friedman, "Fighting Words in a Genteel World," *New York Times*, February 2, 1990, p. A16, quoting the unidentified aide.

necessarily posed by the Soviet Union as a superpower. This view was expressed by both Henry Kissinger and Alexander Haig.[5]

Even within the Bush administration there was some divergence. Secretary of Defense Richard B. Cheney and the Joint Chiefs of Staff, on the one hand, while accepting that there was a diminished threat in Europe, still contended that "fundamental Soviet objectives in the Third World do not appear to have changed," and they believed conflict could still escalate to global war.[6] Director of Central Intelligence William H. Webster, on the other hand, as well as Secretary of State James Baker, took a very different view. Webster testified that "the changes are probably already irreversible in several critical respects," that there was now "little chance that Soviet hegemony could be restored in Eastern Europe," and that even if a hard-line regime were to succeed Gorbachev, it "would have little incentive to engage in major confrontations with the United States" and indeed would even be "unlikely to indulge in a major military buildup."[7]

The course of the year would essentially decide this debate in favor of the administration, and the next two years would decisively favor the Webster-Baker position within it.

## European Security after the Cold War

Bush and Gorbachev had not addressed at Malta the major looming issue of European security in a post–Cold War world. Bush at Malta had even been cautious and evasive on a proposal Gorbachev had advanced in Rome a few days earlier for a summit meeting of the heads of government of the thirty-five members of the Conference on Security and Cooperation in Europe (CSCE). Gorbachev, in turn, still spoke of the "reality" of the existence of two German states as a "decision of history," although he also said in the present tense that "history itself decides" the fate of Europe and the German states. He

---

5.  Kissinger expressed his views on public television's "American Interests" program on January 20, with an account and excerpts cited in Friedman, *New York Times*, February 2, 1990, p. A16. A similar plea for more reliance on military deterrence, based on a belief that the Soviet "strategic interest" had not been redefined, was expressed by Alexander M. Haig, Jr., "Unjustified Euphoria," *Washington Post*, February 11, 1990, p. C7. For a criticism of alleged "softness" in America's effort to help Gorbachev prevail, see Rowland Evans and Robert Novak, "The U.S.-Soviet Love-In," *Washington Post*, February 12, 1990, p. A11.

6.  Patrick E. Tyler, "New Pentagon 'Guidance' Cites Soviet Threat in Third World," *Washington Post*, February 13, 1990, p. A1.

7.  Patrick E. Tyler, "Webster Sees No Revival of Soviet Threat," *Washington Post*, March 2, 1990, p. A1.

stressed the need to avoid "any artificial acceleration" of the process, but he did not say that change was impossible.[8] Bush followed that lead in Brussels the very next day by answering a question about how quickly German reunification might occur with a comment about "not trying to accelerate that process."[9]

For Bush and Baker, only recently ambivalent over sudden stirrings of German interest in unification, the key to future security and the development of East-West relations became achievement of German reunification, with Germany remaining in NATO, and Soviet acquiescence. As 1990 began, attainment of that objective was by no means assured. The rising German interest in reunification might prove stronger than West German ties to NATO if the Soviet Union made German withdrawal from NATO the price for Soviet acquiescence and withdrawal. In the Soviet Union, a strong current of concern arose over the drift of Eastern Europe away from the socialist camp, creating for the first time political opposition to Gorbachev's foreign policy based on "new thinking." The rapidly emerging prospect of absorption of East Germany by the Federal Republic of Germany was ominous enough in political and economic terms. If Germany also remained in NATO, the whole East-West strategic balance would be upset. And the concomitant weakening and possible collapse of the Warsaw Pact would intensify a threat to Soviet security. If Gorbachev were to see the situation in this light, or if the Soviet leadership were to impose this view and if necessary replace Gorbachev, the uncertainties and dangers for Eastern Europe and hence for overall European and American security would be great.

In his State of the Union address, President Bush proposed a substantial reduction of American and Soviet troops in Europe to supplement the reductions in major categories of conventional arms being negotiated at the multilateral talks on conventional forces in Europe (CFE). Bush's proposal called for reducing forces in the central region of Europe to equal levels of 195,000 troops, although the United States would be allowed to keep 30,000 additional troops deployed elsewhere in Europe.[10] For the central region, the United States would only have to cut about 60,000 troops, while the Soviet Union would have to reduce by about 370,000. As for the rest of Europe, the United States would cut about 20,000 troops and the Soviet Union none, since

---

8.    "Remarks of the President and Chairman Gorbachev and a Question-and-Answer Session with Reporters at Malta," December 3, 1989, *Presidential Documents*, vol. 25, (December 11, 1989), p. 1878.

9.    "The President's News Conference," December 4, 1989, ibid., p. 1892.

10.   "Address before a Joint Session of the Congress on the State of the Union," January 31, 1990, *Presidential Documents*, vol. 26 (February 5, 1990), p. 150. Bush did not mention the extra 30,000 U.S. troops beyond the central region (or, in his words, "central and eastern Europe"); it was disclosed in a separate "fact sheet" issued to the press. See "White House Fact Sheet on the President's Conventional Armed Forces in Europe Initiative," ibid., p. 151.

it had no forces except in the central region. The United States, however, would still be left with 30,000 troops, and the Soviet Union would have none in areas beyond the central region. The Soviet Union was already negotiating to withdraw its forces from Czechoslovakia and Hungary and unilaterally cutting its forces in Germany and no doubt could make substantial cuts.[11] The much greater Soviet troop reductions, and the remaining American advantage in Europe as a whole beyond Soviet borders, did not pose a problem of real military significance for Moscow. The discrepancy did, however, draw attention to and exacerbate a serious political problem at home of explaining what appeared to be a one-sided pell-mell Soviet retreat.

Bush had telephoned Gorbachev on the thirty-first, just prior to his address, to tell him about the proposal and to discuss briefly the overall situation in Europe and express hopes for progress in the strategic arms negotiations.[12]

Baker visited Moscow on February 7–9, 1990, and heard first-hand Gorbachev's statement of his concerns over German reunification and above all over a reunified Germany in NATO. While acknowledging legitimate Soviet security concerns, and making clear the American intention not to exploit the situation to the detriment of Soviet security interests, Baker made clear why the United States did not believe the CSCE was capable of serving as the main foundation for European security and why a reunified Germany should remain in the NATO collective security arrangement. He also drew a useful distinction between aspects of the problem that must be resolved only by the people of Germany, and other aspects that should be dealt with by the four residual World War II allied powers. Having already privately sounded out the British, French, and West German leaders, he now prepared the way for a possible "2+4" parallel East and West German and U.S.-USSR-UK-French and German negotiations.[13]

---

11. Agreements were reached in February and March 1990, respectively, on the complete withdrawal of Soviet forces from Czechoslovakia and Hungary by July 1, 1991. This involved about 75,000 troops and five army divisions in Czechoslovakia, and 50,000 troops and three divisions in Hungary. (Another division and about 10,000 personnel had been withdrawn from Hungary in 1989 and early 1990.) In addition, on June 7 at a meeting of the Warsaw Pact Political Consultative Committee a new commission was established to consider a possible new role for the pact; Hungary had already given notice of its intention to leave the military alliance by the end of 1991. The future of the alliance was, at best, uncertain. Poland, however, still with a communist president and communist-dominated lower house, and concerned over possible security risks in a reunified Germany, declined a Soviet offer to discuss Soviet troop withdrawal. And it remained possible that the Warsaw Pact might be refashioned. See chapter 13.

12. This was his first direct telephone call since the initial one the previous January. In arranging the connection, Moscow insisted that Gorbachev actually "initiate" the call.

13. The idea was first advanced by U.S. officials during a visit to Washington by UK Foreign Secretary Douglas Hurd; the idea was then broached on February 2 to West German

German Chancellor Helmut Kohl met with Gorbachev just one day after Baker, and as a result of their talks Gorbachev publicly acknowledged that "the question of unity of the German nation should be decided by the Germans themselves," with due account of the major stake of the international community in ensuring that the positive movement in East-West relations not be adversely affected or "the European balance" upset.[14] At a multilateral East-West summit meeting in Ottawa (on Bush's Open Skies proposal) a week later, on February 13, agreement was formally reached on a 2+4 framework for dealing with German reunification.

Agreement on a framework did not, of course, dispose of the substantial issues, but it did facilitate their resolution. The two Germanies moved rapidly toward unification after an overwhelming vote in favor of unification in East Germany on March 18. As Germany moved during the summer toward economic and subsequent political reunification, parallel negotiations proceeded on the external role of a united Germany.

Gorbachev on February 9, in his meeting with Baker, had offered to accept either 195,000 or 225,000 equal force levels for the United States and the Soviet Union, but not Bush's proposed equal levels of 195,000 in the central region with 30,000 additional troops for the United States in the rest of Europe. Baker agreed to present this counterproposal to Washington. Gorbachev, however, needed to wrap up a deal. Only four days later, at Ottawa, Shevardnadze announced Soviet acceptance of the U.S. proposed manpower reductions, giving the United States the additional 30,000 troops outside the central region of Europe.[15]

---

Foreign Minister Hans-Dietrich Genscher, who had been thinking along similar lines; and on February 6 Baker had a brief talk on it with French Foreign Minister Roland Dumas. Although it was not yet a formally agreed proposal, all seemed favorably inclined. Baker therefore advanced the idea to Gorbachev on February 9, and the initial cautious response was not negative. See Don Oberdorfer, *The Turn: From the Cold War to a New Era, the United States and the Soviet Union, 1983–1990* (Poseidon Press, 1991), pp. 393–97.

For a detailed account of Baker's meetings with Gorbachev and Shevardnadze see Michael R. Beschloss and Strobe Talbott, *At the Highest Levels: The Inside Story of the End of the Cold War* (Little, Brown and Company, 1993), pp. 179–87.

14. See "Meeting of M. S. Gorbachev with H. Kohl," *Pravda*, February 11, 1990. Gorbachev, who only two months earlier had said that history had created two German states and would decide the future, conceded now that history had moved "with unexpected speed."

15. Although some in Washington had been disposed to accept Gorbachev's counterproposal, Bush had rejected it publicly on February 11, and Gorbachev decided to accept the U.S. proposal without delay, as was done on February 13.

Incidentally, even though the U.S. proposal was one-sidedly to American advantage, a few in the Pentagon and on Capitol Hill grumbled over the constraint on American deployments in southern Europe in the future.

At the February meetings, Baker and Shevardnadze also reached agreement on a bilateral deep reduction of chemical weapons to be formalized at the summit. Negotiations on strategic arms reductions, to be discussed shortly, showed some progress but no breakthrough. An attempt to find a new formula for resolution of the continuing civil war in Afghanistan failed.

On February 28, Bush again called Gorbachev and made clear that both he and Chancellor Kohl (who had just visited Washington) believed that a reunified Germany should remain in NATO. Gorbachev again expressed his concerns over such an outcome. They also discussed the situation in Nicaragua, where the Sandinista government had just held, and lost, a free election, and Bush expressed his appreciation for Gorbachev's public pledge of support to the newly elected Nicaraguan government.[16]

Development of economic relations between the United States and the Soviet Union, meanwhile, moved along two different paths.[17] Bilateral talks by senior experts of the two countries on normalizing trade relations began on February 12 and by late May had reached agreement on the technical level. Political issues, however, arose and precluded agreement at the summit.

On a parallel track, meetings undertaken by the seventeen-nation Western Coordinating Committee for Multilateral Export Controls (COCOM) in February and June led to relaxation of controls on a range of technologies. This limited relaxation was partly the result of internal U.S. reevaluations in the light of the changing picture in Eastern Europe and the Soviet Union, and partly the result of complaints and pressures from Western European countries.

On a third track, the United States was less forthcoming. When a new European Bank for Reconstruction and Development (EBRD) was being established to channel assistance to the countries of Eastern Europe, the United States (in March) vetoed EBRD lending to the Soviet Union, which most of the Western European countries had favored. And in June Bush rebuffed a proposal by Chancellor Helmut Kohl to join in providing economic assistance to the Soviet Union, saying that the United States would not object if others wished to provide such aid but would not itself do so until economic reforms were "in place."

---

16. Information from an informed Soviet source, corroborated by Beschloss and Talbott, *At the Highest Levels*, p. 193.

17. The administration's evaluation of the economic reform process in the Soviet Union, and outline of its own policy toward economic relations, was set out in some detail by Secretary Baker in testimony to the House Ways and Means Committee on April 18. See Secretary Baker, "Imperatives of Economic Reform: Changes in Soviet and East European Economies," *U.S. Department of State Dispatch*, vol. 1 (September 3, 1990), pp. 26–31. (Hereafter *State Dispatch*; this publication began with this issue as a successor to the venerable *Department of State Bulletin*, publication of which had unaccountably been discontinued at the end of 1989.)

Baker and Shevardnadze met in Washington on April 4–6 to begin shaping the summit agenda. The most concrete result of the meeting was the public announcement that a summit was planned for May 30 to June 3 in Washington. This was an earlier time than had been foreshadowed at Malta and was responsive to a request from Gorbachev that it would precede his planned Communist Party congress. The discussions of strategic arms reductions were not encouraging, so that the prospect for an agreement by the time of the summit seemed dim. Setting a summit date was significant because it meant a new commitment by President Bush to meet Gorbachev notwithstanding new concerns that had arisen in the United States owing to tension in the Soviet Union over Lithuanian aspirations for independence.

A final preparatory meeting for the forthcoming Washington summit meeting took Baker to Moscow for talks on May 16–19. Again, discussions on strategic arms reductions (to be discussed) were disappointing. Several useful but secondary agreements for the summit were confirmed. But there was no major step forward, either in bilateral negotiations or on the one main remaining issue: terms of German reunification. Baker tried out without success several arguments in support of the American position that a reunified Germany must remain in NATO, contending that this would serve stability and Soviet as well as Western security interests.

Both sides continued to work to resolve differences in order to reach agreement on a strategic arms treaty and to have a successful summit. At the same time, each also had other important interests that did not always coincide. If the rising tension in the Baltic republics caused a domestic political problem for President Bush, it caused a much more severe political issue for Gorbachev and the Soviet leadership. Thus the Politburo-approved instructions for Shevardnadze's meeting with President Bush in Washington in April called for a "preemptive" Soviet demarche on the issue in order "to lead Washington to refrain from possible intentions to encourage more openly separatist forces in the Baltic states."[18] Gorbachev actually met with Lithuanian Prime Minister

18.  In conducting research for this study, I was able in Moscow in 1992 to obtain from the former party Central Committee archives the memorandums submitted to and approved by the Politburo providing instructions for Shevardnadze's talks in Washington in April and talks with Baker in Moscow in May 1990. In both cases, attached to brief top-secret Politburo approval sheets were six-page memorandums for the Politburo, coordinated and signed by Foreign Minister Eduard Shevardnadze, Party Secretary Lev Zaikov, KGB Chief Vladimir Kryuchkov, Minister of Defense Marshal Dmitry Yazov, Politburo member Aleksandr Yakovlev, and leaders of the military-industrial complex (in February Party Secretary Oleg Baklanov and Deputy Prime Minister and head of the Military-Industrial Commission (VPK) Igor Belousov, and in May in their absence Vladimir Koblov). Attached to these memorandums were detailed "Instructions," covering political and also more specific technical arms control and other issues, forty-four pages plus eleven pages of annexes in May, and thirty-six plus eleven pages in April. These memorandums thus reveal in some detail the positions and negotiation guidelines governing the Soviet side and illuminate Soviet objectives and priorities. Although the

Kazimera Prunskiene on the day before he met Baker on May 18, thus opening high-level negotiations. Bush had received Prunskiene in a low-key meeting in Washington on May 3.

The failure in these meetings to move forward on the terms of German reunification is also explained by the fact that the Politburo-approved instructions for the talks of Gorbachev and others with Baker in May flatly stated that the inclusion of a unified Germany in NATO was "unacceptable to us"—an even stronger statement than the April instructions for Shevardnadze's visit to Washington, that "we cannot agree" to the inclusion of a unified Germany in NATO.[19]

---

Soviet instructions sought to keep the focus on disarmament issues, they also reflected the high priority of the issues of the reunification of Germany and the internal Soviet problem of the situation in the Baltic states.

See Center for the Storage of Contemporary Documentation (TsKhSD), Fond 89, Perechen' 9, Dokument 100, *O direktivakh dlya peregovorov Ministra inostrannykh del SSSR s Prezidentom SShA Dzh. Bushem i Gosudarstvennym sekretarem Dzh. Beikerom (Vashington, 4-6 aprelya 1990 g.)* (On Directives for the Negotiations of the Minister of Foreign Affairs of the USSR with US President G. Bush and Secretary of State J. Baker [Washington, April 4–6, 1990]), excerpt from protocol no. 184 of the meeting of the Politburo, April 2, 1990, P 184/25, Top Secret, with attachments 57 pp.; and Fond 89, Perechen' 10, Dokument 61, *O direktivakh dlya peregovorov c Gosudarstvennym sektretarem SShA Dzh. Beikerom v Moskve 16-19 maya 1990 g.* (On Directives for the Negotiations with US Secretary of State J. Baker in Moscow, May 16–19, 1990), excerpt from protocol no. 187 of the meeting of the Politburo of the CC CPSU on May 16, 1990, P 187/31, Top Secret/Special File, with attachments 62 pp. The passage cited is from p. 1 of the "Instructions" for the meeting with President Bush attached to the April memorandum. Also now available is the text of the confidential letter from Gorbachev to Bush hand-carried by Shevardnadze on April 4, approved by the Politburo on April 2: Fond 89, Perechen' No. 9, Dokument 101, *Ob otvetnom poslanii t. Gorbacheva M.S. Prezidentu SShA G. Bushu* (On Comrade M. S. Gorbachev's Letter of Response to U.S. President G. Bush), excerpt from protocol no. 184 of the meeting of the Politburo, April 2, 1990, P 184/28, Top Secret, 1 p. memo plus 6 pp. text.

19. *O direktivakh*, P 184/25, April 2, 1990, appended "Instructions for the Meeting of the Minister of Foreign Affairs of the USSR with U.S. President G. Bush," p. 2; P 187/31, May 16, 1990, "Instructions for the Talks with U.S. Secretary of State J. Baker in Moscow, May 16–19, 1990," p. 30.

In April, the Politburo "Instructions" called for insisting on a German peace treaty, but by mid-May that had been dropped for insistence on various conditions before four-power rights were relinquished. A "transitional period," however, was still sought, and reunification by *Anschluss* or absorption of East Germany was still opposed. The May "Instructions" stated the position on reunified Germany not being in NATO as follows: "Place the question of the military-political status of a future Germany at the center of discussion. Emphasize that for us the inclusion of a united Germany in NATO is unacceptable—politically and psychologically. We cannot agree to what would in that case inevitably be a destruction of the balance of power and stability in Europe. A united Germany must have equal obligations toward the U.S. and other NATO participants and the USSR and states of Eastern Europe." The last sentence may have cushioned the later fallback from this position. Interestingly, it was added in the "Instructions" in place

Before turning to the midyear Washington summit, it is necessary to look into the course of internal Soviet political developments. These were not only the key factors affecting progress in the development of U.S.-Soviet relations, but they were to become crucial to the future of the Soviet Union.

## Internal Soviet Developments and U.S.-Soviet Relations

Each year of the Gorbachev *perestroika* was, in a sense, crucial and each became more difficult. By the end of 1991, internal tensions and conflicts would overwhelm not only Gorbachev but the Soviet Union itself, but throughout 1990, although the danger was recognized, the outcome was not yet clear to anyone.

In retrospect, it is possible to distinguish the growing internal contradictions in terms of three challenges, each crucial, all interrelated. First, and always most immediate, was the familiar political struggle in the upper reaches of the Communist Party leadership and party machine. Second was the new and unfamiliar broader political process unleashed by *glasnost* and *demokratizatsiya*, bringing powerful new political forces into play, often in unforeseen, uncontrolled, and not always constructive ways. Third, and increasingly pressing, was the need for economic reform, a need well recognized but inherently very difficult to carry out, and all the more so given powerful opposition in the political establishment and powerful new rising demands finding diverse expression in the broader political crucible.

Gorbachev was keenly attuned to the political leadership struggles, which he continued in 1990 to wage successfully. He had given deliberate impetus to general political reform, including democratization and movement toward a civil society, but he had failed to appreciate how this process could complicate, and even stymie, management of political and economic reform. And he failed to realize the potential for centrifugal tendencies, especially in the republics, often coupled with resurgent nationalism. Finally, though economic reform became more and more urgent, it also became more difficult to fashion, to decide on, and to implement in the context of political division and political volatility. Meanwhile, the year 1990 saw the Soviet economy slip badly from low rates of growth in the late 1980s to negative growth in all key

---

of another sentence in the Central Committee memorandum, dropped in the actual "Instructions," which would have hardened the Soviet position. It read "That [destruction of the balance of power and stability in Europe] would create a danger for us in the military-strategic situation." Both papers were approved by the Politburo on May 16, but the detailed instructions on this point had probably been drafted in Shevardnadze's Foreign Ministry. See P 187/31, p. 4, and "Instructions," p. 30. For discussion of the Soviet position on developments in Eastern Europe, see the discussion in chapter 13.

indexes.[20] Moreover, temporizing interim reform measures were contributing to the decline. And the economic recession was stimulating political regionalism and giving ammunition to political opponents of *perestroika* who could seek popular unsophisticated support for a return to the good old days.

The year opened with a series of local regional crises. On January 3 Soviet troops had to intervene to quell rioting on the Azerbaijan-Iran border. By January 19–20 after several dozen had died in rioting in Baku, Soviet troops had to intervene in a forceful reestablishment of order that cost several dozen more lives.[21] On February 11 riots broke out in Dushanbe, capital of Tajikistan, over false rumors that scarce apartments were being given to Armenian refugees from Azerbaijan. On May 28 two dozen Armenians were killed in clashes with police in Yerevan. In early June about 150 people were killed in riots in Kirghizia, again requiring intervention by troops.

Less violent but far more significant steps continued to be taken toward independence of the Baltic states. On January 11–13 Gorbachev visited Vilnius and was shocked to find the determination and popular support for independence, reflected in a demonstration by 250,000 Lithuanians. While in Lithuania, he reluctantly conceded the theoretical possibility of secession, though he argued for liberalization within a continuing union. In republic elections in February and March, the Sajudis national front in Lithuania won a resounding victory, 90 of 141 seats, similar fronts in Latvia won a narrow majority, and in Estonia won a near majority, in the Supreme Soviets of those republics.

On March 11, Lithuania declared its independence and elected a noncommunist nationalist, Vytautas Landsbergis, as president. A nonviolent display of Soviet military force in Vilnius was ineffectual. On April 18 Moscow cut off oil deliveries to Lithuania, which was lifted after Lithuania on June 30 agreed to suspend for one hundred days (but not to retract) its declaration of independence. Meanwhile, on May 4 Latvia declared its intention to become independent.

---

20. CIA estimates indicate a decline in GNP from an average annual growth rate of 1.3 in the years 1986–1990 to between -2.4 and -5.0 in 1990. Industrial output during the same period fell from 0.9 to -2.8 and agricultural output declined from 1.8 to -3.6. See James Noren and Laurie Kurtzweg, "The Soviet Economy Unravels: 1985–1991," in *The Former Soviet Union in Transition*, Study Papers submitted to the Joint Economic Committee, Congress of the United States (Washington: Government Printing Office, 1993), vol. 1, p. 14. Official Soviet sources indicated a comparable, though somewhat less precipitous, decline. See *SSSR v tsifrakh v 1990 godu* (The USSR in Statistics in 1990) (Moscow: Finansy i statistika, 1991), p. 40.

21. On January 16, the White House and State Department endorsed Gorbachev's resort to military force to restore order and prevent further bloodshed in Azerbaijan. See Thomas L. Friedman, "Soviets' Response Gets U.S. Support," *New York Times*, January 17, 1990, p. A8. See also "A Talk with the President," *Newsweek*, January 29, 1990, p. 35.

Nationalist sentiments were being increasingly voiced in other quarters too. In January crowds in Moldavia had demonstrated for reunification with Romania. On January 11, Armenia had begun to follow the earlier lead of the Baltic states, not to the extent of declaring independence but in asserting a right to veto Soviet laws. On March 9, the Georgian Supreme Soviet condemned the occupation of the country in 1921 and its subsequent forced incorporation into the Soviet Union. Most significant, in the March elections the Ukrainian nationalist *Rukh* not only showed expected strength in Western Ukraine, annexed only in 1939, but also in urban centers in the heart of Ukraine. Several cities replaced the Soviet flag with the traditional Ukrainian flag, and Ukrainians demonstrated in support of Lithuania's declaration of independence. Incidentally, during 1990 Lithuanians (and some from Latvia and Estonia) launched a concerted political education lobbying campaign for independence in Ukraine, Belorussia, and Moldavia, believing this would place greater pressure on Moscow to grant Baltic independence.[22]

While troubles were erupting on the geographical and political peripheries, Gorbachev's principal attention had to remain on the center. A very important Central Committee plenum met on February 5–7. On the eve of the meeting, an unprecedented popular rally of about 250,000 people demonstrated for democracy in Moscow. At the meeting, Gorbachev, under fire even from some radical reformers (notably Yeltsin), but more so from the conservatives (especially Ligachev), succeeded in gaining approval of a reformist draft "party platform" (in effect, an interim party program) to be adopted by the forthcoming party congress, and he was able once again to move forward the timing of the congress to June-July (which only in September had been moved forward from February 1991 to October 1990). Most indicative of the quickening pace of political change was Gorbachev's successful move to agree on deletion of Article 6 of the USSR Constitution legally establishing the "leading role" of the Communist Party. In December, it will be recalled, Gorbachev had deflected a proposal by radical reformers at the Congress of People's Deputies to delete Article 6, which could have caused a clash between the legislature and the Communist Party. This was, however, a tactical step, and he now moved successfully to have the party itself decide to give up the constitutional provision, easing the way for the legislature to do so later. The platform revised the party's goal from early achievement of "communism" to establishment of "democratic socialism."

---

22. The Belarusian popular front held its founding congress in Vilnius, Lithuania, in June 1989.

    At about the same time, Yugoslavia began to disintegrate. Following elections in April 1990, Slovenia and Croatia began to move toward independence. As they attained independence a year or so later, Macedonia and Bosnia moved to leave the Yugoslav Socialist Federation, and only Serbia and Montenegro were left in a new rump Yugoslavia.

Gorbachev succeeded in getting party endorsement of a stronger presidency of the country. He also called for substantial modifications in leading party bodies to reduce the size of the Central Committee and to change the nature of the Politburo, but those changes were left for the party congress.

Foreign policy issues were debated at the plenum. Ligachev and Vladimir I. Brovikov, a party "apparatchik" serving as ambassador to Poland, led attacks on the new thinking and such developments as the loss of Eastern Europe and the impending "danger" (as Ligachev put it) of reunification of Germany. These attacks were countered by Shevardnadze and Yakovlev, but the issue had been publicly posed, as all the speeches were promptly published.[23]

Shevardnadze, incidentally, had to leave the plenum sessions on February 7 for his meetings with Baker. (Immediately after the plenum Gorbachev had met first with Baker on February 9 and then with Chancellor Kohl on February 10, as earlier noted.)

The March elections (many with runoff elections required because multiple candidacies had yielded no winners on the first round) led to victories for reform candidates in many localities, including Moscow, Leningrad, and Kiev. On March 13, the Congress of People's Deputies agreed (1,771 to 24) to delete Article 6 of the USSR Constitution conferring a leading role on the Communist Party and approved the proposed strengthening of the presidency. Two days later the congress elected Gorbachev as president for a five-year term (by 1,329 to 495). It also approved his proposal for a Presidential Council, to which Gorbachev intended to transfer many of the powers of the old party

---

23. The intention to publish had been made known in advance in order to soften criticisms. See "On the Draft Platform of the CC of the CPSU for the XXVIII Party Congress, Report of M. S. Gorbachev to the Plenum of the Central Committee of the CPSU, February 5, 1990," *Pravda*, February 6, 1990; "Statements Commenting on the Report, February 5 . . . V. I. Brovikov," *Pravda*, February 7, 1990; "Statements . . . February 6 . . . Ye. K. Ligachev," *Pravda*, February 7, 1990; "Statements at the Plenum of the CC CPSU, February 6, . . . E. A. Shevardnadze," *Pravda*, February 8, 1990; "Statements . . . February 6 . . . A. N. Yakovlev," *Pravda*, February 8, 1990; and "Concluding Word by M. S. Gorbachev to the Plenum of the CC of the CPSU, February 7, 1990," *Pravda*, February 9, 1990.

There had, of course, been public commentary by conservative commentators deploring the loss of Eastern Europe, but not by members of the leadership group. For example, Aleksandr Prokhanov, a conservative nationalist writer close to the military high command, had written in January that "the sentimental theory of 'our common European home' had led to the collapse of the Eastern European communist parties, a change in the nature of the states, and the inevitable unification of Germany." Thus, "the entire geopolitical architecture of Eastern Europe, for the creation of which our country had paid an enormous price, had been destroyed overnight." He flatly blamed "the philosophy of new thinking" and the "primacy of universal over class values," which he claimed had "in practice turned to disregard for the interests of the socialist state." See Aleksandr Prokhanov, "Tragedy of Centralism," *Literaturnaya Rossiya* (Literary Russia), January 5, 1990.

Politburo, and a Federation Council, on which the heads of all fifteen constituent republics of the USSR would sit.

Gorbachev declared on April 9 that he would use his expanded presidential powers to institute far-reaching economic reforms, and he continued a
campaign to build public support for a market-oriented economic reform. On
that occasion his economic adviser, Leonid Abalkin, outlined an economic
reform plan calling for widespread privatization and banking and tax changes.
Nonetheless, Gorbachev feared moving too quickly. On May Day, Gorbachev
and the other leaders at Red Square were greeted with jeers by reform-minded
demonstrators when the public was permitted to join the official May Day
parade. When the official economic reform program was launched on May 23,
Prime Minister Ryzhkov, in an act of folly or of deliberate sabotage, undercut
his own program by announcing planned major increases in prices, including a
tripling of the price of bread, for July 1. The predictable result was a wave of
panic buying and shortages. In a speech four days later, Gorbachev unsuccessfully tried to stem the popular alarm. The Supreme Soviet on June 15 rejected
the economic program and price increases and called for a new plan, leaving
economic reform in limbo.

Meanwhile, the beginnings of political parties could be seen in the
development over the first half of the year of two groups, both initially in effect
factions of the Communist Party (though not so termed, since factions were
banned). On the liberal flank was the Democratic Platform, created in January,
and on the conservative side the Russian Communist Party, formally established in June.

On May 29, the eve of Gorbachev's departure for a summit meeting
with Bush in Washington, Boris Yeltsin won a close and hard-fought contest to
become chairman of the Presidium of the Supreme Soviet of the Russian
Federation—in effect, president of Russia.

Internal developments in the Soviet Union also became increasingly
important to the development of U.S.-Soviet relations in several ways. First
they affected and sometimes limited Gorbachev's freedom of action in setting
Soviet policy. Clearly he and Shevardnadze had concerns of their own about the
changing situation in Eastern Europe and the impact of German unification,
but they were also compelled to take account of even greater concerns held and
fanned by others in the Soviet political establishment and public opinion. It was
only after Gorbachev successfully tamed a conservative revolt in the party at the
Twenty-eighth Communist Party Congress in July that he would be able to
agree to the terms for German reunification and a CFE agreement.

Conservative concerns of the military establishment clearly limited
leeway in the START negotiations. After a year of desultory negotiation, new
efforts had been mounted early in the year to try to reach agreement on a
U.S.-Soviet strategic arms reduction treaty (START). On the last day of his
February meetings in Moscow, Baker and his delegation found Marshal Sergei
Akhromeyev and his team ready to move toward a compromise on the sticky

issues of limits on air-launched and sea-launched cruise missiles. The Soviet side agreed to American positions on limiting the number of bombers on which air-launched cruise missiles (ALCMs) would be carried, permitting an undercount of actual ALCM loads by a nominal count for each class of bomber, and the Soviet side agreed to exclusion of non-ALCM-carrying bombers from any ALCM limitation and indeed from any limitation except nominal count of one bomb per aircraft. On sea-launched cruise missiles (SLCMs), the Soviets accepted the long-standing American insistence on not limiting such weapons in the treaty itself. Each side, however, would declare in unverified declarations each year the number of SLCMs it intended to deploy. These compromises were essentially capitulations to American positions that favored the United States. Clearly, Gorbachev and Shevardnadze wanted to reach an agreement even at the cost of unbalanced concessions, and Akhromeyev was reluctantly prepared to go along.

Marshal Akhromeyev was, however, since December 1988 no longer first deputy minister of defense and chief of the General Staff. He was an adviser to President Gorbachev but could no longer speak for the Soviet military, and in the concessions in February he clearly did not. The military vigorously objected, and as a consequence, Gorbachev considered it necessary to permit the General Staff a direct voice not only in deciding such matters but also in participating in the negotiations themselves. Accordingly, when Shevardnadze came to Washington in early April, the Soviet position incorporated several new conditions and partial retreat from the cruise missile agreements of February. A subsequent meeting in Washington two weeks later by Shevardnadze's deputy for arms control, Viktor Karpov, accompanied by Colonel General Bronislav Omelichev, a deputy chief of the General Staff, was unable to break the deadlock. Baker then got authority for modest American compromise steps to meet some of the objections of the Soviet military. He confidentially passed these proposals to Shevardnadze when they met for a 2+4 meeting in Bonn on May 5. When Baker met with Gorbachev in Moscow on May 18, he formally advanced the new U.S. proposals. Gorbachev was flanked by Shevardnadze, Akhromeyev, Omelichev, and Gorbachev's new rising foreign policy adviser, Yevgeny Primakov. Gorbachev was able to negotiate with Baker and resolve most of the cruise missile issues. The Soviet side had to make all the major concessions in reaching the compromises. Even so, Gorbachev and Shevardnadze were under pressure and could not simply make generous concessions on *all* the issues in order to reach a START agreement. And, indeed, a host of other issues remained unresolved, and by May it was clear those could not be decided in time for the forthcoming summit, and therefore probably not in 1990.[24]

---

24. The U.S. administration was unrelenting in pressing its advantage, so eager to "score" with its toughness, that little heed was given to the broader consequences of imposing one-sided compromises on Gorbachev and Shevardnadze. Particularly egregious was

Internal developments in the Soviet Union not only constricted Soviet policy, they also began to affect American policy flexibility and even policy objectives. Beginning with the Lithuanian declaration of independence on March 11, 1990, and limited Soviet economic sanctions in response (a cutoff of oil deliveries), vocal elements in American public opinion began to call for the United States to institute sanctions of one kind or another against the Soviet Union in retaliation. In particular, the normalization of economic relations and economic incentives promised by Bush at Malta had in part to be withheld, although Bush refrained from openly tying such restraint to the situation in the Baltic states. On April 24, 1990, to the surprise of many, he rejected U.S. economic sanctions against the Soviet Union as a response to the Soviet economic measures against Lithuania.[25] A trade agreement and request for most-favored-nation (MFN) status was, however, deferred until Soviet legislation ensured continued emigration (even though emigration from the Soviet Union was so great that the United States instituted some restraints on immigration

---

the question of declarations of numbers of sea-launched cruise missiles (SLCMs), agreed upon in principle in February in a major Soviet concession. Between February and May in negotiations on the number of SLCMs, in an effort to accommodate the United States, the Soviet side had proposed a limit of 760 SLCMs (the declared U.S. program goal was 758, although in practice plans had been scaled back to 637, and only 399 had been funded). Instead of gracefully accepting the generous Soviet proposal, the American negotiators, with Washington approval, in the bureaucratic tradition of hard-nosed bargaining insisted on splitting the difference between the new Soviet proposal of 760 and the last American proposal of 1,000 (an arbitrary number advanced at the time the Soviet Union was calling for zero nuclear SLCMs). Thus a meaningless limit of 880 was set, and the Soviet negotiators—under instructions to settle the matter—could do nothing but capitulate.

This became one of many points to which Soviet military and conservative political opponents later bitterly railed as examples of one-sided Soviet concessions in the START Treaty. And it was. In September 1991, President Bush, seeking a bold initiative, found that the Pentagon was quite prepared to accept even a unilateral withdrawal from deployment of *all* nuclear-armed SLCMs—a move quickly responded to by Gorbachev. Why, then, had the same administration so stubbornly refused until February 1990 even to consider limits on SLCMs, and in May 1990 to insist on imposing an absurdly high ceiling of 880?

The United States also insisted on a similar one-sided concession on air-launched cruise missiles (ALCMs), to exempt an American nonnuclear ALCM called "Tacit Rainbow." That concession was forced from Gorbachev himself in his final presummit meetings with Baker in Moscow on May 18–19, with bitter Soviet military objections that even delayed Baker's departure. On the "Tacit Rainbow" negotiation, see Oberdorfer, *The Turn*, pp. 409–10.

25. National Security Council Soviet affairs expert Condoleezza Rice soon after explained to reporter Don Oberdorfer that Bush did not want to "light a match in a gas-filled room." Ibid., p. 404. This prudence was appropriate; a compromise between the two parties two months later led to an end to Moscow's sanctions against Lithuania without any American action. President Vytautas Landsbergis of Lithuania, however, displaying his characteristically undiplomatic impatience, termed Bush's inaction a new "Munich."

into the United States!), which for other internal Soviet reasons did not occur until the middle of the next year.

The growing trend toward independence in some of the Soviet republics caused a problem for American policymakers. On the one hand, the United States had always championed national self-determination and popular democratic expression of free choice. On the other, the effects of haphazard political disintegration could yield violence, instability, and economic crises. Moreover, ardent local nationalism is not always democratic or respectful of minority rights. The Bush administration therefore declined in 1989–91 to encourage or support disintegrative national separatism in multinational states such as the Soviet Union and Yugoslavia, while urging peaceful resolution of national ethnic and other differences. The Baltic states—Lithuania, Latvia, and Estonia—were a special case for historical reasons (bolstered by the influential sentiment of a substantial American population of Lithuanian descent). The United States had never accepted their forced integration into the Soviet Union in 1940. Nonetheless, the Bush administration took a surprisingly restrained position and called for peaceful negotiation of these republics with Moscow to effect their independence. It was also active behind the scenes in urging this course on both the Soviet and Baltic leaders.[26]

## The Washington Summit

The Washington summit (May 31–June 3, 1990) took place in a world very different from the one that had existed when it had first been announced, about eight months earlier. Some fifteen agreements were concluded, covering a wide range of matters. Most important to enhancing relations was Bush's decision during the summit, reversing his initial intention, to accede to Gorbachev's pleas to sign the trade agreement, even if its submission for

---

26. Bush and Baker warned Gorbachev and Shevardnadze of the negative consequences for American-Soviet relations if there were use of force to quell the Baltic drive for independence and noted that it would kill the proposed trade agreement loosening constraints on U.S. trade with the Soviet Union. They also sought to persuade the Lithuanians to negotiate with Moscow and encouraged Chancellor Kohl and President Mitterrand to send a letter to Lithuanian President Landsbergis on April 26 urging that he suspend the unilateral declaration of independence and negotiate. The administration had successfully rallied a 59 to 36 defeat on March 21 for a Senate resolution introduced by Senator Jesse Helms calling for immediate U.S. recognition of Lithuanian independence, but on May 1 the Senate voted 73 to 24 to withhold trade benefits from the Soviet Union until the embargo on Lithuania was lifted and negotiations by Moscow with Vilnius begun. This particular constraint was voided by the early lifting of the Soviet embargo and initiation of negotiations, but the problem remained unresolved and was to become more acute in early 1991. For a good account of these developments see Beschloss and Talbott, *At the Highest Levels*, pp. 193–212.

congressional approval would be withheld until Soviet legislation permitting emigration was passed. The agreements included some modest and overdue arms control accords on bilateral nuclear testing (protocols on verification permitting ratification of the testing limitations negotiated and signed in 1974 and 1976) and the earlier heralded agreement on bilateral chemical weapons reductions (80 percent of the arsenals of the two sides, without awaiting the comprehensive ban being negotiated in a multilateral forum). Others were more routine: larger exchanges of university students, establishment of cultural centers, cooperation of customs services in narcotics interdiction, joint oceanographic studies, cooperation in peaceful uses of nuclear energy, agreement on the Bering Sea maritime boundary and on a Bering Straits park area, expansion of civil aviation arrangements, and a new long-term grain agreement. The familiar subjects of regional conflicts (eased by the Nicaraguan election) and human rights (eased at the time, until later Baltic repressions) accompanied the arms control accords and these agreements on many aspects of bilateral relations. These traditional four areas of summit discussion as noted had been expanded to add a fifth: transnational world issues including ecology, terrorism, world economic problems, narcotics, health, and increasing attention to international organizations and peacekeeping.[27]

In all, despite disappointing results on START, the 1990 Washington summit showed that U.S.-Soviet relations were essentially normalized and developing new areas of cooperation as well as serving to regulate or settle areas of difference. By 1990 U.S.-Soviet relations could be said to be at least back to the high point of détente of 1972–73, with the prospect—although not assurance—of being more permanent and more cooperative.[28]

One of the most important aspects of the summit was its contribution, not evident at the time, to resolving the major remaining East-West issue: agreement on the terms for the reunification of Germany. Bush again advanced the arguments in support of the position that a reunified Germany should remain in NATO, stressing the necessity and advantages of that situation. He also recapitulated nine points of reassurance that Germany's membership

---

27. Speeches, texts of agreed statements, and official fact sheets on the agreements signed are in *Presidential Documents*, vol. 26 (June 4, 1990), pp. 850–89. The official Soviet compilation of materials, including full texts of all agreements, totaled more than 300 pages. See *Gosudarstvennyi vizit presidenta SSSR M. S. Gorbacheva v Soyedinennyye shtaty, 30 Maya–4 Iyunya 1990 goda* (State Visit of President of the USSR M. S. Gorbachev to the United States, May 30–June 4, 1990) (Moscow: Politizdat, 1990), 336 pp. A shorter version in English is available as *USSR-USA Summit, Washington, May 30–June 3, 1990, Documents and Materials* (Moscow: Novosti, 1990), 112 pp.

28. Shortly after the Geneva summit in 1985, a senior Soviet diplomat had remarked to me that the situation had been "restored to 1979," the still troubled but not yet dead détente prior to the Soviet military intervention in Afghanistan. The five years to 1990 had restored the situation to the flourishing détente of the early 1970s.

would not be adverse to Soviet security and other interests. Although most if not all of these points had been previously stated by West Germany, NATO, or the United States, some required further elaboration. Packaging them as the nine points with U.S. endorsement made more of an impact. Because most of the undertakings would involve German or multilateral agreement, they were formulated in terms of American support and endorsement for them. Several of the points concerned new or renewed German commitments: (1) not to develop or possess nuclear, chemical, or biological weapons; (2) to accept the current border of Germany (that is, no claims to former German territories east of the border of East Germany); (3) to provide financial support for maintaining Soviet troops in eastern Germany for several years, and to pay for new housing for Soviet military troops and their families when they returned to the Soviet Union. Several others involved German and NATO agreement: (4) to accept the continued presence of Soviet troops in eastern Germany for a transitional period of several years; (5) to agree that NATO troops would not be deployed in eastern Germany; (6) and to provide ceilings on the level of German military forces and other countries in central Europe in a follow-on to the CFE Treaty. NATO would also undertake (7) to review and revise its strategy to accord with the new realities in Europe after the Cold War; (8) to accelerate negotiations on short-range nuclear weapons in Europe, after the CFE Treaty was concluded; and (9) to agree on upgrading the CSCE organization to enhance its responsibilities and effectiveness. Though Gorbachev did not agree explicitly that a reunified Germany should be in NATO, he was unexpectedly responsive to the argument that every country should have the right to make such decisions for itself—an application of his own often-reiterated principle of "freedom of choice." Indeed, though clearly several members of Gorbachev's delegation were unhappy with that formula, Gorbachev did not object when shown in advance Bush's closing press conference statement in which, while noting that Gorbachev did not agree that a united Germany should be a member of NATO, he also said that he and Gorbachev were "in full agreement that the matter of alliance membership is . . . a matter for the Germans to decide." Press coverage at the time failed to note that large implied concession and carried stories about the continuing "stalemate" over the issue of German membership in NATO. But for the Bush administration, and less enthusiastically for some of Gorbachev's own entourage, the writing was on the wall.[29]

By mid-1990, many people in the United States and Europe were becoming uneasy over the constantly reaffirmed priority given by the Bush administration to shoring up NATO, in contrast to no more than tepid interest in developing the CSCE or other pan-European security arrangements that would include the Soviet Union and other Warsaw Pact countries. There were

29. Besides the official documents on the summit cited above, very useful accounts based on interviews with Soviet and American participants are found in Beschloss and Talbott, *At the Highest Levels*, pp. 216–28; and Oberdorfer, *The Turn*, pp. 410–30.

concerns that the United States, by appearing to give higher priority to NATO in which the American voice was very strong, was undercutting prospects for early German reunification and for development of pan-European security arrangements embracing Eastern Europe and the Soviet Union.

Subsequently, at a CSCE meeting in Copenhagen on June 5 and a 2+4 meeting in East Berlin on June 22, Shevardnadze sought to convey to Baker the importance of positive public steps by NATO at its forthcoming summit meeting in London to support CSCE and European security arrangements. These would include a nonaggression pledge and West Germany's acceptance of a limit on the armed forces in a reunified Germany (as well as the noncontroversial but important recommitment to abjure nuclear weapons). These matters were covered in the "nine points of reassurance" and were not divergences between the Soviet and American positions, but they remained to be translated from "American endorsement" to allied decision and announcement.

## The Twenty-eighth (and Last) Party Congress

The Supreme Soviet on June 12 approved Gorbachev's report on the Washington summit by a vote of 329 to 2 (with 1 abstention). On the more active foreign policy question of German reunification, however, there was far from unanimity. Ligachev has more recently disclosed that he sent a note to Gorbachev in April 1990 urging a Politburo discussion of the German issue. Later, "taking extreme measures," he wrote directly to other Central Committee members proposing a special plenum be convened to consider events in Eastern Europe. Such a plenum was never held, but clearly the party congress in July would bring the matter to a head.[30]

In the month between the Washington summit and the party congress, two political developments of significance occurred. One was the establishment of a separate Russian Communist Party. All the other republics had their own affiliated communist parties (in past practice, local controlled branches of the Communist Party of the Soviet Union), but Russia's expanse and central role had made a duplicating Russian party seem superfluous. Now that political pluralism within the party was blooming, conservatives losing in the central apparatus controlled by Gorbachev sought an end run by creating a Russian party they hoped to control. The liberals contested. At the founding congress on June 22 the key vote was won by the conservative candidate, Ivan Polozkov, over Yeltsin's candidate, Oleg Lobov, by a vote of 1,396 to 1,066. (Gorbachev had tried only halfheartedly to contest the outcome, and his two preferred centrist candidates were squeezed out by the liberals and conservatives.)

---

30. Ye. Ligachev, "How It Was," *Sovetskaya Rossiya* (Soviet Russia), August 3, 1991.

Ligachev led the attack on Gorbachev's foreign policy, but less expected was a sharp assault by a senior military man, Colonel General Albert Makashov, commander of the Volga-Urals Military District. Makashov slashed at liberals who "twitter on about the fact that no one intends to attack us" and leveled accusations at "the Central Committee, the Politburo, and the government" for not supporting the military sufficiently, for example, by unjustified unilateral force reductions. Moreover, *Red Star*, the official military newspaper, chose to print Makashov's speech in full.[31]

In a related disturbing development, even several conservative voices within Gorbachev's own entourage began to sound critical and cautionary messages publicly. On June 12, Oleg Baklanov, the party secretary responsible for the defense industry, suggested that the Soviet Union was "getting ahead of itself" in its disarmament and other initiatives and not obtaining a "positive response" from the West, which was seeking to exploit the situation in Europe.[32] Two weeks later Marshal Dmitry Yazov, the minister of defense, though less directly critical of Gorbachev's policy, clearly implied his dissatisfaction and concerns that the West still viewed the Soviet Union as the "enemy" and sought to disarm it.[33] Although Yakovlev, Zaikov, and Shevardnadze rebutted these charges, it was disturbing that even the Gorbachev administration itself was openly divided.

Although these signs showed that the old politics was still alive and active, the most significant development of all was a new initiative by Yeltsin in launching an offensive against Gorbachev and the central leadership that had banished him to the periphery of power. After his election as president (chairman of the Supreme Soviet) of the Russian republic, he moved within a few days demonstratively to meet with Lithuanian President Landsbergis—while Gorbachev was in Washington. Then, on June 12, the Russian Supreme Soviet threw down the gauntlet with a declaration of sovereignty. It was one thing if one or even all of the small, peripheral Baltic or Transcaucasian republics avowed sovereignty or even sought to secede; it was quite another for Russia to declare the primacy of its government over the territory and resources of most of the country in a direct challenge to the legitimacy of the Soviet central government and state.[34] Moreover, the Russian action set off a chain of similar

---

31. "We Don't Intend to Surrender," speech of Colonel General A. Makashov, *Krasnaya zvezda* (Red Star), June 21, 1990.

32. "Free Cheese—Only in Mousetraps," interview with Central Committee Secretary Oleg Baklanov, *Rabochaya tribuna* (The Workers' Tribune), June 12, 1990.

33. "What Concerns the Minister," interview with Candidate Politburo Member, Minister of Defense, Marshal D. Yazov, *Rabochaya tribuna*, June 26, 1990.

34. The Russian declaration of sovereignty also stirred some concern and gave impetus to independence sentiments in some of the minority ethnic republics and regions within the Russian Federation. Though Gorbachev may have hoped such regional minority sentiments would reinforce the central Soviet authority as against the Russian republic,

declarations by the other republics—Uzbekistan on June 20, Moldavia (renaming itself Moldova) on June 23, the more important Ukraine on July 16, and Belorussia (soon renamed Belarus) on July 27. Transcaucasian and Central Asian republics followed, with Kirghizia (soon Kyrgyzstan) last on December 12.

This soon led to a second stage of declarations of the supremacy of republic laws over those of the Soviet Union—Russia on October 24, Ukraine the same day, and Belorussia two days later. This soon led to what came to be called "the war of laws," leaving people and Soviet enterprises (as well as foreign investors) in uncertainty as to which laws to obey, as new republic laws began to diverge and contradict union legislation. The action also had a cascade effect *within* republics, as throughout the summer and fall many subordinate "autonomous republics" and provinces (oblasts) began in turn to declare their sovereignty. Karelia in the northwestern Russia was first on August 10, more significant were Tataria (Tatarstan), Bashkiria (Bashkortostan), and Buryatia in August and October, and many others. The process also included entities within other union republics, beginning with Abkhazia in Georgia in August.

This process, touched off by Yeltsin's Russia in June, was not only disruptive of the status quo but also undermined the effort at political reform of relationships between the center and the republics launched that spring with work on a new "Union Treaty." On July 30, a draft Union Treaty that had been under discussion in the Supreme Soviet became the subject of direct negotiation, with participation by all the republics except the Baltics and Georgia. On November 23 a still tentative draft Treaty of Union, for a new "USSR"—a Union of Sovereign (no longer Socialist) Soviet Republics—was published. Final action was expected, and was to come (but with an unexpected result), in 1991.

On July 2 the Twenty-eighth Congress of the Communist Party of the Soviet Union opened. Although no one could know at the time that this would be the last party congress, it was clear that it would be the last of a truly ruling party. There were rumors that Gorbachev would give up the position of general secretary, and he probably did consider it. If so, he must have decided that it

---

he did not encourage independence aspirations. Yeltsin, however, rashly reacted by telling an audience when he visited Tataria (soon Tatarstan), "Take whatever degree of independent authority (*samostoyatel'nost*) you want and can handle. If you want complete authority, take it. If you want to give up some degree of authority do that. . . . Russia will be an earnest defender of the rights that Tataria delegates to Russia." That offer would come back to haunt Yeltsin and Russia later, above all in Tatarstan. (Yeltsin's precise words are not clear; only one partial recording, in English translation, is available; other accounts were by Russian correspondents paraphrasing his words. But the gist was clear. See "Trip by B. Yeltsin. Tataria," *Argumenty i fakty* [Arguments and Facts], no. 32 [August 11–17, 1990]; and Radio Moscow, Domestic Service, 1200 GMT, August 7, 1990, and 1400 GMT, August 7, 1990, and TASS in English, 1539 GMT, August 7, 1990, in FBIS, *Soviet Union*, August 8, 1990, pp. 69, 70.)

would be too risky to allow the party machine to decide upon someone else for the post—it might well go to a conservative who could use the position to fight President Gorbachev within and beyond the party. But the organizational changes in the higher party structure, in addition to many other indications, make clear Gorbachev's intent to shift the party out of the central role in national decisionmaking. The Politburo was expunged and weakened. Of its twenty-four members, only Gorbachev also held a position in the state or government leadership. All the key government leaders who had traditionally been members of the Politburo were excluded. In the outgoing Politburo, numbering nineteen (including nonvoting "candidate" members, a traditional category now dropped), there had been nine central state leaders (for example, the prime minister, the head of the KGB, the defense minister, the foreign minister) and only three regional party chiefs. The new one instead included all the republic and other chief regional party heads (among other things, incidentally, making it impractical to gather for weekly meetings as in the past).

There were spirited debates over foreign and domestic policy and contested elections for the party leadership. Ivan Polozkov, the conservative Russian party leader, knowing that he could not prevail, had in advance removed himself from the running. No significant leader challenged Gorbachev directly, but there was a contest; Gorbachev won with three-quarters of the vote (3,411 to 1,116), while his challenger, Teimuraz Avalyani, received only 501 votes with 4,020 opposing. Ligachev did run for the new post of deputy general secretary, against Gorbachev's selection, Vladimir Ivashko of Ukraine. Ivashko handily defeated Ligachev (3,109 to 776) in a vote more lopsided than others in which conservative positions received more support. Rumors reported that a deal had been cut that both Ligachev and the liberal Aleksandr Yakovlev would be dropped from the leadership, and they were—not only from the Politburo but even from the new smaller Central Committee. The Central Committee, as well as the Politburo, no longer included most government and other national leaders. The party was clearly being shunted aside.

To replace the role of the Politburo, Gorbachev soon unveiled an enlarged Presidential Council. He had already brought his chief of staff, Valery Boldin, over from his position as head of the old Central Committee General Department to head a new Secretariat of the Presidential Council.[35]

Yeltsin did not play a prominent role at the congress. He was due to remain a member of the Central Committee, but before the congress ended he

---

35. Besides offering American expertise on economic management reform, the administration provided unusual advice on organizing a presidential office. White House Chief of Staff John Sununu and a delegation of senior White House aides spent a week in Moscow in August-September 1990, following up on an expression of interest by Gorbachev at the June summit. Dan Balz, "Sununu-Led U.S. Group to Meet with Soviets, Officials Will Discuss Presidential Process," *Washington Post*, August 27, 1990, p. A15.

suddenly announced his decision to resign from the Communist Party. His action soon led several other liberals, including the mayors of Moscow (Gavril Popov) and Leningrad (Anatoly Sobchak), to do likewise. Others, including Yakovlev, while no longer active in the party leadership, nonetheless remained party members.

During the party congress debates, Ligachev and others again attacked Gorbachev and his administration for losing Eastern Europe, on the danger of German reunification, and for weakness on defense and excessive concessions to the United States in arms control negotiations. Gorbachev was on the defensive on these issues, in the sense that the Soviet position was now widely seen as adversely affected in all these respects, but he vigorously stood his ground. He rallied others in the leadership to carry the brunt of the defense, and they did. On arms control concessions, for example, not only Shevardnadze but also Yazov, Zaikov (the senior party secretary for defense affairs), and General of the Army Mikhail Moiseyev firmly defended the Gorbachev administration's line and actions.[36] On Eastern Europe and Germany, Shevardnadze and Yakovlev staunchly defended the administration's actions. The London NATO Declaration, issued coincidentally on the fourth day of the congress, was a help in deflecting charges that NATO was taking advantage of the developments in Eastern Europe.

## German Reunification and the CFE Treaty

At the NATO summit on July 6 the London Declaration picked up and endorsed the points on reassurance to the Soviet Union that Gorbachev and Shevardnadze had been emphasizing to Baker and Bush. The NATO meeting even invited President Gorbachev to address the North Atlantic Council and asked the Warsaw Pact states to establish diplomatic liaison with NATO. It invited the Warsaw Pact members to join in reciprocal pledges of nonaggression and nonuse of force and agree that "we are no longer adversaries." The London Declaration also pledged to reduce nuclear deterrent forces, eliminate nuclear artillery, and "reduce . . . reliance on nuclear weapons"—and "in the transformed Europe" to "adopt a new NATO strategy making nuclear forces truly weapons of last resort." It endorsed the negotiations for confidence-building measures and reductions of forces in Europe and for a CSCE summit later in the year in Paris. The London Declaration encouraged signing a CFE agreement and determining how CSCE institutions could be strengthened by,

---

36. All had been personally involved in the collective leadership decisions on all major arms control issues. Zaikov had headed a special high-level interagency committee on disarmament matters.

among several proposals, establishing a secretariat and a Conflict Prevention Center.[37]

The London Declaration was promptly praised by Shevardnadze and later Gorbachev, who described it "realistic and constructive," attached "extremely great importance" to the nonaggression pledge, welcomed the invitation to direct contacts, and emphasized the announcement of plans to revise NATO "strategic plans and concepts."[38]

President Bush later disclosed that he was the principal architect of the London Declaration. There is no doubt that the NATO allies welcomed the American role both in identifying points of particular interest to the Soviet Union and in moving forward from the earlier more reticent U.S. stance on creating a new security regime in Europe.

Only three days after the successful outcome of the party congress, on July 16, Gorbachev met with Chancellor Kohl and made the final concession on accepting a reunified Germany in NATO, if that were the choice of the German people, in exchange for several concessions from Kohl that, though not constituting a major German or Western sacrifice, did go a long way to contain Soviet concerns. Germany would reduce its armed forces to 370,000 men; German NATO forces and any non-German NATO forces would be excluded from East Germany (explicitly while Soviet forces remained there, but by strong implication even thereafter); Germany would accept and would provide financial support to the Soviet troops in eastern Germany for three to five years and would help pay for their resettlement in the Soviet Union; and finally reunified Germany would reconfirm its obligations not to acquire nuclear, chemical, or biological weapons. The nine reassurances were all reconfirmed.[39]

By September 12 the 2+4 talks concluded with an agreement, hailed in a joint declaration by Baker and Shevardnadze, relinquishing the occupation

---

37. See "London Declaration on a Transformed North Atlantic Alliance," July 6, 1990, *Presidential Documents*, vol. 26 (July 9, 1990), pp. 1041–44; also "Text of Declaration after the NATO Talks," *New York Times*, July 7, 1990, p. 5.

38. "Comments by Soviets on NATO," *New York Times*, July 7, 1990, p. 5.

    Baker had confidentially provided a draft of the London NATO Declaration to Shevardnadze in advance—in itself a sign of how much things were changing—and this helped Shevardnadze and Gorbachev to put a strong positive "spin" on their reaction to it in Moscow.

39. Though Bush had succeeded in his effort to maintain NATO's key role by orchestrating Soviet acceptance of reunified Germany remaining in NATO, Beschloss and Talbott report that "privately he was piqued that in the end Kohl and Gorbachev had worked out the matter on their own." The next day, Bush called Gorbachev ostensibly to brief him on the London summit, but according to sources in reality "his main purpose was to keep the Soviets and Germans from making a habit of bypassing Washington in their diplomatic collaborations." He also "reminded Gorbachev that he [Bush] had been the 'architect' of the NATO declaration." See Beschloss and Talbott, *At the Highest Levels*, p. 240.

rights of the four wartime victors and paving the way for the formal reunification of Germany on October 3.

The CSCE summit in Paris on November 19–21 was the culminating act of the reunification of Europe following the Revolution of '89 in Eastern Europe. The most important accomplishment was the signing of the CFE agreement on reductions of conventional arms of the NATO and Warsaw Pact countries in Europe from the Atlantic to the Urals. Although the original objective of reducing the Soviet military concentration in central Europe and the framework of balancing forces of two alliances had been largely overtaken by events, the CFE agreement nonetheless was of major, even historic, significance. In addition, all member states of the NATO and Warsaw alliances individually signed a joint declaration in which they welcomed "the historic changes in Europe," "the end of the era of division and confrontation," and solemnly declared that they were "no longer adversaries" but would "build new partnerships and extend to each other the hand of friendship," recognizing that "security is indivisible."[40]

Presidents Bush and Gorbachev, who also used the occasion for a further broad exchange of views, were justifiably proud of their role.

As multilateral diplomacy was rapidly winding down the Cold War confrontation in Europe, U.S.-Soviet relations were expanding in bilateral interests and in a new "partnership" toward resolving conflicts around the world.

Apart from private meetings alongside the 2+4 meetings on Germany, Secretary Baker and Shevardnadze met every several weeks. At a meeting in Irkutsk on August 1–2, besides strategic arms reductions, attention was given to the full range of regional conflicts around the globe—Afghanistan, Cambodia, Central America, South Africa, the Horn of Africa, the India-Pakistan dispute, and divided Korea. But no less important than the scope of the agenda was unprecedented congruence of interests. The two men agreed that the time was ripe to work as "partners" in collaboration to resolve these conflicts.

As they were completing these talks, Iraq invaded Kuwait, and Baker and Shevardnadze met again at the Vnukovo airport in Moscow on August 3 to discuss and quickly agree on a joint press statement condemning the Iraqi aggression.[41] The Soviet stand was particularly significant since the Soviet

---

40. "Text of the Joint Declaration of Twenty-Two States," November 19, 1990, *Presidential Documents*, vol. 26 (November 26, 1990), pp. 1871–73; and for texts of the declarations on the CFE Treaty and related White House fact sheet, see *ibid*, pp. 1868–69.

    In addition, the thirty-four CSCE members adopted a new set of confidence- and security-building measures (CSBMs) expanding the system of notifications and observations of military exercises.

41. Soviet officials have said Gorbachev was reluctant but was persuaded of the need to take a prompt and forthright stand in order to validate the "new thinking" pronouncements and contribute to a new world order.

Union had close ties to Iraq. Only a month later, at a quick working summit in Helsinki on September 9, Bush and Gorbachev issued an even more far-reaching joint statement supporting all UN resolutions and acknowledging the possible need for additional action.[42]

The early accord between Baker and Shevardnadze, and then between Bush and Gorbachev, on the need to roll back Saddam Hussein's aggression was of great significance. Gorbachev evidently held higher hopes of being able to do that by diplomacy and was clearly reluctant to see a resort to military force, but nonetheless he was prepared to support the United States and UN consensus in using whatever means proved necessary. This was a reflection of Gorbachev's, as well as Bush's, desire to meet this first post–Cold War military aggression effectively not only on its own merits but as a step in forging "the new world order" about which both presidents frequently spoke. Shevardnadze not only shared this aim but appears to have welcomed the idea that Soviet-U.S. partnership could be boldly cemented by a successful military campaign. Some other advisers to Gorbachev, notably Yevgeny Primakov, did not wish to see America resort to force or to commit Soviet support for it because of concern (exaggerated, as it turned out) over possible adverse impact in the Arab world. Gorbachev permitted Primakov himself to play an important, if unsuccessful, diplomatic role in visiting Baghdad, but when Saddam could not be persuaded, Gorbachev backed the American action.[43]

---

The Soviet Ministry of Foreign Affairs officer serving as Gorbachev's (and Shevardnadze's) English-language interpreter, Pavel Palazhchenko, has reported that at the time the KGB provided an erroneous report to Gorbachev to the effect that the United States was imminently going to strike Iraq. Palazhchenko believes this was deliberate misinformation intended to dissuade Gorbachev from agreeing to the joint statement (from Palazhchenko's yet unpublished memoir).

In one important respect the joint statement apparently went beyond what Shevardnadze had been authorized to agree upon. The joint call for an embargo on arms supply to Iraq had not been accepted by other key members of the Presidential Council, and it appears that Shevardnadze on his own authority included it after Baker's strong importuning. See Beschloss and Talbott, *At the Highest Levels*, pp. 247–48.

42. "Soviet Union-United States Joint Statement on the Persian Gulf Crisis," September 9, 1990, *Presidential Documents*, vol. 26 (September 17, 1990), p. 1344.

43. For a detailed account, especially of Shevardnadze's and Baker's roles, and also Primakov's, see Beschloss and Talbott, *At the Highest Levels*, pp. 247–87; see also Eduard Shevardnadze, *The Future Belongs to Freedom* (Free Press, Macmillan, 1991), pp. 100–08.

In conversations in Moscow in November, when the American military buildup and rhetoric began to seriously portend military action, Soviet officials displayed widely differing views. Some, uninformed on Gorbachev's position, feared a Soviet-American rift if the United States went to war; others were concerned over the divergencies of view in their own country. But a very close associate of Shevardnadze made clear that he expected and welcomed an American-led military victory for the new world order and American-Soviet collaboration in the new post–Cold War era.

On September 9, Bush and Gorbachev met in Helsinki for a brief meeting, on the Persian Gulf crisis. The meeting was arranged on short notice at President Bush's initiative (and close to Moscow for President Gorbachev's convenience) in order to express the solidarity of the two countries—and to reinsure it would continue. The American-Soviet collaboration in seeking to resolve the crisis was advanced in two important respects. First, the United States succeeded in getting Soviet acceptance of language in a joint statement reaffirming support for all the UN Security Resolutions and saying, "Nothing short of the complete implementation of the United Nations Security Council Resolutions is acceptable." It expressed a "preference" "to resolve the crisis peacefully" but reaffirmed that the two countries would be "united against Iraq's aggression as long as the crisis exists," and if current steps did not succeed, to consider further steps to "demonstrate beyond any doubt that aggression cannot and will not pay." Gorbachev had accepted that strong commitment despite efforts by Primakov and some others to water it down.

The second new element in the Helsinki joint statement was an agreement that *after* the objectives of the resolutions had been achieved, not as part of the settlement of that problem, the two countries would then "work actively to resolve all remaining conflicts in the Middle East." In effect, Bush was overturning the entire Cold War policy of attempting to keep the Soviet Union out of the Middle East and agreeing that the two countries should work together to seek a settlement of the Arab-Israeli-Palestinian conflict and other conflicts in the region. Although an "international conference" was not explicitly referred to, it was clearly not excluded (and in the private conversations it had been agreed to pursue a revived international conference). American-Soviet political partnership was developing.[44]

Additional meetings between Baker and Shevardnadze several times in New York during September 26–October 5, Moscow on November 7–8, Paris on November 18–21, New York on November 28, and Washington and Houston on December 9–12 dealt with the strategic arms talks and the Persian Gulf crisis. The last meeting also dealt again with the range of other regional conflicts and the new subject of emergency economic assistance for the Soviet Union.

Meanwhile, other high-level contacts continued to develop. On the military side, Admiral William Crowe, former chairman of the Joint Chiefs of Staff, had visited the Soviet Union in March. General Mikhail Moiseyev, chief of the Soviet General Staff, came to the United States in October. Also in October Secretary of Defense Dick Cheney visited the Soviet Union and had an opportunity to address the Supreme Soviet (as well as to be received by Gorbachev). In November, for the first time, the NATO Supreme Allied

---

44. For the text of the joint statement of Bush and Gorbachev in Helsinki of September 9, 1990, see "U.S.-USSR Statement," *State Dispatch*, vol. 1 (September 17, 1990), p. 92. See also Beschloss and Talbott, *At the Highest Levels*, pp. 260–67.

Commander Europe, General John Galvin, visited the USSR as a guest of Defense Minister Yazov. U.S. and Soviet naval visits were also reciprocated at San Diego in July and Vladivostok in September.

In the economic sphere, Gorbachev, though moving slowly, did meet with Secretary of Commerce Robert A. Mosbacher (and Baker) and fifteen leading American business executives in September. (While in the United States for the June summit, Gorbachev had also arranged a meeting with American business leaders, as well as congressional leaders, to lobby for more trade and investment.) In December a delegation of visitors from the Columbia University Business School also visited the Soviet Union, furthering contact on business management. Finally, although the Houston talks on December 9–12 on possible direct Western economic assistance to the Soviet Union were still exploratory, as the year ended President Bush announced on December 12 that he would waive the Jackson-Vanik amendment in order to make the Soviet Union eligible for export credit guarantees. On December 29 he signed an executive order doing so, and he granted $1 billion in credit guarantees for grain exports. He also proposed a special association of the Soviet Union with the International Monetary Fund and the World Bank, softening the administration's earlier opposition to Soviet membership in these bodies.

## Mounting Crisis in the Soviet Union

The most severe trial of American-Soviet relations in this period was caused by Gorbachev's veering to a more conservative stance on internal economic and political reform, together with intermittent localized repression in the Baltic states and broader efforts to maintain order, from the fall of 1990 to the spring of 1991. Many Americans, although not the Bush administration, took such signs as Shevardnadze's resignation in December 1990 and brutal local repressive acts in Vilnius, Lithuania, and Riga, Latvia, early in 1991, on top of Gorbachev's retreat from the ambitious 500-day economic reform proposal in the fall of 1990, as indications of an abandonment of reform by Gorbachev. That was a hasty and incorrect assessment, as later events were to show, but it did take into account the ups and downs of the very difficult deep transformation of the Soviet society, economy, and polity.

In the wake of his victory in July at the Twenty-eighth Communist Party Congress, besides reorganizing the leadership and shifting the center of gravity of authority from the party to the state, and moving to accommodate German and European unification, Gorbachev turned again to the massive challenge of effecting fundamental economic reform without unleashing social and political revolt. On August 1, Gorbachev met with Boris Yeltsin, and they agreed on an approach to economic reform. A working group of economists was promptly established, chaired by presidential adviser Stanislav Shatalin. By the end of that same month Gorbachev and Yeltsin met again to discuss the emerging "Shatalin plan" for economic reform in a concentrated 500-day period. They also discussed relations between the central authorities and the republics in a nonconfrontational if not congruent exchange of ideas.

September and October were marked by intense debate and maneuver over economic reform. Prime Minister Nikolai Ryzhkov, author of the far more modest and limited reform plan of the previous December, attacked the Shatalin plan—as did Ligachev and many other conservatives. Gorbachev several times reaffirmed his commitment to real reform and to the objectives of the Shatalin plan, even after Ryzhkov's attack. But he also voiced his great concern over disintegrative social and political efforts of rapid implementation of radical reform. He then sponsored a third compromise plan, splicing elements of the Shatalin and Ryzhkov approaches in an "Aganbegyan reform proposal," which the Supreme Soviet endorsed in principle, along with expanding Gorbachev's emergency decree powers on September 24. But the adoption of an economic reform package was deferred to mid-October. A Central Committee plenum was held on October 8–9 to bring along the still powerful party machine. And on October 13 Gorbachev met with the leaders of eleven republics (the three Baltic states and Georgia refused to participate) to discuss the newest economic reform plan. But there was no consensus.

On October 16, Gorbachev presented the new compromise reform plan to the Supreme Soviet. It not only dropped the 500 days but also failed to eliminate the central economic industries or to break up the collective farms, was less far-reaching in privatization, and hedged on price reform. But it was a plan for shifting over time to a less controlled market system. It was tepidly endorsed by Ryzhkov and Shatalin (as well as Aganbegyan and Abalkin), but not by several of the other reform economists, including Shatalin's chief associate Grigory Yavlinsky, who submitted his resignation. On October 19, the Supreme Soviet adopted the economic reform plan 356 to 12 (with 26 abstentions).

Despite the doubts of some reformers about the economic effectiveness of the more cautious approach to reform, and the reluctance of many in the economic management structure, Gorbachev's compromise economic reform plan might have worked. Some Western economists knowledgeable on the Soviet Union indeed believed it was a reasonable program for the situation. Nonetheless, notwithstanding the large (if not enthusiastic) majority in the Supreme Soviet, and neutralization of the party Central Committee, the plan was doomed to failure from the start. The Gorbachev-Yeltsin alliance since the beginning of August collapsed. Yeltsin sharply rejected the plan on October 16 and vowed to implement the unalloyed 500-day Shatalin plan in Russia. How could the union reform be implemented without Russia, or how could Russia alone implement the 500-day plan, in a still single and interdependent economic and political system?

In the same speech, Yeltsin also posed the parallel political issue, calling in effect for a massive transfer of power from the center to the republics.

On October 24 the USSR Supreme Soviet reaffirmed the primacy of the laws of the Soviet Union over those of any individual republic. On the same day, the Russian and Ukrainian Supreme Soviets (and two days later the Belorussian) proclaimed the primacy of the laws of their republics over those of the union. The "war of laws," earlier noted, was joined for both economic and political reform.

Meanwhile there was increasing public concern over a possible military or hard-line coup. At the time the Supreme Soviet reconvened for its full session on September 10, rumors began to spread about unusual troop movements around Moscow. Two regiments of the 106th Guards Airborne Division in Tula were brought up, and the Airborne Troops commander said one was to practice for the November 7 parade, and the other (although in combat gear) was to gather potatoes—a chore for which Soviet troops were often diverted. On September 19 in a television appearance Marshal Yazov himself confirmed the troop movements and gave those two reasons for them. It is still not clear who ordered the movements; it is possible that Gorbachev himself had agreed to a recommendation by Yazov that some troops be held nearby in case there was public disorder when the Supreme Soviet met. There does not appear to have been any preparation for a coup attempt.[45]

In early November, during military movements reportedly (and probably) in practice for the November 7 parade, rumors again circulated of a possible military coup d'état.

On November 11, Gorbachev and Yeltsin met again, for the first time in a month, to try to iron out their differences on economic reform, but by this time the gap was far greater than could be bridged. Then, on November 13, Gorbachev had a startling and unnerving meeting with about 1,100 military deputies to various legislative bodies (including the USSR and Russian Supreme Soviets as well as councils on the local level), in which the growing concern and anger of the officer corps at the deteriorating state of the country, as well as of the military, were brought home to him.

On November 16 Gorbachev presented to the Supreme Soviet, in response to its request, an assessment of the state of the union. It was not effective, too pro forma and too defensive, even petulant, and it was poorly received. Moreover, in contrast, Yeltsin followed with a more statesmanlike speech. There were pleas on the floor for Gorbachev and Yeltsin to get together and work out their differences, but by now they were locked in a power struggle.

---

45. Two and a half years later, Colonel General Yevgeny Podkolzin, by then the commander of the Airborne Troops but in 1990 the chief of staff of those troops, stated in a newspaper interview that the September 1990 troop movements had been authorized by Gorbachev before he went to Helsinki, but that Yazov had not informed the Supreme Soviet when inquiries were made and had made up the story about practice and potato harvesting—as a result of which Podkolzin had the task of fabricating materials to persuade a Supreme Soviet committee of inquiry that those explanations were true. See "VDV [Airborne Troops], As Always, on Guard," *Argumenty i fakty*, no. 12 (March 1993).

Gorbachev returned to the Supreme Soviet the next day with a speech that bristled with action proposals—even if it focused on reorganizing central political institutions. He proposed abolishing the Presidential Council created only a few months earlier, creating a new Security Council, and upgrading the Federation Council (comprising the chairmen of the Supreme Soviets of all the republics) from a consultative to a policymaking body. The plan would also carry further a shift to a presidential form of government and called for creating "presidential prefects" to represent the president in national regions (in effect, to enforce decisions of the center). Even though these proposals were organizational, the fact that they were "doing something" (and Gorbachev's more responsive manner of presentation) caused the speech to be well received.[46]

On November 23, Gorbachev presented the draft Union Treaty, considerably increasing the authority of the republics, as well as formally including their leaders in the central Federation Council. All the eleven republics (less the three Baltics and Georgia) had agreed to presenting the draft, but none was finally committed (and Ukraine withheld its decision until after adoption of a new Ukrainian Constitution). Several reserved the "right" to create armed forces (Russia, Ukraine, Belorussia, Armenia), and all reserved undefined "independence" for conducting foreign relations (in addition to Ukraine, Belorussia, and Moldova opting for "neutrality," and Ukraine and Belorussia for nuclear-free status). The Union Treaty was thus formally launched, with more consensus than many had thought possible, but still with an uncertain future. Underlining this uncertainty was the action of Russia and Ukraine in signing a bilateral treaty four days earlier, on November 19, in a demonstrative common stand against Gorbachev's center. Yeltsin traveled to Kiev to sign it. The treaty contained no secessionist plank, but it also omitted any reference either to the USSR Constitution or to the future Union Treaty.

Gorbachev, meanwhile, remained under fire from both sides of the political spectrum. On November 18, some twenty-three leading liberals (including Oleg Bogomolov, Yury Ryzhov, Galina Starovoitova, and Yury Afanasyev) in effect called on Gorbachev to shape up and push reform or resign.[47] On December 19, fifty-three leading conservatives (including Party Secretary Oleg Baklanov, Leningrad Party chief Boris Gidaspov, retired Mar-

---

46. I was in Moscow at the time, and it was a fascinating experience to see extensive coverage of both USSR Supreme Soviet and Russian Supreme Soviet sessions broadcast on television at night. It was also a most interesting but very discouraging experience to see in contacts with long-time friends and acquaintances among Soviet officials and in the intelligentsia a growing despondence over the recognition that a national tragedy was unfolding that no one could get a grip on and control.

   I also attended the celebration on Red Square on November 7 of the seventy-third anniversary of the October Revolution—no one, of course, then realizing that it would be the last to be celebrated.

47. "The Country Is Tired of Waiting," *Moskovskiye novosti* (Moscow News) (November 18, 1990).

shal Viktor Kulikov, General Mikhail Moiseyev, chief of the General Staff, Admiral Vladimir Chernavin, commander in chief of the navy, General Valentin Varennikov, commander in chief of ground forces, General Yury Shatalin, commander of internal troops, and several leading members of the Academy of Sciences and—listed, but later objecting that he had not signed— Patriarch Aleksei II of the Russian Orthodox Church) appealed to Gorbachev to maintain order.[48]

In a brief address to the Supreme Soviet on November 23, Gorbachev warned of a "paralysis of power" and breakdown of public order and said that "the times are such and the situation in the country is such that something must be done."[49] At a press conference later that day, he sought to stabilize the increasingly volatile situation by a warning and a plea for order. He reaffirmed dedication to *perestroika* and reform, but in light of the deteriorating situation his emphasis was on the danger of the situation getting out of control and leading to bloodshed. He also emphasized his determination to use his new strengthened executive authority not only to advance reform but also to ensure compliance with the law of the land, the laws of the Soviet Union.[50]

In the context of this situation Gorbachev began to lean to the right to stress "law and order." On November 27 Marshal Yazov in a television appearance disclosed that Gorbachev had authorized the use of force if necessary to defend government installations, monuments (some of which had been defaced or toppled in the Baltics), and to protect servicemen (some of whom were being openly harassed). On November 23 the Supreme Soviet passed a resolution against economic sabotage (reviving a term widely abused in Stalinist times), and in late January by presidential decree the KGB was given extensive power to police the economy. On December 2 the liberal Vadim Bakatin was replaced as minister of the interior by former Latvian KGB (and later party) chief Boris Pugo, with Afghan war hero Colonel General Boris Gromov as deputy.

On December 17 the Congress of Peoples' Deputies again convened. In an opening address, Gorbachev warned against "dark forces" of nationalism and demanded popular referenda in each republic on the new Union Treaty, confident that the vast majority in most if not all republics wanted to preserve the union. He also said that the country needed twelve to eighteen months of firm executive rule to prevent its disintegration.[51]

---

48. The letter was made public on December 19 but not published until December 22. "With Hope and Faith—An Appeal to Comrade M. S. Gorbachev, President of the USSR," *Sovetskaya Rossiya*, December 22, 1990.

49. Speech of President Mikhail Gorbachev to USSR Supreme Soviet, Radio Moscow, November 23, 1990, in FBIS, *Soviet Union*, November 26, 1990, p. 26.

50. News Conference with President Mikhail Gorbachev, Radio Moscow, November 23, 1990, ibid., pp. 44–46.

51. "To Move from Words to Deeds, To Decisively Move Forward, Address of M. S. Gorbachev," *Pravda*, December 18, 1990.

On December 20 the congress (and evidently Gorbachev) was shocked by the unexpected resignation of Eduard Shevardnadze as foreign minister, who warned of the danger of dictatorship. Notwithstanding the long-standing friendship and close political ties between Shevardnadze and Gorbachev, Shevardnadze was troubled by Gorbachev's willingness, even if reluctantly, to give more leeway to the conservatives in the administration—and not to defend him more vigorously against the attacks of conservatives on their common foreign policy.[52] In contraposition, KGB Chief Vladimir Kryuchkov in a television appearance on December 11 and again to the congress on December 22 blamed growing difficulties on "anticommunists" both at home and from abroad.

On December 25, the congress approved new executive powers for President Gorbachev and his executive reorganization. It also ordered a national referendum on the new Union Treaty.

On December 27, Gorbachev pushed through his candidate for the new post of vice president, Gennady Yanayev, a conservative nonentity, who was initially rejected and finally approved (1,237 to 563) only after Gorbachev insisted.[53]

As the year ended, there had been a successful transition from turmoil in Eastern Europe to a new united Europe. But the internal problems of the Soviet Union had grown, and the prospects for the coming year were at best

---

52. A senior former Soviet official has told me that Gorbachev had become envious of Shevardnadze's continuing high standing and planned to "kick him upstairs" to the vice presidency, removing him from responsibility for foreign policy and from being the center of public attention. Moreover, Shevardnadze reportedly heard this from a third party before Gorbachev himself had talked with him about it. Shevardnadze did not want to be so treated and decided to preempt Gorbachev by his resignation—which, he also hoped, would have a salutary shock effect in alerting people to the dangerous drift toward conservative law and order priority over reform.

   Another source has said that Gorbachev had suggested to Shevardnadze that he take the vice presidency, but Shevardnadze saw this step as an unwelcome "trap," and aware that Gorbachev now considered his usefulness as foreign minister over, he decided to move first and resign. See Beschloss and Talbott, *At the Highest Levels*, pp. 294–95.

   Shevardnadze was also unhappy that Gorbachev was prepared to make some concessions to the military and conservatives that beclouded foreign policy. He cited in his memoir a case in point. Before signing the CFE Treaty in November 1990, the military had on its own moved thousands of tanks and artillery pieces beyond the Urals in a step not consistent with the spirit of the treaty. Shevardnadze had protested to Gorbachev, who asked his military adviser, Marshal Sergei Akhromeyev, to look into it. Akhromeyev reported back justifying the action as not contravening commitments under the treaty, and Gorbachev dropped the matter—to Shevardnadze's disappointment. See Shevardnadze, *The Future Belongs to Freedom*, p. 214.

53. A senior Soviet official, a few weeks later, described Yanayev to me as "Gorbachev's Quayle—a conservative nonentity, no threat to Gorbachev, and his selection would pacify the right-wing." Yanayev was known personally to Gorbachev from the time both men had been officials in the Komsomol youth organization.

mixed and uncertain. On December 31, in a New Year's address, Gorbachev described 1990 as "one of the most difficult years in our history" and declared "there is no more sacred cause than the preservation and renewal of the Union."[54]

Gorbachev had successfully steered Soviet foreign policy to a historic rapprochement with the West and reintegration of one world. He well deserved the Nobel Peace Prize that he was awarded on October 15. He had also successfully overcome strong opposition in the Soviet leadership in launching political democratization in the country, and he had neutralized the Communist Party as a potential blocking force on political and economic reform and on the new course in foreign policy.

Gorbachev had not, however, been able to control, channel, or even foresee the consequences of *glasnost* and *demokratizatsiya*. He failed to appreciate in full or in time the strong pressures for republic and regional authority and burgeoning national separatism in several republics. And he temporized on economic reform, with less than half measures that actually had a negative effect. Finally, by the end of the year he was facing a growing political tension between reformers and conservatives that could assume unpredictable forms.

As the year ended, Gorbachev had veered to the right for tactical reasons, although he remained determined to press on with *perestroika*. Caution led him to give more and more ground to conservative elements in his administration in order to prevent violence either in seeking or blocking change. He believed they were still committed—as was he—to peaceful change and reform and still under his control. Both assumptions were to prove unwarranted in the fateful year ahead.

Gorbachev's relationship with President Bush was now well established, and he looked forward to welcoming Bush to a Moscow summit in 1991 marked by signing of a START agreement reducing strategic arms. At the same time, some clouds had appeared on this horizon. In particular, the Soviet military, with its relative ascendancy especially after Shevardnadze's departure, had begun to interpret the CFE Treaty in ways that would at the margins reduce the Soviet commitment to reductions in a way that would cause growing concern in the West and would come to require some effort to rein in during the months ahead. Still, on the whole Soviet-American and Soviet-Western relations were on a more solid foundation than in many years.

President Bush had moved in the first two and a half years of his term from cautious circumspection to a new degree of engagement and confidence. This was seen in Bush's refusal to abandon the relationship when internal problems in the Soviet Union raised public doubts in the United States in late 1990 and early 1991. It was also very evident in the cooperation that both sides

---

54. "New Year's Address of the President of the USSR to the Soviet People," *Pravda*, January 1, 1991.

showed in dealing with the Iraq-Kuwait crisis and Gulf war of 1990–91. Without the mutual rapport that had been established, the Soviet cooperation with the United States in providing UN sanctions and a mandate for military action against Iraq could not have been obtained. Though some quarters in both countries continued to voice suspicions about the motives of the other side in the Gulf crisis and war, in fact the two governments were in harmony on the basic course throughout, and the experience of the Gulf crisis helped to strengthen mutual confidence and prospects for future cooperation. So, too, did cooperative American and Soviet approaches in dealing with many other Third World conflicts.[55]

The crowning achievement of 1990 was the decisive replacement of military confrontation between East and West in Europe and the reunification of both Germany and Europe. It was the end of the Cold War. Ultimately, however, Moscow's relations with the United States and the rest of the world would also depend on the outcome of the growing internal crisis in the Soviet Union.

---

55. See chapter 15.

# 11　The Collapse of Communist Rule and of the Soviet Union, 1991

N O   O N E, in Moscow or Washington or anyplace else, could have foreseen at the beginning of 1991 that the year would witness not only the end of communist rule in the Soviet Union but the disintegration of the state itself. The year promised to be a new departure even without such cataclysmic developments. It was the first year of the post–Cold War era, if one marked the end of the old era of confrontation not from the fall of communist rule and Soviet hegemony in Eastern Europe in late 1989, but from the formal end to the division of Germany and of Europe in 1990. Yet it would also turn out to be the last year of the Soviet state, and hence the last year of *Soviet* relations with the United States (and with all states).

As the year opened, Presidents Bush and Gorbachev exchanged now routine annual New Year's greetings to the people of the other country. Gorbachev's greeting noted explicitly that the Cold War was no more, and the two leaders expressed confidence in their future relations.[1] There were, to be sure, concerns and doubts in both countries about the course and even the fate of Gorbachev's *perestroika* in the Soviet Union. And the internal events in that country were the main focus of attention and of influence on Soviet-American relations, together with the one large item of unfinished business, the restoration of an agreed-on global strategic arms balance at lower levels of forces to complement and buttress the dismantlement of military confrontation in Europe agreed upon in 1990.

President Bush also telephoned Gorbachev on New Year's Day, and they discussed the strategic arms talks and the situation in the Persian Gulf.

---

1.　"New Year's Greetings," January 1, 1991, *U.S. Department of State Dispatch*, vol. 2 (January 7, 1991), p. 7, provides the texts of both President Bush's and President Gorbachev's videotaped messages. (Hereafter *State Dispatch*.) President Bush's message is also found in *Weekly Compilation of Presidential Documents*, vol. 27 (January 7, 1991), pp. 2–3. (Hereafter *Presidential Documents*.)

Secretary of State James Baker on January 4 sent a message on the strategic arms issues to Foreign Minister Eduard Shevardnadze (still in his last days in office). These two issues, one on bilateral arms control and the other on bilateral consultation and cooperation in the hot Gulf crisis, were the dominant current foreign policy issues. But internal events in the Soviet Union soon added another element that threatened to eclipse both: use of deadly force by Soviet authorities in Vilnius, Lithuania, on January 13, and in Riga, Latvia, a week later. Eighteen civilians (and two from the security forces) died in the two incidents.

Bush in his first comment described "the turn of events" in Lithuania as "deeply disturbing." He noted that "change in the Soviet Union has helped to create a basis for unprecedented cooperation and partnership between the United States and the Soviet Union. The events that we're witnessing now are completely inconsistent with that course." He declared that "we condemn these acts, which could not help but affect our relationship," but he also wisely wanted to understand the situation there more clearly before responding.[2] Both houses of Congress passed resolutions strongly condemning the Soviet actions in the Baltic republics and recommending that the president consider economic sanctions. But, despite a similar recommendation by his own interagency deputies committee (chaired by Robert Gates), Bush did not impose even symbolic sanctions.

On January 26 Foreign Minister Aleksandr Bessmertnykh, newly in office, flew to Washington. After he had seen the president on January 28, the press was advised that because of the demands of the situation in the Gulf, the planned summit meeting was being put off from mid-February to the middle of the year. This explanation was true, but not the whole truth—obviously, until the situation in the Baltics was cleared up, a summit was not appropriate. Besides assurances on the intention not to use force in the Baltics, Bessmertnykh stressed continuity with his predecessor in policy and Gorbachev's unwavering support for peaceful reform at home and cooperation with the United States in building a new world order. And he agreed to issuance of an important joint statement reiterating Soviet and U.S. commitment to the UN resolutions and coalition efforts to end the Iraqi occupation of Kuwait.[3]

---

2.   "Remarks on Soviet Military Intervention in Lithuania," January 13, 1991, *Presidential Documents*, vol. 27 (January 21, 1991), p. 45.

3.   The text is given in "US-USSR and the Persian Gulf," January 29, 1991, *State Dispatch*, vol. 2 (February 4, 1991), p. 71.

     Bessmertnykh's agreement to a reaffirmation of the Soviet position supporting the UN resolutions against Iraq over Kuwait was a welcome reassurance to Washington. From Moscow's point of view, no less welcome was American agreement to include in the statement renewed commitment to pursue "a meaningful peace process—one which promotes a just peace, security, and real reconciliation for Israel, Arab states, and Palestinians," after the Persian Gulf crisis was resolved. This had not been a quid pro quo, nor even expected, and was seen as a triumph for Bessmertnykh in his first

President Bush delivered his State of the Union address to Congress and the American people the next day. He described the end of the Cold War as a victory for all humanity. While crediting America's leadership as instrumental in making possible "a Europe whole and free," he also stressed that "our relationship to the Soviet Union is important not only to us but to the world. That relationship has helped to shape these and other historic changes." While saying that the United States was "deeply concerned by the violence in the Baltics" and had communicated that concern to the Soviet leadership, the American leaders had received representations that the situation in the Baltics would change. So "We will watch carefully as the situation develops. And we will maintain our contact with the Soviet leadership to encourage continued commitment to democratization and reform. If it is possible," he concluded, "I want to continue to build a lasting basis for U.S.-Soviet cooperation."[4] It would be hard to imagine a greater contrast to the hasty ill-informed shooting from the lip of the Reagan administration's reaction to the shootdown of KAL-007 eight years earlier.

A week later, Bush again noted that "when we see repression in the Baltics, it is very hard to have business as usual," and "we've got to see that no more force will be used against these Baltic States and that there can be peaceful resolution to these questions. Otherwise," he said, "not only will our trade relations be set back . . . but the rest of our overall relationship could undergo a problem. I don't want that." And he gave several concrete examples, first among them that the Soviet leadership had been "steadfast in support of our objectives in the Gulf. And that," he emphasized, "is very, very important." He also noted limitation on arms shipment to the Western Hemisphere, cooperation in ending the conflict in Angola, and "many things" in which it was "to our interest to work closely with the Soviets."[5] The next day, in testifying before the Senate Foreign Relations Committee, Baker made clear that one among these was agreement on a strategic arms reduction treaty (START), as soon as possible, "in our national interest."[6] Baker noted that "we cannot rule out the

---

diplomatic foray as foreign minister. (Based on interview accounts by several Soviet officials involved in foreign relations.)

The statement on the Middle East peace process did raise eyebrows and some hackles in the American press, in addition to partly overshadowing the president's State of the Union address. See Michael R. Beschloss and Strobe Talbott, *At the Highest Levels: The Inside Story of the End of the Cold War* (Little, Brown and Company, 1992), pp. 327–33.

4.   "Address before a Joint Session of the Congress on the State of the Union," January 29, 1991, *Presidential Documents*, vol. 27 (February 4, 1991), pp. 90–91.

5.   "Remarks and a Question-and-Answer Session at a Meeting of the Economic Club," February 6, 1991, *Presidential Documents*, vol. 27 (February 11, 1991), pp. 143–44.

6.   "Foreign Policy Overview and Budget Requests for Fiscal Year 1992," Hearing before the Senate Committee on Foreign Relations, 102 Cong. 1 sess. (Washington: Government Printing Office, 1991), p. 26.

possibility that matters may still turn out for the worse, but at the same time we must be careful not to jump to premature conclusions. The Soviet leadership is at a crossroads."[7]

Gorbachev continued his efforts to persuade Saddam Hussein to withdraw from Kuwait, but on February 21 he telephoned President Bush to tell him that his latest effort had not succeeded. When the U.S.-led coalition opened hostilities on February 23, the Soviet Union supported Desert Storm.[8]

The key to continuing U.S.-Soviet rapprochement remained, however, Soviet internal developments. By mid-March it had become clear that Gorbachev was not going to impose presidential rule or use force to compel submission of the defiant Baltic governments, and that—in Bush's earlier words—the short tragic resort to force in mid-January had, indeed, proved "an anomaly and not a new way of life."[9] Washington remained, however, increasingly concerned over the internal situation in the Soviet Union.[10]

On March 14–17 Baker was in Moscow for discussions with Bessmertnykh (and a meeting with Gorbachev on March 15) on the whole range of issues—the Gulf and Middle East, regional conflicts, a dispute that had arisen over the terms of the Conventional Forces in Europe (CFE) Treaty, and the START issues.[11] By the time of a second round by Baker and Bessmertnykh in Kislovodsk on April 24–25, while some CFE and START issues remained unresolved, agreement was reached on convening a Middle East peace conference that fall.

---

7.   Secretary Baker, "Opportunities to Build a Better World," House Foreign Affairs Committee, February 6, 1991, *Dispatch*, vol. 2 (February 11, 1991), p. 85.

An extensive and thoughtful presentation of the administration's analysis of the situation in the USSR was given to a Senate subcommittee a few weeks later by State Department Counselor Robert B. Zoellick, not prejudging the outcome but sympathetic to Gorbachev's problems and the stakes in U.S.-Soviet relations. See "Soviet Disunion: The American Response," February 28, 1991, *Dispatch*, vol. 2 (March 4, 1991), pp. 144–49.

8.   Immediately before the U.S. attack began, Baker informed Bessmertnykh by phone, and Gorbachev sought a brief delay to try once more, but the attack was already under way.

9.   *Presidential Documents*, vol. 27 (February 11, 1991), p. 143.

On the earlier concerns in Washington over the Baltic situation, and the desire not to undercut Gorbachev, see Beschloss and Talbott, *At the Highest Levels*, pp. 298–325.

10.  In the spring of 1991 the CIA's *National Intelligence Daily* Top Secret report to the president and other senior officials began to print a daily "sitrep" (situation report) on the internal situation in the USSR, with particular attention to the non-Russian republics. A few months later the unclassified Foreign Broadcast Information Service (FBIS) also began to issue a new series of translations of open materials from and concerning "the republics" of the USSR.

11.  For reporting on these discussions, see Beschloss and Talbott, *At the Highest Levels*, pp. 342–44, 350–54.

Although many in Congress had exercised political caution about moving forward on relations with the Soviet Union in the first three months of the year because of the reverberations of the early repressive acts in the Baltic republics, the calls of some on the right for a renewed anti-Soviet stance were not widely supported.[12] The country was not prepared to leave these acts uncondemned, but it was prepared to follow the administration's readiness to display patience in evaluating the course of Soviet policy. As Soviet policy and actions more clearly resumed the path of reform over the months following, as well as showing continued cooperative conduct in world affairs, U.S.-Soviet relations again moved toward rapprochement.

Even during these months of reevaluation, there were many signs of the new developing normal relationship in the post–Cold War world. Apart from now routine trade and other contacts, two are worth noting. One was an embarrassing example of the weight of bureaucratic inertia of the Cold War, of the stickiness of red tape. In January a Soviet prototype compact nuclear reactor for space propulsion, called Topaz II, was brought over and exhibited at a scientific symposium in Albuquerque, New Mexico. There was in fact interest in the United States in possible purchase of such a reactor, which was not available in the United States, and there was interest in Moscow in selling the technology. At this stage the display of the model was merely encouraging for its evidence of a loosening of stringent constraints by the Soviet Union. But when the time came in April to ship the model back to Moscow, the Nuclear Regulatory Commission (NRC) suddenly ruled that U.S. laws prohibited the "export" of such a device to the Soviet Union—even though it was Soviet-made and Soviet-owned, and a model and not even a working reactor. It took a whole month before this absurd and embarrassing situation could be resolved by a

---

12. Although there were many harsh criticisms of the repressive use of force in the Baltics, and some calls for greater support for independence of the Baltic states, the action that briefly caused the sharpest conservative backlash against U.S. cooperation with the Soviet Union was Gorbachev's independent attempt to stave off the U.S. resort to military action in the Gulf and seek Iraq's withdrawal by diplomacy, which was depicted as virtually a betrayal, an attempt to deny the United States the chance to use and display its military power. See E. J. Dionne, Jr., "Gorbachev's New Grist for the Cold War Mill," *Washington Post*, February 21, 1991, pp. A23, A26; and Rowland Evans and Robert Novak, "Same Old Soviets," *Washington Post*, February 22, 1991, p. A23. As one of them, Patrick J. Glynn at the American Enterprise Institute, candidly explained, "It's easier to cope with a world where the Soviets are being the Soviets." Cited in Dionne, *Washington Post*, February 21, 1991, p. A26.

Also within the administration, Secretary of Defense Dick Cheney used the same occasion to argue for a continuing Soviet threat and need for a strong U.S. defense posture and to push for less reliance on Gorbachev and implicitly more on Yeltsin; see Paul Bedard, "Cheney: Cold War Climate Returning," *Washington Times*, February 22, 1991, p. A1.

new NRC ruling (under pressure from the administration) and the reactor returned.[13]

The second incident was much more encouraging as a reflection of the new political relationship. In Somalia, where the United States and Soviet Union had competed for twenty years for the honor of supplying arms to a petty dictator and basing ships in its harbor, civil war had descended into chaos as the year began. On January 5, the entire Soviet diplomatic colony in Mogadishu (39 people) was given quick safe haven in the large walled U.S. Embassy compound, and on the next two days the group was evacuated by helicopter under U.S. Marine cover, together with 242 American and other diplomats, to the USS *Guam* to be taken to safety. That was a poignant example of intimate security cooperation in a regional conflict.

Such complaints as there were over the new relationship came mostly from certain quarters on the Soviet side.

## Gorbachev Leans to the Right

In the last two or three months of 1990 Gorbachev had become very concerned over the signs of gradual breakdown in law and the constitutional order that threatened the unity of the country as well as his course of *perestroika*. He had therefore consciously tacked to the right in an effort to stabilize the situation and had given additional authority to the security and defense forces. This tactical turn continued for the first three months of 1991. It led to a further polarization of political forces and to intense maneuvering to influence Gorbachev and the course of policy. It also led, in the Baltic republics, to tragedy and greatly increased tension.

On January 1, Eduard Shevardnadze issued a new warning, saying that one reason for his resignation had been the fear that there would be a crackdown with use of force. On January 2, the recently created special riot police (OMON, known as the Black Berets) seized the main printing plant in Riga, Latvia, to protect Communist Party property. Five days later, the Ministry of Defense announced on national television the dispatch of paratroops to help secure compliance with the law on military conscription in the Baltic republics,

---

13. The incident received very little press notice in the United States, somewhat more in the Soviet Union. See R. Jeffrey Smith, "U.S. Won't Let Soviets Take Reactor Back Home, Conference Exhibit Trapped in Legal Limbo," *Washington Post*, April 20, 1991, p. A6; and AP, "U.S. Agency to Let Soviets Take Their Reactor Home," *Washington Post*, May 22, 1991, p. A1.

Finally, after a year of sharp debate within the Bush administration, the U.S. Air Force was permitted to buy the Topaz II for a bargain $7.5 million for use in tests under the strategic defense initiative (SDI). See Thomas W. Lippman, "Pentagon Approves Import of Small Russian Nuclear Reactor," *Washington Post*, March 27, 1992, p. A23.

Armenia, Georgia, Moldavia, and the western provinces of Ukraine—the places where separatist nationalist sentiment was strongest and had led to large-scale draft evasion. Secret documents now released show that also on January 7 the Moscow-loyalist Lithuanian Communist Party (the wing that had broken away from the independent Lithuanian Communist Party) had appealed to Gorbachev to disband the republic Supreme Soviet and impose direct presidential rule in Lithuania. Secret records disclose also that on January 8 and eight other occasions during that month Gorbachev's personal administrative chief of staff, Valery Boldin, had met with the Lithuanian loyalist party chief, Mikolas Burociavicus, and with Party Secretaries Oleg Shenin and Oleg Baklanov, Minister of Internal Affairs Boris Pugo (himself a Latvian, and formerly KGB chief, and later party chief, in Latvia), KGB Chairman Vladimir Kryuchkov, and Defense Minister Marshal Dmitry Yazov. There is no indication that Gorbachev was aware of these meetings, although they could have been described as contingency planning meetings. In fact, they were operational planning sessions.[14]

On January 10, Gorbachev sent a message warning the Lithuanian government of the need to "restore in full the force of the USSR Constitution and the constitution of the Lithuanian SSR [Soviet Socialist Republic]," that "the people demand the restoration of constitutional order, reliable guarantees of security, and normal living conditions" and in their absence "are demanding the imposition of presidential rule." This was a not very veiled threat of possible resort to such direct rule. It is clear from many indications, above all what subsequently occurred, that Gorbachev was extremely reluctant either to dismiss (and perhaps arrest) the elected Baltic parliaments and establish his own direct presidential rule or to countenance the use of force that would be entailed and would ensue. His warning may have deterred some further Baltic actions.[15] But it also lent encouragement to pro-Moscow Baltic intransigents

---

14. See Leonid Mlechin, "Vilnius Decided Gorbachev's Fate," *Novoye vremya* (New Times), no. 5 (January 1992), pp. 17–19.

    Party Secretary Oleg Shenin had been the author of a secret Secretariat paper as early as August 29, 1990, which outlined a scheme to bring loyalist communists back to power in Lithuania, although without such drastic measures. The document, apparently genuine, was published in *Nezavisimaya gazeta* (Independent Newspaper), January 29, 1991.

15. Gorbachev's warning was rejected within a few hours by Vytautas Landsbergis, chairman of the Lithuanian Supreme Council, who mockingly said the appeal was directed to a "non-existent" Lithuanian SSR, and he provocatively added that Gorbachev's demand that the USSR Constitution be "restored" was recognition that it was not in fact valid there. See "Gorbachev Sends Warning to Lithuanian Council," Moscow Television, 1200 GMT, January 10, 1991, in Foreign Broadcast Information Service, *Daily Report: Soviet Union*, January 11, 1991, p. 43 (hereafter FBIS, *Soviet Union*); and "Lithuanian President Rejects Gorbachev's Appeal," TASS, 1610 GMT, January 10, 1991, in FBIS, ibid., January 10, 1991, p. 54.

and the conservative security clique in Gorbachev's own administration who were maneuvering to compel Gorbachev's acquiescence, no matter how reluctantly, in a crackdown.

On January 11, a National Salvation Committee of Lithuania announced it would reinstate in full effect the USSR and Lithuanian SSR Constitutions and in effect bid to assume control in the republic.

Soviet troops meanwhile had occupied several buildings claimed by the Lithuanian Communist Party, including the printing plant and the airport and railroad station. On January 9 they occupied, but then withdrew from, the television center.

On January 13 the tragic climax came in a forcible occupation of the television and radio center by troops with tanks, in which fifteen civilians were killed. The National Salvation Committee announced it was taking control of the government. Gorbachev denied any foreknowledge of the action or authorization for use of arms. Though doubted by some, this was true. Interior Minister Pugo and Defense Minister Yazov less plausibly, and less honestly, also disclaimed responsibility. Yazov attempted to justify the action by saying that the National Salvation Committee had asked for help, but he was unable even to identify the membership of the committee or cite any basis for its legitimacy. The local military commander, Major General Vladimir Uskhopchik, also citing only the National Salvation Committee as the political authority, was left holding the bag, but he was not denounced, removed, or even reprimanded.

It is now known from Gorbachev's close associate and press assistant to the president at the time, Vitaly Ignatenko, that Gorbachev had been fed a steady stream of false and misleading information on events and public opinion by his conservative security advisers—Boldin, Pugo, Kryuchkov, and Yazov (and the local Lithuanian and Latvian party chiefs). He confirmed that on January 13, a weekend day, Gorbachev was not even informed of the events there (or of a telephone call from Landsbergis). Only much later did Gorbachev, shaken, learn that the "disturbances" he had belatedly been told about involved tanks and fifteen dead. On January 14, Gorbachev's remaining liberal advisers (Yakovlev, Bakatin, Primakov, Chernyayev, and Ignatenko) met and worked out a plan for Gorbachev to go the next day to Vilnius, acknowledge the injustice, and perhaps even accept Lithuanian independence. Gorbachev was initially receptive, but he later decided against it because the security chiefs were opposed, supposedly on the grounds that they could not guarantee the president's safety if he went there at that time.[16] Gorbachev not only did not go to Vilnius, he did not disassociate himself from the situation and make clear the unacceptability of vigilante salvation committees or military commanders act-

16. Vitaly Ignatenko, "From Vilnius to Foros: Gorbachev's Most Difficult Days," *Novoye vremya*, no. 12 (March 1992), pp. 22–26.

ing without proper authority. It was a serious moral and political failure on his part and contributed to the impression that at the least he did not recognize the growing danger from action by the right, if indeed he was not part of it. Yeltsin, by contrast, flew to Tallin on January 13 and took the politically bold if rhetorical stand of calling on Russian soldiers not to fire on the citizenry.

Nor was this the end. On January 19 a similar National Salvation Committee was established in Riga, Latvia, and on the next day OMON riot police took over the Latvian Interior Ministry by force, leaving five dead. In Moscow, public demonstrations by 100,000 citizens protested the use of force in the Baltics.

On January 23 Gorbachev did, belatedly, express his "most sincere condolences," and said he was "profoundly moved by the tragic turn of the confrontation" in Vilnius and Riga. He called for a thorough investigation of the circumstances connected with the resort to arms and disavowed the action—it was not an expression of presidential policy. He castigated the "irresponsible behavior" and "illegal acts trampling under foot the Constitution itself" by (Baltic) extremists in causing the confrontation. But he also strongly stressed that any "committees" must only "aspire to power through constitutional means, without using violence," and he declared "any attempts to appeal to the armed forces in a political contest are impermissible."[17] The day before he had met with the Latvian leader, Anatolijs Gorbunovs, in an attempt to defuse the situation.

The use of force in a crackdown had clearly been ruled out. By January 30 Pugo announced that the additional troops sent to the Baltic republics were being withdrawn. And Gorbachev decisively rejected dissolution of the elected republic leaderships and resort to direct presidential rule. On February 1 he named delegations to negotiate with the three Baltic republics.

On February 9 Lithuania voted overwhelmingly for independence (90 percent of the 85 percent who voted). On March 3 Latvia and Estonia also voted for independence (by 74 and 78 percent, respectively). Though Gorbachev did not accept those votes as binding (an all-union vote was scheduled for mid-March), he permitted the plebiscites to occur and continued negotiations with the Baltic republic governments.

The hard-line conservative security clique in the Soviet government had failed to convince Gorbachev, or to provoke the situation in a way to force him to crack down in the Baltics. But the group remained in office and in fact was strengthened by a flow of liberals and reformers out of the administration. On January 14 Valentin Pavlov, the conservative former finance minister, was confirmed as the new prime minister. Presidential Council members Aleksandr Yakovlev, Yevgeny Primakov, and Yury Osipyan resigned, as did economic

---

17. "Declaration of President of the USSR M. S. Gorbachev," *Pravda*, January 23, 1991.

reformers Stanislav Shatalin and Nikolai Petrakov, and deputy prime ministers Leonid Abalkin and Stepan Sitaryan were not reappointed by Pavlov.

A Central Committee plenum was held on January 31 to discuss the crisis in the Baltics and the situation overall. Shortly before, Leningrad Party Chief Boris Gidaspov had published a strong antireform interview in *Pravda* and in effect called for backpedaling on democratization and a return to the early *perestroika* of economic "acceleration," the course of 1985–86. He also indirectly attacked Gorbachev for reducing the role of the Communist Party.[18] At the plenum he was joined by Gorbachev's hand-picked deputy general secretary, Vladimir Ivashko, and the chief party ideologist, Aleksandr Dzasokhov, in calling for return to a more active party role in ideology, economic reform, and internal central party control—all of which Gorbachev had deliberately and successfully been curtailing. The criticisms also moved into foreign policy, challenging whether the United States had abused the UN mandate in the extent of its military actions in Iraq. Gorbachev was on the defensive.[19]

Gorbachev continued to support some strong measures to maintain law and order. On January 26 it became known that new Army-police joint patrols would reinforce the usual police (an order signed by Yazov and Pugo on December 29, but not then given a green light by Gorbachev). And on January 26 Gorbachev signed an order giving the KGB broad search authority to uncover corruption and "economic sabotage"—including searches of joint ventures or offices of foreign companies in the Soviet Union.

Economic reform was pursued in confused fashion. On January 22 all bank accounts were frozen and all old fifty- and one hundred-ruble notes were called in for replacement, within ceilings that could wipe out some personal savings, although the objective was to curb black marketing. Eventually the currency "reform" was carried out in a way that did not hurt many people, but it further reduced public confidence in the government and was not effective in its purpose. A month later, a more substantial step was announced with a plan

---

18. "We Are Not Hiding in the Trenches: Interview with Secretary of the CC of the CPSU and First Secretary of the Leningrad Province Party Committee B. V. Gidaspov," *Pravda*, January 12, 1991.

19. "Information Bulletin on the Combined Plenum of the Central Committee and Central Control Commission of the Communist Party of the Soviet Union," *Pravda*, February 1, 1991; "Political Declaration of the Combined Plenum of the Central Committee and the Central Control Commission of the CPSU: 'On the Current Situation and the Tasks of the Party'" ibid., February 4, 1991; and "On the Combined Plenum of the CC and CCC of the CPSU" (record of discussion at the plenum), Ibid., February 4, 1991, and February 5, 1991; quotations from Polozkov, ibid., February 4, 1991.

Polozkov in effect emerged at this plenum as "the new Ligachev"—even reiterating Ligachev's argument for renewed ideological struggle and opposing the substitution of common human values for class struggle in foreign policy.

to dismantle Gosplan, the central planning body, and plans to eliminate most industrial ministries, but still the actual control of enterprises was not affected.

By mid-February, Yeltsin launched a direct attack on Gorbachev, charging him with seeking a personal dictatorship and on February 19 called for his resignation. Four days later, 40,000 people demonstrated at a Democratic Russia rally in Moscow. Gorbachev, visiting in Belarus in late February, warned of possible civil war. On March 1, a series of miners' strikes began that spread and reached 300,000 miners by March 19.

Gorbachev had placed high stakes on the nationwide referendum on a renewed union, scheduled for March 17. He was confident in overwhelming popular support for a union in virtually all republics (save the Baltics). He succeeded in getting agreement on a revised draft Union Treaty (still as a draft subject to approval by the Supreme Soviets of all the republics), and the new draft was published on March 7, before the referendum. It made significant concessions to the republics, sharing with them decisions on national security, defense, foreign policy, and the national budget—all reserved to the union government in the November 1990 draft.

On the same day Gorbachev requested approval by the Supreme Soviet of nine members of the new USSR Security Council: Yanayev, Pavlov, Boldin, Pugo, Kryuchkov, Yazov, Bakatin, Primakov, and Bessmertnykh. (All except Boldin were approved, whereupon Gorbachev simply kept Boldin as his chief of staff.) This slate balanced liberals Bakatin and Primakov with the conservatives Yanayev and Pavlov, and the conservative security forces trio Pugo, Kryuchkov, and Yazov with the liberal foreign minister Bessmertnykh.[20]

Yeltsin meanwhile had succeeded in paralleling Gorbachev's referendum with a vote in the Russian Federation on popular election of a president. He also stepped up his attacks on Gorbachev, on March 9 saying to a Moscow rally, "Let's declare war on the leadership of the country, which has led us into a quagmire."[21] A crowd estimated variously between 100,000 and 300,000 people demonstrated in Yeltsin's support and against Gorbachev. Yeltsin did not specifically denounce the union referendum, but he withheld explicit support, with the result that a positive vote was substantially reduced in the main cities of Russia, although not enough to defeat endorsement of a union. Yeltsin seemed to want the vote for his proposal for popular election of a president of Russia to succeed by a greater margin than Gorbachev's proposition on a union, but for the union vote still to carry.

The referendum on March 17 brought an overall countrywide vote of 76 percent for a renewed union. The figure would undoubtedly have been

---

20. In five months, six of these nine trusted associates would make their abortive coup d'etat: Yanayev, Pavlov, Boldin, Pugo, Kryuchkov, and Yazov.

21. Michael Dobbs, "Yeltsin Urges Reform Forces to 'Declare War' on Kremlin Leaders," *Washington Post*, March 10, 1991, pp. A14–15.

much higher but for Yeltsin's equivocal stand—only slightly more than half of the voters in Moscow and Leningrad voted in favor, and 70 percent voted against in Yeltsin's base at Sverdlovsk, although there was obviously no real opposition to a union in these cities. Russia overall voted 71 percent in favor of the union, Ukraine 70 percent, Belarus 83 percent, and in Kazakhstan, the Central Asian republics, and Azerbaijan the positive vote ranged from 93 percent to 98 percent. The local governments and the vast majority of the population in the three Baltic republics, Georgia, Armenia, and Moldova boycotted the vote on the referendum, showing only pockets of prounion support. In Ukraine, an additional question endorsing Ukrainian "sovereignty" received 80 percent endorsement, at the same time that a renewed union was receiving 70 percent—clearly most Ukrainians did not then see the two as incompatible.

Yeltsin's proposal for election of a president of Russia received some 70 percent of the vote, about the same as Gorbachev's union vote, but favorable percentages were higher in Moscow and many cities. Both he and Gorbachev claimed victory in the outcome. The result probably contributed to their decisions to cooperate in the months ahead on both economic reform and the Union Treaty. One early result was the defeat of a right-wing attempt to unseat Yeltsin in the Russian Supreme Soviet. Conservative Russian Communist Party leader Ivan Polozkov on April 2 gave up on such efforts, and two days later the legislature even gave Yeltsin expanded powers that he had sought.

Before Yeltsin's victory, however, another friction between Gorbachev and Yeltsin had arisen when on March 25 Gorbachev banned public rallies and demonstrations in the capitol for three weeks and placed Moscow police under central Ministry of Interior control. Although the main reason for Gorbachev's action was probably his concern over the controversial introduction of steep price increases over the period March 26 to April 15, Yeltsin and his supporters saw it as curtailing their best way of giving support to Yeltsin on the eve of the confrontation in the Supreme Soviet posed by right-wing attempts to force Yeltsin's resignation. The pro-Yeltsin opposition therefore refused to abide by the ban. Eventually Gorbachev permitted the rallies, while the opposition gave way on holding them at the center near the Kremlin. Thus a compromise was reached, but not without police barricades and considerable tension over a looming possible confrontation. Again, on March 28 more than 100,000 people marched and chanted support for Yeltsin, and they denounced not the hardliners in the Russian Supreme Soviet but Gorbachev. As noted above, Yeltsin won his contest in the Supreme Soviet without the issue even having to be put to a vote.

The hard-liners did not give up, however, on opposing the Union Treaty as a giveaway of central authority, and on April 20–21 a "congress" of the Soyuz (Union) faction denounced the treaty (and Gorbachev) and called for a declaration of national emergency. Gorbachev, meanwhile, again moved on economic reform right after the referendum (on March 19 decreeing retail price and transportation charge increases), and also, especially on his trip to

Japan in mid-April, he strongly defended new thinking in foreign policy and pursuit of a new world order.

On April 22, the anniversary of Lenin's birth (as on January 21, the anniversary of his death), Gorbachev and other leaders placed a traditional wreath at Lenin's mausoleum—for the last time, as events would decree. But this genuflection to the old order, while anomalous and underlining the straddling posture Gorbachev still maintained, was insignificant compared with renewed real steps forward.

## Gorbachev Resumes a Drive for Reform

On the next day, April 23, the "9+1," Gorbachev and the leaders of nine republics (the three Slavic and six Muslim republics), meeting at Gorbachev's dacha at Novo-Ogaryevo, issued a joint statement of their agreement to accelerate approval of the Union Treaty. Yeltsin, as well as the increasingly influential Nursultan Nazarbayev of Kazakhstan, were now strong advocates of the revised Union Treaty. Yeltsin was in some sense the leader of "the nine," but not in the sense that he could control their positions.

On that same day, the Supreme Soviet promptly approved Prime Minister Pavlov's "anticrisis program," combining economic reform, financial stabilization, law and order (a ban on strikes), and a "stick" announcing that those republics that did not join in a renewed union would have to trade with it at world market prices.[22]

On April 24–25, a Central Committee plenum was held to meet the demands of conservative party leaders and organizations (in particular Gidaspov in Leningrad, S. I. Gurenko in Ukraine, and A. A. Malofeyev in Belarus). Gorbachev had held off the plenary party meeting until after his 9+1 Union Treaty accord. He had also reinforced his position by getting a Politburo vote of support the day the plenum opened. But, as he had anticipated, there was a flood of complaints and opposition to market reform, deteriorating economic and political conditions, and foreign policy issues. Among the latter issues were Soviet policy in the Gulf crisis, seen as too supportive of the United States; the CFE Treaty, too one-sided in concessions to the West; the continuation of a threat from NATO, not given due recognition by the Gorbachev administration; and even criticism of a routine Bering Straits demarcation treaty with the United States. The heart of the matter was the reduction of the role of the party as well as of the party's doctrine and policies, reinforced by the threatened loosening of central governmental authority over the republics.

---

22. "Labor, Responsibility, Consolidation: USSR Prime Minister V. S. Pavlov's Report at the USSR Supreme Soviet Session 22 April," *Pravda*, April 23, 1991.

Gorbachev angrily defended his positions and dramatically (if not for the first time) threatened to resign if not given a vote of confidence. As before, he won.[23]

Many party leaders in the republics and provinces, and in Gorbachev's leadership team, must have increasingly come to the realization that the party could not shake Gorbachev's determination; only events and necessary actions in response could lead Gorbachev to swerve or change course. By the same token, many (though not all) reformers took heart at Gorbachev's return to a clear course of reform.

By May 11, Yeltsin publicly proclaimed Gorbachev as an ally of pro-democracy forces and supporter of reforms. Later in the month, Gorbachev visited Kazakhstan and praised Nazarbayev. On the other side, the six separatist nonunion supporters met on May 25 in Kishinev (Chisinau), Moldova, to coordinate their opposition—the three Baltic republics, Moldova, Armenia, and Georgia. Within the Russian Federation, on May 12 all the autonomous republics save one—Tatarstan—endorsed the Union Treaty. By late May, a struggle within the Communist Party of Ukraine was won by Leonid Kravchuk, a supporter of the Union Treaty, against diehard conservatives.

The most important development was the popular election of Yeltsin as president of Russia on June 12 by 57 percent of the vote (mirrored by Popov's 60 percent in Moscow and Sobchak's 70 percent in Leningrad—whose inhabitants also voted a preference for restoring the name St. Petersburg).[24]

Public dissatisfaction with the economic situation, however, persisted. So did unease and unhappiness within the leadership at the new Gorbachev-Yeltsin reform alliance. On June 17, Prime Minister Pavlov took an unprecedented initiative, on his own authority requesting the Supreme Soviet to give his cabinet emergency powers to initiate legislation and issue decrees. His argument was that the president (Gorbachev) could not handle all the responsibilities he had—a transparent excuse for a power grab. In his speech he also attacked the economic reform proposals recently advanced by Grigory Yavlinsky and a Harvard University group calling for a "grand bargain." (In an interview, he attacked more generally the policy of seeking economic assistance from the West.) Pavlov was supported by the security affairs triumvirate—Pugo, Kryuchkov, and Yazov—and by the conservative "Soyuz" deputies. Gorbachev opposed the plan and attacked leaders of the Soyuz faction, but not Pavlov. The Supreme Soviet on June 21 decisively rejected Pavlov's request,

---

23. See "Opening Speech by M. S. Gorbachev, General Secretary of the Central Committee of the CPSU at the Combined Plenum of the CC and CCC of the CPSU, April 24, 1991," *Pravda*, April 24, 1991; other speeches covered in the press and the concluding "Information Report on the Joint Plenum of the Central Committee and Central Control Commission of the CPSU," *Pravda*, April 25, 1991.

24. A year later, with the Soviet Union now history, Yeltsin in a controversial move declared June 12, 1991, a national holiday as the first anniversary of the "independence" of Russia.

264–24, but Pavlov remained in office and Gorbachev even papered over the rift by saying that the request had been "within the framework of *perestroika*."[25] Kryuchkov had delivered a hard-line speech in support of Pavlov to a closed session on June 18, but a long excerpt was released to the media a few days later, blaming the West (including the CIA) for attempting to undermine the Soviet Union by pretending to offer support for *perestroika*.[26]

On June 26 OMON police raided the Vilnius telephone center. There were no casualties, but the action was clearly an attempt again to raise tension and drive a wedge between the democratic reform wing and the Gorbachev administration.

On July 1, a galaxy of nine leading moderate reformers called upon all democratic and reformist forces to unite: Shevardnadze, Yakovlev, Aleksandr Rutskoi (Yeltsin's vice president-elect), Russian Prime Minister Ivan Silayev, industrialist Arkady Volsky, Moscow Mayor Popov, Leningrad Mayor Sobchak, and economic reformers Shatalin and Petrakov. They announced plans to convene a conference in September to launch a new Movement for Democratic Reform and to decide whether a new political party should be established.[27] Presidential spokesman Ignatenko said that Gorbachev considered the action a "positive step," and Yeltsin endorsed it and urged the movement's supporters to become a new political party. A few days later, on July 4, Shevardnadze resigned from the Communist Party. The day before *Pravda* had reported that Gorbachev had said that the conservatives risked a "self-destruction" of the Communist Party from within, and the party could "lose all the political battles and all the elections" that it faced.[28] Yakovlev resigned from the Communist Party on August 16.

On July 5 the Russian Supreme Soviet approved the draft Union Treaty, and on July 12 the USSR Supreme Soviet did so as well. By that time all

---

25. The Supreme Soviet sessions were closed, so reportage was scattered until radio coverage of Gorbachev's speech of June 21 at the conclusion of the debate. See "Gorbachev Addresses Supreme Soviet 21 June," Radio Mayak, June 21, 1991, in FBIS, *Soviet Union*, June 24, 1991, pp. 36–45, and "Pavlov Request Removed from Agenda," Radio Moscow, June 24, 1991, ibid., pp. 45–46.

    Pavlov's general attack on seeking Western economic assistance, which was Gorbachev's policy, was not in his address to the Supreme Soviet but in an interview in *Izvestiya* on the same day, in which he scathingly said that pursuing such a policy would mean, "We will have to stand in line with Israel and Nicaragua." And, he bluntly added, "Whoever wants to do that can, but without me." See "Novo-Ogarevo—Kremlin: The Doors Are Closing," *Izvestiya*, June 18, 1991.

26. On Kryuchkov's speech, see *Sovetskaya Rossiya* (Soviet Russia), June 27, 1991, also in FBIS, *Soviet Union*, June 27, 1991, pp. 23–25.

27. "For a Unification of the Forces of Democracy and Reform, A Group of Well-Known Political Figures Address the People. *Izvestiya* Prints Excerpts," *Izvestiya*, July 2, 1991.

28. "Answering Questions of Concern to Society: From the CPSU Program Commission Session," *Pravda*, July 3, 1991.

the republic legislatures had approved it except for Ukraine, which deferred action until after a vote on independence set for December 1. Kravchuk continued to support a union in principle, but he had become more and more evasive about its terms and noncommittal on the draft, owing to opposition by the nationalist Rukh and his electoral campaign for the presidency, also to be voted on December 1. On July 23, the approved draft was published as the Union Treaty, with announcement on August 2 that signature was scheduled for August 20 (except for Ukraine, and any others tht were not yet ready to sign on that date). Indirectly, the draft entailed virtual recognition of the secession by the three Baltic states and any others that decided not to join, putatively Moldova, Armenia, and Georgia.

Economic reform was also proceeding (although so, too, was continuing economic decline). In votes on July 1 and 5 the USSR Supreme Soviet had taken major steps toward denationalizing three-quarters of Soviet industry, by vote of 303 to 14. On July 8, the nine Slavic and Muslim republics expected to comprise the new union approved a comprehensive compromise economic reform plan (with Yeltsin and Nazarbayev accepting, though favoring a more radical reform). This permitted Gorbachev to announce the support of the nine for the program he would present to the Western Group of Seven in London on July 17. On the eve of that meeting, the Soviet Union also applied for full membership in the International Monetary Fund (IMF), the International Bank for Reconstruction and Development (IBRD, the World Bank), the International Development Association (IDA), and the International Finance Corporation (IFC). At the meeting, Gorbachev had to settle for a promise of special associate membership in the IMF and World Bank, but at least the Soviet Union was moving into the international economic community, as well as proceeding belatedly with real internal economic reform.

Political reform, in addition to the key Union Treaty, was also proceeding. A Central Committee plenum on July 25–26 approved Gorbachev's proposed new reformist draft program for the Communist Party, a major further step toward a social democratic party, forthrightly describing the Leninist-Stalinist-Brezhnevite past "model of socialism" as having proved "bankrupt." Gorbachev declared that "socialism and the market are not only linked, they are indivisible"—a heresy to orthodox communists who still regarded them as incompatible. He called for a party congress later in the year to adopt the revised party program. He also mentioned plans to create a democratic Russian Communist Party as an alternative to the existing conservative one.[29] And he noted that the Communist Party of the Soviet Union (CPSU) had lost more than four million members in the preceding year and a half. Though there was

---

29. Although this was never done, on August 6 at a plenum of the Russian Communist Party, the conservative Ivan Polozkov stepped down and was succeeded by the more moderate Valentin Kuptsov.

heated discussion, it was clear that Gorbachev now had the CPSU Central Committee under control.[30]

Yeltsin, meanwhile, had on July 20 banned all political activity in Russian government-run enterprises and instructed them to "ignore" any order from the CPSU. Although the CPSU Politburo and Secretariat issued a statement condemning Yeltsin's decree, Gorbachev himself was silent, and his spokesman Ignatenko told reporters merely that Gorbachev was concerned that the decree was "introducing elements of tension and confrontation."[31]

On July 29, in a bilateral treaty with Lithuania similar to those Russia was signing with other "sovereign" republics of the union, the March independence declaration was acknowledged, implying Russian acceptance of Lithuanian independence.

Yeltsin's "alliance" with Gorbachev did not mean that program and policy differences did not remain, despite agreement on the Union Treaty and a general program of economic reform. Gorbachev and Yeltsin agreed on four key objectives: political democratization, economic reform, preservation of the union, and new thinking—and acting—in foreign policy. Nonetheless, the two leaders remained strong political rivals, and many in their respective entourages were even more bitterly opposed, some at the extremes opposing even a mutually useful alliance to serve common aims. As a result, tension and competition remained between Gorbachev's union authorities and Yeltsin's Russian ones, not because the latter opposed the union, but because they opposed "the center," which many saw personified in Gorbachev, the Communist Party, and the USSR government.

## The Moscow Summit and the START Treaty

The question of economic assistance by the United States and the West more generally to the Soviet Union, as it again moved toward the daunt-

---

30. "On the Draft New CPSU Program: M. S. Gorbachev's Report to the Central Committee of the CPSU Plenum 25 July," *Pravda*, July 26, 1991; "M. S. Gorbachev's Concluding Speech to the Central Committee of the CPSU Plenum on Discussion of the Draft CPSU Program," ibid., July 27, 1991; and "Resolution of the Central Committee of the CPSU Plenum Dated July 26, 1991: On the Draft CPSU Program and the Tasks of Party Organization in Discussing It," ibid., July 27, 1991.

By coincidence, the last of the "Old Bolsheviks" from 1917, Lazar Kaganovich, 97 years old, died on July 25.

31. See "Yeltsin Decree Abolishes Party Control," Moscow Radio, July 20, 1991, in FBIS, *Soviet Union*, July 22, 1991, p. 71. For Ignatenko's comments see "Presidential Aide Holds Press Briefing," Moscow Radio, July 23, 1991, in FBIS, *Soviet Union*, July 24, 1991, p. 1.

When Yeltsin's decree went into force, on August 4, most institutions did not resist, including even the KGB. The two important exceptions were the political administration in the armed forces and enterprises in the constituent republic of Tatarstan.

ing task of radical economic reform and as political reform and stability again seemed more steady, rose in urgency and in priority. Nonetheless, political prospects within the Soviet Union remained uncertain, and consolidation of the political gains in Europe needed the additional buttress of arms control. The treaty on reduction of Conventional Forces in Europe (CFE) had begun to come unglued almost as soon as it had been signed in Paris, and differences in interpretation had to be resolved before it could be ratified and go into effect. While this was a multilateral treaty and would require multilateral accord, the principal burden of a new negotiation with Moscow on the disputed issues fell on the United States. In addition, in the broader context the Strategic Arms Reduction Treaty (START) between the Soviet Union and the United States remained uncompleted despite advances toward agreement. Thus once again arms control was at the center of negotiating attention both on its own merits and to justify another U.S.-Soviet summit.

As noted earlier, the differences over the CFE Treaty, stemming essentially from Soviet efforts to exploit or create loopholes to cushion the heavier burden of reductions the treaty would impose on Soviet forces, were the subject of renewed discussion by Baker and Bessmertnykh in their meetings in mid-March and mid-April. In early April, Gorbachev had also written to Bush on the CFE problem, and Bush responded, before the April 24–25 meeting of the two foreign ministers. But the main differences remained after that meeting, and another in Cairo on May 12–13 (where Middle Eastern issues, and START problems, were also on the agenda). But a major step forward was taken on May 20–21 when General of the Army Mikhail Moiseyev, the chief of the General Staff, came to Washington with a constructive compromise proposal. Though not yet resolving all the differences, it showed a readiness by the Soviet military to resolve the issue and did provide a foundation for the final resolution.

President Bush called Gorbachev on May 27 to discuss the CFE problem (and START and economic relations). The key agreement was reached on June 1 in Lisbon when Baker and Bessmertnykh were together for the signing of the accords ending the long civil war in Angola. On June 14 at a formal meeting of the CFE signatories in Vienna, the issues were finally resolved by a unilateral statement by the Soviet Union accepting certain obligations "outside" those embodied in the CFE Treaty as they interpreted it, but conceding in substance reductions that met the interpretation taken by the other twenty-one parties to the treaty. The Soviet side preserved "face," but except for token adjustments, by and large it accepted obligations for additional reductions essentially offsetting the loopholes. On principle the Soviet Union (or more to the point the General Staff) had not given way, but in substance on the whole it had.[32]

---

32. It is not necessary for our purposes to review the disputes over the complex CFE provisions in detail. The Soviet Union had moved large quantities of arms from Europe beyond the Urals before the treaty was signed (the last portion perhaps soon after),

Soviet eagerness to resolve the remaining differences over the START Treaty was evident when the two delegations resumed negotiations on April 19. In contrast to the failure by the two sides to move forward when Baker and Bessmertnykh had last dealt seriously with START in mid-March, the Soviets tried now to reenergize the negotiation. The United States, however, wanted to resolve the CFE dispute before tackling the START issues. START was among the subjects discussed by Baker and Bessmertnykh in their mid-May meeting in Cairo, by Bush in his telephone conversation with Gorbachev on May 27, and again by Baker and Bessmertnykh on June 1 in Lisbon, June 7 in Geneva, and June 20 in Berlin. But at the end of June the same three main issues remained that had been present at the beginning of the year: how to deny telemetry encryption of missile tests, how to count missile warheads (especially in "downloading" operational MIRV missiles to carry fewer than the maximum number of warheads with which that missile type had been tested), and how to define the parameters of "new" missile types.[33]

The breakthrough on these last issues came only in mid-July, above all in a visit to Washington on July 11–14 by Bessmertnykh—again accompanied by General Moiseyev, the key man for these decisions. The first two were resolved in the July 11–14 meeting. The last issue was settled on July 17 in a session between Bush and Gorbachev, who were meeting in London for the Group of Seven economic summit. Again the Soviet military had been brought in directly so that it could not criticize or "reinterpret" the decisions made.[34]

Gorbachev had activated the third main subject, economic assistance, in a public plea on May 23 (indicating the scale more precisely than his brief, he acknowledged in answer to a question that he was seeking assistance on the order of $100 billion). Yavlinsky was back as an adviser and was pushing for Western economic assistance. On May 20 the Supreme Soviet finally passed legislation ensuring free travel and emigration, meeting the condition imposed

---

which was avoidance rather than violation (like the distinction between legal tax avoidance and illegal tax evasion). They now undertook to destroy or convert part of those arms (as indeed they had been doing). The principal loophole was a Soviet attempt to exclude the tanks, armored combat vehicles, and artillery of naval coastal defense and marine units (including three former army divisions recently transferred to the navy for coastal defense) on the grounds that naval forces were explicitly not subject to the treaty. In the end, they were permitted to "exclude" the several thousand weapons in these units, but they agreed to reduce an equivalent number of weapons elsewhere, so that the same overall reduction was achieved.

For an overview of the negotiations from March to June, see Beschloss and Talbott, *At the Highest Levels*, pp. 362–70.

33. On these negotiations, see ibid., pp. 370–73, 402–06.

34. While General Moiseyev thus helped to resolve the difficulties, he had earlier played a major role—according to Gorbachev's and Shevardnadze's Foreign Ministry interpreter the main role, greater than Marshal Yazov's—in creating those problems in the first place. Cited from Pavel Palazhchenko's unpublished memoirs.

by the United States for a waiver of the Jackson-Vanik amendment denying export credit guarantees. At the regular meeting of the semiofficial U.S.-USSR Trade and Economic Council in New York May 29–31 a huge Soviet delegation arrived—500 people instead of the usual tens. At the same time, Gorbachev's senior emissaries, Presidential Council member Yevgeny Primakov and First Deputy Prime Minister Vladimir Shcherbakov, came to Washington and met both Bush and Baker—as well as World Bank and IMF leaders. On June 3, Bush announced he would extend the Jackson-Vanik waiver for a full year (formally done on August 2). On June 4, prominent businessman and political figure Robert S. Strauss was named to succeed career diplomat Jack Matlock as American ambassador in Moscow.

Throughout this period, Bush and most of his advisers, while wishing to provide signs of support to Gorbachev in the economic field, were not convinced that any major financial assistance would be effectively used to promote reform. A visit to Washington by Primakov, Shcherbakov, and Yavlinsky at the end of May did not dispel such concerns.[35]

On June 14 a private American study group at Harvard proposed a major U.S. economic assistance program tied to implementation of radical market reform of the Soviet economy, called "the Grand Bargain." The administration, however, remained much more cautious.[36] On June 11 Bush announced a $1.5 billion credit for agricultural purchases. And on June 18 Baker in a speech in Berlin cautiously outlined limited plans for economic assistance to reforms in the Soviet Union. But at first Bush was even resistant to Gorbachev's expressed desire to attend the Group of Seven economic summit in London.

In a telephone conversation on June 21, Bush reported to Gorbachev on the visit by Russian President Boris Yeltsin on June 18–21, during which—in contrast to Yeltsin's earlier 1989 visit—Bush openly received him at the White House.[37]

On July 17–18 the Group of Seven in London held a special 7+1 meeting with Gorbachev, which at least met the latter's wish to make a personal pitch for economic aid. On the eve of the meeting, the Soviet Union had applied for full membership in the IMF (contrary to American advice). But there was no announcement of an aid package, even in general terms, at the

35. See Beschloss and Talbott, *At the Highest Levels*, pp. 376–91.

36. And it remained divided. On June 5, the same day that Gorbachev pleaded for economic assistance in his Nobel Peace Prize lecture in Oslo, Vice President Danforth Quayle sounded a sour note in an interview, harshly dismissing any notion of direct financial aid as a "non-starter." See Bob Woodward, "Quayle Bars Direct Aid to Soviets by U.S. as 'Really a Non-Starter' " *Washington Post*, June 5, 1991, p. A23.

37. There had been much debate and deliberation in Washington over whether and how to receive Yeltsin. See Beschloss and Talbott, *At the Highest Levels*, pp. 345–50, 359–61, 392, 399–400.

end of the meeting, and the IMF soon proffered only special associate membership.

Bush and Gorbachev announced in London on July 17, after their private meeting wrapping up the START Treaty, that they would hold a full summit meeting in Moscow on July 30–31.

Meanwhile, the East-West confrontation in Europe continued to fade. The Warsaw Pact members in February had agreed to disband the military structure of the alliance, and on July 1 the Warsaw Treaty Organization was by consensus of its members dissolved. By that time, Soviet military withdrawal from Czechoslovakia and Hungary had been completed,and withdrawal from Germany and Poland was under way. And in Asia, the gradual improvement in Sino-Soviet relations continued; in May Marshal Yazov visited China in the first visit ever by a Soviet defense minister. Soviet military withdrawal from Mongolia was well under way.

The political-economic map was changing along with the political-military one. On January 1 trade between the countries of Eastern Europe and the Soviet Union was put in terms of world market prices, and a few days later the members of the Council on Mutual Economic Assistance (CMEA, also known as COMECON) decided to dissolve the organization; the Eastern economic bloc went the same way as did the military and political organizations. The Soviet Union, as well as the East European countries, was looking West.

By the time of the Moscow summit, the changing relationship between the United States and the Soviet Union was evident. Friction was greatly diminished. The Cold War was over. Though not yet apparent, it was to prove the last of the superpower summit meetings. Although the meeting was important to Gorbachev and useful to Bush, and a consolidation of great advances in the relationship of the two powers, the context of the changes in the world made it inescapably transitional. Beyond that, this summit would of course become the last of the Soviet summits by virtue of the unforeseen impending sudden collapse of the Soviet Union.[38]

The crowning achievement of the Moscow summit was the signing of the START I Treaty. Yet even that tended to be regarded as finishing up old business rather than representing the future agenda. Indeed, no one foresaw that in less than a year the agreement on reductions of strategic arms that had been so laboriously achieved (negotiated over nearly ten years, resulting in a

---

38. Deputy National Security Adviser Robert Gates, while visiting Canada shortly before the summit, had bragged that the United States was unchallenged and supreme in economic, political, military, and cultural power, adding, "Today, no one questions the reality of only one superpower and its leadership [in the world]." This was not only blunt and undiplomatic via-à-vis the Soviet Union but of highly questionable appropriateness for an American official to say in Canada. See "Gates Tells Canada U.S. Is No. 1," *Washington Times*, May 8, 1991, p. A1.

document of some 700 pages) would be overtaken by an agreement on a further, much deeper reduction.

The START agreement mandated reductions of about 25 percent for the United States and 35 percent for the Soviet Union (owing to differential and nominal counting rules for some types of weapons)—bringing the totals down roughly to where they were when START negotiations began in 1982. The reductions in quick-reaction ballistic missiles within the overall totals, however, were much greater. More important, agreed and reduced ceilings provided greater assurance and predictability and permitted large reductions through unilateral budgetary programming decisions. At the time, the seven years projected for implementing these reductions, though not precluding earlier agreement on further cuts, was assumed to reflect the expectation that negotiations on further steps would be deferred and lengthy. That, at least, was the American expectation.

The two sides agreed without fanfare to resume consultations in October in Moscow on further negotiations on strategic nuclear and space arms control and measures to enhance strategic stability. The Soviet side reaffirmed the tie of the START reductions to continued observance of the ABM Treaty as it had been interpreted in 1972, but the U.S. side avoided this latent issue. The Soviet side also sought agreement on a date for beginning talks on reducing tactical nuclear weapons in Europe but was rebuffed by the United States. Finally, Gorbachev urged setting a date to resume talks on further constraints on underground nuclear tests, but the United States was not prepared to do so.[39]

When the changed political-military situation subsequently led to early new negotiations for much deeper cuts, the START I Treaty of 1991 provided an essential foundation for a START II Treaty, signed in January 1993, calling for cumulative cuts of about two-thirds from the 1991 level. But despite this unexpected opportunity for still further strategic arms reductions, it was correctly recognized in 1991 that arms control and reduction would not retain the salience it had held for the preceding two decades. The danger of war had receded, the arms race had lost its rationale, and the agenda of political consultation and economic issues had become more important for the post–Cold War world.

The new center of gravity was the economic and political situation in the Soviet Union and the role of outside economic support for internal reform. And for this new challenge, while the role of the United States was certainly important, it was not dominant. In this important respect, the bilateral summit in Moscow was but a follow-through to the meeting of Gorbachev with the G-7 in London two weeks earlier. While President Bush did announce in Moscow that the United States was going to ratify the bilateral trade agreement and grant most-favored-nation (MFN) status, as he himself remarked, that merely

---

39. Information from Soviet participants in the summit talks.

"fulfilled thus our Malta goal of normalizing our [bilateral] economic relationship." They had agreed, he noted, that the new agenda was "furthering economic reform in the U.S.S.R., and seeking to integrate the Soviet economy into the international system"—a formidable Soviet task and a formidable multilateral economic-political task.[40]

The American role in this daunting new effort remained modest, and Bush was notably cautious about any new steps beyond the intention to grant MFN nondiscriminatory trade status—promised already the year before and not effected until a year later. A real Western economic aid package, with a modicum of American leadership, also did not appear until the next year. A perceptive commentator, noting the cautious American response on assistance to Soviet economic reform, aptly remarked at the time: "The Bush Administration, after nearly three years, has established a consistent pattern in responding to changes in the [former] Eastern bloc: it rarely catches the first train, but it rarely misses the last one."[41]

At the summit, Gorbachev pressed for relaxation of Western COCOM export controls, noting that the security concerns that had been their justification had now lost their meaning. Some months later COCOM controls were loosened, but although at the summit Bush agreed to consider the matter, he made no concrete commitment. (COCOM was disbanded in 1994.)

The Moscow summit carried further a series of bilateral cooperative programs, in particular in technical economic cooperation and measures to stimulate housing construction.[42] Accords were reached on aviation security against hijacking and on disaster assistance. Most important at least symbolically was a revival of prospects for cooperative space exploration. But the bilateral agenda was essentially normalized.

In the field of global geopolitical concerns, the familiar verbal sparring over regional conflicts in which the two powers were associated with local adversaries was now virtually a thing of the past. One exception was the still not

---

40.  "The President's News Conference with Soviet President Mikhail Gorbachev in Moscow," July 31, 1991, *Presidential Documents*, vol. 27 (August 5, 1991), p. 1080.

41.  Thomas L. Friedman, "Arms Talks: A Warm-Up, Top U.S.-Soviet Issue Is Now the Economy," *New York Times*, June 10, 1991, p. A8.

42.  One American suggestion for expanding contacts was rebuffed. In Baker's last meeting with Bessmertnykh before the London summit, he had proposed introduction of an American Peace Corps presence into the Soviet Union as one agreement that could be concluded at the Moscow summit. This overture was, however, rejected; the Soviet leaders thought it would be demeaning, in effect treating the Soviet Union as a Third World country. The most recent precedent was, in fact, an agreement for the Peace Corps to go into Mongolia.

   The United States continued, however, to pursue the idea with several republics, and in most cases the strong impulse to bring closer ties with the United States overrode such a viewpoint. By 1992 the Peace Corps was welcomed to Russia, Ukraine, and several other successor republics.

fully resolved question of military assistance to the two sides in the civil war in
Afghanistan. Bush also still prodded Gorbachev on further Soviet disengagement from support to Castro's Cuba. Bush did not press for a concrete response
on the question of continuing Soviet military aid to Cuba, but he reminded
Gorbachev that this remained an irritant in U.S.-Soviet relations. He also made
this point publicly in his speech to the Moscow State Institute for International
Relations.[43]

The most salient and important action at the summit in this field was
joint sponsorship for convening an international conference on the Middle East
in October to facilitate settlement of the Israeli-Arab-Palestinian conflict.
Gorbachev supported strongly this initiative and worked to win over Bush from
initial hesitancy prompted by a cautious and uncertain Israeli position. The
United States no longer sought to exclude the Soviet Union from participation
in the Middle East peace process, and Shevardnadze and Baker had been
moving in this direction for some time. Both Bush and Gorbachev proudly cited
their joint efforts in the successful reversal of Iraq's aggression and occupation
of Kuwait. As Bush emphasized, "at every key point in the crisis the United States
and the Soviet Union worked together."[44] Promptly following the summit both
Bessmertnykh and Baker embarked on trips to countries of the Middle East.

Bush noted that cooperation between the two countries had already
brought peace and free elections to Namibia, Angola, and Nicaragua and raised
hopes for resolutions of the conflicts in Cambodia and Afghanistan as well as
the Middle East. The two leaders also called for a negotiated resolution of the
crisis in Yugoslavia.[45] The two foreign ministers, Baker and Shevardnadze, also
issued a joint statement welcoming the progress in resolving the disputes in
Nicaragua, El Salvador, and Guatemala.

In contrast to these steps forward in cooperatively working to resolve
violent regional conflicts, Bush rather unexpectedly added one new point of
divergence to the U.S.-Soviet dialogue by publicly prodding the Soviets on
"Japan's claim—which we support—for the return of the Northern Territories," noting that "this dispute could hamper your integration into the world
economy [owing to Japan's policy of withholding economic assistance as a lever
on this issue], and we want to do whatever we can to help both sides resolve
it."[46] In fact, it was doubtful that an unprecedented public presidential state-

43. "Remarks at the Moscow State Institute for International Relations," July 30, 1991,
    *Presidential Documents*, vol. 27 (August 5, 1991), p. 1067.

44. Ibid., p. 1067.

45. The two presidents issued a joint declaration condemning the violence in Yugoslavia and
    calling for respect for the principles of the Helsinki Accords, by which they meant the
    inviolability of established state borders. Both men were greatly concerned about the
    implications for the Soviet Union of a possible disintegration of the multinational,
    reforming communist federation of Yugoslavia.

46. *Presidential Documents*, vol. 27 (August 5, 1991), p. 1067.

ment of U.S. support for the Japanese position on a disputed issue was either helpful or wise. The United States had for nearly forty years supported the Japanese, its ally, against the Soviet Union when it was an adversary, in part because the United States saw the advantage in keeping tension between Japan and the Soviet Union. Now that the United States wanted to see the dispute resolved and good relations between those two countries, taking such a stand was not the way "to help both sides resolve it." Bush apparently thought the Soviet stand represented merely residual "old thinking," and he was clearly unaware of the extent of Russian public opposition to giving up the islands, to say nothing of the fact that the merits of the issue were by no means only on the side of Japan. The more appropriate thing to do would have been simply to urge both sides to resolve the territorial dispute through negotiation.[47]

Besides the issues of aid to Cuba and the dispute with Japan over the islands, Bush mentioned three other "obstacles" remaining on the path to a "new partnership" with the Soviet Union, all concerning internal Soviet policy. Most prominent and most sensitive was the future of the Baltic states. Bush had, on June 25, submitted a required report to Congress endorsing independence for Latvia, Lithuania, and Estonia, through negotiation, but he had done so quietly.[48] The issue again flared up on the very eve of his visit, when the special OMON police had raided several Lithuanian and Latvian customs border posts on July 28 and 29, an action that embarrassed Gorbachev as well as Bush. On July 30, while Bush was in Moscow, a violent provocation was mounted by unidentified armed men who killed six Lithuanian border inspectors. Gorbachev at once denounced this crime, Pugo denied that this had been an OMON action, and it has at this writing still not been established whether this was (as the Balts and many others assume) a covert operation by some Soviet security force or an act by others (local Russian or native Baltic extremists) seeking to inflame the issue. But even before that act, Bush privately and publicly urged Soviet "good-faith negotiations with the Baltic governments" and "a clear and unqualified [Soviet] commitment to peaceful change."[49]

The second aspect of Soviet domestic policy that Bush raised was military spending. "It's time," he said, "for your military establishment to move to a peacetime footing. It's time to reduce military spending." And he offered

---

47. For further discussion see chapter 14.

   Bush included this new item on the list of issues as a favor to the Japanese, who were lobbying hard for support to their intensified campaign seeking return of the islands, without consideration of the Russian-Soviet position. In the Soviet Union, Bush's intervention on the issue was seen as American pressure taking advantage of Soviet weakness and economic vulnerability.

48. See "Message to the Congress Transmitting the Report on Restoration of the Baltic States Independence," June 25, 1991, *Presidential Documents*, vol. 27 (July 1, 1991), pp. 846–48.

49. Ibid., p. 1067.

"help in converting your military-industrial might to productive, peaceful purposes."[50] Gorbachev was already moving in this direction, especially in 1990–91, but Bush wanted to push the process along.

Finally, in what was in effect a support for *perestroika*, Bush said, "The key challenge—the single most important factor in forging a new partnership between our nations—remains the outcome of the experiment now reshaping [the] Soviet economy—[and] Soviet society." He spoke boldly of how "my country stands ready to assist in this new Soviet revolution," but he also emphasized that while "real reform" of the economy was essential, "the transformation must come from within."[51]

The key step in the internal transformation of the Soviet Union under way when the summit occurred was the progress toward the new Union Treaty. At the very moment when President Bush arrived in Moscow in the late evening of July 29, Gorbachev, Yeltsin, and Kazakhstan's President Nursultan Nazarbayev were hammering out a solution to the last serious disagreement over the treaty, the division of authority between the center and the republics on taxation. They reached agreement about 3:00 a.m., a few hours before Bush began his meetings with Gorbachev. Yet when Gorbachev sought to cement his achievement by a last-minute invitation to Yeltsin and Nazarbayev to join him in one of his meetings later that morning with President Bush, Yeltsin declined.[52] Bush did see Yeltsin that afternoon in his Kremlin office, a meeting arranged earlier as a gesture to the emerging international standing of the republics. In all, Bush successfully steered a middle course that alienated neither Gorbachev nor Yeltsin.[53]

---

50. Ibid., p. 1067.

51. Ibid., p. 1068.

52. After an initial meeting alone, Gorbachev was joined in a Kremlin meeting with Bush by Nazarbayev, Prime Minister Valentin Pavlov, Foreign Minister Alexander Bessmertnykh, and Defense Minister Dmitry Yazov.

    Ukraine's Leonid Kravchuk was not included in the night negotiations, nor present to be invited to participate in a summit meeting, because Ukraine was at this point standing aside from negotiation on the Union Treaty pending a national referendum set for December 1.

53. Bush's agreement to meet in Yeltsin's office added luster to the latter. Bush made clear that dealings with the president of the Soviet Union did not preclude dealings with the presidents of constituent republics, but he also did not elevate the latter to equality. (See especially Bush's comments in a presummit interview with Soviet journalists; "Remarks and an Exchange with Soviet Journalists on the Upcoming Moscow Summit," July 25, 1991, *Presidential Documents*, vol. 27 [August 5, 1991], p. 1057). When Yeltsin pushed for direct ties, to reach bilateral agreements or statements, in accordance with the new division of authority codified in the Union Treaty, Bush suggested waiting until the Union Treaty, not yet signed, had come into effect. In impromptu brief remarks to the press following his talks with Yeltsin, Bush did give him a boost by saying that Yeltsin's recent visit to the United States had been "a big hit," but he also carefully said that it furthered American relations and understanding both with Russia and the Soviet Union.

At the conclusion of the two-day working summit in Moscow, President Bush made another gesture to the awakening republics by visiting Kiev, capital of Ukraine, on his way home. He was very warmly received, reflecting Ukrainian pride at being regarded as a sovereign entity and expectations of support from the United States. President Bush faced a delicate and difficult task in seeking to encourage democracy, economic reform, and freedom while not opening himself to danger of interference in the internal affairs of the Soviet Union. If Bush erred (as some believed at the time, and many thought in retrospect), it was in giving too much weight to advocacy of continuity of a central Soviet state and too little welcome to popular sentiment for independence. His message was sound, if not welcomed by all: that "freedom is not the same as independence" and that "Americans will not support those who seek independence in order to replace a far-off tyranny with a local despotism" or "those who promote a suicidal nationalism based upon ethnic hatred." For the United States to "choose between supporting President Gorbachev and supporting independence-minded leaders throughout the USSR," was, he said, a "false choice." He went out of his way to praise Gorbachev's "astonishing" achievements and to endorse the 9+1 Union Treaty. In all, it was clear that he supported democracy and a greater role for the republics within a continuing union.[54]

Critics in the United States quickly labeled Bush's statement his "Chicken Kiev" speech. It was not welcomed in Kiev, but Bush was in fact taking a courageous stand. In retrospect, the speech was also too strongly supportive of the controversial Union Treaty and not sufficiently in keeping with what proved to be Ukrainian popular support for independence. But at the time, the prospect for the Union Treaty was improving, and no one anticipated the convulsions that would lead to the end of the Soviet Union in four months. In retrospect, clearly it would have been best for Bush not to have made a visit to Kiev at that time.

The Moscow summit of July 1991, nearly twenty years after the first U.S.-Soviet Moscow summit meeting of President Richard Nixon and General Secretary Leonid Brezhnev, was paradoxically less euphoric despite the far greater congruence of positions and more relaxed cooperation. In 1972, and at

---

("Remarks following Discussions with President Boris Yeltsin of the Republic of Russia," July 30, 1991, *Presidential Documents*, vol. 27, p. 1069.)

Yeltsin showed poor form by making President Bush wait seven minutes in his outer office, then stretching an agreed fifteen-minute meeting into forty minutes and trying to arrange an impromptu press conference at the end. See Beschloss and Talbott, *At the Highest Levels*, pp. 412–13.

54. All quotations from Bush's main speech, to the Ukrainian parliament; "Remarks to the Supreme Soviet of the Republic of the Ukraine in Kiev, Soviet Union," August 1, 1991, *Presidential Documents*, vol. 27 (August 5, 1991), pp. 1093–95; for other public statements in Kiev see pp. 1090–97.

subsequent meetings at least until the Malta and Washington summit meeting in 1989–90, even a successful summit was marked by an atmosphere of achievement despite a predominance of competition over cooperation. During the periods of détente in the early to mid-1970s and the latter half of the 1980s, summits had been devoted to creating safe limits for rivalry. By the time of the Malta and Washington summits with the end of the Cold War the meetings were marked by defining a framework for mutual cooperation. By 1991, because the real relationship was so much better, even concord at the summit was becoming routine. The 397 Soviet and 2,059 foreign journalists had little to write about. (Even the pleasant and relaxed sight-seeing by Barbara Bush and Raisa Gorbachev provided no grist for gossipy comments previously evoked by the encounters between Nancy Reagan and Raisa.) Success seemed to threaten summitry with boredom.

Gorbachev's weakened position at home and the Soviet Union's weakened power were evident in the summit, inviting domestic Soviet criticisms of what were portrayed as overbearing American "lectures" on international behavior and internal reform, Soviet kowtowing on the Middle East and Yugoslavia, and excessive Soviet concessions in START and other agreements—even though these were often Gorbachev's political policy preferences and not the product of American pressure.[55] Overall, nonetheless, the summit and its accords were positively assessed in the Soviet Union and the West. The summit certainly did not weaken Gorbachev; nor, however, could it strengthen him in the critical internal struggle that was approaching a climax.

Perhaps the most realistic and persistent comment was made by the former foreign minister, Eduard Shevardnadze: "Now, there are no problems, and relations are going well. I think that this is a natural course. I think that if there is any impact on relations, it will come from domestic unrest in the Soviet Union. If the Soviet Union fails to stabilize the economic and political arenas, this will become a factor that hurts relations. I think this is the only thing that can hinder U.S.-Soviet relations. This is the only thing hampering the dynamic development in relations between the United States and the Soviet Union."[56]

Although subsequent internal developments in the USSR would not harm U.S.-Soviet relations, they certainly would be central in transforming them. But in early August 1991 in the aftermath of the summit, with the long-delayed signing of the Union Treaty set for later that month, the cloud of domestic unrest appeared to be lifting and the course of Soviet external policy and of U.S.-Soviet relations clear.

---

55. For a comprehensive and perceptive analysis of the summit that stresses the influence of Soviet weakness see Joseph G. Whelan, *The Moscow II Summit, July 30–31, 1991: Closing on START and Opening on the New Economic Agenda*, CRS Report for Congress (Washington: Congressional Research Service, 1992), esp. pp. 88–94, 105.

56. "Shevardnadze Interviewed," Tokyo NHK General Television, August 1, 1991, in FBIS *Soviet Union*, August 5, 1991, pp. 10–11.

## Coup and Countercoup

Gorbachev went to his favorite rest home at Foros in the Crimea, one of the dachas maintained for the leadership, for two weeks' rest in mid-August. He was scheduled to return to Moscow on August 19 to be there for the signing of the new Union Treaty on August 20. On the surface, the political scene was quiet.[57] But on the afternoon of Sunday August 18 a delegation unexpectedly arrived to see Gorbachev: Party Secretary and Gorbachev's deputy at the Defense Council, Oleg Baklanov; Party Secretary Oleg Shenin; Deputy Defense Minister General Valentin Varennikov; and Gorbachev's trusted personal chief of staff, Valery Boldin. The delegation informed Gorbachev that the other members of the leadership had agreed that a national state of emergency must be declared and urged him to approve and sign such a directive or resign and turn over his authority to Vice President Yanayev.[58] Gorbachev flatly refused and they left. Gorbachev, cut off from communication with the outside world, remained under house arrest for three days.[59]

The world learned that something had happened when at 6:00 a.m. on August 19 Radio Moscow and TASS announced that President Gorbachev was prevented by "ill health" from exercising his duties and that, in accordance with

---

57. Gorbachev had, in a meeting with Yeltsin and the Kazakh leader Nazarbayev on July 29, discussed the growing tension within the leadership, and with the encouragement of the other two had decided that after the signing of the Union Treaty, he would reorganize the leadership and dismiss a number of the hard-line leaders such as Pavlov and probably Kryuchkov and Pugo. Yeltsin, only half in jest, had looked around to see if anyone was listening to their conversation, which Gorbachev and Nazarbayev had laughed about. In fact, the KGB security chief (General Plekhanov) had bugged the session, thus alerting those about to be purged.

58. Pavlov had called a cabinet meeting on August 17 which discussed the Union Treaty in very deprecating terms, but there was no discussion then of any action to forestall its signature. On August 18, in a meeting at the KGB headquarters, Pavlov, Kryuchkov, Yazov, and Boldin decided that Gorbachev was no longer in control of the situation and that the course they were on would lead to the collapse of the Soviet Union. They then decided to dispatch the delegation to Foros to try to persuade Gorbachev to declare a state of emergency, but if he would not, then they would do so themselves.

59. Although there is no indication that during this captivity Gorbachev read Pushkin's epic *Boris Godunov* (or listened to Mussorgsky's opera based on it), if he had, he would have been astounded at the affinity and applicability of the brooding lament of his predecessor, a seventeenth-century tsar.
    I have attained the highest power,
    For the sixth year now do I rule in peace.
    Yet my tortured soul can find no happiness. . . .
    Here there is conspiracy, there sedition of the boyars,
    Lithuanian plots and secret machinations,
    Hunger and plague, fear and ruin. . . .
    Russia groans in hunger and poverty!

Article 127(7) of the USSR Constitution, Vice President Gennady I. Yanayev was assuming "the duties of president of the USSR." Yanayev made a public address in which he declared a state of emergency and transferred all power to a new State Committee for the State of Emergency in the USSR. Yanayev chaired the committee as acting president, and the other seven members were mostly senior members of Gorbachev's government: Prime Minister Valentin Pavlov, KGB Chairman Vladimir Kryuchkov, Minister of the Interior Boris Pugo, Minister of Defense Marshal Dmitry Yazov, and Deputy Chairman of the Defense Council Oleg Baklanov, and two lesser-known members representing the industrial sector and the agricultural sector, Aleksandr Tizyakov and Vasily Starodubtsev, respectively.[60] The five senior members represented the majority of Gorbachev's Security Council (numbering eight). The Communist Party leadership as such, including Deputy General Secretary Vladimir Ivashko, was not included, although the coup leaders were of course members of the party leadership.

Most if not all of these men had been urging Gorbachev for some time to impose emergency rule. Several had engineered the repressive moves in the Baltic states in January and July, and the attempts to curb public demonstrations in Moscow in March, in attempts to create a situation under which, they hoped, Gorbachev would have to clamp down. They had supported Pavlov's open bid for more power at the Supreme Soviet in June. They had opposed the concessions of power to the republics in the Union Treaty, and the timing of their move now was prompted by a desperate attempt to forestall signing of the treaty. Though acting cautiously and not becoming a member of the committee, Supreme Soviet Chairman Anatoly Lukyanov on August 19 promptly issued a statement criticizing the draft Union Treaty and calling for its revision. The conspirators hoped that Gorbachev would accept their ultimatum and authorize a state of emergency, but if not they were prepared to go it alone, without him and against him. (They may have hoped that even then he would later accept a fait accompli, in which case his health could take a turn for the better, but if not he could be kept in confinement or his health be said to deteriorate.) Just as Gorbachev had seriously underestimated the strength of the conservative convictions and readiness of these associates to act on their own, so too they underestimated his determination not to give in to such pressure. Later attempts by some of the conspirators (and others) to implicate Gorbachev in the plot were absurd. Gorbachev had of course authorized contingency planning for a possible state of emergency, and those plans were now partially implemented. But on earlier occasions, and on this one, he had resolutely refused any pretext to impose emergency rule.

---

60. See items under "Gorbachev Ousted; State of Emergency Imposed," FBIS, *Soviet Union*, August 19, 1991, pp. 8–13.

The conspirators sought to cloak their actions in constitutional legality, but they were inconsistent and made a great error by creating and acting under a new and probably unconstitutional "emergency committee." This fact reinforced the ability of Yeltsin, as the legitimate president of Russia, and others in the military, to obtain the support of or at least neutralize many who, though very reluctant not to obey orders from superiors, were inclined to stand aside and not obey the orders of a cloudy self-constituted committee, especially as it soon became fairly clear that Gorbachev was not ill but in involuntary confinement.

The general reaction throughout the country was to continue with daily life and see what the new developments would bring. Some, at all levels, were suspicious of the claim of Gorbachev's illness, and this suspicion grew. Some were frightened and distressed by this turn of events; others were pleased to see signs of a crackdown for law and order, and perhaps a more predictable and less innovative policy. But most people were simply resigned to wait and see. At high levels, political leaders in republic and regional governmental and Communist Party posts were also inclined to wait and see.

The most obvious and important exception was the active opposition of the leaders of Russia, Kazakhstan, Kyrgyzstan—Yeltsin, Nazarbayev, and Akayev—as well as the leaders of Latvia, Lithuania, Estonia, and Moldova. Most notable in voicing active support were the other leaders in Central Asia and Azerbaijan, the reactionary leader of the breakaway "Dniester Republic" in Moldova, Igor Smirnov, and the Latvian Communist Party leader, Alfred Rubiks. But, again, most moved from apathetic support (based mainly on expectation the coup would succeed) to apathetic opposition with the shift in the tide of events, including leaders in Ukraine, Belarus, Uzbekistan, Armenia, Georgia, and most provinces of Russia.

Most regional Communist Party organizations signified their support for the coup, but many wavered and some stood in opposition. Some of the wavering or supporting republic leaders had to leave the scene soon after, but many stayed on and survived as leaders of the newly independent republics, especially in Central Asia and the Caucasus.

Among civic leaders, the liberal mayors of Moscow and Leningrad were in the forefront of support for Yeltsin and Gorbachev. Also supporting the Soviet Constitution and Gorbachev was Patriarch Aleksei II of the Russian Orthodox Church, although some of his clergy showed early sympathy for the coup.

This is not the place to retell the story of the blunders of the coup conspirators or bravery of those who stood up to their attempts to impose their rule. The failure of the coup conspirators to neutralize President Yeltsin was crucial, but so was the refusal of key military and KGB officers to carry out orders of the committee even though transmitted through their own legitimate channels. It was, in many ways, a tribute to the spirit of openness and legality fostered by Gorbachev over the preceding several years that so many in key positions overcame the traditional tendency simply to obey orders.

The military high command, for example, split even though the minister of defense, Marshal Yazov, was a leading coconspirator as a member of the State Committee for the Emergency. An especially active role in the conspiracy was taken by General Varennikov, deputy minister and commander of ground forces, and by Colonel General Vladislav Achalov, formerly the airborne troops commander who had in December been named to a new position as deputy minister for emergency situations (for example, outbreaks of violence in the Caucasus). Several leading figures in the General Staff were also directly engaged in support of the coup, in particular Colonel General Vladimir Denisov, the chief of the Main Operations Directorate, and briefly and more passively after his return to Moscow the chief of the General Staff, General Mikhail Moiseyev.[61] Active allegiance to the committee was also given by General Ivan Tretyak, the deputy minister in command of air defense forces, and messages of verbal support were sent by several field commanders, in particular the ultraconservative Colonel General Albert Makashov, commander of the Volga-Urals Military District. The commander of the Moscow Military District, Colonel General Nikolai Kalinin, obeyed orders and assumed charge of military actions in the Moscow region (although he was not able to order into action some of the key forces involved, owing to the refusal of their commanders). The only military field command other than the Moscow and Leningrad Military Districts to be ordered into action was the Baltic Military District under Colonel General Fedor Kuzmin, which did obey orders to occupy key points in Riga, Vilnius, and Tallin.

More significant, and more surprising, was the wide extent of increasingly active noncooperation by senior military leaders. Among the deputy ministers, the head of the Soviet Air Forces, Marshal of Aviation Yevgeny Shaposhnikov, the head of the Soviet Navy, Admiral of the Fleet Vladimir Chernavin, the commander of the Strategic Missile Forces, General Yury Maksimov, and the commander of Soviet Airborne Troops, Lieutenant General Pavel Grachev, were stalwart opponents of the coup. Some of them, especially General Grachev, initially carried out orders for preliminary movements of forces, as did Colonel General Kalinin in Moscow and Colonel General Viktor Samsonov, commander of the Leningrad Military District. But Shaposhnikov, Grachev, the deputy minister of interior Colonel General Boris Gromov, and key KGB Special Forces commanders all balked at orders to commit their

---

61. Marshal Sergei F. Akhromeyev, the former chief of the General Staff and at this time an adviser to President Gorbachev, was also implicated in support for the coup, and he committed suicide on August 24. From my personal contacts with him, I have no doubt that he acted, both in supporting the coup and in his suicide, as he stated in his suicide note, because all that he devoted his life to—the Soviet Union, the Soviet Army, and socialism—"was being destroyed."Akhromeyev had especially close ties to Marshal Yazov and General Varennikov, who were classmates in the 1967 graduating class from the General Staff Academy.

forces to action. Similarly, General Samsonov agreed to the request of Mayor Anatoly Sobchak not to enter his troops into Leningrad, despite orders to do so. General Grachev even dispatched one of his airborne forces officers, Major General Aleksandr Lebed, to reassure the defenders of the White House (Russian Parliament building) where Yeltsin and many others were defiantly holding out.

By the third day of the coup, August 21, Marshal Yazov was confronted by demands of the Defense Ministry collegium (comprising his dozen or so deputies) for withdrawal of all troops from Moscow and his own departure from the coup committee. He said that, having committed himself, he could not now abandon the committee, but he acquiesced in orders for the troops to withdraw. The coup attempt was collapsing rapidly.

Orders of the coup conspirators to attack the White House where Yeltsin was defying them and rallying resistance had been foiled by refusal of KGB special forces, MVD (the elite Dzerzhinsky Division of Internal Troops), and Army (Airborne and Guards divisions in Moscow) to strike. Given the confusion and tension, it was little short of miraculous that there were only five people killed in isolated incidents, three young men in Moscow when a tank crew panicked after their vehicle was "blinded," one man from rifle fire in Vilnius, and another in Latvia from being struck by a military vehicle. The broader danger of civil war, if there had been an assault on the White House, was fortunately not unleashed. There was also the theoretical danger to the world from split authority over nuclear weapons.[62] But all in all, the restraint shown by all sides in an exceedingly complex confusion of authority and loyalty was notable.

On the morning of August 22, a delegation was sent by the Russian Supreme Soviet to escort Gorbachev back to Moscow. It was led by Yeltsin's vice president, Aleksandr Rutskoi, a colonel of the Soviet Air Force and Afghan war hero, and members of the Russian KGB and other "muscle" if needed. Another delegation, of coup leaders, including Marshal Yazov and Kryuchkov, also tried to get to Gorbachev to negotiate their pardon in exchange for his return, but they were not received and were instead arrested and returned to Moscow. The coup attempt had completely failed.

President Gorbachev and the Soviet Constitution were rescued, but *perestroika* of the Soviet Union was not. Political and economic reform was of

---

62. From the late afternoon of August 18 to the morning of August 22, the strategic nuclear control coding and communication device in the briefcase that always accompanied the president of the USSR as commander in chief (as in the United States) was in the hands of the coup conspirators. So, too, were the other two complementary control briefcases held by the minister of defense and the chief of the General Staff. Apart from the fact that the coup leaders had absolutely no interest in firing nuclear weapons or threatening to do so, they would in any case have been unable, but only because the commanders in chief of the Strategic Missile Forces, Soviet Navy, and Soviet Air Force all remained loyal to the constitutional order.

course given a new lease on life and boost, but under conditions that involved a more radical political change than was envisaged under even a far-reaching "restructuring." Moreover, the reverberations of saving the constitutional order paradoxically led to the end of that constitutional order within a few months. The coup plotters, in their attempt to prevent controlled change, had unleashed change uncontrollable by central authorities. The collapse of the coup did not restore the status quo, as Gorbachev at first failed to realize; it destroyed the very foundation for central authority that the conspirators had so desperately sought to preserve and reinforce.

The most notable immediate step was the banning of the Communist Party of the Soviet Union (and the communist parties of most republics, including Russia and Ukraine). This was accompanied by a rush to fill the void, by Yeltsin in Russia and by local leaderships of the other republics, in most cases by the communist leaders now shedding party affiliation.

Dramatic as was the collapse of the Communist Party of the Soviet Union (CPSU) after seventy-four years in power, still more fundamental and important was the gradual but inexorable eclipse of the Union Treaty and disintegration of the Soviet Union itself over the four months from August 19 to December 25. Yet this fundamental shift, taken for granted since it has occurred, was not clear at the time. To be sure, there was a spate of declarations of independence by several republics from August 20 to 30. But only in the Baltic states did this lead to early actual secession.

Estonia even before the coup collapsed (August 20) and Latvia immediately after (August 21) rushed to join Lithuania in asserting independence. The Baltic states, having been independent until their coerced entry into the Soviet Union in 1940, were widely regarded as a special case. Yeltsin promptly extended recognition by Russia of the independence of these two states on August 24 (having earlier acknowledged Lithuanian independence). And, notwithstanding Gorbachev's complaint at "overly hasty" action, the countries of the European Community on August 27 extended recognition to the three Baltic states (as Iceland, Sweden, and a few others had already done by then). Even Soviet acceptance of their secession was clearly imminent.

Less expected, and ultimately most significant, Leonid Kravchuk led (or followed) a consensus in Kiev in declaring independence of Ukraine on August 24, subject to confirmation by a national vote on December 1. The conservative leaders of Belarus, though not challenged by an active independence movement, decided to follow suit on August 25 in order to retain power in their hands. By the end of the month Moldova, the three Transcaucasian states—Georgia, Armenia (subject to a referendum), and Azerbaijan, and Uzbekistan in Central Asia, all had declared independence or the intention to seek independence. (Kazakhstan, Kyrgyzstan, Turkmenistan, Tajikistan—and Russia—held back.)

Despite this wave of declarations, there was little movement in these republics to follow through, and no recognition by the USSR, Russia, or the

outside world, except for the Baltic states. Moreover, active negotiation continued on a treaty for a renewed, though now further diluted, union. Yeltsin, for
example, on August 25 reaffirmed that the Union Treaty should be signed,
although by all nine members at one time (unlike the planned August 20
initiation), and therefore should await agreement by Ukraine. He also emphasized that in his view it should be a federation, not merely a confederation.
Gorbachev urged earliest signing, and on August 27 he again threatened to
resign if the Union Treaty was not accepted.

Though the fate of the union would depend on the position to be taken
by the republics (especially Ukraine after its vote on December 1), it also
crucially depended on the closely related continuing political struggle between
Gorbachev and Yeltsin. Ever since Yeltsin had initiated the "parade of sover-
eignties" in June 1990 and assertion of primacy of republic laws in October,
Ukraine and other republics had followed a Russian lead. Though Yeltsin did
not declare Russian independence in the aftermath of the failed coup, he did
seize many of the powers, attributes, institutions, and assets of the central
Soviet regime, a path on which he continued after any need to preempt the
would-be usurpers of power was long gone. And he asserted and exercised
Russian authority in a way that invited and induced the other republics to follow
suit. On August 28, Gorbachev sought, though accepting the extraordinary
need for Yeltsin's decrees assuming overall authority (for example, over the
armed forces, the KGB, and the MVD, on Russian territory) during the coup,
to rein in and again to separate Russian and all-union Soviet affairs. Yet on that
same day Yeltsin barreled on unilaterally to take over the State Bank, Ministry
of Finance, and Bank of Foreign Economic Relations of the USSR.

Yeltsin, indeed, not only played the central political role in defeating
the coup but used the opportunity in effect to mount a countercoup, usurping
the powers of the union presidency and other central union institutions. Although the coup leaders had acted illegally in confining Gorbachev and attempting to exercise his emergency powers, they did not challenge the institutions of the central government, and one of their main aims was to reinforce the
existing structure. Yeltsin, in contrast, tore down the whole existing constitutional structure. And many of Yeltsin's actions were no more legal or constitutional than those of the coupmakers. It was Yeltsin's countercoup, far more than
the inept coup itself, that undercut Gorbachev's efforts to restabilize the status
quo of controlled change under *perestroika* and to legitimize a renewed union.

In the first days after the failure of the coup, Yeltsin deliberately
undercut and even humiliated Gorbachev, most notably during Gorbachev's
televised appearance at the Russian Supreme Soviet on August 23, the day after
his return from Foros. Yeltsin took advantage of the fact that Gorbachev had
not yet been able to inform himself fully on what had happened and publicly
waved in his face documents, incriminating former associates of the president,
which Gorbachev had not yet had an opportunity to read, imperiously telling
him to read them on the spot. Yeltsin then brushed aside ineffectual protesta-

tions of a visibly bewildered Gorbachev and signed in his presence—and that of the millions watching television—a decree suspending activity of the Russian Communist Party.

Gorbachev himself was slow to realize the nature and extent of the changes in the country wrought by the attempted coup, the dramatic defense of the White House, and Yeltsin's countercoup against the reeling central institutions. Gorbachev's initial television address immediately after his return, on August 22, was embarrassingly out of synchronization with events. Perhaps understandably, given the trying personal ordeal he and his family had just experienced, but unwisely in political terms, Gorbachev dwelt unduly on that personal experience and failed to seize the opportunity to lead in a rededication to the future change of the society.[63] Worse still, in answer to questions he sought to salvage what he still saw as a restructured healthy core of the Communist Party and the heritage of the October Revolution. Only two days later, on August 24 (under urging from Aleksandr Yakovlev), did Gorbachev resign as general secretary and urge the Central Committee of the CPSU to dissolve itself.

Yeltsin, meanwhile, had already (on August 23) banned the activity of organizations of the CPSU, including suspending publication of *Pravda* and five other party newspapers. On August 24 Yeltsin took over the archives of the CPSU and the KGB (to keep them from being destroyed). On the next day he seized the property and other assets of the CPSU, noting the dissolution of its Central Committee, and he suspended activity of the Russian Communist Party as well. On November 6 he suspended any activity of the CPSU itself and dissolved all organizational structures, in effect banning the party.

In other republics, the local leadership—in almost all cases comprising the former communist leaders—followed suit and banned or suspended the republic communist parties (for example, Ukraine on August 30). Even before suspending the CPSU and republic communist parties, and with clearer legality, Yeltsin on August 22 (followed by other republican leaders) had issued decrees "departyizing" and depoliticizing all governmental bodies by banning party cells in the armed forces, KGB, internal affairs and other ministries, and enterprises in the Russian Republic.

On most matters where Gorbachev's authority was still in effect, Gorbachev and Yeltsin acted in concert, sometimes also with the Kazakh leader Nazarbayev. Gorbachev had named a few interim replacements for arrested coup conspirators as early as August 22. Yet the next day he had the entire government resign and replaced even some of the just-named ministers, in several cases clearly accepting Yeltsin's nominees. He also replaced the institution of the Cabinet of Ministers with an interim committee headed by Russian Prime Minister Ivan Silayev—pursuant to an unwise suggestion of Yeltsin's,

---

63. For Gorbachev's account of the entire experience see Mikhail Gorbachev, *The August Coup: The Truth and the Lessons* (Harper Collins, 1991).

that further confirmed the not unjustified suspicions of many leaders of other republics that Yeltsin and Russia were taking over the central government.

Gorbachev had sought, as one of his first steps, to restore the process of adoption of the Union Treaty, calling on August 22 for a meeting of the 9+1 the next day. But it soon became clear that if there was to be a new Union Treaty (and union) it would require renegotiation and still greater concessions of authority to the republics. On August 27 Yeltsin, Nazarbayev, and Kyrgyzstan's President Askar Akayev joined Gorbachev in expressing renewed support for a Union Treaty. But it remained unclear what could be done before the Ukrainian referendum on December 1, since the Ukrainians would not discuss political matters before that vote.

Leonid Kravchuk, who only recently had won the leadership of the Communist Party and government in Ukraine, was determined that he should not be outflanked on the nationalist side. The vote on December 1 was not only a popular referendum on independence (not clearly defined), but also popular election of a president of Ukraine, and he faced several rivals. In addition, Kravchuk had been deeply affected by the weakness of his position when General Varennikov, deputy defense minister, accompanied by the generals commanding the three military districts in Ukraine, had on August 19 seen him and demanded support for the coup committee. This experience reinforced other reasons leading him to move quickly to establish Ukrainian control over the military forces on its territory once Ukraine became independent. But Kravchuk also recognized the close economic and other ties between Ukraine and Russia, in particular, and the other republics, and he was not opposed to some continuing association consistent with Ukrainian independence.

Negotiations among Gorbachev and the republic leaders were successful in reaching an agreement, announced on September 2, to work out and sign a new treaty of union, a Union of Sovereign States (SSG). The agreement, while only a commitment to work out a new arrangement, nonetheless was signed by Gorbachev and the leaders of ten republics (all except the three Baltic states, Moldova, and Georgia).

The new agreement was unveiled before a stunned opening session of the Congress of People's Deputies—with Yeltsin seated on the dais next to Gorbachev and Nazarbayev reading the joint statement on behalf of its signers. Moreover, the statement called for radically altering the central authorities to replace the congress and various executive bodies (except the presidency) with three interim councils: a State Council (comprising the 10+1, Gorbachev and the ten republic leaders), a Council of Representatives of People's Deputies (later changed to a renewed Supreme Soviet), and an Interrepublic Economic Council (combining representatives of the center and the republics). Gorbachev undertook the daunting task of persuading the still conservative Congress to give up its authority (in a compromise, the members were to retain some of their personal perquisites). In one of the last of his displays of remarkable ability to ram through a reluctant supporting consensus, Gorbachev succeeded in getting the USSR Congress on September 5 in effect to vote its own demise and to transfer executive and legislative power of the Soviet Union to the three councils—on which the republics had the predominant final voice. The vote was a lopsided 1,683 to 43.

For the next three months, this interim government worked. One of its first acts was on September 6 to recognize the independence of the three Baltic states—Latvia, Lithuania, and Estonia. During these three months a new Union Treaty was hammered out that appeared to offer the basis for a confederation of ten sovereign states (less Moldova and Georgia)—although subject to the position to be taken by the new (or renewed) leadership of Ukraine after its popular referendum of December 1.

Parallel with the efforts to negotiate a new treaty of political union were new negotiations on an economic union. As early as August 29, Russia and Ukraine had declared the need for close economic ties between the two "sovereign states"—still ambiguous, despite reference to "the former union." The next day, Russia and Kazakhstan called for negotiation of an economic union. By September 11 the draft of an economic union was published. On October 1, in a communiqué issued in Alma Ata, the representatives of all twelve republics, including Ukraine, affirmed their intentions to form an economic community. And on October 10, ten of the remaining twelve republics agreed on a text (the absentees were Georgia and Azerbaijan). Gorbachev overstepped in remarks on television on October 12 when he tied this economic treaty with the renewed political Union Treaty still under negotiation and declared Ukraine was an "irreplaceable" member of this union. Although as late as October 15 Ukraine signed another declaration of readiness to sign an agreement with the other republics, when the new economic cooperation (no longer "economic union") treaty was signed on October 18, the eight republic signatories did not include Ukraine. Yet on November 6, Ukraine (and Moldova) did sign, restoring the ten.

On November 25, confidence in agreement on the new draft Union Treaty, minus Ukraine pending its vote, was so high that a champagne ceremony for the initialing was arranged. But at the last moment Yeltsin objected and sought additional powers for Russia at the expense of the center and pushed for the union to be a confederation of states rather than a confederal state. The draft, for example, still had a union president elected by the peoples of all the participating states. So the seven states that had been expected to initial the agreement—Russia, Belarus, Kazakhstan, Kyrgyzstan, Uzbekistan, Turkmenistan, and Tajikistan—merely referred the text to their parliaments. This decision by Yeltsin prevented facing Ukraine with a clear choice between belonging to the union or not—instead, the future of a union was in effect made subject to Ukrainian decision.

Meanwhile, real power was increasingly in the hands of Russia and Yeltsin, rather than the residual union and Gorbachev. By November 30, the USSR government had no funds or source of revenue, and Yeltsin and

Gorbachev agreed to an arrangement under which the operating budgets and resources of Russia and the central government of the USSR were merged. It was announced that many ministries would be abolished. In effect, Russia was now paying the salaries of Soviet officials—a striking sign and a key shift in real power.[64]

## From Gorbachev and the Union to Yeltsin and the Commonwealth

The apogee of support for the new Union Treaty came on December 4, when the Supreme Soviet endorsed the latest draft and recommended its signature to the republics. But this seemingly stellar achievement represented a dead option, like the bright glow still perceived of an already extinguished star. Even before this action, President Leonid Kravchuk of the Ukraine (elected December 1 over several other candidates, with 61 percent of the vote) announced that Ukraine, which had voted 90 percent in favor of independence, had no intention of participating in any renewed union. Gorbachev still urged all, including Ukraine, to sign. At least seven republics—Russia, Belarus, Kazakhstan, and the four smaller Central Asian states—had indicated they were now ready to sign the last draft. Yeltsin and Nazarbayev supported Gorbachev's effort to rally Ukrainian adherence.

Suddenly, on the weekend of December 7–8, Yeltsin and then Kravchuk arrived in Minsk to join Belarusian Supreme Soviet Chairman Stanislav Shushkevich for meetings at a secluded retreat called Belovezhskaya (Bialowieza) Forest. As Yeltsin arrived in Minsk for the meetings, he remarked, "We must discuss very seriously what Union to participate in and what treaty to sign. I believe that we must without fail work out a viewpoint that will prevent our three Slav states from splitting apart, no matter what happens."[65] Gorbachev's press secretary, Andrei Grachev, later said that when Yeltsin had seen Gorbachev shortly before going to Minsk there was no mention of a "commonwealth" agreement among the three states. But he disclosed that Yeltsin had told Gorbachev that "if they [Yeltsin and Shushkevich] did not succeed in drawing Ukraine into the proposed Union they would have 'to think about something else.' "[66] That is exactly what happened.

---

64. Throughout the year, and exacerbated by the political uncertainties, economic performance had sharply declined. During 1991, gross national product in the USSR declined by 17 percent, national income by 15 percent, gross industrial product by 7.8 percent, gross agricultural product by 7 percent, housing starts by 17 percent, and total consumption by 15 percent. Data from the USSR State Committee for Statistics, cited by Radio Free Europe/Radio Liberty, *Research Report*, vol. 1 (March 20, 1992), p. 40.

65. See "Yeltsin's Arrival Statement in Minsk," Radio Moscow, December 7, 1991, in FBIS, *Soviet Union*, December 9, 1991, p. 50.

66. "Not Opposed in Principle," TASS, December 10, 1991, in FBIS, *Soviet Union*, December 11, 1991, p. 12.

Yeltsin had concentrated on wearing down both Gorbachev's power and the power of the central union authorities in the draft Union Treaty. But he also not only wanted a union but was desperate to keep a significant tie with Ukraine (and also Belarus and Kazakhstan, but that was not a problem because they were amenable).[67]

It came as a great surprise and shock to Gorbachev, and to the leaders of the other republics (especially Nazarbayev of Kazakhstan), when on December 8 the three leaders in Minsk unveiled a joint declaration in which they concluded that "the negotiations to draw up a new Union Treaty are deadlocked" and that "the objective process of secession by republics from the USSR and the formation of independent states have become a reality." They declared the establishment of a "commonwealth [or community, *sodruzhestvo*] of independent states," consisting of Belarus, Russia, and Ukraine but "open for accession by all member states of the USSR" and even to "other states that share the aim and principles" of the agreement. They gave a "guarantee to honor international obligations and agreements of the former USSR [sic]" and also "to ensure unified control over nuclear weapons and their nonproliferation."[68] But the powers and even the nature of the "commonwealth" were exceedingly nebulous.

Gorbachev had understood that Yeltsin was going to try to persuade Kravchuk to sign the Union Treaty, or least learn what further amendments Kravchuk might seek. He blamed Yeltsin, after the three-republic announcement of the commonwealth, for abandoning and sabotaging the Union Treaty. Yeltsin bears much of the responsibility for the ultimate failure of the effort to reach a Union Treaty in 1990–91 because of his relentless campaign to build up his own power base, the Russian Republic, and wear down that of Gorbachev, the Soviet Union. But at the Belovezhskaya meeting it is clear that Yeltsin and Shushkevich, unable to move Kravchuk on any version of a "union treaty," moved themselves to reach accord on whatever proved to be a common denominator that would keep Ukraine in some form of association with Russia. To them, that was more important—and preferable—to a union linking Russia and

---

67. Yeltsin occasionally overplayed his hand. For instance, soon after the defeat of the coup, when Yeltsin was riding high in Moscow, he attempted to cow Ukraine into joining a renewed union. On August 26, on Yeltsin's instructions, his press secretary Pavel Voshchanov issued a statement warning that Russia reserved the right to raise the issue of revising borders in cases of large ethnic Russian populations in contiguous republics (explicitly excluding the Baltic states) if the republics did not remain in a union with Russia. While intended to place pressure for continuation of a union, this warning raised strong protests in Ukraine and Kazakhstan. For the text of the statement, see "Yeltsin's Office: Right to 'Revise' Borders," TASS, August 26, 1991, in FBIS, *Soviet Union*, August 27, 1991, p. 71. Although Yeltsin subsequently sought to reassure these republics, he did not repudiate the statement.

68. "Declaration on New Commonwealth," TASS, December 8, 1991, in FBIS, *Soviet Union*, December 9, 1991, p. 48.

Belarus only to the Muslim republics of the south. Gorbachev's bitter disappointment is understandable, but his assessment of what could then be done was less realistic than Yeltsin's.

Gorbachev was not the only one shocked by the prospect of replacement of the Soviet Union by a loose community of the three Slavic republics. Nazarbayev and Akayev, the most intent on reform and union, and the other Central Asian leaders concerned above all over being cut off from Russian economic ties and assistance, were also alarmed. Yeltsin sought to reassure both Gorbachev and Nazarbayev and accepted their joint move to have the Supreme Soviet refer the Belovezhskaya Commonwealth agreement, as well as the draft Union Treaty, to the other republics. On December 13 Kazakhstan and the four Muslim republics of Central Asia met in Ashkabad (now Ashgabat) and agreed on a position welcoming the "desire" of the three Slavic republics to create a commonwealth but contended that it must be given "legal form." They expressed their support if all members (that is, their five republics as well) would join "as equal cofounders of a Commonwealth of Independent States." They set a further meeting in Alma Ata (now Almaty), Kazakhstan, for December 21.[69] The republics had decided they wanted to be included and that the Union Treaty was dead. Yeltsin had removed the alternative of a Union Treaty binding them with Russia and letting Ukraine go its own way.

Kazakhstan has played a particularly important role, not only owing to its size and resources, but also to the fact that it is more closely tied to Russia by geographical, historical, and ethnic ties than the other four republics of Central Asia. Until 1936, Kazakhstan (and Kyrgyzstan) were part of Russia, as autonomous republics within the Russian Federation, much as are Tatarstan and Bashkortostan (Bashkiria) today. Moreover, today the Russian share of the population (38 percent) is nearly as large as Kazakh (40 percent), and the Slavic (plus 8 percent German) share is well over half of the total population. Nazarbayev wanted to retain a multiethnic republic and close ties to Russia because the likely alternative would be a split between the northern (Slavic) and southern (Kazakh) parts of the country. If the four Central Asian republics to the south drifted away, there would also be a gravitational pull apart of the two parts of Kazakhstan. So Nazarbayev sought a continuing union, or if that were not possible, then at least a commonwealth embracing Russia and the Muslim republics of Central Asia.

The military was the other main actor shocked by the commonwealth and prospective abandonment of both the old union and a new one. Gorbachev met with a special conference of senior military men from all over the USSR (a meeting originally scheduled as a purely military annual training review conference) on December 10. He was coolly received and unable to persuade his

---

69. See the "Declaration of Ashkabad Meeting," TASS, December 13, 1991, in FBIS, *Soviet Union*, December 13, 1991, pp. 84–85.

audience that his dogged pursuit of a new Union Treaty would succeed. Yeltsin met with this same conference the next morning, also to a cool initial reception, but with greater success in persuading the officers that the commonwealth was the only path and that he would strive to keep the military unified (their main concern and aim). He also underlined his control over the purse strings, promising to double officers' salaries in the coming year and meet other needs such as housing.[70] Although Gorbachev had from the outset made clear that the dispute over the transformation of the Soviet Union into either a new union or a commonwealth could only be resolved by peaceful political accommodation, and while neither he nor Yeltsin openly "bid" for direct military support, they both recognized the importance of the military constituency. By their unusual meetings under the circumstances they helped to ensure that the military would accept a political resolution of the problem.

The Commonwealth of Independent States was established at Alma Ata on December 21. Not only did the eight Slavic and Central Asian republics join together, but so too did Armenia, Azerbaijan, and Moldova. Only Georgia (mired in internal conflict) stood aside. Moreover, the formal declaration of the eleven successor states explicitly provided that "with the formation of the Commonwealth of Independent States the Union of Soviet Socialist Republics ceases to exist." They also composed a joint message to Gorbachev thanking him "for his great, positive contribution" and "informing" him of the cessation of the Soviet Union and its presidency.[71]

A number of institutions (in the form of interstate ministerial committees) were established, agreement was reached in principle on joint control over nuclear weapons, and "until the question of reforming the Armed Forces is resolved, the command of the Armed Forces is entrusted to Marshal Ye. I. Shaposhnikov."[72] The eight republics also agreed to "support Russia in continuing the USSR's UN membership," including its membership in the UN Security Council.[73] The commonwealth itself was not defined, nor its functions clearly identified, but there was a clear statement that it was "neither a state, nor a super-state structure."[74]

On December 25, Gorbachev resigned as president of the USSR (including transfer of his control over nuclear weapons to Yeltsin). The next day,

70. See "Gorbachev, Yeltsin Ministry [of Defense] Visits Detailed," FBIS, *Soviet Union*, December 12, 1991, pp. 24–26.

71. See the " 'Text' of the Alma Ata Declaration" and other related documents and commentaries, in FBIS, *Soviet Union*, December 23, 1991, pp. 18–41, esp. pp. 27–32.

72. Ibid., p. 31.

73. Ibid., p. 32. Ukraine agreed only because it (and Belarus) were already UN member states, owing to Stalin's insistence in 1945.

74. Ibid., p. 30.

the Supreme Soviet of the USSR met for the last time and dissolved itself.[75] The Soviet red flag with gold hammer and sickle was lowered for the last time over the Kremlin and over the country.[76]

On December 30 the first summit meeting of commonwealth leaders in Minsk began to deal with the myriad of practical problems they faced. Although several issues were agreed in principle, it was clear that a very difficult path lay ahead.


## American-Soviet Relations, the Final Phase

President Bush responded quickly and firmly to the coup. On August 19 he issued a statement saying, "We are deeply disturbed by the events of the last hours in the Soviet Union and condemn the unconstitutional resort to force," and he announced support for Yeltsin's call for restoration of Gorbachev to power.[77] The only direct leverage he could bring to bear was to declare that the United States would not provide promised economic assistance so long as extraconstitutional rule continued, a move paralleled by the European Community, which cut off a previously promised $1 billion in aid until Gorbachev was restored. Bush did, the next day, send Ambassador-designate Robert Strauss to Moscow but only to report on the situation, not to present his credentials to the coup regime.

It was revealed only later that Bush had warned Gorbachev on June 20 of a possible attempt at a coup through Ambassador Jack Matlock, through Secretary Baker to Foreign Minister Bessmertnykh, and directly in a guarded telephone call. This was at the time of Prime Minister Pavlov's overt attempt to gain wider power, and while Gorbachev expressed appreciation for the warn-

---

75. See "Supreme Soviet Adopts Dissolution Resolution," FBIS, *Soviet Union*, December 26, 1991, p. 9; and "Gorbachev Resigns as USSR President," ibid., pp. 20–22.

    With Gorbachev's resignation, only four members of the last Politburo of the CPSU elected in July 1990 remained in power, all now heads of independent states: Nursultan A. Nazarbayev of Kazakhstan, Islam I. Karimov of Uzbekistan, Saparmurad A. Niyazov of Turkmenistan, and Ayaz N. ogly Mutalibov of Azerbaijan (the latter soon to fall from power).

76. The Soviet and Russian flags had coexisted over the Kremlin and many other places since August. Yeltsin had adopted the prerevolutionary White-Blue-and-Red tricolor as the flag of Russia as early as August 22—again leading the other republics (other than the Baltic states); Ukraine had adopted a traditional blue and yellow flag on September 4.

77. See "Statement on the Attempted Coup in the Soviet Union," *Presidential Documents*, vol. 27 (August 26, 1991), p. 1159, and for other related statements on August 19 and 20 see pp. 1154–66.

ing, he was confident he had "everything in hand"—as he did with respect to the open Pavlov challenge, which he rebuffed on June 21, but not with respect to the later action by the same men.[78]

On August 21 Bush spoke to Yeltsin by telephone (and to President François Mitterrand of France, Prime Minister John Major of Britain, and Chancellor Helmut Kohl of Germany, among others). About noon he finally also succeeded in reaching President Gorbachev, whose external communications from Foros in the Crimea had just been reopened. By then the coup crisis was ending.

Bush held back from early recognition of the independence of the Baltic states, despite some domestic criticism, in order not to lean on Gorbachev at a critical time and to give time for prior recognition by the Soviet government. He finally formally recognized the three states on September 2, the same day Gorbachev announced the intention to do so and three days before the new State Council of the USSR did so formally. The United States was thus the thirty-seventh country to recognize the independence of these states, rather than taking a lead. Bush's restraint, while briefly and mildly unpopular at home (and in the Baltic states), was probably wise.

The third CSCE Conference on Human Rights convened in Moscow on September 10, with the Soviet Union now taking an active role in sponsoring human rights.

The CSCE conference gave Secretary Baker the opportunity to see Gorbachev and Yeltsin. Apart from congratulations over defeating the attempted coup, talks were held with each of them on several questions of new concern, such as the new union (then expected), and in particular control over nuclear weapons and conversion of the defense industry. They also were able to resume discussion of the post-Moscow summit agenda of continuing foreign policy issues, including Afghanistan, the Middle East peace process, Soviet relations with Cuba, and the Japanese claim on the "northern territories."[79]

There were two immediate important results of those consultations, and others that came to light only later. The first was an announcement by Gorbachev at his joint news conference with Baker on September 11 that the Soviet Union intended to withdraw the 2,800–man "training" brigade it had maintained in Cuba since 1962. He said the Soviet Union would transform relations with Cuba to normal "mutually beneficial" trade ties and "remove

---

78. See R. Jeffrey Smith, "U.S. Warned Gorbachev of Coup Three Times," *Washington Post*, November 15, 1991, p. A35; Serge Schmemann, "Gorbachev Says Bush Called Him to Give Early Warning About Hard-Line Coup," *New York Times*, November 13, 1991, p. A12; and Beschloss and Talbott, *At the Highest Levels*, pp. 395–98, 400–01.

79. See "New Opportunities in U.S.-Soviet Relations: Secretary Baker, President Gorbachev, President Yeltsin" [statements on September 11], in *State Dispatch*, vol. 2 (September 16, 1991), pp. 681–82. See also Baker's news conference statement when his visit was announced on September 4, ibid., vol. 2 (September 9, 1991), p. 667.

other elements from that relationship" that had been "born in a different time in a different era."[80] Although he indicated there would soon be "discussions with the Cuban leadership," he made clear the Soviet intention to withdraw the token troops. The Cubans had not been consulted and were very angry at this slight, especially because they wanted to use any withdrawal of the Soviet brigade as a bargaining chip to press the United States to withdraw from the base at Guantanamo Bay. Subsequent Soviet (later Russian) negotiations with the Cubans were protracted and inconclusive, and the Russians began a gradual piecemeal reduction toward the ultimate disbanding of the unit. Gorbachev was led to his premature public statement by two pressures: first, Baker had raised the matter, and second in a joint appearance with Yeltsin on American (ABC) satellite television only five days earlier, Yeltsin had replied to a question by saying the brigade would be brought home, and Gorbachev had felt it necessary to concur rather than allow an artificial issue to divide them.

The second immediate step was the joint announcement by Secretary Baker and Foreign Minister Boris D. Pankin (who had replaced Bessmertnykh after the coup attempt) on September 13 that the two countries were ending the supply of arms to the contending parties in Afghanistan as of January 1, 1992, and supported the UN secretary general's negotiations for a transitional coalition rule. Though the UN efforts ultimately did not succeed, the U.S.-Soviet action did lead to the fall of President Najibullah's regime seven months later and at least an end to the international aspects of the Afghan civil war. That civil war had of course been under way long before the Soviet intervention and continued after the fall of the Soviet-supported regime. The September U.S.-Soviet agreement also led to direct Soviet contacts with the *mujahedin*, facilitating a later normalization of relations by Russia and Afghanistan after Najibullah fell.

Another sign of the continuing development of closer U.S.-Soviet ties and thinking was the arrival on September 9 of twenty-two Soviet generals and admirals and six colonels to attend a two-week course on the U.S. system of national security decisionmaking at the John F. Kennedy School at Harvard.

The new broadened American contact with leaders of key individual republics was also in evidence. Secretary Baker traveled to Alma Ata to visit Kazakh leader Nazarbayev on September 16. Nine days later, Kravchuk was received by President Bush in the White House. And a month later (on October 26) Bush, who had first called Yeltsin during the coup crisis, telephoned Yeltsin again to discuss economic investment.

---

80. Ibid., p. 682. (*State Dispatch* regrettably included a misprint using the word "control" instead of "withdraw," as Soviet press and other versions make clear was the word Gorbachev used.)

    Also at that very time there had just been an unprecedented visit to Moscow, and meetings with Foreign Minister Boris Pankin and President Yeltsin, of Jorge Mas Canosa, the leading anti-Castro émigré leader in Miami.

Undersecretary of State Robert Zoellick, a close counselor of Secretary Baker, gave a long and thoughtful statement in testimony before a subcommittee of the House Foreign Affairs Committee on October 2, the main thrust of which was the need for a U.S. policy of active engagement with both the Soviet Union and the constituent republics.[81] Although it may be noted, especially easily in retrospect, that this approach would not hold more than the few months that the Soviet Union remained, it was the appropriate approach for the time and reflected correctly at that point the new reality of the union and the republics as actors with whom it was possible and indeed incumbent on the United States to deal.

President Bush took a significant unilateral initiative advancing arms control. On September 27, in a major televised address from the Oval Office, Bush announced several unilateral steps for redeployment and reduction of American nuclear forces and discontinuation of strategic bomber and some missile alert, called on the Soviet Union to do likewise, and proposed further measures for discussion and possible agreement on reciprocal cutbacks. The far-ranging nuclear retrenchment was inspired directly by the events in the Soviet Union, which jarred Bush and others in the administration into rethinking strategic requirements, and above all into seeking a "fast track" of reciprocal actions rather than protracted arms control negotiations. He noted that "new leaders in the Kremlin and the Republics are now questioning the need for their huge nuclear arsenal," and he was obviously led to do the same. "As a result," he said, "we now have an unparalleled opportunity to change the nuclear posture of both the United States and the Soviet Union."[82] He noted "consultations" with allied leaders Prime Minister John Major, President François Mitterrand, and Chancellor Helmut Kohl (he had called them that morning to advise them of the measures). Although he did not note it publicly, he had also called both Gorbachev and Yeltsin, and each man had reacted positively, although of course not yet with commitment on specific aspects. It was a telling sign of the changing situation that he should have called Yeltsin as well as Gorbachev.[83]

---

81.  "Relations of the United States with the Soviet Union and the Republics," Robert B. Zoellick, *State Dispatch*, vol. 2 (October 7, 1991), pp. 740–48.

82.  "Address to the Nation on Reducing United States and Soviet Nuclear Weapons," September 27, 1991, *Presidential Documents*, vol. 27 (September 30, 1991), p. 1349.
     Although Defense Secretary Cheney had opposed further reductions, General Colin Powell and the other chiefs of staff not only agreed but had recommended most of the specific measures when asked to do so.

83.  The American chargé d'affaires in Moscow (in the absence of an accredited ambassador), James F. Collins, had been able to see Gorbachev at 10:30 a.m. Moscow time to present the U.S. proposals and arrange for Bush to telephone six hours later, so Gorbachev had the opportunity to discuss the subject briefly with the Foreign and Defense Ministries. Bush's call to Yeltsin was made about three hours after his call to Gorbachev.

The key unilateral actions announced in Bush's address were the elimination of all remaining U.S. ground force tactical nuclear weapons; the removal from all U.S. naval ships and submarines, including aircraft carriers, except for strategic ballistic missile submarines, of all nuclear weapons, many to be destroyed and the rest held in secured central storage; removal from alert posture of all U.S. strategic bombers and those missiles, about 600 ICBMs and SLBMs, scheduled for deactivation under the START Treaty; consolidation of operational command of all U.S. strategic nuclear forces, bombers, intercontinental ballistic missiles (ICBMs), and missile submarines in one U.S. Strategic Command; and cancelation of programs for mobile ICBMs and new short-range bomber attack missiles (SRAMs). In all cases, the Soviet Union was "called on" to follow suit with similar steps, but the U.S. actions were not dependent on Soviet response. In addition, Bush proposed two major steps for agreement: to eliminate all land-based ICBMs with multiple warheads (MIRV) and "to join us in taking immediate concrete steps to permit the limited deployment of non-nuclear defenses to protect against limited ballistic missile strikes, whatever their source, without undermining the credibility of existing deterrent forces."[84] He also invited joint discussions to ensure safe handling and dismantling of Soviet nuclear weapons.

It was a bold, but not imprudent, initiative, and it was widely welcomed. Two aspects of the proposed bilateral agreements were controversial. One was the proposal for modifying or abandoning the ABM Treaty (which Bush did not mention) to allow the deployment of ballistic missile defenses, which many people (in the United States, Europe, and the Soviet Union) did not regard as either strategically necessary or stabilizing. The other was the proposal for eliminating all land-based MIRV missiles, which constituted the major part of the Soviet strategic nuclear force, but not of the submarine-launched MIRV missiles that constituted the major part of the U.S. strategic force. Especially in the Soviet Union this was seen as imbalanced, inequitable, and strategically disadvantageous to Soviet security.

On October 5, Gorbachev matched and went beyond Bush's initiative. He seemed to enjoy an "arms race downhill" in reverse. He announced that the Soviet Union too would destroy all ground force tactical nuclear weapons and remove all naval tactical nuclear weapons from ships and land-based naval aviation, destroying some and centrally storing the remainder.[85] He proposed on a reciprocal basis destroying *all* naval tactical nuclear weapons. He also said the USSR would remove from the forces all air defense nuclear warheads to central storage (a category the United States no longer deployed). He then

---

84. *Presidential Documents*, vol. 27 (September 30, 1991), p. 1351.

85. At Malta in December 1989 Gorbachev had proposed elimination of all tactical nuclear weapons with naval forces, only to be firmly rebuffed by Bush.

proposed, on a reciprocal basis, removing all air-delivered tactical nuclear weapons to central storage, something Bush had intentionally not included.

Gorbachev also reciprocated the U.S. actions on removal of all strategic bombers from alert, terminating new mobile missile projects and announcing there would be no increase in the existing SS-24 rail-mobile system, which would be returned to storage. He announced removing 503 ICBMs from alert, including 134 MIRV missiles, and he said that 92 submarine-launched missiles were being removed from the active force, matching the U.S. action. He also said that the Soviet Union would unilaterally further reduce its START-limited warheads from 6,000 to 5,000 and commented that a reciprocal step by the United States would be welcome. And he proposed immediate negotiations to cut strategic offensive weapons beyond START levels by about half.

On the ABM proposal, he said, "We are ready to discuss U.S. proposals on non-nuclear anti-missile systems" and went on to make a more concrete proposal: "We propose to study the possibility of creating joint systems to intercept nuclear missile attacks with ground- and space-based components."

Gorbachev accepted the proposal to enter talks on nuclear safety. But he went much further in also proposing a controlled cessation of the production of all fissionable materials for weapons and declaring a one-year unilateral moratorium on nuclear testing (while hoping to negotiate a permanent ban).

Finally, as Bush had mentioned U.S. plans to reduce its armed forces by 500,000 personnel, Gorbachev announced a further reduction of the Soviet armed forces by 700,000.[86]

Gorbachev ignored the idea of a ban on MIRV land-based ICBMs, leaving to the proposed negotiations for further strategic reductions the task of working out an equitable cut of land- and sea-based strategic missile systems.

The radical reduction of tactical nuclear weapons on land and at sea by both countries meant eliminating large numbers of nuclear weapons even without further negotiations. This was made possible in part by revised technical and strategic considerations, but also in essential part by the end of the Cold War global and European confrontations. It was especially timely because it gave impetus to a Soviet redeployment to Russian centers of thousands of nuclear weapons in outlying republics, and thus reduced the risks of incidents and of nuclear proliferation as republics of the Soviet Union became independent and in some cases laid claim to former Soviet military forces and weapons.[87]

---

86. "Statement of M. S. Gorbachev on Soviet Television," *Pravda*, October 7, 1991; also "Gorbachev Addresses Nation on Disarmament," Moscow Television First Program, October 5, 1991, in FBIS, *Soviet Union*, October 7, 1991, pp. 1–3.

87. It has been reported that the Foreign Ministry in October 1991 recommended to Gorbachev that he take an initiative to remove all Soviet ICBMs deployed outside the Russian Republic, but that the General Staff objected and no action was taken. It is not clear whether the proposal was for unilateral action or for a reciprocal arms control reduction with the United States. In any event, no such initiative was taken.

The September-October Bush and Gorbachev arms control and reduction initiatives thus amounted to a major step beyond the foundation provided by the START Treaty and in turn facilitated a deeper strategic arms agreement between the United States and Russia that would be agreed upon the next year.

Important steps were also taken to advance arms control and peace initiatives in several regions of the globe. On October 17–18 in London the five permanent members of the UN Security Council began talks on curbing arms sales to the Middle East, although with uncertain prospects for success. Baker and Pankin used that occasion to announce that the United States and the Soviet Union would jointly convene a Middle East Arab-Israeli peace conference (and the Soviet Union announced its diplomatic recognition of Israel). On October 30, the Middle East peace conference opened in Madrid.

Meanwhile, on October 23 the United States and the Soviet Union joined China and other sponsoring states in the conclusion of a Cambodian peace settlement. On December 2, the United States and the Soviet Union jointly urged a settlement by the parties in El Salvador, and the subsequent agreement there complemented the earlier Nicaraguan settlement (and the cooling and "normalization" of Soviet-Cuban relations) in dealing with the Caribbean region.

The convening of the Middle East peace talks in Madrid provided an opportunity for yet another meeting of Presidents Bush and Gorbachev on October 29. The main subject of their discussion was not, however, Middle Eastern or other foreign policy issues, although these were discussed (including the worsening situation in Yugoslavia). Arms control was naturally one agenda item, and it was agreed to form working groups, including one on strategic stability. But the main subject of the discussion was the changing situation in the Soviet Union, including reassurances over future central control over nuclear weapons. Economic reform and Western economic assistance were also discussed.

The United States was slowly moving forward on economic normalization. On November 12 the Office of Private Investment Credit (OPIC) approved insurance guarantees for trade with the Soviet Union, overcoming a reluctance of American banks to fund grain credits even with the principal guaranteed. (On October 1 Bush had also granted an additional $585 million in grain credits to cover the margin the banks were unprepared to carry.) On November 20 Bush approved a further $1.25 billion in grain credits and a token $12 million in humanitarian assistance.

From September on, Congress, especially several Democratic leaders but with bipartisan support, had been urging a shift of funds from the Defense Department allocation to provide economic assistance to the Soviet Union and the republics. Although there was originally wide support for transferring up to $1 billion, as proposed by Senator Sam Nunn and Representative Les Aspin, by early November with lack of White House support and growing concerns over the U.S. economy, the measure seemed likely to die. With renewed support also from Republican Senators Richard Lugar and Robert Dole, a bill to transfer $500 million, of which $400 million would be for assistance in dismantling nuclear and chemical weapons, was passed on November 25.

Meanwhile, on November 7-8 at a NATO meeting in Rome a new alliance strategic concept was adopted that added "cooperation" to the twin pillars of defense and détente adopted in 1967. On November 20–21 the first meeting of the U.S.-USSR working group on strategic stability met in Washington.[88]

The United States had begun to carry out its policy of readiness to deal with the republics as well as the Soviet Union central leadership. For example, emergency humanitarian aid had been sent under arrangements made directly with several republics, although coordinated also with Moscow. In a different kind of example, when the United States ratified the CFE Treaty on conventional arms reductions in Europe on November 25 it notified not only Soviet officials but also officials of the Russian and Ukrainian republics.

As the Ukrainian vote on independence on December 1 approached, President Bush overreacted to domestic criticism of his prounion speech in Kiev on August 1 by deciding to make a gesture to the Ukrainian-American constituency. He agreed to receive a group of about fifteen leaders of that community at the White House on November 27. Then, as he prepared for that meeting, he decided to split the difference between divergent recommendations from Secretary of State Baker and Secretary of Defense Cheney. Baker urged that the president not only await the Ukrainian vote but also wait for discussions to ensure Ukraine's readiness to confirm its status as a nonnuclear power before recognition. Cheney, in line with a long-standing Pentagon preference for chipping away at Soviet power, favored an early recognition of Ukrainian independence (as he had, unsuccessfully, urged also for the Baltic states). Bush intended to strike a middle ground by assuring the Ukrainian-Americans that he would "move forward" on recognition after the vote, without yet mentioning timing or conditions. But the message as heard and reported in the press was that the United States would "speed recognition" and "promptly" salute Ukrainian independence.[89] Moreover, two days later, still before the Ukrainian vote, the White House put out the word that it would send a special emissary to Ukraine after the vote on independence.

Bush's action was hasty and ill-considered, in sad contrast to his patient stand on recognition of the Baltic states. Gorbachev's press spokesman issued a statement that made clear that the American president's position, particularly in advance of the vote, was premature and unwelcome and surprising "in view

---

88. The new mood was also reflected in the decision of the editors of the *Bulletin of the Atomic Scientists* in the December 1991 issue to move back the minute hand on their doomsday clock from twelve to seventeen minutes before midnight.

89. See John E. Yang, "Bush Decides to Accelerate Recognition of Ukraine," *Washington Post*, November 28, 1991, p. A1.

of the present level of relations between the two countries and numerous official statements that the U.S. will not be adopting attitudes to such internal affairs of the USSR until the republics arrive at the final decision."[90] Although he did not comment publicly, Yeltsin was also unhappy; his foreign minister, Andrei Kozyrev, had privately requested that the United States not rush to immediate recognition of Ukraine because that would inflame Russian nationalists.

Officials in London, Paris, and Bonn made clear that they had not been consulted or advised before the Bush statement, and that they would not be acting as precipitately on the question of recognition.[91]

Only after the brouhaha in the media over the new American stand did Bush belatedly telephone Gorbachev on November 30 to review the statement he planned to issue after the vote and to assure him that the United States would not regard a Ukrainian vote as a "break from the union." The day after the Ukrainian vote for independence, the White House statement "welcomed" the expression of democracy in the vote (and President Kravchuk's election), and in a misplaced attempt to create a balance, also tied the vote to a "tribute to the defeat of the coup, in which Boris Yeltsin played such a pivotal role." To be sure, in developing its relationship with Ukraine, the statement said, "We also intend to continue our cooperation with President Gorbachev and his government and to strengthen our expanding ties with President Yeltsin and the Russian Government, as well as the other republics." The statement announced the sending of Assistant Secretary Thomas Niles for initial talks to be followed later in the month by a visit by Secretary Baker to Kiev as well as Moscow. The statement noted that the emissary and Baker would discuss ways in which the United States could support Ukraine in its commitment to international obligations, respect for borders, and adherence to norms of the Helsinki CSCE and help Ukrainian leaders "to implement their desire to achieve a non-nuclear status and to ensure responsible security plans."[92]

The general approach was sound, but it was regrettable that President Bush had not waited for the Ukrainian vote and forgone the meeting with Ukrainian-Americans, which triggered hasty, premature, and piecemeal public statements on this sensitive issue.

On December 8, in a CBS television interview, Secretary Baker commented that "the Soviet Union as we've known it no longer exists," although he

90. Francis X. Clines, "Kremlin Indicates Irritation at Bush on Ukraine Stand, Comments on Recognition Seen as Premature and Unwelcome," *New York Times*, November 29, 1991, p. A1.

91. See Stephen Kinzer, "Europe Is Expected to Move More Slowly on Ukraine," *New York Times*, November 29, 1991, p. A20.

92. "Ukrainians Vote for Independence," December 2, 1991, *State Dispatch*, vol. 2 (December 9, 1991), p. 879.

made clear he was not prejudging the form of whatever union or association of republics would develop, and he warned of the risks exemplified by the disintegration of Yugoslavia "with nuclear weapons thrown in."[93] By the time Baker's comment reached the next day's newspapers, another statement, issued in Minsk two hours after Baker spoke, posed the issue much more starkly.[94]

The Minsk Declaration of December 8 by Yeltsin, Kravchuk, and Shushkevich announcing the creation of a commonwealth to succeed the Soviet Union had not yet been received by Baker when he made his remarks. But Yeltsin had called Bush promptly to inform him of the commonwealth, even before he called Gorbachev! This time Washington took a few days to evaluate the situation before making new statements.

On December 12, shortly before departing for visits to the Soviet Union, Russia, Ukraine, Belarus, Kazakhstan, and Kyrgyzstan, Baker gave an address at his alma mater, Princeton University, titled: "America and the Collapse of the Soviet Empire: What Has to Be Done."[95] Baker was speaking at a time of delicate and still unresolved issues within the Soviet Union over the nature of its transformation. While the Soviet Union appeared to be on its last legs, as indeed would soon be confirmed, that was not yet the situation when Baker spoke. Although he could speak of the "collapse of the Soviet empire," he could not yet be sure whether a confederation, commonwealth, or some other associational entity would remain along with the republics. Baker noted as "the most striking characteristic of the post-coup environment" the "dramatic shift of power from the center to the republics." He referred in several passages to the new partners of the United States as "the republics and any common entity" that may be established, a short-lived expedient designation for the fortnight until a commonwealth of the successor states would come to succeed the Soviet Union.[96] Baker's central message was that the United States "will work with those republics and any common entity which commit to responsible security policies, democratic political practices, and free market economies." He noted that some republics were more prepared to take such a course than others, naming five: Russia, Ukraine, Kazakhstan, Armenia, and Kyrgyzstan. This effort to pursue a policy of differentiation based on performance was overlaid by a

---

93. David Hoffman, " 'Soviet Union as We've Known It' Is Gone, Baker Says," *Washington Post*, December 9, 1991, p. A16.

94. Regrettably, Gorbachev received a misleading early press report of the statement to the effect that Baker had said "the Soviet Union no longer exists" without the qualifying words "as we've known it," and he believed he had been unaccountably undercut by the U.S. administration. Information from members of Gorbachev's staff.

95. "America and the Collapse of the Soviet Empire: What Has to Be Done," Secretary Baker, December 12, 1991, *State Dispatch*, vol. 2 (December 16, 1991), pp. 887–93.

96. In the halls of the State Department, this awkward transient appellation, "any common entity," quickly acquired its own acronym, ACE.

second set of countries distinguished by the presence on their territories of nuclear weapons: Russia, Ukraine, Kazakhstan, and Belarus. Both criteria, which largely overlapped in practice, were applied in selecting the five countries that were included on Baker's itinerary.

Baker emphasized the need to assist and to encourage nuclear nonproliferation, including no more than one central nuclear authority in the former Soviet Union. He announced for the first time the administration's intention to use the $400 million appropriated by Congress to assist in the destruction of Soviet weapons of mass destruction.

Much of Baker's attention was also devoted to the need for outside economic assistance, especially humanitarian aid over the winter, at a time of difficult economic and political transition. Although he spelled out several existing, new, and planned American programs, they were all short-term emergency palliatives or contributory technical assistance, helpful but marginal. He called for an international conference of advanced Western countries in January to coordinate assistance, but again he focused on the short-term humanitarian aid that seemed critical at the time.

On the day after Baker's speech, December 13, Yeltsin called Bush to advise him that other republics intended to join the commonwealth. Bush balanced this with a call to Gorbachev to ask his assessment of the internal situation. (On the day before they had also talked about nuclear weapons.) Baker departed the next day for consultations and on-the-spot observation of the situation in key republics and "any common entity" still headed by Gorbachev.

Baker was met in Moscow with a plea by Russia for diplomatic recognition of its independence (and that of Ukraine and Belarus) and in effect support for their commonwealth. Baker naturally did not commit himself or the United States.

In a highly unusual step, coincidental in time with Baker's visit but unrelated, the postcoup chief of what had been the KGB, Vadim Bakatin, called in Ambassador Strauss and, admitting elaborate Soviet bugging of the American Embassy chancery building under construction, presented the ambassador with blueprints and sample devices to permit undoing some of the damage, above all to emphasize the new desire for mutual trust. It was a remarkable closing page in the story of intelligence and counterintelligence duels between the two powers.

Even as Baker was arriving in Moscow, Yeltsin was further isolating Gorbachev, issuing decrees in effect abolishing the Foreign Ministry and Interior Ministry of the USSR, among the few remaining. Baker saw Shevardnadze, again briefly back as Gorbachev's foreign minister since November 19, as he was preparing to go to Brussels to attend the first meeting of the new North Atlantic Cooperation Council (NACC), an "outer" NATO body being established to provide a forum including the foreign ministers of the former Warsaw Pact bloc. The meeting took place, as scheduled, on December 20 with Baker there—but without Shevardnadze, who was told by Yeltsin not to go.

When Yeltsin received Baker on December 16 it was in the St. Catherine's Hall of the Kremlin, where Baker had on previous occasions met President Gorbachev. Moreover, Yeltsin had Marshal Shaposhnikov present as well, underlining that the Soviet defense minister was at his side. They discussed the political and economic situation and agreed on the need to ensure central control over nuclear weapons. When Baker subsequently met Gorbachev, it was a melancholy atmosphere, as the Soviet president was clearly no longer able to manage the course of events.

On December 21, the formation of a commonwealth embracing eleven of the twelve republics of the Soviet Union made clear the imminent demise of that entity. Within a few days the United States, still seeking to pursue a policy of differentiation, decided it would recognize and establish formal diplomatic relations with six of the twelve republics: Russia, Ukraine, Belarus, Kazakhstan, Kyrgyzstan, and Armenia while recognizing independence but withholding establishment of relations with the other six. Although there was a logic to this stand, it also had disadvantages. For one thing it seemed to give too much weight to the four countries having nuclear weapons on their territories—perhaps encouraging them to want to hold on to such a diplomatic asset and influencing others to seek to acquire such an advantage. For another thing, democratic standards were hard to measure; was Kazakhstan really more democratic than Uzbekistan? Any American diplomatic leverage in settling the Nagorno-Karabakh conflict was compromised by choosing Armenia and not Azerbaijan for favored relations. And more generally, most of the excluded republics were Muslim, even though that was not why they were excluded. So within weeks the policy would be abandoned and diplomatic relations established with all republics (except Georgia for a time during its authoritarian and isolationist phase).

Gorbachev's resignation on December 25 was taken as the effective end of the Soviet Union, and President Bush returned from Christmas at Camp David to give a formal address from the Oval Office in which he praised Mikhail Gorbachev's achievements and "sustained commitment to world peace." He also said that Gorbachev's "policies permitted the peoples of Russia and the other republics to cast aside decades of oppression and establish the foundations of freedom. His legacy guarantees him an honored place in history and provides a solid basis for the United States to work in equally constructive ways with his successors."

Bush welcomed the emergence of "the Commonwealth of Independent States" and of a "free, independent and democratic Russia, led by its courageous President Boris Yeltsin." He took the occasion to formally recognize and announce intention to establish diplomatic relations with Russia and the other five favored republics and announce mere recognition as independent states of the remaining six.[97]

In a separate statement Bush gave even greater recognition to Gorbachev's contributions, especially to ending global confrontation and the Cold War.[98] Former President Ronald Reagan also issued a statement saying Gorbachev "will live forever in history."

Thus even as Soviet internal policy was paralyzed by the struggle between Gorbachev and Yeltsin and the disintegration of central (Soviet) control in the months following the coup and countercoup, with a strong assist from the United States Gorbachev had still been able to take important foreign policy steps toward further normalizing and improving bilateral relations, toward resolution of the conflicts and tensions in Afghanistan, Cambodia, the Middle East, and the Caribbean, and not least to orchestrate significant parallel unilateral reductions in nuclear weapons. These nuclear reductions, important in their own right, also greatly facilitated defusing the potential problem of wide dispersal of nuclear weapons in the wake of the dissolution of the Soviet Union.

President Bush's statement on the occasion of President Gorbachev's resignation and the dissolution of the Soviet Union may be taken as the last formal act in the history of U.S.-Soviet relations. Two small but perhaps indicative events in the latter days of the year may also be worth noting. One was a Christmas reception at the Soviet Embassy in Washington on December 19, the first such official Soviet Christmas celebration ever—while at the same time the last reception ever in a *Soviet* Embassy in Washington.[99] The other event, also coincidentally related to the holiday season, was a New Year's celebration, with a Christmas-New Year's tree, held in the Kremlin on December 29 for more than one hundred presidents of large American companies, invited to Moscow in an effort to stimulate trade and investment by a Soviet government that no longer existed by the time they arrived. On this note, the last phase of U.S.-Soviet relations drew to an end.

---

97. "Address to the Nation on the Commonwealth of Independent States," December 25, 1991, *Presidential Documents*, vol. 27 (December 30, 1991), pp. 1883–85.

98. Ibid, p. 1883.

99. On this occasion I took my leave of Ambassador Viktor Komplektov, soon thereafter recalled to Moscow; we had known one another for thirty of the forty-five years of the Cold War.

# IV INTERACTIONS IN THE GLOBAL ARENA

# 12    The Evolving Strategic Relationship: Military Power, Arms Control, and Security

THE STRATEGIC and military relationship between the United States and the Soviet Union was a central consideration influencing policy throughout the Cold War. Its salience in the first several years of the 1980s was greater than usual. By the late 1980s, however, it had diminished greatly, and by 1989–91, was rapidly receding to a peripheral role. Strategic considerations influenced the transformation of political relations over this period, but ultimately political change dominated and transformed the strategic relationship.

In the early 1980s, threat assessments were an important policy consideration, and on both sides serious concern arose not only about the adversary's capabilities but also about his intentions. Negotiated arms control, the ameliorating palliative of the 1970s, was relegated by the Reagan administration to an essentially irrelevant sideline. Political tensions fed upon and in turn generated military effort and concerns. Yet by the late 1980s, Gorbachev's political, military, and arms control initiatives had reduced perceived threats and led to mutual security arrangements, including but not limited to traditional arms control measures, both bilaterally with the United States and multilaterally, which greatly alleviated security concerns even before the Cold War came to an end at the close of the decade.

The strategic relationship has been one important strand of the overall U.S.-Soviet interaction traced in some detail in the preceding chapters. There is no need to recapitulate all of those developments. It may, however, be useful to examine the motivating factors and role of the strategic military and security dimension of the relationship. This can most expeditiously and usefully be done through dividing the subject not into segments such as "military doctrine," "military programs," and "arms control," but into three successive periods: first, a combative unilateral pursuit of security dominated by Reagan's initiative, from 1981 to 1985; second, a period of transition to a more interactive détente in military strategic relationships from 1986 through 1989 in response to initiatives by Gorbachev; and finally a period of growing collaboration and dawning pursuit of common security in the context of the political changes ending the Cold War until the end of the Soviet Union, in 1990 and 1991 (and continuing thereafter in American-Russian relations).

## Strategic Autarky and Confrontation: 1981–85

As President Reagan entered office in 1981, his principal focus—in external and internal policy—was on making America "stand tall" again. One of the principal aims of his administration was to restore what was seen as a depleted and declining military posture to a robust and respected strength. Indeed, one of the first decisions of the administration was to sharply increase defense expenditures—a decision made even before military requirements had been addressed and before anyone knew what the increased expenditures would be used for.[1]

An exaggerated Soviet military threat was soon elaborated and emphasized in statements by top members of the administration, and Secretary of Defense Caspar Weinberger issued a dire detailed unclassified assessment, lavishly illustrated, called *Soviet Military Power*.[2] It presented an ominous picture of a massive Soviet military buildup, but without any indication of countervailing American or other Western military forces or programs, and with data selected and embellished to magnify the impression of a threat. The purpose was to rally public support for the American buildup.[3]

The program to "restore" American military strength, and the accompanying exaggeration of the Soviet military threat, had several causes and purposes. First, for Reagan in particular, it reflected a conviction that the United States had been on the wrong course ever since Nixon pursued détente, and Reagan ascribed not only such things as the Soviet intervention in Afghanistan but also Iran's humiliating year-long imprisonment of hostages from the American Embassy to U.S. failure to have kept up military strength. The

---

1. See the discussion in chapter 1.

2. Department of Defense, *Soviet Military Power* (September 1981), 99 pp. A second edition appeared in 1983, thereafter annually through 1990. Similar, but brief, references to the Soviet military threat also laced Secretary Weinberger's annual reports to the president and Congress.

3. This purpose more broadly affected policy as well. As Assistant Secretary of Defense Richard Perle, an inveterate opponent of arms control, candidly acknowledged in a later interview: "Democracies will not sacrifice to protect their security in the absence of a sense of danger. And every time we create the impression that we and the Soviets are cooperating and moderating the competition, we diminish that sense of apprehension." Roy Gutman, "The Nay-Sayer of Arms Control," *Newsday*, February 18, 1983, p. 6.

military buildup was intended to redress that state of affairs, but it was also intended to send a signal to the Soviet leaders, to U.S. allies, and to the American people that the new administration was not going to let itself be kicked around.

Reagan and Defense Secretary Weinberger referred on several occasions to a "decade of neglect" of American military power, clearly embracing the Nixon and Ford, as well as Democratic Carter, administrations.[4] One reason for this alleged and perceived neglect was believed to be the policy of détente and arms negotiation. The new approach was "confrontational" not because it posed immediate threats to the Soviet Union but because it radically reoriented American security priorities. It was designed to give priority to autarkic reliance on American military power (bolstered by a reinvigorated NATO alliance) rather than pursuit of negotiations, arms control, and cooperative security with the Soviet Union.

Throughout the four years of his first administration, Reagan successfully pressed his major military buildup—or, more accurately, his major increase in military expenditures. By 1985, the rate of increase could no longer be sustained, but Reagan seemed satisfied that strength had been restored. High expenditures continued, in all more than $2 trillion dollars in eight years, although the peak was passed after 1984. Yet the United States did not increase its advantage in missile warheads and ended up deploying only one-quarter of the number of MX missiles planned by the Carter administration. True, Reagan did build 100 B-1 bombers that Carter had canceled, but the aircraft never lived up to the expectations of its advocates. A large, and as it turned out temporary, increase was made in the size of the U.S. Navy (including bringing four World War II vintage battleships out of mothballs and at great expense modernizing them with missiles, before returning them to mothballs). But the fearful "window of vulnerability" depicted in 1980 was closed not by enhanced American defense capabilities or diminished Soviet ones but by the sober realism of the Scowcroft Commission in 1983.[5] The real military relationship remained stable. The United States was not so weak in 1980 as pictured, nor so much stronger by 1984 or 1988; what changed was the official rhetoric and the public impression.

The military buildup did have other effects. For one thing, it contributed mightily to the mountain of national debt—twice what had been accumulated by all thirty-nine predecessors to President Reagan, and to the United

---

4.  For example, Weinberger in his annual report issued in February 1985, though still pressing for a buildup, declared that "we have regained some of the ground lost during a decade of neglect," so that "America at mid-decade is strong and proud, a posture befitting our leadership role in the world." *Annual Report to the Congress, Secretary of Defense Caspar W. Weinberger, Fiscal Year 1986*, February 4, 1985, p. 14.

5.  See *Report of the President's Commission on Strategic Forces*, Washington, April 1983, 29 pp.

States becoming a debtor nation for the first time since 1917. Another unintended effect of the military buildup and accompanying talk about military superiority, along with the politically provocative rhetoric of confrontation, was its impact in Moscow. The Soviet leaders did not change their military effort to match it; indeed they continued a lower level of military buildup, which intelligence reassessment in 1983 showed had begun in 1975–76.[6] There was a modest increase from 1985 through 1988 (the DIA would say it started in 1983), but this reflected procurement programs decided upon earlier (and the increase remained far below the Soviet rate of buildup before 1976—and far below the rate of the American buildup from 1980 on).[7] The American buildup may have caused some delay in Gorbachev's launching a reduction in Soviet military spending and procurement, which began in earnest in 1989, but the Soviet Union did not reverse its plans and emulate the American buildup.

There were also elements in Moscow, especially in the intelligence and military establishments, which became very alarmed at apparent American military intentions. As early as 1981, Yury Andropov (then chief of the KGB) initiated a special intelligence alert to monitor signs of a possible American preparation to launch a nuclear attack on the Soviet Union, an alert intensified in 1983 and ended only in 1984.[8] Marshal Nikolai Ogarkov, chief of the General Staff, led a campaign for a more intensive Soviet military buildup until he was removed from his key position in Moscow in September 1984. Neither

6.  Soviet military spending from the early 1970s to 1983 was estimated to have grown at about a 4 percent to 5 percent increase each year. In 1983, the U.S. intelligence agencies concluded that from 1976 to 1983 the actual rate of increase had been only about 2 percent a year, and procurement of weapons had been level (over the next year or two, the revised estimate put the beginning of this reduced rate of growth at 1975 and revised the growth of procurement to between 0 percent and 1 percent). See "CIA Briefing Paper Entitled 'USSR: Economic Trends, and Policy Developments,'" in *Allocation of Resources in the Soviet Union and China—1983*, Hearings before the Subcommittee on International Trade, Finance, and Security Economics of the Joint Economic Committee, 98 Cong. 1 sess. (Washington: Government Printing Office, 1984), pt. 9, p. 306; and the discussion in Raymond L. Garthoff, *Détente and Confrontation: American-Soviet Relations from Nixon to Reagan*, rev. ed. (Brookings, 1994), chapter 22.

7.  Later intelligence estimates through the decade indicated a slight rise to about 3 percent growth overall a year, and 3 percent for procurement, for the period 1985–88. The year 1989 marked a clear decline by about 6 percent, followed in 1990 by another 6 percent decline, with reduction by about 10 percent each year in procurement, and a continued decline in 1991 (and an even sharper reduction after the breakup of the Soviet Union). For the possible increase in 1983–84, the modest increase in 1985–88, and the decline in 1989–90 see the later annual issues of the annual *Allocation of Resources* series: pt. 10 (1985), pp. 52–56; pt. 11 (1986), pp. 33, 36; pt. 12 (1988), pp. 27–29; pt. 13 (1989), pp. 23, 78; pt. 14 (1990), pp. 57–60, 125–128; pt. 15 (1991), pp. 6, 15, 39–42; and a successor publication, *Global Economic and Technological Change* (GPO, 1991), pp. 23, 194–95.

8.  See the discussion in chapter 3.

country's leadership wanted to press confrontation, however, and fortunately no crisis arose that might have posed much greater dangers in those years.

The Soviet perception of an American threat, even though a misperception, was buttressed by the official American exaggerations of a Soviet threat. Their perception was that the United States was using the "myth of a Soviet threat" to justify a militant American military buildup. This view, not entirely inaccurate, was of course self-serving in that it exonerated Soviet contributions to the arms race. But it also made it more difficult for the Soviet leaders to recognize the role of their own actions in stimulating those of the adversary. Each side tended to assume, and see, the worst motivation by the other, to justify its own actions and deny any justification to the other side, and to discount and disbelieve expressions of concern by the other. Moreover, much of the threat inflation, on both sides, was unconscious, and some of it stemmed from cautious, incomplete, or faulty intelligence.[9] This problem was endemic throughout the Cold War but was aggravated by the Reagan administration's escalation of high-level statements (and a related public campaign) exaggerating the Soviet threat, and by the Soviet response.[10]

9. An amusing example was the use by Soviet military intelligence (GRU), in a secret briefing for senior Warsaw Pact officials, of a purloined copy of the U.S. manufacturer's hyped promotional film on the capabilities of the American *Tomahawk* sea-launched cruise missile (SLCM). Whether the GRU accepted the exaggerated capabilities of the system shown in the film, or was cynically using it for its own purposes, this incident illustrates the reciprocal competitive generation of threats. Information from a senior Soviet military intelligence veteran.

10. On the most general level, statements by President Reagan alleging Soviet military superiority, and by other senior officials alleging dangerous Soviet intentions and capabilities, for example, a window of Soviet opportunity to attack owing to American vulnerability, were inherited from long-standing hard-line critics, such as the Committee on the Present Danger, of several administrations. The claims of a relentless 5 percent annual increase in Soviet military spending, which originated in overcorrection of intelligence estimates in 1976, as noted above was finally found to have been in error all that time (quietly disclosed by CIA testimony to Congress in the fall of 1983). Estimates of Soviet military manpower in Europe, a major issue in the negotiations for mutual and balanced force reductions (MBFR) for years, never publicly corrected, stemmed in part from an intelligence error in assuming 95 percent manning levels when the average was about 85 percent. Soviet chemical warfare stocks overall, and deployments in Eastern Europe, were greatly overestimated, also an error never acknowledged. The attribution of a greater range to the Tu-22M Backfire medium bomber than it had, which underlay the American insistence on counting the airplane as a strategic intercontinental bomber in SALT and START since 1975, was finally quietly acknowledged to have been in error. The same was true of an overestimation of accuracy of the SS-19 ICBM, also a technical intelligence error owing to lack of data, which was finally quietly corrected long after having contributed to the scare over the window of vulnerability. These examples are only illustrative—but none was corrected in open publications such as *Soviet Military Power*.

   A later study by the General Accounting Office based on wide access to classified material concluded that in the 1980s the Department of Defense deliberately engaged

Reagan's emphasis on unilateral American pursuit of security did not include innovative military strategy. The strategic targeting doctrines adopted in the Carter administration were continued.[11] In keeping with Reagan's general approach on reducing the vulnerability of America, civil defense was given a substantial boost in 1982 but soon receded to its customary low profile. Perhaps the most important effort of such strategic elaboration was stimulation of alarm in the Soviet military leadership. There was also a contributing design in both the overall buildup and some specific aspects and strategic conceptions, including the naval buildup and "maritime strategy"; that design was an effort to lead or even compel the Soviet Union to spend itself into the ground. In the words of the classified (but leaked) Defense Guidance in 1982, the United States should develop weapons that were "difficult for the Soviets to counter, impose disproportionate costs, open up new areas of major military competition and obsolesce previous Soviet investment."[12] That call to stimulate an arms race with emphasis on high technology in new areas of competition where the United States had a lead included, as early as 1982, developing "space-based weapons systems," including antisatellite (ASAT) weapons and after 1983 space-based antiballistic missile (ABM) systems.

By the mid-1980s, the increasing cost to the United States of the overall military buildup led to its tapering off. Nonetheless, the idea of channeling the arms race into areas of American advantage remained and as late as 1990 was elaborated into what was called a conception of "competitive strategies" to maximize deterrence and ensure that American "enduring strengths are aligned against enduring Soviet weaknesses."[13]

What about arms control? Strategic arms limitation had in many ways been a key element in the development of détente from 1969 to 1972, and the fate of both remained closely tied through 1979. Both arms control and détente had been placed in suspension in 1980 by the United States.

President Reagan's gut attitude toward international arms control in 1981 was not very different from his negative sentiment toward domestic gun control. Even his attitude toward negotiation on arms control was extremely wary. If the communist leaders of the Soviet Union could not be trusted, were bound to cheat, and regarded treaties as piecrusts to be broken, why negotiate with them at all? Moreover, he was steeped in the common Midwestern view

in a pattern of exaggeration of Soviet capabilities, deception, and misrepresentation of cost and performance of American systems in order to gain congressional authorization and appropriation for desired military programs. See Tim Weiner, "Military Accused of Lies Over Arms," *New York Times*, June 28, 1993, p. A10.

11. See the discussion in chapter 1.

12. Cited in Richard Halloran, "Pentagon Draws Up First Strategy for Fighting a Long Nuclear War," *New York Times*, May 30, 1982, p. 12.

13. *Annual Report to the President and Congress, Dick Cheney, Secretary of Defense,* January 1990, p. 1.

that Americans were too gullible in dealings with Europeans—to say nothing of crafty communists—so the United States would probably lose its "made in the U.S.A." shirts. He believed Presidents Nixon, Ford, and Carter had succumbed to Moscow's blandishments at the cost of American security.

Reagan decided early in his administration not to ratify what he had earlier called the "fatally flawed" SALT II Treaty, signed by President Carter in June 1979. But he went much further. He also did not try to amend it and was flagrantly uninterested in resuming the SALT negotiations. Senior members of his administration made clear that priority would be given to building up American military power, and then perhaps to negotiating arms limitations— from a position of strength.

The Soviet leaders had expected the Reagan administration to take a tough stand on SALT II. They braced themselves for expected demands for renegotiation. At first they tried to discourage anticipated attempts to amend the treaty by emphasizing that it was already the result of balanced compromises by both sides and that, as a solemnly signed treaty, it should not be reopened. Then they began to stress the value of the treaty, without ruling out some additions or changes. But they had no response to the lack of interest in any SALT treaty displayed by the new administration, even though initially it decided to take no actions contrary to the unratified treaty (and the expired SALT Interim Agreement of 1972) for the time being.

Throughout most of 1981 Ambassador Anatoly Dobrynin, in private meetings with Secretary of State Haig, kept urging a resumption of the strategic arms talks. Haig would only repeat the need first for Soviet restraint in the Third World (and in Poland).[14] When finally the United States showed an interest in negotiation, it was at first only in the field of intermediate-range nuclear forces (INF), and the reason for that American interest was the rising public opposition in Western Europe to the planned deployment of U.S. missiles. Only by at least appearing to work for arms limitation on a negotiating "track" could public support in the West be maintained so that NATO could go forward on a second, a deployment track established by the 1979 NATO alliance decision. And when the United States was ready to resume strategic arms talks (redubbed strategic arms reduction talks, or START, to stress reduction—and to shed the old acronym), it was again obvious that it was attempting to head off rising American public support for a freeze on the deployment of all nuclear weapons.

The INF and START negotiations from 1981 through 1983 have been well-chronicled in detail[15] and are reviewed briefly below. The internal policy

---

14. See Alexander M. Haig, Jr., *Caveat: Realism, Reagan, and Foreign Policy* (Macmillan, 1984), pp. 102–09.

15. See Strobe Talbott, *Deadly Gambits: The Reagan Administration and the Stalemate in Nuclear Arms Control* (Alfred A. Knopf, 1984).

debates and decisions within the Reagan administration were more revealing, and ultimately more significant, than the negotiations between the United States and the Soviet Union. Not only was there constant bureaucratic infighting, but the general policy line of the Reagan administration and its leadership style ensured that the American position precluded agreement.

In the INF negotiations the Reagan administration opted for the propaganda high ground by proposing a "zero option" for intermediate-range missiles. Although this proposal shored up political support in NATO countries for continuing preparations for deployment, the principal purpose of the administration, it also killed the prospect for serious negotiation and agreement. Although on the surface the proposition was equitable and admirable (in aiming at "eliminating a whole class of armaments"), it was heavily loaded to Soviet disadvantage. Though it would have meant NATO would not proceed with the newly planned deployment of 572 U.S. missiles in Europe, it would have meant the Soviets' not only eliminating all their recent deployments of SS-20 missiles but also rolling back twenty years of strategic history and dismantling hundreds of older Soviet intermediate-range missiles deployed since the late 1950s. It would also have limited only land-based missiles, exempting all sea-based missiles and aircraft, so that the United States would have retained the option of an unlimited increase in those systems capable of striking the Soviet Union. Further, by restricting the proposed constraints to U. S. and Soviet systems, all British and French nuclear strike systems were excluded. Not only would existing missile and bomber systems be untouched, but future expansion would be unlimited, and announced plans of the British and French for deploying warheads with multiple independently targeted reentry vehicles (MIRVs) would make their forces larger in number of warheads than the Soviet INF missile forces and give them more than double the number of planned American missile warheads. Finally, the U.S. and NATO proposal called for limiting all Soviet intermediate-range land-based missiles wherever deployed, not just those facing Europe. In short, on all counts the proposal was loaded to Western advantage and Soviet disadvantage, and it was clearly not a basis for negotiation aimed at reaching agreement.

The American policy community (with the possible significant exception of President Reagan himself) well understood the nonnegotiability of the zero option when it was proposed. Indeed, some civilian leaders in the Pentagon and hard-liners in the White House had successfully pushed its adoption for that very reason.[16]

---

16. For the most complete review of the INF negotiations see ibid., pp. 21–206. See also Jonathan Haslam, *The Soviet Union and the Politics of Nuclear Weapons in Europe, 1969–87* (Cornell University Press, 1990), pp. 106–40; and Paul H. Nitze, *From Hiroshima to Glasnost* (Grove Weidenfeld, 1989), pp. 366–98.

Secretary of State Haig opposed the zero option on the grounds that, as he put it in his memoir, "proposal of the Zero Option would, as it has, generate the suspicion that

The reasons for the failure of the INF negotiations, however, went deeper than an American position tailored to be unacceptable to the Soviet Union. The basic interest of NATO in American INF deployments in the first place had been to ensure a coupling of U.S. conventional and tactical nuclear forces in Europe with U.S. intercontinental nuclear forces. For that purpose, *some* U.S. deployment was needed. To be sure, the zero option itself violated that premise, and that fact was troubling to some NATO strategic analysts. But since the real purpose, and the only realistic outcome, of advancing the zero option was to preclude agreement and to ensure deployment, that theoretical inconsistency did not trouble many people. But the Soviet aim in INF was to head off any deployment of U.S. intermediate-range missiles in Europe, inasmuch as they would constitute strategic weapons against targets in the Soviet Union itself. Thus the aims of the two sides were irreconcilable, even if moderate positions had been advanced. The Soviets offered increasingly substantial reductions in their missile force in exchange for nondeployment of the American missiles, eventually offering to reduce the number of SS-20s facing Europe by nearly half and to reduce the total number of missile launchers to less than one-fourth what it was or had been before the new SS-20 deployments. That would reduce the number of warheads to less than half the current number, a level that again would be lower than it was before the SS-20 deployment began. But by 1983 the United States was only interested in proceeding with deployment, not in reducing Soviet forces, even if that resulted in a more favorable overall balance.

When the NATO deployment began in November 1983, the Soviet Union broke off the talks. The Soviet and American (and British and French) nuclear forces remained to be taken into account in unilateral decisions and in possible future negotiations.

START, too, was fated to fail in this period. Although each side initially took a position loaded to its advantage, that could have reflected bargaining tactics. There was no fundamental incompatibility in the aims of the two sides comparable to that in the INF talks, although there were other heavy impediments to successful negotiation. First, there was the legacy of SALT II. In framing an arms control position, the Reagan administration intentionally ignored the SALT II limitations and set out to do better for the United States.

---

the United States was only interested in a frivolous propaganda exercise, or worse, that it was disingenuously engaging in arms negotiations simply as a cover for a desire to build up its nuclear arsenal." Haig, *Caveat*, p. 229.

Ken Adelman, later director of the Arms Control and Disarmament Agency, in 1981 attended (as a stand-in for UN Ambassador Jeane Kirkpatrick) the NSC meeting that led Reagan to decide on the zero option. He has stated that the deciding factor was a disingenuous suggestion by Secretary Weinberger (who had advanced the zero option because he was sure the Soviet side would reject it) that the president might win the Nobel Peace Prize for the zero option. See Kenneth L. Adelman, *The Great Universal Embrace: Arms Summitry—A Skeptic's Account* (Simon and Schuster, 1989), p. 240.

Since the SALT II provisions represented the results of seven years of hard bargaining, it was unlikely that the Soviet Union would make appreciably greater concessions. Nevertheless, the United States proposed deeper reductions, skewed in a fashion that would eviscerate the heart of the Soviet strategic force, entailing a reduction by two-thirds in Soviet large missiles. Although overall equal levels would nominally be equitable, the more detailed subceilings bore much more heavily on the Soviet forces. Even more important, none of the planned major improvements to the U.S. strategic force—the large MX intercontinental ballistic missile (ICBM) with multiple independently targeted reentry vehicles (MIRVs), the B-1 bomber, the Trident submarine-launched ballistic missiles (SLBMs) and submarine force—would have been banned or even curtailed. While the Soviet Union was being asked to give up most of its best forces, the United States could modernize its best forces and slough off older systems planned for retirement in any case.[17]

The Soviet approach, while also slanted in its favor, attempted to preserve and build on the foundation of SALT II. In effect, the Soviets attempted to negotiate SALT III, proposing sizable reductions from the SALT II ceilings. (The basic limit of 1,800 strategic nuclear delivery vehicles was close to the 1,800–2,000 level proposed by the Carter administration in March 1977—and the 1,900 level proposed by the Nixon administration in August 1970—although other terms of the proposal differed.)

START did not begin until mid-1982. By the summer of 1983 both sides had made some modifications in their positions, but the gap remained very great.[18] In particular, the United States was not ready to accept curtailment of its buildup of counterforce capabilities comparable to the drastic reductions sought in Soviet counterforce capabilities. Although the U.S. proposals were nominally equal, they would have applied unequally. For example, the proposed limit of 5,000 missile warheads for each side would have meant a sizable and equitable cut of about one-third in the arsenals of both sides. But a subceiling of 2,500 warheads on land-based missiles, and further sublimits of 210 on MX-sized ICBMs (for example, the Soviet SS-18 and SS-19 and U.S. MX) and of 110 on very large ICBMs (the Soviet SS-18), would have meant a cut of more than half in Soviet ICBM warheads and two-thirds in SS-18 and SS-19 warheads, while the United States could have deployed additional ICBM warheads, including the then-planned 100 MX missiles. Moreover, all other U.S. strategic modernization programs could have continued: Trident II SLBMs, bomber-based ALCMs, submarine-based sea-launched cruise missiles

---

17. See Talbott, *Deadly Gambits*, pp. 233–76. Haig admitted that the U.S. START proposal was "a non-negotiable package . . . a two-faced proposal which was clearly going to fall of its own weight and did." See Roy Gutman, "Bad Tidings: The World According to Haig," an interview with the former secretary of state, *Newsday Magazine*, August 12, 1984, p. 16; and Haig, *Caveat*, p. 223.

18. Talbott, *Deadly Gambits*, pp. 277–342.

(SLCMs), and the Pershing II medium-range ballistic missile (MRBM) and ground-launched cruise missile (GLCM) European-based systems. Overall, though the proposal would have alleviated the vulnerability of American land-based intercontinental missiles, it would have greatly increased the vulnerability of Soviet land-based missiles. As a Soviet general remarked to me in 1983, "You [the United States] want to solve *your* vulnerability problem by making *our* forces vulnerable."[19] And he was right.

The natural conservatism on both sides, evident throughout the SALT negotiations of the 1970s, remained. Both tried to get maximum reductions in the forces of the other side, but without being willing to make comparable sacrifices in their own forces and capabilities. Both were wary about constraining future options. In the past that contradiction had been resolved by reaching agreements that did not seriously reduce the strategic forces of either side. Critics of the SALT I Interim Agreement and SALT II Treaty were correct in saying they did not do enough to curb improvements or to reduce military forces. U.S. attempts to impose drastic changes on the Soviet military force, while keeping its own intact and enhanced, were obviously unacceptable to the Soviet Union. And Soviet attempts to do the same to the United States, or, failing that, again to make relatively larger but still ineffective cuts on both sides, largely for cosmetic effects in order to reach an agreement, were not acceptable to the Reagan administration (although they probably would have been to any of its three predecessors).

Indeed, the interest of the Reagan administration as a whole (and it was rent by disagreements among its chief components) in strategic arms limitation remained very uncertain. The argument continued to be made, and perhaps even believed by some (including President Reagan), that only as American military power was "restored" (that is, expanded and enhanced) would the Soviets have an incentive to negotiate seriously (that is, to accede to U.S. terms). That approach was either naive or feckless.

When the Soviet leaders decided to break off the INF talks at the end of 1983, they also suspended the START negotiations. The reason was a conviction that, after a year and a half of nonstart START, the United States was not seriously interested in negotiating a mutually acceptable agreement. They also believed that the shock in the West of ending the two negotiations would cause a reappraisal and might jar the United States into undertaking a more serious negotiating effort. Instead, the Reagan administration was able to claim that it remained as interested in arms limitations as ever and that the Soviets were solely to blame for the breakdown caused by their walkout. Whatever the merits of the respective charges, the U.S. position seemed more justified in the West because the Soviet Union had walked out.

---

19. Interview with Colonel General Nikolai F. Chervov, chief of the Treaty and Legal Department of the General Staff (responsible for arms control), Moscow, September 29, 1983.

In another important area of arms control, control over nuclear weapons testing, public opinion in the West was more indifferent and the Reagan administration ignored the limited constraints of the Threshold Test Ban Treaty (limiting tests to under 150 kilotons) signed in 1974 and the treaty on Peaceful Nuclear Explosions signed in 1976 and did not submit them for ratification. (President Carter had also not done so, because he hoped to negotiate a comprehensive test ban, CTB.) Reagan rebuffed Soviet attempts to resume negotiations on a CTB, suspended in 1980, and indeed in July 1982 he took a firm decision—for the first time since the Eisenhower administration—to oppose a CTB.

An important new element entered the picture in 1983, one that would cast a long shadow over all subsequent strategic arms negotiations and possible limitations. President Reagan, in a dramatic and unexpected embrace of the concept of strategic ballistic missile defense in a speech in March 1983, resurrected a whole additional dimension of the arms race.[20] While both sides had continued to conduct research and development work on ABM systems, the ABM Treaty of 1972, of indefinite duration, had for a decade successfully removed uncertainties arising from strategic defense from the mutual deterrent arms equation. Suddenly it was back. While the technology was uncertain and distant, the very idea of Star Wars, as the president's idea was quickly dubbed, captured wide public attention. It also stirred considerable disquiet. The president's initial idea was to substitute assured defense for deterrence by assured retaliation. Later discussion of his concept, officially termed the strategic defense initiative (SDI), blurred this aim and tended instead to stress a high-priority research and development of exotic ballistic missile defense systems that might complement, rather than replace, strategic offensive forces intended to deter.[21] The concept, and the concrete technical schemes envisaged, remained uncertain. Nevertheless, the United States soon (in 1984) launched a $26 billion, five-year SDI research and development program.

Many in the United States (and in Western Europe) questioned the desirability, as well as the technical prospect, of a pursuit of strategic defense. The very idea challenged the underpinnings of mutual deterrence, which had been the foundation for U.S. and NATO policy long before SALT. Moreover, while the administration argued (not completely convincingly) that its whole

20.  President Ronald Reagan, "National Security. Address to the Nation," March 23, 1983, *Weekly Compilation of Presidential Documents*, vol. 19 (March 28, 1983), pp. 442–48. (Hereafter *Presidential Documents*.)
     See the discussion in chapter 3.

21.  President Reagan issued a National Security Decision Directive (NSDD)–172 on "presenting the Strategic Defense Initiative" on May 30, 1985. This document in fourteen single-spaced pages offered a detailed rationale and discussion of the strategic context and objective of the SDI but straddled the issue of deterrence versus defense. Secret. (Declassified November 27, 1992.)

development program would be compatible with the ABM Treaty, no one could dispute that the avowed purpose of the SDI was to find effective means of ballistic missile defense, the deployment of which (and at least some testing) would require amendment or abrogation of the ABM Treaty.

Soviet reaction was strongly negative. The Soviet leader, Yury Andropov, personally responded to the Star Wars speech with a resounding denunciation of the reopening of the issue of ballistic missile defense and reaffirmation of mutual deterrence and the ABM Treaty. Soviet scientists, like most American ones, saw no prospect of a truly effective defense against an enemy first strike, as President Reagan had described his goal. What they did see was the possibility, and American lead, in developing a partially effective defense that, while not protection against the full force of an enemy first strike, its avowed purpose, might be considered adequate against a degraded *retaliatory* strike. Thus the SDI complemented suspiciously well what they already saw as a concerted long-term American plan to develop a first-strike capability.

The SDI was thus seen as an ominous alternative to arms control, predicated on removing the most effective existing arms limitation agreement, the ABM Treaty, and prejudicing the prospects for any strategic offensive arms limitation.[22] It also contributed to the Soviet decision to abandon the START charade in November 1983.

---

22. Besides a large volume of published Soviet commentary, several important studies were prepared under the auspices of the Committee of Soviet Scientists in Defense of Peace, Against the Nuclear Threat, by a study group cochaired by Academician Roald Z. Sagdeyev, director of the Institute of Space Research of the Academy of Sciences, and Dr. Andrei A. Kokoshin, deputy director of the Institute of USA and Canada, and composed of a number of leading scientists and some senior military consultants. Their first report was drafted in 1983, but not published until April 1984 (in only 170 copies); see *Strategicheskiye i mezhdunarodno-politicheskiye posledstviya sozdaniya kosmicheskoi protivoraketnoi sistemy s ispol'zovaniyem oruzhiya napravlennoi peredachi energii* (Strategic and International Political Consequences of the Creation of a Space-Based Anti-Ballistic Missile System Utilizing Directed Energy Weapons) (Moscow, 1984), 43 pp. Two later studies were also issued, with wider circulation. See *Udarnyye kosmicheskiye vooruzheniya i mezhdunarodnaya bezopasnost'* (Space Strike Weapons and International Security) (Moscow: Novosti, 1985), 75 pp.; and *Shirokomasshtabnaya protivoraketnaya sistema i mezhdunarodnaya bezopasnost'* (A Large-Scale Anti-Ballistic Missile System and International Security) (Moscow: Novosti, 1986), 91 pp.

In February 1985, the KGB headquarters (the Center) also sent a Top Secret message to key stations abroad, including London. Oleg Gordievsky, the designated deputy chief of the KGB station (*rezidentura*) in London, supplied that message to British Intelligence, and it has now been published. It showed that Soviet concerns over use of the SDI to develop offensive as well as defensive arms were genuine, whether realistic or not. It also showed keen interest in any information on possibilities for inclusion of elements of the SDI and antisatellite arms (ASAT) in arms negotiations. Finally, the KGB report also stated that with the aid of the widescale ABM system that the SDI program was designed to create, "the Americans expect to be able to ensure that United States territory is completely invulnerable to Soviet intercontinental ballistic

Why did President Reagan, in an unusually personal decision, launch the strategic defense initiative? There had been interest in some quarters in the Pentagon in resuscitating ballistic missile defense and in antisatellite weapons and even space-borne weapons. The impetus for Reagan's decision, however, came from a small coterie of military-industrial scientists, most prominently Edward Teller.[23] But most important of all was Ronald Reagan's own vision.

The idea of unleashing American technological genius to provide a total defense of the country appealed to Reagan's nostalgic, even atavistic, deep-seated desire to see America again invulnerable, self-reliant, freed from the shackles of interdependence, with its fate no longer tied to mutual security, to mutual vulnerability through mutual deterrence. President Reagan's dream was indeed, as he proclaimed at the outset and often thereafter, even when only he still believed it, that his SDI would make nuclear weapons "impotent and obsolete." His commitment was not based on science but on faith, so scientific-technical and military-technical arguments (to say nothing of political-military ones) were irrelevant and his vision unchangeable. The vision was a mirage. But it had a significant impact.

The SDI alarmed the Soviet political and military leaders because it threatened to reverse the trend toward reducing military outlays and curtailing the arms race. Nonetheless, they did not respond by adopting new programs including major increases in military spending nor did they abandon arms reduction negotiations. Although they studied possible countermeasures to the

---

missiles, which would enable the United States to count on mounting a nuclear attack on the Soviet Union with impunity." See Christopher Andrew and Oleg Gordievsky, *Instructions from the Centre: Top Secret Files on KGB Foreign Operations 1975–1985* (London: Hodder and Stoughton, 1991), pp. 106–115, quotation on p. 112.

At the same time, while taking the threat of the SDI very seriously, the KGB was also wary (and eager to obtain any information) about whether it was a giant "sting" operation, in Soviet parlance "a large-scale disinformation operation of the Reagan administration calculated to obtain, in exchange for abandoning [the program,] concessions from the USSR in the field of nuclear weapons." (Ibid., p. 114.) This suspicion is of particular interest, even though it is not known whether the KGB obtained any information to support that possibility. It was disclosed in the United States in 1993, however, that while the SDI was a serious program, there was a highly secret disinformation effort undertaken in conjunction with the program in an attempt to mislead the Soviet Union into massive outlays against unreal threats. Although some of the reports of manipulating American SDI tests for that purpose may not have been valid, Secretary of Defense Les Aspin after an internal investigation did confirm that "there was a deception program aimed at the Soviet Union," part of a "category of highly secret activities called special access programs." Transcript of Secretary of Defense Les Aspin's press conference of September 9, 1993, p. 3; and see R. Jeffrey Smith, "3 'Star Wars' Tests Rigged, Aspin Says; Scheme to Mislead Soviets Went Awry," *Washington Post*, September 10, 1993, p. A19.

23. The best account is found in William J. Broad, *Teller's War: The Top-Secret Story Behind the Star Wars Deception* (Simon and Schuster, 1992).

SDI, the American program never came close enough to fruition to even permit identifying the nature of the strategic defense system that would need to be countered, so that actual Soviet military spending was little affected. The studies by Soviet scientists had also led to the conclusion not to attempt to emulate the SDI program beyond the existing research effort. The decision to proceed in the START negotiations and to agree on strategic arms reductions was difficult but was made. Expectations that some American advocates of the SDI may have had that the initiative would bleed the Soviet economy were not met. Nonetheless, it did add to growing tensions, and to growing Soviet suspicions of American aims, and made more difficult the pursuit of arms control and normalization of relations.

Coincident with the drive for the SDI and rising inclination to abandon the unsigned but observed SALT II strategic arms limitations was a mounting campaign accusing the Soviet Union of violating several arms control agreements.[24] First advocated without success by hard-liners who temporarily were in charge of the Arms Control and Disarmament Agency (ACDA) in 1981, the autonomous General Advisory Committee on Arms Control and Disarmament (GAC), similarly dominated by hard-liners with access to classified information, prepared a massive compilation of charges titled "A Quarter Century of Soviet Compliance Practices under Arms Control Commitments: 1958–1983," submitted to the president on December 2, 1983. Right-wing senators and press commentators pressed for months for its release, and Congress finally succeeded in amending the Defense Authorization Act passed in October 1984 to call on the president to release the GAC report, at least in a "sanitized" unclassified version, and he did so that month. It was a mish-mash of charges, some serious, many ambiguous, and not a few frivolous or false. But even earlier, Senators Jesse Helms and James McClure had succeeded—in the aftermath of the KAL-007 incident—in amending the ACDA authorization act in December 1983 to require the president to submit a "report on the record of the compliance or noncompliance" of the Soviet Union to existing arms control agreements to which it was a party. The "President's Report to the Congress on Soviet Noncompliance with Arms Control Agreements" was submitted on January 23, 1984. While it was far more modest than the GAC Report, it did raise seven cases of "serious concern" about Soviet compliance (in addition to gratuitously being titled a report on Soviet "noncompliance").

The Defense Authorization Act (for fiscal year 1985) passed in October 1984, besides its provision on the release of the GAC report, called for another presidential report, which was submitted on February 1, 1985. The next Defense Authorization Act, passed in November, mandated annual reports by the

---

24. For the best overall discussion of the issue of compliance, including a detailed review of most of the concrete issues raised in the 1980s, see the report of an expert working group sponsored by Stanford University and Global Outlook. Gloria Duffy, ed., *Compliance and the Future of Arms Control* (Ballinger, 1988).

president on Soviet compliance to begin in December 1985, so the practice was thereafter institutionalized. (All of these presidential reports, through 1991, continued to be prejudicially titled reports on "Soviet noncompliance.") The February 1985 report reiterated the seven charges from 1984 and added six more, although many were admittedly "ambiguous," "suggesting" possible intentions to violate, or with information "insufficient to assess compliance." But the overall impact, as intended, was to raise doubts about Soviet trustworthiness.

Not least among the pernicious effects of these reports on noncompliance was the degrading of a serious matter into a politicized exercise in Cold War polemics. For example, one of the issues raised in 1985 and thereafter was alleged Soviet violation of the 1963 Limited Test Ban Treaty. Some Soviet underground nuclear tests over the years had vented radioactive matter into the atmosphere, which had been detected beyond the border of Soviet airspace. Although technically that was a violation of the 1963 treaty, when the treaty was negotiated it had been explicitly recognized that some unintentional venting might well occur. There was no dispute that the Soviet Union had never tested in the atmosphere, which would constitute a direct and deliberate violation, over the more than twenty years the treaty had been in effect. Moreover, while the United States had (with airborne sensors much improved since 1963) detected radioactive matter beyond Soviet air borders, Soviet airborne sensors may not have, so Soviet denials might in many cases have been genuine, even if American charges also were. Finally, the United States had also unintentionally vented radioactive matter into the atmosphere, which had on some occasions been detected beyond U.S. airspace borders; indeed, it was the first country to have done so (in 1964). Thus while the Soviet Union had technically violated the nuclear testing treaty, so had the United States.[25] Yet none of these considerations was even mentioned in the president's reports on Soviet noncompliance.

One unfortunate effect of the administration's hatchet job on Soviet noncompliance was that the few deliberate Soviet violations were mixed in with the ambiguous and contrived allegations of violation, and attempts to deal with them were undercut by the devaluation of the process of assessment of compliance, negotiation on clarification of the issues, and encouragement of discontinuance of any actions inconsistent with agreements.

The most clear-cut case of a violation was the Krasnoyarsk radar, a large phased-array radar discovered under construction near Krasnoyarsk in central Siberia in American reconnaissance satellite photography in July 1983. The Krasnoyarsk radar, though not an ABM radar, was an early-warning radar subject to a corollary constraint under the ABM Treaty limiting the deployment of such radars to locations on the periphery of the national territory and oriented outward. Evidently filling a gap in Soviet early-warning coverage to the northeast, its location far inland in Siberia was not consistent with the

---

25. See Duffy, *Compliance*, pp. 52–54.

treaty. The Soviet response, however, was to claim that the radar was for space-tracking, allowed under the treaty at any location. Though not convincing, the Soviet position could also not be demonstrably refuted. Moreover, some in the American administration claimed that the radar was part of a "pattern" of preparation for possible Soviet breakout from the ABM Treaty, and even that it was an ABM radar. With successive reports on Soviet noncompliance, this latter argument was elaborated, with the transparent objective of preparing the ground for possible American abandonment of the ABM Treaty. The Soviet decision to place an early-warning radar near Krasnoyarsk was taken for reasons of cost rather than to prepare for breakout from the ABM Treaty, but it was a deliberate violation.[26]

The compliance issue rested on understandable concerns in a situation in which security rested on arms control agreements between untrusted and untrusting adversaries even to a modest extent. Yet issues had arisen in the 1960s and 1970s and been adequately resolved. There were a few clear violations—on both sides, and a larger number of cases of ambiguities and exploitation of ambiguities and loopholes, which fed these concerns on both sides. Concern was, however, magnified in the Reagan administration by the combination of a negative attitude toward arms control and toward existing arms control restraints (especially the ABM Treaty after 1983), and a confrontational posture toward the Soviet Union. This confrontational stance and charges of violations were reciprocated by the Soviet leadership in the first half of the 1980s.[27]

---

26. The decision was taken in September 1979 by the Politburo, amending earlier plans that would have placed the radar at Norilsk, a treaty-compliant location. The decision was made deliberately, for reasons of cost, on urging by Defense Minister Dmitry Ustinov, despite objections by the chief of the General Staff, Marshal Nikolai Ogarkov, and his deputy General Sergei Akhromeyev, who argued that the decision would give the United States grounds for charging a violation. See Marshal S. F. Akhromeyev and G. M. Kornienko, *Glazami marshala i diplomata* (Through the Eyes of a Marshal and a Diplomat) (Moscow: Mezhdunarodnyye otnosheniya, 1992), p. 256, supplemented by interviews.

27. Although many of the Soviet charges of violation were clearly tit-for-tat reprisals, and no more serious than many of the American charges, some had merit. Ironically, the same provision of the ABM Treaty giving rise to the controversy over the Krasnoyarsk radar raises a serious question about the consistency with the treaty of two large American phased-array radars deployed in Thule, Greenland, and Fylingdales Moor, England, as replacements for earlier mechanically steered radars located there. See Duffy, *Compliance*, pp. 89–103.

Arguably, the American SDI program was the greatest violation of all. Certainly in an American court of law anticipatory breach of contract is judicially actionable, and the stated purpose of the SDI program in the 1980s was to develop an effective nationwide defense against ballistic missiles so that it could be deployed, an action not consistent with the ABM Treaty under any interpretation. Several concrete aspects of the SDI program provoked Soviet charges of violation, and some may have been. See ibid., pp. 113–30.

In the fall of 1984, partly in response to a Soviet initiative to open talks to ban space weaponry, the administration raised the idea of "umbrella talks" to cover a flexible combination of arms limitations on various strategic offensive and defensive arms. The Soviet reaction, to the surprise of many in Washington, was favorable—though cautious. The new approach provided a new way not only to resume strategic arms and INF talks without either side having to back down on the issues that stalemated INF and START from 1981 through 1983, but also an avenue for addressing the SDI and ASAT issues. Agreement was reached in a meeting in early January between Secretary of State George Shultz and Foreign Minister Andrei Gromyko to resume negotiations in March 1985. Nevertheless, the nuclear and space arms talks (NST), as they were formally called, were from the start stymied by the issue of strategic defenses and space arms, with Soviet insistence on preservation of the ABM Treaty and persistent pursuit of a ban on all weapons in space, and the United States adamantly against anything that would constrain the SDI. The stalemate was confirmed at the summit meeting between Reagan and Gorbachev at Geneva in November 1985.

The renewal of arms negotiations in 1985 also intensified the efforts of those who opposed maintaining existing agreements and reaching new ones. The most serious example was the assertion by the Reagan administration of a new "broad interpretation" of the ABM Treaty that would permit wider leeway for the SDI without taking on the domestic battle and international onus entailed in abrogating the treaty. Originated and sponsored by hard-line advocates of the SDI in the Defense Department, despite an express provision in the treaty text, Article V(1), that "Each party undertakes not to develop, test, or deploy ABM systems or components which are sea-based, air-based, space-based, or mobile land based," under the "broad interpretation" the parties *would* be allowed to develop and test such ABM systems if they were based on new physical principles. This self-serving interpretation was not thoroughly examined or agreed upon within the administration before it was prematurely publicly expressed in a television appearance by National Security Adviser Robert McFarlane on October 6, 1985. McFarlane, unlike Weinberger and his assistant secretary Richard Perle, was attempting not to gut the ABM Treaty but to provide negotiating leverage for the president. The whole matter backfired. In the end, the administration insisted on the validity of the new broad interpretation but announced its intention (soon made mandatory by an alarmed Senate) to abide by the traditional interpretation in the SDI program.[28]

Among other things, no attempt had been made to discuss the interpretation with the other treaty partner, the Soviet Union, whose leaders vigor-

---

28. The full account of the reinterpretation fiasco, and the issues underlying it, is given in Raymond L. Garthoff, *Policy versus the Law: The Reinterpretation of the ABM Treaty* (Brookings, 1987).

ously rejected the broad interpretation and reaffirmed the traditional one. The whole matter arose only weeks before the first Reagan-Gorbachev summit.

So, too, did a "leaked" letter from Secretary Weinberger to Reagan, warning him not to agree at the summit to any Soviet proposal to reaffirm the traditional interpretation of the ABM Treaty or to agree to continue to observe the SALT II Treaty, never ratified but in practice observed by both countries since 1979. At the Geneva summit, President Reagan did not indicate any "give" on these issues. He continued to favor negotiation of a strategic arms reduction treaty, but he showed no interest beyond that in arms control and no willingness to curtail the SDI in any way.

At the outset, this period of strategic confrontation from 1981 through 1985 was described as a period dominated by President Reagan's initiative in disengaging from the limited pursuit of cooperative security and reliance on unilateral means of assuring security. On the whole, the Soviet leadership did not do well in meeting that challenge. Given the Reagan administration's position, the stubborn attempt in these years by Brezhnev and succeeding Soviet leaders to stick with the general incrementalist approach to arms control which both sides had followed in the 1970s was frustrated. Not only was the SALT pattern unsuccessful in START and INF negotiations, but attempts to resuscitate negotiations in other areas such as antisatellite and nuclear testing talks failed. So, too, did efforts to raise new proposals. Notably, in 1981 and 1982—before Reagan's SDI initiative—the Soviet Union introduced into the UN General Assembly proposals to ban space weapons. In 1984, even the lackluster Konstanin Chernenko attempted to open negotiations on a "code of conduct" of the nuclear powers to deal with the danger of nuclear war (which, incidentally, Leonid Brezhnev, Yury Andropov, and Chernenko all forthrightly said would be "madness" and could have no winner, long before Gorbachev and Reagan included such a statement in the communiqué at the Geneva summit in November 1985).

Nor were occasional Soviet attempts to stimulate arms control by unilateral steps successful. Brezhnev in June 1982 had announced a unilateral Soviet pledge not to be the first to resort to nuclear weapons, but the action was disparaged in the West and in any case "no first use" continued to be rejected as a NATO policy.[29] From 1981 to 1986 several Soviet unilateral moratoriums and proposals for a joint moratorium on INF deployment, which would have frozen a situation to Soviet advantage, were, not surprisingly, rejected or ignored. But when in August 1985 Gorbachev introduced a unilateral moratorium on nuclear testing (later extended four times until early 1987) with a call for the United States to join in a moratorium and in negotiations on a test ban,

---

29. In fact, considerable evidence shows that the Soviet pledge on no first use was not mere propaganda but a genuine strategic policy. See the discussion in Raymond L. Garthoff, *Deterrence and the Revolution in Soviet Military Doctrine* (Brookings, 1990), pp. 80–89.

under conditions in which neither side would have enjoyed an advantage, there was also no positive American response.

## Taming the Strategic Relationship: 1986–89

Although Gorbachev welcomed the renewal of high-level dialogue in the Geneva summit after a lapse of more than five years since the preceding one, he was frustrated by Reagan's adamancy on the SDI, which in turn limited his options for pursuing strategic and INF arms reductions. More basically, the SDI not only made arms control much more difficult but it again focused attention on the military factor and the adversarial dimension of the Soviet-American relationship and of world politics more generally. Gorbachev was determined not only to reduce tensions but to demilitarize the international environment, above all the East-West relationship (and the internal Soviet economic and political system), and turn toward more reliance on the cooperative pursuit of common security. So he set about to undertake a series of steps, some internal and some unilateral, and others proposals for external and necessarily bilateral or multilateral actions. His gradual success in this endeavor marked the dominating element in the sharp change in the strategic relationship from 1986 through 1989.

Gorbachev's first step was a speech on January 15, 1986, proposing a comprehensive framework for arms reductions, with a target of eliminating all nuclear weapons by the year 2000. That goal was widely regarded as unrealistic and probably propagandistic, contributing to the general failure to recognize that Gorbachev had laid out a comprehensive framework that also provided for more limited measures, including a separate INF agreement, more realistic deep strategic reductions (which were eventually agreed on in START I and II), conventional force reductions in Europe (CFE), and a comprehensive nuclear test ban.[30]

One of the standard Western objections to almost any Soviet nuclear arms control proposal was the Soviet and Warsaw Pact preponderance in conventional arms in Europe. This was one of the arguments, apart from impracticality, raised after Gorbachev's January initiative. But on April 18 Gorbachev, and on June 11 the Warsaw Pact formally, offered new approaches for reductions in conventional arms. The Western reaction, however, was to

---

30. "Declaration of the General Secretary of the CC of the CPSU M. S. Gorbachev," *Pravda*, January 16, 1986.

    For a contemporary account noting these broader purposes and possibilities, see Raymond L. Garthoff, "The Gorbachev Proposal and Prospects for Arms Control," *Arms Control Today*, vol. 16 (January–February 1986), pp. 3–6.

assume these were propaganda utterances. In retrospect, it is clear that they were not.

While Gorbachev was wrestling with the problem of regenerating movement toward strategic arms reductions in the context of American pursuit of the SDI, Reagan on May 27, 1986, pulled another leg out from under the shaky structure of strategic arms control by declaring that "in the future the United States must base decisions regarding its strategic force structure on the nature and magnitude of the threat posed by Soviet strategic forces and not on standards contained in the SALT structure, which has been undermined by Soviet noncompliance."[31] While this language, and the overall balance of his remarks, was sufficiently ambiguous to prompt contradictory press and congressional commentary, what it meant was the policy of not undercutting the constraints of the unratified SALT II Treaty, accepted since 1981 by his administration, would be abandoned whenever that was considered expedient.[32] Reagan made clear that his "priority" was fulfillment of the strategic force modernization program (including a second 50 MX Peacekeeper ICBMs he was then lobbying for) over any arms control restraints, although it would have been possible to accommodate the planned program within the SALT II ceil-

---

31. "SALT Restraints. Statement by the President," May 27, 1986, *Presidential Documents*, vol. 22 (June 2, 1986), p. 709.

32. One reason Reagan's message was ambiguous was that he announced in it his decision to decommission two Poseidon submarines, for the present keeping the United States below the SALT II ceiling. (He had been told it would be too costly to keep them in service.) Another reason was that he had left a theoretical loophole to review his decision if the Soviet Union changed its practices on compliance by the time the United States would be in a position to exceed the SALT II limits that fall in its ALCM buildup.

  The Reagan administration had slipped into accepting the SALT II limits in a curious way. The Department of State released a statement on March 3, 1981, stating, "While we are reviewing our SALT policy, we will take no action that would undercut existing agreements so long as the Soviet Union exercises the same restraint." The statement explicitly disavowed a casual statement by Secretary of the Navy John Lehman earlier that same day to the effect that the United States should not feel bound by the SALT I and II agreements as it built up its military power. Secretary Haig, without White House clearance, issued the statement both to make clear to Lehman and others that he was the "vicar" of foreign policy and because he believed (as did the Joint Chiefs of Staff) that on balance there were some advantages to the United States in Soviet observance of the SALT restraints. (See Walter Taylor, "Haig Says U.S. Will Observe SALT Limits," *Washington Star*, March 5, 1981, p. A6. For reasons unknown, the statement was not subsequently published in the *Department of State Bulletin*.) In September, Haig and Gromyko reportedly agreed that both sides would exercise reciprocal restraint so as not to undercut the existing agreements. Then in May 1982, President Reagan made a more authoritative restatement of the same position, declaring as the United States prepared to enter START negotiations, "As for existing strategic arms agreements, we will refrain from actions which undercut them so long as the Soviet Union shows equal restraint." See "Memorial Day, 1982," May 31, 1982, *Presidential Documents*, vol. 18 (June 7, 1982), p. 730. That position stood for the next four years.

ings, and the Joint Chiefs of Staff recommended doing so. Reagan sought to blame the change on what he termed a Soviet "pattern of noncompliance" with existing arms control agreements (although not claiming that they had exceeded the SALT II levels, which they had not). Although he argued that Soviet noncompliance "increasingly affected our national security" (which most observers would have challenged, given the marginal effects of the Soviet violations, actual and alleged), he went beyond that to say that the pattern of Soviet noncompliance "raised fundamental concerns about the integrity of the arms control process itself."[33] That was questionable, but his claim to this effect certainly raised further doubts about the future of the arms control process.

At a special meeting of the Standing Consultative Commission (SCC) charged with monitoring the SALT agreement, held in July in response to a Soviet request, the United States declared its intention to discontinue further discussion there of the SALT I Interim Agreement, by then long expired, and the unratified SALT II Treaty, leaving only the ABM Treaty to be monitored in the future. In the next annual President's Report on Soviet Noncompliance, in March 1987, the administration had it both ways: it devoted several pages to justifying its abandonment of the SALT II restraint and to reiterating the panoply of charges of violations of the SALT I and SALT II agreements, before stating that they would no longer be reviewed in the full body of the report.[34]

There is no need to repeat an account of the slow-moving strategic arms negotiations, and the sudden burst of promise at the Reykjavik summit in October 1986, before the SDI again prevented agreement. After the summit meetings in Geneva and Reykjavik, General Secretary Mikhail Gorbachev came to recognize this personal entrancement of the president with the SDI, but he could not break its thrall. It became a cruel irony of fate that President Reagan's desire to banish the nuclear specter on the one hand opened up the prospect for nuclear disarmament, while foreclosing it with the other through stubborn dedication to the quixotic pursuit of his SDI illusion. Reagan's insistence on negotiating nuclear arms reductions rather than mere limitations, a cynical slogan of his associates in the early 1980s, suddenly came to life in his personal encounter of another kind at Reykjavik. Although the prospect of agreement on eliminating all strategic nuclear weapons, or even all nuclear weapons, came within reach at Reykjavik, it could not be grasped because he still held tight to the beguiling image of self-attained strategic independence through the SDI.[35]

---

33. "SALT Restraints. Statement by the President," May 27, 1986, *Presidential Documents*, vol. 22 (June 2, 1086), pp. 707–08.

34. "The President's Unclassified Report on Soviet Noncompliance with Arms Control Agreements," White House, March 10, 1987.

35. If the SDI-ABM Treaty issue had not derailed the agreement by the two presidents to eliminate all (or all strategic) nuclear weapons, senior advisers and military leaders would no doubt have prevailed in converting *complete* elimination into a long-term

Soon after, President Reagan reasserted his priorities in militantly defending his handling of the Reykjavik meeting. "We can either bet on American technology to keep us safe, or on Soviet promises. And each has its own track record," Reagan said. "I'll bet on American technology any time." He also bragged, in the same speech (on the campaign trail for the congressional midterm elections) that "today we're dealing with the Soviet Union from a position of strength."[36]

What was clear to Gorbachev was the need for the Soviet Union to take the burden of breaking the stalemate. That could not, however, be done easily or quickly. Yet by the end of 1987, as a result of far-reaching Soviet concessions, the INF Treaty had been signed, and strategic arms control was gaining a new lease on life.

Although final conclusion of a multilateral agreement reducing major conventional arms in Europe was not reached until 1990, the key steps toward one were Gorbachev's December 1988 announcement of substantial unilateral Soviet reductions along with proposals and agreements in 1989 for disproportionate reductions in Soviet and Warsaw Pact forces. These would establish a balance with Western forces at a lower level.

Similarly, negotiations between 1987 and 1989 brought a breakthrough on banning chemical weapons. Again, an important bilateral Soviet-American accord on deep reductions was signed in June 1990 as a way-station to a worldwide ban signed in January 1993, initially by 137 countries. But the impetus came from Soviet concessions in the late 1980s, beginning with Soviet announcement in April 1987 of a unilateral cessation of chemical weapons production and restriction of all chemical weapons to Soviet territory.

Soviet urgings for a comprehensive nuclear test ban continued to be rebuffed by the United States throughout this period, but the Soviet Union was ready to agree on any steps in that direction, and Shultz and Shevardnadze in September 1987 agreed on resumption of negotiations on measures to strengthen verification for the partial agreements signed in 1974 and 1976 but never ratified. Soviet officials had contended that no additional verification was necessary, but they acceded to the American position. As a result of these negotiations in the late 1980s, additional protocols on verification measures were signed in June 1990 and ratified soon thereafter.

There was also further progress in confidence- and security-building measures (CSBMs). The earliest steps had been taken in July 1984, when the United States and the Soviet Union agreed on upgrading the twenty-one-year-old "hot line" crisis communications link between the two presidents. Fittingly,

---

objective, dependent among other things on adherence by all nuclear powers and very far-reaching verification controls, but there would probably have been very sharp reductions in the years ahead.

36. "Rapid City, South Dakota," October 29, 1986, *Presidential Documents*, vol. 22 (November 3, 1986), p. 1484.

that was a useful measure even—or especially—between adversaries in times of tension. Similarly, in June 1985 the Standing Consultative Commission—almost ignored in the early 1980s (Weinberger had proposed its abolition)—was used to sign an agreement on a "common understanding" on procedures of notification in case of a nuclear accident or "unauthorized" nuclear explosion. Surprisingly, given the American administration's attitude toward the ABM Treaty, a technical "common understanding" on interpreting that treaty's constraints on utilization of air defense radars at ABM test ranges was also signed at the SCC meeting in June 1985.[37]

In 1984, Senators Sam Nunn and John Warner had provided bipartisan sponsorship for a proposal, endorsed by the Senate, for creation of Nuclear Risk Reduction Centers in Washington and Moscow. At first, the administration was cool to the idea. After five months of interagency deliberation, the administration formally endorsed the idea, although with two important changes that diluted the value of the proposed centers. The original proposal called for joint U.S.-Soviet manning of such centers in both Washington and Moscow. At the insistence of the Department of Defense, the administration approved only national manning; the center in Washington would have only U.S. personnel, and the Moscow center only Soviet personnel. In addition, consideration of contingency planning to meet possible use of nuclear weapons by "unauthorized parties," that is, international terrorist groups, was dropped.

In September 1985 Nunn and Warner visited Moscow and raised the idea with Gorbachev in an unusual display of congressional diplomacy. Gorbachev reacted positively to the idea. At the Geneva summit meeting in November, Reagan and Gorbachev agreed to proceed with formal talks on the matter. In May 1986, negotiations began in Geneva, and by May 1987 agreement was reached on a draft accord.[38] Finally, on September 15, 1987, an agreement on establishing Nuclear Risk Reduction Centers was signed by Secretary Shultz and Foreign Minister Shevardnadze.[39]

---

37. The 1985 SCC "Common Understandings" were confidential, although the fact of their agreement was known. In 1993 the United States and Russia declassified the texts; they are most conveniently available in *Arms Control Today*, vol. 23 (March 1993), p. 19.

38. In a move to defuse lingering Pentagon suspicion of the idea, the U.S. delegation had Assistant Secretary of Defense Richard Perle and NSC staff officer Colonel Robert E. Linhard as cochairmen. The U.S. delegation had never met as a body before its first meeting with the Soviet delegation, and the lack of organization continued. After the first round of negotiations in May 1986 concluded, no delegation report was submitted; finally, the Department of State on its own authority sent an information cable to interested parties. Nonetheless, the second (August 1986) and final (May 1987) sessions successfully proceeded.

39. The centers formally began operation on April 1, 1988. The U.S. center is located in the Department of State and headed by a Foreign Service officer; the Moscow center is in the General Staff headquarters and headed by a one-star general.

In some ways an even more interesting bilateral agreement was reached in June 1989 after nine months of negotiations between delegations from the U.S. Joint Chiefs of Staff and the Soviet General Staff. Called the Agreement on the Prevention of Dangerous Military Activities, it dealt with four kinds of incidents: unintentional straying into the national territory of the other side; activity where one of the parties has designated an area of "special caution" (as in the Persian Gulf); hazardous uses of laser devices; and peacetime jamming interference with command and control communications. The agreement reflected the unease and unhappiness of the military in both countries with incidents that occurred in the early and middle 1980s and stemmed from discussions in the first meetings of U.S. and Soviet chiefs of staff (Admiral William Crowe, Jr., chairman of the Joint Chiefs, and Marshal Sergei Akhromeyev, chief of the General Staff) in Washington in December 1987, and Defense Secretary Frank Carlucci with Defense Minister Marshal Dmitry Yazov in Bern in March 1988. The agreement was signed by Admiral Crowe and General Mikhail Moiseyev (Akhromeyev's successor).[40]

Bilateral arms control negotiations between the Soviet Union and the United States in this period culminated in the INF Treaty in December 1987, with continuing progress on START (and pro forma strategic defense and space talks). Progress in multilateral negotiations on conventional arms in Europe (MBFR) remained elusive in the late 1980s, although talks in the Conference on Disarmament in Europe (CDE) on confidence- and security-building measures were more successful than had been generally anticipated. This success was owing to a much greater readiness on the Soviet side to accept obligations on providing information and for on-site verification. (Generous limits on the size of exercises, and insistence on exclusion of air and naval activities, were owing to Western, not Soviet, reluctance to undertake more far-reaching constraints.) By September 1986 the CDE had successfully concluded a significant agreement.[41]

In March 1989, new negotiations on conventional forces in Europe (CFE) began, replacing the moribund MBFR Talks. The CFE differed from MBFR in many ways, including a broader participation (all the member states of NATO and the Warsaw Pact with forces in Europe) and geopolitical area (Europe from the Atlantic to the Urals). Most important was a new spirit and approach, evident from the outset. In 1989 these talks made great strides toward an agreement reached the next year. Thus conventional forces, as well as strategic nuclear forces and chemical weapons, were the subject of promising negotiations by the end of the decade.

---

40.  The most complete account of the negotiations and background of the agreement is Kurt M. Campbell, "The U.S.-Soviet Agreement on the Prevention of Dangerous Military Activities," *Security Studies*, vol. 1 (Autumn 1991), pp. 109–31.

41.  See chapter 13. On the INF negotiations from 1984 through 1987, see also Haslam, *The Soviet Union and the Politics of Nuclear Weapons*, pp. 141–74.

There was thus a substantial turn-around from no real arms control negotiations in 1984 to several major agreements and promising progress on others by 1989. The single most significant factor underlying this important shift was the determination of Soviet leader Mikhail Gorbachev to overcome the military confrontation between East and West. Political agreements reducing the risk of war, or reducing the burden of escalating armaments, were important means for effecting this change. Such agreements, reached through international negotiation, required internal deliberations and decisions in capitals. These decisions in turn required conceptions of security and military requirements for security compatible with negotiated constraints. Although such decisions are political, they are highly dependent on political-military determinations in which military views are highly important, be it in Moscow, Washington, or other capitals. In the period here under review, from 1986 through 1989, and beyond, the crucial decisions had to be made in Moscow because the most significant changes and concessions making possible the taming of the strategic relationship were made there.

As earlier discussed, Gorbachev was responsible for initiating and persisting in a far-reaching change of Soviet conceptions of security and military doctrine during this period. He publicly declared in the authoritative Political Report to the Twenty-seventh Congress of the Communist Party of the Soviet Union in February 1986 that the whole conception of security must be changed. The heart of Gorbachev's argument was the conclusion that no nation can any longer find security in military power, either in defense or deterrence. "The character of contemporary weapons," he said, "does not leave *any* state hope of protecting itself by military-technical means alone, for example by creating even the most powerful defense." And, though mutual deterrence is more effective than defense, "security cannot indefinitely be based on fear of retaliation, that is on doctrines of 'deterrence' or 'intimidation.' " Rather, "The task of insuring security increasingly is a political task, and can be resolved only by political means." Moreover, security cannot be absolute for any country and can only be mutual, specifically for the Soviet Union and the United States, and "if one takes international relations as a whole, it can only be universal." Finally, building on his discussion of global interdependence, he concluded by calling for the "creation of a comprehensive system of international security"— military, political, economic, and humanitarian.[42]

One important element in Gorbachev's new understanding of security was that, especially between major powers, it could not be enhanced at the expense of the security of another. As earlier noted, at his first summit meeting

---

42. For further discussion see chapter 6. All quotations are from M. S. Gorbachev, *Politicheskii doklad tsentral'nogo komiteta KPSS XXVII s"yezdu Kommunisticheskoi partii Sovetskogo Soyuza* (Political Report of the Central Committee of the CPSU to the 27th Congress of the Communist Party of the Soviet Union) (Moscow: Politizdat, 1986), pp. 81–83.

with President Reagan in Geneva he had said that the Soviet Union did not want to see the United States disadvantaged because that would lead to distrust and instability, and he repeated that thought publicly in his press conference there. He also expressed this view on other occasions to Reagan and Shultz, but though he was told privately that the Americans agreed, no American leader ever reciprocated and publicly stated that the United States wanted the Soviet Union to enjoy no less security than did the United States.[43]

Although this change affected foreign policy in many ways, and arms control policy, it also deeply affected military policy and military doctrine and strategy. Gorbachev encouraged the application of his "new thinking" to military doctrine, and he opened the subject to public discussion and participation by civilian experts in the field, stimulating the military as well to propose new approaches.[44]

The late Marshal Sergei Akhromeyev, then chief of the General Staff, later wrote that the military leadership understood that the governing military doctrine of the Soviet Union was not in keeping with the new political thinking and began to change it. In the fall of 1986, he personally set forth the main elements of the new doctrine, which had been worked out with leading generals of the General Staff, at a special meeting of the professors of the General Staff Academy. By the end of 1986, the new doctrine was formally adopted by the Defense Council.[45]

---

43. Gorbachev had repeated his statement publicly after the Geneva summit (see chapter 5). Gorbachev's similar statement to one by Shultz in October 1987 elicited Shultz's statement that he agreed. For the most complete available account of private meetings see "From Gorbachev's Archive: Meeting of M. S. Gorbachev with U.S. Secretary of State G. Shultz on October 23, 1987," *Miroyaya ekonomika i mezhdunarodnyye otnosheniya* (The World Economy and International Relations), no. 10 (October 1993), p. 80. Shultz does not refer to this in his abbreviated account of their meeting, but there is no reason to doubt its accuracy.

44. See Raymond L. Garthoff, "New Thinking in Soviet Military Doctrine," *Washington Quarterly*, vol. 1 (Summer 1988), pp. 131–58; and Garthoff, *Deterrence and the Revolution in Soviet Military Doctrine*, chapter 4.

Initially, civilian scholars in the security and arms control field wrote primarily in academic and international relations publications, joined by retired and a few active duty military men. By 1988 and after, there was greater cross-fertilization of thinking, including the first lectures and roundtable discussions by a few civilians (including the future Russian deputy defense minister Andrei Kokoshin) at the General Staff Academy. Also, beginning in 1986 military men began to discuss arms control matters in the professional military journals, in particular the confidential General Staff journal, *Military Thought*. Information based on a review of the files of *Military Thought* and interviews, especially with Colonel General Nikolai Chervov, Major General Valentin Larionov, and Andrei Kokoshin.

45. Akhromeyev and Kornienko, *Glazami marshala i diplomata*, pp. 121–26. This meeting at the General Staff Academy and the late 1986 Defense Council adoption of the new doctrine had never been publicly disclosed before Akhromeyev's posthumous memoir.

The most striking change was the inclusion in military doctrine, not only in foreign policy, of the objective of the prevention of war. Previously, military doctrine had only addressed ways of waging a war if one should occur. The new doctrine also changed the objective from victory over the enemy, if war should come, to preventing his victory and terminating the conflict. This had significant implications for military strategy and force structure. It meant a change from long-standing plans even in a defensive war to assume the offensive and drive West to the English Channel; the new defensive doctrine called for three weeks of defensive warfare along the border during which a political solution would be sought. Needless to say, such a radical change was not made easily.[46] This change in strategy also permitted the drastic reductions in offensive capabilities that in turn made possible Gorbachev's unilateral move in December 1988 and the later deep CFE Treaty reductions in Soviet and Warsaw Pact forces.

The first official unveiling of the new military doctrine and strategy was in a Warsaw Pact statement in May 1987.[47] This declaration also included a proposal for joint Warsaw Pact–NATO consultation on military doctrine of the two alliances—a constructive proposal, although one initially treated coolly and with great caution in the West.

Although these momentous changes in Soviet security policy and military doctrine and strategy were taking place, there were no parallel—or reciprocating—changes in the U.S. or NATO doctrine. There was of course no corresponding NATO strategy of major forward offensive operations in the event of war, although some steps in this direction had been under way in the NATO alliance. Thus, for example, the American concept of "airland battle" led to NATO adoption in November 1984 of a concept of prompt deep attacks on follow-on forces of the Warsaw Pact (FOFA). The U.S. Army had adopted a new basic operations manual (FM 100-5, *Operations*) in 1982 that seemed to mirror the Soviet doctrine of that period—it accented the role of the offensive, to destroy the enemy's fighting force, with victory as the objective. Most of these changes in NATO and U.S. doctrine had occurred in 1982–84, but they were not followed in the period 1985–89

---

I was told in July 1988 about the fact that the new military doctrine had been developed in 1985–86 by Marshal Akhromeyev and by Colonel General Nikolai Chervov, chief of the Legal and Treaty Department (responsible for arms control matters) of the General Staff.

46. See Garthoff, *Deterrence and the Revolution in Soviet Military Doctrine*, pp. 101–08, 149–85; and Akhromeyev and Kornienko, *Glazami marshala i diplomata*, pp. 122–25, 175–80.

47. "On the Military Doctrine of the Member States of the Warsaw Pact," *Pravda*, May 30, 1987.

by changes corresponding to the application of new thinking to Soviet military doctrine.[48]

The overall strategic relationship between East and West, the strategic military balance between the United States and the Soviet Union, and the European theater balance between NATO and the Warsaw Pact, remained essentially stable throughout the 1980s. What changed were strategic doctrine, a toughening in the West in the first half of the decade to more closely match the long-standing Soviet and Pact approach, a Western action overestimated in wary Soviet evaluations, and a "softening" in the East in the second half of the decade, warily underestimated in Western evaluation. Thus besides significant conceptual changes, especially in the Soviet Union in 1986–87 and thereafter, there remained on both sides more sluggish and cautious perceptual changes reflecting long-ingrained suspicions and many misperceptions.

The Secretary of Defense's annual Reports to the President and the Congress represented perhaps the most "authoritative" statements, if also among the most bleak. At about the time Gorbachev came to power, Secretary Caspar Weinberger displayed his inability to empathize in rejecting as "inherently incredible" the "theory" of the Soviet leaders' concern over their own security as a source of their military doctrine, simply on the presumptive grounds that "their military buildup has been continuous, regardless of whether or not they faced any conditions they could conceivably call a threat." He added that "regardless of the underlying motivation for the Soviet military buildup, postwar history demonstrates a Soviet willingness to take advantage of any perceived weaknesses in the global politico-military balance. A prudent American defense policy cannot rest on unproven and scarcely credible theories of relatively benign Soviet motivations."[49] A year later, paradoxically in the same month that Gorbachev at the party congress was proclaiming his new approach to common security, Weinberger was appealing to keep up the American military buildup, which he saw as "redefining the terms of the U.S.-Soviet relationship" because "the United States is now beginning to deal from strength." Still, he argued—with no evidence at all—that it might not be enough to build forces the United States would regard as sufficient for deterrence—"all the evidence we have suggests that preparing to deter an attack

---

48. For a review of how these and other American and NATO developments, in strategic as well as European theater applications, appeared ominous to military men in Moscow, see Raymond L. Garthoff, "Soviet Perceptions of Western Strategic Thought and Doctrine," in Gregory Flynn, ed., *Soviet Military Doctrine and Western Policy* (London and New York: Routledge, 1989), pp. 197–327, esp. 242–71.

The U.S. Army did radically modify its doctrine in a revised FM 100-5, but not until June 1993 (a 1986 revision merely refined the "airland battle" concept).

49. *Annual Report to the Congress, Caspar W. Weinberger, Secretary of Defense, Fiscal Year 1986*, February 4, 1985, p. 22.

only by assembling forces adequate to deter us under similar conditions could provide too little to deter the Soviets." The bottom line was simple: "We can buy the forces required to secure freedom and peace"—"or we can meanly conclude that it is too great an effort, falter and thus yield to the forces of totalitarianism and tyranny."[50]

A year later, after the new Soviet military doctrine had been adopted and only shortly before it was officially announced, Secretary Weinberger in his last Report to the Congress simply ignored the mounting evidence of significant change. Indeed, he described the Soviet buildup as "all the more ominous" because it was coupled with "military writings which continue to reflect their belief that the USSR could prevail in a nuclear war" and "a Soviet belief that nuclear war may, under certain conditions, be fought and won."[51] Yet the United States had access to classified Soviet writings, as well as public ones, that refuted that claim. And ignoring Gorbachev's often reiterated view, which he had expressed jointly with President Reagan at Geneva in November 1985, that a nuclear war could not be won and must never be fought, Weinberger chose instead to cite Lenin as author of an "avowed Soviet policy" of promoting world communist revolution. Again, for good measure, he noted that while "scholars" (but apparently not government analysts) "continue to debate the question of Soviet motives and objectives, . . . a prudent American defense policy cannot rest on theories of Soviet motivation, but must respond to the facts of Soviet policy and military capability."[52] Yet he was unabashedly selective with the "facts"—such as the claim, increasingly untrue, that in the Soviet Union, "there is no public opinion to impose any restraints," and that because the Soviet Union had used military force to invade Afghanistan, there was a proven propensity, a "willingness to use military force to invade and coerce other countries" that "can be applied elsewhere as well."[53]

By early 1988, when Gorbachev's new thinking was becoming ever more clearly a guide to Soviet policy, Secretary of Defense Frank Carlucci still signed a report claiming that the past year had seen "an intensifying Soviet public relations campaign designed ostensibly to portray a new Soviet commitment to peace." Moreover, "despite this 'new look,' Moscow is continuing its arms buildup and expanding its political and military influence wherever and whenever the opportunity presents itself." Where? When? "While it is hard to find fault with the [Gorbachev] rhetoric," Carlucci continued, "we would be far

50. *Annual Report to the Congress, Fiscal Year 1987, Caspar W. Weinberger, Secretary of Defense*, February 5, 1986, pp. 3, 38, 5.

51. *Annual Report to the Congress, Fiscal Year 1988, Caspar W. Weinberger, Secretary of Defense*, January 12, 1987, pp. 54–55.

52. Ibid., p. 23.

53. Ibid., p. 24.

more reassured by supporting actions."[54] This, one must note, was written after such supporting actions as the conclusion of the INF Treaty and announcement of Soviet withdrawal of forces from Afghanistan. While Carlucci at least dropped Weinberger's specious claim that Soviet military doctrine continued to avow the winnability of nuclear war, he did so grudgingly as well as belatedly: "Recent Soviet declaratory statements appear to reject their previously held concepts of nuclear warfighting while disclaiming a preemptive nuclear strategy," but he claimed the United States had "not seen, however, corresponding changes in Soviet force posture." Moreover, this change was also said to be "in line with their new 'peace offensive' "—with the deprecating implication that it should be discounted if not ignored. "Regardless of Gorbachev's stated intentions," he concluded, American "policy decisions must be made in light of these growing [Soviet military] capabilities. Intentions can change overnight."[55] Even by 1989, with the Soviet Union's announcement of unilateral force reductions overall and in Eastern Europe, its withdrawal from Afghanistan, and other steps, Secretary Carlucci still stressed "caution" and claimed that "there is no evidence that Gorbachev and his allies will abandon communism or their drive to expand Soviet influence," and he said that "we must be guided by realism, not wishful thinking. The West's security preparations must be based not on Kremlin declarations, but on actual Soviet military capabilities."[56]

The first in a new annual series of unclassified issuances of *Joint Military Net Assessments* (replacing the former Joint Chiefs of Staff [JCS] annual publication *U.S. Military Posture*), supplementing the Secretary of Defense's annual reports, released in June 1989, was straightforward in noting, "Recent trends in Soviet rhetoric imply a gradual but fundamental change in doctrine and strategy, moving from a position requiring overwhelming military superiority to one emphasizing defensive sufficiency." Still, the *JMNA* noted that more time was required "before reaching definitive conclusions about Soviet intentions" and restated the long-standard claim that the Soviet Union had "forces far in excess of what might be required for defense."[57]

---

54. *Annual Report to the Congress, Fiscal Year 1989, Frank C. Carlucci, Secretary of Defense*, February 18, 1988, p. 23.

55. Ibid., pp. 23–25.

56. *Annual Report to the Congress, Fiscal Year 1990, Frank C. Carlucci, Secretary of Defense*, January 17, 1989, p. 3.

57. Joint Chiefs of Staff, *1989 Joint Military Net Assessment* (Washington, 1989), p. ES-2. There was, however, no analysis in support of that claim.

    This claim, never substantiated, had become standard polemical rhetoric on both sides. For example, General Mikhail Kozlov, then deputy chief of the Soviet General Staff, a decade earlier claimed NATO's forces "far exceed requirements for defense and bear a distinctly offensive character." See General of the Army M. Kozlov, "A Bloc for Aggression and War: The Offensive Character of the Armed Forces of NATO," *Krasnaya zvezda* (Red Star), November 20, 1979.

The public relations documents also slowly underwent a cautious change. *Soviet Military Power* from 1986 through 1989 continued to accent heavily "the threat." Only in September 1989 did that year's issue drop the subtitle "An Assessment of the Threat" and substitute "Prospects for Change." Discussions of Soviet military doctrine lagged seriously and simply ignored and implicitly denied the important changes under way.[58] Incidentally, the Soviet Ministry of Defense dropped its parallel publication, *Whence the Threat to Peace*, after its 1987 edition.

The strategic relationship was thus undergoing an important but gradual transformation by the end of 1989. The intercontinental strategic balance was very stable, and both recent American concerns over a window of vulnerability opened by Soviet ICBMs and Soviet concerns over a new window of vulnerability created by the American SDI had receded. The strategic forces of the two sides were much too large and did have characteristics that tended to sustain the qualitative arms race, but the START negotiations offered promise of at least capping and moderating the strategic arms competition. In the European theater, Soviet and Warsaw Pact forces were being reduced, and the new CFE negotiations were on track to yield a balance of forces between the two alliances that would effectively eliminate the earlier Warsaw Pact preponderance and capability for a rapid westward offensive in the event of war.

Thus the strategic relationship was being "tamed." More generally, there were at least signs of a gradual movement toward creating some elements of a common security regime, in particular several bilateral U.S.-Soviet strategic, and multilateral European, confidence- and security-building measures. Moreover, advances in all these areas had come about through actions taken on Gorbachev's initiative.

Then came the sudden Revolution of '89 in Eastern Europe. Though encouraging for the future, the immediate effect was to remove the foundations from the carefully calculated balance of alliances in Europe. Would the Soviet

---

58. Each year after 1981, the secretary of defense held a news conference introducing the new edition of *Soviet Military Power*. In doing so in April 1988, Secretary Carlucci not only disparaged what he referred to as "considerable speculation" that the Soviets were changing their military doctrine but claimed that Soviet contingent preparations for nuclear war "contradict . . . Soviet protestations that they share President Ronald Reagan's view that nuclear war can never be won and must never be fought"—implicitly charging Gorbachev with deception in signing the joint statement to that effect at Geneva in 1985 and ignoring that the United States as well as the Soviet Union was making a wide range of preparations for the contingency that a nuclear war might occur despite all efforts to prevent it and despite recognition that it could not be won. Carlucci also made the off-the-cuff comment, "It seems to me the jury is still out on whether *perestroika* and *glasnost*, to the extent they exist (are) in the Western interest." See "Soviet Military Power," news conference by Secretary of Defense Frank C. Carlucci, April 29, 1988, *Defense Issues*, vol. 3 (Department of Defense, 1988), pp. 1, 2, 4.

Union see the consequences of the revolutionary shift in Eastern Europe as undermining its pursuit of common security?

## *Toward Common Security: 1990–91*

Mikhail Gorbachev was no longer in control of the situation, and he as well as the West would in 1990–91 be reacting to developments rather than driving them. Nevertheless, although Gorbachev concluded he had to make tactical concessions to rising domestic opposition in the course of internal economic and political restructuring, he persisted in pursuit of a new strategic relationship with the West.

The most immediate decision in late 1989 had been *not* to resist the toppling of communist governments in Eastern Europe. The next step was accommodation of the desire of Czechoslovakia and Hungary for withdrawal of all Soviet troops from those countries, promptly agreed on in February and March 1990, to be completed by the end of June 1991. Poland later—after the reunification of Germany with reconfirmation of its existing eastern borders— decided it also wished to see Soviet forces leave, and agreement in October 1991 led to withdrawal by October 1992. East Germany had formally withdrawn from the Warsaw Pact in 1990 on the eve of its merger into the Federal Republic, and it had been agreed that Soviet forces in eastern Germany would leave by the end of 1994. After some partial steps, the Warsaw Pact itself was dissolved on July 1, 1991.

One consequence of the rapid erosion and dissolution of the Warsaw Pact in 1990–91 was that individual national force levels already established in negotiating the CFE Treaty no longer represented a balance of equal forces between NATO and a counterposed alliance. Moscow, which had controlled up to two-thirds of the conventional arms in Europe, would now control not half, as had been envisaged in 1989, but only about a third of the military forces between the Atlantic and the Urals. Yet Gorbachev and Shevardnadze succeeded in keeping on track the negotiations leading not only to the CFE (and to additional CSBMs, including establishment of a Conflict Prevention Center in Vienna), but also to acceptance of the reunification of Germany within NATO.

By the end of 1991, the North Atlantic Cooperation Council (NACC) was established, on NATO initiative, bringing into association with NATO all of the former Warsaw Pact members, including the Soviet Union (and separately the three Baltic republics, by then independent).

Gorbachev had set out to dismantle the confrontation of military alliances in Europe, the division of Europe, and the Cold War—and he did.

The strategic forces of the Soviet Union and the United States were finally placed again under a cap at lower levels in the START I Treaty signed in

Moscow in July 1991. Further reciprocal unilateral nuclear arms reductions (especially of tactical ground force and naval weapons) in September 1991, on the initiative of President Bush and warmly welcomed and reciprocated by Gorbachev, further lessened both arsenals and tensions in the strategic relationship.

The changes in Soviet military doctrine continued, with reductions in military production and forces as well.[59] The Warsaw Pact appeal of May 1987 for discussion of military doctrine led, somewhat belatedly because of Western caution and a new geopolitical context, to international seminars on military doctrine in January-February 1990 and October 1991. Bilateral visits and other contacts by military leaders and representatives of various countries proliferated in these years, further breaking down the hostile insulation of the Cold War era.

Meanwhile, the Soviet Union continued to reduce, and in most cases to terminate, military arrangements and arms supply to Cuba, North Korea, Vietnam, and other countries during these two years (as well as completing the withdrawal of Soviet troops from Mongolia and Cuban troops from Angola). The Soviet Navy departed Cam Ranh Bay in Vietnam, and the token Soviet brigade in Cuba began to return home.[60]

The United States and NATO, at first slowly and cautiously, also responded to the changed strategic relationship. The United States took the lead in helping NATO to begin a recasting of its strategic concept and outlook in the London NATO summit in July 1990, carried further in Rome in November when the NACC was established. Subsequently U.S. forces in Europe and most European national armed forces began a build-down.

The United States even began to adjust its strategic forces employment plans. The strategic war plan, the Single Integrated Operational Plan (SIOP), was modified in October 1990 and again in mid-1991, although very cautiously (only in mid-1991 dropping from the target lists the leaderships of the Eastern European and Baltic states).[61] In July 1990 the U.S. Air Force terminated the constant airborne fall-back command flights known as "Looking Glass." Ever since February 1961, such flights with a Strategic Air Command (SAC) general officer aboard had continuously been airborne to provide a command authority who could unleash a retaliatory destruction of the Soviet Union even if the president (and the United States) had been obliterated.

---

59. The CIA estimated that real Soviet defense spending for the three-year period 1989 through 1991 declined by more than 25 percent. Reductions were across the board but most sharp in weapon procurement. See *The Former Soviet Union in Transition*, vol. 2, study papers submitted to the Joint Economic Committee, Congress of United States (GPO, 1993), p. 705.

60. See chapter 15. Very limited use of facilities at Cam Ranh Bay continued.

61. For a rare unclassified but informed discussion, see R. Jeffrey Smith, "U.S. Trims List of Targets in Soviet Union," *Washington Post*, July 21, 1991, p. A1.

Least responsive and most laggard were American public statements by Defense Department leaders. Secretary Dick Cheney in January 1990 only conceded that the fall of communist dominoes in Eastern Europe "*may* reduce the division of Europe and hold the *long-term* potential for bringing freedom." He argued, "Even if the Soviet threat recedes permanently—and it has certainly not yet done so—American power will still be required." To be sure, he acknowledged that "U.S.-Soviet and East-West relations have improved markedly since the early 1980s" and that "cooperative aspects of the U.S. relationship with the Soviet Union are growing," but he still warned that "the United States must be prepared to remain in long-term competition with the Soviet Union."[62] By January 1991, Cheney was prepared to say that "the past two years have seen dramatic changes in the security environment, particularly in the Soviet Union and Eastern Europe" and that "the persistent threat of the Cold War—a massive invasion into Western Europe" had been "rendered unlikely."[63] By February 1992, Cheney claimed victory in the Cold War, among other reasons because of "our refusal to be intimidated by the enormous build-up in Soviet military power" and "our willingness to match that build-up." And, in an assertion it would be difficult to document from the record, he retroactively claimed foresight: "Long before the collapse of the Soviet Union, the United States had already begun to shape its military planning on the assumptions of a sharply reduced Soviet threat."[64]

The JCS *1990 Joint Military Net Assessment* was slow to grasp (or at least to voice) the changing strategic situation. Changes in the Soviet Union and Warsaw Pact were seen as presenting "both opportunities and challenges." For example, "Perceptions of a lessening Soviet threat . . . will bring demands for decreased military spending," but "the Soviet Union's restructured military will be formidable" and "despite their current problems [in March 1990], the Soviets are unlikely to weaken significantly their strategic position."[65] By March 1991, the JCS was prepared to acknowledge "the demise of the Cold War," a "fundamental shift in relations between the United States and the Soviet Union," and that "forty years of Cold War confrontation have given way to a new world order."[66] Still, despite recognition of the need for "a reassessment and a fundamental review of the parameters that have shaped U.S. national military strategy," the first results were not impressive: "The Soviet Union

62. *Annual Report to the President and the Congress, Dick Cheney, Secretary of Defense*, January 1990, p. 1, and covering letter to the President and Congress. Emphasis added.

63. *Annual Report to the President and the Congress, Dick Cheney, Secretary of Defense*, January 1991, p. v.

64. *Annual Report to the President and the Congress, Dick Cheney, Secretary of Defense*, February 1992, pp. vi, 1.

65. Joint Chiefs of Staff, *1990 Joint Military Net Assessment* (Washington, 1990), p. ES-3.

66. Joint Chiefs of Staff, *1991 Joint Military Net Assessment* (Washington, 1991), p. 1-1.

remains the one country in the world capable of destroying the United States with a single devastating attack" even though "the rationale for such an attack is difficult to construe." And "Whatever the future Soviet state may look like, it still will have millions of well-armed men in uniform," and for all the Soviet overall reduction of its forces and retraction of its never more than token military presence around the globe, "The United States, as the leader of the Free World, must maintain the conventional capability to globally counterbalance the might of the Soviet Union's huge conventional forces, in conjunction with our allies."[67] The 1992 JMNA—probably the last in the series—although thickest of all, had dropped its former centerpiece, a net assessment of a global war between NATO and the Soviet Union (Warsaw Pact); rather it examined a major regional crisis and other contingencies.[68]

The 1990 edition of *Soviet Military Power*, for the first time issued without a press presentation by the secretary of defense, attempted to set a middle course between "those who are determined to believe that the Soviets no longer threaten Western interests" and "those who regard the Soviet threat as largely unchanged." Admitting "ambiguity of the threat," *SMP* nevertheless argued that "prudence demands that we focus on the most dangerous challenge to our national security," and evidently the victim of its own propaganda that insisted threats are based on "capabilities" and not a compound with intentions, it could do little but reiterate that "the military might of the Soviet Union is enormous" and even less presciently that "all evidence indicates that this fact will not change."[69] But this was to be the last edition of *Soviet Military Power*. By 1991, the draft of a new edition was scrapped except for a more or less factual account called simply *Military Forces in Transition*.[70] And that was the last issuance of its kind.

This review of the changing strategic relationship between the United States and the Soviet Union from 1981 through 1991 has focused heavily on perceptions and depictions of the relationship because those images and their propagation were salient. The actual strategic balance was not only stable but also had remarkably little impact on developments. Even the more volatile views of possible changes in that balance, though much more influential, were significant far more for the ways they were used to serve various domestic political purposes (and to a lesser extent foreign policy purposes) than for any real anticipated influence on the balance.

The successful conclusion of a START I Treaty in July 1991 did fill a gap that had been left by the repudiation of the SALT II Treaty. Together with

---

67.  Ibid., pp. 1–3, 1-4.

68.  Joint Chiefs of Staff, *1992 Joint Military Net Assessment* (Washington, 1992), pp. 1-1, 1-2.

69.  Department of Defense, *Soviet Military Power, 1990*, preface.

70.  Department of Defense, *Military Forces in Transition, 1991*.

the INF and CFE Treaties, it complemented the ABM Treaty (which had barely survived its battering during the SDI years) in establishing a broad arms control regime and a foundation for deeper cuts—as shown by the START II Treaty signed in 1993. Yet for all of its virtues, the vaunted reductions under START I would not quite bring actual strategic force levels back down to those existing in 1981.

The restoration of an agreed arms control regime was also an accomplishment after the damage brought about by sharp practices, exploitation of ambiguities, and a few outright violations of arms control agreements (by both sides, most blatantly by the Soviet Union)—and by overdrawn, polemical exaggeration of the issue (engaged in by the United States and in turn by the Soviet Union) during the period.

Similarly, hard-ball negotiating strategy and tactics weakened the arms control process and its results, in this period most successfully practiced by the United States inasmuch as the Soviet Union after 1985 was more interested in reaching agreements and even ready to concede more than its share to reach them. For example, after successfully protecting the tremendous American (and Western) superiority in naval forces from Soviet efforts to include naval arms control in the CDE and other CSBMs, in the CFE, and in START, the United States suddenly showed that it had been holding back for no real strategic reason, when in September 1991 President Bush unilaterally withdrew all nuclear weapons from U.S. naval ships (except for strategic ballistic missile submarines). That was a statesmanlike move, and of course the Cold War was over. But there had been no good reason less than two years earlier at Malta, when Gorbachev was declaring the Cold War over, for Bush to brusquely dismiss Gorbachev's proposal at that time to eliminate all naval tactical nuclear weapons. And as late as May 1990 the United States had insisted on keeping the right to deploy 880 nuclear-armed SLCMs (when the United States had 350 SLCMs and SLCM program goals had already been cut back to 758) simply because the Soviet negotiators were over a barrel, and 880 was the mathematical median between an arbitrary U.S. figure of 1,000 and a Soviet offer to accommodate the declared U.S. program of 758 by a ceiling of 760.[71] This, too, of course was reversed in September 1991 when all nuclear-armed SLCMs were removed.

Though arms control, including expanded confidence- and security-building measures, had an important role to fill, the changes in political alignment (and even sovereignty) and military deployments and capabilities had even more important roles in creating a new security environment. The new security environment in Europe, and in the world, did not by any means exclude new dangers and problems. Indeed the reversal of the Cold War counterbalance of alliances permitted some old conflicts to reassert themselves

---

71. See chapter 10, footnote 24.

and new ones to arise, notably, the civil wars in former Yugoslavia and the Iraqi aggression against Kuwait and UN response. The fact that the U.S.-led international force that defeated Iraq had UN backing, including support by the Soviet Union, former ally and arms supplier to Iraq, bore impressive witness to the revolutionary change in the global strategic relationship.

Common security had become much more than a slogan by the final days of the American-Soviet strategic relationship. Gorbachev had, as early as 1986, avowed a new approach to defining—and attaining—security. From 1987 to 1991, he undertook many unilateral and negotiated measures to help bring about a new cooperative security approach. Although his parallel efforts to transform the internal Soviet system failed, he did take the key steps to bring about a new international order, one that may be termed "interactionist," as contrasted with confrontational, and one that was geared to shared and common security. The INF, START I, and CFE Treaties, and the important parallel reciprocated Soviet and U.S. unilateral sweeping withdrawal from deployment of all land and naval tactical nuclear weapons in the fall of 1991, were major steps. So was the resolute Soviet defense of the ABM Treaty throughout the period of efforts by the SDI-minded Reagan administration to evade or gut it. The foundation was laid for the START II reductions agreed upon in January 1993 and the moratorium on nuclear weapons testing (and prospective ban as this book is written in 1994). Arms control, so near death during most of the 1980s, came to life as never before late in the decade as cooperative security began to become a reality.

There was, however, far more to the new security approach than arms control and reductions. Important changes in Soviet military doctrine and strategy aimed at preventing or terminating a war, rather than at attempting to win a war, were one significant element. Most important of all was the establishment of new Soviet political-military relationships with the United States and Europe (East and West), less dramatically with China, and change effected through retrenchment and disengagement from the whole Third World.

Russia is the principal successor to the Soviet Union, but among the significant distinctions between them is a radically new and different geostrategic situation. Russia in its new borders most closely resembles geographically not prerevolutionary Russia of the World War I era, but Russia of the seventeenth century. The strategic difference is less startling but also significant. Not only is there a neutral and independent belt of states in the old "Eastern Europe," but also in the new "farther eastern" Europe—Ukraine, Belarus, Moldova, and the Baltic states. And there is a new belt of independent states across Transcaucasia and Central Asia. These newly independent states, formerly part of the Soviet Union (and earlier of the Russian Empire), are now collectively termed in Russia "the near abroad" and are seen as a sphere of special strategic significance to Russia. The Moscow Military District became the Western frontier district. At this writing it remains to be seen whether the new neighboring state of Ukraine will give up all aspirations to become a nuclear power. Russia itself has been having difficulty in maintaining armed forces far less than half as large as those of the Soviet Union.

Under the circumstances even such important and well-established elements of military doctrine as no first use of nuclear weapons came under challenge, not from advocates of expansion, but from those who feared Russia could not provide nonnuclear defense and deterrence. Russian military doctrine and strategy will not revert to earlier Soviet terms, but they must now be fashioned to meet the new situation of Russia. New attention, for example, is also being given to peacekeeping roles for the Russian Army in its own environs and abroad. All of these matters were posed, but not ultimately settled, in a new document setting forth "The Basic Provisions of the Military Doctrine of the Russian Federation," approved in November 1993. Future Russian, cooperative Russian-American, and world security arrangements are beyond this present discussion, but it must be noted that new challenges, beyond the cooperative security framework that had applied in Gorbachev's Soviet Union from 1988 through 1991, have arisen.

# 13 Europe and American-Soviet Relations

EUROPE HAD BEEN a central arena of the emergence of the Cold War in the late 1940s and remained the central locus of confrontation even as peripheral areas around the globe also became enveloped in the conflict. Europe was also the leading element in the détente of the 1970s.[1] During the reinvigoration of American-Soviet tension in the early 1980s, Europe again came to be an important area of conflict in a complex way. Yet by the latter years of the decade, new processes were rapidly developing that led beyond a new détente to the sudden ending of the confrontational division of Europe and of the Cold War. How did this come about?

## Western Divergence over Détente

The disjunction between the collapse of American-Soviet détente and the continuation of an East-West détente in Europe intensified in the early years of the 1980s. The first effects were felt in 1980, in the wake of the Soviet military intervention in Afghanistan, when the United States abandoned détente and Europe did not.[2] During 1981–82 a similar discrepancy attended the responses of the United States and Western Europe to the Polish suppression of the Solidarity movement in December 1981 and thereafter.

Though less clear-cut and dramatic, an uneasy compromise was also required in NATO policy statements and in coordinating the positions of the NATO countries for the Conference on Security and Cooperation in Europe

---

1. See Raymond L. Garthoff, *Détente and Confrontation: American-Soviet Relations from Nixon to Reagan*, rev. ed. (Brookings, 1994), chapters 4, 14.

2. Ibid., chapter 27.

(CSCE) follow-through conference in Madrid (1981–83), the Conference on Disarmament in Europe (CDE) in Stockholm (1984–86), and other CSCE follow-through meetings. The most central and politically important issue straining U.S.-West European relations from 1981 through 1983 was the internal debate over deployment of American intermediate-range missiles in Europe and attendant concerns over the conduct of the INF arms talks. Potentially even more important was a growing divergence over arms control in general as a measure to alleviate the tensions and risks of war between East and West. The Western Europeans felt much more strongly and positively about arms control than the Reagan administration. This gap, though muffled, gave rise to doubts in Europe about the U.S. commitment to arms control and concern about the U.S. preference for a unilateral arms buildup, including the strategic defense initiative. To the Europeans, the SDI threatened the ABM Treaty and the whole process of East-West arms control and stirred fears of American strategic decoupling and isolationism as well. At the same time, there was a growing American sentiment that the Europeans were not doing their share to carry the common defense burden and were too readily inclined to take a soft détente attitude and to be too eager for arms control.

Finally, underlying all these concerns and differences was a growing estrangement over what the tasks, if not the purposes, of the alliance should be. The NATO alliance withstood and outlived many internal "crises" over several decades of the Cold War. It overcame the specific issues of the early 1980s reasonably well. Nonetheless, if the United States had remained on a confrontational-containment course while Western Europe pursued détente in relations with the Soviet Union and the Soviet bloc in Eastern Europe throughout the 1980s, the impact on the alliance might have become severe. The United States, however, returned to a détente policy (even while abjuring the word) for the second half of the decade.

The European allies, to be sure, had not been happy with the United States unilaterally taking some steps toward détente and arms limitation with the Soviet Union in the 1970s. That feeling was, however, nothing compared with their unhappiness and concern over unilateral U.S. pursuit of a course of quasi confrontation in the first half of the 1980s. The harsh rhetoric emanating from the top officials of the Reagan administration in the early 1980s, including hostile remarks about the Soviet system by President Reagan himself that seemed to place in question the very possibility of dealing with the Soviet Union, was disquieting to many Europeans. Particularly distressing were remarks criticizing détente itself—to which NATO, including the United States, had solemnly subscribed since December 1967.[3] For example, the Europeans found shocking an off-the-cuff statement by Secretary of Defense Caspar Weinberger to a group of NATO defense ministers in 1981, a statement

---

3.   Ibid., chapter 4.

reported widely in the European press: "If the movement from cold war to détente is progress, then let me say we cannot afford much more progress."[4] The meeting of NATO foreign ministers in May 1981 was the first occasion under the new U.S. administration that called for a formal statement of alliance policy. In preparing and negotiating the ministerial communiqué (a process that, as was traditional, preceded the actual meeting), the U.S. representatives tried to omit any reference to détente, but the Europeans balked. They could all agree on criticizing the Soviet Union, especially for the occupation of Afghanistan. But the European allies insisted on reaffirming the aim of détente. Finally the United States reluctantly acceded to a formulation that reaffirmed the goal of a "more constructive East-West relationship" and stated that the allies would "maintain a dialogue with the Soviet Union and will work together for genuine détente and the development of East-West relations, whenever Soviet behavior makes this possible." They also agreed "to encourage Soviet restraint and responsibility."[5]

Again in May 1982, at the meeting following the imposition of martial law in Poland, the United States sought to have the aim of détente deleted. Again the allies (led by the West Germans) insisted on its retention. Thus the May 1982 communiqué reaffirmed the aims of "genuine détente" and a "more constructive East-West relationship" to be achieved through "dialogue and negotiation." Moreover, "arms control and disarmament, together with deterrence and defense," were recognized as "integral parts of Alliance security policy."[6] These themes were reiterated in subsequent alliance communiqués, including a special alliance declaration in May 1984 that reaffirmed the Harmel Report of 1967.[7]

---

4.   Cited in Walter Isaacson, "Softly, with a Big Stick," *Time*, April 27, 1981, p. 28. The occasion was a meeting of the Nuclear Planning Group. Weinberger deliberately chose to make disparaging comments about détente on several other occasions during that same visit to Europe, his first as secretary of defense, on which he was accompanied by Undersecretary Fred C. Iklé and Assistant Secretary Richard Perle. On one occasion he contended that the Iron Curtain had been reinforced "during the last few years—the period in which we were engaged in the process called detente." See George C. Wilson, "Weinberger Sent Mixed Signals in European Tour," *Washington Post*, April 14, 1981, p. A12.

5.   "Final Communique, May 5, 1981," *Department of State Bulletin*, vol. 81 (July 1981), pp. 39–40. (Hereafter *State Bulletin*.) The background to the communiqué decision has been provided by participants.

     The term "genuine détente" implied doubt whether current Soviet behavior reflected full adherence to détente, a point on which the European allies agreed after Afghanistan. This phrase was first used in the NATO communiqué in December 1980. Nonetheless, alliance support for détente was reaffirmed.

6.   "Final Communique, May 18, 1982," *State Bulletin*, vol. 82 (August 1982), p. 67. So did a special NATO summit meeting in June 1982; see "NATO Summit Declaration, June 10, 1982," ibid., pp. 9–10.

7.   "Washington Statement on East-West Relations, May 31, 1984," *State Bulletin*, vol. 84 (July 1984), pp. 11–13. See chapter 4. The Harmel Report, named for a NATO study

While formal NATO statements thus glossed over differences in evaluation and approach, these divergent views continued to crop up in statements by leaders. President Reagan stunned allied leaders in an impromptu statement at the close of a formal NATO summit meeting in Bonn in June 1982 when he said the Soviet Union was "at war with us."[8]

By contrast, Foreign Minister Hans-Dietrich Genscher of West Germany, in an article in *Foreign Affairs* in 1982, vigorously reaffirmed "the European view" that the "policy of a balance of power must continue to be supplemented by détente" and the alliance policy as set forth in the Harmel Report.[9] Later, Genscher even called for a revival of the U.S.-Soviet détente established in the Nixon-Brezhnev summit of 1972.[10]

These divergences in American and West European views of détente and approaches to East-West relations resurfaced and found expression well into the 1980s as the United States and Europe dealt with various developments. For example, European concerns over the Reagan Doctrine of robust competition in the Third World were well reflected in the anguished remarks of President Richard von Weizsäcker of the Federal Republic of Germany, speaking at a commencement ceremony at Harvard University in 1987. Speaking of the Third World, he said, "Have we not time and again misinterpreted the social struggle of those nations primarily as a problem of our own security? How long will we carry on seeking and supporting military solutions there? When will the East *and the West* put an end to the wretched 'zero-sum game' of their proxy wars on the soil of third countries?"[11]

---

group proposed by Belgium Foreign Minister Pierre Harmel to study future tasks of the alliance, was approved by the NATO members in December 1967. Its chief contribution was a broadening of the alliance mission to embrace détente as well as defense.

8.  See Roy Gutman and Jim Klurfeld, "Reagan Remark on Cold War Stunned Allies," *Newsday*, July 11, 1982, p. 4. There is no official text of the remarks, which Secretary Haig described as "an ad-libbed, if you will, or unstructured, personal intervention." This spontaneous personal expression by the president was precisely what so shocked the allies.

9.  Hans-Dietrich Genscher, "Toward an Overall Western Strategy for Peace, Freedom and Progress," *Foreign Affairs*, vol. 61 (Fall 1982), p. 43, and see pp. 42–66.
    This was an important article; informed German sources have advised me that it was drafted by the policy planning department of the German Foreign Ministry.

10. This call appeared in a ten-page statement or White Paper, justifying German pursuit of détente, issued by Genscher in August 1984. See John Tagliabue, "Bonn Defends Ties to East: Says They Help Ease Strains," *New York Times*, August 7, 1984, p. A6.

11. See Anthony Lewis, "When We Could Believe," *New York Times*, June 12, 1987, p. A31. Emphasis added.

## The Polish Crisis, 1981–83

As the Reagan administration was entering office, a potential crisis over Soviet military intervention in Poland, feared in December 1980, was dissipating. The internal political crisis in Poland, however, continued and intensified. During 1981 the Reagan administration and the NATO allies continued to issue warnings against Soviet military intervention.[12] As the NATO ministerial communiqué in May 1981 put it, "Poland must be left free to resolve its own problems."[13] Then, on December 13, 1981, General Wojciech Jaruzelski and a Military Committee of National Salvation took over from the Communist Party and government in what was virtually a military coup, and did act, imposing martial law. Jaruzelski acted under conditions of disintegrating political authority, moreover in a situation in which the Soviet Union might at some point intervene with its own military forces if the Polish leadership did not.[14]

---

12. On his first day as secretary of state, Haig sent a letter to Gromyko warning against Soviet intervention in Poland. Gromyko replied through Dobrynin eight days later (at Haig's first meeting with him) warning against American interference in Poland (see Alexander M. Haig, Jr., *Caveat: Realism, Reagan, and Foreign Policy* [Macmillan, 1984], pp. 242, 104).

13. *State Bulletin*, vol. 81 (July 1981), p. 39. While the communiqué went on to say that "any outside intervention would have the gravest consequences for international relations," it was clear that it meant any overt and direct, in particular military, intervention by the Soviet Union.

    Similarly, in a Department of State policy statement on Eastern Europe to Congress in June 1981, Assistant Secretary Lawrence Eagleburger had stated that the United States would "continue to refrain from words or actions which would complicate the resolution of Poland's problems by the Poles themselves." Lawrence S. Eagleburger, "U.S. Policy Toward the USSR, Eastern Europe, and Yugoslavia," statement before the Subcommittee on Europe and the Middle East of the House Foreign Affairs Committee on June 10, 1981, *State Bulletin*, vol. 81 (August 1981), p. 76.

14. The Polish leaders had been trying to deal with the political standoff between themselves and Solidarity and the people and had been fending off Soviet pressures for the entire year since December 1980, but the situation had continued to deteriorate.

    Since 1989 there has been a debate in Poland about whether General Jaruzelski was acting in Poland's interests in heading off a Soviet intervention by his own initiative or whether he served Soviet rather than Polish interests. Jaruzelski has argued that in view of what he then knew he could not have acted in any other way, and that Polish martial law was the lesser evil. He recalled Brezhnev's repeated double-edged warnings that Moscow "would not leave Poland to its own fate." In particular, he was influenced by a chilling discussion with Soviet Defense Minister Marshal Ustinov in September 1981 in which he said, "The Soviet Union would no longer tolerate the situation, that it threatened the security of the whole Warsaw Pact," and along with Afghanistan and the hostile Chinese stance Poland represented a "third front." He also said that Marshal Viktor Kulikov, the commander in chief of the Warsaw Pact command, similarly had told

When the Poles acted, without direct Soviet action or military intervention, the Western powers suddenly found they had been deterring the wrong contingency. Although Soviet responsibility was widely suspected, and

---

him: "If this continues, my hand will not shake." See John Darnton, "Jaruzelski Is Now Sorry He Ordered Martial Law," *New York Times*, March 4, 1993, pp. A1, A12.

Similarly, some former Soviet military commanders have said that by December 1981 if the Poles themselves did not crack down on Solidarity with martial law, the Soviet Army was prepared to take over. For example, see the interviews with the late General Viktor Dubynin, then chief of the General Staff of the Russian Army, who in 1981 had been one of the division commanders whose troops were slated to move into Poland, in "General Dubynin: Thanks to the Poles for Putting Up with Us for 47 Years," *Novoye vremya* (New Times), no. 26 (June 1992), pp. 28–29; and another interview in *Gazeta Wyborcza* (Electoral Gazette), March 14, 1992, p. 1. On the other hand, the chief Soviet intelligence officer in Poland at the time, Lieutenant General Vitaly Pavlov of the KGB, has asserted that Yury Andropov had told him that the Soviet leadership was determined not to intervene with Soviet forces and that he had so informed the Polish leaders, including General Jaruzelski. See Vitaly Pavlov, "Intelligence [Operations] Not Allowed," *New Times*, no. 24 (June 1993), p. 25. General Anatoly Gribkov has affirmed that Jaruzelski, through Polish chief of the General Staff F. Sivitski, had tried from December 9 through 11 to get General Kulikov to persuade the Soviet leaders to make a public declaration of their support to the Polish leadership to back up martial law. See General of the Army A. I. Gribkov, "The 'Brezhnev Doctrine' and the Polish Crisis at the Beginning of the '80s," *Voyenno-istoricheskii zhurnal* (Military Historical Journal), no. 9 (September 1992) pp. 51–52.

Reportedly, the Politburo debated the question of military intervention several times during the year, each time deciding at that point not to intervene. A final key Politburo meeting of December 10, 1981, discussed the still equivocal but crystalizing plans of General Jaruzelski for imposition of martial law and military rule, and again decided in any case not to intervene with Soviet troops.

The record of that meeting of December 10, 1981 (and the records of several meetings on the Polish crisis) has now been declassified. It reveals that Party Secretary Konstantin Rusakov reported that the Polish Politburo had unanimously voted to impose martial law, and that Jaruzelski intended to announce it to the people in a patriotic address as head of a military government, not as a party action. Yury Andropov, however, said that Jaruzelski remained uncertain and reluctant on introducing martial law. Mikhail Suslov said that Jaruzelski was playing a two-faced game with them, but that under any circumstances they should not send Soviet troops in. Konstantin Chernenko summed up the consensus on not intervening with Soviet troops, and Brezhnev concluded on that note. The document is in the former Central Committee archive, TsKhSD, Fond 89, Perechen' 66, Dokument 6, *Zasedaniye Politbyuro TsK KPSS 10 dekabrya 1981 goda* (Meeting of the Politburo of the CC CPSU, December 10, 1981), agenda item no. 1, "On the Question of the Situation in Poland," Top Secret, Special File, only copy, 11 pp. (statements cited from pp. 4, 5, 9–11).

Jaruzelski may or may not have believed the Soviet leaders would eventually intervene if he did not stabilize the situation, even if on several occasions in 1980 and 1981 they had decided not to do so. There was no Soviet ultimatum compelling him to impose martial law, but the shadow of possible Moscow intervention under some circumstances was not absent when he reluctantly made the decision to do so.

the shadow of Soviet power was clearly ever present in the background, the Soviet Union did not, as had been feared, intervene directly.[15]

In response to martial law in Poland, the Western countries called off planned meetings to renegotiate Poland's huge hard-currency debt and announced that no new commercial credits would be extended. This action was primarily intended to demonstrate dissatisfaction with the Polish political repression of Solidarity, but it was also a form of economic retrenchment that fell short of calling the Polish debt into default. The United States went further than its European allies in its demonstrative punitive gestures by banning U.S. government-sponsored shipments of agricultural products, denying Polish fishing rights in American waters, and suspending landing rights to the Polish national airline. Most-favored-nation (MFN) trade status for Poland was suspended ten months later, and the United States also blocked Poland from receiving assistance from the International Monetary Fund (until late 1984).

The United States also imposed economic sanctions on the Soviet Union, an action that the European allies did not join. There was an ironic element in the American move. The United States had threatened punitive action if the Soviet Army moved into Poland. Then, when it did not do so, the United States imposed sanctions anyway. Some of the unilateral actions were clearly demonstrative, such as denying landing rights to the Soviet airline Aeroflot and not renewing the scientific exchange agreement. Others were more concrete economic measures: the Kama purchasing commission (which bought parts for a huge truck factory built in the early 1970s) was closed; negotiations on a new maritime agreement were suspended; and negotiations on a new grain sales agreement were postponed. Most significant, the United States suspended sales of oil and gas technology and validation of export licenses for high technology.

Although these actions were authorized by the president as a response to Soviet pressures on Poland, hard-line advocates of a confrontational approach within the administration had been urging these same measures for

---

15. As became publicly known only in June 1986, a key Polish General Staff officer directly involved in planning the martial law crackdown, Colonel Ryszard Kuklinski, had been supplying information on Polish and Soviet military plans to the United States and defected just one month before the crackdown. He had not known the date martial law would be declared, but he knew it would be a Polish military move, not a Soviet one. For his own account, see "The Crushing of Solidarity," *Kultura* (Culture), Paris, no. 4 (475) (April 1987), pp. 3–57, translated and reprinted in *Orbis*, vol. 32 (Winter 1988), pp. 7–31.

   General Jaruzelski, in a later account, stated that because Kuklinski had known all the plans, the Polish leadership assumed that the failure of the U.S. government to act meant a tacit if reluctant American approval for Polish action, in preference to Soviet military intervention. See Paris AFP, April 17, 1992, in Foreign Broadcast Information Service, *Daily Report: Eastern Europe*, April 20, 1992, p. 17. (Hereafter FBIS, *Eastern Europe*.)

some time for quite different reasons: to place the Soviet economy under greater pressure and reduce even indirect contributions to Soviet military capacity. Haig has commented that some of the National Security Council (NSC) members regarded the Polish action as "an opportunity to inflict mortal political, economic, and propaganda damage on the U.S.S.R.," as well as to "control Soviet behavior toward Poland," and even to apply economic sanctions that could bring the Soviet Union "to her knees."[16] As Haig has noted, it was highly questionable that such a course could succeed. It was also an approach that risked provoking a Polish uprising that the United States could not have aided.

Six months later, in June, the administration—overriding the objections of Secretary Haig—expanded economic sanctions by banning the sale of American equipment and technology for construction of the Soviet gas pipeline to Western Europe. Worse still, this ban included American technology manufactured by Western European firms under U.S. license. Moreover, this action followed only days after an alliance summit meeting at Versailles at which the allies had understood that the United States would not seek to impose such extraterritorial restraints on trade but would instead accept a general agreement to tighten the terms of credit to the Soviet Union.[17]

The Europeans were incensed, and furious on other grounds as well, not the least of which was the illegality of the action in their view (and in the view of virtually all international lawyers). They also saw no relation between the U.S. moves and what had occurred in Poland or any other Soviet action, nor could they foresee any favorable consequences. The ban indirectly involved, moreover, a punitive sanction against the Western countries.[18] Finally, to make matters worse, just a month later the United States unilaterally decided to sign a new grain sale agreement with the Soviet Union. It looked as though the United States wanted its European allies to bear the burden of a policy of economic warfare they did not accept, while the United States would retain its lucrative trade in grain. Again, too, the United States, as with its sanctions against Iran in 1979 and against the Soviet Union in 1980 after Afghanistan, gained a reputation for breaking contracts and for unreliability as an economic

---

16. Haig, *Caveat*, p. 240.

17. For Haig's account of these events see ibid., pp. 303–16. As earlier noted, the president made this decision at a meeting scheduled by William Clark for a time when Haig was absent (pp. 312–13).

    For a detailed account, see Antony J. Blinken, *Ally vs. Ally: America, Europe, and the Siberian Pipeline Crisis* (Praeger, 1987).

18. A member of the White House staff told me that, in fact, Reagan had decided on the pipeline embargo in a fit of anger when he could not promptly reach French President François Mitterrand. Reagan's decision occurred after Mitterrand had spoken out, implying that the United States was acceding to a European position, following the NATO Versailles meeting.

partner. The main U.S. rationale for seeking to prevent construction of the pipeline was to protect the Europeans from possible Soviet pressure in the form of a potential future threat to withhold gas once the Europeans were (marginally) dependent on it. Yet here was the United States exerting very real economic pressure on its Western allies. Moreover, the Western European powers were confident they could understand and defend their interests against the Russians—or, if need be, against the Americans.

Some Europeans concluded that the Reagan administration was behaving so vehemently over the gas pipeline not because it was concerned about the vulnerability of Western Europe, as it claimed, nor even because it wanted to put economic pressure on the Soviet Union. Rather, the pipeline represented a major East-West economic link that supported European détente, one not shared by the United States, and it thus reduced U.S. leverage over Western Europe on questions of policy toward the Soviet Union.

Finally, five painful months later, the extended trade sanctions of June 1982 were removed. The allies accepted a vague agreement to be vigilant in East-West trade, to keep it economically sound and not one-sidedly to Soviet advantage. In the United States, the administration justified the resolution of the impasse with the allies over sanctions as representing a new consensus on a *tougher* general trade policy toward the Soviet Union, which it was not.[19] Thus ultimately the trade sanctions, rather than modifying Soviet, or West European, behavior, created a problem resolved only by modifying the U.S. position.

No serious new problems in coordinating Western economic relations with the Soviet Union or Eastern Europe arose in the mid–1980s, but a persisting divergence remained, marked by more restrictive American practice and continuing U.S. pressure on its allies. Moreover, this coincided with persisting U.S.-European frictions over the General Agreement on Tariffs and Trade (GATT) and other trade relations from 1982 to 1986.

On the question of sanctions over Poland, the moderation of the Polish regime and its end to martial law and release of political prisoners gradually led to a partial relaxation of American sanctions in 1984.[20] Even when the United States was pressing for tough economic sanctions against the Soviet Union over Poland in 1982, however, it did not suspend the INF talks that had just begun.

---

19. See George P. Shultz, *Turmoil and Triumph: My Years as Secretary of State* (Charles Scribner's Sons, 1993), pp. 135–43.

20. Later, in 1986, the Polish government released all remaining political prisoners and largely dismantled the martial law regime still partially effective in 1984–86. Removal of the remaining sanctions, denial of most-favored-nation (MFN) trade status and eligibility for credits, was long debated within the administration and finally announced on February 19, 1987. According to informed administration officials, the main opponent of lifting these sanctions in 1986 was, surprisingly, Secretary of State George Shultz, rather than ideologues in the White House. He wished to use them as leverage for Polish internal liberalization.

The START talks on strategic arms reduction, while delayed by three months, also began in mid–1982.

## The Struggle over INF, 1981–83

The decision to deploy new American intermediate-range missiles in Europe, taken by NATO in December 1979, had always enjoyed only tepid support by Western publics. In the new context of growing American-Soviet confrontation, aggravated by European unease over the posture of the Reagan administration, the theater nuclear deployments, now dubbed intermediate-range nuclear forces (INF), became a controversial issue in the early 1980s.

The U.S. agreement to open arms limitation talks on the INF, announced to the allies at the May 1981 NATO ministerial meeting, prevented what otherwise could have become a serious split over the deployment of INF missiles undermining confidence between the United States and its allies. The global-zero proposal, though it initially attracted European praise, increasingly came to be regarded as the nonnegotiable propaganda platform it then was. At the same time, the West generally considered the steadfast Soviet objection to any deployment of U.S. missiles as equally intransigent and unacceptable. Thus, despite increasing dissatisfaction at the failure of the INF talks over their two-year life (November 1981–November 1983), by breaking off the talks the Soviet Union took the lion's share of the blame in the eyes of Western publics.

One episode did cause a flare-up of concern in the alliance before it subsided. When in July 1982 the American negotiator, Ambassador Paul Nitze, worked out with his Soviet counterpart, Ambassador Yuly Kvitsinsky, a possible compromise agreement in an informal celebrated "walk in the woods," without authorization from Washington, the proposed compromise was turned down by both Washington and Moscow. As word of this development leaked out, the U.S. administration was criticized in some quarters in Europe for repudiating the attempt. Serious division within the alliance was spared only by the parallel Soviet rejection. Which side had turned the compromise down first was not possible to determine, and the blame was seen as shared.[21]

The INF talks did not lead to an agreement; indeed, they stimulated additional Soviet deployments as an avowed countermeasure. They were, however, successful in another respect. The mere fact that they had taken place was sufficient to reduce to politically manageable levels popular opposition in Europe to the NATO deployment. It began on schedule in December 1983.

---

21. Strobe Talbott, *Deadly Gambits: The Reagan Administration and the Stalemate in Nuclear Arms Control* (Alfred A. Knopf, 1984), pp. 116–51.

The process of deployment was not seriously impeded by residual public opposition.

Despite genuine Soviet concern over the military implications of the short-time-to-target Pershing II missiles in particular, the INF deployment was not strongly supported in Washington, or in NATO, for its military value. Rather, it was seen initially—on both sides of the Atlantic, and in Washington by both the Carter and Reagan administrations—as a step to shore up alliance unity. It was also seen, especially in Europe, as a step to reinforce deterrence by "coupling" American conventional and strategic forces. The real European concern was strengthening the American commitment, and the real U.S. interest was demonstrating that commitment. Nonetheless, a measure that had been intended to brace unity became a source of friction and division, especially in Europe. Deploying NATO INF had become a problem, not a solution.

The widespread popular opposition to the INF deployment in the early 1980s frequently assumed broader antinuclear, anti-American, and anti-alliance overtones. It led the Social Democratic Party in Germany, especially after it lost the elections in March 1983, to oppose the INF deployment that to a large extent its leader, Helmut Schmidt, had inspired. At the grassroots all three parties in Germany were affected by the shift in popular opinion against the INF deployment, even though the West German governments under both parties continued to support deployment. In Great Britain, too, the opposition Labour Party moved toward rejecting any nuclear weapons, American or British, in the country. Although public opposition tended to subside once the deployment began and the INF talks ended, it did not die.

The NATO governments supported proceeding with the negotiation and deployment tracks as they had agreed in 1979. The stronger American interest in deployment and the growing European interest in arms limitation, in response to public pressures, did, however, cause frictions. Moreover, by 1983 the U.S. government had turned a measure originally designed to accede to European desires into an alliance loyalty test administered by Washington. The predominant view in the Reagan administration from the outset was that the INF talks were essentially a matter not of arms control, but of "alliance management."[22] To many Europeans, this approach looked like alliance manipulation by Washington. Moreover, the goal became not the satisfaction of European preferences, but success in deployment despite arms talks, European public disaffection, and—in particular—Soviet opposition.

The Soviet leaders, as noted earlier, undertook a major campaign to influence Western public opinion against deployment. They placed the INF issue in the political forefront and made it a much more decisive political-military factor than it inherently was. In doing so, they only increased the signifi-

---

22. This phrase has been attributed to Richard Burt, first director of politico-military affairs and then assistant secretary for European affairs in the Department of State during this period. See ibid., p. 62.

cance of their failure. By making support for INF deployment a touchstone of political intentions and détente, they damaged East-West political relations (especially with West Germany, the key country). The Soviets were heavy-handed in their attempt to influence the West German election in 1983, and their efforts backfired. Overall, deployment became a defeat for the Soviet Union of larger political dimensions than it would otherwise have been.

At the same time, INF deployment was less clearly a victory for the United States and NATO. Deployment was not an end in itself, or merely a victory in overcoming Soviet opposition, although both came to predominate as aims in Washington. The purpose of the deployment had been to reinforce deterrence, to reassure the allies, and to enhance allied unity over the long run. All of these aims were, to some degree, casualties. The 1983 NATO victory was pyrrhic.

## Strategic Arms Negotiation: SDI, INF, and START, 1983–91

The American initiative on strategic ballistic missile defense, the strategic defense initiative (SDI) or, popularly, Star Wars, in March 1983 disturbed many Europeans for several reasons. First, it was a sudden, unilateral pronouncement by the United States on a subject of long-standing central importance to the alliance, on which the expressed alliance consensus was diametrically the opposite of the president's stand. Second, it represented a direct long-term challenge to the ABM Treaty, strongly endorsed by the alliance on its merits and generally acknowledged as the most significant arms limitation agreement to date. Third, it posed difficult potential problems either if the defense technology were provided to Europe (posing problems of strategy as well as cost), or if it were not. The very idea of such strategic defenses seemed applicable only to the United States. If so, the SDI would potentially decouple the security of the United States from the security of Western Europe. Moreover, it threatened to stir up an arms race that would undercut the British and French nuclear deterrents. Last, but far from least, it seemed to represent a turning away from arms control and reduction of East-West tensions by the United States in favor of unilateral U.S. pursuit of a new military technological will-o'-the-wisp with isolationist overtones. The absence of consultation only reinforced this impression.[23]

Over the several years from the time of President Reagan's speech launching the SDI, European views on the SDI became more moderate for several reasons. As it became clear that the United States, at least throughout

---

23. See Louis Deschamps, *The SDI and European Security Interests*, Atlantic Paper no. 62, Atlantic Institute for International Affairs (London: Croom Helm, 1986).

the Reagan administration, would seriously pursue the SDI, Western European governments chose to refrain from directly taking issue with the U.S. government. As the United States dangled apparently attractive opportunities for European gain from participation in SDI research, the major Western European allies (and Japan) joined in direct support. At the same time, though muting their direct criticism of the whole idea of the SDI and even participating in research on it, they remained skeptical of the attainability of the avowed aim, doubtful of its strategic merit, and concerned over its impact on arms control and political détente between East and West. They welcomed the resumption of talks when the new Nuclear and Space Talks (NST) began in March 1985, and they hoped a compromise agreement would restore the shaky strategic arms limitation regime established by SALT. Finally, American dedication to the SDI tempered over time, and the nature of the program was gradually but significantly changed.

The agreed formulation of an NST objective of "preventing an arms race in space" was, however, interpreted by the Soviet side as meaning that no weapons in space should be developed or deployed, while the United States sought to gain Soviet agreement to space weaponry for ballistic missile defense. The issue intensified, and the prospect of any compromise was severely set back when in October 1985 the American administration advanced a highly questionable new interpretation of the ABM Treaty that would permit testing of ABM systems in space. The strong objection of the NATO allies contributed to a rapid temporizing retreat by the administration to the position that it would continue to base its actual SDI program on the traditional more restrictive interpretation. It did not, however, repudiate the new interpretation and left open the possibility of reverting to it at any future time of its choice.[24]

The Geneva summit meeting of Reagan and Gorbachev in November 1985 again papered over the continuing gap between the two sides over SDI, but did call for renewed efforts and set a goal of a 50 percent reduction in strategic offensive arms. Again, the Geneva NST failed to advance over the next year.

Meanwhile, in May 1986 the American administration chose to announce that the United States would no longer consider itself bound to continued observance of the never ratified SALT II Treaty and the expired SALT I Interim Agreement. The European reaction (and an unexpectedly wide American reaction) was strongly negative. The fact that the constraints on planned American military programs were marginal, and that the Soviet Union had been dismantling a far greater number of older strategic weapons than the United States in order to maintain the SALT limits, pointed up the gratuitous political nature of the American abandonment of the existing agreements.

---

24.  See the discussion in chapter 12.

The unilateral repudiation of the SALT offensive agreements, coupled with the attempt to impose a unilateral reinterpretation gutting the legally binding ABM Treaty, convinced many in Europe that the United States, and not the Soviet Union, posed the greatest threat not only to further progress in arms control, but to its very survival.[25]

Western European support for East-West arms control, and especially U.S.-Soviet strategic arms limitations, was strong but not unalloyed with some concerns. When U.S.-Soviet strategic arms control negotiations had, for the first time in fifteen years, broken down in November 1983, the first concern of the Europeans was to see a resumption of talks at least to keep confrontation from monopolizing the relationship. When talks had been resumed, in 1985, there was hope for gradual progress in reducing arms and at least for maintaining strategic arms limitations—again, above all to prevent an unmitigated political confrontation and arms race. Only when, unexpectedly, the possibility of a sudden far-reaching step toward eliminating nuclear weapons appeared at the Reykjavik summit in October 1986 did the contradicting impulses in European thinking come into play.

On the one hand, the Western Europeans were disappointed that an agreement on strategic arms limitations had not been reached, and that the problems of INF missiles, the SALT II Treaty constraints, and the SDI remained. On the other hand, they were shocked that President Reagan had, even if tentatively and conditionally, agreed to an elimination of all strategic nuclear weapons in a span of ten years, and only slightly less concerned that he had proposed—and reaffirmed after Reykjavik—that all ballistic missiles should be eliminated within ten years. The allies had not been consulted on this proposal, and there was great concern over the impact of any such sudden change in the strategic balance on deterrence. Thus, while not in favor of an unlimited pursuit of the SDI, they were grateful that at Reykjavik the stalemate over testing weapons in space had at least prevented an agreement on extensive nuclear disarmament while Soviet conventional arms remained unconstrained.

Even though no agreement had been reached, the Western Europeans were disturbed that the American president had without their prior knowledge, much less advice or concurrence, taken the stand he had on a matter vital to them. Again, European interests seemed neglected by the American president. The fact that the president acted partly on impulse, and partly on the basis of a decision from which not only they but the professional military leaders of the United States had been excluded, was profoundly unsettling. This diminished confidence remained even though no agreement or arms reductions were

---

25. Though NATO governments did not go so far, even they were disturbed by the American policy. For example, at the NATO ministerial meeting in Estoril, Portugal, in June 1985 Shultz heard many of his colleague foreign ministers, unpersuaded by American arguments and allegations of Soviet violations, urge the United States to maintain the SALT II limits.

made. At the same time, the Europeans (and Americans) now realized for the first time the need to think through their own interests in deep arms reductions, and possible elimination of nuclear weapons, as serious possibilities. What would the effects be on deterrence? And was there an alternative to deterrence as a means to ensure security, the ultimate objective? These were central questions for the alliance as a whole, and after Reykjavik more and more people in Western Europe and in the United States saw a need to consider these questions carefully, and together. Finally, despite the improbability of any early agreement the matter assumed some urgency since it remained in play in continuing negotiation between the United States and the Soviet Union, and had importance not only in its own right in terms of rethinking the aims of arms control and defense policies, but also as a key question affecting East-West relations.

During the last months of 1986 the United States sought to move ahead on those areas where the Soviet Union had made concessions at Reykjavik, while standing fast on no ABM constraints and no linkage of the INF to strategic force reductions. The Soviet side responded by again tying the INF to strategic forces, and strategic offensive forces to ABM and space weapons constraints, stressing that all concessions at Reykjavik had been made as parts of a package. On February 28, 1987, Gorbachev broke the impasse by agreeing to proceed with negotiation of a separate INF agreement based on the Reykjavik zero levels for the United States and USSR in Europe, and one hundred INF warheads for each outside of Europe, in the United States and USSR respectively.

Negotiations continued in the separate strategic and space weapons talks with gradual advances, but for the whole of 1987 attention and efforts were focused by both sides principally on the INF negotiation. Gorbachev had concluded that only an INF agreement was feasible, and he was determined to restore the bilateral arms control process through a successful negotiation and agreement. What remained of the strategic arms control regime established in the 1970s, the ABM Treaty, was in peril, and the United States in 1986 had abandoned the previously bilaterally observed expired SALT I and unratified SALT II limitations. By mid-April, first to Secretary Shultz in Moscow, and then in a public speech, Gorbachev indicated readiness to meet a new Western European concern over "shorter range INF," or SRINF (those with a range of 500–1,000 km in addition to the longer-range INF, or LRINF (a range of 1,000–5,500 km) missiles, previously the sole subject of INF negotiation. Although the United States had no weapons deployed in the SRINF category while the Soviet Union did, Gorbachev was ready to negotiate the elimination of those systems. Thus Gorbachev accepted what came to be called the "double-zero option" for missiles in Europe, zero LRINF and zero SRINF. The European reaction was ambivalent, welcoming the Soviet reductions but with some unease over the rapid steps toward nuclear arms reduction in Europe without comparable movement to reduce conventional arms in which the East had a numerical preponderance.

On July 23, Gorbachev went still further, agreeing to global-zero LRINF and SRINF missiles, giving up all Soviet INF missiles deployed in Asia as well as Europe. This simplified verification and was welcomed in China and Japan.

Although several other issues were involved in the negotiation, the only one of particular interest in Europe arose when the Soviet Union, which had made almost all the concessions, insisted on elimination also of seventy-two Pershing IA SRINF held by Germany, with nuclear warheads provided by the United States. After only a few weeks, under rising public pressure and a boost from his own coalition foreign minister, Hans-Dietrich Genscher, Chancellor Helmut Kohl announced on August 26 that Germany would eliminate its SRINF when the United States and Soviet Union did so. That left the American warheads for the system, obviously no longer relevant, but which the Soviet Union insisted be removed under the agreement. Initially, the United States objected, but a few weeks later acceded.

Although there was some restlessness in the NATO political-military bureaucracy, the European countries welcomed the success of the negotiation when the INF Treaty was signed by President Reagan and General Secretary Gorbachev on December 8, 1987.

Strategic arms reduction talks continued to inch forward in 1988 but did not approach agreement. In the aftermath of the INF agreement, however, and with anticipation of a U.S.-Soviet strategic arms agreement before long, some Europeans began to express concern over the continuing disparity in conventional forces and arms in Europe. Almost exactly a year after the INF Treaty was signed, Gorbachev again took the initiative, in his UN speech on December 7, 1988, to announce significant Soviet unilateral force reductions, especially in offensive tank forces in Eastern Europe, and a large overall reduction in Soviet conventional forces. When that was followed by the successful negotiation of the Conventional Forces in Europe (CFE) Treaty signed in November 1990, providing for asymmetrical reductions of NATO and Warsaw Pact forces, entailing far greater reductions on the Eastern side, there remained no concern over U.S.-Soviet strategic arms reductions except to wish their earliest successful conclusion.

As noted, subsiding American interest, and consequently subsiding Soviet concern, in the SDI also kept that from remaining of high interest in Europe.

The START I Treaty, with modest reductions and extensive verification, was finally completed and signed on July 31, 1991. It brought the levels of strategic weapons back down to about what the levels were when the START reductions had begun in 1982, a modest step but one in the right direction. It was useful in helping, together with the ABM Treaty, the INF Treaty, and the

CFE Treaty, to establish a solid arms control regime. But by that time, with the end of the Warsaw Pact and the Cold War the political-military complexion of Europe had drastically changed.

## Eastern Europe in American and Soviet Policy in the 1980s

Policy toward the communist countries of Eastern Europe was low in the interest and priorities of the Reagan administration in 1981, except for concern about possible Soviet intervention in Poland. Relations with those countries, in contrast, always stood very high in the priorities of the Soviet Union.

Poland was of critical importance to the Soviet Union in 1980–81,[26] and the Soviet leaders helped to establish the conditions under which General Wojciech Jaruzelski's regime was able in December 1981 to impose martial law and contain the deteriorating state of communist rule in Poland without direct Soviet intervention.

Apart from the deepening Polish internal political crisis, temporarily resolved by martial law and the dissolution of Solidarity, there were widespread economic difficulties throughout Eastern Europe in 1981–82. The most prominent and critical case was Poland with a hard-currency (mostly Western) debt of some $25 billion dollars in 1980 and a sharp drop in productivity and production in 1980–82. But this was only the most dramatic case. Romania, East Germany, Czechoslovakia, and Hungary suffered from curtailed East-West credit and trade. These economic problems caused the countries of Eastern Europe to turn more toward the Soviet Union, but it too was facing difficulties. The Soviet Union was thus not able to capitalize on the troubled state of East-West trade in ways that would tie the countries of Eastern Europe more closely to itself. It had to reduce energy exports to Eastern Europe by 10 percent. Nonetheless, it was required to increase its hidden subsidies to other countries in Eastern Europe in order to prevent the emergence of political instability and to provide sufficient direct economic aid to Poland to prevent an economic and political collapse.

---

26. For an interesting analysis see Sidney I. Ploss, *Moscow and the Polish Crisis: An Interpretation of Soviet Policies and Intentions* (Westview Press, 1986).

     The developments in Poland were also closely watched by others in Eastern Europe, with thin hope by liberal circles in several countries, but with concern in the East German leadership over both the volatile situation to their east and the possible repercussions of its suppression or spread, and alarm in the leadership of both Czechoslovakia and Romania over its possible spread to their own peoples. Concern on these grounds was also felt to some degree in the Soviet Union itself, especially by the leadership of the Ukraine and in the Baltic States.

Soviet policy was clear: to ensure continuing communist rule in the countries of the Warsaw Pact, to foster economic viability and integration, and to enhance political unity in support of Moscow's policies. It was a traditional policy of a traditional leadership under Brezhnev.

Some more open-minded Soviet cooperation with their Eastern European communist allies on relationships with the West began in the period of détente in the mid- to latter 1970s, continued for a time, but tapered off in the early 1980s. Confidential joint research studies on East-West European cooperation were undertaken in the late 1970s and early 1980s by Soviet and East European academic experts under a program headed by Academician Oleg T. Bogomolov, code-named Star. A parallel program on the normalization of Soviet-American relations in the context of their relationships with the countries of Eastern Europe, code-named Moment, was headed by Academician Georgy Arbatov of the Institute of the USA and Canada. Many of the recommendations of these groups, however, were not accepted by the Soviet and East European governments, and authors of some of the studies were even labeled "revisionists" and disciplined. These efforts ground to a halt. They did, however, lay the basis for much that would come later.[27]

During 1981–82 the Soviet Union and the countries of Eastern Europe were coping with their economic problems and slowly stabilizing the situation in Poland. As discussed earlier, the Reagan administration had focused first on possible military intervention in Poland and then sought unsuccessfully in the aftermath of martial law in Poland to force its Western European allies into punitive economic warfare. This course of action was pursued without benefit of a considered policy. Not until twenty months into the administration's first term was a policy toward Eastern Europe adopted.

Among the disparate elements in the Reagan administration were hard-liners in the White House and the Pentagon who were inclined to treat the countries of Eastern Europe and the Soviet Union as a whole, as "the communist enemy," all under Moscow's rule. From that perspective, there was no need for American policy or more than nominal relations with any of the "satellite" countries of the Soviet bloc. Others, especially in the Department of State, believed that a continued policy of "differentiation" among the communist countries was necessary for an effective policy, whether of détente or confrontation. The only policy statement of this first year and a half was a presentation by the then-Assistant Secretary of State for European Affairs Lawrence Eagleburger, testifying before a House subcommittee in June 1981. He reaffirmed the approach of tailoring American relations with each country and in terms of the relations of the Eastern European states with the USSR on the basis of two criteria: the degree to which the countries of Eastern Europe

27. For the first public disclosure of these programs see Igor Orlik, "Russia and Eastern Europe: Problems and Prospects," *Mezhdunarodnaya zhizn'* (International Affairs), no. 7 (July 1992), p. 35, with additional information from interviews.

"pursue independent foreign policies and/or more liberal domestic policies."[28] This approach, with variations in interpretation and adaptation, had been U.S. policy for nearly two decades.[29] There were ruffled feathers in the White House staff after this testimony because it had not been cleared and did not yet constitute an agreed-on administration position.[30] The issue was, however, considered sufficiently theoretical that the statement was not repudiated or countered, although the divergent views continued.

Only in August 1982 was a formal new policy guidance established in NSDD-54, and it marked at least a partial victory for the pragmatists of the State Department over the ideologists with an undifferentiated hostility: "differentiation" was reaffirmed.[31] There remained, however, ample opportunity for issues to arise over the degree of "forward thrust" of American effort to reduce Soviet hegemony in Eastern Europe and encourage political pluralism.[32]

The first public articulation of the new policy was in a speech by Vice President George Bush in Vienna in September 1983, after he had visited Hungary, Romania, and Yugoslavia.[33] Bush frankly stated: "Our policy is one of differentiation; that is, we look to what degree countries [of Eastern Europe] pursue autonomous foreign policies, independent of Moscow's direction, and to what degree they foster domestic liberalization—politically, economically, and in their respect for human rights." He specified that "the United States will engage in closer political, economic and cultural relations with those countries such as Hungary and Romania which assert greater openness or independence. We will strengthen our dialogue and cooperation with such countries." And, he went on, "We will not, however, reward closed societies and belligerent foreign

---

28. Eagleburger, *State Bulletin*, vol. 81 (August 1981), pp. 73–78, quotation from p. 76.

29. For an interpretive survey, see Raymond L. Garthoff, "Eastern Europe in the Context of U.S.-Soviet Relations," in Sarah Meiklejohn Terry, ed., *Soviet Policy in Eastern Europe* (Yale University Press, 1984), pp. 315–48.

30. When I inquired of a knowledgeable National Security Council official about policy toward Eastern Europe, and referred to the Eagleburger testimony, I was told that it represented only a State Department position that had not been reviewed or approved by the White House.

31. See also the discussion in chapter 1. During the interagency review and preparation of National Security Decision Directive (NSDD)–54, consideration was given to the more stringent criterion of both greater independence and internal liberalization, but that idea was rejected.

32. Even Secretary Shultz, recently in office when the policy was adopted and representing the more moderate view, described it as "our policy designed to move countries of Eastern Europe away from the Soviet Union by adjusting our behavior toward those countries, depending on the degree to which they might take positions at variance with Moscow." See Shultz, *Turmoil and Triumph*, p. 40.

33. Other aspects of this speech have been discussed in chapter 3.

policies—countries such as Bulgaria and Czechoslovakia which continue to flagrantly violate the most fundamental human rights, and countries such as East Germany and, again, Bulgaria which act as proxies to the Soviets in the training, funding and arming of terrorists and which supply advisers and military and technical assistance to armed movements seeking to destabilize governments in the developing world." Bush drew a line, though ambiguously, when he further said: "The United States does not seek to destabilize or undermine any government, but . . . we support and will encourage all movement toward the social, humanitarian and democratic ideals," without even saying such "movement" itself must be peaceful. Finally, Bush made clear that the United States did not regard the wartime Yalta agreement as dividing Europe into spheres of influence, and he said that in that accord the Soviet Union had "pledged itself to grant full independence" to the countries of Eastern Europe, and that "the Soviet violation of these obligations is the primary root of East-West tensions today."[34]

The confrontational tone of high-level American statements on Eastern Europe continued in 1984. In January, while attending the opening of the Conference on Disarmament in Europe (CDE) in Stockholm, Secretary Shultz stressed: "Let me be very clear: the United States does not recognize the legitimacy of the artificially imposed division of Europe. This division is the essence of Europe's security and human rights problem, and we all know it."[35]

In August, President Reagan, in a speech directed at Polish-Americans on the fortieth anniversary of the Warsaw Uprising, declared that "passively accepting the permanent subjugation of the people of Eastern Europe is not . . . acceptable" and that the United States did not accept "the division of Europe into spheres of influence."[36] He also spoke of the countries of Eastern Europe as "captive nations." Finally, he said that what had happened in Poland with the emergence of Solidarity was a sign that "the tide is turning."[37] Secretary Shultz echoed this theme a few days later in an address to the Veterans of Foreign Wars. Not only did he find the tide of history turning against Soviet domination in Eastern Europe, but turning with the United States as a result of

---

34. "The Vice President: Address at the Hofburg, Vienna," September 21, 1983, *State Bulletin*, vol. 83 (November 1983), pp. 22, 21, 20.

   Bush also overrode State Department advice and gratuitously insulted the Russians and unnecessarily riled U.S.-Eastern European relations; see chapter 3.

35. "Secretary Shultz Visits Europe," statement at the CDE, Stockholm, January 17, 1984, *State Bulletin*, vol. 84 (March 1984), p. 35.

   This statement by Shultz made a strong negative impression on Eastern European officials, and they referred to it for months.

36. "Fortieth Anniversary of the Warsaw Uprising," August 17, 1984, *Weekly Compilation of Presidential Documents*, vol. 20 (August 20, 1984), pp. 1133, 1132. (Hereafter *Presidential Documents*.)

37. Ibid., p. 1133.

the crusading American policy. "Our policies are working," he said. "Gradually, but inevitably, Communist oppression is losing the contest" in Central America and around the world. "The tide of history is with us. The values that Americans cherish—democratic freedom, peace, and the hope of prosperity—are taking root all around the world."[38] The title and theme of Shultz's address was "Diplomacy and Strength," and with "our willingness to act decisively in moments of crisis," we could help turn this "tide of freedom."[39] He specifically promised that while "we may not see freedom in Eastern Europe in our lifetime," "someday it will happen." And he recalled Czechoslovakia in 1968, Hungary in 1956, and East Germany in 1953, as well as Poland in the early 1980s.[40]

American policy formulation and articulation, and rhetorical support for a crusading spirit, did not seem to find expression in these years beyond some step up in propaganda efforts. Eastern Europe had receded from a prominent position in Washington after the suppression of Solidarity and the spent efforts at economic retaliation.

From the Soviet perspective, however, these indications of an American crusading zeal were perceived as much more ominous. In the first place, anything potentially affecting Eastern Europe was of high priority. Beyond that, the importance accorded propaganda was much higher in Moscow. And finally the responsibilities of the new White House committee on "public diplomacy" established by NSDD-77 in January 1983 were understood to constitute what the Soviets call "active measures," going beyond propaganda to include a wide range of covert actions.[41] The chief of the Central Committee International Information Department, Leonid Zamyatin, in 1984 stressed that despite signs of American interest in dialogue, the pursuit by the United States

---

38. "Diplomacy and Strength," August 20, 1984, *State Bulletin*, vol. 84 (October 1984), p. 19.

39. Ibid., pp. 20, 19.

40. Ibid., p. 20.

   Secretary Shultz has acknowledged in his memoir that shortly before this spate of speeches he had proposed to Reagan "a new level of U.S. activism" and more vigorous application of "differentiation" in U.S. policy toward Eastern Europe. See Shultz, *Turmoil and Triumph*, p. 479.

41. The Soviet leaders clearly had an exaggerated notion of the "active measures" to be undertaken by the Clark Committee, but they were not entirely wrong. See chapter 3. For Soviet accounts, see S. Losev, "'Public Diplomacy'—A Doctrine of International Brigandage," *Mezhdunarodnaya zhizn'*, no. 4 (April 1983), pp. 78–87; R. Ovinnikov, "A 'Crusade' to the Brink of Nuclear War," *Mezhdunarodnaya zhizn'*, no. 5 (May 1983), pp. 97–106; and Yury B. Kashlev, *Konveier dezinformatsii i litsemeriya* (Conveyor of Disinformation and Dissimulation) (Moscow: Znaniye, 1985), 64 pp.

   The Soviet leaders were also aware that the United States had been actively involved in the early 1980s not only in intelligence collection but also in covert action, particularly in Poland. See the discussion in chapter 1.

of an intensified political warfare campaign had now been raised to "the status of state policy" and was controlled as never before by the White House. He described this campaign as combining "a strategy of a global assault on socialism as a social system with the tactics of a differentiated approach to individual socialist countries" with the aim "to weaken and divide them." Furthermore, the campaign was said to prosecute this "ideological war" not only with propaganda, but with "blackmail, disinformation, and acts of provocation and terror."[42] The Soviet leaders therefore directed particular efforts to reinforcing the cohesion of the Soviet-led bloc in Eastern Europe.

Beginning in mid–1983 the Soviet leaders began a campaign aimed at greater ideological discipline and conformity in the bloc. This campaign was related not only to a growing sense of tension and increased danger felt in Moscow,[43] and the perceived American crusading attack on the countries of Eastern Europe, but also to internal debates within the Soviet political establishment. From 1983 into 1986 there ensued a remarkable series of recurring transnational ideological-political debates in Eastern Europe and the Soviet Union. Without reviewing these debates comprehensively, it is useful to illustrate their scope.

In April 1983 *Pravda* twice injected itself into a feud within the Finnish Communist Party that Moscow had avoided entering for years. Now it supported a conservative dogmatist faction against moves by the "Eurocommunist" majority to oust the "Stalinists" (as the majority group called them). This followed a personal visit by conservative Politburo member Grigory Romanov to Helsinki where he had in effect supported the conservative Finnish comrades.[44] A few weeks later, a Soviet article strongly criticized the relatively liberal Polish deputy prime minister, Mieczysław Rakowski, in effect for being too soft on Solidarity. Yet another article criticized Dumitru Popescu, a member of the ruling Political Executive Committee of the Romanian Communist Party, for distorting Marxist-Leninist theory, escalating a charge in April against a lesser Romanian writer. Both the Poles and the Romanians reacted to these criticisms by stubbornly defending their positions and rejecting the Soviet charges.[45]

---

42. Leonid Zamyatin, "Washington's New Orientation?" *Tribuna* (The Tribune), Prague, no. 44 (October 31, 1984), p. 3.

   This Soviet perspective was also evident in conversations with Soviet party officials concerned with international affairs.

43. See the discussion in chapter 3.

44. M. Kostikov, "At the District Conferences of the Communist Party of Finland," *Pravda*, April 21, 1983, and M. Kostikov, "For the Unity of the Communist Party of Finland," *Pravda*, April 26, 1983.

45. The attack on Rakowski, not by name but clearly identifying him (as the former chief editor of *Polityka* [Politics]), appeared in Andrei Ryzhov, "When One Loses Orientation: On the Pages of the Warsaw Weekly *Polityka*," *Novoye vremya* (New Times), no. 19

In a speech in June 1983 General Secretary Yury Andropov indicated little tolerance for ideological or political deviations in Eastern Europe, stressing the need for "strengthening cooperation and cohesion" in the bloc.[46] Andropov's pronouncement—described in a subsequent *Pravda* editorial as a "thesis" of the Central Committee plenum—was echoed in other authoritative Soviet statements.[47] This stress on conformity was also clear at the time of a visit to Moscow in July by Hungarian leader János Kádár. Despite Kádár's repeated careful references to autonomy, Andropov (and their joint communiqué) ignored that idea.[48]

Throughout this period there was considerable maneuvering over a still-tentative summit meeting of the Council on Mutual Economic Assistance (CMEA, also called CEMA and COMECON). Also, during this period the Soviets convened a special meeting of "leading party and state figures" in Moscow—in effect, the leaders of the Warsaw Pact, but for reasons never disclosed not described as such. This meeting discussed countermeasures to the increasingly imminent NATO initiation of operational deployment of INF missiles. The Soviets failed at this meeting to get East European support for their own tough position or countermeasures, including moving some Soviet missiles forward into Eastern Europe.[49]

At this juncture the Chinese actively resumed contacts with the Eastern Europeans and sought expanded relations. East Germany seemed

---

(May 6, 1983), pp. 18–20. The attack on Popescu appeared in a book review by Pimen Buyanov in *Literaturnaya gazeta* (Literary Gazette), May 4, 1983. The first in the series, criticizing Romanian writer Vasile Iota, was in E. Bagramov, "A Class Approach or an Eclectic Theory of Factors?" *Novoye vremya*, no. 16 (April 15, 1983), pp. 18–19. The rebuttals appeared in a series of indirect replies in *Polityka* (May 14, 1983), including an interview with Rakowski himself, but only one of them mentioned the Soviet article and deflected its criticism indirectly. The Romanians were much more blunt, rebutting the Soviet criticism on factual and theoretical grounds (Pompilu Marcea, in *Romania Literara* (Literary Romania), May 12, 1983, and Vasile Iota, in *Contemporanul* (Contemporary Times), June 3, 1983). The Czechs (and, from a less approving angle, the Yugoslavs) also picked up the Soviet criticism of Rakowski.

46. "Speech of Comrade Yu.V. Andropov, General Secretary of the Central Committee of the CPSU at the CPSU Central Committee Plenum Held on June 15, 1983," *Pravda*, June 16, 1983.

47. "Unity and Cohesion," editorial, *Pravda*, June 24, 1983; see also the important address of Party Secretary Mikhail Zimyanin, "A Party of Revolutionary Activities, Speech of Comrade M.V. Zimyanin," *Pravda*, July 30, 1983.

48. "Joint Soviet-Hungarian Communiqué," *Pravda*, July 24, 1983.
        Despite this Soviet firmness on ideological discipline in the socialist bloc, somewhat greater leeway was accorded internal economic decisions. A senior Soviet party official has told me that on this same visit Kádár raised with Andropov the matter of some additional internal Hungarian economic reform measures, as if seeking approval, and Andropov waved the question away, saying "That's your affair."

49. "Meeting in Moscow," *Izvestiya*, June 29, 1983.

especially receptive and eager to build ties. At the Sixth National People's Congress in Beijing in June Premier Zhao Ziyang referred to the "socialist" character of the East European regimes, an acknowledgment not yet accorded by the Chinese to the Soviet Union.[50]

An extraordinary meeting of party secretaries charged with ideological affairs was convened in September 1983 in Moscow, chaired by the second-ranking Politburo member and party secretary Konstantin Chernenko.[51] It was used by the Soviets not only to press for ideological conformity, but also to bring up some other issues. One was countermeasures to NATO INF deployment, on which the June summit meeting had not been entirely successful, and again on this occasion the attempt was inconclusive. There was also a clear indirect reference to the American exploitation of the KAL issue ("the latest events" show that U.S. circles "will not hesitate to use provocative actions to poison the international atmosphere even further," in the *Izvestiya* account of the meeting).[52] This was pointed at Romania, which had been neutral in its brief treatment of the KAL issue, and Hungary, which had given only lukewarm support to the Soviet position (perhaps because Vice President Bush was then due for his visit to both countries).

Bush's provocative Vienna speech was made the day following the Moscow meeting of Soviet and Eastern European party secretaries.

Amidst burgeoning political tensions between East and West, and to a lesser extent within the Eastern bloc, there was clear improvement in the economic condition of Eastern Europe. The year 1983 had seen a transition from a downward trend toward an improvement, and 1984 was to prove if not a boom at least a time of economic recovery (more slowly, though gradually, even in Poland). There remained, however, economic tensions among the Eastern states.

The prime ministers of the CMEA met in mid-October 1983 in East Berlin. Soviet Prime Minister Nikolai Tikhonov was fairly blunt in threatening to withhold supplies of fuel and raw materials from countries that did not rally to the Soviet position, but important differences remained. For the most part, the issues were economic; the Soviets pressed especially hard for improved quality of goods shipped from Eastern European countries to the Soviet Union. Some issues did, however, directly relate to East-West relations. Despite pressures for greater (as well as better) intra-CMEA ties, for example, Hungary

---

50. See chapter 14 for further discussion of Chinese diplomatic activity in Eastern Europe in the 1980s.

51. The seriousness of the occasion of the previous extraordinary meetings of Eastern bloc party secretaries underlies the importance of this one; the last had been in December 1980 when they met to discuss the Polish crisis, and the preceding one had been in 1968 at the time of the Czechoslovak crisis preceding Soviet-led bloc military intervention.

52. "Conference of Central Committee Secretaries of the Fraternal Parties of the Socialist Countries," *Izvestiya*, September 22, 1983.

held out for expanding its trade with the West. In a special meeting of only the top leaders, the Soviet Union did finally win acceptance of its long-sought CMEA summit meeting.[53]

The central focus of Soviet attention, and East-European as well, during the last three months of 1983 was the impending NATO INF missile deployment. Although the Eastern Europe countries had wholeheartedly supported the Soviet position calling for negotiated constraints on INF missile deployments in 1979–83, when that policy had failed by the end of 1983 they were much more reluctant to support the new Soviet line of punitive constraint on East-West relations, which was especially directed against West Germany as the main perceived supporter of the United States and central host to the new missile deployments. They were also very reluctant to see tit-for-tat new Soviet deployments of missiles in Eastern Europe.

On October 27, the Soviets unilaterally announced (in an authoritative interview of Andropov by *Pravda*) the contingent Soviet response if NATO deployment of INF missiles should proceed as planned. Though offering a further reduction in Soviet SS-20 missiles facing Europe from 243 to "about 140" if agreement could be reached not to make the deployment, Andropov now threatened to break off the INF arms negotiation if the deployment did occur.[54] Also, separately, two days earlier the Ministry of Defense had announced preparations to deploy "operational-tactical" missiles of lesser range in Czechoslovakia and East Germany as part of the necessary "countermeasures."[55] Then, on November 24, a statement was issued in Andropov's name announcing that with the beginning of NATO INF deployment the Soviet Union was withdrawing from the negotiations and implementing its planned countermeasures.[56]

The Eastern European reaction showed the extent of disarray in the communist camp. The Romanians on the next day issued a formal party-government statement criticizing the United States and the Soviet Union and appealed to the Soviet leaders to "reconsider" their decisions on countermeasures.[57] Hungary, while unenthusiastically supporting the Soviet position, also

---

53. "Communiqué on the 37th Meeting of the CMEA Session," *Pravda*, October 21, 1983.

54. "Replies of Yu.V. Andropov to Questions from the Newspaper *Pravda*," *Pravda*, October 27, 1983. The NATO deployment, he said, would "make it impossible to continue the talks."

55. "In the USSR Ministry of Defense," *Pravda*, October 25, 1983.

56. "Statement by Yu.V. Andropov, General Secretary of the Central Committee of the CPSU and Chairman of the Presidium of the Supreme Soviet of the USSR," *Pravda*, November 25, 1983.

57. "Declaration of the Executive Political Committee of the Central Committee of the Romanian Communist Party, State Council and Government of the Socialist Republic of Romania," AGERPRESS, November 25, 1983, in FBIS, *Eastern Europe*, November 28, 1983, p. H1.

referred to the Romanian declaration and its call for an East-West summit and failed to criticize the United States.[58] Though Bulgaria endorsed the Soviet stand, and although there were no plans to deploy Soviet missiles in Bulgaria, a few weeks later Todor Zhivkov chose to reaffirm a proposal for a Balkan nuclear-free zone. Perhaps he wanted insurance against being asked to accept a Soviet deployment, in any event his action struck a jarring note as the Soviet Union was undertaking new nuclear-armed missile deployments.[59] Most striking was the East German reaction. Both East Germany and Czechoslovakia had earlier reported indications of popular unhappiness over the prospect of new Soviet missile deployments. But now Party Chief Erich Honecker publicly commented that the new deployment in his country was "no cause for jubilation" and expressed his intention to "limit the damage as much as possible" in East-West relations.[60] Although the East Germans were not in a position to prevent the Soviet deployment, these statements were remarkably out of key with the Soviet position. Czechoslovak Prime Minister Lubomír Štrougal was reported to have said that in his country "no one jumped for joy" over the introduction of Soviet missiles in the counterdeployment there.[61]

Only days later, in early December, the annual meeting of the Warsaw Pact defense ministers took place, in Sofia. At the meeting, the Soviet Union pressed for increased military efforts by all the Eastern European communist countries. Marshal Ustinov publicly repeated this call in a speech two days after the meeting, saying that all Warsaw Pact members were "required to strengthen" their defense capabilities in light of the NATO buildup.[62] The Romanians, at least, objected to the Soviet plan, and later demonstratively did not increase their defense budget. The Warsaw Pact defense ministers also failed to endorse the Andropov statement on countermeasures, a blow to Soviet efforts to put pressure on the European NATO countries over the INF issue.[63]

---

58. "Guaranteeing the Security of the Socialist Community Is the Goal of the Soviet Union," *Népszabadság* (Popular Freedom), November 27, 1983.

59. *Rabotnichesko delo* (The Workers' Cause), December 12, 1983.

60. Speech by Erich Honecker delivered at the Seventh SED Central Committee plenum, November 26, 1983, *Neues Deutschland* (The New Germany), November 26–27, 1983.

61. Cited by Bradley Graham, "Soviet Missile Plan Disconcerts Bloc Allies," *Washington Post*, December 20, 1983, p. A1. Štrougal's remarks were not published in Czechoslovakia, as Honecker's had been in East Germany.

62. "With a Friendly Visit," *Pravda*, December 10, 1983; and "Meeting of Combat Friendship: Soviet Military Delegation in Bulgaria," *Krasnaya zvezda* (Red Star), December 10, 1983.

63. The meeting ended on December 7. A Bulgarian News Agency (BTA) account of the closing speech by General of the Army Dobri Dzhurov, who as Bulgarian defense minister was the host of the conference, reported Dzhurov as saying that the participants had "unanimously supported" Andropov's statement on countermeasures. This attempt failed; the published version of Dzhurov's speech the next day and the conference

The annual meeting of ideological affairs party secretaries took place in Moscow only two days after the defense ministers' meeting. In an unprecedented action, Romania boycotted the meeting. Although that was a severe blow to bloc unity, the absence of the Romanians did at least permit the Soviet leaders finally to squeeze an indirect endorsement of the Soviet position from the others. Even without the Romanians, however, the session was characterized as only "business-like" (a term usually used to describe negotiations with adversaries), and while the members present attached "great importance" to the Andropov statements of November 24 and September 28, they did not directly endorse them. No statement of support was given for the Soviet missile deployments or other counter-measures mentioned in the Andropov statement of November 24.[64]

The latter part of 1983 and early 1984 marked the peak of East-West tensions, and emergence of only thinly veiled tensions within the Eastern bloc. At this juncture came the transition in the Soviet leadership from Andropov to Chernenko. A more conciliatory tone also began to be sounded in American policy pronouncements directed to the Soviet Union, although not toward Eastern Europe. The year 1984 became one of transition in East-West relations, but passed without dramatic developments. Disagreements within the Eastern camp on political, ideological, economic, and military matters, though not becoming acute, remained.

Soviet attempts to curtail East-West détente and create punitive tensions in the West succeeded to a degree, but at an unexpected and disproportionate cost in frictions in the Eastern bloc. The dissatisfactions over military countermeasures in late 1983 faded in time, but new dissatisfactions arose over continuing political countermeasures. The Soviet-orchestrated boycott of the Los Angeles Olympics in May brought reluctant conformity by the East Europeans (except maverick Romania), but generated considerable negative popular reaction. Soviet attempts to force Eastern European political sanctions against West Germany were successful in blunting several well-publicized planned developments—notably, compelling in September the indefinite postponement of planned and announced visits to West Germany by East German leader Erich Honecker and Bulgarian leader Todor Zhivkov.[65] But in the broader sense the Soviet campaign failed. East Germany not only did not

---

communiqué were silent on the Andropov statement. BTA Release, December 7, 1983; *Narodna armiya* (The People's Army), December 8, 1983; *Rabotnichesko delo*, December 8, 1983; and *Pravda*, December 8, 1983.

64. "Meeting of Central Committee Secretaries of the Fraternal Parties of the Socialist Countries, *Pravda*, December 10, 1983.

65. Honecker had met with West German Chancellor Helmut Kohl for the first time at Andropov's funeral in February 1984, and in an unprecedented talk they had agreed on the need for a continuing dialogue. But in September Moscow told Honecker he must postpone his planned trip, and Chernenko's next ranking party secretary, Mikhail Gorbachev, went to Sofia to persuade Zhivkov, too, not to go to the Federal Republic.

suspend its dialogue and interaction with West Germany, but continued to develop it. Permitted emigration to the West, for example, was stepped up in early 1984 despite clear Soviet disapproval (and reached 33,000, four times the 1983 level). In July agreement on a major West German loan of $683 million to East Germany was concluded despite known Soviet objection.[66]

A CMEA summit was held in Moscow in June 1984, the first since 1969. Though by no means resolving the many issues in CMEA production and trade relations, it did assist in keeping efforts to deal with them on track. In addition, for the first time the CMEA leaders declared a willingness to conclude agreements with their Western European counterpart, the European Community (EC). While the CMEA summit marked a qualified success for Soviet efforts to establish greater economic and general cohesion in the Eastern bloc, it did nothing to curb the growing divergence over several political and ideological issues.

At the summit, for example, the Soviets called for a "drawing together" of the bloc members, but the Eastern Europeans virtually all stressed differences and the need to take differences into account. The final statement omitted the call for "drawing together."[67] Chernenko, in a statement commenting on the summit, called the exchange of views at the meeting "frank" as well as fruitful, a code word for disagreement.[68]

In fact, new ideological and political issues arose. Hungary, for example, supported the East German position on continuing to develop ties between the two German states (including reprinting key East German articles even after *Pravda* had attacked them).[69] But Hungary went much further. Mátyás Szürös, the party secretary for international relations, in January published an article that affirmed a role for small countries in bridging East-West tensions and suggested that interests of members of the Warsaw Pact no longer always coincided.[70] The conservative Czechs promptly sharply criticized this "revisionism," but the East Germans approvingly reprinted a further interview by Szürös in which he repeated his stand.[71] The orthodox senior deputy chief of the Soviet

---

66. The arrangements for the loan, and the large permitted emigration to the West, were closely related. See "E. Germany Lets 33,000 Migrate, Kohl Announces," *Washington Post*, August 18, 1984, p. A6.

67. "On the CMEA Countries' Economic Summit Meeting," *Pravda*, June 15, 1984.

68. "Speech of Comrade K. U. Chernenko," *Pravda*, June 15, 1984.

69. For example, see Tibor Thurzo, "Sense of Responsibility and Activity," *Népszava* (Voice of the People), July 28, 1984; *Népszabadság*, August 2, 1984, and Jeno Bocher, "East German Foreign Relations: A Multilateral Dialogue," *Magyarország* (Hungary), August 5, 1984.

70. Mátyás Szürös, "The Reciprocal Effect of National and International Interests in the Development of Socialism in Hungary," *Társadalmi Szemle* (Social Review), no. 1 (January 1984), pp. 13–21.

71. Michal Stefanak and Ivan Hlivka, "The National and the International in the Policy of the Communist Party of Czechoslovakia," *Rudé Právo* (Red Truth), March 30, 1984; and

Central Committee department for liaison with the parties of the socialist countries, Oleg Rakhmanin, under an established pseudonym (O. V. Borisov), strongly criticized positions taken by the Hungarians.[72] But the Hungarians did not recant and persisted in their position. The Hungarian deputy minister of foreign affairs responsible for bloc relations, István Roska, declared in a published interview in early 1985 that "the member states [of the Warsaw Pact] are independent and sovereign countries that, without exception, respect the principle of noninterference in each others' internal affairs."[73] Again, East Germany promptly published that interview in its press.[74]

A very tough Soviet attack followed three months later in *Pravda*, again by the hard-line Central Committee official Rakhmanin (under another established pseudonym, O. Vladimirov). The *Pravda* article warned against attempts to revise bloc relations, stressed cohesion, and attacked the concept of a separate role for small states, and it emphasized that the "main criterion is the interests of socialism," rather than the interests of any individual state. He attacked "covert, and even open, Russophobia and anti-Sovietism."[75] The article was reprinted the next day by the Czechoslovak and Bulgarian party newspapers.

Yet the "debate" continued. Equally important, a parallel internal Soviet debate on these same issues continued and even intensified. Presumably one reason that party and government officials and spokesmen in Eastern Europe felt able to voice their views despite strong Soviet criticisms was an awareness that Soviet thinking, and the internal political balance in the Soviet Union, was in flux. For example, while in 1984 General Secretary Konstantin Chernenko, Prime Minister Nikolai Tikhonov, Defense Minister Dmitry Ustinov, and Central Committee official Oleg Rakhmanin were stressing West German revanchism and trying to organize an East European cold shoulder on relations with the West, other Central Committee officials such as Nikolai Shishlin and Vitaly Kobysh, *Izvestiya* political observer Aleksandr Bovin, and *Literaturnaya gazeta* political observer Fedor Burlatsky, with implicit higher-level backing, were pressing for détente with Western Europe and ignoring the alleged revanchist danger.

Under the Gorbachev leadership in 1985–86 the debates continued. "Vladimirov's" tough *Pravda* article of June 1985, for example, came some

Mátyás Szürös interview "Common Goals, National Interests", reprinted in *Neues Deutschland*, April 12, 1984, from *Magyar Hirlap* (Hungarian Journal), April 4, 1984.

72. O.V. Borisov [Oleg B. Rakhmanin], "Union of a New Type," *Voprosy istorii KPSS* (Questions of History of the CPSU), no. 4 (April 1984), pp. 34–49.

73. "Socialist World Order—Hungarian Diplomacy," Interview with Deputy Foreign Minister István Roska, *Népszava*, March 2, 1985.

74. *Neues Deutschland*, March 4, 1985.

75. O. Vladimirov [Oleg B. Rakhmanin], "The Guiding Factor of the World Revolutionary Process," *Pravda*, June 21, 1985.

three months after Gorbachev's accession. But a spate of other Soviet articles quickly took issue with Rakhmanin's view. Oleg Bogomolov, director of the Institute on Economics of the World Socialist System, accepted the Eastern European stress on national differences in an article in the party's chief political-theoretical journal *Kommunist*.[76] Bovin defended the role of small states, and Central Committee officials Nikolai Shishlin and Georgy Shakhnazarov, and others, argued against the Vladimirov position.[77] Most far-reaching was a public call by Yury Novopashin of Bogomolov's institute to renounce "great power ambitions" and "hegemonistic pretensions."[78]

Gorbachev himself had stated, in his first speech as general secretary, that his "first commandment" was to strengthen the "fraternal friendship" of "the countries of the great socialist community."[79] Moreover, he accompanied this by deed. In contrast to Andropov's neglect of the Eastern European leaders upon his accession to power, and Chernenko's routine meetings with each, Gorbachev called a meeting of the socialist camp party chiefs on March 13 while they were still in Moscow for Chernenko's funeral.[80] At this meeting, it is now known, in remarks not subsequently published, Gorbachev told the Eastern European leaders that they should act individually on their own authority as equals. Although this message was initially welcomed, these leaders later came to understand that with greater freedom came greater responsibility: they could not rely upon Moscow to shore them up. At first, however, they did not realize that Gorbachev really meant what he was saying.[81]

---

76. O. Bogomolov, "The Concordance of Economic Interests and Politics under Socialism," *Kommunist* (Communist), no. 10 (July 1985), p. 91. The same issue of *Kommunist* also featured an article spelling out in detail the Hungarian economic approach; see Károly Nemeth, "In the Interests of Building a Developed Socialist Society," ibid., pp. 70–81. Nemeth was a deputy to General Secretary János Kádár.

77. Aleksandr Bovin, Radio Budapest, August 31, 1985, in FBIS, *Soviet Union*, September 6, 1985, p. CC1; and, see N. Shishlin, "Toward the 27th Congress of the CPSU: The First Commandment," *Novoye vremya*, no. 35 (August 23, 1985), pp. 9–11 (excerpted at length the day after its publication by the Hungarian party newspaper *Népszabadság*, August 24, 1985); and Georgy Shakhnazarov on "Program of Our Life," Moscow Television, November 26, 1985 in FBIS, *Soviet Union*, November 27, 1985, pp. BB1–2.

78. Yu. S. Novopashin, "Political Relations of the Countries of Socialism," *Rabochii klass i sovremennyi mir* (The Working Class and the Contemporary World), no. 5 (September-October 1985), pp. 55–65.

79. "Speech by Comrade Gorbachev, General Secretary of the Central Committee of the CPSU at the CC CPSU Plenum on March 11," *Pravda*, March 12, 1985. This reference by Gorbachev to his "first commandment" was cited by Nikolai Shishlin for the title of his own article five months later; see footnote 77.

80. "A Friendly Meeting," *Pravda*, March 14, 1985.

81. The principal source for Gorbachev's statement and East European reactions is Anatoly Chernyayev, then a deputy chief of the Central Committee International Department

The first major development was a formal meeting of the Warsaw Pact party leaders in Warsaw in April, at which agreement was announced to extend the Pact for another twenty years.[82] There had been hints, especially by the Romanians, that perhaps a ten-year renewal was sufficient, but the Soviet leaders were determined on a twenty-year extension and made clear they would not permit any change in the Pact.[83] There were indications that the leaders in Moscow did agree to provide more oil to Romania as a "sweetener." Ceauşescu had also privately solicited an invitation to the United States, perhaps to increase his bargaining power, but not because he believed he had any alternative to continued membership in the Pact. The United States, however, declined to invite a visit by President Ceauşescu.[84]

In December 1985 the CMEA adopted a Comprehensive Program for Scientific and Technical Progress. In November 1986, after the regular CMEA meeting, another summit meeting was held in Moscow, aimed at further enhancing economic "integration" of the member countries' economies, especially in the high-technology field. But these efforts did not eliminate diverging interests nor diminish Eastern European interest in also further developing economic ties with the West.

By the time of the party congress in early 1986, Gorbachev had moved toward a position more agreeable to the East Europeans. Gorbachev, in the Political Report of the Central Committee to the congress, called for bloc unity but said that "unity has nothing in common with conformity," a formulation granting much leeway for expression of national differences.[85] But there were indications that important differences still remained in the Soviet political

---

and soon to become Gorbachev's principal foreign affairs aide. Discussion with Chernyayev on February 25, 1993.

82. "Communiqué on the Meeting on the Top Party and State Figures of the Member States of the Warsaw Pact," *Pravda*, April 27, 1985.

83. The Romanians, while signing, still attempted to assert some independence. The party newspaper, in reporting the meeting, stressed Romania's "national independence" and again declared that both blocs needed new arms control initiatives. Dumitru Tinu, "In the Interests of Peace and Security in Europe and Throughout the World—At the Conclusion of the Summit Meeting of Party and State Leaders of the Member Countries of the Warsaw Pact," *Scinteia* (Spark), April 28, 1985.

84. Information from knowledgeable U.S. officials.

    In May 1985 the American ambassador to Romania, David Funderburk, a political appointment to the post in 1981, resigned and sharply criticized the Romanian regime, urging most-favored-nation trade status (MFN) be revoked. Also in May 1985 it was announced that five Romanian diplomats in West Germany had been expelled for involvement in a plot to bomb the office of Radio Free Europe. American-Romanian relations had declined considerably by this time.

85. "Political Report of the Central Committee of the CPSU to the 27th Congress of the Communist Party of the Soviet Union, Report of the General Secretary of the CC of the CPSU Comrade M.S. Gorbachev," *Pravda*, February 26, 1986.

establishment.[86] For example, while Gorbachev in the Political Report of the Central Committee did not refer once to the hallowed slogan of the conservatives, "socialist internationalism," the party program, approved at the same time, did mention the term.[87] In the fall of 1986, the hard-line Oleg Rakhmanin (Borisov, and Vladimirov) was removed from his Central Committee position and replaced as first deputy chief of the department of the Central Committee for liaison with the socialist countries by the much more liberal Georgy Shakhnazarov.[88] Differences of view nonetheless were evident through 1986 in Moscow and with the Eastern Europeans (who, as earlier noted, had widely diverging views).[89]

An important change in Soviet policy came in late 1986. Several informed Soviet sources in later years have referred to a key Politburo meeting, which approved a memorandum submitted by Gorbachev, calling for a "restructuring" of Soviet policy toward Eastern Europe.[90] Signs of the new policy

---

86. In discussions in Moscow just after the congress, when I asked a senior Central Committee official why more had not been said about Soviet relations with Eastern Europe, he told me the matter was "too sensitive," and an editor of *Pravda*, when asked why the paper had not commented more on the socialist community, said the subject was "too controversial."

87. As noted in chapter 6, the revised party program was already in draft and had been worked over for more than two years before Gorbachev came to power; the Political Report, while also a consensus document approved by the Politburo, had been drafted *de novo* and could more freely express Gorbachev's positions.

88. Shakhnazarov had long been the head of a department in the Institute of State and the Law of the Academy of Sciences as well as a Central Committee consultant and official. He was one of those who had taken issue with the Vladimirov *Pravda* article in 1985 (see footnote 77).

89. The Eastern Europeans were generally pleased with the stand taken by Gorbachev and the party congress, with its thrust on change and criticism of dogmatism, and saw their position enhanced. For example, see Mátyás Szürös, "The Program of Acceleration," *Népszabadság*, March 8, 1986. This was not, however, the view of most of the older senior leaders, set in their ways and afraid of change.

For a good study of Eastern European thinking and interaction with the Soviet Union in this period, see Karen Dawisha, *Eastern Europe, Gorbachev, and Reform: The Great Challenge*, 2d ed. (Cambridge University Press, 1990).

90. Among others, then-Party Secretary Yegor Ligachev has confirmed this Politburo meeting, saying that there had been no serious disagreement, in particular over recognition of the need for freedom of choice by the East Europeans and renunciation of any Soviet military intervention. (Conversation between Ligachev and the author, November 11, 1991.) The meeting and memorandum were also confirmed by the first deputy chief of the Central Committee department for liaison with the socialist countries, A. S. Kapto, at a Ministry of Foreign Affairs conference; see A. S. Kapto "Priority of Our Relations with the Socialist Countries," reprinted in *Mezhdunarodnaya zhizn'*, no. 10 (October 1988), p. 29. See also Ronald Asmus, "Evolution of Soviet-East European Relations under Mikhail Gorbachev," Radio Free Europe RAD Background Report 153 (August 22, 1989), p. 2.

were soon evident. First among them was an important secret conversation of the Eastern European party leaders in Moscow on November 10–11, 1986, following a routine and publicized meeting of government leaders of the CMEA in Bucharest. Carrying further what he had first told them in March 1985, Gorbachev now told the Eastern European leaders that they must "restructure" their rule and gain legitimacy, and that the Soviet Union could no longer be expected to keep them in power.[91]

The new Soviet policy line was soon reflected in public statements. Gorbachev took the occasion of a visit to Prague in April 1987 to state that "the entire system of political relations among the countries of socialism can and must [*mozhno i dolzhno*] unswervingly be built on the basis of equal rights and mutual responsibility. No one has the right to claim a special position in the socialist world. Independence of each party, its responsibility to its people, the sovereign right to decide questions of the development of the country—all these are for us unconditional principles."[92] Two weeks later in Budapest the conservative second-ranking party secretary Yegor Ligachev made clear his endorsement of the changed policy line, emphasizing that "every country looks for solutions independently, *not as in the past*. It is not true that Moscow's conductor's baton, or Moscow's hand is in everything . . . every nation has a right to its own way."[93]

Although emphasizing the independence of each of the Eastern European nations, Gorbachev and his colleagues assumed and believed that they (as the Soviet Union) would continue to adhere to a socialist system. They also recognized, however, the need for *perestroika* not only in the Soviet Union, but also in each of the countries of Eastern Europe. Indeed without the necessary reform, risks would arise. They were, however, convinced that democratic political reform, as launched in the Soviet Union at the Central Committee plenums of January and June 1987, would also be adopted in the countries of Eastern Europe, and there too would help to advance necessary economic reform. Indeed, they expected and hoped for mutual advantages. As Gorbachev said in Bucharest in May, "In developing perestroika, the CPSU naturally proceeds from the concrete conditions of the Soviet Union, from our under-

---

91. I first learned of this "secret speech" by Gorbachev from Aleksandr Tsipko, at the time a Central Committee official concerned with Eastern Europe, in July 1990; it was subsequently confirmed by another Soviet official. The meeting had been referred to in passing by Kapto in his July 1988 report to the Ministry of Foreign Affairs conference (*Mezhdunarodnaya zhizn'*, no. 10 (October, 1988), pp. 29–30). The meeting was also attended by Fidel Castro of Cuba, Truong Chinh of Vietnam, and Jambyn Batmonh of Mongolia as the heads of CMEA governments.

92. "Meeting of Czechoslovak-Soviet Friendship, Speech of Comrade M. S. Gorbachev," *Pravda*, April 11, 1987.

93. Budapest Television, April 26, 1987, in FBIS, *Eastern Europe*, April 27, 1987, p. F6. Emphasis added.

standing of the theory of socialism, taking into account the needs and will of the Soviet people. At the same time we study with intent interest the experience of friends, their trials in the realm of theory and practice of socialist construction, and we strive to utilize widely all that suits our conditions," and vice versa.[94] A few months later, a Central Committee official told me that under the new relationship, the socialist countries were now seen as "multiple laboratories for economic reform."[95]

   Perhaps most telling of all was the off-the-cuff remark of Soviet Foreign Ministry spokesman Gennady Gerasimov, who when asked in April 1987 by a Western correspondent what the difference was between Dubček's suppressed Prague Spring of 1968 and Gorbachev's *perestroika* of 1987, quipped "19 years" (and again, when asked about that remark in August 1988, he said "I'll amend that now. The difference is 20 years.)"[96]

   Thus by 1987 a new course was being pursued by the Soviet Union in "restructuring" its relationship with the countries of Eastern Europe and seeking to get those countries to restructure themselves.[97] There was a tremendous potential for change below the surface within those countries, indeed greater by far than Gorbachev and the Moscow leadership then understood, but there was also great resistance by the leaderships in Eastern Europe—mostly led by an older generation less inclined to change and justifiably fearful of the consequences. East German leader Honecker was now able to make his visit to West Germany in September 1987, three years after he had been compelled to postpone it. In December 1987 Gustáv Husák was replaced in Prague by the only slightly less rigid Miloš Jakeš, and in May 1988 in Budapest the feeble János Kádár was replaced by Károly Grósz. In August 1987 Wojciech Jaruzelski (on the basis of an understanding with Gorbachev in April) publicly reopened the issue of the Katyn massacre of 1940 and denounced Soviet deportations and repressions in World War II. Most Eastern European leaderships, however, used their new freedom to ward off Soviet-style *perestroika*, *glasnost*, and

---

94. "Enrich and Enliven the Life of the Working People, Meeting of Romanian-Soviet Friendship, Speech of Comrade M. S. Gorbachev," *Pravda*, May 27, 1987.

95. Nikolai Shishlin, in an interview conversation on December 3, 1987.

96. Both of these daring remarks were not reported in the Soviet or Czechoslovak press, only by Western correspondents present.

97. Throughout this period, Shevardnadze was attempting, with little success, to change the long-standing pattern of sending veteran party officials rather than professional diplomats as Soviet ambassadors to the Eastern European states. Although the Politburo normally only "approved," with little attention, ambassadorial appointments, those to the socialist countries were "decided" by the Politburo, on advice of the party Secretariat rather than the Foreign Ministry. Gorbachev may have been disinclined to change the practice because he hoped to rejuvenate the Eastern European parties and lead them into *perestroika*, but those sent continued to be not new thinkers but old-line veterans of the party machine. For Shevardnadze's desire to send diplomats see Eduard Shevardnadze, *The Future Belongs to Freedom* (Free Press, Macmillan, 1991), pp. 113–14.

*demokratizatsiya* rather than to emulate it. And not all changes of leadership or policy were reformist. In the summer of 1988 Todor Zhivkov sacked his presumed heir, the more reform-minded Chudomir Aleksandrov, not long after Aleksandrov had visited Gorbachev in Moscow,[98] and a few months later Jakeš forced the retirement of Prime Minister Lubomír Štrougal, the most reform-minded of the Czechoslovak leaders. Nonetheless, the process of reform and change had been launched, and as most countries in Eastern Europe failed to keep pace with change in the Soviet Union, their leaderships were becoming even more isolated and weak rather than staving off inevitable change. The most dramatic sign of popular support for *perestroika* and pressure from below was the chants of young East Germans clashing with the police in East Berlin in mid–1987, saying, "The wall must go!" coupled with "Gorbachev! Gorbachev!"[99]

As Gorbachev's *perestroika* within the Soviet Union departed more and more clearly from orthodox Marxist-Leninist tenets and practice, the conservative Eastern European leaders became increasingly concerned about the spillover effects and pressures for change in their countries. The gap between them became more pronounced after Gorbachev's increasing assertion of common human values over class values, beginning with his address on the seventieth anniversary of the October Revolution in early November 1987.[100] Ironically, Gorbachev remained confident that the peoples of Eastern Europe—and the Soviet Union—had embraced "the socialist choice" and merely needed enlightened leadership and opportunity for free expression of

---

98. Zhivkov, a crony of Brezhnev and 76 years old in 1988, never got along well with Gorbachev. They first met in 1979, when Gorbachev as a new young party secretary accompanied Brezhnev and Chernenko, then newly appointed a member of the Politburo, to Sofia. (I was at the time in Sofia as the American ambassador.) Zhivkov fawned over Chernenko as well as Brezhnev but ignored Gorbachev. In 1985, Zhivkov told a visiting Western minister of state jokingly that the Soviet Union was really a colony of Bulgaria—sending raw materials and buying their manufactured goods. In 1987 he told visiting U.S. Deputy Secretary of State John Whitehead that "this boy"—Gorbachev—was not going to tell him what to do (according to someone present). And in 1988, Zhivkov indiscreetly rushed, after the Andreyeva article and prior to the *Pravda* rebuttal, to tell a Sofia audience (in a not published speech) that "now we can drop this nonsense about *glasnost*" (from a reliable Bulgarian source). In October 1987, however, Gorbachev had summoned Zhivkov to Moscow and criticized the Bulgarian's announced plans for a sudden economic reform.

99. Serge Schmemann, "Rallying Cry of East Berliners: 'Gorbachev!' " *New York Times*, June 10, 1987, p. A7.

100. "October and Perestroika: The Revolution Continues, Report of General Secretary of the CC of the CPSU M. S. Gorbachev to the Jubilee Joint Session of the Central Committee of the CPSU, the Supreme Soviet of the USSR, and Supreme Soviet of the RSFSR, Dedicated to the 70th Anniversary of the Great October Socialist Revolution, in the Kremlin Palace of Congresses, November 2, 1987," *Kommunist*, no. 17 (November 1987), pp. 30, 34, 38–40.

that choice. The hardened East European old-line communist leaders more realistically recognized the inherent threat to them and to their communist parties.

In contrast to the intimate and active Soviet engagement with the issue of relations with Eastern Europe in the mid–1980s, the U.S. role was generally inactive. Formal setting of policy by the new administration in 1982 had been followed in 1983 and 1984 by occasional rhetorical reiterations of American dedication to freedom for Eastern Europe, including Vice President Bush's Vienna speech and the 1983 visit by Bush to Hungary and Romania as well as Yugoslavia. But these policy declarations seemed more directed at American ears than at affecting the situation in Eastern Europe. Only the Soviet leaders were inclined to exaggerate the scope of American covert efforts to serve the rather provocative public calls for freedom. When it came down to concrete policy steps, other considerations prevailed. For example, while Hungary was singled out for praise by Bush and Shultz, and although Hungary was engaged in a struggle within the Soviet bloc to vindicate a modest ameliorative role in East-West relations, the United States in COCOM refused to permit a Hungarian arrangement with ITT to modernize the telephone system of the country (on the grounds that the technology could be applied to military communications as well). The whole conception, to say nothing of the demonstrable reality, of divergent views among communist leaders and communist countries did not usually penetrate above the level of embassy and intelligence analysts to affect the decisions of American policymakers.

After the Reagan-Gorbachev summit meeting in Geneva, the administration did decide to renew its visible interest in Eastern Europe by another high-level visit, this time by Secretary Shultz—the first by a secretary of state since a visit by Secretary Cyrus Vance in 1978. In a news conference in Washington before his departure in December 1985, Shultz said that "the division of Europe is artificial, unnatural and illegitimate," and in West Berlin he called that city a symbol of an "unnatural and inhuman" division of Europe, and he said that the United States does "not accept incorporation of Eastern Europe . . . into a Soviet sphere of influence."[101] These, however, were his most inflammatory remarks, and in general Shultz was much less militant than Bush had been. In Budapest, he noted the possibility of wider and more productive ties with Eastern Europe if the series of Reagan-Gorbachev meetings were fruitful—for the first time linking the prospects for improved American ties with Eastern Europe to U.S. relations with Moscow. This may have occurred as a result of Kádár's emphasis on the value of improving American-Soviet relations for giving the Eastern Europeans more room for maneuver, a point Shultz had perhaps not previously realized.

---

101. "The Secretary: News Conference of December 6 [1985]," *State Bulletin*, vol. 86 (February 1986), p. 50; and "Berlin and the Cause of Freedom," December 14, 1985, *State Bulletin*, vol. 86 (February 1986), p. 31.

Shultz's trip also included several stops in Western Europe, and the secretary sought on several occasions to indicate an identity of American and Western European views on relations with Eastern Europe. There was some appreciation in Western Europe that Shultz's statements on the whole were less inflammatory, and some hope that the United States would begin to take a more active interest in relations with the countries of Eastern Europe. There was, however, no identity of views. The Western Europeans continued to see the countries of Eastern Europe as individual if not fully independent nations, and not to see them only in terms of their relationship to Moscow. The Europeans were also less hostile to the government of Poland, and more critical of that of harshly authoritarian Romania, than was the United States.[102]

After Shultz's trip, the United States again became absorbed in other matters and American relations with Eastern Europe again receded from the stage. Shultz did, however, see a need for a more flexible American engagement with Eastern Europeans seeking change. Accordingly, in the summer of 1986 he assigned general oversight of relations with Eastern Europe to Deputy Secretary John Whitehead.[103]

In November, Whitehead visited Hungary and Yugoslavia, in the first of what became six trips to countries of Eastern Europe in the years 1986–88, visiting each of the Warsaw Pact countries at least twice. In January 1987, after a Polish amnesty for many imprisoned members of Solidarity, Whitehead visited Poland (and several other countries in Eastern Europe), and in February Reagan lifted the remaining sanctions imposed on Poland in 1981 (some had been dropped in January 1984). On his return, Whitehead told Shultz that "things are changing" in Eastern Europe.[104] In November 1987 Whitehead became the highest American official ever to visit East Germany.

In September 1987, Vice President George Bush visited Poland. At first, recalling the undesirable diplomatic fallout from Bush's remarks in 1983 after his last visit to Eastern Europe, the State Department tried diplomatically

102. For an informed news article that carries much of the flavor of Western European reactions, see James M. Markham, "Allies Pleased by Shultz Visit to East Europe," *New York Times*, December 20, 1985, p. A10.

103. Shultz, *Turmoil and Triumph*, pp. 692–95.
    The State Department also began the commendable practice of sending U.S. diplomats and officials to consult with Eastern European countries before and during international conferences and negotiations such as the CSCE and CDE conferences, or for courtesy briefings, for example, after the Geneva and Reykjavik summit meetings.

104. Shultz, *Turmoil and Triumph*, pp. 873, 1003. Shultz had earlier, in November 1986 at the CSCE foreign ministers meeting, authorized his staff (Rozanne Ridgway and Thomas Simons) to meet with the Poles and "encourage them to initiate internal changes that moved away from the Soviets." Ibid. In Poland, Whitehead had successfully insisted that he meet Lech Wałęsa, or he would not see General Jaruzelski. Jaruzelski, incidentally, told Whitehead: "Someday you in America will realize who is the real Polish patriot who has kept his country alive all these years." Ibid., pp. 874–75.

to derail the vice president's interest in traveling there.[105] Zbigniew Brzezinski was used as an intermediary to see whether a real visit to "the Polish people" would be feasible, and he concluded that it would. That finding removed the State Department's nominal reason for questioning the proposed visit, and it took place. Fortunately, Bush was moderate and cautious in his statements.[106] He met Lech Wałęsa, but quietly. He met requests for debt relief and new loans with recommendations for economic reform.[107]

Deputy Secretary Whitehead continued in 1988 the increased attention to Eastern Europe. Besides his personal visits to countries in the region in February and October, he outlined American policy in a speech in January. He restated the policy of differentiation, relating American development of ties to the appropriate relationship with each country, with most attention to trade. Reflecting the Washington view, he described Soviet policy in cautious terms, noting that "the Soviets' true motives" in Eastern Europe remained subject to "discussion," but oblivious to the important changes under way, he warned, "Let us be clear, the long-run Soviet interest in maintaining a hegemonic relationship with Eastern Europe has not changed." Whitehead pleaded in his speech that a new "opportunity to help effect real change in a direction favorable to our interests" was at hand, and that the United States should not squander it, but the government did not act on that premise, remaining more true to Whitehead's somewhat wistful recognition that "we have had a tendency in the United States to focus on Eastern Europe only at times of crisis."[108] And despite Whitehead's energetic personal engagement, there was no new or active American policy approach.

In the Soviet view, however, as earlier noted, the United States was active not only in overt and covert propaganda, but also in political and military preparations for destabilizing and eventually interfering in Eastern Europe and even in the Soviet Union itself with the aim of rolling back communist rule.

---

105. See chapter 3.

106. Bush was less cautious in some statements to accompanying American news reporters; he was criticized in the American press for slighting American workers by saying they ought to send Soviet tank mechanics to Detroit "because we could use that kind of ability," and for crass political thinking when after Wałęsa's high praise of him, Bush cracked, "How many relatives does he have in Iowa? That's the only thing I want to know." See Rowland Evans and Robert Novak, "Bad Jokes, Good Policy," *Washington Post*, October 7, 1987, p. A21.

107. David Hoffman and Jackson Diehl, "Bush Presses Poland for Reforms," *Washington Post*, September 27, 1987, p. A34; Hoffman and Diehl, "Bush Sees Jaruzelski, Wins No Shift of Stance," *Washington Post*, September 28, 1987, pp. A15, A21; and Hoffman, "Chanting Polish Crowds Provide Bush with Footage for '88 Campaign," *Washington Post*, October 4, 1987, p. A18.

108. Deputy Secretary [John C.] Whitehead, "The U.S. Approach to Eastern Europe: A Fresh Look," January 19, 1988, Current Policy 1044 (Washington: Department of State, 1988).

While the Soviet Union's propaganda, and probably to a large extent even its own assessment, was grossly exaggerated, it was not wholly fictitious. The American public diplomacy and Project Democracy programs, for example, included smuggling portable radio and video transmitters to Solidarity in Poland through the AFL-CIO's Free Trade Union Institute. Radio Free Europe was not only used to transmit American-originated propaganda, but also as a channel for playing back into Poland and other communist countries underground materials sent out of those countries through official American as well as other channels. Polish emigre groups were funded. Some 10,000 balloons carrying containers of anti-Soviet, pro-Solidarity propaganda leaflets were reportedly released from Bornholm Island, Denmark, to ride prevailing winds into Poland. In 1987 Congress openly appropriated $1 million in July and a second $1 million in December for aid to Solidarity. American funds paid for the legal defense of arrested Solidarity leaders and fines imposed for illegal publishing.[109] Finally, some of those and other less identifiable and covert activities in support of Solidarity had been carried out under a collaborative U.S.-Vatican covert action program since 1982.[110]

Although such actions were seen in the United States as justified by the constraints of communist societies, they were not unreasonably regarded as subversive by the Soviet and Eastern European governments.[111] Such activities were seen in Moscow in ominous conjunction with statements by President Reagan and other senior officials ever since 1981. A speech by Reagan in November 1986, not especially noted in the United States, had special impact.

---

109. For informed press accounts, see Rowland Evans and Robert Novak, "Solidarity Rides the Airwaves," *Washington Post*, April 24, 1985, p. A25; and Robert Pear, "U.S. Helping Polish Underground with Money and Communications," *New York Times*, July 10, 1988, pp. 1, 14.

110. See the discussion in chapter 1 and the extensive account by Carl Bernstein, "The Holy Alliance," *Time*, February 24, 1992, pp. 28–35.

111. For a detailed Soviet account of alleged Western, and especially American, covert actions to stimulate and support Solidarity before and after the imposition of martial law, see Vadim Trubnikov, *Krakh 'operatsii Poloniya', 1980–1981gg.* (The Collapse of 'Operation Polonia', 1980–81) (Moscow: APN, 1983), 253 pp. Described as a "documentary account," this volume presented some true, and some probably untrue, allegations. A similar Polish account was published in Russian translation as *Neob"yavlennaya voina protiv Pol'shi: podryvnaya deyatel'nost' zapadnykh spetssluzhb* (The Undeclared War against Poland: Subversive Activities of Western Intelligence Services) (Moscow: Politizdat, 1984), 221 pp. See also the official Polish "white paper," *Polityka Stanów Zjednoczonych Ameryki wobec Polski w swietle faktów i dokumentów (1980–1983)* (The Policy of the United States of America toward Poland in the Light of Facts and Documents, 1980–83) (Warsaw: PAI, 1984), 271 pp; and A. G. Dmitrenko, *Proval "strategicheskogo eksperimenta": Politika SShA v otnoshenii Pol'ski v 70–80-e gody* (The Downfall of a "Strategic Experiment": U.S. Policy toward Poland in the 1970s and 80s), L'vov: Vyshcha shkola, 1988), 192 pp. There were many other Soviet and Polish propaganda tracts on the subject.

The occasion was the thirtieth anniversary of the Hungarian revolution of 1956, and Reagan paid homage to the Freedom Fighters, but he went further: he seemed to say that the United States had made a mistake by not intervening in 1956, and that it would not make that mistake again. In his words, "As we look back now over three decades of Soviet adventurism around the world, can anyone truly say it was in fact in our interest to stand by, hands folded, at the dying of the light in Hungary? And would it be today in our interest to stand by and watch the dying of the light in Afghanistan. . . . I say no. Not then. Not now. Not ever. Yes, it is in our interest to stand with those who would take arms against the sea of darkness."[112] Most Americans would understand this to be emotional or eloquent rhetoric, but not a policy commitment. But in Moscow leadership circles this speech was apparently taken to represent a dangerous call for extension of the Reagan Doctrine, previously applied only in the Third World, to Eastern Europe.[113]

Besides the rhetoric of American political leaders, there were also more ominous statements by less senior but official voices that were given serious attention in the East. For example, an American Defense Department official in 1983 stated, "The Reagan administration sees the steady growth of Soviet military power over the past decade and more as the greatest threat . . . to hopes for recovery of freedom in the Baltic states and other subjugated nationalities of the current Soviet empire." He thus implied that even Soviet defensive military power to protect its existing borders was illegitimate, and that the Soviet Union itself was only a "current," and not necessarily enduring, country. Moreover, he went on to state, "Our [the Americans'] objective must be to loosen the Soviet hold on Eastern Europe and the Baltic States." And he related this to the American policy of differentiation in remarkable terms, "differentiation in favor of those who are trying to be free."[114] That kind of statement made more threatening the restatement by President Reagan and other leaders of the American reservation on the 1940 incorporation of the three Baltic states (Latvia, Lithuania, and Estonia) into the Soviet Union.

Similarly, at a conference hosted by the West German military journal *Wehrkunde*, Undersecretary of Defense Policy Fred C. Iklé (formerly of the Committee on the Present Danger), said NATO should reconsider its stated

---

112. "Ethics and Public Policy Center. Remarks at the 10th Anniversary Dinner," November 18, 1986, *Presidential Documents*, vol. 22 (November 24, 1986), p. 1581.

    In this speech Reagan also spoke of an American lead in a technological revolution and said "this new position of strength for the West is the backdrop for the talks we've been having with the Soviets" (p. 1582).

113. I was told by two Soviet officials, Georgy Arbatov only a few weeks after Reagan's speech, and Central Committee official Valentin Falin three years later, how great had been the impact in Moscow of this speech by Reagan.

114. "Address by Leon K. Pfeiffer, Special Assistant, Deputy Assistant Secretary of Defense for European and NATO Policy," *Baltic Bulletin*, Los Angeles, May 1983, pp. 6, 12.

policy of maintaining a defensive posture in a conflict: "Should we assure Soviet planners that they do not need to worry about a counterinvasion?" he asked.[115] Whatever the merits of that argument, it seemed provocative to the Soviets, especially when advanced in a public forum in West Germany sponsored by a tough-line unofficial German military group. And at the same conference, the NATO Supreme Allied Commander, Europe, General Bernard Rogers, was reported as saying that NATO had plans to help Eastern Europeans who might rebel against Soviet forces in a European conflict.[116]

This Soviet concern stemmed from the initial ominous evaluations of the Reagan administration's policy as early as 1981–82. Thus the leaked top secret Defense Guidance in 1982 not only proclaimed the aim of eroding support for communist rule within the Soviet sphere in Eastern Europe, but also called for building up special military capabilities so that in wartime "to exploit political, economic and military weaknesses within the Warsaw Pact and to disrupt enemy rear operations, special operations forces will conduct operations in Eastern Europe."[117]

In one instance, a direct American military contact with a Warsaw Pact country caused serious concern in Moscow. In March 1984, despite some frictions between the United States and Romania, General John W. Vessey, Jr., chairman of the Joint Chiefs of Staff, visited Romania in the first visit by an American military chief to Eastern Europe since World War II. The visit was so successful that General Vessey and Romanian military leaders even discussed hypothetical war scenarios, an unprecedented occurrence between members of the two confronting military alliances.

Against the background of their own suspicions, such indications of American interest in liberation of the peoples of Eastern Europe—and parts of the Soviet Union—may even have made the American indifference to improving relations with the existing governments in Eastern Europe seem designed and ominous, rather than negligent or of low priority. Moreover, some American steps were retrogressive. For example, during the 1970s the United States had gradually concluded agreements with each of the countries of Eastern Europe removing the reciprocal discriminating travel restrictions imposed on diplomats in the Cold War years.[118] Then in December 1985 the United States reimposed travel restrictions on Bulgaria, Czechoslovakia, Poland, and East Germany as of January 1986 (and, on the principle of differentiation, merely warned the Hungarians and Romanians against spying, while not applying the

---

115. See "U.S. Aide Faults NATO Strategy," *New York Times*, March 3, 1986, p. A2.

116. Ibid.

117. Quoted from the text of the guidance by Richard Halloran, "Pentagon Draws Up First Strategy for Fighting a Long Nuclear War," *New York Times*, May 30, 1982, p. 12.

118. As American ambassador to Bulgaria at the time, in 1977 I signed the last of the series of agreements abolishing these reciprocal discriminatory travel restrictions.

restrictions to them). A few months later, those countries affected responded with comparable restrictions. The matter was not significant, but symbolically it seemed to resurrect Cold War practices.

While American relations with Eastern Europe thus followed a low and bumpy road through the 1980s, Western European ties with the East continued to develop. The Western Europeans continued to chafe and resent American efforts not only to apply COCOM strategic trade controls harshly on their trade with Eastern Europe (while pressing for exceptions for U.S. military trade with China), but also because the Europeans saw trade as an important instrument for improving relations, for détente, an aim they continued to hold. The United States, however, sought to constrain trade not only for strategic reasons but also for policy reasons stemming from a drive to stimulate economic and political difficulties in the East, an aim the Western Europeans did not share. By August 1984, the exasperated West German economics minister, Martin Bangemann, said at a press conference in Bonn that the West German government "will not tolerate" further tightening of controls on trade with the East.[119]

Foreign Minister Hans-Dietrich Genscher, in a comment implicitly directed at the United States, called on the Western countries to pursue a policy "free of domestic political ups and downs," and he explicitly called on the United States to revive the agreement reached by Nixon and Brezhnev in 1972.[120] This statement, in August 1984, paralleled the East German resistance to Soviet pressures to curtail trade and other relations with the West. And in language almost identical to that of the Hungarians (supported by the East Germans and, more discreetly, the Bulgarians) in the East, Genscher's official statement declared: "The middle-sized and smaller states that form the vast majority of the community of nations can help assure, by common efforts, that the rivalry between the superpowers does not tear the system of international relations from its hinges."[121]

The Reagan-Gorbachev summit meeting in Geneva in November 1985 was welcomed by European states East and West for its hope of a restoration of better relations between the United States and the Soviet Union, especially for the opportunity it gave them to pursue increased and improved East-West ties.

Relations between the two German states remained both the bellwether and the most important single relationship between Eastern and West-

---

119. Quoted by William Drozdiak, "Europe Chafes at U.S. Moves To Curb Exports," *Washington Post*, August 12, 1984, pp. A1, A15.

    For fuller discussion, see Henry R. Nau, "International Technology Transfer," *Washington Quarterly*, vol. 8 (Winter 1985), pp. 57–64; and Jan Feldman, "Trade Policy and Foreign Policy", ibid., pp. 65–75.

120. See Tagliabue, *New York Times*, August 7, 1984, p. A6.

121. Ibid. See also the important article by Genscher two years earlier in *Foreign Affairs*, vol. 61 (Fall 1982), pp. 42–66.

ern Europe. Germany was also the Soviet Union's principal Western trading partner. And because of the central West German role in agreeing to the deployment of American INF missiles, that country had been the chief target of Soviet anger and pressure from 1983 through 1985. The turning point toward an improvement in relations came with a meeting between Genscher and Gorbachev in Moscow in July 1986. Although important differences were recognized, including disagreement over INF missiles, there was also agreement on several other issues, including support for the SALT II and ABM Treaties.[122] A clear shift in Soviet policy followed, and East-West ties more generally were substantially relieved of the Soviet pressures of 1983–85 stirred by reaction to the INF deployment.

In July 1986, French President François Mitterrand also visited Moscow. Gorbachev, putting the blame on the United States for creating recent tensions, remarked, "Europeans are sick and tired of nerve-racking confrontation and tension. They need the air of détente." And Mitterrand, rather than defending the United States, agreed, "Europe must again become the master of its own destiny." Gorbachev noted that the visit was almost precisely twenty years after President Charles de Gaulle's "historic visit"; and Mitterrand in turn noted that French-Russian relations went back ten centuries, and their futures must be "complementary."[123]

Particularly important in terms of the still-unforeseen developments soon to come, a visit by West German Chancellor Helmut Kohl to Moscow in October 1988 took the last remaining chill off the cool Soviet-German relationship of the early to mid–1980s.

The improvement in Soviet relations with Western Europe was pursued primarily on its own merits. The Soviet leaders also sought, of course, to influence the United States indirectly through this process. The commonly expressed Western view that the Soviet Union was just trying to divide the West, to split the Western Europeans from the United States, was however a distortion. It was most convincing to those Americans (and West Europeans) who did not wish to see improved East-West European ties because they undercut a policy of isolating, weakening, and confronting the Evil Empire of the East. But the Soviet leaders saw their purpose quite differently: they would have preferred to see Western Europe and the United States together, not divided, in pursuit of a policy of East-West détente. This was expressed by the

---

122. For a contemporary news analysis, see Gary Lee, "Soviet, German Talks End 3 Years of Chilly Ties," *Washington Post*, July 22, 1986, p. A15.

123. Michael Dobbs, "Gorbachev Turns Anew to W. Europe; Renewal of Détente Gets Top Billing at Banquet for Mitterrand," *Washington Post*, July 8, 1986, p. A9, cited these statements except Gorbachev's reference to de Gaulle's visit. That reference, and also the other statements by Gorbachev cited, were given in a TASS verbatim broadcast of Gorbachev's speech, "Mikhail Gorbachev's Speech at Dinner in Honor of François Mitterrand," July 7, 1986, in FBIS, *Soviet Union*, July 8, 1986, pp. G3–6.

Soviet political observer Aleksandr Bovin in an interview with an East European journal. "We understand perfectly," he said, "that notwithstanding all the contradictions we are not in a position to cut those numerous close ties that bind Western Europe and the United States. We never set ourselves unrealistic objectives. And we are striving precisely to resolve real questions. Since Western Europe and the United States are allies, and in our opinion the elements of common sense in European politics are stronger, we are attempting to get Western Europe to influence the United States in order to make American policy more sober, reflecting contemporary reality to a greater extent. . . . Détente is in the interest not only of the USSR, but also of Western Europe and, of course, of the whole world."[124]

Importantly, multilateral East-West negotiations, especially in the CSCE framework, allowed the Eastern European countries to take an active role in East-West negotiations and to "spread their own wings" a little. Eastern European officials frequently noted this advantage.[125] Indeed the CSCE process conferred legitimacy on the Eastern European pursuit of "European" aims and increased East-West contacts, gave the Eastern Europeans a greater diplomatic role, and strengthened the European security focus of Eastern European and even Soviet policy in the 1980s.

Gorbachev's policies toward Eastern and Western Europe were increasingly coming together. From the outset, his overall world view and framework of new thinking were grounded in a reassessment of processes in an interdependent world. This was clearly evidenced in early pronouncements, and most fully in his report to the Twenty-seventh Party Congress in early 1986. Though Gorbachev remained a convinced socialist (a communist, in his own view), he rejected the Leninist-Stalinist division of the globe into two confrontational camps destined to inexorable conflict until one, the progressive socialist world, would win out over the other, the tired capitalist world that would be left on the trash heap of history. And this ideological revisionism (which he regarded as renewal) had important policy implications. First of all, "peaceful coexistence" between the states of the two systems—which had long ago already moved from being an interim tactic by a relatively weak Soviet state under Lenin and Stalin, to becoming under Khrushchev and Brezhnev an imperative of the nuclear age for an indefinite future—was not sufficient. Gorbachev saw the need for integration of the Soviet Union and the socialist world with the surprisingly resilient and successful new capitalist world. Sec-

---

124. Interview of *Izvestiya* Political Observer Aleksandr Bovin by Petko Bluskov and Vasil Asparukhov, "Conversation in the Otechestven Front Correspondents' Room in Moscow," *Otechestven Front* (The Fatherland Front), Sofia, June 26, 1986.

125. Many Eastern European party officials and senior diplomats emphasized this point in conversations with me and with others. It was also occasionally acknowledged in articles; for example, Mátyás Szürös, "Hungary and the Helsinki Process," *Valóság* (Truth), July 1986, pp. 1–7.

ond, for Europe, it implied an end to the confrontation between two political and military alliances and the creation of one Europe, a common dwelling place for Europeans in the West and the East (and extending not only from the Atlantic to the Urals, but from Vladivostok through Europe to San Francisco). Third, for Eastern Europe it also meant moving to free development by each state of its own institutions and policies, in conjunction with the merging of East and West, and an end to Soviet hegemony and discipline (at the extreme by military intervention).

In Gorbachev's pronouncements from 1985 through 1989 there was not only an increasingly explicit spelling out of those views and policy positions, but also the contours of a further development of his thinking. Increasingly, he seemed to regard as ineluctably related, even as facets of the same entity, the attributes of being "civilized," "European" (even sometimes "Western"), "efficient," and—"socialist," socialism taken as a system dedicated to advancing the welfare of the people, with little regard for traditional dogmatic definition of the term.

Within the Soviet Union, he sought to "restructure" (really, to reconstitute) a radically revitalized Communist Party led by those who saw the new realities and imperatives as he did (men like Shevardnadze, Yakovlev, Yeltsin until he became too impatient and ambitious, Ligachev until he became too tied to the past). But in addition, as well as to help along the revitalization of the Communist Party (at least until 1990, when he finally began to despair of the party ever reforming itself), Gorbachev moved to bring popular participation into the political process through *glasnost* and *demokratizatsiya*.

Gorbachev also kept discussions within the leadership focused on a combination of broad generalities and very specific steps, not on the intermediate strategic level where debate could have been the most divisive. Thus he avoided raising such issues as the future of the Warsaw Pact until 1990. Marshal Akhromeyev, in his posthumous memoir, has noted that he as chief of the General Staff and Marshals Sokolov and Yazov as successive defense ministers by 1987 were concerned about the future of the Warsaw Pact and the possible collapse of the security system in Eastern Europe. In the summer of 1987 Yazov and he submitted a paper on that subject to Gorbachev with the plan that it be discussed with the military leaders, but although Gorbachev examined the paper, he did so without the presence of the military leaders and without discussing the matter with them.[126]

On the world and European arena, Gorbachev had to persuade the Western powers that an end to the Cold War and division of Europe was in their interests, and that it was now feasible because the Soviet Union too sought that outcome. In Eastern Europe he had to persuade hard-bitten leaders of the

---

126. S. F. Akhromeyev and G. M. Kornienko, *Glazami marshala i diplomata* (Through the Eyes of a Marshal and a Diplomat) (Moscow: Mezhdunarodnyye otnosheniya, 1992), p. 69.

old communist school to step down, new Gorbachevian leaders to step up, and the peoples of those countries to forget the errors and excesses of past communist rule and to welcome and support *perestroika* and a new socialist path.

Gorbachev sought to reach Western and Eastern Europeans with the slogan of a "European common home" (at the same time reassuring both Americans and West Europeans that this was not meant to exclude the United States). On an official visit to Britain in December 1984, three months before becoming general secretary, Gorbachev had, unexpectedly for almost all observers, quickly gained the confidence of the not easily charmed Prime Minister Margaret Thatcher. ("Gorbachev," she told the press, and later President Reagan, "is a man we can do business with.") He also coined an expression, not much noted at the time, which he was later to make a major theme. "Europe," he said, "is our common home. Home, and not a 'theater of military operations.' "[127] He used the expression again shortly before he became party leader in a domestic speech and in the fall of 1985 on the eve of a visit to France.[128] He spelled the idea out a little more fully in his earlier mentioned speech in Prague in April 1987 (he had chosen Prague because it lies almost exactly in the geographical center of Europe).[129] But he made his most full exposition, fittingly by place and time, at the Council of Europe in Strasbourg in July 1989. As he then noted, "The Cold War is passing into history." He related the conception of a common European home to replacement of a balance of power by a balance of interests, and replacement of deterrence (restraint of others) by self-restraint. Finally he emphasized both freedom of choice by each country and the impermissibility of any interference in the affairs of others.[130]

As earlier noted, the parallel concept of central relevance to Soviet-East European relations was the shift from socialist solidarity (proletarian internationalism) to freedom of choice by each country of its basic political and economic system, its leaders, and its policies. This theme was given an authoritative ideological cachet in Gorbachev's report to the Nineteenth Party Conference in June 1988. He defined one of the attributes of "socialism" as a system not only "strengthening collaboration and mutual cooperation with fraternal

---

127. "Speech of M. S. Gorbachev to the British Parliament," *Pravda*, December 19, 1984.

128. "A Policy Course of Unity and Solidarity, A Meeting of Voters with M. S. Gorbachev," *Pravda*, February 21, 1985; and "Address by M. S. Gorbachev on French Television," September 30, 1985, *Pravda*, October 2, 1985.

129. *Pravda*, April 11, 1987. For his comment on selection of Prague, see Mikhail Gorbachev, *Perestroika: New Thinking for Our Country and the World* (Harper and Row, 1987), pp. 194–95.

130. "The All-European Process Moves Forward, Visit of M. S. Gorbachev to the Council of Europe, Speech of M. S. Gorbachev," *Pravda*, July 7, 1989. In Russian, there is a nice juxtaposition of two words with the same root in the phrase replacing deterrence (*sderzhivaniye*) with restraint (*sderzhannost'*).

socialist countries" but also "managing normal civilized relations among *all* peoples and states on the basis of democratic principles of equal rights, non-interference in the affairs of one another, and recognition of the sovereign right of peoples to determine their own destiny."[131]

In his speech to the UN on December 7 Gorbachev again stressed what he referred to as "the compelling necessity of the principle of freedom of choice . . . a universal principle to which there should be no exception."[132] In Kiev in February 1989 he referred specifically to freedom of choice for all socialist states, and in West Germany in June he referred to "freedom to determine their destiny" and to "self determination" of peoples. In July at Strasbourg he again referred to freedom of choice for all countries.[133]

In parallel with these affirmations of the rights of others to decide their destiny was the complementary acknowledgment of "the impermissibility of interference in internal affairs irrespective of the pretext," as Gorbachev put it in an important declaration in Belgrade in March 1988.[134] This was only the most authoritative of a number of Soviet disavowals in 1987–89 of the so-called Brezhnev Doctrine used to justify the Soviet-led intervention in Czechoslovakia in 1968.[135]

---

131. "Moving to the Realization of the Decisions of the XXVII Congress of the CPSU and the Tasks of Deepening Perestroika, Report of the General Secretary of the CC of the CPSU, Comrade M. S. Gorbachev," *XIX vsesoyuznaya konferentsiya Kommunisticheskoi partii Sovetskogo Soyuza, 28 iyunya—1 iyulya 1988 goda, stenograficheskii otchet* (19th All-Union Conference of the Communist Party of the Soviet Union, June 28-July 1, 1988, Stenographic Account) (Moscow: Politizdat, 1988), vol. 1, p. 91. Emphasis added.

132. "M. S. Gorbachev's Speech at the United Nations," *Pravda*, December 8, 1988.

133. "Perestroika—A Cause of All Peoples of the Country, Speech of M. S. Gorbachev at a Meeting with Workers in Kiev," *Pravda*, February 24, 1989; "Joint Declaration [signed by Gorbachev and Kohl]," *Izvestiya*, June 15, 1989; and *Pravda*, July 7, 1989.

134. "Soviet-Yugoslav Declaration," *Pravda*, March 19, 1988.

135. The Soviet Union never acknowledged the existence of a "Brezhnev Doctrine," although in 1968 *Pravda* had sought to justify action (intervention) taken as "an international duty" of "the entire community of socialist states" to "safeguard" socialism in any of its members, as "the fate of the socialist gains" of each state is part of the "common cause of the entire community." ("The Defense of Socialism Is a Supreme International Duty," *Pravda*, August 22, 1968.) In October 1987, the editors of the Soviet press agency Novosti in an interview with the leading Czechoslovak newspaper said, "As far as the so-called Brezhnev Doctrine is concerned: It is only a legend thought up and cultivated in the West" and then cited Gorbachev's April Prague speech on equality and no "special standing" for any socialist country. See "The Soviet Union—Past, Present and Future," interview with Novosti, *Rudé Právo*, Prague, October 31, 1987. In an interview with editors of the *Washington Post* shortly after the Belgrade declaration, Gorbachev was asked whether intervention such as in Czechoslovakia in 1968 could reoccur, and he replied flatly that "interference is unacceptable from any country" as well as reaffirming his Belgrade stand. See Robert G. Kaiser and David Remnick, "The

As earlier noted, the context for this sharp change in Soviet policy toward Eastern Europe, the fruits of which would become evident in 1989 and 1990, included the attempt to encourage *perestroika* within the communist countries of Eastern Europe in parallel with the internal transformation of Soviet society, as well as to carry out a *perestroika* of relations between the Soviet Union and these countries.

The change extended to envisioning, and working toward, a reintegration of Eastern Europe, including the Soviet Union, with the West. The change in Soviet policy was also reflected in small but telling organizational changes. For example, in March 1988, a new academic Institute of Europe—not of Western or Eastern Europe—was established. In October 1988 the Central Committee department for relations with the socialist countries was abolished and merged into the International Department.

Some other steps were also taken in developing relations with the West. Bilateral relations with Western powers, as noted earlier, were given additional attention. And in June 1988 formal ties were established between the Council for Mutual Economic Relations and the European Community, perhaps more important in political than in economic terms (as trade and other economic relations remained on a bilateral commercial basis).

The move toward a real reintegration of Europe presupposed a dismantling of the military confrontation along the center of Europe, which was already a firm Soviet intention in 1986–88, although public affirmations of Soviet desire were not taken at full value by the West until the CFE negotiations in 1989–90. The real beginning of Western recognition came only after Gorbachev announced significant unilateral Soviet force reductions in Eastern Europe in his UN speech of December 7, 1988.[136]

---

Gorbachev Interview: Gorbachev—Master Juggler, Careful Politician," *Washington Post*, May 22, 1988, p. A30.

As noted earlier (in chapter 8), Gorbachev had also tried to get a statement affirming freedom of choice and impermissibility of foreign interference in his joint statement with President Reagan at the close of the Moscow summit in June 1988. The wary U.S. administration, however, rejected the language as too akin to the language of the despised American-Soviet détente of the 1970s.

136. Soviet officials told American counterparts, and other Americans with whom they were in contact, as early as 1986, of the new Soviet approach and even plans, but these messages were regarded with caution or even seen darkly as "disinformation" by the most suspicious administration officials.

The late Ambassador Lev Mendeleyevich, then chief of policy planning in the Foreign Ministry, told me in April 1988 that conventional arms reductions in Europe was among their top priorities, that relations with the Eastern European countries were being shifted toward normal bilateral state relations, that Shevardnadze was attempting to replace party leaders with professional diplomats as ambassadors to the Eastern European countries, and that the Soviet leadership was serious about changing the overall relationship with the West to give meaning to the expression an "all-European home." I was told of such changes by a number of Soviet officials from 1986 on.

Thus, Soviet policy changes toward Eastern Europe, though considered necessary in their own right and to bolster *perestroika* in the Soviet Union itself, were also integral to the broader changes sought in East-West relations, especially for the European security, confidence-building, and arms reduction efforts already under way but in need of reinvigoration.

## European Security, Confidence Building, and Conventional Forces Reduction (CFE)

The development of East-West relations in the 1980s was buffeted by the many challenges in American-Soviet relations, in the world, and in Europe itself that have been reviewed. Détente did not flourish in the decade after the Helsinki accord. American-Soviet relations deteriorated sharply. Nonetheless, something that could still be called détente survived in Europe.

The development of formal security and arms control in the first half of the 1980s was sluggish. The broader development of the framework of "European security and cooperation" that had been established at Helsinki in 1975 stalled. By the mid–1980s, however, a change was occurring and the process was revived and even revivified.

The CSCE review conference in Belgrade in 1977–78 had been dominated by acrimonious exchanges over the question of human rights, but they were mild compared with the strong exchanges at the next review conference in Madrid. Convened in November 1980, the meeting lasted until September 1983—a year longer than the original CSCE negotiation of 1973 to 1975. Its main achievement was agreement on a Conference on Confidence- and Security-Building Measures and Disarmament in Europe (CCSBMDE, usually shortened to CDE).

Although the CDE was held pursuant to agreement reached at the Madrid CSCE conference, it had origins in several independent initiatives. President Giscard d'Estaing of France had first proposed a CDE at the UN Special Session on Disarmament in May 1978. The Warsaw Pact foreign ministers made a similar proposal in May and again in December of 1979. Meanwhile, the EC foreign ministers had endorsed the idea in November 1979, and the NATO foreign ministers cautiously endorsed it in December 1979, as a possibility to be considered at the forthcoming Madrid CSCE meeting. The United States was initially rather cool to the idea, and even though it had participated in the NATO limited endorsement and in joint development in NATO of a package of possible "confidence- and security-building measures" (CSBMs) in 1979–80, when the Madrid meeting began in November 1980 the United States was still reserved about the idea.

By late 1980, the Carter administration had decided to support a CDE and agreed to introduction of the NATO package of CSBMs at Madrid, but it withheld formal commitment to a CDE to leave final decision to the incoming administration. On February 16, 1981, in one of his first foreign policy decisions, although one then regarded as routine, President Reagan agreed to a CDE as long as it was integral to the CSCE process, would not conflict with the MBFR negotiations, and would work out "militarily significant," "politically binding," and "verifiable" CSBMs covering the whole of Europe.[137]

Although the Soviet Union and the Warsaw Pact had proposed a disarmament conference in Europe, their concept had been rather different. They stressed "military détente" through political declarations and commitments (such as nonuse of force and no first use of nuclear weapons), rather than military-technical and verification arrangements. Nonetheless, only a few days after Reagan's decision, the Soviet leadership (General Secretary Brezhnev in his report to the Twenty-sixth Party Congress on February 23) had publicly accepted application of such measures to the whole of Europe including the USSR to the Urals. And at Madrid by July 1983 both the Soviet Union and the United States accepted a compromise mandate for the CDE proposed by a caucus of neutral and nonaligned states. On the initiative of West German Foreign Minister Genscher, supported by several European countries uneasy over the deepening chill in East-West and U.S.-Soviet relations that winter, the Stockholm conference opened in January 1984 with a meeting of the foreign ministers. The meeting of Gromyko and Shultz was cool, though that was an improvement over their heated exchange in Madrid in September. Gromyko's speech was harsh, and Shultz's was considered tough by the Soviets and East Europeans. Nonetheless, by coincidence on the eve of the meeting President Reagan delivered his speech of January 16 proffering "constructive cooperation" with the Soviet Union. Although his words were not addressed to the CDE, that forum in a way became a possible test of the ability of the two superpowers and their allies to resume constructive cooperation.

The CDE opened in Stockholm in January 1984. Its initial mandate was to build on and extend beyond the modest confidence-building measures in the 1975 Helsinki Final Act. (A possible later stage of the CDE, to address more far-reaching measures including disarmament, was also envisaged.) The main issues and problems that rapidly emerged were predictable. The Soviet Union and its Warsaw Pact allies (with the partial exception of Romania, which often acted alone) stressed political and declaratory commitments. The West-

---

137. John Borawski, "The Stockholm Conference on Confidence and Security Building Measures in Europe," *Arms Control*, vol. 6 (September 1985), p. 121, and see this article for a good account of the origins and development of the CDE negotiations through mid–1985. See also the useful monograph by the first U.S. representative to the CDE conference, James Goodby, *The Stockholm Conference: Negotiating a Cooperative Security System for Europe*, Occasional Paper no. 6 (Department of State, Foreign Service Institute, n.d. [1987]). For a review by a former British member of the CDE conference at Stockholm, see John Freeman, *Security and the CSCE Process: The Stockholm Conference and Beyond* (St. Martin's Press, 1991).

ern powers stressed concrete measures providing information on forces, annual forecasts of future military exercises, notification of exercises and force movements, opportunities for observers of military exercises, and verification measures including on-site inspection of suspected noncompliance. When the Warsaw Pact came around to also presenting its military-technical CSBMs, they placed more reliance on limiting exercises and less on other aspects. The Warsaw Pact also continued to press for nonuse of force, no first use of nuclear weapons, no use of chemical weapons, nuclear-free zones in northern and central Europe and the Balkans, and reductions in military spending. The neutral and nonaligned countries jointly offered a compromise set of proposals and played a very useful role throughout in effecting compromise agreements.

There is no need to review the course of the negotiations that ensued from January 1984 to September 1986, when a document with rather far-reaching CSBMs was unanimously agreed on.[138] All in all, while both sides (or, in some cases, more accurately "all parties") contributed to the compromise, the Soviet Union and Warsaw Pact moved further in meeting the Western positions. The Soviet leaders even agreed that a large area in the USSR would be included despite the fact that the territory of the United States was excluded. The Soviets also accepted far-reaching verification, including on-site inspection.

Although the United States and NATO sought more extensive information on and observation of military exercises, as well as verification, once the Soviet Union and Warsaw Pact countries moved to include military confidence-building measures they sought greater constraints than did NATO. For example, they wanted to limit field exercises to no more than 40,000 troops, and to include independent air and naval exercises in the European region, while the West opposed those constraints. Most differences were simply bargained through reciprocal compromises; for instance, NATO originally sought forty-five days advance notice of exercises whereas the Warsaw Pact proposed thirty days—the compromise was forty-two days; a difference between 6,000 or 20,000 military personnel participating as the level requiring advance notification became a compromise of 13,000. One of the most important Western compromises was the agreement to include a reaffirmation of a pledge on nonuse of force, first foreshadowed in President Reagan's speech to the Irish Parliament in June 1984. In October 1985, shortly before the Geneva summit meeting with Reagan, Gorbachev announced Soviet acceptance of the Western proposal for advance annual forecasts of planned exercises. Also at that juncture the East agreed to move into a more effective "working phase" of negotiations. Later, in January and July 1986 Gorbachev agreed to omit naval and air exercises. Toward the end, the Soviets agreed to far-reaching verification in-

---

138. For a detailed and informed account in addition to those cited above, see John Borawski, *From the Atlantic to the Urals: Negotiating Arms Control at the Stockholm Conference* (Washington: Pergamon-Brassey's, 1988).

cluding on-site inspections (in August 1986, first disclosed by Gorbachev to President François Mitterrand in July). The West met that compromise by agreeing to reduce the number of such inspections and to the use of host-country aircraft as part of the inspection process.

As this capsule summary of highlights in the negotiation shows, both sides compromised, the East to a somewhat greater extent. The direct role of President Reagan and General Secretary Gorbachev in publicly indicating major concessions was another feature of the process. So, too, was the relationship to progress in developing Soviet-U.S. relations. At the Geneva summit meeting, the CDE was the only ongoing negotiation to which the two leaders could point as showing progress. And the CDE was successfully concluded in September 1986 not only in time for the CSCE meeting at Vienna, but also immediately preceding the Reykjavik summit.

The successful CDE negotiation not only gave added impetus to improving East-West relations, but also gave more of a voice and some reassurance to the Eastern Europeans, who had made independent contributions. The agreed notifications and restrictions on military exercises considerably curtailed any possible Soviet use of such exercises to place political pressure on any Eastern European country, and they also increased the political cost of any future Soviet military intervention.

The CDE stood as the most successful new CSCE enterprise since the Helsinki Final Act in July 1975. While several less important brief meetings (called forums, experts' meetings, or seminars) on cultural affairs (at Budapest, October-November 1985), on peaceful settlement of disputes (Montreux in 1978 and Athens in 1984), on science (Hamburg in 1980), and on the Mediterranean (Valletta in 1980 and Venice in 1984) had been modestly successful, those on humanitarian affairs remained the most contentious. One on human rights in Ottawa in mid–1985 failed to come near agreement. A meeting on "expansion of human contacts" in Bern in the spring of 1986 was, if the most successful of these other meetings, yet not fully successful.

The United States had pressed hardest to have the Bern meeting. The six-week session in April-May 1986 for the first time saw considerable real progress on problems such as family reunification and expansion of contacts and exchanges (in addition to the exchanges of charges of noncompliance on human rights that had marked all the Helsinki follow-up meetings). Again, both sides compromised, and ultimately a neutral and nonaligned countries' compromise draft document emerged that was almost universally seen as a good step forward. All but one of the thirty-five states supported the Bern Document—but, owing to the CSCE rule of unanimity, the failure of even one country to accept it meant that the draft document could not be adopted. The solitary holdout was the United States.

Washington's refusal to approve the Bern Document, reportedly despite a recommendation by the American delegation, was based on the weak grounds that it was too "modest" and "weak," and that "the real problem remains the problem of compliance with existing documents" rather than producing new ones.[139] Coming on the last day of six weeks in which the United States had pushed for and contributed to a new document, this was an embarrassingly inadequate argument. The Western Europeans and nonaligned were disappointed and angered by the American action. Foreign Minister Genscher of West Germany personally appealed to Secretary Shultz. But the White House was more moved by rumblings on the right in conservative quarters in the United States, who feared that any accord with the Soviet Union in the human rights field would dilute and disorient a confrontational posture on this issue directed at the Soviet Union.

The Soviet Union had a field day in criticizing the United States. *Pravda* was able to pontificate that "the history of the Helsinki forums knows of no other occasion when *both* the West and the East have requested the United States to think things over, to accept a compromise, and not to wreck an agreement that had been so difficult to reach."[140] The American stand seemed to justify Soviet charges that the United States was only interested in anti-Soviet (and anti-East European) propaganda on human rights.

The most damaging aspect of the White House decision not to join in the consensus document, however, was its impact on the Europeans. Allowing all other participants, NATO, neutral and eastern, to reach a consensus and then pulling the rug out from under them on the last day was diplomatically incompetent. Beyond that, not only Soviet charges but Western suspicions of American interest in exploitation of the human rights issue rather than support of gradual real progress in amelioration and improvement seemed only too clearly justified. Finally, the president was seen as demonstrating that he was more interested in satisfying extremist American sentiments, in U.S.-Soviet political warfare, or both, than in considering the interests of the European countries, even its European allies, moreover in a European forum on security and cooperation. Not only were American and Western European interests seen to diverge, but European interests were seen as ranking low in American priorities and as subject to easy sacrifice.[141]

---

139. From a statement by Ambassador Michael Novak, a neoconservative political appointee as head of the U.S. delegation at Bern, on May 27, 1986, at the concluding session; see Thomas W. Netter, "U.S. Rejects Accord at Rights Meeting, Calling It Too Weak," *New York Times*, May 28, 1986, p. A12; see also "Bern Meeting Concludes: U.S. Withholds Consensus on NNA Document," *CSCE Digest* (June 1986), pp. 6, 8.

140. V. Bol'shakov, "Washington Again Says 'No,' " *Pravda*, May 28, 1986. Emphasis added.

141. The Bern conference was barely mentioned in the American press, and apart from a few paragraphs in the *New York Times* article cited above there was virtually no reference to the U.S. stand. This very fact was in marked contrast to the European press and public attention to the meeting and the CSCE process more generally. The administration's decision was clearly not in response to any measurable popular American sentiment against such agreements, but it was facilitated by indifference and seemed to some Europeans to reflect an underlying American disinterest in European affairs.

The culminating development in the CSCE process in the mid–1980s was the third overall conference reviewing developments since the Helsinki Final Act. The foreign ministers of the thirty-five members (all European states except Albania, and the United States and Canada) met in Vienna on November 4, 1986, in a new round of talks that continued until January 19, 1989. As in Belgrade in 1977–78 and Madrid in 1980–83, all aspects of the CSCE Final Act and other evolving negotiations were on the agenda, including the question of a broadened mandate for renewed negotiations on confidence- and security-building measures and disarmament in Europe. The Soviet Union, at the outset, showed a new self-confidence by proposing that a conference on human rights be held in Moscow.

A notable European security endeavor in the early 1980s outside the CSCE framework, indeed outside the framework of official participation, was the Palme Commission. Popularly named for its chairman, former Swedish Prime Minister Olof Palme, an Independent Commission on Disarmament and Security Issues was formed in 1980. It was composed of distinguished public figures and former political leaders, including former Secretary of State Cyrus Vance from the United States and Academician Georgy Arbatov from the Soviet Union. While the Palme Commission had global representation and interests, it gave special attention to European security issues. A report called "Common Security: A Programme for Disarmament" was issued in 1982. It received considerable attention in Europe and also indirectly influenced political thinking in the Soviet Union, but it received little attention in the United States.[142] New confidence- and security-building measures were to be designed to reduce the risk of military confrontation and conflict, and they were to be extended to "the whole of Europe" from the Atlantic to the Urals.

The mutual and balanced force reductions (MBFR) negotiation under way in Vienna since 1973 continued, with minor changes of position by both sides. The Soviet walkout from START as well as INF talks at the end of 1983 was not carried over to the MBFR talks, although progress in MBFR continued to prove elusive. In 1985 and 1986 both sides made minor concessions, but a basic stalemate remained stemming largely from a discrepancy over claims about the number of Soviet (and Polish) forces. In February 1986 the Warsaw Pact countries tabled a draft MBFR treaty. While there was agreement over eventually reaching a common ceiling on forces at the levels of 900,000 military personnel, including 700,000 ground forces personnel, on each side in the MBFR Central European zone (East and West Germany, Poland, and Czecho-

---

142. The title of the report, as issued in English, is given above. An edition published in the United States was given a different subtitle; see *Common Security: A Blueprint for Survival*, with a prologue by Cyrus Vance (Simon and Schuster, 1982). A limited Soviet edition was also published in Russian (in 5,000 copies), titled *Bezopasnost' dlya vsekh: programma razoruzheniya* (Security for All: A Program for Disarmament) (Moscow: Progress, 1982), 278 pp.

slovakia), both sides were suggesting only minor, token cuts in U.S. and Soviet forces (5,000 versus 6,500 U.S., and 11,500 Soviet) as a first step. And in the Western proposal this minor cut would have to be accompanied by far-reaching verification measures, including on-site inspections.

The Warsaw Pact did, however, independent of the MBFR negotiations, propose extensive reductions in conventional forces and arms throughout Europe from the Atlantic to the Urals. Gorbachev first proposed such reductions in general terms in a speech in East Berlin on April 18, 1986.[143] When the Warsaw Pact leaders met in June of that year in Budapest they formally proposed initial reductions of 100,000 to 150,000 troops on each side in the next year or so, followed by cuts totaling roughly one-fourth of the forces each alliance maintained in Europe, about 500,000 on each side.[144] NATO replied six months later, in the "Brussels Declaration on Conventional Arms Control" in December 1986, agreeing to negotiate a new mandate for European conventional arms control.[145] Thus by the close of 1986 it seemed clear that there would be Europewide arms control talks to succeed the successful CDE and to supplant the failed MBFR. Talks on a new mandate for arms reduction negotiation began on February 17, 1987, and successfully concluded on January 10, 1989.

By the time the Vienna CSCE conference ended on January 19, 1989, agreement had thus been reached on a mandate for new negotiations on conventional arms control in Europe, soon called Conventional Forces in Europe (CFE), and for renewed Negotiations on Confidence- and Security-Building Measures (NCSBM). As before, the NCSBM talks included all thirty-five CSCE members; the new CFE talks would comprise all twenty-three states who were members of NATO and the Warsaw Pact, although as individual members, not as alliances. On March 6, the CSCE foreign ministers convened again in Vienna to inaugurate the two new forums, which opened on March 9, 1989.[146] By the time the new talks opened, it was clear that the prospect for agreement on conventional arms reductions was good. Despite not inconsequential differences to be worked out, Foreign Minister Shevardnadze had made clear in a speech on March 6 Soviet readiness to agree to asymmetrical reductions, meaning disproportionately much greater Soviet and Warsaw Pact reductions, to reach equal force levels in categories of major conventional arms. This had been implied in several speeches by Gorbachev and others in

---

143. "11th Congress of the Socialist Unity Party of Germany, Address of Comrade M. S. Gorbachev," *Pravda*, April 19, 1986.

144. "Warsaw Pact Appeal to the NATO States and All European Countries Concerning a Program for Reducing Armed Forces and Conventional Arms in Europe," *Pravda*, June 12, 1986.

145. "Brussels Declaration on Conventional Arms Control (11 December 1986)," *NATO Communiqués 1986* (Brussels: NATO Information Service, 1986), pp. 31–32.

146. In the meantime, the ill-starred MBFR talks, in session since 1973, met for formal disbanding on February 2, 1989 (appropriately without fanfare).

1987 and 1988, but Western governments were suspicious of such generosity. By May 23, concrete proposals in the negotiations offered sharp Warsaw Pact cuts. The negotiations continued to make progress throughout 1989, raising hopes for an agreement possibly as early as the end of 1990.

The most fundamental line of development of East-West relations in Europe was not, however, focused on formal security undertakings or multilateral enterprises. European relations, and even an East-West European détente, continued through the development of an organic network of ties through trade, travel, and bilateral contacts of all kinds among the countries and peoples of East, West, and neutral Europe. These ties proved more durable and meaningful than the more dramatic political designs for détente. And, as noted, they had contributed to a divergence between the United States and its Western European allies in the early 1980s, later repaired.

Détente in Europe throughout the 1980s also continued to attenuate to some degree the dependence of the Eastern European countries on the Soviet Union. Not only the fact of Soviet military predominance and the political-military obligations of the Warsaw Pact, but also the considerable economic dependence of Eastern European countries contributed to maintaining the hegemonic role of the Soviet Union in the socialist community. Nonetheless, the area of autonomous decision and the development of a European relationship that transcended the ideological and political division of the two camps continued to develop throughout the 1980s.

By late 1983 and 1984 this phenomenon of East-West rapprochement of the European countries resting uneasily between the Soviet Union and the United States assumed some unexpected forms, as has been discussed. Eastern Europe was reluctant to join the Soviet campaign of stirring up East-West tensions. Curtailing ties with West Germany and accepting the deployment of Soviet missiles in Eastern Europe were particular stumbling blocks. Originally the Soviet leaders had strongly pushed the development of East-West détente, specifically a rapprochement between East and West Germany, to influence Western policy. By 1984, after Moscow had decided to cool that approach, it was clear that even such stalwart and close allies as East Germany and Bulgaria had developed a strong desire to maintain their détente ties. Under the policies of the Gorbachev leadership in Moscow after 1985, Soviet-East European alignment in support of thawed East-West détente overcame these differences.

Increasingly, the NATO alliance and the Warsaw Pact alliance became less than a principal focus in East-West relations. Thus even when the United States adopted a more confrontational stance toward the Soviet Union after Afghanistan, especially under the Reagan administration, and when the Soviet Union sought in 1983–84 to heighten tensions as a reaction to the NATO INF deployment, the countries of Europe—East and West—continued to pursue a general policy of détente.

Nevertheless, by the latter half of the 1980s, uneasy coexistence between European détente and American-Soviet confrontation had shown Europeans in the East and the West that to an important extent East-West relations were not divisible. While European détente had survived, it had been seriously constrained by the continuing tension between the superpowers. The United States continued to press for limits on economic relations by its Western European allies against the countries of the East; the Soviet Union imposed limits on the political relations of its Eastern European allies with the West. As a senior West German official put it: "As long as both superpowers do not improve their relations, Europeans in East and West have only a very small margin [in which] to cooperate." Probably alluding to the postponement of the visit by the East German leader, he added, "We have already experienced just how small our room for maneuver really is."[147] This comment incidentally reflected a tendency to see the position of the Europeans as one—when they spoke of "our room for maneuver," they meant all Europeans, East and West.

Even more fundamental and ultimately most decisive for the future of East-West relations in Europe were the revolutionary internal changes taking place within the Eastern bloc, above all in the Soviet Union itself. These changes were to lead in rapid succession to two revolutions ending the division of Europe: one in Eastern Europe in 1989–90, as the Soviet Union let it go its own way, and soon after in the Soviet Union itself, leading by the end of 1991 to the dissolution of that state.

## The Revolutions of '89 and '91 and the New Europe of the 1990s

In earlier chapters a central place has been given to the events in Europe in 1989–90, and they need not be reviewed at length. It is, however, useful to examine now the ways in which those developments reflected, affected, and ultimately profoundly transformed American-Soviet relationships with each other and with Europe.

The events of 1989 showed that the "restructuring" of Soviet relations with the Western countries, and with the socialist countries of Eastern Europe, was real. On one level, the Soviet Union controlled and directed efforts through a combination of unilateral measures and mainly multilateral negotiations to dismantle the East-West confrontation. Gorbachev's unilateral force reductions in Eastern Europe announced at the UN in December 1988 were followed by further steps throughout 1989. As earlier noted, in January, the Vienna CSCE conference ended with agreement to pursue two new sets of talks, and in March these new parallel negotiations opened: the Conventional Forces in Europe (CFE) negotiations among the twenty-three member states

---

147. Cited by William Drozdiak, "Visiting Kohl Seeks Link to Arms Talks," *Washington Post*, November 30, 1984, p. A24.

of NATO and the Warsaw Pact for reciprocal arms reductions, and separate talks among all thirty-five members of the CSCE on military confidence– and security-building measures (CSBMs) in Europe. Those two negotiations succeeded in less than two years in reaching major agreements, signed in Paris in November 1990. Without reviewing their course here, it should be noted that from the outset both sides worked constructively and made compromises, but the key steps were early moves by the Soviet Union. In January 1989 the Warsaw Pact had unilaterally submitted new and essentially accurate comprehensive data on its arms, overcoming the main blockage that had stymied the old MBFR talks for years. In May Shevardnadze announced Soviet agreement to equal levels of arms for the two alliances in Europe to the Urals, implying a huge asymmetry in reductions at the expense of the Soviet Union and Warsaw Pact. In May 1989, Gorbachev had accepted reductions to equal levels 10 percent below the existing lower (NATO) level and national ceilings entailing deep cuts by the Soviet Union (despite some later Soviet transfer of arms to Asia), in exchange for a cap on theoretical increases by West Germany.

These early signs confirmed that the new negotiations promised real achievement in winding down the arms race and deflating Western perceptions of a conventional arms threat. The talks also contributed to gradual Western recognition that Gorbachev was indeed serious about dismantling the military confrontation between East and West. This process reached its culmination in the Paris Charter, the CFE Treaty, and other agreements signed in November 1990.

Important as these steps were in defusing and lowering military sources and reflections of tension, even more significant were the political changes stimulated by the new Soviet policy. Above all, the dizzying succession of changes in the countries of Eastern Europe throughout 1989 ending in the collapse of communist rule in all of the Eastern European countries of the Warsaw Pact in effect also marked the end of the political confrontation between East and West. This Revolution of '89 led to the reunification of Germany and the formal all-European agreements of 1990 that consolidated the end of the Cold War. Only shortly thereafter, a "Revolution of '91" not only ended communist rule in the Soviet Union, but resulted in the collapse of the Soviet Union itself. Combined, these developments marked the end of an era and the birth of new relationships among the countries of Europe, east and west, Russia and the other successor states to the former Soviet Union, and the United States.

Several key aspects of this momentous change merit closer attention. First is the extent and nature of Soviet encouragement, and benign nonintervention, in the internal changes in Eastern European countries in 1989 culminating in the Revolution of '89. As noted, since 1985 Gorbachev had been preparing the ground for shifting political power in Eastern Europe from the old authoritarian bureaucratic leaders to the new reforming socialist leaderships responsive to popular consent. He persisted even as the prospect of continued socialist orientation diminished.

In February 1989, the Polish leadership opened roundtable talks with the leaders of formerly outlawed Solidarity. By April they had agreed on free elections for 35 percent of the Sejm (Lower House) and all of the Senate. By June, election of the 100 members of the honorific Senate in Poland yielded an astonishing 99 victories for Solidarity, and a complete sweep of the 161 freely contested seats in the Sejm by Solidarity. On August 22, at the critical juncture as the Polish leaders were deciding to share power, Gorbachev advised Polish party leader Mieczysław Rakowski that national reconciliation was indeed the only path. While reaffirming Soviet support for the Polish Party, he made clear that Rakowski should not block the turnover of power to a coalition government led by Solidarity.[148] This marked the first peaceful ouster of a ruling communist government, occurring moreover in the most important country of Eastern Europe.

Meanwhile, in May in Hungary the reformist communist leadership had literally and symbolically started to tear down the Iron Curtain by removing barbed wire barriers on its border with Austria. In June, Imre Nagy, victim of suppression of the 1956 revolution, was reinterred with honor, and three weeks later his now-retired successor, János Kádár, died. In September, under conflicting pressures, Hungary opened its border with Austria to thousands of East Germans on their way West, deepening a growing crisis in East Germany. And in October, Hungary officially became simply a "republic" rather than a Soviet-style "people's republic," and the communist party, seeking to shake off the burden of its past, renamed itself from the Socialist Workers Party to the Hungarian Socialist Party.

Gorbachev and the Soviet leadership not only permitted, but encouraged, this liberalization and moves toward popular rule. It is still not entirely clear whether and when Gorbachev saw the likelihood that reformist, *perestroika*-oriented, communist leaderships would fail and be followed by noncommunist governments, but this prospect became increasingly evident. Lieutenant General Leonid V. Shebarshin, named the head of KGB foreign

---

148. Many sources report Gorbachev's telephone call to Rakowski, although none has been able to confirm the precise terms Gorbachev used. For example, see Charles Gati, *The Bloc That Failed: Soviet-East European Relations in Transition* (Indiana University Press, 1990), p. 168. Rakowski's account, in his draft memoir, was made available to Don Oberdorfer; see Don Oberdorfer, *The Turn: From the Cold War to a New Era, the United States and the Soviet Union, 1983–1990* (Poseidon Press, 1991), pp. 360–61.

The Polish decision was not, however, made by Rakowski alone, and General Wojciech Jaruzelski, the party chief until July when he was elected president of Poland, stated that the basic decision to share power was made in Warsaw, and *that* was "the historic achievement of Gorbachev. . . . We didn't have to ask his assent for this or any other solution." (See Stephen Engelberg, "Jaruzelski, Defending Record, Says His Rule Saved Poland," *New York Times*, May 20, 1992, p. A1.) That is true. But Gorbachev lent his behind-the-scenes support to the Polish leader's decision by making sure that Rakowski understood that any other path would not find favor in Moscow.

intelligence in January 1989, has said that the first major assessment he read upon assuming that office was an estimate that the "chances for survival of the [Warsaw Pact] allied regimes were small."[149] While Gorbachev may have hoped that the regimes in Eastern Europe could transform themselves or at least give way to "socialist" successors, he knew that there was a substantial risk that the process would get out of hand. Yet he saw the alternative of hard-line repression as both doomed for the long run and incompatible with his objectives for liberalization at home and for ending the Cold War in Europe. And even conservatives in the leadership, notably Yegor Ligachev, had agreed as early as 1986–87 that the Soviet Union must not resort to force in an effort to control the situation. No matter how uncertain the prospect, only a course seeking to build popular support held any possibility of success, and Gorbachev persisted.[150]

Gorbachev's decision to press ahead with political liberalization in the countries of Eastern Europe was not reversed even as, at the same time, serious ethnic, nationalist, and emerging separatist tendencies caused a wave of difficulties in the Soviet Union. Drawing a firm line against any secession from the Soviet Union, even by the formerly independent Baltic states, Gorbachev saw this as a different problem.

On April 9, 1989, disturbances in Tbilisi, Georgia, were brutally suppressed with twenty killed. In May and June rioting flared up in several places in Central Asia. In July there were violent actions again in Georgia, by Abkhazians. Most perplexing to Gorbachev was the steady growth of expression of independence sentiment in the Baltic states, leading Lithuania and Estonia in May, and Latvia in July, to declare their "sovereignty." In August, an impressive turnout of an estimated 1 million Balts created a "human chain" reaching from Vilnius 430 miles through Riga to Tallin, protesting the fiftieth anniversary of the Molotov-Ribbentrop agreement assigning the Baltic states to the Soviet sphere of influence and laying the foundation for Stalin's coercion of the entrance of the three republics into the USSR in June 1940. At a Central Committee plenum on September 19–20, the leadership still assumed the problem was one of finding the right balance within the union.

---

149. L. V. Shebarshin, *Ruka Moskvy: Zapiski nachal'nika sovetskoi razvedki* (The Hand of Moscow: Notes of the Chief of Soviet Intelligence) (Moscow: Tsentr–100, 1992), p. 237.
     Shebarshin also remarked that on a familiarization visit to Prague in May 1989, the Czechoslovak intelligence service was demoralized by events and the regime's attempts to maintain the status quo, while Soviet Ambassador Viktor Lomakin, a former career party official, unable to comprehend what was going on in Czechoslovakia, had oriented his thinking on the views of local hard-liners and was unreceptive to other views. Ibid., pp. 238–39.

150. Secretary Baker, in early September, reportedly remarked privately, "Gorbachev's obviously riding a tiger, but it's almost as though he's spurring the tiger on." Cited in Michael R. Beschloss and Strobe Talbott, *At the Highest Levels: The Inside Story of the End of the Cold War* (Little, Brown and Company, 1992), p. 102.

Gorbachev visited East Germany in early October and is reported to have told Honecker yet again to reform, warning him, "Those who are late will be punished by life itself."[151] Publicly, Gorbachev withheld any sign of support for Honecker and called for *perestroika*. When, two days later, crowds in Leipzig grew to unmanageable size, the security forces did not move against them; the security and military leaders—notably Egon Krenz—refused to fire on the people. By October 17, Honecker was ousted by his own Politburo, and replaced by Krenz.[152] (Krenz later revealed that the East German leader had advised Gorbachev two days before Honecker's removal.)[153] On November 9, the new East German leadership (reportedly after calling Gorbachev) opened the gates and permitted the Berlin Wall to be torn down. The foremost symbol of the Iron Curtain division of Europe was no more.[154]

---

151. See Hannes Adomeit, "Gorbachev and German Unification: Revision of Thinking, Realignment of Power," *Problems of Communism*, vol. 39 (July-August 1990), p. 6.

    Honecker was unresponsive, and in Gorbachev's unsmiling presence publicly said that "the GDR enters the threshold of the year 2000 with confidence that the future belongs to Socialism." "Address of E. Honecker," *Pravda*, October 7, 1989.

    Gorbachev had not wanted to go to East Berlin, but the Politburo had insisted that he make a final try to persuade Honecker to recognize reality and change. This visit persuaded Gorbachev that Honecker must go, and it might be too late to save the GDR. When the crowd chanted against Honecker, Polish Prime Minister Mieczysław Rakowski, who knew German and was also present, turned to Gorbachev and told him, "This is the end." (Reported by Anatoly Chernyayev in a discussion on February 24, 1993.) After Gorbachev returned to Moscow, he stated that Honecker's days were numbered and that they must prepare for German reunification. See Valery Boldin, *Ten Years That Shook the World: The Gorbachev Era as Witnessed by His Chief of Staff* (Harper Collins Basic Books, 1994), p. 143.

152. Honecker's removal and Krenz's succession was formalized by the Central Committee the next day, October 18.

153. See Kevin Costelloe, "Men Who Succeeded East Germany's Boss Bares Plot Details," Associated Press, May 2, 1991; and Volker Warkentin, "Ex-Commitment Leader Krenz Testifies at Comrade's Fraud Trial," Reuters, May 2, 1991.

    Soviet troops in East Germany had received orders from the Ministry of Defense in Moscow not to leave their barracks and not to interfere in East German affairs. Former Central Committee official Valery Musatov, cited from an interview by Gabriel Partos, *The World That Came In from the Cold* (London: Royal Institute of International Affairs, 1993), p. 246.

154. In January, Honecker had vowed that the Berlin Wall would "still be standing in 50 or even 100 years" (*Neues Deutschland*, January 20, 1989). In that same month, Aleksandr Yakovlev, in Germany, had distanced Gorbachev's Soviet Union from the Berlin Wall, saying, "We didn't build this wall—this isn't our wall" (cited in *Der Tagesspiegel* [Daily Mirror], January 10, 1989). And Gorbachev himself in May, while visiting the Great Wall of China, answered a question by an American reporter about the future of the Berlin Wall by saying, "We must work to improve the international atmosphere and I hope that would create conditions when all unneeded walls [that is, the Berlin Wall] would disappear." (From a Western correspondent present.)

On the day after the Berlin Wall came down, the veteran communist leader with the longest incumbency, Todor Zhivkov of Bulgaria, also fell, removed from power by his colleagues. His successor, the long-time foreign minister, Petar Mladenov, had only a few days earlier stopped in Moscow on his way to and from Beijing, returning to Sofia only on November 9. Perhaps Zhivkov merely feared that his ouster had been planned in Moscow and, in trying to stave it off, brought it about.[155]

Before the month was over, on November 24, Miloš Jakeš, the hard-line leader of Czechoslovakia, resigned, a week after the Czech propaganda chief, Ján Fojtík, had been summoned to Moscow and told that the Soviet Union would repudiate the 1968 invasion of Czechoslovakia, thus removing any foundation for the regime.[156]

In December, immediately following his summit meeting at Malta with Bush, Gorbachev convened a meeting in Moscow of the Warsaw Pact leaders. All except of course Gorbachev himself, and Romania's Nicolae Ceauşescu, were new since the last summit meeting of the Warsaw Pact in Bucharest five months earlier. Gorbachev described his meeting with Bush and the further improvement in relations. He said that the United States was no longer an enemy, although the Warsaw Pact was still necessary to oppose those who still favored confrontation. He asked the views of the others, but none wanted to speak up except Ceauşescu, who struck a lonely and discordant note arguing that NATO was growing stronger and that the Warsaw Pact must become stronger too and oppose the anticommunist policies of the West. Gorbachev reiterated the need to eliminate the legacy of the Cold War. All present, except Ceauşescu, also agreed to condemn the 1968 invasion of Czechoslovakia and to reaffirm the principles of sovereignty and noninterference and resolution of all

---

155. Mladenov had a sharp argument with Zhivkov on October 23 and had submitted his resignation as foreign minister and Politburo member in a letter on October 24 addressed to all the top party leadership organs—the Politburo, Central Committee and Central Control and Auditing Committee—in which he strongly criticized Zhivkov's record. Nonetheless, Zhivkov did not accept the resignations and insisted Mladenov proceed with a long scheduled visit to China (which meant transiting Moscow twice). Mladenov was in China on November 5–8, and on either or both stops en route he presumably consulted with Soviet leaders, possibly including Gorbachev. He had long-standing close relations with them (as foreign minister ever since 1971), and there is no doubt they shared the view that Zhivkov should be replaced. (Gati is in error in saying that Gorbachev brought Mladenov to Moscow the day before the Bulgarian action; Gati, *The Bloc That Failed*, p. 187.) But whatever the nature of such Moscow discussions, Zhivkov's fate was decided by an alliance of key Bulgarian leaders, including especially General Dobri Dzhurov, the defense minister. The domestic events in East Germany were no doubt foremost in their thinking on November 10 when they compelled Zhivkov's resignation.

156. See Robert G. Kaiser, *Why Gorbachev Happened: His Triumphs and His Failure* (Simon and Schuster, 1991), pp. 306–07.

disputes solely by political means. The Brezhnev Doctrine was formally buried.[157]

In Romania, the last of the old communist regimes faced the outbreak of a national revolt after troops fired on demonstrators in mid-December, and on December 22 Nicolae Ceauşescu was overthrown, fled, and was captured. He was tried by a military field court martial, and on December 25 his execution was announced. There have been reports that some of those who deposed and succeeded Ceauşescu, and who had long been plotting, had been in touch with Gorbachev and had expected Soviet support. In this instance there is no clear evidence that Gorbachev had advance knowledge.[158] He had, however, made clear on his last visit to Romania that he believed in *perestroika* for all the countries of Eastern Europe. Ceauşescu had, however, understood how brittle his own authority was and feared to make any change. In August, alarmed by the rapid retreat of the communist leadership in Poland (and unaware of Gorbachev's encouragement of that process), Ceauşescu had privately called for Warsaw Pact military intervention in Poland, but of course he received no support from Moscow or elsewhere.[159]

Throughout this year culminating in the Revolution of '89, Gorbachev had continued to reaffirm the principle of freedom of choice by each people. As discussed earlier, he restated that ideal at the Sorbonne and in Strasbourg in July, and in Rome at the end of November (while en route to Malta to meet with President Bush). The Warsaw Pact summit meeting in early December reaffirmed that "history had confirmed" the need "to observe strictly the principles of sovereignty, independence, and noninterference." And the 1968 military intervention in Czechoslovakia was repudiated and condemned.[160]

Gorbachev and his policies did come under fire from conservative critics in the Soviet party leadership, especially at the Central Committee plenum in February 1990. There, both Ligachev and a former career party official then serving as ambassador to Poland, Vladimir Brovikov, sharply at-

---

157. Based on an account by an Eastern European participant; see Oberdorfer, *The Turn*, pp. 384–86.

158. Unidentified "intelligence sources" are cited as saying that Silviu Brucan, one of the plotters and later the new foreign minister, had been in Moscow just a month before the uprising. See Jack Anderson and Dale Van Atta, "Soviet Hand in Bucharest," *Washington Post*, September 22, 1991, p.C7. I have not, however, been able to confirm that report.

      For the fullest review of available evidence on the several Romanian plots and possible connections with the Soviet Union, see James F. Burke, "Romanian and Soviet Intelligence in the December Revolution," *Intelligence and National Security*, vol. 8 (October 1993), pp. 26–58.

159. Disclosed by Sergei Tarasenko, close foreign policy aide to Shevardnadze, in a discussion on February 25, 1993.

160. "Declaration of the Leaders of Bulgaria, Hungary, the GDR, Poland and the Soviet Union," *Pravda*, December 5, 1989.

tacked the loss of communist control in Eastern Europe. Similar charges were made at the party congress in July. But the critics had no alternative policy. Even Ligachev had agreed that there must be no Soviet military intervention.[161] Under these circumstances, the most the Soviet leaders could do was to swim with the rapid flow of events during 1989.

The United States was even more disposed to flow with the current of events. When the Bush administration entered office at the beginning of 1989, as noted in an earlier chapter, the president decided to review and reconsider policy toward the Soviet Union, a process that lasted for several months. A similar review and delay marked policy toward Eastern Europe. Although this review did not result in any significant changes, it helped to head off what might have been a serious mistake.

Even before the new administration entered office, Henry Kissinger approached Bush (on December 18, 1988) with a proposal for a secret diplomatic approach to the Soviet leadership to strike a deal based on the balance of power: if the Soviet Union would permit more leeway and liberalization in Eastern Europe, the United States would undertake not to take advantage of that situation to act against the legitimate security interests of the Soviet Union in the area. Bush, who was accompanied only by Brent Scowcroft (his choice to become national security adviser, the post he had held under President Ford in 1975–77, after serving as the deputy adviser under Kissinger in 1973–75), was intrigued by the idea. He authorized Kissinger, who was about to visit Moscow as part of a Council on Foreign Relations delegation, to take a letter from him to Gorbachev. The letter did not spell out the proposed deal, but rather Bush's reaffirmation of intent to develop relations, although only after an assessment of the relationship and policy options—in all, a minimal and even hedged commitment. But the letter from Bush gave a certain cachet of authority to Kissinger's role and his oral message proposing the confidential exchanges and negotiation on "managing" the situation in Eastern Europe in such a way that the interests of the Soviet Union and the United States were met. Gorbachev's advisers (and probably Gorbachev himself) were of two minds on the Kissinger proposal, but Gorbachev at least kept open the possibility, even of resurrecting the old Kissinger-Dobrynin confidential "back-channel." On January 28, Kissinger reported to Bush (now accompanied by Baker as well as Scowcroft). No decision was made at that time, and Bush's policy review tended to put off the matter. Baker was probably influenced by the strong opposition of

---

161. Besides implying such agreement in several later writings, Ligachev confirmed to me that he had, in 1989 as earlier, agreed that there must be no Soviet military intervention. Interview, November 11, 1991.

   Shevardnadze, responding to attacks at the party congress, denied that the changes in Eastern Europe were contrary to Soviet interests (on which there were clearly contrary views), and then went on to say that "even if what was happening in Eastern Europe were at variance with our interests, even then we would exclude any interference in the affairs of these states." No one directly challenged that proposition. See E. A. Shevardnadze, "We Will Live in a New Europe," *Izvestiya*, July 4, 1990.

professional diplomats in the State Department, who pointed out the risks of legitimizing a slipping Soviet role in Eastern Europe in exchange for processes already under way and the likelihood of strongly negative reaction by Europeans, East and West, to any kind of U.S.-Soviet negotiation behind their backs over the future of Europe.

On March 28, Baker disclosed the idea in a frank on-the-record interview with a correspondent of the *New York Times*, as an idea with some possible merit but also drawbacks. The disclosure, whether intended as a trial balloon or a decoy to attract fire, brought strong protests and objections from Eastern and Western Europeans, as the State Department experts had predicted. The idea of a Kissingerian diplomatic game was dead.[162]

A sensible core idea underlay the proposal: that the United States and the Soviet Union should each behave in ways that did not inflame developments under way in Eastern Europe or stimulate concerns in Moscow that the West would seek to take advantage of such developments. That the two powers should consult about the situation was quite a different matter from a secret negotiated deal. The consultative approach was taken and was successful.

Bush unveiled the meager results of his policy review on relations with Eastern Europe on April 17 (in a speech before a heavily Polish-populated American city, Hamtramck, Michigan), by coincidence on the same day as the formal legalization of Solidarity in Poland.[163] He was, however, cautious and modest in proposals for aid to the new steps of liberalization in Eastern Europe, initially proposing only $125 million over three years. Congress, responding to intervening events, raised that figure to $938 million by the time that it authorized the expenditure (in November).

Bush was restrained in his later speeches. In Mainz, West Germany, in June he did rhetorically urge, "Let Europe be whole and free."[164] In July, Bush visited Poland and Hungary, but he was circumspect in his statements (in sharp contrast to his inflammatory remarks when as vice president he had visited the region six years earlier.)[165] He spoke about the desire of the United States for constructive cooperation with the East European countries pursuing reform and held out general indications of aid for them.

While—appropriately—not articulated in these terms, the policy that Bush and Baker were now implementing was based on the judgment (later

---

162. Beschloss and Talbott, *At the Highest Levels*, pp. 13–16, 19–21, 44–46.

163. "Encouraging Political and Economic Reforms in Poland," April 17, 1989, *State Bulletin*, vol. 89 (June 1989), pp. 3–5.

164. "President's Address, Mainz," May 31, 1989, *State Bulletin*, vol. 89 (August 1989), p. 38. He also noted the removal of Hungarian border barriers and urged, "Let Berlin be next" (p. 39).

165. See chapter 3. Bush had also been less inflammatory on a later visit as vice president in 1987.

proved correct) that there were favorable prospects for liberalization and even democracy in Eastern Europe, which could be attained with the acquiescence of the Soviet Union, rather than by challenging it directly.[166] Indeed, as a result of this trip Baker suggested and Bush agreed to seek an earlier "interim" summit meeting with Gorbachev. On July 18 on his way back to Washington Bush wrote to Gorbachev proposing such a meeting. This was the origin of the summit meeting in Malta in early December.

On several occasions during the year, most notably on July 29 when Baker met with Shevardnadze in Paris, the United States coupled warnings against the adverse consequences for American-Soviet relations if Moscow were to resort to force to prevent change in Eastern Europe with assurances that the United States (and by implication the West) would not seek to take advantage of the situation in ways adverse to the security interests of the Soviet Union. The Soviets, in this instance Shevardnadze, gave reassurances that the Soviet Union would not resort to force.[167] These exchanges and the American reassurances were helpful to Gorbachev and Shevardnadze not only in overcoming their own concerns, but also in arguing their case with others in the leadership (even though the hard-liners would not be reassured by any American rhetoric). These mutual reassurances were again exchanged at the Malta summit, as the Revolution of '89 was completing its initial sweep of Eastern Europe.

As a symbolic indication of the changing relationships between the two alliances, just three weeks after Malta Shevardnadze visited NATO headquarters in Brussels—at which time he suggested that NATO (and the Warsaw Pact) "at this crucial stage in the European process can play an important role in stabilizing Europe."[168]

The year 1990 witnessed five developments directly concerning Europe and American-Soviet relations: consolidation of the shift to noncommunist rule in the countries of Eastern Europe; changes in the relationship of those countries with the Soviet Union, and the effective neutralization of the Warsaw Pact and the CMEA; the reunification of Germany; the codification of the

---

166. Indeed, in the unexpectedly most significant action during his Eastern European trip, Bush made clear to General Jaruzelski that the United States was not interested in winning a contest with the Soviet Union over Poland, but in contributing to an evolutionary process there, as Jaruzelski had been doing and might continue to do. Jaruzelski reportedly was so encouraged by Bush's words that, contrary to his earlier inclination, he decided to run for president. He won the office. President Bush thus may have been responsible indirectly for Jaruzelski's subsequent constructive role in a transition from communist rule in Poland. See Beschloss and Talbott, *At the Highest Levels*, pp. 88–89.

167. Oberdorfer, *The Turn*, p. 360; confirmed to me independently by a knowledgeable American source.

168. See Edward Cody, "Shevardnadze Visits NATO, Warns Against Reunification," *Washington Post*, December 20, 1989, pp. A1, A30. As the article title noted, Shevardnadze also expressed concerns over German reunification, particularly over its relationship to NATO and the acceptance by a reunified Germany of its eastern borders.

reunification of Europe, marked by the Paris CSCE summit meeting; and the agreement on significant reduction of conventional arms, especially those of the Soviet Union. All were interrelated to some extent. Together, they marked a decisive shift away from the Cold War configuration of Europe, even though in most cases they began processes that would take time to develop fully.

The year 1991 continued the process of rapidly evolving change with three main developments: the further shift in relationships between the Soviet Union and the countries of Eastern Europe marked by the end of the Warsaw Pact (and the CMEA) and major withdrawals of Soviet forces (entirely from Czechoslovakia and Hungary, in part and continuing from Germany and Poland); coupled with the extension of a NATO relationship to the members of the former Warsaw Pact, including the Soviet Union; and finally the travail within the Soviet Union during the year, culminating in the overthrow of the rule of the Communist Party after seventy-four years, and by year's end the collapse and dissolution of the Soviet Union itself. Mention should also be made of two other developments: one, the disintegration and outbreak of civil war within former Yugoslavia, exemplifying a major European crisis not stemming from the Cold War confrontation, yet not controllable by any of the institutions of the newly reunified Europe; and the other, the failure of Western Europe to meet its own expectations to unify. Instead the region had to face new challenges of redefining its long-term relationship with the eastern and southern parts of the reunified Europe, now stretching to Vladivostok and including much of Central Asia.

The United States and the Soviet Union were now increasingly on the same side, rather than in adversarial conflict. To be sure, there was still a need to reconcile different interests, but even when differences existed, there was a common desire to resolve them. To some extent, this was only a further development of tendencies already under way but not yet complete in 1990 and 1991. Still, cooperation was now becoming the hallmark of American-Soviet relations.

Bush and Baker, as they had promised, did not seek to use the opportunities that were there to exploit the collapse of Soviet hegemony in Eastern Europe either by moving to extend NATO forward to the Soviet borders or by trying to exploit the widening fissures within the Soviet Union. Only in relatively minor ways did the United States take advantage of Soviet weakness, for example, in extracting marginal advantages in negotiating the remaining differences on the START I Treaty signed in mid–1991.

On the most critical issue, the reunification of Germany, though the positions of the two countries initially differed significantly (above all on the question of a united Germany remaining in NATO), they worked cooperatively to resolve the problem by working out a series of provisions to reassure the Soviet leadership and public that their security would not be jeopardized.

Although Gorbachev and other Soviet leaders were prepared to relinquish control over Eastern Europe, and even reluctantly to see reform-minded communist governments supplanted by noncommunist ones, they had not been prepared to see East Germany absorbed into West Germany, and they were worried by the prospect.[169] On November 10, the day after the Berlin Wall came down, Gorbachev sent a rather alarmed message to President Bush (and to Prime Minister Margaret Thatcher and President François Mitterrand) emphasizing that "history had decreed" that there were two German states (a comment he had also made earlier to West German President Richard von Weizsäcker, at a time when the issue was much less active). Gorbachev was really concerned that events could get out of control, and though he did not contemplate using the large Soviet military forces in East Germany, he feared that by their presence they might become involved, for example, in response to uncontrolled civilian actions against them. This would also make more difficult the general shift to a new European and international order.[170] The Soviet leaders, some much more alarmed than Gorbachev and Shevardnadze, were also much concerned about how a reunited Germany might in the future throw its weight around. Finally, the sudden rise of a renascent reunited Germany, coupled with the collapse of the whole socialist camp, evoked wide public concern in the Soviet Union, much stronger than the apprehension over the change of regimes in Eastern European countries.

Reassurance that the security interests and rights of the Soviet Union and other three postwar occupation powers would be taken into account in the reunification of Germany was provided through the negotiations of the 2+4 (two German states and four wartime victors) in 1990. The reaffirmation of

---

169. Anatoly Chernyayev, Gorbachev's foreign affairs aide, has described how soon after he began working directly for Gorbachev, in early 1986, he had put "the German question" on an agenda of important issues, and Gorbachev had asked him "Why?" Gorbachev smiled and said that matter would only arise "later," implying much later. Chernyayev in a discussion on February 24, 1993.

Shevardnadze claimed in his memoir and in several interviews that as early as 1986 he had concluded that the question of German reunification would arise "in the near future as the main and decisive issue for Europe." Shevardnadze, *The Future Belongs to Freedom*, p. 131; and (for the quotation cited above) see his interview with Fedor Burlatsky, "His Resignation Above Life . . .," *Literaturnaya gazeta*, April 10, 1991. This appears, however, to be at least an overstatement. Former First Deputy Minister of Foreign Affairs Georgy Kornienko (under Shevardnadze at that time, after years under Gromyko) has stated that nothing on the record supports that claim of Shevardnadze, and much contradicts it. He noted that in 1986, contrary to all the advice of the professional diplomats, Shevardnadze insisted on changing the long-standing ministry organization under which one office handled German affairs, West, East, and Berlin. Shevardnadze thought East Germany should be handled with the other socialist states of Eastern Europe, and he shifted responsibility for it, breaking up the handling of German affairs. See Akhromeyev and Kornienko, *Glazami marshala i diplomata*, pp. 262–64.

170. On Gorbachev's message to Bush and other Western leaders, see Oberdorfer, *The Turn*, p. 365; and Beschloss and Talbott, *At the Highest Levels*, p. 137. Gorbachev's concerns over both the immediate situation getting out of control and the transition to a new order being derailed were described to me by Aleksandr Bessmertnykh and by Gorbachev's foreign policy aide, Anatoly Chernyayev, in a discussion on February 24, 1993.

acceptance of Germany's eastern borders, reaffirmation of nonnuclear weapon status, a reduction of and ceiling on German military forces, and nonextension of other NATO forces into eastern Germany contributed greatly to allaying Soviet concerns, as did the parallel moves to enhance pan-European security arrangements through the further CSCE and CFE arms reduction agreements concluded in November 1990.[171]

The sudden leadership and governmental changes in Eastern Europe in late 1989 posed several problems and challenges for the Soviet Union. A Politburo meeting on January 2, 1990, decided to commission the Foreign Ministry, the Ministry of Defense, the KGB, and the International Department of the Central Committee to analyze and prepare recommendations to the Politburo on three questions: arms control and security matters (in light of the changed situation); the position the Soviet Union should take "in relation to cooperation and establishing contacts with the leadership of the new structures of authority" in the Eastern European countries "taking account of the processes taking place there"; and "the line of the CPSU and measures for support of the Communist and workers' parties in the Eastern European countries."[172] The memorandum prepared under the third item, later adopted by the Politburo, in the Central Committee archive has also become available. It laid out the sorry status of the communist parties, most of which in its own words were "in a state of deep ideological crisis and organizational disarray."[173] Without reviewing this fascinating document in detail, it is worth noting that it ascribed the fall from power, sharp loss of membership, and other disastrous consequences to their failure to change earlier from the old "administrative-command model of socialism." It noted that all, with the possible exception of the Bulgarian party, would now be opposition parties, as well as that all had to some degree become left socialist or social-democratic parties and abandoned communist positions. The recommended course for the Soviet Union was, in effect, to accept the new reality, maintaining

---

171. See the discussion in chapter 10.

172. TsKhSD (The Center for the Storage of Contemporary Documentation; holder of the archives of the former Central Committee), Fond 89, Perechen' 9, Dokument 62, *O sobytiyakh v Vostochnoi Yevrope i pozitsii CCCP* (On the Events in Eastern Europe and the Position of the USSR), excerpt from protocol no. 175 of the meeting of the Politburo of the CC CPSU of January 2, 1990, P 175/U, Top Secret. This document was recently declassified, and I obtained a copy at the TsKhSD.

173. TsKhSD, Fond 89, Perechen' 9, Dokument 103, *O linii KPSS i merakh v podderzhku kommunisticheskikh i rabochikh partii v vostochnoyevropeiskikh stranakh* (On the Line of the CPSU and Measures of Support to Communist and Workers Parties in the Eastern European Countries), excerpt from protocol no. 184 of the meeting of the Politburo of the CC CPSU on April 5, 1990, P 184/38, Top Secret. Discussion above and following is based on the eight-page International Department memorandum of the same title adopted by the Politburo and attached to the cover memorandum, quotations from pp. 1, 2.

contact with the parties and not abandoning them and even providing some material support indirectly to help them survive. But the Soviet Union could no longer align with the former communist parties or against other parties. Indeed, the Soviet leaders were also urged not to delay in also establishing contact with other new parties and forces, such as Solidarity in Poland, the Civic Forum in Czechoslovakia, and the National Salvation Front in Romania. Above all, no efforts were to be made to attempt to restore the former communist parties to power.

Documentary information is not available on most other decisions that were taken in 1990 on readjusting politically to the new situation. It is known that besides agreeing on terms for the reunification of Germany through absorption of East Germany into the Federal Republic, the Soviet Union moved to accommodate the political changes in the other former communist-ruled countries of Eastern Europe. Meetings of the Warsaw Pact continued (with East Germany formally withdrawing before its demise through merger), as did meetings of the CMEA through 1990 and into 1991, although it was clear that the nature of each would change, and it became clear that both would soon be phased out.

The Soviet leaders were faced with growing internal difficulties, including a spillover effect from Eastern Europe in the Baltic republics, as they decided how to deal with the suddenly changed relationship in Eastern Europe. Nonetheless, they had made the basic decision without even posing it to themselves: they would accommodate the Revolution of '89, not try to reverse or undercut it. This momentous change had occurred much more suddenly and precipitously than they had hoped, brushing aside and bypassing the more gradual reforms and changes under enlightened socialist-communist leadership that the Soviet leaders had sought. These revolutionary changes, however, had occurred peacefully and without a direct confrontation with the Soviet Union or the half-million Soviet troops deployed in most of the countries of Eastern Europe. The Soviet leaders were confident that "objective" factors (such as geographic location and extensive economic ties) would lead any governments in these countries to need and to maintain close cooperative ties with the Soviet Union. Shared security interests were also foreseen, including the fact that these countries remained outside the unifying European Community. Some would also want reassurance against a resurgent and reunifying Germany. Such judgments were in part well founded, although there was a tendency to exaggerate them and to underestimate the negative burden that past Soviet hegemony placed on any continuing institutional association and actual dependence on the Soviet Union.

Finally, Gorbachev and some of the other Soviet leaders, though by no means all, while shaken by the sudden and drastic nature of the shift, did see the outcome as the fruition of establishment of a "common European home" and the end of counterpoised military alliances that they had sought.

Continued Soviet-East European bilateral diplomatic dialogue, economic interaction, and even the cooperation in gradual loosening and discarding of institutional (Warsaw Pact and the CMEA) ties kept a process of read-justment and normalization going, rather than leading to a rift in relations.[174]

The top secret Politburo-approved instructions for negotiations with the United States in the high-level April and May 1990 meetings leading to the Washington summit, now available in the former Central Committee archive, reflect very well Soviet concerns and policy at that time. The instructions providing guidance to Shevardnadze for his talks with Bush and Baker in April called for him to raise the subject and "to lay out our evaluation of the processes in Eastern Europe, accenting the fact that the major changes in the Eastern European countries have created a new situation on the continent, opened additional possibilities for accelerating the all-European process, and overcoming the alienation of the two parts of Europe." Apart from some concern expressed over what were seen as American attempts to give a political angle to economic assistance, the main paragraph of the leadership's guidance to Shevardnadze could have been written in Washington, so parallel was the thinking in the two capitals:

Emphasizing the impermissibility of any kind of interference, direct or indirect, from outside in the internal affairs of the countries of Eastern Europe, and the unconditional right of their peoples to freedom of choice, [you should] at the same time call for collaborative efforts with the United States to ensure favorable external conditions for the democratic development of the deep transformation in these countries. In concrete terms, [you should] direct attention to the necessity of opposing attempts to raise territorial questions and inflame nationalistic sentiments, which encourage claims against neighboring countries and are capable of causing complications on both the domestic and international levels.

The guidance also sought preservation of the "existing security mechanisms and structures in Europe in the period of establishment of new all-European structures of collective security." These would include direct NATO–Warsaw Pact ties "in the interests of strengthening mutual confidence on the continent"— and, unwritten, in an attempt to shore up the Warsaw Pact for a while longer.[175]

---

174. In parallel, the Eastern European countries, reflecting the rapid disappearance of a Soviet-led bloc, increasingly took positions on international issues and in international forums, as well as in bilateral relations, differing from those taken by the Soviet Union. The first dramatic example was a vote in the UN Human Rights Commission on March 6, 1990. A U.S. initiative criticizing human rights in Castro's Cuba, still opposed by the Soviet Union, was cosponsored by two Eastern European observers—Poland and Czechoslovakia—and was voted for by the two Eastern European voting members of the commission—Hungary and Bulgaria. See "E. Europeans Join West in Rights Vote on Cuba," *Washington Post*, March 7, 1990, p. A30.

175. See TsKhSD, Fond 89, Perechen' 10, Dokument 61, *O direktivakh dlya peregovorov Ministra inostrannykh del SSSR s Prezidentom SShA Dzh. Bushem i Gosudarstvennym sekretarem Dzh. Beikerom (Vashington, 4–6 aprelya 1990g.)* (On Directives for the Negotiations of the Minister of Foreign Affairs of the USSR with U.S. President G. Bush and Secretary of State J. Baker (Washington, April 4–6, 1990), P 184/25, Top Secret,

At the same time, as discussed in an earlier chapter, the Soviet leaders sought from November 1989 to June 1990 (formally until mid-July) to stretch out the process of reunification of Germany. Above all they wanted to prevent a reunited Germany from being a member of NATO. They failed on this last point, but they did succeed in getting Western agreement to place several important constraints on future German military power (overall force levels and continued nonnuclear status) and a transition period for withdrawal of Soviet forces from Germany without NATO forces moving in.[176]

The problems of German reunification under terms that met minimum Soviet security concerns, and of the gradual decoupling of the Eastern alliance institutions led to the articulation of two competing views in Moscow by early 1991. One, emanating from the International Department of the Central Committee, and approved by the party Secretariat, emphasized the existence of threats to Soviet interests and the need to vigorously use Soviet leverage to ensure continuing Soviet influence in the area.[177] The other, expounded by the Foreign Ministry, was more satisfied with the outcome and saw more benefit, and even achievement, in the new situation, and saw far less of a threat to Soviet interests.[178]

One or two key examples can illustrate the differences in outlook and policy direction. "The Changes in Europe and New Approaches to Ensuring Security: Building a 'Common European Home,' " is the revealing title of a chapter in the Foreign Ministry review. It declared that "the experience of 1990 demonstrated the timeliness and practical significance of the concept of 'a common European home' advanced by the Soviet Union." Its upbeat opening sentence held that "the year under review [actually, November 1989 through December 1990] saw a breakthrough in the sphere of political ways and means of ensuring the national security of the USSR in the European sector in the

---

p. 24 of the Directives. The same position, more briefly put, was contained in the instructions approved for the talks with Baker in Moscow May 16–19. See chapter 10, footnote 18, for full identification of these later instructions.

176. See chapter 10.

177. The International Department memorandum was adopted by the Secretariat of the Central Committee. Originally secret, it was soon declassified and published for guidance to party organizations. See TsKhSD, Fond 89, Perechen' 20, Dokument 22, *O razvitii obstanovki v Vostochnoi Yevrope i nashei politike v etom regione* (On the Development of the Situation in Eastern Europe and Our Policy in That Region), P15/2, January 22, 1991, Secret, 8 pp., also published, in *Izvestiya TsK KPSS* (Bulletin of the CC of the CPSU), no. 3 (March 1991), pp. 12–17.

178. The Foreign Ministry analysis, also prepared in January 1991, was part of a larger annual report on foreign policy over the year. See *Vneshnepoliticheskaya i diplomaticheskaya deyatel'nost' SSSR (noyabr' 1989g. - dekabr' 1990g). Obzor MID SSSR* (Foreign Policy and Diplomatic Activity of the USSR, November 1989-December 1990. A Survey by the Ministry of Foreign Affairs of the USSR), printed in full in *Mezhdunarodnaya zhizn'*, no. 3 (March 1991), pp. 40–54.

context of formation of a fundamentally new model of security on the continent." Three key factors were seen as responsible for this development: first, "the historic, truly revolutionary turn by the Soviet Union to a new conception of national security, to guaranteeing human rights and democracy, to market [economic] relations based on equality for all forms of property, and to a government based on law." Second, "the radical changes in Europe are based on a dismantling of the old structures in the countries of Central and Eastern Europe . . . under conditions of the free choice of their path by the peoples, their striving for independence, and including the possible transformation of the social-economic system." And third, "the transition in relations between the USSR and the United States from confrontation to partnership and cooperation, and also the rapprochement of the USSR and Eastern European countries with the states of Western Europe."[179] The Foreign Ministry survey then reviewed all the accomplishments of the year in the Paris Charter of the CSCE, the CFE Treaty, establishment of ties with the Council of Europe, Euratom, and the European Parliament, and cited many similar developments, including the negotiated terms of the reunification of Germany.[180]

The memorandum prepared by the International Department, by contrast, emphasized the potential dangers and risks for Soviet security in the changing situation in Eastern Europe and stressed the need for hard-headed Soviet use of the limited leverage it had (including economic dependencies of Eastern European countries on the Soviet Union) to exercise its influence. It did not seek to reverse the Revolution of '89, but it depicted the consequences as diminishing, rather than enhancing, Soviet security. The difference in outlook was also exemplified by the following statement: "For securing the interests of the USSR in Eastern Europe the existing and potential interparty ties of the CPSU has considerable value." The document referred not only to ties with the former communist parties but also argued that it would be "expedient to put on a systematic basis ties with other parties of the democratic spectrum, taking account of their role and weight in social-political life." That point of view and recommendation for an active role by the Communist Party in developing such new ties were completely absent in the Foreign Ministry analysis. But the International Department analysis also did posit the objective of developing "good, neighborly mutual relations with the states of the region," not least because that was seen as the best way to prevent them from becoming "sources of anti-Sovietism, so that they would not become an external catalyst for national separation and centrifugal tendencies in the Soviet Union." Above all, the paper argued that a guiding precept of Soviet policy must be that "under no circumstance should the Eastern European region become an actual or potential threat to the military security of the Soviet Union. Under any turn of events the countries of the region must remain free of foreign bases and armed forces." A further objective to serve these concerns,

---

179. *Mezhdunarodnaya zhizn'*, no. 3 (March 1991), pp. 40–41.

180. Ibid, pp. 41–54.

and closer to the Foreign Ministry view, was the prevention of conflicts within the region and its development as an area of stability and cooperation "as an indispensable condition for advance of a united European area with participation of the Soviet Union in that area."[181]

In a sense, these were compatible and complementary approaches, although with strikingly different outlooks and emphases. Both were representative of elements in the hybrid Gorbachev leadership. They were also, in part, signs and instruments of a continuing competition for influence. The International Department's memorandum probably represented a bid to take back some of the "turf" that had been shifting into the bailiwick of the Foreign Ministry at a time when conservatives in the party machine may have hoped to recoup some of their slipping clout in the aftermath of the resignation of Eduard Shevardnadze in December 1990.[182]

One of the most important ways that the Soviet Union could retain or regain some positive influence in Eastern Europe and credibility as a partner for the future was by accepting and living with the revolutionary changes. That course also required a similar readiness by the new governments of the Eastern European countries to facilitate the many and often difficult readjustments

---

181. *Izvestiya TsK KPSS*, no. 3 (March 1991), pp. 12, 15.

182. For example, the argument that the CPSU could still play a useful role in contacts with the new parties emerging in Eastern European countries would support a role for the International Department.

In an interview in November 1990, Valentin Falin, the head of the International Department, had told me about the report they had recently prepared on Eastern Europe. He also told me that the International Department had sunk in esteem and clout, that he had forty vacancies that he could not fill because good people were not willing to go there, and that the department was going to be cut by half even though it had just absorbed the former department for liaison with the socialist countries (predominantly Eastern Europe).

Nonetheless, there was rivalry and competition between the International Department and the Foreign Ministry. It surfaced in the general public press in the same month as the larger unpublished studies, in two articles in *Pravda* by the deputy head of the International Department responsible for Eastern Europe, Valery Musatov, and the deputy foreign minister for European affairs, Yuly Kvitsinsky. The articles reflected the main difference over whether the changes in Eastern Europe caused a security threat to the USSR. See Valery Musatov, "Eastern Europe: A 'Typhoon' of Change," *Pravda*, March 13, 1991; and Yu. A. Kvitsinsky, "Eastern Europe: What Is Coming with the Changes?" *Pravda*, March 18, 1991.

Incidentally, even the "conservative" party officials recognized that there had been a need to place relations with the Eastern European countries on a new basis of real equality, and they continued to support the efforts that had been undertaken. Musatov, for example, in an essay in an academic publication noted approvingly the key meeting of Gorbachev with the Eastern European leaders in November 1986, and also that, in practice, the old leaderships of the Eastern European countries had (except for Kádár and Jaruzelski) greeted the new Soviet approach "with lack of understanding" and "active non-agreement." See V. L. Musatov, "Eastern Europe: The Process of Change," *Novaya i noveishaya istoriya* (Modern and Contemporary History), no. 2 (March-April 1991), p. 28.

implied and required. By and large, both sides did contribute to such a process of mutual accommodation to change.

In terms of institutional change, the most visible and basic developments were the step-by-step dismantling of the political, economic, and security bonds of the former bloc.

At a CMEA meeting of heads of government in Sofia in January 1990, Prime Minister Nikolai Ryzhkov, more aware than some of his new Eastern European colleagues that the Soviet Union had been subsidizing the others for some years, announced that all Soviet trade with the other countries would have to be placed on a world market (hard-currency denominated) basis as of January 1991. Bilateral negotiations on economic relations followed, and the CMEA was liquidated by common consent on June 28, 1991. During 1991, Soviet trade with Eastern Europe declined by about 60 percent. The process of readjustment would require years.

The Warsaw Pact as an instrument of Soviet hegemonic control of its political, ideological, military, and economic bloc in Eastern Europe was shattered by the Revolution of '89. The only question was whether it could continue, and for how long, to serve as a mechanism for coordinating Soviet and Eastern European policies and actions in various spheres of foreign and security policy. Warsaw Pact foreign ministers, meeting in Prague in March 1990, for example, agreed on supporting a Czechoslovak proposal for a pan-European Commission for Security in Europe that would build on the CSCE. While agreeing on this initiative, the others all declined to support a Soviet proposal for a joint statement opposing NATO membership for a reunited Germany. On the eve of the reunification of Germany a few months later, East Germany in one of its last acts formally withdrew from the Warsaw Pact.

The only question was whether the Warsaw Pact would be considered sufficiently useful by its Eastern European members as an interim new consensual security coordination body, or whether it was so burdened by its past role as a tool of Soviet domination as to be considered a liability to be shed as soon as possible. During 1990 that remained an open question, but by early 1991 it was clear that the Pact was no longer regarded as anything but a burden. After a decent interval of gradual dismantling of functions, on July 1, 1991, the Warsaw Pact was formally dissolved.

Throughout 1990 and 1991, there was a consensus in the Soviet leadership on each step of the dissolution of the Pact. Then-Foreign Minister Bessmertnykh has said that Marshal Yazov, the defense minister, and others in the Politburo raised no objection and made no attempt to prevent or make more difficult the process of disengagement, and they cooperated in working out the arrangements.[183]

---

183. Bessmertnykh himself was centrally involved in 1991, but said this cooperation had also existed while Shevardnadze was foreign minister throughout 1990. Interview with Aleksandr Bessmertnykh, February 24, 1993.

At the beginning of 1990 both Czechoslovakia and Hungary requested early withdrawal of all Soviet troops from their territory, and negotiations led to rapid agreement in February and March 1990, respectively, on complete withdrawal of Soviet forces by June 1991. Here, too, in Moscow deliberations there was no objection in principle or on the policy, despite an earlier Soviet military stand on maintaining such deployments.[184]

The Soviet leaders even asked the Poles in early 1990 if they too wished talks on Soviet withdrawal—but at that time, with the issue of German reunification and recommitment to accepting the eastern borders of Germany unresolved, not only General Jaruzelski but also Solidarity Prime Minister Tadeusz Mazowiecki did not want to see Soviet troops go. In September Polish leaders changed their minds, and only after very difficult negotiations on terms from November 1990 to October 1991 was agreement reached that all Soviet troops in Poland would leave by October 1992 (except up to 6,000 logistical personnel to help in continuing withdrawals from Germany that could remain until 1994).

While there was no policy disagreement in Moscow over the agreements to withdraw Soviet forces from Eastern Europe, including the largest contingent by far—some 350,000 troops in East Germany at the time of reunification—the political pressure to accept a timetable for rapid withdrawals from a number of countries all at once did cause severe logistical and other problems for the Soviet armed forces. The need to move, and relocate in the Soviet Union, nearly 1 million service personnel, dependents, and civilian employees in just a few years caused serious problems and considerable distress and dissatisfaction in the armed forces.[185] The detailed negotiations over claims

---

184. Anatoly Chernyayev, Gorbachev's foreign affairs aide, has told me that the Hungarians had first cautiously raised the question of Soviet troop withdrawal in 1988, when decisions were being made for some reduction in Soviet forces (as announced in December 1988). He stated that Yazov had spoken out then against full withdrawal—and although the issue was then set aside, Gorbachev had in the Politburo discussion told Yazov he had better be thinking about where in the Soviet Union to put those troops; he saw the need coming for their complete withdrawal. Interview with Anatoly Chernyayev, February 24, 1993.

The Foreign Ministry, by contrast, as early as the mid–1980s had studied the question of withdrawal of Soviet forces from the Eastern European countries other than Germany. Interview with Sergei Tarasenko, who had directly participated, February 24, 1993.

185. In January 1989, before the start of Gorbachev's announced reduction of 50,000 Soviet troops in Europe, there were 375,000 in East Germany, 73,500 in Czechoslovakia, 62,500 in Hungary, and 58,000 in Poland, in all about 570,000 and 330,000 dependents and civilian employees, totaling 900,000. Another 60,000 troops were being withdrawn from Mongolia at the same time.

During the two years 1990–91, 130,000 troops and 55,000 civilians were withdrawn from East Germany, and all 125,000 troops and 88,000 civilians from Czechoslovakia and Hungary.

by both sides for compensation (for example, for buildings built by the Soviet forces versus costs of environmental cleanup), and charges for transportation (especially by Poland) also caused hard feelings.

Without fanfare, Soviet nuclear weapons were removed from Czechoslovakia, Hungary, and Poland in early 1990 and from East Germany later in 1990–91.

Besides Soviet military retrenchment, the Soviet intelligence services also had to curtail their former close ties with the countries of Eastern Europe. Czechoslovakia, Hungary, and East Germany cut back their ties early in 1990 to such matters as coordination on counterterrorism and monitoring narcotics trafficking. A Central Committee Secretariat meeting in March 1990 approved a memorandum, "On Changing the Regulation for Representatives of the KGB of the USSR with the Security Organs of the NRB [Peoples Republic of Bulgaria], VR [Hungarian Republic], MNR [Mongolian Peoples' Republic], PR [Polish Republic], and ChSSR [Czechoslovak Socialist Republic]." Even revised ties with East Germany and Romania were not envisaged.[186] By March 1991 KGB representation and formal ties with Polish Intelligence ended, and later in 1991 KGB ties with Czechoslovak Intelligence were also terminated.[187]

Along with the dismantling of older ties, the Soviet leadership did work to build new ones, as envisaged by both the "hard" International Department and "soft" Foreign Ministry variants of a new Eastern European policy line. On April 5, 1991, Gorbachev and Romanian President Ion Iliescu signed a Treaty of Cooperation, Good-Neighborliness and Friendship, replacing the "Brezhnevite" treaty of 1970. Although the agreement was intended by the Soviet leaders to be the first of a new series of bilateral treaties, instead it languished and was never

---

186. St 113/102g (113th Secretariat Meeting), March 16, 1990, 7 pp. I consulted this document and an attached reference memorandum submitted by KGB chief Vladimir Kryuchkov, held in the Special File and apparently not yet declassified, in the former Central Committee archive (TsKhSD) in January 1993.

187. Shebarshin, *Ruka Moskvy*, p. 239, cited the end of ties with the Czechoslovaks; other sources have disclosed the ending of ties with Poland.

Incidentally, the Soviet leaders (and still more the Soviet intelligence establishment) were concerned with a parallel initiation of U.S. intelligence contacts with former Warsaw Pact countries of Eastern Europe. I had occasion to ask Director of Central Intelligence William H. Webster about this (on June 18, 1991), and he assured me that contacts were discreet and nonprovocative vis-à-vis the Soviet Union. Other informed sources, on a background basis, told me that by the spring of 1991 the CIA had established good ties with the intelligence services of Czechoslovakia, Poland, and Hungary, and after September 1991 with Bulgaria. (Contacts with Yugoslavia and Romania, by contrast, remained minimal and strained.) Of course, learning former secrets of the Warsaw Pact was considered fair game, especially because much was revealed after East Germany was absorbed into the Federal Republic. The Soviet intelligence services were concerned not only about the leakage of former Warsaw Pact secrets, but about contacts that could facilitate penetration of the Soviet intelligence services, Soviet forces in Germany, and the Soviet Union itself.

ratified. Bulgaria, Poland, Hungary, and Czechoslovakia declined to sign similar proposed treaties because of concern that the text committing the parties not to enter any alliances with third parties against the other signatory could be used not only to prevent, for example, their joining NATO some time, but even to keep them from joining the European Community or any other group that a future Soviet government might consider directed against its interests.

The failure to obtain Eastern European friendship treaties of this kind showed the limits of the International Department's approach. In fact, new bland bilateral treaties would have been signed in 1992—the first, with Hungary, had already been completed by December 1991—but the end of the Soviet Union meant that Russia (and Ukraine and some other successor republics) in due course concluded such treaties during 1992. Meanwhile, the Soviet Union continued normal bilateral diplomatic relations with its former allies.

As the Soviet Union was adjusting to the new realities of Eastern Europe with painful and far-reaching changes, the United States and its NATO partners also faced uncertainties and a need to change their individual and collective Western relationships with the new regime in Eastern Europe. Secretary Baker toured Eastern Europe in February 1990 and laid out U.S. policy in a speech in Prague. He reiterated the American view that he had expressed in Berlin in December 1989: that a new security architecture for Europe should be based on both an expanded CSCE role and the CFE conventional arms agreement then under negotiation, and a continuing key role for NATO. He did not, however, explain how NATO, a Western alliance, could serve as a vehicle for ensuring security of the Eastern European countries. His other main themes were the need for the Eastern European countries to develop democratic political institutions and free market economies. American and other Western economic assistance was affirmed, but without the proposal of any major new programs.[188] It sounded an appropriate note of encouragement and a still vague promise to assist.

By mid–1990, Deputy Secretary of State Lawrence Eagleburger was named "coordinator of U.S. assistance to Eastern Europe," and the United States began to shift eighty diplomats from posts elsewhere around the world to augment the modest traditional American official presence in Eastern Europe. Although the Soviet Union was adjusting to dealing with friendly but wary ex–allies, the United States was faced with eager disciples seeking aid, rather than with allies of an adversary. Although the United States did institute modest bilateral political as well as economic assistance programs, including Peace Corps, U.S. Information Agency, and National Endowment for Democracy programs, the major effort was directed to participation in multilateral economic assistance programs, and to fashioning multilateral security arrangements that could encompass the pan-European CSCE and the Western NATO alliance.

---

188. "From Revolution to Democracy: Central and Eastern Europe in the New Europe," February 7, 1990," *U.S. Department of State Dispatch*, vol. 1 (September 3, 1990), pp. 10–14.

The so-called Group of 24 advanced Western countries (from East Asia as well as Western Europe and North America) had been established in July 1989 to coordinate assistance to Poland and Hungary, which were already embarked on economic reform. In December the Group of 24 decided in principle to consider expanding their assistance to other countries of Eastern Europe, and in July 1990 they formally included Czechoslovakia, Bulgaria, Yugoslavia, and East Germany (the latter for only its short remaining existence). Romania was not yet included because of recent repression of political demonstrations, but it was later added. Yugoslavia was included in mid–1990 because of political reforms in some constituent republics and early economic reform, before internal strains sundered the country. In November 1991 newly independent Latvia, Lithuania, and Estonia, and newly "democratic" Albania, were also included.

In May 1990, a European Bank for Reconstruction and Development (EBRD) was established by the countries of the European Community, Japan, and the United States (with initial capital of $12 billion) to lend primarily to private or privatized enterprises in Eastern Europe and to aid environmental cleanup.

In all, from mid–1989 through the end of 1991 some $45 billion of economic assistance (mostly loans, with 80 percent provided by Western European countries) had been pledged, although actual disbursements by that time came to only $9 billion.[189]

The second major area of Eastern European concern, and American and Western efforts to provide reassurance, was pursuit of new security arrangements. At the July 1990 London NATO summit, the alliance, besides announcing new strategic guidelines, invited the Eastern European countries—and the Soviet Union—to establish regular diplomatic liaison with NATO for mutual consultation, and to develop military contacts. At the CSCE Paris summit in November, the countries of NATO and the Warsaw Pact issued a joint declaration that they were "no longer adversaries" but would "build new partnerships and extend to each other the hand of friendship."[190]

The Paris CSCE summit also approved new negotiations on confidence- and security-building measures, and creation of a Conflict Prevention Center. The CPC was established in Vienna in March 1991, initially with a modest mandate (implementing agreed-on CSBMs) but with potentiality for wider use. The Soviet Union had urged its creation and sought a wider role for it.

At the next North Atlantic Council meeting in Copenhagen in June 1991, on the eve of the already announced dissolution of the Warsaw Pact, the NATO countries spoke of "intensified" diplomatic and military contacts and exchanges, encouragement of greater contacts of parliamentarians of Eastern Europe with the

---

189. Paul L. Montgomery, "Aid to East Europe Put at $45 Billion," *New York Times*, November 12, 1991, p. D9, reporting on the Group of 24 meeting then taking place.

190. "Text of the Joint Declaration of Twenty-Two States," November 19, 1990, *Presidential Documents*, vol. 26 (November 26, 1990), p. 1872.

North Atlantic Assembly, and participation in some peripheral NATO programs for civil cooperation (for example, on problems of the environment).

A further real step was taken at the Rome NATO summit in early November 1991, when the creation of a new institution at ministerial and other levels, the North Atlantic Cooperation Council (NACC), was announced. The process of cooperation was now described as "dynamic." (The idea of such an NACC, reaching "from Vladivostok to Vancouver," had been proposed by Secretary Baker and German Foreign Minister Genscher on October 2). On December 20, 1991, only a few days before the end of the Soviet Union, the foreign ministers of all the former NATO and Warsaw Pact adversaries (also including the three newly independent Baltic states) met in Brussels for the inaugural NACC meeting. They adopted a North Atlantic Cooperation Council Statement on Dialogue, Partnership and Cooperation and agreed on annual meetings at the ministerial level. A special meeting was held on March 10, 1992, to admit Russia and the other ten former Soviet republics of the Commonwealth of Independent States (the one remaining, Georgia, was also included soon after) in place of the now defunct Soviet Union. On June 5, 1992, the first full ministerial meeting of the now thirty-seven members of the NACC (including Albania, and with Finland as an observer) met in Oslo.

In an interesting parallel development to the NACC, the Western European Union (WEU) held a ministerial meeting in Bonn only days later (June 19, 1992), augmented by the foreign and defense ministers of all the Eastern European (and three Baltic) states but not including Russia and the other eleven republics of the former Soviet Union. The WEU sometimes sought to present itself as a possible alternative to NATO as the security arm of the European community. The United States, not a member, was wary of this approach. The Eastern European states clearly, however, gave precedence to the NACC with the United States (and Russia) participating.

It is clear that most Eastern European members of the NACC would prefer full membership in NATO, but that had not been offered (and was not in 1994, when the issue was posed), and is not likely to be at least for some time. It was clearly desirable to include Russia, and therefore also to include at least Ukraine and the other European republics of the former Soviet Union, in the NACC. In the end, all former republics of the USSR were included. The result in some ways almost duplicates the pan-European membership of the CSCE— and makes the organization more formal and honorary than effective as an action group. The Helsinki CSCE summit on July 10, 1992, endorsed the NACC as being "in harmony with the goals of the CSCE."[191]

Meanwhile, several East (Central) European states had also sought to coordinate their cooperation with one another more closely, not as an alliance,

---

191. For a good summary of the NACC see Guido Gerosa, "The North Atlantic Cooperation Council," *European Security*, vol. 1 (Autumn 1992), pp. 273–94.

but at least as a consultative bloc. In mid-February 1991 President Lech Wałęsa of Poland, President Václav Havel of Czechoslovakia, and Prime Minister József Antall of Hungary met in a summit meeting of "the Triangle" (as they came to be called) at Visegrad, Hungary, and agreed to continue meetings at various levels to coordinate and lobby for their common interests. [192] At their second meeting, in October, they welcomed the Genscher-Baker proposal for what became the NACC. But they continued to meet to coordinate their diplomatic efforts (after 1993 becoming a "Quadrangle," including the Czech Republic and the Republic of Slovakia, after Czechoslovakia split). But they did not see their group as a substitute for the CSCE, NACC, or closer future ties with NATO.

Thus the liberalization in Eastern Europe sponsored by Gorbachev in the latter half of the 1980s led eventually to the liberation of the countries of Eastern Europe from communist rule and from Moscow's enforced embrace. The United States had encouraged and greatly welcomed these developments, but rather than attempting to push the process, it wisely stood aside and let Gorbachev bring them about. And in the final two years of transition into the post-Cold War world in 1990–91, both the United States and the Soviet Union showed great discretion in easing the dramatic shift of Eastern Europe out of the former bloc and into a new broadened "Europe free and whole," which President Bush had but envisioned on the eve of the Revolution of '89. Finally, in the aftermath of the Revolution of '91, Russia, Ukraine, Belarus, and the other successors to the former Soviet Union were also incorporated into the emerging structure of the new Europe.

In contrast, the parallel descent of the former Yugoslav Federation, and the inability of the various multilateral European entities to deal effectively with it, was only the most dramatic of many signs showing that a new order would be difficult to build. The new Europe would be subject to many difficult and challenging new stresses despite, and perhaps in some cases because of, the absence of the discipline of East-West confrontation in Europe during the Cold War.

---

192. Visegrad had also been the site of a similar coordinating meeting in 1335 of King Charles I of Hungary, King John of Bohemia, and King Casimir III (the Great) of Poland.

    An earlier meeting of the same countries in Bratislava, on April 9, 1990, had not led to agreement, but the situation had changed by early 1991 (and so had some of the leaders).

    For a useful analysis of the 1991 situation see Joshua Spero, "The Budapest-Prague-Warsaw Triangle: Central European Security After the Visegrad Summit," *European Security*, vol. 1 (Spring 1992), pp. 58–83.

# 14    Asia and American-Soviet Relations

EUROPE CONTINUED TO THE END to be the principal theater of competition in the rivalry between the United States and the Soviet Union. Asia, especially China (and increasingly Japan as well), also remained important in the 1980s. The importance of the triangular relationship among the United States, the Soviet Union, and China, however, was much less significant in the 1980s than it had been in the 1970s.[1] A review of the course of developments from 1981 through 1991 shows why that was so. Similarly, the general importance of Japan and other countries in East Asia rose, and changes in both Soviet and American policy changed the overall pattern of the two powers' involvement and competition. Now of course Russia is the successor to the Soviet Union in post–Cold War Asia, and new relationships are being developed, though built on the foundation of the past.

Triangular diplomacy among the United States, the Soviet Union, and China during the period 1978–80 had entered a new phase marked by a close Sino-American rapprochement and complete collapse of the U.S.-Soviet détente of the 1970s. The triangular relationship was further affected in 1981–82 by continuing deterioration of U.S.-Soviet relations, by ambiguities in U.S.-Chinese relations, and by the stirrings of Soviet interest in improving relations with China. But before reviewing Sino-American and Sino-Soviet relations, it is useful to look at a turn in Chinese policy in that period that affected both relationships.

---

1.    For a detailed review of the development of American, Soviet, and Chinese relations and interrelationships from 1969 through 1980, see Raymond L. Garthoff, *Détente and Confrontation: American-Soviet Relations from Nixon to Reagan*, rev. ed. (Brookings, 1994), chapters 6, 7, 8, 20, 21, 27.

## Chinese Policy

During 1981, Deng Xiaoping, the key Chinese leader despite his modest formal post as vice premier, and the driving force in the rapprochement with the United States from 1978 on, strengthened his position. At a key party plenum in June 1981 he engineered the replacement of party chief Hua Guofeng by Hu Yaobang. Nonetheless, powerful elements wary of the turn toward the United States remained influential in the Chinese political system. Throughout the 1980s, under Deng's astute guidance, a continued shift in all levels of the party, state, managerial, and military leadership gradually brought more forward-looking and less doctrinaire cadres into positions of authority. The "four modernizations," and above all market-oriented economic reform on a vast scale, developed. Nonetheless, conservative views on many issues of domestic and foreign policy remained, including reservations on policy toward the United States.

China launched a shift of foreign policy toward greater independence and reassertion of its position, including in areas that diverged from or contradicted U.S. positions. Several pronouncements signaled this shift. In June 1981 a prominent resolution revived the "three worlds" theory, in which China—pursuing an "independent and self-reliant" foreign policy—also identified itself with the Third World as distinct from, and to an important extent in opposition to, both the Western and Soviet worlds.[2] Soon thereafter another article continued this theme, directly attacking U.S. policy toward the Third World, especially the Reagan administration's support for Israel, South Africa, South Korea, and Taiwan.[3]

In 1981 China voted with the United States on only 10 percent of the votes in the UN General Assembly (in contrast with 33 percent in 1979), and with the Soviet Union on 76 percent. As the Chinese correctly argued, this did not reflect a turn to a pro-Soviet alignment but to a more Third World position.

China, in 1980, had taken a line similar to that of the United States in warning that the Soviet Union and Cuba were seeking to use the situation in El Salvador to advance their influence. But as early as March 1981 China switched to support the position of the Salvadoran guerrillas (and throughout supported Nicaragua) against what it saw as efforts by the United States to use the

---

2.   "Resolution on Certain Questions in the History of Our Party since the Founding of the People's Republic of China," Xinhua, June 30, 1981, in Foreign Broadcast Information Service, *China*, July 1, 1981, pp. K7, K32. (Hereafter FBIS, *China*.)

     Also in June 1981 China used its position in the Security Council to block selection of a European—East or West—as secretary general of the United Nations, vetoing the Western and Soviet bloc candidate.

3.   Mei Zhenmin, "U.S. Relationship with the Third World," Xinhua, July 8, 1981, in FBIS, *China*, July 9, 1981, pp. B1–2.

situation to advance its interests.[4] China staunchly supported Nicaragua (verbally) and criticized the U.S. support for the contras. Similarly, China strongly opposed the U.S. occupation of Grenada in 1983.

In general, at least rhetorically the Chinese supported Third World national liberation movements (including the PLO). They similarly supported newly liberated countries, such as Angola and Mozambique, against what were seen as foreign-supported insurgencies. In two cases the Chinese strongly opposed indigenous governments regarded as foreign puppets and actively aided the opposing insurgents: in Afghanistan and Kampuchea (Cambodia).

China also sought to identify itself in support of the Third World in other ways. For example, in December 1982–January 1983 Premier Zhao Ziyang visited ten countries of Africa—the first trip there by a Chinese leader of his rank since Zhou Enlai had visited many of the same countries in 1963–64. In the UN General Assembly, China sought to champion the economic plight of the Third World and contrasted American and Soviet wasteful pursuit of an arms race.

China did not support the Solidarity movement in Poland. Chinese concern over uncontrolled spontaneous political movements in communist countries overrode its satisfaction at seeing the Soviet Union further burdened. And when the United States instituted sanctions against Poland and the Soviet Union after the Poles instituted martial law and suppressed Solidarity in 1981, not only did China not join in, but on the contrary it boosted its trade with Poland. The Chinese did not regard General Wojciech Jaruzelski as a Soviet puppet, and they wished to aid him to maintain power.

Divergences with the United States in world politics were not limited to the Third World. Indeed, American policy toward China continued to be regarded with some suspicion. In February 1982 then Vice Premier (and later President) Li Xiannian commented in an interview that "the United States is not a friendly country."[5] Usually the Chinese simply stressed the hegemonic rivalry of the two superpowers and did not identify China with either, but rather with the Third World. In August Foreign Minister Huang Hua said, "China will never cling to any superpower. China will never play the 'U.S. card' against the Soviet Union, nor the 'Soviet card' against the United States. We will also not allow anyone to play the 'Chinese card.' "[6] And at the Twelfth National Congress of the Communist Party of China on September 1, 1982, General Secretary Hu Yaobang stressed that China "never attaches itself to any big power or

---

4. This shift is well documented by Jonathan D. Pollack, *The Lessons of Coalition Politics: Sino-American Security Relations*, R-3133-AF (Santa Monica, Calif.: Rand, 1984), pp. 79–80.

5. Allen S. Whiting, "Reading Tea Leaves: China-Soviet Détente," *New York Times*, May 18, 1982, p. A23.

6. Xinhua, August 20, 1982, in FBIS, *China*, August 23, 1982, p. A1.

group of powers, and never yields to pressure from any big power."[7] He was also highly critical of both the United States and the Soviet Union.

Clearly, by the time of the Twelfth Party Congress the Chinese leadership had decided to move to a detached independent position between the United States and the Soviet Union. In theory, the Chinese would remain equidistant between the two powers. In practice, they would probably continue to be closer to the United States or at least more wary of the Soviet Union. But ties with the Soviet Union would soon be reactivated. The Chinese also chose to distance themselves from the United States to a greater degree than they had in the period from 1978 to 1980; above all they wanted to avoid a dependent position within a U.S.-led coalition. When the Chinese sought a united front against the Soviet Union from 1971 through 1979, their primary purpose had been to prevent a Soviet-American coalition against them. That accomplished as a result of the collapse of the Soviet-American détente, China could now afford independence. Moreover, the Chinese believed that the Reagan administration in the early 1980s was overdoing confrontation with the Soviet Union, just as they believed the United States had overdone détente in the 1970s.[8]

Besides the change in American-Soviet relations there was a revised Chinese perception of the balance of power between the two superpowers. In the second half of the 1970s the Chinese saw a trend toward growing Soviet military power. In the first half of the 1980s they saw the United States as again becoming the stronger. They also concluded that despite such shifts there was a generally stable balance between the two. This view also provided a better base for China to maneuver without having to lean to one side or the other to help ensure the balance.

The Chinese shift may also have reflected differences within the leadership. Hu Yaobang, whose influence had grown, may have given a less central role to the United States in his conception of China's balanced policy than did Deng Xiaoping. It is, however, difficult to tell, since Deng's position on triangular diplomacy had certainly changed by the early 1980s from what it had been in the late 1970s.

As noted earlier, one of the main areas of divergence and conflict in Chinese and American policy after 1980 concerned the Third World. Moreover, as the Chinese restored more normalcy to their relationship with the Soviet Union and sought to establish greater identification with the Third World, they stated their position in terms designed to make their policy clear. At the Cancun summit meeting in 1981, Premier Zhao Ziyang lumped the two superpowers together and said that in their rivalry they were both menacing

---

7.   Hu Yaobang, "Create a New Situation in All Fields of Socialist Modernization: Report to the 12th National Congress of the Communist Part of China, September 1, 1982," *Beijing Review*, vol. 25 (September 13, 1982), p. 29.

8.   This opinion was not publicly stated by the Chinese, but it was frequently implied and was explicitly told to me by a senior Chinese official in 1984.

international security.[9] An article in October 1982, shortly after the party congress, explicitly noted that China stood with the United States in opposition to the Soviet Union on the issues of Afghanistan and Kampuchea, while it stood with the Soviet Union in opposition to the United States on Israeli aggression and South African apartheid. But, the article concluded, "This does not mean that China 'allies' with the United States under some circumstances or becomes a Soviet partner under other circumstances. This precisely proves that . . . China is independent of all [both] the superpowers."[10] And in his speeches to the UN General Assembly in September 1983 and again in September 1984 Foreign Minister Wu Xueqian criticized the United States and the Soviet Union with equal harshness, in 1984 attacking the Soviet Union on Afghanistan and the United States on Grenada.[11]

As part of an effort to demonstrate solidarity with the peoples of the world, China again stressed its version of peaceful coexistence. On the thirtieth anniversary of the formulation of the Five Principles of Peaceful Coexistence, Premier Zhao Ziyang argued that these principles, first endorsed by the Bandung Conference in 1955, "have, in fact, been accepted by the international community as the basic guideline in handling international relations."[12]

China also increased its ties with the world community. It strongly backed further development of international law such as the Law of the Sea Convention in 1982 (along with the Soviet Union and most of the nations of the world, except the United States). China joined the Committee on Disarmament in Geneva in 1980, occupying a place for China left vacant ever since the committee had been established in 1962. In 1980 China joined the International Monetary Fund (IMF) and the World Bank (replacing the Republic of China on Taiwan). In 1982 China announced it would voluntarily increase its budget share allotment to the United Nations. In 1983 it joined the International Atomic Energy Agency (IAEA).

China continued through the 1980s to concentrate on internal affairs rather than extensive foreign relations and to concentrate on internal economic development while restraining recurrent pressures for greater internal political

---

9. Xinhua, October 27, 1981, in FBIS, *China*, October 27, 1981, p. J3.

10. Liaowang, quoted by Xinhua, October 20, 1982, ibid., October 21, 1982, pp. A1-2. Cited by Harry Harding, ed., *China's Foreign Relations in the 1980s* (Yale University Press, 1984), p. 199, and see his discussion on pp. 195–201.

 For a study stressing the historical roots of Chinese foreign policy independence as adapted to the ideology of Marxism-Leninism and to current geopolitical realities, see Mark Mancall, *China at the Center: 300 Years of Foreign Policy* (Macmillan Free Press, 1984), especially pp. 445-502.

11. Renmin Ribao (People's Daily), September 29, 1983, in FBIS, *China*, September 30, 1983, pp. A1–7; and "China's Stand on World Situation Outlined," *Beijing Review*, vol. 27 (October 8, 1984), pp. 16–25.

12. "Premier Zhao Ziyang on Five Principles," *Beijing Review*, vol. 27 (July 30, 1984), p. 16.

liberalization. Political dissent and occasional open demonstrations were suppressed; the Tiananmen Square repression was only the largest case. Changes in the political leadership, throughout this period dominated by Deng Xiaoping (despite his nominal "retirement" from the party Central Committee in November 1987), were nonetheless also a continuous balancing act among several prestigious elder party (often military) leaders and younger political and economic leaders. In September 1985 Deng engineered a large-scale retirement of older conservative party and military leaders (including ten of twenty-four Politburo members). But in January 1987, his "liberal" heir apparent Hu Yaobang was ousted and replaced by Zhao Ziyang. Yet after the massive and bloody suppression of demonstrations at Tiananmen Square in June 1989, Zhao too was replaced. But throughout this period Deng steered a conservative course with respect to the exercise of political power, though he consistently pushed for substantial economic reform.

The independent foreign policy course laid out at the Twelfth Party Congress in 1982 was reaffirmed at the Thirteenth Party Congress in October-November 1987. Not only did it mean developing relations with both the United States and the Soviet Union, but also with Japan, the countries of the Association of South East Asian Nations (ASEAN), and even South Korea. Negotiations were concluded with Britain on the transition of Hong Kong in (and after) 1997, although by the late 1980s Hong Kong was already the most important Chinese trading partner (even ahead of Japan), as well as a conduit for investment and trade with Taiwan (and for circumventing direct Chinese trade quotas, for example, with the United States). Foreign economic investment, especially in a series of special economic zones at cities along the coast, was welcomed. The common element in these expanded ties was their direct support to the primary aim of internal economic development under firm political control.

After Tiananmen, Chinese policy for the remainder of 1989 was focused almost exclusively on crisis management in China. During 1990 and the first eight months of 1991 attention shifted to also include efforts to repair the damage to China's standing in the West. After the abortive conservative coup and successful anticommunist countercoup in Moscow, from August 1991 into 1992 China's leaders turned their priority to debating the causes of the Soviet collapse and determining ways to ensure that the same fate would not befall them.

Nonetheless, despite primary attention to internal development, important steps were taken during the 1980s in China's relationships with the United States and the Soviet Union.

The Chinese turn in foreign policy to a more active independent role had broader ramifications, but it included a reordering of relationships with the other members of the strategic triangle: the United States and the Soviet Union.[13]

---

13. For a perceptive early commentary, see Allen S. Whiting, "Assertive Nationalism in Chinese Foreign Policy," *Asian Survey*, vol. 23 (August 1983), pp. 913–33.

## U.S.-Chinese Relations

The approach of the Reagan administration to China, as it entered office in 1981, exhibited a sharp contradiction.[14] On the one hand, the new administration advocated a continued, even intensified, effort to build American-Chinese relations on the basis of a strategic geopolitical alignment directed against the Soviet Union. This course was essentially a continuation of the policy advanced by Zbigniew Brzezinski, President Carter's national security adviser, and conducted from 1978 through 1980. It was energetically pursued by Secretary of State Alexander M. Haig, Jr. It also appealed to the anti-Soviet inclination of President Reagan and other members of his administration. On the other hand, it conflicted head-on with a second course, based on another sentiment strongly held by Reagan and a number of his colleagues: a strong sympathy for the Republic of China on Taiwan, and a distaste for close ties with the Communist People's Republic of China, especially at Taiwan's expense. Reagan and many right-wing conservatives had levied strong criticism at the Carter administration on this score.[15] Reagan was pressed to hold to this position by his national security adviser, Richard Allen. At the extreme were those with an ideological aversion to close collaboration with any communist country, even in order to use one against another.

Policy toward China was not a priority for the new administration. Haig, however, decided to preempt the issue. Even in his congressional confirmation hearings before the inauguration, Haig had stressed the "compatibility and . . . convergence" of American and Chinese "strategic" interests.[16] On February 6 he had the Department of State spokesman declare the administration's intention to base its policy on the U.S.-Chinese normalization communiqué of December 15, 1978.[17] This move, unexpected and not cleared, led the White House to make background comments stressing the counterpoint—the president's intention to act in strict accordance with the Taiwan Relations Act. This pattern of public contradiction was repeated frequently in the months following.

---

14. For a fuller account of the development of U.S.-China relations in the 1980s, see Harry Harding, *A Fragile Relationship: The United States and China since 1972* (Brookings, 1992), pp. 107–296.

15. During the election campaign in 1980, Reagan even commented in interviews with Robert Scheer that the Sino-Soviet split represented only "an argument over how best to destroy us" and not "because of any apparent difference in their belief in Communism or Communism's mission to conquer the world." See Robert Scheer, *With Enough Shovels: Reagan, Bush and Nuclear War* (Random House, 1982), pp. 242, 247.

16. "Major Points in the Senate Foreign Relations Committee's Questioning of Haig," *New York Times*, January 11, 1981, p. 26.

17. See Bernard Gwertzman, "Reagan and the World," *New York Times*, February 8, 1981, pp. A1, A16.

The Reagan administration on assuming office was surprised to learn the scope and extent of American-Chinese relations, especially the secret collaboration on intelligence.[18] The momentum of developing relations was evident in increasing contacts. During 1981, 80,000 Americans visited China, and 16,000 Chinese visited the United States; by mid-1982, 8,000 Chinese students were at American universities, and 1,500 Americans were resident in China.[19]

A serious problem quickly intruded, one that would continue to plague American-Chinese relations. Taiwan, eager to determine if the Reagan administration would change course, pressed for new advanced combat aircraft from the first days of the new administration.[20] Although the administration did not deal with the problem for some time, it was plainly there. Both Taiwan and China wanted to learn where they stood with the new administration.

Haig, with some support from Vice President George Bush, who had served as the U.S. representative in Beijing in 1973–75, persuaded Reagan to authorize him to visit China. In mid-June 1981 Haig went to Beijing to set American policy firmly on course and to strengthen American-Chinese ties as a weapon in maneuvering with the Soviet Union. He also hoped to overcome Chinese doubts and quiet the Taiwan issue.

Haig's visit to Beijing was generally regarded as a step toward improving relations and moving beyond early frictions over the status to be accorded Taiwan by the United States. Haig naturally treated the trip as a success. And in one indirect respect it was. As Haig said in his memoir, "The trip was an opportunity to drive the bureaucracy and the Administration toward the policy I had been struggling to establish."[21] In advance of the visit, Haig had succeeded in getting the president to approve a change in the trade status accorded China: it was placed in the category of a friendly but not allied country. This change permitted the transfer of somewhat more advanced technology and dual-use items having military as well as civilian applications, and allowed China to request the purchase of items on the munitions list, including defensive weapons, from commercial U.S. sources.[22] (In 1980 Secretary of Defense Brown had held out the possibility of that status, and Minister of National Defense Geng Biao had submitted a list of desired items, but no action had been taken on the requests.)

In Beijing Haig publicly announced with great éclat the U.S. readiness to sell defensive weapons to China. His statement annoyed both the Chinese

18.  See Pollack, *The Lessons of Coalition Politics*, p. 74.

19.  See Allen S. Whiting, "Sino-American Relations: The Decade Ahead," *Orbis*, vol. 26 (Fall 1982), p. 697.

20.  Pollack, *The Lessons of Coalition Politics*, p. 74.

21.  Alexander M. Haig, Jr., *Caveat: Realism, Reagan, and Foreign Policy* (Macmillan, 1984), p. 205.

22.  Ibid., pp. 204–05.

leaders and the White House and Pentagon. Haig had been authorized to tell the Chinese of the decision, but not to announce it publicly. For their part, Deng and other Chinese leaders did not want to appear to have agreed to a strategic relationship with the United States while the Taiwan issue remained unresolved. This impression and the Chinese unhappiness were enhanced when Haig also announced a forthcoming visit by General Liu Huaqing, deputy chief of staff of the Chinese Army, to discuss arms purchases. Again, this announcement had not been authorized by the Chinese, and when they did confirm the planned visit, they studiously omitted any reference to possible arms purchases.[23] Haig failed to note the Chinese dissatisfaction in his memoir. When he complained of the White House reaction, including President Reagan's promise to carry out the Taiwan Relations Act, made at a press conference on the last day of the secretary of state's visit, Haig failed to note that the president's statement was prompted by Haig's public overexuberance about arms sales to China. Reagan, like Deng, did not want a domestic constituency to think the unsettled Taiwan issue had been cast aside.[24]

During Haig's visit to China, intelligence on the situation in Kampuchea (Cambodia) and Afghanistan was exchanged, continuing in a more restricted way exchanges (or more accurately, earlier American disclosures) by Henry Kissinger and Zbigniew Brzezinski. It was also leaked to the press as the visit ended that the United States and China had earlier established intelligence facilities in Xinjiang to monitor Soviet strategic military testing activities.[25] The Chinese, by contrast, remained discreet on this whole aspect of the relationship (for example, the presence of Zhang Zhunzi, the chief of military intelligence, as a member of the Chinese delegation was not mentioned by Xinhua, the New China News Agency).

Overall, nonetheless, Haig's visit was a failure. He had played a major card, arms sales, at the wrong time. The Chinese, rather than being impressed, saw the United States as trying to bind them into an anti-Soviet alignment under American direction and on American terms, including on the Taiwan issue. Deng Xiaoping was moved to say publicly, "The United States thinks that China is seeking its favor. In fact, China is not seeking any country's favor." While expressing the hope that Sino-American relations would develop further, he even felt it necessary to say, "If worst comes to worst and the relations retrogress to those prior to 1972, China will not collapse. . . . The Chinese people . . . will never bow and scrape and beg for help. . . . When U.S. Secretary

---

23. The visit was later postponed and finally canceled.

24. Ibid., pp. 205–08; and Pollack, *The Lessons of Coalition Politics*, pp. 83–88.

25. See Philip Taubman, "U.S. and Peking Jointly Monitor Russian Missiles," *New York Times*, June 18, 1981, pp. A1, A4. The information was attributed only to "senior American officials." For background on the negotiation of the arrangement in 1978–79, see Garthoff, *Détente and Confrontation*, chapters 20 and 27.

of State Alexander Haig came to China, I told him the same thing. . . . China and the United States should cooperate on an equal footing."[26]

Haig had thought the Chinese would be so tempted by the prospect of American arms sales and strategic cooperation against the Soviet Union that they would acquiesce in American arms sales to Taiwan. He was wrong, as he should have known from soundings taken when former President Ford visited China in March and from Chinese reaction to speculation in the U.S. press after leaks that the United States intended to permit arms sales.[27]

Meanwhile, President Reagan himself in one of his first encounters with the Chinese was incensed when, at the Cancun global economic summit meeting in October 1981, Premier Zhao Ziyang routinely called the United States an "imperialist" power.[28] More substantively, the Cancun meeting also illustrated sharply a growing rift between the United States and China over the Third World.

The Soviet leaders observed the American effort to build a stronger strategic cooperation with China and the growing Chinese restraint. They drew conclusions for Soviet policy on both counts.

Over the next year American relations with China continued to be strained over the Taiwan issue. This was clear when Vice President Bush visited China in May 1982, hoping but not succeeding to parlay his personal association into closer relations. Instead, the Chinese sought to use the visit to press Bush for a change in the U.S. position on Taiwan. The main question became whether the United States would supply an advanced FX fighter-bomber to Taiwan, but the FX also served as a symbol of broader concerns.[29] The Chinese postponed indefinitely the planned visit by General Liu Huaqing. Even after the United States decided in January 1982 not to supply the F-5G, it reaffirmed continued coproduction of the F-5E and supply of some used F-104Gs. Only on August 17, 1982, was agreement reached in a joint U.S.-Chinese com-

---

26. Interview with Deng Xiaoping, *Ming Bao*, Hong Kong, August 25, 1981, in FBIS, *China*, August 25, 1981, p. W6.

27. Pollack noted that a Chinese Foreign Ministry spokesman explicitly rejected this proposal on June 10, shortly before Haig's visit, and also noted earlier rejections. See *The Lessons of Coalition Politics*, pp. 81–83. Lieutenant General Brent Scowcroft, who accompanied Ford, confirmed to me that soundings were taken on that visit, and that Deng Xiaoping took the initiative in raising and rejecting the idea of U.S. supply of arms to both China and Taiwan.

28. Information from a member of the U.S. delegation who witnessed the president's personal anger at the routine Chinese statement. Zhao undoubtedly regarded the term as descriptive and factual, rather than an epithet. The Chinese speech was, however, very critical of U.S. as well as Soviet policy. The principal real issue raised by Zhao was the continuing U.S. arms sales to Taiwan.

29. See A. Doak Barnett, *U.S. Arms Sales: The China-Taiwan Tangle* (Brookings, 1982), p. 28. Barnett's study gives an excellent review of the problem in its broader context through the spring of 1982.

muniqué that essentially settled the Taiwan arms sales issue for the next decade, although even then the two sides immediately interpreted the joint statement differently.[30]

By that time Secretary of State Haig, who had struggled to advance U.S. relations with China in pursuit of alignment against the Soviet Union, had left the scene.[31] After nearly two years under the Reagan administration, the United States, in its relations with China, was more or less back to the same point it had been at when the administration first assumed office. Haig attributed great significance to the role of China in the world alignment of political forces, especially in containing Soviet expansion.[32] He had not, however, been successful in establishing American policy toward China on the line he sought, although he did help to prevent a greater worsening of American-Chinese relations.

In September 1982 former President Richard Nixon visited China, where he was received with high honor, and in October Henry Kissinger also revisited Beijing. The Chinese sent word back through them to the Reagan administration that China was interested in improving relations.

American policy and diplomatic communication with China developed more regularly in 1983 and 1984, even though Secretary of State George Shultz, who had succeeded Haig, gave lower priority to relations with China and rejected the ideas of a "China card" and a geopolitical "triangle."[33] Several high-level visits continued. Shultz visited Beijing in February 1983;[34] Secretary

---

30. Pollack, *The Lessons of Coalition Politics*, pp. 94–95. See also George P. Shultz, *Turmoil and Triumph: My Years as Secretary of State* (Charles Scribner's Sons, 1993), pp. 381–82.

    The August 1982 understanding led to continuing U.S. arms arrangements with Taiwan at roughly the same level, until during the presidential election campaign in September 1992 President Bush suddenly stepped up the quality and quantity of U.S. military aircraft provided in order to keep open the F-16 production line in electorally critical Texas.

31. In his memoir, Haig stated that "more than any other thing" during his tenure as secretary of state, the question of policy toward China marked a growing rift between him and President Reagan. Paradoxically, in his view, his departure in mid-1982 then became "the single act that made possible the solution of this critical question" in the August 1982 accord on arms sales to Taiwan. Haig, *Caveat*, pp. 195, 215.

32. See ibid., pp. 194–95.

33. Shultz explained his views well in his later memoir. He noted that he considered it "a mistake to place too much emphasis on a relationship for its own sake. A good relationship should emerge from the ability to solve substantive problems of interest to both countries." At the same time, he also believed that "when the geostrategic importance of China became the conceptual prism through which Sino-American relations were viewed, it was almost inevitable that American policymakers became overly solicitous of Chinese interests, concerns, and sensitivities." Shultz, *Turmoil and Triumph*, p. 382.

34. The Chinese were very guarded in their evaluations of the Shultz visit and continued to stress "obstacles," despite tentative agreement on an exchange of visits by the respective heads of government.

of Commerce Malcolm Baldrige in May; the president's science adviser, George Keyworth, also in May; and Secretary of Defense Caspar Weinberger in September 1983. Minister of Foreign Affairs Wu Xueqian visited the United States in October 1983, and Minister of National Defense Zhang Aiping in June 1984. The most important political visits were those by Premier Zhao Ziyang to Washington in January and by President Reagan to Beijing in April 1984.

Although no major issue comparable to the question of arms sales to Taiwan arose over those years, the effects of that disagreement remained and lesser new irritants arose. For example, in the first three months of 1983 a conflict of interests arose over trade, especially over U.S. curbs on imports of textiles, an important issue when Shultz visited Beijing in February.[35] Soon after, in April 1983, a Chinese tennis star defected to the United States, leading China to sharply curtail cultural contacts for about a year.[36] In May the editor of a Hong Kong communist newspaper was sentenced to ten years' imprisonment as a U.S. spy.[37]

There were, however, some steps forward. In May 1983 the United States further relaxed constraints on technology transfer. China was raised to the same general category (category V) as the Western European countries,

---

Shultz had no illusions about what his visit could achieve. He saw the visit, and those of others to follow, as reestablishing relations on a more solid footing rather than subject to the previous pendulum swings. See Shultz, *Turmoil and Triumph*, pp. 385–93.

35. Michael Weisskopf, "Chinese Trade Issues Seen Snagging Shultz," *Washington Post*, January 31, 1983, p. A12; and Christopher S. Wren, "China, Upset by U.S. Trade Curb, Halting Import of 3 Commodities," *New York Times*, January 20, 1983, pp. A1, D11.

    Reagan in January 1983 clamped down on quotas of thirty-three Chinese textile products, leading to a Chinese boycott of American cotton and soybeans. The United States also rebuffed Chinese efforts to waive COCOM trade restrictions.

36. See "19 Events with U.S. Canceled by China," *New York Times*, April 8, 1983, pp. A1, A8.

    Americans failed to appreciate the strong Chinese reaction to the defection of Hu Na, which was seen as an "insult" and affront to Chinese "national dignity and state sovereignty." (*Renmin Ribao*, April 9, 1983.) Moreover, an official Ministry of Foreign Affairs protest note described it as a "grave political incident." (Xinhua, April 6, 1983.) President Reagan unwittingly contributed to the ruffled nationalistic Chinese sentiments when he off-handedly said he would rather adopt Hu Na than send her back, and *People's Daily* chose to interpret the remark as seeking to divide her from her family, a repudiation of interest in human rights. (*Renmin Ribao*, April 19, 1983.)

    Two and a half years later, another minor incident again showed Chinese sensitivity even where there was no official American action. In November 1985, University of California campus police in Berkeley arrested a Chinese research scholar believed to be a peeping tom at a dormitory. He was soon released when it appeared he was not the culprit, and an apology was given for the error, but the Chinese again protested and called it a "grave incident."

37. Christopher S. Wren, "China Jails a Hong Kong Editor as a Spy for U.S.," *New York Times*, May 16, 1983, pp. A1, A3.

Australia, Japan, and India. Each sale still had to be decided case by case, but the symbolic significance was considerable, and the change permitted greater leeway in trade.[38]

Secretary of Defense Weinberger's visit in September 1983, and the return visit by Defense Minister Zhang Aiping in June 1984, restored a low-key military security relationship (despite unrequited efforts by Weinberger to stir up a more militant anti-Soviet stance).[39] In August 1984, Secretary of the Navy John Lehman visited China and sought to establish contacts between the two navies. The new relationship could perhaps best be called selective strategic cooperation: exchanges of military visits, and limited intelligence and policy-planning meetings, but no major arms sales and a reserved attitude in defining areas of congruence on strategic interests.[40] In addition, without public disclo-

---

38. Pollack, *The Lessons of Coalition Politics*, p. 108.

39. Throughout the visit, Chinese commentary consistently stressed the role of military contacts in advancing mutual understanding and improving general bilateral relations and downplayed any suggestion of strategic collaboration—in striking contrast to treatment of Secretary Harold Brown's visit in 1980. Weinberger's anti-Soviet remarks and enthusiastic comments on common Sino-American strategic interests were ignored in Chinese reporting. And when American correspondents asked Premier Zhao Ziyang about strategic cooperation, he replied by emphasizing that China "follows an independent foreign policy" and "does not attach itself to any big power." *Renmin Ribao*, September 28, 1983, in FBIS, *China*, September 28, 1993, p. B3.

     Weinberger's account of his visit makes clear his attempt to build ties to China based on presumably shared anti-Soviet interests. See Caspar W. Weinberger, *Fighting for Peace: Seven Critical Years in the Pentagon* (Warner Books, 1990), pp. 255–81, for his 1983 visit, and pp. 282–83, for Zhang Aiping's return visit in 1984. Weinberger commented on why he felt he could establish rapport with the Chinese premier: "Zhang Aiping was unquestionably a Communist, but he was an anti-Soviet Communist" (p. 270).

40. In internal U.S. military contingency planning, the possibility of wartime U.S.-Chinese collaboration against the Soviet Union remained. Secretary Weinberger's secret Defense Guidance issued in March 1982, and subsequently leaked to the press, included in the context of a possible U.S.-Soviet protracted global war the statement, "Encouragement and, if possible, logistic support will be provided to China's military initiatives that would fix [that is, tie down] Soviet ground, air and naval forces in the USSR's far eastern territories." Quoted from a leaked copy of the Defense Guidance in "U.S. Arms Plan Bared," *Chicago Tribune*, January 17, 1983, p. 1. Earlier partial leaks from the Defense Guidance in May and June 1982 had not included this passage. In other speeches and reports Weinberger also stressed common anti-Soviet security interests of the United States and China; for example, see *Department of Defense Annual Report, Fiscal Year 1983*, p. II-20. In a public speech in December 1983 Weinberger described China as "a potentially decisive factor in the global balance of power." See "Remarks Prepared for Delivery by the Honorable Caspar W. Weinberger, Secretary of Defense, to Washington Press Club, Washington, D.C., Tuesday, December 13, 1983," news release, Office of Assistant Secretary of Defense (Public Affairs), Washington, December 13, 1983, p. 3.

sure, targets in China were dropped from the U.S. nuclear war strike plan (SIOP) in late 1982.

One area in which a shared strategic interest continued and cooperation prospered until 1989 was the clandestine supply of arms to the anti-Soviet *mujahedin* fighting in Afghanistan. By 1983, because of loose coordination through Pakistan after 1980, the United States was purchasing Soviet-designed weapons made in China that were then given to the *mujahedin*.

Both the United States and China made some efforts and compromises to improve relations in 1983-84.

Premier Zhao Ziyang's visit to the United States in January 1984 was the most important since Deng Xiaoping's visit five years earlier. Chinese commentary described the visit as "a major event in the history of Sino-U.S. relations" because it took place at "a critical juncture" in those relations. Although important differences, especially over Taiwan, were noted, the visit was said to have clarified respective positions and to have been "fruitful" and "positive," and "laid a good foundation for furthering relations."[41]

The visit by President Reagan to China was of particular importance. He seemed to marvel at his discovery that China was a multicolored tapestry and not merely a sea of red. Indeed, on his return trip President Reagan—who had expressed vehement hostility to "Red China" for more than thirty years— spoke exuberantly about his experience in "*so-called* Communist China" (and expressed optimism that the Chinese were embracing capitalist principles in their economic reform).[42] He also seemed not to have noticed that his efforts to forge an anti-Soviet alliance, which he (and his immediate advisers) assumed would be a bond, were in fact rebuffed and his anti-Soviet statements censored by the Chinese. The principal achievement, rushed for the summit visit, was an agreement on cooperation on peaceful uses of nuclear energy that included American assistance in the development of Chinese nuclear power reactors.[43] On closer reading and following further discussions after the summit meeting, the agreement turned out not to provide the minimum necessary assurances against nuclear proliferation to third powers, and opposition was so strong that it could not be submitted to Congress until after more than a year of further discussion. Yet Reagan, in terms approaching the enthusiasm of the earlier

---

41. Editorial, "A Significant Visit," *Renmin Ribao*, January 18, 1984, in FBIS, *China*, January 18, 1984, pp. B3–B5.

42. Cited in Robert G. Kaiser, "Another Western 'Barbarian' Honors the Middle Kingdom," *Washington Post*, May 6, 1984, pp. F1, F2. Emphasis added. Deng Xiaoping could scarcely have appreciated this compliment, which supported the charges of his Chinese political opponents, not all of whom had been removed from the party leadership.

43. Three other minor agreements were concluded on cultural exchanges, extension of an American course in management techniques, and a guarantee against double taxation of American corporations operating in China.

convert Nixon over his summitry with the communist powers, described the developing relationship between China and the United States as "one of the principal events of post-war diplomacy" and expressed the hope that "this important, new friendship of ours will mature and prosper."[44]

U.S.-China relations by 1983–84 were thus back on a track of normal development, although still plagued by occasional eruptions of the basically unsettled differences over Taiwan.[45] They did not, however, return to the situation that had prevailed from 1978 into 1980. For one thing, China did not occupy so central a place in the thinking of the U.S. leaders from 1981 on (with the exception of Haig during his tenure, and he was frustrated in his attempt to set policy). In different ways Kissinger, with his image of a flexible triangular balance of power, and Brzezinski, with his aim of a more active American-Chinese collaboration against the Soviet Union, had both given a more salient role to China than did the Reagan administration. Reagan's belated enthusiasm after his visit in the spring of 1984, and Shultz's interest, also largely derived from his own visit, were not rooted in a geopolitical conception of world politics and were in no way as important as Nixon's and Carter's. Moreover, the Reagan administration (including Haig) implicitly assumed that China had a greater stake in improving relations than did the United States, and that the United States could therefore dangle the prospect of arms sales but otherwise ignore Chinese interests, including Taiwan.

One sign of the changed American view of the role of China was a statement by Secretary Shultz a month after his visit. In it he ascribed to China a regional role more than a global one, as well as a role in "resisting Soviet aggression." The Chinese did not take kindly to either characterization, especially because in the same speech Shultz made clear the far more important role of Japan in American thinking (as had President Reagan) and also reiterated a comment by the president in saying that "progress in U.S.-China rela-

---

44. "Remarks at a Ceremony for the Signing of Four Agreements between the United States and China for the President's Departure from Beijing," April 30, 1984, *Weekly Compilation of Presidential Documents*, vol. 20 (May 7, 1984), p. 613. (Hereafter *Presidential Documents*.)

Secretary Shultz was far more sober in his evaluation, although he believed the visit had been successful not only for American-Chinese relations, but also "as a training ground and confidence builder for President Reagan's subsequent dealings with the Soviets across ideologies." Shultz, *Turmoil and Triumph*, pp. 395–99, quotation from p. 398.

45. For example, Deng Xiaoping privately warned Secretary Weinberger during his 1983 visit that American policy toward Taiwan could lead to an "eruption" in Chinese-American relations. He confided this to Japanese visitors nearly a year later. See "Deng Warns of 'Eruption' in U.S.-China Ties Over Taiwan," *New York Times*, October 12, 1984, p. A8.

tions need not come at the expense of relations with our other friends . . .
including . . . the people of Taiwan."[46]

The Chinese reciprocated by downgrading their relations with the
United States. And some elements of early common interest attenuated. Most
notably, Chinese successes in raising domestic grain production sharply curtailed a need for grain imports. As a result of this combination of political and
economic circumstances, the Chinese by the end of 1984 failed to meet the
terms of a four-year grain agreement with the United States (underbuying by
some $475 million worth of grain, 3.8 million metric tons of the 6 million
annually required by the agreement). The agreement was then permitted to
lapse.[47]

In early 1984 two Chinese were arrested attempting to spirit out of the
United States high technology banned for export. Of much greater seriousness,
although it did not directly affect the development of relations, was the arrest
in November 1985 of a veteran CIA analyst of Chinese origin, Larry Wu-Tai
Chin, who had served as a Chinese spy since 1952.

During 1985–88 the pattern of relations continued basically on the
track established in 1983–84. In July 1985 President Li Xiannian visited the
United States, and the peaceful nuclear cooperation agreement prematurely
announced well over a year before on the occasion of President Reagan's visit
to China was finally signed. In October 1985 Vice President Bush revisited
China, and in May 1986 Vice Premier Yao Yilin came to the United States. As
noted in the following discussion, these exchanges paralleled similar high-level
reciprocal Soviet and Chinese visits in the mid-1980s.[48]

American and Chinese military visits, not yet paralleled in Sino-Soviet
relations, also continued. In January 1985 General John W. Vessey, Jr., chairman of the Joint Chiefs of Staff, visited China.[49] Tentative agreement was
reached for a visit by U.S. Navy destroyers to Shanghai. By April, however, the

---

46. "The U.S. and East Asia: A Partnership for the Future," March 5, 1983, *Department of
State Bulletin*, vol. 83 (April 1983), pp. 32, 33, and see pp. 31–34. (Hereafter *State
Bulletin*.) President Reagan had said that "the United States-Japanese relationship
remains the centerpiece of our Asian policy." See "American Legion. Remarks at the
23rd Annual Washington Conference," February 22, 1983, *Presidential Documents*, vol.
19 (February 28, 1983), p. 274.

47. See Lena H. Sun, "U.S. Protests China's Reneging on Grain Deal," *Washington Post*,
December 22, 1984, p. A17.
   Besides reduced need, China had complained about the high price and presence
of pesticides in the grain. Finally, the Chinese made known their unhappiness at
unilateral U.S. imposition of import quotas on certain Chinese textile exports.

48. The Chinese were careful to reassure the United States that their improvement in
relations with the Soviet Union was not at the expense of relations with the United States
and would remain far short of renewed alliance.

49. During his visit, General Vessey was shown Chinese Army exercises in the Shenyang
Military District of Manchuria, near Soviet Siberia.

planned U.S. naval port call ran aground on the shoals of the U.S. refusal to confirm that the ships did not have nuclear weapons on board. General Secretary Hu Yaobang himself said the ships would not carry nuclear weapons, and the United States was then on the spot—particularly since it was embroiled at that very time in a serious dispute with New Zealand over that country's new policy of denying port calls to ships with nuclear weapons, which clashed with the long-standing American policy of refusing to confirm or deny the presence of nuclear weapons on any ship.[50] The issue dragged on for months; the ships did not visit China until November 1986. The Chinese portrayed the Vessey visit as a step in developing Chinese-American bilateral relations, not as increasing strategic collaboration.

Chief of the General Staff Yang Dezhi's return visit to the United States in May 1986 saw a similar round of visits to military facilities and further discussion of possible military equipment sales. The possibility of joint exercises of military forces in the future was discussed.[51] Yang Dezhi also visited the headquarters of the U.S. commander in chief Pacific, Admiral Ronald Hays, in Hawaii.

American interest in selling such technology as radar and avionics had already reversed the usual situation in COCOM, with the United States now seeking most of the exceptions to bars on sales to communist countries. In October 1985, in time for Vice President Bush to announce during his visit to China, the United States had obtained its allies' agreement to expedite such approval. Nonetheless, sales of military technology moved slowly.

In October 1986 Secretary of Defense Weinberger again visited China. No major development of relations was made, but there was further "slow but steady progress" (in Weinberger's words) in military technology sales.[52] The major sale by this time was advanced avionics equipment for the Chinese F-8 fighter plane, which did not involve American state-of-the-art electronics, but was a big boost for the Chinese, and at an estimated $500 million by far the largest sale of military equipment. A month later, the U.S. Navy fleet visit to Qingdao marked the first such visit since 1949 (when U.S. Navy ships departed from stationing at that same port, then known in English as Tsingtao). Weinberger formally announced this ship visit while in Beijing (although he had been upstaged, intentionally or otherwise, by a prior low-key Chinese announcement).

---

50. Although this might have been inadvertent, there is reason to believe that the offending statement by Hu Yaobang was deliberately placed in his speech by officials in the Ministry of Foreign Affairs who wished to sabotage the pace of military cooperation by making the naval visit less likely.

     China had welcomed and supported New Zealand's policy of denying port visits to nuclear-armed ships when that issue arose in January 1985.

51. In fact, a modest but symbolic joint naval "passing exercise" had, by arrangement, occurred on January 12, 1986, near Hong Kong. A U.S. destroyer and frigate met and engaged in drills and joint actions with a Chinese destroyer and accompanying oiler.

52. Weinberger, *Fighting for Peace*, pp. 284–87.

Political and strategic aspects of the U.S.-China relationship did not, however, rise or return to the 1978–80 high point. The one area of a continuing increase was in trade. By the mid-1980s Sino-American trade had become far more important than the trade of either with the Soviet Union. In 1985 U.S.-China trade turnover had reached more than $7.7 billion, four times USSR-China trade ($1.9 billion) and well over two and a half times U.S.-Soviet trade ($2.9 billion).

In a speech summing up U.S. policy toward China in December 1986, Assistant Secretary for East Asia and Pacific Affairs Gaston J. Sigur, Jr., sought to emphasize "consensus" (notably lacking in 1981), "consistency" (also lacking in 1981), and "stability" (applied both to U.S. policy and to its aim in China—"a politically stable, modernizing China is in a better position to resist outside [Soviet] pressure and intimidation and is less likely to be a disruptive factor in Asia").[53] The most arresting element in Secretary Sigur's remarks was his reassertion of a shared American and Chinese concern over "Soviet actions that threatened international peace and security." Though he did not specify any actions, he went on to discuss Gorbachev's Vladivostok speech as a threatening development—"We believe," he said, implying a consensus, that the speech is "only the beginning of a new round of Soviet activism in Asia. Moscow may attempt to increase its influence in the region through subtle tactics designed to overcome the suspicions most Asians have of Soviet intentions." But he expressed confidence that "our friends and allies in the region are not impressed by empty rhetoric . . . . They will judge Moscow by its actions rather than its words." He then adopted as his own the three Chinese-designated obstacles to improved relations: Soviet withdrawal from Afghanistan, Vietnamese withdrawal from Kampuchea, and a rollback of the Soviet military buildup along the Chinese borders since the 1960s. He also called for reduction in SS-20 deployments in Asia and reduction of military support for North Korea and concluded, "I am not optimistic that the Soviet Union will take *any* of these steps." It was a very poor prediction, as the Soviet Union within the next three years took *all* of those steps. "In contrast," in his words, "the United States was engaged in a close and positive dialogue with friends and allies throughout the region," including China.[54] Again, the "contrast" betrayed residual hard-line assumptions about Soviet policy that were already obsolete. Some months later, Sigur was still listing as the primary element in the U.S. "consensus" that "our long-range foreign policy goals in East Asia require us to meet the Soviet strategic and geopolitical challenge in the

---

53. Gaston J. Sigur, Jr., "China Policy Today: Consensus, Consistence, Stability," December 11, 1986, *State Bulletin*, vol. 87 (February 1987), p. 50.

54. Ibid. Emphasis added.

area," and "that to do so we must preserve a commonality of interests with major Asian states such as China."[55]

American policy, however, was already shifting. When Secretary Shultz visited China for six days in March 1987, and more briefly in July 1988, he stressed Chinese economic reform and U.S.-China economic relations.[56] Sino-Soviet relations were discussed, but although there was some shared skepticism about how far the Soviet Union was prepared to go in implementing its new thinking, the main point was American acceptance that an improvement in Sino-Soviet relations would be in the interests of all. By mid-1988 Undersecretary for Political Affairs Michael H. Armacost, noting that "Sino-Soviet relations are already improving," predicted further normalization and accepted this as being in the interests of both countries, and by clear implication of the United States as well.[57] And in Beijing in July 1988 Secretary Shultz praised the fact that "the success of our experience is now reflected in the parallel efforts of our two countries to reduce tensions with the Soviet Union."[58]

By the mid- to late 1980s both positive and negative developments in Sino-American relations were based on other considerations than the fading triangular geopolitical one. One positive element, U.S. arms sales to China, did have roots in the old shared anti-Soviet policies. But increasingly important was friction over U.S. objections to Chinese sales of arms to other countries, above all missiles to Iran (but also to Pakistan and Saudi Arabia). In October 1987 that issue led to mild sanctions for about six months (a "temporary hold on further liberalization of COCOM controls" on trade with China),[59] and in turn to Chinese bristling over American "political blackmail" and "hegemonism," posing a "threat to stable Sino-U.S. relations."[60]

By 1987 the Chinese began to blame the United States more strongly than the Soviet Union for the arms race, and they supported the Soviet position against the American SDI.[61]

55. Gaston J. Sigur, Jr., "U.S. Policy Priorities for Relations with China," April 22, 1987, *State Bulletin*, vol. 87 (July 1987), p. 42.

56. See "Secretary Visits Asia: Dalian," March 3, 1987, *State Bulletin*, vol. 87 (May 1987), pp. 6-10. See also J. Stapleton Roy, "China: Reform and Future Prospects," statement before the Senate Foreign Relations Committee on September 17, 1987, *State Bulletin*, vol. 87 (December 1987), pp. 51–54.

57. Michael H. Armacost, "China and the U.S.: Present and Future," June 1, 1988, *State Bulletin*, vol. 88 (August 1988), p. 71.

58. "Secretary's Trip to East Asia and the Pacific, Banquet Toasts (Excerpts), Beijing," July 14 and 15, 1988, *State Bulletin*, vol. 88 (October 1988), p. 29.

59. Armacost, *State Bulletin*, vol. 88 (August 1988), p. 71.

60. Huan Xiang, "Sino-U.S. Relations Over the Past Year," *Beijing Review*, vol. 31 (February 17-28, 1988), pp. 29–31.

61. For one of the earlier indications, see Huang Tingwei and Song Baoxian, "Disarmament: New Aspects of an Old Issue," *Beijing Review*, vol. 30 (January 19, 1987), pp. 24–25.

Apart from bilateral frictions (despite advances) in trade, American criticisms of Chinese human rights abuses also became a more prominent issue. Disturbances in Tibet, especially after a well-publicized visit of the exiled Dalai Lama to the United States in the fall of 1987, were held against the United States by China's leaders, and subsequent suppression of the Tibetans in turn angered Americans. (Congress was far more inclined to react than the administration; the Senate unanimously voted strong condemnation in the fall of 1987, but the administration did nothing more than "reaffirm our strong commitment to respect for human rights in Tibet as elsewhere in the world" (rhetoric, not deeds, to apply Sigur's distinction in a less comfortable context).[62]

Another element of friction was increased American awareness, if not increased Chinese activity, with respect to espionage in the United States. Two Chinese diplomats in Washington were arrested and declared persona non grata in December 1987. A number of other cases of Chinese espionage in the latter 1980s were not publicized by the United States in order not to damage American-Chinese relations further.

On the other side of the relationship, a court hearing in the United States compelled the disclosure of a secret Defense Department security guideline under which China (along with the Soviet Union, Vietnam, Cuba, and others) was listed as a hostile country.[63] Given all the public protestations of friendship, this secret listing caused some public consternation in China (even if it may have come as no real surprise to the leadership). The Foreign Ministry noted that such a listing was "contrary to numerous official statements by the American Government."[64]

U.S.-China relations nonetheless continued on the general path of normal development to mid-1989.[65] The new Bush administration, if anything, gave a boost to the relationship. One of President Bush's first trips abroad was to China in February 1989. He drew on his earlier service there in the early 1970s and was upbeat on the state of U.S.-China relations.[66] There were, however, no new initiatives. Moreover, the visit was marred by China's prevention of contact with a dissident, which underlined the human rights issue. Nonetheless in the spring of 1989 there remained a widespread feeling in the

62. Armacost, *State Bulletin*, vol. 88 (August 1988), p. 71.

63. Richard Halloran, "Secret Is Out on Listing China as a Hostile Country," *New York Times*, January 25, 1988, p. A20.

64. The Soviet armed forces' newspaper *Red Star* published with evident satisfaction a brief notice of the Chinese Foreign Ministry's objection to the U.S. designation. See "Events, Facts: China," *Krasnaya zvezda* (Red Star), January 28, 1988.

65. For the final, and positive, statement from the Reagan administration, by Secretary Shultz, see "U.S., China Celebrate Decade of Diplomatic Relations, Secretary's Toast," December 15, 1988, *State Bulletin*, vol. 89 (February 1989), p. 25.

66. "President's Trip to Japan, China, and South Korea," *State Bulletin*, vol. 89 (May 1989), pp. 10–17.

United States on China still bordering on euphoria, though less so than in the mid-1980s.[67]

A watershed in relations, for the United States, came with the brutal suppression of peaceful demonstrators on Tiananmen Square on June 3-4, 1989, with hundreds killed. The euphoria was dashed. Nonetheless, President Bush was notably restrained, not going much beyond rhetorical objection, despite wide public and congressional indignation. Further military contacts were promptly suspended, and two weeks later (on June 20) it was announced that all high-level exchanges of U.S. government officials with China were being suspended.[68] That sanction was, however, promptly undercut by the secret dispatch of National Security Adviser Brent Scowcroft and Deputy Secretary of State Lawrence Eagleburger to Beijing only two weeks later—although the visit did not become known for half a year. In October, former president Richard Nixon broke the ice with a visit to Beijing, and in November Henry Kissinger visited. Deng Xiaoping suggested to Nixon that the United States was implicated in stirring up the unrest in China and told him that it was up to the United States to improve relations.[69] Then, in a surprise move, Scowcroft and Eagleburger visited Beijing in early December in what was still believed to be the first break in a six-month ban on high-level official contacts. It was seen and described as a "risky gamble" and was highly controversial, provoking a wave of congressional criticism. Then, in the midst of that debate, came the stunning disclosure (based on a Chinese leak) that the two officials had also gone to Beijing in early July, making a mockery of the public sanction on no official contacts.

When the Chinese lifted martial law in Beijing in January 1990, the United States dropped its principal sanction of a ban on World Bank loans to China. But the public debate continued, including heated argument over renewal of most-favored-nation trade status in May, although the administration prevailed in granting it. In November, Foreign Minister Qian Qichen was received in Washington for talks with Baker, and even briefly by President Bush, but with no visible result.[70]

---

67. As Harry Harding has perceptively observed, this euphoria about China was not an enthusiasm of liberals, but of American conservatives—beginning with President Bush. See Harding, *Fragile Relationship*, pp. 169–72.

68. See "Demonstrations in China" (State Department and White House statements, May 18 through June 20, 1989), *State Bulletin*, vol. 89 (August 1989), pp. 75–77.

69. Nicholas D. Kristof, "Better Relations Depend on U.S., Deng Tells Nixon," *New York Times*, November 1, 1989, p. A8.

70. The reception of Qian was a "reward" for the Chinese UN vote authorizing use of force in the Persian Gulf crisis with Iraq. (The Chinese had abstained rather than vote for the resolution but that permitted its passage.) According to the earlier understanding, that would merit meeting Secretary Baker, but not President Bush, but at the last moment Bush decided he wanted to receive Qian. See Harding, *Fragile Relationship*, pp. 271–73.

During 1991 relations continued to follow a wavering pattern of ups and downs. The same issues continued: Chinese sales of military technology to Middle Eastern countries; human rights issues, including export of products made by prisoners ("slave labor"); trade violations, such as Chinese infringement of copyrights and computer software; and the high Chinese trade surplus with the United States, curtailing imports and pushing textile exports. The United States again was visited by the Dalai Lama in April, and he was received by President Bush. China also curtailed academic exchanges in 1990–91. In November, Secretary Baker visited Beijing, in what was conceded to be a gamble and proved to be one that was lost. He got only vague assurances on curbing military technology exports. But not much had been lost in making the effort (in contrast to the two disastrous Scowcroft-Eagleburger missions).

China, however, did announce it would adhere to the Nuclear Nonproliferation Treaty (NPT). China's acquiescence also made possible UN Security Council support for the Gulf War against Iraq. In all, relations from June 1989 to the end of 1991 (and beyond) were marked by new tensions and mixed relations between China and the United States, but with virtually no relevance any longer to relations of either power with the Soviet Union (or, after the end of 1991, Russia). The triangle was gone.

Overall, American-Chinese relations assumed a far more routine nature after the early 1980s than in the rapidly changing 1970s, and there were several reasons. First, American policy contributed to the sharp change in triangular geopolitical relationships in the 1980s. The second important new element contributing to this situation in the 1980s was, as earlier discussed, a change in Chinese policy. Third was a changed Sino-Soviet relationship, stemming from a Chinese reevaluation of the triangular relationship and a Soviet reassessment and desire to reduce tensions and improve relations.

## Sino-Soviet Relations

In 1981–82 the Chinese decided to resume direct talks with the Soviet Union to enhance China's position in triangular diplomacy while maintaining independence. In the 1970s the Chinese had wanted a more confrontational relationship between the United States and the Soviet Union and had therefore opposed détente between them. One important reason for this position was to reduce the ability of the Soviet Union to place pressure on China. Another was precisely to increase the opportunity for China to play a more active role in triangular diplomacy, and that aim required improving relations with the Soviet Union, as well as with the United States, to gain increased leverage with both superpowers. Finally, this changed triangle would permit China—"the Middle

Kingdom"—to pursue its more independent policy in the world, especially in the Third World.

China's intention became crystal clear when it called for renewed Sino-Soviet border talks within three days of the conclusion of Secretary of State Haig's visit to China in June 1981.[71] The Chinese had, however, as already noted, earlier outlined three "obstacles" or conditions for any serious improvement in relations with the Soviet Union: Soviet withdrawal from Afghanistan, Vietnamese withdrawal from Kampuchea, and a rollback of the Soviet military buildup along the Chinese borders since the end of the 1960s (including withdrawal of Soviet forces from Mongolia). These were stiff terms, and the Soviets initially saw them as precluding real improvement unless the Chinese were in practice to modify their stance. Eventually, however, the Soviet Union was to yield on all three.

Soviet policy toward China was also moving. The Soviets had taken the initiative on several occasions in 1981 and 1982 in attempting to resume the Sino-Soviet dialogue broken off by China in early 1980 (soon after it had begun) in reaction to the Soviet intervention in Afghanistan. At the Twenty-sixth Party Congress, on February 23, 1981, Brezhnev expressed a desire for improved relations with China and proposed working out confidence-building measures; the Chinese promptly rejected the idea.[72] Again on September 25, 1981, in an unpublicized message, the Soviets proposed holding the suspended border talks. The Chinese did not reply for three months, suggesting prolonged deliberation.[73]

In February 1982 Prime Minister Nikolai Tikhonov warily said that the Soviet Union would not "walk away from concrete steps directed toward improving relations" if talks were held "on the basis of equality and in the spirit of mutual understanding," but he stressed "this process must not be one-sided."[74] The next month in Tashkent Brezhnev went much further in a conciliatory direction, saying, "We have never considered normal the state of hostility and estrangement between our countries," and "We are prepared to come to terms, without preconditions, on mutually acceptable measures to improve Soviet-Chinese relations on the basis of mutual respect for each other's interests." Brezhnev also said that the Soviets did not "deny the existence of a socialist

---

71. Littuichan, *Renmin Ribao*, in FBIS, *China*, June 18, 1981, pp. C1–7.

72. *Pravda*, February 27, 1981; and Xinhua, March 15, 1981, in FBIS, *China*, March 16, 1981, pp. C1–2.

73. See Gerald Segal, *Sino-Soviet Relations after Mao*, Adelphi Paper 202 (London: International Institute for Strategic Studies, 1985), p. 10. This monograph is a useful review for this period.

74. "Replies of Chairman of the Council of Ministers of the USSR N. A. Tikhonov to Questions from the Editors of the Newspaper 'Asahi' (Japan)," *Pravda*, February 17, 1982.

system in China," a point that had not been conceded for nearly two decades, although he then went on to criticize Beijing's "association with the policy of the imperialists around the world" that "contradicts the interests of socialism."[75] In a speech in Baku in September Brezhnev repeated the Soviet interest in improving relations, as he did at a meeting with military leaders in Moscow in October shortly before his death. Significantly, on this latter occasion he linked Soviet interest in improving relations with China to the deterioration in Soviet relations with the United States.[76]

The Twelfth Party Congress in September 1982 removed the previous thesis that the Soviet Union was "the main source of danger of a new world war," and the concomitant proposition on the need for creating a global united front (that is, with the United States) against "Soviet hegemonism." Nonetheless, Moscow was still seen as posing a "serious threat" to Chinese security that needed to be removed before full normalization of relations. More specifically, Hu Yaobang cited the three obstacles and said that normalization of relations with the Soviet Union was dependent on the Soviets' taking "practical steps to lift their threat to the security of our country."[77] But the Chinese, while maintaining the three obstacles (or conditions) in principle, soon set them aside in practice to the extent of agreeing to hold semiannual "consultations" on normalization by deputy ministers (called "special representatives"). These talks began in Moscow in October 1982, between Deputy Foreign Ministers Leonid F. Ilychev and Qian Qichen. In the talks, when the Chinese raised the three conditions, the Soviets refused to discuss them on the grounds that they involved third countries. Nonetheless, dialogue had been resumed.[78]

These Chinese moves to improve relations with the Soviet Union accompanied the steps it took to improve the now strained relations with the United States (the Taiwan arms communiqué, it will be recalled, had been signed on August 16, 1982). China was not shifting from the United States to the Soviet Union. It was applying the Nixon-Kissinger strategy of gaining

75. "Speech of L. I. Brezhnev," *Pravda*, March 25, 1982. Brezhnev also emphasized that the Soviet Union had always supported the Chinese position on Taiwan, in an attempt to rub salt in the Sino-American wound over this issue.

76. "Kremlin Meeting of Military Leaders," *Pravda*, October 28, 1982.

77. Hu Yaobang, *Beijing Review*, vol. 25 (September 13, 1982), p. 31.

78. This process of rapprochement in 1981–82 may have been assisted by a well-placed contact in the Soviet Ministry of Foreign Affairs. A Chinese former intelligence officer has said that such a high-level MFA official in the late 1970s and early 1980s maintained discreet contact with an officer at the Chinese Embassy to "explain" Soviet policy. Though the Chinese were wary, this source proved well-informed and reliable, and able to advise on events in advance. He claimed to have played a role in arranging Brezhnev's Tashkent speech and influencing the broader Soviet shift of policy. Personal communication to the author from the Chinese former intelligence officer.

leverage in triangular diplomacy by improving relations with both the other powers.

Soviet policy in 1982 also shifted from a predominantly antagonistic line toward China, punctuated by occasional calls for improving relations, to a stance predominantly devoted to seeking a rapprochement. This shift was reflected in the termination during 1982 of Soviet publication of a serial book collection of polemics and critical commentaries on Chinese policy called "A Dangerous Course." First published in 1969, eleven volumes were released, with the final one signed to press on December 30, 1981, and issued early in 1982.[79] Similarly, polemic articles attacking Chinese military policy, which had characterized the Soviet military professional literature, ended in 1982.[80]

Brezhnev's successors urged improvement in relations. Foreign Minister Huang Hua was received briefly by Andropov and spent ninety minutes with Gromyko on the occasion of Brezhnev's funeral in November 1982. Andropov, in his first major address as the new party leader, referred to his predecessor's speeches in Tashkent and Baku and, as if to deny speculation about differences in Moscow, stressed "the convictions of all our party, its striving to look forward" in seeking improved relations. He also noted, "We pay close attention to every positive response to this from the Chinese side."[81] In August 1983 Andropov said that "certain positive trends have been perceptible in our relations recently," although "the present level of bilateral relations is still far from the level that, we are convinced, should exist between such major and moreover neighboring powers."[82]

The actual course of Sino-Soviet relations in 1983–84 remained on a more normal basis than was the case before 1982, but still involved little more than the semiannual consultations by deputy foreign ministers and modestly improved trade. Irritants continued. For example, a squabble over alleged

---

79. The series collected the principal authoritative commentaries from leading Soviet political journals and newspapers roughly annually and was published by the State Political Publishing House in editions of 50,000 (after the first volume, in 1969, which had been issued in 200,000 copies). Each book was some 250–350 pages in length. The last was: *Opasnyi kurs* (A Dangerous Course), vypusk odinnadtsatyi (issue no. 11) (Moscow: Politizdat, 1981), 352 pp.

80. The confidential journal of the Soviet General Staff, *Voyennaya mysl'* (Military Thought), had, for example, published nine sharp political-military attacks in the years 1978–82, ending in November 1981, and thirteen informational surveys of aspects of Chinese military affairs, ending in March 1982. The journal *Zarubezhnoye voyennoye obozreniye* (Foreign Military Review), which had published a dozen articles on Chinese political military and military affairs in 1981–82, carried its last polemic in March 1982 and its last informational article in September 1982.

81. "Speech of General Secretary of the CC CPSU Yu. V. Andropov at the plenum of the CC CPSU, November 22, 1982," *Kommunist* (Communist), no. 17 (November 1982), p. 20.

82. "Yu. V. Andropov's Answers to Pravda Questions," *Pravda*, August 27, 1983.

Chinese claims to Soviet territory erupted in the press in January 1983, spurred by a Soviet article.[83] More significant, although it did not become an issue impeding the development of relations, was growing Chinese attention to the Soviet deployment of SS-20 intermediate-range ballistic missiles in Asia within range of China (108 had been deployed by 1983; ultimately 171 were deployed by 1985-86, before the entire force was dismantled under the INF Treaty of 1987).

During the early to mid-1980s, the Soviet Union and China undertook to allay perceived threats to the other side. The Soviets, for example, reduced the frequency of military exercises along the Chinese border. And the Chinese, as part of their drastic reduction and modernization of the Chinese Army begun in 1985, cut back the forces deployed along the Sino-Soviet border.

The Soviets tried to keep relations with both China and the United States from deteriorating, in part to prevent a return to closer Sino-American ties. They also sought to prevent China from succeeding in its effort to consolidate a position at the apex, or balance, of the triangle, but they had little leverage. One small sign of their tandem approach with the other two powers can be seen in the fact that the senior specialists on China and the United States in the Foreign Ministry in Moscow were both raised to deputy minister rank at the same time.[84]

The semiannual rounds of talks by deputy ministers continued, but without significant advances. In March 1983 the Soviets proposed a nonaggression pact, but the Chinese turned down the idea. In August 1983 Andropov again suggested the value of confidence-building measures, but the Chinese were not responsive. A visit by Soviet First Deputy Prime Minister Ivan V. Arkhipov, scheduled for May 1984, was postponed by the Soviets because of a renewed Vietnamese-Chinese border battle in April—and perhaps because of pique at President Reagan's visit to Beijing. The Chinese and Soviet foreign ministers, Wu Xueqian and Andrei Gromyko, did meet for six hours in New York in September 1984 to carry the dialogue forward.[85]

The two countries also agreed to increase trade. In a politically significant small move, in April 1983 the Sino-Soviet border was opened in one region

---

83. Observer, "What Is the Purpose?" *New Times*, no. 3 (January 1983), pp. 12–14. The Chinese promptly rebutted the charges. "A Reply to the 'Observer' of the Soviet New Times Weekly," *Shijie zhishi* (World Affairs), no. 3 (January 1983), in FBIS, *China*, January 24, 1983, pp. C1–3.

84. This double promotion—of Viktor G. Komplektov, head of the USA Department, and Mikhail S. Kapitsa, head of the First Far Eastern (China) Department—occurred in December 1982.

     Soon after, China also promoted the head of its Soviet and East European Affairs Department, Yu Hongliang, to vice foreign minister.

85. This became an annual meeting thereafter, the next meeting a year later introducing Eduard A. Shevardnadze who had by then replaced Gromyko as foreign minister.

to limited local trade. Other such local trade arrangements followed during the next few years. From 1983 to 1984 trade doubled, reaching some $1.2 billion (about one-fourth of Sino-U.S. trade). One reason for the increase was Chinese recognition that its industrial plant and economic planning system remained largely geared to the Soviet system. But the Chinese also continued to turn to Japan and the West for new technology, while the Soviets held back on selling advanced technology, awaiting an improvement in overall relations.

The Chinese continued in the early and mid-1980s to improve ties to the countries of Eastern Europe. The breakthrough was a visit by Hu Yaobang to Romania and Yugoslavia in May 1983.[86] The Soviet reaction was much less alarmist than it had been to earlier moves to develop contacts in the late 1970s, especially to the visit by Hua Guofeng to Eastern Europe in 1978. Such visits became normal, and by June 1987 led to the highest-level visit in three decades when party leader Zhao Ziyang visited Poland, East Germany, Czechoslovakia, Hungary, and Bulgaria.[87]

By the end of 1984, Sino-Soviet relations began to move forward from the modest plateau reached in 1982–84. In September Foreign Ministers Gromyko and Wu had a meeting in New York referred to in relatively positive terms in both Moscow and Beijing. In December 1984 Arkhipov did visit Beijing, the highest-ranking contact since Aleksei Kosygin met with Zhou Enlai at the Beijing airport in 1969. He was well received and on his eight-day stay visited several economic installations and met several of the top Chinese leaders.[88] Agreements were reached on economic, scientific, and technological cooperation, and it was agreed to establish a Sino-Soviet Commission on Economic, Trade, Scientific, and Technological Cooperation. Of special note, the Soviet envoy was addressed by Vice Premier Yao Yilin as "Comrade" Arkhipov, a politically significant change from the practice of a quarter of a century of estrangement. Nonetheless, he was also reminded of the three obstacles to fully developing relations.

Shortly before Chernenko's death, in March 1985, the first Chinese parliamentary delegation visited Moscow. On the occasion of Gorbachev's selection to succeed Chernenko, Secretary General Hu Yaobang sent Chinese Communist Party congratulations, and this message and the reply constituted

---

86. There were also visits that year by lower-ranking Chinese officials to all the Warsaw Pact countries: Deputy Foreign Ministers Qian Qichen visited Hungary, Poland, and East Germany, and Ma Xusheng visited Bulgaria and Czechoslovakia.

87. Other notable visits in this period included trips to China in 1986-88 by Eastern European leaders Wojciech Jaruzelski of Poland, Erich Honecker of East Germany, Todor Zhivkov of Bulgaria, János Kádár of Hungary, and Miloš Jakeš of Czechoslovakia. In early 1987, Chinese Foreign Minister Wu Xueqian also visited Czechoslovakia, Poland, and Bulgaria.

88. Arkhipov had been a leading figure among Soviet economic specialists working in China in the 1950s, and he drew upon this experience and rapport.

the first exchange of greetings between the two communist parties since the early Khrushchev years.[89] Politburo member Peng Zhen, in visiting the Soviet Embassy in Beijing to pay condolences on Chernenko's death, referred to his successor as Comrade Gorbachev, repeating the use of a fraternal party address first accorded to Arkhipov four months earlier. Then Vice Premier Li Peng, representing China at the funeral, referred to the Soviet Union as a socialist country (reciprocating for the first time Brezhnev's reference to socialist China three years earlier). Gorbachev, in his first speech as the new party leader, called for "serious improvement" in relations with China which, "with reciprocity," he believed should be quite possible.[90] Beijing responded by referring to Gorbachev's "positive approach." Gorbachev also twice received Li Peng and his delegation—in contrast to Chernenko's failure to receive Vice Premier Wan Li at all when he attended Andropov's funeral the year before.

Gorbachev indeed sought to improve relations with China. In an early foreign policy initiative that also had broader objectives, he sought in May 1985 (during a visit by Indian Prime Minister Rajiv Gandhi) to revive Brezhnev's proposals of a decade earlier for an Asian collective security arrangement, but with a significant difference: China (along with India) was proposed as a key member, rather than being the unnamed target of the earlier proposal. He seemed to have in mind a pan-Asian compact and continuing forum similar to the Helsinki CSCE process in Europe. The initiative did not yield any early results, but it helped to lay the foundation for a later improvement. At about the same time, in a negative coincidence (unplanned unless by Vietnam), the Vietnamese-Chinese border again erupted in local fighting.

In July 1985 Vice Premier Yao Yilin, in Moscow returning Arkhipov's visit, signed a new five-year trade pact, as had been envisioned in the December talks in Beijing, calling for a further substantial increase in trade. Soviet technicians also reappeared in China for the first time since 1960 to assist in modernizing seventeen factories originally supplied by the Soviet Union in the 1950s, as well as seven new ones.

On July 27, 1985, without publicity, the Soviet Union shut down a clandestine anti-PRC Chinese-language radio (Ba Yi; "August 1," Chinese Army day) beamed at China for more than two decades. This removed a major irritant to the Chinese.

Toward the end of the year several other developments left the trend in developing relations uncertain. In December, Deputy Foreign Minister Mikhail Kapitsa visiting Beijing obtained tentative Chinese agreement to an

---

89. A message from General Secretary Brezhnev in 1976 congratulating Hua Guofeng on his selection as party chief and expressing condolences on Mao Zedong's death was rejected by the Chinese because of the absence of CCP-CPSU party ties. Neither party had even attempted to address the other directly from the mid-1960s until that time.

90. "Speech of General Secretary of the CC of the CPSU Comrade M. S. Gorbachev to the Plenum of the CC CPSU, March 11, 1985," *Pravda*, March 12, 1985.

exchange of visits by the foreign ministers during the coming year. The Soviets unwisely leaked this news to the press, with the result that the Chinese felt it necessary to say that such visits should await progress on dealing with the three obstacles, making the prospect of the meetings much less likely. And in Moscow, although Gorbachev received Vice Premier Li Peng, Soviet officials said the meeting was not very successful. Gorbachev is reported to have been rebuffed when he sought renewal of party-to-party contacts and urged Chinese attendance at the forthcoming Soviet party congress.

Also in December, a Soviet commercial jet airliner was hijacked to China. The plane and crew were, however, promptly returned, and the Chinese tried the hijacker (the copilot, a Soviet citizen of Central Asian origin).

The Chinese did not send a delegation to the Twenty-seventh Party Congress in Moscow in February–March 1986. At the congress, Gorbachev singled China out for unusual attention (it was the only socialist country referred to by name, and he devoted two paragraphs to it). In warm terms he said: "One can speak with satisfaction of the definite improvement in relations of the Soviet Union with its great neighbor—socialist China."[91]

In March, Arkhipov again visited Beijing and met Premier Zhao Ziyang, although he received a cooler reception than he had fifteen months earlier. In April a new and more senior Soviet ambassador, Oleg Troyanovsky, was sent to Beijing, and a number of other important personnel changes were made.[92]

Besides spurning Soviet efforts to develop party relations, the Chinese also rejected several other proposals. In January 1986 they again declined a Soviet proposal for a nonaggression pact. In April they rejected a proposal by Foreign Minister Shevardnadze for a summit meeting, saying it was "unrealistic." (This Soviet proposal may have stemmed from a Chinese overture for a summit meeting, reportedly conveyed to Gorbachev in December, which would however have been conditioned on progress in overcoming the three obstacles.)

It seems clear that by 1985 the Chinese leaders decided that the Soviet Union wanted to improve relations but not to concede on the three obstacles. Although the Chinese were prepared for normalization of state relations with the Soviet Union and mutually advantageous trade, they concluded that if they were to have leverage to get any Soviet movement in the three areas of

---

91. Gorbachev, *Pravda*, February 26, 1986. Emphasis in the original. This statement was greeted by applause.

92. Igor Rogachev replaced the much older and hard-line Mikhail Kapitsa as deputy foreign minister overseeing China affairs; Mikhail Titarenko replaced the older less flexible Mikhail Sladkovsky as the head of the Far Eastern Institute; and "new thinker" Georgy Shakhnazarov replaced the hard-line Oleg Rakhmanin as deputy chief of the Central Committee department for liaison with socialist countries.

contention, they would have to hold in check further steps to develop relations until there was some Soviet movement on them.

The Soviet leaders in turn clearly wished to improve relations with China, but at first they were not prepared to sacrifice security interests they believed were served by their alliance with Vietnam, continued military presence in Afghanistan (although as early as 1985 they were reviewing that commitment), and military deployment in the Far East including along the Chinese border.

In a major speech on Soviet policy in Asia and the Pacific at Vladivostok in mid-1986, Gorbachev referred to "a noticeable improvement" in relations with China "in recent years," and said, "I would like to confirm that the Soviet Union is prepared, at any time and at any level, in the most serious way to discuss with China questions of additional measures to create an atmosphere of good neighborliness."[93] He disclosed agreements reached or pending for cooperation in developing the Amur River basin and for constructing a rail link between Xinjiang and Kazakhstan (meeting a Chinese request), and he proposed cooperation in space exploration, including the training of Chinese astronauts. Most important, without referring to the Chinese "three conditions," he made gestures on two of them. First, he announced a token reduction of six regiments, about 10,000 men, from the 108,000-man Soviet contingent in Afghanistan, and he reaffirmed Soviet interest in a negotiated settlement that would permit complete Soviet military withdrawal.[94] He also disclosed that the Soviet Union and Mongolia were considering withdrawal of "a considerable number of Soviet troops from Mongolia."[95] Finally, he stated that the Soviet Union was prepared to discuss with China "concrete steps aimed at a balanced reduction of the level of ground forces" of the two countries along their border in the Far East.[96] On Kampuchea he could say little except to note that the problem "depends on the normalization of Chinese-Vietnamese relations" and that "we can only express our interest in seeing the border between these socialist states again becoming a border of peace and good neighborly relations,

---

93. "Speech by Comrade M. S. Gorbachev at a Ceremonial Meeting Devoted to the Presentation of the Order of Lenin to Vladivostok," *Pravda*, July 29, 1986.

94. Ibid. The withdrawals from Afghanistan were not only minor, they were offset by other reinforcements, so there was probably little if any net reduction.

95. Ibid. There had been about 65,000 Soviet troops in five divisions deployed in Mongolia since the beginning of the 1970s. The Soviets in January 1987 announced that, pursuant to Gorbachev's speech, they were withdrawing one division, which they did. As will be noted, they withdrew all forces by 1992.

96. Ibid. Soviet officials have told me that the Soviet Union had privately proposed mutual reductions in the early 1980s, but the Chinese were not prepared to agree. Tacit mutual reductions had occurred, but in 1986 the Chinese still did not wish to negotiate modestly reduced levels, as that would involve Chinese consent to the remaining Soviet levels of forces.

and a comradely dialogue renewed with unnecessary suspicions and distrust removed. The moment for this now seems propitious."[97]

The Chinese reaction to Gorbachev's overture was guarded and stressed the need to deal with the Vietnamese occupation of Kampuchea (Cambodia).[98]

The Soviets continued to seek an improvement in relations. Deputy Prime Minister Arkhipov had, without publicity and allegedly for acupuncture treatment, arrived in Beijing just before Gorbachev's speech. He remained there two weeks. Deputy Prime Minister Nikolai Talyzin, head of Gosplan, visited Beijing in September, principally to discuss economic relations. He proposed several areas of collaboration including the renovation of facilities built earlier with Soviet assistance, and new construction, including peaceful nuclear power stations.[99]

During 1986, the Soviet Union also broadened the area of consultations with China, especially in bilateral meetings on issues arising in Soviet-

---

97. Ibid. The Soviets wanted to see an improvement in Chinese-Vietnamese relations, even though Vietnam would then to some degree become less dependent on alliance with the USSR, and to see a settlement of the Kampuchean stalemate on virtually any basis. But in 1986 they still valued their alliance ties with Vietnam and the military base at Cam Ranh Bay too much to put pressure on the Vietnamese. A leading Soviet Far Eastern affairs scholar told me in early 1986 that the Chinese were more ready to resolve the issues than the Vietnamese, who remained "very belligerent," but that while the Soviets wanted to see Chinese-Vietnamese relations improve, they felt they had to defer to the Vietnamese.

98. The first public Chinese reaction was a statement by Foreign Minister Wu Xueqian on August 13, in which he said simply that the Chinese had "taken note" of Gorbachev's statement "made in Vladivostok (Haishenwai)," thus interjecting the Chinese name for the Chinese fishing village they claim existed on the site before the Russian colonization of the area. Wu also stressed the need still to overcome the three obstacles and in particular stressed Kampuchea. See "China and the World: Foreign Minister Wu Xueqian on Sino-Soviet Relations," *Beijing Review*, vol. 29, (August 18, 1986), p. 9.

   In September Deng Xiaoping questioned whether the Soviet leadership was firmly and unanimously set on improving relations. He also emphasized the obstacle of Kampuchea. But he said, for the first time, that if that obstacle were overcome, he would be happy to meet with Gorbachev. Xinhua, September 6, 1986, and "Deng on Sino-Soviet, Sino-U.S. Relations," *Beijing Review*, vol. 29 (September 15, 1986), p. 5.

   According to Deputy Foreign Minister Igor Rogachev, Deng Xiaoping had also earlier responded through the Romanians as an intermediary, making clear his readiness for a summit meeting but only if the Soviet Union had moved on the three obstacles. Cited from an interview with Rogachev by Don Oberdorfer, *The Turn: From the Cold War to a New Era, The United States and the Soviet Union, 1983-1990* (Poseidon Press, 1991), pp. 237–38.

99. Excerpts from a Politburo decision on August 25, 1986, detailing instructions for Talyzin and making very clear the broader purposes of cultivating Sino-Soviet relations were made public in April 1991. See "Relations with China: The Beginning of a Turn (Documents from 1986)," *Izvestiya TsK KPSS* (Bulletin of the Central Committee of the CPSU), no. 4 (April 1991), pp. 93–95.

American arms control negotiations. (The United States had been consulting with China intermittently since the early 1970s, and systematically since 1984.)

In the semiannual deputy foreign ministerial meetings in October 1986, the new Soviet representative, Deputy Foreign Minister Igor Rogachev, did obtain Chinese consent to resume the border negotiations broken off after the Soviet intervention in Afghanistan seven years before. He was reportedly treated, however, to a vigorous Chinese onslaught on the issue of Kampuchea.[100]

Unexpected and unintended difficulties continued to arise from time to time. On July 12, a border incident left one Chinese guard dead, but both countries sought to play down the incident. Neither published the fact, and when it leaked out in the Japanese press a month later both Chinese and Soviet officials called it "an isolated incident" and an accidental encounter.[101] In September, an unarmed Soviet submarine-launched ballistic missile went far off course and apparently landed in Manchuria.

In October 1986, the Soviet Union for the first time in twenty years ceased jamming Russian-language radio broadcasts beamed by Radio Beijing to the Soviet Union. (China had stopped jamming Soviet broadcasts in Chinese in 1982.) Soon after, the Soviet Union ceased propaganda broadcasts to China by its own Radio Peace and Progress and closed the last remaining clandestine radio broadcasting to China.

In February 1987 the talks on disputed border areas began, resuming negotiations that had been in abeyance since 1969. Rogachev's agreement in principle had probably been given after Soviet indications of readiness to make concessions on the issue, and in January Gorbachev had (at the same time he announced withdrawal of one division from Mongolia) publicly declared that the Soviet Union would accept the principle of the Thalweg (mid-channel) border division, meaning most of the disputed river islands would go to China.

On the whole, however, Gorbachev's Vladivostok initiatives were slow to be picked up by China (and by other Asian states). On the first anniversary of his speech, Gorbachev sought to reactivate discussion especially of arms control and confidence-building measures through a well-publicized interview with an Indonesian newspaper, *Merdeka*.[102] The most important new position that Gorbachev advanced was an important unilateral Soviet concession: he agreed to eliminate all Soviet intermediate-range missiles in Asia in the Intermediate-

100. The Italian communist newspaper published a leaked report, attributed to conversations with Chinese and Soviet sources, of tough exchanges between Rogachev and Qian Qichen. See S. Ginzberg, "How Negotiations Stalled on Cambodia," *L'Unita*, October 15, 1986.

101. See Daniel Southerland, "China Calls Border Clash an 'Isolated Incident'" *Washington Post*, August 24, 1986, p. A23.

102. See "Answers of M. S. Gorbachev to Questions of the Indonesian Newspaper 'Merdeka,'" *Pravda*, July 23, 1987.

range Nuclear Forces (INF) Treaty being negotiated with the United States. Previously in the negotiation, focused on Europe, the United States had agreed that the Soviet Union could retain one hundred missile warheads in Asia. The treaty, eliminating all intermediate-range missiles, was signed in December 1987, and the missiles were subsequently destroyed.

By the end of the year Gorbachev again floated the idea of a Sino-Soviet summit, but was rebuffed. The Chinese wanted to see more movement on overcoming the three obstacles.

Gorbachev was beginning to face some restlessness from conservative party leaders in the Soviet Union at his generous concessions on various international issues. By 1988 many in the Soviet leadership believed that Sino-Soviet relations were sufficiently normalized that one-sided concessions on the three obstacles were not justified. Gorbachev, however, had very good, even compelling, reasons to move in all three areas even if China had not posed them as conditions to further improvement in bilateral relations.[103]

In February 1988 Gorbachev announced the goal of withdrawing all Soviet troops from Afghanistan in one year. In April successful international negotiations over Afghanistan confirmed such withdrawal by February 1989, and by that date the last Soviet troops left.[104] That obstacle was essentially removed.

As early as October 1986, in the semiannual consultations, the Soviet side had for the first time agreed to discuss the issue of Vietnamese troops in Kampuchea among "regional issues." The Chinese had stressed the Vietnamese-Kampuchean issue as the "key" obstacle throughout 1987 and into 1988. The Soviets agreed to direct discussions in a special meeting in late August 1988, and though no agreements were reached the Chinese were sufficiently impressed with Soviet seriousness that they agreed to the next step toward a summit, a visit by Foreign Minister Qian Qichen to Moscow in December.

In May 1988 Hanoi announced withdrawal of 50,000 troops, about half of their total, from Kampuchea by the end of the year, with subsequent further reductions promised.

Gorbachev resumed a full-scale effort to move forward Asian, including Chinese, relations in a second major speech on Asian affairs at Krasnoyarsk in central Siberia on September 16, 1988. He again expressed readiness to move toward a summit meeting with China. Also, as in the earlier Vladivostok speech of 1986 and *Merdeka* interview of 1987, Gorbachev outlined several broad areas for Asian-Pacific cooperation, including regional economic and security measures. While repeating in more general terms his earlier call for an

---

103. See the discussion in chapter 15.

104. See the discussion of Afghanistan in chapter 15. China ceased providing support to the *mujahedin* in Afghanistan as soon as the Soviet troops had withdrawn.

Asian security arrangement, he now proposed beginning with tripartite discussions of the Soviet Union, China, and the United States.[105]

In early December 1988, in his address to the UN General Assembly, Gorbachev announced a major two-year unilateral arms and troop reduction program. While largely focused on Europe, it also included a substantial reduction of twelve army divisions and 200,000 men in Asia, including reductions along the Chinese border. He also announced that "most" (later specified as 75 percent) of the Soviet troops remaining in Mongolia would be withdrawn by the end of 1990.[106]

Thus by December 1988 the Soviet Union had taken major steps to meet the Chinese on all three of the obstacles to improving relations. The Chinese reciprocated. When Foreign Minister Qian Qichen came to Moscow that month, in the first visit by a Chinese foreign minister since 1957, he brought authorization allowing a joint announcement in Moscow of a visit by Gorbachev for a summit meeting in Beijing in the first half of 1989. When Shevardnadze made a return visit to Beijing in February, the date for the summit was announced for May 15.

In the interim between Shevardnadze's visit and the summit meeting, the last Soviet troops left Afghanistan, Soviet troops began to leave Mongolia, and Hanoi announced that all remaining Vietnamese troops would be out of Cambodia by the end of September 1989. The three obstacles were essentially now overcome. Other factors that had led to a serious rift between the two former socialist allies long before these three obstacles had arisen had also been overtaken by time, events, and important changes in the two countries in their outlook and policies over the three decades since the last Sino-Soviet summit. The ideological gulf that had converted an initial presumptive solidarity into bitter rivalry and perceived direct challenges had faded and become less relevant, as each had turned to dealing with its own national problems and to acceptance of membership in the existing world community rather than to competition in efforts to lead a "world revolution."

Thus in their meetings, their joint communiqué, and their internal commentaries both did see, and did regard as a significant achievement, that Gorbachev's summit marked "the normalization of interstate relations between the Soviet Union and China."[107] Although that may seem a modest accomplishment, it brought to an end three decades (or more) of often tense, and never "normal," relations. The communiqué emphasized that "the normalization of

---

105. "Time for Action, Time for Practical Work, Speech of M. S. Gorbachev in Kransnoyarsk," *Pravda*, September 18, 1988.

106. "M. S. Gorbachev's Speech at the United Nations," *Pravda*, December 8, 1988.

107. "Joint Soviet-Chinese Communiqué," *Pravda*, May 19, 1989. (Also, "USSR-PRC Joint Communiqué on Summit Issued," TASS, in FBIS, *Soviet Union*, May 18, 1989, pp. 16–18.)

Soviet-Chinese relations is not directed against third countries and does not infringe upon the interests of third countries," a point repeated by both sides (and conveyed earlier to the United States by both sides). Both countries also abjured any ambitions or claims to "hegemony" in the Asian-Pacific region or anywhere in the world.

Not mentioned in the official communiqué, but noted in speeches and press commentary, was the parallel normalization of relations between the communist parties of the two countries.[108] Each country, and party, was watching with interest and some concern the reform program being carried out in the other (as well as those under way in Eastern Europe). They did include in the communiqué the comment that "the sides consider it useful for the two countries to exchange information and experience in the field of building socialism, restructuring and reform, as well as opinions on issues of mutual interest that concern bilateral relations and the international situation." And, to acknowledge differences, they noted that "disagreements on these or other matters should not impede the development of relations between the two sides."[109]

In the international sphere, there were no new agreements or steps, but there was reaffirmation of ongoing bilateral efforts to resolve border issues, reduce armed forces along the border, and develop economic and other ties. There was also reaffirmation of efforts to resolve regional conflicts, especially in Cambodia, and a somewhat surprising Chinese agreement to a Soviet proposal to call on the United Nations to take an increased role in security matters such as resolving regional conflicts, and for the United Nations and other international forums to deal with "the solution of global economic, social, demographic and ecological problems, crucial for preserving and developing world civilization, and for the quality of life."[110] Nonetheless, on the whole there was a general underlying divergence in perceptions of the world; the new thinking under Gorbachev did not find a parallel in Chinese policy.

The most dramatic, and of course unexpected and unwelcome, aspect of the summit, stealing some of its thunder, was the presence of a million young Chinese in the streets protesting China's domestic policies. Gorbachev naturally avoided direct contact with the demonstrators and minimized comment on the affair, but in his public statements he did reaffirm the need for democratic participation while counseling patience and discipline. The Chinese leaders had to alter the program of summit events slightly, and they waited until the day after Gorbachev had departed the country before declaring martial law on

---

108. For example, see the authoritative unsigned editorial "A Totally New Level: Or the Results of M. S. Gorbachev's Visit to the PRC," *Pravda*, May 21, 1989; and less prominently in the editorial "Mission of Peace and Good-Neighborliness," *Izvestiya*, May 20, 1989.

109. "Joint Soviet-Chinese Communiqué," *Pravda*, May 19, 1989.

110. Ibid.

May 19. A massive and bloody crackdown followed in the Tiananmen Square massacre on June 3-4.

The Gorbachev summit in retrospect became the high point of Sino-Soviet relations, consolidating a major advance from the past. It did not, however, form the intended foundation for new advances beyond normalization of relations. This was inevitable despite discreet official silence from Moscow on the crackdown and despite continuing contacts and negotiations. The growing Chinese interest in Soviet reform was checked and led to a Chinese campaign against "peaceful evolution" and a return to emphasis on greater self-reliance and stiffened political orthodoxy. (Peaceful evolution meant not only Western concepts of gradual change to a market economy but also the policies of *perestroika*.) Chinese economic reform did, however, continue. This new Chinese line dampened enthusiasm for any great increase in people-to-people contacts. Following the sudden collapse of communist rule in Eastern Europe in November, this Chinese disenchantment with the failure of communist reform, and the growing internal difficulties within the Soviet Union in 1989-91, led to a new barrier to both popular and party ties, even as state relations continued to develop normally.

Thus the period from May 1989 to August 1991 marked a new phase in relations, though not quite what had been anticipated. After some hiatus, official relations picked up with the visit of Prime Minister Li Peng to Moscow in April 1990 (again, a first in twenty-six years). Li Peng's visit saw the signing of a broad ten-year agreement on economic, scientific, and technical cooperation, and a first agreement on cooperation in space research. It also led to an agreement (apparently weak on specific commitments) on reduction of troops along the border. The Soviet Union and Mongolia had, the month before, agreed that all Soviet troops would be out of the country by the end of 1992.

General Xu Xin, deputy chief of the General Staff, accompanied Li to Moscow, and in meetings with Soviet military leaders arranged to begin regular exchange visits of military leaders. The first independent military delegation in thirty years was one led by Soviet Rear Admiral Vladimir Khuzhokov, visiting Beijing in June. In July, a delegation of Soviet military veterans of military assistance missions in China in the 1930s, service in Manchuria in 1945, and military advisers in the 1940s and 1950s, visited China. Other reciprocal visits followed, leading to visits in 1991 by the respective chiefs of staff, General Mikhail Moiseyev and General Chi Haotian. Marshal Dmitry Yazov became the first (and last) Soviet minister of defense ever to visit China, in May 1991.[111]

---

111. One analyst has sought to make the case that Soviet military and political conservatives wanted in 1990–91 to build a Soviet-Chinese alliance against the United States and the West and claimed that Marshal Yazov on his visit to Beijing in May 1991 "reportedly" called for such a Sino-Soviet alliance against the West. See Hung P. Nguyen, "Russia and China: The Genesis of an Eastern Rapallo," *Asian Survey*, vol. 33 (March 1993),

No less important were meetings and visits in 1990 and 1991 by senior military and military industrial specialists pursuing China's new interest in purchasing Soviet weaponry, in particular advanced fighter aircraft.[112]

By 1991 relations had stabilized at a level that led to a summit meeting in Moscow reciprocating the visit by Gorbachev two years earlier. In preparation, Deputy General Secretary of the CPSU Vladimir Ivashko visited Beijing in February and Foreign Minister Aleksandr Bessmertnykh in April. Then on May 15-19, 1991, General Secretary Jiang Zemin visited Moscow—thirty-four years had passed since the last visit by a Chinese leader, Mao Zedong in 1957.

The official communiqué on the meeting called it "a continuation of the summit meeting between M. S. Gorbachev and Deng Xiaoping in May 1989" (excising any reference to Zhao Ziyang).[113] As the communiqué put it, both sides "highly assess the important significance of the normalization of Soviet-Chinese relations" and "expressed satisfaction that a new page is being opened in relations" between them. Besides reconfirming the usual range of political, economic, technical, and military contacts and ties, they agreed that despite differences in their internal development, "there are no universal patterns for carrying out reforms or for implementing *perestroika*." They also agreed that reforms were "necessary to reveal the potential of socialism," but that an important condition of reform was "the maintenance of stability in the state and society," and of course that "each people has the right to decide the affairs of its own country in keeping with its specific conditions."[114]

In international affairs, the two states also promised to "continue to foster the process of normalization of the world situation," especially "to make efforts together with all states of the world to institute a new world order."[115]

---

pp. 285–301. Although a few conservatives may have thought in such terms, it is unlikely that Yazov did.

112. The most senior were First Deputy Prime Minister Yury D. Maslyukov, chairman of Gosplan, and Deputy Prime Minister Igor S. Belousov, chairman of the Military-Industrial Commission.

These discussions, continued by the successor Russian government, led in 1992 to delivery of twenty-four Su-27 fighter aircraft, with training of Chinese air force pilots in Russia, and by the end of that year to contracts for military purchases totaling $1 billion.

Chinese interest, particularly in acquiring advanced fighter aircraft, was stimulated by the abandonment in the spring of 1990 of efforts to strike a deal for upgrading Chinese fighters with advanced U.S. technology.

113. Gorbachev's official host in 1989 had been President Yang Shangkun, and the senior real summit partner Deng Xiaoping, but his nominal counterpart was General Secretary Zhao Ziyang, who had been dismissed and replaced by Jiang Zemin after the Tiananmen Square crisis.

114. "Joint Soviet-Chinese Communiqué," *Pravda*, May 20, 1991 (see also FBIS, *Soviet Union*, May 21, 1991, pp. 16–19, slightly different translation).

115. Ibid.

There were few concrete agreements, the most important being an agreement on most of the eastern section of the Sino-Soviet border, the 4,300 kilometers from the Mongolian border to the Korean border, signed by the foreign ministers on May 16. But the focus was precisely on consolidating and furthering the overall normalization reached in 1989. Gorbachev, in a dinner speech, emphasized that the basis for relations was intrinsic, but also that good relations contributed to international stability, and in a renunciation of triangular diplomacy he said Sino-Soviet relations "are not some kind of a card in a geopolitical game. No!"[116]

The challenge to the new normalization at the end of the 1980s came not from new geopolitical maneuvering by either country, or by any other. Three months later came the August coup attempt in Moscow, and by the end of the year the dissolution of the Soviet Union. There are many indications that the Chinese leaders would have welcomed success for the coup, but they avoided premature commitment and relations were not directly affected. The swift collapse of the Communist Party of the Soviet Union, and soon of the Soviet Union itself, was a serious shock. The Chinese leaders were more than ever convinced that they had been correct to combine economic reform with a continuing tight hold on political orthodoxy, and also that they had acted correctly in suppressing anarchy at Tiananmen Square.

Internal Chinese documents, including minutes of a Politburo meeting on August 28, that have been published in Hong Kong confirm other indications of strong Chinese criticism of Gorbachev's policies, regrets that the coup failed, hostility to Boris Yeltsin, and determination to guard against dangerous internal Chinese tendencies and influences from the Soviet Union (and, later, from Russia and the other successor states).[117]

China promptly recognized Russia and the other eleven successor states to the Soviet Union on December 27, 1991. For most purposes, Russia as the continuing neighboring great power is the successor, and interstate relations have continued on a normal basis (there are of course no longer interparty relations). The border agreement signed in May 1991 by the Soviet government was ratified in February 1992 by the Russian government. Former Soviet Deputy Foreign Minister Igor Rogachev was named the new Russian ambassador to China, and that was well received. By March 1992 Russian Foreign Minister Andrei Kozyrev visited Beijing, in the first of a series of high-level visits, followed by President Boris Yeltsin in December 1992.

---

116. "Opening a New Page," *Pravda*, May 16, 1991.

117. "CPC Internal Documents View USSR Changes," FBIS, *China*, February 7, 1992, pp. 5–17; full texts of He Po-shih, "What Does CPC Say Internally in Wake of Changing Situation in Soviet Union?" *Tangtai* (The Present Age), Hong Kong, no. 10 (January 15, 1992), pp. 41–52. The authenticity of these documents has not been challenged.
   On a visit to China in February 1992, the author's discussions with Chinese specialists on Soviet affairs also confirmed these general outlines.

At the same time, China has been concerned over the appearance of independent states in Kazakhstan and Kyrgyzstan that may prove powerful attractions to kin living in neighboring Xinjiang province of China.[118] Border area military reductions talks with the Soviet Union, last meeting in November-December 1991, reconvened in March-April 1992 with a Russian delegation, but by the next session in July-August 1992 and thereafter China faced a joint delegation of representatives of Russia, Kazakhstan, Kyrgyzstan, and Tajikistan; all shared the common inherited border with China, and they decided to provide a single joint delegation. By late 1992 a general agreement had been reached. Nonetheless, unresolved territorial disputes remain on the borders of Kyrgyzstan and Tajikistan with China's Xinjiang province.

Despite the new complexities in Central Asia, and a new ideological difference between communist China and noncommunist Russia, since the end of 1991 Russia has succeeded the Soviet Union on the foundation of the relationship that had been established with China. And after three troubled decades, the Soviet Union and China by 1991 had normalized their relations as both came to see that their relationship was a mix of common and competing bilateral interests, without a broader framework of either alliance or hostility. The course of relations in the future will of course depend on developments in both countries as well as between them, and in the broader geopolitical environment, above all in the northern Asian-Pacific region.

## Japan and East Asia

Increasingly, relations among the United States, the Soviet Union, and China became part of the action on a broader Asian-Pacific arena rather than a geopolitical triangle. The most important additional actor has been Japan. Although U.S.-Japanese relations have remained close, Japan developed its relations with China after 1978, and Soviet-Japanese relations were unfrozen under Gorbachev, although full normalization was not achieved.

As China launched its independent foreign policy in 1982, within and beyond the strategic triangle, one direction it turned was toward Japan. In November 1983 Chinese-Japanese relations reached a new level with a visit by General Secretary Hu Yaobang to Japan, followed by a return visit to China by Prime Minister Yasuhiro Nakasone in March 1984. During Hu's visit, there was discussion of the Soviet deployment of SS-20 missiles in Asia, threatening both

---

118. There were reports of violent demonstrations, suppressed, in Xinjiang in October 1991. Moreover, emigre Kazakhs and Uigurs in the two neighboring now independent republics are again becoming active. There are about 6 million Uigurs (related to the Uzbeks), 1 million Kazakhs, and 140,000 Kyrgyz in Xinjiang.

China and Japan.[119] But while Chinese-Japanese relations were not tense, they were also not active in the 1980s.

Soviet leaders in the early 1980s had made some overtures to Japan to improve relations, notably on the occasions of the Twenty-sixth Party Congress in February 1981 and in Brezhnev's speech in Tashkent in March 1982—both better remembered for the parallel approaches to China. But Japan joined the United States in economic sanctions against the USSR after Afghanistan and Poland in 1980-82 and did not respond to the vague Soviet overtures. The Soviet Union showed no readiness to deal with the one subject of interest to the Japanese—the disputed islands north of Japan.

In New Delhi, on the occasion of the funeral of Indian Prime Minister Indira Gandhi in November 1984, Prime Ministers Tikhonov and Nakasone met briefly. More significant was a meeting under similar circumstances between Nakasone and the new Soviet leader Gorbachev in Moscow in March 1985. While the Soviets continued to be harshly critical of Japan (with more than the usual number of commentaries in 1985 on the fortieth anniversary of the end of World War II), and especially critical of military ties to the United States, by year's end agreement had been reached for an exchange of visits by foreign ministers in the year ahead.

A visit to Japan by Foreign Minister Shevardnadze in mid-January 1986 was the first at that level in a decade.[120] Though considered mutually useful, the visit did not break any new substantive ground in relations. It may, however, have been regarded by the Gorbachev leadership as a reconnaissance of possibilities for the future, as well as a step toward general improvement of relations. Gorbachev, in his major address on Soviet policy toward Asia and the Pacific in July 1986, referred to Japan as "a power of paramount importance." He said that "signs of a change for the better" were appearing in relations with Japan, and he not only referred to the visits by the foreign ministers (Japanese Foreign Minister Shintaro Abe had visited Moscow in May 1986, reciprocating Shevardnadze's visit) but also disclosed that a Soviet-Japanese summit meeting was "on the agenda."[121]

Soviet-Japanese relations, however, remained through the 1980s (and beyond) constrained by the difficult dispute over the four islands north of Hokkaido, considered by the Japanese as their "northern territories" (as they were before 1945), and by the Soviets as part of the Kuril Islands obtained by

119. Xinhua, November 30, 1983, citing Chinese Foreign Minister Wu Xueqian in FBIS, *China*, December 1, 1983, p. D3.

120. Gromyko, who had last visited Japan in 1976, generally regarded that country as little more than a political-strategic appendage of the United States; the change occurred after his move from the foreign ministry.

121. *Pravda*, July 29, 1986. The Japanese soon thereafter announced that an invitation had been extended for a visit by Gorbachev to Japan in January 1987, although the visit did not occur until April 1991.

wartime agreement with the United States and occupied by the Soviet Union in August-September 1945. Moreover Japan renounced claims to the Kuril Islands in its 1951 San Francisco Peace Treaty (even though the Soviet Union did not sign that treaty). The Soviets saw the territories primarily as of strategic significance to their naval bastion in the Sea of Okhotsk, an economic asset (fishing and minerals), and politically important as an element of the overall "final" territorial settlement in Asia and Europe after World War II.[122]

Without reviewing here the merits of the Soviet and Japanese positions, it should be noted that each has a case in light of history, equity, and international law—although the ultimate resolution of the issue will no doubt have to involve a political accommodation.[123] The Japanese leadership began to harden its position by courting previously apathetic public reaction in Japan with a rising campaign in the 1970s and 1980s, including the inauguration of the first of an annual Northern Territories Day on February 7, 1981, at the height of East-West confrontation.[124]

The first sign of slightly warming relations was Gorbachev's Vladivostok speech, shortly after which some Japanese were permitted in August 1986, for the first time in a decade, to visit family burial shrines on the disputed islands (carefully balanced by a contrived visit of Russians to the graves of some deceased Russian visitors in Japan). Moscow also sent a new and capable envoy to Tokyo in July, Ambassador Nikolai Solovyev.

The path to better relations remained difficult, with new problems arising. In the summer of 1987 when Japan agreed to participate in research under the aegis of the American SDI program, the Soviet Union protested, and the image of U.S.-Japanese military partnership against Soviet interests was reinvigorated. In August, two Japanese (a diplomat and a business executive) in Moscow were caught in espionage and expelled. The Japanese retaliated in kind. In December a Soviet reconnaissance bomber aircraft was fired upon

---

122. On September 2, 1945, the day the Soviets completed occupation of the islands, Stalin declared that "henceforth, the Kuril Islands . . . shall not serve as a means to cut off the Soviet Union from the ocean or as a base for a Japanese attack on our Far East." "Address of Comrade I. V. Stalin to the People," *Pravda*, September 3, 1945. On February 2, 1946, the Soviet Union formally annexed the islands, retroactive to September 20, 1945.

123. In a word, there is a strong case for Russia to relinquish the islands of Shikotan and the Habomais in a peace settlement, but the Japanese case for regaining the southern Kuril Islands of Kunashir and Iturup (Etorofu) is weak. That is no doubt why Japan has shied away from turning the issue over to the International Court of Justice—a trump card the Russians may yet play. For further discussion see Raymond L. Garthoff, "A Diplomatic History of the Dispute," in Vladimir Ivanov, ed., *Moscow and Tokyo after the Cold War: The Territorial Dispute Revisited* (Washington: U.S. Institute of Peace, 1993).

124. February 7 was the date of signature of the Treaty of Shimoda in 1855, the first Russian-Japanese treaty, which had set the border between the Kuril Islands of Iturup and Urup—where the Japanese would now like to reestablish the border.

when it intruded over Okinawa, a more vigorous Japanese response than usual, but there was also an unusual Soviet acknowledgment, explanation of navigational error (notable even if contrived), and apology.

Gorbachev continued his overtures for improved relations, in particular in his Krasnoyarsk speech in September 1988 (although qualified by criticism of the "persistent buildup" in military cooperation with the United States). In December 1988 Shevardnadze again visited Japan, and on this occasion for the first time he accepted recognition of a territorial dispute, and the two sides agreed to establish a working group on a peace treaty (and another on discussion of Cambodia and other regional conflicts). When Foreign Minister Sosuke Uno paid a return visit to Moscow in May 1989, Shevardnadze subtly indicated that the U.S.-Japan Security Treaty was no longer seen as a bar to improving relations. In November Aleksandr Yakovlev visited Japan on an advance probe for a visit by Gorbachev. He spoke vaguely about seeking some "third way"—compromise—on the islands.

A new and complicating element entered the picture with a visit to Japan by Boris Yeltsin in January 1990, during which he proposed a long-term (fifteen to twenty years) five-stage gradual resolution of the issue of the disputed islands, by "compromise," although in effect he was holding out the prospect of gradual Russian concessions. He followed this with a visit to the southern Kurils in August, by which time the issue was hotly disputed in Soviet public debate.

Some frictions remained. For example, apart from frequent Soviet coast guard detentions and fining of Japanese fishing poachers near the disputed islands (which are an especially rich fishing area), Soviet seizure in May 1990 of a flotilla of ocean-going North Korean fishing boats illegally fishing in Soviet waters further north led to the discovery that a number of them were Japanese ships and crews who by collusion were flying the North Korean flag. Nonetheless, in May Foreign Minister Taro Nakayama told the Diet that the Soviet threat (long hyped by the Japanese government) was "receding." And in September the Japan Defense Agency's annual White Paper on defense dropped the long-standard characterization of Soviet military activity as a "threat."[125] In September 1990 Shevardnadze visited Tokyo for the third time, to prepare the way for a summit meeting. In December the first Japanese astronaut entered outer space as a passenger on a Soviet space flight.

Gorbachev's summit meeting in Tokyo finally came in mid-April 1991, nearly five years after he had begun to push for it. It was a success, if only by virtue of coming about. But it was not a great success and did not decisively advance relations, owing to a continuing stalemate over the disputed islands. In Japan, the very few voices (notably a former deputy prime minister, Shin

---

125. This was agreed to by the Japan Defense Agency only after government assurances that dropping all reference to a Soviet threat would not be used to justify further reductions in defense appropriations.

Kanemaru) who attempted to modify the Japanese position were brought into line. Japan was very firm on reacquiring all the disputed islands,[126] and though in early 1991 the Japanese evinced some readiness to be flexible on the timing of reversions, they showed no flexibility on demanding Soviet acknowledgment of Japanese sovereignty over them. Also by the time that the question of international economic assistance for the Soviet Union arose in 1990–91, Japan had set a firm policy: no economic aid or investment until the issue of the "northern territories" was settled on its terms.

Meanwhile, debate in the Soviet Union was affected by this Japanese stance. Some were attracted to the prospect of obtaining Japanese economic rewards for "a few rocks in the ocean," while others in patriotic terms denounced on principle any "sell-out" of Russian patrimony and land for Japanese gold and criticized willingness to give up a permanent treasure and legacy for at best ephermal short-term gains (they also questioned whether the promised rewards would really materialize). Rumors circulated in early 1991 that Gorbachev had already signed a deal to give up the islands for $200 billion. These unfounded rumors were denied, but they helped to poison the atmosphere when in March the ruling Liberal Democratic Party leader Ichiro Ozawa visited Moscow and did discuss the economic assistance to be expected if the island dispute was resolved. Rumors were printed (and denied) that he had offered $26–$28 billion (the figures were from a Liberal Democratic Party study of what investment might be undertaken).

The nationwide referendum in March 1991 on maintaining a union was accompanied by a vote taken in the territory of the disputed islands on the question of their cession to Japan. The vote in the district composed of all the disputed islands except Iturup was 68.8 percent opposed, 21.5 percent in favor, and 7.8 percent "other" views.[127] (In the district composed of the northern Kurils and Iturup, 87 percent voted against.) This vote, though having no legal effect (as it turned out, neither did the national vote on the union), showed the unsurprising opposition of the majority—as well as the more surprising fact that more than one-fifth of the population in this economically depressed area were ready to take a chance on Japanese rule, a proportion that increased substantially in the next few years.

---

126. Usually the disputed islands are referred to as four: Iturup (Etorofu, in Japanese), Kunashir (Kunashiri), Shikotan (or Shpanberg to some Russian nationalists, for the name of an early Russian explorer; Shikotan-to in Japanese), and the Habomai group (actually five small islands between Shikotan and Hokkaido, Japan). The population of these islands totaled about 17,000 Japanese civilians; they were expelled to Japan in 1947–49, and the Russian population there now for the last fifty years numbered about 25,000 civilians (and 10,000 military) in 1991, of whom about 7,000 civilians and 1,000 military were on Shikotan, with no civilians and only two small border guard posts on the Habomai group.

127. The voting results were cited in Vitaly Guly and Valery Sharov, "The Southern Kurils: The View from Two Shores," *Literaturnaya gazeta* (Literary Gazette), March 20, 1991.

As a result of the increasing internal tension, and rising voice of the Russian republic, Gorbachev and Shevardnadze not only decided not to move on the issue of the islands, but also to include Russian republic and local Far Eastern political leaders in the official summit delegation. Russian Foreign Minister Andrei Kozyrev, and Sakhalin (and Kurils) Governor Valentin P. Fedorov, were among those included.[128]

Thus the long-awaited Gorbachev summit marked only a very limited step toward normalization of relations.[129] And in effect it closed the book on Japanese-Soviet relations. No new steps were taken, although debate continued apace in the Soviet Union, until the union dissolved. Russia then acquired the issue and the daunting task of seeking a resolution. President Yeltsin, by the time he canceled a planned visit to Tokyo in September 1992, faced much the same dilemma as Gorbachev. There was no "Yeltsin" over his shoulder, but there was a wide array of political critics at home, as well as an uncompromising Japan.

The Japanese were slow in 1987–89 to see the opportunities presented by Gorbachev's new thinking. By the time they did, they were overbearing and overconfident. Although they correctly saw Soviet (and later Russian) economic decline and vulnerability, and growing need for Japanese economic assistance, they failed to see the predictable greater difficulty for any leader in Moscow to take a step bound to be politically risky and costly as public opinion mounted in an increasingly democratic environment.[130] What Gorbachev could have done in 1987–88 he could no longer do in 1990–91, nor could Yeltsin in 1992–93 (leading him to postpone twice a visit first planned for September 1992 until October 1993).

As noted earlier, the United States—unwisely—entered the Japanese-Soviet (Russian) dispute at the Moscow summit in July 1991, supporting the Japanese stand.[131] While this support earned Japanese gratitude, it was resented in the Soviet Union as American pressure at a time of Soviet weakness and vulnerability.[132] And it certainly did not help Japan and the Soviet Union

---

128. Fedorov stridently led the opposition to any territorial concession, while seeking some collaborative Japanese investment. Although included in the Tokyo summit delegation, he left in a huff and returned home early because he was not included in some talks between Gorbachev and Prime Minister Toshiki Kaifu.

129. Gorbachev's visit to Japan was April 16–19, the expected height of the cherry blossom season, but in 1991 the blossoms came early and by the time of the visit were largely gone—seen by the Japanese as a fitting symbol of the disappointing outcome.

130. For a detailed analysis of Japanese perceptions and policy, see Gilbert Rozman, *Japan's Response to the Gorbachev Era, 1985–1991: A Rising Superpower Views a Declining One* (Princeton University Press, 1991).

131. See chapter 11. President Bush had even earlier raised in passing the question of the disputed islands at Malta in December 1989 and Washington in June 1990, to no avail, but he went further—and went public—at the Moscow summit.

132. Even in a liberal pro-Western Soviet newspaper, after noting that Bush had unexpectedly raised the issue in his first public speech after arrival, the commentators concluded,

advance toward resolution of the issue. Indeed, in part it reflected residual American geopolitical "old thinking." For forty years the United States had supported the Japanese as the U.S. ally against a Soviet adversary—and, at the same time, helped to keep alive a source of tension between Japan and the Soviet Union that kept Japan dependent on the United States. In the new world order it was in the American interest to see the dispute resolved and good relations established between Japan and Russia. Reinforcing an overbearing Japanese stand while pressuring a weak but proud Soviet (Russian) leadership seeking a compromise was not the way to help resolve the problem. Yet the Bush, and later the Clinton, administrations continued to support the Japanese positions.

In contrast, Britain, France, and Germany avoided identification with the Japanese position on the disputed islands and turned down Japan's repeated efforts to get endorsement for their position from the European Community and the Group of 7. The most Japan could obtain was support for a peaceful negotiated resolution of the issue, which of course was also the Soviet (later Russian) position.

Little need be said of U.S.-Japanese relations, save that the political and military alliance remained very strong, while growing economic competition led to new frictions throughout the period. This also led to some impingement on security cooperation, particularly when Congress sought to place sharp curbs on collaboration in sharing U.S. military technology in 1989. Also despite the American attempt to support Japan on the dispute with the Soviet Union over the islands, a gap did arise over Western efforts to assist the Soviet Union and Russia and the other republics in their difficult transition from centralized socialism to a market economy and political democracy. In contrast to the efforts by the United States and the Western European powers, Japan remained aloof and unprepared to shoulder its share of the burden in support of a common objective. It gave priority to its particularist interest in acquiring the islands.

Besides new relationships among the Soviet Union, China, the United States, and Japan, the four powers also interacted in new ways with their neighbors in East Asia, especially North and South Korea, and Vietnam, and to a more peripheral extent with Mongolia and the countries of the Association of South East Asian Nations (ASEAN).

---

"This fact shows that Bush came to Moscow not simply as the president of the United States but also as the fully empowered representative of the seven largest Western powers that lay claim to leadership in the world today, and that President Bush is prepared to put pressure on the Soviet Union in fields that affect the interest not only of America but also of its allies." A. Vasilyev and S. Ivanov, "G. Bush: 'Wonderful Day, Wonderful City'," *Komsomolskaya pravda* (Komsomol Truth), July 31, 1991. See also S. Kondrashov, "Political Observer's Opinion: What Did George Bush Take Away? And What Did He Leave Behind?" *Izvestiya*, August 3, 1991.

North Korea had for years been closer to China than the Soviet Union, though quite independent. But in 1978–80 it observed with concern the Chinese rapprochement with the United States and Japan, and with greater satisfaction, saw the contrary turn in Soviet relations with the United States. The North Koreans were also moved by the U.S. decision in 1981 to supply F-16 fighter bombers to South Korea to seek more modern aircraft than its aging MiG-21s, stimulating a competition between the Soviet Union and China over supplying arms. The Soviets were reluctant to provide more advanced aircraft, and the Chinese offered their F-7s (Chinese-version MiG-21s). In June 1983 the heir-apparent in North Korea, Kim Jong-Il, visited China with much fanfare.

The Soviets then moved to head off closer North Korean–Chinese ties. The veteran North Korean leader, Kim Il-Sung, for the first time in twenty-three years visited Moscow in May–July 1984. Soon after, in exchange for Soviet overflight rights (for reconnaissance, and flights to Vietnam), the Soviets agreed to provide two squadrons of MiG-23s. The Soviet Union was by this time the largest trading partner of North Korea. In October 1986 Kim again visited Moscow.

Kim Il-Sung soon—for the first time in five years—also visited Beijing, in May 1987. The Sino-Soviet competition for influence continued, but with both powers disinclined to give North Korea more than minimal support.

Both the Soviet Union and China were, however, for the first time balancing their relations with North Korea with growing ties to South Korea. China participated in the Asian Games in Seoul in 1986, and the Seoul Olympic Games in 1988, despite North Korean opposition. Chinese trade with South Korea also began to expand. The Soviet Union too was increasing its trade with the south and in April 1989 opened a trade mission in Seoul. Soviet historians began to acknowledge for the first time that North Korea had invaded South Korea in 1950.

In June 1990, during his visit to the United States, Gorbachev met with South Korean President Roh Tae Woo, and three months later in September the Soviet Union and Republic of Korea established diplomatic relations. China, rather than seeking to bind North Korea to itself more closely, moved along the same path as had the Soviet Union and also established diplomatic relations with South Korea in August 1992.

Meanwhile intermittent North Korean–South Korean contacts settled into a series of meetings of prime ministers beginning in September 1990. Both Koreas entered the United Nations in September 1991, a step previously blocked by North Korea and its Soviet and Chinese allies. Finally, the high-level North and South Korean meetings led in December 1991 to signing the Treaty on Reconciliation, Nonaggression, and Cooperation, and a joint declaration banning nuclear weapons on the Korean peninsula. This latter agreement was especially important because a series of disclosures in early 1991 had raised world concerns over a massive secret North Korean nuclear weapons development program, not unlike that of Iraq. While the joint declaration did not remove that concern, it led in turn to an IAEA safeguards agreement and verification monitoring by outside experts. It appeared that North Korea had indeed been embarked on a secret nuclear weapons program, but (although not acknowledging this fact) was moving to close the program down. Subsequent North Korean backsliding on the issue of IAEA inspections, however, kept the issue alive.

The United States, closely aligned with South Korea and having no relations with North Korea, had virtually no direct influence on these developments, although it sought to encourage North–South Korean contacts. The United States also pressed for verifiable North Korean commitments not to pursue a nuclear weapon capability. In this connection, the American withdrawal of nuclear weapons from South Korea in late 1991 was a helpful step.

North Korea was important as a communist country geographically as well as politically between China and the Soviet Union. By the early 1990s it had to modify its political stance, having moved from a position as beneficiary of Sino-Soviet competition to one of isolation.[133] After some promising initial steps toward a constructive adjustment of its policies, North Korea again turned intransigent and continued to pose a danger to the security and peace of the region.

A second, less important, communist country, the People's Republic of Mongolia, also was located between the two great communist powers. While closely tied to the Soviet Union, it too was a constant factor in Chinese calculations. In 1983 there were indications of an unusual Mongolian restiveness with the signs of improving Sino-Soviet relations. Though Mongolia had been a dependency of the Soviet Union since the early 1920s, it had its own interests. In the spring of 1983, apparently on their own initiative and perhaps intending to complicate Soviet-Chinese relations, the Mongolians expelled some 8,000 long-time Chinese residents. By mid-1984 two probably related developments turned events in the other direction. In July a Sino-Mongolian border delimitation agreement was signed, and in August the veteran Mongolian party leader, Yumjaagiyn Tsedenbal, was replaced by the younger and more flexible Jambyn Batmonh.

As earlier noted, Soviet military presence in Mongolia was one of the three obstacles posed by China in the early 1980s to improvement of relations with the Soviet Union. And, as also noted, Gorbachev gradually reduced and then moved in March 1991 to eliminate that presence by 1992. Beginning in December 1988, a Mongol variant of *perestroika* was launched.

In March 1989, Foreign Minister Tserenpiliyn Gombosuren paid the first official visit of a foreign minister to Beijing in the forty years since the establishment of diplomatic relations. Other high-level visits ensued, and Mongolian-Chinese relations were normalized. Mongolia also joined the nonaligned

---

133. For a useful analysis by leading Russian and South Korean analysts, see Il Yung Chung, ed., *Korea and Russia: Toward the 21st Century* (Seoul: Sejong Institute, 1992).

Group of 77 and several other international bodies. In May came the first visit to Mongolia by a Japanese foreign minister, and Japanese investment followed.

The United States, which had several times in the 1960s and 1970s considered establishing ties with Mongolia, had stepped back each time because of not wishing to antagonize first the Republic of China on Taiwan, and later the People's Republic of China. Under the changed conditions of the latter 1980s, in January 1987 the United States did establish relations, although until late 1991 with minimal presence and without a resident ambassador.

On the heels of the revolutionary changes in Eastern Europe, Mongolia followed. Large popular rallies in January 1990 called for democracy and reform. By March the party leader and the Mongolian Politburo called for an end to the monopoly on power of their own party. A new party leader was elected, Gombojavyn Ochirbat, and Batmonh soon lost his other position as president to Punsalmaagiyn Ochirbat. In July, in the first free elections ever, the newly reformed Communist Party won, but it invited the opposition into the government and formed a coalition government. Buddhism reasserted itself quickly.

In August 1990, and again in July 1991, Secretary Baker visited Ulaanbaatar. A Peace Corps contingent was sent to teach English and use of computers. President Punsalmaagiyn Ochirbat visited Washington in January 1991, the first visit of a Mongolian chief of state to the United States, and a scientific and technological cooperation agreement was signed.

Though the Soviet Union and the Western powers including Japan welcomed the changes in Mongolia, sentiment in China was mixed. While the withdrawal not only of Soviet military presence, but virtually of Soviet presence and influence of any kind, accorded with one Chinese interest, the birth of a truly independent Mongolia and nonconforming "communist" and noncommunist coalition at its leadership posed a potential challenge to other Chinese interests. Mongolia could now stand as an attractive alternative to the Mongols of China's adjoining province of Inner Mongolia. This same consideration also began to influence Russian thinking, as some Mongols began unofficially to talk about a "Greater Mongolia" embracing not only the free republic and Inner Mongolia, but also Tuva, Buryatia, and Altai in Siberia.

Far more complex was the readjustment of Soviet, Chinese, and American interests in Indochina. The Vietnamese used their alliance with the Soviet Union concluded in November 1978 to confront the Chinese, but at the same time to limit Soviet influence in Laos and Kampuchea (Cambodia). In December 1981 the Vietnamese replaced the first Kampuchean party leader, Pen Sovan, who had sought to gain some leeway by establishing closer ties to the Soviets, with Heng Samrin, who had headed the puppet government from the outset in 1979.[134] Nonetheless, Soviet-Vietnamese relations, and Soviet eco-

---

134. See Leif Rosenberger, "The Soviet-Vietnamese Alliance and Kampuchea," *Survey*, vol. 27 (Autumn/Winter 1983), pp. 221–23, and more generally pp. 207–31. See also Pao-min Chang, "The Sino-Vietnamese Conflict Over Kampuchea," ibid., pp. 175–206.

nomic and military assistance to Vietnam, remained important to both sides at least through the mid-1980s. The continuing tense Vietnamese-Chinese conflict, to which both contributed, also meant that the Soviet improvement of relations with China was limited as long as Moscow supported Vietnam.

As the Soviet Union began, cautiously, to seek improved relations with China starting in 1982, the Vietnamese directly and indirectly sought to frustrate that design. Without noting the many instances, one important example was the successful Vietnamese pressure to postpone the planned visit of First Deputy Prime Minister Arkhipov to China in mid-1984, and then engineer Soviet association with an anti-Chinese attack. But Gorbachev was more persistent, although for a long time unprepared to override Vietnam on the question of Cambodia. One reason was the benefits Moscow saw in continued Soviet military presence in Vietnam.

The American establishment of diplomatic relations with China in 1978 and other steps of rapprochement—and even some direct encouragement—clearly facilitated the Chinese military attack on Vietnam in 1979.[135] This in turn led to greater Vietnamese dependence on the Soviet Union, and to the Vietnamese grant to the Soviet Union of the large naval base at Cam Ranh Bay (which had been a major U.S. naval facility during the Vietnam War). The United States, as well as ASEAN and China, refused to recognize the Vietnamese-sponsored and -supported Heng Samrin regime established in Kampuchea in 1979. In 1981, in the "Haig-geopolitical phase" of the new administration's policy, there were hints of more direct collaboration with China to put military pressure on Vietnam, but they faded away.[136] The United States, nonetheless, gradually increased assistance to the anti-Vietnamese Kampuchean rebels covertly during the 1980s, and openly after 1985.

Throughout the first half of the 1980s, the Soviets steadily built up their military presence in Vietnam. In 1979, following the Chinese attack on that country, the Vietnamese leaders agreed to Soviet military use of bases that they had rejected when it had earlier been requested (first in 1975, and again in 1978). Only after Vietnamese need for Soviet support had become so clear was this decision reluctantly made. From a naval port visit in early 1979, an expanding and more permanent Soviet presence began in 1980. By the mid-1980s the Soviets had established a headquarters at Cam Ranh Bay with major communications intelligence intercept facilities, a naval flotilla, usually of about twenty-five ships, several tens of Tu-95 Bear reconnaissance and Tu–142 Bear antisub-

---

135. See Garthoff, *Détente and Confrontation*, chapter 2.

136. John H. Holdridge, the assistant secretary of state for East Asian affairs, told a group of American business executives in Beijing in June 1981: "We will seek, if we can, to find ways to increase the political, economic and, yes, *military pressure* on Vietnam, *working with others* [that is, China] and in ways which will bring about, we hope, some changes in Hanoi's attitude toward the situation." Cited in "Regaining the Strategic Initiative," *National Security Record*, no. 38 (October 1981), p. 3. Emphasis added.

marine warfare aircraft and Tu-16 Badger medium bombers, and a squadron of twenty MiG-23 fighters for local air defense. The aircraft also used facilities at Da Nang. While no match for the U.S. bases and forces in the Philippines, the Soviet Union had broken the American monopoly on a superpower military presence stationed in the southeast Asian area.

The principal factor in a gradual but significant change in Soviet attitudes and policy toward Vietnam was the application of "new thinking" to determination of Soviet policy after 1986.[137] For one thing, improving relations with China was increasingly seen as more important than continuing to give priority to Vietnamese preferences. For another, Vietnam was a costly drain on Soviet resources, and, moreover (as the Soviets complained) much was wasted or misspent. Finally, confrontation with the United States, and related military-strategic considerations, declined and then became a negative factor. The military base at Cam Ranh Bay became much less useful.

At his speech at Krasnoyarsk in September 1988, Gorbachev proposed as balanced measures a U.S. withdrawal from its naval base at Subic Bay in the Philippines and Soviet withdrawal from its base at Cam Ranh Bay. The United States had no interest in such a trade and saw the offer mainly as an attempt to complicate ongoing U.S.-Philippine negotiations over renewal of the Subic base rights. Gorbachev had not really expected the offer to be accepted. It was, however, significant as an indication that Moscow was preparing to give up the base at Cam Ranh, and at least some Soviet officials wanted to try to get some dividend from that move. Soviet sources have subsequently revealed that the proposal had not been cleared first with the Vietnamese, who resented the unilateral Soviet action. The Soviet Union then did move to reduce sharply its military presence at Cam Ranh during 1989 and 1990. In tandem, the Soviet Union cut and then ended military assistance to Vietnam and spurned Vietnamese efforts to obtain military assistance as "rent" for the base it was vacating.

During 1988, several other important developments occurred in or affected the region. From a bad beginning with a new Vietnamese-Chinese naval clash over the disputed Spratly Islands in March, the Vietnamese made their first overtures for improved relations with China in mid-1988, leading to official bilateral talks in Beijing in January 1989 for the first time in ten years. Vietnam also sought to open talks with the United States in mid-1988, offering assistance in tracing Americans still missing in action from the Vietnam War. Finally, as noted, in May 1988 Vietnam had announced withdrawal of 50,000 troops from Kampuchea that year. In April 1989, Hanoi promised to withdraw its remaining troops (another 50,000) by September 1989, and it did so.

Sino-Soviet talks on Cambodia (renamed from Kampuchea in April 1989) had also begun in the summer of 1988, as did—for the first time—direct

---

137. One of the last supporting moves of "old thinkers" was a reassurance (soon overtaken by events) given to the Vietnamese by Yegor Ligachev, attending the Vietnamese Sixth Party Congress in Hanoi in December 1986.

talks in July between the Hun Sen government in Phnom Penh and the three opposition groups. Negotiations on Cambodia continued with intermittent progress and reverses for the next three years. All three great powers contributed. The Soviet Union had urged Vietnamese withdrawal, and then (for the time being) picked up the burden of assisting the Cambodian government. Beginning in 1988 the United States began to seek to persuade China to reduce its support for the Khmer Rouge. The United States finally shifted its position sharply in mid-1990, dropping exclusive support for the notorious Khmer Rouge-dominated three-party opposition coalition and agreeing to deal also with the government in Phnom Penh.

September 1990 saw a breakthrough in talks among the Cambodian factions, soon after an agreement on the outline of a plan to end the Cambodian civil war had been agreed on by the UN Security Council—including, of course, China as well as the Soviet Union and the United States. September also saw the first high-level U.S.-Vietnamese meeting since 1973, when Secretary Baker met with Foreign Minister Nguyen Co Thach. That same month saw the first secret high-level Vietnamese-Chinese talks between the top party and government leaders, including Jiang Zemin and Nguyen Van Linh.

All of these paths to normalization of relations and settlement of the Cambodian conflict found fruition in 1991. Further secret Sino-Vietnamese meetings led to an official summit meeting in Beijing in November 1991 between party leaders Jiang Zemin and Do Muoi, and Prime Ministers Li Peng and Vo Van Kiet, who agreed on full normalization of Sino-Vietnamese relations. While U.S.-Vietnamese talks did not lead to full normalization of relations, by October 1991 Baker met with Vietnamese Foreign Minister Nguyen Manh Cam and indicated readiness to work toward that goal. The occasion for their meeting was the successful conclusion of the Cambodian peace talks leading to an agreement by all parties in Paris on October 23, 1991. A few days earlier, Cambodia had dropped rule by its Communist Party and embraced both a multiparty political system and a market economic system. Coincident with the Paris accord the United States lifted its embargo on trade with Cambodia. The United States had recently opened an embassy and sent a chargé d'affaires to Laos and now was also ready to send one to Cambodia.

Thus by the end of 1991, while absorption of the still-armed Khmer Rouge faction remained to be accomplished, Cambodia was no longer the arena for several overlapping international proxy conflicts.[138] Indochina in gen-

---

138. Although all Cambodian factions, including the Khmer Rouge, had accepted the Paris peace agreement, implementation over the next two years was very difficult. New negotiations among the parties led to elections in May 1993 and election by a new national assembly of a coalition government headed by the most durable political figure, Prince Norodom Sihanouk, in June 1993. The Khmer Rouge, however, did not participate in the coalition government and remained a law unto itself and a threat to the country.

eral was no longer the cockpit of U.S.-Soviet, Sino-Soviet, Sino-Vietnamese, and other confrontations, although U.S.-Vietnam relations were not fully normalized, and of course some conflicts of interest among various parties remained. The Soviet Union had largely withdrawn from the region by the time it expired.

In parallel with the easing of Sino-Soviet and Sino-Vietnamese relations, and resolution of the Cambodian conflict, relations of the Soviet Union and China with the other countries of Southeast Asia, in particular the six members of ASEAN, was normalized. Foreign Minister Shevardnadze both illustrated and conveyed the new Soviet approach by an unprecedented tour of Southeast Asian states in March 1987, including Thailand, Indonesia, and Australia as well as the communist states of Indochina. This process continued. At the twenty-fifth anniversary meeting of ASEAN in Manila in July 1992, Vietnam and Laos were welcomed to membership (with Cambodia expected to be included later), and along with the American, Japanese, Australian, and New Zealand foreign ministers, those of Russia and China were also present as invited observers. The American and Soviet bases at Subic Bay and Cam Ranh Bay were in the final stages of being phased out. In many ways, that meeting in Manila represented the kind of new cooperative and demilitarized relationship among the countries of Asia and the Pacific that Gorbachev had called for in 1986 and 1988.

For several years the Soviet Union had been quietly and gradually developing trade and diplomatic relations with several of the smaller nations of the Pacific and southeast Asia.[139] Some of these initiatives were not successful, as when the Soviets miscalculated the staying power of President Ferdinand Marcos in the Philippines and issued statements of support for him and against U.S. "interference" in his final losing days in power. On the whole, however, the Soviet Union had been able, by not trying to do too much, to benefit from the irritations of several smaller Pacific nations who saw the the American role as overbearing.

In late 1986 the Soviet Union had applied for membership in the Pacific Economic Cooperation Conference, and early in 1987 applied to join the Asian Development Bank.

The Soviet Union also extended its commercial, and especially fishing, interests into the Pacific Ocean region. As early as August 1985 the Soviet Union purchased one-year fishing rights in the water of Kiribati (the former Gilbert Islands)—leading the United States to outbid and purchase the same fishing rights the next year. But the Soviet Union persisted, reaching agreements in 1987 for fishing rights around Vanuatu (formerly the New Hebrides)

---

139. One sign of the growing Soviet attention to the area was the establishment in June 1986 of a Department of Pacific Ocean Affairs, and in April 1991 of a Department of General Problems of the Asian-Pacific Region, in the Ministry of Foreign Affairs.

and Papua New Guinea. The Soviet Union also established diplomatic relations with Fiji, Vanuatu, and Kiribati in the late 1980s.

In September 1990 the Soviet Union hosted an international conference on the Asian-Pacific region, at which Shevardnadze reaffirmed Soviet interests in continued normalization of relations and development of economic and other areas of cooperation. By this time, however, Soviet resources were pinched and there was little wherewithal for concrete initiatives.

## Asia in American-Soviet Relations

During the first half of the 1980s, the effects of the geopolitical triangular balance among the Soviet Union, the United States, and China played a significant but declining role. From 1986 on, other complex interrelationships among those three powers and other countries increasingly came to dominate the scene, and by the beginning of the 1990s U.S.-Soviet (and then U.S.-Russian) relations, and the roles of China, Japan, and others were completely altered by the disappearance of the Cold War lines of confrontation.

The Soviet leaders welcomed the frictions in American-Chinese relations in 1981–82 because that weakened the anti-Soviet alliance they had seen develop in 1978–80. On the whole, they took with equanimity the gradual improvement in Sino-American relations after 1983, although clearly they hoped to place their relations with China at least on a par with those of the United States. They were even prepared to take the drastic actions sought by China to overcome all of the three obstacles it had posed as necessary for a real improvement of relations. Soviet analysts of both American and Chinese affairs continued in their assessments in the 1980s to emphasize basic long-term stresses in the Sino-American relationship,[140] although other Soviet observers varied in their judgments. From the standpoint of Soviet-American relations, the China factor continued to trouble the Soviet leaders, but much less so after 1981 than it had in the late 1970s. There was also an interesting change in Soviet concern. In the period 1978–80 Soviet analysts and officials, in conversations and in published articles, warned the Americans of the unreliability of building a relationship with China and the costs to American-Soviet relations. By 1983-84 they were warning the Chinese about the dangers of becoming an appendage to the United States and sacrificing Chinese relations with the Soviet Union.

The United States sought to maintain good relations with China, but was not prepared to satisfy the Chinese position on Taiwan. Though seeing advantage in latent Sino-Soviet mutual suspicion in the 1980s, the United

---

140. For example, see A. Ye. Bovin, "Washington-Beijing: A Contradictory Partnership," *SShA: Ekonomika, politika, ideologiya* (USA: Economics, Politics, Ideology), no. 8 (August 1984), pp. 17–26.

States did not seek to exacerbate those differences or to prevent an improvement in Soviet-Chinese relations.

The general outcome of the shift in triangular diplomacy from the 1970s to the 1980s was the American loss of its position as the balancing element. Nixon and Kissinger had improved U.S. relations with both of the other powers and gained leverage with both. Carter and Brzezinski lost much of this leverage by aligning with China. Reagan exacerbated relations with both, and lost leverage with both, in 1981–82 (despite Haig's efforts to sustain Brzezinski's approach). By 1983 the United States was seeking to ameliorate relations with China and, after 1985, to some extent with the Soviet Union too. But in the 1980s the heyday of triangular diplomacy had passed.

Soviet long-standing "national, state interests" in the Asian-Pacific area generally were strongly emphasized in Gorbachev's key speech in Vladivostok in July 1986. Apart from the extensive overtures to China and more limited ones to several other states, he stressed that "our approach to that part of the world is based on recognition and understanding of the realities existing there," but he said that the Soviet Union was "in favor of building new and equitable relations with Asia and the Pacific." To that end, he proposed (more formally than he had in a precursor statement to the Twenty-seventh Party Congress in February 1986) a conference along the lines of the Helsinki (CSCE) conference, to be attended by "all countries gravitating toward the Pacific Ocean."[141] This proposal did not, however, meet with any early favorable response. Even Asian countries on good terms with the Soviet Union, notably India, were cool to this idea.

Gorbachev sharply criticized past American actions in the Far East, in particular the Vietnam War, and also the military buildup since the mid-1970s that, he said, was turning the Pacific Ocean into "an arena of political-military confrontation."[142] Nonetheless, he conceded that the United States was a major Pacific power and that "without its participation one cannot solve the problem of security and cooperation in the Pacific Ocean area." He also declared that in developing "mutually beneficial cooperation" with the United States there were "quite a few opportunities both in the Far East and in the Pacific Ocean."[143]

In Krasnoyarsk two years later, frustrated by the absence of real movement on relations in Asia and the Pacific, especially with the United States,

---

141. *Pravda*, July 29, 1986.

Soviet scholars and diplomats in Moscow told me in March 1986 that Gorbachev's Political Report to the Party Congress signaled a greater Soviet focus on the Asian-Pacific area and predicted further interest.

142. Among the kinds of things that Gorbachev had in mind were a series of major U.S. amphibious exercises in the Alaska-Japan region in 1986–87. A few months after he spoke, a foray by a battle group headed by the missile battleship USS *New Jersey* sailed into the Sea of Okhotsk in September 1986 and out via straits in the Kuril Islands. The Soviets regarded the action as provocative.

143. *Pravda*, July 29, 1986.

Gorbachev repeated: "We are looking hard for points of contact on the problems of the Asia-Pacific region with the United States. And we often ask: Why do we not have mutual understanding here, in contrast to other important spheres of world politics? Our state interests do not appear to clash. . . . So what is the problem?"[144]

The problem was that the United States did not yet see advantage or need to engage the Soviet Union in that region, in contrast to Europe. In Europe, there had been a more clearcut line of confrontation throughout the Cold War, which had divided the continent, and by the end of the 1980s an opportunity was perceived, and seized, to dismantle that division. In Asia, the multiple political divisions were far less congealed and there was no overall movement or dramatic denouement as in Europe in 1989-90. Nonetheless, the situation did change substantially in Asia as in Europe during the years 1988-91, and by the end of the Soviet period, Asia and the Pacific had also to some extent become an area of increased cooperation. The lingering unresolved dispute between the Soviet Union, and later Russia, with Japan over the contested islands did remain as an obstacle, not directly in U.S.-Soviet relations, but indirectly to some extent because it precluded full Russian-Japanese normalization. But it was difficult to find other areas of significant divergence remaining in the early 1990s.

New problems, however, persist and will arise to challenge both countries as well as other powers in the region. The North Korean reluctance to end its nuclear weapons program or at least to permit effective international verification poses a potentially divisive and dangerous situation. Although Russia and the United States share an interest in preventing North Korean acquisition of a nuclear weapons capability, and have worked in cooperation, a complex chain of developments involving unpredictable South Korean and Japanese reactions to a nuclear-armed North Korea could present new problems and divergent American and Russian responses. Any currently unexpected but not inconceivable tensions between Russia and Japan or China could pose issues for American policy.

The greatest restraint on a more active Soviet (then Russian) role in Asia by the early 1990s was not the blocking action of any adversary or even unresolved conflict of interests—it was that the implosion of the Soviet Union forced that country, and Russia as its successor, to devote its attention and resources inward to deal with the formidable problems of economic and social transition and recovery. Although liberated from the confining thinking and engendered conflicts of the former Soviet political worldview, Gorbachev's policy by 1990-91 and his successor's were simply confined by lack of means to engage economic or other opportunities in Asia and the Pacific, as well as elsewhere in the world. That situation is likely to prevail for some time. But not forever.

---

144. *Pravda*, September 18, 1988.

# 15 Competition in the Third World

AN APPARENT SHARPENING of the competition between the superpowers in the Third World in the second half of the 1970s was one of the most important factors in the collapse of détente.[1] The Soviet Union, not without reason, saw a continuing very active American role in that competition. But more significant in its impact on their relationship was the American perception, also not without reason, of an increasingly active and expansionist policy by the Soviet Union. The U.S. concern, however, prompted an exaggerated response. In the 1980s, the Soviet presence markedly diminished while the U.S. role increased. A closer look at the perceptions of the two sides and the realities of their competition in the Third World in the 1980s is now appropriate.

## The Haig Doctrine, 1981–82

President Reagan entered office with the conviction that "the Soviet Union underlies all the unrest that is going on" in the world. Secretary of State Haig, while far more knowledgeable about world politics, also had a simplified and magnified image of the Soviet Union's exploitation of circumstances and situations around the world for its own advantage. Moreover, for other reasons too, Haig placed the subject of Soviet involvement and expansion of influence in the Third World at the center of American-Soviet relations.[2]

---

1. See the discussion in Raymond L. Garthoff, *Détente and Confrontation: American-Soviet Relations from Nixon to Reagan*, rev. ed. (Brookings, 1994), chapters 7, 8, 11, 15, 19.

2. See the discussion in chapter 1.

The first region to attract American concern and charges of Soviet expansionism was Central America and the Caribbean. In actuality, throughout the 1970s the Soviet Union—and to a lesser extent even Cuba—had shown great restraint in supporting revolutionary movements of the left in the Caribbean and Latin America. Both Moscow and Havana primarily provided discreet training, including paramilitary training in Cuba and the Soviet Union, for some Latin American (as well as Arab and African) revolutionaries. Only their verbal support, and such noncommittal political support as that entailed, was unsparing. Considering the strong declaratory stand of the Soviet Union and Cuba in support of national liberation and progressive change, this support was unsurprising except that it was so limited.

After the overthrow of the Allende government in Chile in 1973 and the suppression of local terrorists in Argentina and Uruguay, most of Latin America became relatively stabilized usually under authoritarian regimes until opposition to repressive right-wing dictatorships in several countries of Central America and the Caribbean basin erupted into armed struggle late in the decade. The most significant was the left-to-moderate liberal opposition coalition led by the Sandinistas that eventually overthrew the Somoza regime in Nicaragua in July 1979. Even there, greater external support was given by such noncommunist countries as Panama, Costa Rica, Venezuela, and Mexico than by the Soviet Union and Cuba. The Soviets remained very guarded in their support even after the Sandinista-led victory.[3] Moreover, it has been reported that Castro himself counseled the Sandinistas not to adopt too radical a course and not to alienate American support, as he had done. Indeed, Castro's regime in Cuba was highly dependent on Soviet support, amounting to some $8 million a day by the end of the decade (as became painfully clear when that direct and indirect economic subsidy ended in the beginning of the 1990s). Moscow in the early 1980s did not desire to subsidize Nicaragua in addition to Cuba (and Vietnam).

The turn to violence next in El Salvador led to a reformist coup d'état in October 1979. Within a few months, however, right-wing military elements within the ruling junta gained a predominant role, and most of the liberal and moderate political elements left the government, some eventually joining the guerrilla opposition for lack of any alternative. During the 1970s the small Communist Party of El Salvador had, on Soviet advice, declined to join other

---

3. The communists (called the Nicaraguan Socialist Party) had made their peace with the Somoza regime and were not part of the Sandinista-led insurgent coalition. The Soviet Union had begun to shift its support from the communists to the Sandinistas only in 1977.

    The Soviet Union held back from full commitment or support even after the Sandinista victory until March 1980, by which time the United States had made clear it would accept the outcome—and by which time the United States was arming the insurgents in Afghanistan.

groups in armed resistance. Only in 1980 did it begin to participate, and even then it remained one of the smallest components. The United States continued to support the junta and to encourage economic reform, although violence from the extreme right and left led to increasing polarization that united the moderate opposition with the radical left.

On the eve of the change of American administrations in January 1981, the Soviet Union and Cuba shifted course and began to supply arms on a more substantial scale to the Salvadoran revolutionaries. This shift did not occur because the Soviet leaders had decided to abandon détente; they were trying, at the same time, though presumably without high expectations, to restore a measure of détente into relations with the incoming American administration. One reason for the shift was simply that the Soviet leaders believed progressive revolutions were morally right and historically inevitable under conditions of rising popular dissatisfaction with repressive authoritarian rule and economic exploitation. Given that this view also existed earlier, it could not have been the cause for a change in policy. Still, this perspective, while it should be obvious, is rarely acknowledged. A second reason is that the Soviet leaders believed that the prospects for the revolution in El Salvador to succeed, even if not imminently, were on the rise. Moscow (and Havana) wanted to be seen by potential revolutionaries everywhere, and especially in the immediate region, as ready to support progressive change, in contrast to the United States. This was an important factor in the situation: American policy was clearly swinging to support the existing authoritarian regimes in Central America. By channeling arms through Nicaragua to El Salvador the Soviets and Cubans could probably ensure American identification with efforts at forcible repression in El Salvador—and perhaps also lead the United States to develop closer ties with the authoritarian regimes in Guatemala and Honduras. Such U.S. actions would alienate many in such countries as Mexico and Costa Rica, as well as in Western Europe, who favored progressive change. The United States, as it ostentatiously set aside the banner of human rights in 1981, would again be cast in the role of external Yanqui policeman in a region with a long history of resentment against American intervention. Meanwhile, the Soviet and Cuban role was indirect and could even be denied. There were no Soviet or even Cuban soldiers with the revolutionary forces, while American military men had resumed instruction in internal military policing and suppression operations in El Salvador.

A Salvadoran guerrilla "final offensive" in January 1981 failed. Soon after, the Soviet leaders began to revert to their skepticism over whether there was a revolutionary situation in Central America. This outlook reinforced their caution and contributed to keeping their involvement in the region thereafter low key.

There may also have been a more subtle consideration in the Soviet decision to provide some indirect assistance to revolutionaries in Central America. The Soviet leaders may have wished to demonstrate to Washington that just as the United States and its friends such as Egypt were quietly supplying arms (including weapons of Soviet origin) to the resistance in Afghanistan in the Soviet Union's backyard, so too could the Soviet Union and its friends such as Cuba quietly supply arms (including American-made M-16 rifles acquired in Vietnam) to the revolutionaries in El Salvador. This action would, besides serving the other purposes noted earlier, at a minimum show Washington that two could play the same game. It might even lead to a tacit agreement by both powers to curtail or cease such actions. That would be a deal Moscow would have been only too ready to make. In view of its stance of principled support for the cause of progressive revolutionary change in Central America, it could not acknowledge such a deal publicly, but that would not be necessary since it had not acknowledged supply of arms in the first place.

The Soviets also hoped the elected leftist government in Jamaica represented a sign of progressive advance in those countries having democratic processes. The left-wing coup in Grenada in 1979 by the pseudo-Marxist New Jewel movement of Maurice Bishop had also been welcomed, although warily. The Soviets only cautiously supported Castro's efforts to bring Grenada into the outer circle of Soviet-aligned progressive states and carefully refrained from close identification or commitment. Contrary to later U.S. claims, the evidence acquired on Grenadan contacts with the Soviets shows how little support the Soviets gave to Grenada (and how little confidence they had in its leaders). As shall be shown, Moscow did not attempt to use Grenada as a base to expand communist rule in the area. Similarly, the Soviets welcomed warily the leftward turn of Lieutenant Colonel Desi Bouterese, the dictator in Suriname who took power in a coup in 1980, and kept him at arm's length.

The United States, in parallel with its support for the government of El Salvador, took an increasingly hostile position toward Nicaragua. On April 1, 1981, the United States cut off aid to Nicaragua. From August to November Assistant Secretary of State Thomas Enders negotiated with the Nicaraguans over terms to secure a halt to Nicaraguan support for the guerrillas in El Salvador. But increasingly the administration shifted its objective to one of bringing pressure on the Sandinistas to share power within Nicaragua and to curtail their ties with Cuba and the Soviet Union.

As early as March 9, 1981, President Reagan had issued a secret "Presidential Finding on Central America" that instituted a covert action program to interdict arms supply via Nicaragua to the guerrillas in El Salvador. After a key National Security Council (NSC) meeting on November 16, he issued NSDD-17, authorizing a considerable expansion in covert support for paramilitary Nicaraguan forces (popularly called the contras, a diminutive of *contrarevolutionarios*) and providing an initial $19 million. The CIA armed, trained, and supported a force of contras that grew from a few hundred in mid-1981 to some 15,000 troops in the field by the mid-1980s. They operated into Nicaragua primarily from bases in Honduras and to a lesser extent from Costa Rica.

An NSC document of April 1982 that later leaked into the public domain defined the American objectives for these covert operations and a much wider range of political, economic, and other activities. The objectives were much broader than interdicting arms supply into El Salvador, the initial public justification, and applied in varying ways to the whole of Central America. Basically the unpublicized U.S. aim was "to eliminate Cuban/Soviet influence in the region." Moreover, this objective was to be accomplished "in the short run." In the longer run the aim was to "build politically stable governments able to withstand such influences." This action program was predicated on the conclusion that the United States has "a vital interest in not allowing the proliferation of Cuba-model states" in the region.[4]

In 1982 the administration announced a Caribbean initiative, intended as an economic-aid carrot to rally countries in the region to American policy, as well as to enhance their viability and resistance to leftist revolution. In 1983 the administration appointed a prestigious commission chaired by former Secretary of State Henry Kissinger, primarily to rally the support of the American public for the policy of resisting communist encroachment in the region. Neither device was notably successful in deflecting attention from the internal conflict in El Salvador and the incursions into Nicaragua.

While El Salvador and in time Nicaragua were the main focus of action in the region, the principal target of American concern at the outset was Cuba. Many members of the Reagan administration shared an animosity toward Castro's Cuba. Moreover, Cuba was seen not only as a tool of successful Soviet expansion of influence in Africa, but also as the potential source of expanded communist influence in the Western Hemisphere, especially the Caribbean basin. Both Reagan and Haig frequently referred to Cuba as a Soviet proxy.

Haig early in the administration recommended to President Reagan that, in his own words, the president "lay down a marker on the question of

4.   The leaked NSC Planning Group document, "U.S. Policy in Central America and Cuba through F.Y. '84, Summary Paper," April 1982, was printed in full in "National Security Council Document on Policy in Central America and Cuba," *New York Times*, April 7, 1983, p. A16. This document included references and details on the Presidential Finding of March 9, 1981, and National Security Decision Directive (NSDD)–17 of November 1981. A second presidential finding followed on December 1, 1981, authorizing paramilitary operations against the Cuban pressure and Cuban-Sandinista "support structure" in Nicaragua aiding the Salvadoran insurgents.

Incidentally, the United States had to rebuild hastily its intelligence network in the area. In the late 1970s, as part of a curtailment of CIA activities, the CIA station in El Salvador had been closed, and the one in Nicaragua had been reduced to a minimum. (Information from a former senior CIA official.)

In early 1983, the CIA planned to carry out a covert operation to overthrow Lieutenant Colonel Bouterese in Suriname, but the operation was canceled after objection from the congressional oversight committees. See Bob Woodward, *Veil: The Secret Wars of the CIA, 1981–1987* (Simon and Schuster, 1987), pp. 240–41.

Cuba."[5] When the president did not do so, Haig did. Several times in February he referred, as earlier noted, to the need to deal with the problem of external assistance to the guerrillas in El Salvador "at the source"—and "clearly it's Cuba."[6] Not only did Haig's strident stance alarm the Cubans and give Moscow concern, but Secretary of Defense Weinberger and the Joint Chiefs of Staff also did not want to become needlessly involved in a war with Cuba. Haig's proposal to consider a naval blockade of any shipments of arms from Cuba was rejected by the president after strong objections from the Pentagon. As Haig said later, he was "virtually alone" in the administration on this issue.[7]

The incoming Reagan administration had been surprised to learn of a secret diplomatic channel of communication that the Carter administration had developed to Castro. In February the Cubans quietly sought to continue it, but they were turned down. By November 1981, however, Haig availed himself of an offer by the Mexican government and met with Cuban Vice President Carlos Rafael Rodríguez. This contact was followed by a secret visit to Havana by General Vernon Walters, the former deputy chief of the CIA and now a special roving ambassador, who met with Castro. These exchanges did not, however, lead to any improvement in relations.[8] The Reagan administration even rebuffed a significant Cuban overture. Soon following Haig's meeting, in December the Cubans told the chief of the American diplomatic interests section in Havana that they had stopped supplying arms to Nicaragua—and this was borne out by U.S. Intelligence. But the administration ignored the move and indeed in April tightened economic sanctions.[9]

Cuban aid to Nicaragua, including again military assistance, remained at a level that annoyed Washington without provoking it. There was, however, concern and displeasure in the administration, recurrently expressed publicly, over increased Soviet supply of arms to Cuba. In 1981 the general volume of

5. Alexander M. Haig, Jr., *Caveat: Realism, Reagan, and Foreign Policy* (Macmillan, 1984), p. 98.

6. "Secretary Haig Interviewed for French Television," *Department of State Bulletin*, vol. 81 (April 1981), p. 15. (Hereafter *State Bulletin*.)

7. Haig, *Caveat*, p. 129, and see pp. 123–31.
   The administration was not, however, averse to "rattling" the Cubans in various ways—even literally by sending SR-71 reconnaissance aircraft over Cuba and deliberately rubbing it in by sonic booms reminding the Cubans of these intrusions. See Patrick E. Tyler, "SR-71 Plane Roars Into Retirement," *Washington Post*, March 7, 1990, p. A4, citing Reagan administration officials.

8. Ibid., pp. 132–37. See also Don Oberdorfer, "Nicaraguan Leader Blasts U.S. at U.N., Offers Negotiations: Diplomacy Up, but Optimism on Result Is Not," *Washington Post*, March 26, 1982, pp. A1, A23; and John M. Goshko, "U.S. and Cuba Open Official Negotiations," *Washington Post*, July 13, 1984, pp. A1, A27.

9. See Wayne S. Smith, *The Closest of Enemies: A Personal and Diplomatic Account of U.S.-Cuban Relations Since 1957* (W. W. Norton and Company, 1987), pp. 253–60.

arms began to rise substantially, and in early 1982 included a second squadron of MiG-23 fighters. This stirred up again the question of a possible violation of the American-Soviet understanding reached after the Cuban missile crisis in 1962 (and clarified and expanded in 1970), as had the delivery of the first squadron in 1978.[10] CIA Director William Casey in 1982, and President Reagan in 1983, both made casual (and unwarranted) charges that the Soviets had violated the 1962 understanding by supplying these arms to Cuba.[11] These were, however, only offhand statements reflecting a general propensity to assume Soviet violation rather than considered charges, and they were not followed up.

Haig charged that the quantity of arms in Cuba "far exceeds" what Cuba needed for defense against "any potential threat emanating from this hemisphere."[12] That assertion could only be true if he meant the United States would never go to war against Cuba—a veiled threat he had made. To both Moscow and Havana, the buildup of arms in Cuba did reinforce deterrence of a possible American attack. Moreover, the Soviet leaders were not prepared to commit themselves to come to Cuba's aid if it were attacked, and they believed the supply of arms was a politically useful reassurance to Castro as well as a way of making that extreme eventuality less likely.

Soon after the Reagan administration came into office, according to later Cuban revelations, Fidel Castro sent his brother, Defense Minister Raúl Castro, to Moscow where he met with General Secretary Leonid Brezhnev, Defense Minister Dmitry Ustinov, and Party Secretary Boris Ponomarev (in charge of relations with socialist countries). Raúl briefed the Soviet leaders on Havana's great concern over the danger of an American attack or other action against them, but according to Raúl (disclosing his mission over a decade later, after the fall of the Soviet Union), Leonid Brezhnev bluntly replied, "We cannot fight in Cuba because it is 11,000 kilometers away. If we go there, we'll get our heads smashed." Raúl said he and Fidel found this Soviet response "difficult to endure in silence," but they continued in public to refer to "strengthening bonds of friendship" in order to "disorient the enemy."[13]

In commenting on Reagan's decision early in his term, "despite some sentiment among his advisers to do otherwise," "to abide strictly by the understandings on the status of Cuba reached by the U.S. and the U.S.S.R. in the

---

10. See Garthoff, *Détente and Confrontation*, chapter 18.

11. "The Real Soviet Threat in El Salvador—and Beyond," Interview with CIA Director William J. Casey, *U.S. News and World Report*, vol. 92 (March 8, 1982), pp. 23–24; and Francis X. Clines, "President Accuses Soviet on '62 Pact," *New York Times*, September 15, 1983, p. A11.

12. "The Secretary: Question-and-Answer Session following ABA Address," August 11, 1981, *State Bulletin*, vol. 81 (September 1981), p. 15.

13. Raúl Castro's interview appeared in *El Sol de Mexico* in April 1993 and was reported in Yevgeny Bay, "Soviet Union-Cuba: 'The Pandora Affair'—Havana's Leadership Reveals Secrets of Relations with Moscow," *Izvestiya*, April 27, 1993.

aftermath of the Cuban missile crisis," Haig seriously misstated their nature. He said in his memoir that "these understandings did not include the right of Moscow and Havana to inspire, train, equip, and arm insurgencies in Central America or anywhere else in the world."[14] Nor, of course, did they include any such right for the United States. These understandings also did not place any agreed limitations on such a right by either side. American policy, however, was clearly aimed at inspiring the maximum concern, and hence restraint, in all links in the chain—Moscow, Havana, and Managua. Haig therefore took the occasion of an early encounter with the Nicaraguan ambassador to reply to an expression of confidence that there would be no change in relations by saying that the United States was not only prepared to cut off economic assistance (as it did within weeks of coming to office), but "to do other things as well"—which it soon began to do by arming and supporting anti-Sandinista counterrevolutionary insurgents, the "contras."[15]

The American neuralgia over Cuba, and especially over Soviet military presence in Cuba, was given another brief boost of a different kind in March 1982 when Brezhnev seemed to threaten stationing Soviet nuclear missiles in Cuba. In opposing the NATO plan to deploy new American intermediate-range missiles in Western Europe, Brezhnev had stated that would create "a real additional threat to our country" and would "compel us to take retaliatory steps that would put the other side, including the United States itself, its own territory, in an analogous position."[16] Other Soviet spokesmen had earlier sought to evoke a Western understanding of their concern over "nonstrategic" missiles based within range of strategic targets in the Soviet Union by noting the American concern in 1962 over comparable Soviet missiles in Cuba. Brezhnev clearly wished to do the same. But he did not mention Cuba, and he could at least as easily have been suggesting some other deployment, such as Soviet sea-based missiles capable of striking targets in the United States.[17] *Pravda*, a few days later, refuted a statement by Secretary of Defense Weinberger rashly attributing on the basis of Brezhnev's speech a Soviet "intention" to deploy

---

14. Haig, *Caveat*, p. 98.

15. Ibid., p. 100. Haig recorded with satisfaction: "Ambassador Delia was shocked by my blunt words, but these were carefully chosen. I knew that they would be repeated in Havana and Moscow as soon as she could get back to her embassy's code room."

16. L. I. Brezhnev, Speech to the 17th Congress of Trade Unions of the USSR, March 16, 1982, *Pravda*, March 17, 1982.

17. One ambiguous early hint that this might be what the Soviets had in mind appeared in an article by Vitaly Zhurkin, in which he had raised the question of "how the strategic situation would look for the United States if it forced the other side to develop and to deploy adequate weapons systems, for instance medium-range missiles, *close to American shores*." V. Zhurkin, "In Pursuit of the Impossible Goal: The 'New U.S. Nuclear Strategy'" *Literaturnaya Gazeta* (Literary Gazette), September 17, 1980. Emphasis added.

nuclear missiles in Cuba, but then went on to ask: "how should the Soviet Union react, following Weinberger's logic, to American attempts to deploy in the immediate vicinity of the Soviet Union" similar nuclear missiles?[18] The Soviet purpose clearly was not to probe for possible deployment of their missiles in Cuba, but to attempt to dissuade the American deployment in Europe.

Though El Salvador and Cuba were most directly in the limelight in 1981, the administration also devoted great attention to the other prominent alleged Soviet proxy, Qadhafi's Libya.[19] In May the United States closed the Libyan mission in Washington because of links to suspected terrorism. In July a leak disclosed that the administration had proposed three covert operations in Africa, including Libya, but that the House Intelligence Committee had objected. A campaign of disinformation and attempts to frighten Qadhafi was, however, undertaken. In August, the Sixth Fleet entered the Gulf of Sidra (claimed as coastal waters by Libya) coinciding with Egyptian military exercises near the Libyan border. On August 19 two patrolling U.S. Navy F-14 interceptors shot down two Su-22 Libyan jet fighters that had unwisely attacked them over the Gulf of Sidra. President Reagan triumphantly announced, "Let friend and foe alike know that America has the muscle to back up its words."[20] Also in August and again in October reports appeared of a U.S. plan to "destabilize" Qadhafi's rule in Libya.[21] In November and December 1981 there was in turn a scare prompted by reports that Qadhafi had sent a hit team to assassinate President Reagan or some other senior American leader.[22] No substantiation for the report was found.[23]

---

18. "There Can Be No Double Standard," *Pravda*, March 20, 1982.

19. For example, see Haig's repeated references in *Caveat*, pp. 96, 109, 110, 172, 220.

20. "U.S.S. Constellation: Remarks during a Visit to the Aircraft Carrier," August 20, 1981, *Weekly Compilation of Presidential Documents*, vol. 17 (August 24, 1981), p. 891. (Hereafter *Presidential Documents*.)

    The encounter had been anticipated, indeed provoked, and the American airmen had practiced interceptions of Libyan aircraft.

21. See Don Oberdorfer, "U.S. Has Sought to Pressure Qadhafi," *Washington Post*, August 20, 1981, pp. A1, A17.

    These may have related to real plans, or they may have been intended to contribute to the disinformation plan for harassing Qadhafi. In October, the leading Libyan political exiles formed a National Front for the Salvation of Libya.

22. Philip Taubman, "U.S. Officials Say FBI Is Hunting Terrorists Seeking to Kill President," *New York Times*, December 4, 1981, pp. A1, A27.

23. Indeed, several years later the British *New Statesman* obtained a secret U.S. Customs Service document, dated November 28, 1981, listing the fourteen members of the alleged Libyan terrorist hit team. The list was composed of well-known Lebanese politicians of the Amal party, bitter opponents of Qadhafi, and should have been immediately recognized for the canard it was. See Duncan Campbell and Patrick Forbes, "Investigations: Tale of Anti-Reagan Hit Team Was Fraud," *New Statesman*, August 16, 1985, p. 6.

The United States also in early 1981 provided covert funding to Hissen Habre, who was challenging Libyan-supported President Goukouni Oueddei of Chad. In June 1982 he defeated him. Although the Soviet Union was not involved, Qadhafi was seen as a Soviet proxy and Goukouni as a Qadhafi proxy.[24]

The Reagan administration also addressed the Soviets directly with its concerns over what it saw as Soviet proxies. Haig constantly raised this subject with Dobrynin in the early months of 1981 in his quest for Soviet acceptance of "restraint and reciprocity" in the Third World. As Haig notes in his memoir, Dobrynin told him, "All I ever hear from you . . . is Cuba, Cuba, Cuba!"[25] Haig sought to ensure that the Soviet leaders would get the message of U.S. seriousness by seeing to it that "every official of the State Department, in every exchange with a Soviet official, emphasized American determination that the U.S.S.R. and its clients—especially Fidel Castro and Qadhafi—must moderate their interventionist behavior."[26] Dobrynin denied knowledge of any untoward behavior by Castro. As for Qadhafi, as Haig has noted, "Dobrynin made it clear that Libya was an American problem," not a Soviet responsibility.[27]

Haig's efforts to impress American concern on the Soviets had an effect. Haig has acknowledged that the United States "began to receive signals in return . . . that the Soviets were telling their friends to slow down support to insurgencies and urging restraint in their dealings with the United States." Although Haig did not identify the friends, he had Nicaragua in mind. But although those signals were indeed being sent, for some reason in his memoir Haig referred to this intelligence as "rumors, which I did not altogether credit."[28] He did not want to acknowledge this restraint, as it did not jibe with his ongoing and strident campaign about a Soviet threat to the Central American and Caribbean region.

In one instance, the Soviet Union was seen not as manipulating proxies but as the direct aggressor: Afghanistan. In Afghanistan, the only Third World country rent by a civil war and immediately adjoining the Soviet Union itself, the Soviet leaders had reluctantly decided to intervene directly with Soviet military forces.[29] President Jimmy Carter had reacted with strong rhetoric and a wide range of sanctions, including covert supply of arms to the insurgents, known as the *mujahedin*. The Reagan administration continued, and gradually increased, this covert assistance. In March 1982, and periodically thereafter, the United States also charged the Soviet Union with employing lethal myco-

---

24. See Woodward, *Veil*, pp. 96–97, 157–58, 215; and see Jay Peterzell, *Reagan's Secret Wars* (Washington: Center for National Security Studies, 1984), pp. 45–54.

25. Haig, *Caveat*, p. 107, and see pp. 108–10.

26. Ibid., p. 110.

27. Ibid., p. 109.

28. Ibid., p. 108.

29. See Garthoff, *Détente and Confrontation*, chapter 26.

toxins in Afghanistan (and more extensively in Laos and Cambodia) in violation of the convention banning use of chemical and biological weapons.[30]

The Soviet occupation of Afghanistan continued to be pressed in domestic rhetoric, in international forums, and in bilateral discussions with the Soviet leadership.[31] In relative terms, however, it was given less attention in such dialogue owing to the new emphasis on the Central American and Caribbean region. When the United Nations, after two years of shuttle diplomacy opened the way, convened negotiations in June 1982 for a settlement of the conflict in Afghanistan, the United States displayed minimal interest.

Beginning with Haig's conversations in 1981, but especially in 1982–83, with talks at the assistant secretary of state level, several rounds of unpublicized U.S.-Soviet diplomatic exchanges took place that dealt with regional issues and potential crises in southern Africa, the Middle East (in particular the Iran-Iraq war), and Afghanistan. These quiet diplomatic discussions, persisting throughout the decade, were one of the most successful aspects of American diplomacy with the Soviet Union in the 1980s. One main reason was their confidentiality. Another was the interest on both sides in pragmatically probing "rules of engagement" in the regional geopolitical competition. To cite an example, both the United States and the Soviet Union not only warned the other not to exploit the Iran-Iraq war, but also used the opportunity to explain some of their own activities in the region (including U.S. military preparations for contingent action to ensure world access to the Persian Gulf), as those actions might have been subject to misinterpretation by the other side.[32]

Higher-level exchanges on key regional issues occasionally served the same purpose. The Hot Line was used in the Lebanese situation to help prevent misinterpretations. Most important, in September 1982 Secretary of State George Shultz confidentially warned Foreign Minister Andrei Gromyko of serious adverse consequences if MiG aircraft were delivered to Nicaragua, that such

---

30. Secretary of State Alexander M. Haig, Jr., "Chemical Warfare in Southeast Asia and Afghanistan," report to the Congress, March 22, 1982, Current Policy Special Report no. 98 (Department of State, 1982), 32 pp.

    The mycotoxin (specifically tricothecene toxin), commonly called "yellow rain," was said to have been "positively identified" in Laos and Cambodia, and later in Afghanistan, but the allegations as to Soviet (and in Southeast Asia Vietnamese) use of weapons to deliver the toxins was challenged by many and never proved, and presence of the toxin was later generally considered to have natural causes.

31. For example, the U.S. Congress declared March 21, 1982, "Afghanistan Day," initiating an annual commemoration of the struggle of the Afghan people for freedom.

32. Information from informed U.S. officials. Soviet officials, however, have said that the United States failed to inform them in these talks of U.S. Middle East arms sales.

    By the fall of 1982, while not directly colluding, both the United States and the Soviet Union were "tilting" toward Iraq in order not to see a victory by Iran, judged then to be the greater potential threat to the respective interests of both superpowers.

a move would be "unacceptable" to the United States.[33] Despite many earlier signs that the Soviet bloc had intended to provide such aircraft, they were not sent.

The United States also undertook actions, for example, some U.S. programs in Central America and the Caribbean basin, which were not directly related to the Soviet Union, but that would advance American influence while curtailing that of the Soviet Union.

The Middle East was the other prime area of attention. Initially, the administration (Haig) had a curiously naive belief in the possibility of creating a "strategic consensus" to weld "our friends"—Israel and the Arab states—together.[34] This unreal scheme was predicated on the fact that all were America's friends and all shared a desire not to see Soviet influence in the region expand. So far, so good. But the conception ignored the divisions over the Palestinian issue and the exigencies of internal and external relationships and imperatives of the countries. The proposition collapsed of its own weight, but not before causing difficulties, including a bitter battle in Congress over the sale of the airborne warning aircraft surveillance system (AWACS) and other air defense systems to Saudi Arabia. That issue also adversely affected U.S.-Israeli relations. So, in reverse, did Israeli bombing of the Iraqi nuclear reactor in June 1981.

The Israeli invasion of Lebanon in June 1982, on a very thin pretext of retaliation for a terrorist action in London (by an anti-Palestine Liberation Organization Arab splinter group, it soon turned out), opened a wide range of new problems for Israel, Syria, the PLO, Lebanon, the United States, and the Soviet Union. Secretary of State Haig had, knowingly or not, given what the Israelis considered a green light to proceed with their plan. But he was, coincidentally, removed from office almost immediately after the Israeli invasion began, and the administration took an increasingly negative attitude toward the deep Israeli thrust all the way to Beirut.[35]

---

33. See George P. Shultz, *Turmoil and Triumph: My Years as Secretary of State* (Charles Scribner's Sons, 1993), p. 121. Before issuing this warning Shultz had been careful to ascertain that if the MiGs were delivered, the United States would destroy them. (I had noted this confidential démarche on the MiGs in the first edition of my book *Détente and Confrontation* in 1985, p. 1061.)

President Reagan later bluntly reaffirmed this point to Soviet leader Mikhail Gorbachev when they first met, in Geneva in November 1985. A well-informed senior State Department official told me that Reagan said words to the effect that the Soviets could play around in Nicaragua, but if they ever really created a threat to America there the United States would smash it. The Soviet leaders had no intention of building a military base in Nicaragua, but the warnings no doubt reinforced caution on their arms supply and other support for the Sandinistas.

34. See, for example, "Relationship of Foreign and Defense Policies, Secretary Haig's Statement before the Senate Armed Services Committee on July 30, 1981," *State Bulletin*, vol. 81 (September 1981), p. 17.

35. For a perceptive analysis, see George W. Ball, *Error and Betrayal in Lebanon: An Analysis of Israel's Invasion of Lebanon and the Implications for U.S.-Israeli Relations*

The United States landed Marines to help arrange the evacuation of the PLO from Beirut in August, after a cease-fire was arranged, and then withdrew them. But after the Lebanese right-wing Christian Phalange massacred Palestinian refugees in the Shatila and Sabra camps in September in Israeli-controlled territory, and evident Israeli failure to provide security despite a written American pledge to the PLO based on firm Israeli assurances to the United States, the U.S. Marines (together with French and Italian contingents) were brought in.[36] Unlike the European contingents, however, the United States began, through naval gunfire and air action in the interests of local security, to participate haphazardly in the Lebanese civil war.

The Soviets provided Syria with extensive replacements of arms to make up for the losses suffered in the Syrian-Israeli fighting in Lebanon, but made clear to Syria that their commitment did not include any direct Soviet action to assist the Syrians beyond the borders of Syria. While the Soviet Union lost standing by not assisting the PLO in any way, it avoided any direct involvement even after the United States intervened. It did, however, reportedly use the Hot Line in 1982 to warn about the consequences of U.S. intervention in Lebanon.

The Soviet leaders were quite concerned in 1982 over the U.S. military involvement in Lebanon because of what they believed it meant. They could not imagine that the United States would commit the U.S. Marines unless Washington had decided to use force as necessary to meet a broader American aim, which they assumed must be establishment of a U.S. satrapy in Lebanon. The later military withdrawal four months after the tragic and humiliating loss of 241 U.S. Marines in a terrorist truck-bombing in October 1983 was ascribed not to American goodwill or even prudence, but to adverse domestic repercussions in the United States.

In southern Africa, the United States began in 1981 to pursue a new policy called "constructive engagement" (with the Republic of South Africa), aimed at persuading the South Africans to give Namibia independence, and to use the leverage of "covert" South African military pressure in Southern Angola to effect a compromise settlement of the civil war in Angola. Just as the Reagan administration was entering office, a conference on Namibia (Southwest Africa) under UN General Assembly Resolution 435/78 failed, but many people believed the new administration had too hastily decided that an agreed-on 1978 Western plan, which the South Africans had accepted, needed to be revised to make it more acceptable to them. The main new element introduced by the United States was tying Namibian independence to withdrawal of Cuban

---

(Washington: Foundation for Middle East Peace, 1984).

The Israeli invasion of Lebanon definitively ended the quixotic search for a "strategic consensus" among the disparate friends of the United States in the region.

36. Ibid., pp. 55–59.

troops from Angola—which was the primary American interest. A decade later this "constructive engagement" was to succeed, but the Reagan linkage seems to have delayed settlement of both issues.[37]

A second step the new administration took on Africa was to seek congressional action in 1981 to rescind the Clark amendment of 1976 that banned U.S. covert military assistance to the insurgents in Angola. The opposition group UNITA (National Union for the Total Independence of Angola), headed by Jonas Savimbi, was a rebellion against the Marxist regime in Luanda ever since the civil war in 1975–76, with military assistance from South Africa. Though a separate issue, any American renewal of aid to Savimbi would in a sense be another form of U.S. "constructive engagement" with South Africa as well as a challenge to the Soviet- and Cuban-supported Angolan government. Congress (the House, not the Senate), however, declined to remove the Clark amendment restriction, even though the administration claimed it merely wanted to remove what Haig termed a "disabling restraint" on the executive branch.[38]

In fact, William Casey had already in 1981 begun working on support of covert operations through third parties, and one of the first cases was inducing Saudi Arabia secretly to fund the Angolan rebels (and the *mujahedin* in Afghanistan), in part as a quid pro quo for American sale of AWACS to Saudi Arabia.[39]

Apart from occasional ritual references to Soviet "intervention" in Ethiopia, Angola, and Mozambique, the administration did not in the initial years seek directly to counter Soviet activities in those countries. The United States did not, however, seriously consult with the Soviet leaders on most African issues, although there were exploratory talks in 1982 by Assistant Secretary Chester A. Crocker with his Soviet counterpart on the situation in southern Africa.

The United States engaged in several covert operations in those years, short of support for armed insurgencies. One was the successful crushing of the underground communist Tudeh party in Iran in 1983. Based principally on

---

37. For a useful account of the "constructive engagement" policy by its principal author and the official responsible for its implementation, see Chester A. Crocker, *High Noon in Southern Africa: Making Peace in a Rough Neighborhood* (W. W. Norton and Company, 1992).

38. Secretary Haig, in answering press questions, even said repeal of the Clark amendment would "not prejudge" any decision to pursue actions banned by it, "not at all"; "it does not suggest for a moment that anyone is going to engage in the internal intervention in Angolan affairs." See Secretary Alexander M. Haig, Jr., "Question-and-Answer Session following Address before ASNE [the American Society of Newspaper Editors]," April 24, 1981, *State Bulletin*, vol. 81 (June 1981), pp. 9–10.

39. Neil A. Lewis, "Saudis Linked to Donations to Angola Rebels," *New York Times*, July 2, 1987, p. A5. This account was derived from remarks by Saudi Prince Bandar, among other sources.

information from a KGB defector, Vladimir A. Kuzichkin, the United States supplied the Iranians with detailed information which they verified and used to destroy the Tudeh and the Soviet intelligence network in Iran.[40] This was an unusual active measure to reduce potential Soviet influence even in an area where the United States was excluded from influence.

## The Reagan Doctrine, 1983–88

During the years 1983 through 1985, an important new dimension of American policy toward the competition in the Third World unfolded. There was no sudden or single pronouncement or action effecting this shift, which was grounded in the American support for the contras and the *mujahedin* in 1981–82.[41] Symbolically, the American occupation of Grenada in October 1983, together with major increases in aid to the insurgents in Nicaragua and Afghanistan, marked the change. It was articulated more fully in 1985 and expanded in scope.

In an address to the conservative Heritage Foundation in early October 1983, President Reagan applied the crusade against communism that he had announced before the British Parliament in June 1982 to the global geopolitical competition. Claiming that hopes for détente in the late 1970s had "ended in Soviet expansionism in three continents" and the occupation of Afghanistan, he posed the issue in all-encompassing ideological-moral terms: "the struggle now going on in the world is essentially the struggle between freedom and totalitarianism, between what is right and what is wrong." Posed in such Manichean terms, the policy prescription was clear: "The goal of the free world must no longer be stated in the negative, that is, resistance to Soviet expansionism. The goal of the free world must instead be stated in the affirmative. We must go on the offensive with a forward strategy for freedom."[42] And those taking up arms against communist rule were called "freedom fighters," deserving of Western support.[43]

---

40.  See Bob Woodward, "CIA Curried Favor with Khomeini, Exiles; Sources Say Agency Gave Regime List of KGB Agents," *Washington Post*, November 19, 1986, pp. A1, A28.

41.  Indeed, as early as March 1981 CIA Director William Casey had proposed to the National Security Planning Group covert support to resistance movements all over the world: Afghanistan, Cambodia, Cuba, Grenada, Iran, Laos, Libya, and Nicaragua. See Joseph E. Persico, *Casey: From the OSS to the CIA* (Viking, 1990), p. 264.

42.  "Heritage Foundation. Remarks at a Dinner Marking the Foundation's 10th Anniversary," October 3, 1983, *Presidential Documents*, vol. 19 (October 10, 1983), p. 1383.

43.  Steven R. Weisman, "President Calls Nicaragua Rebels Freedom Fighters," *New York Times*, May 5, 1983, p. 1.
     Some members of the administration had used the term earlier, in particular CIA Director Casey in a speech at Georgetown University on April 13, 1983.

The administration gave renewed effort to develop a policy and "doctrine" in its second term. In his 1985 State of the Union address, President Reagan proclaimed, "we must not break faith with those who are risking their lives—on every continent, from Afghanistan to Nicaragua—to defy Soviet-supported aggression."[44] Secretary Shultz soon followed with a major speech on "America and the Struggle for Freedom,"[45] in which he spelled out much more fully what was soon called (though never officially) "the Reagan Doctrine."[46]

The purpose of the Reagan Doctrine was to provide a coherent conceptual framework for explaining American policy, for welding together lofty moral goals of support for freedom, democracy, and human rights with more concrete political-military aims of rolling back Soviet-supported "Marxist" regimes in Afghanistan, Nicaragua, Angola, Ethiopia, and Cambodia (to note those frequently mentioned in the mid-1980s, all mentioned in Shultz's speech). It was predicated on the judgment that there was a shift in the balance of power to American advantage (and that of "the Free World"), and Soviet disadvantage. Shultz, in this and other speeches, referred explicitly to the Soviet conception of the "correlation of forces," and noted that while the correlation of power might have favored the communists in the late 1970s, it no longer did. "Today," he said, "the Soviet empire is weakening under the strain of its own internal problems and external entanglements." That was, indeed, true. Shultz also credited a change in American strength and will "to resist the spread of Soviet influence, and to protect freedom." He explicitly saw the Free World, with active American leadership, now able to turn the tide and "challenge the Brezhnev Doctrine," which held that once communist rule had been established it must not be permitted to be rolled back. Finally, it was also acknowledged that "the outcome of this struggle will affect not only the future of peace and democracy" but also "our own vital interests." Thus the moral high road was seen as also serving American interests, a politically winning combination for domestic consensus and support. "When the United States supports those resisting totalitarianism, therefore, we do so not only out of our historical sympathy for democracy and freedom but also, in many cases, in the interests of national security. . . . In many parts of the world we have no choice but to act, both on moral and strategic grounds."[47]

---

44. "The State of the Union," February 6, 1985, *Presidential Documents*, vol. 21 (February 11, 1985), p. 146.

45. "America and the Struggle for Freedom," February 22, 1985, *State Bulletin*, vol. 85 (April 1985), pp. 16–21. See also Shultz's article, "New Realities and New Ways of Thinking," *Foreign Affairs*, vol. 63 (Spring 1985), pp. 705–21.

46. The term was coined by columnist Charles Krauthammer in "The Reagan Doctrine," *Time*, April 1, 1985, p. 55. (The term had at least one earlier use, but did not then catch on; see an unsigned editorial called "A 'Reagan Doctrine'?" in the *Washington Post*, May 7, 1983, p. A22.)

47. Shultz, *State Bulletin*, vol. 85 (April 1985), pp. 17, 18.

While spokesmen of the Reagan administration occasionally claimed credit for having stopped Soviet expansionism, there had of course been no cases of Soviet-supported regimes coming to power, still less of direct or indirect Soviet interventions, since Afghanistan at the very end of the 1970s, nor any signs that there would have been—no matter what American administration or policy. While still thinly claiming some credit for increased American strength and will, the relevant change was what Shultz rightly noted as "the new phenomenon we are witnessing around the world—popular insurgencies *against* communist domination."[48]

The heart of the Reagan Doctrine, as President Reagan said two years later (when he also first acknowledged it as a "doctrine"), was "helping democratic insurgents in their battle to bring self-determination and human rights to their own countries"—a doctrine for waging "regional conflicts" in the Third World. And he referred to its application in Afghanistan, Nicaragua, and later Angola ("the most recent extension of this policy"). Yet he still referred to it more broadly not only as an attempt to move beyond "containment," but also as the pursuit of "a forward strategy for world freedom."[49] As he put it in another speech, his administration had "declared the principal objective of American foreign policy to be not just the prevention of war but the extension of freedom. . . . And that's why we [have] assisted freedom fighters who are resisting the imposition of totalitarian rule in Afghanistan, Nicaragua, Angola, Cambodia, and elsewhere."[50]

Another new feature of the Reagan Doctrine was its justification for, in effect, indirect or even direct American military intervention in Third World regional (or civil war) conflicts on the basis of "the inherent right of individual and collective self-defense against aggression—aggression of the kind committed by the Soviets in Afghanistan, by Nicaragua in Central America, and by Vietnam in Cambodia."[51] This argument was dubious and was rejected by the International Court of Justice in the case of American mining of Nicaraguan ports in 1984, but it continued to be asserted.

The Reagan Doctrine in theory was broader than in practice. Ideologues on the right emphasized this in urging American arms assistance not only to the "freedom fighters" in Nicaragua, Afghanistan, and (from 1986) Angola, but also to those in Mozambique and Ethiopia. Yet the administration limited serious support to Afghanistan, Nicaragua, and Angola. Even in Cambodia assistance was—wisely—kept limited in view of the weakness of the noncom-

---

48. Ibid, p. 18. Emphasis in the original.

49. "Los Angeles, California. Remarks at a Luncheon," August 26, 1987, *Presidential Documents*, vol. 23 (August 31, 1987), p. 966.

50. "Meeting with Soviet General Secretary Gorbachev in Reykjavik, Iceland," October 13, 1986, ibid., vol. 22 (October 20, 1986), p. 1377.

51. Shultz, *State Bulletin*, vol. 85 (April 1985), p. 19.

munist rebel forces and their alliance with the savage Khmer Rouge; aid to Cambodia (then called Kampuchea) was an initiative of Congress rather than the administration. Certainly there was no inclination to provide aid in a "forward strategy for world freedom" to the opposition against any of the right-wing dictatorships that enjoyed normal or even favored relationships with the United States.[52]

In one important case, Cuba, the Reagan Doctrine was silent, and policy was negative on any attempt to stir up insurgency again (as had been done in the early 1960s). This was a striking change at least of rhetoric from the Haig Doctrine.[53]

Two aspects of the globalism of the Reagan Doctrine as it was stated did cause concern in Moscow. First was the possible application of the doctrine,

---

52. The administration did accept the overthrow of Ferdinand Marcos in the Philippines and Jean Claude (Baby Doc) Duvalier in Haiti, both in February 1986, but only at the last moment, and without enthusiasm. Secretary Shultz has described his great difficulty in persuading President Reagan to recognize Corazon Aquino, who had won election as president, and to ease Marcos into departing. As Shultz noted, even at the end Reagan was "still deeply disturbed at the thought of the fall of a longtime friend and anti-Communist ally." (Shultz, *Turmoil and Triumph,* p. 636, and see pp. 628–29.) Earlier, Vice President George Bush on a visit to the Philippines in 1981, soon after Marcos's controversial "victory" in elections boycotted by all his opponents after their campaigns had been curbed, had gushed to Marcos in a public statement, "We love your adherence to democratic principles and to the democratic processes." See Department of State, *American Foreign Policy: Current Documents 1981* (1984), p. 1049. The next day, the State Department press spokesman when asked about that statement commented that the State Department had not contributed to the vice president's remarks.

   Similarly, according to Shultz, Reagan saw such dictators as General Augusto Pinochet in Chile as merely "authoritarian" and "a friend of the United States and bulwark against Communism"; Shultz did not agree. See Shultz, *Turmoil and Triumph,* p. 970. Some in the administration openly equated anticommunism with democracy. To cite an egregious example, Lieutenant General Robert Schweitzer, promoted after he had been relieved from the NSC staff early in the Reagan administration (see chapter 1, footnote 13), at a reception in October 1985 as the U.S. representative to and president of the Inter-American Defense Board, presented General Pinochet with a ceremonial sword and whitewashed his coup, gratuitously saying, "It was in response to the repeated demands of the people that Your Excellency and the army acted on September 11, 1973, to remove a Marxist-Communist regime." He then went on to express understanding for Pinochet's efforts to make "the transition of your great nation toward a democracy free of the twin scourges of terrorism and subversion . . . each one of our countries has its own distinct way." So much for universal human rights and democratic ideals. Cited in *Harper's Magazine,* May 1986, p. 18.

53. The principal reason was the lack of appropriate "assets" in Cuba; the real change from the Haig era was the subsiding of rhetorical threats against Cuba. In fact even the assets Washington thought it had were an illusion. In mid–1987, as the result of the defection of a very senior Cuban intelligence officer, the United States learned that virtually all of its intelligence network in Cuba since the early 1960s had been controlled by Cuban counterintelligence.

and of American covert arms support for insurgencies, in Eastern Europe.[54] Though no serious consideration was ever given to that course of action, and there were no insurgencies, the Soviet (and some Eastern European communist) leaders were concerned. After all, Reagan and Shultz referred to the doctrine in global terms—U.S. support for forces fighting for freedom "everywhere," "in all continents"—and were never precise about the conditions under which the United States regarded armed action as legitimate. Most ominous, Eastern Europe and even the Soviet Union itself were not excluded from the goal of freedom everywhere; indeed, Shultz's key speech launching the Reagan Doctrine, for example, even included them: "We should support the forces of freedom in communist totalitarian states"—"just as we want freedom for people anywhere else." Moreover, he emphasized that "the United States will never accept the artificial division of Europe into free and not free." To be sure, most, although not all, other indications were that the United States did not contemplate going beyond political means in "the Second World."[55] Today, it seems unremarkable, except for having been prescient, to have taken a stand on principle for freedom of the Eastern European countries. In the mid-1980s, coupled with ambiguous indications of American definitions of collective self-defense as justification for clandestine arms shipments to insurgents against governments recognized by the United States (such as Nicaragua), rather than furthering the proclaimed goal such American policy statements made it more difficult for a Soviet leader seeking to allow freedom of choice in Eastern Europe—as Mikhail Gorbachev was doing in the last half of the 1980s.[56]

Gorbachev and the Soviet leadership did not really believe the United States was intending to try to stir up armed insurgencies in the Soviet Union and Eastern Europe. But their second concern was on the mark: they did see the Reagan Doctrine (or American policy of "neoglobalism," as they usually called it) as directed not only against the regimes in Afghanistan, Nicaragua, Angola, Ethiopia, and Cambodia, but against the Soviet Union as well. Many published sources could be cited on the Soviet reaction, but a much more authoritative secret Central Committee document from mid-1986 is now available from the archives. Its authors (who included Shevardnadze, Dobrynin, and Yakovlev) concluded: "Although the immediate target of the policy of 'neoglobalism' now is mainly countries of the Third World, above all those with progressive regimes, its spearpoint is directed in practice against the Soviet Union and socialism as a whole." The Reagan Doctrine was seen to have as its real objective "not only to stop the further spread and consolidation of positions

---

54. See chapter 13.

55. The United States did, for example, extend covert nonmilitary support to Solidarity in Poland. See chapter 13 for further discussion.

56. See chapter 13.

of socialism in the world, but also to 'exhaust' the USSR and its allies . . . wearing it down in conflicts in different regions of the world."[57]

Most actions taken by the United States under the Reagan Doctrine, other than the references to it in speeches, were at least initially, and in some cases extensively, covert. Later, congressional action (especially on support for the Nicaraguan contras) came to involve extensive public debate. But many activities were kept secret, although with much eventual leakage. Most of these activities involved covert American financing and supplying of weapons, equipment, and training. There did, however, remain some ambiguity about possible direct American military participation—although, in fact, none occurred. At the time, however, this was less clear, as when Secretary of Defense Weinberger in 1986 addressed a U.S. military conference on low-intensity warfare at length on insurgency and counterinsurgency and the role of American "special operations forces." Besides saying the United States "must decide if our interests justify intervention" in any given case, he also spoke ambiguously about how U.S. interests would be determined. For example, "We must decide whether an existing leadership is better or worse for its people and our interests than possible alternatives." Earlier, in 1982, Weinberger had also advanced the concept of "horizontal escalation," whereby the United States might react to a challenge in one place by forceful initiation of a counteraction elsewhere. And in 1983, Weinberger had elevated the Third World-oriented Rapid Deployment Joint Task Force (created in 1980 under the Carter Doctrine) to become U.S. Central Command, at least nominally equal to the European, Atlantic, and Pacific Commands, and promoting its commander to similar four-star status. Now, Weinberger's general theme—sounded in typical hyperbole in his introductory sentences—was that war was all around us, and "in virtually every case, behind the mask is the Soviet Union and those who do its bidding." Moreover, "if it is proper and just that we should help those who wish to remain free, then we can hardly turn our backs on those who have lost their freedom and want it back. It is certain that we cannot co-exist with the so-called Brezhnev Doctrine."[58]

---

57. From the Center for the Storage of Contemporary Documentation (TsKhSD), the former Central Committee archive. TsKhSD, Fond 3, Opis 102, Dokument 230, *O merakh po usileniyu nashego protivodeistviya amerikanskoi politike 'neoglobalizma'* (On Measures to Strengthen Our Counteractions to the American Policy of "Neoglobalism"), resolution (*postanovleniye*) of the Central Committee of the CPSU, July 31, 1986 (p. 1 of the Resolution; p. 172 of the archive file). (The final approved Resolution is also stamped August 1, while the typescript is dated July 31, 1986.)

58. "Remarks Prepared for Delivery by the Honorable Caspar W. Weinberger, Secretary of Defense, at the Conference on Low-Intensity Warfare," January 14, 1986, Office of the Assistant Secretary of Defense (Public Affairs), Washington, January 14, 1986, pp. 1, 3, 4, 6.

To cite one other example, despite public assurances by the president in 1983 that no use of American troops against Nicaragua was "planned," a secret report to Congress

Whatever intended or unintended ambiguities surrounded American intentions on U.S. implementation of the Reagan Doctrine, there was a still wider blurring of responsibility. A substantial number of American and international privateers were at work debating, organizing, and in some cases participating in paramilitary activities around the world. For example, in June 1985, before Congress had revoked the Clark amendment banning U.S. assistance to the rebels in Angola, a global "alliance" of anticommunist insurgents, calling themselves Armed Movements Fighting Against Soviet Expansionism, met in Jamba, Angola, Savimbi's rebel stronghold. Guerrilla leaders from Afghanistan, Nicaragua, Angola, and Laos participated. The conference was sponsored by the private Washington-based Citizens for America, a conservative lobbying group chaired by Lewis Lehrman. Jonas Savimbi announced that the first goal of the alliance (which one might have supposed would be to coordinate and press its efforts) would be "to make the people of the United States understand the struggle." But there was an even more unusual feature of the affair: President Reagan had sent a message of support to the conference, saying the rebels' goals "are our goals"—a rash moral commitment, as well as an ill-considered political action.[59] Three months later, when the World Anti-Communist League held its eighteenth annual convention in Dallas, President Reagan again sent greetings and a message saying: "I commend you all for your part in this noble cause. Our combined efforts are moving the tide of history toward world freedom." Before commending them "all," Reagan would have been well advised to learn that the conferees included people closely tied to the right-wing death squads in Honduras, Guatemala, and El Salvador, rapacious rebels in Mozambique, representatives of *Soldier of Fortune* magazine, and others not all devoted to the "noble cause" Reagan had in his vision.[60]

---

in May 1985 included a statement, later leaked to the press, that the use of American forces in Nicaragua "must realistically be recognized as an eventual option, given our stakes in the region, if other policy options fail." Cited in Shirley Christian, "Reagan Aides See No Possibility of U.S. Accord with Sandinistas," *New York Times*, August 18, 1985, pp. A1, A16.

59. Alfonzo Chardy, "Rebels of 4 Nations Form Antileftist Front: Groups' Meeting in Angola Organized by U.S. Lobby," *Washington Post*, June 6, 1985, pp. A29–30. The Soviet press gave the meeting, and Reagan's letter, some attention.

    I was told by White House staff that Reagan sent the letter because he liked the general objective, and because Lehrman, who was an old friend and New York Republican supporter, had asked him to; the Department of State was not consulted about the letter.

60. See Charles R. Babcock, "Dallas Hosts Anti-Communist League," *Washington Post*, September 17, 1985, p. A14; Sidney Blumenthal, "The Contra Conclave: 'Freedom Fighters' Gather in Washington," *Washington Post*, July 17, 1986, pp. B1, B3; Jack Anderson and Joseph Spear, "Anti-Communist League Unleashed," *Washington Post*, August 9, 1986, p. F11.

    One of the contra representatives present, Mario Calero, told a television team: "We need money without any strings attached, without any humanitarian baloney."

The Reagan Doctrine appealed especially to the ideological anticommunists in the administration, and to Reagan's ideological sentiments, but it was also useful to those with more concrete political and strategic aims, such as Secretary Shultz, who sought to press the Soviet Union to cease supporting Marxist regimes, but also to work for resolving regional conflicts. It was also welcomed by those like William Casey and others who wished to bolster covert operations, and by Secretary Weinberger and others who opposed negotiation with the Soviet Union and wanted to keep an atmosphere of threat that would bolster large defense fundings.

The articulation of a "doctrine" and policy as a struggle between forces of Good and Evil carried within it the seeds of serious difficulties. First of all, it did not reflect reality. The governments of Nicaragua, Angola, Afghanistan, Cambodia, Ethiopia, and Mozambique were led by self-styled Marxists, and all were in some degree authoritarian, but they varied greatly in their faults and virtues. Moreover, all were indigenous regimes. The insurgents were also a varied mix (some of whom, especially in Ethiopia and Cambodia, and arguably Angola, were also Marxists). By defining all insurgents as anticommunists and defining anticommunist as prodemocracy, the United States government credited fundamentalist *mujahedin*, contras, and Angolan tribal warriors as "freedom fighters," fighting for democracy and human rights, when that was simply not true. Yet President Reagan even called the contras "the moral equal of our Founding Fathers."[61] Very often the most important distinguishing attribute of these fighters was simply a struggle for power, or against traditional foes, or the experience of privation, not pro- or antidemocratic values. Within a few years, the same governments in Afghanistan, Angola, Cambodia, and Mozambique gave up their Marxism. Those in Nicaragua and Cambodia gave up power, in Nicaragua after conducting and losing a free election in 1990. In Angola, after a free election in 1993 the loser—our "freedom fighter" Savimbi, supposedly dedicated to democracy—was the one to resume a war. In Afghanistan, the victorious "democratic" *mujahedin* after 1992 fought with at least as much enthusiasm against one another as they had against the previous regime. Human rights (of women, in particular) were often *less* respected.

The second flaw of the doctrine was cultivation of a double standard in American thinking. Secretary Shultz bridled when news reporters asked him to define the difference between a terrorist and a freedom fighter—to him the difference was essential.[62] But contra freedom fighters fought very much as did Salvadoran insurgents, or any other rural guerrilla force. And when the United

---

61. "Conservative Political Action Conference," March 1, 1985, *Presidential Documents*, vol. 21 (March 11, 1985), p. 245. This speech was drafted by Anthony Dolan, who got the idea for the comparison to the Founding Fathers from William Casey. See Persico, *Casey*, p. 431.

62. See "Question-and-Answer Session," February 22, 1985, *State Bulletin*, vol. 85 (April 1985), p. 21; and see Shultz, *Turmoil and Triumph*, p. 645.

States itself trained contras in planting explosives, sabotage, techniques for silent killing, and other tradecraft indistinguishable from terrorist activity, it could not really sustain the distinction. The United States employed Ramon Medina in training contras and in general as a "counterterrorist" expert in Central America; whence his expertise? As Luis Posada Carriles, his real name, he was a terrorist who is still wanted by Venezuela for planting a bomb that blew up a Cubana de Aviación civil airliner in October 1976, killing seventy-three people. Perhaps the United States did not consider that a terrorist act because it was, after all, an anti-Castro action; in any case he was not only not turned over to Venezuela, but put on the American off-the-books payroll. Regrettably, many such examples could be cited.

A third, related flaw in the Manichean framework of the Reagan Doctrine was the logical bar to negotiation and compromise. Angels do not compromise with the Devil. In practice, with difficulties, the United States (and other parties) did negotiate and resolve many of these conflicts. In some cases material support for insurgents may have contributed to more favorable outcomes. But in no case did a good versus evil approach contribute anything constructive.

The fourth serious shortcoming of the Reagan Doctrine was its effect of giving priority to the one objective of weakening Soviet-aligned governments without weighing the cost to other American interests and objectives. For example, it meant setting aside American efforts to press Pakistan to give up its nuclear weapons program; because the United States needed Pakistan to channel arms to the *mujahedin*, sanctions could not be threatened (even those required under existing U.S. law). It meant compromising not only efforts, but principles, on human rights in several countries: El Salvador, Pakistan, South Africa, Zaire (used as transit for supply to UNITA in Angola), and others. It meant overlooking deep involvement in the drug trade by U.S. "proxies," the *mujahedin*, and others involved in the supply effort to the contras. Finally, it meant misdirecting economic assistance, providing disproportionate aid (real assistance, and euphemistic but still costly distortions of local economies for building military infrastructures) to countries such as Pakistan, China, Honduras, and El Salvador. The American share in the international arms trade also went up in those years.

Fifth, these covert operations meant political associations and political debts that were discreditable and later sometimes embarrassing and incalculable. For example, one of the first associations in contra recruitment and training in 1981–82 (before the Falkland Islands War) was with the Argentine generals whose repressive rule in Argentina was overlooked. Later, one channel to support the contras was General Manuel Noriega of Panama, who had for some time been on the CIA payroll. Similarly, in Afghanistan U.S. arms mostly went to Islamic fundamentalists, many of whom had fought against the precommunist Afghan governments and now contribute to the postcommunist civil strife. Moreover, some of the international *mujahedin* from Arabia and elsewhere who fought in Afghanistan and were armed (by Pakistan) with U.S. arms, were within a few years even fighting in Bosnia and post-Soviet Azerbaijan and Tajikistan, as well as in postcommunist Afghanistan.

Finally, the Reagan Doctrine framework of subordinating all else to "freedom fighting" incurred the extensive and deeply debilitating consequences of widespread violations of the law—of American law and international law. None of the expositions of the Reagan Doctrine raised the question of legality of the actions being advocated and undertaken, for good reason.[63] The actions could not be justified. There is no need to recall the many instances revealed in the Iran-contra scandal alone, and there were many more than those disclosed.

The "public diplomacy" propaganda and active measures program launched by the U.S. administration in 1983 and run from the NSC was focused in part on the Third World.[64] The State Department established the Office of Public Diplomacy for Latin America and the Caribbean, mainly to influence public opinion in the United States to support the contras. The office sought to circumvent the ban on such activity by the United States Information Agency (USIA), although USIA officers were included on its staff. It was terminated in late 1986 after the Iran-contra scandal broke and a year later was found by the General Accounting Office to have been a violation of the law banning publicity and propaganda activities in the United States.[65] The Defense Department had a similar operation in the Office of Public Support Programs under the deputy undersecretary for policy.[66]

---

63. Earlier, in a speech seeking to justify initial support for the contras for the narrow "defensive" purpose of preventing the flow of arms to El Salvador, the president did make a dubious claim of legitimacy, contending that purpose was "in conformity with American and international law." See "Central America. Address Delivered before a Joint Session of the Congress," April 27, 1983, *Presidential Documents*, vol. 19 (May 2, 1983), p. 611.

64. See chapter 3. This program, although also directed to Eastern Europe, was especially active in seeking to gain support for the contras and other U.S. programs in Central America and the Caribbean (for Eastern Europe, see chapter 13).

65. See Joe Pichirallo, "NSC Oversaw Office in State Department," *Washington Post*, September 19, 1987, p. A18; Richard L. Berke, "State Department Linked to Contra Publicity," *New York Times*, October 5, 1987, p. A3; Pirachello, "Ex-Head of State Dept. Office Denies Illicit Propaganda Role," *Washington Post*, October 11, 1987, p. A16; and Joanne Omang, "The People Who Sell Foreign Policies," *Washington Post*, October 15, 1985, p. A21.

   One small example from their work illustrates its quality. A September 1985 report called "Revolution Beyond Our Borders" quoted Sandinista leader Tomas Borge as having said in 1981, "This revolution goes beyond our borders," but it omitted the sentence following, in which Borge went on to say, "This does not mean we export our revolution. It is sufficient that they follow our example." Omang, *Washington Post*, October 15, 1985, p. A1.

66. One of the papers prepared by their office on "The Strategic Importance of Central America for the United States," by Colonel Nestor G. Pino-Marina, in 1985 was replete

The Reagan Doctrine characterized American policy toward the key regional (mostly civil war) conflicts in the Third World, which provided the main bone of contention between the United States and the Soviet Union during the remaining years of the Reagan administration.

The burgeoning U.S. covert action program and support to antigovernment insurgents being sent into Nicaragua in the early 1980s gradually became publicly known and proved controversial. President Reagan throughout staunchly defended support to the contras, but congressional support waxed and waned. The administration, or at least parts of it, attempted to keep an active diplomatic track going, hoping that the contra pressure would lead the Sandinistas to compromise by backing off on their support to the Salvadoran insurgents and attenuating their own military ties with Cuba and the Soviet Union. Secretary Shultz, and his successive assistant secretaries for Latin American affairs Thomas O. Enders and Langhorne A. Motley, worked with the Central American states in the Contadora process, and with the Nicaraguans directly, but they were opposed at every turn by Casey of the CIA, and William Clark and NSC staffers in the White House.[67] Meanwhile, throughout 1983 and 1984 the anomaly of a widely publicized and openly debated and funded "covert" operation to overthrow the recognized government of a country with which the United States was not at war became even more bizarre. The turning point leading in October 1984 to a congressional cutoff of funding was the mining by CIA agents—with White House authorization—of Nicaraguan ports with deaths and damage to ships of other countries.[68] The Senate voted 84 to 12 to condemn the mining, and the House soon followed, 281 to

with such scare-propaganda as maps depicting SS–20 intermediate-range missile coverage of North America from Nicaragua, and alleging an existing Nicaraguan military buildup of 120,000 men, with dire warnings that "America must not be mislead [sic] by the Soviets or its [sic] regional surrogates" (p. 22). Colonel Pino-Marina, by the way, a key U.S. Army adviser on Central America and the Caribbean, was a graduate of the Cuban cadet school under Batista, a member of the Bay of Pigs brigade in 1961, and one of its veterans given U.S. citizenship and entrance into the U.S. Army under special dispensation after the collapse of that Cuban venture. His qualifications for advising on U.S. policy toward the region were mixed.

67. See Shultz, *Turmoil and Triumph*, pp. 305, 400–04.

68. Bob Woodward and Fred Hiatt, "CIA Views Minelaying Part of Covert 'Holding Action': Stepped-Up Role Seen after U.S. Elections," *Washington Post*, April 10, 1984, pp. A1, A15; Fred Hiatt and Joanne Omang, "CIA Helped to Mine Ports in Nicaragua," *Washington Post*, April 7, 1984, pp. A1, A24; Persico, *Casey*, pp. 371–80; and see *The Mining of Nicaraguan Ports and Harbors*, Hearing and Markup before the Committee on Foreign Affairs, House of Representatives, 98 Cong. 2 sess., on H. Con. Res. 290, April 11, 1984 (Washington: Government Printing Office, 1984).

Secretary of State Shultz was "astonished" when he learned of the mining. He had been privy to a proposal for such action in 1983 and had successfully opposed it. Later, he was not informed when the matter was again considered and decided on. See Shultz, *Turmoil and Triumph*, pp. 306–08, 404–06.

111.[69] Although that action was not binding on the administration, Congress also soon moved to cut off all funds for covert support for the contras.[70] The final blow was the revelation that the CIA had prepared for the contras a manual on the conduct of operations that included only thinly veiled language on selective terrorism and assassination.[71] The contras continued their operations with other sources of support, including large sums from unofficial U.S. sources,[72] and money contributed by other countries at official American request, sometimes in violation of American law. Eventually, illicit Iranian arms sales revenues were channeled to this support, which when revealed in November 1986 became the Iran-contra scandal.

For all of the American escalation of support for the contras, the insurgents were unable to make serious inroads in Nicaragua, or establish a secure base area, much less to challenge the government. American support and the Honduran sanctuary kept them in action, however, and the Sandinista army could not extirpate them. A stalemate developed.

In El Salvador, while the guerrillas had suffered a major setback on their premature offensive on the eve of the Reagan administration, they had sufficiently broad popular support to maintain a continuing insurrection. Although Haig's plans for an early victory also failed, continuing U.S. support and military assistance kept the Salvadoran government in control. As in Nicaragua, a military stalemate developed in El Salvador over the decade: neither the government nor the guerrillas could defeat the other.

The U.S. government continued to impute a responsibility for the civil war in El Salvador to Soviet, Cuban, and Nicaraguan instigation, though with-

---

69. Joanne Omang and Don Oberdorfer, "Senate Votes, 84–12, to Condemn Mining of Nicaraguan Ports: Administration Tries to Defend Its Position," *Washington Post*, April 11, 1984, pp. A1, A16; and T. R. Reid and Joanne Omang, "CIA Funds Run Short for Covert Operations: House Joins Senate to Condemn U.S. Participation in Minelaying," *Washington Post*, April 13, 1984, pp. A1, A18.

   Nicaragua also took the case to the International Court of Justice (the World Court) in the Hague, and although the U.S. government denied competence of the Court, it heard the case and on November 26, 1984, found the United States guilty of illegal activity in the mining and other belligerent activities.

70. Martin Tolchin, "Senators, 88 to 1, Drop Money to Aid Nicaragua Rebels," *New York Times*, June 26, 1984, p. A1; Philip Taubman, "White House Quits Rebel Aid Battle," *New York Times*, July 25, 1984, p. A1; and Taubman, "House Votes to Deny Help to Nicaraguan Insurgents," *New York Times*, August 3, 1984, p. A3.

71. "CIA Said to Produce Manual for Anti-Sandinistas," *New York Times*, October 15, 1984, p. A7; "Excerpts from Primer for Insurgents," *New York Times*, October 17, 1984, p. A12; Joel Brinkley, "C. I. A. Primer Tells Nicaraguan Rebels How to Kill," *New York Times*, October 17, 1984, p. A1; and see Persico, *Casey*, pp. 417–18.

72. Lou Cannon, Don Oberdorfer, and George Lardner, Jr., "Private U.S. Groups Raise Funds for Contras," *Washington Post*, September 10, 1984, p. A22; and Fred Hiatt, "Private Groups Press 'Contra' Aid: Millions Raised in U.S.," *Washington Post*, December 10, 1984, pp. A1, A19.

out the shrill vehemence of 1981–82, but the only demonstrable connection was occasional interception of small shipments of arms brought in from Nicaragua.

The American invasion of Grenada in October 1983 represented a rare instance of U.S. readiness to use its own military power directly to eliminate a communist-aligned regime, under unusual circumstances where that could be done expeditiously. While not typical in this direct and overt use of American military power, the Grenada operation (codenamed Urgent Fury) was quite in keeping with the aims of the Reagan Doctrine: it rolled back communist rule.

President Reagan had, in several earlier speeches, noted construction of a 10,000-foot airfield runway in Grenada that he suggested could be used to support Soviet or Cuban military aircraft. "Grenada," he noted, "does not even have an air force. Who is it intended for?" His conclusion was that "the Soviet-Cuban militarization of Grenada, in short, can only be seen as power projection into the region."[73] Though such an airfield might have been used occasionally by Soviet military aircraft, the reason Grenada needed a long-runway airport was to compete with other nearby islands for foreign tourists able to land on Boeing 747s.[74]

The American decision to move militarily on Grenada was a sudden one, when internal conflict in the Grenada regime caused some concern about the safety of the large number of American students there, and about a possibly more radical turn threatening to neighboring island states, especially after Prime Minister Maurice Bishop and several other leaders were killed in a coup on October 19, 1983. An American invasion force of some 7,000 men, supplemented by token forces from several eastern Caribbean island states, suddenly landed on October 25, and soon overwhelmed the 600-man Grenadan army

---

73. See, in particular, "National Security, Address to the Nation," March 23, 1983, *Presidential Documents*, vol. 19 (March 3, 1983), p. 445.

74. Trinidad and Barbados, for example, each had airports with runways of 10,500 to 11,000 feet, permitting Boeing 747s from North America to land.

    Among the Grenadan documents captured after the American invasion, records of a Central Committee meeting in July 1983 make clear that the airport was regarded as a key investment project to develop the tourist industry, along with seven planned new hotels. Moreover, while Reagan said the airport was being built by the Cubans "with Soviet financing and backing," in fact the Soviet Union did not finance it. In March 1981, the Reagan administration had persuaded the European Community not to provide financing for the airport. Grenada had to seek financing from Algeria, Libya, Venezuela, and some Western European countries. The project was managed by a reputable British firm, Plessy Airports, which confirmed that it was being built to standard commercial specifications.

    Finally, it was the United States that financed completion of the airport in 1984–85 (for some $19 million). President Reagan landed on the new airport when he paid a visit in early 1986, at which time he noted its value for the tourist industry.

and 636 Cuban construction personnel (most Army reservists) led by 43 Cuban military professionals.[75]

When President Reagan announced the invasion on October 25, he said the action was being taken for three reasons: "First, and of overriding importance, to protect innocent lives, including up to a thousand Americans, whose personal safety is, of course, my paramount concern. Second, to forestall further chaos. And third, to assist in the restoration of conditions of law and order" (later paraphrased to say the restoration of democratic institutions) in Grenada.[76] These same objectives were cited in a letter sent to the leaders of the two houses of Congress in compliance with the notification on deployment of the armed forces called for in the War Powers Act.[77] He also stressed the request for assistance from the Organization of Eastern Caribbean States (OECS). The chairman of the OECS, Prime Minister Eugenia Charles of Dominica, was present when he made his announcement. Later, the administration cited an appeal from Governor General Sir Paul Scoon of Grenada, which it was said could not be cited on October 25 because his safety had not then yet been assured.[78] In the initial statements, nothing was said about a Cuban or Soviet threat or even connection to the events in Grenada, and the United States informed both Moscow and Havana that the action was not directed against them. Secretary Shultz advised the State Department spokesman that this was "not an East-West confrontation" and that "we must keep our statements in line with our legal position: our action was undertaken at the request of the Organization of Eastern Caribbean States and its central purpose was to rescue the American students."[79]

These justifications for action were weak in substance and dubious in legitimation of the action—whatever its moral and political merits and favorable consequences.

The American students were not in danger, but if they or the U.S. government had in prudence wished to evacuate them, they could easily have done so. Administration arguments rest heavily on the assertion that the airport

---

75. It is not necessary here to review the complex American decisionmaking process or the sometimes confused military operation itself. According to the official reports, 18 Americans were combat fatalities and 116 wounded, along with 24 Cuban deaths and 59 wounded, and 45 Grenadans (mostly civilians) dead and 337 wounded.

76. "Situation in Grenada," October 25, 1983, *Presidential Documents*, vol. 19 (October 31, 1983), p. 1487.

77. "United States Forces in Grenada. Letter to the Speaker of the House and the President Pro Tempore of the Senate," October 25, 1983, ibid, p. 1493.

78. Deputy Secretary of State Kenneth W. Dam, "The Larger Importance of Grenada," Current Policy 526 (Department of State, 1983), p. 2.

79. Shultz, *Turmoil and Triumph*, pp. 335–36.

was "closed to general commercial traffic."[80] That assertion is misleading; the airport was open. Four commercial charter planes left the day before the invasion, including one chartered by Canada to evacuate twenty-nine Canadians who wished to leave. Scheduled airline service had stopped not because of any interference by the Grenadan authorities, but because the OECS—who had just asked the United States to intervene—banned all flights to Grenada through their airports, cutting it off. The administration also claimed that a "shoot-to-kill' nighttime curfew prevented the students' movement. Yet the curfew had been lifted the day before the invasion, and the fact that it would be had been announced on October 21, before the invasion decision was made.

The key element in the administration's justification was the appeal from the OECS. Yet under the OECS Treaty decisions by its members must be unanimous, and only five of the seven parties participated—one of those absent of course being Grenada. Even if the request of the OECS (or rather five of its members) had been legally valid, there is also a serious question about whether the United States (and Jamaica and Barbados) was entitled to join them, inasmuch as the charter of the Organization of American States (OAS), to say nothing of the UN Charter, bans intervention.[81]

The later additional justification, the appeal from Governor General Scoon, was made not to the United States but to the OECS; moreover, it was oral and passed through an intermediary (on October 24, two days *after* the U.S. decision to invade). The United States on October 27 was given a letter "dated October 24" but evidently signed later by Scoon. In any event, while the governor general represented an element of legitimacy, he was the representative of the Queen of England—and the queen's first minister, Margaret Thatcher, emphatically objected to the proposed invasion of Grenada, a Commonwealth country.

An inconclusive debate later rumbled in political-legal circles for some time, but the administration was not politically challenged at home.[82] Few Americans were even aware that the UN Security Council voted 11 to 1 against the U.S. action (Britain abstaining, France opposing), requiring rare American use of its veto. Nor that most of the U.S. allies in NATO and the OAS criticized the U.S. action. The military campaign was short, with only 18 American

---

80. Assistant Secretary of State Langhorne A. Motley, "The Decision to Assist Grenada," testimony before the House Armed Services Committee, January 24, 1984, Current Policy 541 (Department of State, 1984), p. 2.

81. There was also a technicality, in that St. Lucia, on behalf of the other OECS members, had never completed the registration of the 1981 OECS Treaty with the United Nations, so that it was not valid vis-à-vis other countries.

82. Most Democrats supported the action or remained silent after public reaction proved strongly favorable. The most thorough and trenchant criticism was given by Congressman Les Aspin; see "A Look at the Grenada Invasion," *Congressional Record*, vol. 130 (January 23, 1984), p. E49.

combat deaths, the American students were safe and sound, and the action was welcomed not only in the United States but also by the people of Grenada and the neighboring East Caribbean islands. It was at least locally a success.

On October 27, President Reagan delivered a rousing address to the nation on both the tragic terrorist attack killing 241 Americans in Beirut and the successful military operation in Grenada. Secretary Shultz's cautions were thrown to the winds. The same objectives in Grenada, to be sure, were reiterated and even elaborated. For example, in reaffirming the government's "responsibility to go to the aid of its citizens, if their right to life and liberty is threatened," Reagan went on to say, "The nightmare of our hostages in Iran must never be repeated."[83] No doubt President Reagan was concerned about the safety of the American students and was concerned over a possible hostage situation. He also elaborated on the need to restore law and order, saying, "Grenada was without a government, its only authority exercised by a self-proclaimed band of military men."[84] In fact, though the new leaders of Grenada were ruthless in dealing with their former leader and his supporters, and there was widespread public discontent (prompting the curfew), there had been virtually no disorder or bloodshed since October 19. General Hudson Austin, the minister of defense and new strongman, was not head of "a self-proclaimed band," and the government, now led by Deputy Prime Minister Bernard Coard, while lacking in legitimacy, was no more illegitimate or ineffective than a number of other states that the United States had not invaded.

The same justification for the intervention also continued to be offered. But a new and quite different kind of political and geopolitical justification, more in line with the real reason for the intervention, was also introduced.

The new theme of Reagan's address was a slashing attack on the Soviet Union and Cuba, and an attempt to justify the American action as a necessary countermeasure. By tying this justification to a military operation to "restore democracy" to Grenada, the Reagan Doctrine was manifest in a sharply etched way, even more so than the more typical cases of its application in supporting proxy insurgents against what were depicted as Soviet-bloc proxy regimes.

Reagan said the Cubans working on the airport turned out to be larger in number and "a military force," which, he said, "makes it clear a Cuban occupation of the island had been planned."[85] The American troops did discover larger stocks of small arms and other weapons than they had expected,

---

83. "Events in Lebanon and Grenada. Address to the Nation," October 27, 1983, *Presidential Documents*, vol. 19 (October 31, 1983), p. 1501.

84. Ibid.

85. Ibid. This claim of a planned Cuban occupation of the island, for which there was absolutely no evidence, was soon dropped. The U.S. command, having raised its estimate of Cuban personnel from 600 to 1,100 by October 27, soon had to acknowledge that there were 784 Cubans in all, including 636 construction workers and 43 professional military men.

and the secret documents (seventeen tons of documents were seized and studied) revealed plans for a total of some 10,000 rifles, 4,500 submachine and
machine guns, 80 artillery and 48 antiaircraft artillery. guns, no tanks, and two
transport airplanes. The documents showed Grenada had plans for a total force
of some 7,200 men, of whom however three-fourths would be reservists.[86] But
President Reagan described the warehouses of guns as "enough to supply
thousands of terrorists." Grenada, Reagan said, "was a Soviet-Cuban colony,
being readied as a major military bastion to export terror and undermine
democracy. We got there just in time."[87]

And in a curious juxtaposition, Reagan undercut the credibility of his
claims on Grenada by gratuitously tying them to the situation in Lebanon,
unlike in virtually all respects including the one he advanced. "The events in
Lebanon and Grenada, though oceans apart," he said, "are clearly related. Not
only has Moscow assisted and encouraged the violence in both countries, but it
provides direct support through a network of surrogates and terrorists. It is no
coincidence that when the thugs tried to wrest control over Grenada, there
were 30 Soviet advisers and hundreds of Cuban military and paramilitary forces
on the island." This thesis of a connection rested in part on Reagan's belief that
the new leaders were "more radical" than Bishop, which was true, and "more
devoted to Castro's Cuba," which was not.[88] Reagan also referred to the airport,
which the Grenadans "claimed was for tourist trade, but which looked suspiciously suitable for military aircraft, including Soviet-built long-range bombers."[89] But the heart of Reagan's case against the Soviet Union was not even
circumstantial; it was mythical and ideological.

The State Department, for example, in several publications reported
that the American invasion force had found "almost 900 Cuban, Soviet, North
Korean, Libyan, East German, and Bulgarian personnel, including 'permanent'
military advisers."[90] That sounds impressive, an ominous phalanx of communists
and radicals (Libya). Who were they? There were 49 Soviet personnel, 17
Libyans, 10 North Koreans, 10 East Germans, and 3 Bulgarians—almost all the

---

86. See Department of State and Department of Defense, *Grenada: A Preliminary Report*
(1983), pp. 18–30.

87. Presidential Documents, vol. 19 (October 31, 1983), p. 1501.
    Casey also hyped the alleged subversive threat from Grenada in giving background
to journalists even though the CIA experts had convincingly argued to him that no such
threat existed. See Persico, *Casey*, pp. 354–56.

88. Ibid., pp. 1500–01. Shultz in his memoir also still believed the new Grenadan leaders,
Bernard Coard and Hudson Austin, were "very much in the Cuban camp." See Shultz,
*Turmoil and Triumph*, pp. 341, 325. This was not the case.

89. Ibid., p. 1500. Even in his memoir a decade later, Secretary Shultz still said the airport
"obviously was for military use, not for 'tourism.' " Shultz, *Turmoil and Triumph*,
pp. 341, 324.

90. GIST, *Grenada Collective Action* (Department of State, 1984), p. 1.

staffs of their respective embassies. Of the 784 Cubans, 636 were airfield construction workers, 19 diplomatic staff, 29 health and education advisers, 43 military, and various other categories. What was so ominous about those "almost 900" people from six countries? As for the "permanent" military advisers, that applied to some of the 43 Cubans distinguished from others who were on two- to four-month temporary rotational duty, nothing more.

The charge of "terrorist" purposes and subversive export of revolution had no foundation. None. The secret documents indicate that all the arms were provided only for Grenadan defense and indeed included clauses banning transfer to any third party. They were all compatible with defense of the island, none with special applicability for use against other countries (with no maritime or air transport), and many clearly not useful for such purposes (such as antiaircraft defense guns and 50 warning sirens). In the security field, the Grenadans had requested training by the Soviet Union for three counterintelligence officers and one intelligence officer.

The most frequently cited reference, the only one that might be taken to imply a Soviet interest in expansion of communism, was a remark by Marshal Nikolai Ogarkov to his counterpart, Major Einstein Louison, chief of staff of the Grenadan Army. From Louison's memorandum of the meeting (in March 1983), Ogarkov had commented that "over two decades ago, there was only Cuba in Latin America [as a progressive country], today there are Nicaragua, Grenada and a serious battle is going on in El Salvador." He noted American attempts "to prevent progress, but there were no prospects for imperialism to turn back history." He warned that Grenada, being so close to the United States, must be "vigilant," and that the Soviet Union would "contribute to raising the combat readiness and preparedness of the Armed Forces of Grenada," but he was noncommittal when Louison asked about a pending request for fuel, spare parts, uniforms, and the like. He was giving Louison a pep talk and certainly not an assignment to carry a revolution forward beyond Grenada. Indeed, he even put Major Louison down; as Louison himself noted in his memorandum, "Marshal Ogarkov replied rather jokingly [to the request for supplies] that students should be concerned with studies"—Louison was completing a six-month course in Moscow as a tactical infantry officer.[91]

It was true that the Grenadans had concluded that to get Moscow's attention they must strive to be useful to the Soviet Union. For example, Grenada and Cuba (but not Nicaragua) voted against the UN General Assembly resolution condemning the Soviet invasion of Afghanistan. One of the captured documents, a report to Grenada from its ambassador in Moscow, W. Richard

---

91. Paul Seaburg and Walter A. McDougall, eds., *The Grenada Papers* (San Francisco: Institute for Contemporary Studies, 1984), pp. 190–91. Also in Jiri Valenta and Herbert J. Ellison, eds., *Grenada and Soviet/Cuban Policy: Internal Crisis and U.S./OECS Intervention* (Westview Press, 1986), p. 310. Both volumes provide extensive documentary collections, the latter offering more varied commentary.

Jacobs, in July 1983, included his observation that "by itself, Grenada's distance from the USSR, and its small size, would mean that we would figure in a very minute way in the USSR's global relationships. . . . For Grenada to assume a position of increasingly greater importance, we have to be seen as influencing regional events. We have to . . . be the sponsor of revolutionary activity and progressive development in this region at least." But this did not mean exporting subversion and revolution. "At the same time, we have to develop and maintain normal state to state relations with our neighbours." His concrete recommendation was to try to steer Suriname into Soviet-Cuban alignment: "If we can be an overwhelming influence on Suriname's international behaviour, then our importance in the Soviet scheme of things will be greatly enhanced."[92]

The United States sought to gear up a major public relations or propaganda campaign based on the captured documents, but it was not very successful despite several books and many articles enthusiastically following the administration's line because anyone who familiarized himself with the materials soon discovered that objectively they did not support the administration's contentions.[93] One of the weakest arguments advanced, that the arms shipped to Grenada were in excess of needs for defense, was absurd on the face of it—they had just proved woefully inadequate.

The Soviet Union and Cuba, needless to say, condemned the American invasion, but they did not display any other reaction.[94] Incidentally, on October 26, as the State Department was negotiating arrangements with Havana on the possible surrender and return of the Cubans on Grenada, CIA Director William Casey called Deputy Secretary Kenneth Dam and told him that he, Casey, had arranged with General Manuel Noriega to fly from Panama to Havana, and he was there ready to act as the U.S. representative. Secretary Shultz, understandably annoyed at this unauthorized and unwanted action, passed word back to Casey to "forget it."[95]

---

92. In Seaburg and McDougall, *Grenada Papers*, pp. 207–08; and Valenta and Ellison, *Grenada*, pp. 332, 334.

93. Among those commissioned to exploit the materials was the ubiquitous Michael Ledeen, expert on terrorism and disinformation, whose name has appeared in a number of connections.

94. Fidel Castro was harder on the Cuban officer he had sent, a few days before the invasion, to rally resistance. Colonel Pédro Tortoló Comas, who had headed Cuban military advisers in Grenada from 1981 until the spring of 1983, was ordered to lead a fight to the death. When Tortoló and his men surrendered (after twenty-four deaths and fifty-nine wounded), they were repatriated. It was later learned that Castro cashiered Tortoló, reducing him in rank from colonel to private, and sent him and the nearly forty other surviving military professionals who had surrendered to expiate their failure to "fight to the death" by serving—and perhaps dying—in Angola.

95. Shultz, *Turmoil and Triumph*, p. 337.

The Grenada operation, as earlier noted, was a success politically in the United States, and at least at the time in Grenada. American combat forces were gone within two months, although 250–300 military police remained another year and a half. The effect on American-Cuban relations was negative, but that did not change the situation. There were several "bonus" effects for the United States. Lieutenant Colonel Desi Bouterese in Suriname promptly (on October 26) ordered the Cuban ambassador and approximately 100 Cuban personnel out of the country and suspended all agreements with Cuba. Nicaragua exhibited considerable concern—which Washington policymakers welcomed. Castro found it necessary to note that Cuba could not go to the aid of Nicaragua if it were attacked. The Cubans, too, soon withdrew about 1,000 personnel from Nicaragua (and later, when it was called for in the ongoing Central American peace talks, withdrew all Cuban military advisers from Nicaragua). They did not want to give the United States any pretext for intervention. Soon after the Grenada operation the French passed along Syrian concern over a possible American attack—which Secretary Shultz told the French would not happen, but not to tell that to the Syrians—let them sweat it out.[96]

It is more difficult to draw a balance for Soviet-American relations. On the one hand, the American resort to arms in Grenada reinforced restraints against Soviet support for "client" states in the Third World. On the other hand, it is difficult to picture how that would have made a difference, given their existing caution. As an American military action puncturing "the Brezhnev Doctrine" the invasion was not likely to set a new pattern, and indeed it remained unique. But in Moscow it was seen as a dangerous indication that the United States was unpredictable, and prone to use military power. And the fall of 1983, it will be recalled, was the time of greatest Soviet alarm and Soviet-American tension in two decades.

Other direct uses of American military power were few, although far more frequent than such actions by the Soviet Union or any other major power. The next incident of consequence was three years later in a familiar setting for flare-ups of conflict: Libya. The United States had been engaged in proxy local wars with Libya involving Chad and the Sudan (and indirectly Egypt) in the mid–1980s. In March 1986, in a replay of the American-Libyan clash of 1981, the United States carried out a naval exercise again in the Gulf of Sidra. Predictably, American aircraft were fired upon, this time by SA-5 long-range antiaircraft missiles recently acquired from the Soviet Union. The United States had planned for this contingency and promptly attacked the SA-5 radars, and for good measure preemptively sank three Libyan patrol craft. Libya unwisely declared a "state of war." Without announcement, it also began to activate a terrorist reprisal. On April 5, a Libyan-directed terrorist bomb in a Berlin discotheque killed two people and injured dozens more including more

---

96. See ibid., pp. 339–44.

than fifty Americans. On April 14, the United States launched bombing attacks (with F-111s from British bases, as well as carrier aircraft) on terrorist facilities and military targets in Libya, including against "headquarters" for terrorist actions that looked suspiciously like an effort to kill Qadhafi (and did kill his young adopted daughter).[97]

The Soviet Union did not consider Libya an ally and was concerned over Qadhafi's erratic behavior. Nonetheless, the Soviets were long-time arms suppliers (and Libya was a paying client), and they had traditionally supported "anti-imperialist" regimes. After the March attacks, the Soviet Union postponed a scheduled meeting of Shevardnadze with Shultz in Washington and strongly criticized the American move, but did nothing more.

The second major regional conflict involving the American-Soviet rivalry, Afghanistan, as in Central America, developed into a military stalemate. The "limited contingent of Soviet troops," as the Soviet government called its forces in Afghanistan, was increased from 75,000 to 108,000 men in 1981–82 but was not further increased despite the fact that a Soviet force that size, bolstering the Afghan Army, clearly could not defeat the *mujahedin* with their bases of operations in Pakistan (and to a much lesser extent in Iran). Yet the *mujahedin* insurgents were equally unable to defeat the Afghan government and Soviet forces. This stalemate persisted despite massive infusions of arms on both sides. The United States alone poured more than $2 billion into material support for the insurgents during the 1980s, and Saudi Arabia gave hundreds of millions. The Soviet Union provided arms and munitions on an even larger scale.

The Reagan administration gradually increased its support, particularly after 1985. President Reagan signed a National Security Decision Document (NSDD)–166 in March 1985, setting the objective of driving the Soviet forces out of Afghanistan "by all means available," escalating the aim from the previous guidance in an intelligence "finding" by President Carter in 1980 calling for such support to the insurgents merely to "harass" Soviet forces in Afghanistan.[98] Secretary Shultz supported CIA Director Casey in pushing to get this increased objective and increased funding.[99] He wanted to keep the pressure on Moscow both to negotiate and to withdraw.

---

97.  Ibid., pp. 680–87. Shultz noted Secretary Weinberger's delaying tactics on the reprisal strike in March, and early closeout of the naval exercise.

98.  Several journalists reported on the "covert" U.S. program; the most full and informed wrap-up account is Steve Coll, "Anatomy of a Victory: CIA's Covert Afghan War: $2 Billion Program Reversed Tide for Rebels," *Washington Post*, July 19, 1992, pp. A1, A24, and "In CIA's Covert Afghan War, Where to Draw the Line Was Key," *Washington Post*, July 20, 1992, pp. A1, A12.

99.  Shultz noted his role in his memoir; see Shultz, *Turmoil and Triumph*, p. 1087.
     Congress willingly supported funding for the Afghan insurgents, sometimes authorizing and appropriating larger sums than requested, in contrast to the controversial off-and-on-again funding of the contras.

The American-led support of the *mujahedin* was a multinational effort. Pakistan was the key, as the base for the rebels and as the conduit. The Pakistani Inter-Service Intelligence Agency (ISI) handled the supply arrangements and all relations with the various insurgent groups. The ISI favored and gave preferential treatment and the lion's share of arms to Islamic radicals such as Gulbuddin Hekmatyar, hardly the most promising freedom fighter. Besides Pakistan, Egypt was an early and continuing source of Soviet-type weapons and financial assistance. China was another contributor, although by the mid-1980s the United States was paying China about $100 million a year for Soviet-type weapons for the Afghans.[100]

In March 1986, the United States decided after long deliberation to take the risks in upgrading the weaponry supplied to include its most advanced hand-held antiaircraft missile, the Stinger. Those missiles went into action in September and downed many Soviet and Afghan aircraft and helicopters (including at least one civilian passenger plane).[101] They also were illegally diverted to other countries, Iran acquiring some from Afghan insurgents, and China some from Pakistan. By the early 1990s, the CIA was trying to buy back Stingers at inflated prices from various Afghan groups. A few were used in 1992 against Uzbek (nominally Tajik) aircraft in a spillover of Islamic insurgency from Afghanistan to the newly independent formerly Soviet republic of Tajikistan.

The United States also provided funding for training anticommunist Afghans in "public relations" propaganda in the West, as well as providing a transmitter for Radio Free Afghanistan (the Voice of Free Afghanistan), broadcasting clandestinely from Pakistan after October 1985. And, as part of the military support, besides arms and training for advanced weapons such as the Stingers, the CIA also collaborated with the ISI in training Afghans in urban sabotage and terrorist operations and supplied sniper weapons and C-4 plastic explosives.[102]

The most dangerous American action, apparently undertaken by William Casey on his own authority in October 1984 (even before NSDD-166), was encouragement for Afghan insurgents to make raids into Soviet territory for military harassment, sabotage, and subversive propaganda (including distribution of the Koran) in Uzbekistan and Tajikistan. When this program became known to others in Washington, it was curtailed. Once encouraged, however,

100. Coll, *Washington Post*, July 19, 1992, pp. A1, A24; and July 20, 1992, pp. A1, A12.

101. There was considerable resistance to the decision to supply Stingers in the Pentagon and from some officials in the CIA. The idea appears to have originated in the State Department and was pushed by Secretary Shultz. See Shultz, *Turmoil and Triumph*, p. 692.

102. See Coll, *Washington Post*, July 20, 1992, p. A12.

the Afghan insurgents themselves occasionally mounted raids into Soviet territory.[103]

The United States also participated, without much high-level attention
or interest, in the UN-sponsored Afghan-Pakistan negotiations in Geneva from
1982 to 1988. Throughout this period, except for a few senior officials in
1987–88, there was no expectation that the Soviet Union would ever agree to
withdraw. Moreover, many in Washington preferred to see them stay and
"bleed." The focus was entirely on waging the war in Afghanistan to wear down
the Soviets. This high-level inattention to the negotiations later led to some
difficulty in the final negotiation in 1988.

Along with the intensification of American military support to the
*mujahedin* in Afghanistan after 1985 under the Reagan Doctrine, congressional
approval was finally obtained in July 1985 to repeal the Clark amendment,
permitting resumption of arms supply to the insurgents in Angola. The issue of
whether to do so was debated for several months, but the administration
succeeded in getting authorization to do so, as was announced in January 1986,
when Savimbi visited Washington and was received by President Reagan, who
proudly dubbed the ex-Maoist guerrilla a "freedom fighter."[104] While military
assistance was provided on a much more limited scale than to the Afghan
insurgents, a decision to provide Stinger antiaircraft missiles to the insurgents
in both countries was made at the same time (March 1986).

As earlier noted, in practice the Reagan Doctrine was much more narrowly focused than its sweeping moral, ideological, and geopolitical terms suggested. Nicaragua was the first key target in time and remained important largely
because of the domestic political resonance of the Monroe Doctrine coupled with
bipartisan political neuralgia over Castroite Cuban influence. But it was also
increasingly divisive, controversial, and eventually—even before Iran-contra—a
political liability. Afghanistan remained the most politically supported application,
with Congress appropriating even more funds than the administration requested.
The rationale was essentially anti-Soviet, fed in part (especially in the early years)
by fears of further Soviet expansion in the region, and in part (especially in later
years) by its appearance as a good opportunity to impose a heavy drain and burden

---

103. Most of these raids took place in 1986–87 and led to Soviet retaliation in air strikes on
*mujahedin* bases along the Afghan border in Pakistan, leading to further Pakistani-en-
couraged raids into Tajikistan. The Soviet Union did not publicize these raids into its
territory. See Coll, *Washington Post*, July 19, 1992, pp. A1, A24; information also from
Soviet sources in interviews. There were occasional disclosures by *mujahedin* to the
Western press; for example, see Bryan Brumley, "Fighting Spills Over into Soviet
Territory," *Washington Times*, February 24, 1987, p. A7.

104. "America's Agenda for the Future," February 6, 1986, *Presidential Documents*, vol. 22
(February 10, 1986), p. 175. President Reagan received Savimbi on January 30; Secretaries Shultz and Weinberger had earlier seen him. Savimbi's UNITA, and its supporters, had hired an American public relations firm for $600,000 to dress up his image in
the American press for this visit.

on the Soviet Union at fairly low cost to the United States. Angola combined anti-Cuban and anti-Soviet motivations with particular pressures from the political right wing, which welcomed the common front with South Africa.

In contrast, despite logic and protestations from the right, Mozambique (which was not host to Soviet or Cuban troops, although those countries gave some economic and arms support including advisers) the administration continued to pursue a diplomatic course, calling for negotiated settlement. The American strategy, as Shultz later put it, was "to befriend Samora Machel [then president of Mozambique] and draw him away from the Soviet camp."[105] South Africa and Mozambique signed an agreement in March 1984 under which the rebel Mozambique National Resistance (RENAMO) would be assimilated, and South Africa would cease assisting it, but that accord broke down in practice. As Secretary Shultz has confirmed, William Casey was throughout these years pursuing a contrary policy of his own, encouraging South Africa to continue to provide covert assistance to RENAMO despite the diplomatic accords.[106] There was occasional sharp debate within the administration, especially in 1985 when Reagan met rather reluctantly with Machel—until he was charmed into liking him and reaffirming the policy of weaning Mozambique away from the Soviets, after Machel regaled Reagan with anti-Soviet jokes and derogatory anecdotes about communism.[107] In 1987 domestic right-wing pressures in the United States for application of the Reagan Doctrine in Mozambique again mounted, but the administration continued to rebuff them.

Ethiopia would have seemed an appropriate target for the Reagan Doctrine, with Soviet arms and military advisers and Cuban troops (up to some 17,000 at the peak, in 1978). Yet the administration declined to engage itself. In the absence of countervailing American support for the insurgents, the Cubans unilaterally withdrew three-quarters of their troops in 1984–85, leaving only one 2,500-man brigade and about 500 advisers. (There were also about 1,500 Soviet military advisers, several hundred East German security advisers—and several hundred Israeli paramilitary advisers.) This contrasted markedly with the great increase in Cuban troops in Angola in 1986–88 to match American military assistance to the UNITA insurgents, showing that at least in the short run American aid did not reduce the Cuban presence.

In some other cases, the United States either cut off military assistance (as in Somalia in 1987–88, owing to congressional action), or intervened clandestinely in covert political action (as reportedly in Mauritius and Madagascar). But these events were not directly related to the Reagan Doctrine.

In Cambodia (called Kampuchea during the 1980s), overt American assistance began on a small scale in 1985 as a congressional, not an administra-

105. Shultz, *Turmoil and Triumph*, p. 1113.

106. Ibid., pp. 1113, 1116.

107. Ibid., pp. 1116–17.

tion, initiative. Although directed only to the small noncommunist resistance forces, those were joined in a coalition with the notorious Khmer Rouge against the Vietnamese- (and Soviet-) supported government in Phnom Penh. Persistent reports suggest, however, that the CIA had covertly been funding the noncommunist groups since 1982, so American support may simply have become more open.[108] This aid continued through the 1980s and was in accordance with the policy of our allies in the Association of South East Asian Nations (ASEAN), but it was a dubious venture since the probable successor if the insurgents had won would have been the odious Khmer Rouge. During the 1980s, the Soviet Union was not directly involved but supported its ally Vietnam, which had stationed large forces in Cambodia to contain the insurgency there.

The Reagan Doctrine (and its Haig Doctrine precursor) dominated the principal regional conflicts of the Third World during the 1980s, especially those in which the Soviet Union and United States had an interest. There were, of course, many other conflicts in which the two powers were not involved (or in which only one or the other was tangentially involved), such as the Polisario Saharan war with Morocco, and civil strife in India, Sri Lanka (formerly Ceylon), Myanmar (formerly Burma), Indonesia in East Timor, and others. Even without the interventions of the Soviet Union and the United States, conflicts would certainly have occurred in Afghanistan, Central America, Africa, Southeast Asia, and the Middle East. Nonetheless, the Soviet-American rivalry and duel for influence made its mark on those conflicts in which the superpowers chose to involve themselves, as well as on their bilateral relations. This process was not new, but the turn it took in the 1980s was an American challenge to the Soviet Union and those regimes aligned with or beholden to it.

The Iran-contra scandal in the United States, from November 1986 through 1987 and to some extent through the remainder of the Reagan presidency in 1988, diminished the luster of the Reagan Doctrine. Though arms continued to be supplied to the insurgents in Afghanistan and Angola, the decline of the Reagan Doctrine in the last years of the Reagan administration was paralleled by the rising influence of Soviet initiatives under Gorbachev's leadership. By 1988, the latter were dominant, and a new phase ensued in Third World aspects of the American-Soviet relationship.

## The Soviet Role: On the Defensive, 1980–87

From the Soviet perspective, in the first half of the 1980s the United States had turned to a broad policy of more active use of counterrevolutionary insurgent forces in its attempt to roll back history. This had begun under the

---

108. For example, see Charles R. Babcock and Bob Woodward, "CIA Covertly Aiding Pro-West Cambodians," *Washington Post*, July 8, 1985, pp. A1, A18.

Carter administration in 1980, after the Soviet occupation of Afghanistan. Then beginning in 1981 the Reagan administration stepped up U.S. assistance to insurgents in Afghanistan, stimulated a new insurgency in Nicaragua, and indirectly supported other reactionary powers in aiding the insurgencies in Cambodia, Angola, Mozambique, and Ethiopia. In short, virtually all the gains by revolutionary forces in the latter half of the 1970s were being subjected to a vigorous counterattack in the first half of the 1980s. Moreover, the Soviet Union was overextended and not in a favorable position to aid those regimes (except in Afghanistan, where the Soviet Union had a direct and dominant role, although it was still unable to suppress the insurgency). As the USSR acquired more allies, clients, friends, and involvements in the Third World in the latter half of the 1970s, it became more mindful of the status quo, and as these six Soviet-aligned countries of "socialist orientation" experienced insurgencies in the 1980s, the Soviet Union became a *counter*insurgency power.

The Soviet evaluation of the moral and historical role of the governments in these countries was subjective. But its evaluation by the early 1980s that the wheel of fortune had turned against these movements once in power was objectively founded. So was the perception of the U.S. role, although with some exaggeration in the Soviets' own assessments, especially in its propaganda. Early in this period the Soviet leadership did try to deal with "the American threat" to Third World countries by a diplomatic initiative, but it was stillborn and had only fleeting propaganda impact. In an attempt to reassert a détente approach, or at least to make it more politically costly to the United States not to do so, Brezhnev in April 1981 proposed a "code of conduct" toward the Third World patterned on the noninterference promises of the Helsinki Final Act applying to Europe. But it was ignored by the United States.[109]

The absence of Soviet support to new progressive revolutions elsewhere after 1979 was in the first instance based on the sharp decrease in new indigenous revolutionary situations in a postcolonial Third World. And the Soviet Union was overextended as a result of its commitment in Afghanistan and its direct support to Vietnam and Cuba and, to a much lesser extent, Ethiopia (and still less in Nicaragua and Angola, where more direct support was given by Cuba, and in Mozambique). Soviet preoccupation first with Poland, then the issue of intermediate-range nuclear (INF) missile deployment in Europe, deepening internal economic problems, and serial transitions in the Soviet leadership itself further reduced any inclination to wider involvement in the geopolitical competition in the Third World, even before Gorbachev brought a whole new evaluation and worldview into Soviet policy after 1985.

---

109. "In a Friendly Situation, Speech of L. I. Brezhnev," *Pravda*, April 28, 1981. The occasion was a visit to Moscow by Libya leader Muammar Qadhafi, and the Soviets also sought to deflect his requests for Soviet support by such an international initiative.

Soviet attention to the Third World reflected several interests apart from ideological inclination to support "progressive" political change. First of all was the belated recognition by many in the Soviet establishment from 1980 on that the Soviet support for anti-imperialist progressive revolutions in the Third World in the latter half of the 1970s had played a major role in souring many in the West, above all the United States, on détente. This view was openly voiced only after 1987, but it was increasingly given weight by the new Soviet leadership after 1985. It became a powerful counterweight to ideological commitments, even though for some time it usually found expressions through revised ideological evaluations rather than in directly and openly overriding ideological considerations.

Although generally overestimated in Western evaluations, the leaders in Moscow did have strategic political, military, and geopolitical interests. Cuba and, in the 1980s, Nicaragua were important in breaking the American monopoly over the Western Hemisphere and providing a political entree to the Soviet Union. While strategic interest was curbed by prudence and the Soviet-American understandings of 1962 and 1970 limiting Soviet military presence and activities in Cuba (and by extension, in Nicaragua and in general in the area), Cuba still provided a valuable intelligence post (for communication intercepts) and a modest opportunity for naval and air reconnaissance. Similarly, limited regional naval and air reconnaissance presence was established in Vietnam (especially at Cam Ranh Bay), Ethiopia (first at Massawa, later the Dahlak Islands in the Red Sea), Yemen (Aden), and Angola (Luanda port and airport). Together with port calls in friendly countries such as India, Syria, Mozambique, and Mauritius, this thin net of facilities helped support a politically useful (if strategically limited) military presence, and pretensions to being a global power.

Another set of Soviet interests was economic. Although the two countries given the bulk of economic assistance (Cuba and Vietnam) were a considerable net drain, they did provide some useful raw materials (nickel and sugar from Cuba). But on the whole the Soviet Union was constrained and, with a few exceptions such as these, was never the source of more than modest economic aid. The Soviet Union did carry on normal commercial trade with most countries of the Third World, especially in the Middle East and South Asia, particularly where barter deals—including arms sales—could be arranged. Arms exports were substantial, much larger than economic aid. Where possible, the Soviet Union got hard currency or the equivalent for arms (as from Libya), but more often it had to settle for countertrade. Finally, the major part of the arms exports was on credit, especially to the new radical Marxist regimes in Africa and the Middle East, intended mainly to buy political influence, with likelihood of eventual repayment remote.

Third World countries in turn fell into several distinct categories: semiallies (Cuba, Vietnam), friendly major regional powers (India), radical nonaligned friends (Syria, Iraq, South Yemen, Libya), the new radical revolutionary regimes (Nicaragua, Angola, Ethiopia, and Mozambique), and lesser radical states sharing little but ideological "antiimperialism" (Grenada, Suriname, the Congo, Guinea-Bissau, Equatorial Africa, Benin, and the like).

Cuba and Vietnam, as independent states, pursued their own policies, notwithstanding their close relationships with the Soviet Union. Neither was directly threatened by internal insurgents or external enemies (except Vietnam from China in the late 1970s and the early 1980s). Cuba was, however, concerned over what it saw as a possible serious threat from the United States in the early 1980s. Both countries were directly involved with their own military forces in civil wars abroad, Cuba in Ethiopia and Angola and Vietnam in Cambodia, and therefore would necessarily be involved in conflict settlement in those three countries. By the mid-1980s the Soviet Union advised both Cuba and Vietnam to withdraw their military forces, while urging the governments of Ethiopia, Angola, and Cambodia (Kampuchea)—as well as Afghanistan—to negotiate political settlements with their insurgent adversaries through "national reconciliation."

In other aspects of their relationship, Cuba and the Soviet Union drifted further apart from 1984 on. In April 1986, soon after Gorbachev had launched his reforms, Castro launched his own brand of "reform," called rectification, which amounted to the opposite of the Soviet *perestroika*. Instead of gradual liberalization of the system, Castro's rectification meant tightening up against any political liberalization, and more autarkic insulation from the outside world. Over the next four years *glasnost* in the Soviet Union led to increasingly pointed unofficial, and occasionally even more guarded official, criticisms of the large hidden Soviet subsidies to Cuba, and what was seen as Cuban squandering of them, including unnecessarily large military expenditures. The Cubans reacted angrily, even with a riposte by Vice President Carlos Rafael Rodríguez in *New Times* to several articles that had appeared there.[110] At this same time, 1986–87, the Soviet Union began to curb oil shipments and reduce the above-world-market price it paid for Cuban sugar; in December 1986 Castro had to announce an austerity program, which in later years became much more severe. This Soviet retrenchment was not intended as a sanction against Cuba; it was the unavoidable by-product of the Soviet Union's efforts to make its activities cost-effective and to balance its books. But the impact was correctly seen in Havana as reflecting a lower priority for Cuba in Soviet policy.

---

110. See Vladislav Chirkov, "How Are Things, Compañeros?" *New Times*, no. 1 (January 12, 1987), pp. 18–19; Chirkov, "An Uphill Task," ibid., no. 33 (August 17, 1987), pp. 16–17; and Carlos Rafael Rodríguez, "A Difficult but Steady Ascent," ibid., no. 41 (October 19, 1987), pp. 16–17. At that time, *New Times* (*Novoye vremya*) appeared in eight foreign language editions, including Spanish, as well as in Russian, and was widely read in Cuba—until the authorities banned its circulation there after these and other critical articles appeared.

The next year, Rodríguez was reported to have remarked that *Moscow News* was more hostile than *Radio Marti*, the American propaganda station beamed at Cuba.

By 1988 Soviet-Cuban trade declined by 12 percent—the first real reduction in twenty years. Both sides increasingly failed to meet commitments when they could sell at higher price on the world market (Soviet oil and Cuban nickel), and they quarreled in the socialist bloc Council on Mutual Economic Assistance (CMEA). The Soviet Union did, reluctantly, continue to fund and build a nuclear power reactor that could ease Cuban energy needs. Cuban-Soviet divergences on various international questions also greatly increased, especially as the Soviet Union moved toward closer relations with the United States with the summit meetings of 1985 through 1988. One of the signs prepared for Gorbachev's planned visit to Havana in December 1988 (postponed owing to the earthquake in Armenia, and Gorbachev's early return from New York) had said "Cuba, the Last Bastion of Socialism." Relations continued downhill thereafter.

Soviet relations with Vietnam, discussed elsewhere, also showed increasing friction as the 1980s brought reduced Soviet interest and material support for Vietnam, and Soviet advice to reform the economy.[111]

Syria was sometimes dangerously counterposed to Israel (especially when both were in Lebanon). Libya was involved in intrigues and conflicts in several neighboring countries and potentially with Egypt and the United States. Iraq was, from 1980 to 1987, at war with Iran; despite the 1972 Soviet Treaty of Friendship and Cooperation with Iraq, the Soviet Union took a neutral stance on the war.

The Soviet leaders sought in the early and mid–1980s to stabilize the situation by restraining friends and associates from actions that could bring American or other (for example, Israeli, in the case of Syria and the PLO) armed attacks. As already noted, the Soviet leaders had made clear to Cuba that Soviet military forces could not protect the island country. They had also made this clear to Nicaragua, and the limits of Soviet aid were made even more clear when in 1983 the Soviet Union reversed its earlier decision to send MiG-21 fighter planes to that country, after receiving the American threat to destroy them if they were sent. Similarly, in 1984, after the American mining incidents, Cuba asked the Soviets to send a naval flotilla to waters near Nicaragua just to signal Soviet support for the Nicaraguans. Moscow refused, again indicating to Cuba and to Nicaragua the sharp limits on Soviet backing.[112] The Soviet Union did of course continue to supply arms to Cuba, including a second squadron of

---

111. See the discussion in chapter 14.

112. Congressional Research Service, *The Soviet Union in the Third World, 1980–85: An Imperial Burden or Political Asset?*, report prepared for the House Committee on Foreign Affairs, September 23, 1985 (GPO, 1985), p. 435. It has also been reported that the Soviet refusal so piqued Castro that he therefore declined to attend Soviet leader Chernenko's funeral in March 1985 (after having gone to Brezhnev's in 1982 and Andropov's in 1984).

MiG-23s in 1982 and a third squadron later. These remained below the threshold of the American constraint on arms for Cuba.

From the mid-1980s on the Soviet Union supported the various regional Contadora and Central American (Arias) proposals for negotiated settlement of the Nicaraguan and Salvadoran conflicts. The Soviet Union, and from 1984 Cuba too, urged the Salvadoran guerrillas to be more flexible and to negotiate with the government and advised the Nicaraguan government to support the regional initiatives for negotiated settlements.

The Soviet role was necessarily circumscribed and circumspect in advising the independent radical states such as Syria and Libya that could come into direct conflict with the United States. As noted earlier the Soviets had made clear to Syria in 1982 (and thereafter) that they would not come to Syria's defense in any conflict in Lebanon, reaffirming the position that they had taken in 1967 and 1973—only if Damascus itself were threatened would they interpose forces. Soviet support for the PLO was even more restricted. As the Soviet reactions to American military actions against Libya in 1981 and 1986, and in occupying Grenada in 1983, made clear, the Soviet Union was not prepared to give more than moral and rhetorical support to Third World countries that came under Western attacks.

More generally, the lowered Soviet interest in the Third World was evident in the reduced attention given to "progressive" revolutionary change in the region in Leonid Brezhnev's Report to the Twenty-sixth Party Congress in 1981, and the still sharper reduction of attention to the Third World as a whole given by Mikhail Gorbachev at the Twenty-seventh Party Congress in February 1986.[113] Even in the beginning of the 1980s, it was clear that overall Soviet interest and involvement in the Third World was diminishing, quite apart from reinforcing constraints prompted by the more militant American stand.

From 1980 into the latter half of the decade, the principal Soviet effort was an attempt—overall ending in failure—to consolidate the gains by radical (normally Marxist) regimes who had come to power in the Third World in the mid- to late 1970s. Direct Soviet involvement was minimized, and efforts were made to promote settlements—on terms favorable to their protégés—in the civil wars in Soviet-affiliated or client states: Nicaragua, Angola, Ethiopia, Mozambique, Cambodia—and above all Afghanistan. Especially after 1985, Moscow increasingly counseled its protégés under the gun to seek "national reconciliation," that is, political compromise with their adversaries and political settlements of their conflicts.

Only in Afghanistan, on the border of the Soviet Union and directly affecting its security, had Soviet military forces been directly committed. And even there, despite the stakes, the Soviet military force was limited to 108,000 men—one-fifth of the size of American forces committed to the war in

---

113. See the discussion in chapter 6.

Vietnam.[114] Although efforts were made to defeat the insurgents, the principal objective remained the more modest aim of preventing their victory over the Soviet-supported Afghan government in Kabul and its control of the major cities and lines of communication. The initial expectation when the decision was made to intervene in December 1979, that the mere presence of Soviet troops in garrison would bolster a new Afghan government and army so that they could quickly defeat the insurgency, proved wrong. The Soviet leaders did seek to promote a compromise settlement of the conflict, even in the mid-1980s, but until decisions to withdraw were made in 1985–86, the Soviet political-military strategy in practice amounted to just carrying on a war neither side could win (at least not within the constraints on force commitment that the Soviet leadership had set). Because they had initially failed to see the resiliency of the insurgency and the weak popular base of the government, the Soviet leaders had not foreseen a protracted war in which external military assistance could play a significant role in keeping the insurgency alive. From 1980 on, the Soviet leaders knew they were stuck with the situation but did not know how to deal with it—they were reluctant to pull out, because that would have been a clear political defeat and would have entailed new risks of an American advance, but they also remained determined not to get in deeper.

Although the fact is little acknowledged, the Soviets prompted the Afghan government to begin probing for a negotiated settlement with Pakistan and Iran as early as May 1980, and then they turned to the United Nations. In February 1981 Secretary General Kurt Waldheim named a special negotiator, Javier Pérez de Cuéllar, who began shuttle diplomacy. Pérez de Cuéllar soon after became the new secretary general, and the assignment went to Diego Cordovez, another respected senior Latin American diplomat. Talks began in Geneva in June 1982 and continued intermittently until agreement was reached in April 1988. The Soviet Union worked for a settlement that would permit its withdrawal and a political settlement reconciling the Kabul government with other Afghan political forces including the *mujahedin* insurgents, underwritten by Pakistan and the United States as well as by the Soviet Union.[115]

---

114. Marshal Akhromeyev, the late chief of the General Staff (and in 1979 senior deputy chief) has stated that the original authorized deployment ceiling was 75,000 men, raised in 1981–82 to 108,000. See S. F. Akhromeyev and G. M. Kornienko, *Glazami marshala i diplomata* (Through the Eyes of a Marshal and a Diplomat) (Moscow: Mezhdunarodnyye otnosheniya, 1992), p. 167. Actual strength reached a peak of 120,000. See B.V. Gromov, *Ogranichennyi kontigent* (The Limited Contingent) (Moscow: Progress, 1994), p. 345.

115. The most informed accounts of the negotiations will be the forthcoming volume by Diego Cordovez and Selig Harrison, to be published by Oxford University Press, and the book by a former Pakistan diplomat, Riaz M. Khan, *Untying the Afghan Knot: Negotiating Soviet Withdrawal* (Duke University Press, 1991). For background see also Amin Saikal and William Maley, eds., *The Soviet Withdrawal from Afghanistan* (Cambridge University Press, 1989).

External support for the various *mujahedin* insurgents, mainly channeled through Pakistan by the United States, Saudi Arabia, Egypt, and China, and also from Iran, certainly contributed to their ability to frustrate Soviet efforts to win a military victory, although it is uncertain whether they could have been stamped out. External assistance was not enough to bring them victory, even when fairly advanced arms such as Stinger antiaircraft missiles were provided. In retrospect, it is clear from Soviet sources, including archives now available, that the Soviet objective was to disengage honorably and leave a friendly nonaligned Afghanistan, not to incorporate Afghanistan or any part of the country into the Soviet Union, and not to use it as a permanent Soviet military base and springboard for further expansion, as was depicted in American official pronouncements and general discussion from December 1979 through the 1980s.

As noted earlier, the United States mounted a massive "covert" military supply effort to the Afghan insurgents, totaling some $2 billion during the 1980s, and escalating in 1985–87 to include some attacks on Soviet territory and some subversive propaganda infiltration of Tajikistan and Uzbekistan. That raised a new and serious concern in Moscow about overall American intentions toward the Soviet Union.[116] It also reinforced the conclusion in Moscow that there could be no military victory in Afghanistan, although that conclusion had probably been reached in 1980–81, before American and other external military assistance became a major factor. The Soviet leadership as a whole, despite the unwise optimism of the small group of leaders who in late 1979 decided on the intervention, had early recognized the crucial lack of a foundation of political support in Afghanistan for the Kabul government. Most of the Soviet leaders also realized that the introduction of alien Soviet military forces had weakened, rather than bolstered, support and further reduced the legitimacy of the communist regime.[117]

From 1980 through 1986 the Soviet effort to deal with the Afghanistan dilemma combined three strands: first, a military commitment sufficient to hold the main cities coupled with attempts to weaken the insurgents elsewhere; second, political efforts to bolster the regime by buying off some tribes and seeking to broaden the base of support of the government by enlisting broader noncommunist national groups and leaders and downplaying communist social programs; and third, efforts for an international negotiated settlement. Their aim was to withdraw Soviet military force, but under conditions that would

---

116. I recall being told of this at the time (early 1986) by a highly alarmed Soviet official. The Soviet authorities were suppressing information about the raids because they did not want to create an expectation that they would undertake sharp reprisal actions.

117. Marshal Akhromeyev, for example, wrote that "by 1981 it had become clear if not to all, at least to the majority of sober realists in the Soviet leadership that there could not be a military solution of the problem," long before external assistance became a major factor. See Akhromeyev and Kornienko, *Glazami marshala i diplomata*, p. 47.

leave a nonhostile, nonaligned, and neutral Afghanistan. From time to time, depending on changes in the internal Afghan and international situations and changes in Soviet leadership evaluations, the emphasis shifted. Andropov wanted in 1983 to resolve the issue, but he knew it would be a long and arduous process. He lacked an effective policy or policy framework for anything beyond more of the same efforts.[118] Occasional efforts to advance new military tactics, especially more aggressive use of small elite special forces better trained for counterinsurgency after 1984, were also pressed in an attempt to strengthen the Afghan government's negotiating position.

A fascinating window into Andropov's thinking and the workings of the Politburo on this subject is now available in the top secret minutes of a Politburo meeting of March 10, 1983. Gromyko reported on behalf of the Politburo's Commission on Afghanistan, a senior Foreign Ministry, Defense Ministry, KGB, and Central Committee International Department group established in 1980 that he chaired. He noted how slowly the Afghan government was stabilizing the situation and asked for 300 million rubles for further support. He also noted that because the talks with Pakistan in Geneva under UN auspices were going so slowly, "we must do all we can to find mutually acceptable variants for political settlement [*uregulirovanniya*]," although that would be a long drawn-out process.[119] Andropov, however, was not inclined to authorize a more forthcoming negotiating stance or, on the other hand, such large outlays. He asked that the commission's recommendations be reworked and made more of "a political document," by which he made clear that he meant "it must be laid out much more flexibly." Gromyko and Boris Ponomarev at once said it would be reworked. Andropov also suggested an early meeting with Babrak Karmal. Vasily Kuznetsov, Nikolai Tikhonov, and Mikhail Gorbachev all chimed in to reply "Right [*pravilno*]." That was the depth of the Politburo

---

118. When UN negotiator Diego Cordovez went to Moscow in March 1983, Andropov received him and strongly encouraged the UN effort. Cordovez was also struck by Andropov's candid admission that the continued Soviet presence in Afghanistan was hurting the Soviet Union in several ways: loss of life, unnecessary large expenditures, regional tension, setback to relations with the West, and loss of Soviet prestige with Islamic countries and in general in the Third World. See Khan, *Untying the Afghan Knot*, p. 107. See also Akhromeyev and Kornienko, *Glazami marshala i diplomata*, p. 48. The next month, the Soviet Union sent a special diplomatic representative to be an observer at the Geneva talks. Khan, *Untying the Afghan knot*, p. 113.

   Andropov also told Afghan leader Babrak Karmal in July 1983 that he could not count on having Soviet troops in Afghanistan indefinitely and should broaden his domestic political support. While Karmal did nothing, this statement was a clear indication that even Andropov, one of those responsible for the 1979 decision to intervene, was thinking of withdrawal. See Akhromeyev and Kornienko, *Glazami marshala i diplomata*, p. 48.

119. TsKhSD, Fond 89, Perechen' 14, Dokument 29, *Zasedaniye Politbyuro TsK KPSS 10 marta 1983 goda* (Meeting of the Politburo of the CC CPSU, March 10, 1983), Top Secret, only copy (working transcript), pp. 12–14, quotation on p. 12.

discussion. With the amendments Andropov had made, the commission's report was, as usual, approved—but no real decision had been made except to do more of the same.[120]

Andropov's thinking, however, reflected well the basis for the Politburo's approach through the first half of the 1980s. First of all, he spoke of "with what difficulty and how carefully" they had decided to send troops into Afghanistan in 1979 (which he, as one of the four men then responsible, presented in 1983 in a decidedly "revised" fashion).[121] He then went on: "In resolving the Afghan problem we must proceed from existing realities. What do you want? It's a feudal country, where tribes have always ruled in their own territory, and the central authority has far from always extended to each village. The essence of the matter is not in the position of Pakistan. American imperialism is giving us battle here, understanding well that on this sector of world politics it has lost its positions. Therefore we can't retreat. Miracles on earth don't happen. Sometimes we get angry at the Afghans because they don't act consistently and work slowly. But let's remember our own struggle with the bandits [*basmachestvo*] in Central Asia. After all, practically the whole Red Army was concentrated then in Central Asia and the struggle with the *basmachi* lasted until the mid '30s. Hence in relation to Afghanistan both exactingness and understanding are needed."[122] Clearly, the Afghan problem was not going to be solved under Soviet leaders of the old school like Brezhnev and Andropov.

The key turning point, it is now known, came early under Gorbachev, in 1985–86, although this did not become evident until Gorbachev's public announcement in February 1988 of a specific plan for withdrawal within a year if the Geneva talks succeeded. Gorbachev later disclosed that, soon after the April 1985 plenum of the Central Committee, the Politburo had carried out a

---

120. Ibid., pp. 13–14.

121. Ibid., p. 13. Andropov said: "You remember with what difficulty and how carefully we decided the question of the entry of our troops into Afghanistan. L. I. Brezhnev insisted on an individual vote by name of members of the Politburo. The question was considered by a plenum of the Central Committee." In fact, there was no Politburo meeting, much less decision by vote, until two weeks after the decision to send troops had been made in an informal meeting by Brezhnev, Ustinov, Andropov, and Gromyko on December 12, 1979, recorded only in a handwritten note by Chernenko as Brezhnev's chief of staff. (The document is in TsKhSD, Fond 89, Perechen' 14, Dokument 31.) There was no Central Committee plenum until six months later, in June 1980, when that body "approved" the Politburo decision. By all accounts, the December decision was difficult, but not carefully considered. Andropov was attempting to cover the shortcomings of the 1979 decision to which he had been party—and that attitude also influenced his stubbornness about considering any new policy course that would acknowledge the failed consequences of the 1979 decision.

For further discussion of the 1979 decision, see Garthoff, *Détente and Confrontation*, rev. ed., chapter 26.

122. Ibid., p. 13.

"hard, impartial analysis of the situation [in Afghanistan] and already at that time began to seek a way out of the situation." He emphasized how difficult the task had proved and asserted the need for a more flexible "genuine national" leadership in Afghanistan and international negotiations to ensure that Afghanistan would be "an independent, neutral, and nonaligned state," which would "meet the interests of Afghanistan," as well as "our state interests."[123] More is now known about this period from former Soviet officials. In March 1985, just after his confirmation as general secretary and before the famous April plenum, Gorbachev discussed with Anatoly Chernyayev and Georgy Arbatov the priority policy issues with which he must deal. Afghanistan was on the list, as seventh or eighth; when Arbatov suggested it be moved to first place, Gorbachev agreed. In several of the early Politburo meetings when Afghanistan was on the agenda, Gorbachev drew the attention of his colleagues to the effect of the war on the domestic situation by reading out loud some of the numerous letters from soldiers or their families asking, "Why are we here?" and "We're here to fulfill an international duty and we're killing people."[124] Even earlier, Gorbachev had encouraged Marshal Akhromeyev, after he had visited Afghanistan in the spring of 1984, to tell the Politburo his frank judgments that the war was being waged against the people of Afghanistan and could not be won, and that Karmal and even Najibullah had proved unable to rally the Afghan people.[125]

The UN negotiator, Diego Cordovez, said that "from the time Gorbachev came in, things began to change. It was immediate and very significant. In May [when the talks resumed], only two months after he took over, they came up with a number of ideas on how the negotiations should move forward."[126] In June 1985, after a three-year hiatus, the Soviets reactivated Soviet-American regional security talks on Afghanistan at the level of deputy foreign minister. In August, First Deputy Foreign Minister Georgy Kornienko took a new active role in bilateral discussions with Pakistani Foreign Minister Yaqub Khan.[127]

Some analysts have assumed or concluded from continuing active Soviet military operations in Afghanistan and substantial supply of arms to the Afghan government forces during the years 1985 through 1988 that the Soviet leadership under Gorbachev was still trying to gain a military victory. As noted earlier, most Soviet military and foreign affairs officials had concluded well before 1985 that a military solution was not feasible. Though evidence is

123. "Revolutionary *Perestroika*—An Ideology of Renewal, Speech of General Secretary of the Central Committee of the CPSU M. S. Gorbachev, at the Plenum of the CC of the CPSU, February 18, 1988," *Pravda*, February 19, 1988.

124. Anatoly Chernyayev, in a discussion with the author on February 26, 1993.

125. Ibid.

126. Don Oberdorfer, *The Turn: From the Cold War to a New Era, the United States and the Soviet Union, 1983–1990* (Poseidon Press, 1991), p. 238.

127. See Khan, *Untying the Afghan Knot*, p. 138.

lacking, it is possible that in the spring of 1985 Gorbachev was willing to let those who believed military action could bring about victory, or at least an improved position for negotiating from strength, do what they could over the next six to eight months. There was, however, no increase in Soviet force levels.

On October 17, 1985, the Politburo discussed the problem of Soviet policy toward Afghanistan and decided in principle to withdraw Soviet forces as soon as feasible, while leaving a friendly government in power.[128] That decision was not greatly different from an outcome any Soviet leader would have accepted at least from 1982 on, but what was different was the readiness to face up to the need to resolve the matter and the decision to take action to do so. At the Twenty-seventh Party Congress in February 1986 Gorbachev publicly referred to the situation in Afghanistan as "a bleeding wound" and asserted Soviet desire to withdraw its troops "in the nearest future," opening up public discussion and preparing the way for withdrawal.[129]

Other informed Soviet sources have also referred to the decision in 1985 to withdraw from Afghanistan, and it was reflected in many steps that were taken in the next three years despite a continuation of the war. A Ministry of Foreign Affairs report in 1989 said the decision to withdraw from Afghanistan had been made in December 1985; that may represent a later Politburo confirmation of the earlier decision or have been the date of some internal ministry application of the October 1985 Politburo decision.[130]

Before the October 1985 Politburo meeting, Gorbachev met secretly with Babrak Karmal and told him bluntly to shape up his government because "We have to think together about withdrawal of the Soviet troops from Afghanistan." Karmal's visage darkened, and he said that if the Soviet Union took the troops out, "next time you will need to bring in a million soldiers." This description of the meeting was given later by Najibullah, Karmal's successor,

---

128. The most authoritative documentation for this decision is a reference to it by Gorbachev in a later Politburo meeting in November 1986. The record of the October 1985 meeting remains Top Secret, but the November 1986 record has been consulted in the former Central Committee archive in Moscow. (See footnote 134.) See also Anatoly Chernyayev, *Shest' let s Gorbachevym* (Six Years with Gorbachev) (Moscow: Progress, 1993), pp. 57–58.

129. M. S. Gorbachev, *Politicheskii doklad tsentral'nogo komiteta KPSS XXVII s"yezdu Kommunisticheskoi partii Sovetskogo Soyuza* (Political Report to the Central Committee of the CPSU to the 27th Congress of the Communist Party of the Soviet Union) (Moscow: Politizdat, 1986), pp. 88–89.

Shevardnadze later disclosed that the sentence on the need to withdraw from Afghanistan was almost dropped from the report in last-minute revisions, but he urged its restoration. See Eduard Shevardnadze, *The Future Belongs to Freedom* (Free Press, Macmillan, 1991), p. 47.

130. "The Foreign Policy and Diplomatic Activity of the USSR (April 1985-October 1989), A Survey Prepared by the USSR Ministry of Foreign Affairs," *Mezhdunarodnaya zhizn'* (International Affairs), no. 12 (December 1989), p. 12.

who was present. Najibullah claimed to have told his colleagues after the session that Karmal's reaction was wrong. Although that may have been a self-serving invention by Najibullah, a Soviet observer present at the meeting carefully noted reactions among the Afghan officials and reported that only Najibullah had seemed to agree with the idea and that Najibullah himself had probably reached the conclusion that the situation could only be settled after all foreign troops had left.[131] Several months later, in May 1986, Najibullah replaced Babrak Karmal as party general secretary, although the latter remained as president.

The Soviet leadership first disclosed its intention to withdraw to the American leadership at the Geneva summit meeting in November 1985. Gorbachev raised the subject of Afghanistan in the summit discussion and spoke about withdrawal "as part of a general political settlement between us." Reagan, however, ignored this comment, which had not been foreseen in his script, and merely made his earlier planned statement listing Afghanistan with Nicaragua and Cambodia as examples of Soviet trouble-making.[132] Secretary Shultz told other members of the U.S. delegation that he had sensed that Moscow might be reevaluating its position on Afghanistan.[133]

Diplomatic negotiation moved very slowly over the next year, and the United States increased the scale and the effectiveness of its arms supply to the Afghan insurgents. Babrak Karmal, too, was cautious in moving toward "national reconciliation," interpreting that agreed-on objective in a much more restricted way than did Gorbachev. In November 1986 another key Politburo meeting took several important decisions on Afghanistan. Gorbachev complained that in the year since their October 1985 meeting there had been no progress toward settling the matter. He said the Soviet Union must end the war in one or, at most, two years, and he later proposed withdrawing half the Soviet troops in 1987 and the other half in 1988. He also called for "broadening the political base of the regime with account for the real distribution of power." Najibullah would replace Karmal, who had become entirely ineffectual. Najibullah should be invited to Moscow the next month. Finally, Gorbachev also stressed the need to begin direct talks with Pakistan and to ensure that Soviet withdrawal would not be followed by the Americans coming into Afghanistan.[134]

---

131. B. Pyadyshev, "Najibullah, President of Afghanistan," *Mezhdunarodnaya zhizn'*, no. 1 (January 1990), p. 20. Ambassador Pyadyshev interviewed Najibullah, quoted his comment, and added the information about the Soviet diplomat's observation.

132. See Shultz, *Turmoil and Triumph*, p. 601.

133. See Oberdorfer, *The Turn*, p. 153; and Kenneth L. Adelman, *The Great Universal Embrace: Arms Summitry—A Skeptic's Account* (Simon and Schuster, 1989), p. 141.

134. TsKhSD, Fond 89, Perechen' 14, Dokument 41, *Zasedaniye Politbyuro TsK KPSS. 13 noyabrya 1986 goda* (Session of the Politburo of the CC of the CPSU, November 13, 1986), Top Secret, only copy (working transcript), 31 pp. "On Further Measures on Afghanistan" (pp. 24–31); quotations from pp. 25, 31. I consulted this document, trans-

This Politburo record is of particular value because it is an unvarnished transcript, not merely a decision document based on the meeting. Among its revealing sidelights on Soviet-American relations is a comment by Andrei Gromyko: "As for the Americans, they are not interested in settling the situation in Afghanistan. On the contrary, it's advantageous to them to have the war drag out," to which Gorbachev commented, "That's right." When Gorbachev expressed his concern that the Americans not move into Afghanistan after the Soviet troops moved out, Marshal Akhromeyev had said, "They won't go into Afghanistan with armed forces," and Anatoly Dobrynin had added, "We can reach an agreement with the Americans on that." There was full agreement that "the strategic objective," as Gromyko stressed, was to "bring the war to an end" and get Soviet troops back home. In the middle of their discussion, Shevardnadze had remarked: "Now we are reaping the fruits of decisions not thought through in the past."[135]

In the United States, the Soviet decision to withdraw, publicly announced by Gorbachev in February 1988, has frequently been assumed to be related to the American supply of arms, especially the Stinger antiaircraft missile (the decision to supply was made in March 1986, and the first successful firing in Afghanistan in September 1986). But in this Politburo discussion of November 1986 there was no mention of the Stinger or indeed of American arms supply in general. There was discussion of Afghan army and security force levels and reiteration of a conclusion reached years before that a military solution was not feasible; as Viktor Chebrikov remarked: "The military way has not given a resolution for the past six years." And as Gorbachev emphasized, "We laid down a line for settling the Afghan problem in a meeting of the Politburo in October of last year."[136] They needed to press ahead more vigorously with that line.

And they did. Babrak Karmal was ousted as president one week later, on November 20. On December 12 President Najibullah visited Moscow, where Gorbachev told him flatly: Soviet troops would be withdrawn within one and half to two years, and he had better shore up his position with real "national reconciliation" during that time.[137]

Meanwhile, the Politburo Commission on Afghanistan under Shevardnadze as chairman, with Yazov, Chebrikov, and Yakovlev as members,

---

ferred from the so-called presidential or Kremlin archive, in the former Central Committee archive. It has now also been printed in a Russian historical journal: see "Secret Documents from the Special File: Afghanistan," *Voprosy istorii* (Questions of History), no. 3 (March 1993), pp. 22–26.

135. *Zasedaniye*, pp. 25, 31, 25, 27; and *Voprosy istorii*, no. 3, (March 1993), pp. 23, 26, 23, 24.

136. *Zasedaniye*, pp. 27, 31; and *Voprosy istorii*, no. 3 (March 1993), pp. 23, 25.

137. Pyadyshev, *Mezhdunarodnaya zhizn'*, no. 1 (January 1990), p. 21; and Akhromeyev and Kornienko, *Glazami marshala i diplomata*, p. 149.

became more active.[138] Soviet diplomacy redoubled efforts, especially with Pakistan and the UN negotiations. The Soviets found it difficult to engage the United States, although the Americans continued to advocate a neutral, non-aligned independent Afghanistan, which the Soviets also sought as a bar to American inroads. There were of course differing desires and expectations about the nature of the future Afghan government.

In mid-September 1987, Shevardnadze finally told Shultz confidentially what they had told Najibullah nine months earlier: the Soviet Union was determined to pull its troops out of Afghanistan, perhaps in less than a year, in all probability before the end of the Reagan administration, and it wanted American assistance with the international negotiations to facilitate withdrawal and to prevent a radical fundamentalist Islamic regime.[139] Gorbachev had told Shultz in April, when the secretary was in Moscow, that the Soviets wanted to withdraw, and even earlier Soviet officials had said as much to Ambassador Arthur Hartman.[140] But Shevardnadze now was saying the decision was firm. The defensive "holding" role in Afghanistan was giving way to active steps to resolve the problem of Soviet withdrawal, and if possible also the civil war.

In Africa, the Soviet leaders in the first half of the 1980s simply tried to bolster the regimes in Ethiopia, Angola, and Mozambique. This included Soviet military advisers, including direct advisory assistance in the conduct of the wars in Ethiopia and Angola, although in Angola the Cubans played a more central role. In Ethiopia, the Cubans had from the outset distanced themselves from the Ethiopian campaign against the Eritreans (with whom the Cubans had an earlier sympathetic relationship when they were fighting against the old regime in Addis Ababa). In 1984–85, as earlier noted, the Cubans withdrew three-quarters of their military personnel (partly also because neither the Ethiopians nor the Soviets would pay their upkeep).

---

138. Akhromeyev and Kornienko, *Glazami marshala i diplomata*, p. 166.

139. See Shultz, *Turmoil and Triumph*, p. 987; and Oberdorfer, *The Turn*, pp. 234–35.

140. Shultz, *Turmoil and Triumph*, pp. 870, 895.

In February 1987 Gorbachev was said, by a KGB intermediary, to have asked that President Reagan be told that American assistance in "national reconciliation" of the various contending Afghan groups would help Soviet withdrawal, and to have hinted that the Soviet Union might then be able to help in settling some other regional conflicts. The oral message was relayed by Radomir Bogdanov, a KGB officer serving as a deputy director of Arbatov's Institute of the USA and Canada to Suzanne Massie, the American writer known to the Soviets to be consulted by Reagan. The policy message accorded with real Soviet policy on Afghanistan, but the "message" appears to have been a KGB contrivance directed at trying to induce American interest in helping the Soviet Union to extricate itself from Afghanistan by offering a carrot. The Soviet leadership intended, and did, work to resolve other conflicts in any case. The provenance of the message was suspect in Washington, and if anything it probably reduced receptivity to the real Soviet interest in working out a way to withdraw. See ibid., p. 872.

Besides avoiding any new commitments in Africa, the Soviet Union reduced earlier ties. For example, from 1983 to 1988 the Soviet Union reduced the number of African states receiving military assistance (mostly minor) from twenty-two to seven. More important, while increasing military assistance to Angola in 1987–88 after the United States had begun supplying arms to Savimbi, and while maintaining support to Mengistu in Ethiopia, as earlier noted the Soviet leaders from 1985 on urged their friends to compromise, pursue "national reconciliation" with other groups, and seek to settle their disputes by political means. This was the Soviet message to Ethiopia, Angola, Mozambique, the South West African Peoples' Organization (SWAPO) in Namibia, and the African National Congress (ANC) in South Africa. For those in power and confronting insurgencies (Ethiopia, Angola, and Mozambique), this meant giving up some of the power they held. And both for them, and for the Soviet Union, it meant diluting the "progressive," socialist nature of the countries. But it could also mean survival and in any case seemed the only realistic course. For the Soviet Union, it would relieve the leadership from a costly economic and political burden.

In the Middle East, the Soviet Union diluted ties to the few radical states with which it had been associated by seeking to build new ties to others. For example, the Soviet Union balanced its 1979 Treaty of Friendship and Cooperation with the People's Democratic Republic of Yemen (South Yemen) by concluding a similar treaty with the Yemen Arab Republic (North Yemen) in October 1984. In July 1984 the Soviet Union resumed diplomatic relations with Egypt. In September and November 1985, the Soviet Union established diplomatic relations for the first time with Oman and the United Arab Emirates. In 1984 the Sheikdom of Kuwait and the Kingdom of Jordan made their first arms purchases from the Soviet Union. All these steps offered possible broadening of Soviet influence, and certainly broadening of Soviet contacts, diluting the Soviet relationship to the radical Arab states. When a coup within the leadership of South Yemen occurred in January 1986, there were widely voiced suspicions in Washington that Moscow had engineered to bring a more pliant leader to power there. In fact the Soviet leaders were as surprised as anyone, and Soviet as well as Western personnel were quickly evacuated (by Soviet and British ships). The United States, for good measure, warned the Soviets to keep out of the situation—and they in turn urged the United States to stay out. Neither intervened (or ever had any intention to do so).

In 1985 and 1986 the Soviets broadened their contact in the Middle East in another, especially important, way. They opened quiet diplomatic conversations with Israel, looking toward eventual resumption of diplomatic relations (broken since 1967).

In 1987 an attempt by the Israelis and Jordanians to set in motion an Arab-Israeli negotiation on peace in Palestine, encouraged by the United States, failed. Nonetheless, it had included the idea of joint U.S. and Soviet sponsorship of a resumption of a UN international conference as the framework for negotiation by the parties—not unlike what did occur later. But in 1987 the United States decided to go along with such a procedure, which necessarily would involve the Soviet Union in the peace process and thus required American judgment that the Soviet Union would act constructively. Shultz and Shevardnadze consulted in April 1987 and reached an agreement. Although the initiative failed for other reasons, it had revealed a readiness and interest by both the U.S. and Soviet governments in cooperative action to try to help settlement of the long-standing Arab-Israeli conflict.[141]

Overall, the Soviet leadership sought to maintain or expand its role in the Third World, in particular in South and Southwest Asia, not by commitments to radical regimes but by more broadly based contacts. For example, in February 1986, First Deputy Foreign Minister Georgy Kornienko visited Iran, and agreements were signed resuming civil air flights and setting up a joint economic commission on natural gas exploitation, important as signs of a restoration of some degree of normalcy, and of Soviet balancing between Iraq and Iran. (The United States was, unsuccessfully, attempting to do the same thing through clandestine diplomacy and intelligence sharing with Iraq and arms transfer to Iran.)

In May 1985, Prime Minister Rajiv Gandhi visited Moscow, and in November 1986 Gorbachev visited India, maintaining traditional close ties. Gorbachev's visit to India was his first to any Asian or Third World country, and while there he signed a joint "Delhi Declaration," embodying a code of new thinking on peaceful coexistence for the Third World. It was scarcely noted in the United States but was widely publicized in that part of the world. Gorbachev reaffirmed these positions on a second visit two years later. In a marked departure from Soviet policy, Gorbachev encouraged India to improve relations with Pakistan and China and did not attempt to bring India into semialignment against the West.

At about this same time, the Soviet Union began low-key efforts to improve relations with other established Third World middle powers, which it had neglected while giving attention to the "progressive," but less stable and more impoverished, radical states.

Thus practical political and economic considerations began to be given greater weight, and ideological ones less emphasis, reflecting the new view of the world signaled in Gorbachev's party congress report in February 1986. The Soviet Union was less on the defensive and was shifting toward normal relationships based on mutual interest, or as Soviet spokesmen put it, on "a balance of interests" rather than a balance of power or a shared ideology. There still remained, however, the need to liquidate the regional conflicts and civil wars into which the Soviet Union had earlier fallen or jumped.

---

141. See ibid., pp. 936–49, especially pp. 937, 939, 944–45.

As this period of transition was under way, a new flare-up of conflict arose that helped to point the way to cooperation rather than confrontation with the West in meeting such crises. The Iran-Iraq war had been an unusual case of a conflict in which both the Soviet Union and the United States had steered clear of direct involvement and of treating it as in any way an East-West conflict. In later 1986, international shipping through the Persian Gulf to neutral Kuwait began to come under attack from Iran. Kuwait, which had good relations with the United States and, secretly, also with the Soviet Union, raised with the other members of the Gulf Cooperation Council the idea of seeking superpower protection for shipping in the Gulf. In early 1987, council members approached the United States and the Soviet Union, suggesting "reflagging"— nominal registration of Kuwaiti ships under the American or Soviet flags—in order to underline a commitment to their protection by the two powers. The Soviet Union, seeing an opportunity to develop a cooperative security role with the United States, agreed. The issues for American policymakers were not only whether to assume the commitment to military protection, but also whether to agree to a Soviet role. Many, including some in the administration, argued against that. Nonetheless, the operation was undertaken, and was successful, contributing to UN Resolution 598, supported by both the Soviet Union and the United States, and by August 1988 acceptance by Iran and Iraq of a cease-fire. The operation was not only successful in its specific terms and in contributing to an end to the eight-year-old war, but as Secretary Shultz later commented, "The United States and the Soviet Union were on the same side of a security issue for the first time since the beginning of the cold war."[142]

## The "Gorbachev Doctrine," From Competition to Cooperation, 1988–91

During the first three years of his leadership, Gorbachev moved gradually to dampen down regional conflicts in which the Soviet Union was involved or which it could influence, but he did not disengage or cut off existing involvements.[143] Nonetheless, from early on, he had begun to articulate an

---

142. Ibid., p. 934, and see pp. 925–35, for his account of the whole episode. This was a rare occasion when Secretary of Defense Weinberger for somewhat different reasons (he did not share Shultz's positive interest in seeing U.S.-Soviet cooperation develop) also supported the operation. For his account see Caspar W. Weinberger, *Fighting for Peace: Seven Critical Years in the Pentagon* (Warner Books, 1990), pp. 387–428.

  Shultz exaggerated; the two superpowers had cooperated in some other regional conflicts, notably in the Middle East in October 1973 (see Garthoff, *Détente and Confrontation*, chapter 11), and in reaching arms control and confidence-building agreements. Nonetheless, it was a useful step in expanding security cooperation.

143. One reason that Gorbachev had to move slowly was the lack of a consensus on a new policy in the leadership at that time. By 1988 besides other changes in the Politburo (and

approach that one may call the Gorbachev Doctrine, although he never used that term. In his Twenty-seventh Party Congress speech of February 1986 he had emphasized the need for peaceful political resolution of disputes and development of a comprehensive international system of common security. He emphasized freedom of choice by each nation, mainly in the context of Europe but applicable everywhere.[144]

On September 17, 1987, in a major article keyed to the opening of the annual session of the UN General Assembly, Gorbachev emphasized again the need for a comprehensive system of international security, including the need to resolve regional conflicts, and above all urging use of the United Nations and other international diplomatic means. He called for increased efforts at conflict resolution, use of UN peacekeeping forces, intensified international cooperation against terrorism, a UN headquarters "Hot Line" to the capitals of permanent members of the UN Security Council, and assuring human rights.[145] Moreover, the Soviet Union began to do things to give substance to this approach, such as acknowledging and starting to pay for UN peacekeeping operations that it had previously denounced. (Soviet cooperation in the escorting of Kuwaiti ships has been noted.)

In the economic sphere, the Soviet Union began to reorient its whole relationship with the Third World, sharply reducing ideological and even power-influence considerations (with a few exceptions) and increasing the importance of economic criteria. About two years after this process had begun, Gorbachev formalized it in a decree in July 1990, which stated that Soviet economic relations with the developing countries of the Third World would be based "on the principles of mutual benefit and mutual interests, guided by international standards and practices," meaning above all equal economic benefit for the Soviet Union from trade. The relationship would also be in keeping with "real possibilities," that is, economic constraints on the Soviet Union.[146] Besides cutting subsidies to Vietnam and Cuba, the Soviet Union renegotiated the Egyptian debt. The Soviet Union also began to seek a role in the General

---

the sidelining of Andrei Gromyko) key originators of the course traditionally pursued in the Third World and even in the early 1980s were gone, notably Mikhail Suslov, who died in 1982; Boris Ponomarev, head of the International Department of the Central Committee since 1955 (and earlier first deputy since 1948), who was retired in early 1986; and Rostislav A. Ulyanovsky, deputy head of the International Department dealing with Third World countries, had also retired.

144. See chapter 13.

145. M. S. Gorbachev, "The Reality and Guarantees of a Secure World," *Pravda*, September 17, 1987.

146. "Decree of the President of the Union of Soviet Socialist Republics, On Introducing Changes into the Foreign Economic Practice of the Soviet Union," July 24, 1990, *Pravda*, July 25, 1990.

Agreement on Tariffs and Trade (GATT) and the International Monetary Fund (IMF).

The Soviet Union also took measures to normalize relations with other countries. Soviet-controlled clandestine radio broadcasts to Iran and to China were terminated (in September and November 1986, respectively). Many of these steps were of course intended to restore ties and influence, but they also bore witness to the Soviet recognition that security was indeed comprehensive and not merely military and was better served by cooperation rather than confrontation.

To some extent, the new cooperative internationalism advanced by Gorbachev reflected awareness of the limits on Soviet ability to influence the course of events, but it went beyond that. Gorbachev saw the world political process as complex, far beyond the traditional Soviet view of a simple zero-sum game of two camps competing for world domination. He was the first Soviet leader to see the world in post-Leninist terms.

The Gorbachev Doctrine was not merely prudent disengagement from overcommitments but had the objective of contributing to a new world order, a comprehensive international security system. Gorbachev worked to try to resolve regional conflicts, not merely to avoid new commitments and cut losses on earlier Soviet involvements. Thus in his last four years, the Soviet Union moved to obtain international (and in civil wars national) cooperation in resolving conflicts based on a balance of interests. The Soviet Union disengaged from its military occupation in Afghanistan. It encouraged the Cubans to withdraw their forces from Ethiopia and Angola, the Vietnamese to withdraw from Cambodia, the Nicaraguans to hold free elections and make peace, the Salvadoran insurgents to lay down their arms and join in a political process, and the Cambodian factions to resolve their conflict. It helped to reactivate the Middle East peace process and joined the UN effort to roll back Iraqi occupation of Kuwait. These and other activities in the Third World took place in parallel with the steps in Europe leading to the end of the division of Europe and of the Cold War.

The keystone and highest priority was Afghanistan. On February 8, 1988, Gorbachev announced Soviet agreement to withdraw all Soviet forces from Afghanistan within ten months from the time the agreements then under negotiation in Geneva were signed.[147] He had finally "bitten the bullet," and despite the reference to the negotiations in effect he had put Soviet withdrawal on an irrevocable course.[148] Gorbachev credited the Afghan leadership publicly

---

147. "Statement of the General Secretary of the Central Committee of the CPSU M. S. Gorbachev on Afghanistan," *Pravda*, February 9, 1988.

148. Georgy Kornienko, in 1987–88 one of the key second-echelon advisers on Afghanistan policy (as first deputy chief of the Central Committee's International Department, along with Shevardnadze's first deputy, Yuly Vorontsov, KGB first Deputy Vladimir Kryuchkov, and Yazov's first deputy, Marshal Sergei Akhromeyev), argued for an earlier pullout and for forcing Najibullah to form a real coalition government, but he was

with making the withdrawal possible, arguing that "the policy of national reconciliation is a reflection of new political thinking in Afghanistan" and saying that "success of the policy of national reconciliation has already made it possible to begin withdrawing Soviet troops." He argued that the establishment of a coalition government was "a purely internal Afghan issue," but the Geneva negotiations could help the process of peaceful Afghan national reconciliation. Further, reflecting his confidence in the earlier negotiated obligations of the external powers, he noted, "The Geneva obligations will close the channels for outside assistance to those who hope to impose their will on the whole nation by armed force."[149] Finally, "when the Afghan knot is untied, it will have the most profound impact on other regional conflicts too"—the Middle East, the Iran-Iraq war, in southern Africa, in Kampuchea (Cambodia), and in Central America.[150]

Intensive negotiations proceeded to work out the net of specific agreements: two bilateral agreements between Afghanistan and Pakistan, two more which the Soviet Union and the United States were also to sign as "witnesses," and finally a Declaration on International Guarantees to be signed by the United States and the Soviet Union. On April 14, 1988, this package of what were called "the Geneva accords" was signed, to go into effect on May 15, with Soviet military withdrawal to be completed by February 15, 1989.[151]

Before the accords were signed, however, several issues arose that needed to be resolved. One was a Pakistani attempt, finally abandoned at American urging, to reopen the question of constituting a new coalition govern-

---

opposed by Shevardnadze. He has given his account in G. M. Kornienko, "How the Decisions Were Taken on Introducing Soviet Troops into Afghanistan and Withdrawing Them," *Novaya i noveishaya istoriya* (Modern and Contemporary History), no. 3 (May-June 1993), pp. 107–18.

149. Ibid.

150. Ibid.

Before Gorbachev's speech, and even after it, many senior officials in Washington (especially in intelligence) continued to argue that the Soviets would not withdraw. Robert Gates and his top Soviet affairs expert, Fritz Ermarth, were among the most adamant, and they reaffirmed a national intelligence estimate to that effect. The DIA was equally confident the Soviets would stay. The State Department analysts, and lower-level expert analysts at the CIA, did not agree. These differences stemmed in part from erroneous assessment of Soviet military interests in Afghanistan, and even more basically from failure to recognize that Gorbachev and his Soviet Union were implementing "new thinking" and had new objectives. Gates and his colleagues also believed that the Najibullah regime would quickly collapse, and they did not believe the Soviet leadership would take actions such as withdrawal of Soviet troops because it would risk that result. See Shultz, *Turmoil and Triumph*, pp. 1087–88.

151. For the full texts, and official statements on the occasion, see Khan, *Untying the Afghan Knot*, pp. 315–37. See also "Key Sections of Accords on Afghanistan as Signed in Geneva," *New York Times*, April 15, 1988, p. A12.

ment. But the main issue concerned continuing supply of arms by the external powers to the Afghan insurgents and government.

Just as the Soviet Union moved decisively and publicly to withdraw, the United States reneged on its key commitment. In December 1985 the United States had agreed that when all Soviet troops were withdrawn, the parties (including Pakistan and the United States) would cease supplying arms to the insurgents. Yet when Shevardnadze said this publicly in January 1988, Shultz took issue; only in March, after Gorbachev's public commitment on withdrawal, did it become clear to Moscow that the United States had changed its position; now Soviet withdrawal was not enough, there must be "symmetry" on arms supply: if the Soviet Union could continue to supply arms to the Afghan government, the United States must have the right to supply arms to the insurgents.[152] Although on its merits this was not an unreasonable position, it was unreasonable to change to it when the deal was being finalized.

The fact is that in 1985 no one in Washington believed the Soviet Union was serious about withdrawing its troops, and as Shultz has acknowledged, in early 1988 "as the possibility of Soviet withdrawal became increasingly real," the position the United States had earlier agreed to seemed less of a good deal. Moreover, President Reagan, previously unaware of the stand his administration had taken, did not like the idea of the United States cutting off aid to "freedom fighters" before the communist Afghan government was toppled. The proposed arrangement also came under public criticism in the United States. And it was Shultz's correct judgment, hinted at in his memoir, that the Soviet leaders were by early 1988 hooked on withdrawal and were simply in no position to resist the U.S. demand for symmetry on arms supply. Gorbachev felt "betrayed," as Dobrynin told Ambassador Jack Matlock, but he was indeed in no position to do anything but accept the outcome. The result was a charade in which the accords said that Pakistan would not supply arms to the insurgents, and the United States guaranteed the accords, but with an "understanding" on the side that the supply of arms would continue.[153]

---

152. See Shultz, *Turmoil and Triumph*, pp. 1087–91; and Khan, *Untying the Afghan Knot*, pp. 140, 269–77.

   Shultz waffled in his account. Although he has acknowledged that in December 1985 "our negotiators in Geneva had taken the position" that our assistance to the *mujahedin* would cease, the U.S. negotiators had agreed to the provision after authorization from Washington, sent by the Department of State with White House clearance, even if not engaging the president's and perhaps not Shultz's attention. Shultz did concede that "the Soviets regarded this, not surprisingly, as a shift in our position" (p. 1087).

153. Shultz, *Turmoil and Triumph*, pp. 1087–91. Shultz noted that when President Reagan asked President Zia in a telephone conversation how Pakistan would handle the fact that they would be violating the agreement by channeling U.S. arms, Zia replied that they would "just lie about it," as they had been doing for eight years. Zia added that "Muslims have the right to lie in a good cause" (ibid., p. 1091). Reagan seemed satisfied.

This was far less than ideal—and the signing "ceremony" for the Geneva Accords was remarkably cold and formal, with not even the usual handshakes. Nonetheless, the Soviet withdrawal of forces did have a formal if thin international cover. Half of the Soviet troops were withdrawn in the first three months, and the last on schedule on February 15, 1989. Contrary to the expectations of most American officials, and indeed probably of most Soviet officials, the Afghan government of Najibullah successfully fended off *mujahedin* attacks for another three years.[154] During most of this time, the Soviet Union continued to send large supplies of weapons.[155] In September 1991 the United States and the Soviet Union agreed as of December 31 to cut off all arms aid to any Afghans, finally realizing "negative symmetry." In April 1992 the Najibullah government fell, although shifting alliances and intermittent armed conflict reigned among the successors.[156]

The Soviet initiative on Afghanistan in February 1988 was followed by others dealing with other regional (and civil) conflicts.[157] Virtually all involved

---

154. The U.S. government was so sure that the Najibullah regime would quickly fall that it demonstratively closed its embassy in Kabul shortly after the completion of the Soviet military withdrawal. It thus deprived itself of a valuable listening post and faced the new problem of deciding which shifting coalition government it should acknowledge (among a succession of weak ones) by reestablishing a diplomatic mission.

155. The Russian government in 1992 declassified a number of records of Politburo meetings and decisions of 1989 on supporting the Najibullah regime. A Politburo meeting of January 24 considered, but rejected, one course of action that would have required leaving one division of Soviet troops disguised as Afghans to secure the main route to Kabul. Over a dozen other top-level memoranda from January 1989 through March of 1990 detail the extensive supply of weaponry, including large numbers of Scud missiles. An Afghan suggestion of recruiting foreign volunteers was not opposed, especially if they came from other Muslim countries, but the idea of any "volunteers" from the Soviet republics was rejected.

   The January 24 meeting is in the former Central Committee archive: TsKhSD, Fond 89, Perechen' 10, Dokument 16, *O meropriyatiyakh v svyazi s predstoyashchim vyvodom sovetskikh voisk iz Afganistana* (On Measures in Connection with the Forthcoming Withdrawal of Soviet Troops from Afghanistan), excerpt from protocol no. 146 of the meeting of the Politburo, January 24, 1989, P 146/vi, Top Secret/Special File. This document, which I consulted in the archive, has now also been published, under the heading "Secret Documents from the Special File: Afghanistan," *Voprosy istorii*, no. 3 (March 1993), pp. 26–32.

   The discussion of foreign volunteers is in the report of the 158th session of the Politburo on May 12, 1989, archive reference: TsKhSD, Fond 89, Perechen' 10, Dokument 35; also in *Voprosy istorii*, no. 3 (March 1993), pp. 32–33.

156. It is ironic that Najibullah's regime remained in power longer than Gorbachev's, longer than the Soviet Union itself.

157. The Soviet leaders had very much in mind that their initiative in disengaging from military intervention and assisting in the political resolution of the Afghan conflict could contribute to the resolution of other such conflicts. A Politburo-approved policy paper in August 1989 credited their Afghan withdrawal with having given a boost to UN efforts

complex multilateral negotiations, as well as difficult efforts at persuasion and the phasing out of existing Soviet commitments. Nonetheless, the pattern over the four years through 1991 was impressive.

The second major regional conflict wrapped around a civil war that had led to Soviet-American proxy confrontation was Angola. Here, too, as 1988 began, the Soviet and Cuban side moved toward resolving the conflict. On January 29 Cuba agreed, in exchange for a place at the negotiating table, to withdraw all of its troops from Angola as part of the peace settlement process. When Shultz raised the subject of Angola in April when he was in Moscow, he found Gorbachev and Shevardnadze discouraged but interested in seeing progress toward resolving the issue. At the Moscow summit four weeks later Shultz and Shevardnadze agreed to set as a target an agreement on Angola and Namibia by September, the tenth anniversary of UN Resolution 435.[158]

The Soviet leaders had been trying to persuade the Cubans and the Angolans to agree on Cuban withdrawal and "national reconciliation" with Savimbi. Although they did agree on complete Cuban withdrawal, the timing and a schedule for withdrawal were other matters. Both sides had built up large forces, and the South Africans were active in Savimbi's region. After failure of an Angolan government offensive in 1987, UNITA advanced and laid siege to Cuito Cuanavale, which lasted through the first three months of 1988. At this time, in March, Assistant Secretary Crocker met with South African Foreign Minister Roelof (Pik) Botha in an attempt to enlist South African cooperation in a settlement, but the request was rebuffed. The Soviets urged the Cubans to give up Cuito Cuanavale and in effect the south of Angola, but the Cubans refused. A Cuban-led counteroffensive relieved the city and forced UNITA back. In June the Cubans and Angolans attacked South African forces at the Calueque Dam, long conceded to them. Those reversals and South African public discontent with their casualties led the South Africans to be more ready to compromise in the negotiations. On July 20, the main points of an overall agreement on Namibia and foreign disengagement from Angola were readied, and a cease-fire took place in August. By the end of August the South Africans completed a withdrawal from Angola, and by the end of September a two-year Cuban withdrawal was agreed on in principle. On December 13, 1988, an accord was finally signed, in the presence of Assistant Secretary Crocker and Soviet Deputy Foreign Minister Anatoly Adamishin. A week later, on December 22, foreign ministers signed an accord on creation of Namibia (which then

---

to settle other regional conflicts and increasing release in political means to resolve conflicts. See TsKhSD, Fond 89, Perechen' 9, Dokument 26, *O strategicheskoi linii SSSR primenitel'no k OON i svyazannym s nei mezhdunarodnym organizatsiyam* (On the Strategic Line of the USSR with Respect to the UN and Related International Organizations), excerpt from protocol no. 164 of the meeting of the Politburo, August 28, 1989, P 164/177, Secret, p. 3.

158. See Shultz, *Turmoil and Triumph*, pp. 1124–25.

emerged as an independent state in March 1990), and a tripartite Angolan-South African-Cuban treaty contained reciprocal obligations including a schedule for complete Cuban military withdrawal by mid–1991.[159]

The December 1988 accords in effect reduced the Angolan conflict from a "regional conflict" with outside parties to a civil war, although warfare resumed (with intermittent new short-lived cease-fires), with continuing supply of arms by the external powers, for two and a half years more.[160] The United States, the Soviet Union, and Portugal (as the official mediator) cooperated in trying to bring the MPLA government in Luanda and UNITA in the south into an agreement on power sharing or "national reconciliation." By the end of May 1991 all Cuban troops had been withdrawn. Finally, on May 31, 1991, the Estoril peace accord was signed, and the United States and Soviet Union agreed to cease supplying arms. The government and UNITA agreed to reduce greatly and to merge their armed forces. Shortly after, the MPLA disavowed Marxism-Leninism and converted to social democracy. Angola at least had a chance.[161]

---

159. See Crocker, *High Noon in Southern Africa*; and Shultz, *Turmoil and Triumph*, pp. 1125–29. Although Shultz does not mention it, the United States on December 21 also deferred normal diplomatic relations to Angola until the government made peace with UNITA.

   The Cubans, by rejecting U.S.-encouraged Soviet advice on pulling out of Cuito Cuanavale and by successful counteroffensive operations, though not defeating UNITA, did help to persuade South Africa to agree to a cease-fire and withdrawal in August, and to the Angola-Namibia accords.

   The Cuban commander after October 1987 was the experienced General Arnaldo Ochoa Sanchez, previously the senior Cuban adviser in Ethiopia and Nicaragua. He may have acted in defiance of instructions from Castro, as well as from the Soviets. In 1989, after his return to Cuba, he was arrested, tried, and executed on corruption and drug-smuggling charges—although many believed the Castro brothers saw the renowned general as a potential threat to their power. See William A. De Palo, Jr., "Cuban Internationalism: The Angola Experience, 1975–1988," *Parameters*, vol. 23 (Autumn 1993), pp. 67–71.

160. In the United States, there was some renewed debate over whether to keep sending arms to Savimbi, but the program continued. The Soviet Union also continued to send arms to the Angolan government, including making an arrangement whereby the Cubans left behind for the Angolans their own substantial arms as Cuban troops withdrew, and the Soviet Union replaced those weapons with others sent directly to Cuba; this involved leaving in Angola more than 1,000 tanks, 200 infantry fighting vehicles, 500 artillery pieces, 70 air defense missile complexes, and 44 combat aircraft. See TsKhSD, Fond 89, Perechen' 10, Dokument 20, *O kompensatziya* (On Compensating the Republic of Cuba with Arms from the Soviet Union for Those Left by Cuban Troops in the Peoples' Republic of Angola), excerpts from protocol no. 147 of the meeting of the Politburo, February 7, 1989, Top Secret/Special File, attached memorandum (same title) no. 318/3/3–00144, January 31, 1989, from Shevardnadze, Yakovlev, Yazov, Kryuchkov, and Katushev, p. 1.

161. In October 1992 national elections were held in Angola. President José Eduardo dos Santos and the MPLA were reelected by a strong plurality, though less than a majority; Jonas Savimbi and UNITA, however, refused to accept the results and quickly mounted

The next continuing conflict in Africa was in Ethiopia. Gorbachev told Colonel Mengistu Haile Mariam when he visited Moscow in July 1988 that he should work toward a negotiated settlement with the Eritreans and Ethiopian rebels. Mengistu did not take well to this advice, which was delivered again more bluntly by Politburo member Viktor Chebrikov in Addis Ababa in January 1989. With the end of the Ethiopian-Somali state of war in April 1988, and with Soviet encouragement, the Cubans moved in 1989–90 to withdraw their one remaining brigade and then their military advisers. By early 1990 the Soviet Union had withdrawn its military advisers from the combat areas and was reducing their number. Arms shipments continued in 1989–90 under an existing military assistance agreement (although by a Politburo decision of November 1989 promised heavy weapons deliveries were suspended),[162] and when the military agreement expired in 1990 it was not renewed.

Besides urging Mengistu to work out a political settlement based on "national reconciliation," in sharp contrast to a few years earlier the Soviet Union also recommended that he seek to improve his relations with the United States and other Western countries. There was a resumption of U.S.-Ethiopian contacts in 1988–89, but no real change in the relationship. Ethiopia did reestablish diplomatic relations with Israel (which was already providing military advisers), but this did not—as Mengistu hoped—lead to an improvement in relations with the United States.

In May 1991 Mengistu fled, the Soviet Union evacuated the base at the Dahlak Islands, and the United States played a role in negotiating the takeover of power by the rebel groups. The United States, which had stopped supplying arms to Somalia and Sudan in 1989, did not restore a military relationship with Ethiopia.

The third country in Africa torn by civil war, Mozambique, had not become a regional conflict involving Soviet and American proxies, although there were Soviet (and some Cuban and East German) military advisers, and

---

a larger armed force than the government. The civil war resumed. The freedom fighters proved not to be champions of democracy after all. In May 1993, very belatedly, the United States finally recognized the weakened Luanda government and established relations and soon thereafter began to supply nonlethal military equipment to the government.

162. TsKhSD, Fond 89, Perechen' 10, Dokument 45, *O nashei dal'neishei Iinii v otnoshenii Efiopii* (On Our Future Line in Relation to Ethiopia), excerpt from protocol no. 172 of the meeting of the Politburo, November 17, 1989, P 172/1, Top Secret/Special File, pp. 1–2. While suspending heavy weapons shipments, and withdrawing advisers from the north of the country, at this point a new five-year plan for military cooperation was still envisaged, although with a much reduced military role. See also TsKhSD, Fond 89, Perechen' 10, Dokument 44, *O nashikh shagakh v syazi s obrashcheniyami Mengistu Khaile Mariama* (On Our Steps in Connection with the Appeals of Mengistu Haile Mariam), excerpt from protocol no. 165 of the meeting of the Politburo, September 19, 1989, P 165/30, Top Secret/Special File, 4 pp.

South African covert support for the insurgents. In June 1989, the Soviet Union informed the Mozambicans that it would phase out its military advisers over the remaining year and a half of the existing military cooperation agreement and then terminate military assistance (most of the advisers were pulled out during 1989 although some military assistance continued during that period).[163] The Soviet Union continued to press for a new accord of Mozambique with South Africa and urged the United States to do the same. In mid-1989 South Africa declared it was providing no assistance to the rebels. In December 1990 the Soviet Union and the United States joined several other countries agreeing to supply observers to help police a cease-fire agreement. Talks between the government and rebels continued from 1990 until October 1992, when an agreement was reached. A cease-fire was put into effect, although the political situation remained unsettled and uncertain.

The third major regional conflict that had troubled Soviet-American relations was Nicaragua. The Soviet role was indirect but continued the pattern. For several years the Soviet leaders had urged the Sandinistas to work with the Contadora and Central American peace efforts and to seek national reconciliation with the contras and disaffected elements of the population. The March 1988 cease-fire was a result of the efforts long under way, in particular of the Central American presidents, working with the United States as well as with Nicaragua.

When the Bush administration came into office in January 1989, one of its first important foreign policy steps was to abandon the attempt to keep alive American funding of the contra military operations in Nicaragua. This was done in recognition of the important successes of the peacemaking effort and the consequent deadline in political support in the United States for any further contra funding. The Sandinistas in turn agreed to free elections in a year, in February 1990, in exchange for demobilization of the contras.

In May 1989 Gorbachev in confidential correspondence informed President Bush that since the end of the previous year the Soviet Union had ceased supply of arms to Nicaragua.[164] At a meeting in Moscow with Foreign Minister Eduard Shevardnadze soon after that, Secretary of State James Baker

163. See TsKhSD, Fond 89, Perechen' 10, Dokument 48, *O voyenno-tekhnicheskom sotrudnichestve s Narodnoi Respublikoi Mozambik i ob ukreplenii material'noi bazy VVS po pros'be chlena Politbyuro TsK partii Frelimo M. Matsin'ye* (On Military-Technical Collaboration with the People's Republic of Mozambique and on the Strengthening of the Material Base of the Air Forces in Accordance with the Request of M. Matchine, Member of the Politburo of the CC of the Frelimo Party), excerpt from protocol no. 175 of the meeting of the Politburo, December 19, 1989, P 175/31, Top Secret/Special File, 5 pp.

164. Michael R. Beschloss and Strobe Talbott, *At the Highest Levels: The Inside Story of the End of the Cold War* (Little, Brown and Company, 1993), p. 59.

For a review of Soviet-Nicaraguan relations from 1989 through 1991 see Jan S. Adams, *A Foreign Policy in Transition: Moscow's Retreat from Central America and the Caribbean, 1985–1992* (Duke University Press, 1992), pp. 109–31.

told him that if the Sandinistas won the forthcoming elections fairly, the United States would accept their legitimacy. The Soviets in turn exerted strong efforts to persuade the Sandinistas of the need for free elections.[165] The Soviets, and the Sandinista leaders, believed that the opposition would make a good showing but that the Sandinistas would win.[166] When the opposition won the elections, the Soviets—and the Sandinistas—accepted the result. Secretary Baker was in Moscow a week later, preparing for the forthcoming Moscow summit, and in the joint communiqué on that meeting Shevardnadze joined in pledging to respect the results of the elections (and privately the Soviets confirmed they would not supply arms to the Sandinistas).[167] In an internal Politburo discussion two months later, the Soviet leaders decided to maintain a political dialogue with the new government, to work out a plan for economic cooperation, to limit military cooperation to assistance in maintenance and repair, and to keep up "friendly" party relations between the Communist Party of the Soviet Union (CPSU) and the Sandinistas. They also decided to work with the United States in helping to resolve the problem of assimilating the contras (seeing that as the main political task). Finally, they saw the first signs of a move by the parties toward serious negotiations in El Salvador, which should be supported, and agreed to try to bring the Cubans along on a new approach to Nicaragua and El Salvador.[168]

The process of negotiating a settlement among the parties in El Salvador was very difficult and long, but not owing to any lack of support for a

---

165. In October 1989, Foreign Minister Shevardnadze went to Nicaragua in the first (and last) high-level Soviet visit. (When Gorbachev had visited Cuba in April 1989, he had conspicuously not visited Nicaragua.) Shevardnadze stressed the need for national reconciliation and absorption of the contras and their sympathizers through participation in the political process.

166. This is a fairly evident conclusion from the fact that the elections were held and were fair. A Politburo assessment made just before the elections, now in the Russian archives, confirms that this was the view of the Soviet leaders. The recommendation to the Politburo, and accepted by it, had called for commitment to accept the outcome, in part to induce Washington to make a similar commitment. The Politburo also decided to urge the victorious Sandinistas to maintain a policy of "national reconciliation." See TsKhSD, Fond 89, Perechen' 9, Dokument 80, *O nashei linii v syazi s predstoyashchimi vyborami v Nikaragua* (On Our Line in Connection with the Forthcoming Elections in Nicaragua), excerpts from protocol no. 179 of the meeting on the Politburo, February 17, 1990, P 179/20, Top Secret, pp. 2, 3. The recommendations had been submitted by Shevardnadze and Aleksandr Yakovlev.

167. Beschloss and Talbott, *At the Highest Levels*, p. 193.

168. TsKhSD, Fond 89, Perechen' 9, Dokument 117, *O nashei linii v otnoshenii Nikaragua pri novom pravitel'stve v etoi strane* (On Our Line in Relation to Nicaragua under a New Government), excerpt from protocol no. 185 of the meeting of the Politburo, April 13, 1990, P 185/20, Top Secret, pp. 1–2, and appended note, pp. 1–6. The proposals approved by the Politburo had been submitted jointly by Shevardnadze, Yakovlev, and Kryuchkov on April 6 (memorandum 324/05, Top Secret/Special File).

settlement by the Soviet Union. As the Politburo discussion of April 1990 showed, the Soviet leaders sought to use whatever influence they had with the Cubans as well as directly with the Salvadoran insurgents. Eventually, an accord was reached in January 1992.

At this juncture it may be appropriate to look briefly at the development of Soviet-Cuban relations. In all, relations in the 1985–87 period had been good, but there was some friction as the Soviets moved to put economic relations on a cost-effective basis, that is, to reduce their hidden subsidies to Cuba. Gorbachev visited Cuba in April 1989, but it became very clear to both sides that a wide gap existed between their views on internal policies and on foreign policy. The Cuban leaders continued to see a threat from the United States, while Gorbachev was urging Castro to improve relations with the United States.[169] Though no record of Gorbachev's discussions with Castro is available, it is known that they became acrimonious. There is available information from later discussion of these matters between Castro and the Soviet ambassador, Yury V. Petrov.

In June 1990 Ambassador Petrov saw Castro to brief him on the Soviet-American summit meeting and Gorbachev's latest pronouncements. Castro said he wanted "civilized relations" with the United States, but the U.S. government was not ready for good relations. The United States, he said, was seeking to squeeze Cuba and was aided in that effort by the Soviet constraints in their economic relations with Cuba. Castro also told the Soviet ambassador that for four months Cuba had sent not even a single weapon to the Salvadoran rebels, but he did not want to make a public declaration of that fact as the Americans wished.[170]

A new economic agreement between the Soviet Union and Cuba signed in December 1990 sharply cut back on Soviet subsidization of trade, for example, bringing the price paid for sugar down to about the world market price. By that time, the number of Soviet economic advisers had been cut from more than 3,000 in 1989 to about 1,000 at the beginning of 1991.

In September 1991 Gorbachev told Secretary Baker that the Soviet military presence in Cuba would be withdrawn—a statement made to the Americans and made publicly—even before the matter had been brought up with Castro.[171] The Cubans were not pleased to see the token Soviet brigade

---

169. Though not directly pertinent, the American invasion of Panama in December 1989 again raised an alarm in the Cuban leadership.

   On Soviet-Cuban relations from 1989 through 1991 see Adams, *A Foreign Policy in Transition*, pp. 76–106.

170. TsKhSD, Fond 89, Perechen' 8, Dokument 62, *Zapis besedy c Fidelom Kastro, 20 Iyuniya 1990 g. (Iz dnevnika Petrova, Yu. V.)* (Memorandum of Conversation with Fidel Castro, June 20, 1990. From the [Official] Diary of [Ambassador] Yu. V. Petrov), June 29, 1990, Secret, pp. 2–4.

171. David Hoffman, "Soviet Brigade to Leave Cuba, Gorbachev Says," *Washington Post*, September 12, 1991, pp. A1, A34.

leave, but they were furious at the unilateral Soviet decision and public announcement without any consultation. The Cubans dragged out subsequent talks and the schedule for phased departure of the 2,800-man brigade. Withdrawal began in late 1991 and was completed by June 1993. By the time the Soviet Union dissolved at the end of 1991, there were only a few hundred civilian advisers left in Cuba.[172]

The final regional conflict in which the United States had applied the Reagan Doctrine was the civil war in Cambodia. In the summer of 1988 and following, multilateral talks on Cambodia developed (bolstered by the initiation at about that same time of bilateral talks between the Soviet Union and China, Vietnam and China, and the United States and Vietnam).[173] In May 1988, after considerable Soviet urging, Vietnam announced withdrawal of 50,000 troops (about half the total) from Cambodia that year. In April 1989 Vietnam further promised to withdraw all of its troops by September. That was apparently done, although some units were subsequently reintroduced in 1990 without official acknowledgment for brief campaigns in support of the government.

The Soviet Union in turn phased out its military assistance program to Vietnam and began to withdraw its forces from the base at Cam Ranh Bay in 1989. The Soviets also proposed a moratorium on any supply of arms to the Cambodians, but the United States and China did not agree.

A Cambodian peace conference opened in Paris in July 1989 but collapsed after only a few weeks owing to sharp discord among the several Cambodian factions.

In July 1990 the United States dropped its support for the noncommunist guerrillas and supported a coalition of all parties including the government in Phnom Penh, which it had previously tried to exclude. In August there was a "breakthrough" as far as concurrence of the external powers (the United States, the Soviet Union, China, and Vietnam) on a coalition, but it took more than a year to bring the Cambodian parties to an agreement in October 1991. The October 1991 accords effectively ended the "regional" conflict, even though the civil war was not yet really settled. It was an example that once Cold War exploitation and sponsorship ended, local rivalries continued. After the signing of the Cambodian peace accords, the United States opened talks with Vietnam

---

Gorbachev's precipitate public statement was prompted by an off-the-cuff comment by Russian President Boris Yeltsin; Gorbachev did not want at that critical juncture to have even the appearance of a policy rift on this issue.

172. After tense relations, in November 1992 the Russian government signed four agreements with Cuba: an economic and trade agreement, establishment of a commission to discuss repayment of the large Cuban debt, a merchant shipping agreement, and an agreement on military-technical cooperation. The latter involved resumption of supply of spare parts for weapons that Cuba already had in exchange for continued functioning of the Russian intelligence monitoring station in Cuba.

173. See chapter 14.

on normalizing relations, and China and Vietnam began to normalize their long-strained relationship.[174] American and Soviet leaders continued to consult from time to time on the lingering Cambodian problem but in a cooperative rather than adversarial framework.

The Middle East continued to be the scene of several old and new conflicts, and a subject for continuing consultation between the Soviet Union and the United States, but there were no proxy conflicts to resolve. The two powers continued to seek to get Israeli-Arab peace talks going. In February 1989 Foreign Minister Shevardnadze visited Pakistan and made an extensive two-week trip through Iran and the Gulf area, the first such visit by a Soviet foreign minister in nine years. The nature of the Soviet approach to the region was changing. Although not severing ties to the radical states (Syria, Iraq, Libya, South Yemen, and the PLO), the Soviet Union cut back on arms deliveries and began to withdraw military advisers from Yemen in 1989–90. Most important, it moved to improve relations with the other states in the region. Steps were taken to improve relations with Egypt, Jordan, Saudi Arabia, and the Gulf states. Efforts were also made in 1989 to improve ties to Iran, balancing that with continued ties to Iraq. Building on the establishment of diplomatic relations with Oman and the United Arab Emirates in 1985, the Soviets now established relations with Qatar (1988) and Bahrain (1990) and opened reciprocal embassies with Saudi Arabia (1990). The Soviet Union welcomed the merger of the two Yemens in 1990. At the same time, in line with Gorbachev's statement in 1987 that the absence of ties with Israel (since 1967) "could not be considered normal," a pattern of relationships developed into full diplomatic recognition in October 1991.

The Soviet Union agreed in 1986 to pay its share of funding for the UN International Force in Lebanon (UNIFIL), supported the Iran-Iraq cease-fire in 1988, supported UN Security Council Resolution 658 of 1990 on a referendum to resolve the Western Sahara (Polisario versus Morocco) conflict, and in September 1991 supported UN repeal of the 1975 resolution equating Zionism with racism.

After the Iraqi occupation of Kuwait, the Soviet Union joined the UN consensus condemning Iraq, imposing sanctions, and by January 1991 (in UN Security Council Resolution 678) authorizing "all necessary means," that is, military operations, to force the Iraqis out of Kuwait.

Finally, in October 1991 in one of the last major diplomatic acts of the Soviet Union, President Gorbachev joined President Bush in convening a Middle Eastern peace conference in Madrid.[175]

---

174. See chapter 14.

175. The Soviet role was constructive and not unimportant, but it was essentially passive. The United States played the key part in bringing the Israelis and Arabs together. The Soviets wanted to see the near Eastern peace process succeed, and they wanted the symbolic role of appearing as a coconvening great power with the United States, so they were ready to go along with a process managed from Washington. For the American

In the South Asian subcontinent, the Soviet Union also diluted its former unconditional support for India in the interests of seeking to bolster international stability. Notwithstanding a renewal in August 1991 for twenty years of the 1971 Soviet-Indian Treaty of Peace, Friendship, and Cooperation, in November 1991 the Soviet Union supported a Pakistani proposal in the UN General Assembly for a South Asian nuclear-free zone despite Indian objection.[176]

By 1991 and after, the "nonaligned movement," once politically a factor to be reckoned with, was in effect defunct. Without a bipolar confrontation of the two worlds of East and West, there was no longer anything for the Third World to be nonaligned with.

In sum, in the Third World the Soviet Union moved energetically in its unilateral diplomatic activities, in conflict resolution, and in cooperative security measures including notably the "grand coalition" giving a UN mandate in the Gulf War to drive Iraq from Kuwait.

It would be a mistake to see the more spectacular Soviet moves, such as withdrawal from Afghanistan, as merely Soviet retrenchment, disengagement from costly and unpromising involvements in Afghanistan, Nicaragua, Angola, Ethiopia, and Mozambique. That was one element in the picture, but only one. There was a much broader and deeper shift from ideologically motivated attachments to a few countries to broad normalization of economic and political relationships around the world, in the Third World, in East Asia, and in Europe East and West.[177] Even more significant was the parallel and overlapping shift from geopolitical and geostrategic attachments made under a strategy of confrontation with the West, to normalized relations based on a desire to cooperate with the United States and other former foes from the Cold War.

The American role in relation to the Soviet reorientation and broad readjustment of its role in the Third World was essentially reactive. The measures undertaken under the Reagan Doctrine in general were continued and met success: the Soviet withdrawal from Afghanistan, the Vietnamese withdrawal from Cambodia, and the Cuban withdrawal from Angola and Ethiopia, leading eventually in several cases to the fall of those governments (in Afghanistan and Ethiopia), or their merger in coalitions (Cambodia), or defeat at the polls (Nicaragua). But the insurgents did not come to power, except in

---

role, see William B. Quandt, *Peace Process: American Diplomacy and the Arab-Israeli Conflict since 1967* (Brookings and University of California Press, 1993), pp. 383–412.

176. After the collapse of the Soviet Union, while Russia and India sought to maintain good relations, the "special relationship" that India had enjoyed with the Soviet Union dissolved. In January 1992 by common consent negotiations began for a new treaty to replace the one extended just the year before, with more anodyne security and economic provisions.

177. See chapters 14, 13, respectively, for Asia and Europe.

Afghanistan, where a new civil war flared among the victors. Election of a staunch opposition leader in Nicaragua led not to a contra victory but to "national reconciliation" with the Sandinistas and the contras. The regime in Angola shed its Marxism-Leninism, but after free elections remained in power—though still facing an armed insurgency. The Reagan Doctrine defeated its intended target, a Soviet policy of expansionism in the Third World, but that target was no longer there. Brezhnev's policy of selective opportunistic expansionism had been abandoned even before Reagan came to power. Residual Soviet involvement was repudiated and liquidated under the Gorbachev Doctrine—and, moreover, almost certainly would have been even if the Reagan Doctrine had never been adopted.

The American response to Gorbachev's reorientation of Soviet policy was reactive, cautiously encouraging, but wary. Secretary Shultz, and later President Bush and Secretary Baker, eventually came to recognize and welcome Gorbachev's policy revolution vis-à-vis the Third World (and the world as a whole). But it was a gradual and cautious reaction, not welcomed by all in Washington. As late as 1990, incredibly, the internal Defense Guidance of the Bush administration recognized no change in Soviet "fundamental objectives" in the Third World.[178] To be sure, others in the administration (CIA Director William Webster and Secretary James Baker) did not share that stubborn dedication of Defense Secretary Richard Cheney and deputy NSC adviser Robert Gates to "the Soviet threat." But the administration was slow to fully accept the nature of the Gorbachev revolution affecting foreign policy in the world as well as Soviet-U.S. relations. Soviet support for the American-led Gulf War against Iraq in 1991 was the final proof.

Thus one may say that if, in its own terms, the Reagan Doctrine triumphed, no less so did the Gorbachev Doctrine, with more far-reaching consequences: not just the clearing of some battlefields of the Cold War but of ending the Cold War. The Gorbachev Doctrine represented a shift of policy and performance disengaging by choice from the whole global confrontation with the United States, to a policy predicated on cooperative security and normalized relationships with other countries. By the end of the Gorbachev (and Soviet) eras, the Soviet Union and the United States had indeed become global partners to a degree that was unthinkable just a few years earlier.

---

178. See the leaked guidance, in Patrick E. Tyler, "New Pentagon 'Guidance' Cites Soviet Threat in the Third World," *Washington Post*, February 13, 1990, pp. A1, A9.

# V  CONCLUSIONS

# 16    Retrospect and Prospect

THIS VOLUME DEALS with the final phase of the Cold War and the last stage of the existence of the Soviet Union. It brings to the end both the story of the Cold War and the final period of American-Soviet relations, from 1981 through 1991. It offers an occasion to look back not only at that final decade but also at the Cold War as a whole. At the same time, notwithstanding a new situation and new conditions, this period in continuing history represents the foundation for the American-Russian relationship in the future.

## *Looking Back: The Cold War in Retrospect*

The fundamental underlying cause of the Cold War was the belief in both the Soviet Union and the United States that confrontation was unavoidable, imposed by history. Soviet leaders believed that Communism would ultimately triumph in the world and that the Soviet Union was the vanguard socialist-communist state. They also believed that the Western "imperialist" powers were historically bound to pursue a hostile course against them. For their part, American and other Western leaders assumed that the Soviet Union was determined to enhance its power and to pursue expansionist policies by all expedient means to achieve a Soviet-led communist world. Each side thought that it was compelled by the very existence of the other to engage in zero-sum competition, and each saw the unfolding history of the Cold War as confirming its views.[1]

---

1.    An earlier version of the discussion in this section of the chapter appeared in Raymond L. Garthoff, "Why Did the Cold War Arise, and Why Did It End?" *Diplomatic History*, vol. 16 (Spring 1992), pp. 287–93, and as a chapter in Michael J. Hogan, ed., *The End of the Cold War: Its Meaning and Implications* (Cambridge University Press, 1992), pp. 127–36.

The prevailing Western view was wrong in attributing a master plan to the Kremlin, in believing that communist ideology impelled Soviet leaders to expand their power, in exaggerating communist abilities to subvert a Free World, and in thinking that Soviet officials viewed military power as an ultimate recourse. But the West was not wrong in believing that Soviet leaders were committed to a historically driven struggle between two worlds until, in the end, theirs would triumph. To be sure, other motivations and interests, including national aims, institutional interests, and even personal psychological considerations, played a part. These influences, however, tended to enhance the ideological framework rather than weaken it. Moreover, the actions of each side were sufficiently consistent with the ideological expectations of the other side to sustain their respective worldviews for many years.

Within the framework of ideological conflict, the Americans and the Soviets waged the Cold War as a geopolitical struggle, based more realistically on traditional balance-of-power politics than on world class struggle or global containment and deterrence theory. If ideology was the only thing driving the superpowers in the Cold War, why is the conflict seen as arising from the ashes of World War II rather than as stemming from the October Revolution of 1917? The answer is clear. In 1917 and during the next twenty-five years the Soviet Union was relatively weak and only one of several great powers in a multipolar world. By the end of World War II, however, Germany and Japan had been crushed, Britain, France, and China were weakened, and the enlarged Soviet Union, even though much weaker than the United States, seemed to pose an unprecedented threat by virtue of its massive armies and their presence deep in Central Europe. Under these circumstances, Josef Stalin's reassertion in 1946 and 1947 of the division of the world into two contending camps seemed more valid and more threatening than ever before.

So the Cold War had essential ideological and geopolitical dimensions. A Manichean communist worldview spawned a Manichean anticommunist worldview. Each side imputed unlimited objectives, ultimately world domination, to the other. Each side looked to the realization of its ambitions (or its historical destiny) over the long term and thus posited an indefinite period of conflict. But even though both sides envisioned a conflict of indefinite duration, and even though policy decisions were pragmatic and based on calculation of risk, cost, and gain, the hazard of a miscalculation always existed. And that could be fatally dangerous, given the historical coincidence of the Cold War and the first half-century of the nuclear age. Nuclear weapons, by threatening the existence of world civilization, added significantly to the tension of the epoch; the stakes were utterly without precedent and beyond full comprehension.

Nuclear weapons also helped to keep the Cold War cold, to prevent a third world war in the twentieth century. Nonetheless, in the final analysis and despite their awesome power, nuclear weapons did not cause, prevent, or end the Cold War, which would have been waged even if such weapons had never existed. The arms race and other aspects of the superpower rivalry were, however, driven in part by ideological assumptions. As a result, while the Cold War and the nuclear arms race could be attenuated when opportunities or constraints led both sides to favor a relaxation of tensions, neither could be ended until the ideological underpinnings of the confrontation had also been released. This occurred under Mikhail Gorbachev's leadership, which saw a fundamental reevaluation in Moscow of the processes at work in the real world, a basic reassessment of threats, and finally a deep revision of aims and political objectives. The United States and the West in general were cautious but eventually recognized this fundamental change and reciprocated.

The West did not, as is widely believed, win the Cold War through geopolitical containment and military deterrence. Still less was the Cold War won by the Reagan military buildup and the Reagan Doctrine, as some have suggested. Instead, "victory" came when a new generation of Soviet leaders realized how badly their system at home and their policies abroad had failed. What containment did do was to successfully preclude any temptations by Moscow to advance Soviet hegemony by military means. It is doubtful that any postwar Soviet leadership would have deliberately resorted to war. That was not, however, so clear to many at the time. Deterrence may have been redundant, but at the least it was highly successful in providing reassurance to the peoples of Western Europe. For over four decades it performed the historic function of holding Soviet power in check, or being prepared to do so, until the internal seeds of destruction in the Soviet Union and its empire could mature. At that point, however, Mikhail Gorbachev and the transformation of Soviet policy brought the Cold War to an end.

Despite the important differences among them, all Soviet leaders from Lenin until Gorbachev had shared a belief in an ineluctable conflict between socialism and capitalism. Although Gorbachev remained a socialist, and in his own terms even a communist, he renounced the Marxist-Leninist-Stalinist idea of inevitable world conflict. His avowed acceptance of the interdependence of the world, of the priority of all-human values over class values, and of the indivisibility of common security marked a revolutionary ideological change. That change, which Gorbachev publicly declared as early as February 1986 (though it was then insufficiently noted), manifested itself in many ways during the next five years, in deeds as well as words, including policies reflecting a drastically reduced Soviet perception of the Western threat and actions to reduce the Western perception of a Soviet threat.

In 1986, for example, Gorbachev made clear his readiness to ban all nuclear weapons. In 1987 he signed the INF Treaty, eliminating not only the Soviet and American missiles deployed since the late 1970s but also the whole of the Soviet strategic theater missile forces that had faced Europe and Asia for three decades. What is more, the treaty instituted an intrusive and extensive system of verification. In 1988 Gorbachev proposed conventional arms reductions in Europe under a plan that would abandon the Soviet Union's numerical superiority, and he also launched a substantial unilateral force reduction. In

1988–89 he withdrew all Soviet forces from Afghanistan. At about the same time, he encouraged the ouster of the old communist leadership in Eastern Europe and accepted the transition of the former Soviet-allied states into noncommunist neutral states. By 1990 Gorbachev had signed the CFE Treaty accepting Soviet conventional arms levels in Europe to the Urals that were much lower than the levels for NATO. By that time he had not only accepted Germany's reunification but also the membership of a unified Germany in NATO. Within another year he had jettisoned the Warsaw Pact and the socialist bloc and agreed in START I to verified deep cuts in strategic nuclear forces.

Although Gorbachev had not expected the complete collapse of communism (and Soviet influence) in Eastern Europe that occurred in 1989 and 1990, he had made clear to the Twenty-seventh Congress of the Soviet Communist Party as early as February 1986 that a new conception of security had to replace the previous one, and that the confrontation of the Cold War had to end. No longer speaking in Leninist terms of contending socialist and capitalist words, Gorbachev spoke instead of one world, an "interdependent and in many ways integral world." He denied that any country could find security in military power, either for defense or deterrence. Security, he said, could only be found through political means, and only on a mutual basis. The goal, he asserted, should be the "creation of a comprehensive system of international security" that embraced economic, ecological, and humanitarian, as well as political and military, elements. Hence, the Soviet decision to give new support to the United Nations, including collective peacekeeping, and to join the world economic system. Hence, the cooperative Soviet efforts to resolve regional conflicts in Central America, Southern Africa, the Horn of Africa, Cambodia, Afghanistan, and the Middle East, not to mention the Soviet Union's support for the collective UN-endorsed action against Iraq in 1991. And hence Moscow's willingness to countenance the dissolution of the Eastern European alliance and socialist commonwealth, which had been fashioned to meet security requirements and ideological imperatives that had now been abandoned. These moves were all prefigured in the new approach that Gorbachev laid down in early 1986.

In the final analysis, only a Soviet leader could have ended the Cold War because it rested on the Marxist-Leninist assumption of a struggle to the end of two social-economic-political systems, the capitalist world and the socialist (communist) world. Gorbachev set out deliberately to end the Cold War. Although earlier Soviet leaders had understood the impermissibility of war in the nuclear age, Gorbachev was the first to recognize that reciprocal political accommodation, rather than military power for deterrence or "counterdeterrence," was the defining core of the Soviet Union's relationship with the rest of the world. He accepted the idea of building relations on the basis of a "balance of interests" among nations, rather than pursuing maximization of the power of one state or bloc on the basis of a "correlation of forces," a balance of power. The conclusions that Gorbachev drew from this recognition, and consequent

Soviet actions, finally permitted the Iron Curtain to be dismantled and the global confrontation of the Cold War to be ended.

Gorbachev, to be sure, seriously underestimated the task of changing the Soviet Union, and this led to policy errors that contributed to the failure of his program for the transformation of Soviet society and polity. His vision of a resurrected socialism built on the foundation of successful *perestroika* and *demokratizatsiya* was never a realistic possibility. He knew deep economic reform was necessary, and he tried; he did not find the solution. A revitalized Soviet political union was perhaps beyond realization as well. The reasons for Gorbachev's failure were primarily objective, not subjective; that is, they were real obstacles he was unable to overcome—internal opposition, powerful inertia, intractable problems of economic transformation, and the politically charged problem of redefining a democratic relationship between a traditional imperial center and the rest of the country, *not* unwillingness or inability to give up or modify his ideological presuppositions and predispositions.

In the external political arena, however, Gorbachev both understood and successfully charted the course that led to the end of the Cold War, even though in this area, too, at first he had an exaggerated expectation of the capacity for reform on the part of the communist governments in Eastern Europe.

As the preceding discussion suggests, the American role in ending the Cold War was necessary but not primary. There are several reasons for this conclusion, but the basic one is that the American worldview was derivative of the communist worldview. Containment was hollow without an expansionist power to contain. In this sense, it was the Soviet threat, partly real and partly imagined, that generated the American dedication to waging the Cold War, regardless of what revisionist American historians have to say. These historians point to Washington's atomic diplomacy and to its various overt and covert political, economic, paramilitary, and military campaigns. Supposedly designed to counter a Soviet threat, they argue, these initiatives actually entailed an expansion of American influence and dominion.

The revisionist interpretation errs in attributing imperial initiative and design to American diplomacy, but it is not entirely wrong. American policymakers were guilty of accepting far too much of the communist worldview in constructing an anticommunist antipode, and of being too ready to fight fire with fire. Indeed, once the Cold War became the dominant factor in global politics (and above all in American and Soviet perceptions), each side viewed every development around the world in terms of its relationship to that great struggle, and each was inclined to act according to a self-fulfilling prophecy. The Americans, for example, often viewed local and regional conflicts of indigenous origins as Cold War battles and acted on that assumption. Like the Soviets, they distrusted the neutral and nonaligned nations and were always more comfortable when countries around the world were either their allies or the satellites and surrogates of the other side. Thus, many traditional diplomatic relationships not essentially attendant on the superpower rivalry were swept into the vortex of the Cold War, at least in the eyes of the protagonists—and partly in fact as a result of their actions.

It is true that the Cold War led in some instances to constructive American involvements. The Marshall Plan is a prime example, not to mention American support for some democratic political movements, and for the Congress for Culture Freedom and the liberal journal *Encounter*. But other overt and covert involvements were more frequently less constructive, and often subversive, of real liberalism and democracy. Apart from the loss of American lives and treasure in such misplaced ventures as the Vietnam War and in the massive overinvestment in weaponry, one of the worst effects of forcing all world developments onto the procrustean bed of the Cold War was the distortion of America's understanding and values. By dividing the globe into a communist Evil Empire controlled by Moscow and a Free World led by Washington, American policymakers promoted numerous antidemocratic regimes into rewarded members of the Free World as long as they were anticommunist (or even rhetorically anticommunist). Washington also used the exigencies of the Cold War to justify assassination plots, to negotiate deals with war lords, drug lords, and terrorists, and to transform anticommunist insurgents, however corrupt or antidemocratic, into "freedom fighters." Alliance ties, military basing rights, and support for insurgencies were routinely given priority over such other American objectives as the promotion of nuclear nonproliferation, economic development, human rights, and democracy.

Parallel Soviet sins were at least as great. While Soviet foreign assistance to socialist and "progressive" countries was sometimes constructive (building of the Aswan Dam, for example, or economic assistance to India), it was also skewed by the ideological expectation of moving the world toward communism and by expectations of Soviet geopolitical advantage in the Cold War. Often dictatorial regimes, "marxist" or "socialist" only according to the cynical claims of their leaders, provided the basis for Soviet support, as with Siad Barre in Somalia, for example, or Mengistu in Ethiopia. The Soviet Union also engaged in many covert political operations and lent support to national liberation movements (some authentic, others less so) that sometimes included elements engaged in terrorism. On both sides, then, ideological beliefs combined with geopolitical considerations to fuel a Cold War struggle that left many victims in its wake.

Although the decisive factor in the end of the Cold War was a change in these beliefs, it is worth repeating that the Soviet leaders could discard a long-encrusted and familiar ideology only because of a powerful transformation in the way Gorbachev and some colleagues perceived reality, and because they were ready to adapt domestic and foreign policies to the new perception. Over time, the extent and depth of these changes became inescapable and their validity compelling. Earlier I noted some of the cumulative changes in Soviet foreign policy that brought the Cold War to an end. The critical culminating event was the Revolution of '89.

The year between the destruction of the Berlin Wall in November 1989 and the European conference in Paris in November 1990 saw the removal of the most important concrete manifestation of the Cold War—the division of Germany and Europe. The division of Europe had symbolized the global battle between the two ideological and geopolitical camps in the years immediately after World War II. When that division came to an end, the consequences for the international balance of power were so substantial that even the most hardened cold warriors in the West were forced to acknowledge that the Cold War had ended—even before the collapse of communist rule in the Soviet Union or of the Soviet Union itself. Moreover, the Revolution of '89 in Eastern Europe was decisive not only in demonstrating that the ideological underpinnings of the Cold War had been removed but also in shifting the actual balance of power. The removal of Soviet military power from Eastern Europe dissolved the threat to Western Europe and also restored a reunified Europe to the center of the world political stage. Russia and even the United States, though still closely linked to Europe, have now become less central.

## Looking Back: The Final Years of the Cold War

The changes in leadership of the United States and the Soviet Union in the early 1980s came at a time of urgent need in both countries to redefine their relationship after the collapse of the détente of the 1970s. The particular combination was inauspicious. The new American president in January 1981 was vigorous and ideological, had clear authority, believed in the need for a more assertive stand, and had very little awareness of international politics. The Soviet leadership, by contrast, was old and weak. (Kosygin and Suslov died, and Brezhnev was dying as the new leadership came into office in Washington, and then Andropov and in turn Chernenko each were in office barely more than a year before passing away.) Not until Mikhail Gorbachev assumed office in March 1985 was the troubled succession really completed. Moreover, during the first half of the 1980s this leadership was not only transitional but bureaucratically constrained, ideologically ossified, and set in its ways with respect to international politics. Although this combination might seem to have given the United States an advantage, that conclusion is doubtful. Its main effect was to preclude constructive negotiation and collaboration. Moreover, while the posture of the Reagan administration from 1981 through 1983 was confrontational, and not only in rhetoric, its policy was more equivocal and fragmented. Even so, it too was ill-prepared to engage in constructive negotiation and collaboration.

U.S. actions from 1981 through 1983 were not sufficiently aggressive to be described as a policy of confrontation (which is not to say that the results would have been desirable if it had been). Yet the Reagan policy was too gratuitously hostile to serve usefully in an effective competition. It was neither a policy of combining the carrot and the stick, as in the early and mid-1970s, nor even of applying the stick while offering the carrot as in the late 1970s (as Haig had sought to do). Rather, it seemed to represent a provocative brandishing of a stick that was enough to annoy and alarm the Soviet bear but not enough to cage him. Nor did the United States offer any positive incentives to the Soviet leaders no matter what they did. The Reagan administration policy was primarily a unilateral approach focused on American self-doubts and on building American military power to redress a perceived but largely nonexistent weakness.

Reagan's policy after 1984, however, while pursuing "realistic" negotiation on arms control (that is, "negotiating from strength" on the basis of positions conservatively favoring American interests), and even seeking to engage Moscow in a broader dialogue, could not resist recurrent confrontational rhetoric and an escalating application of the Reagan Doctrine that sought to roll back radical left and communist rule in a number of countries in the Third World.

Even on the basis of its apparent objectives, the Reagan administration dissipated many of its advantages, especially in its first term. It lost much of the consensus of the American public on the need for a defense buildup by a mindless spending spree. The administration reduced, rather than rebuilt, allied confidence. The gap between the United States and Western Europe increased, despite a conservative swing in West Germany and Great Britain (and in the policies of France), and the successful weathering of the issues of the deployment of intermediate-range nuclear (INF) missiles, and then their elimination.

Although the Reagan administration did launch U.S. policy, and especially policy toward the Soviet Union, on a new path, it also borrowed much from other approaches. Even its slogans (which were, unexpectedly, often the best guide to policy) were largely borrowed. "Peace through strength" was the term Ford had turned to after shelving the word détente (in his primary contest with Reagan in 1976). "Reciprocity" was borrowed from Carter and Brzezinski; "negotiation" and "dialogue" from Nixon and Kissinger. The confrontation rhetoric was the most original, though much (a "crusade," negotiation from "positions of strength") was vintage 1950s. It was also the least useful for any purpose except to satisfy internal political-psychological drives and to mollify a hard-line constituency. It created a new barrier that could only be partly dispelled by its partial abandonment after 1984.

Most of the foreign policy successes of the administration involved the later neutralization of problems the administration itself had generated. China policy, for example, got back on track by 1983–84 after travails largely caused by the Reagan administration's agitation of the Taiwan issue in 1980–81. Relations with the West Europeans were restored in 1983–84 after being aggravated by U.S. assaults on European détente and economic interests in 1981–82. The United States disentangled itself and withdrew its surviving Marines from Lebanon in early 1984 after ensnaring itself there in 1982 in the first place. The deepening involvements in Central America from 1981 through 1985 slowly moved on to a path toward resolution in the latter half of the 1980s only because Congress kept the administration from excessive commitments to covert warfare. But during 1985–88 the United States still assumed a far more active role in seeking to upset communist rule in Nicaragua, Afghanistan, Angola, and Cambodia (Kampuchea), under the Reagan Doctrine.

To understand the policy of the Reagan administration toward the Soviet Union, one must first understand the nature of the administration, especially Reagan's role. Reagan was unusually detached and distant from the daily implementation (and formulation) of policy, even though he ultimately determined its direction. Haig, failing to understand this arrangement so different from the Nixon administration, rather than becoming Reagan's "vicar" for foreign policy soon fell by the wayside. Shultz understood and persisted quietly in pursuing a low-key policy of engagement. Reagan was in many ways like a ceremonial monarch, entirely dependent on his viziers and courtiers for his limited knowledge of what was going on in the outside world—and even in his own domain and court. For example, he was disbelieving when a reporter at a news conference informed him that the United States under his administration had become the world's greatest debtor nation. Similarly, ignorance and absence of interest in knowing the facts, rather than deliberate design, on the part of Reagan and many of his entourage led to unprecedented irresponsibility with respect to many charges against the Soviet Union. The message and "the script," based on his presumptions, were more important to him than the facts. Yet this indifference to reality not only impeded understanding but also undercut understanding between him and the Soviet leaders. For example, Reagan could not understand why Gorbachev would not believe him when Reagan offered to share the fruits of his strategic defense initiative (SDI)—unaware that not one of his own cabinet officers, members of Congress, or allied governments believed that either.

The Soviet Union rhetorically reconfirmed the détente policy of the 1970s, even though it was clearly dead, at the Twenty-sixth Party Congress in March 1981 under Brezhnev. It was reaffirmed by his interim successors until Gorbachev at the Twenty-seventh Party Congress in February 1986 began to institute a new approach. In response to the first Reagan administration from 1981 to 1984, the Soviet leaders modified their expectations, all in the same general negative direction, although differences arose among them on specific issues. The changing world scene also led to some modification of views, and by the mid-1980s differences had emerged within the leadership and the broader political establishment. Overall, from the Twenty-sixth Party Congress in 1981 until the Twenty-seventh in 1986, Soviet leaders and observers less frequently referred to a favorably shifting correlation of forces in the world. Developments in the world were going less favorably for the Soviet Union in the 1980s than in the 1970s, and one major and central example was in relations with the United States. But there was no basic reassessment until Gorbachev launched one in 1985–86.

As the Soviets appraised American policy during the first half of the 1980s they concluded that the turning point, in what they saw as a continuing process of change in the United States since 1976, was not the beginning of the Reagan administration in January 1981 but the sharp shift by President Carter in January 1980. From the standpoint of the Soviet leaders, first Carter and then Reagan had kicked over the card table, when all they had been doing (in their view) was playing the game—and not necessarily even winning, much less cheating. They were angered and perplexed. They naturally tended to see a dark design by the American leaders—a turn to militarism.

When the Soviet leaders described the change as a turn to "militarism" that term was not simply an epithet, but represented the common element in what they saw as mutually reinforcing changes in four crucial aspects of American policy toward the Soviet Union, and a fifth with respect to Soviet interests in the Third World.

First, the U.S. political line was seen as having shifted decisively, after several years of growing inclination, to an abandonment of détente. President Carter's across-the-board reaction to the Soviet intervention in Afghanistan was not recognized as having been caused by that event, but at most precipitated by it (most Soviet analysts described Afghanistan as but a pretext). Carter abandoned détente in practice in January 1980; Reagan disavowed détente explicitly. But Reagan then went on to replace the quest for political cooperation mixed with containment with a crusade against the communist system. In the Soviet view, a principal reason that détente was dropped by the United States was to stir up a more militant anti-Soviet atmosphere to gain public and congressional support for a major military buildup and assertion of global American hegemony.

Second, then, was the U.S. military program launched by President Carter in 1980, and again intensified by Reagan. In fact, the U.S. and NATO military buildup was traced to 1978, but only with the intermediate missile deployment decision in December 1979 and major U.S. military budget increases in 1980 was it really under way. In expenditures, if less in capabilities, it grew greatly until the mid-1980s. And this put pressure on the strained Soviet economy in its attempt to ensure continued parity.

Third was an ominous change in U.S. military doctrine, abandoning mutual deterrence based on parity and substituting a drive for superiority in war-waging capabilities in order to provide escalation dominance at all levels of nuclear and nonnuclear engagement. Presidential Directive (PD)–59 under Carter in 1980 was the touchstone, although the process had begun with the

Schlesinger Doctrine in 1974. Again, the NATO missile deployment decision was seen as related to the war-waging capabilities sought to implement PD-59. Moreover, the American turn to seek war-waging superiority came after an explicit Soviet modification of military doctrine and renunciation of superiority and winnability of war in the nuclear age. The Reagan administration added the strategic defense initiative (SDI), seen as an attempt to neutralize the Soviet deterrent and give the United States a commanding superiority.

Fourth, rounding out the other three, was U.S. abandonment of arms control with the shelving of the SALT II Treaty by Carter in January 1980, confirmed by its explicit rejection by Reagan in 1981. The fact that the Carter administration faced serious difficulties in ratification even before Afghanistan was seen as largely owing to its own actions (in particular, stirring up a storm over a small Soviet military contingent in Cuba after years of ignoring its presence). Moreover, the Carter administration was prepared (even suspiciously ready) to pay for ratification with a major increase in military outlays. Finally, the Carter administration was seen as intent on circumventing the purposes of the treaty by its MX deployment program and the NATO intermediate missiles in Europe, the latter nominally to match Soviet SS-20 missiles but seen as really intended as a precursor element in an across-the-board buildup of counterforce war-waging capabilities. The Carter administration even before Afghanistan had also backtracked in both the comprehensive nuclear test ban and antisatellite arms control talks.

The Reagan administration abandoned all arms control efforts, only going through the motions of INF and START negotiations in 1982–83 to satisfy Western public opinion sufficiently to keep support for the INF deployment in Europe and for massive military programs at home. In 1983 came the challenge of a technological end run through the SDI. By 1985 the United States demonstratively abandoned the de facto acceptance of the SALT II force levels and sought to undermine the ABM Treaty by spurious reinterpretation. Again, after the Soviet Union had developed a serious interest in negotiating strategic arms limitations in the SALT process, the United States dropped out.

The fifth change was in U.S. resort to military force in the Third World to block or roll back what the Soviets regarded as progressive revolutionary change. The Carter Doctrine was seen as only the first step in an intensification of American reliance on military means to secure what were called "vital interests" but seemed to extend to any area, even where U.S. interests earlier had been minimal. It was a repudiation of the Nixon Doctrine and reflected an end to the "Vietnam syndrome" and restraint. And the Carter Doctrine was a robust challenge that sought to roll back the modestly favorable shift in the correlation of forces that the Soviet leaders had seen in this arena.

The Reagan administration took this legacy of a shift in American policy and drove it home. Reagan himself, and by and large the American people, saw the Reagan administration from 1981 through 1985 as pursuing a policy of peace through strength, containment of Soviet expansion, "restoration" of military power that had languished, a peaceful assertion of democratic values in an ideological challenge, and readiness to negotiate (from a strong position). But from Moscow it appeared that the Reagan administration sought to acquire military superiority in order to roll back a changing correlation of forces in the world, to negotiate if at all by exerting pressure, for a political-economic-ideological offensive against socialism and the USSR under the shadow of growing military power, and thus to attempt to reassert American dominance in the world against the Soviet Union. Finally, the Soviet Union was charged with being a focus of evil and an Evil Empire—in other words, the legitimacy of the very existence of Soviet rule and of the socialist system was challenged.

Even as the Reagan administration became less strident in its rhetoric, and more ready to negotiate, it also articulated the Reagan Doctrine on the reversibility of socialist revolutions and acted to encourage (and even instigate) insurgencies aimed at overthrowing Third World regimes aligned with the Soviet Union, and to call for democratic (noncommunist) government in the socialist commonwealth (Soviet bloc) itself. Thus in 1982–88 American assistance to groups seeking to overthrow the regimes in Nicaragua and Afghanistan increased in openness and in scale, and the United States began a more direct role in supporting similar efforts in Angola and Kampuchea.

The Carter administration after vacillation and then the Reagan administration with undisguised enthusiasm were seen to have chosen confrontation over détente and a striving for military superiority over mutual arms limitation.

As the Soviet leaders assessed the possibilities for improving or even stabilizing relations with the United States, still a Soviet aim, they thus remained skeptical. The one element they regarded as potentially the most significant but still quite uncertain was that political realities in the United States and the world might lead "realists" in U.S. ruling circles to shift back to a policy akin to what Nixon came to call "hardheaded détente," represented most closely by the positions held first by Haig and later Shultz, and at least rhetorically by Reagan after 1984. The Soviets were acutely aware of their own very limited ability to influence U.S. realities, but some among them saw at least a possibility that internal American economic and political constraints, and what they believed remained the long-term trends in the world historical process, would compel realists in Washington to see—as Nixon and Kissinger had—a better prospect in swinging with the historical trend than attempting to buck it. At the same time, they had a more sober and less optimistic evaluation of the pace of change in the global correlation of forces, and so they did not expect early or far-reaching change in American policy. Moreover, advocates of a more confrontational policy continued to have a role in the administration and to have a powerful if diminishing voice in U.S. policy throughout the Reagan administration.

The NATO alliance weathered both the deployment of the American missiles (and the Soviet demonstrative counterdeployments) and the imposition of unwise economic sanctions. Finally, President Reagan was reelected in 1984, not particularly because of the popularity of his policy toward the Soviet Union, but at least not weakened perceptibly by it. Indications in 1984 of an interest by the Reagan administration in improving relations with the Soviet Union remained to be tested.

The increased American readiness to resort to use of military power around the world was seen in El Salvador, Nicaragua, Lebanon, Libya, and Grenada (and later Panama). Use of American military force had been indirect in Central America and ineffective in Lebanon. Nonetheless, this return to pre-Vietnam gunboat diplomacy (exemplified, in a way, by the return of the four vintage 1945 battleships, and literally in the *New Jersey*'s gun bombardment of the Shiites and Druze in Lebanon in 1983) reflected greater American reliance on military means. In most cases, the Soviets believed such imperialist use of force locally in the Third World rebounded politically to the disadvantage of the West. At the same time, such action also undercut Soviet influence at least in the short run and did damage to the argument within the Soviet political establishment that continued Soviet advocacy of great-power détente aided, or was even compatible with, progressive revolutionary change in the world. The Soviets, too, had reason for wanting "restraint and reciprocity" in superpower behavior in the Third World.

The Soviet leaders were prepared to deal with the United States on the geopolitical issues in the competition in the Third World. Their view of the problems, and of both the American role and their own, differed greatly from those held in Washington. These differences in perception, and clashes in interests and competition for influence, made agreement neither easy nor stable. But some points could be negotiated or, more often, clarified and ameliorated by less formal but authoritative and concrete dialogue. Thus, for example, the Soviet Union did not provide MiG fighters to Nicaragua, despite clear indications in 1981–82 that it had planned to do so. Similarly, while the United States and several Muslim countries provided arms to the anticommunist guerrillas in Afghanistan via Pakistan, the quantities and types of weapons (even though Stinger antiaircraft missiles were provided from 1986 on) were kept below a threshold that could have provoked Soviet retaliation or interdiction attacks in Pakistan.

One cardinal point stood out and, in the view of the Soviet leaders, required serious attention by both the United States and the Soviet Union, regardless of fluctuations in the correlation of forces: containing the risks of nuclear war. Even if the prospect of détente in any broader sense was deferred, coexistence in its fundamental meaning was at stake. Although not anticipating that the United States would choose resort to war, the Soviet leaders did see increased dangers of situations getting out of control. For that reason, as well as economic pressures and resource constraints, Soviet leaders from Brezhnev on were seriously interested in negotiated arms limitations and reductions. But they were also determined not to accept unequal limitations, above all not under pressure from a United States they believed was intent on gaining and using military advantage precisely to compel Soviet acceptance of inferiority. The Soviet leaders, though seeking arms limitations on what they would regard as equal terms, were also determined not to settle for less. It took Gorbachev to rise above such considerations.

The debate over arms control in Moscow in the first half of the 1980s was no longer, as in the 1960s and early 1970s, whether arms control and mutual arms limitation were in its interests. That battle had been decided at the start of the 1970s in favor of arms control. In the early and mid-1980s the question in Moscow was whether there was any real prospect of U.S. interest in arms limitations on a mutually advantageous basis. It was not the advisability of arms control, but its attainability given the American stance, that was in serious doubt.

Given the uncertain prospect for effective arms limitations, the question of military requirements in an intensified arms competition assumed particular importance. Decisions made during the eleventh five-year plan, covering the period 1981–85, amended the original plan laid down in the late 1970s on the basis of an expectation of a continuing SALT process and continuing incremental limitations beyond the SALT II Treaty. But these were ad hoc adjustments, and many issues remained unresolved. Moreover, not only were the remaining restraints of the SALT I Interim Agreement and SALT II Treaty precarious, so too was the ABM Treaty and the whole prospect for mutual arms control. Decisions in 1985 on the twelfth five-year plan for 1986–91 and, in the late 1980s for the planned thirteenth for 1991–96, thus prompted intense consideration and debate, affecting the conjunction of economic, military, foreign policy, and internal political interests and competing demands.

Despite the huge Reagan military buildup in the first half of the 1980s and the threat of the American SDI, Soviet defense spending continued from 1985 through 1988 to remain roughly constant as a share of Soviet gross national product (GNP). From 1989 through 1991, when Gorbachev was politically able to do it, Soviet military spending and procurement were cut sharply. The American impetus to the arms race, and still more the domestic influence of the Soviet military-industrial complex, kept Soviet expenditures from being cut earlier but did not lead to a matching increase.[2] As the Soviet leaders in the mid-1980s contemplated the possible requirements to meet future American deployment of a strategic antimissile defense, they decided on an asymmetrical rather than a matching response. Even that would only have to occur to meet the contingency of an actual American deployment of ABM defense. The nature of the countermeasures would depend on the precise nature of the American deployment program. But as the 1980s progressed the SDI seemed less and less likely to yield a deployable defense system. Thus while the Soviet

---

2.   See chapter 12 for further discussion and source information.

leaders in the mid-1980s were genuinely worried about a situation arising in which they would have to increase spending to offset an American strategic antiballistic missile defense, that prospect and that concern diminished. Moreover, the contingent future nature of any response, as well as its asymmetrical nature, neutralized and prevented the heavy burden on the Soviet defense budget and economy that the United States had expected and sought.

In retrospect, clearly the United States overrelied on deterrence and on intimidation in arms control. There was no consideration whatsoever by the Soviet leadership of any actions that the American military buildup deterred. Nor were the Soviet leaders in the first half of the 1980s intimidated into any political, military, or arms control concessions because of the American policy of negotiation from positions of strength. That this was the intention of the American leadership was not secret. For example, in the speech in which he introduced the SDI President Reagan had bragged of negotiating for strategic arms reductions from a "position of strength" based on enhanced strategic forces.[3] Similarly, Secretary of State George Shultz spoke of how he and President Reagan were "determined to make American strength serve the cause of serious negotiations on behalf of American interests."[4]

To be sure, in the late 1980s the Soviet leadership under Gorbachev did make concessions to many tough American positions in arms reduction negotiations: it settled for no more than its own unilateral reaffirmation of the ABM Treaty in its restrictive interpretation, it conceded many points in the strategic arms reductions talks (START) in order to get agreement, and it accepted the one-sided zero option for the Intermediate-range Nuclear Forces (INF) Treaty. These have often been cited as examples of Soviet capitulation to American firmness in negotiation and negotiation from a position of strength based on a military buildup the Soviet Union could not match. Yet if the Soviet leaders had not wanted such an outcome, they were not forced to accept it; they could simply have done without those arms control agreements. Moreover, they did not simply cave in to meet tough American positions. Gorbachev repeatedly took the initiative to go beyond American positions, to make greater sacrifices of Soviet military advantages than those called for by the United States, both in unilateral actions and in pushing the United States to go further in negotiations. He used the early Reagan propaganda stance on zero INF missiles rather than giving in to it (and he added the second zero for shorter-range INF missiles even though there too the Soviet Union had to destroy a far larger number of weapons). Gorbachev was ready to accept, and even to seek, a reduced Soviet weight in the balance of military power because he under-

3.   President Reagan, "National Security," address to the nation, March 23, 1983, *Weekly Compilation of Presidential Documents*, vol. 19 (March 28, 1983), p. 447.

4.   George P. Shultz, *Turmoil and Triumph: My Years as Secretary of State* (Charles Scribner's Sons, 1993), p. 119.

stood the broader political and even historical gains from overcoming the action-reaction arms race, irrespective of whether the arms competition was in pursuit of strategic advantage or merely to ensure a strategic deterrent balance. He sought not mutual deterrence, but mutual assurance. His goal was to end the arms race and the Cold War that spawned it, not merely to stabilize a perpetual deterrent balance (and still less to seek a phantom strategic superiority).

Finally, insofar as the Soviet leaders saw American policy as directed to challenging the legitimacy of the Soviet system and undermining Soviet rule at home and hegemony in the socialist commonwealth (Soviet bloc), they were strongly inclined to take a firm and hard line in response. Moscow believed that this was the aim of the Reagan administration. There were, however, divided views within the Soviet establishment over the ability of the Reagan administration to effectively pursue that course.

Despite their long-term ideological expectations, the Soviet leaders in the 1980s did not have aspirations for creating a new wave of change in the world. They especially did not want to commit their own resources, prestige, and security to such ventures. The Soviet leaders thus remained to a great extent in a reactive and defensive posture on relations with the United States, although they sought to present themselves—and even to see themselves—as holding the initiative and waiting for the United States to come around to reality. This reactive posture characterized Soviet—and in this case, also American—engagement around the globe in the 1980s as the two powers competed for influence in the Third World, in Europe, and in relations with China.

The years 1984 and 1985 were transitional from the renewed confrontation of 1980–83 to renewed engagement and negotiation. The year 1984 marked the final year of drifting Soviet policy and a year of virtual hiatus in Soviet-American relations. Reagan had sharply, though not completely or consistently, turned from a confrontational stance to at least a rhetorical position seeking renewed engagement. But neither he, nor the coasting Soviet leadership, had the vision or the means to do more than recognize and step back from the dangers of unmitigated confrontation that had become sharp by late 1983.

The year 1985 was also transitional, as a new Soviet leader from a younger generation was getting his bearings and preparing to execute a sharp change in Soviet policy, foreign and domestic. The Reagan administration coasted on a mixed policy marked by renewed competition in the Third World and reengagement in negotiation on arms control issues, though the administration was acting without a clear aim or strategy beyond rolling back communist influence while trying to reduce tension with Moscow. The American policy, though not so described or even recognized, represented exactly what the American critics of détente had charged (with some justification, but much exaggeration) to be a Soviet abuse of détente in the 1970s: cosmetic negotiations on arms control combined with a major military buildup and a vigorous assertive policy to reduce the influence of the other side around the world.

The Geneva summit in late 1985 and the Reykjavik summit in 1986 were the most significant steps and signs of a changing relationship, which by 1987 and 1988 under Gorbachev's leadership had led to what might fairly have been described (although for political reasons was not) as a successful renewed détente.

The years of transition were, in a sense, reflections of both the success, but also the dead end, of Reagan's initial policies. By 1984 the Soviet Union had been defeated in its efforts to prevent NATO INF deployment and had maneuvered itself into taking the onus of breaking off for a full year all bilateral arms control negotiations with the United States (for the first time since SALT began in 1969). When negotiations resumed in 1985, the Soviet Union was unable to make any headway in meeting its security interests or in moving toward any agreement except on one-sided American terms. If the deadlock were to be broken, it would require concessionary Soviet initiatives.

In my earlier volume *Détente and Confrontation*, analyzing the rise and fall of the détente in American-Soviet relations in the 1970s, I adopted from other political scientists a categorization of three schools of thought in American approaches to dealing with the Soviet Union (with analogues in Soviet policy advocacy).[5]

Those in the first school of policy, dominant in American policymaking in the early 1980s for the first time since the formative years of Cold War containment strategy in the 1950s, were called the essentialists. Ronald Reagan was the first president to come to office as a classical essentialist, that is, he saw the Soviet Union, in his words, as "an Evil Empire," led by leaders committed to an ideology sanctioning any means to attain its immutable aims, including absolute power and a communist world. The Soviet system was seen as totalitarian and exceedingly powerful and dangerous. Such an approach could not envisage anything but a protracted conflict, with no possibility for real accommodation and little if any positive value in negotiation. The appropriate America policy was therefore confrontation with the Soviet Union, building American military power, and rallying the Western alliance and the whole Free World under American leadership to face the global communist menace.

The second school focused on Soviet behavior, rather than the essence of the Soviet system and its ideology. Though regarding the Soviet Union as an adversary, the advocates of this approach perceived the Soviet threat as primarily geopolitical. Although they saw a Soviet aim to expand Soviet influence in

---

5. See Raymond L. Garthoff, *Détente and Confrontation: American-Soviet Relations from Nixon to Reagan* (Brookings, 1985), pp. 1119–22. I cited there a useful discussion that both articulated these schools and discussed the wider literature: Alexander Dallin and Gail W. Lapidus, "Reagan and the Russians: United States Policy toward the Soviet Union and Eastern Europe," in Kenneth A. Oye, Robert J. Lieber, and Donald Rothchild, eds., *Eagle Defiant: United States Foreign Policy in the 1980s* (Little, Brown and Company, 1983), pp. 191–236, including its bibliographical references.

the world, they also regarded the Soviet Union as prudent and opportunistic, and responsive to incentives and to risks and costs. Hence, while skeptical of accommodation, the practitioners of this approach, who may be called mechanists or pragmatists, saw opportunities for U.S. policy to be used to manipulate American power and negotiation to influence and even to "manage" Soviet foreign policy behavior.

Advocates of the third, or interactionist, approach saw the sources of Soviet-American conflict not only as rooted in conflicting aims and ambitions, and in geopolitical more than ideological terms, as did the mechanists, but also as stemming from the dynamics of the competition itself. The conflict was driven by mutual perceptions and misperceptions as well as conflicts of interest. As with the mechanists conflict was seen more in geopolitical than ideological terms. Adherents of this approach varied in assessments of Soviet intentions and capabilities, but they tended to find an important reactive element in Soviet policy and interactive element in Soviet-American relations. Also pragmatists, interactionists agreed with mechanists that Soviet behavior was subject to external influence, but saw much wider possibilities for change and for American influence. They tended to find greater diversity in internal Soviet politics and therefore greater potential for evolution of the Soviet system. They also believed there was a greater learning process and feedback in foreign relations and greater interaction between the actions and policies of the two sides. While the mechanists relied on linkage and leverage with sticks and carrots (incentives and penalties) orchestrated by the United States to manage Soviet behavior, the interactionists saw less efficacy in attempts by the United States to manipulate Soviet policy and more need to deal with the Soviets directly on the basis of a balance of respective interests. Soviet policy was viewed not only as pursuing Soviet aims and objectives, but also as realistic and reactive and influenced by experience. Interactionists saw possibilities, and a need, for negotiation of common constraints, arms control, and rules of the game or a code of conduct to contain geopolitical competition. They also saw less opportunity and greater risks in unilateral American actions to impose constraints on the Soviet Union from a position of strength.

Although in practice many variations existed within these approaches, clearly the détente policy of Nixon and Kissinger, the diluted détente policy of Brzezinski, and the post-détente policy advocated by Haig, then Shultz, and later Baker and Bush were within the mechanistic school. In the Carter administration, policy controversy stemmed from tension between the mechanistic geopolitical approach of Brzezinski and the interactionist approach of Vance. In the Reagan administration, Reagan set a confrontational tone with his essentialist declarations about the Soviet system as the focus of evil, although he proved less consistent in practice, and the tension of his administration shifted to a tug of war between mechanists and essentialists. Haig and Shultz were the main exponents of the mechanist approach, and William P. Clark, Richard Pipes, William Casey, Donald Regan, Caspar Weinberger, Richard Perle, and Jeane

Kirkpatrick were among the most prominent essentialists. But what counted was Reagan himself, and he moved from being an essentialist in 1981–83 to becoming a mechanist after 1985 and ultimately even an interactionist. George Bush, too, and James Baker, from an initial mechanist position when they entered office in 1989, after nearly a year began, belatedly, to act more as interactionists, though still with mechanist tendencies, in 1990 and 1991.

Leonid Brezhnev, Yury Andropov, Konstantin Chernenko, and their colleagues including the durable Andrei Gromyko, while all burdened by essentialist ideological views, were nonetheless in practice mechanists. In contrast, Mikhail Gorbachev, and some of his closest colleagues, including Eduard Shevardnadze and Aleksandr Yakovlev, were interactionists.

Although Ronald Reagan personified and dominated the years of confrontation, 1981 through 1983, Mikhail Gorbachev dominated the interactionist years of Soviet-American relations from 1986 through 1991. Moreover, the Soviet Union under Gorbachev moved from what had been a weak reactive posture in 1981–84 to assume the initiative from 1987 through 1989. By 1990–91, while U.S. policy remained largely reactive, so too did Gorbachev's leadership—but now both powers were reacting to events in Eastern Europe and the Soviet Union over which Gorbachev was losing control, undercutting his ability to maintain the initiative with the United States.

In the post–Cold War years, under President Boris Yeltsin in Russia and both President Bush in 1992 and subsequently President Bill Clinton, American-Russian relations have continued to be based on an interactionist pattern.

In retrospect, it is clear that the single most significant factor not only in turning American-Soviet relations back from confrontation to détente and even beyond during the decade of the 1980s was the impact of Mikhail Gorbachev.[6] Given the policies pursued by Reagan and later Bush, without Gorbachev American-Soviet relations throughout the 1980s and into the 1990s would almost certainly have continued on the same basic course as they did in 1984–85, with minor variations in a pattern of continuing competition. What made the difference was Gorbachev's determination to change the whole Soviet relationship with the world, to enter into the interdependent real world rather than continue a conflict between "two worlds," socialism and capitalism. Gorbachev was not merely an advocate of renewed détente. Détente, after all,

---

6.  There are several useful biographies of Gorbachev that help to answer the question that immediately arises: how could the Communist Party of the Soviet Union bring to the fore a man who held such unorthodox convictions, and how for that matter could he have acquired them? See Gail Sheehy, *Gorbachev: The Making of the Man Who Shook the World* (London: Heinemann, 1991); Dusko Doder and Louise Branson, *Gorbachev: Heretic in the Kremlin* (Viking, 1990); Zhores A. Medvedev, *Gorbachev* (W. W. Norton and Company, 1986); and Robert G. Kaiser, *Why Gorbachev Happened: His Triumphs and His Failure* (Simon and Schuster, 1991).

was an easing of Cold War tensions between adversaries. Gorbachev did not merely want to reduce tensions; he set out to end the Cold War, to create a "common European home," to turn down decisively the arms race and demilitarize the East-West relationship, and to disengage from Soviet involvement in a geopolitical-ideological struggle in the Third World. To do this he was prepared to sacrifice Soviet political hegemony and military preponderance in Eastern Europe, to make disproportionate concessions in arms control (INF, START, and CFE), to withdraw Soviet troops from Afghanistan and Soviet support for Cuban troops in Angola and Ethiopia and Vietnamese troops in Cambodia, to work for resolution of regional conflicts and greater international cooperation in and through the United Nations and in many other ways, and to make "socialist" regimes everywhere stand or fall on the basis of accomplishment and popular mandate. He also was determined to press for radical transformation of the whole Soviet social-political-economic system. He advocated steps relevant to his changed international course: reducing military forces and outlays, reducing secrecy and control, meeting international standards of human rights, and reforming the Soviet economy so that it could enter the international economic system.

Not all of these far-reaching changes were fully worked out conceptually or in policy terms when Gorbachev first came to power, but the general direction and even many of the concrete manifestations were, and others followed. The "stagnation" of the Brezhnev years was an important impulse for change, but much more was required, above all a recognition of the failure of the Soviet system and of Soviet leaders to understand the world beyond their borders. Andropov, aided by the vantage point of many years' exposure to the relatively unvarnished internal reporting of the KGB, understood the deepening stagnation of the Soviet system and at least some of its flaws. He was prepared, but was too ill and too short-lived to do more than launch a modest beginning at an internal renewal.[7] But Andropov did not understand the depth of the systemic failure of the Soviet system, nor did he understand the massive errors of the Soviet perception of the outside world. Here his KGB exposure was double-edged; while in some ways it may have given him greater sophistication (as he had displayed even earlier in the Central Committee staff in the 1960s), it also contributed to his incorrect evaluation of Western, especially American, intentions. He was among those most negatively affected by Reagan's confrontational posture in 1981–83, especially toward the end of his life. He continued to believe in the clash between two worlds (ever present in

---

7. Andropov reportedly had in the late 1970s created a special department in the KGB to prepare critical evaluations of the Soviet internal, especially economic, situation. In 1982, as a party secretary, shortly before taking office as general secretary, he also sponsored more than a hundred studies of economic, political, and social problems, undertaken in 1982–83 with the assistance of several junior members of the leadership, including Mikhail Gorbachev and Nikolai Ryzhkov, as they both later confirmed.

the intelligence arena), and he did not believe that negotiation and accommodation with the current leaders of the United States were possible.

Konstantin Chernenko was not prepared by intellect or experience to understand the internal or external situation in ways other than those he had long shared with his patron, Leonid Brezhnev. Chernenko was unprepared to take any major change in internal or external policy, although his earlier experience supporting Brezhnev's détente policy in the 1970s did help condition him at least to reopen Soviet-American negotiation, especially on arms control. During his brief tenure, he broke the ice of the deep freeze Andropov had put on relations late in 1983.

Mikhail Gorbachev, by all indications, entered office in March 1985 with great self-confidence and also with awareness that the tasks he faced were formidable. He understood, better than Andropov, if still incompletely, the need for a deep transformation, indeed a reformation, of the Soviet system and of socialism (what came to be called *perestroika*). He also understood something that none of his predecessors had, that their whole conception of the outside world was archaic and distorted and actually contributed to their international isolation and reduced their security. Though his views on these internal and external tasks were not fully formed, and indeed still suffered from serious shortcomings, he had an openness to change rare in any political leader, and especially in one brought up in the Soviet system.

Initially, indeed from 1985 to 1988 and to some extent to the end (1991), Gorbachev thought it possible to reform and revitalize the ideology of socialism, the Soviet social-economic-political system, the Communist Party, and the Union of Soviet Socialist Republics. But as he found various of his initial premises invalid, he changed them and was prepared to change his stand. He did not swim with the tide, although at times (especially from October 1990 to April 1991) he made tactical concessions on the pace of reform. He remained throughout an advocate of "socialism" and of democracy, which he regarded as mutually reinforcing. But he came eventually to see that the Communist Party of the Soviet Union was not able to reform itself. At first he had counted on a reformed party to lead *perestroika*; later he successfully neutralized the party as a potential obstacle, engineered its loss of a monopoly of power, and shunted it to the sidelines in 1990. He was not, as has sometimes been alleged, a prisoner of devotion to the Communist Party or to socialism in its Marxist-Leninist form. Gorbachev was ultimately stymied not by limits on his vision or his readiness to revise his understanding and his programs, but by opposition and ultimately by his inability to control the forces unleashed by his destruction of the old order. Hence, eventually the Soviet socialist system, the Soviet Union itself, and Gorbachev fell.[8]

---

8.   There is a burgeoning literature on the causes of the collapse of the Soviet system and state, and postmortems evaluating the failure of Western Sovietology to predict that outcome (or in most cases even to hold positions to be compatible with it). One of the

Despite the ultimate failure of Gorbachev's attempt to reform the Soviet system, one should not overlook the extent of his achievement. He made the crucial major decisions to replace rule by a monopoly party political machine with democratically elected leaders—President Boris Yeltsin of Russia, after all, was elected under the Gorbachev administration (and even against Gorbachev's preferences, bearing strong witness to the political revolution Gorbachev had brought about). Gorbachev had two crucial failures: temporizing and failing on economic reform, and failing in time to recognize and to accommodate centrifugal regional and national-ethnic tendencies. First of all he was never able to find a way to dismantle the command economy and give free play to the market without social chaos. Also, while he was able to neutralize and sideline the Communist Party at the center, and make national and international policy, he could not overcome the entrenched interests of the party-administrative-economic bureaucracy or implement a political-economic revolution throughout the country. Second, he was slow to recognize the power of rising national and ethnic political sentiment, and coupled with it the tendencies, even in regions where there was no ethnic national factor, toward revolt against the continued dominance of even a reforming Moscow "center." Whether a confederal union was still possible in August 1991 is not clear, but that is moot; it is evident that after the failure of the August coup attempt, and the success of the Yeltsin countercoup against Gorbachev and the central (Soviet) government, Ukraine could not be kept in a union and hence there would be none.

Gorbachev's principal achievement in the internal sphere was the gradual disestablishment of the ruling totalitarianist Communist Party and establishment in its stead of the foundation for a civil society.

Even more significant was Gorbachev's historic achievement in bringing an end to the Cold War. That success did not carry over to help deal with the internal crisis; indeed it marginally weakened Gorbachev's position internally. But in the longer run, it may be seen to have been more closely related than was evident. Gorbachev often characterized his efforts in external relations as bringing the Soviet Union to be part of "the civilized world," which required ending the Cold War confrontation. At the same time, he also sought, with more success than is usually acknowledged, to transform his country into a "civil society." Important steps such as the moves to demilitarize the external relationship and the internal economic and social system served both objectives. So, too, did the abolition of the "image of the enemy," depiction of an external threat based on ideological grounds and used to justify internal repression and secrecy as well as militarization and external hostility. Thus both the

most useful discussions is Alexander Dallin, "Causes of the Collapse of the USSR," in *Post-Soviet Affairs*, vol. 8 (October–December 1992), pp. 279–302. For generally conservative viewpoints, see "The Strange Death of Soviet Communism: An Autopsy," an entire special issue of *National Interest*, no. 31 (Spring 1993).

internal and external achievements of Gorbachev had a direct impact on American-Soviet relations and laid the foundation for subsequent American-Russian relations.

It is important to give more attention than was given by the United States at the time to the conceptual articulation of the "new thinking" under Gorbachev from 1985 through 1988. This reevaluation of world processes (parallel with the reevaluation of internal processes) and reevaluation of threats, opportunities, and real interests in the world underlay the significant steps implementing new thinking from late 1987 through 1991. These later steps were more evident to the West, but they had their foundation in the new thinking that had been percolating for many years but first came to be espoused by the leadership under Gorbachev, soon after he became the leader. The new thinking was first notably expounded in Gorbachev's Report to the Twenty-seventh Party Congress in early 1986.

The "new thinking" under Gorbachev, while evolutionary in its sources and origins, was revolutionary in its aims and impact.[9] It combined idealist assumptions about the international order with pragmatic approaches to resolving concrete problems, as Gorbachev's arms control policies illustrated well. It also reflected and facilitated a learning process, as past failures prompted rethinking and new approaches. Transnational influences were also evident, for example, in the impact of the experience of international contact and discussion through the Palme Commission, the meetings of the unofficial Pugwash and Dartmouth movements, and other intellectual cross-fertilization begun earlier and continued in the 1980s.

It is especially important to recognize two significant aspects of the adoption of new thinking by Gorbachev and a few of his close associates. First, the acceptance of new thinking, and its application to policy and action, was by no means the only course that could have been followed—indeed, it was far from the most likely. Along with ingrained caution and bureaucratic lag, this unpredictability of the new thinking above all in the ideologically long-hide-bound Soviet Union was one reason for the slow Western readiness to accept it as real. The second, related, significant feature of the new thinking was its voluntary nature. Gorbachev and his coterie of close associates (above all Aleksandr Yakovlev and Eduard Shevardnadze) chose to shift Soviet policy from competition to cooperation, to end the Cold War and to rely on cooperative security, to shift from a conflict of adversarial camps to building a better structure of a single interdependent world. In part this shift represented long-belated recognition of realities, but it went beyond that to choose to pursue a liberal foreign policy based on idealist assumptions—despite a slow and cautious Western, and especially U.S., response. If the Soviet Union had only been

---

9. I am indebted for this felicitous expression to Robert Herman, whose doctoral dissertation now in progress at Cornell University will make a substantial contribution to understanding the origins and development of new thinking in the Soviet Union.

adjusting to Soviet weakness and to resurgent American strength, as Reagan and many Americans believed, it would have cut its losses where it was overextended, perhaps including Afghanistan and to some extent elsewhere in the Third World, but it would have "dug in" and stood its ground as it surely could have done in Eastern Europe, in the arms competition, and in many other areas. The Berlin Wall, the Warsaw Pact, the Soviet SS-20 intermediate-range missiles—and the Soviet Union—would still be in place. For the new thinking embraced both foreign and internal policy. Although the restructuring of the Soviet Union failed, the restructuring of international relations succeeded. But of course it required interaction, above all with the United States, and that did not come easily.

What about the interaction, the effects of Soviet actions on American policy, and of American policy on that of the Soviet Union? This study presents massive evidence of such effects. In summing up, it is useful to note and consider some of the more important ones. On the whole, as earlier noted, the initiative rested mainly with Reagan from 1981 to 1985 and then passed to Gorbachev. In brief, Reagan's action and rhetoric during these years led the Soviet leaders to dig in on confrontational lines and raised serious doubts in Moscow about whether any other kind of relationship with the United States was even possible. Dialogue and negotiation fell into minimal use, sustained only by diplomats on both sides (including Secretary Shultz) who retained modest hopes.

Gorbachev did not set about to reinvigorate his diplomacy, especially toward the United States, on the basis of any expectations or illusions about the American position. As an interactionist, however, he (and his colleague Eduard Shevardnadze, whom he soon installed as foreign minister in place of the too-experienced Andrei Gromyko) set out to take a stand and moved to "create facts" to which the United States (and other Western powers) would have to react. If that required far-reaching proposals, and even far-reaching and one-sided concessions in negotiation or unilateral actions to change the situation, Gorbachev was prepared to act accordingly. And he did.

Some American observers, above all those with an essentialist viewpoint or a stake in the Reagan administration and its reputation, have contended that Gorbachev's remarkable pliancy was a response to and justification for the Reagan administration's hard line of the previous four or five years. Gorbachev gave way on the INF, accepting the Reagan administration's notoriously one-sided zero option (which even such a hard-liner as Secretary Alexander Haig had seen as "a frivolous propaganda exercise or worse").[10] It was acknowledged that Brezhnev, Andropov, and Chernenko had not responded to the Reagan confrontational line and military buildup, but Gorbachev's conces-

10. Alexander M. Haig, Jr., *Caveat: Realism, Reagan, and Foreign Policy* (Macmillan, 1984), p. 229.

sions were seen as belated reactions to them. Yet Reagan's crusading line, tough arms control stance, offensive on human rights, and the SDI and other military programs had made Soviet movement toward accommodation more difficult rather than more likely. Reagan's line gave ammunition to Soviet hard-liners, not to those seeking compromises based on a balance of interests.

Gorbachev pressed ahead with his unilateral actions and concessionary negotiations not owing to the Reagan hard line and military buildup, but despite it. He was determined to change the name of the game. Although it is true that the Reagan military buildup and pursuit of the SDI posed a military challenge that the Soviet Union was economically and technologically hard pressed to meet, Gorbachev's response was not temporizing competition or prudent accommodation. Instead he persisted with an ultimately successful campaign that he would have pursued in any case to deprive the arms race of a political foundation and to sharply devalue the military factor in Soviet-American and East-West relations. Gorbachev understood that the Soviet Union could not afford to match or overmatch the United States militarily, but more important he understood that it did not need to. He understood that both countries, and the world, would be better off without a Cold War military confrontation and permanent arms race. He did not lose the arms race, he called it off. Indeed, the Reagan military buildup was seen in Gorbachev's Moscow as compelling evidence that not only could the Soviet Union not gain from such competition, but that even the United States could not, and that the continuing competition was fruitless as well as unnecessary.

The tough negotiating posture of the United States under Reagan and Bush from March 1985 through the START I Treaty signed in July 1991 required Gorbachev to make the lion's share of concessions. The first major concrete step was the larger reductions under INF, including a rollback not only of the SS-20 buildup of the late 1970s and early 1980s, but of the large SS-4 and SS-5 deployments of the late 1950s and 1960s, and in Asia as well as Europe. But while the cuts were painful to many military leaders and others who disliked seeing unbalanced Soviet reductions, Gorbachev had broader objectives. First of all, he revalidated arms control, which had suffered not only neglect and abuse at Reagan's hand in the treatment of the SALT II Treaty and the illegal unilateral "reinterpretation" of the ABM Treaty, but also the drumbeat of charges of Soviet cheating—mostly unsubstantiated—levied by the Reagan administration. Those charges raised serious questions not only about past Soviet compliance, but about the value of any arms control and reduction agreements. When that same administration signed a major new arms agreement, the INF Treaty, the whole arms control process was restored, as Gorbachev had calculated. In addition, Gorbachev was working to dismantle the whole East-West military confrontation, and the INF Treaty greatly reduced Western concerns. Initially, to be sure, there remained in Western Europe concerns about the conventional forces balance, or rather imbalance in Soviet and Warsaw Pact favor. But Gorbachev met that concern by unilateral

Soviet reductions and by taking negotiating positions that gave up the huge Soviet and Warsaw Pact numerical superiorities in conventional arms all the way to the Ural mountains. Again, one-sided military concessions were made because Gorbachev's purpose was to dismantle the military confrontation in Europe and, together with political change in Eastern Europe, as he had said as early as 1984, to make Europe a "common home," rather than "a theater of military operations."[11]

The continued tough bargaining by Reagan and Bush in an obsolete zero-sum negotiating mode made it more difficult for Gorbachev, not all of whose colleagues were convinced new thinkers. But he successfully persisted. Not only was the START I Treaty signed in July 1991, but Gorbachev was prepared at any time from 1986 on to reach the even deeper reduction in strategic arms than that finally reached by Bush and Yeltsin in START II in January 1993. But he was frustrated by the American administration not only on deep cuts of strategic arms, but also on cessation of nuclear testing, on tactical and naval nuclear weapons (until Bush's belated dawning new thinking in September 1991), and on ensuring the ABM Treaty and preventing an arms race in outer space.

The Reagan administration, and generally the Bush administration, also continued through the 1980s to "hang tough" and force Gorbachev to make virtually all the concessions not only in arms negotiations but also in other fields, for example, on the terms of withdrawal from Afghanistan. Rather than facilitating Gorbachev's revolution by cooperation, the Reagan and Bush administrations made the task more difficult by such tactics, before eventually welcoming the result they had wanted but had done so little to bring about.

There was one notable exception. While the Reagan administration had pressed its public calls for change in Eastern Europe (and even supplemented them with covert action), in the crucial "endgame" the Bush administration in 1989–90 deliberately held back from pushing the process of change in ways that would have made it more difficult for Gorbachev to accept the process that led to the Revolution of '89. The "captive nations" of Eastern Europe were not liberated by American political and propaganda pressures over several decades, nor even by the brave persistence of local patriots. They were released only when Moscow, under Gorbachev's enlightened recognition of the necessity to allow freedom of choice, withdrew the Brezhnev Doctrine and the resort to Soviet military power to preserve hegemony. Bush and Baker wisely did what they could to facilitate that Soviet change by not attempting to push its pace, nor crowing over its achievement.

The failure and collapse of the Soviet system also pose the question of judging the effect of the indictments of that system that had been voiced by American leaders, especially in the Reagan administration. Did such rhetoric

---

11. "Speech of M. S. Gorbachev at the British Parliament," *Pravda*, December 19, 1984.

and posture help bring about the end of the Cold War? In retrospect, as criticisms and even as predictions such statements appear to be justified by the historical outcome. Yet it would be a serious error to judge their effect, and their appropriateness at the time, by that standard. Nor did anyone at the time, in the early and mid-1980s, expect or foresee that within a decade the Cold War, communist rule, and the Soviet Union itself would come to an end. Indeed, U.S. administrations, though flaying the faults and fundamental weaknesses of the Soviet system, placed greater emphasis on its power and continuing long-term threat to the world. Even well into the Gorbachev transformation, strong voices in Washington were warning that even a successful *perestroika* would merely make the Soviet Union a more formidable adversary.

The crusading spirit evidenced by American leaders and their indictment of the Soviet system were largely irrelevant to the outcome even though the American campaign did reflect some truths about the Soviet Union's fundamental flaws. The principal diplomatic and political effect of the American campaign was negative; it helped to sustain an adversarial confrontation based substantially on reciprocal fears. Once a historic transformation began *within* the Soviet system, the effects of Western (above all American) challenge were more complex, but still predominately negative. Western criticism played some positive role in demonstrating that if the Soviet Union wanted to join and be a respected member of the world community it would have to accept certain standards in its internal as well as its international behavior. And Gorbachev placed a high priority on meeting what he repeatedly referred to as civilized, common human values. Adversarial attacks, however, made it harder for Gorbachev to liberalize Soviet internal and international behavior because the powerful domestic conservative forces with which he was in constant struggle objected that he was giving in to American pressures, sacrificing Soviet interests, and kowtowing to the West. He persisted anyway, but his task was harder.

The West had contained the Soviet Union, though Soviet expansionist ambitions were far less evident in reality than its own ideological design or Western fears suggested. The Soviet system was eventually brought down by its inherent failings and in the final analysis by Gorbachev's recasting of the entire Soviet relationship to the outside world—a radical revision undertaken not in reaction to anything that Reagan did, but in response to the recognition that the world was not cast in the Marxist-Leninist mold. In foreign policy as well as policy at home, Gorbachev's revolution was above all a conscious effort to break away from a failed system. Gorbachev succeeded in breaking the internal grip of the old Soviet system over the people, but he failed in the attempt to create a new economic and political system in time to prevent the breakup of the Soviet Union before it could be transformed into a renewed union (less some peripheral republics), and this failure also swept him from political leadership. But before that happened, he had succeeded in disengaging the Soviet Union from its support for leftist regimes in the Third World, and in dissolving the enforced Soviet hegemony over Eastern Europe and the division of Europe.

Above all, Gorbachev succeeded, beyond anyone's imagination, in bringing the Cold War to an end. He may not have done so alone, but what happened would not have happened without him; that cannot be said of anyone else.

## *Looking Forward: American-Russian Relations in the Post-Soviet Era*

American-Russian relations in the new era remain mixed, although with more cooperation and especially with less competition than characterized U.S.-Soviet relations during the Cold War. It is possible that relations, already advanced well beyond détente, will move toward an entente, though that outcome will depend on several things that cannot yet be confidently predicted, especially future internal developments in Russia.

If U.S. policy decisions in the Cold War on how best to meet perceived Soviet challenges in a competitive context were complex and sometimes divisive, new decisions on how best to serve American interests in a context of building cooperation with Russia are sometimes no less difficult and controversial. So, too, are Russia's decisions on its interests and policy.

During the final phase of the Gorbachev period, Soviet-American relations exhibited far more cooperation than competition. The Gulf War was the most striking and significant example, but far from the only one. Cooperation helped in resolving a range of regional conflicts (Nicaragua, El Salvador, Ethiopia), or at least in removing international competition from those where civil wars lingered or reerupted (Afghanistan, Angola, Cambodia). The United States and the Soviet Union moved far in bilateral strategic arms control and reductions (START and reciprocated unilateral cuts), as well as in multilateral arms control (CFE, banning chemical weapons, and preventing further nuclear nonproliferation).

The Cold War had ended. There were virtually no conflicting positions at the final U.S.-Soviet summit meeting in July 1991. No doubt, if a restructured Soviet Union had survived, some differences would in due course have emerged. But examples such as the Gulf War showed not only a new absence of conflict but positive cooperation in building the new world order of which both Presidents Bush and Gorbachev frequently spoke.

The sudden, rapid collapse of the Soviet Union and emergence of Russia and eleven other successor states loosely tied by compact into a Commonwealth of Independent States (CIS) was an easy transition for the United States and the rest of the world, notwithstanding many uncertainties. Russia and the other successor states quickly reassured the world community that they would accept the obligations and commitments of the Soviet Union—to the United Nations, the CSCE, all arms control agreements, and economic obligations. There was uneasiness over whether Ukraine, Kazakhstan, and Belarus would accept a continued central authority over nuclear weapons and the commitment to their dismantlement mandated by the START Treaty. The initial acceptance by all, however, of a central Commonwealth control of all nuclear weapons, and an early agreement at Lisbon to sign a protocol of adherence to the START Treaty and to join the Nonproliferation Treaty (NPT) as nonnuclear weapon states, seemed to resolve that problem. Later, Ukraine toyed with the idea of becoming a nuclear power. By 1994 the problem seemed to be successfully resolved, assuming Ukraine does not upset the arrangement midcourse.

Russia was the principal successor of the Soviet Union, not only by virtue of size, population, and control of the major resources of the former union, but as the member of the UN Security Council and as the sole successor nuclear weapons state under the NPT. The new Russian government also absorbed most of the former assets (and liabilities) of the Soviet Union except for those elements physically located in the other newly independent republics. Moscow, the Kremlin, vast Russia spanning eleven time zones—all were familiar.

Finally, although the Russian government set out to distinguish itself from its Soviet predecessor, it did so by attempting to paint its Soviet anteced-ent in dark colors, to undercut the image of Gorbachev's new thinking abroad and *perestroika* at home. Yeltsin had of course been driving for power for two years on a platform of liberalism, reform, and the shedding of all remaining vestiges of communist institutions and ideas. The new Russia aspired to be, if different, even *more* pro-Western, pro-cooperative, and more consistent in its "new thinking" than Gorbachev's policies had been. This new posture was partly self-justification for Yeltsin's role in bringing down Gorbachev's reform-ing Soviet Union, partly manifestation of a real desire to take a new path, and partly emphasized to persuade the West that it should reward the new Russia with desperately needed economic assistance.

The new Russian posture of demonstrative cooperation, a stance that can best be termed as ingratiating accommodation, lasted about a year to a year and a half. This happened to coincide with the last year of the Bush administra-tion in the United States and the beginning of the Clinton administration, but it was initially adopted—and later displaced—largely for reasons of a shifting political situation in Russia. In one respect, however, American-Russian (and more widely Western-Russian) relations did make a difference. There was much debate, some promise, but little delivery of Western economic assistance to Russia. The ultracooperative, ingratiating Russian policy toward the West did not yield the economic assistance expected (whether realistically is another question). In the West, the promise of economic assistance was tied to im-plementation of far-reaching Russian economic reform, which the Russians did not believe they could undertake without massive assistance, leading to a circular process in which little was done.

In the United States, for the first year and a half (1992 to mid-1993) almost the only question raised about relations with Russia was the matter of economic assistance: should it be given, how much, how, when, and for what. On all other international matters, Russia was either disengaged or following an American lead, essentially continuing the policy of the last year of the Gorbachev Soviet era. American policy toward Russia was not a partisan issue; it did not figure in the 1992 election campaign and though the Clinton administration was somewhat more forthcoming on aid than the Bush administration had been, it is not clear that a renewed Bush administration would not also have continued its slow movement in the same direction. There was bipartisan interest in encouraging democratic political reform, market-economy economic reform, and continued nuclear arms reductions in Russia—and the other successor states. But there was also bipartisan caution about apparent largesse in economic aid to anyone when the American economy was still in recovery, as well as caution about providing assistance that might simply be consumed rather than contribute to structural reform. As a result, actual economic assistance by the United States was heavily concentrated in two areas: support for American business in assistance roles, and support for nuclear disarmament, with a lesser additional expenditure for direct support of development of free enterprise in Russia. But major economic support was channeled through the large multilateral economic and banking institutions and was held back pending evidence of structural economic reform.

President Yeltsin, and many in his administration and in the inherited legislature—the intermittent Congress of People's Deputies and the standing Supreme Soviet—were in favor of economic reform. The decline of the Soviet economy that began in earnest in 1990 and worsened in 1991 was followed by an even more precipitate fall in 1992 in Russia and the other republics. All the problems of the Soviet economy were inherited but were made much more severe by new stresses caused by the breakup of the political, and therefore also managerial, infrastructure and supply channels of the formerly integrated Soviet economy.

But if there was universal recognition that something had to be done, and wide recognition that some kind of "reform" was needed, there was no consensus on what that reform should be. Western advice, by individual experts as well as by the IMF, was strongly focused on drastic macroeconomic change—closing industries, mines, enterprises that were not cost effective, tailoring reform to the desired economic results. Russian political, as well as economic managerial, leadership had differing views on what was economically desirable, but there was wide consensus on what was *not* feasible: doing what the Western economists advised, suddenly putting millions of Russians out of work with neither a social welfare net nor infrastructure for retraining, moving, rehousing, or reemploying them. The Russian leaders looked not only at the expected final economic result, but at the unavoidable immediate and intermediate social and political cost, if not chaos, of trying to get from here to there. Meanwhile, the economy continued to slide. Steps were taken, especially in privatization and in freeing the currency. But each step taken, or not taken, was controversial.

Internal political life became very active. Although institutions, such as political parties in a Western mold, were slow to develop, widely fragmented political competition thrived. Economic controversies spawned political controversies, and personal political rivalries and shifting alignments made the political competition fluid, and ultimately dangerous. Tensions rose between the somewhat autocratic Yeltsin administration and the increasingly independent legislature. Tensions also rose widely among the eighty-nine constituent republics and regions of the Russian Federation and the Moscow center. Meanwhile, the constitution was still the obsolete Soviet constitution of 1977 patched together with numerous piecemeal amendments but without coherence.

The intensification of the political struggle led Yeltsin increasingly to resort to what may most charitably be called "extraconstitutional" methods of governance, as he sought to defend the path to democracy by autocratic measures. The political conflict led ultimately to Yeltsin's dissolving the legislature and using force against it in October 1993 when some of its members attempted to provoke an uprising. That was followed by renewed rule by decree of Yeltsin, then by adoption of his proposed new constitution and election of a new legislature in December 1993. The election disturbingly showed a strong public support for conservative and hard-line nationalists, above all the extremist Vladimir Zhirinovsky.

Against this background of intensifying internal political conflict in 1993 Russian foreign policy underwent a significant change, with important implications for Russian-American relations.

The change in Russian foreign policy from 1992–93 to 1993–94 can most succinctly be described as a turn from a more self-effacing and passive role seeking entry into the international community to a more assertive pursuit of national interests. In part, this may have been the result of a gradual need to pay more attention to the outside world after the initial imperative concentration on internal problems. In part, it probably reflected a tactical move by Yeltsin to fend off increasingly effective charges by political opponents on the right and left that he was kowtowing to the West, selling out Russian interests for economic assistance that, to boot, Russia was not even receiving. In part, it represented a gradual clarification and definition of Russian national identity, previously submerged not only through nearly seventy-five years of communist rule but several centuries of a Russian empire that embraced most of the other now newly independent adjoining states, constituting what has come in Russia to be called "the near abroad." Finally, the change in Russian policy was also the result of a process of learning from experience.

As earlier noted, in its first year or so Russia sought to pursue a policy based on the "new thinking" advocated by Gorbachev. It wanted to differentiate itself from his policies by seeking to apply the new thinking more consistently and more thoroughly than he had done. Gorbachev had advocated, and done much to pursue, an idealistic acceptance of transnational goals such as common security and cooperative internationalism. Moreover, Gorbachev had moved the Soviet Union from the position of a superpower heading one of two global contending camps to dissolution of that camp and substitution of a position of partnership with the other superpower in the creation of a new world order in what was now seen as the one and only interdependent world.

Yeltsin had never shown interest in Gorbachev's new thinking and vision of the world, either to endorse or to criticize it. He had occasionally sought to take a stand going beyond Gorbachev on certain issues (such as settling the Kuril Islands territorial dispute with Japan or withdrawing the token Soviet Army brigade stationed in Cuba), but he had not identified these positions as new thinking. His foreign minister, Andrei Kozyrev, had been a protégé of one of the leading progenitors of the new thinking from the 1970s, former deputy Soviet foreign minister Vladimir Petrovsky. Kozyrev had then been an important new thinker in the collegium of the Soviet Foreign Ministry under Eduard Shevardnadze, before leaving to become Yeltsin's first Russian foreign minister in 1990 (the constituent Soviet republics had long had nominal foreign ministries).

Foreign policy was not Yeltsin's strong suit. It had not been central to his political rise or to his interests (not unlike President Clinton). Nor was he (like President Bush) strong on what Bush had called "the vision thing" for the post–Cold War world. And the internal political struggle in Russia and pressing needs to avert domestic crisis were necessarily his highest priorities. So Yeltsin let Kozyrev articulate the new Russian positions of "more" new thinking in 1992. Few situations could be found in practice where the new Russian foreign policy could be changed to be more thorough new thinking. (And some attempts, such as the attempt to pick up the old American tongue-in-cheek proposal for developing a joint strategic antiballistic missile system, backfired. The Russians learned that the United States had never intended to share such a system and moreover was moving rapidly to abandon the idea of such a system altogether. The project was scaled back to studying the idea of coordination in exchanging early-warning information as a confidence- and security-building measure.)

Within a year or so Russia had nothing to show for its embrace of idealistic internationalism. There was also no dividend for new thinking in terms of economic assistance from the West. Moreover, Russia was not given a share in world economic or political management. It had given up arms clients and lost most of its share of one of its few potential hard-currency earning exports, arms. A similar problem arose when the United States objected in 1992 to some uranium fuel sales on the world market at lower prices which the United States termed "dumping." That problem was largely resolved when, in February 1993, an agreement was reached for U.S. purchase of 500 metric tons of highly enriched uranium over a twenty-year period at the market price (a total deal amounting to about $12 billion). The agreement was conditioned on Russia sharing with Ukraine, Kazakhstan, and Belarus for their "equitable" share from fissionable materials in nuclear warheads removed from their territory. In another case widely publicized in Russia, the United States seemed overbearing in exerting heavy pressure that compelled Russia in 1993 to give up a sale of civilian space booster technology to India. Only reluctantly did the United States later agree in December 1993 to giving Russia a share in a cooperative (though U.S.-dominated) peaceful space program.

From the Soviet Union being an embarrassingly obvious junior partner in the Gulf War with Iraq and in the sponsorship of Arab-Israeli peace talks, Russia became a largely ignored nonpartner in later American-led decisions on possible sanctions against Serbia or the Bosnian Serbs. Some of these things rankled in the Yeltsin administration (never a very cohesive or established group). More important, they became the source of strong attacks from various quarters along the Russian political spectrum.

Thus what some Russians now call "the romantic period" in Russian-American relations, in 1992, gave way in 1993–94 to a more balanced synthesis of the globalist new thinking with assertive defense of national interests. Such a synthesis was clear in revisions of a foreign policy "concept" first drafted by the Foreign Ministry in 1992 but amended after comments and criticisms by members of the parliament and others in the government. Published in January 1993, a "Foreign Policy Concept of the Russian Federation" established guidelines for the full range of foreign policy. Although this document gave first place to relations with the countries of the Commonwealth of Independent States (CIS), among other nations and regions of the world, relations with the United States were given highest priority. "For the foreseeable future, relations with the United States will retain a prominent place on the scale of Russia's foreign policy priorities, corresponding to the position and weight of the United States in world affairs." Moreover, "Russia will strive toward the stable development of relations with the United States, with a view toward strategic partnership, and in the future—toward alliance." At the same time, "the absence of antagonistic contradictions in our relations with the United States does not mean a total absence of conflict. However, possible differences of opinion will not lead to confrontation if both countries proceed from the commonality of their long-term national interests and follow a realistic course." Accordingly, "the expansion of interaction and the development of partnership should not only not erode the independent role of Russia or cause harm to its interests, but should be based on a strict consideration of our priorities." The defensiveness of this formulation reflected the wide domestic criticisms in Russia of Yeltsin's and Kozyrev's earlier openly internationalist and pro-American policy course in 1992. So, too, did the further injunction to oppose any American attempts to turn the United States into "the sole superpower," in effect relegating the Russian partner to a satellite.[12]

---

12. *Kontseptsiya vneshnei politiki Rossiiskoi federatsii* (Foreign Policy Concept of the Russian Federation), Document no. 1615/IS, Ministry of Foreign Affairs of the Russian Federation, January 25, 1993), 58 pp. Quotations above from the translation in *Foreign*

A considerable backlash had developed in the Soviet Union as early as 1988–91, and in Russia in 1992–93, in reaction against what was widely perceived as a "pro-American" foreign policy insufficiently taking account of Russian interests. Although this perception was exaggerated (sometimes consciously but often not), it had a basis in fact. Although this charge was levied by political opponents against Mikhail Gorbachev (and his aides Eduard Shevardnadze and Aleksandr Yakovlev), and later against Boris Yeltsin (and his foreign minister, Andrei Kozyrev), it has had a broader resonance.

Many Russians believe that the United States sought to break up the Soviet Union and succeeded. Many believe that the United States covets Russian resources and is seeking to support privatization, U.S. investment, and expanded trade not to help Russia, or even for mutual benefit, but to exploit American power and Russia's weakness and tribulations. Many see the United States treating Russia as a defeated enemy and as wanting to keep Russia weak. Some who initially believed that the West, above all the United States, was promising more assistance and could have done more to help Russia back on its feet are now disillusioned.

This view is basically wrong, but nonetheless it has a following. Moreover, many Americans have tended to regard Russia as defeated in the Cold War, and to assume it is, or should be, ready now to accept U.S. tutelage and docilely follow a U.S. lead, or at least accept a junior role in a partnership.

Even Russian liberals have now concluded that the world is a less idealistic place, that new thinking not only must be moderated because of domestic political criticism but also that it should be leavened with greater defense of Russian national interests. Some who once wanted to show they could do more than Gorbachev now criticize him for having been too forthcoming.

One area of change has been in Soviet military doctrine. The Russian military establishment, desperately pressed to maintain less than half of the former Soviet military structure, has been struggling to survive. Even so, with a talented senior staff steeped in strategic doctrine and theory it has worked to develop a new military doctrine to meet the drastically changed requirements, and resources and constraints, of the new Russia. Without discussing that problem here, it is necessary to note that articulation of a revised military doctrine finally approved in November 1993 had important implications for Russian policy that relate to the agenda of Russian-American relations. A major change in Soviet strategy had been made in the Gorbachev period, a change too little appreciated in the West. The traditional, long-standing contingent strategy called for Warsaw Pact advance against NATO if war should come (only by Western attack or provocation in Soviet scenarios) in an "offensive defense."

Broadcast Information Service, *Daily Report: Central Eurasia, Foreign Policy Concept of the Russian Federation*, March 25, 1993, pp. 1, 8, 9. A later version was prepared but not publicly released.

This was changed in concept in 1986–87 to a "defensive defense" along the dividing line in Central Europe pending political resolution and termination of any conflict.[13] The new posture of balanced forces of the two alliances foreseen when the CFE Treaty was first negotiated was considerably weakened in 1990–91 when the Warsaw Pact collapsed. Nonetheless, particularly given the end of the Cold War and the even more remote possibility of East-West war in Europe, the Soviet Union still could assume a "defensive defense" along its Western borders (as in 1939–41). The dissolution of the Soviet Union changed that. Although the prospect of a war with NATO remained extremely improbable, there were new uncertainties about the whole constellation of political and military power in the expanded Eastern Europe west of Russian borders. The Moscow Military District became a border district for the first time in more than three hundred years.

Under these drastically changed and yet fluid political-military conditions, Russian military strategists abandoned the "defensive defense" of Gorbachev's new thinking for "flexible response," with whatever combination of defensive and offensive actions against whatever adversary might be required (and feasible). Similarly, the late Brezhnev period "early new thinking" innovation of no first use of nuclear weapons was abandoned.[14] Conventional defense, with greatly shrunken Russian forces, was no longer assured and defensive resort to nuclear weapons might be required against a superior conventional invasion force (to use the example often orally cited by Russian military men, China).

Thus Russia by 1993–94 had shifted its military doctrine to resemble that of NATO—flexible response with possible first use of nuclear weapons if necessary to meet a superior conventional attack. This shift occasioned some reaction in the West, but rather little (because, paradoxically, the earlier Soviet doctrinal changes to defensive defense and non-first use of nuclear weapons had not been given the credence they deserved). The changes were not ominous; they reflected readjustment with realism to a new situation where the "new thinking" of the Gorbachev period no longer applied.

In terms of strategic weapons, there is little difference or friction between Russian and American interests. The START II Treaty has yet to be ratified, but will probably be accepted as the next step in bilaterial strategic arms reduction. There is a growing interest in both countries, with some steps already taken, to remove strategic nuclear forces from the high alert levels of the past to postures less risking of accident and less inclined to possible decisions under crisis pressure for early, even preemptive, use.

---

13. See the discussion in Raymond L. Garthoff, *Deterrence and the Revolution in Soviet Military Doctrine* (Brookings, 1990), pp. 94–185.

14. Ibid., pp. 80–89.

Both powers are now more concerned about the possibility of nuclear weapons in the hands of other countries than they are about one another's arsenals, and nuclear and missile nonproliferation is a priority for both. Agreement on a global comprehensive nuclear weapons test ban and cutoff of further fissionable materials for weapons is now an avowed aim of both countries and a practical prospect.

In one instance, the new Russian military situation posed an issue for the United States and other countries stemming from an existing arms control agreement reached under other circumstances. The CFE Treaty not only posed ceilings on major conventional arms, but also regional subceilings on the "flank" areas. No longer a flank area supplementing a Warsaw Pact (or even Soviet)–NATO theater, the Northern Caucasus area is now seen from Moscow as a new potentially threatening front. But Russia (and Ukraine, which has a parallel constraint and a parallel interest in alleviating it) now wants to modify the constraints on quantitative levels of tanks, armored personnel vehicles, and artillery in that region. (The actual constraint covers both the southern and northern flanks taken together, but the problem arises from the situation in the south.) To date, the United States and most CFE participants strongly oppose any amendment or reinterpretation of the CFE Treaty, not only because of doubt that Russia and Ukraine need to increase their forces in that area, but because there is a strong concern over reopening the multilateral treaty. Nonetheless the problem may have to be addressed, and the changed geopolitical and geostrategic situation should be taken into consideration.

Most Russians, naturally, see Russia as a great power with security interests in its neighborhood. The failure of the CIS to develop as a real community in the first year, and in particular its failure to maintain a common military and security framework, contributed to the conclusion that Russia must provide for its security, including through agreements providing for stationing of some Russian forces in other republics. There is, however, virtually no support for the idea of using Russian military power to reestablish a Russian empire.

The Russian policy shift in 1993–94 was not to the right, nor to rebuilding an empire. In part, it was a corrective to somewhat naive expectations of an American embrace and partnership on the basis of new thinking. An assertion of Russian security interests in the near abroad is entirely understandable. To acknowledge such an interest need not and should not mean giving Russia a free hand to do whatever it might wish there. But so far the record is more reassuring than some have realized.

The role of the Russian Army in the "near abroad" has become an issue in American thinking about Russia, if not yet an issue in American-Russian relations. The foremost and most politically sensitive concern in the United States for the first two and a half years was the presence of Russian (formerly Soviet) troops in the Baltic states. The process of negotiation between Russia and the Baltic states was protracted and difficult, but agreement was reached leading to withdrawal of all Russian military forces from Lithuania by August 1993 and from Latvia and Estonia by August 1994. Among the issues raised by Russia were the rights of retired former Soviet military personnel in Latvia and Estonia as residents (there was no problem in Lithuania since all there were given the choice not only of continued residence but of citizenship). While Russia used troop withdrawal for bargaining leverage on that issue, and on a few other related issues such as setting aside competing claims for Soviet-built military infrastructure versus past environmental damage by the Soviet military presence, it did not attempt to use its military presence to subvert or even to influence the internal political affairs of the Baltic states. The protracted negotiation and gradual withdrawal was also determined in part by the need to find housing for the 140,000 military personnel and their families in Russia (a problem compounded by the coincident large withdrawals from Germany and Poland).

In only one exceptional case did the question of a continued Soviet military presence in the Baltic states become a real issue, an early-warning radar installation at Skrunda in Latvia. In that case, the United States, committed to cooperation with Russia on reciprocal strategic early-warning systems as well as committed to helping to arrange troop withdrawal from the Baltics, helped to broker a compromise resolution under which the Soviet Union could continue to operate the station for four years after withdrawal of its forces.[15]

In 1992 most of the former Soviet military forces in the "near abroad" were converted into armies of the new independent republics (all except the Black Sea Fleet in Ukraine, and most forces in Belarus, Kazakhstan, Kyrgyzstan, and Turkmenistan). The others were taken into the new Russian armed forces created in May 1992 (after abandonment of plans for unified CIS armed forces): the forces in Germany and Poland, the Baltic states, the Transcaucasian states, Tajikistan, and part of the forces in the other Central Asian states. Withdrawals of these forces in 1992–93 were completed in Poland, Lithuania, and Azerbaijan and proceeded in Latvia, Estonia, Armenia, and Belarus. There were some withdrawals also in Moldova and Georgia, although other troops remained there.

Local secessionist or civil wars developed in five places: Nagorno-Karabakh, the Armenian enclave in Azerbaijan; South Ossetia in Georgia; Abkhazia in Georgia; the Transdniester (Dniester Republic) in Moldova; and Tajikistan. In none of these cases did the former Soviet armed forces begin hostilities, although eventually they became at least indirectly involved. In the Nagorno-Karabakh situation both Azerbaijan and Armenia received a share of arms of the former Soviet forces located in those republics, which were with-

---

15. Russia would have an additional eighteen months to dismantle the installation. The agreement, reached on March 15, 1994, at the time of this writing had not yet been ratified by the Latvian Saeima (parliament), nor had agreement yet been reached on the amount of annual rent for the lease.

drawn (entirely from Azerbaijan, and all but one Russian division from Armenia, which remained at Armenian request, but not near the area of hostilities).
In Georgia, the government received some weapons from disbanded Russian
units, and various parties to civil war obtained some former Soviet arms mainly
by raiding garrisons. In South Ossetia, by agreement of the parties a small joint
Russian-Georgian-Ossetian peacekeeping force effectively maintained a truce
after a cease-fire. In Abkhazia, the Abkhazians with some unofficial or masked
Russian assistance (and assistance by anti-Russian mountain tribal irregulars)
defeated the Georgians in 1993. Georgia requested Russian military assistance
to stabilize its own situation, and agreed to maintain about 20,000 Russian
military troops in Georgia (including two small divisions that had remained
along the Turkish border). In Tajikistan, after initial neutrality in a Tajik civil
war, the one Russian Army division and border guards then became the nucleus
of a CIS peacekeeping force (together with Uzbek, Kazakh, and Kyrgyz detach-
ments). In Moldova, Russian units on the left bank were withdrawn and some
arms turned over to Moldova, but the headquarters and one understrength
division of the Russian (ex-Soviet) 14th Army remained in the breakaway
self-declared Dniester Republic, and gave it indirect and at times even direct
support. This was the most egregious case of interference in the internal affairs
of another country (inasmuch as Russia had recognized Moldova within its 1991
borders, and even if the local Russian commander acted largely on his own).

Russian political interests in the near abroad would not have led to
sending military forces beyond its borders, but their existing presence there has
contributed to concerns if not to local tensions. The principal Russian interest
in the near abroad is not, however, expansionist but adjustment to the consequences of the sudden disintegration of the Soviet Union—and Russian empire. The economic ties remain, and are even more critical to other republics
than to Russia, although they are ties of interdependence. Suddenly, ties among
people who had shared one national history, sometimes for generations, have
been sundered. Some 25 million Russians live beyond the borders of the
Russian Federation (and large numbers of Ukrainians and others as well live
beyond the borders of their republics). While this does not give Russia a right
to claim the territories where they live, nor a right to intervene, it is natural for
a new Russian state as it defines its own identity to wish its ethnic national
compatriots abroad not to be discriminated against.

The numerous human, as well as economic and other, ties among all
the states of the former Soviet Union have contributed to greater viability of the
CIS than it was expected to have. Nationalism undercut the earliest hopes of
Yeltsin and many others, especially in Russia (recall, for example, the fielding in
the 1992 Olympics not of Russian and other national teams, but of a "Unified
Team"). Despite early predictions that the CIS would serve merely as a transi-
tory arrangement for a civilized divorce and gradual disaggregation of ties, and
despite its failure to establish a united strategic nuclear command, it has
recovered with new recognition (sometimes reluctantly) of continuing common

interests. Continuing ties of national interest have led more recently to a new lease on life for the CIS in the security as well as economic fields. All four states that earlier stood apart from or left the Commonwealth—Moldova, Georgia, Armenia, and Azerbaijan—are back in. In part, to be sure, this may be the result of Russian pressure, but it would not have occurred without the existence of essential common interests and interdependence. One area of common interest, for example, is guarding the outer borders of the former Soviet Union, especially in the south facing Afghanistan, Iran, and Turkey. Russia continues by agreement to play a major role in that border guard role along those borders (excepting only Azerbaijan, but also including the Central Asian borders with China).

By early 1994, although American public opinion was not really engaged, political commentary had begun to focus on alleged Russian "neoimperialism" in the near abroad as part of a budding political debate between the Clinton administration's support of the Yeltsin government (as had the Bush administration), and challengers who argued that Russia was seeking to expand into territories of the former Russian and Soviet empires in the near abroad. As noted above, the Russian Army became involved in a few cases, although only because troops were already there. Russia has not in any instance used the political and military opportunities to expand by accepting adjoining areas that have sought to secede from other republics—South Ossetia, Abkhazia, or (not directly adjoining) the Dniester Republic. Nor did Russia, for example, use its military presence to acquire or even lay claim to the Russian-populated northeastern area of Estonia. Finally, the Russian government has not encouraged the Russian-populated and secessionist-minded Crimea to leave Ukraine.

Russian peacekeeping forces in Moldova-Dniester, introduced with reluctant Moldovan consent, have kept the cease-fire since August 1992. The truce in South Ossetia has held since June 1992. A first truce in Abkhazia was broken by the Georgians, a second by the Abkhazians, but a third with Russian help has held since October 1993. In the absence of alternatives—the United Nations, the CSCE, and NATO have all declined to provide peacekeeping forces—the Russian and CIS role has been constructive. Although it would be preferable to provide a broader and more politically detached peacekeeping force, to date none has been available. (All observations in this paragraph are as of mid-1994.)

Part of the problem in American reaction has been a more assertive tone in Russian political pronouncements with respect to the near abroad. The strong showing of conservatives, former communists, and hard-line Russian nationalists in a protest vote in the December 1993 elections had a reinforcing double effect. First, it increased concerns in the United States (and in Eastern Europe and the new states of the former Soviet Union) over possible future Russian policy. Compounding that has been the turn to stronger statements about the defense of Russian national interests in the region, especially the near abroad, by Yeltsin, Kozyrev, and other spokesmen of the present Russian government, military, and parliament. The fact that Russian policy had been little changed only prompted still stronger rhetoric, which in turn invited alarm in Eastern Europe and the West. In particular it provided ammunition to those in the United States who had been seeking something with which to attack the Clinton administration, and its Russian policy was seen in the American political arena as one possibly vulnerable element.

Thus while Russia turned in 1993–94 to more firm, sometimes strident, defense of Russia's national security interests, questions were raised in the United States about whether there would remain as close a coincidence of Russian and American interests as had earlier been assumed. The early Russian deference to American leadership under Yeltsin in 1992 (begun under Gorbachev in 1991) was of course never a viable pattern for the relationship or foundation for a real partnership. But this had begun to become an American impression by 1993.

Renascent American concerns about apparent or potential Russian neoimperialism in its near abroad was also accompanied by the independent Russian political and diplomatic stand on Bosnia and Serbia. Unlike the earlier Gulf War and Arab-Israeli negotiations, where Russian and American policies had coincided and the United States had taken the lead, on the Bosnian crisis Russia took its own stand. It also sought a negotiated settlement, and as the external power with the greatest potential for influencing the Serbs to cooperate it played a constructive role, but on its own initiative and on a different tack.

In February 1994 the Ames spy case caused a remarkable flurry of attention in the American press and Congress. Though it was despicable for a trusted American veteran CIA officer, Aldrich Ames, to become a Soviet (and remain a Russian) spy, the brief flareup of calls for reassessing American relations with, and especially economic assistance to, Russia was preposterous. Ames after all had given away not American policy secrets, but secrets about American spies in Russia. It was absurd to imply that the United States had a right to recruit Russians to give it Russian secrets, but bad form for the Russians to defend themselves by recruiting an American to learn about those spies for the United States in Russia.[16] That such uproar could occur showed the fragility of the new American-Russian relationship of partnership.

While changing American views on Russia were in part responsive to perceived changes in Russian policy, or at least changes in rhetoric, they also stemmed to an important extent from what many American political figures saw as a new opportunity to take positions that had not been popular during the romantic period in 1992–93 (or even since 1990). There were three categories

---

16. There has, incidentally, been rising concern in the Russian intelligence services and government over a considerable increase in foreign intelligence activities in Russia, and in the other countries of the former Soviet Union, sometimes in collaboration with them, directed against Russian targets.

of critics of American policy toward Russia: cold warriors, geopoliticians, and politicians. The hard-line cold warriors had been reluctant to give up an enemy, and since the end of the Cold War had been seeking a new adversary against whom to rail. The geopoliticians had been reluctant to give up the game. Some, including Zbigniew Brzezinski and sometimes Henry Kissinger, have suggested building up counterweights to Russia in Ukraine and other border states—contesting, in effect, the "near abroad" with a forward neocontainment strategy.[17] The politicians have simply wanted to hit Clinton, and have seen Clinton's policy toward Russia, which had been held up as a self-proclaimed administration success in 1993, as vulnerable after the December 1993 elections and faltering economic reform to possible failure and succession of a more militant Russian nationalistic government.

In addition to these negative American reactions to changing Russian policy, there is a more healthy belated recognition by others in and out of the government that Russia is an independent country and great power with its own national interests. While some critics have suggested that Russia is a rival, rather than a partner, some in the Clinton administration, in particular Secretary of Defense William Perry, have described the relationship as a "pragmatic partnership," and as he noted, "Russia can be both our partner and our rival and both at the same time" and "the new Russia will have interests different from our interests. Even with allies like France and Japan, we have rivalry and competition alongside our partnership, and so it will be with Russia."[18]

The new Russian realism is entirely compatible with development of good relations between the two countries. The challenge, for both countries, is to build a real partnership serving the national interests of both countries, cooperating in pursuit of congruent and common interests, accommodating differences where interests or objectives diverge, and reconciling or neutralizing interests that conflict. While objective differences in power and global interests make infeasible a partnership of equals, what is possible and is needed is a partnership of peers.

It is also important to realize that while American-Russian relations remain a mix of cooperation and competition, as with U.S.-Soviet relations during the Cold War, the basic framework is essentially different. No longer are the two powers engaged in a fundamentally zero-sum contest, and no longer is there fear of war.

---

17. See Zbigniew Brzezinski, "The Premature Partnership," *Foreign Affairs*, vol. 73 (March-April 1994), pp. 67–82; and Henry Kissinger, "Be Realistic about Russia," *Washington Post*, January 25, 1994, p. A19.

    Brzezinski's son, Ian Brzezinski, is in fact resident in Kiev as an adviser to the Ukrainian government.

18. Transcript of address by Secretary of Defense William J. Perry, George Washington University, March 14, 1994, pp. 2, 9, 4.

Russia wants not to be taken for granted, and to be recognized as one of the great powers in the world with its own national interests, albeit no longer as a global superpower nor with global ideological pretensions. The United States can and should accept that approach, and should help Russia fully enter the international community with equality and dignity. That acceptance of Russia's role will of course entail responsibilities as well as privileges for Russia, for example, with respect to the conduct of peacekeeping operations and controls on the export of technology for weapons of mass destruction.

The United States under the Bush and Clinton administrations has sought to advance the processes of democratization and development of a market economy in Russia. Support for pursuit of those objectives is sound, but the United States (and other outside entities such as the Group of 7 and the IMF) are not in a position to insist upon (or even to know with sufficient confidence) what is the most effective and appropriate course of political and economic reform. The Russian people and its elected leadership must make its own choices and decisions, even if that includes its own mistakes. The United States also should recognize that desirable as are those reform objectives, internal stability of Russian society and the Russian state is also a priority objective. American visions of reform should not be set as a central indicator in determining even American policy toward Russia, much less as a criterion for judging American relations with Russia.

Russia must recognize its international responsibilities and the appropriate constraints on pursuit of its interests. The United States, for its part, needs to be more understanding of Russian pursuit of its national interests. American relations with Russia require recognition that each country seeks to further its own national interests, and that these interests will not always coincide. The reconciliation of diverging interests, moreover, is a task for both countries. The United States should not, for example, attempt or even appear to be freezing Russia out of legitimate competition in world trade in the few areas where it is able to compete (for example in peaceful uses of space). Helping Russia to obtain a fair share of market access may be more important than direct economic and financial aid.

The United States should recognize the central role of Russia in the CIS, and that Russia has vital interests in the "near abroad," while helping Russia—and the other countries of the former Soviet Union—to develop on the basis of the independence of the new states.

The United States and other Western European powers should continue to encourage pan-European security arrangements through the CSCE and NATO's Partnership for Peace. It would be a serious mistake to isolate Russia from this process even unintentionally, for example by taking into full NATO membership countries of the former Warsaw Pact (to say nothing of former republics of the Soviet Union) without equal opportunity for Russia to join. No attempt should be made to build anti-Russian containment through building up Ukraine or other border states as counterweights to Russia.

The United States must not only develop a new relationship with Russia, but also give due attention to the other successor states, especially Ukraine and Kazakhstan (not only, although importantly, to ensure that they acquiesce in the continued dismantling of strategic nuclear weapons on their territory). Russia is the most important successor of the Soviet Union, and its intrinsic importance should command greater attention. The successful building of democratic institutions, a prosperous economy, and stability in Russia is also the best guarantee for the security of its neighbors. The other successor states are of varying intrinsic importance, but should be given due attention, also on their own merits and with respect to their individual qualities. The United States shares with them all an interest in preserving peace and stability in the central Eurasian region.

As an American writing primarily for an American readership, I have placed the emphasis on American policy toward Russia, while also discussing Soviet policy interests. The profound transformation under way in Russia is another, objective, reason for concentrating on developments in and concerning Russia in evaluating American-Russian relations. It is, however, important also to bear in mind that a less obvious and less disrupted transformation is also under way in the adaptation of American policy. The United States, with a strong tradition of seeing a missionary democratizing role in the world, a tendency reinforced by the end of the Cold War and collapse of communism and at least for the present a new role as the only superpower, may seek to dominate the American-Russian relationship more than it should. The Bush and Clinton administrations have both shown a mix of "realist" and "idealist" tendencies combined but focused on a central role for the United States (and by no means only in relation to Russia). The United States must not only be sensitive to Russian (and other) interests and roles in the world, but also to weighing its own role with due regard to others.

The relationship between the United States and Russia will continue to occupy a place of importance in international politics. It will, nonetheless, be relatively less important than the former U.S.-Soviet relationship above all because of the rising significance of Europe and Japan and of multilateral problems, decisions, and agreements, in all spheres, including arms and arms control as well as political and economic issues. Awareness of this reality is reflected in the decisions and actions of the United States and Russia in their own relations, as well as in their respective broader policy agendas.

## *Looking Forward: International Relations in the Post–Cold War Era*

History, including the history of international relations, inexorably moves forward. The Cold War was an important episode, but with roots in earlier history and with ramifications that continue to influence the post–Cold

War world. The world is returning to multipolarity in a system of great and lesser powers. Related to this development is a shift to wider security concerns and therefore a shift in the elements of world power. Military power is by no means without continuing, and in the most ominous sense, ultimate influence. Nor has its use ended. But military force as a means of registering and influencing power has declined, while other factors—above all, economic ones—have become more important. One consequence is an increase in the relative weight of Japan and the European Union (especially with a unified Germany) and a decrease in the relative weight of the United States as well as Russia. A new pattern of relationships is emerging between these countries and the rest of the globe (until recently called the Third World, although regarded mainly as an arena for competition between the two worlds led by the superpowers). Some observers expect economic and sociopolitical North-South tension to replace the ideological and politico-military East-West confrontation of the Cold War.

Economic relationships are changing and growing in salience. To the extent that they have been related to political relationships fashioned in the crucible of the Cold War, they require redefinition. Underlying economic trends have also greatly reduced the postwar dominance of the United States and have seen great increases in the economic role of Japan, Germany, four East Asian smaller powers (South Korea, Hong Kong, Taiwan, and Singapore), and most recently, China. European integration has slowed, but the Common Market is absorbing most of the European Free Trade Association (EFTA) countries. The collapse of the Soviet political and economic bloc, including the Council on Mutual Economic Assistance (CMEA), has led the former communist countries of Eastern Europe to seek not only to reform and revive their own economies, but also to orient themselves toward, and attempt to integrate with, the West. The same is true of many of the new states that were formerly republics of the Soviet Union, including Russia itself and Ukraine, Belarus, and the Baltic states.

Russia seeks to become the eighth member of the conference of Western economic leaders constituting the Group of 7, and while there is no longer any political bar to such a role, the Russian economy is still deeply disrupted and in need of reform and resuscitation.

There has been some debate over whether, indeed, the United States remains as the only global superpower (and, if it is, how long it will remain one). The definition of "great powers" or other differentiation among those states that do have greater power and influence than most states will not be easy to determine. Under virtually any definition, however, Russia almost certainly remains in the category of major powers, despite its present economic weakness and shaky political status. Ukraine, with a population, territory, and armed forces comparable in size to France or Britain (and still anguishing over giving up claims to the nuclear missiles on its territory) also aspires to being recognized as a great power, although the prospect for that is at best distant even if economic crisis and political divisions are overcome.

Military power will be less salient in world politics, but will remain a factor and on occasion will be used. The Gulf War, waged against Iraq in 1991 by a U.S.-led coalition and supported by the Soviet Union, was the first significant case, although probably atypical. That experience did illustrate the enormous change in relations between the former Soviet Union and the West.

The possible proliferation of nuclear and other weapons of mass destruction and the efforts to deal with that danger are important elements of the new political agenda—again, in contrast to the nuclear confrontation between East and West during the Cold War. The potential impact of the dangers of nuclear proliferation is considerable. Although there have been favorable developments in the world arena (concerning Argentina, Brazil, and South Africa, and French and Chinese adherence to the Non-Proliferation Treaty [NPT]), there have also been new challenges (Iraq and North Korea, and putatively Iran). The case of North Korea is potentially dangerous, not only because of the still tense relations between North and South Korea, but also because it could stimulate a change of policy toward acquisition of nuclear weapons by South Korea and Japan. There also remains the anomalous status of the undeclared nuclear powers: Israel, India, and Pakistan.

Since the disintegration of the Soviet Union there has been the new problem of possible attempts by Ukraine (and initially Kazakhstan) to become instant major nuclear powers by establishing and keeping control over strategic nuclear weapons systems of the former Soviet Union located on their territory. If Ukraine were to take full control and claim status as a nuclear weapons power, there would be substantial deterioration of Ukrainian-Russian relations, even if probably not direct armed hostilities. Such a move by Ukraine would also pose a severe challenge to the United States, which had negotiated an agreement with Ukraine to divest itself of all nuclear weapons, and to the other Western powers. It could have negative effects on the stability of Eastern Europe and could contribute to reopening in Germany the question of its nonnuclear status. Overall, it would weaken support for the Non-Proliferation Treaty (NPT), which is due for renewal in 1995. Fortunately Ukraine has been moving (since early 1994) toward permitting all the nuclear weapons on its territory to be removed to Russia for dismantling in exchange for compensation for the nuclear materials in the warheads as well as security assurances from the nuclear powers.

The less dramatic and acute but also important area of curbing the spread of nuclear and missile delivery technologies requires effective efforts not only of Russia, but also of Ukraine and several other republics of the former Soviet Union. It is of course a worldwide problem and also concerns China, Israel, and other potential suppliers of relevant technologies.

Above all, there will be a return to the more traditional pattern of shifting blends of cooperation and competition among all nations, including former Cold War allies as well as former adversaries. Countries will pursue their own perceived interests in a more open international context. They will engage not only in new forms of cooperation but also in shifting rivalries and conflicts similar to those that preceded the Cold War. In short, the world will resume a pattern of political relationships free of bipolar superpower and coalition rivalry. Nations can hope for a new more stable and serene world order, and strive to fashion one, but it will not come into being easily.

Numerous local and regional conflicts that were largely subsumed into the global confrontation of the Cold War now assume their own places in the world order—or disorder—and new ones will arise. As earlier noted, new sources of potential conflict lie in the former, now-shattered Soviet empire. The disintegration of the former Yugoslavia has sparked severe internecine conflicts, notably in Bosnia-Herzegovina. Other examples of persistent if less acute tensions remain in Eastern Europe. And of course conflicts elsewhere in the world continue, now in the absence of Cold War superpower involvement, for example, in Afghanistan, Angola, and Cambodia. Others will arise. Thus there is a new challenge to the world community to develop the potential for wider pursuit of cooperative security.[19]

American-Soviet consultations and cooperation permitted UN agreement to deal with the first major post–Cold War armed conflict, the Iraq invasion of Kuwait and the subsequent Persian Gulf War defeating Iraq, in 1990–91. Russian-American consultation, though not always agreement, has also been one element in the complex diplomatic overlay to the even more complex internal war in Bosnia. In many, though not in all, future instances of regional conflict both American and Russian interests will be engaged, usually but not always in cooperation. Russia continues to play a role beyond its periphery, as in cosponsoring with the United States the Arab-Israeli peace process. In the future, however, Russia will not be greatly involved in most of the Third World. It is a question for American policymakers whether and what role the United States will play in particular situations.

International organizations, in particular the United Nations and its many affiliates, will undoubtedly play a larger role. This has already been seen by the more vigorous role of the United Nations in the Gulf War, in facilitating resolutions of many regional conflicts (including Afghanistan, Southern Africa, Cambodia) and humanitarian interventions (Somalia, Bosnia). No longer is its security role trammeled by the veto of Cold War antagonists in the Security Council. Nonetheless, the United Nations and other international organizations have no ultimate power; they are the instruments of a community of sovereign states. For this reason it would be an error simply to project a straight-line growth of influence.

The United Nations, and especially for security issues the Security Council, must therefore reflect necessary political consensus of relevant states,

---

19. For a comprehensive review of this problem and potential solutions, see Janne E. Nolan, ed., *Global Engagement: Cooperation and Security in the 21st Century* (Brookings, 1994).

and increasingly that means that it must come to reflect the real distribution of power in the world. The Security Council should include Japan and Germany; in order to obtain the necessary broad consensus of the majority of states, it will also probably be necessary in some fashion to ensure adequate representation from South and Southeast Asia, Africa, and South America, without making the Council unworkably large.

Most discussions have involved projection and extrapolation from the present situation. This is an appropriate, indeed necessary, starting point, but it alone is not sufficient. Nearly half a century ago World War II had clearly closed one chapter in contemporary history, and the prospective era, what became the Cold War, soon became clear in its outline (although its duration and whether it would remain "cold" were not then known). Today, by contrast, it is not yet clear what will be the dominating, defining element of the era before us. It is, nonetheless, necessary to ponder the possible course of world politics over the next half century.

It is also necessary to rethink international relations theory in the light of the denouement of the Cold War as well as what can be envisaged of the current era. The end of the Cold War in one respect represented a triumph of "new thinking" idealism over mechanist realism. This success was, at the same time, blurred by the decline and fall of the Soviet empire for other, internal, reasons. Was Soviet abandonment of the Cold War merely a retreat and defeat owing to weakening capabilities, or was it a victory for enlightened thinking? The record leads to the conclusion that it was a choice rather than a necessity. Nonetheless, it was also conditioned by realist constraints. As noted, Russian policy initially sought to apply idealistic international "new thinking" even more consistently than had Gorbachev. Yet within a year or so Yeltsin found that the exigencies of internal politics and public opinion as well as of world politics compelled a reinvigoration of realist attention to national interests and a synthesis or amalgam of internationalist and nationalist, moralist and realist, considerations.

The United States, for its part, celebrated victory in the Cold War without appreciation of a need to review its own policy premises, except to think in terms of taking a lead in efforts to establish a new post–Cold War world order. To a large extent its idealistic self-image was, if anything, seen as vindicated by the outcome. The early success of American leadership in the Gulf War initially sustained optimism that a "new world order" was being born. The Bosnian, Somalian, and Haitian debacles, and frustration over the North Korean nuclear weapons program, soon introduced reminders of the complexities of the new world.

The nature of the global new order will be influenced by policies of the United States and Russia, but at the same time the policies of the two powers will be influenced by the evolution of the world order. The international political system and international environment will reflect changes in the balance of power among many states. Even established factors such as geography, history, and natural resources are not truly constants, as the disintegration of the Soviet Union and need for Russia and its other successors to establish their identity and define their interests remind us. Similarly, perceptions of threats and opportunities by both the United States and Russia, and by each in relation to other states as well as to each other, will be dependent on many factors.

The future will also see development of international relations on the foundation of the internal political evolution of states, especially of the major states, as well as on the evolution of the international system.

Though the nature of the future international system cannot yet be clearly defined, the world must certainly escape the confines of the Cold War framework. The history of the preceding periods, pre–World War I, and the interwar period, as well as the Cold War itself, must now be reexamined.

The Cold War is not only the most recent phase of history, it also constitutes the foundation for the future, and the end of the Cold War is the stepping-stone to whatever lies beyond. It has been my purpose in this volume, and in its predecessor (now revised to benefit from reflection on the end of the Cold War), to contribute to understanding this recent past.

# A Commentary on Sources

THE ACCOUNT in this book has been extensively documented in footnote references, and a comprehensive bibliography would be redundant. It would also be too long to be useful, given the wide range of subjects covered because of their relationships to the overall theme. At the same time, it may be useful to discuss briefly the types of sources available and to note the most important ones dealing directly with the central subject of American-Soviet relations in the 1980s.

First is the public record, by which I mean the publicly reported course of events and published statements of various kinds primarily by leaders, official institutions, and other prominent speakers, commentators, and analysts of the two countries. In short, the record of events, of pronouncements, and of expressions of view on both sides. Contemporary and subsequent official compilations of statements and other documents are an important category of data. For example, in the United States, there are the *Weekly Compilation of Presidential Documents* and the *Department of State Bulletin* (until 1990, subsequently *U.S. Department of State Dispatch*), and numerous other official publications (such as the annual *American Foreign Policy Current Documents*), and congressional hearings. In the Soviet Union, many collections of documents and of statements by various leaders were published, including from 1987 through 1991 the official *Bulletin of the Ministry of Foreign Affairs of the USSR* (*Vestnik ministerstva inostrannykh del SSSR*). The press is of course an important source, although it is necessary to distinguish between established facts and attempts to determine facts, as well as between official and unofficial views.

A second source is the testimony of participants in the policy process, through memoirs or interviews. For the period covered in this book, the memoirs of President Ronald Reagan (*An American Life*, Simon and Schuster, 1990); Secretary of State Alexander M. Haig, Jr. (*Caveat: Realism, Reagan, and Foreign Policy*, Macmillan, 1984); and especially the memoir of Secretary of

State George P. Shultz (*Turmoil and Triumph: My Years as Secretary of State*, Charles Scribner's Sons, 1993) are of particular value. Many memoirs of others in the Reagan and Bush administrations are also useful. Kenneth Adelman, Max Kampelman, Jeane Kirkpatrick, Paul Nitze, and Edward Rowny have dealt with certain aspects of foreign policy. A number of other members of the Reagan administration have written accounts that are less directly related to foreign policy and relations with the Soviet Union but that illuminate the internal political life of that administration. President George Bush and Secretary of State James Baker will probably also publish memoirs of their period, and Ambassador Jack Matlock is writing a book on the Reagan administration's policy toward the Soviet Union, based on his experience.

On the Soviet side, there are no major substantive memoirs on Soviet-American relations covering the period, although there are a number of memoirs that contribute to our understanding of the Soviet system and policymaking (by the late Foreign Minister Andrei Gromyko, former Foreign Minister Eduard Shevardnadze, and many former Soviet leaders and officials including Sergei Akhromeyev, Georgy Arbatov, Valery Boldin, Anatoly Chernyayev, Valentin Falin, Georgy Kornienko, Yuly Kvitsinsky, Yegor Ligachev, and Anatoly Sobchak). Of these, the memoirs of Anatoly Chernyayev, Gorbachev's foreign affairs aide and speechwriter from 1986 through 1991, based on and citing his contemporary journal and records of many meetings, are especially useful. (To date not available in English: *Shest' let s Gorbachevym* [Six Years with Gorbachev], Moscow: Progress, 1993). Former President Mikhail Gorbachev has written a major memoir that will soon be published. Another volume, of collected transcripts of Gorbachev's meetings with foreign leaders, will also be a valuable source of reference.

Former American and Soviet officials are often available for interviews, the reticence of the latter now generally gone since the dissolution of the Soviet state. Senior and key second-level officials are frequently both better informed about important details and more inclined to speak out frankly about bureaucratic infighting than are the top leaders. In the case of the present volume, I have benefited greatly from knowing most of the American and Soviet officials involved (below the level of the top leaders), in several cases for many years. Some made background information available off the record through the period covered by this account. (Unlike the situation with respect to my earlier study, *Détente and Confrontation*, I was retired from government service through this period and not directly involved.)

Information from memoirs and from interviews and conversations can be very useful, especially in providing leads to pursue in further research or in illuminating points of view or the background to events. Such information is, however, subject to many possible sources of error: selective memory, mistaken recollections, limits of access or awareness at the time, unintentional—and sometimes intentional—bias. Often people involved in the same event have widely differing recollections. Still, carefully used, testimony of participants or witnesses can add usefully to documentary sources in the public record.

In a special category are accounts written by journalists or contemporary historians drawing heavily on interviews. Several interesting books dealing with the Soviet Union during this period, especially the Gorbachev years, are available. On American-Soviet relations, two works are unusually well informed: Don Oberdorfer, *The Turn: From the Cold War to a New Era, the United States and the Soviet Union, 1983–1990* (Poseidon Press, 1991), and dealing with the years 1989 through 1991 Michael Beschloss and Strobe Talbott, *At the Highest Levels: The Inside Story of the End of the Cold War* (Little, Brown and Company, 1993). There are at present no other histories of American-Soviet relations examining this final decade.

Despite the recency of the period covered, a number of formerly secret official documents of both countries have already been declassified, and these have been used and cited in this study. In the case of documents of the former Soviet Union, the dissolution of that state has led the Russian authorities to declassify many formerly secret and top secret documents from the 1980s through 1991, although that has been done in a somewhat haphazard fashion. Some of these materials, however, cited throughout this study, do make a valuable contribution, particularly in the discussion of Soviet policy toward Afghanistan and the Third World, and Eastern Europe, but also on some aspects of Soviet-American relations more directly. In addition to the National Archives of the United States and its presidential libraries, the National Security Archive in Washington has the most complete file of relevant declassified American documents. In Moscow, the Center for the Storage of Contemporary Documentation houses the archives of the former Central Committee of the Communist Party of the Soviet Union, including documents sent to the Central Committee from various ministries and agencies. Its files are only accessible in part, but are very useful. It is also the depository for declassified documents from the Presidential Archive (also called the Kremlin Archive), including Politburo documents from the period through August 1991, in a special file (Fond 89).

# Index

The Great Transition

Soviet politics, 204n, 316, 323, 350, 361, 438, 458, 461, 484, 390, 391, 420, 428, 439; telephone calls to Bush, 489, 490, 496; Ukraine, 440, 479, 482, 484–85, 495; Union of Sovereign States, 481; Union Treaty, 455, 457, 460, 470, 479, 482, 483–85; U.S.-Russian relations, 769, 779, 790; visit to Lithuania, 453; visits to U.S., 383, 464. *See also* Russia
Yemen, 21, 718, 731, 746
Yepishev, Aleksei A., 77, 79n
Yerevan, 419
Yugoslavia, 420n, 425, 468, 493, 540, 560, 608, 618n, 620, 622, 796. *See also* Eastern Europe
Yurchenko, Vitaly S., 225m 231

Zagladin, Vadim, 81–82, 122n, 139n, 222, 262

Zaikov, Lev, 416n, 429, 432
Zaire, 21n, 700
Zaitsev, Mikhail M., 210
Zamyatin, Leonid, 9n, 68, 81, 173–74, 192, 562
Zakharov, Gennady F., 281, 285, 311n
Zhang Zhunzi, 631
Zhang Aiping, 634, 635
Zhao Ziyang, 565, 625, 626–27, 628, 632, 634, 635n, 636, 649, 651, 659. *See also* China
Zhirinovsky, Vladimir V., 781
Zhivkov, Todor, 399, 567, 568, 576, 603
Zhou Enlai, 625, 649
Zhukov, Georgy, 78n
Zhurkin, Vitaly, 262n, 685n
Zia ul-Haq, 737n
Zoellick, Robert, 386n, 488n, 490